The End of the Maoist Era

The End of the Maoist Era

Chinese Politics During the Twilight of the Cultural Revolution, 1972-1976

Frederick C. Teiwes and **Warren Sun**

An East Gate Book

M.E.Sharpe
Armonk, New York
London, England

An East Gate Book

Copyright © 2007 by M.E. Sharpe, Inc.

All rights reserved. No part of this book may be reproduced in any form
without written permission from the publisher, M.E. Sharpe, Inc.,
80 Business Park Drive, Armonk, New York 10504.

Library of Congress Cataloging-in-Publication Data

Teiwes, Frederick C.
  The end of the Maoist era : Chinese politics during the twilight of the Cultural Revolution,
1972–1976 / by Frederick C.Teiwes, Warren Sun.
    p. cm.—(Politics of transition in China, 1972–1982)
  "An East Gate Book."
  Includes bibliographical references and index.
  ISBN-13: 978-0-7656-1096-6 (cloth : alk. paper)
    1. China—Politics and government—1949–1976. 2. China—History—Cultural
Revolution, 1966–1976. I. Sun, Warren, 1949– II. Title. III. Title: Chinese politics during
the twilight of the Cultural Revolution, 1972–1976.

DS777.75.T434 2007
951.05′7—dc22   2006024507

Printed in the United States of America

IBT (c)   10   9   8   7   6   5   4   3   2   1

To friends in China who lived through these years

CONTENTS

TABLES

ABBREVIATIONS

Organizations

CCP	Chinese Communist Party
CYL	Communist Youth League
GPD	General Political Department
MAC	Military Affairs Commission
MFA	Ministry of Foreign Affairs
NPC	National People's Congress
PLA	People's Liberation Army
PRC	People's Republic of China
SPC	State Planning Commission

Publications and Publishing Agencies

AJCA	*The Australian Journal of Chinese Affairs*
AS	*Asian Survey*
BNC	*Bainianchao* [Hundred Year Tide]
CQ	*The China Quarterly*
CRDB	*The Chinese Cultural Revolution Database CD-ROM*
DDWX	*Dang de wenxian* [The Party's Documents]
DDZGSYJ	*Dangdai Zhongguoshi yanjiu* [Contemporary China History Studies]
FBIS-CHI	Foreign Broadcast Information Service-China
GMRB	*Guangming ribao* [Brightness Daily]
HQ	*Hongqi* [Red Flag]
IS	*Issues & Studies*
NCNA	New China News Agency
PR	*Peking Review*
RMRB	*Renmin ribao* [People's Daily]
SPRCM	*Selections from People's Republic of China Magazines*
SPRCP	*Survey of People's Republic of China Press*
ZGDSCKZL	*Zhonggong dangshi cankao ziliao* [CCP History Teaching Reference Materials]
ZGDSZL	*Zhonggong dangshi ziliao* [Materials on CCP History]

PREFACE

This volume grew out of, and forms part of, a larger study of the elite politics at the highest levels in Beijing which shaped China's dramatic transition during the 1972-82 decade. This transition took the People's Republic from the ideologically charged and often turbulent pseudo-revolution at the end of the Maoist era, through a period best described as an effort at restoration of the pre-Cultural Revolution norms and practices of the communist regime, toward a set of policies and approaches breaking with many pre-1966 orthodoxies that was, by the mid-1980s, labeled "reform." In its original conception, the study was to focus initially on the period following the death of Chairman Mao Zedong and the arrest of the so-called "gang of four" in September-October 1976 through to the Third Plenum of the Cenral Committee in December 1978, a meeting widely, if in important respects inaccurately, regarded as both the key turning point in a post-Mao succession struggle between the dead Chairman's anointed successor, Hua Guofeng, and the restored old revolutionary, Deng Xiaoping, as well as marking a clear start on the policies of "reform [of internal structures] and openness [toward the outside world]." Thereafter, the study would examine the emerging new dynamic in ideology, policy and leadership arrangements through to Hua's complete demise at the Twelfth Party Congress in 1982.

The original plan naturally included an overview assessment of elite politics at the very end of Mao's lifetime, specifically the efforts in 1975 under the stewardship of Deng Xiaoping to rectify the excesses of the Cultural Revolution, Deng's subsequent decline and fall in late 1975-early 1976, the designation of Hua as the successor, and the purge of the so-called "gang" within a month of Mao's death. Such an assessment was and is clearly essential to understanding the personalities, political relationships and interests, and policy preferences of the key actors in the post-Mao period, and thus to providing an adequate analysis of the dynamics of the transition. In the course of our research, however, we realized that more than a background chapter was both possible and necessary. First, a rich vein of diverse new materials, notwithstanding significant gaps, presented the opportunity for a fine-grained detailed account of not only 1975-76, but of the immediately preceding years. Second, the existing scholarly literature contained remarkably little on the elite politics of the late Maoist era. While contemporary articles and a very few monographs from the period itself or immediately thereafter appeared, these efforts were inevitably limited by the severe restrictions on sources then available. Subsequently, little systematic scholarly effort was applied to the elite politics of this period once China opened up in the 1980s and researchers could apply their skills to less opaque areas. By and large, the limited new scholarship addressing the leadership politics of the years in question consisted of overview pieces, sections of books developing analytic schemes for leadership politics over a longer period, and aspects of studies on particular leaders, policy areas or localities. Finally, the period following Lin Biao's demise in September 1971 to Mao's death was the only part of the Maoist era we had not examined in detail in previous works. This was no longer an acceptable situation as our research deepened.

Our initial decision to skip the 1972-76 period, apart from background treatment of 1975-76, reflected a paradox. On the one hand, the central message of our past studies, the unchallenged dominance of Mao Zedong in elite politics, had become increasingly accepted by the scholarly community—albeit with some exceptions and qualifications. It seemed time to move on to a new challenge and provide a coherent, detailed interpretation of the necessarily different political dynamics when the Chairman was no longer around. On the other hand, the accepted wisdom of the field, earlier versions of which we have repeatedly challenged in our studies of the pre-1972 period, was in various respects closer than usual to the reality of Chinese communist elite politics for the post-Lin Biao years, notwithstanding a failure to understand the depth of Mao's dominance. As widely argued, the legacy of the Cultural Revolution did indeed sharply divide the Politburo, a conflict mirrored throughout the Party. The chief protagonists at the top for most of this period were the radicals identified, somewhat misleadingly by Mao himself, as a "gang of four," against leading figures of the pre-Cultural Revolution leadership, notably Zhou Enlai and Deng Xiaoping, although the relationship of Zhou and Deng was considerably more complex than normally depicted. A third group, best termed establishment beneficiaries of the Cultural Revolution and ultimately led by Hua Guofeng, also played a distinctive role, but its distinctiveness was less due to policy orientation or even collective political interest than to its members' relative lack of status in the history of the communist revolution. Finally, Mao did, in a sense, sit above the conflict, repeatedly shifting support among various individuals and groups in the top body and wider elite, although he was much more engaged in the actual direction of the Party-state than is often assumed. Thus notwithstanding the broad strokes in which conventional wisdom is more or less accurate, in many nuances it is wide of the mark, and an accumulation of such nuances adds up to a significant departure from the actual conduct of leadership politics. It is these nuances, and the larger story they tell of how various forces maneuvered around a dominant Mao, that made this study imperative.

The present book, then, becomes the first volume in our larger project on the transition from revolution through restoration toward reform. We envision two further volumes—*Volume II: Hua Guofeng, Deng Xiaoping and the Road to the Third Plenum, 1976-78*, covering the high tide of restoration, and *Volume III: Between Restoration and Reform, 1979-82*, on the period up to the 1982 Twelfth Party Congress. Our research for these projected studies has been extensive if unfinished, especially for Volume II. While our findings are of course subject to modification, elaboration, and even reversal as further evidence becomes available, we are able to sketch in broad outline our present findings here, findings that provide a first glimpse of how the leadership politics of late Maoism affected the developments of the post-Mao era.

Volume II will challenge the dominant view of the period up to the Third Plenum as involving both a relatively clear-cut policy conflict between lingering Maoism and emerging "reform," as well as an on-going power struggle between Hua and Deng. Our research on this period indicates that this view is as fundamentally flawed as the earlier orthodoxy of a pre-Cultural Revolution "two line struggle" between Mao and his alleged leadership "opponents," or the still widely-believed view of Lin Biao as an ambitious politician who used the Cultural Revolution to further his power objectives, ultimately challenging the Chairman himself. For the immediate post-Mao period, conventional wisdom depicts the alleged succession struggle as linked to pronounced ideological and policy divisions between "neo-Maoists" around Hua and Deng's reform group, with Deng emerging victorious at the Third Plenum due to a combination of failures in Hua's policy program, the construction of an attractive alternative program by Deng, and Deng's skill in building a broad anti-Hua coalition. Our research findings to date provide the basis for a radically different picture: Hua's policies were based on the necessarily limited measures implemented by Deng in 1975, but now substantially extended following Hua's coup against the radicals and the declaration of the end of the Cultural Revolution at the mid-1977 Eleventh Party Congress, and there is little evidence of policy conflict between the two men; Hua never challenged Deng's emerging authority, based on high revolutionary status, while both men had to contend with the legacy of the still greater authority of Mao; developments at the pre-1978 plenum work conference which weakened Hua were not orchestrated by Deng but caught both men by surprise; and there was no conscious "reform" program advanced at the work conference or plenum, while many precursors of reform had already been introduced under Hua's active leadership. In sum, elite politics was complex, but it was not polarized. As a major participant recently recalled, "The contradiction and struggle did not form into two opposing armies; that wasn't the situation then."[1]

Volume III will take up the story after the Third Plenum which, our above arguments notwithstanding, marked significant departures in elite politics. Deng's preeminence became more obvious, Hua's role declined, and policy explorations became bolder, although the current orthodoxy of "reform and opening" emerging from the plenum is greatly overstated. The complexity of the new period produced a more diverse scholarly assessment, making it more difficult to speak of a conventional wisdom. Nevertheless, some fairly common

---

[1] *Deng Liqun guoshi jiangtanlu* [Record of Deng Liqun's Lectures on National History] (5 vols., Beijing: Zhonghuarenmingongheguo shigao bianweihui, 2000), vol. 3, p. 358.

themes emerged in the literature. With China developing reform approaches, elite politics was assertedly marked by a cyclical pattern of advance and retreat reflecting the fortunes of different factions. While the balance strongly shifted to Deng's "reform coalition," Hua still offered resistance to specific reform measures and struggled to retain his position, finally succumbing in 1980-81 when key younger members of Deng's anti-Hua coalition, Hu Yaobang and Zhao Ziyang, took over Hua's leading Party and government posts respectively in the context of a Deng-led attack on Mao's historical position. Deng also had to maneuver against other contending groups, while overarching all of this, in various interpretations, was a subtle struggle for preeminence between Deng and Chen Yun, where the influence of each waxed and waned in response to circumstances. Although elements of these views have to be taken seriously, as in the earlier periods, various specific findings sit uneasily with such commonly-held interpretations: Hu and Zhao had good relations and compatible positions on key issues with Hua; Chen Yun completely respected Deng's position as leader; and Deng's consistent position concerning the historical verdict on Mao was to protect the late Chairman's prestige, even while acknowledging his mistakes and undermining his policy legacy. More broadly, our research indicates that Deng's role in this piecemeal reform process was essentially unchallenged for reasons of revolutionary prestige and the decisive leadership he provided. When he changed course, it was not because positions were forced on him; it rather reflected his pursuit of consensus and policies that worked. How this worked out in specific cases, and the subtleties of leadership interaction, will be the subject of further investigation.

The present study has had to contend with enormous but not fatal problems of methodology and sources. While acknowledging, as an anonymous reviewer of our analysis of the 1976 Tiananmen incident published in *Pacific Affairs* observed, that the sources available on this most difficult late Mao period present a mix of "fact" and "fiction," we nevertheless believe that rigorous attention to detail and careful evaluation of evidence takes us toward the "truth" of at least the broad dynamics of elite politics, even as definitive analyses of particular events remain elusive. Of course, as amply demonstrated in our research for previous studies of the Maoist era, this is an enduring problem, but one particularly difficult for the "Cultural Revolution decade." A combination of major gaps in archival material, in part because such material never existed, in part because key evidence was destroyed, restricted access for even high-ranking Party historians to the evidence that remains, making detailed knowledge of specifics especially hard to come by, constraints created by an official line in the most authoritative publications, a broader literature that does indeed mix "fiction" with "facts," and a culture of secrecy during the period itself whereby even high-ranking participants remained ignorant of major developments and often took rumors as credible. Our task, before reaching overall conclusions, was to assess a variety of sources and specific claims, detective work involving literally thousands of judgments concerning specific evidence and events. These judgments have been based on the nature of the sources and assessments of their inherent bias, cross-checking other sources dealing with the same event, but keeping in mind that Chinese sources frequently repeat one another without independent consideration, detailed examination of specific historical contexts, linguistic analysis of documents, and pursuing elusive questions in interviews with well-placed and reliable Party historians.

Specific types of sources, and a few particularly important examples, deserve brief comment. Official sources, notably biographies of Mao and Zhou Enlai, and chronologies of Zhou and Deng Xiaoping, are generally authoritative, although not infallible, for the factual information they provide. The problem is with what is not included, with the general effect of shielding Party leaders from negative information, in the present circumstances being more protective of Deng than Mao. Memoirs and reminiscences (*huiyilu*) by high-ranking elite figures are often revealing, but more in fragments than as sustained coverage of the period, with many memoirs glossing over the difficult 1966-76 period, including particularly significant episodes involving the authors, as well as generally adhering to accepted views of heroes and villains.[2] A much more comprehensive quasi-memoir used extensively in this study is the account by Deng's daughter Mao Mao of her father's "Cultural Revolution years,"[3] a book that in fact was heavily vetted by the Party's Central Documents Research Office, a process that both provided information beyond Mao Mao's knowledge and kept the story within the parameters of the official view. Yet her book provides information that could only be known to Deng's family members and close staff and reveals insights at variance with what is normally assumed.

Beyond this, there is a range of publications including serious, if constrained, academic studies of varying quality by Party historians, writings by informed authors outside of China not subject to official controls, and various market-driven unofficial genres, notably reportage literature (*jishi wenxue*) providing detailed journalistic descriptions of events that are not completely reliable. The outstanding example of an informed study produced outside of, and indeed banned in China, is the biography of Zhou Enlai by Gao Wenqian.[4] A former member of the Zhou section of the Central Documents Research Office, writing and publishing in the United States, and using materials he had examined as a Party historian, Gao has produced an extremely valuable book, but one flawed

---

[2] For a thoughtful discussion of the limitations of memoirs, see Joshua A. Fogel, "Mendacity and Veracity in the Recent Chinese Communist Memoir Literature," in Timothy Cheek and Tony Saich, eds., *New Perspectives on State Socialism in China* (Armonk: M.E. Sharpe, 1997).

[3] Mao Mao [Deng Rong], *Wode fuqin Deng Xiaoping: "wenge" suiyue* [My Father Deng Xiaoping: The "Cultural Revolution" Years] (Beijing: Zhongyang wenxian chubanshe, 2000).

[4] Gao Wenqian, *Wannian Zhou Enlai* [The Later Years of Zhou Enlai] (New York: Mingjing chubanshe, 2003). For a critical discussion, see Warren Sun's review in *The China Journal*, no. 52 (2004).

by gaps in the story, inadequate referencing, occasional indiscriminate use of sources, and a clear bias against Mao that, however justified at some level, diminishes objective analysis. Moreover, Gao's access to sensitive materials, while significant, was less than he has claimed, and this undoubtedly contributed to some of the mistaken conclusions in the book. Overall, however, Gao provides important materials that, if not providing a startlingly new view of Zhou Enlai, confirm skepticism concerning the Premier, while illuminating various critical developments during 1972-76.

We have made extensive use in Chapters 7 and 8 of a prime example of reportage literature, the two-volume study of "Deng Xiaoping in 1976" by the pseudonymous Qing Ye and Fang Lei,[5] a study providing the most detailed accounts of the Tiananmen incident and the purge of the "gang of four" later in the year. This source, the collaborative effort of a senior Party historian and a literary writer, presents dramatic blow-by-blow accounts of events that are clearly embellished, including several outright fabrications, and as such is undoubtedly the most questionable of our major sources. While skeptically examining each assertion for credibility, we accept Qing and Fang's general reconstruction of events and key specific claims for a number of reasons: compatibility with other sources and the logic of the situations described, the inclusion of important documents that can be verified by other means, and our personal knowledge of the authors. The senior author is a Party historian with exceptional access by virtue of both professional and family circumstances, someone who has both seen extremely sensitive documents and interviewed many of the leading figures of the period. Other senior Party historians acknowledge the status of this scholar, and accept the study as significant, various reservations notwithstanding. While we cannot vouch for everything in its reconstruction of 1976, and accept that some of the material we have used may be erroneous, on balance we believe this source provides exceptionally valuable insights into elite politics at the very end of Mao's life.

In addition to documentary collections published in China, we have also made major use of Party documents and leaders' speeches issued by organizations outside China. This requires caution since, for example, documents issued on Taiwan have in the past sometimes proven bogus. Our main source of such externally-provided documents is the Cultural Revolution collection, under the general editorship of Song Yongyi and issued in CD-Rom format by The Chinese University of Hong Kong, a collection significantly more extensive than the various printed collections of Cultural Revolution materials and involving leadership-level documents generally missing from earlier collections.[6] Based on

---

[5] Qing Ye and Fang Lei, *Deng Xiaoping zai 1976* [Deng Xiaoping in 1976] (2 vols., Shenyang: Chunfeng wenyi chubanshe, 1993). Concerning the deliberate fabrications included in these volumes, our understanding, based on interviews with the senior author, is that they were included both for commercial reasons and to mislead the authorities as to the identity of the original sources.

[6] Song Yongyi, chief ed., *The Chinese Cultural Revolution Database CD-ROM* (hereafter *CRDB*)

close scrutiny of the language, issues, circumstances, and larger political context raised in the various texts, we estimate that at least 90 percent of the documents in the collection are genuine. Our confidence in the collection, subject to the analysis of individual documents, is also based on our knowledge, as a result of discussions with the compilers, of how the documents were selected and secured, plus our ability to verify independently many of the most important items in the collection.

As in previous studies, a final major source has been interviews with Party historians and participants in elite politics.[7] Naturally, in using such sources we have considered any apparent bias of the interviewee, the basis upon which the source obtained information and drew conclusions, consistency with available written and other oral sources, and our assessment of the reliability of the individual concerned, often based on repeated contact over the years. While we have encountered more contentious views among oral sources concerning developments in 1966-76 than for earlier periods, overall we see no reason to alter our previous judgment that the Party historians we have interviewed are on the whole modest and serious individuals with high standards of historical evidence. These scholars are not happy without a solid factual basis for their conclusions, are skeptical of their sources, and candid about the limitations of their knowledge, an empirical approach that creates considerable confidence in their specific information and interpretive conclusions. Former participants, understandably, often display biases reflecting their roles in the events and personal loyalties, but such interviews have nevertheless provided important information and insights into the events under study.

Utilizing these diverse sources, we have done our best to distinguish "fact" from "fiction" in the following pages, noting alternative views, gaps in the record, and uncertainties and conflicting claims concerning specific developments. As already indicated, we cannot guarantee the accuracy of our analysis of every event, nor the adequacy of our characterizations of every leader. But we are bold enough to believe that we have corrected many misleading perceptions of elite politics at the end of the Mao era, have significantly advanced an accurate reconstruction of that politics, and have identified the basic dynamics of leadership interaction during these dramatic years.

Although many people have contributed to this study, not for the first time Chris Buckley must be singled out. Chris was with the project from the beginning, contributing to the research in manifold ways. He read widely in the emerging Chinese literature, providing us with summaries of the most valuable sources and securing copies of such materials from the diverse Beijing market. He also facilitated our contacts with a wide range of scholars and individuals involved in

(Hong Kong: The Chinese University Press, 2002). For a comprehensive discussion, see Warren Sun's review in *The China Journal*, no. 50 (2003).

[7] For a somewhat out-of-date overview of the interview process, see Frederick C. Teiwes, "Interviews on Party History," in Cheek and Saich, *New Perspectives on State Socialism in China*.

the events of the period, and on various occasions conducted revealing interviews on our behalf. Apart from shrewd comments on draft chapters, he was deeply involved in a stimulating three-way discussion by email concerning the meaning of information uncovered, both for the present study and the projected Volumes II and III. In short, Chris' contribution has been immense.

Others have helped in various ways, including assisting with research materials, exchanging ideas, commenting on draft chapters, providing research assistance, or relating personal experience, such as concerning the events on Tiananmen Square in April 1976. We thank Matt Brazil, William Burr, Timothy Cheek, Chen Yizi, David Denny, Joseph Fewsmith, Keith Forster, Gao Wenqian, David Goodman, Nancy Hearst, Jonathan Howe, Jean Hung, Richard Kraus, Li Dezhen, Kenneth Lieberthal, Lin Yousu, Roderick MacFarquhar, Pei Bolin, Elizabeth Perry, Kathleen Peterson, Tony Saich, Michael Schoenhals, Stuart Schram, David Shambaugh, Song Yongyi, Lyndon Storey, Su Shaozhi, Robert Suettinger, Pamela Tan, Julia Tong, Wang Bengxu, Xu Bing, Michael Yahuda, Yan Jiaqi, Zhang Yunlin and David Zweig for these diverse contributions. We also thank a number of (mainly American) officials who dealt with key actors in our story during their official duties and have provided their reflections: Stephen Fitzgerald, Chas Freeman, the late William Gleysteen, James Lilley, the late Michel Oksenberg, Stapleton Roy and Richard Solomon. Keith Forster, in addition to his direct personal contribution, is also acknowledged for the single most helpful scholarly work on the period, his study of the dramatic and complex developments in Zhejiang. We are also further grateful to Tim Cheek for permission to use an updated version of our article on the 1976 Tiananmen incident that originally appeared in *Pacific Affairs* in the Summer 2004 issue.

In our recent studies, we have consistently offered special thanks to the many Party historians and other oral sources who have provided us with many insights into and much information on the topics of our investigations. It is our regret that this very large number of individuals must necessarily remain anonymous. Our thanks are no less heartfelt for being repeated again in the context of our endeavor to understand the last years of the Maoist era. Despite the inherent limitations of interviews noted above, we once again come away impressed with the intellectual seriousness and basic honesty of the great majority of our interview sources.

Institutional support was, of course, essential for the successful conduct of our research. Above all, we gratefully acknowledge the long-standing generous financial support of the Australian Research Council. Party history institutes in Beijing graciously arranged access to individual scholars, and the Contemporary China Research Institute, with Cheng Zhongyuan and Du Pu making special efforts, further provided valuable logistic support. Other institutions around the world facilitated our research through access to library resources, opportunities to interact with other scholars as well as Chinese historians temporarily overseas, and with many support services that assisted our research and writing. We especially thank the Contemporary China Centre at the Australian National University, Harvard University's Fairbank Center for East Asian Research, the Hoover Institution Library, the Rockefeller Foundation's Bellagio Center, the Modern Chinese History Library of the Academia Sinica, Taipei, and the Universities Service Centre at The Chinese University of Hong Kong. Naturally, our home universities, the University of Sydney and Monash University, have provided ongoing and varied support that we also gratefully acknowledge.

In the process of producing the study presented here, particular thanks are owed to Nancy Hearst who proofread the manuscript, and to Miguel Yamin and Jacqui Owen who skillfully prepared the camera-ready pages. At M.E. Sharpe, Patricia Loo and Angela Piliouras provided essential support for the project, as well as necessary technical and editorial advice and coordination.

Finally, it is traditional to thank our families for their support of our scholarly efforts. We do so again, with a special recognition that this project has been particularly long, the demands on our energies especially demanding, and their support all the more valued because of these circumstances.

Sydney and Melbourne
April 2006

The End of the Maoist Era

INTRODUCTION

Regarding the Cultural Revolution, the overall assessment is: basically correct, [but] some shortcomings. Now we must consider the deficient aspects. It is a 70/30 distinction, 70 percent achievements, 30 percent mistakes, [but] opinions on this do not seem to be unanimous. The Cultural Revolution committed two mistakes, 1. knocking down everything, 2. widespread civil war. In knocking down everything a part was correct, for example concerning the Liu [Shaoqi and] Lin [Biao] cliques. A part was mistaken, for example [knocking down] many old comrades. These [old comrades] also have faults, and can be criticized a bit. It doesn't matter whether the experience of war has already lasted more than ten years. [Even] widespread civil war, grabbing guns, shooting off most of them, fighting a bit, is also physical training. But beating people to death, not giving first aid to the wounded, this is not good.

> —Mao Zedong's assessment of the Cultural Revolution, November 1975[1]

Wang Dongxing: The Chairman in some periods criticizes these people [e.g., Deng Xiaoping—the authors], in other periods he criticizes those people [Jiang Qing *et al.*—the authors] in order to bring about a consensus on the line, [he] doesn't want the criticism to knock them over.
Chairman Mao: Right, it isn't to knock people over, only to correct mistakes, bring about unity and produce good work. My criticism of Jiang Qing is also like this.

> —Exchange between Wang Dongxing and Mao during Mao Yuanxin's report to the Chairman on a meeting to "help" Deng Xiaoping, November 4, 1975[2]

Comrade [Zhang] Yufeng: How are you! Now I would like to present a report to the Chairman that I wrote on the night of the 16th [of June 1975, concerning my mistakes and crimes during the 40 years from the Zunyi conference to today]. Please use your discretion [in passing it on to the Chairman]. Make sure that you only read it to him when he is feeling good and relaxed, has a full stomach, and has had a good sleep. Be sure not to read it to him when he is tired. Please, please.

> —Zhou Enlai's letter to Mao's secretary, Zhang Yufeng, June 16, 1975[3]

The Cultural Revolution was clearly the defining issue of Chinese Communist Party (CCP) leadership politics during the last years of Mao's life. While the movement's essential features of chaotic and often violent mass activism and fractured official organizations had largely, if hardly completely, ended by the time of the Ninth Party Congress in April 1969, the official designation of the entire 1966-76 period as the "Cultural Revolution decade" captures an essential reality. For the remainder of the decade, and especially after the flight and death of Mao's personally designated successor, Lin Biao, in September 1971, the achievements and shortcomings of the Cultural Revolution were high in the consciousness of elites and populace alike. At the same time, the official view throughout remained that consolidating and continuing the Cultural Revolution were the core of the Party's political line.

Most important in terms of the political course of the post-Lin Biao period, Chairman Mao Zedong was obsessed with *his* Cultural Revolution throughout these last years. As is well known, in 1976 Mao observed that he had achieved two things in his life, defeating Chiang Kai-shek and launching the Cultural Revolution, but while most applauded the first, many opposed the second which was still an unfinished project. This, in fact, was a sentiment he had expressed on various earlier occasions beginning in 1972.[4] But Mao's anxiety concerning people negating the Cultural Revolution in the future and his tenacious commitment to the movement were balanced by an acute awareness of its faults as seen in the first quotation above. Moreover, even as Mao asserted the movement was 70 percent correct, he was profoundly and often primarily concerned with rectifying the 30 percent errors that threatened its long-term viability. While the sources of his contradictory actions were often obscure and influenced by long-standing personal prejudices and emotional reactions, their underlying basis has been

---

[1] *Jianguo yilai Mao Zedong wengao* [Mao Zedong's Manuscripts since the Founding of the State], vol. 13 (January 1969-July 1976) (Beijing: Zhongyang wenxian chubanshe, 1998), p. 488. This source conflates a series of Mao's statements between October 1975 and January 1976. Other sources, however, place most of this statement in early November. See Chen Donglin and Du Pu, eds., *Zhonghuarenmingongheguo shilu* [True Record of the PRC], vol. 3, part 2, *Neiluan yu kangzheng—"wenhua dageming" de shinian (1972-1976)* [Civil Disorder and Resistance—The "Cultural Revolution" Decade, 1972-1976] (Changchun: Jilin renmin chubanshe, 1994), p. 1291; and Mao Mao, *"Wenge" suiyue*, p. 418.

[2] *Mao Zedong zhuan (1949-1976)* [Biography of Mao Zedong, 1949-1976] (2 vols., Beijing: Zhongyang wenxian chubanshe, 2003), vol. 2, p. 1756. We identify the people referred to on the basis of Mao's actions in the second half of 1975.

[3] Cited in Gao Wenqian, *Wannian Zhou*, p. 13. Zhou's accompanying letter to Mao (see *ibid.*, pp. 11-13) expressed the Premier's remorse and shame for his errors and crimes, and indicated his willingness to provide a summary report in order to maintain his integrity. Before an operation for cataracts in July 1975, Mao was functionally blind, with the result that Zhang Yufeng read documents to him.

[4] See *Mao zhuan*, vol. 2, p. 1645. The full quotation of Mao's 1976 statement is given at the start of the Conclusion, below, p. 595.

well characterized by the Chairman's official biographers: "Concerning various concrete issues, [Mao] could correct errors that caused serious consequences, including by adjusting certain important policies, but he would not allow criticizing and correcting the guiding ideology of the 'Cultural Revolution'."[5] This study examines how Mao's conflicted view of the Cultural Revolution played out in the political developments of 1972-76, and in the process it reveals a dynamics of leadership politics during this period of great conflict and stress that, in critical respects, is different from what is commonly believed.

This places the Chairman at the center of the unfolding drama, something again captured well by Mao's biographers: "[In these years] many big unforeseen events in China's political situation were all intimately linked to the state of Mao Zedong's thinking."[6] Yet Mao's central role in the politics of this period has seldom been adequately reflected in Western scholarship. Although the Mao of 1972-76 has rarely been presented as under sustained attack or as vulnerable to opposition forces as erroneously claimed in (previous) consensus views on earlier periods,[7] to the extent a conventional wisdom can be posited for a period largely under-examined, and where relevant works appeared over a long period and thus drew on significantly different sources,[8] it falls far short of understanding Mao's power and impact in these last years of his life. The existing literature, with rare

---

[5] *Mao zhuan*, vol. 2, p. 1648.

[6] *Ibid.*, p. 1649.

[7] Most significantly, the earlier consensus acceptance of the alleged "two line struggle" between Mao and his "opponents" before the Cultural Revolution, which is systematically rebutted in Frederick C. Teiwes, *Politics and Purges in China: Rectification and the Decline of Party Norms 1950-1965*, 2nd edition (Armonk: M.E. Sharpe, 1993), and the imagined sharp conflict with Lin Biao. On the Lin Biao case, see Frederick C. Teiwes and Warren Sun, *The Tragedy of Lin Biao: Riding the Tiger during the Cultural Revolution, 1966-1971* (London: C. Hurst & Co., 1996), especially the Introduction, for a point by point comparison of our interpretation and the commonly accepted view. See also the summary below, pp. 32-34.

[8] During the period itself and shortly thereafter, the events were analyzed in contemporary journal articles, as well as in a small number of monographs—notably Kenneth G. Lieberthal, *Sino-Soviet Conflict in the 1970s: Its Evolution and Implications for the Strategic Triangle* (Santa Monica: Rand Report R-2342-NA, July 1978); idem with the assistance of James Tong and Sai-cheung Yeung, *Central Documents and Politburo Politics in China* (Ann Arbor: Michigan Papers in Chinese Studies, no. 33, 1978); and Jurgen Domes, *China after the Cultural Revolution: Politics between Two Party Congresses* (London: C. Hurst & Co., 1975), Part Three. These studies were necessarily based largely on open PRC publications and leaked documents. With China opening up and the discipline of Party history revived in the 1980s, new documentary sources and the possibility of interviews presented rich material for analysis. Unfortunately, little in-depth work has been done on the period. Of the work done, of particular note are: Barbara Barnouin and Yu Changgen, *Ten Years of Turbulence: The Chinese Cultural Revolution* (London: Kegan Paul International, 1993), ch. 7, the study most clearly grasping the extent of Mao's overwhelming authority; Roderick MacFarquhar, "The Succession to Mao and the End of Maoism, 1969-82," in idem, ed., *The Politics of China, Second Edition: The Eras of Mao and Deng* (New York: Cambridge University Press, 1997); Keith Forster, *Rebellion and Factionalism in a Chinese Province: Zhejiang, 1966-1976* (Armonk: M.E. Sharpe, 1990), chs. 6-10; and Lowell Dittmer, *China's Continuous Revolution: The Post-Liberation Epoch, 1949-1981* (Berkeley: University of California Press, 1987), chs. 5-7.

exceptions, variously depicts a weakened Mao,[9] someone forced to maneuver for support,[10] or at best someone deliberately withdrawn and only reacting to the actions of others.[11] While there is something in the last of these views, the others are completely wide of the mark. Most fundamentally, to varying degrees existing works fail to address in a detailed, sustained and analytically persuasive way how and why the Chairman shaped the unfolding events of the period, a shortcoming which we intend to rectify.

As always, given Mao's near-complete dominance[12] of other leaders of the People's Republic of China (PRC), a situation graphically reflected in Zhou Enlai's letter to Zhang Yufeng quoted above and demonstrated repeatedly in the following analysis, the question becomes the nature of the interaction of these leaders with the Chairman, and how they conceived their interests, developed their strategies, and acted in an environment in which Mao was both unchallengeable and not long for this world. In these years, furthermore, potentially countervailing institutions interests were exceptionally weak due to a combination of the lingering effects of the organizational disruption of 1966-68, the repeated emphasis on Cultural Revolution ideology, and the divergent forces placed very consciously by Mao in leading bodies and lower organizations alike.[13] At the very top, leaders had to be attuned not only to the Chairman's explicit instructions, but also to his often dimly perceived preferences. In one sense, this was nothing new as Mao had frequently been ambiguous concerning his views and willing to make reversals of his own recent positions, something that became an increasingly vexing feature of leadership politics since the Great Leap Forward.[14] But in another sense, given both the radical yet contradictory nature of Mao's goals during the "Cultural

---

[9] See, e.g., Dittmer, *China's Continuous Revolution*, pp. 123, 192, who sees Mao "retiring from active politics" at the start of the period, and increasingly irresolute and ineffectual toward its end.

[10] See Jing Huang, *Factionalism in Chinese Communist Politics* (Cambridge: Cambridge University Press, 2000), pp. 325-47, who pictures Mao in this as earlier periods as dependent on balancing major constituencies or "mountaintops" in order to sustain his position.

[11] See, e.g., the account in Kenneth Lieberthal's fine textbook, *Governing China: From Revolution Through Reform* (New York: W.W. Norton, 1995), pp. 117-19, which, as many other analyses, focuses on other actors, with Mao largely reduced to "interven[ing] periodically ... to tip the scale in one direction or the other, but ... never permit[ing] either side to gain decisive advantage."

[12] We qualify Mao's dominance as "near-complete" simply because, given their individual interests and preferences, other leaders to a greater or lesser degree pushed their own views within what they perceived to be the Chairman's limits of tolerance, even on rare occasions engaging in a form of symbolic defiance. A case in point was Xu Shiyou's objections to Wang Hongwen's promotion at the Tenth Congress; see below, p. 99. But in the end, virtually everyone obeyed Mao, or at least did not challenge his instructions, even when their most fundamental interests were under attack.

[13] The classic pre-Cultural Revolution case of Mao overriding institutional interests was the Great Leap Forward following a period in the mid-1950s when, with the Chairman's clear consent, such bureaucratic interests clearly played a major role in shaping policy. See Frederick C. Teiwes with Warren Sun, *China's Road to Disaster: Mao, Central Politicians, and Provincial Leaders in the Unfolding of the Great Leap Forward, 1955-1959* (Armonk: M.E. Sharpe, 1999).

[14] On Mao's repeated ambiguity in the comparatively predictable pre-Cultural Revolution period, see

Revolution decade" and his increasing remoteness from his colleagues for reasons of health, the problem of correctly understanding the Chairman reached new heights. What, then, were the key features of Mao's interactions with his colleagues and the larger system at the end of his life?

This is not the place to attempt a detailed analysis of why Mao launched the Cultural Revolution. Suffice it to say that the Chairman was set on his unprecedented course by some combination of genuine distress over perceived "revisionist" tendencies in the Party and society, a feeling that traditional rectification efforts to deal with these problems were ineffective, dissatisfaction with specific policies, negative assessments of the performance and even loyalty of particular colleagues, the need for scapegoats given his inability to admit responsibility or cope with the consequences of his failed policies since the Hundred Flowers and Great Leap, and a clearly unfounded sense that power was somehow slipping from his hands.[15] Once launched, the Cultural Revolution was a watershed in Mao's leadership in various respects. In terms of basic orientation, Mao advocated far more extreme approaches to dualities in his thinking than in even his most radical pre-1966 phases—political purity over any semblance of specialist knowledge, mass activism and anti-authoritarian attitudes virtually negating organizational constraints, and ideological objectives overriding considerations of economic development and social stability. Most telling was that Mao, whose earlier career had earned him Stuart Schram's apt description as a "natural Leninist,"[16] was now willing to destroy the CCP as a functioning nationwide organization in his quixotic quest for ideological purity. Beyond this extremism, there was much that the Chairman was unable to explain, leaving an almost incoherent guide to action for leaders and masses alike, as in his injunctions to "fight self" and "support the left." For the top leadership, moreover, a much more threatening situation emerged than that before the movement. Not only were long-standing Party norms violated along with the fracturing of the CCP's organizational structure, but personal vulnerability was infinitely greater than in the past as evidenced in the physical abuse and deaths of three Politburo members—Liu Shaoqi, Peng Dehuai and He Long.[17] While this situation changed after the Lin Biao affair, it was clearly an inhibiting memory for all top leaders in 1972-76.

Teiwes, *Politics and Purges*, pp. xvii, xx, xxii-xxvi, xxxii, xxxvi, xxxix, xliii-xlv, liii, lvii-lviii, lx-lxi, 196, 218, 302, 308, 311, 385, 389-90, 394, 433ff, 447, 462-63, 466, 498n33.

[15] For further discussion, see *ibid.*, especially pp. xxxvi-xliv and ch. 11; and Frederick C. Teiwes, "Politics at the 'Core': The Political Circumstances of Mao Zedong, Deng Xiaoping and Jiang Zemin," *China Information*, vol. XV, no. 1 (2001), pp. 14-22.

[16] Stuart R. Schram, *The Political Thought of Mao Tse-tung* (revised and enlarged ed., New York: Frederick A. Praeger, 1969), p. 35.

[17] See Frederick C. Teiwes, *Leadership, Legitimacy, and Conflict in China: From a Charismatic Mao to the Politics of Succession* (Armonk: M.E. Sharpe, 1984), ch. 3, for an overview of Party norms. Chapter 1 of the same book examines the (less extreme) manifestations of dualities in Mao's thinking

After the Ninth Congress, and particularly after the Lin Biao affair, Mao's ambiguity reverted, in a sense, to pre-Cultural Revolution days. That is, the more moderate sides of his "dialectical" thinking that had been fundamentally ignored in 1966-68—national development, social discipline, organizational control, and the critical principle of Party leadership—were now again on the agenda. Exactly how these were to be reconciled with Mao's continuing devotion to Cultural Revolution values could never be entirely clear, and, as we will document, even when the Chairman gave comparatively clear instructions there was always the danger of misreading his intentions and overstepping the mark. Leaders long familiar with Mao's ways and intent on retaining his favor were acutely aware of the danger. Thus, in 1975, after Mao criticized the Politburo radicals and entrusted Deng Xiaoping with arguably the strongest grant of authority anyone received over the entire 1972-76 period, Zhou Enlai warned Deng: "The Chairman is still observing, don't get overexcited, don't confront [the radicals] head to head."[18] The dilemma was how to push one's own objectives within the context of Mao's stated general view.[19]

Ironically, given that Mao's Cultural Revolution had done so much to fracture Party unity and had placed mutually hostile groups in the emerging post-1968 official structures including on the top bodies of the regime, one of the Chairman's pervasive concerns throughout 1972-76 was to uphold leadership unity. This objective, expressed in the November 1975 exchange between Mao and Wang Dongxing quoted at the start of this Introduction, was reflected in the Chairman's statements and actions throughout the period. While one can never be confident of Mao's complete motivations in his injunctions to fractious Politburo members to unite,[20] it appears he considered radicals such

---

during the pre-Cultural Revolution period. With regard to personal vulnerability, before 1966 no Politburo member died from other than natural causes apart from the 1954 suicide of Gao Gang (see Frederick C. Teiwes, *Politics at Mao's Court: Gao Gang and Party Factionalism in the Early 1950s* [Armonk: M. E. Sharpe, 1990], pp. 121ff), while only Rao Shushi, Peng Dehuai and Zhang Wentian had been ousted from their official positions, with the latter two formally remaining on the Politburo. While Peng Dehuai's death has been attributed to mistreatment during the Cultural Revolution, he actually passed away in 1974 when such mistreatment had generally ceased.

[18] Interview with Party historian specializing on the period, January 2000. Cf. Gao Wenqian, *Wannian Zhou*, pp. 575-76, 580-81. For a similar statement by another acute observer of the Chairman, see Chen Yun's remarks from the same period, below, p. 305.

[19] Apart from trying to fathom Mao's wishes, and at most cautiously test the limits of his tolerance, some leaders also attempted to play on Mao's perceived prejudices and peculiarities, with mixed results. Zhou Enlai engaged in such ploys, as in recommending positions against his own views on the calculation that the rebellious side of Mao would reject bureaucratic advice. A case in point concerned inviting the US table tennis team to China in March 1971. In this case, Zhou submitted and endorsed Ministry of Foreign Affairs arguments against an invitation as premature, and Mao adopted the contrary view. On the other hand, in an apparent attempt to pander to Mao, Zhou appointed his "niece," Wang Hairong, Vice Minister of Foreign Affairs in August 1973, a move that earned Mao's anger, but not a reversal of the appointment. *Mao zhuan*, vol. 2, pp. 1630-31; interview with senior Party historian, February 2000; and interview with Party historian specializing on Zhou, December 2002. Cf. below, p. 12n25.

as Jiang Qing and Zhang Chunqiao, old revolutionaries like Zhou Enlai and Deng Xiaoping, and younger products of the Party establishment such as Hua Guofeng and Ji Dengkui, as representing the various orientations and skills that would be required for consolidating the Cultural Revolution. In attempting to forge unity among these forces, Mao was, if anything, more out of touch with reality than in his quest to somehow merge the diverse strands of Cultural Revolution rebelliousness and national development. For someone who had so shrewdly judged the requirements of fostering Party unity earlier in his career,[21] Mao's belief (to the extent he held it) that forces so bitterly opposed in 1966-68 could somehow put aside their animosity and cooperate on a lasting basis suggests a striking naïveté, or at best a forlorn hope. But while the objective was unattainable, Mao's insistence on unity still had important consequences by placing significant limits on the struggles of the contending groups. Without the Chairman's initiative or endorsement, no one could openly attack anyone else, and much of the conflict was driven underground. More broadly, in contrast to the Cultural Revolution proper, no top leader was physically abused, those in Mao's periodic disfavor basically retreated to the sidelines without further consequences, and even Deng Xiaoping, the only Politburo member formally ousted in the entire period, remained under Mao's protection.

Political succession was another of Mao's major concerns throughout his last years. In the broadest sense, the Cultural Revolution placed major emphasis on the need to cultivate a generation of "revolutionary successors" to keep China on its anti-revisionist course. In terms of a successor to the Chairman himself, the post-Lin Biao period marked a new dynamic. Previously, from the mid-1940s to the eve of the Cultural Revolution, Liu Shaoqi held this position, an arrangement broadly supported within the elite. With the start of the Cultural Revolution, Mao elevated a reluctant Lin Biao to the successor position, taking the unusual step of writing the arrangement into the new Party constitution adopted at the Ninth Congress.[22] Following Lin's flight and death, Mao never again publicly acknowledged a successor, but the issue was clearly on his mind and resulted in some unusual arrangements. At various times Mao placed his senior colleagues, first Zhou Enlai and later Deng Xiaoping, in such powerful positions that power would have been in their hands had he passed away earlier. But he also looked for a successor to take over in the longer term, and by 1972 he had settled on the

---

[20] Additional considerations often cited are an inability to choose among different groups, and a conscious plan of balancing contending forces to reinforce his own position.

[21] In particular, during his rise to power in the revolutionary period. See Frederick C. Teiwes, "Mao and His Lieutenants," *The Australian Journal of Chinese Affairs* (hereafter *AJCA*), no.19-20 (1988), pp.35-44; and idem with Warren Sun, *The Formation of the Maoist Leadership: From the Return of Wang Ming to the Seventh Party Congress* (London: Contemporary China Institute Research Notes and Studies, 1994), especially pp. 40-52, 66-67.

[22] On Liu and Lin as successors, see Teiwes, "Mao and His Lieutenants," pp. 56-67; Teiwes with Sun, *Formation*, pp. 34-40; and Teiwes and Sun, *Tragedy*, pp. 57-65.

youthful Shanghai worker rebel, Wang Hongwen. As we shall see in Chapter 1, this was well understood within the leadership and dutifully supported by Zhou Enlai and other senior leaders. Mao's concerns did not stop there, however, and he promoted and observed other younger officials. In an effort to create a wider corps of successor generation leaders, he selected a number of figures from the establishment for key Party and state posts, notably Hua Guofeng, Ji Dengkui, Wu De and Li Desheng.[23] Mao also promoted young radicals including Xie Jingyi and Chi Qun to positions outside the Politburo in expectation of important future roles—but no one was more significant than his nephew, Mao Yuanxin. Finally, in 1976, in the context of the Tiananmen crisis, with Zhou dead, Deng perceived as having adopted the wrong line, and Wang considered a disappointment, Mao placed Hua in positions which guaranteed him the status of successor. Overall, throughout this period, Mao's preoccupation with the succession produced an ongoing reassessment of his colleagues, and contributed to the volatile course of elite politics.

While Mao's concern with leadership unity, the coming succession, and the contradictory requirements of consolidating the Cultural Revolution were central to the conduct of elite politics, another factor shaping Politburo contention derived from the Chairman's varying involvement in different issue areas. In the broadest terms, Mao's domestic focus was on the superstructure, those very areas of education, culture and ideology that had been at the core of the Cultural Revolution. This, as all top leaders realized, was an area of particular sensitivity, especially prone to conflict within the Politburo, and vulnerable to the Chairman's intervention from above. In contrast, while Mao clearly had various preferences which became features of policy, he largely left economic policy and the more practical aspects of government administration to experienced leaders versed in the pre-1966 system. This, of course, left such officials with more leeway to pursue their preferences, and less scope for radical interference given both the radical group's lack of credentials in these areas and Mao's comparative aloofness. Of all issue areas, however, Mao's greatest concern and tightest control was exercised over foreign affairs. His chief implementers and assistants in this sphere were Zhou Enlai and then Deng Xiaoping, both of whom basically shared his policy orientation throughout this period. Beyond that lay a paradox. While there were virtually no differences within the foreign affairs leadership on matters of substance, and in effect the business of the foreign policy establishment was simply to carry out Mao's orders, this sphere was particularly volatile due to a combination of Foreign Ministry factionalism dating from the Cultural Revolution and involving attitudes toward Zhou Enlai, the Chairman's

---

[23] Hua *et al.* were identified by Party historians specializing in the 1970s as leaders Mao was cultivating as potential successors; interviews, September 1994 and February 2000. Hua, Ji and Wu (the last of whom, according to a senior Party historian, Mao had considered one of China's four most talented provincial leaders along with Wang Renzhong, Tao Lujia and Zhao Ziyang), all impressed the Chairman during his pre-Cultural Revolution travels to their localities.

own complicated view of Zhou, and his intense focus on developments in this area. Thus the paradox addressed in this study: an area of no real policy conflict was front and center in some of the crucial developments in leadership politics.

A final factor profoundly influencing elite politics was the declining state of the Chairman's health. In early 1972, already 78 and in frail health, Mao suffered congestive heart failure creating a "health crisis." While Mao's health was a state secret from even Politburo members, a group of leaders headed by Zhou now formed a special group to oversee his medical treatment. After a slight improvement, the group was dissolved after a year, but Mao's fragile condition was apparent at the Tenth Party Congress in August. From that time on, Mao never attended a Central Committee meeting, and only rarely Politburo meetings, last participating in May 1975. In the meantime, a new leadership group to supervise his medical care was set up in 1974 and remained in place until his death. Clearly, Mao's health was in accelerated decline, and by late 1975 his ability to communicate with foreign guests was seriously affected. Such meetings, with Mao barely intelligible, then decreased until ending in May 1976. Finally, in late June the Chairman's condition became critical, apparently eliminating his remaining capacity to control events, even as the authority of his line remained sacrosanct.[24]

The consequences of Mao's parlous health were not limited to increasing remoteness from his colleagues. The situation also enhanced the significance of his personal assistants, particularly three junior figures who conveyed the Chairman's instructions to the rest of the leadership and reported back on the activities of those leaders. In the process, the dynamic of leadership politics was further altered. At the start of the period, the "two ladies" (*liangwei xiaojie*)— Mao's niece, Wang Hairong, and one of his Foreign Ministry interpreters, Tang Wensheng (Nancy Tang)—performed the liaison role. By 1970-71 they began to serve as go-betweens to the Foreign Ministry where they both held positions, and consequently to Premier Zhou. By 1973-74, their role seemed to expand to incorporate liaison functions to the leadership as a whole, although this was not formalized.[25] It is unclear when they completely ceased carrying out this

---

[24] *Mao zhuan*, vol. 2, p. 1617, lists the first medical group as consisting of Zhou, Wang Hongwen, Zhang Chunqiao and Wang Dongxing. We believe this implausible since Wang Hongwen only arrived in Beijing in September 1972, and was clearly outranked by Zhang at that point. It is likely that the writers confused this group with the 1974 group, and that Ye Jianying was probably the fourth member of the 1972 group. For overviews of Mao's health, see *ibid.*, pp. 1615-17, 1638, 1642-43, 1664-65; Zhang Yufeng's account of Mao's declining health from 1971, "Anecdotes of Mao Zedong and Zhou Enlai in Their Later Years," *Guangming ribao* [Brightness Daily] (hereafter *GMRB*), December 26-7, 29-30, 1988, and January 1-6, 1989, in Foreign Broadcast Information Service-China (hereafter FBIS-CHI), 89-017, pp. 16-19, and 89-019, pp. 30ff; Barnouin and Yu, *Ten Years*, pp. 245-46, 286, 289-91; and Li Zhisui, *The Private Life of Chairman Mao: The Memoirs of Mao's Personal Physician* (London: Chatto & Windus, 1994), pp. 542-52, 581ff, 614ff. We have severe reservations about Li Zhisui's book (see Frederick C. Teiwes, "Seeking the Historical Mao," *The China Quarterly* [hereafter *CQ*], no. 145 [1996]), but believe his claims about Mao's health are generally reliable.

function, but by October 1975, Mao Yuanxin, the Chairman's nephew and a key radical in Liaoning, was authoritatively acting as his liaison to the Politburo. An enormously important role was played by these individuals, although, as we shall see, the impact of the "two ladies" was very different from that of Mao Yuanxin. But in both cases leaders were extremely sensitive to their importance,[26] and no one dared to challenge their reports of Mao's views, even when doubts existed concerning the accuracy of their representations. Apart from their influence on specific developments, of especially great significance in Mao Yuanxin's case, the larger lesson of their roles is simply as further and particularly dramatic evidence of Mao's dominance. How else can one explain informal references to these people as representing supreme authority, of having "access to heaven" (*tongtian*)?[27]

This, then, was the context in which Politburo leaders operated in 1972-76: an authoritative Chairman holding contradictory views who repeatedly shifted his emphasis, someone concerned with Party unity and succession arrangements, but increasingly remote and usually only reached through go-betweens of limited formal status yet with great reflected authority. How did groups on the Politburo navigate this difficult terrain? What can be said of the background, interests and conflicts of these forces? Although conventional understandings correctly grasp important aspects of the central leadership equation, in key respects existing scholarly views misread leadership politics at the end of Mao's life. In the following overview discussion, we take a first step toward understanding the nature and dynamics of the key top-level players in Beijing.

The Protagonists in the Politburo, 1972-76

Conventional wisdom concerning the nature of conflict within the Politburo in the post-Lin Biao period essentially posits three leadership groupings or factions, roughly categorized as radicals, Cultural Revolution beneficiaries drawn from the pre-1966 establishment, and senior revolutionary veterans.[28] While broadly accurate in a descriptive sense, this distorts reality in several respects. First, as we examine in greater detail throughout this study, the establishment beneficiaries,

---

[25] According to a senior Party historian specializing in Zhou Enlai. Interview, December 2002. Of the "two ladies," Wang Hairong held the higher bureaucratic position within the Foreign Ministry as well as the family connection to Mao, while Tang Wensheng served as Mao's main English-language interpreter for most of the 1972-76 period. A variety of oral sources with personal experience of the "two ladies" view Tang as the "brains" of the duo, and claim that Wang, apart from speaking little English, demonstrated little talent generally. Although commonly referred to as Mao's niece, Wang Hairong was actually the granddaughter of Mao's cousin, and she addressed the Chairman as "granduncle."

[26] Zhou Enlai was especially attentive to the "two ladies." E.g., see below, pp. 29-30.

[27] See, e.g., the reference to Wang Hairong in October 1975, in Zhang Hanzhi *et al.*, *Wo yu Qiao Guanhua* [Qiao Guanhua and I] (Beijing: Zhongguo qingnian chubanshe, 1994), p. 82.

[28] Other terminology has been used: e.g., Barnouin and Yu, *Ten Years*, pp. 292-93, adopt "radicals, moderates and veteran cadres." In addition to the issues discussed below, there is the further problem

notionally in the middle and facing threats from both sides, in fact were aligned to the old revolutionaries in both policy and historical senses throughout the period, even if the alignment was obscured by the need to obey whatever position Mao declared. Moreover, their antipathy to the radicals was not just due to stupid politics on the part of the radicals who assertedly failed to make a "natural" alliance with Hua Guofeng and other beneficiaries.[29] Nor should it be seen as simply due to specific conflicts generated by Jiang Qing in particular against most of these comparatively junior figures since the early 1970s.[30] More fundamentally, these leaders were part of the Party and army establishment that had been threatened in the gravest sense by the radicals since 1966. In addition, they had an instinctive respect for the revolutionary status of the old guard, as well as specific pre-1949 loyalties in individual cases. In certain periods, junior beneficiaries outranked some of their more senior colleagues,[31] but they seemed more comfortable in their traditional subordinate roles. Tellingly, in early 1976, with Deng in trouble, Hua, Ji Dengkui and Chen Xilian recommended to Mao that while they could do concrete work, it was necessary to appoint a "major responsible person" to coordinate State Council affairs,[32] someone who, we believe, could only have been Li Xiannian, the most senior government leader available at that time.

Second, while the beneficiaries have often been considered "waverers"

---

of assigning individuals to the three categories. Thus Barnouin and Yu categorize Li Desheng as a "veteran cadre" in contrast to Chen Xilian as a "moderate" vacillating between the two contending forces, even though in terms of age, military background, and Party status as of the 1970s, there was not a great deal to choose between them. Clearly, the categorization was influenced by subsequent official verdicts, Chen as a "whateverist" who was removed from the Politburo in 1980, in contrast to Li who continued to serve until 1985 and was never criticized for alleged opposition to Deng Xiaoping. The irony is that Chen was actually more senior than Li; see below, p. 103n187. In terms of our usage here, we define old revolutionaries as senior figures from the revolutionary period who achieved Politburo rank before the Cultural Revolution. This group included aged and infirm Politburo members such as Zhu De and Liu Bocheng, while its only figures playing active political roles were Zhou Enlai, Ye Jianying, Li Xiannian and, subsequently, Deng Xiaoping. This distinction, however, blurs the fact that (especially military) beneficiaries such as Chen Xilian and Li Desheng were, by any realistic standard, veteran revolutionaries with up to two decades of service to the cause before 1949.

[29] See MacFarquhar's argument in "Succession," pp. 299-300.

[30] For example, Jiang's 1974 attack on the Hunan opera *Song of the Gardener* that Hua had sponsored (see Ting Wang, *Chairman Hua: Leader of the Chinese Communists* [London: C. Hurst & Co., 1980]), pp. 96-97), her spring 1975 private denunciation of Ji Dengkui, Wang Dongxing and Wu De as spies or former Guomindang members (Wu De, "Guanyu fensui 'sirenbang' de douzheng" [On the Struggle to Smash the "Gang of Four"], *Dangdai Zhongguoshi yanjiu* [Contemporary China History Studies] [hereafter *DDZGSYJ*], no. 5 [2000], p. 58), and Jiang's frequent rebukes of Chen Xilian at Politburo meetings during the period (interview with senior Party historian, January 2000).

[31] Not only did Hua assume the number two and then number one position over the entire older generation in 1976, in 1973-74 he and others outranked and, before 1974, actually had a greater political role than Deng Xiaoping.

[32] Mao Mao [Deng Rong], *Wode fuqin Deng Xiaoping, shangce* [My Father Deng Xiaoping, vol. 1] (Beijing: Zhongyang wenxian chubanshe, 1993), p. 449. Another indication of "normal" status expectations was Chen Xilian's subsequent credible claim that he had been loyal to Deng before

between sharply opposed radical and old guard forces, in fact virtually everyone wavered according to Mao's demands. Thus in March 1974, the redoubtable Deng himself, in a criticism meeting chaired by Wang Hongwen, joined in to attack Tao Lujia, then head of the Science and Technology Commission for National Defense, for resisting the anti-Lin Biao and Confucius campaign.[33] Moreover, a case can be made that Zhou Enlai was the worst waverer, the leader most likely to tack excessively in whatever direction Mao required.[34] On the other hand, Mao's underlying support for Jiang Qing caused the leading old revolutionaries to pull their punches where she was concerned. "Not opposing Jiang Qing" was, along with not reversing verdicts on the Cultural Revolution, one of Mao's conditions for Deng's return, while by Jiang's account Deng had been "very kind and understanding" toward her for most of 1974, and Deng also limited attacks on her subsequently.[35] In short, supine political behavior was not limited to the beneficiaries, just as thinly veiled animosity toward the Politburo radicals was not the sole preserve of the old revolutionaries.

The situation is even more complicated, and also reflective of the overarching significance of Party status, when we consider the case of Kang Sheng, a Politburo member since 1934, who was disgraced in the post-Mao period as one of the arch villains of the Cultural Revolution, and almost invariably listed as part of the "radical camp" in analyses of the period.[36] Although Kang was very ill and played a negligible direct role in Party affairs in the post-Lin Biao years,[37] the evidence

---

Mao's death with one exception; see below, p. 485. It can also be seen in Li Desheng's respectful winter 1974 visit to his old Second Field Army leader Deng, where Deng praised Chen's fighting abilities in a patriarchic manner; Li Desheng, "Weiren de danshi yu xionghuai" [The Guts and Heart of a Great Man], in *Huiyi Deng Xiaoping* [Remember Deng Xiaoping] (Beijing: Zhongyang wenxian chubanshe, 1998), vol. 1, p. 112.

[33] "Wang Hongwen, Zhang Chunqiao tingqu Guofang Kewei pi Lin pi Kong huibaohui" [Wang Hongwen and Zhang Chunqiao Listen to the Science and Technology Commission for National Defense's Criticize Lin and Confucius Report-back Meeting] (March 8, 1974), handwritten manuscript held at the Menzies Library, the Australian National University.

[34] A view expressed by a senior Party historian with extensive access to the personalities of the period; interview, January 2000.

[35] Yao Jin, ed., *Yao Yilin baixitan* [Evening Chats with Yao Yilin] (Beijing: Zhongguo shangye chubanshe, 1998), p. 189; and below, pp. 186, 245.

[36] Whether Kang was as unmitigatedly evil as almost invariably depicted is beyond the scope of our analysis, although Deng Liqun, who was not beholden to Kang, would claim in the post-Mao period that he was not as bad as portrayed. See *Deng Liqun guoshi jiangtan*, vol. 3, p. 341. For the conventional view, see John Byron and Robert Pack, *The Claws of the Dragon: Kang Sheng— The Evil Genius Behind Mao—and His Legacy of Terror in People's China* (New York: Simon & Schuster, 1992). On Kang as aligned to the radicals and opposed to Zhou Enlai, see MacFarquhar, "Succession," pp. 259, 278, 284, 287. What can be concluded from the following discussion is that Zhou and Deng either did not know of Kang's misdeeds (something especially implausible in the case of Zhou), or that they did not consider them particularly significant given the atmosphere Mao had created.

[37] While Kang attended the Tenth Congress in 1973, he never again attended Central Committee

strongly suggests close, even very close, personal relations between Kang on the one hand, and Zhou Enlai and Deng Xiaoping on the other, both historically and in the several years preceding Kang's death in December 1975 after an extended illness. We examine in subsequent chapters Kang's few known activities in 1972-75, activities indicative of his good relations with Zhou and Deng. In the case of Deng, this reflected not only what Deng's daughter has described as "a close [post-1949] working relationship," with involvement in the early 1960s polemics against the Soviet Union perhaps the most significant work connection, but also seemingly warm family relations before the Cultural Revolution.[38] The relationship with Kang was, if anything, even stronger in the case of Zhou Enlai, a relationship described by a specialist on Zhou as "extraordinarily close." This was demonstrated in April or May 1975, when Kang, deep into his own terminal illness, insisted on being carried by stretcher to the equally dying Zhou to discuss the traitorous behavior of Jiang Qing and Zhang Chunqiao (see below).[39] All of this suggests that the ties of history, which in both relationships went back to the late 1920s, and the sense of being part of the real pre-1949 revolution, overrode political postures and even crimes in the post-1966 period.

What is especially remarkable about Kang's contact with Deng and Zhou in 1972-75 was that the central issue of their interaction concerned the aforementioned activities of Jiang Qing and Zhang Chunqiao. Contrary to accepted notions of the "radical camp," and notwithstanding a shared political orientation and cooperation with Jiang and Zhang during the Cultural Revolution, Kang's overriding concern in his last years seemingly was to expose them as traitors during the pre-1949 revolution. As a result, he confidentially denounced them to Deng and Zhou, and sought their assistance in bringing the matter to Mao's attention.[40] By extension, there could be no doubt about his preferences regarding current political struggles. Although Kang's approach to Mao in late 1975 to denounce Deng remains to be explained (see Chapter 6), his true attitude was apparently expressed in an order to his people that they be loyal to Deng. For his part, in the post-Mao period, even as official attention turned to Kang's crimes and he was posthumously expelled from the Party, Deng seemingly remained silent on the Kang Sheng issue.[41]

Examining the core radical group, the so-called "gang of four," reveals

---

or Politburo meetings. See *Mao zhuan*, vol. 2, p. 1664. He did, however, attend a National Day reception in 1974.

[38] Mao Mao, *Wode fuqin*, vol. 1, pp. 179-81; and Roderick MacFarquhar, *The Origins of the Cultural Revolution 3: The Coming of the Cataclysm 1961-1966* (New York: Columbia University Press, 1997), pp. 360-61.

[39] Lin Qing, *Zhou Enlai zaixiang shengya* [Zhou Enlai's Career as Prime Minister] (Hong Kong: Changcheng wenhua chuban gongsi, 1991), pp. 316-21; and interview, April 2001.

[40] Mao Mao, *Wode fuqin*, vol. 1, pp. 179-81; idem, *"Wenge" suiyue*, pp. 433-34; and below, pp. 73-74, 233.

[41] Interviews with Party historian specializing on the period, June 1999 and February 2000; and

further complexities. Given the distortion of the political characters of both the virtuous and villainous in CCP historiography—and the lamentable tendency of Western observers to adopt these stereotypes—we should take some pause when considering the extremist, disruptive, and politically incompetent official image of these individuals. While there are exaggerations in this portrayal, the evidence as a whole points to individuals with a highly radical agenda, who conducted political activities that contributed significantly to disorder, and who, to varying degrees at different times, displayed a combative attitude toward other leaders that would inevitably bring about a struggle they could not win in a post-Mao context. The main problem, apart from exaggeration and misrepresentations of specific events, concerns the extent to which there actually was a "gang of four" in the sense of a tightly integrated faction.[42] Indeed, the "gang of four" terminology, which came as a surprise to most of the elite following the arrest of the radicals in October 1976 even as it quickly became widely accepted, derived from Mao's use of the phrase on perhaps as few as two occasions.[43] That the four leaders held common perspectives and interests, and undertook some major coordinated action is undeniable, but tensions and differences among the four were also palpable. Examining these conflicts and their impact on elite politics is a major aspect of our unfolding story.

The potential for conflict can be seen in the respective backgrounds of the four. Jiang Qing, an abrasive and often spiteful personality, had little claim to prominence apart from being the Chairman's wife.[44] Indeed, shortly before the Cultural Revolution, Zhang Chunqiao spoke of cultivating Jiang in order to get

---

below, pp. 400-401. The information on Kang's order to his subordinates comes indirectly from this reliable oral source, reportedly originally from someone very close to Kang. Deng's silence is further suggested by a review of his *Selected Works* which avoid any mention of Kang.

Similarly, Deng apparently never criticized another Cultural Revolution villain, Xie Fuzhi. Xie, who died in 1972 after allegedly being responsible for various persecutions during the Cultural Revolution, was also posthumously expelled from the CCP in 1980. Xie had been a valued subordinate in Deng's Second Field Army, as indicated in the account of Deng's pre-1949 career by his daughter. Deng Maomao [Deng Rong], *Deng Xiaoping, My Father* (New York: Basic Books, 1995), pp. 286, 360, 367, 399, 413, 414, 418, 424. For his part, Xie offered only the most superficial obligatory criticism of Deng in 1966. Interviews with specialist on the Cultural Revolution, January and February 2000.

[42] It is worth noting that Mao initially warned Jiang Qing *et al.* against *forming* "a small faction of four people," and several of his subsequent comments seemed to suggest that he hoped he could dissuade Wang Hongwen in particular from acting as part of such a faction. See below, pp. 192, 211, 231. It is also undoubtedly the case that, by placing the four on the Politburo, Mao enhanced their sense of common interests that was not completely reflected in previous events, although this did not by any means always override their differences.

[43] See the summary of Mao's critical comments concerning the radicals in Hua Guofeng's Political Report to the Eleventh Party Congress in 1977, in *Peking Review* (hereafter *PR*), no. 35 (1977), pp. 26-29. This summary lists two occasions, in December 1974 and May 1975, when Mao used the term, as well as a similar July 1974 reference to "a small faction of four."

[44] While it might be objected that this needlessly accepts official CCP views that in turn reflect a cultural bias toward women in positions of power, there is little evidence to contradict the basic

close to Mao.[45] For his part, Zhang was a true *xiucai*, or high standard Party intellectual of the pre-1966 period, a theorist whose views were taken seriously by Mao since at least 1958, although there apparently was little actual contact between Zhang and the Chairman before the Cultural Revolution. Zhang had also demonstrated considerable political and administrative skills as both a propaganda official before 1966, and then as the main municipal leader in Shanghai during the Cultural Revolution.[46] Yao Wenyuan, while lacking the depth and breadth of Zhang's experience, was also a theorist of some note and sophistication.[47]

In sharp contrast, Wang Hongwen came from the factory floor, albeit as a minor Party official rather than a true worker, with a poor educational background that not only limited his capacity to master Marxism-Leninism, but was also reflected in his overall cultural level, a factor so important to intellectuals like Zhang and Yao.[48] Apart from undoubted tensions resulting from Zhang and Yao (and also Jiang) looking down on the poorly educated Wang, their interactions in Shanghai had been complicated. Early in the Cultural Revolution Wang, who was a shrewd and forceful actor in the revolutionary politics of Shanghai, had thrown the support of his rebel Workers' General Headquarters behind Zhang, providing him, and subsequently the Politburo radicals generally, with what Elizabeth Perry and Li Xun have termed "some claims to a social base," and in turn Wang's organization received Zhang's blessing as the preeminent worker rebel group. But while this mutual support was important for both men in

---

picture. Ironically, some sympathy for Jiang can be found in the portrait by Mao's doctor, Li Zhisui, who, despite deep antipathy, described how her difficult personality and behavior were shaped by being totally dependent on Mao, seeing him infrequently and having to put up with his sexual affairs, being rejected sexually herself by the 1960s, fearing complete abandonment, and having little to do before the Cultural Revolution. See Li, *Private Life*, pp. 140-45. The most sympathetic account by her hand-picked American biographer, Roxane Witke, *Comrade Chiang Ch'ing* (Boston: Little, Brown and Company, 1977), picks up on many of these features and describes Jiang "as a person of extraordinary courage, as a woman leader at a time of transition" (p. 10), but also notes a "fundamentally antagonistic" political style (p. 6).

[45] Elizabeth J. Perry and Li Xun, *Proletarian Power: Shanghai in the Cultural Revolution* (Boulder: Westview Press, 1997), p. 8.

[46] On Mao's 1958 reaction to Zhang's ideas on "bourgeois right," see Bo Yibo, *Ruogan zhongda juece yu shijian de huigu* [Reflections on Certain Major Decisions and Events] (Beijing: Zhonggong zhongyang dangxiao chubanshe, 1993), vol. 2, p. 752. On Zhang's handling of Shanghai during the Cultural Revolution, see Andrew G. Walder, *Chang Ch'un-ch'iao and Shanghai's January Revolution* (Ann Arbor: Michigan Papers in Chinese Studies no. 32, 1978), especially chs. VII-VIII; and Perry and Li, *Proletarian Power*, *passim*. More generally, Mao regarded Zhang as "very capable," considering him a possible replacement for Zhou Enlai or even as a successor to Lin Biao, and thus ultimately to himself. Interviews with senior Party historians, March 1998 and January 2000; and below, p. 18n50.

[47] See Merle Goldman's account of Yao's contributions to the pre-Cultural Revolution ideological debates, "The Chinese Communist Party's 'Cultural Revolution' of 1962-64," in Chalmers Johnson, ed., *Ideology and Politics in Contemporary China* (Seattle: University of Washington Press, 1973), pp. 225-26, 230-32.

[48] See Barnouin and Yu, *Ten Years*, pp. 248-49; and Perry and Li, *Proletarian Power*, pp. 18, 149.

Shanghai politics, there were ample instances of divergent interests and tensions in this local context.[49] One can further speculate that Mao's choice of Wang as his successor by 1972 would have been a blow to Zhang, who apparently had been considered previously.[50] In any case, once posted to Beijing, Wang was out of his depth with the consequences of repeated tension with his fellow radicals and a general unhappiness with life at the Center. Overall, with the other radicals (as well as Politburo members generally) having difficulty with Jiang's personality, there is sufficient evidence of specific past and ongoing conflicts and dislikes to qualify substantially the notion of a tightly cohesive faction.[51] Apart from these conflicts, even stronger evidence comes from the behavior of the "gang" in the period from Mao's death to their arrest in October 1976. As we shall see in Chapter 8, contrary to official assertions that they planned to seize power, the radicals repeatedly differed among themselves and did not develop a coordinated strategy, despite their undoubted common interests as Mao's soldiers for defending the Cultural Revolution.

If the common interests of the "gang of four" did not always produce coordinated action or defuse corrosive tensions, there were similar questions concerning the group's relationship to radicals below the Politburo level. Broad common interests did not generally translate into local activities being orchestrated by the Politburo radicals. Given the organizational dislocation of the period, local rebels largely acted according to their own circumstances with limited direction from Beijing, while clashes of specific interests with the four leaders at the Center were not uncommon. Of particular significance, the "gang" was attuned to Mao's shifting attitudes in ways impossible for lower-level radicals. At the extreme, this required these central politicians to carry out his orders to curb local disorder, as in Wang Hongwen's involvement in the 1975 crackdown on Zhejiang rebels (see Chapter 4). Even more telling for the overall course of elite politics, the Chairman placed great hope in "new radicals," young activists emerging in 1966-68 distinct from Jiang Qing, Zhang Chunqiao and Yao Wenyuan, activists he expected not only to protect the Cultural Revolution, but also to have independent substance. Wang Hongwen was a prototype of this

---

[49] See Perry and Li, *Proletarian Power*, pp. 20-23, 29-30, 34-36, 44-47, 91, 124-25, 129-30, 142-43, 145, 152-54, 160, 163-64, 166.

[50] See Wang Nianyi, *1949-1989 nian de Zhongguo: Dadongluan de niandai* [China 1949-1989: The Years of Great Turmoil] (Henan: Henan renmin chubanshe, 1988), pp. 387-88; Teiwes and Sun, *Tragedy*, p.110n15; and Barnouin and Yu, *Ten Years*, pp. 247-48. The consideration of Zhang apparently happened not long after the Ninth Congress.

[51] For example, Jiang supported an attack on Zhang in early 1968 (see Teiwes and Sun, *Tragedy*, pp. 50-51); Wang supported the "Lin Biao clique" in moves ultimately aimed at Zhang during the 1970 Lushan plenum (*ibid.*, p. 145); and in June 1975 Mao claimed that Jiang had complained to him about Wang ("Tong Deng Xiaoping guanyu piping 'sirenbang' de yici tanhua [jielu]" [Extract from a Talk with Deng Xiaoping concerning Criticizing the "Gang of Four"] [June 1975], in *CRDB*, p. 1.

force, but one who disappointed Mao in large part by failing to establish such an independent identity. As suggested previously, below the Politburo others played important roles, none more so than Mao Yuanxin. Indeed, as we will explore in Chapters 6 and 7, Mao Yuanxin's impact on CCP elite politics in the final year of Mao's life exceeded that of the so-called "gang."

At the center of the elite configuration stood the relationships of Mao, Zhou and Deng. These relationships went back 45 to 50 years,[52] and, as within the top leadership generally, produced a sense of family with all the attendant personal tensions and expectations that overlay political interaction. This was further intensified by Mao's profoundly judgmental nature, his hopes, disappointments and resentments concerning his colleagues. With regard to Zhou, the Chairman's attitude appears to have been shaped by two long-held beliefs: that Zhou was ideologically weak, having adopted the wrong "line" in the early 1930s concerning revolutionary strategy, in 1937-38 when he followed Wang Ming's policies on the anti-Japanese struggle, and in 1956-57 by advocating the cautious economic policies of "opposing rash advance,"[53] but at the same time that he had been totally loyal since the start of the 1940s and possessed vitally important administrative skills. Indeed, Zhou's notorious propensity to self-abasement before the Chairman to demonstrate his loyalty was again on display in late 1973 when Mao asked for 40 to 50 minutes of self-criticism, and the Premier responded with seven hours worth.[54]

Zhou's display emphasized another key feature of the relationship—for all of Mao's ostensible efforts to contain criticism of the Premier during this period, it was the Chairman who launched it in the first place. Indeed, Mao was often truculent in his criticism, for example, asking in December 1973, "Who is colluding with foreigners, who wants to be the emperor?" The result was apparently the worst period of the Premier's life. As we shall see in Chapter 2, the reasons for this attack are complicated, including Mao's anger that Zhou had had continued discussions with Henry Kissinger without consulting him, and his earlier dissatisfaction with foreign affairs work. But arguably, the most important factor was Mao's resentment of Zhou's prestige both domestically (because of his identification with the rehabilitation of old cadres and anti-leftist measures) and internationally (where much foreign commentary credited the Premier with being the architect of the Sino-American rapprochement). A similar jealousy was perhaps manifest when Mao prevented the attendance of foreign dignitaries at

---

[52] In the cases of Mao and Zhou and Zhou and Deng, contact dated from 1924 and 1923 respectively, while Mao and Deng first crossed paths in 1927.

[53] On these matters, see Teiwes with Sun, *Formation*, pp. 7-8, 43-46; and idem, *China's Road to Disaster*, ch. 1 and pp. 73-75, 92, 98-99.

[54] Interview with Party historian specializing on the period, February 1998. For earlier examples of Zhou's abject self-criticism, see Teiwes with Sun, *Formation*, p. 46; and idem, *China's Road to Disaster*, pp. 97-98, 245-46, 249-50, 253-57.

Zhou's memorial service in 1976.[55]

In contrast to his continuous use of Zhou with apparent deep-seated disdain, Mao had long regarded Deng as a favorite, and by the latter 1950s hinted at a future successor role for his colleague, presumably as next in line after Liu Shaoqi.[56] Even during his disenchantment with Deng during the Cultural Revolution as he removed his favorite from power, the Chairman still had a future role in mind for his wayward colleague, as shown in his repeated (at least ten times) declarations distinguishing Deng from Liu.[57] With Lin Biao's demise, and Deng having performed his own self-abasement in appealing to Mao for the opportunity to work, Deng's return was only a matter of time. We examine the process in Chapter 1. Deng's rehabilitation was arguably related to Mao's long-standing attitudes toward Zhou, and Deng's further rise was linked to Mao's new discontent with the Premier, particularly in late 1973 (see Chapter 2). Perhaps the most succinct expression of the Chairman's contrasting attitudes toward Deng and Zhou can be seen in Li Xiannian's comment concerning Wang Hairong and Tang Wensheng: "These two young ladies were bad to Premier Zhou but nice to Deng Xiaoping." Whatever personal tensions existed between the "two ladies" and Zhou, such behavior can only be explained as reflecting the views and carrying out the instructions of "heaven."[58]

In any case, Deng's return to power was a gradual process. He was on

---

[55] Wang Nianyi, *Dadongluan*, p. 471; Zong Daoyi, "1973 nian Zhou Enlai shenbian de shita: yanliang" [The World Turns Cold to Zhou Enlai in 1973], *Zhonghua ernü* [Sons and Daughters of China], October 2001, pp. 10-15; Mao Mao, *"Wenge" suiyue*, pp. 287-88, 439-40; Barnouin and Yu, *Ten Years*, pp. 262-64; idem, *Chinese Foreign Policy during the Cultural Revolution* (London: Kegan Paul International, 1998), pp. 36-39; interview with scholar specializing on Zhou Enlai, March 2001; interview with a well-connected historian of China's foreign affairs, July 1999; and below, p. 436. Zhou's virtual equal seniority in CCP revolutionary history was arguably another source of jealousy, but as we discuss in Chapters 6 and 7, there were larger issues at play concerning the Cultural Revolution at the time of Zhou's death.

[56] In his memoirs, Khrushchev reports that Deng was the only CCP leader about whom Mao was consistently positive, while during the Great Leap Mao referred to himself as the "main marshal" and Deng as "vice marshal." See Strobe Talbott, trans. and ed., *Khrushchev Remembers: The Last Testament* (Boston: Little, Brown and Co., 1974), pp. 252-53; and Teiwes with Sun, *China's Road to Disaster*, p. 149. According to several PRC sources, in the late 1950s Mao explicitly told Khrushchev that Deng would be the "second generation leading core" after Liu. Guo Dehong and Tang Yingwu, eds., *Zhonggong dangshi gaoceng renwu pingzhuan, shang juan* [Critical Biographies of Senior Figures in CCP Party History, Volume 1] (Changchun: Jilin wenshi chubanshe, 2000), p. 45; and Gao Yi, *Lishi xuanze le Deng Xiaoping* [History Chose Deng Xiaoping] (Wuhan: Wuhan chubanshe, 1999), pp. 184-85. See also MacFarquhar, *Origins 3*, pp. 640-41n14.

[57] Wang Li's memoirs of his conversations with Mao, cited in Xue Qingchao, *Lishi zhuanzhe guantou de Deng Xiaoping* [Deng Xiaoping at the Turning Points of History] (Zhengzhou: Zhongyuan nongmin chubanshe, 1996), p. 220. Cf. below, p. 25.

[58] For Li's observation, see *Deng Liqun guoshi jiangtan*, vol. 3, p. 323. A personal grudge by Wang and Tang toward the Premier concerned a 1972 incident when Zhou implemented Mao's order to replace Tang with another interpreter, but the "two ladies" believed it was Zhou's initiative. Barnouin and Yu, *Foreign Policy*, p. 38 (Yu being the pseudonym of a Foreign Affairs Ministry insider); and

something like probation for about eight months after returning to work in March 1973 while Mao observed his behavior, a situation also contributing to Deng's relatively good relations with the radicals in this initial period. Determining Deng's precise role and influence from spring 1973 to October 1974 is difficult due to source limitations,[59] but it appears his duties, probably largely in foreign affairs, were comparatively light to late 1973. But in the context of the harsh criticism of Zhou and the rotation of military region commanders, Deng's role became much more significant with his appointment to the Politburo and the Party's Military Affairs Commission (MAC) in December, although his precise military role in 1974 remains elusive. Some analysts have misinterpreted the undoubted importance of bringing Deng into People's Liberation Army (PLA) affairs by viewing his assignment as necessary to reassure the military and guarantee its cooperation with the reshuffle.[60] As discussed in Chapter 2, the rotation was orchestrated single-handedly by Mao and carried out by Zhou and Ye Jianying, with total obedience from the concerned commanders but no role by Deng.[61] In fact, the rotation set the stage for Mao's agenda of further tightening the screw on the military through the Criticize Lin Biao and Confucius campaign. Little wonder, then, rather than defend the army, the limited evidence indicates that Deng participated in the criticism of PLA leaders, although undoubtedly with different ultimate objectives than those of the radicals. Deng's foreign affairs activities also expanded, most famously in leading China's delegation to the United Nations in April 1974. Meanwhile, he played a growing, if again elusive, role in State Council affairs and economic work.[62] All of this demonstrates increasing prominence in the first half of 1974, but it took a confluence of

---

interview with Foreign Affairs official involved in the incident, November 2002.

[59] Most significantly, the major chronologies of Deng's post-1966 career, *Deng Xiaoping sixiang nianpu (1975-1997)* [Chronology of Deng Xiaoping's Thought, 1975-1997] (Beijing: Zhongyang wenxian chubanshe, 1998), and *Deng Xiaoping nianpu (1975-1997)* [Chronology of Deng Xiaoping, 1975-1997] (2 vols., Beijing: Zhongyang wenxian chubanshe, 2004), start with 1975. Interviews also produced only bits and pieces of information, and data from both written and oral sources on Deng's military role are especially fragmentary. It is further notable that the detailed chronology of Zhou Enlai, *Zhou Enlai nianpu (1949-1976)* [Chronology of Zhou Enlai, 1949-1976] (3 vols., Beijing: Zhongyang wenxian chubanshe, 1997), vol. 3, pp. 585-677, records no personal meetings between the Premier and Deng after their March 1973 encounter to October 1974.

[60] See, e.g., MacFarquhar, "Succession," pp. 290-91. For a somewhat different twist also suggesting Mao's dependence on Deng, see Huang, *Factionalism*, pp. 334-35.

[61] There was, of course, considerable irony in the Premier's role since it was precisely the time when Mao launched a severe attack on Zhou, but it was also consistent with past cases of Zhou micromanaging Mao's policies. Cf. e.g., Zhou's management of the dispersal of senior leaders from Beijing during the war scare of October 1969; Teiwes and Sun, *Tragedy*, p. 113. As for Deng, although there are questionable claims that he proposed the rotation (see below, p. 140n70), there is no evidence of any role in the actual implementation of the transfers.

[62] Mao Mao, *"Wenge" suiyue*, p. 315, provides a rare claim of her father's participation in a variety of economic tasks over the first 18 months after his return to work, but gives no indication of the timing of these assignments, or the division of responsibilities and authority between Deng and Li Xiannian,

factors—Mao's continuing if toned down unhappiness with Zhou, the Premier's permanent hospitalization with terminal cancer in June that necessitated his *de facto* replacement, and the Chairman running out of patience with the political and economic disruptions of summer 1974—to place Deng unambiguously at the center of CCP politics. Deng's October nomination by Mao as First Vice Premier set the stage for his assumption of the top government post in all but name in January 1975.

The Zhou-Deng relationship was also complicated. Despite Deng's claim that he regarded Zhou as an elder brother, this was hyperbole at best. One historian engaged in Zhou Enlai studies rejected such a proposition with a vigorous "no, no." Other oral sources conved a similar, if toned-down sense of so-so relations, observing that, on the one hand, Zhou had played a prominent role in attacking Deng during the early stages of the Cultural Revolution, and, on the other, during the post-Mao period Deng was apparently critical of Zhou's relatively spineless performance during the Cultural Revolution, at least within small circles. Of course, as with all things at Mao's court, the situation was not straightforward. As Deng explicitly acknowledged, Zhou had no choice but to do things against his wishes, and it is clear that the policy preferences of the two men were very compatible. As one source put it, Zhou understood that Mao considered Deng "his man," and that bringing Deng back in 1973 was for the purpose of taking the Premier's place, but at the same time he also understood and appreciated that Deng's thinking was different from the Chairman's.[63]

Whatever the reservations of the two leaders, their relationship involved more than similar policy preferences. Clearly, both men hoped for a post-Mao period in which the power of the radicals was at least marginalized, at best eliminated. Although Zhou was concerned that Deng was insufficiently cautious in pushing consolidation efforts in 1975, he reportedly enjoined Ye Jianying to make sure that

---

the Politburo's ranking economic specialist. Mao Mao reports that both Li and Deng assisted the ill Premier with State Council daily work, but when Zhou entered hospital quarters on June 1, Deng was placed in charge of daily work. See Cheng Zhongyuan and Xia Xingzhen, *Lishi zhuanzhe de qianzou: Deng Xiaoping zai yijiuqiwu* [The Prelude to the Historical Turning Point: Deng Xiaoping in 1975] (Beijing: Zhongguo qingnian chubanshe, 2004), p. 25n1.

[63] *Selected Works of Deng Xiaoping (1975-1982)* (vol. 2, Beijing: Foreign Languages Press, 1984), pp. 329-30; and interviews with historians specializing in Zhou or the period, April 1998, April 1999, and July 1999. See also Philip Short, *Mao: A Life* (New York: Henry Holt, 2000), p. 587. A Hong Kong report, *Zhengming* [Contention], March 1, 1999, pp. 23-26, claims that Deng made some scathing criticisms of Zhou's Cultural Revolution "insincerity and lack of principle" at Party meetings in 1978 and subsequently. When questioned about this, a Party historian felt that such criticisms might be genuine, but they could only have been made in a small circle, not in an open meeting.

Additionally, Henry Kissinger, *Years of Renewal* (New York: Simon & Schuster, 1999), pp. 163-64, notes that in an April 1974 conversation at the United Nations, Deng deliberately distanced himself from Zhou, but this may have been no more than accommodating the political wind of the time. More telling was Deng's post-Mao remark (p. 160) that although Zhou had eased the fate of many during the Cultural Revolution, "he had never actually tried to reverse the policies which had caused the suffering in the first place."

the radicals never seized power.[64] It is plausible, however, that despite his desire to prevent a radical power seizure, Zhou would not have favored a confrontation with them after Mao's death, instead opting for some sort of arrangement that would not have humiliated the Chairman's wife.[65] What the more abrasive Deng, who apparently thought he had been acting with sufficient restraint, would have done in similar circumstances is also a matter for speculation, but he was denied the opportunity as his actions turned Mao against him and led to his dismissal. This left the decision to act against the radicals in the hands of Hua Guofeng who, contrary to the general view, acted decisively to effect their arrest, a "quick and clean" solution that Deng could only applaud from the sidelines.[66]

These, then, were the main actors during the twists and turns of leadership politics in Mao's last years. In the following pages we examine in detail how the various players acted within the broad constraints described above. To repeat our main argument, to an extraordinary, even astonishing degree, the Chairman dominated this process even as his very life ebbed, and with it his capacity for detailed control. He was indeed "heaven" for all elite actors in 1972-76.

---

[64] *Zhou nianpu*, vol. 3, p. 724. Although some sources place Zhou's remark in December 1975, the authoritative *Zhou nianpu* only indicates that it occurred sometime during that year. On Zhou's worries about Deng's insufficient caution, according to a specialist on Zhou, the Premier kept urging Deng to do things in a more skillful way; interview, March 2001. It is also of interest that very few expressly hostile statements by Zhou concerning the radicals have been reported in the voluminous post-Mao material on the Premier. In any case, his concerns notwithstanding, in September 1975 Zhou told Deng that he had done a better job in 1975 than Zhou himself earlier. *Zhou nianpu*, vol. 3 p. 721.

[65] This was precisely the view of some officials close to Zhou who, in conversations with American diplomat Stapleton Roy during the early post-Mao period, concluded that it was good that Zhou was no longer around at the time of Mao's death since, as a compromiser by nature, he would have been unlikely to take decisive action against the "gang." Interview with Ambassador Roy, June 1999.

[66] For Deng's praise of the "quick and clean solution," see Wu De, "Guanyu fensui 'sirenbang'," p. 64.

Chapter 1

COMING TO TERMS WITH LIN BIAO: "ULTRA-LEFT" AND "ULTRA-RIGHT" ON THE ROAD TO THE TENTH PARTY CONGRESS, 1972-73

In our country there are people who curse us, saying we are completely leftist. Which people are our "leftist faction"? They are those who wanted to knock down the Premier today, Chen Yi tomorrow, Ye Jianying the next day. This so-called "left" faction is now in jail. For several years there was chaos under heaven, fighting in various places throughout the nation, widespread civil war. The two sides fired guns, all together one million guns. This army faction supported this faction, that army faction supported that faction, [all] fighting. Power was seized by that "left" faction. ... The chief backstage backer [of the "left" faction] is now no longer with us, [he is] Lin Biao.

> —Mao Zedong on Lin Biao as the Cultural Revolution's "leftist" chieftain during a meeting with the Sri Lankan Prime Minister, June 28, 1972[1]

In July 1967 Mao Zedong had a private talk with me alone in Wuhan. I reported to the Chairman, "You've said many times that Liu and Deng must be distinguished, but now the slogan is 'Down with Liu, Deng, [and] Tao [Zhu]'." Mao Zedong immediately answered: "Liu Shaoqi and Deng Xiaoping are different. Xiaoping can administratively (*wen*) match Shaoqi and Zhou Enlai, and militarily (*wu*) he can match Lin Biao and Peng Dehuai. If Lin Biao's health doesn't hold out, then it will be Deng Xiaoping who comes forward."

> —Wang Li, a younger radical from the Central Cultural Revolution Group, recalling in 1991 a conversation with Mao at the height of the Cultural Revolution[2]

[At the time of the Tenth Party Congress], Chairman Mao placed his hopes on the comrades of the Politburo, especially Wang Hongwen, Zhang Chunqiao, Jiang Qing and Yao Wenyuan. I remember that not long after the Tenth Congress, Chairman Mao summoned us to [his] swimming pool residence [in Zhongnanhai] for a talk. He called on the Politburo to assist them. At that time, Chairman Mao pointed out the window to some green vegetables in the vegetable patch: "[Cultivate them] just like [those vegetables] are growing."

> —Wu De's recollection of Mao at the time of the Tenth Congress[3]

Lin Biao's attempt to flee the country and his resulting death on September 13, 1971, came as a shock to the people of China, to Party officials from the basic levels to the Politburo, and to Mao Zedong. For the people and cadres of China, as they gradually became aware of the "incident" over the following months,[4] the affair raised doubts not only about "Chairman Mao's best student and successor," but also concerning the Cultural Revolution which saw Lin's elevation, and the Chairman himself. If the Cultural Revolution had been hard to understand, the great majority seemingly accepted its premise, or at least the legitimacy of the regime which had inflicted it upon them. The Lin Biao incident shattered that illusion for many, leading people to at least question Mao's judgment, or to conclude bitterly that it was all a power struggle among the highest rulers.[5] Politburo members and other high-ranking officials were equally shocked, even those who had been aware of Mao's mounting displeasure with Lin since the Lushan Central Committee plenum in summer 1970. As for Mao, a senior Party historian is undoubtedly on the mark in concluding that despite his developing distrust of Lin, the Chairman would not have expected an act of betrayal as when Lin boarded the fatal flight that crashed in the Mongolian desert.[6]

In the following section we examine the devastating physical and emotional impact of Lin's perceived betrayal on Mao, as well as his and the leadership's immediate responses. Here the broader political impact of the incident deserves initial comment. Since the Ninth Congress, Mao had placed the CCP on a road of winding down the Cultural Revolution and correcting its excesses. This was, to be sure, a limited course correction, but the direction was clear. While we doubt the speculation of a Party historian that without the Lin Biao incident the

---

[1] Chen and Du, *Shilu*, vol. 3, part 2, pp. 834-35. Zhou Enlai, along with Tang Wensheng and Wang Hairong, was present at the meeting.

[2] Ji Xichen, *Shi wu qianli de niandai yi wei "Renmin ribao" lao jizhe de biji* [An Unprecedented Era: The Notes of an Old *People's Daily* Reporter] (2 vols., Beijing: *Renmin ribao* chubanshe, 2001), p. 626.

[3] Wu De, "Guanyu fensui 'sirenbang'," p. 52.

[4] It took more than three weeks after his demise before Lin's name and image were completely removed from the PRC media, and his death was officially announced only in July 1972. Starting shortly after the event, various levels of the CCP from the top down were informed of the bare outline of what had happened as the top leadership struggled to provide a coherent story. In December 1971 and January 1972, the first two batches of material on Lin's case were distributed within the Party, with a third batch to follow in July 1972.

[5] The importance of the Lin Biao incident in undermining the credibility of the regime and Mao is clear from many discussions with Party historians, intellectuals, ordinary cadres and other citizens. Cf. An Jianshe, "Gaoju pipan jizuo sichao de qizhi" [Hold High the Banner of Criticizing the Ultra-left Ideological Trend], in idem, ed., *Zhou Enlai de zuihou suiyue 1966-1976* [Zhou Enlai's Last Years, 1966-1976] (Beijing: Zhongyang wenxian chubanshe, 2002), pp. 197-98. For a brief discussion of regime legitimacy, including during the "Cultural Revolution decade," see Frederick C. Teiwes, "The Chinese State during the Maoist Era," in David Shambaugh, ed., *The Modern Chinese State* (Cambridge: Cambridge University Press, 2000), pp. 157-59.

[6] An Jianshe, "Pipan jizuo sichao," p. 198.

Cultural Revolution might simply have faded away, his observation that the affair introduced new complexities into the situation is valid. Mao, wrongly and disingenuously attributing the excesses of the Cultural Revolution to Lin, but rightly recognizing the threat of those excesses to his larger objective, now initiated or endorsed more flexible policies and more far-reaching attacks on "left" deviations than those carried out earlier after the Ninth Congress and particularly after he first criticized Lin at the Lushan plenum. On the other hand, as his biographers observe, Mao was aware that "after the Lin Biao incident many people developed basic doubts about the 'Cultural Revolution'," not to mention the Chairman's own credibility, and as a result he became "very concerned with how the [movement] would be viewed in the future" and determined to defend its essential validity. These two considerations, while theoretically compatible, resulted in increased tension as *both* aspects took on new salience, each backed by forces with a history of conflict within the Politburo.[7]

In this chapter, after reviewing the initial reaction to Lin's demise, we address the key developments of the early post-Lin Biao period beginning with the more far-reaching attack on "left" deviations—i.e., on a so-called "ultra-left ideological trend" (*jizuo sichao*), an attack that dominated throughout most of 1972, and still had significant influence in the first half of 1973. Key aspects of this effort were rectifying problems in economic construction and cadre policy, in the latter case by accelerating the rehabilitation of veteran revolutionaries ousted in 1966-68. In December 1972, however, Mao redefined Lin's essential deviations as "ultra-rightist" (*jiyou*) in nature, leading to a revival of praise of the "new born things" of the Cultural Revolution and criticism of revisionism as the main task. After examining the politics of the shift from the "ultra-left" to "ultra-right" definitions of Lin's essence, we discuss the most significant rehabilitation of an old revolutionary, that of Deng Xiaoping. This is followed by an analysis of the major organizational developments of the period—the effort to restore the Party and reassert its role as the key coordinating organization of the regime, the further revival of state bureaucratic organs, the reappearance of official mass organizations, and the linked gradual withdrawal of the PLA from civilian affairs. Particularly notable was the creation of an urban militia under civilian Party control, a force that would play a significant if usually exaggerated role in elite politics. We next turn to the crucial, largely overlooked, role of foreign affairs in leadership politics preceding the August 1973 Tenth Party Congress. Finally, we examine the process leading to the Congress and its outcomes, notably a strong reaffirmation of the Cultural Revolution, a continuation of the mixed personnel policy of rehabilitating veteran cadres and promoting youth, and the confirmation of Wang Hongwen as the presumptive future successor.

---

[7] *Mao zhuan*, vol. 2, p. 1644; An Jianshe, "Pipan jizuo sichao," pp. 199-200; and interview, December 2003. According to An Jianshe (p. 207), at the time of the Ninth Congress Mao observed that the Cultural Revolution had entered its concluding stage.

These events have been analyzed elsewhere, although usually in condensed form and seldom addressing the significance of the foreign affairs question. How does our interpretation of developments up to the Tenth Congress differ from what has been generally accepted? While there is enough diversity in the limited existing literature to warn against characterizing any particular view as conventional wisdom, there nevertheless are two generally accepted propositions. First, that Zhou was the driving force of the attack on "ultra-leftism," making 1972 "Zhou Enlai's year."[8] Second, that the Premier's brief dominance was a new stage in an ongoing struggle with the Politburo radicals that allowed him to damage their cause, but also led to their counterattack and a new political balance in 1973.[9] What of Mao in all this? Most accounts paint the Chairman as relatively passive in the attack on "ultra-leftism," endorsing rather than initiating Zhou's efforts, a view stated forcefully by senior Party historian Liao Gailong in 1980: "Following Lin Biao's death ... [Mao] allowed [Zhou to restore the Party's traditions, liberate cadres, rehabilitate and revive the national economy]."[10] As for the shift in emphasis from criticizing the "ultra-left" to opposing the "ultra-right," Mao is given a much more central, albeit reactive, role in responding to the urgings of Jiang Qing and Zhang Chunqiao, and concluding that the anti-leftist tide had gone too far.[11] As our subsequent analysis will demonstrate, while there is something in these accepted understandings, they underestimate Mao's impact, and do not adequately capture the elite politics of the period.

Before examining specific events, some general observations concerning the preceding issues are in order. First, it is undeniable that in 1972 Zhou Enlai played a more critical role in CCP elite politics than ever before. Apart from his driving role in various policies, for the first time since 1949 Mao placed Zhou in charge of the Party Center, and together with his close relationship to Ye Jianying, who was simultaneously given responsibility for the PLA, Zhou now had enormous influence over all three traditional pillars of regime authority—the Party, State Council and army. Indeed, if Mao's doctor is to be believed, during his health crisis of early 1972, a despairing Chairman commented to Zhou that if he could not make it, "everything [will] depend on you."[12] Yet Mao, not Zhou, determined

---

[8] See MacFarquhar, "Succession," pp. 282-83. Cf. the more extreme account of Dittmer, *Continuous Revolution*, pp. 124-25, who speaks of Zhou as guiding 18 months of an "engineering" policy approach after Mao abdicated in his favor.

[9] A forceful expression of this view is William A. Joseph, *The Critique of Ultra-Leftism in China, 1958-1981* (Stanford: Stanford University Press, 1984), ch. 5. In contrast, Dittmer, *Continuous Revolution*, p. 124, argues that Zhou and the radicals joined ranks in the initial post-Lin period.

[10] Liao Kai-lung [Liao Gailong], "Historical Experiences and Our Road of Development" (October 25, 1980), trans. in *Issues & Studies* (hereafter *IS*), November 1981, p. 98. Liao went on to say that Mao soon became vexed with Zhou's efforts, reversed them, and subsequently launched the campaign against Lin Biao and Confucius in order to oppose Zhou.

[11] See MacFarquhar, "Succession," p. 283.

[12] Li Zhisui, *Private Life*, p. 551. On this source, see above, p. 11n24.

CCP policy concerning leftist practices: criticism of such practices predated the Premier's enhanced role, and attacks on left phenomena continued after the diminution of Zhou's power at the end of 1972. Zhou remained utterly dependent on Mao while the Chairman lived. As Party historian An Jianshe observed, the Premier's efforts in the struggle against "ultra-leftism," "cannot be separated from Mao Zedong's understandings at the time."[13] Zhou's dependence on Mao can be seen in two striking developments in 1972. One concerned something all too familiar in Zhou's career—several sessions of self-criticisms in May and June 1972. In contrast to various past and several future cases, these were not offered when the Premier was under attack. In fact, his typically excessive self-criticisms allowed him to rebut long-standing rumors that, under the alias of Wu Hao, he had deserted the Party in the early 1930s. Party leaders—as was also the case with Jiang Qing and Zhang Chunqiao—were deeply vulnerable to suspicions of betrayal during the revolutionary struggle, the type of charge that was used falsely, with Zhou's complicity, to expel Liu Shaoqi from the Party in 1968. In this case, by authorizing Zhou's self-criticism, Mao allowed the Premier to clarify the circumstances of this threatening issue, and then banned further discussion of it. But the larger lesson was clear: it was Mao, and Mao alone, who could provide such an opportunity, but in a context where self-examination of one's faults was mandatory—something carried out to excess by the Premier even at the time of his greatest clout.[14]

An even more remarkable example of Zhou's own perception of his utter dependence on Mao was a virtually unknown incident during Nixon's groundbreaking visit to China in February 1972. Again, this was not only a time when Zhou exercised great authority, but it also concerned a sphere where Zhou's value to Mao was at an all-time high. The matter in question was Nixon's arrival in Beijing and the famous handshake between the President and Premier. The point at issue is that the photograph of the handshake which appeared in the *People's Daily* the next day was, in one significant respect, faked. In that photo the trailing interpreter, who in fact was Ji Chaozhu, was replaced by the image of Wang Hairong, Mao's niece and one of the "two ladies." This substitution puzzled people in the Ministry of Foreign Affairs, and remained a source of speculation and contention over the following three decades. The enemies of the "two ladies" concluded that they had somehow brought about the switch, but it is virtually certain that this was the work of Zhou Enlai. Not only would it have taken someone of Zhou's status to bring about such a switch, but it was the Premier's practice to vet all photos and film of such occasions. The interpretation

---

[13] An Jianshe, "Pipan jizuo sichao," p. 207.

[14] See *Zhou nianpu*, vol. 3, p. 529; Chen and Du, *Shilu*, vol. 3, part 2, p. 828; Gao Wenqian, *Wannian Zhou*, pp. 374-77; and Yan Jiaqi and Gao Gao, *Turbulent Decade: A History of the Cultural Revolution*, trans. and ed. by D. W. K. Kwok (Honolulu: University of Hawaii Press, 1996), pp. 145-47. Li Fuchun and others reportedly urged Zhou not to make so many self-criticisms, to no avail. See Quan Yanchi, *Zouxia shengtan de Zhou Enlai* [Zhou Enlai Down to Earth] (Hong Kong: Tiandi tushu youxian gongsi, 1993), pp. 367-68.

of this strange event, we believe, is inescapable: in highlighting a member of the Chairman's family, Zhou was trying to send a message that Mao was the architect of this momentous development. How widely that message was understood is another matter, but the Premier undoubtedly hoped it would be read that way by Mao. That Zhou would be concerned with such a detail at a time of both his greatest powers and one of the pivotal events in PRC foreign policy speaks volumes.[15]

As throughout his last years, Mao's dominance, together with his emphasis on unity, also constrained conflict within the Politburo. Simply put, leadership conflict had to stop short of explicit attacks, except when stipulated by the Chairman. It is clear that at no point during his control of Party and government affairs in 1972 did Zhou confront the radicals. As Mao's biographers put it, the Premier knew the struggle was complex and his method was to avoid direct conflict with Jiang Qing et al.[16] This, of course, did not obviate significant gains for Zhou in terms of preferred policy directions and enhanced organizational clout, or corresponding setbacks for the radicals. But it meant the radicals' official status was untouched; they still had scope to raise objections, and, in specific areas, to exert real authority. Moreover, whenever the Chairman shifted his view, their influence could increase dramatically. Yet while Jiang Qing apparently always had greater leeway to criticize Zhou than vice versa,[17] the radicals were also inhibited. Thus, as we shall see, when the radicals raised the critical issue of the definition of Lin Biao's sins at the end of 1972, for all their passion and political self-interest, they approached the matter with a certain delicacy until Mao spoke. In contrast, when Zhou came under direct and harsh attack in summer 1973 for alleged foreign affairs errors, the initiative came from Mao himself. This, then, was the political context from the death of Lin Biao to the Tenth Party Congress.

---

[15] A lesser factor might have been a desire to curry favor with the "two ladies" who were becoming increasingly important in their liaison role, and had Mao's ear. The photo appeared in Renmin ribao (hereafter RMRB) [People's Daily], February 22, 1972, p. 1. A film of the same event clearly shows Ji Chaozhu behind Zhou; in any case, Wang Hairong, unlike Tang Wensheng, had very poor English at best and would not have been assigned such a critical role. The incident was first brought to our attention by a Foreign Ministry insider in an interview, November 2002. Zhou's review of photos and film of such events was confirmed by a leading Party history authority on Zhou (interview, December 2002), while the referral of photographs to the Premier on the specific occasion was recounted in the memoirs of the official photographer. See Du Xiuxian, Hongjingtou—Zhongnanhai sheying shiyan zhong de guoshi fengyun [Red Camera—National Affairs Storms in the Eyes of a Zhongnanhai Photographer] (Shenyang: Liaoning renmin chubanshe, 1998), vol. 1, pp. 290-92.

[16] Mao zhuan, vol. 2, p. 1647.

[17] Cf. Mao's restriction on Deng Xiaoping concerning criticism of Jiang Qing; above, p. 14. Concerning criticism of Zhou, according to an authoritative CCP source, there was an understanding that Jiang was free to criticize the Premier as long as he worked. Interview, April 1986. While overstated in our view, there is nevertheless a certain credibility in this claim given Mao's attitude toward and treatment of Zhou.

Responding to the Lin Biao Crisis

The shock and uncertainty created by the Lin Biao affair were manifested in various ways within the high-ranking elite. One indication was the infrequency of appearances by leaders, major editorials, reported national conferences and provincial Party committee meetings, while important official occasions were either not observed or celebrated in an unprecedented low-key manner. Thus not only was the normal grand parade cancelled and replaced by lesser festivities in Beijing's parks on National Day immediately following Lin's demise in 1971, but the same procedure was followed for May Day and National Day in 1972 and 1973 as well.[18] The limited number of editorials reflected uncertainty over what to tell the public, and little by way of a clear ideological overview was presented.[19] Meanwhile, the leadership grappled with providing a coherent explanation of the Lin affair within the Party. Early characterizations of Lin as a "bourgeois ambitionist," who manipulated the cult of Mao and engaged in "organizational sectarianism" in the PLA, were soon joined by accusations of a plot for a military coup and plans to assassinate the Chairman, as well as claims of Mao-Lin conflict since at least the Ninth Congress.[20] Subsequently, of course, these matters were joined by questions of Lin's ideological orientation, whether it was "ultra-left" or "ultra-right." Apart from the general uncertainty enveloping the top elite, the disorientation of individual leaders in the wake of the Lin Biao incident was also apparent. Zhou Enlai was a case in point. Apparently unnerved by Lin's abortive attempt to flee the country, before his own flights the Premier would carefully check the flight plans and then anxiously peer out of the plane's window to make sure it was on course and not heading toward a forbidden destination.[21]

The most telling disorientation was that of Mao. Contrary to what one would expect had Mao just won an ongoing power struggle with his deputy, the

[18] See *Mao zhuan*, vol. 2, p. 1605; Thomas W. Robinson, "China in 1972: Socio-Economic Progress Amidst Political Uncertainty," *Asian Survey* (hereafter *AS*), January 1973, pp. 10-11; and idem, "China in 1973: Renewed Leftism Threatens the 'New Course'," *AS*, January 1974, p. 7. While the parades were not resumed during the remainder of Mao's life, on National Day in 1974 and 1975 receptions were held bringing together most of the leadership, as opposed to the leaders being dispersed to various parks.

[19] The lack of a clear line can be seen in the 1972 *RMRB* New Year editorial which spent nearly half its space on international affairs and presented a smorgasbord of Mao quotes on domestic matters, while in July *Hongqi* (hereafter *HQ*) [Red Flag], the Central Committee's theoretical journal, commented on the "bewilderment" affecting people during the current struggle. *PR*, no. 1 (1972), pp. 8-11; and Robinson, "China in 1972," p. 10.

[20] See Harry Harding, Jr., "China: The Fragmentation of Power," *AS*, January 1972, p. 13; and Robinson, "China in 1972," pp. 7-10.

[21] See the recollections of Zhou's pilot, Zhu Ruiai, "Wo wei Zongli fei zhuanji" [I Flew the Premier's Charter Plane], in Cheng Hua, ed., *Zhou Enlai he ta de mishumen* [Zhou Enlai and His Secretaries] (Beijing: Zhongguo guangbo dianshi chubanshe, 1992), p. 481. According to Li Zhisui, *Private Life*, p. 549, another top leader, Kang Sheng, was clinically depressed after the Lin Biao incident.

Chairman was reportedly initially temperamental and then certainly depressed after Lin's demise. Perhaps most authoritative, Mao's biographers describe the Lin Biao affair as a blow to his spirit and health, with his depression seemingly contributing to the major health crisis of early 1972. Mao was withdrawn for much of 1972, rarely speaking, something that in all likelihood should only partially be attributed to his health.[22] To the extent he "allowed" Zhou Enlai to push opposition to "ultra-leftism," this emotional disorientation was undoubtedly a factor, although probably not the main one. There was also, as we shall see, an element of remorse over how various veteran revolutionaries had been treated in the Cultural Revolution, even though Mao could not quite accept his own responsibility. Moreover, according to one frequent visitor to the Chairman throughout this last period of his life, the impact of September 13 meant an emotional change extending beyond 1972. In this person's view, the Lin Biao incident was a turning point mentally as well as physically, in that from this point on Mao was more suspicious, felt totally isolated, was very emotional, and "not normal at all."[23] While perhaps overstated, Mao was prone to tears and upset, an emotional fragility that undoubtedly added to the difficulty of anticipating his reactions.

Before examining the reactions of Mao and the leadership in greater detail, it is necessary to review briefly the true nature of Lin Biao's rise and fall, and contrast it to the story pieced together by the regime in 1971-72 and more or less maintained to this day. While we have not undertaken detailed research on Lin Biao since our study a decade ago, new PRC material and the rare outside scholarly study essentially confirm our earlier findings.[24] Bluntly put, the official version is a gross distortion, and in key respects a fabrication, the worst ever concocted by CCP historiography. Gross distortions concern Lin's alleged plans for a military coup and Mao's assassination. Although many uncertainties remain, it appears that in early 1971 a group of young officers around Lin's son, Lin Liguo, at most considered some responses, including military action, to Mao's increasingly

---

[22] See *Mao zhuan*, vol. 2, pp. 1610ff. While there is little doubt concerning Mao's depression, an oral source goes further and claims that, at the time of Lin's flight, Mao initially refused to believe it, and, when the matter was confirmed, lashed out at Zhou Enlai and Jiang Qing for "cheating" him with exalted praise similar to that which Lin had used. An exceptionally temperamental Chairman then dismissed his work staff and had to be calmed down by his daughters and his secretary, Zhang Yufeng. Interview, September 1994.

[23] Interview, November 2002.

[24] The most relevant PRC materials on the Lin Biao affair are analyses by Wang Nianyi, He Shu, Jin Chunming, Yu Ruxin and Chen Xiaoya. These works can be found in Ding Kaiwen, ed., *Chongshen Lin Biao zuian* [The Lin Biao Case Reassessed] (New York: Mingjing chubanshe, 2004). The most important scholarly study since our 1996 book is Jin Qiu, *The Culture of Power: The Lin Biao Incident in the Cultural Revolution* (Stanford: Stanford University Press, 1999). The virtue and limitation of this study are that Jin, the daughter of Lin Biao "clique member" General Wu Faxian, was able to provide detailed inside information, but from the perspective of her family's desire to absolve Wu.

relentless pursuit of Lin, but without Lin's knowledge. Similarly, in the last days before September 13, Lin Liguo apparently canvassed the assassination option, again probably without his father's awareness. Indeed, it is plausible that Lin's actual act of betrayal—his fleeing China—was in fact against his will and effected by his family while he was groggy from sleeping tablets. Lin's wife, Ye Qun, and Lin Liguo clearly panicked at a time when Mao had indicated that he wanted to confront Lin, but Lin's own involvement in the "September 13 incident" seems marginal at best. Moreover, there is little to suggest any serious planning for either a military takeover or a threat on Mao's life by the young hotheads around Lin Liguo.[25]

Whatever may have happened in the last months of Lin Biao's life, a more fundamental distortion, one repeated in much Western scholarship, concerns the nature of Lin's objectives and role during his period as Mao's successor. According to this view, Lin was an ambitious politician who strongly pushed radical Cultural Revolution policies, but who, by seeking to strengthen army power, subsequently ran afoul of a threatened Chairman, leading to a bitter power struggle. Thus ideologically Lin was the "ultra-leftist" politician claimed by the CCP in 1972. In reality, however, Lin was a leader in poor health fundamentally uninterested in political power, which he described as a "tiger" not to be ridden, and he tried to avoid elevation to the successor role, but could not resist Mao's demand. Rather than being a leading proponent of Cultural Revolution extremism, on the rare occasions he expressed his own views, they were for moderation and national development. In this respect, Lin was a "rightist"—although hardly the "ultra-rightist" officially proclaimed in 1973. To the extent that our views have altered since our earlier analysis, it lies here: we are even more convinced that Lin disapproved of the Cultural Revolution, but this was an attitude he held privately. Lin's basic strategy was to avoid engagement, to mouth excessive praise of Mao, to "do no more than follow in [the Chairman's] wake," and, as he advised a close colleague [Tao Zhu], "be passive, passive and again passive." Throughout these difficult years, Lin maintained mutually respectful relations with Zhou Enlai, but experienced difficult and sometimes abrasive encounters with Jiang Qing,

---

[25] Teiwes and Sun, *Tragedy*, pp. 1-2, 3n7, 5, 39, 152n100, 155-56, 160; Sun Wanguo [Warren Sun], "Gu you Dou'e, jin you Lin Biao" [There Was Dou'e in the Past, There Is Lin Biao in the Present], *Mingbao yuekan* [Ming Pao Monthly], no. 7 (1996); Jin Chongji, ed., *Zhou Enlai zhuan, 1949-1976* [Biography of Zhou Enlai, 1949-1976] (2 vols., Beijing: Zhongyang wenxian chubanshe, 1998), vol. 2, p. 1037; and interview with senior military historians, March 1998 and January 2005. For the orthodox account of the coup and assassination plots, which actually suggests how haphazard any such plotting was, see Yan and Gao, *Turbulent Decade*, pp. 314-17, 322-26. The emphasis on a military coup in the CCP account was apparently derived from Mao's assertion, after hearing a report that a scrap of paper with the numbers "571" was recovered from the crash site of a helicopter carrying some of Lin Liguo's associates, that "571 [which can be a homonym for 'military uprising'] is the most crucial piece." *Wu De koushu: shinian fengyu wangshi—wo zai Beijing gongzuo de yixie jingli* [Wu De's Oral Account: Past Events during the Ten Years' Storm—Some Experiences from My Work in Beijing] (Beijing: Dangdai Zhongguo chubanshe, 2004), p. 139.

especially after the Ninth Congress. Indeed, the crisis at the Lushan plenum derived from tensions between Jiang and the civilian radicals around her on the one hand, and the central PLA command and Ye Qun on the other. Lin's fatal mistake was to allow himself to be drawn into this dispute which resulted in Mao deciding in favor of Jiang, and then saw him launch a year-long critique of Lin and his associates. Rather than counterattack, Lin repeatedly sought the opportunity to explain himself to Mao. But the Chairman, much as in the case of Deng Xiaoping five years later, rebuffed the approaches of a long-standing favored subordinate.[26]

Lin Biao had indeed been, along with Deng Xiaoping, the most favored of the Chairman's colleagues.[27] This probably goes some way toward explaining Mao's reported initial refusal to accept that Lin had fled, and then his forgiving attitude toward those who had been "taken in" by Lin, even ordering that Lin's secretaries should be given new work. Of course, whatever Mao may have truly thought of Lin after his "betrayal," this posture had the advantage of claiming that he too had been deceived, and Lin's (real and imagined) transgressions had nothing to do with him. Thus on November 14, to a delegation from the Chengdu region, Mao not only suggested that no one could have known that Lin was a counterrevolutionary, he also blamed the harsh attacks on the so-called "February adverse current" in 1967 on Lin. In fact, Lin may have sought to ameliorate the situation, and he only joined in the attack once Mao's anger with the marshals and vice premiers who had objected to Cultural Revolution excesses became obvious, but now Mao claimed that "at the time I wasn't clear [on the matter]." Similarly, at the end of December, when a high-ranking officer of his security detail, Zhang Yaoci, tried to make a self-criticism concerning his relations with Lin Biao and Ye Qun, the Chairman replied, "You didn't know about Lin Biao, neither did I."[28] Whatever Mao's precise motivation at the time—seemingly some combination of resentment that a cherished colleague had betrayed him, the political need to deny knowledge and culpability for the excesses of the Cultural Revolution, the refusal to admit to himself that he might be at fault for those excesses, and genuine remorse over some of the suffering endured by old comrades during the movement—the situation now created the opportunity to blame Lin for all the shortcomings of the previous five years. In any case, all of this was conducive to applying the "ultra-left" label to his dead comrade.

In the briefings that followed September 13, Zhou Enlai and Mao took leading roles. With Zhou presumably managing the process, "high-ranking cadres" were

---

[26] See Teiwes and Sun, *Tragedy*, pp. 1, 6-9, 46-55, 134ff, 152ff and *passim*; Guan Weixun, *Wo suo zhidao de Ye Qun* [Ye Qun according to My Knowledge] (Beijing: Zhongguo wenxue chubanshe, 1993), pp. 242-43; and below, pp. 413-15.

[27] See Teiwes, "Mao and His Lieutenants," pp. 63-65.

[28] See *Mao zhuan*, vol. 2, pp. 1608-1609; and above, p. 32n22. On actual developments concerning the "February adverse current," see Teiwes and Sun, *Tragedy*, pp. 75-79.

informed of Lin's demise on September 18, and the news was transmitted to the prefecture and PLA division levels on the 28th. The Chairman spoke to small audiences on apparently three occasions before the end of the year. Apart from claiming that few could have known Lin's evil nature, and that he certainly had not, Mao argued Lin had taken no heed of his warnings concerning Cultural Revolution excesses such as pushing the cult too far and attacking other PLA marshals, that the few plotters must be distinguished from those simply confused by Lin's status, and the appropriate policy toward those making mistakes was the traditional "save the patient" approach. Although Mao apparently did not use the term "leftist," apart from a clear inference that Lin was acting in a "leftist" manner in his alleged July 1966 letter to Jiang Qing that was now fabricated and released, this was clearly the gist of the specific mistakes cited by the Chairman. The situation was not so clear, however. As the story of the military coup emerged, it was difficult to categorize such an alleged act as "left" or "right." Moreover, when the partially fabricated "571" coup outline was circulated internally, first in November and then more widely in January, it included probably genuine attacks on Cultural Revolution policies that could only be seen as coming from the "right." It was these aspects, we believe, that hardened Mao's perception of Lin as a rightist opponent of the Cultural Revolution, even though he would endorse the leftist interpretation for the time being. From the outset, when the notebook on which the "571" document was based was discovered shortly after September 13, Ji Dengkui opposed distribution, but this was seemingly unrelated to the ideological cast of the document. Instead, Ji objected to the unflattering picture of Mao it contained, a cursing of the Chairman that should not get exposure. In any case, Mao overruled Ji's concern, and ordered the document's release.[29]

Inevitably, a new power equation quickly emerged after September 13. Not only had the successor perished in the Mongolian desert, but Ye Qun, another Politburo member as well as Lin's wife, was also killed. Beyond this, four additional close associates of Lin, all Politburo members and heads of

---

[29] See *Mao zhuan*, vol. 2, pp. 1605-10; Ma Qibin *et al.*, eds., *Zhongguo Gongchandang zhizheng sishinian (1949-1989)* [The CCP's Forty Years in Power, 1949-1989] (revised ed., Beijing: Zhonggong dangshi chubanshe, 1991), pp. 344, 346; and Wu De, "Lushan huiyi he Lin Biao shijian" [The Lushan Conference and the Lin Biao Affair], *DDZGSYJ*, no. 2 (1995), p. 56. On Mao's 1966 letter, see Teiwes and Sun, *Tragedy*, pp. 58, 60-63; Chen Xiaoya, "Mao Zedong gei Jiang Qing de xin zhenwei bian" [Is Mao's Letter to Jiang Qing Authentic or Fake?], in Ding Kaiwen, *Chongshen Lin Biao zuian*, pp. 614-20; and Jin Chunming, *Jin Chunming zixuan wenji* [Jin Chunming's Self-selected Collected Works] (Chengdu: Sichuan renmin chubanshe, 2002), pp. 124-27.

Concerning the "571" materials, our assessment is that no such document had been prepared by Lin Liguo *et al.*, and that those sections dealing with detailed coup plans were apparent fabrications. However, it is likely that much of the content directed at Mao personally and the Cultural Revolution did derive from discussions among Lin Liguo and associates, and that these sections were constructed on the basis of interrogations of the surviving members of the group, as well as from the notebook discovered after September 13.

PLA service arms or operational departments—Huang Yongsheng, Wu Faxian, Li Zuopeng and Qiu Huizuo—were soon arrested, although the lack of clarity concerning their culpability was indicated by the initial leniency in dealing with them, including Mao's conciliatory remark that they were old comrades who should be allowed mistakes, as well as by the fact that none of the so-called "four generals" were charged with plotting a coup at their 1980-81 trial.[30] Thus in one fell swoop more than a quarter of the Politburo and the core of the central military command had been eliminated. Beyond that, the need to identify and purge the "remnants" of Lin Biao's "clique" was a particular concern to Mao, but given the "save the patient" rectification emphasis and the recognition that people could easily be "deceived," the process was conducted cautiously in central and provincial organs over the next two years.[31] But the immediate task was to fill the gaping holes at the highest levels.

As already emphasized, Zhou Enlai was the lynchpin of the new arrangement. This was inevitable given his Party status, wide public prestige, administrative talent, demonstrated trustworthiness in the detailed implementation of Mao's plans over many years, and his vital role in the Chairman's foreign policy objectives with the crucial rapprochement with the United States in progress. Thus Zhou was given formal responsibility for the Party Center at the start of October, if indeed he had not already been exercising it on a *de facto* basis since September 13 or even earlier.[32] At the same time, his control over the State Council was enhanced. Although Premier throughout 1966-71 and playing a key role in governmental affairs, his authority had been diluted by factionalism within ministries, and then by the imposition of "military representatives" to bring a semblance of order to these bureaucracies. It would be no easy task to regain control from both radical factions and PLA representatives, but Zhou moved quickly to strengthen his hand at the top. On October 2, he gained Mao's approval for the appointments of Li Xiannian, Hua Guofeng and others to assist with State Council work.[33]

Li and Hua were shrewd choices, both in terms of Mao's apparent favor and

---

[30] See Teiwes and Sun, *Tragedy*, pp. 39, 160n116.

[31] See Robinson, "China in 1972," p. 10; Dittmer, *Continuous Revolution*, p. 182; and Frederick C. Teiwes, *Provincial Leadership in China: The Cultural Revolution and Its Aftermath* (Ithaca: Cornell University East Asian Papers, 1974), pp. 115-18, 126-27. It is difficult to be precise about the extent of the purge, especially concerning how many of those who were removed from office were actually linked to Lin Biao, but roughly one-quarter of the 1969 Central Committee members, mainly consisting of military personnel, were not reelected at the Tenth Congress, and up to 17 percent of provincial Party secretaries had apparently been removed in the September 1971-August 1973 period. Of these provincial leaders, a disproportionate number had served in Lin's Fourth Field Army before 1949, although this was far from a sweeping purge of officers with this connection.

[32] *Mao zhuan*, vol. 2, p. 1605. While it is unclear who had formal and *de facto* responsibility for the Party Center since 1966, it is unlikely that, even as number 2 leader, Lin would have performed these duties except in a *pro forma* way, given his poor health and general desire to avoid administrative tasks. Moreover, with Mao's estrangement from Lin after the Lushan plenum, it is likely that by summer 1971 at the latest Zhou would have been shouldering this responsibility.

administrative experience. Li Xiannian, as a pre-Cultural Revolution Politburo member, had long worked closely with the Premier on economic policy. In a striking parallel to Zhou, Li was regarded with a certain disdain by Mao but nevertheless valued for his expertise, and apart from Zhou and Kang Sheng, he was the only pre-1966 civilian Politburo member reappointed at the Ninth Congress. Li performed various economic roles before and after the Ninth Congress, and presumably was now given overall supervision of economic policy. Beyond his economic work, Mao's trust in Li was demonstrated in April 1971 when he added Li (together with Ji Dengkui and General Zhang Caiqian) to the MAC Office (*Junwei banshizu*) that monopolized military authority under Lin Biao, as a way of diluting Lin Biao's power in the army.[34] The case of Hua was of course different, with Zhou having little previous work contact with the younger official, although Hua seems to have already been in Beijing, perhaps working on agriculture, before the Lin Biao incident. While Hua was known for his broad administrative competence, more importantly he was someone who had earned Mao's favor for both his talent and loyalty. Thus, at a crucial juncture in August 1971, Mao both chided Hua to develop a "political nose" to go with his administrative skills, and entrusted him to brief Zhou on his concerns about Lin, suggesting recognition of not only broad experience, but also political potential. It was testimony to the Premier's understanding of both Mao and Hua that he now assigned Hua critical responsibilities as deputy head of the State Council's group in charge of administrative affairs (*yewuzu*).[35]

Second only to confirming Zhou Enlai's stewardship of the "first front" of leadership,[36] was reorganizing military power. On October 3, the MAC Office was disbanded and replaced by a new MAC Council (*Junwei bangong huiyi*) headed by Marshal Ye Jianying, a completely reliable Mao loyalist despite his distaste for the Cultural Revolution, who was now also placed in charge of MAC daily work. Given Ye's long-standing personal closeness to Zhou, this clearly strengthened Zhou's hand in the PLA. But even more than his association with Ye, Zhou's clout was directly mandated by Mao who instructed the MAC that

---

[33] *Mao zhuan*, vol. 2, p. 1606.

[34] Teiwes and Sun, *Tragedy*, pp. 121-22, 153; and interview with senior Party historian, January 2000. According to our oral source, Mao disdainfully described Li as too timid during his December 1974 Changsha discussions with Zhou Enlai concerning State Council leadership.

[35] See Ma Qibin, *Sishinian*, p. 344; and Wang Dongxing, *Mao Zedong yu Lin Biao fangeming jituan de douzheng* [Mao Zedong's Struggle Against the Lin Biao Counterrevolutionary Clique] (Beijing: Dangdai Zhongguo chubanshe, 2004), p. 100.

[36] The concept of "two fronts of leadership," with Liu Shaoqi, Zhou, Deng Xiaoping and others on the "first front" managing the daily affairs of the Party-state, and Mao on the "second front" considering issues of ideology and overall policy direction, emerged in the 1950s, and was implemented by the early 1960s. For further discussion, see Roderick MacFarquhar, *The Origins of the Cultural Revolution 1: Contradictions among the People 1956-1957* (New York: Columbia University Press, 1974), pp. 152-56; and Teiwes, *Politics at Mao's Court*, pp. 32, 115-18.

the Premier must participate in handling big issues. The new MAC Council included Li Xiannian, Li Desheng, Ji Dengkui, Wang Dongxing and, particularly interesting (see below), Zhang Chunqiao, but arguably more important initially was the selection of officials to take over central military organs previously led by Lin's associates. On Zhou's recommendation, the previous day Mao approved the appointment of PLA veterans Li Desheng, Yu Qiuli and Zhang Caiqian to control three of these headquarters departments, a measure apparently superseding the immediate post-September 13 dispatch of Li Desheng to the air force, with Li Xiannian and Hua Guofeng sent to oversee the MAC as well as the navy and PLA logistics.[37] A final personnel arrangement, setting up a ten-person Central Special Case Group (*zhongyang zhuan'anzu*) to investigate the Lin Biao affair, established a body that, while not strictly a military organ, necessarily delved deeply into PLA affairs. Also created on October 3, and headed by Zhou, the group involved a mixture of leaders, including radicals Jiang Qing, Zhang Chunqiao and Yao Wenyuan, younger establishment figures Ji Dengkui, Li Desheng and Wu De, and Mao's faithful security chief, Wang Dongxing. Ji and Wang were placed in charge of the group's daily work, work that Mao directed closely.[38] These personnel arrangements are summarized in Table 1.

A number of things stand out in these arrangements. First, while few appointments went to senior old revolutionaries, enormous power was invested in Zhou Enlai, Ye Jianying and Li Xiannian, veteran pre-1966 leaders who had jaundiced views of the Cultural Revolution, but who were absolutely loyal to Mao. Apart from this, they already had Politburo status, while other senior revolutionaries such as Deng Xiaoping would have to be gradually reintegrated into the leadership. Second, the role of younger establishment beneficiaries of the Cultural Revolution is striking, and suggests both a confidence in them and a concern for the future succession on Mao's part. Hua Guofeng, Ji Dengkui and Li Desheng in particular were given vital assignments. In May 1973, moreover, Hua and Wu De, along with Wang Hongwen, were formally co-opted into the work of the Politburo, a status Ji already had as an alternate member since the Ninth Congress. Indeed, Ji, who would play an increasingly vital role in Party organizational affairs in the following years, had been singled out by Mao at the Congress as a model "revolutionary cadre" emerging from the Cultural Revolution. Of course, Ji was a model who had suffered at the hands of rebels

---

[37] *Mao zhuan*, vol. 2, p. 1606; Ma Qibin, *Sishinian*, pp. 343-44; Wu De, "Lushan huiyi he Lin Biao shijian," p. 55; Jin Chongji, *Zhou zhuan*, vol. 2, p. 1041; and Gao Wenqian, *Wannian Zhou*, p. 352. Yu Qiuli had been serving as a civilian since 1958, but he, Li Desheng and Zhang Caiqian had all received military honors as generals in 1955.

[38] *Mao zhuan*, vol. 2, p. 1606. This body included all Beijing-based Politburo members except Ye Jianying and Li Xiannian, and the aged or infirm Zhu De, Liu Bocheng and Dong Biwu. The state of Kang Sheng's health at this juncture is unclear, although it apparently deteriorated sharply after the Lin Biao incident. Cf. above, p. 31n21.

Table 1: Post-Lin Biao Appointments, October 1971

Official	Existing positions, 9/71	New assignments, 10/71
Zhou Enlai	CCP VC; Premier	Party Center daily work; CSCG head; oversee MC
Kang Sheng[a]	CCP VC	CSCG
Ye Jianying*	Politburo; MAC VC	MC head; MAC daily work
Xie Fuzhi[b]	Politburo	MC
Jiang Qing	Politburo	CSCG
Zhang Chunqiao	Politburo	MC; CSCG
Li Xiannian	Politburo; Vice Premier; MAC Office	State Council/assist Zhou; MC
Yao Wenyuan	Politburo	CSCG
Li Desheng*	Politburo alternate; head PLA GPD; 1st Secretary Anhui	MC; PLA headquarters control; CSCG
Ji Dengkui	Politburo alternate; MAC Office	MC; CSCG daily work
Wang Dongxing	Politburo alternate	MC; CSCG daily work
Wu De	CC; 1st Secretary Beijing	CSCG
Hua Guofeng	CC; 1st Secretary Hunan	State Council/assist Zhou
Yu Qiuli**	CC; SPC leader	PLA headquarters control
Chen Shiju*	CC; Commander PLA Engineering Corps	MC
Zhang Caiqian*	CC; PLA Deputy Chief-of-Staff; MAC Office	MC; PLA headquarters control
Liu Xianquan*	CC; 1st Secretary Qinghai	MC
Wu Zhong*	CC alternate; Commander Beijing Garrison	CSCG

Sources: *Mao zhuan*, vol. 2, p. 1606; *Lijie Zhonggong zhongyang weiyuan renming cidian 1921-1987* [Personnel Dictionary of Successive CCP Central Committees, 1921-1987] (Beijing: Zhonggong dangshi chubanshe, 1992); Malcolm Lamb, *Directory of Officials and Organizations in China: A Quarter-Century Guide* (Armonk: M.E. Sharpe, 1994); He Husheng *et al.*, *Zhonghuarenmingongheguo zhiguanzhi* [Records of PRC Officials] (Beijing: Zhongguo shehui chubanshe, 1993); and Wolfgang Bartke, *Who's Who in the People's Republic of China* (Armonk: M.E. Sharpe, 1981).

Key: *=PLA officer; **=former PLA officer; VC=Vice Chair; CSCG=Central Special Case Group; MC=MAC Council; GPD=General Political Department; CC=Central Committee; SPC=State Planning Commission.
a. Kang was in poor health, and died in 12/75. b. Xie was seriously ill, and died in 3/72.

during the movement, but was judged to have reformed in the process.[39] Finally, Wang Dongxing, already an alternate Politburo member, was strategically placed both in terms of guiding the investigation of the Lin affair and as a MAC Council member. Since Wang, as chief of Mao's security detail, was the top leader with the most access to Mao, these arrangements were clearly important for the Chairman's ability to keep on top of developments, even as his fragile health restricted that capacity.

But what of the radicals? There is a logic in the claims of Party historians such as An Jianshe that the demise of Lin Biao, notwithstanding the conflict between the radicals and Lin's camp, marked a setback for both the Cultural Revolution and their own fortunes. Doubts about Cultural Revolution excesses could only encourage doubts about their role in causing those excesses. When, in November 1971, Mao ordered that the "February adverse current" not be mentioned again, claiming that it was Lin Biao's fault, he couldn't erase from the minds of the top leadership the fact that Jiang Qing and Zhang Chunqiao, not the deceased Lin, were the chief antagonists of the vice premiers and marshals who were objecting to extremism. As An Jianshe put it, the radicals had no way to distinguish their theoretical position from Lin Biao's posture—although a more accurate observation would note that it was the predominant rhetoric, which Zhou Enlai among others voiced, that was indistinguishable. In these circumstances, it is understandable that Jiang Qing rarely appeared in public for a long period, and no Cultural Revolution-style exhortations were published in the official media.[40] But crucially, in sharp contrast to 1974-75, Mao offered no criticism of the radicals.

The new personnel arrangements, while not generous to the radicals, hardly eliminated their influence. Of particular note, Zhang Chunqiao, recently considered by Mao as a possible successor, was now placed on the MAC Council in addition to his duties in the Party Center and on the special case group investigating Lin Biao. As we shall see in the following section, even in the economic area, at a time when the attack on "ultra-leftism" was dominant, Zhang was able to sideline key policy documents on the economy. More striking was Zhang's new clout in the PLA, something enhanced not only by his position on the MAC Council, but also by the fact that he was placed in overall control of the navy. The defining issue concerned Lin Biao's influence in the navy, an influence that had been exercised by one of the "four generals," Political Commissar Li Zuopeng. In the immediate post-September 13 context, Commander Xiao

[39] On Ji Dengkui, see David M. Lampton with the assistance of Yeung Sai-cheung, *Paths to Power: Elite Mobility in Contemporary China* (Ann Arbor: Michigan Monographs in Chinese Studies, 1986), pp. 41-47; and Ji Pomin, "Ting fuqin Ji Dengkui tan wangshi" [Listening to My Father Ji Dengkui Talk on Past Events] (November 6, 2003), www.nanfangdaily.com.cn/zm/20031106/ji/jswshb/200311060680.asp. In speaking of younger establishment beneficiaries, we refer to a range of ages, from 48 in the case of Ji to 58 in the case of Wu De.

[40] See An Jianshe, "Pipan jizuo sichao," pp. 200-202.

Jingguang was given responsibility for conducting navy work, and in early 1972 the navy's Party committee held a meeting in which its leaders engaged in criticism and self-criticism concerning Lin Biao. Xiao, who had served in Lin's Fourth Field Army, apparently was under some suspicion, particularly concerning his role at the 1970 Lushan plenum in support of Lin. In any case, in early 1972, Mao had already shown his concern by personally rehabilitating Su Zhenhua, the pre-1966 political commissar, and then appointing him as the service's first deputy commander in May. As a result, Su was not only one of the earliest Cultural Revolution victims to be recalled after September 13, but even more unusual, he was almost immediately restored to real power.[41]

A new, more intensive enlarged meeting of the navy's Party committee convened under Xiao's leadership in July to deal with Lin Biao. Whatever suspicion existed concerning Xiao, in its first stage the meeting avoided focusing on him. In September, however, backed by a Mao comment that the meeting had become one-sidedly "entangled in historical [i.e., pre-Ninth Congress] issues," Zhang Chunqiao, backed by the other Politburo radicals,[42] began to attack Xiao's conduct of the navy meetings and his mistakes since the Ninth Congress. In November, the MAC Council under Ye Jianying basically approved the Party committee's concluding report on the meeting which did not single Xiao out for criticism, while Zhou Enlai, wanting to wind down matters, instructed that the meeting should not go on for too long. Zhang Chunqiao, however, objected, overturned (*tuifan*) the report, effectively seizing Ye's leadership on the matter, and attacked both the meeting and Xiao Jingguang. Zhang claimed the meeting had "negated the Cultural Revolution," and he ordered criticism of Xiao for having "boarded [Lin's] pirate ship," as seen in not voting for the Politburo radicals at the Ninth Congress[43] and in his speeches at Lushan where the main target was none

---

[41] See *Xiao Jingguang huiyilu (xuji)* [Memoirs of Xiao Jingguang, continued] (Beijing: Jiefangjun chubanshe, 1988), pp. 286-91; and Chen and Du, *Shilu*, vol. 3, part 2, p. 828. While it is simplistic to link PLA leaders to one top military figure, and Su as well as Xiao had served under Lin Biao, his primary identification appears to have been with Deng Xiaoping's Second Field Army. Su was replaced in 1967 by Li Zuopeng, who had been both second political commissar and the deputy commander in charge of navy daily work. On Li, see Teiwes and Sun, *Tragedy*, pp. 38, 40. Su's unusually quick restoration to real power can be seen in comparison to Hu Yaobang, who was rehabilitated at the same time, but who had to wait until 1975 for a significant role. Cf. Deng Xiaoping's probation period after his return to work; above, pp. 20-21.

[42] Jiang Qing was especially notable in this regard, but of particular interest is that Wang Hongwen, having just arrived in Beijing, was already participating in not only the navy meeting, but also in related Politburo and MAC Council meetings, well before his formal right to participate in the Politburo was approved.

[43] This question is indicative of the confusion and distortions of the period. Xiao apparently had not voted for Zhang Chunqiao and Yao Wenyuan in the 1969 Politburo elections, later claiming he did not sufficiently understand their circumstances. He did, however, vote for Jiang Qing out of respect for Mao, although she claimed in 1972 and 1973 that this was not true. Interestingly, Xiao did not vote for Ye Qun, his navy colleague Li Zuopeng, Wu Faxian or Qiu Huizuo, i.e., the occupants of the very "pirate ship" he had allegedly boarded. See *Xiao Jingguang huiyilu*, pp. 300-301, 307-308.

other than Zhang himself. Zhang not only succeeded in dragging out the meeting for another three months, he also personally revised the final report to criticize Xiao's mistakes, and the report was quickly distributed by the Party Center. Although Mao had already rebuffed Zhang and Jiang's effort to have Xiao dismissed, and Xiao formally retained his post, navy power had passed to Su Zhenhua. Mao's role in these developments is unknown apart from his terse September comment and his subsequent refusal to dismiss Xiao, but we assume that at some point Zhang obtained the Chairman's at least tacit support for the broader attack on the navy leadership. At minimum, the combination of Mao's concern with the navy, and his own new authority in the military, gave Zhang significant power in an area in which he had no previous experience or credentials.[44]

The sum total of the new situation was that however much Zhou's leverage had been increased in the aftermath of the Lin Biao incident, Zhang Chunqiao and the radicals still had a position of latent and indeed real power in the immediate post-Lin Biao period. Their position was further enhanced with the arrival of Wang Hongwen in Beijing in September 1972, an arrival clearly signaling much greater things for the young worker rebel in the future. Similar to developments in the navy case, this latent power would become increasingly manifest as the Party's debate over the nature of Lin Biao's errors unfolded during the "criticize Lin and rectification" (pi Lin zhengfeng) campaign which had been launched in December 1971.

The Critique of the "Ultra-Left"

The fact that criticism of "ultra-left" tendencies was the dominant feature of public discourse for the year or so after the Lin Biao incident is well known. Several additional factors must be kept in mind when examining this critique of Cultural Revolution excesses. First, as has been recognized,[45] the attack on leftist phenomena was an extension and deepening of the dominant trend since the Ninth Congress, and especially the Lushan plenum, both junctures where Mao alone—and certainly not Zhou—was in a position to set the course of regime policy. Second, despite the clear implication that Lin Biao, i.e., "swindlers like Liu Shaoqi," was a leftist, there was no explicit theoretical statement that this was the case. Mao's June 1972 identification of Lin as the backstage backer of the "left faction" to the Sri Lankan Prime Minister was kept secret, even if it was known

---

[44] See ibid., pp. 293-313; Chen and Du, Shilu, vol. 3, part 2, pp. 838-39; and Teiwes and Sun, Tragedy, pp. 144ff. Xiao's effective replacement by Su, already seen when Su was placed in charge of a small group to handle Xiao's case at the navy meeting, was confirmed when Su became first secretary of the navy Party committee after the meeting concluded. The tension between the two men was later manifested in 1978, when Su delayed the reversal of the 1973 decision criticizing Xiao. Xiao Jingguang huiyilu, pp. 300, 311-12.

[45] See, e.g., MacFarquhar, "Succession," p. 282, who speaks of Zhou "renewing his year-old campaign to stabilize administration and encourage production," and observing that "leftism seemed to be on the retreat as early as 1970."

in the inner circle. Moreover, the central conference on criticism of Lin in May-June avoided attacks on "ultra-left" thought,[46] nor was criticizing "ultra-leftism" a slogan used in key propaganda statements. Rather, the concept appeared in articles attacking concrete excesses in a wide range of specific contexts, and was used carefully by Zhou Enlai in internal meetings.[47] The difficulty of the matter was due not only to the fact that a military coup was neither "left" nor "right," but also to the Party's historic preference for the left. In this context, the closest thing to a theoretical position was the assertion that enemies of the CCP such as Lin adopted both guises, combining their "unchanging [bourgeois] class nature" with "ever-changing tactics," sometimes rightist, sometimes "ultra-leftist." Thus even in this period of strong criticism of Cultural Revolution excesses, a large residue of the movement's ideology shaped political discussion.[48]

It is against this background of a longer-term trend of criticizing leftist errors, together with the ambiguous theoretical overview, that the relative roles of Mao and Zhou must be assessed. If Zhou was the driving force in implementing the anti-"ultra-left" agenda, to what extent was he initiating measures and manipulating Mao's shock over Lin Biao, and to what extent was he carrying out the Chairman's broad directions, while testing the limits of Mao's intentions? The answer is by no means clear, but either way, as An Jianshe observes, Zhou's actions cannot be separated from the Chairman's understanding of the situation.[49] What can be said, as the preceding indicates, is both that Mao's specific claims regarding Lin Biao in the initial months after September 13 painted Lin as committing leftist mistakes, and as late as June 1972 he specifically labeled his dead successor as the "leftist chieftain" of the Cultural Revolution period. But whether this simply opened up possibilities for Zhou to exploit, or whether the Chairman himself was a more active force in the expanded attack on leftism, requires analysis. Such analysis, in turn, requires discriminating treatment of different areas—not only of critical cadre and economic policy issues, but also concerning diplomatic work and the particularly sensitive culture, education and science spheres. Since much of the content of the critique of "ultra-leftism" in these spheres has been well covered in the literature,[50] our focus will be on the political process.

Liberating Cadres. Despite the emphasis on Zhou Enlai's role in official sources and foreign scholarship alike,[51] the rehabilitation of senior cadres was unambiguously *the* area where Mao's initiative drove the attack on "ultra-

---

[46] Chen and Du, *Shilu*, vol. 3, part 2, pp. 827-28.

[47] This was emphasized in an interview with a leading Party history authority on the "ultra-left" issue, December 2002. This authority speculated that for most of 1972 Mao, or even the radicals, may not have paid much attention to Zhou's use of "ultra-leftism." Another sophisticated Party historian speculated that Mao may indeed have referred to Lin as an "ultra-leftist," and Zhou then ran with the label; interview, December 2002.

[48] See Joseph, *Critique*, pp. 126, 130-31.

[49] An Jianshe, "Pipan jizuo sichao," p. 207. An's reference is to Zhou's criticism of the "ultra-left" before September 13, but it can be taken to apply throughout.

leftism." In the most discriminating CCP accounts, in contrast to other areas, Zhou's efforts concerning cadre liberation carry such comments as "according to Mao Zedong's intent," or acting "under Mao Zedong's concern." The crucial evidence, however, is not only that the Chairman, when he did comment on the affairs of state in 1972, predominately addressed this question, but even more that virtually from day one following the Lin Biao affair he addressed cadre issues. As we have seen, Mao emphasized the "save the patient" approach to those deceived by Lin, even expressing unhappiness at the lack of applause for those making self-criticisms during a meeting as 1971 ended and 1972 began. This approach, of course, stood in sharp relief to the Cultural Revolution tendency to "strike all" and "suspect all," a tendency now sharply denounced as "ultra-leftist." But what was especially significant was that, in a series of comments from October 1971 to the start of 1972, the Chairman spoke positively of old cadres who had suffered during the Cultural Revolution, notionally at the hands of Lin Biao. The classic case was his November reference to the "February adverse current," significantly uttered when one of the victims of the incident, Ye Jianying, entered the room. While suggesting remorse, Mao's comment, that the matter should no longer be spoken of and placing the blame on Lin, was still ambiguous. Not only did he himself shirk any culpability while Jiang Qing *et al.* escaped criticism, but there was no "reversal of the verdict" (*pingfan*) on the case itself. Nevertheless, together with his other comments, Mao had opened the door to favorable consideration of the plight of victims of the Cultural Revolution.[52]

As in other areas, there was a pre-September 13 background to the lenient cadre policy reemphasized after Lin's demise. Even during the chaotic days of 1967-68 there had been periodic warnings against excesses, and the very concept of "revolutionary cadres"—i.e., those officials who had been tested in the cauldron of the Cultural Revolution and had notionally transformed their thinking, and then joined PLA officers and mass representatives in a "three in one alliance" to run the newly emerging governing structures—reflected the reform approach. Hua Guofeng and Ji Dengkui were stellar examples of this type. After the Ninth Congress, the approach was extended with the gradual return to work of those ousted a few years earlier, including significant numbers of former vice ministers, as well as provincial-level leaders. This process continued apace, so that by 1972, at many local levels, more than 90 percent of cadres criticized during the Cultural Revolution had reportedly returned to their original posts. A further subtle change

---

[50] See the detailed discussion in Joseph, *Critique*, ch. 5.

[51] See, e.g., Yan and Gao, *Turbulent Decade*, p. 409; and Barnouin and Yu, *Ten Years*, p. 253. There is a certain irony in treating Yan and Gao's book here and elsewhere as representing CCP views since its relentless criticism of the Cultural Revolution earned official disfavor in the 1980s, but in terms of specific claims and overview, it basically, and uncritically, adopts the Party line on the 1966-76 period.

[52] See *Mao zhuan*, vol. 2, pp. 1608, 1610, 1619, 1622; and An Jianshe, "Pipan jizuo sichao," pp. 199-201, 211, 233.

was the redefinition of the "three in one alliance" in 1970 as involving "the old, the middle-aged, and the young," a formula conductive to the return of more senior cadres, although one also sensitive to Mao's concern for new blood in official institutions. But at the time of Lin Biao's demise, and notwithstanding the election (in fact demotion) of veteran figures such as Marshal Chen Yi and former Party Vice Chairman Chen Yun to Central Committee membership in 1969, very few ousted senior leaders had returned to significant roles, and many continued to suffer various forms of "persecution."[53] Following September 13, Mao's actions gave new hope.

By the end of 1971 some old cadres and their families sent letters to Mao and Zhou complaining of unjust suffering and seeking redress. The Premier, "under Mao's concern," acted to use the opening and address the difficulties facing old cadres in this immediate period, for example, in seeking out and bringing to Beijing the wife of one of Lin Biao's alleged major victims, the late Marshal He Long who had died of "persecution" in 1969, and then organizing her to write a letter to the Center that he passed on to Mao.[54] The crucial development, however, was Mao's well-known gesture of attending the January 1972 funeral of Chen Yi, another key figure of the "February adverse current." In an apparent last minute decision, Mao, despite his own poor health, attended the ceremony in what came to be regarded as an implicit personal apology for the suffering of Chen and other senior cadres during the Cultural Revolution. The details of this event are revealing in several respects. First, in his cautious manner, Zhou prepared a funeral oration carefully balancing Chen's merits and shortcomings, shortcomings that could only be seen through the prism of the Cultural Revolution. Mao, however, ordered that Chen's merits and faults not be assessed. At the funeral itself, Chen's wife attempted to apologize for her dead husband, telling Mao that Chen had not fully understood things when he opposed the Chairman in the past, but Mao interrupted, declaring Chen a "good man." He further observed to Prince Sihanouk, who also attended the funeral, that "Lin Biao opposed me, Chen Yi supported me," and commented that "the February adverse current was Commander Chen's action against Lin Biao." Clearly, in a striking reflection of Mao's political and even spiritual dominance, what was important to those who had suffered in the Mao-initiated onslaught of the late 1960s was that the Chairman validated their contribution to the Party's cause. The immediate consequence was that Mao had given an unmistakable hint that old cadres, including those who had committed serious mistakes in the

---

[53] See An Jianshe, "Pipan jizuo sichao," p. 207; Robinson, "China in 1972," p. 11; Harding, "Fragmentation of Power," p. 3; Hong Yung Lee, *From Revolutionary Cadres to Party Technocrats in Socialist China* (Berkeley: University of California Press, 1991), p. 105; and Teiwes, *Provincial Leadership*, pp. 18-19, 30-38, 76-81, 95-98.

[54] An Jianshe, "Pipan jizuo sichao," p. 211; and interview with senior specialist on Zhou, December 2002. On the He Long case and Lin's problematic role, see Teiwes and Sun, *Tragedy*, pp. 32-38.

Cultural Revolution, were good and should be liberated. As a result, the trickle of letters from old cadres seeking redress now increased greatly.[55]

The course of cadre policy had been set, but concern for veteran cadres was only part of it. Key subsequent developments included: Ji Dengkui, apparently now overseeing organizational work, in a March 1972 talk emphasized the twin objectives of liberating old cadres and promoting new ones; an April *People's Daily* editorial vetted by Zhou on the "save the patient" policy also linked the two aspects, declaring that both veterans and new cadres emerging from the Cultural Revolution were the Party's treasures and could be given work regardless of earlier mistakes; attention to the abuse of imprisoned old cadres, leading to Mao's denunciation of fascist methods in December 1972; and the further extension of traditional cadre policies as a result of a March 1973 Politburo meeting. At the Politburo meeting, which was held in the context of more letters from old cadres, Mao declared his objective was to achieve "stability and unity," while after the meeting Zhou approached the Chairman concerning the situation of various ousted senior officials. This drew Mao's comment that his Cultural Revolution objective had been only to get at bureaucracy (*guanliaozhuyi*), not to give veteran leaders a hard time. With this opening, Zhou argued the case for implementing more thoroughly the long-established cadre policy, producing Mao's approving comment, "you do it." Under the Premier's proposal to deal with easy cases first, the Central Organization Department undertook the examination of 300 cases, with Zhou personally taking charge of Politburo handling of the issue, and Hua Guofeng as well as Ji Dengkui apparently playing important roles. Organizationally, high-ranking Party cases from top provincial officials up were handled by the Organization Department, military cases of the army commander level and above by the PLA's General Political Department (GPD), and State Council cases from the vice minister level by the Premier's Office. The very top cases such as that of He Long, however, were excluded from the authority of these bodies and dealt with exclusively at the very highest level.[56]

The key aspect of the policy was the rehabilitation of senior CCP figures. This was implemented "batch by batch" throughout 1972-73, and indeed beyond to the second half of 1975. The process and content of this "liberation"[57] of

[55] *Mao zhuan*, vol. 2, pp. 1611-15; Zhang Yufeng, "Anecdotes of Mao and Zhou," in FBIS-CHI-89-017, pp. 17-19; and interview with senior specialist on Zhou, December 2002.

[56] "Ji Dengkui zai Guowuyuan huibao ganbu huiyishi de jianghua jingshen" [The Spirit of Ji Dengkui's Speech at the Time of the State Council Report-back Cadre Conference] (March 31, 1972), in *CRDB*, p. 1; *RMRB*, April 24, 1972, p. 1; An Jianshe, "Pipan jizuo sichao," pp. 211, 221; *Mao zhuan*, vol. 2, pp. 1619, 1654; "Deng Xiaoping guanyu qicao guoqing sanshi zhounian jianghua gao de tanhua jiyao" [Summary of Deng Xiaoping's Talk on the Draft Speech for the 30th Anniversary National Day Celebration] (September 4, 1979), in *CRDB*, p. 1; and Xie Guoming, "175 wei jiangjun jiefang neimu" [The Inside Story of the Liberation of 175 Generals], in An Jianshe, *Zhou Enlai*, p. 357. Xie Guoming describes a very similar exchange between Mao and Zhou at a December 1972 meeting in Zhongnanhai to what is recounted here as occurring at the March Politburo meeting.

[57] The actual measures involved in Mao's comments on cadre policy were actually quite varied, from

senior cadres further indicated Mao's control. First, the decisive steps were the Chairman's comments on the letters from these officials or their families. Moreover, the slow pace of rehabilitation leading to significant power—with the significant exception of Su Zhenhua—reflected Mao's penchant for assessing behavior and ideological "progress." The choice of individuals rehabilitated also pointed to Mao's personal judgments and specific needs. Of the 15 or so most prominent senior individuals receiving Mao's favor in the period up to the Tenth Congress, nearly half arguably had either previous close working relations with Mao, or had been highly assessed by him earlier in their careers.[58] The Chairman's judgment can also be seen in the different roles assigned to "liberated" leaders, nowhere more clearly than in the cases of two pre-Cultural Revolution Politburo Standing Committee members certified for work by Mao in mid-1972—Chen Yun and Deng Xiaoping. We examine Deng's return to work later in this chapter and in subsequent chapters. As for Chen Yun, someone whose economic expertise would have been exceptionally valuable, in contrast to the favored Deng, while Mao lived he never rose above low profile State Council duties in 1973-74, and subsequently the largely symbolic role of National People's Congress (NPC) Vice Chairman from 1975. Mao's 1962 opinion that "this man has always been a rightist" probably explains Chen's relegation to marginal duties.[59] Finally, a number of high-ranking PLA officers from Field Armies other than Lin Biao's Fourth, officials who tended to assume real power earlier than liberated civilian leaders, was a sign of Mao's concern to offset any lingering Lin influence in the military.[60] In short, particularly in the most high profile cases, from the start

---

authorizing a review of cases, better treatment, and return to work, but rarely involving a formal *pingfan* of the concerned cases. Mao's general approach was to bring people back to work first, and deal with their historical problems later. See *Mao wengao*, vol. 13, pp. 286, 287, 290, 294, 300, 301, 302, 304, 307, 308-309, 324, 334, 339, 340, 345-46, 351, 355, 360.

[58] While our list of prominent individuals is somewhat arbitrary based largely on Mao's comments in *Mao wengao*, vol. 13, the former category includes Wu Lengxi and Yang Chengwu who accompanied Mao on important trips to the provinces in 1958-59 and 1967 respectively. Among those whom Mao had earlier highly appreciated were Hu Yaobang (see Yang Zhongmei, *Hu Yaobang: A Chinese Biography* [Armonk: M.E. Sharpe, 1988], pp. 39-40, 47, 52-53, 83-86) and Wang Jiaxiang (see Teiwes with Sun, *Formation*, pp. 47, 49-52). In another sense, the rehabilitations of Tan Zhenlin and Chen Zaidao, who had suffered as a result of the "February adverse current" and Wuhan incident respectively in 1967, suggests personal remorse on the Chairman's part. See Teiwes and Sun, *Tragedy*, pp. 80ff.

[59] See *Mao zhuan*, vol. 2, p. 1621; David M. Bachman, *Chen Yun and the Chinese Political System* (Berkeley: China Research Monograph no. 29, 1985), pp. 78, 80-81; and *Chen Yun wenxuan, disanjuan* [Selected Works of Chen Yun, vol. 3] (Beijing: Renmin chubanshe, 1995), pp. 216-29.

[60] Most notably, Yang Chengwu, deputy PLA Chief-of-Staff by the end of 1974, from the North China Field Army, Chen Zaidao and Yang Yong of the Second Field Army (along with Su Zhenhua) who had military region posts by mid-1973, and Liao Hansheng of the First Field Army, who seemingly had to wait until 1975 for a top position as political commissar of the Nanjing Military Region. In this respect, the argument of Huang, *Factionalism*, pp. 325ff, concerning the importance of "mountaintops" carries some weight, although his assertion of Mao's *dependence* on such factions is well wide of the mark. Cf. above, p. 6n10.

Mao's hand was dominant in rehabilitations that were arbitrary, biased and limited. What was arguably more important than his role in high profile cases *per se* was the increased attention to traditional cadre policy that opened the way to further rehabilitations beyond those that had transpired before September 13.

The subtleties of Mao's dominance, Zhou's role, the constraints under which the Politburo radicals operated, and the atmosphere of the process can be seen in the rehabilitation of 175 PLA generals under the auspices of the GPD. In a process seemingly initiated after Mao angrily reacted to the "false case" against He Long in December 1972, the GPD was given the task of drawing conclusions on the circumstances under which these generals were "knocked down" during the Cultural Revolution, the original units had to concur—which was often difficult given the continued presence of those involved in the original action—and finally each case had to be reviewed and decided by the Politburo. With Mao's comment, the He Long matter suddenly became an "easy case," and efforts to clear it up and restore He's reputation proceeded, although not without bureaucratic delays. More broadly, at the same point Mao asked "how could so many cadres be knocked down" when his intention was merely to educate them, thus setting the stage for further rehabilitations.[61] As for Zhou Enlai, he encouraged the work of the GPD behind the scenes, chaired all Politburo meetings dealing with individual cases, said relatively little, avoided recriminations with the radicals who sometimes fiercely contested specific cases, and in the end succeeded in lowering the temperature and securing the liberation of those at issue. While rehabilitation was naturally a godsend for those affected, it could be a fraught process for those victimized in 1966-68. In one case, a general was so nervous that he did not dare to sit down when questioned by the GPD, and in another the general concerned asked whether he would be allowed to wear his uniform and collar insignia when summoned to see the Premier.[62]

As seen dramatically in the He Long case, once Mao expressed a view on a case, the outcome was not in doubt, even if the process was sometimes drawn out. Undoubtedly because liberating cadres was clearly Mao's policy, there is little evidence of resistance from the Politburo radicals to the policy as such, although there were often objections to individual cases. Nor was there any sign of a change in policy when Lin Biao's sins were redefined as "ultra-right" at the end of 1972. Moreover, when the radicals objected, there apparently were few, if any, cases where they prevented rehabilitation.[63] Zhou, who became vulnerable

---

[61] Xie Guoming, "175 wei jiangjun," pp. 357-58. In contrast to He Long, the other top military case, that of Peng Dehuai, received neither sympathy from Mao nor action from the responsible authorities. Even the delay in handling He's case where a formal *pingfan* was at issue reflected Mao's dominance, since various officials were unwilling to act without his explicit authority.

[62] Xie Guoming, "175 wei jiangjun," pp. 358ff. Once someone had been liberated, there was often a drawn out process to place him in an appropriate unit. In addition to the difficulty of returning to the unit from which an officer had been ousted, status considerations often complicated the process.

[63] A case in point concerns Chen Zaidao, the most prominent victim of the Wuhan incident in 1967.

in other areas with the redefinition of Lin's sins at the end of 1972, continued to implement cadre liberation well into 1973, and perhaps beyond, gently but decisively overriding radical obstruction. Zhou clearly played an essential role, one that may have involved some subtle manipulation of Mao, as in his late 1971 "preparatory work" with He Long's widow. But as Deng Xiaoping noted in 1979, while everyone understood the Premier's efforts to protect old cadres, it was a case of "if Chairman Mao didn't speak, Premier Zhou would not have been able to protect anyone."[64] While the judgment that Zhou never took a step without Mao's prior consent is undoubtedly too harsh,[65] the Premier's indefatigable work to restore the traditional cadre policy and liberate old cadres was completely dependent on Mao. As we examine later in this chapter, Zhou's dependence was further seen in his involvement in the other aspect of the Chairman's cadre policy—the promotion of the young, as personified in the case of Wang Hongwen.

Readjusting the Economy. Economic policy was a quite different area, one in which Mao had acknowledged his lack of credentials in the 1950s. This did not, of course, prevent him from seizing control of the economy and plunging China into the disaster of the Great Leap Forward. The Great Leap disaster, however, chastened Mao to the extent that he never again devised or took charge of a radical developmental strategy, but he remained central to economic developments in ways beyond the fact that his approval was necessary for any policy initiative. Mao's specific policy preferences, notably devolution of authority to the localities, continued to be emphasized, albeit in more moderate ways than during the leap forward, and with mixed results.[66] More significant was the destructive impact of the Chairman's preoccupations with other matters, strategic as well as ideological. The effort to build an industrial "third front" inland to counter potential military attacks from the United States and/or the Soviet Union led to a massive misallocation of resources in the mid-1960s, and the post-Ninth Congress "new leap forward" driven by Mao's insistence on war

---

Despite "fierce conflict" in the Politburo, Zhou prevailed. Whether the radicals were aware that Mao and Zhou had already discussed the case is unclear, but in the end they were forced to admit defeat. See Xie Guoming, "175 wei jiangjun," p. 358. On the question of radical obstruction more generally, see Ji Dengkui's recollection of a wider range of rehabilitations in 1972-73; *Mao zhuan,* vol. 2, pp. 1695-96.

[64] See "Deng Xiaoping guanyu guoqing sanshi zhounian jianghua" (September 4, 1979), p. 1. While the specific remark undoubtedly referred to the early stage of the Cultural Revolution, the point applied equally to Zhou's post-Lin Biao efforts.

[65] See Gao Wenqian, *Wannian Zhou,* p. 524, on Zhou's extreme caution in handling He Long's rehabilitation. Zhou advised Ji Dengkui not to rush on He's case before he was absolutely sure of Mao's intention.

[66] See Harry Harding, "China: Toward Revolutionary Pragmatism," *AS,* January 1971, p. 58; and Liu Suinian and Wu Qungan, eds., *China's Socialist Economy: An Outline History (1949-1984)* (Beijing: *Beijing Review,* 1986), pp. 370-71.

preparations against the Soviets caused great waste and economic dislocation.[67] But clearly, the most destructive impact on the economy was produced by the Chairman's treasured Cultural Revolution, not simply by giving higher priority to revolution in the injunction to "grasp revolution and promote production," but by his willingness to accept vast economic damage as an acceptable cost in the effort to transform society.[68] By the Ninth Congress, however, Mao believed the time had come to repair the damage, a process inevitably involving the revival of economic practices that had been harshly attacked in 1966-68.

This effort developed into the critique of "ultra-left" economic practices following the Lushan plenum and the subsequent attacks on "sham Marxists," i.e., Lin Biao's Lushan ally, Chen Boda, in the "criticize Chen and rectification" (pi Chen zhengfeng) campaign from September 1970. The central features of the effort were attacks on "anarchism" (wuzhengfuzhuyi) in the workplace that had undermined production, as well as on non-economic work, and the related effort to restore orthodox systems and work processes, i.e., approaches that were indisputably within the practice of state socialism but had run afoul of radical currents in 1966-68. As is well known, the most prominent aspects of the critique and the measures to rectify the situation included: restoring reliable national economic plans, enforcing "rational" enterprise management regulations to combat anarchism, opposing rural egalitarianism including attempts to impose Dazhai-style brigade accounting regardless of local conditions, requiring attention to specialist expertise in contrast to one-sided "phony politics," emphasis on the efficient use of resources and quality in production, and upholding the socialist principle of "to each according to his work."[69]

These policies largely involved a readjustment, moving economic practice away from disorganization toward settled patterns in a process which deepened on a more across the board basis after September 13. In one area, however, the post-Lin Biao policy change was more dramatic: the decisions to import foreign goods and technology and develop flexible methods of credit. This revived an approach of the immediate pre-Cultural Revolution period which had been out of bounds since 1966, but on Mao's initiative was placed on the policy agenda shortly after Lin's demise. Subsequently, in the context of Nixon's visit and the availability of Western resources for infrastructure development, Mao specifically endorsed a draft State Planning Commission (SPC) report advocating the import of complete sets of equipment and new technology from the West in early 1972. A year later, in January 1973, he similarly approved a SPC proposal for aggressive

---

[67] See Barry Naughton, "The Third Front: Defence Industrialization in the Chinese Interior," CQ, no. 115 (1988); and Teiwes and Sun, Tragedy, pp. 115ff.

[68] On the economic costs of the Cultural Revolution, see Michael Schoenhals, ed., China's Cultural Revolution, 1966-1969: Not A Dinner Party (Armonk: M.E. Sharpe, 1996), pp. 62-66.

[69] See Liu and Wu, China's Socialist Economy, pp. 378-82; and Fang Weizhong, Zhonghuarenmingongheguo jingji dashiji (1949-1980 nian) [Chronology of Economic Events in the PRC, 1949-1980] (Beijing: Zhongguo shehui kexue chubanshe, 1984), pp. 487-90.

importation of advanced equipment that resulted in the largest expenditure of funds in this area since imports from the Soviet Union in the 1950s. As a senior specialist on economic policy in the 1970s has observed, it was the Chairman who opened up the policy of borrowing from the West that would expand dramatically in the post-Mao period.[70]

Despite the efforts to rebalance economic practice and the new opening to the international economy, the anti-left thrust of policy both before and after Lin Biao's demise was significantly complicated by Mao's strategic and ideological concerns. As indicated above, war preparations since the Ninth Congress seriously dislocated the economy through the pursuit of unrealistic high targets, including the doubling of steel output during the Fourth Five-Year Plan (1971-75). This resulted in the phenomenon of the "three excesses"—too many workers and employees, an overly high wage bill, and excessive urban sales of food grains. Although this problem had been recognized by the SPC and Zhou Enlai as early as the year-end 1970 national economic conference, little effective was done about it, not only in 1971 when it could be conveniently blamed on Lin Biao, nor in 1972 when Zhou's influence over the economy was at its height. Despite the Premier's efforts, massive capital construction continued and "the problem grew from bad to worse." With Mao's international concerns somewhat easing, it was only in 1973 that a *slight* decrease in spending on national defense and defense industries was approved. In short, the structural pressures placed on the economy by the demands of war preparations seriously compromised the efforts at readjustment despite the gains achieved by the criticism of "ultra-left" practices.[71] Meanwhile, the impact of the critique itself was attenuated by the absence of a clear overall ideological message. Before September 13, An Jianshe argues, Mao's insistence on the Cultural Revolution meant no great results could be achieved, as discordant propaganda led cadres to evade action against left tendencies for fear of being labeled "right deviationists." But even with the heightened anti-"ultra-left" emphasis subsequently, the continuing assertions of the correctness of the Cultural Revolution inevitably resulted in confusion, limited awareness, and a lack of thoroughness in dealing with problems.[72]

---

[70] Liu and Wu, *China's Socialist Economy*, pp. 383-84; Lawrence C. Reardon, "Learning How to Open the Door: A Reassessment of China's 'Opening' Strategy," *CQ*, no. 155 (1998), pp. 480ff; *Mao zhuan*, vol. 2, p. 1622; interview with leading PRC economist, January 2001; and interview with senior Party historian, January 2005.

Mao's initiation of the policy arose in August-September 1971 and was typically bizarre: enquiring of a maid about the fabric of her dacron clothing, the Chairman learned it was not easily available in China, and then set in motion the large-scale importation of Western technologies and production lines for scarce products. As a result, the January 1972 SPC report under the supervision of Li Xiannian, Hua Guofeng and Yu Qiuli called for importing synthetic polyester fiber equipment, as well as chemical fertilizer. See Cheng Zhensheng, "Li Xiannian yu qishi niandai chu de daguimo jishu shebei yinjing" [Li Xiannian and the Large-scale Importation of Technology and Equipment in the Early 1970s], *Zhonggong dangshi yanjiu*, no.1 (2004), p. 73.

[71] See Liu and Wu, *China's Socialist Economy*, pp. 370-77; Fang Weizhong, *Jingji dashiji*, pp. 469, 471, 486, 489, 496; and Teiwes and Sun, *Tragedy*, pp. 122-23.

What does this tell us about the roles of Mao and Zhou in combating "ultra-leftism" in the economy, apart from how the Chairman's foreign policy and ideological preoccupations complicated the Premier's task? As a leading specialist on Zhou Enlai observed in an interview, Mao was the key and Zhou's task was not simply to win his support for the attack on the "ultra-left," but the Chairman's support was a prerequisite for any effort. While the Chairman had endorsed curbing economic excesses since the Ninth Congress, his role after September 13 in this area was clearly different from that in dealing with cadre liberation. With Mao having set the general direction, the process was for specialist bodies such as the SPC, often with Zhou's deep involvement, to draft measures that went to the Politburo for discussion and summary, and then to Mao for approval. Mao's contribution was comparatively remote in response to recommendations coming to him. In historical accounts, or in the speeches of officials at the time, apart from approving specific measures, Mao is simply described as "very concerned" about the economy, or as urging Party leadership over economic work. The Chairman had entrusted Zhou with managing the economy, while the Premier compiled scattered Mao comments on economic issues to give political weight to his initiatives. Beyond this, of particular interest is the Chairman's approval of the new opening to the world economy, arguably an area especially requiring his personal authority. In terms of Mao's specific input, the most detailed account concerns his May 1973 criticism of planning work as "not on track," with emphasis on the need for greater reliance on the localities. More importantly, he observed that correcting economic problems was all well and good, but more attention needed to be given to the superstructure. This would mean trouble for the economy as well as politics in the year ahead, especially as the subject of "ultra-leftism" became taboo from late spring 1973.[73]

Where did this leave the Politburo radicals with regard to economic policy in 1972 and the first half of 1973? The answer is mixed, and revealing as a result. Basically, they were forced to go along, both as a result of their own lack of knowledge in the area and more importantly due to Mao's stance. As Mao's biographers have observed, given their awareness of the Chairman's support of economic policy initiatives, Jiang Qing and Zhang Chunqiao said little about economic work and simply wrote "approve" on official documents. This situation also played into Zhou Enlai's hands in his attempt to extend the critique of "ultra-leftism" more generally. Similar to his "easy case" approach to liberating cadres,

---

[72] See An Jianshe, "Pipan jizuo sichao," pp. 208, 213-14; "Quarterly Chronicle and Documentation," *CQ*, no. 52 (1972), p. 771; and Joseph, *Critique*, pp. 125, 128.

[73] *Mao zhuan*, vol. 2, pp. 1622-23, 1646; "Wang Bicheng zai Yunnan shengwei he Kunming junqu dangwei ganbu xuexiban shangde jianghua" [Wang Bicheng's Speech at the Cadre Study Class of the Yunnan Provincial Committee and the Party Committee of the Kunming Military Region] (February 6, 1972), in *CRDB*, p. 5; An Jianshe, "Pipan jizuo sichao," pp. 221-22; Chen and Du, *Shilu*, vol. 3, part 2, pp. 914-15; and interview, December 2002.

Zhou started by focusing on the economy, an area where the damage caused by Cultural Revolution excesses was "easy to see," then building up a momentum that he hoped could be extended into the more sensitive areas of culture, education and science.[74]

Nevertheless, in two significant cases widely cited in post-Mao attacks on the "gang of four," Zhang Chunqiao was able to interfere in economic matters. The first instance, very early in the post-Lin Biao period, concerned the summary document of the December 1971-February 1972 national planning conference which criticized various leftist practices. Zhang successfully objected to distributing the summary as a central document, ostensibly because it was too long, but "in fact" because he judged the criticisms as directed at the Cultural Revolution. A year later, after the next national planning conference, he again prevented the circulation of the meeting's summary, this time on the basis that it had not been unanimously approved by all the participating local delegations. In policy terms, Zhang's actions do not appear to have had a major effect, as the spirit of the documents was passed on by the participants and the anti-left measures continued to be implemented. From Zhang's perspective, he was forced to object (even after the redefinition of Lin Biao as "ultra-right") on largely technical grounds, but he was successful in preventing the most authoritative distribution of Zhou's policy efforts. What role, if any, Mao had in Zhang's actions is unknown. But as in other respects, by placing Zhang in such an influential position, Mao had enhanced the potential for policy disruption.[75]

The ironic result of Zhou's efforts in the economic (and other) spheres was that, on the one hand, they neither amounted to "Zhou's year" in 1972, nor went very far in righting the economic situation. While credited with creating a basis for consolidation efforts under Deng Xiaoping's leadership in 1975, Zhou's measures fell considerably short of what Deng was able to accomplish.[76] On the other hand, Zhang Chunqiao and the other radicals had minimal impact on actual economic policy, even as the political tide turned against Zhou in the first half of 1973. Mao's quibbling about planning and the localities in May 1973 was essentially over a matter of emphasis and could be accommodated. But what was threatening was the Chairman's shift of emphasis to the superstructure which opened the field for the radicals. As we shall see in subsequent chapters, it was less policy change than the disruption of political movements—especially the campaign to "criticize Lin Biao and Confucius" in the first half of 1974—which threatened the economy, and it was only the Chairman's reaction to the resultant

---

[74] *Mao zhuan*, vol. 2, p. 1646; and An Jianshe, "Pipan jizuo sichao," p. 234.

[75] See An Jianshe, "Pipan jizuo sichao," pp. 212, 220; and *History of the Chinese Communist Party: A Chronology of Events (1919-1990)*, compiled by the Party History Research Centre of the Central Committee of the Chinese Communist Party (Beijing: Foreign Languages Press, 1991), pp. 354-55, 359.

[76] See the discussion in An Jianshe, "Pipan jizuo sichao," pp. 232ff.

disruption and his November 1974 instruction to "boost the national economy" that provided the political bedrock for Deng's 1975 efforts.

Reviving Diplomatic Work. While not having the same prominence as cadre policy and economic work, an important part of the critique of "ultra-leftism" was directed at the foreign affairs sector. As with foreign policy matters throughout the 1972-76 period, concrete policy alternatives were not at issue. Instead, with Zhou Enlai taking the lead, the effort was to repair the diplomatic apparatus and methods so that the PRC could conduct an active foreign policy in accord with Mao's new post-Cultural Revolution international line. In 1967-68, similar to the economy but arguably even more dramatically, China's foreign interests were sacrificed to the pursuit of ideological purity. While not quite "no foreign policy" since the war in Vietnam and the worsening Sino-Soviet conflict were high on Mao's agenda, China nevertheless entered a period of extreme isolationism. In part, officially encouraged anti-foreign sentiment produced popular extremism, most notoriously the burning of the British mission in August 1967—an act denounced by Mao as anarchism. Meanwhile, factional chaos within the Ministry of Foreign Affairs (MFA) undercut its capacity to function, while Chinese diplomats abroad spread Maoist propaganda over the protests of local governments. Beyond this, in a decision that could only have been approved by Mao, all Chinese ambassadors save one were recalled to Beijing for ideological study. Overall, no foreign government or political party—whether imperialist, revisionist, or even an extreme left splinter group—could escape PRC disdain if it refused to toe the Maoist line of the moment.[77]

As indicated, in 1967 Mao had already reacted to anarchism in foreign affairs as well as other sectors. In the British mission case, he purged several lesser members of the Central Cultural Revolution Group, but left unscathed Jiang Qing who had inflamed the broader context, and of course avoided his own fundamental responsibility.[78] By early 1969, moreover, the Chairman adopted a new foreign policy approach including the initial delicate moves that would lead to the rapprochement with the US, moves initially kept within a very narrow circle, yet eventually requiring professional expertise. More generally, Mao introduced a new foreign policy framework of rallying a broad coalition of international forces—essentially nation-states of any stripe from European

---

[77] See Thomas Robinson, "China Confronts the Soviet Union: Warfare and Diplomacy on China's Inner Asian Frontiers," in Roderick MacFarquhar and John K. Fairbank, eds., *The Cambridge History of China, Vol. 15, The People's Republic, Part 2: Revolutions within the Chinese Revolution* (Cambridge: Cambridge University Press, 1991), pp. 231-54; Barnouin and Yu, *Chinese Foreign Policy,* pp.10-28, 66-78, 155-60; Ma Jisen, *The Cultural Revolution in the Foreign Ministry of China* (Hong Kong: The Chinese University Press, 2004), especially chs. 7-8; and Melvin Gurtov, "The Foreign Ministry and Foreign Affairs in the Chinese Cultural Revolution," in Thomas W. Robinson, ed., *The Cultural Revolution in China* (Berkeley: University of California Press, 1971).

[78] See Gurtov, "Foreign Ministry," pp. 347-52; and Teiwes and Sun, *Tragedy,* pp. 82-89.

democracies to the Greek military junta to third world dictatorships—against the two superpowers. This strategy required ample diplomatic resources, and an approach to the outside world far removed from Cultural Revolution invective directed at anyone who failed to worship at the Chairman's shrine.[79]

Driven by Mao's new policies, although surely reflecting his own preferences, Zhou set out to bring order to the MFA. According to one important ministry figure, by 1971 the Premier achieved tight control and a good political environment, "almost as good as before the Cultural Revolution," while other ministries were still in chaos. Yet Zhou continued to hammer away at the need for a professional approach in repeated talks over the two years before and after September 13. This was helped by propaganda against Chen Boda for his association with the so-called "May 16 group" that was blamed for disruption in the MFA in 1967-68, and of course by the ongoing criticism of anarchism. Concerning Zhou's own actions, in April and May 1971 he criticized "ultra-leftism" at several conferences dealing with foreign affairs work, leading the Central Committee's International Liaison Department to alter propaganda unsuitable for foreign audiences. In August 1972, the Premier addressed Chinese ambassadors to foreign countries, attacking anarchism and chauvinism while criticizing the MFA, *People's Daily* and the Xinhua News Agency for failing to repudiate thoroughly "ultra-leftism." At the end of November, Zhou told a meeting on foreign affairs work that these issues still had not been cleared up, and he then approved the report of the meeting which criticized anarchism and "ultra-left" thought. This step fed into the growing dispute over the nature of Lin Biao's errors (see below), causing Zhou in effect to reverse himself in mid-December following Mao's redefinition. In that reversal, however, while declaring Lin's political line "definitely ultra-rightist," the Premier claimed that his (presumably still valid) August remarks only referred to Lin's "ultra-leftism" in foreign affairs. That Zhou still felt able to attack the problem in foreign affairs work was further seen at the start of 1973 when he approved a foreign affairs conference draft criticizing "ultra-leftism" and anarchism, and then at separate meetings called for proper treatment of foreign experts working in China.[80]

While Mao's intense interest in foreign policy suggests without clearly demonstrating that he played a more active role in the actual process of reviving diplomatic work than in readjusting economic policy, the burden again fell on Zhou Enlai. Moreover, similar to the economy and cadre policy, the basic policy

---

[79] See Joseph Camilleri, *Chinese Foreign Policy: The Maoist Era and its Aftermath* (Oxford: Martin Robertson, 1980), chs. 5-6; Jonathan D. Pollack, "The Opening to America," in MacFarquhar and Fairbank, *Cambridge History of China*, vol. 15, pp. 407-26; and Teiwes and Sun, *Tragedy*, pp. 123-26.

[80] See An Jianshe, "Pipan jizuo sichao," pp. 206, 213, 217-18, 220; Yan and Gao, *Turbulent Decade*, pp. 410, 414-15; *Mao zhuan*, vol. 2, pp. 1646-47; *History of the Party*, p. 359; *Zhou nianpu*, vol. 3, pp. 541-42, 568, 574, 577, 583; Gao Wenqian, *Wannian Zhou*, p. 393; Joseph, *Critique*, p. 124; and interview, November 2002.

approach of correcting Cultural Revolution excesses continued well into 1973 despite the redefinition of Lin Biao as an "ultra-rightist" at the end of 1972. Indeed, interference by the Politburo radicals in diplomatic work *per se* seemed even less than concerning the economy and cadre liberation. The reason foreign affairs played a role in the theoretical turnaround was because, in addressing anarchism in this sphere, Zhou wittingly or not raised a much more fundamental issue going to the root of assessing the Cultural Revolution.

Into Sensitive Territory: Culture, Education and Science. Inevitably, dealing with "ultra-leftism" in the culture, education and science spheres, and policy toward intellectuals generally, would be more fraught than efforts to correct excesses in handling cadres, economic work and foreign affairs. This, of course, goes to the heart of the *Cultural* Revolution, a movement seeking to transform the superstructure, that originated in universities and secondary schools, and reflected Mao's deep personal ambivalence concerning intellectuals. In addition, and to an extent not replicated in other areas, an alternative set of policies—the so-called "new born things of the Cultural Revolution" including model revolutionary plays and educational reforms—existed upon which a new order theoretically could be built. In education, a number of new policies were implemented as schools and universities resumed operation after the Ninth Congress: priority to politics in the classroom, drastically simplified curricula, measures challenging the authority of teachers, admissions policies strongly favoring "red classes" and eschewing national entrance examinations, and emphasis on experience in society rather than book learning.[81] Thus more was involved than simply rectifying anarchism and extremism as officially sanctioned radical programs complicated efforts to revive intellectual life.

A further complicating factor was the authority of the Politburo radicals in the culture-education-science area. This was not entirely formal, although Zhang Chunqiao was in charge of at least one key conference in this period. Rather, it derived from the leading roles of these leaders in 1966-68, notably Jiang Qing as "the standard-bearer in literature and art circles." In bureaucratic terms, with the responsible pre-1966 organizations[82] dissolved, more junior radical figures assumed major roles in the coordinating bodies established in 1971, notably Chi Qun as deputy head of the State Council Science and Education Group, and Yu Huiyong as deputy head of the State Council Culture Group. The heads of these bodies, however, were not radicals—former Vice Minister of the State Science and Technology Commission Liu Xiyao for the Science and Education Group, and Politburo member Wu De for the Culture Group. But the clout of the radicals was palpable. In his recollections, Wu De claimed great difficulty in

---

[81] For a sympathetic contemporary view of the "revolution in education," see John Gardner and Wilt Idema, "China's Educational Revolution," in Stuart R. Schram, ed., *Authority, Participation and Cultural Change in China* (Cambridge: Cambridge University Press, 1973).

[82] The Ministry of Culture, Ministry of Education, and State Science and Technology Commission.

carrying out his responsibilities, particularly due to clashes with Jiang Qing over trivial matters. As a consequence, Wu sought some insurance by recruiting Wang Mantian, Wang Hairong's aunt and thus Mao's relative, to the Culture Group to facilitate access to the Chairman, while the radicals sometimes backed off from disputes given their uncertainty concerning Mao's views. Overall, however, Jiang Qing was able to override her Politburo colleague. Even with Zhou Enlai present, Jiang rebuffed Wu's request to transfer a former Ministry of Culture cadre to the group to compensate for his own ignorance of artistic matters, and set two restrictions on Wu's work by banning such transfers and limiting bureaucratic support to her eight model productions.[83]

Reflecting Zhou Enlai's "first easy then difficult" approach, his attention to the culture-education-science spheres deepened from the middle of 1972. Nevertheless, moves to counter "ultra-left" phenomena and revive educational institutions pre-dated September 13, even though they were caught up in the special sensitivity of the area. Among Zhou's efforts in culture, education and science before summer 1972 were: in the first half of 1971, he criticized "ultra-leftism" affecting specialists and lamented the scarcity of books about Chinese and foreign history, as well as attempting to defend intellectuals more generally; following the Lin Biao incident and throughout the first half of 1972, he issued directives to relevant departments on overcoming leftist tendencies and affirmed the Hundred Flowers, the classic "pro"-intellectual policy; and, overall, he emphasized the importance of professional proficiency and raising educational standards, and worked for the reopening of universities, albeit universities ostensibly serving worker-peasant-soldier students.[84]

The so-called "two assessments" of education in the 17 years before the Cultural Revolution illuminate Zhou's efforts before mid-1972, the political sensitivity of the area, and the fact that some moderation of leftist policies occurred prior to Lin's demise. Approved at the April-July 1971 national education conference held under the control of Zhang Chunqiao and Chi Qun, these assessments asserted that "[in the 17 years after 1949], Chairman Mao's proletarian revolutionary line has not been implemented in the main, as a result of which the bourgeoisie has exercised dictatorship over the proletariat; [and] the great majority of intellectuals [trained in these 17 years] still remain basically bourgeois in their world outlook; in other words, they are still bourgeois intellectuals."[85] While the common view that the "two assessments" were a

---

[83] Wu De, "Cong Guowuyuan wenhuazu dao sijie Renda" [From the State Council Culture Group to the Fourth NPC], *DDZGSYJ*, no. 1 (2002), pp. 77-79; Chen Donglin and Du Pu, eds., *Zhonghuarenmingongheguo shilu* [True Record of the PRC], vol. 3, part 1, *Neiluan yu kangzheng— "wenhua dageming" de shinian (1966-1971)* [Civil Disorder and Resistance—The "Cultural Revolution" Decade, 1966-1971] (Changchun: Jilin renmin chubanshe, 1994), p. 704; and Lamb, *Directory*, pp. 519-20, 526-27.

[84] See An Jianshe, "Pipan jizuo sichao," pp. 205-207, 212, 234; *Mao zhuan*, vol. 2, p. 1646; Ma Qibin, *Sishinian*, pp. 339, 349; and Yan and Gao, *Turbulent Decade*, pp. 409, 411.

major victory for the radical viewpoint is not strictly wrong, the reality was more complicated. The 1971 conference was convened on Mao's authority, and clearly the participants were concerned with the Chairman's views, but there is little information on his concrete role apart from approving the eventual document emerging from the meeting. The initial draft proposed at the conference by Shanghai delegates and said to be the view of the Shanghai Municipal Party Committee—and thus Zhang Chunqiao, Yao Wenyuan and Wang Hongwen who all held leading positions on the committee—was considerably harsher, declaring that traitors, spies and capitalist roaders had monopolized power in the educational sphere. This led to intense opposition at the meeting, with participants pointing out that Mao and the Party Center had approved the educational line. Chi Qun attacked these participants, questioning their standpoint, while Mao's nephew and Liaoning representative Mao Yuanxin claimed such objections negated "new born things of the Cultural Revolution." Under Zhang Chunqiao's direction, the conference essentially denied any positive contributions by intellectuals.[86]

In these circumstances, Zhou addressed the conference's leading small group on July 6. Whether the Premier had any prior discussions with Mao is unknown, but he clearly did not feel inhibited from challenging the position the conference had reached, albeit within limits. Apparently speaking with some authority, Zhou presented a considerably more positive assessment, arguing that "Chairman Mao's red line *also* illuminated the educational line," "the great majority of intellectuals accept Party leadership and serve socialism," and concrete analysis of teachers and students must be discriminating.[87] This led to some back peddling on Zhang Chunqiao's part, as he now said the problem of the leading power during the 17 years had not been solved, and Mao's line had not been implemented. This resulted in a somewhat compromise version of the "two assessments" submitted to the Center later in July which held that during the 17 years Mao's line had not been implemented *in the main*, but acknowledged, notwithstanding their bourgeois world view, "most teachers support socialism and want to serve the people."[88]

By the time of the State Council Science and Education Group's May-June 1972 symposium on the educational revolution in universities and foreign language institutes, the situation had evolved further. The sketchy available accounts of this meeting make no mention of either Zhang Chunqiao or Chi Qun, but note that it was held while Zhou was in charge of the daily work of the Party Center. While ostensibly criticizing both the rightist and "ultra-leftist"

---

[85] As trans. in *History of the Party*, p. 352. This version, which is basically faithful to a number of authoritative sources, is nevertheless harsher than what can be deduced from *Mao wengao*, vol. 13, p. 239 (see below).

[86] Chen and Du, *Shilu*, vol. 3, part 1, pp. 705-706.

[87] *Ibid.*, p. 705 (emphasis added).

[88] *Ibid.*; and *Mao wengao*, vol. 13, p. 239.

crimes of Lin Biao, the meeting offered an opportunity to express concern with the damage caused to higher education by the Cultural Revolution, and the practical measures endorsed by the symposium were designed to address the resulting problems: lifting educational standards, emphasizing instruction in basic theories, cultivating talented individuals for scientific research, and implementing the Hundred Flowers policy toward intellectuals.[89]

While this represented a shift toward combating left excesses, it was in the following months that education and science came to the fore in the form of deepening conflict within the Politburo. While impossible to isolate from other developments such as Zhou Enlai's August comments to diplomatic personnel, and an October *People's Daily* article on anarchism "according to the spirit of Zhou Enlai's many speeches," or from various initiatives in the educational realm,[90] much of the radical concern came from efforts concerning science and involving Beijing University's renowned physicist, Zhou Peiyuan. Zhou Peiyuan became in effect the spearhead of the effort to reorient higher education away from the Cultural Revolution's extreme emphasis on practical, vocationally-oriented curricula and back toward basic theoretical enquiry. Growing out of a July 1972 meeting with the Premier, Zhou Peiyuan prepared an article on the need for more attention to theoretical research in the natural sciences. Aware of the article, seemingly because the Premier informed the State Council Science and Education Group of Zhou Peiyuan's concerns, Zhang Chunqiao and Yao Wenyuan sought to derail the project, organizing a collection of critical opinions, delaying publication, and finally diverting the article from the *People's Daily* to the less authoritative *Guangming Daily*, where it was published on October 6. Once published, they organized opposing views in Shanghai. More pointedly, with Zhang Chunqiao allegedly commenting that "some people use the renowned physicist to oppress us," Zhang and Yao sent people to investigate the background of the article, declaring that Zhou Peiyuan had a behind-the-scenes supporter who must be criticized, "no matter how powerful [he] is." The unknown factor was Mao who received Zhou Peiyuan in November, listened to his opinions on higher education and the urgent needs of the nation's science, but only commented that "this matter has great relevance," and it was something for the Science and Education Group, the Beijing Municipal Party Committee, and the Party Center to examine, with the Center deciding on a course of action.[91]

---

[89] Chen and Du, *Shilu*, vol. 3, part 2, pp. 824-25; Ma Qibin, *Sishinian*, p. 349; Barnouin and Yu, *Ten Years*, pp. 252-53; and Yan and Gao, *Turbulent Decade*, p. 411.

[90] For example, the inauguration of English lessons on Beijing radio, efforts to improve the standard of teaching materials, calls for all related institutions to publish academic magazines, and convening the first conference on science and technology since 1966. See Yan and Gao, *Turbulent Decade*, p. 411.

[91] *Ibid.*, pp. 410, 412-13; An Jianshe, "Pipan jizuo sichao," pp. 214-17; and *Mao zhuan*, vol. 2, pp. 1657-58.

These developments presumably influenced the reclassification of Lin Biao as an "ultra-rightist," but as in other areas there was no immediate sign of a sharp reversal of policy in the first half of 1973. Indeed, the continuing drift toward standards was seen in the adoption and implementation of a "cultural examination" as a prerequisite for university admission, albeit a process linked to recommendation of worker-peasant-soldier students by the masses. By the second half of 1973, however, with Jiang Qing *et al.* "making educational circles the first target of attack," heavy propaganda on a number of exemplary cases pointed in precisely the opposite direction, both before and after the Tenth Congress. The most famous, and most telling, was the case of the "blank examination paper." Zhang Tiesheng, an educated youth working in a rural commune in Liaoning, sat for the regional examination after passing his commune's preliminary exam. After performing badly on several sections, Zhang turned the paper over and wrote a letter criticizing the whole process, claiming only selfish bookworms could succeed while people such as himself who truly served the people were disadvantaged. This case was seized upon by the Politburo radicals as a heroic example of "going against the tide"—a phrase that would become a key concept at the Tenth Congress. Perhaps more significant than the activities of the radicals in Beijing was the role of Mao Yuanxin in bringing the case to prominence in Liaoning, and thus nationally. Mao Yuanxin even reportedly modified Zhang Tiesheng's letter for propaganda purposes. The turn in propaganda effectively called a halt in efforts to repair the educational system until mid-1975.[92]

From "Ultra-Left" to "Ultra-Right." Although the circumstances and pace varied by area, throughout the first half of 1972 the dominant trend was criticism of "ultra-leftist" excesses. Indeed, even before September 13, Jiang Qing and Lin Biao himself had criticized "ultra-leftism," albeit assertedly with ulterior motives. After September 13 to mid-1972, as we have seen, the radicals largely kept quiet as criticisms of left excesses in various spheres unfolded, undoubtedly because of their understanding that these criticisms and related measures had Mao's backing. From mid-1972, however, "the struggle deepened" as Zhou Enlai attempted to extend the effort into more difficult areas and build on the momentum already achieved. The Politburo radicals felt that they were under attack, and this was a correct assessment in the sense that their preferred policy orientation was under heavy pressure. Yet Zhou never directed personal attacks on them, and, as seen particularly in the case of Zhang Chunqiao and the navy, Mao had given the radicals considerable resources to defend their interests. The developing conflict, particularly in August-November, set the stage for the Chairman's December redefinition of Lin Biao as an "ultra-rightist."[93]

---

[92] See Yan and Gao, *Turbulent Decade*, pp. 411, 417-20; *GMRB*, November 30, 1976, in *Survey of People's Republic of China Press* (hereafter *SPRCP*), no. 6251 (1977), pp. 66-73; and An Jianshe, "Pipan jizuo sichao," pp. 221-23.

[93] See An Jianshe, "Pipan jizuo sichao," pp. 207-208, 212, 216-17.

We have already noted some of the key developments fueling the conflict in the second half of 1972: Zhou's August talks to diplomatic personnel, the circumstances surrounding Zhou Peiyuan's October article, and the late November foreign affairs meeting. Zhou's early August talks, including a separate effort criticizing central propaganda organs for insufficient exposure of leftist problems, increased the tension within the leadership, although perhaps not as much as sometimes claimed. Jiang Qing, true to form, reportedly expressed disgust, although the circumstances have not been specified. A more restrained reaction came from Zhang Chunqiao and Yao Wenyuan, who expressed reservations and argued that criticism of Lin Biao [i.e., the "ultra-left"] should not be excessive. Indeed, over the next two months, the mixed message of opposing both right and left continued, with a tug of war apparently going on over the precise media line. In this context, the National Day joint editorial[94] was drafted under Zhou's authority, although Yao excised its call to "criticize right and 'left' deviations, [but] especially the ultra-left trend." This incident also points to the ambiguous authority in the media sphere. While, in his capacity of directing the Party Center's daily work, Zhou's writ seemingly extended into this area, Yao had specific responsibility for propaganda work. This further complicated the relations between the two men; in the specific case we surmise that Zhou accepted the deletion in order to avoid a direct clash. But such a clash soon emerged on October 14 when the *People's Daily*, a little over a week after Zhou Peiyuan's essay in *Guangming Daily*, published three articles on the particularly explosive theme that "anarchism is false Marxism," thus implicitly questioning the entire rationale of the Cultural Revolution. These articles, reportedly written in the spirit of Zhou's speeches since August, produced a major internal struggle that fed into the late November meeting that also highlighted anarchism.[95]

As a leading Party historian has argued, the October articles on anarchism were not only less severe criticisms than they might have been, but were also contradictory even if their purpose was clear. As with so much of the criticism of leftist phenomena over the previous few years, the issue was clouded by the assertion that anarchism was the product of a revisionist line, the work of "swindlers" who used this "ultra-left" manifestation to cover up their "rightist counterrevolutionary essence." The thrust, William Joseph has observed, was to treat "ultra-leftism" as a tactical problem, not as a symptom of an erroneous line, as was the case with revisionism. Such qualification and obfuscation notwithstanding, giving anarchism a full page of theoretical consideration in the Party's daily took the issue beyond criticism of specific manifestations in

---

[94] Of the *People's Daily*, *Red Flag* and the *PLA Daily* (*Jiefangjun bao*).

[95] *Mao zhuan*, vol. 2, p. 1646; *History of the Party*, p. 358; and Joseph, *Critique*, pp. 129-32. On the question of authority in the propaganda area, a central organization and propaganda group was established under the Politburo in November 1970 with Kang Sheng as head, but with Jiang Qing and Zhang Chunqiao as the key members. By 1972, however, Kang's role appears minimal.

different areas. The background to the articles goes back to March 1972 when Hua Guofeng, Li Xiannian and Yu Qiuli undertook an investigation tour of Heilongjiang to look into long-standing problems in three Harbin factories, and advocated criticism of anarchism in response to the chaotic conditions they found. This, in turn, led the writing group of the Heilongjiang Party Committee to produce an article on the meeting of the three central leaders with local officials, under the title "Anarchism is the Counterrevolutionary Tool of Marxist Swindlers." This text then found its way to the theoretical department of the *People's Daily*, headed by the paper's future editor, Hu Jiwei, where it was reworked by several theoreticians including Mao's old traveling associate, the recently liberated Wu Lengxi, with the main responsibility taken by Wang Ruoshui. With Zhou Enlai apparently not directly involved, and Zhang Chunqiao and Yao Wenyuan away in Shanghai, this then became the lead article of the three published on October 14.[96]

If Zhang and Yao's absence allowed the *People's Daily* theoretical department to arrange publication of the articles on anarchism, articles which plumbed theoretical issues with analyses of Lenin and Bakunin, once published a major conflict ensued. Judged by several senior Party historians as a more critical turning point for the escalating conflict than any previous development, the articles were seen as expressing the views of old cadres about Red Guard rebels during the late 1960s. In Shanghai, Zhang and Yao reacted immediately, seeking information on who was responsible at the *People's Daily*, organizing an internal issue of Shanghai's *Wenhui Daily* which recounted the views of the "masses" that the articles were "poisonous weeds" negating the Cultural Revolution, and bringing direct pressure on the *People's Daily* staff—an alleged campaign of suppression to "bludgeon people who mentioned opposing the 'left' [and] set the limits and tone of criticism." It was in this context that, at the end of November, Zhou approved the report of the foreign affairs meeting criticizing anarchism and "ultra-left" thought. It was also at this point, following various media items on the rightist essence of Liu-type "swindlers" that the radicals went one step further in the December 1 issue of *Red Flag*, with an article declaring that "[the swindlers] have consistently been ultra-right."[97]

It is unclear what role, if any, Mao played in this increasingly tense state of affairs. He would surely have been aware of what was appearing in the

---

[96] *RMRB*, October 14, 1972, p. 2; An Jianshe, "Pipan jizuo sichao," pp. 215-16; Joseph, *Critique*, pp. 130-32; Yan and Gao, *Turbulent Decade*, p. 414; Hu Jiwei, "Bingxue qiqing, jinshi qijian: zhuisi Wang Ruoshui Tongzhi" [As Pure as Ice and Snow, as Strong as Metal and Stone: Reminiscences of Comrade Wang Ruoshui], *Zhengming* [Contention], April 2002, p. 51; and interview with senior Party historian, December 2002. While Zhou may not have been directly involved, given his meticulous work style and responsibility for the Party Center, it is almost certain he would have seen the articles in advance.

[97] Hu Jiwei, "Bingxue qiqing," p. 51; Joseph, *Critique*, pp. 132-33; Yan and Gao, *Turbulent Decade*, p. 414; *Mao zhuan*, vol. 2, p. 1646; *HQ*, no. 12 (1972), p. 12; and interviews with senior Party

pages of the *People's Daily*, but whether he had spoken explicitly on the matter to either Zhou or the Politburo radicals is unknown, although one must assume that both Zhou and the radicals had reason to hope that he was sympathetic to their concerns. Significantly, there was a certain tentativeness on both sides. According to a senior source with access to the document, while the foreign affairs meeting's report criticized anarchism, it only raised the issue once, and in the context of the special circumstances in the MFA dating back to the attack on the British mission in 1967 that Mao himself had denounced. It did not generalize about the essence of Lin Biao, and thus could be seen as a relatively safe report for Zhou to endorse on November 30. Indeed, the next day, according to another senior source, Zhang Chunqiao also expressed his agreement with the report, although he simultaneously expressed reservations on the theoretical issue: "I wonder whether or not the main problem at present is still ultra-left thought, and whether criticizing Lin is criticizing ultra-leftism and anarchism." The next day, December 2, Jiang Qing was more forthright, but to a degree still tentative: "I *personally* believe that we should criticize ultra-rightism, which was what the traitor Lin Biao really represented. [What we] should be talking about is the victory of the Cultural Revolution."[98]

The issue came to a head, in an eerie foreshadowing of an even more significant change of course almost three years later,[99] when a lower-level figure within the *People's Daily* sought guidance from Mao on the confusion in propaganda work. Wang Ruoshui, who had played a central role in the October 14 articles, wrote to the Chairman on December 5 (in what was actually one of a series of letters) asking about the different views expressed in the *People's Daily* and *Wenhui Daily*, noting candidly the different opinions of Zhou as opposed to those of Zhang Chunqiao and Yao Wenyuan. In this letter Wang expressed his own view, which was to back strongly the Premier's efforts to curb "ultra-leftism." Whether Mao would have remained aloof from the conflict without Wang's letter cannot be known, but his apparent November support of Zhang Chunqiao's criticism of the navy leadership suggests the Chairman's views were in flux. In any case, the missive either forced him to intervene in the Politburo conflict, or provided the excuse to make clear his own opinion. On the 6th, Mao summoned Jiang Qing and instructed her to transmit Wang's letter to Zhou, Zhang Chunqiao and Yao Wenyuan, urging that they talk it over and solve the problem. Jiang proposed to Zhou that they first talk and unify their understanding, a proposal the Premier accepted. On the same day, however, Zhang and Yao claimed that Mao said Lin

---

historians, December 2002.

[98] Yan and Gao, *Turbulent Decade*, pp. 414-15; *Mao zhuan*, vol. 2, pp. 1646-47; An Jianshe, "Pipan jizuo sichao," pp. 217-18; and interviews with senior Party historians, December 2002. The italics in Jiang's statement, which indicate the matter had not been settled by the Chairman, are added.

[99] I.e., Liu Bing's October 1975 letter to Mao that contributed to the Chairman's removal of Deng Xiaoping from power. See below, pp. 388ff.

"had always been a rightist," a claim that would be verified in 11 days' time. The Chairman had set in motion a process that changed not only the definition of Lin, but the tone of Politburo interaction as well.[100]

On December 17, Mao convened a small meeting of Zhou, Zhang and Yao, declared that Wang's letter was erroneous, decreed that criticism of "ultra-leftism" should be reduced a bit, and redefined the nature of Lin's "line": "It is ultra-rightist. [Lin was] a revisionist, a splitter, carried out plots, and betrayed the Party and country." Two days later, when convening a meeting of *People's Daily* editors to convey Mao's verdict on Wang Ruoshui's letter together with Jiang, Zhang, Yao and other Politburo members, the Premier conceded the situation, acknowledged that the October 14 articles had been erroneous, that Lin Biao had indeed promoted an "ultra-rightist" political line, and claimed his previous "ultra-left" characterization of Lin was limited to foreign affairs. Zhou's humiliation was not limited to these admissions at this and subsequent meetings in December. He now clearly lost any authority over the propaganda sphere, thus greatly complicating his efforts across the board. At a personal level, in what would be a recurring situation for the Premier, the radicals adopted a very harsh posture toward Zhou, acting cold and indifferent, and paying no attention to him—all in front of lower-ranking officials. Clearly, as a Party historian observed, this was impossible without Mao in the background. We can only speculate whether the radicals were merely taking advantage of Mao's position on the issue, or reflecting a newly expressed attitude concerning Zhou on the Chairman's part, but decades later Wang Ruoshui recalled his amazement as he began to form the view that Mao really didn't like Zhou.[101]

Why Mao altered course in December 1972 can only be a matter of conjecture. Mao's personal attitude toward Zhou was arguably a factor, especially in view of Wang Ruoshui's approving reference to the Premier's efforts. Moreover, as argued above, Lin Biao's personal preferences were to moderate the Cultural Revolution, so it follows that Mao's true opinion was that Lin was indeed a rightist, however much the circumstances in September 1971 made it convenient to focus on leftist mistakes. But such possible considerations were undoubtedly less important than Mao's fundamental commitment to the Cultural Revolution and the evolution of the critique of "ultra-leftism" into more sensitive areas in the latter part of 1972. In particular, by focusing on anarchism and treating the issue at a theoretical level, the October 14 articles tread on territory of extreme sensitivity to Mao, especially since the inference could be drawn that the Cultural

---

[100] Yan and Gao, *Turbulent Decade*, p. 415; *Mao zhuan*, vol. 2, pp. 1647-48; An Jianshe, "Pipan jizuo sichao," pp. 218-19; Hu Jiwei, "Bingxue qiqing," pp. 51-52; and above, pp. 41-42.

[101] *Mao zhuan*, vol. 2, p. 1648; Yan and Gao, *Turbulent Decade*, pp. 415-16; *Zhou nianpu*, vol. 3, pp. 567-68; An Jianshe, "Pipan jizuo sichao," pp. 219, 235; Barnouin and Yu, *Ten Years*, pp. 254-55; Wang Ruoshui, "Zhou Enlai jiuzuo douzheng de shibai" [Zhou Enlai's Defeat in His Effort to Rectify Leftist Excesses] (January 22, 2001), http://www.cnd.org/HXWZ/ZK01/zk247.gb.html; and interviews with Party historians, December 2002 and January 2005.

Revolution caused anarchy, while Wang Ruoshui's letter graphically displayed conflict in the Politburo. Whether Mao would have acted in late 1972 or 1973 without these articles or Wang's letter is moot, but, we believe, their absence at best would have delayed a reaction.

Whatever Mao's precise motives for his December decision, a number of things can be said about the critique of "ultra-leftism." First, the claim of sophisticated Party historian An Jianshe that the Lin Biao incident forced Mao to reconsider the reasons for the excesses of the Cultural Revolution is misleading. As An and others acknowledge, attacks on "ultra-leftism," by Jiang Qing and Lin himself among others, predate September 13. While the needs of the moment, particularly to rally people disillusioned with the Cultural Revolution, dictated the continuation and deepening of criticism of leftist errors, there is nothing to indicate any significant reconsideration of the fundamental issue on Mao's part, apart from his heightened awareness of the threat to his legacy. Significantly, it was not long after the Lin Biao affair in February or March 1972 that the Chairman, apparently for the first time, reflected on the Cultural Revolution as the second great achievement of his life. Second, the entire effort to criticize "ultra-leftism," even at its height in 1972, was relatively tame. Overall, it amounted to little more than the consolidation measures normal in CCP history following intense political campaigns. From Mao's perspective, he was quite prepared to correct a range of practical questions, but would not allow any reconsideration of the movement at a theoretical level. Zhou Enlai, acutely aware that Mao's support was a prerequisite and proceeding cautiously, tried to keep within these boundaries. But actions such as the October 14 articles and Wang Ruoshui's letter, where he seemingly had at best an indirect role, pushed the issue further than he presumably wanted, even allowing for the fact that in objective terms these too were limited actions.[102]

Finally, as we have noted in all the specific areas examined above, the redefinition of Lin Biao did not end efforts well into the first half of 1973 to correct left deviations, or to introduce new programs to bring greater order in those spheres. Indeed, even when addressing *People's Daily* editors on December 19, 1972, Zhang Chunqiao indicated that some such efforts were still necessary, observing that "I don't mean to oppose completely criticism of ultra-left thought." But, as throughout, the CCP's propaganda line had a critical impact on practical work, Zhou now lost his authority in this area, and the new emphasis was clearly reflected in the joint New Year editorial citing the absolute necessity for the *current* Cultural Revolution, and emphasizing the task of criticizing revisionism. The ensuing propaganda efforts sought to explain away "ultra-leftism" as a tactical ploy of the "swindlers" and a matter of secondary importance, and strongly defend the "new born things" of the Cultural Revolution, although, as Joseph

---

[102] An Jianshe, "Pipan jizuo sichao," pp. 198-99; *Mao zhuan*, vol. 2, pp. 1644-45, 1648; and interview with senior specialist on Zhou Enlai, December 2002.

argues, its criticism of "ultra-rightism" was noticeably unspecific and abstract. By mid-year, with the Tenth Congress approaching, criticism of "ultra-leftism" had become taboo, "Liu-type swindlers" were ever more consistently labeled "ultra-rightist" in essence, praise of heroes "going against the tide" became a major media theme, and work in areas such as the economy was complicated by the emphasis on "combating rightist restoration."[103] This further turning away from the critique of 1972 was undoubtedly linked to Mao's ongoing discontent with Zhou Enlai and to his desire to promote younger rebels emerging from the Cultural Revolution, notably Wang Hongwen, matters we consider later in this chapter.

The Return of Deng Xiaoping

Although not the first liberated cadre to return to work, and someone who was required to wait about eight months after his posting as a vice premier in March 1973 for truly significant power, Deng Xiaoping was clearly the most important official to be rehabilitated from the moment he received Mao's initial blessing in August 1972. The significance of Deng's rehabilitation was due to both his high status before 1966 as one of Mao's select "close comrades-in-arms" and CCP General Secretary, and his symbolic Cultural Revolution role as the "number two capitalist roader within the Party" after Liu Shaoqi. The latter role necessitated careful preparations for his return in terms of explanations for the general public, as well as for high-level and rank-and-file Party members. In contrast to his usual terse comments on letters concerning others seeking rehabilitation, Mao expounded on Deng's virtues:

> The errors committed by Deng Xiaoping are grave. But he should be distinguished from Liu Shaoqi. (1) In the Central Soviet [in the early 1930s] he was purged as one of the four criminals Deng, Mao [Zetan, Mao's brother], Xie [Weijun], Gu [Bai], he was boss of the so-called Mao faction (*Mao pai*). ... (2) He does not have historical problems. That is, he did not surrender to the enemy. (3) His work with Liu Bocheng in battle was skilled and successful. As well, after entering the city [with the establishment of the PRC] he was not lacking in good deeds, for example, he led the delegation for the Moscow negotiations [in 1963], and he did not bow to Soviet revisionism. I've said all this many times before, and now I'm saying it again.[104]

Thus, grave errors notwithstanding, Deng rated highly on many of Mao's essential criteria of personal loyalty, a clean revolutionary record, substantial military (*wu*) achievements, and firmness against the Soviet revisionists. In addition, his

---

[103] See Yan and Gao, *Turbulent Decade*, p. 416; An Jianshe, "Pipan jizuo sichao," pp. 219, 235; *PR*, no. 1 (1973), pp. 9-11; Joseph, *Critique*, pp. 132-37; "Quarterly Chronicle and Documentation," *CQ*, no. 55 (1973), pp. 600-602; and Liu and Wu, *China's Socialist Economy*, p. 386.

[104] *Mao wengao*, vol. 13, pp. 308-309.

work "in the city" indicated the type of administrative (*wen*) skill that would be increasingly required given Zhou Enlai's recently diagnosed cancer. There is little doubt that in bringing Deng back Mao was at least considering Deng as a potential replacement for Zhou, whether simply out of administrative need, or, more likely, also reflecting his long-standing reservations concerning the Premier.[105]

As we saw in the Introduction, the Chairman's favoritism toward Deng was long standing. Its origins lay in the revolutionary period, specifically from the late 1930s when Deng served as a loyal and efficient enforcer of Mao's "line." The crucial step was Deng's appointment as political commissar of the 129th Division in early 1938, a step reflecting both Mao's confidence in Deng and his reservations concerning this army, part of which had been commanded by his inner-Party enemy, Zhang Guotao. This force eventually became the Second Field Army, and it is significant that at the end of 1973, Mao specifically called for the promotion of officers from this "mountaintop" to counter those from Lin's Fourth Field Army. Beyond his role as Mao's enforcer, an important factor for future Mao-Deng relations was Deng's military accomplishments as a leader of Liu Bocheng's Second Field Army, notably at the crucial Huai-Hai battle in 1948. This not only resulted in enormous prestige for Deng within the Party and army generally, leading to proposals that he be named a PLA marshal in 1955, it also earned the admiration of Mao who had long been fascinated with military heroism. It is no coincidence that Mao's two favorite colleagues were Lin Biao, widely seen as the greatest of all Red Army generals, and Deng.[106] His battlefield skills made Deng a rare talent indeed, someone who combined *wen* and *wu*. Mao noted this explicitly as early as 1951: "Whether it's politics or military affairs, Deng Xiaoping is top class."[107] Deng was, in Mao's mind, an all rounder destined for great things, and in appointing him General Secretary at the Eighth Party Congress in 1956, the Chairman raised Deng well above his previous Party status.[108]

While necessarily speculative, arguably another important factor binding Mao and Deng—one that also applied in the Mao-Lin case—was their respective

---

[105] Deng's rehabilitation as based on the need to replace Zhou's skills is widely cited; see, e.g., *Mao zhuan*, vol. 2, p. 1649. For somewhat different discussions of Mao's criteria for top leaders, see Teiwes, "Mao and His Lieutenants," pp. 56ff; and idem, "Politics at the 'Core'," pp. 22-26.

[106] See Benjamin Yang, *Deng: A Political Biography* (Armonk: M.E. Sharpe, 1998), pp. 81-83, 86ff; Frederick C. Teiwes, "The Paradoxical Post-Mao Transition: From Obeying the Leader to 'Normal Politics'," in Jonathan Unger, ed., *The Nature of Chinese Politics: From Mao to Jiang* (Armonk: M.E. Sharpe, 2002), pp. 70-71; David S. G. Goodman, *Deng Xiaoping and the Chinese Revolution: A Political Biography* (London: Routledge, 1994), pp. 117-19; Schram, *Political Thought*, pp. 22-24, 125-26, 157; and below, p. 143.

[107] Gao Yi, *Lishi xuanze*, p. 184.

[108] Deng, now promoted to sixth in the leadership, had been an ordinary Central Committee member ranked 28th at the Seventh Congress in 1945. In comparison, Peng Zhen, who now became Deng's deputy in the Central Secretariat, was a Politburo member in 1945.

age and seniority, and the deference implied. Whereas Liu Shaoqi and Zhou Enlai, who had roughly equal Party seniority to Mao and were only five years younger than the Chairman, might have been perceived as "equals," Deng (and Lin) were another six to nine years Mao's junior and dependent on him for their rise through the Party's ranks. This undoubtedly led to great respect in exchanges with Mao, perhaps along the lines of the teacher-student relationship so significant in Chinese culture.[109] Such interaction was inevitably more congenial to Mao than the fraught relationships with Liu and Zhou, notwithstanding their total loyalty to the Chairman. Thus when Mao referred to Deng in late 1973 as "a needle hidden in cotton," i.e., someone whose soft exterior covered a decisive and determined leader, he was expressing admiration for his colleague's toughness without the complication of near equal seniority.[110]

What went wrong in the Mao-Deng relationship before the Cultural Revolution? This is not the place for an extended analysis, nor have we undertaken focused, in-depth research into this issue. Nevertheless, the interpretation offered by an authoritative Party historian on Deng's predicament and response in the immediate pre-1966 period appears credible. In this interpretation, Deng shared the discomfit of other "first-front" leaders with Mao's ideological drift in the early 1960s, and (like them) avoided confrontation, but unlike Liu Shaoqi, he subtly reduced his activities to minimize potential conflict with Mao. This resulted in Deng's deputy in the Secretariat, Peng Zhen, often taking the leading role, but also in a reduction in Deng's reporting to the Chairman. While undoubtedly Deng's organizational prominence, combined with Mao's need for scapegoats for China's perceived revisionist course, led to the label of "number two capitalist roader,"[111] arguably it was Mao's disappointment with Deng's distancing and his reluctance to speak out on the issues the Chairman had raised, rather than any of Deng's positions *per se,* that sealed his fate. But because of their past history, Mao's behavior was complicated. On the one hand, he repeatedly noted the distinction between Liu and Deng from early in the Cultural Revolution, and even sympathetically edited the draft of Deng's October 1966 self-criticism. On the other hand, at least before the Ninth Congress, he allowed the attack on the "Liu-Deng line" to proceed and authorized Deng's removal from his official positions, even as he made sure that Deng had the physical protection that he deliberately denied to Liu.[112]

---

[109] The teacher-student relationship was explicitly argued for Mao and Lin by a senior oral source, but this source was not questioned in these terms concerning Deng. Interview, March 1986. Cf. Teiwes, "Mao and His Lieutenants," pp. 63-64.

[110] See *Mao zhuan,* vol. 2, p. 1674; and Teiwes, "Mao and His Lieutenants," pp. 59-60, 63, 70.

[111] The only active and truly powerful figure at the Center who survived the Cultural Revolution purges was the subservient and indefatigable Zhou Enlai. Similarly, with few exceptions, the top Party officials in each province were ousted. See Frederick C. Teiwes, "Provincial Politics in China: Themes and Variations," in John M.H. Lindbeck, ed., *China: Management of a Revolutionary Society* (Seattle: University of Washington Press, 1971), p. 151.

As we have seen, Mao's behavior toward Deng during the Cultural Revolution was even more remarkable. If Wang Li is to be believed, the Chairman contemplated replacing Lin Biao with Deng at the height of the movement's chaos in 1967. Other signs of ongoing favoritism were Mao's reported rejection of Lin Biao and Jiang Qing's alleged 1968 proposal to expel Deng from the CCP, Zhou Enlai's opinion (surely reflecting his perception of Mao's attitude) that it would have been possible for Deng to attend the 1970 Lushan plenum, and above all Mao's assignment of one of his closest functionaries, Wang Dongxing, to guarantee Deng's security and needs during his exile in Jiangxi in 1969-72. Wang served an invaluable service for Deng during this period and, as we shall see, later in the Mao era. The remarkable account of Deng's life during this difficult period by his daughter Mao Mao is, in many respects, a description of the Mao-Deng relationship, with Wang as the crucial intermediary. Wang had the responsibility of making sure nothing happened to the Chairman's chastised favorite, a task he carried out beyond the letter of his assignment. Although he dismissed Deng's thanks when Deng returned to work in 1973 on the basis that he was simply carrying out Mao's wishes, Wang had done much more. He not only saw to every household request of the Deng family, he conveyed Deng's correspondence to Mao, and advised Deng on the proper approach to the Chairman. Wang Dongxing was an essential factor in Deng's personal and political well-being, but, as he candidly acknowledged, this was as a reflection of the Chairman's intent.[113]

If Mao's parental-style mixture of punishment and protection is clear, how can we characterize Deng's attitude and behavior toward his leader? We can only assume that for much of a career marked not only by his own rise but also by Mao's almost unimaginably successful leadership of the CCP, Deng admired Mao's strength of leadership and appreciated his ever more awesome power. Yet there apparently was a loyalty that went further and extended into the post-Mao period. We shall examine this complex matter in our Volume II; for now it is sufficient to note his 1979 statement as the process of reevaluating Mao began—"[All] lines, principles and policies formulated by Chairman Mao were correct, our mistakes came from not insisting on Chairman Mao's line, principles and policies."[114] More telling, and more to the point for the period of Deng's

---

[112] Teiwes, "Mao and His Lieutenants," pp. 68-69; Wang Li, *Wang Li fansi (xia)* [Wang Li's Reflections, vol. 2] (Hong Kong: Beixing chubanshe, 2001), pp. 635-37; Xue Qingchao, *Lishi zhuanzhe guantou,* p. 220; interview, March 1986; and above, p. 25.

[113] See Yan and Gao, *Turbulent Decade*, p. 454; Zhang Zuoliang, *Zhou Enlai de zuihou shinian: yiwei baojian yisheng de huiyi* [The Last Decade of Zhou Enlai's Life: Recollections of a Medical Care Doctor] (Shanghai: Shanghai renmin chubanshe, 1997), pp. 233, 275; Mao Mao, *"Wenge" suiyue,* especially pp. 132, 270; and below, pp. 490-91. Given Mao's attitude, we are skeptical of Yan and Gao's claim that Lin Biao and Jiang Qing sought Deng's expulsion in 1968.

[114] See below, p. 595, for a fuller quotation and source. It can be argued that this was simply a calculated stance designed to counter negative views on Mao that would strain Party unity, but we believe it reflected something more personal as well.

exile, he *privately* expressed support for the Chairman to his family in remote Jiangxi. When Deng's children, recently arrived from Beijing, complained about the chaos of the Cultural Revolution, he chastised them for their lack of faith in the movement.[115] Loyalty on the part of Mao's colleagues, however, had another aspect: subservience and self-humiliation. While Deng may or may not have gone to the lengths of Zhou Enlai,[116] the effort to portray him as someone almost uniquely willing to stand up to Mao, particularly over the question of the Cultural Revolution in 1975, does not bear scrutiny (see Chapter 6). Clearly, Deng had repeatedly bent to Mao's will, as in July 1962 when he changed his tune on the spot concerning the color of cats once Mao's contrary attitude became clear, in October 1966 when his self-criticism was clearly more self-abasing than that of Liu Shaoqi on the same occasion, and in providing a July 1968 self-criticism as required by the special case group handling his case despite the lack of any evidence, on the "assumption that this had been ordered by the Center [i.e., Mao]." And crucially, Deng stood ready to reaffirm his 1968 promise that he would never reverse verdicts on the Cultural Revolution.[117]

This, then, was the background when the Lin Biao affair presented a political moment that Deng could not afford to miss. Having received news of September 13 via a briefing in the factory where he worked in Jiangxi, Deng's first step was a November 1971 letter, the first of many, sent directly to Mao. Deng condemned Lin and Chen Boda, declared that Lin deserved his downfall, pledged absolute support for Mao and expressed joy for the country, and reported on his own progress over the past two years. Deng said he had observed Mao's instructions,

---

[115] Mao Mao, *"Wenge" suiyue*, p. 162.

[116] The evidence is mixed. Foreign assessments by those who encountered Chinese leaders in these years are generally kinder to Deng, usually suggesting he showed no particular deference to Mao. On the other hand, Kissinger, *Years of Renewal*, p. 142, speaks of Chinese officials (seemingly including Deng) being "extraordinarily deferential" in Mao's presence. However, William Gleysteen, who accompanied Kissinger on an October 1975 meeting with Mao and Deng, reported that he perceived a non-deferential posture on Deng's part that stood him out from the other Chinese present. Interview, June 1999.

As for Chinese sources, a reliable oral source reports a conversation with one of the most important members of Mao's household, who pictured Deng begging Mao's forgiveness on many occasions. In general terms, while Deng's behavior appears less groveling than that of Zhou, it seems nowhere near as intrepid as that of Deng Zihui or Peng Dehuai. On Deng Zihui, see Frederick C. Teiwes and Warren Sun, eds., *The Politics of Agricultural Cooperativization in China: Mao, Deng Zihui, and the "High Tide" of 1955* (Armonk: M.E. Sharpe, 1993), pp. 11-15. On Peng Dehuai, see Frederick C. Teiwes, "Peng Dehuai and Mao Zedong," *AJCA*, no. 16 (1986).

[117] See Teiwes with Sun, *Road to Disaster*, pp. 225, 227-28; Liu's and Deng's October 1966 self-criticisms in *Collected Works of Liu Shao-ch'i 1958-1967* (Hong Kong: Union Research Institute, 1968), pp. 357-64, and *Chinese Law and Government*, Winter 1970-71, pp. 278-90; Mao Mao, *"Wenge" suiyue*, pp. 75-77; and "Deng Xiaoping xiegei Zhonggong zhongyang de 'wode zishu' (zhailu)" [Extracts from Deng Xiaoping's "My Self-statement" Written to the CCP Center] (June 20, 1968), in *CRDB*, p. 3. Deng's famous comment on cats, "it doesn't matter if a cat is black or white as long as it catches the mouse," has long been regarded as the epitome of his pragmatic approach in contrast to Mao's ideological bent.

engaged in reform through labor, was absolutely observing his guarantee to the Party Center concerning the Cultural Revolution, and finally expressed the wish that he could make some contribution to the Party. This was modestly put in terms of some technical work, and linked to expressions of excitement at the progress of the socialist motherland and the heartfelt wish that the Chairman could live forever.[118] The decisive response came from Mao at the time of Chen Yi's funeral in January 1972 when, in the course of praising Chen, the Chairman also spoke favorably of Deng. Mao declared that Deng's mistakes, in contrast to those of Liu Shaoqi, were "contradictions among the people," thus clearly indicating the possibility of a future role. Although official accounts have exaggerated the impact of Zhou Enlai in these developments, Zhou did suggest to Chen's children that they pass on Mao's remarks about Deng, thus contributing to the process of liberating cadres generally, and expectations concerning Deng's return specifically.[119]

The letter which led to Mao's comment on Deng's virtues was written on August 3, 1972. According to a leading authority on Deng, this letter had more or less been authorized by Mao in advance, and Deng was expected to declare formally where he stood (*biaotai*). Deng drafted his letter after hearing his fourth briefing on the Lin Biao incident. The message was similar to his November letter: support for the campaign against Lin, self-criticism of his mistakes and crimes, and an even clearer request for work. Deng elaborated with various "exposures" of Lin, and pitched his appeal for work as a means through which he could "correct my errors and return to the Chairman's proletarian revolutionary line." Deng was still modest about a suitable work assignment, noting that he could do investigation and research (which was all that Chen Yun would be allowed to do), said his health was good enough so that he could work another seven or eight years, and he would wait quietly for Mao's instruction. On the 14th, Mao had the letter circulated to "various comrades of the Center" along with his own comments. This, of course, was a signal, but Mao did not commit himself to any job for Deng, thus tossing this sensitive issue into the collective lap of the Politburo.[120]

Of particular interest are the respective responses of Zhou Enlai and the Politburo radicals. Zhou's response can only be described as very cautious. Following Mao's August comment, Zhou convened the Politburo, but, allegedly because of the attitude of Jiang Qing *et al.*, it was difficult to reach a conclusion. Four months later, rather than making a proposal himself, Zhou contacted

---

[118] Mao Mao, "*Wenge*" *suiyue*, pp. 207-11; and interview with leading specialist on Deng, November 2002.

[119] See Yan and Gao, *Turbulent Decade*, p. 453.

[120] "Deng Xiaoping gei Mao Zedong de xin" [Deng Xiaoping's Letter to Mao Zedong] (August 3, 1972), in *CRDB*, pp. 1-2; Mao Mao, "*Wenge*" *suiyue*, pp. 234-36; *Mao zhuan*, vol. 2, p. 1621; Ji Xichen, *Shi wu qianli de niandai*, vol.1, p. 19; and interview with specialist on Deng, November 2002.

Ji Dengkui and Wang Dongxing to ask them to consider a post for Deng. On December 27, Ji and Wang made recommendations concerning Tan Zhenlin as well as Deng, in Deng's case that he be appointed a vice premier. Zhou's cautious response was to proceed with Tan's case first, on the grounds that Mao's views would have to be sought before anything could be done concerning Deng. Zhou then consulted Mao, who quickly agreed to Deng's posting, and the formalities were completed with a Party Center decision on March 10, followed by the transmission of the decision to lower levels together with Deng's June 1968 self-examination and his August 1972 letter reaffirming his promise never to reverse verdicts on the Cultural Revolution.[121] What of the radicals in these circumstances? While the vague statement that their "attitude" made it very difficult to conclude Deng's rehabilitation implies obstruction, this appears overstated at best. Indeed, a senior Party historian working on Deng claims that while Jiang Qing may have been unhappy with the idea of Deng's return initially, there is no evidence of determined opposition given Mao's stance. Indeed, she (like Mao) may have seen Deng as someone who could be used against Zhou, and for more than a year after Deng's return her relations with him were reportedly good. In any case, as noted in the Introduction, one of the stipulations that Deng accepted for his return to office was the pledge not to oppose Jiang.[122]

When Deng arrived in Beijing in late February 1973, now saying he could work for another 20 years rather than the seven or eight he mentioned in his August letter to Mao, he was obviously a very significant figure, but one who would be granted limited powers. The first leader to visit Deng after his arrival was Wang Dongxing, thus underlining both Mao's attention to the arrangement and Wang's own go-between role. Subsequently, on March 28, Zhou Enlai, accompanied by Li Xiannian, met with Deng, and subsequently reported to Mao on his mood and

---

[121] *Mao zhuan*, vol. 2, pp. 1650, 1652; "Zhonggong zhongyang guanyu huifu Deng Xiaoping Tongzhi de dang de zuzhi shenghuo he Guowuyuan fuzongli de zhiwu de jueding ji fujian (1. Deng Xiaoping Tongzhi de xin; 2. Deng Xiaoping Tongzhi de 'Wo de zishu' [zhailu])" [CCP Center's Decision on Restoring Comrade Deng Xiaoping's Party Organizational Life and State Council Vice Premier Duties and Appendices [1. Comrade Deng Xiaoping's letter; 2. Comrade Deng Xiaoping's "Self-statement" (extracts)]] (March 10, 1973), in *CRDB*, pp. 1-6; and Mao Mao, *"Wenge" suiyue*, pp. 272-73. Tan Zhenlin, a pre-1966 Politburo member, had also come to the fore through letters to Mao, and the night before approaching Ji and Wang, Zhou had been told by Mao that Tan could return to work. Tan's subsequent positions as a Central Committee member and NPC Vice Chairman were largely window dressing, however.

[122] Interview with specialist on Deng, November 2002; above, p. 14; and below, p. 186. Mao Mao, *"Wenge" suiyue*, p. 272, claims that a February-March 1973 Politburo meeting concerning Deng's return and work assignment met strong resistance from the radicals, resulting in "sharp struggle." We find this claim implausible given the clarity of Mao's position by this time, although it is conceivable there were differences over Deng's precise duties.

According to a Hong Kong source, lower-level radicals in Shanghai were not so restrained and continued to refer to Deng as the "number two capitalist roader" after the decision was made, leading Zhang Chunqiao to reprimand them for their lack of sophistication. *Mingbao yuekan*, no. 6 (1996), p. 39.

health. On the 29th, Zhou accompanied Deng to see the Chairman, who offered Deng words of encouragement and reportedly was extremely happy to find him in good health and spirits. This was followed by a Politburo meeting in which Deng's concrete work was discussed and, to his surprise at the speed of the arrangement, Deng was given the task of assisting with foreign affairs. It was also decided that on relevant important issues, Deng would participate in Politburo discussions. This, however, by all accounts did not amount to a great deal in practice. At this stage, despite his military credentials, Deng had no role in the PLA. Even in foreign affairs he does not appear to have participated in policy-making to any marked extent. Perhaps most indicative of his low-key role, of the fact that he was indeed on some form of probation, was the limited interaction he had with Zhou Enlai, much less Mao. Apart from the March encounters with Zhou and a long talk in April discussed below, Deng seemingly had little meaningful contact with Zhou from shortly after his return until late in 1973, when Mao placed him in direct conflict with the Premier (see Chapter 2). Throughout this period, Deng was still waiting for Mao to grant him real power.[123]

While this was the general circumstance of Deng's situation after he returned to work, two encounters in spring 1973, with Kang Sheng and Zhou Enlai respectively, reportedly dealt with the "historical problems" of Jiang Qing and Zhang Chunqiao. Deng's daughter, Mao Mao, who accompanied Deng on his visit to Kang but not his seemingly subsequent visit to Zhou, is the source for these encounters. On the latter occasion, Deng and his wife, Zhuo Lin, went to see the Premier on April 9. According to Mao Mao, based on her father's recollection many years later, during this lengthy meeting Zhou stated that Zhang Chunqiao had been a traitor to the Party, but Mao would not allow an investigation, and the Premier cautioned them against spreading news about the matter. With regard to this account, it is notable that Zhou, unlike Kang, did not raise the even more sensitive case of Jiang Qing. Even with this qualification, Mao Mao's version of the event should be treated with some skepticism. A very authoritative Party historian specializing on the period has expressed doubt given Zhou's character and caution. In his view, the issue affected the most sensitive of all matters, the Premier's relations with Mao, and it is questionable he would raise it, especially since a third party in Deng's wife was present. For these reasons, he concluded such a conversation was very unlikely, even though he regarded Zhou's tentative raising of the question with Mao in December 1974 as more credible (see Chapter 3). We would add, moreover, some doubt that Zhou would address the

---

[123] Mao Mao, "*Wenge*" *suiyue*, p. 270; *Mao zhuan*, vol. 2, p. 1650; *Zhou nianpu*, vol. 3, pp. 585ff; interview with Party historian specializing on the period, April 1999; and interview with senior specialist on Deng, November 2002. Note that while Deng could participate in Politburo discussions on relevant (presumably foreign policy) topics, he was not given the right to attend regularly, a right granted to Wang Hongwen, Hua Guofeng and Wu De in May 1973. According to a source close to Ye Jianying's family, Ye and Deng also had little contact in 1973-74. Interview, March 1997.

matter even with Deng alone, given that Deng was not close to the Premier. Our best guess is that to the extent Zhang Chunqiao was discussed, perhaps in light of the common perception at the time that Zhang would be the next premier, it was in a more guarded manner than Deng's recollection suggests. In any case, the issue would not go away, in large part due to the ongoing efforts of Kang Sheng.[124]

Mao Mao's account of the meeting with Kang Sheng is more graphic and more credible, especially since she herself was present. Described only as taking place after his return to Beijing, Deng took Zhuo Lin and Mao Mao to see Kang, a family friend as well as work colleague before 1966, for an apparent courtesy call. Kang was already in an emaciated state, but "as soon as he saw my parents, the first thing that came out of [his] mouth was curses concerning Jiang Qing and Zhang Chunqiao, [curses that were] brutal and vehement." It was apparently on this occasion that Kang first informed Deng of his charges about Jiang's and Zhang's traitorous activities during the revolutionary period. Whether these charges were accurate or not,[125] Kang subsequently urged Zhou Enlai to act on them, and in 1975 involved Deng in a scheme to pass them on to Mao. Looking back on the spring 1973 visit a quarter-century later, Mao Mao observed that if anyone else had cursed Jiang and Zhang it would have been understandable, and Kang's harsh condemnation could only show how malicious the relations between Kang and the "gang of four" had become. At the time, Deng and his family were surprised at Kang's outburst and didn't know how to respond; after all, they had only just returned to Beijing and were largely ignorant of the state of elite politics. More significant is that the sheer sensitivity of the matter would have argued for extreme circumspection, but it did not inhibit Kang's outburst. The incident was seemingly indicative of the extraordinary trust Kang placed in his old comrade, and the depth of his hatred of Jiang and Zhang. In any case, the encounter gave Deng an invaluable insight into leadership politics during a period when he maintained good relations with Jiang, while biding his time for more important assignments from Mao.[126]

---

[124] Mao Mao, "Wenge" suiyue, p. 275; interview, December 2002; and below, pp. 232-33. Zhou's own wife, Deng Yingchao, who he famously kept in the dark concerning sensitive issues, was also present.

[125] In a dispassionate review of the charges of treason against Zhang, a Party historian who had researched the issue reported that while three other accusations concerning a society he joined as a youth, questions of whether his initial CCP membership was bogus or not, and essays he had written in the 1930s attacking Lu Xun were based on distortions of history, Zhang's wife had indeed been a traitor during the revolutionary period, but Zhang had subsequently covered this up. Interview, December 2002. Accusations against Jiang Qing seemingly focused on her alleged confession denouncing communism when imprisoned in 1934-35. See Ross Terrill, The White-Boned Demon: A Biography of Madame Mao Zedong (London: Heinemann, 1984), pp. 60-61, 408.

[126] Mao Mao, "Wenge" suiyue, pp. 433-34; idem, Wode fuqin, vol. 1, pp. 180-81; above, p. 15; and below, pp. 233, 366-67.

Organizational Developments: The Party-State, Mass Organizations, and the PLA and the Militia

Organizational developments from the Lin Biao incident to the Tenth Congress paralleled and were indeed part of the process of opposing "ultra-leftism," and then coping with the December 1972 redefinition of Lin's sins. Moreover, as with the issues canvassed above, these efforts to deal with Cultural Revolution excesses go back to the Ninth Congress. The key aspects of this process were the revival of the central institutions of the Party-state, the ministries and commissions of the State Council which had been seriously disrupted in 1966-68, and the structure of Party committees from the provincial to basic levels that had collapsed. Equally significant was the attempt, enshrined in the documents of both the Ninth and Tenth Congresses, to restore the integrating principle of the system—"unified leadership" (*yiyuanhua lingdao*), i.e., Party authority over all other institutions.[127] Closely related to these developments was the question of the institutional role of the PLA. During the Cultural Revolution, the army had been thrust into activities it never sought, and the issue now became how to return the military to its traditional defense role. This was complicated by both the intrinsic difficulty of withdrawing to the barracks after the disorder of the late 1960s, and by the fallout from Lin Biao's demise. But, by 1973, a pattern of withdrawal was gaining momentum. Finally, 1973 saw the revival of official mass organizations, notably the trade unions, women's federation and Communist Youth League (CYL), all institutions of the pre-1966 system, but now influenced by Cultural Revolution ideology and reemerging as the rhetoric of opposing restoration escalated. Of these organizations, the most notable was the militia, both for its relationship to the PLA, and because of exaggerated claims that it had become a "second armed force" at the service of the Politburo radicals in their quest for power.

These developments must be seen against the background of the severe institutional disruption of 1966-68, and the organizational and personnel legacies

---

We do not have a definitive interpretation of the reasons for Kang's animus toward Jiang and Zhang, but several considerations can be offered. First, the conventional linking of Kang to the "gang" and especially Jiang was always overstated. While Jiang, Zhang and Yao Wenyuan were intimately involved in Mao's buildup to the Cultural Revolution from early 1965, it was more than a year later before Kang understood Mao's objectives. Second, it is likely that competition between Kang and Zhang for the mantle of the Party's leading theorist produced tension if not enmity. Indeed, according to an oral source, in 1971 Mao referred to Zhang as "a hero from Shandong, a rare thinker in our Party," an assessment he apparently never conferred on Kang, also a Shandong native. Further, with Kang and the "gang" all residing at Diaoyutai, there may have been opportunities for more than the usual personality clashes. Finally, there are some indications that, in comparative terms, Kang may have been less radical than Zhang, notably by giving strong support to Zhou's efforts against "ultra-leftism." Teiwes, *Politics and Purges*, pp. lx-lxi, 460-64, 505n108; and interviews with Party historians, January 2000 and December 2002.

[127] See the organizational principles section of the 1969 and 1973 Party constitutions; *HQ*, no. 5 (1969), p. 37, no. 9 (1973), p. 27.

of that disruption. The new organizational reconstruction revolved around the three components of the original Cultural Revolution version of the "three-way alliance": the PLA, which, from 1967, was drawn into the dominant governing role in the localities as other institutions collapsed, and assumed a vital role as "military representatives" providing authority and a degree of order in central ministries; "revolutionary cadres" in central and local institutions, who provided administrative experience while upholding the fiction of ideological tempering during the movement; and "mass representatives," i.e., activist student Red Guards, worker rebels, and rebel faction leaders from bureaucratic organizations who had challenged the pre-1966 structure to greater or lesser degrees. Apart from tense relations among these groups, the situation during both the high tide of the Cultural Revolution, and the subsequent rebuilding of institutional structures, was also complicated by intense conflicts within each of these categories, conflicts that frequently resulted in violence and death in the 1960s.[128] A further complication was that even while the general trend involved harsh crackdowns to curb anarchy, the largely military authorities were denied *carte blanche* in dealing with rebels who often held positions in the Revolutionary Committees set up in 1967-68, as well as retaining their own networks and rebel organizations, however marginalized they became in 1969-72. In short, while the tide was running against "revolutionary rebels" as the rebuilding process unfolded, they retained some legitimacy in the emerging system, and thus a position from which future influence and power could be claimed.[129]

With the exception of a few especially vulnerable bodies like the Ministry of Education,[130] State Council organs did not suffer the dissolution that befell the Party apparatus after 1966. However, ministries were generally rent by factional fighting, many leaders were pushed aside, leaving only "leading members" and "military representatives" visible to outsiders, and regular operations were

---

[128] For outstanding studies exploring such conflict in two localities, see Perry and Li, *Proletarian Power*, especially ch. 5, on Shanghai; and Forster, *Rebellion*, especially ch. 2, on Zhejiang.

[129] See Richard Baum, "China: Year of the Mangoes," *AS*, January 1969, pp. 14-16; Perry and Li, *Proletarian Power*, pp. 172-75; Anita Chan, Richard Madsen, and Jonathan Unger, *Chen Village: The Recent History of a Peasant Community in Mao's China* (Berkeley: University of California Press, 1984), ch. 5; Forster, *Rebellion*, pp. 101-105; and Teiwes, *Provincial Leadership*, pp. 76-80, 95-96. The crackdowns included Mao's summer 1968 dispatch to the countryside of Red Guards who had "failed" him with their violent factional-fighting, and especially brutal treatment including executions of leftist extremists during the 1968-69 "cleansing of class ranks" and the 1970-72 "one strike, three antis" campaigns. The "one strike" was against counter-revolution, and the "three antis" were graft and embezzlement, speculation and profiteering, and extravagance and waste. Both campaigns had many facets and could be used by radical as well as conservative forces depending on local conditions, but the basic orientation was law and order and Cultural Revolution rebels were prominent targets.

[130] The ministry was abolished in June 1966, and it is likely that the Ministry of Culture was also abolished about the same time. The State Council groups on science and education and on culture established in 1971 were not replaced by ministries until 1975.

severely curtailed. While key bodies such as the SPC continued to function throughout the Cultural Revolution, in various cases it was only *circa* 1970-73 that reports of ministerial activities began to reappear, and ministers and vice ministers were identified. During this period, shortly after Mao called for rebuilding the state structure, a significant administrative reorganization took place in June 1970 involving the abolition and merging of ministries, a simplification reducing State Council organs from 90 to 27, and at the same time Party core groups were established to enforce "unified leadership." This revival of the PRC's most professional organizations only reached fruition when a full ministerial structure and leadership was approved at the January 1975 NPC (see Chapter 3). What is striking is that, in an area where notionally it should have been comparatively easy to revive earlier patterns, there was no full-scale return to pre-1966 staffing, even with the stepped-up rehabilitation of cadres in 1973-74. For one thing, younger cadres, who had risen in prominence during the Cultural Revolution, obtained significant although subordinate positions in the reemerging structure. For another, PLA officers often retained leading roles. Thus when Party core groups were set up in mid-1970, military men held at least half of these posts. Even in 1975 when the new State Council was unveiled, a bit more than one-quarter of the newly appointed ministers had been career military men before the Cultural Revolution.[131] This, however, paled in comparison to the PLA presence in the restored Party structure.

While the Party Center called for restoring "unified leadership" as early as October 1967, a message frequently repeated over the following years and featured in the New Year editorials of 1972 and 1973, realizing this objective was a slow and difficult process. The immediate task in 1967-68 had been, on the contrary, to supersede the shattered Party committee system with Revolutionary Committees that combined Party and administrative functions in slimmed down single bureaucratic units, a new structure dominated by the PLA at the provincial and other territorial levels. It was only in November 1969 that the first county Party committee was set up, and a year later there were still only 45 such committees in the PRC's 2,185 counties. Although the Central Cultural Revolution Group, which had effectively usurped the functions of the Center's various departments, was dissolved in December 1969, thus signaling the revival of more orthodox

---

[131] See Chen and Du, *Shilu*, vol. 3, part 1, pp. 599-600; He Husheng, *Zhiguanzhi*, pp. 156-88; Lamb, *Directory*, sections C, D and G; and Dittmer, *Continuous Revolution*, p. 183n24. Of the 23 Party core group heads appointed in 1970, at least 12 were PLA officers, and it is likely that most if not all of the remaining four heads in the machine building ministries traditionally led by army cadres had the same background. Only four core group heads were clearly serving in civilian positions before 1966, while the circumstances of seven are unknown. In 1975, the eight career PLA ministers appointed at the NPC included Ye Jianying as Minister of Defense, who clearly was in a different category. Moreover, four other military figures were responsible for machine building ministries. The three ministries normally under civilian officials but now with PLA ministers were Metallurgy, Agriculture and Forestry, and Commerce.

organizational patterns, when a new coordinating body in the form of a central organization and propaganda group was set up nine months later, it was led by some of the same Cultural Revolution radicals.[132] Several of these radicals, Kang Sheng and Zhang Chunqiao, as well as Xie Fuzhi, also held the leading posts in the Party rectification leadership group set up in April 1970 to guide the task of Party rebuilding. At the Party Center, several functional departments reappeared in 1969-72, while a similar elaboration of CCP organization surfaced at lower levels once Party committees were reestablished. The most significant development, however, was the creation of new Party committees at the provincial level from December 1970 to August 1971. This process resulted in even greater military dominance than that achieved in the Revolutionary Committees set up during the chaos of 1967-68, a situation still largely in place at the time of the Tenth Congress. Given the control of the existing (largely military) provincial leaders, the personnel outcomes of the process were predictable.[133]

The conflicts involved in reestablishing the Party structure flowed directly from the interaction of the three forces brought into leading positions during 1967-68. The combination of high-handedness and lack of civilian administrative experience on the part of PLA officers (see below) brought them into conflict not only with rebel groups who were often forcefully suppressed, but also with retained or restored "revolutionary cadres." These cadres, for their part, not only had to take orders from military men lacking knowledge of their specialist areas, they also were in a frequently poisonous relationship with the mass representatives who had criticized them as representing the bourgeois line, and who remained dubious that they had genuinely reformed. This left such cadres in a bind, unsure whether carrying out their duties would leave them vulnerable to future charges of revisionism. For their part, the rebel "mass representatives" had reason to be fearful of Party rebuilding at a time when the emphasis was on law and order, on discipline rather than "ultra-democracy," and they were being marginalized even within the Revolutionary Committees. The very process disadvantaged them, since existing Party members (the great majority of whom had joined before 1966) had voting rights, while most rebels were outsiders. In an attempt to bring "the masses" into the process, an "open door" approach was initially adopted in 1969, in which mass organizations participated in criticizing existing

---

[132] Kang Sheng headed the group, with Jiang Qing and Zhang Chunqiao playing key roles. Cf. above, p. 61n95.

[133] See Perry and Li, *Proletarian Power*, p. 158; *PR*, no. 1 (1972), p. 11, no. 1 (1973), p. 11; Forster, *Rebellion*, pp. 95, 103; Teiwes and Sun, *Tragedy*, pp. 127-33; Lamb, *Directory*, pp. 52, 54; Frederick C. Teiwes, "Before and After the Cultural Revolution," *CQ*, no. 58 (1974), pp. 335-36; and Teiwes, *Provincial Leadership*, pp. 30-33, 91-98, 115-21. Fifty-seven percent of all new provincial secretaries, and 69 percent of first secretaries, were PLA officers, compared to 38 percent of Revolutionary Committee vice chairmen and 62 percent of chairmen at the time of the Ninth Congress. Note that the heavy military share of Party secretaries was achieved during precisely the period when Lin Biao's star was in decline. At the time of the Tenth Congress, the figures for army leaders were 47 percent of all secretaries, and 66 percent of first secretaries.

Party members and the admission of new ones. The resulting obstruction due to objections of "the masses" led to a less open process from 1970, during which only a few mass representatives were invited to the actual decision-making sessions and, as under the traditional "mass line," there was no right for outsiders to attend Party meetings. The result was not only a (gradual) speeding-up of the rebuilding process, but also a situation in which, to the extent the case of Zhejiang is typical, those mass representatives now gaining prominent positions in the Party and other official organs were not the leading rebels of 1966-68, but more malleable types.[134]

As indicated, the role of the army was central to Party rebuilding, not only in the resulting PLA personnel appointments at the provincial and lower territorial levels,[135] but also in terms of the process and the political dynamics once Party committees were set up. In most places, the process was guided by the PLA through such devices as military representatives dominating "Party core groups" within the Revolutionary Committees, and the use of "three supports and two militaries" (sanzhi liangjun)[136] army personnel who had been dispatched to bureaucratic and production units to curb Cultural Revolution chaos in 1967. In addition, even when Party committees were established in localities, authoritative orders on civilian matters often came directly from provincial military districts and multi-province military regions. Deng Liqun observed many years later that even as Party committees were being restored, cadres liberated, and Party life revived within organizations, territorial Party committees and administrative units were still required to report to the PLA for approval of their actions. All of this, and particularly the dictatorial methods frequently adopted by army officers, was a problem well before the Lin Biao incident, but became conflated with the Lin issue. Immediately after the Ninth Congress, Mao called attention to the high-handedness of the PLA as the key problem in the localities, and several media and study campaigns from fall 1969 through summer 1970 emphasized defects in work and the obligation of the army to obey the Party. By the end of this period, and especially after the Lushan plenum, Mao had become concerned with Lin's military power, but no unusual actions were taken to curb PLA power *per se* as opposed to undermining Lin. As we have seen, military clout even increased in terms of representation on the new provincial Party committees.[137]

---

[134] See Graham Young, "Party Building and the Search for Unity," in Bill Brugger, ed., *China: The Impact of the Cultural Revolution* (Canberra: Australian National University Press, 1978), especially pp. 42-56; Domes, *China after the Cultural Revolution*, ch. 3; Perry and Li, *Proletarian Power*, pp. 158-61, 179; and Forster, *Rebellion*, pp. 101-106, 113.

[135] According to reports on Hubei and Yunnan, the proportion of PLA officers as heads of county Revolutionary Committees reached 97-98 percent. Presumably, similar proportions applied when Party committees were set up. See Teiwes and Sun, *Tragedy*, p. 128n47.

[136] I.e., support of industry, agriculture, and the broad masses of the left; military control and political and military training.

[137] See Forster, *Rebellion*, pp. 101-102; Domes, *China after the Cultural Revolution*, pp. 52-53;

Following September 13, the question of getting the military out of politics became more salient even as the (imagined) threat from Lin passed. In terms of the general problems caused by the PLA's role in civilian affairs, in addition to an emphasis on the need for the army to be cautious and undergo rectification, some specific measures were taken, notably an August 1972 circular on the "three supports and two militaries." This circular decreed that such detachments should, under the changed circumstances, obey the relevant local Party committees according to the principle of "unified leadership," and once Party committees were established in their departments, schools and factories, they should return to their military units. Moreover, military organs from the provincial to county levels were to accept the leadership of territorial Party committees at the same level, in addition to the authority of PLA Party committees. For his part, Mao commented that once the troops left specific areas, they should no longer interfere in the affairs of those localities. The extent to which any of this happened, as Deng Liqun's reflection indicates, was far from universal, and arguably impossible to implement on a wide basis given the still fragile political situation since the Cultural Revolution. Rather than a general return to the barracks after the Lin Biao incident, the main priority was to deal with Lin Biao's presumed followers. Thus the most extensive removals of military personnel took place within the central PLA apparatus, with a much more modest cleaning out of Fourth Field Army veterans at the provincial level. While the percentage of military-connected Central Committee members at the Tenth Congress represented a significant decline from the Ninth Congress, to a large extent it simply reflected the removal of Lin's presumed supporters. The question of the military's role in the overall system remained unresolved. Mao would only address the "back to the barracks" issue in a decisive fashion in late 1973 (see Chapter 2).[138]

Apart from efforts to restore pre-1966 Party, government and army operational patterns, the post-September 13 period also saw the revival of official mass organizations eclipsed during the Cultural Revolution: the trade unions, women's federation, and CYL.[139] In 1972, basic-level organizations at least of the Youth League were revived in various localities, and the following year provincial-level trade union, women's federation and CYL bodies were established at congresses held in virtually all provinces and major cities. The 1973 New Year

---

Deng Liqun guoshi jiangtan, vol. 3, p. 325; and Teiwes and Sun, *Tragedy*, pp. 128-33. The measures Mao took against Lin after Lushan were, most prominently, the so-called "throwing stones, mixing in sand, and digging up the cornerstone": i.e., criticism of Lin's top supporters, adding presumed loyalists to MAC bodies dominated by Lin's group, and reorganizing the leadership of the Beijing Military Region. See MacFarquhar, "Succession," pp. 265-68.

[138] See Chen and Du, *Shilu*, vol. 3, part 2, pp. 847-48; and *Deng Liqun guoshi jiangtan*, vol. 3, p. 325. PLA officers comprised 32 percent of the Tenth Central Committee, compared to 44 percent of the Ninth Central Committee. Robinson, "China in 1973," p. 3.

[139] The CYL is different from the other organizations in that it does not attempt to cover

joint editorial provided a clear signal by calling for the consolidation of the mass organizations step by step, and emphasized that this was another area in which the Party's "unified leadership" was to be implemented. In the context of the post-Cultural Revolution situation, however, this was an ambiguous stipulation. As we have seen, Party leadership was designed to reduce the PLA's role, but in 1973 local Party committees were still dominated by the military. Even more significant, these revived official mass organizations would draw on the new blood emerging during the chaos of 1966-68, thus leading to judgments that the new mass organizations formed part of the support base of the Politburo radicals. It certainly was the case that these bodies recruited Cultural Revolution activists, in the process institutionalizing the interests of these presumptive young radicals. Moreover, in various places rebel organizations such as Red Guard congresses continued to exist outside the new official structures, and were able to bring pressure on them. Yet the case was not clear-cut, as can be seen by examining the worker activists heading the trade unions. In Shanghai, Ye Changming, an associate of Wang Hongwen in the struggles of the 1960s, led the trade union federation. But in Zhejiang, union leadership was assumed by Jiang Baodi, a female textile worker not noted for rebelliousness, despite belonging to the more radical worker faction. And in Beijing, the unions were chaired by model worker Ni Zhifu—a figure subsequently trusted to play a key role in curbing worker resistance in Shanghai after the arrest of the "gang of four."[140]

The final mass organization revived in this period under the principle of unified Party leadership, one directly led by the trade unions in the cities, was the militia. As noted, the militia question is of particular importance for two reasons. The first concerns the relationship of the militia to the professional military, to which it had been subordinate in its pre-1966 version.[141] The second, larger issue

---

comprehensively a category of people, but instead is a selectively-recruited body with the aim of providing future members for the CCP itself. In addition, there were less developed efforts in 1973-74 to revive a lesser mass organization of the pre-1966 period, the Poor and Lower-Middle Peasant Association. See "Organizing China's Peasants: A Rural Upsurge?" *Current Scene*, September 1974, pp. 14-15.

[140] See Dittmer, *Continuous Revolution*, pp. 185-87; Robinson, "China in 1973," pp. 15-16; *PR*, no. 1 (1973), p. 11; Forster, *Rebellion*, pp. 108-109, 117, 120-26; Perry and Li, *Proletarian Power*, pp. 146, 163-69; and "Ni Chih-fu—Member of the CCPCC Politburo," *IS*, January 1978, pp. 91-93. In Shanghai, Wang Hongwen himself formally chaired the new body. The complexity of the situation is further indicated by the fact that under Ye Changming's leadership the Shanghai unions actually maintained a good deal of independence from the municipal committee—even though that committee was formally led by the Politburo radicals and in fact by their followers.

[141] While this had been the situation on the eve of the Cultural Revolution, the relationship was more complex over the entire PRC period to that date. In the immediate post-1949 period, urban militias were under the leadership of the trade unions, before being abolished in 1953. Rural militias, however, were under PLA command and continued to be so after 1953. During the Great Leap, and stimulated by the 1958 Taiwan Straits crisis, a great expansion of the militia took place nationwide under the rubric of "everyone a soldier," with urban militias reestablished under direct PLA supervision. For a detailed account of the development of militias in the PRC and earlier, see Elizabeth J. Perry,

concerned the overall significance of the urban militia, the so-called "second armed force," for conflict within the Politburo. The official post-Mao account, often reflected in Western analysis, is that the "gang of four" built up this "second armed force" to counter not only an unsympathetic PLA, but also to support a bid for power following Mao's death, while the Shanghai militia planned an "armed rebellion" after the arrest of the "gang." In fact, the evidence concerning the elite politics aspects of the militia story prior to the Chairman's passing is particularly sparse, while what is known about events in September-October 1976 suggests different conclusions (see Chapter 8).[142] Here we review developments up to the time of the Tenth Congress, also including the September 1973 *People's Daily-Liberation Army Daily* joint editorial that launched a new militia campaign. Unsurprisingly, the crucial actor setting the course of the militia, both during the Cultural Revolution and in the run-up to the Tenth Congress, was Mao.

Mao's initial post-1966 impact on the militia came as a consequence of the Cultural Revolution's broad-ranging attack on authority. With chaos spreading in 1967, many existing militia organizations were marginalized or simply collapsed, sometimes replaced by factory militias. At the same time, in many places rebel groups clashed directly with the PLA, attacking military facilities and abusing officers, but Mao's reaction was to view army efforts to restore order as representing the "right," and to encourage the rebels, asking in July 1967, "why don't we arm the left?" As the situation further deteriorated in summer 1967, Zhang Chunqiao seized on this remark to propose to the Chairman the creation of a new force of armed workers to replace the conservatively-inclined existing militia. This created a new vehicle of proletarian power in Shanghai with a force led by Wang Hongwen's Workers' General Headquarters. Mao gave his approval with some constraints, and by early August "arming the left" became a key short-term central policy. Shanghai, however, was different from other places due to Mao's strong support for Zhang and the new municipal leadership. Elsewhere, rebel groups, conceiving themselves the "left," and now receiving or seizing weapons from PLA depots, engaged in much more violent action. From late summer 1967, however, local PLA forces were granted greater scope to crack down on anarchy as Mao criticized "ultra-left" excesses and ordered the end of distributing arms to the masses and the return of those in rebel hands to the army. Over the subsequent period to the Ninth Congress, Shanghai's new armed workers' force supported the radical local Party authorities, and was allowed to retain its weapons. In other places, however, surviving old militias often backed

---

Patrolling the Revolution: Worker Militias, Citizenship, and the Modern Chinese State (Lanham: Rowman and Littlefield, 2006).

[142] For overviews of official charges against the "gang" with regard to the militia, see *A Great Trial in Chinese History: The Trial of the Lin Biao and Jiang Qing Counter-revolutionary Cliques, Nov. 1980-Jan. 1981* (New York: Pergamon Press, 1981), pp. 25-26, 191-95; and New China News Agency (hereafter NCNA), December 28, 1976, in *SPRCP*, no. 6254 (1977), pp. 284-85.

more conservative forces, particularly in rural areas where the established local authorities had weathered the storm.[143]

A new emphasis on militia building began in 1969, precisely the time Mao emphasized war preparations for a possible clash with the Soviet Union. The Chairman now approved a document abolishing paramilitary organizations, and restoring the pre-1966 militia system, thus reestablishing PLA supervision. Moreover, the emphasis was on military tasks. Although Shanghai was able to resist ceding the leading role to the military, the summer 1970 national militia work conference emphasized patriotism rather than class struggle in the militia training curriculum, while the "people's war" aspect of militia tasks was emphasized in June 1972 on the tenth anniversary of Mao's 1962 instructions on militia building. While the revived militia was considered "a new born thing of the Cultural Revolution," in 1969-72 its structure and function, at least according to national policy, mirrored the pre-Cultural Revolution situation. The militia had political and production tasks, but its primary role was to repel aggression through the traditional system of integration with the PLA.[144]

By 1972, however, the Lin Biao affair was weighing on Mao's mind, and contributing to enhanced efforts to reaffirm the traditional principle that "the Party controls the gun." While part of this effort was directed at negating the clout of Lin's presumed supporters, larger concerns undoubtedly influenced the Chairman as well. While we doubt that he was concerned with threats to his own authority—and events at the end of 1973 (see Chapter 2) would demonstrate that any such concerns were unnecessary—Mao sought greater balance in the political system, seemingly to prevent a future situation after he was gone in which the PLA could override his long-term objectives, specifically to maintain the legacy of the Cultural Revolution. There was no question of the army's loyalty to Mao personally, but after coping with the chaos of 1967-68, many PLA leaders clearly had reservations about the movement itself. Thus, when the Chairman reoriented Party policy at the end of 1972, he emphasized guarding against revisionism, and a redefinition of the mission and leadership of the militia soon followed. In a series of steps begun in spring 1973 and laid out in the September *People's Daily-Liberation Army Daily* joint editorial, a new urban militia was in effect created, an armed force which emphasized political, class struggle objectives,

---

[143] See Perry and Li, *Proletarian Power*, pp. 161-62; Perry, *Patrolling the Revolution*, pp. 214ff; Michael Schoenhals, "'Why Don't We Arm the Left?' Mao's Culpability for the Cultural Revolution's 'Great Chaos' of 1967," *CQ*, no. 182 (2005), pp. 280ff; James C. F. Wang, "The Urban Militia as a Political Instrument in the Power Contest in China in 1976," *AS*, June 1978, p. 544; and Teiwes and Sun, *Tragedy*, pp. 72-75, 81ff. One case in which Mao specifically authorized the arming of a rebel group occurred in Jilin, where the group concerned was linked to his nephew, Mao Yuanxin.

[144] See Perry and Li, *Proletarian Power*, p. 162; Perry, *Patrolling the Revolution*, pp. 243-45; Wang, "Urban Militia," pp. 544-45; and "Quarterly Chronicle and Documentation," *CQ*, no. 51 (1972), pp. 586-87. The ability of Shanghai leaders to keep PLA jurisdiction nominal was undoubtedly aided by Zhang Chunqiao's position as political commissar of both the Shanghai Garrison and Nanjing Military Region, as well as his national standing.

and which was placed under the authority of territorial Party committees rather than the PLA. Among the many tasks listed in the editorial, including production and public security functions, none was more important than "strengthening the dictatorship of the proletariat and preventing the restoration of capitalism." But this was far from a total shift of emphasis—the militia was still required to counter imperialist threats, and its new armaments in Shanghai were suited to repelling foreign attacks, particularly by air. Moreover, although the Party's unified leadership was heavily stressed, the PLA still had some vaguely defined role in militia work as part of a coordinated defense effort.[145]

While the record is fragmentary, it is nevertheless clear that, as in his comment on "arming the left" in 1967 and his heavy emphasis on war preparations from 1969, Mao again was the decisive force in reshaping this "new born thing of the Cultural Revolution." In March 1973, local radical leaders in Shanghai received a phone call from Wang Hongwen who reported that the Chairman had been making many enquiries concerning the city's militia, in particular wanting to make sure that it had adequate weapons, and as a result had ordered the MAC to dispatch 200,000 guns to Shanghai. Then in May, Mao entrusted Wang and Zhang Chunqiao with the task of rebuilding the Shanghai militia, a directive that prefigured the September editorial in emphasizing arming the workers, preparing for war, consolidating the dictatorship of the proletariat, and preventing the restoration of capitalism. The authority and initiative came from Mao, yet the new militia orientation clearly supported the Politburo radicals as it reflected the Chairman's preoccupations of the time—not merely clipping the wings of the PLA, but also his emphasis on relying on the working class, his preference for Shanghai, the model city for Cultural Revolution radicalism, as opposed to the more bureaucratic environment of Beijing,[146] and his insistence on promoting young successors to the revolutionary cause, Wang Hongwen being the case *par excellence*. The Shanghai experience quickly became a model that received massive publicity and was emulated throughout China in the latter part of 1973.[147]

The radicals, for their part, saw the militia as a resource to be cultivated, but it was a resource given to them by Mao and thus legitimate in the context of the time, notwithstanding post-Mao attempts to portray their actions as behind the Chairman's back. Whether specific incidents, such as Wang Hongwen's reported September 1973 remark that a national militia headquarters was needed and he

---

[145] See "Urban Militia—A New Force?" *Current Scene*, January 1974; Wang, "Urban Militia," pp. 545-51; *PR*, no. 40 (1973), pp. 6-7; *Shanghai minbing douzheng shi ziliao* [Materials on the History of the Shanghai Militia Struggle] (Shanghai: Shanghai minbing douzheng shi ziliaozu, 1981), vol. 22, pp. 42, 45, 46; and Perry, *Patrolling the Revolution*, p. 245.

[146] Mao's preference for the localities over Beijing was long-standing. For examples from the 1950s, see Teiwes with Sun, *China's Road to Disaster*, pp. 58, 61, 194-98.

[147] See *Shanghai minbing douzheng shi ziliao*, vol. 22, pp. 43-44, 46, 51-56; Perry, *Patrolling the Revolution*, pp. 246-49; and "Urban Militia—A New Force?" pp. 22-24.

would take charge of it, were the radicals' own proposals or reflections of Mao's ideas is uncertain,[148] but the basic project of developing the urban militia was hardly illicit. In any case, the new militia would remain a potential flashpoint for the remainder of Mao's life.

Zhou Enlai's Setback on the Foreign Affairs Front, May-July 1973

As argued in the Introduction, no area commanded more of Mao's attention and control than foreign affairs, but foreign policy produced virtually no divisions of substance over the entire 1972-76 period. Indeed, when asked about policy differences in this period, one of the most significant MFA figures at the time laughed and said, "What policy debate? It was just a matter of doing what Mao decreed."[149] Yet the foreign affairs sector was also a sphere of intense conflict since the start of the Cultural Revolution, and some of the key developments in elite politics in the post-Lin Biao period paradoxically concerned events in this sector. Inevitably, in 1972-73 Zhou Enlai was at the center of such developments. Although Mao's close collaborator in the Sino-US rapprochement and the Nixon visit in early 1972,[150] and the essential implementer of foreign policy over the following year, in spring 1973 Zhou became embroiled in an issue that would produce the Chairman's severe rebuke and seriously damage the Premier's standing. It was not, of course, related to any genuine dispute over policy direction. Instead, the precipitating factor was an analytic report on the June Nixon-Brezhnev summit prepared by the MFA, a report that Zhou approved.

Some additional background is required. First, of all the areas in the government he headed, by 1971 Zhou exercised the greatest authority over the MFA, in no small part due to the strategic objective of Sino-American rapprochement and the task of restoring the ministry as an effective diplomatic instrument. As noted earlier, in the undoubtedly exaggerated assessment of one important insider, the ministry now functioned almost as well as before 1966. But factions that could be traced back to the disruptions of 1967 remained, and, in the

---

[148] See *A Great Trial*, p. 191. In our view, it is unlikely that Wang would have raised the national headquarters issue without Mao's at least tacit approval. According to a leading military historian, no national headquarters was ever established. Interview, January 2005. Cf. below, pp. 258-60.

[149] Interview, November 2002. The single example of a policy difference within the MFA cited by this source, a debate in 1975 over whether the Soviet Union should be considered a revisionist country or, in a novel view, a socialist country domestically but a hegemonist internationally did not amount to a dispute over concrete policy alternatives.

Western studies in the 1970s, notably Lieberthal's sophisticated *Sino-Soviet Conflict*, understandably utilized the existing public sources to hypothesize competing foreign policy approaches which did not in fact exist as real alternatives in the policy process. Writing a decade later, Robert S. Ross correctly concluded that Mao so dominated foreign policy that there was no room for conflict, at least as far as strategic (as opposed to foreign economic) policy was concerned. See his "From Lin Biao to Deng Xiaoping: Elite Instability and China's U.S. Policy," *CQ*, no. 118 (1989), pp. 277-84, 295. See also Barnouin and Yu, *Chinese Foreign Policy*, pp. 52-53.

[150] On the intense Mao-Zhou interaction during Nixon's visit, see *Mao zhuan*, vol. 2, pp. 1639-40.

view of several ministry figures of the period, in the 1970s the underlying source of MFA conflict was attitudes toward Premier Zhou. This was naturally linked to Mao's ambiguous view of Zhou and his periodic criticisms of the Premier during these years. Also involved by 1973, and over the entire period to Mao's death, was the complicated relationship of the "two ladies"—Wang Hairong and Tang Wensheng, activists during the Cultural Revolution, but largely in support of Zhou—to the MFA's leading professional, Qiao Guanhua, who would become minister in late 1974, and his wife, Zhang Hanzhi. Described by a ministry official of the period as involving "conflict within cooperation," but over time becoming "cooperation within conflict," the essential issue was power, and both sides were vulnerable to charges of failing to show proper respect to the Premier. Tensions also existed among the various top-level ministry professionals in ways that often remain obscure but point to an even more complex situation. In addition, as in so many other units, tension between young cadres who benefited from the Cultural Revolution and their more experienced seniors corroded organizational cohesion and provided fuel for new conflicts. Finally, Jiang Qing's hostility toward Zhou played into and animated the other tensions within the ministry.[151]

In short, for all of the Premier's dominance in the MFA in 1971-72 and into 1973, he remained vulnerable to the legacy of Cultural Revolution factionalism and, above all, to any possible shift in Mao's attitude. That such a shift had taken place over the nature of Lin Biao's mistakes at the end of 1972 was clear, although its extent and implications were not, nor was it obvious that the Chairman's disenchantment would extend to the foreign affairs sphere. It is necessary to be clear that the absence of real debate over foreign policy was fundamentally because Mao's dominance excluded such debate, rather than being due to any absolute consensus. As for Zhou Enlai, one senior Party historian argued that in general terms he was undoubtedly less optimistic than Mao about the potential of world revolutionary forces, but this scholar considered the two men's views largely the same.[152] In any case, there is no indication of any difference between Mao and Zhou over the desirability of Sino-American rapprochement and its implications for China's position *vis-à-vis* the Soviet Union.

The problem was that Mao was not completely predictable, even in an area like foreign affairs where he provided clearer guidelines and more continuous attention than elsewhere. When MFA officials were asked by Zhou in May or June 1973 to prepare an analysis of the visit of Soviet leader Leonid Brezhnev to the US in the second half of June, two basic reference points had to be considered. One was Mao's theoretical perspective emphasizing the struggle of a wide range of international forces, nation-states of all stripes as well as oppressed peoples, against *both* superpowers—the Soviet Union and the United

---

[151] Interviews, November 2002. On Cultural Revolution developments, see Ma Jisen, *The Cultural Revolution in the Foreign Ministry*, pp. 178ff and ch. 8; and Gurtov, "Foreign Ministry."

[152] Interview, December 2002.

States. This perspective, which would be formally unveiled by Deng Xiaoping as Mao's "theory of the three worlds" at the United Nations in spring 1974, had been unfolding for a number of years and was clearly in place by 1973. The theory depicted great international turmoil with the disintegration of reactionary forces accelerating, tarred the two superpowers (the first world) with the same brush as hegemonists seeking to dominate the world, and identified the PRC as part of the third or developing world in resisting both, albeit with Moscow the more unbridled of the two threats. On the question of the relationship of the two superpowers, the theory held that it involved both collusion and contention, but conflict was fundamental while cooperation simply provided a breathing space to prepare for a new fight.[153] In reality, the Chairman's theory overlapped with, but differed from, the central dynamic of the PRC's evolving foreign policy. In Mao's actual strategic approach, the second reference point, cultivating Sino-US relations, stood at the core of a policy that increasingly became, in many respects, little more than an attempt to play the American card against the Soviet Union.

As Henry Kissinger observed after his February 1973 discussions with Mao and Zhou, it was only then, after a year and a half of private high-level exchanges, that the USSR became "the centerpiece and completely permeated our talks." In his February 17 meeting with Kissinger, Mao graphically summarized his strategic assessment: "we should draw a horizontal line [through] the US-Japan-[China]-Pakistan-Iran-Turkey and Europe." This "horizontal line" rationale remained the basis of PRC foreign policy until the mid-1980s. Mao's basic idea was that China should seek to mobilize an anti-Soviet coalition of nations from Japan through the Middle East to Europe, with the US as the superpower lynchpin of the effort. During the February discussions there was, on the one hand, an atmosphere of a community of interests, a sense that, as Mao put it, "we can work together to commonly deal with a bastard." Yet for all the common perceptions exchanged with Kissinger, Mao and Zhou also revealed considerable suspicion that the US would collude with Moscow to the disadvantage of China. Both leaders expressed generalized worries that the US might help the Russians "whether purposely or not," and even wish to divert Soviet attention from Europe to the east. At his rhetorical extreme, Mao speculated that the US would be happy to see the Soviet Union invade China as a means of bringing down the Soviets: "you can let them get bogged down in China, for [up to] four years. And then you can poke your finger at the Soviet back." One immediate concern, the precise matter that would be the central issue of Brezhnev's forthcoming visit, was the

---

[153] In addition to Deng's UN speech, key expressions of the general viewpoint can be found in Qiao Guanhua's October 1972 speech to the UN and the 1972 National Day joint editorial, as well as in Mao's brief February 1974 comment in a meeting with a visiting African leader. See *PR*, no. 40 (1972), pp. 9-10, no. 41 (1972), pp. 4-10; and Barnouin and Yu, *Chinese Foreign Policy*, pp. 152-53, 214-26. The second world consisted of the developed countries of Europe, Canada, Australia and Japan that assertedly sought independence from superpower exploitation.

Soviet initiative for a nuclear understanding that, as Kissinger observed in his report to Nixon, was anathema to the Chinese.[154]

The nuclear understanding, formalized as the Prevention of Nuclear War Agreement during the Brezhnev visit, was clearly a source of great concern to the PRC. The agreement, which in reality was of limited significance, was questioned by Zhou and other Chinese officials in both the lead-up to the visit and subsequently. On the whole, however, Kissinger and David Bruce, the head of the new US Liaison Office in Beijing who arrived in May, found the Chinese taking the development in restrained fashion. On the American side, Kissinger and Nixon went to great lengths to inform the Chinese of progress in the negotiations with the Soviets, explain that the purpose of the agreement was to buy the US time and limit Soviet freedom of action, repeatedly reassure them that no agreement would be made that was harmful to PRC interests, and, after the visit, dramatically revealed Brezhnev's proposal for joint action (precisely the kind of superpower condominium China feared) to prevent development of the PRC's nuclear force capability, along with US rejection of the idea. Perhaps most indicative of the Chinese attitude was Zhou's exchange with Bruce on June 25, near the end of Brezhnev's visit. The meeting had been arranged at Bruce's urgent request in what was another American reassurance effort. Apart from raising possible US support of a Soviet attack, Zhou commented that such agreements were not reliable (a "scrap of paper," as he would call it ten days later to a US Congressional delegation), and it would give the "impression of two great powers dominating the world." Nevertheless, Zhou was, according to Bruce, "speaking more in sorrow than anger," and went on to indicate that China would continue on its current course, a course that clearly included practical measures with Washington. Mao appeared satisfied if ambiguous concerning Zhou's report on the meeting, the next day commenting that "Now that backs are stiffened, Bruce will be comfortable."[155]

The fateful MFA report originated in these circumstances. It was completed shortly after the Brezhnev visit, and following Zhou's approval published within the MFA on June 28. The project involved some of the highest figures in the ministry, including Minister Ji Pengfei and Vice Minister Qiao Guanhua. The

[154] William Burr, ed., *The Kissinger Transcripts: The Top Secret Talks with Beijing and Moscow* (New York: The New Press, 1998), pp. 86, 88, 89, 94, 99-100, 112-14, 115-16. See also Henry Kissinger, *Years of Upheaval* (London: Weidenfeld and Nicholson and Michael Joseph, 1982), ch. 3. On the shift away from the "horizontal line" policy in the mid-1980s, see *Xu Xiangqian zhuan* [Biography of Xu Xiangqian] (Beijing: Dangdai Zhongguo chubanshe, 1991), p. 554.

[155] See Burr, *Kissinger Transcripts*, pp. 124-49; Kissinger, *Years of Upheaval*, pp. 274-300; *Zhou nianpu*, vol. 3, p. 601; and Zong Daoyi, "153 qi Xinqingkuang he Jixin'ge diliuci laifang gei Zhou Enlai dailai dailai de zhengzhi zainan" [Zhou Enlai's Political Disaster Due to (Foreign Ministry Bulletin) no. 153 on the New Situation and Kissinger's Sixth Visit to China], *Zhonghua ernü*, September 2001, p. 6. The other key issue in Sino-US relations in this period was the deteriorating situation in Cambodia where, despite differing interests, the two sides unsuccessfully sought to cooperate in certain respects.

chief drafter was Zhang Zai, an official from the American and Pacific Division where Tang Wensheng also worked, and Zhang reportedly was a particular friend of Tang. Thus while the actual preparers of the report were lower-level officials, those involved more generally had direct experience with the February Kissinger mission (Ji and Qiao sat in on his meetings with Zhou, and the "two ladies" were present for all the encounters with Mao and Zhou). While the full report is unavailable, and its nuances can only be surmised, it did adopt a critical posture toward the US, concluding that the Nixon-Brezhnev summit had been "full of deception," and that "the atmosphere of US-Soviet world domination is even stronger." The article met with universal approval within the MFA. Zhou praised it as "worth considering" before ordering its publication in the ministry's bulletin, while Tang Wensheng reportedly expressed extravagant support. The remarkable fact is that none of those with direct knowledge of Mao's attitudes thought anything was amiss. They were rudely shocked a few days later when Mao, briefed on the report by the "two ladies," reacted furiously. When Zhou learned of the Chairman's reaction from Wang Hairong on July 3, he immediately had the article recalled and destroyed. There followed the usual round of self-criticisms by Zhou and the ministry, but the ramifications were more significant than normal.[156]

What was the nature of Mao's furious reaction, and what explains it? How exactly Mao responded when briefed on the article by the "two ladies," or what influence they possibly had on his attitude,[157] is unclear. The Chairman's views are largely known from his comments to Wang Hongwen and Zhang Chunqiao, whom he summoned on July 4, apparently to vent his anger not only about the report, but also concerning a whole series of perceived inadequacies in the work of the MFA and various "shitty documents," including the Premier's speeches. With regard to the Nixon-Brezhnev article, Mao's fundamental substantive objection was that it was unrealistic, that its view of increasing US-Soviet collusion mistook the superficial for the substance.[158] Although he did not state it clearly, for Mao the underlying reality was that Soviet-American conflict continued to validate his "horizontal line" policy. The Chairman's commitment

---

[156] See Zong Daoyi, "153 qi Xinqingkuang he Jixin'ge diliuci laifang," p. 7; and Burr, *Kissinger Transcripts*, pp. 86, 103, 109.

[157] According to a significant MFA figure of the time who was hostile to Wang and Tang, they took the initiative not only to emphasize alleged differences in Zhou's position as opposed to Mao's, but also called the Chairman's attention to Western praise of the Premier as the architect of Chinese foreign policy. Interview, November 2002. While we are skeptical of such claims, believing any negative comments concerning Zhou by the "two ladies" would have been in response to Mao's attitude, the question of Western praise of the Premier may have been crucial (see below).

[158] An example of Mao's realism in this talk was his insistence that US strategic policy was shifting toward Europe. Here he seemed to be criticizing an earlier MFA report that he mentioned in an early June meeting with Vietnamese leaders, i.e., contrary to this report's emphasis on Asia and the Pacific, US strategy focused on Europe and the Middle East. *Mao zhuan,* vol. 2, pp. 1655-56.

to realism was demonstrated in a rebuke to excessively ideological positions, whether expressed in the report or elsewhere. Mao attacked the position of no compromise as un-Marxist, and declared himself "the bad type of person who specializes in colluding with US imperialism, Japan and West Germany," as well as being a right opportunist. At the same time, the Chairman expressed annoyance that his theory of the world undergoing big turmoil, big splitting and big reorganization had been replaced by references to US-Soviet deception and strengthening superpower domination. Apart from showing sensitivity over his own formulations, in this particular complaint Mao departed from the realism of his actual policy that relied on a tacit alliance with America, since his theory linked big turmoil to deepening revolutionary struggle that would inevitably weaken the United States. Beyond this, Mao complained about the MFA's wrong predictions, specifically concerning Tanaka's accession to power in Japan, and more broadly that the ministry never discussed big issues with him, but simply submitted trivial matters for his approval. This, Mao warned, would lead to revisionism if not stopped.[159]

While we believe other factors were more significant than the report itself, it is difficult to judge how reasonable or otherwise Mao's reaction was without the full text. A case might be made that Mao was at least partially justified in that Zhou and the MFA bureaucrats had not fully absorbed his "horizontal line" policy, and that he had reason to be discontented with other ministry work such as erroneous analyses of Tanaka's political prospects and his attitude toward China. Yet the report on the Nixon-Brezhnev summit seemingly went little further than Mao's own expressed doubts about possible deceptions in the US-Soviet relationship, only noting an increased "atmosphere" (qifan) of condominium, and only claiming superpower agreement for the time being. Moreover, the report almost certainly made no recommendations for a change in Mao's policy. What was without doubt unfair in the Chairman's intemperate outburst was the failure to acknowledge the dilemma facing Zhou and the foreign affairs officials given the PRC's internal political context. As in so many other Mao-created political circumstances, the authors of the report presumably felt it safer to err on the side of criticizing American motives than risk the label of right opportunism that Mao would apply to himself. What foreign affairs bureaucrat would have the temerity to debate big policy issues that remained in Mao's hands alone? Indeed, the episode of the article on the Nixon-Brezhnev summit demonstrated precisely how unpleasant the consequences could be when major matters were broached. It is most likely, in the opinion of several senior Party historians, that Mao's reaction at root had little to do with foreign policy issues or MFA performance *per se*. In their view, this was simply an opportunity to get at the Premier, in part due to the

---

[159] Mao Zedong, "Tong Wang Hongwen, Zhang Chunqiao de tanhua jiyao"[Summary of a Talk with Wang Hongwen and Zhang Chunqiao] (July 4, 1973), in *CRDB*, pp. 1-2. Wang Hairong and Tang Wensheng were note takers on this occasion.

belief that Zhou was unreliable concerning the Cultural Revolution, but perhaps even more as a reflection of the jealousy noted in the Introduction. Although the timing is unclear, it was probably during this period that Mao reacted furiously when Wang Hairong and Zhang Yufeng read him Western reports praising Zhou's diplomacy. Thus in one action, the Chairman gave vent to his anger, and made clear that he was in charge of PRC foreign policy.[160]

Whatever the reason for Mao's fury, once Zhou became aware of it through Wang Hairong, he wrote the Foreign Ministry on July 3, ordered the recall and destruction of the article, and assumed full responsibility for the error. After their July 4 meeting with the Chairman, Zhang Chunqiao informed Zhou of Mao's comments, and instructed him to hold a Politburo meeting. On the 5th, Zhou convened the Politburo, and after Zhang relayed the Chairman's comments, the Premier recounted Mao's criticisms of foreign affairs work since late June, and made an initial self-criticism. He also forwarded to Mao his letter of the 3rd to the MFA along with the ministry's self-examination report of the 4th, drawing on Mao's comment that the Premier's mistake was "a chronic shortcoming" rather than an isolated incident, but that it wasn't limited to Zhou. Study meetings were subsequently convened at the MFA from July 12, with leading personnel criticized concerning Mao's complaints, which resulted in seemingly intense struggle sessions until early August. Ji Pengfei, as the MFA leader, was criticized for various shortcomings, and the ministry was labeled an independent kingdom that, ironically, had committed rightist errors. Particularly heavy criticism was directed at Qiao Guanhua who was accused of running a "pirate ship," a reference to his leading role in overseeing the Nixon-Brezhnev report. Qiao was also required to speak to the Politburo where he apparently was very critical of Zhou. In August, however, the struggles abated, and Qiao was assigned to participate in drafting the foreign affairs section of the Tenth Congress work report which predictably, if paradoxically, adopted a strident tone concerning the US. While the report followed Mao's July critique by emphasizing that superpower contention was absolute, Europe was the focus of that contention, and the Soviet Union was the greater threat, it still accused the Americans of seeking to divert the Soviet Union eastward toward China, and even of wanting to "devour" the PRC, thus hardly presenting the US as a reliable security partner. Qiao was then elected to the Central Committee at the Congress, and in September-October led the Chinese delegation to the annual United Nations session of world leaders.[161]

---

[160] Interviews, January 2005; and above, pp. 19-20. A senior Party historian reported seeing a document in which Tang Wensheng claimed Wang Hairong and Zhang Yufeng read Western reports concerning the Premier to a furious Mao, but he could not be precise about the time. One of our interviewees also speculated that another factor in Mao's irritation involved Qiao Guanhua's personal relationship with Zhang Hanzhi; see below, p. 225.

[161] See *Zhou nianpu*, vol. 3, pp. 603-604; *Mao wengao*, vol. 13, pp. 356-57; *Mao zhuan*, vol. 2, p. 1656; Zong Daoyi, "153 qi Xinqingkuang he Jixin'ge diliuci laifang," pp. 7-9; Ma Jisen, *The Cultural Revolution in the Foreign Ministry*, pp. 359-62; Zhang Hanzhi, *Kuaguo houhou de dahongmen*

The most significant victim of the affair, of course, was Zhou Enlai. He was soon involved in the study sessions on MFA shortcomings and continuing discussions in the Politburo. On July 14, Zhou vetted a revised MFA article analyzing US-Soviet relations along Mao's lines, and on the 15th submitted it to Mao together with a note that he would prepare a separate self-examination. Mao responded that no further self-criticism was required, but meanwhile Zhou's reputation took a battering at the MFA. In a large-scale study group of 128 people organized by Wang Hairong, Mao's harsh criticism of the Premier's words as "bullshit" was quoted, although the Chairman was not explicitly cited as the source, and it subsequently circulated widely in the foreign affairs system.[162] But the most significant indication of Zhou's damaged position had already taken place with Mao's meeting with Wang Hongwen and Zhang Chunqiao on July 4. More important than Mao's grossly unfair attitude toward Zhou's handling of foreign policy[163] was the very fact that Wang and Zhang, but not Zhou, were summoned to hear the Chairman's complaints. The key here, as with Wang Li in 1967, is that Mao was instructing radicals to take an interest in foreign affairs, telling them to learn foreign languages so they would not be deceived by the senior cadres of the MFA and dragged onto their "pirate ship." While Wang, at least, did attempt to learn English, and as the presumptive successor was presumably expected to know enough to provide an eventual guiding hand for foreign policy, there is little evidence of any concrete involvement in foreign affairs by him (or Zhang) beyond participation in Mao's meetings with visiting leaders from September 1973 to May 1974.[164] Instead, the person increasingly influential in the foreign affairs sector was Deng Xiaoping. But Mao's July remarks did create a basis for radical interference in foreign affairs, and indicated how far Zhou had fallen in Mao's eyes. In all likelihood, this was simply a further, albeit dramatic,

---

[Stepping into the Large Scarlet Gate] (Shanghai: Wenhui chubanshe, 2002), pp. 127-28; and PR, no. 35-36 (1973), pp. 22-23. Of course, the Tenth Congress report was, unlike the report on the summit, a public and thus ideological document, but by the same token it complicated Mao's diplomatic strategy by potentially causing concern in Washington.

[162] See Zhou nianpu, vol. 3, pp. 604-605; Mao wengao, vol. 13, pp. 357; and Ma Jisen, Waijiaobu wenge jishi [True Record of the Foreign Affairs Ministry during the Cultural Revolution] (Hong Kong: The Chinese University Press, 2003), p. 330.

[163] In the actual conduct of foreign policy from the Kissinger visit to mid-year, there is no indication that the Premier was out of step with Mao, or ever criticized by him. Even with regard to the Nixon-Brezhnev article, although Zhou allegedly "highly" praised it, his actions seemed more restrained in simply saying it was "worth considering" and having it published internally.

[164] See Mao Zedong, "Tong Wang Hongwen, Zhang Chunqiao de tanhua," p. 1; and Xu Jingxian, Shinian yimeng: qian Shanghai shiwei shuji Xu Jingxian wenge huiyilu [Ten Years One Dream: Cultural Revolution Memoirs of Former Shanghai Municipal Secretary Xu Jingxian] (Hong Kong: Shidai guoji chuban youxian gongsi, 2004), p. 286. Concerning Wang Li, Wang claimed that "Our Great Leader Chairman Mao instructed me to poke my nose into foreign affairs work. Premier Zhou was present when the Chairman gave this instruction." See Zong Daoyi, "Wang baqi jianghua yu Waijiaobu duoquan naoju" [Wang's August 7 Speech and the Farce of Usurping Power in the Foreign Ministry], Zhonghua ernü, December 2001, p. 36.

step in Zhou's disfavor since the end of 1972. It was also another step in the rise of the radicals, particularly their soon-to-be ranking colleague on the Politburo, Wang Hongwen, the first named of the leaders summoned on July 4 despite his lower formal status.

Wang Hongwen and the Tenth Congress

The Tenth CCP Congress held from August 24 to 28, 1973, was unique for Party congresses in the Maoist era. It was not only held within the time period laid down by Party statutes, it actually convened ahead of schedule in contrast to the grossly overdue Eighth and Ninth Congresses.[165] Moreover, it was exceptionally short, its five days comparing to the 24 of the Ninth Congress, as well as being the first Party congress since 1928 that Mao did not address the body. Yet another unique feature is that the Congress was held entirely in secret, the delegates only informed of its start at the last minute, and arrived at Beijing's Great Hall of the People by underground passage to avoid attention.[166] Yet in some respects the Congress was predictable, particularly its radical message on consolidating and continuing the Cultural Revolution. While outside observers were struck by the prominence given to the claim that "going against the tide is a Marxist-Leninist principle," a proposition ascribed to Mao and written into the new Party constitution, those following recent CCP propaganda with regard to Zhang Tiesheng should not have been overly surprised.[167] Also expected was an official verdict on the Lin Biao affair. Personnel arrangements were less predictable, but to some degree calculable with the retention of all Politburo members save Lin Biao's group. Zhou Enlai's position as the ranking Party Vice Chairman was unsurprising, although it masked a significantly weakened position. More broadly, the new Politburo and Central Committee marked the continuing shift of power from military to civilian hands. Of all the arrangements, the most startling to the outside world, the Chinese population, and rank-and-file Party members— but not to the inner circle—was the selection of Wang Hongwen as Party Vice Chairman and third-ranking leader overall. We first examine Wang's rise, before turning to Congress preparations starting in May and the related problems for Zhou, and finally to the Tenth Congress itself.

Wang Hongwen's emergence as the successor would have been a major surprise not only for Wang himself, but for the other Politburo radicals as well. As suggested in the Introduction, Wang demonstrated political talent to advance

---

[165] According to the rules, congresses were to be held at five-year intervals, but the Eighth Congress convened 11 years after the Seventh, and the Ninth nearly 13 years after the Eighth.

[166] One consequence of this situation was the amusing story of a delegate who would be elected to the Central Committee, but whose only pair of trousers was being washed when he was urgently summoned to Beijing—thus earning him the title of "wet pants Central Committee member" in unofficial Party lore. Interview with leading Party historian, March 1986. Cf. below, p. 106.

[167] See Robinson, "China in 1973," pp. 9-10; *PR*, no. 35-36 (1973), pp. 26, 31; and above, p. 60.

his own and his faction's cause in the early stage of the Cultural Revolution. The key to success was his alliance with Zhang Chunqiao, albeit an alliance with its own internal tensions and one in which Wang demonstrated independence. Wang was insightful enough to understand that he would be subordinate to Zhang, given Mao's backing of the latter, but he also pushed his group's interests in ways that sometimes led to direct clashes with his superior. Indeed, after Wang moved to Beijing in fall 1972, sometimes sharp clashes within the remaining Shanghai leadership reflected the contrasting provenance of the respective protégés of Wang and Zhang—with Third Secretary Wang Xiuzhen, a worker colleague of Wang's in the Workers' General Headquarters, frequently in conflict with Second Secretary Xu Jingxian, one of the leading figures in the Writers' Group, the intellectual faction that was Zhang's most trusted support base. This, of course, reflected a fundamental Cultural Revolution tension between radical intelligentsia and mobilized workers. But it also demonstrated that, contrary to some belief, Wang Hongwen was hardly Zhang's cat's-paw. This arguably was one of the factors attracting Mao to the young Shanghai worker cadre.[168]

Wang fit almost perfectly Mao's abstract criteria for a successor, criteria he laid out more generally for future leaders up to the level of Party vice chairman and Politburo Standing Committee member from the time of the Ninth Congress, and especially after the 1970 Lushan plenum and September 13: youth, and worker-peasant-soldier background. Wang fulfilled all these requirements. Only 38 at the time of his elevation at the Tenth Congress, Wang came from a peasant family, had served as a soldier in Korea, and, although not an actual production worker, as a factory cadre he could be considered a member of the proletariat.[169] And, of course, he was a rebel activist during the Cultural Revolution. In cultivating Wang for leadership, Mao demonstrated both new and familiar patterns. What was new was that the Chairman had fixed upon someone with whom before 1966 he had no contact or even knowledge. In this, Wang was different from Hua Guofeng or Ji Dengkui, both of whom had impressed Mao since the 1950s, and as mid-rank Party leaders came from a very different milieu from Wang's. Yet the process of Wang's emergence in the Chairman's eyes was typical in other ways. Once Mao took notice of Wang, there followed a period of observation, an assessment of the candidate's qualities and how he behaved. This was similar not only to Mao's attention to Hua and Ji, but, in the context of 1973, to Deng Xiaoping during his period of probation.

Wang apparently came to Mao's notice at the height of the Cultural Revolution in summer 1967. The Chairman had repaired to Shanghai from Wuhan, after

---

[168] See Perry and Li, *Proletarian Power*, pp. 15-16, 21-23, 47-49; Li Xun, *Da bengkui: Shanghai gongren zaofanpai xingwangshi* [The Great Collapse: The Rise and Fall of Worker Rebels in Shanghai] (Taipei: Shibao wenhua chubanshe, 1996), p. 507; MacFarquhar, "Succession," p. 289; and above, pp. 17-18.

[169] See *Mao zhuan*, vol. 2, p. 1655; and Barnouin and Yu, *Ten Years*, p. 248.

contributing to the events in the central Chinese city that led to an upsurge of violence and subsequently to his denunciation of "ultra-leftism." In Shanghai, Mao saw Wang on television and was favorably impressed with the young man. The Chairman's first face-to-face encounter with Wang occurred over a year later on the Tiananmen rostrum during the 1968 National Day celebrations in what might be characterized as a job interview. Subsequently, when the Central Committee met in plenary session later in October, Wang was invited to attend on Mao's personal initiative. During the plenum, Mao asked Wang to stand so everyone could see him, a move identical to his highlighting of Hu Yaobang during the revolutionary period. At the Ninth Congress, Wang was leader not only of the Shanghai delegation, but also of the East China discussion group, spoke to the Congress as the representative of the entire nation's working class, attended Mao's small-scale meetings, and was elected to the Central Committee. By this time, Mao's intention to cultivate Wang would have been clear to Zhang Chunqiao, although he undoubtedly could not have imagined this would involve elevation to the status of putative successor at the Tenth Congress.[170]

At the August-September 1970 Lushan plenum, although initially praising Lin Biao's speech which raised the state chairman issue, and furthered moves against Zhang Chunqiao, once Mao's position became clear, Wang quickly supported the Chairman's view that there should not be a state chairman, and supplied material to Jiang Qing and Zhang. Wang and Xu Jingxian were then secretly received by Jiang, who told them that "we have great hopes for you," a message the Shanghai radicals understood as coming from Mao. The Chairman's hopes and confidence were further seen as the Lin Biao affair came to a head. During his August-September 1971 southern tour, only days before Lin fled, Mao summoned Wang, together with Nanjing Military Region Commander Xu Shiyou, to his train in Shanghai to inform them of his intention to confront Lin after his return to Beijing. Shortly after September 13, Wang, but not Xu, was called to the capital for emergency consultations in the wake of Lin's flight and death, and sent back to Shanghai to deal with Lin's military followers in the city.[171]

This, then, was the background when Wang received a telephone call from Zhang Chunqiao in early September 1972, telling him to hand over his Shanghai duties to others and prepare to come to Beijing immediately for study. Wang was surprised, feeling this was very sudden, while others in Shanghai saw it as a sign that Wang was destined for Politburo membership. What is striking is that upon his arrival in the capital on September 7, it became quickly apparent that Wang was earmarked for something greater than the Politburo. Zhou Enlai took special care of Wang, arranging for him to live in the Diaoyutai Guesthouse where the other radicals resided. Wang subsequently met with Mao quite a few

---

[170] Xu Jingxian, *Shinian yimeng*, pp. 276-82; and, regarding Hu Yaobang, interview with leading Party historian, March 1986.

[171] Xu Jingxian, *Shinian yimeng*, pp. 282-84; and Teiwes and Sun, *Tragedy*, p. 145.

times, with the Chairman again asking about his background and experience, exploring Wang's views on various topics, and enjoining him to "study Marxist-Leninist books, and attend certain meetings to learn different things."[172] Although Wang reportedly had a hard time with theory, he was extremely busy attending a wide range of meetings, in particular those conducted by Zhou. The Premier had been assigned by Mao to help Wang, and Wang's attendance at Zhou's meetings was mandatory. Of particular note was the range and intensity of the meetings that Wang attended, a situation that, as Zhang Chunqiao noted, placed Wang in an even more central position than his radical colleagues and former superiors in Shanghai:

> Hongwen is even busier than me and Yao Wenyuan in Beijing. We only participate in Politburo activities and meetings of the Center. But he attends all the Premier's meetings, the State Council's, the MAC's, even the SPC's, he is invited to attend all of them. Moreover, he needs to vet more documents than we do. The Premier has instructed that every system must report to him.[173]

Notably, this included the military, where Wang's role would be formalized in early 1974. By the end of 1972, Wang's status as successor was revealed to a PLA audience, when central leaders attended the last day of a Beijing Military Region Party Committee meeting. Ye Jianying noted that Mao had talked about the problem of a successor since 1964, introduced Wang citing his peasant, Korean War and worker background, and declared that "the Chairman has noticed him, he has to be cultivated." Zhou then further explained that it was Mao's intention to choose a young man between the ages of 30 and 40 of worker-peasant background "to be vice chairman of the Party and MAC." Thus the most prominent veteran leaders of the Party and army forcefully endorsed the young Shanghai radical, something which would not be unnoticed four years later when PLA officers came under criticism for being uncritical toward Wang. Meanwhile, Mao himself was satisfied with Wang's progress, commenting to Zhang Chunqiao that Wang's background and experience were superior to their own.[174]

It is no surprise, then, that Wang played a key role in the process leading up to the Tenth Congress. Zhou Enlai was also involved, although against the background of his weakening position. It goes without saying that Mao was the critical actor, and hardly surprising that preoccupation with the Cultural Revolution was the key factor in his thinking. By early 1973 the Chairman was clearly in defensive mode, worrying about people rejecting the movement and concerned that it be affirmed at the Tenth Congress. At a late March Politburo meeting, Mao,

[172] Xu Jingxian, Shinian yimeng, pp. 284-86; and Barnouin and Yu, Ten Years, pp. 248-49.

[173] Xu Jingxian, Shinian yimeng, pp. 286-87.

[174] See ibid.; Barnouin and Yu, Ten Years, p. 249; and interview with military historian, January 2005. PLA officers following the arrest of the "gang of four" complained particularly of Ye introducing Wang as the successor, something that presumably occurred on more than this occasion.

unconvincingly, objected to views in society that the Cultural Revolution had failed: "How can anyone say this? The Cultural Revolution seized Liu Shaoqi's clique, and also Lin Biao's clique. This is a great victory. Without the great revolution, how could Liu and Lin have been exposed and toppled?" With Mao providing the basic guidelines and overseeing the process, the Politburo discussed the Tenth Congress and established work organs to deal with it. In addition to Mao's concern with reaffirming the Cultural Revolution, the anomaly of Lin Biao's name being in the existing Party constitution, as well as the need to deal with his case officially, hastened the convening of the Congress ahead of schedule. A Party Center work conference from May 20 to 31 took up preparations for the Tenth Congress as its main agenda, with Zhou Enlai in charge of the meeting.[175]

The Premier's position had clearly been undermined by Mao's redefinition of Lin Biao's line at the end of 1972, as seen in the dismissive behavior of Jiang Qing and Zhang Chunqiao toward him on that occasion. Nevertheless, Zhou remained responsible for Party Center work, and the degree of the shift in policy orientation remained unclear, with Zhou continuing to push some anti-"ultra-left" measures, and even Zhang stating that he was not entirely against dealing with "ultra-left" errors. Mao's explicit criticism of Zhou had not yet reached the level of his July 4 disparagement of the Premier's "shitty speeches," but the May conference marked a clearer turn in the CCP's official posture. Subsequently, "ultra-leftist" shortcomings largely disappeared from public discussion as Tenth Congress preparations focused on the Cultural Revolution message, and preparatory arrangements enhanced the clout of the radical forces. With Zhou in the chair, the May meeting endorsed Mao's proposals for revising the Party constitution,[176] the participation of Wang Hongwen, Hua Guofeng and Wu De in Politburo work, and the liberation of 13 senior cadres, nearly all of whom would be elected to the Tenth Central Committee.[177]

Undoubtedly, the most significant development at the May conference was the placing of the Politburo radicals, including Politburo member-in-waiting Wang Hongwen, in charge of Tenth Congress preparations. Zhang Chunqiao, Wang and Yao Wenyuan were placed in effective control of both the political report to the

---

[175] See *Mao zhuan*, vol. 2, pp. 1653-54; and Chen and Du, *Shilu*, vol. 3, part 2, pp. 914-15. In Mao's mind, the Cultural Revolution had not ended completely. In June 1973, in response to a question from the President of Mali, Mao said there was "still a bit of a tail" in the movement. The other agenda items for the May conference were to discuss the Lin Biao and rectification campaign, and the 1973 national economic plan.

[176] Notably to delete references to individuals (i.e., Lin Biao) as the successor, and add references to certain recent Mao directives. Chen and Du, *Shilu*, vol. 3, part 2, p. 914.

[177] *Ibid.*, p. 915. The 13 were: Tan Zhenlin, Li Jingquan, Wang Jiaxiang, Ulanfu (past Politburo members who received no new operational posts), Li Baohua, Liao Zhigao, Jiang Hua, Jiang Weiqing, Tao Lujia (pre-1966 provincial Party leaders who soon received provincial or central posts), Qin Jiwei, Li Chengfang, Fang Qiang (PLA officers who soon assumed military or military-related posts), and (posthumously) former Anhui leader Zeng Xisheng.

Congress and the new constitution. Although Zhou Enlai officially headed the drafting group for the political report, and Kang Sheng the group responsible for the revision of the constitution, Zhang, Wang and Yao were in charge of the actual drafting. The extent to which the Premier's role was solely formal from the outset is unclear; in the event, Zhou reported on the progress of the political report to Mao in person in mid-June, and sent a draft on July 7, in both cases gaining the Chairman's basic approval. In any case, in his meeting with Wang and Zhang on July 4, Mao began by declaring, "You two are responsible for the work report and constitution." At some point, perhaps during the May conference, Mao also called for a third document, presumably to be drafted by the radicals as well, a report on the Lin Biao affair that the Chairman stipulated should not be loaded with "trivial details," but should just make clear that Lin was plotting. This document apparently never materialized, but the message was incorporated into the political report. Zhou's marginalization was further indicated by the fact that it was a matter of debate as to who would actually deliver the work report, with Zhang proposing Wang in July, and Mao, for unclear reasons, deciding only a few days before the Congress that the task would fall to the Premier despite his minimal input into the document. While the process of choosing Tenth Congress delegates and Central Committee members had clearly been under way since the May gathering, Wang Hongwen's new status was underlined in early August when he was named to head a group in charge of Congress personnel selection.[178] Table 2 underlines the radical grip on Congress preparations by summarizing the membership of the three groups.

Several additional developments in the last days before the Congress deserve attention. First, Jiang Qing proposed that Mao's recent criticisms of Confucius be included in the political report. The unfolding of the anti-Confucian issue will be discussed in Chapter 2 in the context of the "criticize Lin [Biao] and Confucius" campaign. Suffice it to say here that Mao had made several comments attacking Confucius since March 1973, notably during his sharp critique of the MFA in July, and, even though he did not explicitly draw the link, it is likely that some people already sensed a connection between Confucius and Zhou Enlai. In any case, Zhou now opposed Jiang's proposal on the grounds that time was too short to implement it, and Mao did not contradict him. Soon afterward, Zhou complained about the number of articles criticizing Confucius, saying that there was no Party document on the matter, and thus suggesting that Mao had not taken a clear position.[179] About the same time, at an August 22 Politburo meeting, a dispute broke out over the Congress Presidium, the body notionally presiding over the gathering. It was initially proposed that the Presidium have four vice

---

[178] *Mao zhuan*, vol. 2, pp. 1658-60; Mao Zedong, "Tong Wang Hongwen, Zhang Chunqiao de tanhua," p. 1; *Zhou nianpu*, vol. 3, pp. 606, 609, 614; and Chen and Du, *Shilu*, vol. 3, part 2, pp. 914-15.

[179] See *Mao zhuan*, vol. 2, p. 1659; and below, pp. 122-23.

Table 2: Preparatory Groups for the Tenth Congress, Spring-Summer 1973

Political Report Group	Constitution Revision Group	Personnel Group[a]
Zhou Enlai[b]	Kang Sheng[c]	Wang Hongwen
Zhang Chunqiao[d]	Wang Hongwen[d]	Zhou Enlai[b]
Wang Hongwen	Jiang Qing	Kang Sheng[c]
Yao Wenyuan	Zhang Chunqiao[d]	Ye Jianying
Ye Jianying	Yao Wenyuan[d]	Zhang Chunqiao[e]
Li Xiannian		Ji Dengkui[e]
		Li Desheng[e]

Sources: *Mao zhuan*, vol. 2, pp. 1658-60; *Zhou nianpu*, vol. 3, p. 609; and Chen and Du, *Shilu*, vol. 3, part 2, pp. 914-15.

a. Authoritative sources differ on the makeup of the personnel group, with *Zhou nianpu*, vol. 3, p. 609, having Wang assisted by Zhang Chunqiao, Ji Dengkui and Li Desheng, and *Mao zhuan*, vol. 2, p. 1660, listing Zhou, Kang Sheng and Ye Jianying as Wang's deputies. We believe the Zhang-Ji-Li group was in charge of actual work, while Zhou, Kang and Ye were formally responsible.
b. Limited role.
c. No practical role due to serious illness.
d. Responsibility for drafting.
e. Apparently in charge of actual work.

chairmen: the Premier, Wang Hongwen, Kang Sheng and Ye Jianying. Xu Shiyou, however, objected, arguing that there should only be one vice chairman, clearly meaning the Premier. Subsequently, he shifted his argument to advocating that only the three old cadres be selected. Xu, who in his capacity as Nanjing Military Region commander had difficult relations with Wang Hongwen, was apparently also reflecting the doubts of many veteran figures concerning Wang's elevation. Xu was countered both by Zhou's explanations of Mao's views on Wang, and Zhang Chunqiao's assertions that Xu was opposing the Chairman's opinion. This forced Xu's retreat, but the fact that Xu and others did not applaud Wang's report on the constitution suggested that they remained unconvinced and, more fundamentally, were dissatisfied with the Cultural Revolution itself.[180]

---

[180] *Mao zhuan*, vol. 2, pp. 1661, 1663. The interesting questions are why Xu was so bold as to raise the issue, and why he was able to get away with his dissenting actions. While one can speculate that Mao's anti-intellectual biases provided some leeway for the poorly educated but totally loyal soldier, in fact the Chairman had been critical of Xu, complaining both during his August-September 1971 southern tour preceding the Lin Biao affair, and at the time of *pi Lin zhengfeng* criticism in May 1973, of Xu's lack of affection, and in at least the latter case forced a self-criticism. See Li Wenqing, *Jinkan Xu Shiyou (1967-1985)* [A Close Look at Xu Shiyou, 1967-1985] (Beijing: Jiefangjun wenyi chubanshe, 2002), pp. 209-10, 247-48.

A final pre-Congress development occurred on the very eve of the Congress at a Politburo meeting on the 23rd. In view of the poor health of many old cadres, Deng Xiaoping suggested the possibility of their serving as advisers. Mao seized on the idea to propose a Central Advisory Commission, the same structure Deng would create in 1982, to accommodate such cadres, and said that he (Mao) would become chairman of such a body. Clearly feeling that the Chairman's unambiguous authority must be fully maintained, Zhou immediately objected, as did everyone else, and Mao then dropped the proposal. Mao's motives were unclear, although the Chairman's biographers credit his genuine worries over his health and, more ambiguously, the "complicated [political] situation." In any case, the instinctive reaction of the Chairman's Politburo colleagues told the essential story—he would in any case exercise ultimate power as long as he lived, and any apparent willingness to push him to the sidelines, even in response to his own suggestion, was too dangerous to embrace.[181]

Despite claims that Mao's approach to the Tenth Congress encompassed his wish to deal with the problems created by the Cultural Revolution as well as to reaffirm the movement, once the Congress opened there was little indication of attention to such problems apart from a strong restatement of the principle of "unified leadership." There were no speeches by responsible leaders discussing policies in functional areas, and the political report delivered by Zhou devoted a single paragraph to the economy, largely repeating past policy slogans.[182] In contrast, more than half the report dealt with the Lin Biao affair, basically denouncing Lin as a plotter of both a military *coup d'état* and the assassination of the Chairman without, as *per* Mao's order, providing revealing detail. One of the few new claims in the report, an ironic revelation in view of Zhou's current situation, was that Lin had been forced to read the Ninth Congress work report (largely drafted by Zhang Chunqiao and Yao Wenyuan) that emphasized continuing the revolution under the dictatorship of the proletariat, rather than his own preference for developing production. This was linked to a larger proposition, in both the work report and Wang Hongwen's report on the new constitution, that the line of the Ninth Congress remained the Party's guiding ideology. The centerpiece of that line was the summing up and justification of

---

[181] See *Mao zhuan*, vol. 2, p. 1666; and *Zhou nianpu*, vol. 3, p. 615. Note the similarity of the dilemma to that of Mao's top colleagues in the early 1960s, when he notionally retired to the "second front," leaving daily operations to his associates, but still exercised absolute authority. See Teiwes, *Politics and Purges*, pp. xxxvi-xliv, 478-79. Also note that this is Deng's only recorded attendance at a Politburo meeting before the November-December 1973 criticism of Zhou (see Chapter 2).

[182] Such as the Great Leap injunctions for "greater, faster, better and more economical results" and "walking on two legs," and the early to mid-1960s policies of "taking agriculture as the base" and "learning from Daqing and Dazhai." Potentially more relevant, but still vague policy directions, included strengthening planning and coordination, and improving rational rules and regulations, both aspects of the critique of "ultra-leftism" in the economy. *PR*, no. 35-36 (1973), pp. 24-25. On Mao's claimed intention, see *Mao zhuan*, vol. 2, pp. 1654, 1657.

the Cultural Revolution, a justification which now became the underlying *raison d'être* of both reports to the Tenth Congress and the revised constitution. While sketchy on actual guidance for superstructure reforms, with the work report only calling for continuing the revolution in literature and art, education and public health, the three documents were heavy with rhetorical flourishes which could only raise anxiety among officials unhappy with the turmoil of 1966-68. These included: the injunction to emulate rebellious behavior by "daring to go against the tide"; stipulating in the constitution that "[Cultural] Revolutions like this will have to be carried out many times in the future"; quoting Mao that "every seven or eight years monsters and demons will jump out [again]"; and the observation that "two line struggles within the Party ... will occur ten, twenty or thirty times [in the future]." These exhortations provided little concrete guidance, but they could only inhibit resistance to radical pressure.[183]

Mao's wishes were reflected as strongly in the personnel arrangements overseen by Wang Hongwen, and approved at the Congress and the subsequent First Plenum of the new Central Committee on August 30. This was seen not simply in individual appointments, but in the broader criteria Mao had laid down for the new leadership as a whole. The Chairman's formula of "combining the old, middle-aged and young" was stipulated in the new constitution as a requirement for Party leadership bodies at all levels; more specifically, Mao directed that it be applied to the five vice chairmen of the Party. With Zhou and Kang Sheng continuing in this position, the new appointees exactly fit this formula: Ye Jianying (b. 1897), General Li Desheng (b. 1916), who not only met the age criteria, but also Mao's stipulation that the middle-aged person "be able to fight," and, of course, Wang Hongwen (b. 1935). Mao's class criteria could also be seen in the new bodies chosen at the Tenth Congress. The priority given to the working class in the new constitution, a priority colorfully reflected in Mao's comment on the eve of the Congress that the CCP should be renamed the "Party of Mr. Worker," was seen not only in Wang Hongwen's elevation, but in the appointments of Ni Zhifu and Wu Guixian as alternate Politburo members, and in the selection of many worker Central Committee members. In calling for the selection of workers and peasants, Mao noted that their cultural level might be a bit low, but this could be overcome. To this end, in the months before the Tenth Congress, future Politburo member Chen Yonggui, the peasant leader of Dazhai brigade who had caught Mao's attention before the Cultural Revolution, attended classes in Beijing to improve his understanding of Marxism-Leninism and study the Congress documents.[184]

---

[183] *PR*, no. 35-36 (1973), pp. 17-33. For further discussion of the reports and constitution, see the sensitive contemporary analysis by Richard Wich, "The Tenth Party Congress: The Power Structure and the Succession Question," *CQ*, no. 58 (1974), pp. 243-47. On Lin and the Ninth Congress work report, see Teiwes and Sun, *Tragedy*, pp. 104-10.

[184] *PR*, no. 35-36 (1973), p. 27; *Mao zhuan*, vol. 2, p. 1655; Gao Wenqian, *Wannian Zhou*, p. 486; *Li Desheng huiyilu* [Memoirs of Li Desheng] (Beijing: Jiefangjun chubanshe, 1997), p. 455; and

As noted above, all of the sitting Politburo members not caught up in the Lin Biao affair were retained, and, in addition, all the similarly uninvolved Ninth Congress alternate members were promoted to full membership or, in the case of Li Desheng, to even higher rank. Despite the emphasis on Party building since 1969, a central Party Secretariat was not reestablished, nor was there an elaboration of Party Center organs. The Politburo Standing Committee was enlarged to nine from the previous five members; in addition to Mao and the five vice chairmen, Zhang Chunqiao, and Party elders Zhu De and Dong Biwu were included. In Table 3 we offer an overview of the new Politburo somewhat different from earlier scholarly constructs.[185]

The categories here are essentially based on revolutionary status, and the possibility of achieving Politburo membership without the Cultural Revolution. "Old revolutionaries" were not necessarily older than establishment types who only achieved Politburo status after 1966;[186] the defining quality in the usage here is having achieved that rank by the Eighth Congress in 1956. Although classifying Kang Sheng as an old revolutionary runs against conventional usage, it was indeed the case in terms of Kang's career and, as we have seen, affected his relations with Zhou and Deng. "Establishment officials" (a slightly different usage from establishment beneficiaries in order to include the rehabilitated Su Zhenhua) were mostly plausible future Politburo members given career backgrounds and/ or associations with Mao, although it would have been remarkable if more than one or two would have been promoted in the normal course of events. In contrast, with the possible exception of Zhang Chunqiao, whose theoretical talents had impressed Mao since the late 1950s, the "pure" Cultural Revolution products had no chance of rising to the heights without the disruption of the late 1960s. Beyond this, Li Desheng, who could be considered to have been helicoptered into the top echelon, fits uneasily into our reconstruction. Although certainly a figure from the PLA establishment, Li was of considerably lower rank than fellow Politburo members Xu Shiyou and Chen Xilian, and clearly would not have risen to the Politburo without having caught Mao's attention for his efforts in dealing with Cultural Revolution strife in Anhui, notionally "in support of the left" in 1967-68.[187]

From this perspective, several things can be said with some confidence. The position of the old revolutionaries had not been strengthened and, in view of Mao's increasingly negative opinion of Zhou, was actually weakened. As with many old cadres elected to the Central Committee, elderly figures Zhu De, Dong Biwu and Liu Bocheng were symbolic inclusions on the Politburo, and were

---

interviews with Party historians, November 2002. While Mao had set the criteria for Li Desheng's elevation, it was Zhou who nominated him for the post. On Mao's interaction with Chen Yonggui in 1964, see Teiwes, *Politics and Purges*, pp. 432-33.

[185] See Teiwes, *Leadership*, p. 114; Huang, *Factionalism*, p. 327; and Robinson, "China in 1973," p. 5.

[186] Thus Xu Shiyou (b. 1906) was older than Li Xiannian (b. 1909).

Table 3: The Tenth Congress Politburo, August 1973

Old revolutionaries	Establishment officials	"Pure" CR products
Active officials	*Beijing based*	*Radicals*
Zhou Enlai VC	Li Desheng* VC	Wang Hongwen VC
Ye Jianying* VC	Ji Dengkui	Zhang Chunqiao SC
Li Xiannian	Hua Guofeng	Jiang Qing
	Wu De	Yao Wenyuan
	Wang Dongxing	
	Su Zhenhua*a A	
Inactive figures	*Regionally based*	*Non-radicals*
Kang Shengb VC	Chen Xilian*	Chen Yonggui
Zhu De* SC	Xu Shiyou*	Ni Zhifu A
Dong Biwu SC	Wei Guoqing*c	Wu Guixian A
Liu Bocheng*	Saifudind A	

Sources: *Zhonghuarenmingongheguo dang zheng jun qun lingdao renminglu* [Name Lists of PRC Party, Government, Military and Mass Organization Leaders] (Beijing: Zhonggong dangshi chubanshe, 1990), p. 5; and sources to Table 1, above, p. 39.

Key: *=PLA figure; VC=Vice Chair; SC=Standing Committee; A=alternate member.
a. Su was purged in the CR, but was one of the first officials rehabilitated in 1972.
b. Kang was in very poor health, and died in 12/75.
c. Guangxi Party chief Wei might be considered a civilian, but his past, current and future posts were all closely tied to the military.
d. Seypidin Azizi, a Uighur, presumably a symbolic national minority figure on the Politburo.

given no real work. Only Zhou, Ye Jianying and Li Xiannian had genuinely significant functions at the Center.[188] While the four radicals did not receive new operational posts, their influence in the lead-up to the Congress and at the Congress itself was abundantly clear, and they assumed significant Politburo authority over various sectors.[189] Of particular interest was Zhang Chunqiao's selection

[187] Both Xu and Chen were military region commanders by 1955 and 1959 respectively, while Li was only an army commander at the start of the Cultural Revolution. Also, in the military honors handed out in 1955, Xu and Chen were named full generals (*shangjiang*), while Li was appointed two grades lower as a major general (*shaojiang*). Moreover, Li first met Mao at the 1968 Central Committee plenum. On Li's performance in Anhui, see Cheng and Xia, *Deng zai yijiuqiwu*, p. 8.

[188] Su Zhenhua (b. 1912) would also qualify if we use Mao's age-based definition as laid down at a spring 1973 Politburo meeting, i.e., people over 60. *Li Desheng huiyilu*, p. 455.

[189] While no Politburo responsibilities were revealed at this time, over a year later Wang Hongwen referred to Politburo duties that probably dated from this time: Zhang Chunqiao for Party affairs and Volume 5 of Mao's *Selected Works*, and Yao Wenyuan for publishing and propaganda. *Mao zhuan*, vol. 2, p. 1712. Wang himself, as the putative successor, presumably had some broader oversight responsibilities.

as Congress Secretary-General, a post indicating significant power in the past. When the local Shanghai radicals learned of this assignment, they concluded that Zhang, who was widely regarded as the likely next Premier, would be promoted to at least the Standing Committee, a promotion duly conferred.[190] Taken together with Wang Hongwen's clear anointment as the successor, the Congress can only be regarded a significant radical victory. Yet their enhanced clout derived more from specific tasks assigned by Mao than from organizational posts, and from his present, but always changeable, preference for their ideological views. Although we have and will continue to argue that it is a mistake to overemphasize the commonality of the four leaders' interests, at the Tenth Congress the four radicals were drawn together by both ideology and function—in part due to their rise as "pure" Cultural Revolution products, and in part because of the anti-restorationist duties Mao handed them.

The crux of the matter was that formal positions did not equate with stable power. Mao could alter the equation at any time, both in terms of policy direction and individual status, as would be seen in the elevation of Deng Xiaoping, newly restored to Central Committee membership at the Congress, to the Politburo at the end of the year, and then to Party Vice Chairman in January 1975. But official positions did confer status, and positioning for possible further advancement as Mao's priorities changed, and subsequently as the post-Mao period unfolded. In this regard, two individuals largely overlooked in contemporary analyses, Ji Dengkui (b. 1923) and Hua Guofeng (b. 1921), are particularly notable. These figures were key civilian "middle-aged" establishment beneficiaries promoted or appointed to full Politburo membership. They were already performing significant functions in the Party and State Council, and would assume even more prominence when the State Council was reorganized at the Fourth NPC in 1975. While as vulnerable to Mao's whims as any other leader, arguably their continuing organizational roles, together with their essentially moderate views, stood them in good stead in developing broader acceptance within the elite. More generally, the younger establishment types as a group had a larger role in the new Politburo, as well as more operational posts, than any other category, especially when ill health and political inexperience are taken into account. While PRC sources emphasize "old cadres" as balancing the radicals in Mao's design,[191] to a considerable extent it was these "middle-aged" figures, with their responsibilities for practical work, who provided a counterpoint to the radical project of upholding the Cultural Revolution legacy.

Politburo appointments, however, only give some indication of Mao's design which can be seen even more dramatically in the make-up of the new Central Committee. The broad outlines have long been noted: PLA representation fell

---

[190] See Xu Jingxian, *Shinian yimeng,* p. 271. At the three previous congresses, the secretary-general post was filled by Ren Bishi in 1945, Deng Xiaoping in 1956, and Zhou Enlai in 1969.

[191] See, e.g., Mao Mao, *"Wenge" suiyue,* p. 294.

from 43 to 30 percent, with much of the loss born by presumptive followers of Lin Biao; civilian cadres, including those recently liberated, increased from 29 to 33 percent; while "mass representatives" grew substantially from 28 to 37 percent, although this was heavily skewed to alternate members.[192] To superimpose Mao's "old-middle-aged-young" formula on these figures, one result (mirroring the Politburo situation) was the prominence of the "middle-aged" compared to the "old" when we look at civilian cadres. As observed previously, although various senior figures now returned to the Central Committee, few truly senior cadres assumed any positions of real power in Beijing. It can even be argued that Deng Xiaoping would be the *only* such figure to emerge from the new appointees to the Tenth Central Committee. In contrast, "middle-aged" figures such as Zhao Ziyang (b. 1919), Guangdong's first secretary before 1966 and now again a leading Party figure in the province, and Tao Lujia (b. 1917), Shanxi's pre-Cultural Revolution leader who would soon take a leading role in the PLA's Science and Technology Commission for National Defense, attained Central Committee status either in recognition of positions already held, or as an indication that actual power was not far off. Importantly, a fundamental alteration of Party norms was at work here, a norm shattered by the Cultural Revolution, but not restored despite attention to traditional procedures in the two reports and constitution: respect for seniority and revolutionary status. While never an explicit formal norm, such respect was a crucial underpinning of the pre-1966 value system, and, as we have already argued, an instinctive reflex among many of the "middle-aged" figures whose careers were now advanced.[193]

The more dramatic assault on seniority obviously came from the workers and peasants who made up more than a third of the Central Committee, and were represented on the Politburo by Wang Hongwen, Chen Yonggui, Ni Zhifu and Wu Guixian.[194] These people were clearly an essential part of Mao's design for the future—leading examples of the millions of revolutionary successors called for at the Congress. While analysts tended to lump such mass representatives with the Politburo radicals, a tendency shared by old revolutionaries in the days following Mao's death as they worried that the "gang of four" might obtain a majority if their fate were put to a Central Committee vote (see Chapter 8), the actual situation was much more complex. The largely younger figures from the factory floor and villages might have had overlapping ideological perspectives and political interests with the established Politburo radicals and Wang Hongwen, but their interests were not identical, they operated at lower levels, and they had little knowledge of political developments at the Center. In terms of Central

---

[192] Figures based on Lee, *Revolutionary Cadres to Party Technocrats*, pp. 99, 117.

[193] See *PR*, no. 35-36 (1973), pp. 25, 27-28, 32. On formal and informal Party norms, see Teiwes, *Leadership*, ch. 3.

[194] Although 18 to 24 years older than Wang, Ni and Wu, Chen Yonggui lacked seniority in terms of Party membership and major official posts.

Committee membership, many of the worker and peasant inductees whom Mao ordered cultivated were largely representational and symbolic, holding few operational posts. Beyond that, many were more traditional representatives of the "masses" such as model workers than particularly adventuresome Cultural Revolution activists. This can be seen in the cases of alternate Politburo members Ni Zhifu (b. 1933), a model worker who developed a drilling device in the 1950s, and female textile worker Wu Guixian (b. 1938). Both had benefited from the Cultural Revolution, but were more notable for post-1968 organizational activities than rebel mobilization. Nor was the older peasant leader, Chen Yonggui (b. 1914), although linked to Mao's left policy impulses before 1966, identified with the radicalism of 1966-68, and in the immediate future Chen would develop extreme animosity toward Zhang Chunqiao, although he maintained cordial relations with Wang Hongwen (see Chapter 7).[195]

One of the striking features of the process producing this flood of workers and peasants into the Central Committee was its last-minute rushed nature. Although Mao had been talking of the need to bring people of worker and peasant background into the central leadership since the Ninth Congress, the directive to select large numbers of workers and peasants from the grass roots for committee membership was apparently sudden. The demand to increase greatly the proportion of worker members in particular changed the previous emphasis on workers, peasants and soldiers, and workers now filled Central Committee slots formerly held by PLA officers. Wang Hongwen, as head of the Congress personnel group, called on lower levels to nominate candidates according to the new spirit. In the case of Shanghai, with the municipal delegation already in Beijing, Wang told his local colleagues that their existing list, arrived at through the normal unit-based selection process, was no good. The city had to come up with a new list of workers and peasants immediately, something that was only accomplished by Wang's middle of the night phone call to the Shanghai organization chief. In his exchange with the delegation, Wang complained that he had asked earlier for a list of 100 people, and when the delegation head replied they had no idea the request concerned the Central Committee, Wang further complained that they should have figured it out as he was bound from speaking openly on a top secret matter. The episode thus illustrated the haste of the whole effort, the limited input of Wang and his group which seemingly simply conveyed Mao's demands to lower levels, the inevitable complete surprise of those selected, and the guarded communications between the Politburo radicals and their Shanghai followers. The last-minute nature of the decision was further indicated by the convening of a central study class, with Wang, Li Desheng and Ji Dengkui in leading roles, to train the new worker-peasant recruits *after* their election to the Central Committee.[196]

---

[195] See Dittmer, *Continuous Revolution*, p. 183; Lee, *Revolutionary Cadres to Party Technocrats*, pp. 114-21; Wang Xueliang, "Mingren Wu Guixian de gushi" [Stories of Celebrity Wu Guixian], *Dangshi wenyuan* [Party History Literary Gallery], no. 11 (2005), pp. 24-27; "Ni Chih-fu," pp. 91-93; and below, p. 502.

Another notable outcome of the process was that prominent leading rebels on the Ninth Central Committee—with Nie Yuanzi, the Beijing University intellectual who wrote the first "big character poster" in June 1966, the outstanding example—were now dropped, while other famous rebels like Zhejiang's Weng Senhe failed to obtain a seat. Despite the injunction to "go against the tide," the personnel selections, which in this respect were probably more deliberate than the sudden decision on worker-peasant members, suggested that unfettered rebelliousness, the type that resulted in anarchy, was not what was sought. Although the Central Committee reportedly contained "not a few rebels," new members seemingly had to demonstrate some degree of discipline and respect for organizational norms. Apart from the cases of Ni, Wu and Chen, Wang Hongwen himself, although a bold rebel leader not adverse to violence in 1960s Shanghai, in certain respects can be seen as this type of more restrained rebel. To a substantial extent, this was a consequence of his alliance with Zhang Chunqiao. With Zhang crucially backed by Mao, radical authority could be established in Shanghai and violence was much less a factor than elsewhere in China. Wang thus became part of the new "revolutionary" establishment from an early point in time, and it is probably no coincidence that his old factory was the first unit in the country to reestablish a Party committee in 1969.[197]

A final aspect of the emerging personnel situation bears comment. Mao was, in effect, attempting to build a cohort of "new radicals." Apart from worker-peasant-soldier inductees to the Central Committee, there was a small number of well-connected young people who, by 1970, had assumed important roles and would continue to play a significant part in the unfolding elite politics to the end of Mao's life. Not all were appointed to the Central Committee in 1973, but all had links to the Chairman: Xie Jingyi, now a full Central Committee member, from Mao's Zhongnanhai staff who would attend at least some Politburo meetings; Tang Wensheng, Mao's interpreter and one of the "two ladies," made a Central Committee alternate, reportedly on Jiang Qing's recommendation; Wang Hairong, the Chairman's niece and the "second lady"; Chi Qun, who served in Mao's security unit and played a key role at Qinghua, one of the "two universities" in which the Chairman took special interest; and Mao's nephew Mao Yuanxin, who would be the most significant of all through his crucial role in the

---

[196] See *Mao zhuan*, vol. 2, pp. 1655, 1665; Xu Jingxian, *Shinian yimeng*, pp. 267-68; and Hao Jiansheng *et al.*, *Yang Gui yu Hongqiqu* [Yang Gui and the Red Flag Irrigation Canal] (Beijing: Zhongyang bianyi chubanshe, 2004), pp. 307-309.

[197] See *Mao zhuan*, vol. 2, p. 1664; Forster, *Rebellion*, pp. 118-19, 132-33; idem, "Spontaneous and Institutional Rebellion in the Cultural Revolution: The Extraordinary Case of Weng Senghe," *AJCA*, no. 27 (1992); Perry and Li, *Proletarian Power*, pp. 18-21; and Wich, "Tenth Party Congress," p. 235. We are not suggesting that these choices were entirely of Wang's own volition, and there is evidence that he and Zhang Chunqiao made special efforts to assure that Weng Senhe was a delegate to the Congress. What we are suggesting is that personnel decisions were made with knowledge of Mao's preferences, and at the time of the Tenth Congress these excluded extreme rebels from 1966-68, precisely the types of persons attacked as anarchists and "ultra-leftists."

1975 demise of Deng Xiaoping.[198] While all of these "new radicals" had been Cultural Revolution activists in some sense, like Wang Hongwen none had been truly destructive of order. Indeed, Chi Qun played a key role in restoring order at Qinghua when dispatched by Mao in 1968. One could also ask whether the "two ladies" were truly radical in their views, rather than simply being caught up in conveying Mao's orders and attitudes.[199] In any case, the Chairman undoubtedly saw a role for these people in keeping alive the revolutionary flame, and, as events would demonstrate, he did not expect them to act as puppets of the Politburo radicals.

The Tenth Congress, in both ideology and personnel, reflected Mao's absolute dominance, but also great fragility. The fragility began with the Chairman's health, as seen in the fact that, a few interjections apart, Mao did not speak for the first time since assuming unchallenged Party leadership in the 1940s, and his difficulty in movement meant that, contrary to practice, the delegates left the hall before he was assisted out himself.[200] As for the CCP as an institution, concerning theory and policy, Mao had provided some ringing rhetoric, but little in the way of clear guidance for the future. In organizational terms, the Party's structure was still a work in progress, the political role of the PLA was not fully resolved, and although the overdue NPC session was promised, it would not eventuate for another 16 months when a new State Council would finally be ready. Regarding personnel and leadership, relations fell abysmally short of the theme of unity that was supposed to be the objective of both the Ninth and Tenth Congresses.[201] This goes beyond tensions between radicals and old revolutionaries that have long been emphasized in the literature. Even more fundamentally, it extends to the atmosphere initially created by the Cultural Revolution, and now sustained by Mao's continuing insistence on the correctness of the movement—an atmosphere that constrained informal contact among leaders and the necessary trust for effective action, even within presumptive groupings. Thus the Tenth Congress occurred in the midst of an extended period when the two leading lights of the old revolutionaries—Zhou Enlai and Deng Xiaoping—seemingly had no significant contact. We have also seen the emergence of Wang Hongwen in a manner suggesting less than total identification with any radical "gang." While we are not questioning the overlapping interests of the now four Politburo radicals, the fact that it was the Premier who was assigned to "care for" Wang, and that

---

[198] Neither Wang, Chi or Mao attained Central Committee status, in the cases of the Chairman's niece and nephew apparently because of his desire to avoid the impression of nepotism.

[199] Indeed, in May 1967 Wang and Tang wrote Mao defending Zhou from radical attacks in the MFA; Ma Jisen, *The Cultural Revolution in the Foreign Ministry*, pp. 142-43. See also above, p. 20; and below, p. 131.

[200] *Mao zhuan*, vol. 2, p. 1664.

[201] The Tenth Congress work report gave prominence to Mao's call at the Ninth Congress to "Unite to win still greater victories," while Wang Hongwen's report painted a glowing picture of veteran cadres and young successors learning from each other. *PR*, no. 35-36 (1973), pp. 17, 32.

Wang's new status eclipsed that of Zhang Chunqiao, are indicative of tensions and complexities that will be seen again in coming chapters.

Although there were clear differences between the predominant critique of "ultra-leftism" for more than a year after the Lin Biao affair and the revived radical themes of the Tenth Congress, the actual shifts in political direction were in major respects less dramatic than usually believed. The post-September 13 policy direction, while deepened due to Mao's need to explain away his own mistakes, and by Zhou's skill in using false accusations blaming Lin Biao for Cultural Revolution excesses to extend attacks on leftist practices, essentially continued the post-Ninth Congress orientation without providing any clear theoretical rationale or consequent reassurance. Policy adjustments in the economy and superstructure were, in most respects, modest, while claims concerning the liberation of cadres—an area under Mao's near-total control—greatly overstate the reality. This was not yet a broad-based rehabilitation of Cultural Revolution victims; it was most significant in the PLA where the underlying motive was to counter Lin's remaining influence by rehabilitating cadres from other "mountaintops." Similarly, the turn to the left in late 1972 and 1973 was less sharp than sometimes imagined. Modulated attacks on "ultra-left" phenomena continued in the first half of 1973, and even after they disappeared from public discussion, many policies were essentially unchanged. But the ideological climate had changed, and, significantly, Mao's assessment of Zhou Enlai had hardened. The stage was set for a more far-ranging alteration of course through the campaign against Lin Biao and Confucius—a movement some would see as a "second Cultural Revolution."

Chapter 2

"THE SECOND CULTURAL REVOLUTION," FALL 1973-SUMMER 1974

At the time of the [November 1973 enlarged Politburo meetings criticizing Zhou Enlai], before receiving a briefing from Wang Hairong and Tang Wensheng, Mao Zedong asked whether Deng Xiaoping had spoken. ... [Having only recently returned to work and not yet a Politburo member, Deng had been silent, but after others spoke he gave a speech a few days later.] Once the speeches started, he had no choice but to criticize Zhou Enlai as Mao Zedong had demanded of each participant. ... When [the "two ladies"] reported Deng Xiaoping's speech to Mao Zedong, Mao happily said: "I knew he would speak" ... [and] wanted Deng brought to him immediately.

—Deng's daughter's account of his behavior and Mao's reaction, late 1973[1]

Comrades, you must have recently read the articles criticizing Lin Biao and Confucius, and know that Qinshihuang was cursed for 2,000 years for making a revolution replacing an exploiting system with another exploiting system. Will our Great Cultural Revolution [also] be cursed? Certainly some people will curse it. And even ten years or several decades later, there will be some people who curse it and come out to reverse the verdicts on Liu Shaoqi and Lin Biao.

—Wang Hongwen to the Central Study Class shortly before the launch of the campaign to criticize Lin Biao and Confucius, January 14, 1974[2]

In the 1974 criticism of Lin Biao and Confucius, when the "gang of four" criticized "Zhou Gong" [the Duke of Zhou, i.e., Zhou Enlai], the Chairman felt this was unacceptable. Afterward the Chairman convened a meeting [of the Politburo on July 17—the authors], and personally arranged to sit between Premier Zhou on his right and Ye Jianying on his left. [Holding hands with Zhou and Ye], the Chairman said, you [the radicals] cannot conduct this sort of criticism against [Zhou and Ye] again.

—Deng Liqun's account of Mao's criticism of Jiang Qing *et al.* for their attacks on Zhou and Ye, summer 1974[3]

As throughout the entire post-Lin Biao period, the Cultural Revolution continued to be the central issue of elite politics in the year following the Tenth Congress. Mao was acutely aware of widespread dissatisfaction with the movement, whether by people who saw it as a dark, fearful night, by officials bent on revenge after being attacked by rebels, or even by those who felt its objectives were good but that it did not have to be carried out in such a chaotic manner.[4] In the immediate wake of the Lin Biao affair until late 1972, the Chairman's approach to protecting his Cultural Revolution was to focus on correcting what he later termed the 30 percent errors of the movement. But after concluding that the consolidation efforts under Zhou Enlai had gone too far, in 1973 Mao's emphasis shifted to a strident reaffirmation of its alleged 70 percent positive achievements. As we have seen, this was the essence of the Tenth Congress, even though the policy and political implications of this stance were far from clear.

The key question was the status of the *current* Cultural Revolution. In mid-1973, Mao declared the movement still had a bit of a tail, while the sense that it was winding down was also implicit in references at the Party Congress to periodic resurgences in the future, as much as seven or eight years away.[5] Moreover, following the Congress there was little indication that any such upsurge was an immediate prospect. Yet in January 1974, following closely upon Mao's crucial steps to launch new and more thoroughgoing criticism of Zhou, and to impose a rotation of military region commanders, the campaign to criticize Lin Biao and Confucius (*pi Lin pi Kong*) was launched, a movement that would be termed a "second Cultural Revolution" by Wang Hongwen and, by Zhang Chunqiao, a "second seizure of power."[6] This movement, however, fell far short of the chaotic conditions of 1966-68, with very few senior officials removed from office, and violent clashes between populace and authorities, or among

---

[1] Mao Mao, *"Wenge" suiyue*, pp. 288-89. Mao Mao claimed that "after a very few words [Deng] changed the subject and spoke of the international strategic situation." However, according to Gao Wenqian, *Wannian Zhou*, pp. 472-73, although Deng's criticism of Zhou was brief, the weight of his remarks was heavy and fully in accord with Mao's line. See also below, p. 137.

[2] "Wang Hongwen zai zhongyang dushuban de baogao" [Wang Hongwen's Report at the Central Study Class] (January 14, 1974), in *CRDB*, p. 4.

[3] *Deng Liqun guoshi jiangtan*, vol. 1, p. 368. The reference to holding hands, apparently on this occasion, comes from "Geng Biao guanyu zhua sirenbang qingkuang de jianghua" [Geng Biao's Speech concerning the Circumstances of Seizing the Gang of Four] (October 16, 1976), in *CRDB*, p. 2. Our deduction concerning the date is based on other comments by Mao critical of the radicals at the July 17 Politburo meeting.

[4] See "Wang Hongwen zai zhongyang dushuban," pp. 2-4, on currents of dissatisfaction with the Cultural Revolution. On Mao's awareness, see above, pp. 27, 96-97.

[5] See above, pp. 97n175, 101.

[6] See An Jianshe, "Mao Zedong yu 'pi Lin pi Kong' ruogan wenti kaoshu" [Commentary on Certain Questions concerning Mao Zedong and "Criticizing Lin Biao and Confucius"], *Dang de wenxian* [The Party's Documents] (hereafter *DDWX*), no. 4 (2000), p. 61; Zhonggong Shanghai shiwei dangshi yanjiushi, ed., *Zhongguo Gongchandang zai Shanghai 80 nian (1921-2001)* [The CCP's 80 Years in

mass factions, decidedly limited in comparison to the earlier period. In addition, the campaign was supposed to be under the leadership of Party committees at all levels.[7] Nevertheless, there were obvious similarities: sharp criticism of sitting authorities, wall posters naming Politburo members, demonstrations and associated political activism by mass groups, factional strife including armed clashes, the promotion of rebellious behavior with "going against the tide" equated to Mao's Cultural Revolution dictum that "to rebel is justified," the recruitment of young rebels into official power structures, and undeniable costs in terms of economic production and social stability. Mao acknowledged the link in August when he effectively called off the movement with the observation that "the Cultural Revolution has already lasted eight years [and] it is now time to establish stability." At the end of 1974, moreover, he observed it was not quite right to consider the criticism of Lin Biao and Confucius a "second Cultural Revolution." But neither comment suggested disapproval of *pi Lin pi Kong*, something Mao never expressed.[8] Rather, the time had come for a temporary pause, with future Cultural Revolutions still in prospect.

While it is clear that Mao dictated the twists and turns of the period, there is nevertheless considerable uncertainty as to his precise role in shaping the Lin Biao-Confucius campaign. Although the *People's Daily* in February 1974 declared that the movement was "initiated and led by Chairman Mao," post-Mao CCP sources have portrayed Mao as more distant from its initiation and conduct. In this interpretation, the sudden emergence of the campaign in

---

Shanghai, 1921-2001] (Shanghai: Shanghai renmin chubanshe, 2001), p. 673; Perry and Li, *Proletarian Power*, pp. 177-78; Forster, *Rebellion*, p. 166; and Ann Elizabeth Fenwick, "The Gang of Four and the Politics of Opposition: China, 1971-1976," Ph.D. dissertation, Stanford University, 1984, pp. 254-55.

Zhang Chunqiao's idea of the "second power grab" contrasted the first upsurge during the Cultural Revolution as "from the bottom up," while the current 1974 effort was "from the top down." See the summary discussion in *Shanghai "wenhua dageming" shihua* [Historical Narrative of the "Great Cultural Revolution" in Shanghai] (3 vols., Shanghai: 1992), pp. 668-702.

[7] While Party committee authority over the Cultural Revolution had been asserted in the Sixteen Articles of August 1966, this soon became non-operative as the committees themselves disintegrated. Notional Party committee authority remained in place throughout the Lin Biao and Confucius campaign although, as examined later in this chapter, there was considerable pressure on Party committees that sometimes produced paralysis.

[8] *Mao wengao*, vol. 13, p. 402; and "Zhou Enlai zai Zhengzhiju Changwei huishang zhuanda de Mao Zedong tanhua yao dian (jielu)" [Extract from Zhou Enlai's Transmission at a Meeting of the Politburo Standing Committee of the Main Points of Mao Zedong's Talk] (the end of 1974 to the start of 1975), in *CRDB*, p. 1. While *pi Lin pi Kong* continued to dominate the media for the remainder of 1974, the campaign's intensity decreased markedly as it essentially became a study movement, and it concluded by the time of the new movement to study the theory of the dictatorship of the proletariat in February 1975 (see Chapter 4). See John Bryan Starr, "China in 1974: 'Weeding Through the Old to Bring Forth the New'," *AS*, January 1975, p. 9; and An Jianshe, "Mao Zedong yu 'pi Lin pi Kong' ruogan wenti," p. 57.

Mao's ongoing positive attitude toward *pi Lin pi Kong* was indicated by his December 1974 comment affirming that Jiang Qing and the radicals had made contributions to the movement, even as he warned them against forming a "gang of four." Wang Nianyi, *Dadongluan*, pp. 510-11.

January came virtually as a surprise to Mao, who had no prior knowledge of some of the early critical events. Also, the Chairman assertedly had a much more educational intent than what actually eventuated, and duly criticized the "gang of four" for the disruptive features of the movement. This issue will be examined in more detail below, but for now some initial observations are in order. First, Mao's direct responsibility for specific developments in the campaign cannot be determined on the basis of the available evidence. There are significant gaps in the sources, undoubtedly due in part to efforts to maximize the "gang's" culpability while minimizing Mao's, but also reflecting the limits on access to materials by even senior Party historians. Beyond that, official sources contrast Mao's asserted limited involvement to his personal leadership in the early stages of the Cultural Revolution, claiming that he rarely expressed views on the new movement during this period.[9] The circumstantial evidence, however, indicates that Mao was broadly and decisively responsible: he had raised and pursued the Confucius issue since spring 1973, linking it to both Lin Biao and Zhou Enlai; the development of key *pi Lin pi Kong* critiques and the "three-month movement" in October-December, both precursors of the 1974 campaign, took place at the "two schools"—Beijing (Beida) and Qinghua Universities—that were under Mao's direct control; and the key targets of the campaign, Zhou Enlai and the PLA, were precisely the targets singled out by the Chairman at the end of 1973. Notwithstanding the degree to which the radicals may have exceeded his wishes guiding *pi Lin pi Kong*, or his changing assessments as the campaign unfolded, Mao's preoccupations and actions in late 1973 created the movement's central dynamic.

These developments took place against the background of a changing but still murky power equation within the leadership. This, in turn, was linked to the ongoing health problems of Mao and Zhou Enlai. As we saw in Chapter 1, Mao's serious condition in 1972 had improved to the point that the special leadership group overseeing his health was disbanded by spring 1973. Although still ill, the Chairman's condition remained stable until spring 1974 when near blindness, pulmonary problems and motor neuron disease led to the establishment of a second medical group in mid-June. Meanwhile, Zhou's condition was, if anything, even more serious. With his cancer worsening, in the first half of 1974 during his political trials in the Lin Biao-Confucius campaign the Premier was in and out of the hospital and had several operations before finally entering hospital quarters permanently on June 1. In this period the Premier still carried a heavy work load, including discussions with visiting foreign leaders, an area in which Deng Xiaoping's role was becoming more prominent. The relationship between Zhou's illness and Deng's rise is an important if elusive question, one entangled with Mao's obvious preference for Deng, and Zhou's own presumed wish to see

---

[9] See *PR*, no. 6 (1974), p. 5; An Jianshe, "Mao Zedong yu 'pi Lin pi Kong' ruogan wenti," pp. 58-60; and *Mao zhuan*, vol. 2, pp. 1680-83, 1685.

Deng assume his responsibilities. Indeed, the official claim is that Zhou delayed his permanent move to the hospital until after Deng returned from his April visit to New York as head of the PRC delegation to the United Nations. Nevertheless, and more predictably, Wang Hongwen formally took over Zhou's responsibilities for chairing Politburo meetings and Party Center daily work in June.[10]

In certain respects, the emerging political equation was clear: despite his notional position as number two in the regime and his significant duties, Zhou Enlai was weakened further by new intense criticism from late 1973, the Politburo radicals, the "green vegetables" that Mao cultivated at the Tenth Congress, exercised significant and at times overbearing authority, various establishment beneficiaries of the Cultural Revolution accumulated administrative power in their organizations, and Deng Xiaoping assumed important new responsibilities. But a great deal was not clear-cut as events unfolded. To start with Zhou Enlai, although suffering through the worst political crisis of his life, in contrast to the Tenth Congress political report that he delivered but had no role in drafting, the Premier drafted reports for Mao on the work of the Politburo during the initial post-Congress months, reports countersigned by Wang Hongwen, and played a central role in preparations for the anticipated NPC session.[11] Zhou apparently was also able to deal with the administrative tasks of the State Council throughout the entire period without much interference.[12] Moreover, notwithstanding Mao's displeasure with Zhou's foreign policy performance in both spring and fall 1973, the Premier continued to be deeply engaged in foreign affairs, including accompanying foreign leaders to all 18 audiences granted by Mao from September 1973 to May 1974. This, coincidentally, presumably provided Zhou with more direct contact with the Chairman than any radical leader including Wang Hongwen, who attended two fewer of Mao's meetings with foreigners. Moreover, in late January Zhou was named the ranking figure of the Politburo's seven-person small group responsible for the Lin Biao-Confucius campaign.[13] The bottom line, however, was that Zhou simply had to endure immense political pressure, whether three weeks of intense Politburo criticism in November-December, esoteric media attacks throughout the *pi Lin pi Kong* campaign, or hectoring over minor issues by Jiang Qing in the Politburo.

---

[10] See *Mao zhuan*, vol. 2, pp. 1617, 1690-91, 1693; Zhang Yufeng, "Anecdotes of Mao and Zhou," in FBIS-CHI-89-019, pp. 33-34; Yan and Gao, *Turbulent Decade*, pp. 425, 440; and Barnouin and Yu, *Ten Years*, p. 286. Wang was carrying out these duties at least sporadically if not more frequently earlier as a result of both Zhou's political decline and his worsening health. See Zhang Zuoliang, *Zhou Enlai de zuihou shinian*, pp. 312, 328-29.

[11] See *Mao zhuan*, vol. 2, pp. 1666-67, 1679.

[12] See Chen and Du, *Shilu*, vol. 3, part 2, pp. 1014, 1025, 1047, 1054-55, 1060, 1063-65, 1071, 1074-75, 1082-83, 1098-99, for reports of State Council conferences and notices where there is no indication of radical involvement outside of the culture and education spheres.

[13] See below, p. 148.

The enhanced clout of the Politburo radicals was seen most clearly in their stewardship of the new campaign, although their performance in this area also drew Mao's criticism. But outside the campaign arena, their bureaucratic control was limited to the areas they had largely dominated since the start of the Cultural Revolution—the media, culture and education. Thus while *pi Lin pi Kong* criticism extended into economic issues and the movement disrupted the work of various ministries, there is little to indicate significant radical influence on economic policy making *per se*. Indeed, given the enhanced power of the radicals, it is striking that there are no reports of incidents corresponding to Zhang Chunqiao blocking distribution of national planning conference proposals in 1972 and 1973.[14] Moreover, despite Mao's July 1973 injunction to Wang Hongwen and Zhang Chunqiao to learn foreign languages so they could intervene in foreign affairs, the "gang of four" (as distinct from the deeply involved "two ladies") seemingly played little more than a cosmetic role in this sphere.[15] One crucial area, however, where Wang and Zhang gained new, or more precisely continuing authority, was the military. On January 18, 1974, the same day that the first batch of *pi Lin pi Kong* materials was released, they were named members of a new MAC six-person small group, the body now responsible for major PLA issues.[16] The extent of their influence in the PLA given their lack of military experience is problematic, but their appointment arguably enhanced their militia-building efforts, and in the context of early 1974, Wang and Zhang were clearly bolstered in conducting the Lin Biao-Confucius movement in the army.

A critical question concerns the functioning of the radicals as a faction. The official claim is that it was precisely in this period that the "gang of four" formed, a claim undoubtedly linked to Mao's introduction of the notion of a four-person faction in July 1974. It must be emphasized, however, that Mao warned against *forming* such a faction, rather than asserting that one already existed, and throughout the year his strictures had been predominately directed at Jiang Qing, with the other three leaders enjoined to be careful in cooperating with her. Indeed, it is striking that, as in the Cultural Revolution itself, the Chairman granted his wife great power at the same time that he distanced himself from her

---

[14] Liu and Wu, *China's Socialist Economy*, pp. 385-90, blame the "gang" (and Mao) for production setbacks in the first half of 1974, solely in terms of the disruptions caused by *pi Lin pi Kong* and the larger inhibitions to dealing with economic problems caused by the rejection of the critique of "ultra-leftism." No new radical policy initiatives are cited. See also Joseph, *Critique*, p. 139; and above, pp. 52-53.

[15] While Wang attended all but two of Mao's 18 receptions of foreign leaders from September 1973 to mid-1974, this was largely to bolster his profile with foreign and domestic audiences, and he apparently played no role in the business end of the visits where Zhou and (later) Deng were the key interlocutors. Jiang Qing met with visitors on eight seemingly social occasions, while Yao Wenyuan only rarely attended formal occasions. Zhang Chunqiao, although almost never mentioned, joined Zhou and Li Desheng in accompanying a Vietnamese delegation to meet Mao in November 1973.

[16] See below, p. 148. On Wang and Zhang's earlier MAC involvement, see above, pp. 39ff, 96.

personally, now rejecting her efforts to meet him face-to-face.[17] But this still leaves the question of the nature of the ties among the four Politburo radicals. The task of challenging the system as leading members of the Central Cultural Revolution Group in 1966-69 engendered common political interests, albeit not without tension, among Jiang, Zhang and Yao Wenyuan, while Wang was part of the new Shanghai ruling group with Zhang and Yao in a relationship marked by conflict as well as mutual dependence. And as noted previously, Wang's dramatic promotion over the others from late 1972 introduced the potential for further tension.

This is not to claim that there is clear evidence of conflict among the four radicals during *pi Lin pi Kong*, evidence which exists for other periods.[18] Nevertheless, a number of considerations should be taken into account when considering charges that they acted as a coordinated illegitimate faction throughout the movement. First, exchanges of notes among the four during the campaign[19] can be seen as a natural consequence of their duties for running the campaign as the key members of the responsible seven-person *pi Lin pi Kong* small group. The extent to which such activities amounted to acting behind the back of Mao and the Politburo as claimed is unclear given the highly prejudicial nature of the evidence, as well as uncertainties concerning whether other members of the seven-person small group were informed of the issues, and the nature of reporting by the group to the full Politburo when the campaign was discussed. In contrast to 1967-68, in 1974 the Politburo continued to function and the Lin Biao-Confucius movement was frequently on its agenda.[20] Another unknown concerns the relationship of Wang Hongwen and Zhou Enlai. There is no doubt that Wang played a leading role in orchestrating the movement which targeted the Premier as one of its two main targets, but the nuances of Wang's actions are obscured in official sources, much as is the case with Deng's criticism of Zhou

---

[17] See *Mao zhuan*, vol. 2, pp. 1683-86. Jiang moved out of Mao's household in September 1966, and from spring 1972 was no longer granted casual access. In March 1974, Mao rebuffed her repeated appeals for a meeting. Of course, much of this undoubtedly flowed from strictly personal friction, for example, the oft-reported claim that Jiang demanded money from Mao in October 1973. See Yan and Gao, *Turbulent Decade*, p. 427.

[18] There is, however, a tantalizing case of possible tension between Jiang and Wang in September 1973. In one of the petty incidents so characteristic of Jiang, she reportedly pushed herself forward in front of two Party vice chairmen after an army drama performance, and then took offense when she was not introduced and they were. The vice chairmen concerned were not named, but the logic of the situation suggests they were Wang and Li Desheng. See Yan and Gao, *Turbulent Decade*, p. 435.

[19] See, e.g., "Zhonggong zhongyang guanyu 'Wang Hongwen, Zhang Chunqiao, Jiang Qing, Yao Wenyuan fandang jituan zuizheng (cailiao zhi yi)' de tongzhi ji fujian" [CCP Central Committee Notice and Attachment concerning "Proof of the Crimes of the Wang Hongwen, Zhang Chunqiao, Jiang Qing, Yao Wenyuan Anti-Party Clique (first batch of materials)"] (December 10, 1976), in *CRDB*, p. 6.

[20] The Politburo discussed the campaign on at least nine occasions from January to mid-July. *Zhou nianpu*, vol. 3, pp. 648, 649, 650, 651, 653, 654, 673.

in November. While speculative on our part, given Zhou's attention to and close working relationship with Wang after his arrival at the Center in 1972, and even more in view of the Premier's apparent effort as death approached in late 1975 to wean Wang away from Jiang Qing, it is plausible that some element of mutual regard existed between the two men. Indeed, according to a well-placed senior scholar in Zhou studies, Wang demonstrated a respect for the Premier that stood out in comparison to the three other radicals.[21]

Finally, although we have no direct evidence of tension among the Politburo radicals during this period, information concerning conflict among their respective followers in Shanghai is available. Cultural Revolution tension between radical intellectuals who were Zhang Chunqiao's most reliable supporters, and the worker rebels led by Wang Hongwen, again exploded precisely as the Lin Biao-Confucius movement was launched in January 1974. On this occasion, the workers' organization descended from Wang's rebel headquarters convened a meeting on the new campaign where Xu Jingxian, Shanghai Second Party Secretary and Zhang's leading literati supporter, delivered the keynote address that the worker rebels regarded as an insufficiently radical interpretation of the new movement, subsequently forcing Xu to apologize before the Shanghai Revolutionary Committee. The wounds between intellectual and worker radicals in Shanghai were further reopened several months later by a passing reference in a literati journal to an incident in November 1966 when Zhang Chunqiao commented disparagingly on Wang's claims of the achievements of the worker rebels. On this occasion, after some bitter exchanges, Zhang intervened and the workers' union was compelled to offer a confession. Later in the spring, as worker rebels attacked rehabilitated officials, Party First Secretary and veteran cadre Ma Tianshui appealed to Zhang for assistance, resulting in the union being instructed to curb the rebels. These incidents not only demonstrate the conflict among the Shanghai followers of Wang and Zhang, they more generally cast doubt concerning any national radical faction tightly organized from the Center. Although rebels throughout China could potentially gain a great deal from the leadership of the Politburo radicals over the movement, much of the factional activity was generated from below, while many of the linkages to the Center went through the key individuals rather than to a collective "gang of four."[22]

The last, and in many ways most elusive figure in the new power equation, was Deng Xiaoping. Clearly, Deng gained significant new responsibilities in this period, most notably appointment to the Politburo and MAC in December 1973. His prominence on the national and world stage was given a considerable boost when he was selected to head the PRC delegation to the United Nations special

---

[21] *Ibid.*, p. 657; interview, January 2005; above, pp. 95-96; and below, p. 412n71.

[22] See Perry and Li, *Proletarian Power*, pp. 22-23, 181; and Fenwick, "Gang of Four," pp. 220ff. Fenwick emphasizes the "gang's" building of a factional network, but her detailed discussion suggests the loose nature of the ties.

session in April 1974, yet many of his actual activities have been shrouded in secrecy. Moreover, despite official efforts to depict Jiang Qing as hostile to Deng, and the contemporary suspicions of some involved in the *pi Lin pi Kong* effort that Deng was a target, by Jiang's own testimony she and Deng maintained good relations throughout the period.[23] And notwithstanding the claim that Zhou delayed his withdrawal to hospital care until Deng returned from the UN, there is only limited information illuminating the relationship between the Premier and Deng before fall 1974. We will consider the puzzle of Deng's role at the end of this chapter, after examining developments immediately after the Tenth Congress, Kissinger's November 1973 visit and Mao's related dissatisfaction with Zhou, the November-December Politburo meetings criticizing Zhou and stipulating the rotation of military region commanders, and providing a comprehensive assessment of the Lin Biao-Confucius campaign.

After the Tenth Congress: The National People's Congress, the "Three-Month Movement," and Escalating Criticism of Confucius

While the Tenth Congress strongly defended the Cultural Revolution, it did not provide clear directions for the immediate future. Certainly, radical themes dominated public discourse, with both the National Day and New Year joint *People's Daily*, *Red Flag* and *PLA Daily* editorials emphasizing the necessity for the Cultural Revolution, protecting and developing the movement's "new born things," cultivating revolutionary successors, "going against the tide," and focusing on the superstructure.[24] Over this period, moreover, criticism of Confucius and his contemporary representatives escalated well beyond the level that raised Zhou Enlai's concern around the time of the Congress, while the reassertion of Cultural Revolution educational reforms was at the center of the "three-month movement" at the "two schools," Beida and Qinghua. Yet at the same time, there were indications of a more traditional political order, first and foremost in the repeated emphasis on the unified leadership of Party committees. In concrete organizational terms, this second tendency found its manifestation in preparations for the Fourth NPC, an issue that quickly rose to the top of the Politburo's agenda.

Plans for the NPC meeting originated in tandem with preparations for the Tenth Congress. Much as the Party Congress dealt with leadership issues in the Party structure, the NPC would fill vacant state posts and also reorganize the government structure in its first meeting since 1965. Detailed information is sparse, but the process can be traced to the May 1973 work conference that

---

[23] See Yue Daiyun and Carolyn Wakeman, *To the Storm: The Odyssey of a Revolutionary Chinese Woman* (Berkeley: University of California Press, 1985), p. 327; and below, p. 186.

[24] See *PR*, no. 40 (1973), pp. 8-9, and no. 1 (1974), pp. 6-8. Regarding "going against the tide," the media devoted attention to both the celebrated blank examination student, Zhang Tiesheng, and new models of rebellious behavior. See Yan and Gao, *Turbulent Decade*, pp. 419-20, 425.

authorized the Tenth Congress. The same meeting also considered convening the NPC, and estimated that this could be accomplished before the National Day celebrations on October 1. Presumably, some preliminary work was under way even as the focus was on the Party Congress, possibly involving preliminary personnel considerations by the Tenth Congress personnel small group led by Wang Hongwen. The political work report at the Tenth Congress work declared that the state body would be convened soon, and not long afterward Zhou and Wang reported to Mao on NPC arrangements. On Mao's instructions, the Politburo met on September 12 to discuss the issue, and calculated that preparatory work should be completed by October 5, leading the Premier to report optimistically to Mao on the prospects. The National Day editorial spoke positively about "greeting" the NPC, while in mid-October the Politburo basically passed the draft government work report. In this period various localities and work units consulted on NPC elections, and a first draft name list for the Congress Presidium and NPC Standing Committee went to the Politburo for discussion and approval. At this point, it appeared convening the NPC was imminent; moreover, there were no indications — or post-Mao reports — of significant conflict. Particularly striking, while State Council personnel appointments would be a centerpiece of the Fourth NPC and logically a source of contention, and with Wang Hongwen now explicitly placed in charge of the organization small group for the NPC, the evidence is simply lacking of moderate-radical divisions in fall 1973 over staffing the prospective government.[25]

The situation changed dramatically on October 21, the day after Zhou again reported optimistically to Mao on convening the Congress. On the 21st, Minister of Public Security Li Zhen committed suicide, producing a tense atmosphere in Beijing. The Politburo believed that homicide was a possibility, and special measures were adopted to increase vigilance.[26] There is no available record of NPC preparations after this point, but official sources place greater weight on the discontinuation being a consequence of the "gang of four's" activities directed at Zhou Enlai. Allegedly seeing the Premier as the main obstacle to their seizing power and the Fourth NPC as an opportunity, from the time of the Tenth Congress, using

---

[25] *Mao zhuan*, vol. 2, pp. 1666-67; *Zhou nianpu*, vol. 3, pp. 621, 628; and *PR*, no. 35-36 (1973), p. 25, no. 40 (1973), p. 7. The organization small group also included Li Desheng, Li Xiannian, Ji Dengkui, Wu De and Wang Dongxing. Other small groups appointed on September 12 were for the revision of the state constitution (Kang Sheng as nominal chair, Zhang Chunqiao as acting chair, Jiang Qing, Ji Dengkui, Su Zhenhua and Ni Zhifu), and for the government work report (Zhou Enlai as chair, Wang Hongwen, Ye Jianying, Zhang Chunqiao, Yao Wenyuan, Li Xiannian and Hua Guofeng). Clearly the radicals were well represented on these groups, but arguably less dominant than in the small groups responsible for the Tenth Congress.

[26] *Mao zhuan*, vol. 2, p. 1667. While it was subsequently determined that Li did commit suicide, the reasons are unclear. A leading Party historian still regards the case as unresolved, despite the general acceptance of the suicide verdict; interview, January 2005. In the event, the case was examined by Hua Guofeng, assisted by Ji Dengkui and Wu De. This may have led to Hua being named Minister of Public Security when the NPC finally met in January 1975. See *Zhou nianpu*, vol. 3, p. 629.

articles criticizing Confucius (see below), the "gang" reportedly launched attacks on Zhou, other important leaders, and old cadres recently restored to work. This is a less than convincing explanation for derailing the NPC, however, especially given the apparent lack of major contention over Congress arrangements to mid-October. Moreover, even January's New Year editorial, which went beyond calling for a deepening of the criticize Lin and rectification movement to link Lin Biao and Confucius, still spoke of "greeting" the Congress. By this time, however, Mao's new criticism of Zhou and the rotation of military region commanders had intervened, and the launching of *pi Lin pi Kong* within the month clearly ended any possibility of convening the NPC.[27]

Overlapping the aborted effort to hold the Fourth NPC was increasing attention to the superstructure, particularly efforts to reassert the "new born things" of the Cultural Revolution, none more so that its educational reforms. Despite the National Day editorial, subsequently echoed in the New Year editorial, emphasizing study rather than mass mobilization, a campaign unfolded at Beida and Qinghua Universities from October to December (and into early 1974)—the so-called "three-month movement"—to "oppose the rightist resurgence" (*fan youqing huichao*) by ferreting out "exponents on top" and removing its "social base below." Post-Mao accounts have variously described this campaign as an assault on Zhou Enlai, and as the basis for launching *pi Lin pi Kong*. With the objective of conveying the spirit of the Tenth Congress and enforcing its "line," the "three-month movement" undermined any lingering efforts to combat "ultra-leftism" in education, and it became a model widely emulated in other universities. In post-Mao accounts, moreover, primary responsibility for this allegedly unsanctioned initiative has been laid at the doorstep of Jiang Qing, with Chi Qun at Qinghua the most prominent figure on the scene. In this context, it is worthwhile to recall that whatever the relationship between Jiang and Chi Qun, Chi had been a member of Mao's guard unit in Zhongnanhai and had been dispatched by the Chairman to Qinghua in 1968 to restore order. Moreover, as Deng Liqun would observe many years later when discussing Deng Xiaoping's error of getting involved in Qinghua matters in fall 1975, the "two schools" were among the very few organizations where Mao insisted on direct control. And, in contrast to his remarks concerning *pi Lin pi Kong* excesses, there is no record of the Chairman ever objecting to developments at the "two schools" during the last months of 1973.[28]

Various aspects of the campaign have been ably summarized by Ann Fenwick, and illuminated by the testimony of Beida academic Yue Daiyun. Conducted

[27] *Mao zhuan*, vol. 2, pp. 1667-68; An Jianshe, "Mao Zedong yu 'pi Lin pi Kong' ruogan wenti," p. 57; and *PR*, no. 1 (1974), p. 7.

[28] See *History of the Party*, p. 361; An Jianshe, "Pipan jizuo sichao," pp. 222-23; *PR*, no. 40 (1973), pp. 8-9, no. 1 (1974), p. 7; Fenwick, "Gang of Four," pp. 227, 229-30; Joseph, *Critique*, p. 140; and below, p. 390. According to Yue Daiyun, when she returned to Beida in early 1974, the campaign was still running. Yue and Wakeman, *To the Storm*, pp. 315-17.

by Chi Qun, the even more important Xie Jingyi,[29] and their followers at the two universities, the movement reasserted the radical educational stance of the 1971 "two assessments." Targeting educational personnel who were dissatisfied with the Cultural Revolution and the revolution in education, the movement produced policy, structural and leadership change. Moderate policy adjustments over the previous several years were now discarded or weakened: Qinghua's "restorationist" 1972-73 teaching plan was abandoned, Zhou Peiyuan's early 1973 program for strengthening basic theoretical research was shelved, and school-run factories and manual labor were reemphasized at the expense of laboratory work. This was accompanied by structural changes that abolished faculty organizations concerned with raising teaching and research standards, and replaced them with new politicized structures placing academics under the supervision of students and worker-PLA propaganda teams. Finally, with large numbers of people criticized at the "two schools," substantial numbers assertedly subjected to public struggle, and some dismissed from their jobs and/or expelled from the Party, opportunities for advancement opened up as followers of Chi and Xie assumed leading positions in department and school Party committees.[30]

The movement reportedly engendered antagonism between students and teachers reminiscent of the Cultural Revolution, but overall the campaign resembled the directed political movements of the pre-1966 era. Anyone who had criticized "ultra-leftism" or had been involved in the changes cautiously introduced by Zhou Enlai was suspect, and the thoughts and actions of teachers and cadres since 1971 were subject to investigation for any inclination of feudalism, capitalism, or revisionism. With meetings organized in each department by propaganda team leaders, students were encouraged to expose teachers who led young people in an academic direction that neglected politics. This, of course, inhibited efforts to revitalize academic life, but it hardly achieved genuine ideological reform. A striking case in point was the so-called ambush of 600 plus professors who were called in at the end of the year and given an "examination without preparation," with more than 90 percent failing. This was designed to deflate their arrogance toward Zhang Tiesheng's blank examination paper, and demonstrate that one examination was not a fair test of ability. But rather than reduce the teachers'

---

[29] Although under Chi in the Qinghua structure, Xie was a Central Committee member, a Beijing Party secretary, and apparently attended Politburo meetings. In November 1974, Jiang Qing proposed that Xie have the right to attend Politburo meetings, and she was present for at least Mao's last Politburo meeting in May 1975. See below, pp. 221, 296.

[30] See Fenwick, "Gang of Four," pp. 227-29; An Jianshe, "Pipan jizuo sichao," p. 222; and above, pp. 57-60. While most sources indicate an intense campaign, this may be an overstatement. According to an intellectual who experienced the movement at Beida and confirmed various phenomena discussed here, the campaign was less disruptive than pictured, was probably basically aimed at figures at the Center rather than on campus, and largely dealt with a few "dead tigers" like Zhou Peiyuan. He acknowledged, however, that as a non-Party member at the time, a harsher process could have been under way within the Party without his knowledge. Interview, January 2005.

sense of superiority, it only served to heighten their dissatisfaction. Chi Qun organized the exercise, but neither he nor the "gang of four" were the ultimate instigators of the ambush. In a display of personal control, that initiative came from Chairman Mao.[31]

The "two schools" played a central role in another important development during the post-Congress period—the intensification of criticism of Confucius and linking the sage to Lin Biao. Before examining these developments, it is necessary to trace the emergence of Confucius as a political issue since spring 1973. While Confucius was the subject of sometimes politically-charged debates in the years before 1966, as John Bryan Starr has intimated, Mao's views had tended to the middle ground which encompassed both a rejection of Confucian traditionalism, and an acknowledgement of his contribution to Chinese culture. During the Cultural Revolution, Mao criticized Confucian thought while Red Guards strongly attacked Confucius in the general onslaught against the "four olds," but the issue did not lead to a formal Party decision or feature prominently in leadership politics. While the new criticism starting in 1973 lent itself to the crucial issue of attitudes toward the Cultural Revolution, it arguably arose almost by chance from the discovery, in investigations after Lin Biao's demise, that Lin had written scrolls, made marginal notes on texts, and kept a diary praising Confucian views. This, and perhaps the negative references in the "571" documents to Qinshihuang, China's unifying emperor to whom Mao had likened himself, may have encouraged the Chairman to dwell on the link between Lin and Confucius. In any case, at the May 1973 conference preparing for the Tenth Congress, Zhou reported Mao's view that, when criticizing Lin Biao, it was also necessary to criticize Confucius. Subsequently, Mao wrote poems critical of leading historian Guo Moruo for his early scholarly works that rebuked Qinshihuang, and in early July, in his talk largely devoted to criticizing Zhou Enlai, the Chairman suggestively told Wang Hongwen and Zhang Chunqiao that Lin and the Guomindang followed the dictates of Confucius, and opposed the Legalist school of thought associated with Qinshihuang. Finally, on August 5, Mao again raised the issue with Jiang Qing, giving her his most recent poem concerning Guo Moruo, and declaring that throughout past dynasties, the politicians who made progressive contributions were all Legalists.[32]

---

[31] See Fenwick, "Gang of Four," pp. 227, 229; Yue and Wakeman, *To the Storm*, pp. 314-17; Yan and Gao, *Turbulent Decade*, pp. 425-26; and Chen and Du, *Shilu*, vol. 3, part 2, pp. 1007-1008.

[32] See Starr, "China in 1974," pp. 2, 6-7; An Jianshe, "Mao Zedong yu 'pi Lin pi Kong' ruogan wenti," pp. 55-56; Chen and Du, *Shilu*, vol. 3, part 2, pp. 915, 930, 938; Yan and Gao, *Turbulent Decade*, p. 422; and *Mao wengao*, vol. 13, pp. 361-62.

While we believe the "571" coup outline document was concocted, it is likely that various contents were based on actual discussions among Lin Liguo and his associates as revealed by post-September 13 investigations (see above, pp. 32-33). In any case, Mao and Lin had expressed differing views on Qinshihuang as early as 1958 when Lin interjected during a Mao speech to note the emperor's tyranical behavior, but Mao responded with an essentially positive evaluation, observing that the CCP had eliminated many more opponents than Qinshihuang. *Mao Zedong sixiang wansui*

Coincidentally or not, within days of Mao's talk with Jiang Qing, the *People's Daily* published the first of two articles by Guangzhou professor Yang Rongguo criticizing Confucius for having sought to restore slave society in opposition to the more progressive feudal system.[33] Yang's articles introduced through historical analogy the critical issue of the restoration of the pre-Cultural Revolution system, quoted Mao on summing up history to guide contemporary movements, and alluded critically to the Duke of Zhou. At this stage, however, the discussion was largely academic—albeit with the political edge common in PRC debates. That it was not a first-order political issue is indicated by the fact that Zhang Chunqiao's draft of the Tenth Congress work report made no reference to criticizing Confucius, and Jiang Qing's last minute effort to insert such a reference was opposed by Zhou and ignored by Mao. Nevertheless, Mao's interest in the subject was growing. According to Party historian An Jianshe, in the second half of 1973 the Chairman paid close attention to the discussion and frequently expressed his own views not only in praise of Qinshihuang and against Confucius, but also linking the issue to past inner-Party opportunists and contemporary ideological trends. Against this background, criticism of Confucius and alleged Confucianists such as Liu Shaoqi and Lin Biao intensified significantly in the peak national press from September. Other developments pointed to the importance of the new effort: a new radical journal that quickly took up the issue, *Study and Criticism* (*Xuexi yu pipan*), was launched in Shanghai in mid-September and distributed nationally, and writing groups in various organizations developed the themes that would dominate the theoretical side of the *pi Lin pi Kong* campaign. Among the prominent writing groups were those based in the Shanghai and Beijing municipal Party committees, the State Council Culture Group, *Red Flag*, and the Central Party School. But most significant was the newly established group at Beida and Qinghua bearing a homonym for "two schools" (*Liang Xiao*).[34]

The establishment and activities of *Liang Xiao* illuminate the complexity of the situation in late 1973, and indeed into the Lin Biao-Confucius campaign. Formed as the "three-month movement" started, the writing group's work continued both through that campaign and *pi Lin pi Kong*, and beyond. As described by Yue Daiyun on the basis of the experience of her husband, Tang Yijie, one of the leading figures of the group, the circumstances could not have been more different from those faced by other professors at the "two schools." Rather than suffering criticism from students and propaganda teams, the carefully

---

[Long Live Mao Zedong Thought], Red Guard collection of Mao's talks and speeches ([Taipei]: n. pub., 1969), vol. 1, p. 195.

[33] Whether Yang's articles were a direct consequence of Mao's meeting with Jiang, in all likelihood they were an orchestrated response to the Chairman's various comments on Confucius since May.

[34] See An Jianshe, "Mao Zedong yu 'pi Lin pi Kong' ruogan wenti," p. 56; Yan and Gao, *Turbulent Decade*, pp. 422-25; Dittmer, *Continuous Revolution*, p. 198; Fenwick, "Gang of Four," pp. 231-34; "Quarterly Chronicle and Documentation," *CQ*, no. 57 (1974), pp. 207-209; and above, p. 98.

selected members of *Liang Xiao*, a dozen academically learned and politically sophisticated scholars later expanded to 32 in spring and summer 1974, were relieved of other duties to focus on preparing materials critical of Lin Biao and Confucius. The group had unusual privileges of luxurious quarters and ample work space, special foods, and access to materials. A remarkable aspect of the situation of these scholars, representatives of the "stinking ninth category" of intellectuals so abused during the Cultural Revolution, was their harmonious relationship with key radical figures. Chi Qun kept the scholars informed of Mao's latest instructions, thus facilitating their writing tasks. Perhaps most striking was the generally positive impression group members gained of Jiang Qing through several brief encounters: Jiang professed concern for the masses, engaged in manual labor, had good calligraphy, and appeared to want to learn humbly from the professors. Another feature of Yue's account is its failure to report any awareness that Zhou Enlai was the target of *pi Lin pi Kong*, with Tang Yijie wondering whether Deng Xiaoping was under attack. Instead, with Zhou forwarding relevant documents to the group, Tang had the impression that the Premier endorsed its work, notwithstanding the use of the Duke of Zhou as a negative model. The extent of general elite awareness that Zhou was under attack is uncertain, but foreign policy developments in November 1973 soon confirmed for those in the inner circle that the Premier was as vulnerable as ever to Mao's dissatisfaction.[35]

Another Kissinger Visit, More Problems for Zhou Enlai

When Henry Kissinger arrived in Beijing on November 10, 1973, much had changed internationally and in the domestic politics of both the United States and China. The most dramatic change concerned US domestic politics. Rather than representing a triumphantly reelected President Nixon as on his previous visit in February, Kissinger now attempted to present a message of policy continuity for an administration in political free fall due to the Watergate scandal. Mao and Zhou were concerned as well as mystified over the Watergate developments, although seemingly expecting Nixon to prevail. Kissinger, in turn, had his own concerns about the Chinese leadership. While perceiving a possible decline in Zhou's authority, as well as his nervousness over the Confucian issue, Kissinger's basic concern was with the future, given the advanced years and questionable health of both Mao and Zhou.[36]

---

[35] See Yue and Wakeman, *To the Storm*, pp. 323-27. See also MacFarquhar, "Succession," p. 287n145, who reports that another leading member of *Liang Xiao* claimed that he at no time wrote or supervised articles consciously aimed at the Premier. At a more general level, there were reports that the issue was hotly debated by Beida students; see "Quarterly Chronicle," *CQ*, no. 57 (1974), p. 208, while recent discussions with well-connected intellectuals, ordinary cadres, and members of the public produced a range of recollections from "everyone knew and we talked about it among ourselves," to "I suspected Zhou was the target, but didn't dare talk about it," to "I had no idea." Interviews, July 2004 and January 2005.

Kissinger, of course, had no way of knowing the current state of play within the CCP leadership, particularly as it affected Zhou. As we have seen, in February Zhou was already on the defensive following Mao's redefinition of Lin Biao as an "ultra-rightist," but matters deteriorated further for the Premier from May as he was largely excluded from preparations for the Tenth Congress, and then as a consequence of Mao's anger over the MFA assessment of the Nixon-Brezhnev summit. In the post-Tenth Congress period, Zhou had a more central role in the abortive preparations for the NPC, but, as top-level leaders if not necessarily wider circles understood, at the same time he was the target of the intensifying criticism of Confucius. Most relevant for the events at hand, Mao's July criticism of Zhou and the MFA and the subsequent criticism sessions within the ministry weakened Zhou's authority over the foreign affairs bureaucracy which was now increasingly in the hands of the "two ladies." Zhou's vulnerability was tellingly reflected in his immediate response to Jiang Qing's request for the distribution of a foreign affairs bulletin to Zhang Chunqiao and Yao Wenyuan in the midst of Kissinger's visit. Nevertheless, the Premier remained Mao's indispensable instrument for dealing with the outside world, especially when it came to Sino-US relations. Significantly, in contrast to all but one other of Mao's audiences with foreign leaders in the period through mid-1974,[37] Wang Hongwen was absent for Kissinger's reception. For actual negotiations, Zhou was in charge during seven or more meetings with Kissinger, on at least one occasion as lone interlocutor, with Ye Jianying involved in military discussions, Foreign Affairs Vice Minister Qiao Guanhua (rather than Minister Ji Pengfei) attending some meetings during the four day period, and Tang Wensheng of the "two ladies" omnipresent as interpreter. Given Mao's attitude toward him, the Premier was unusually cautious in dealing with Kissinger, taking special care to adhere to the Chairman's oral instructions—all to no avail.[38]

---

[36] On the US domestic context, see Patrick Tyler, *A Great Wall: Six Presidents and China, An Investigative History* (New York: Public Affairs, 1999), pp. 166-67. Kissinger, *Years of Upheaval*, p. 696, recalls Zhou losing his composure when he (Kissinger) raised the Confucius issue at the final banquet. Kissinger drew parallels between Confucian and contemporary culture in terms of education and regulating conduct. Zhou rejected the parallel in agitated fashion, and, revealingly, made sure that Tang Wensheng had a detailed record of his response. Mao had referred to "worship of Confucius" during his meeting with Kissinger the previous day; Burr, *Kissinger Transcripts*, p. 195.

[37] The November 19 meeting with South Vietnamese Liberation Front leaders; see below, p. 130.

[38] See Burr, *Kissinger Transcripts*, pp. 166ff; *Zhou nianpu*, vol. 3, p. 633; Kissinger, *Years of Upheaval*, pp. 687-89; and Gao Wenqian, *Wannian Zhou*, pp. 458-59. Tang Wensheng attended important exchanges on November 10, 13 and 14, and probably on other occasions, without Wang Hairong present; see Burr, pp. 170, 203, 206, 209. Ji Pengfei, as Kissinger's bureaucratic equivalent, attended the November 12 audience with Mao, earning the Chairman's displeasure for his inarticulateness when asked a question, as seen later in Mao's disparaging comment that Ji had "sunk deep into my sofa but could not even break a fart." Ji, by all accounts a diplomat of limited talents, was already in Mao's disfavor after a lackluster foreign trip in the summer, based on a report by Wang Hairong. See Ma Jisen, *The Cultural Revolution in the Foreign Ministry*, pp. 378-79; and Burr, p. 186. Burr, p. 203, lists "Vice Minister [presumably of Defense] Chai Hongging" as present

As far as international events and bilateral US-China relations are concerned, developments over the preceding eight months were paradoxical. Notwithstanding the Nixon-Brezhnev summit, in terms of Mao's fundamental concern, opposition to the Soviet Union under the Chairman's "horizontal line" concept, the American performance in preventing Soviet military involvement in the October Arab-Israeli war coincided exactly with PRC objectives, even if two weeks earlier Huang Zhen, head of the PRC Liaison Office in Washington, had emphasized support for the Arabs as Chinese rhetoric required. When Mao met with Kissinger on November 12, in a remarkable three-hour performance leading US Liaison Office head David Bruce to remark, with arguably minimal exaggeration, that it was "the most extraordinary and disciplined presentation he had ever heard from a statesman," the Chairman set the record straight. Observing that Huang Zhen did not understand the importance of US resistance to the Soviet Union, Mao expressed his full approval of US tactics in the Middle East. Throughout the long exchange, Mao further approved Kissinger's broad international strategy, and exchanged generally reinforcing views on various specific issues and foreign leaders. It is understandable, then, despite later analysis questioning his motives, that Kissinger reported in positive terms on the "deepening [common] strategic perspectives" resulting from his trip. But the paradoxical aspect of the situation was also in clear view during the discussion with Mao—the normalization of diplomatic relations was increasingly bogged down given Nixon's political weakness, not to mention the inherent difficulties of the issue. Mao raised the matter, but at the same time declared it less important than the international situation, and observed that "we are in no hurry" and willing to wait 100 years for both Taiwan and diplomatic relations with the US. The message was that there would be little progress on normalization, but that this would not undercut larger US-China strategic cooperation.[39]

For both immediate political reasons—the desirability of a foreign policy success to bolster Nixon's deteriorating position—and the more long-range goal of strengthening US-China relations for a post-Mao and post-Zhou future, Kissinger came with proposals designed to further the normalization process and give concrete substance to US-China strategic cooperation. These proposals dealing with Taiwan and intelligence sharing would, contrary to Kissinger's intention, ensnare Zhou in a new crisis. As with other concrete bilateral issues,[40] getting beyond broad anti-Soviet perspectives was a more fraught prospect. Precisely

---

with Ye at the important late evening meeting on November 13, but we have been unable to identify anyone likely to be the person indicated by this garbled name.

[39] See Burr, *Kissinger Transcripts*, pp. 158-59, 167, 181, 183, 186-88; and Tyler, *A Great Wall*, pp. 174-75.

[40] The outstanding case in the period between Kissinger's February and November visits concerned diplomatic coordination to secure a settlement in Cambodia, an issue that led to much friction in the summer and the cancellation of an earlier Kissinger trip, as the apparent willingness on both sides to work together was overwhelmed by conflicts of interests and events on the ground. As Qiao

what happened on these questions is unclear, both because, as per Kissinger's practice of tightly controlling information, the US record is incomplete, and the official Chinese account, which touches directly on Zhou's alleged mistakes, is vague. However, widely accepted accounts found in recollections and Chinese reportage literature assert that, with regard to Taiwan, Mao believed Zhou showed weakness by acknowledging that there were two possibilities for solving the issue, by peaceful or military means, when fighting was the only possibility. In this version, Zhou's "weakness" was conveyed or misrepresented to Mao by the "two ladies," and Tang Wensheng also played a key role in informing the Chairman of Zhou's alleged overly accommodating behavior regarding Kissinger's proposals on intelligence sharing. In this latter case, another cause of Mao's anger reportedly was the Premier's willingness to continue discussions on these proposals on the morning of November 14, despite the fact that he had been unable to consult the Chairman during the night, most likely because Mao was asleep. While elements of this version are undoubtedly true, the story is clearly more complicated.[41]

The Taiwan issue was the less substantial in every sense. Rather than coming to Beijing with realistic proposals for achieving normalization, a prospect impossible in the current US political climate, on November 11 Kissinger offered reassurances of support for "one China," promises of a reduced American presence in Taiwan, and a reaffirmation of the intention to complete full normalization by the end of Nixon's second term in 1976. All of this, described by Kissinger as a more "flexible" approach than the Japanese formula of cutting diplomatic ties with Taiwan, amounted to the US maintaining its recognition of the Republic of China, and Kissinger raised the possibility of adapting the 1972 Shanghai communiqué to provide a way for diplomatic relations. It was, in fact, a *de facto* "two Chinas" proposal, as Tang Wensheng realized when Zhou and Tang reported to Mao. When Zhou probed Kissinger further the next afternoon about the meaning of his proposal, its essential "two Chinas" solution for the time being became clear. Zhou then dropped the matter, but Mao picked it up later that afternoon. After the Chairman's odd observation concerning the presence of diplomatic representation by the defunct Baltic states in the US, remarks that, in his memoirs, Kissinger interpreted as Mao hinting at a possible Taiwan solution, the Chairman clearly ruled out Kissinger's feelers by declaring China could wait 100 years for formal ties unless the US adopted the Japanese formula. Mao, according to his biographers, was unhappy with the dubious US attitude, and his ruminations about the Baltic states were arguably intended to send a different

---

Guanhua commented to Kissinger at the UN in October, both countries had erred in getting involved in Cambodia which "very definitely [is] only a side issue." See Kissinger, *Years of Upheaval*, pp. 678-82.

[41] See Barnouin and Yu, *Chinese Foreign Policy*, p. 37; Gao Wenqian, *Wannian Zhou*, pp. 462-63; and Ma Jisen, *The Cultural Revolution in the Foreign Ministry*, p. 362.

message—while the Soviet Union might put up with such an affront to national unity, China would not.[42]

Taiwan and normalization were essentially finessed for the remainder of Kissinger's visit. Various concrete problems including the disposition of rowdy marine guards at the US Liaison Office, the sudden appearance of a US Navy cruiser in the Taiwan Straits, US plans to provide Taiwan with the capability to produce its own fighter jets, and the State Department's approval of additional consulates in Taiwan complicated but did not derail the talks. While the view that the PRC was not content to let normalization remain on the back burner expressed by Qiao Guanhua to Kissinger in October undoubtedly reflected the Chinese leadership's frustration at the slow progress, Kissinger was essentially correct in claiming that Zhou accepted the limits of what was feasible. In the end, the communiqué on the visit agreed to upgrading the two countries' liaison offices, and reaffirmed the "one China principle."[43] None of this, however, related to Mao's ostensible unhappiness with the Premier concerning Taiwan. Apparently at some point during his discussions with Kissinger on the 11th, Zhou made his observation concerning the two possibilities for the reunification of Taiwan. This surely was reported to Mao who, when meeting with Kissinger, declared his own view: "I do not believe in a peaceful transition [with the Taiwan counterrevolutionaries]." At this point Mao aggressively asked Foreign Minister Ji Pengfei (who seemingly had not been involved in the Zhou-Kissinger meetings) for his opinion, but the undoubted target was the Premier.[44] While Zhou would soon be charged with "capitulationism" with regard to this and intelligence sharing, Mao's insistence that fighting was the only possibility and Zhou was succumbing to nuclear blackmail was disingenuous, to say the least, given the basic PRC policy at the time of allowing Taiwan to remain on the back burner. However accurate Mao's view of a peaceful settlement may have been, acknowledging two theoretical possibilities was simply in accord with the needs of the US-China relationship that the Chairman had made the centerpiece of his foreign policy.

Intelligence sharing and other military cooperation were more significant American proposals. To provide momentum for the Sino-US relationship, and seemingly because he regarded a Soviet attack on China as a more realistic possibility than he had in the past, at the very outset of his visit Kissinger raised the possibility of discreet strategic assistance to the PRC based on studies that had been conducted within the US government. The idea, initially flagged to Zhou and Ye Jianying following the welcoming banquet on November 10, was for a secret relationship whereby the US would provide China with intelligence

---

[42] See Burr, *Kissinger Transcripts*, pp. 168, 173, 176, 185-87; Tyler, *A Great Wall*, pp. 167-69; Kissinger, *Years of Upheaval*, pp. 688, 691-92; and *Mao zhuan*, vol. 2, p. 1669.

[43] See Burr, *Kissinger Transcripts*, pp. 168, 173-74, 178, 201-202, 204-205; Tyler, *A Great Wall*, pp. 166, 169-70; and Kissinger, *Years of Upheaval*, pp. 684, 688.

[44] Burr, *Kissinger Transcripts*, p. 186.

from its advanced technical resources to reduce PRC exposure to Soviet attack, what became a proposal to establish a hotline. The offer was made on the basis of strengthening the PRC's defense capacity which was in the American interest, and no reciprocity was required. Kissinger proposed further discussions in a small group involving himself and Zhou or their delegates. Zhou, after seeking Mao's instructions, replied that China would not take up the matter now, but left open future discussions. The matter appears to have rested there until Kissinger unexpectedly again raised the issue with Zhou following the final banquet on November 13. Neither Mao nor Kissinger had directly discussed the matter during their meeting on November 12, although Kissinger repeated his previous day's assessment to Zhou that now he saw a greater possibility of a Soviet attack, particularly to destroy China's nuclear capability. But while acknowledging the possibility, Mao seemed more impressed with the contradiction between Soviet ambitions and capabilities, and the obstacles to any Russian attack.[45]

When Kissinger met with Zhou, Ye and each side's military experts from 10 p.m. to past midnight on November 13, although other items were discussed, including various bilateral problems, the coup in Chile, and developments in Indochina, security cooperation was the key issue. According to the truncated American record, Kissinger pursued his effort to develop a tacit alliance by offering the supply of equipment and other services in the event of war, and especially by early warning of a Soviet attack. Kissinger elaborated on how US satellite technology could provide information on missile launches, and then transmit it rapidly by a hotline ostensibly established for other functions. Zhou noted that "there are some things that would be useful to us," but wanted to study the matter before a final consultation on the morning of Kissinger's departure. In the intervening period, part of which was taken up with drafting the communiqué with Kissinger, the Premier, apparently unwilling to wake a potentially irritable Chairman, failed to consult with Mao. From 7.35 a.m. the next morning, Zhou and Kissinger met a final time for nearly an hour. While other issues were again on the agenda, in this exchange Zhou observed that China had to prepare for the worst and the hotline proposal could provide "intelligence of great assistance," although he was concerned that China not be seen as a US ally. Kissinger presented two draft documents on the hotline and an accidental war agreement, but the Premier wanted more time to study the matter before further consultation—in the American transcript mentioning Marshal Ye as the main person together with himself for future bilateral discussions. According to Mao's biography, however, when avoiding a positive answer to Kissinger's proposals, Zhou stated that he would report to Mao who would "decide everything."[46]

---

[45] See Burr, *Kissinger Transcripts*, pp. 169-71, 183-84.

[46] See *ibid.*, pp. 203-205, 209-12; Gao Wenqian, *Wannian Zhou*, pp. 462-63; and *Mao zhuan*, vol. 2, p. 1670.

Nothing came of Kissinger's proposals as the Chinese side never raised them again despite Zhou's expressed interest. One can only speculate about the reasons. Did the potential costs of discovery outweigh any benefit? Was Mao indeed confident that the Soviets would not launch an attack on China's nuclear facilities? Or was the Chairman simply allergic to close military cooperation, much as in the same mode as when he rejected Khrushchev's proposal for a joint fleet in 1958, a matter he mentioned to Kissinger on the 12th? For our purposes, the more important question is why did Mao react so negatively toward Zhou's performance on the issue. As indicated above, one explanation concerns Zhou's failure to consult during the early hours of November 14, and his decision to go ahead in canvassing the question in the morning without explicit approval. Another is that Zhou's interest in the proposal was seen as undignified, as being both too fearful of nuclear war and too grateful to the US, a view, according to various accounts, wrongfully presented to Mao by Tang Wensheng, leading the Chairman to conclude that the Premier and Ye had been weak in their dealings with the Americans. In any case, together with the Taiwan issue, Zhou was soon the target of Mao's ire. After being criticized by the Chairman on November 17, Zhou convened the Politburo that evening, relayed Mao's criticisms, and gave a detailed account of his talks with Kissinger. Jiang Qing attacked Zhou's "right-deviationist capitulationism" at the Politburo meeting, and the next day the Premier twice wrote to Mao to report on the Politburo meeting and engaged in further self-examination.[47] The Premier's central operating role in foreign policy was still apparent on the 19th, when he participated in Mao's reception of a South Vietnamese Liberation Front delegation, with Zhang Chunqiao replacing Wang Hongwen at the meeting for unknown reasons.[48] Nevertheless, Zhou's vulnerability was dramatically underscored on November 21 when the Politburo began enlarged meetings to criticize him and Ye Jianying that lasted well into December.

The record is too murky to support a definitive analysis, but several matters bear consideration. First, there is little to indicate that Zhou went too far on either the Taiwan or hotline issues. In the former, the Premier's actions were well within existing policy, and whatever notional "concessions" emerged from the discussions, both Mao and the entire Politburo endorsed the communiqué on the visit.[49] As for the hotline, while Mao had put off discussions on cooperation after Kissinger's initial approach, he seemingly did not entirely rule them out. Zhou

---

[47] See Burr, *Kissinger Transcripts*, pp. 197, 205-207; *Deng Liqun guoshi jiangtan*, vol. 3, pp. 121, 313; Tyler, *A Great Wall*, p. 171; Ma Jisen, *The Cultural Revolution in the Foreign Ministry*, p. 362; Fan Shuo, *Ye Jianying zai feichang shiqi 1966-1976* [Ye Jianying in an Extraordinary Period, 1966-1976] (2 vols., Beijing: Huawen chubanshe, 2002), vol. 2, p. 410; *Zhou nianpu*, vol. 3, p. 634; Zong Daoyi, "1973 nian Zhou Enlai," p. 10; *Mao zhuan*, vol. 2, p. 1670; and Gao Wenqian, *Wannian Zhou*, pp. 460-63.

[48] *PR*, no. 47 (1973), p. 3. Li Desheng, as well as the "two ladies," was also present.

[49] *Mao zhuan*, vol. 2, p. 1670. According to a senior scholar specializing on Zhou Enlai, the available

may have showed too much interest for Mao's taste when Kissinger unexpectedly raised the matter a second time, but far from acting without authority, Zhou was acutely aware that the Chairman would "decide everything." Second, the tendency to blame the "two ladies"—more accurately Tang Wensheng as the interpreter for Zhou's encounters with Kissinger—for prejudicing Mao against the Premier is most likely misplaced. On at least one occasion, following Kissinger's initial proposals on Taiwan, Zhou and Tang briefed Mao together; moreover, according to a Party historian specializing on the period, the Premier vetted Tang's reports to the Chairman. A more plausible account is provided by the former highly-placed CCP specialist on Zhou, Gao Wenqian. According to Gao, after Kissinger departed on November 14, Mao called in Tang and Wang Hairong to review the record of the Zhou-Kissinger talks. But rather than receiving erroneous reports as officially claimed, it was Mao who directed the "two ladies" to spread claims that during the negotiations Zhou had been fearful of Soviet atomic bombs, failed to consult the Chairman, and accepted the US nuclear umbrella.[50]

This leads to the final conclusion that, as in mid-year but arguably to an even greater extent, Mao was being unpredictable, but also unfair, even vindictive, toward Zhou Enlai. Neither a comment acknowledging a possible peaceful solution to the Taiwan issue—a proposition at the core of the 1972 US-China Shanghai communiqué—nor seeking clarification concerning the hotline proposal in a non-committal manner can be reasonably described as "capitulationism."[51] As with the reasons for abandoning further interest in the hotline proposal, we can only speculate about Mao's harsh response directed at the Premier. Did he, as in 1958, viscerally react against a perceived dilution of national sovereignty, and blame the messenger? Was this simply another manifestation of Mao's dissatisfaction with Zhou since his rejection of the critique of "ultra-leftism" in December 1972? Or was it, as many foreign affairs insiders in China believe, a reflection of the Chairman's jealousy over Zhou's high international standing? Indeed, well-placed, sophisticated Party historians believe the fallout from Kissinger's visit had little to do with policy or procedures, and everything to do with Mao's larger attitudes toward Zhou.[52] Whatever the reasons, Zhou now faced an exceptionally testing time.

American record of Zhou's talks with Kissinger is basically correct and demonstrates that the Premier did not make any major mistakes. Interview, December 2002.

[50] Gao Wenqian, *Wannian Zhou*, p. 463; and interview, November 2002. While there is evidence of Wang and Tang's resentment toward Zhou for (wrongly) perceived personal slights, the larger picture is complex as they tended to back the Premier within the MFA during the Cultural Revolution. See above, pp. 20n58, 108. In the present context, in any case, we believe the importance of US-China relations would have dictated accurate reporting by Tang.

[51] As one senior historian of PRC foreign policy put it, not refusing more clearly was transformed into "capitulationism." Interview, January 2005. It is worth noting that, in a fundamental sense, Mao's criticism of Zhou was the opposite of what it had been in July; see above, pp. 89ff.

[52] Interviews, January 2005. On Mao's jealousy, see Barnouin and Yu, *Chinese Foreign Policy*,

Zhou Enlai and the PLA under Threat: The Politburo Meets, November-December 1973

For someone with long working experience with Mao, Zhou Enlai was surprisingly slow to grasp the peril of his situation. When Mao summoned Zhou together with responsible MFA personnel on November 17, he criticized the communiqué on the Kissinger visit (despite having approved it), and complained about the purported American desire to provide a nuclear umbrella. Zhou naturally made an immediate self-criticism, but seemingly found it difficult to understand why Mao was making such a big fuss and demanding that he convene the Politburo that evening to criticize the conduct of the negotiations with Kissinger. Zhou may have focused on the fact that Mao, however unfairly, was at least dealing with foreign policy issues, and provided his own observation that "when struggling [with the Americans] it is easy to be 'leftist,' when cooperating [with them] it is easy to be rightist." But the signals were there, notably in the Chairman's demand that "whoever carries out revisionism must be criticized," and his encouragement of the MFA people present to have the courage to act on this injunction.[53]

Mao laid down the theme for the evening's Politburo meeting: Zhou and Ye's revisionist line. The focus became Zhou's alleged capitulationism in foreign affairs, with Ye dragged in for his participation in the military discussions with the US which was characterized as "right-inclined weakness." While the tone had been set by Mao, Jiang Qing, who grasped the Chairman's meaning, was particularly vociferous on the capitulation theme. Zhou, in Gao Wenqian's interpretive account, could not believe that such excessive criticism was Mao's intention, instead thinking it was just a manifestation of Jiang's unreasonableness, and hoped the Chairman would stop her. But with Jiang continuing, it was more than Zhou could bear, leading him to exclaim that while he had made many mistakes, he would not wear the hat of "right capitulationism." In writing his report on the Politburo meeting the next day, the Premier made a self-examination of his errors, concluding that he "had not done enough" in the Kissinger negotiations. This self-criticism was judged insufficient by Mao, leading to a second letter in which Zhou adopted a more severe tone, not only acknowledging his revisionism, but also calling on middle-aged and young cadres to dare to critique the revisionist thinking and rightist errors of old cadres like himself. Even this seemingly did not go far enough for Mao who, according to Gao, was determined to undermine thoroughly the Premier's foreign policy prestige.[54]

Mao now ordered a series of enlarged Politburo meetings, chaired by Wang Hongwen and starting on the 21st, in which Zhou and Ye would be severely criticized for their "right-deviationist errors" in dealing with the Americans. Mao controlled every aspect of these meetings, determining the participants as well

---

pp. 35-36.

[53] Gao Wenqian, *Wannian Zhou*, pp. 463-64; and *Mao zhuan*, vol. 2, p. 1670.

[54] Gao Wenqian, *Wannian Zhou*, pp. 464-65; and Zong Daoyi, "1973 nian Zhou," p. 10.

as the topics and tone of the sessions. With the focus on foreign policy, leading MFA figures were required to attend—the so-called "four elders" (Minister Ji Pengfei, Vice Ministers Qiao Guanhua and Zhong Xidong, and US Liaison Office head Huang Zhen), and "four beauties" (including the "two ladies," Wang Hairong and Tang Wensheng, and Qiao Guanhua's wife, Zhang Hanzhi),[55] plus Geng Biao from the Party Center's International Liaison Department. The most important invitee, however, was Deng Xiaoping who, as we have seen, joined in the criticism of Zhou to Mao's delight. The mechanism for Mao's control was the "two ladies," with Tang Wensheng starting the meetings by introducing the agenda, relaying the Chairman's new directives on the criticism of Zhou and his recent instructions on foreign affairs work, in statements that reportedly lasted up to eight hours. The tenor of the criticism conveyed was extremely tough, adopting phrases that Mao had used in attacking Liu Shaoqi and Lin Biao, and producing great tension throughout the Politburo. As this unfolded, Zhou realized that the problem was not the difficulty of getting along with Jiang Qing, but that the entire critique was according to Mao's design.[56]

In addition to the input of the "two ladies," the proceedings, which apparently were particularly intense from November 25 to December 5, were orchestrated by a six-person "help [Zhou] small group" dominated by Jiang Qing, and also including Wang Hongwen, Zhang Chunqiao, Yao Wenyuan, Wang Dongxing and Hua Guofeng. This group, with Wang Dongxing providing another direct link to Mao, met with the "two ladies" in the mornings at the Diaoyutai State Guesthouse before the Politburo sessions to discuss Mao's plan for the day, and in the evenings to discuss how Wang and Tang would report the day's proceedings to the Chairman. Reportedly, Wang Dongxing and Hua no longer attended after several meetings, leaving the four radicals to plan tactics, and thus create the context for the alleged formation of the "gang of four."[57]

As indicated, the criticism in the Politburo reached extreme heights, with Zhou not only accused of revisionism and capitulationism, but also of establishing an "independent kingdom" in the MFA, betraying the country, and being willing to serve as a puppet emperor if the Soviet Union invaded. Jiang Qing famously characterized the situation as the 11th line struggle within the Party (Liu Shaoqi being the 9th, and Lin Biao the 10th), and, reflecting on the situation in early 1972 when a seriously ill Mao spoke of the possibility of Zhou taking over, accused the Premier of being impatient to seize the Chairman's authority. The participants reportedly found this last charge difficult to believe, and most of them sympathized with Zhou, but everyone was required to speak, and all followed Mao's script. Jiang Qing apparently believed Mao had the same fate in mind for Zhou as that

---

[55] The fourth "beauty" or "flower" (*hua*), or "little" (*xiao*), has been variously identified as Qi Zonghua or Luo Xu, also young female MFA cadres.

[56] Gao Wenqian, *Wannian Zhou*, p. 466.

[57] *Ibid.*, pp. 466-68.

suffered by Liu and Lin, but the Chairman's objectives proved more limited. While intent on undermining Zhou's prestige, Mao seemingly was unwilling to create another shock to the system by purging the Premier so soon after the Lin Biao affair. He intervened on December 9, calling a halt to the criticism and expressing satisfaction with what had transpired. In his view, only two mistakes had been committed: the claim that an 11th line struggle was underway, and the accusation that Zhou was impatient to seize authority. To round out the latter point, Mao claimed that in fact it was Jiang Qing who was impatient.[58]

Zhou Enlai suffered grievously during these Politburo sessions, physically and emotionally. Zhou's already serious health situation deteriorated further, but arguably the political pressure was worse. This, of course, was familiar ground for any Party member under severe criticism, and a situation Zhou himself had endured on more than one occasion in the past. As the accusations mounted, Zhou had no scope to respond, and he was subjected to social isolation as previously frequent visitors now avoided him and displayed a cold demeanor. No one dared to keep him informed of developments, and the only leaders to show any concern were Ye Jianying, who might have been expected to do so considering his long-term closeness to the Premier, and the fact that he too was under criticism, although much less,[59] and surprisingly, given conventional preconceptions, Ji Dengkui. Moreover, while the conditions facing a leader under severe criticism were familiar, Zhou's situation was worse than what he had endured in 1958 when sharply attacked for "opposing rash advance." Denied the opportunity of a face-to-face self-criticism before Mao, Zhou was forced to write out his self-examination. In contrast to 1958 when the Premier was allowed the assistance of his secretary in preparing his statement, he was now denied all help. His pleas to the "two ladies" for a bit of help given his advanced age, blurred vision and trembling hand apparently went unanswered. While feeling deeply wronged, Zhou prepared his self-criticism, which would last seven hours rather than the 40 to 50 minutes Mao suggested, uncertain as how to assess the situation. The only approach he could adopt was to add to the accusations against himself in an effort to appease Mao. Zhou ended the self-examination by declaring that responsibility for the work of the Politburo should be assumed by others, a step recalling his offer to resign in 1958. For his part, despite the fact that he had earlier complained about Jiang Qing leaking Politburo discussions outside the body, the Chairman now added to Zhou's humiliation by having the contents of

[58] See *ibid.*, pp. 466-69; Wang Nianyi, *Dadongluan*, p. 471; and Barnouin and Yu, *Ten Years*, p. 264. Mao's willingness to criticize Jiang even in the midst of the intense onslaught against Zhou was also seen in his approving comment on a letter he had received critical of her, and its circulation to the Politburo on November 25. See *Mao wengao*, vol. 13, pp. 367-68.

[59] While there is evidence of Mao's dissatisfaction with Ye throughout 1973-76, one of China's leading military historians believes the Chairman's discontent was never strong, and at this point the overwhelming target was Zhou who, in his view, had been exercising primary leadership over the PLA. Interview, January 2005.

the Politburo sessions discussed in the MFA and MAC, and news of the Premier's errors soon circulated in the capital's political circles.[60]

While the requirements of the moment meant that everyone had to join in the attack on Zhou, what can be said about individual performances? The task is difficult because the records of the meeting were destroyed, reportedly in the post-Mao period at the request of Zhou's widow, Deng Yingchao, and more fundamentally because the information would be embarrassing to various leaders, none more so than Deng Xiaoping. Nevertheless, some evidence can be assessed and conclusions drawn. To start with the Politburo radicals, there can be no doubt of Jiang Qing's leading role and shrill performance. Beyond that, however, things are less clear. Of the other radicals, only Yao Wenyuan is singled out in official accounts as taking a prominent role, something arguably further suggested by Jiang's proposal that, since Zhou and Ye were not up to the task, she and Yao, along with Wang Dongxing, should be added to the Politburo Standing Committee. Apart from some formulaic accusations, Zhang Chunqiao's involvement was not noted, except for one report that he joined Jiang in criticizing temporary adjournments caused by Zhou's illness as political resistance. As for Wang Hongwen, the only available information concerns formal roles such as chairing the meetings and participating in the "help [Zhou] small group," as well as organizing a large print edition of the Politburo discussions for Mao. When Mao determined to end the criticism of Zhou and reject Jiang's proposal for promotions to the Standing Committee, he called in Zhou and Wang separately to inform them of his decisions. Given the incomplete record caution is required, but on the face of it there is no evidence that Wang in particular was any harsher in criticizing the Premier than other participants in the Politburo meetings.[61]

The presumptive younger radicals, Wang Hairong and Tang Wensheng, obviously played a central role at the Politburo meetings as Mao's liaison officers. They inevitably set the critical agenda, a role which arguably led Li Xiannian to reflect that Wang and Tang were "bad to Premier Zhou but nice to Deng."[62] Despite evidence of some personal tension between the "two ladies" and the Premier, and the fact that following Mao's death they were subject to

---

[60] Gao Wenqian, *Wannian Zhou*, pp. 467-68, 472, 474-75; and Zhang Zuoliang, *Zhou Enlai zuihou shinian*, p. 314. On the criticism of Zhou in 1958, see Teiwes with Sun, *China's Road to Disaster*, pp. 73-74, 97-99. Of course, Zhou had himself participated in the same sort of unconscionable behavior toward other leaders, most notoriously in his written comment that Liu Shaoqi deserved to be put to death. See Sun Wanguo, "Gu you Dou'e, jin you Lin Biao," p. 108.

[61] Gao Wenqian, *Wannian Zhou*, pp. 477, 458; *Mao zhuan*, vol. 2, p. 1671; Wang Nianyi, *Dadongluan*, p. 471; *Zhou nianpu*, vol. 3, pp. 634-35; *Ye Jianying zhuan* [Biography of Ye Jianying] (Beijing: Dangdai Zhongguo chubanshe, 1995), pp. 620-21; and Chen and Du, *Shilu*, vol. 3, part 2, p. 994. Official sources generally only report Jiang nominating herself and Yao for the Standing Committee, but *Ye zhuan* also cites Wang Dongxing.

[62] See above, p. 20. According to a senior specialist on Zhou Enlai, it is unclear whether the "two ladies" attended Politburo meetings apart from those in November-December 1973. Interview, December 2002.

investigation and criticism for actions against Zhou, on balance leading Party historians and MFA veterans conclude that any harsh treatment of the Premier, as in these circumstances, was largely a function of carrying out Mao's wishes. Overall, they believe, Wang and Tang's attitude toward Zhou was one of great respect. In any case, in December 1973, once Mao decided to terminate the criticism, he sought to absolve himself by making Wang and Tang shoulder responsibility for the Politburo excesses. When receiving the King of Nepal on the 9th, Mao pointed to the "two ladies," claiming that these "small generals" were provoking the situation, that they wanted to purge the Premier and, astoundingly, himself. While Mao's official biographers treat this as the Chairman's strong support of Zhou, Gao Wenqian's characterization as a "dirty trick" appears closer to the truth. Mao was not through with Zhou, but it suited his purposes to cool things down. After having Wang and Tang criticize Zhou, the Chairman now gave him a way out, leaving the "two ladies" to complain privately that Mao was making a reputation for himself, while they were left to clean up the mess.[63]

In certain respects, the case of Vice Minister of Foreign Affairs Qiao Guanhua and his wife, MFA interpreter Zhang Hanzhi, was similar to that of the "two ladies." As leading ministry figures, Qiao and Zhang were required to attend the Politburo meetings and join in the criticism of Zhou, although, in the view of a senior Party historian, like Wang and Tang they shared a fundamental respect for the Premier, a respect based on Qiao's work as a foreign affairs professional under Zhou since the revolutionary period. Moreover, there is little to suggest any policy tension in the early 1970s between Qiao and Zhou. Indeed, as we saw in Chapter 1, Qiao had been severely criticized as a result of Mao's displeasure in summer 1973 with the Foreign Ministry report on the Nixon-Brezhnev summit. While this incident indicated Qiao's professional closeness to Zhou, it also underlined his vulnerability when the Premier, and by extension the MFA's performance, came under attack in November.[64]

The response of Qiao and Zhang to this vulnerability was what came to be regarded as overly harsh attacks on Zhou at the November-December meetings. In the absence of a detailed record, it is difficult to judge how different Qiao's and Zhang's efforts were from the attacks of others, but Zhang's own memoir refers to their "first great mistake," a mistake marked by "excessive words" that assertedly left them distressed, but which they deemed necessary for survival. Moreover, they were perceived at the time by some within the MFA as having overstepped some vaguely defined line, as being too enthusiastic in attacking the Premier in an effort to save their own skins, and subsequently adopting an arrogant attitude toward other long-term foreign affairs associates of Zhou. A complicating factor

---

[63] Gao Wenqian, *Wannian Zhou*, pp. 475-76; *Mao zhuan*, vol. 2, p. 1671; interview with senior Party historian, December 2002; and interview with MFA veteran, September 2003.

[64] Interview with specialist on foreign affairs, July 1997; and above, p. 91. For further discussion of Qiao and Zhang's relationship with Zhou, see below, p. 225.

was a related perception, that Qiao had aligned himself with Jiang Qing. While Li Xiannian's late 1976 claim that Qiao and Zhang had been targeted quite early by the "gang of four" and had decided to go along may be overstated, it is likely that Jiang began to cultivate them by the time of the attacks on the Premier's foreign policy leadership in 1973, and arguably Jiang's nomination of Qiao for a vice premiership in 1974 reflected her approval of his late 1973 criticism of Zhou. Yet the Premier himself, according to Zhang Hanzhi, was understanding of Qiao's and Zhang's actions, perhaps as a simple acknowledgment of the fundamental requirement of elite politics.[65]

This requirement also shaped the performance of Deng Xiaoping—a performance more skillful than Qiao's, or at least one better protected by his high revolutionary status. While Deng could not have known Mao's full intention for Zhou as he sat in on Politburo meetings seemingly for the first time since his return to work, he certainly understood that he would have to join in the criticism in a sufficiently robust manner to earn the Chairman's approval. Accordingly, in his comparatively brief but tough speech, Deng not only followed closely Mao's criticisms of Zhou, he also pointed to the Premier's alleged ulterior motives. While Jiang Qing's claim that Zhou was impatient to displace Mao has been widely attacked in official accounts, Deng in effect argued the same thing. Deng pointed to the Premier and said, while others who might wish to replace Mao are too distant to have a chance, you are close enough to contemplate the possibility. Deng's talk thus added to the accusations against the Premier, leaving him all the more unable to respond. As Deng would have understood, this was Mao's test for him, and the Chairman's happy and excited reaction was the clearest indication that he had passed with flying colors. When summoned after his speech, Deng had a long talk with Mao, and it is clear that another part of the leadership puzzle had fallen into place for the Chairman. With a loyal follower having proved himself in Mao's eyes, Deng was now ready for important posts and eventually replacing the Premier. With Zhou's illness worsening, that decision would have to be faced soon regardless of Mao's feelings toward the Premier, and Deng was the obvious candidate combining administrative skills, political loyalty, and an emotional compatibility with Mao. That process began after a short recess in the Politburo meetings.[66]

---

[65] Zhang Hanzhi, *Wo yu Qiao Guanhua*, pp. 65-66, 88; Li Lianqing, *Waijiao yingcai Qiao Guanhua* [Foreign Affairs Bright Talent Qiao Guanhua] (Nanjing: Jiangsu renmin chubanshe, 2000), p. 265; "Li Xiannian, Chen Yun, Tan Zhenlin zai sijie Renda Changwei disanci huiyishang de jianghua" [Speeches of Li Xiannian, Chen Yun and Tan Zhenlin at the Third Session of the Fourth NPC Standing Committee] (December 2, 1976), in *CRDB*, p. 1; Gao Wenqian, *Wannian Zhou*, p. 467; interview with senior Party historian, December 2002; and interview with MFA veteran, September 2003. Qiao and Zhang's second, greater mistake is examined in Chapters 6 and 7. While Zhou may have forgiven Qiao and Zhang, the Premier's wife, Deng Yingchao, reportedly never did. See Wen Xiang, "Mao Zedong, Qiao Guanhua, Zhang Hanzhi, Zhou Enlai" [Mao Zedong, Qiao Guanhua, Zhang Hanzhi and Zhou Enlai], *Boxun* [Well-informed News] (March 9, 2004), http://www.peacehall.com/news/gb/pubvp/2004/03/200403090141.shtml.

What did Mao intend with the Politburo onslaught against Zhou, and why did he initiate it? This, of course, is unknowable in any precise sense, and anything we offer must be speculative. Mao himself may have been unsure how far he would push the matter when launching and continuing to fuel the unrelenting criticism of the Premier. It is unlikely that Jiang Qing would have introduced the concept of an 11th line struggle without at least the belief that this was Mao's intent, and others on the Politburo thought it at least possible. According to an Internet source, Ye Jianying and Li Xiannian sought advice from Mao via Wang Dongxing concerning how to conduct such a struggle. Moreover, one well-placed Party historian claims that Mao had commented on Zhou's alleged desire to grab power before Jiang raised this damning issue, and he seemingly alluded to it even after stopping the direct criticism of Zhou with the rhetorical question, "who wants to be the emperor?" Perhaps most suggestive of the possibility that the Chairman was seriously considering a full purge of Zhou is the testimony of his nephew, Mao Yuanxin. Based on his involvement in small group discussions in spring 1973, Mao Yuanxin subsequently concluded that in undertaking the *pi Lin pi Kong* campaign, the Chairman was trying to prevent the reversal of the 9th line struggle, i.e., to defend the Cultural Revolution, to complete the 10th line struggle against Lin Biao, and at the same time was considering whether a verdict could be reached on the 11th line struggle.[67] Mao may have backed off to avoid further political upheaval, but it is likely that he was seriously entertaining Zhou's purge.

Mao Yuanxin's experience in the spring 1973 small group provides further insight into why the Chairman adopted such a harsh posture toward the Premier. The reasons cited earlier for Mao's strong reaction to Zhou's handling of the Kissinger talks remain relevant—a cumulative dissatisfaction with the Premier's performance since late 1972, a genuine, if unreasonable, perception of undignified behavior in negotiations with the US, and jealousy over Zhou's domestic and international prestige. Yet the virulence of the treatment meted out suggests something deeper as well. We noted in the Introduction Mao's belief that, whatever Zhou's administrative abilities, and however much his loyalty could be relied on, he was ideologically weak. With the Chairman perceiving the critique of "ultra-leftism" a danger to his Cultural Revolution, on his instructions Mao Yuanxin convened the small group discussions to delve into Zhou's past, and to review and revise nine articles his uncle had written during the Yan'an rectification criticizing doctrinairism and empiricism. Two of these

---

[66] Gao Wenqian, *Wannian Zhou*, pp. 469-73; interview with senior scholar on Zhou, January 2005; and above, p. 110. The scholar cited, and several other Party historians, while having reservations about Gao Wenqian's book, confirm the accuracy of his account of the November-December Politburo meetings.

[67] Gao Wenqian, *Wannian Zhou*, pp. 517-18; Wang Nianyi, *Dadongluan*, p. 471; Fan Shidong, "Qiliu nian Beijing gongting zhengbian zhenxiang" [The Truth about the 1976 *Coup d'Etat* in Beijing], http://www.boxun.com/hero/fansidong/24_1.shtml; interview, March 1998; and below, p. 142n75.

articles focused on empiricism, with Zhou Enlai named the representative of this erroneous tendency, although in the 1973 revision Liu Shaoqi's name was substituted. The Chairman still could not let the issue go, however. In June 1974, the very moment when Jiang Qing was intensifying attacks on the "inner-Party Confucius," he again called for a new revision of the nine articles, a step further increasing the pressure on Zhou. When he decided in July to moderate attacks on the Premier, Mao signaled this by indicating that the nine articles were no longer needed and could be withdrawn. But Zhou remained vulnerable, whether to the attack on empiricism in early 1975 (see Chapter 4) or in the *Water Margin* campaign later that year (see Chapter 5). The pressure could be perversely turned on or off at the Chairman's pleasure, but Mao himself was caught in the emotions of his long-standing complex relationship with Zhou. Even after the Premier's death, on his own deathbed Mao again called for revising the nine articles and further criticism of Zhou Enlai.[68]

In mid-December 1973, in any case, Mao gave Zhou some respite, although the Premier was still the object of the Chairman's complaints when the Politburo reconvened on the 12th. Taking personal charge of the Politburo, Mao broadened the criticism of Zhou and Ye beyond the Kissinger visit and foreign affairs, charging that "the Politburo [led by Zhou] doesn't discuss political affairs, and the MAC [under Ye] doesn't discuss military affairs or politics." This second phase of the November-December Politburo meetings, starting with the full session on December 12, followed by Mao's meetings with relevant Politburo members and leaders of the Beijing, Shenyang, Ji'nan and Wuhan Military Regions on the 13th, 14th and 15th, and then his reception of participants at an MAC conference on the 21st (and subsequent implementing Politburo sessions in his absence), focused on the PLA. The Chairman addressed broader issues than defects in the work of the MAC. As we saw in Chapter 1, rhetorical attention had been given to the problem of military dominance in the localities since the Ninth Congress, and the Lin Biao affair added urgency to the matter, yet little had been done to address the question systematically. While various officers associated with Lin's armies in the past had been sidelined, and even loyal generals from other military "mountaintops" such as Xu Shiyou were forced to make self-criticisms, at the time of the Tenth Congress the PLA still dominated local Party committees and retained a strong presence in central ministries. One concrete measure, the urban militia under local Party authorities broached by Mao in spring 1973, had developed into a major organizational effort after the Party Congress. Another move reducing PLA clout was abolishing the MAC's National Defense Industry Office in September, and replacing it with a new body of the same name under the State Council. But the decisive step was introduced by Mao on December 12 when, in an unprecedented move that took nearly everyone by surprise, he proposed that the commanders of eight military regions exchange positions with

---

[68] Gao Wenqian, *Wannian Zhou*, pp. 516-19, 606; and above, p. 19.

each other, thus breaking the local political dominance of these figures, who were also serving as ranking provincial Party secretaries in their areas.[69]

Although acknowledging having considered the problem for a number of years, in raising the rotation of military region commanders on December 12, Mao claimed that the plan was Ye Jianying's idea, and said he had also sought out the Premier and Wang Hongwen for their approval. The evidence further indicates that he had also consulted Ji Dengkui, but apparently not Deng Xiaoping.[70] Yet in another surprise move, Mao now proposed Deng's return to the Politburo and MAC, again citing Ye Jianying as suggesting the arrangement. While we can only speculate, Ye's initiative is probably best understood as reflecting his understanding of Mao's appreciation of Deng,[71] and of the Chairman's unhappiness with Ye's own performance. Over the four days from the 12th to the 15th, Mao explained the rationale for the rotation. He made clear his dissatisfaction with PLA interference in local affairs, declaring ridiculous the situation of local Party bodies being forced to obtain approval of decisions from army authorities, and calling for the rectification of such Cultural Revolution distortions by restoring local civilian power. Mao further complained about the domination individual commanders gained from their long service in a particular locale, a situation making them "slippery" and unaccountable, and stripping political commissars of any useful function since the commanders had the final say. In this, according to a senior Party historian, Mao was mindful that these appointments often stretched back to the army "mountaintops" of the revolutionary period. Mao's concern, in this scholar's view, was not that the "mountaintops" were a threat to himself, but that such "independent kingdoms" would create dangers for unity after his passing.[72]

---

[69] See *Mao zhuan*, vol. 2, pp. 1672-76; Wang Nianyi, *Dadongluan*, pp. 471-72; Li Wenqing, *Jinkan Xu Shiyou*, pp. 246-48; and above, pp. 83-84. Xu Shiyou's self-criticism was demanded in May 1973, with Li Desheng conveying Mao's concerns, and delivered at the central *pi Lin zhengfeng* conference. The complicated situation involving these generals, who were reelected or, in Li's case, promoted at the Tenth Congress, but then rotated at the end of 1973, and finally caught up in *pi Lin pi Kong* criticism, is discussed below.

[70] See Cheng and Xia, *Deng zai yijiuqiwu*, p. 6, on Mao acknowledging consultation with Ye, Zhou and Wang, but not Deng. Regarding Ji, Mao also commented that rotation was a "Henan people's invention," which would point to Ji as both a former Henan official and the Politburo member responsible for organization. Xue Qingchao, *Lishi zhuanzhe guantou*, p. 300. Gao Gao and Yan Jiaqi, *"Wenhua dageming" shinianshi, 1966-1976* [A Ten-year History of the "Great Cultural Revolution," 1966-1976] (Tianjin: Tianjin renmin chubanshe, 1986), p. 529, however, claim that the rotation plan was proposed by Deng. In any case, whoever first floated the idea, it almost certainly would have been based on a reading of Mao's wishes.

[71] Another indication of Ye's reading of Mao's attitude occurred sometime in the latter part of 1973, presumably before the December Politburo sessions. Ye approached Deng to seek his opinion on how to prepare for the long delayed MAC conference, a conference that would be finally held in 1975 (see Chapter 4). Yu Shicheng, *Deng Xiaoping yu Mao Zedong* [Deng Xiaoping and Mao Zedong] (Beijing: Zhonggong zhongyang dangxiao chubanshe, 1995), p. 263.

[72] *Mao zhuan*, vol. 2, pp. 1672-73; Mao Zedong, "Guanyu dajunqu silingyuan duitiao deng wenti de

A clear implication of Mao's initiative, although one not explicitly raised in his known remarks, was to strengthen centralization. In the context of the emerging Confucian-Legalist discussion, prominent articles during the two months before the Politburo meetings emphasized the significance of Qinshihuang's rule in setting up China's first highly centralized political system. Qinshihuang's success, moreover, was attributed to his political line, thus diminishing purely military contributions to the Qin dynasty's formation, and by extension highlighting the need for PLA leaders to adhere to Mao's Cultural Revolution line. With the *pi Lin pi Kong* campaign under way, moreover, considerable media attention focused on the threat to central political authority posed by strong regional warlords.[73] The irony, of course, was that the regional commanders were completely loyal and subordinate to Mao, but the breakdown of coherent central authority caused by the Chairman's own Cultural Revolution policies greatly exacerbated the potential for "independent kingdoms" inherent in lengthy postings.

While Mao's concern with localist tendencies and excessive PLA interference in politics should not have caused surprise, his rotation plan, coming on the heels of the intense criticism of Zhou Enlai, undoubtedly heightened anxiety within the military. The Chairman, now personally conducting the proceedings, worked to create a less tense atmosphere. In contrast to the harsh attacks on the Premier, Mao provided a mixture of reassurance, cajoling, appeals to discipline, and "a bit of" self-criticism—but in a context of his own firm authority and still threatening themes. On the 12th, even before introducing the rotation plan, he proposed Deng's return to the Politburo and MAC, thus presenting PLA leaders with a figure of high military prestige, "a marshal [and] your old commander," a step sometimes seen in Western analysis as a virtual *quid pro quo* for military acceptance of the transfers. Throughout the ten-day period from the 12th to 21st, while making his dissatisfaction with current arrangements known, Mao largely used the bland observation that service in a single locale for many years was "not very good," asked for opinions, and reassured the affected commanders that they would not lose their Politburo or Central Committee positions, and would keep the same rank despite their transfers. Mao also expressed sympathy for the problems inevitably involved in the sudden shifts, and enquired about the specific situations of individual commanders. He further acknowledged the harsh treatment suffered by some of the Red Army's outstanding generals during the Cultural Revolution, famously referring to Zhu De as a "red commander" in contrast to the "black commander" label applied by the Red Guards. Finally, he

---

tanhua yaodian" [Main Points of Talks on the Question of Transferring Military Region Commanders] (December 12, 1973 [sic]), in *CRDB*, p. 1; *Deng Liqun guoshi jiangtan*, vol. 3, p. 314; and interview, July 2001. Huang, *Factionalism*, pp. 328ff, emphasizes "mountaintops" in his analysis of the period, but, erroneously in our view, sees them as a potential threat to Mao.

[73] See *RMRB*, September 28, 1973, p. 2; *HQ*, no. 11 (1973), pp. 30-40; Fenwick, "Gang of Four," p. 210; and J. P. Jain, *After Mao What? Army Party and Group Rivalries in China* (London: Martin Robertson, 1976), p. 88.

engaged in his "bit of" self-criticism regarding the cases of He Long, Luo Ruiqing, Yang Chengwu and others. This, predictably, was similar to his offerings after the September 13 incident: Lin Biao was really at fault, but now the Chairman went further and accepted some responsibility for paying one-sided attention to Lin.[74]

If these initiatives were reassuring, Mao also demanded obedience and introduced unsettling themes. Discipline was stressed, with Mao repeatedly requiring the singing of the revolutionary Red Army song, "The Three Main Rules of Discipline and Eight Points of Attention," during these meetings. The Chairman also foreshadowed war, civil as well as foreign, declaring himself fit for such trials, and wanting to know who else was similarly willing to fight. In this, Mao targeted Zhou, going on to ask, "who is colluding with foreigners [and] wants to be the emperor?"[75] Also unsettling was the mixed message concerning the two types of personnel receiving Mao's attention in the post-Lin Biao period, but who remained in underlying conflict: revolutionary veterans and young Cultural Revolution activists. While the Chairman's solicitude toward the regional commanders and higher-ranking figures such as Zhu De would have been reassuring, his post-Tenth Congress personnel policy called for cultivating younger cadres. During the December meetings Mao endorsed letters from young rebels Li Qinglin and Zhang Tiesheng, pointed to his promotion of Wang Hongwen, and warned against looking down on such youthful pioneers. In a similar vein, Mao had already rebuffed a rumor that "old marshals must return to their posts, [and] little soldiers must go back to their barracks," altering it to "old marshals should toe the line, little soldiers should be promoted." Beyond this, the Chairman declared he would act if the Politburo and MAC didn't change their ways. Most threatening, he revived his warning on the eve of the Cultural Revolution by calling attention to the danger of "China turning revisionist."[76]

In this mix the promotion of Deng Xiaoping was clearly significant. In addition to nominating Deng for Politburo and MAC membership, appointments dutifully approved by the Politburo on December 22, Mao added to the importance of the new arrangement with comments that went further than his praise 16 months

---

[74] See *Mao zhuan*, vol. 2, pp. 1672-77; Mao Zedong, "Guanyu dajunqu silingyuan," pp. 1-2; Wang Nianyi, *Dadongluan*, p. 472; *Deng Liqun guoshi jiangtan*, vol. 3, p. 320; MacFarquhar, "Succession," pp. 290-91; and above, pp. 35, 44ff.

[75] Wang Nianyi, *Dadongluan*, p. 471; and Gao Wenqian, *Wannian Zhou*, p. 473. While clearly referring to Zhou, Mao's use of "wanting to be the emperor" could be taken in two ways. It could suggest support of Jiang Qing's attack on the Premier for impatience to take over, notwithstanding Mao's rejection of the notion a few days earlier. Or, it conceivably could be related to Zhou's alleged willingness to serve as a puppet emperor if the Soviets invaded.

[76] See *Mao zhuan*, vol. 2, pp. 1672-77; Mao Zedong, "Guanyu dajunqu silingyuan," pp. 1-3; Wang Nianyi, *Dadongluan*, pp. 471-72; "Yao Wenyuan dui *Hongqi* bianjizu zhaojiren tan pi Kong ji zhuanda Zhuxi zhishi" [Yao Wenyuan Talks to the *Red Flag* Editorial Group Convener about Criticizing Confucius and Conveying the Chairman's Directives] (December 3, 1973), in *CRDB*, p. 1; and "Wang Hongwen zai zhongyang dushuban," p. 3.

earlier in the lead-up to Deng's return to work. Now the Chairman went beyond Deng's past contributions to address his abilities. Mao's comments pointed to a figure of substance: Deng "handles affairs in a relatively decisive manner," and "looks gentle but is firm, like a needle in cotton." Mao further observed that some people feared Deng—i.e., the cotton may not always have been in evidence, but the steel was. Overall, the Chairman evaluated Deng by the same 70/30 standard he applied to Stalin, the Cultural Revolution, and himself.[77] Another suggestive pointer to Deng's new prominence was Mao's statement that it was necessary to promote more officers from the Second Field Army, as well as from the Fourth Front Army, which both belonged to Deng's "mountaintop."[78] Yet while the Chairman clearly indicated Deng's importance, his actual role was far from clear. Although Mao spoke of him as the secretary-general of the Politburo (*mishuzhang*) or the body's adviser (*canmouzhang*), as well as a military adviser (*junshi*) to the MAC, this fell short of specific responsibilities, and in fact Deng was simply assigned to "participate in" the work of the two bodies.[79] Deng assumed more specific, if still largely hidden duties in 1974.

What was the political meaning of Deng Xiaoping's December 1973 promotion? As suggested, Deng's elevation was probably designed in part to reassure PLA leaders on the eve of their forced transfers, and it is also likely that Mao saw Deng as someone who could control the various "mountaintops." Of particular significance, in view of his quite separate military history, is that Deng was an optimal choice for the task of further expunging Lin Biao's influence in the PLA, a key objective of Mao's since September 13. But any suggestion that Deng's promotion was somehow necessary to insure implementation of the rotation order is dismissed by Party historians. Simply put, there was no question of the notionally powerful regional commanders doing anything other than salute and carry out the Chairman's orders. The rotation was carried out in strikingly short order, with the affected commanders, unaccompanied by any staff except a single secretary, moving to their new posts within ten days of formal Politburo approval of the scheme on December 22. Moreover, Deng apparently played

---

[77] *Mao zhuan*, vol. 2, p. 1674; Mao Zedong, "Guanyu dajunqu silingyuan," p. 2; Wang Nianyi, *Dadongluan*, pp. 471-72; interview with senior Party historian, November 2002; and above, p. 66. Moreover, when indicating his own fault in listening to Lin Biao in the case of Luo Ruiqing, Mao also noted Deng's doubts about the case at the time.

[78] See Chen Shiqu, *Cong Jinggangshan zoujin Zhongnanhai: Chen Shiqu huiyi Mao Zedong* [From Jinggangshan to Entering Zhongnanhai: Chen Shiqu Remembers Mao Zedong] (Beijing: Zhonggong zhongyang dangxiao chubanshe, 1993), p. 323. The Fourth Front Army led by Mao's revolutionary period opponent, Zhang Guotao, was later reorganized into the Second Field Army. During the December meetings Mao was particularly solicitous of the Fourth Front Army's post-Zhang Guotao head, Marshal Xu Xiangqian.

[79] See *Mao zhuan*, vol. 2, pp. 1672-73. At one point (*Mao zhuan*, vol 2, p. 1674), Mao also used the term *zong canmouzhang* (chief-of-staff). This has led both Western and Chinese sources to claim Deng was appointed PLA Chief-of-Staff at this point, but this clearly was not the case. The post remained unfilled until Mao decided to appoint Deng in October 1974 (see Chapter 3).

no role in the transfers, even when his old Second Field Army subordinates were involved. Indeed, Deng seemingly was as surprised as anyone at his MAC assignment despite his pre-1949 military achievements, having only presumed that he would take up State Council and foreign affairs responsibilities following his return to work. On the basis of available information, it appears Zhou and Ye were in charge of practical arrangements for the transfers, while Wang Hongwen and Zhang Chunqiao dealt with political aspects of the scheme.[80]

The rotated regional commanders (with the exception of Chen Xilian who soon assumed greater responsibilities in the MAC) were losers under the new arrangement—by virtue of being divorced from their familiar surroundings and "mountaintops," by being subject to criticism in their former bailiwicks by discontented officers no longer under their control, by having to deal with established, unfamiliar political commissars in their new postings (thus creating the checks and balances that Mao sought), because they did not receive provincial Party positions in their new areas as civilianization of the CCP apparatus accelerated, and not least because apparently all of them were subjected to strong criticism as the *pi Lin pi Kong* campaign unfolded in the military regions and subsequently at the Center. There was no bigger loser than Li Desheng. Only four months after being made Party Vice Chairman at the Tenth Congress, Li was dispatched from his Beijing Military Region post to the Shenyang Military Region in an exchange with Chen Xilian, another Second Field Army veteran. Moreover, unlike half the rotated commanders, Li had not been in his Beijing Military Region post for many years, having only taken up the position in January 1971.[81] Also telling, on Mao's order Li was required to give up his concurrent position as GPD head, a post he had assumed when Lin Biao was Minister of Defense. Finally, a year later the Chairman forced Li to resign formally as Vice Chairman in favor of Deng.[82] What explains this sudden reversal in Li Desheng's fortunes?

Li Desheng's case has been one of the most mysterious of the late Maoist era. Once ensconced in Shenyang, apart from the loss of his Vice Chairmanship,

---

[80] *Li Desheng huiyilu*, pp. 467-68; Mao Mao, *"Wenge" suiyue*, p. 293; *Zhou nianpu*, vol. 3, p. 639; Fan Shuo, *Ye Jianying zai feichang shiqi*, vol. 2, pp. 387-89; and interviews with Party historians, January 2000, July 2001 and November 2002.

[81] Chen Xilian (Shenyang), Xu Shiyou (Nanjing), Yang Dezhi (Ji'nan), and Han Xianchu (Fuzhou), had all served at least 14 years in their posts, while Li, Zeng Siyu (Wuhan), Pi Dingjun (Lanzhou), and Ding Sheng (Guangzhou) had served six years or less. Mao explicitly acknowledged the short tenures of Li, Zeng and Ding. *Mao zhuan*, vol. 2, p. 1675. An anomaly was the case of Pi Dingjun who, although only in Lanzhou for four years, now returned to Fuzhou where he had previously served in lesser posts. The three other military region commanders who were not rotated—Qin Jiwei (Chengdu), Yang Yong (Urumqi), and Wang Bicheng (Kunming)—were all recent appointees. See "Quarterly Chronicle and Documentation," *CQ*, no. 57 (1974), pp. 206-207; and He Husheng, *Zhiguanzhi*, pp. 578-82.

[82] Mao Zedong, "Guanyu dajunqu silingyuan," p. 1; and Ji Pomin, "Ting fuqin Ji Dengkui tan wangshi."

Li remained largely unaffected by the twists and turns of elite politics during the remainder of Mao's life, as well as throughout the post-Mao period to his retirement in the mid-1980s. In our view, the most likely explanation for this is that once removed from Beijing, Li was not directly involved in the maneuverings at the Center, and thus was spared the unjust label of "neo-Maoist" that befell his fellow Second Field Army veteran, Chen Xilian. But that is a story for our Volume II. In late 1973, however, Li was very much center stage. His promotion at the Tenth Congress met Mao's stipulation for a "middle-aged" vice chairman "who can fight," but more significantly it reflected the Chairman's confidence in Li for critical tasks since his appointment as GPD head in spring 1970. Li's importance as Mao turned against Lin Biao was seen at the Lushan plenum in summer 1970 when, with Chief-of-Staff Huang Yongsheng in trouble, he was dispatched to Beijing in the middle of the plenum to take over Huang's duties in the MAC, and four months later by his appointment as Beijing Military Region Commander as part of the effort to "dig up the cornerstone" of Lin's power in the PLA. Moreover, as noted in Chapter 1, following the September 13 incident, Li played a key role in assuring control over the central military apparatus.[83]

After the Tenth Congress, however, in the context of intensifying leftist themes, the work of the GPD become vulnerable to criticism, and when the *pi Lin pi Kong* campaign unfolded in early 1974, resistance to the movement within the GPD was a major issue. During the January 25 mobilization meeting, Xie Jingyi attacked the GPD, specifically criticizing an October instruction from the "department head" that "was not in accord with the spirit of the Tenth Congress." Thus the explanation of Li's demotion as a consequence of a struggle over the GPD between Li and the Politburo radicals, who assumed leadership of army political work after Li's transfer, undoubtedly captures the major factor in Li's decline. Yet Li's fate was also linked to accusations that, despite his role in containing Lin Biao, Li had joined "Lin's pirate ship." This accusation, which in fact also points to the conflict over the GPD, will be examined further in our analysis of the Lin Biao-Confucius campaign in the PLA.[84]

Apart from Li Desheng, the rotation of military region commanders foreshadowed the PLA becoming a key target of the *pi Lin pi Kong* campaign as it unfolded in the first eight months of 1974. With Mao apparently seeking a thorough investigation of army problems, both the central military apparatus and regional and lower-level commands were subject to searching criticism, criticism that was particularly intense in the central PLA departments (see below). Moreover, the PLA shakeup was linked to the post-Tenth Congress militia-building program that now intensified in conjunction with the Lin Biao-Confucius effort. By early 1974 delegations from every province and military region were visiting

---

[83] *Li Desheng huiyilu*, pp. 401, 407; and above, pp. 38, 80n137.

[84] Wang Nianyi, *Dadongluan*, pp. 486-87; *Li Desheng huiyilu*, pp. 407ff, 416ff, 455, 484-85; interviews with Party historians, November and December 2002; and below, pp. 170-71.

Shanghai to study Wang Hongwen's local model, while Shanghai expanded its militia organization, budget and armaments. At this juncture, Shanghai leader Wang Xiuzhen explicitly linked the rotation of commanders, *pi Lin pi Kong*, and militia building as measures to "guard against revisionism"—a linkage fully reflecting Mao's aims.[85] Finally, the December transfers prefigured the new military leadership arrangement in January: the MAC six-person small group. While Ye Jianying headed the group, as well as being responsible for MAC daily work and serving as Party secretary of the army's General Staff Department, his authority presumably was suspect given both the December meetings and the criticism directed at him during *pi Lin pi Kong*. Two other members, Chen Xilian and Su Zhenhua, were professional officers and Second Field Army veterans, while Deng Xiaoping ranked fourth in the group. The second and third positions, however, which arguably were more significant than Ye's in the context of the moment, were held by Wang Hongwen and Zhang Chunqiao in yet another indication of Mao's post-Lin Biao determination to have a radical presence at the top of the army command. These posts further provided Wang and Zhang with formal military office to support their conduct of the Lin Biao and Confucius campaign in the PLA.[86]

Pi Lin pi Kong: The Campaign to Criticize Lin Biao and Confucius

Despite Mao's criticism of Confucius since spring 1973 and the intensifying attacks on the sage, including references to Lin Biao, after the Tenth Congress, at the start of 1974 CCP plans simply called for deepening the criticize Lin Biao-rectification campaign. In early January, Zhou submitted to Mao a report (countersigned by Wang) on Politburo deliberations that only referred to the *pi Lin zhengfeng* movement, thus echoing the New Year *People's Daily*, *Red Flag*, and *PLA Daily* joint editorial. That editorial, however, also declared criticizing Confucius a component part of the criticism of Lin Biao, and toughened circumstances were immediately apparent in sensitive quarters.[87] Despite claims

---

[85] See *Shanghai minbing douzheng shi ziliao*, vol. 22, pp. 52-56; and above, pp. 83-84. Despite the post-Mao effort to picture the "second armed force" as an illicit "gang of four" scheme to oppose the PLA, as we saw in Chapter 1, Mao provided the impetus for the urban militia. It is also of note that after his arrest Wang Hongwen refused to accept claims that the militia was designed to promote the radicals' seizure of power, arguing that his statements warning against PLA unreliability followed Mao's concerns and were directed at Lin Biao's followers. Against the clearly exaggerated claims attacking the radicals on this issue, there is some circumstantial support for Wang in contemporary internal and public statements linking the militia program to the struggle with Lin. See *Feiqing Yuebao* [Chinese Communism Monthly] (Taipei); vol. 17, no. 10, p. 39, no. 12 (1974), p. 18; *HQ*, no. 8 (1976), p.73; *Zhanwang* [Outlook] (Hong Kong), no. 347 (1976), pp. 17-18; "Guowuyuan, Zhongyang junwei zhuanfa 'Shanghai chengshi minbing qingkuang diaocha' de tongzhi" [The State Coiuncil and Central MAC Issue a Notice on "Investigation of the Circumstances of the Shanghai Urban Militia"] (November 19, 1973), in *CRDB*, p. 1; and "Quarterly Chronicle and Documentation," *CQ*, no. 57 (1974), pp. 210-11.

[86] See below, Table 4, p. 148.

by his biographers that Mao had not (explicitly) advocated a large-scale *pi Lin pi Kong* campaign at this stage, the buildup, and the Chairman's instigation, were clear by the turn of the year. On December 29, Wang Hongwen unnerved cadres at the Center by reporting what had only been known by the Politburo and a few others—that the Chairman had repeated his challenge on the eve of the Cultural Revolution to prepare for a struggle with revisionism. On January 14, Wang again raised Mao's challenge to the Central Study Class, emphasized the need to defend the Cultural Revolution and refute the wrong line that had taken hold in many places, and stated that a mass movement would soon appear throughout the country. This was two days after Wang and Jiang Qing wrote to Mao proposing the distribution of materials criticizing "the doctrines of Lin Biao, Confucius and Mencius," materials prepared under Jiang's direction at the two universities answering directly to the Chairman. Significantly, although official sources claim the preparation of these documents by the *Liang Xiao* writing group was undertaken without the knowledge of Zhou or the Politburo, no similar claim was made concerning the Chairman. In any case, Mao's approval of Wang and Jiang's proposal on January 18, which was emphasized by his personal drafting of central Document no. 1 (1974) conveying that approval, resulted in the rapid development of the new movement.[88]

While the events that subsequently unfolded may not have been under Mao's detailed management, the claim of Party historian An Jianshe that the Chairman was less involved than in the early stage of the Cultural Revolution, even though substantially true in light of his poor health, ignores the fundamental similarity between the two periods. As in 1966-67, Mao set a process in train, and then periodically intervened to adjust the course of the ensuing movement. To borrow Shaoguang Wang's insightful observation concerning the first year of the Cultural Revolution, throughout 1974 Mao once again undertook an "emergency salvage" role, both to push forward and rein in a movement he did not fully understand. Through mid-January, however, the Chairman instigated and lent his immense authority to launching the *pi Lin pi Kong* effort, with little sign of imposing any restraint.[89]

---

[87] A much stricter regime was applied to Lin Biao's daughter, Lin Doudou, in the days immediately following the editorial. Interview with source close to Lin's family, January 2005.

[88] See *Mao zhuan*, vol. 2, pp. 1679-81; *PR*, no. 1 (1974), p. 7; Forster, *Rebellion*, pp. 141, 286n52; "Wang Hongwen zai zhongyang dushuban," pp. 1-2 and *passim*; minutes of the January 25, 1974 mobilization meeting in the Australian National University collection (see below, p. 151n96); and An Jianshe, "Mao Zedong yu 'pi Lin pi Kong' ruogan wenti," pp. 57-58.

[89] Ibid., p. 58; and Shaoguang Wang, "The Structural Sources of the Cultural Revolution," in Kam-yee Law, *The Chinese Cultural Revolution Reconsidered: Beyond Purge and Holocaust* (Basingstoke, Hampshire: Palgrave Macmillan, 2003), p. 83. For a thumbnail sketch of adjustments during the early phase of the Cultural Revolution, see Teiwes, *Provincial Leadership*, pp. 16ff.

Media publicity for the Lin Biao-Confucius campaign began in late January following large mobilization rallies in Beijing on January 24 and 25. On January 31, the Politburo established the seven-person small group to oversee the movement, a group nominally led by Zhou Enlai, but containing the four radicals, and apparently dominated by Jiang Qing who would be praised in central documents as well as within leftist circles for her personal leadership. When the decision to create the *pi Lin pi Kong* small group was taken on January 31, the Politburo also decreed that the MAC small group, which had been set up two weeks earlier to deal with pressing military issues[90] and included Wang Hongwen and Zhang Chunqiao, would deal with the movement in the army, thus creating a situation parallel to that of the Central Cultural Revolution Group and PLA Cultural Revolution Group seven years earlier. Table 4 gives the full membership of the two groups:

Table 4: Guiding Bodies for the Lin Biao-Confucius Campaign, January 1974

Seven-person small group for *pi Lin pi Kong*[a]	Six-person MAC small group[b]
Zhou Enlai	* Ye Jianying
# Wang Hongwen	# Wang Hongwen
# Zhang Chunqiao	# Zhang Chunqiao
# Jiang Qing	Deng Xiaoping
# Yao Wenyuan	* Chen Xilian
Hua Guofeng	* Su Zhenhua[c]
Wang Dongxing	

Source: *Zhou nianpu*, vol. 3, pp. 644, 648.
Key: * pre-Cultural Revolution PLA leader; # Cultural Revolution radical.
a. Formed January 31.
b. Formed January 18.
c. Added to original group on January 20.

By this time, however, the movement had already gained momentum with Party Center notices on January 22 and 25 adding weight to the distribution of materials on the 18th. Some of the momentum would be attributed in post-Mao accounts to the "gang of four's" actions "behind the back" of the Politburo and Mao, using individual authority—especially by Jiang Qing who wrote letters, sent materials, and dispatched agents, notably Xie Jingyi and Chi Qun, to the MAC,

---

[90] On these issues and Deng Xiaoping's role, see below, p. 180.

leading organs of the navy and air force, several military region commands, and individual military and other units—to propagate the new campaign. Whatever formal authority Jiang did or did not have for these efforts, a comprehensive official mobilization was under way in the provinces and military regions from late January, with the ranking Party secretaries, including such decidedly non-radical rehabilitated leaders as Zhang Pinghua in Hunan and Zhao Ziyang in Guangdong in charge. All work units were required to set up *pi Lin pi Kong* small groups, campaign offices and study classes were established at and above the county level, media coverage greatly expanded, and meetings and rallies were held across the nation in official organizations, universities, factories and communes. Clearly, a centrally authorized intense political campaign was under way.[91]

The January Mobilization Meetings. The most noted events during January, events allegedly organized by the radicals without the prior approval of either Mao or the Politburo, were two mobilization meetings held during spring festival on the 24th and 25th, the first for military units in Beijing, and the second for cadres of the State Council and Party Center. While, by and large, only post-Mao accounts broadly attacking the radicals are available for the military meeting, detailed material exists on the January 25 rally. The two meetings symbolically targeted the sources of Mao's discontent in the November-December Politburo meetings: the PLA and Zhou Enlai (the responsible person for both the State Council and Party Center). In addition, there was a third, much less noted, but in some respects even more significant mobilization meeting on the 27th. This meeting was called by the Politburo, attended by the Central Study Class, GPD and *PLA Daily* staff, and featured Jiang Qing calling on journalists to be "liaison officers" who would report on the development of the campaign. Given that the Politburo recognized that the movement was uneven, these "liaison officers" were granted great power, including direct access to the Center, and the authorities at all levels were ordered to respond to their demands.[92]

Although relatively little is known about the January 24 gathering, Jiang Qing's central role is clear. Her letter to the MAC on that day led to the rally of 10,000 military cadres that immediately followed. Indeed, she had already arranged for a similar rally for the navy on the 23rd (see below). Interestingly, Jiang's letter was addressed to four of the six members of the newly formed MAC small group—Ye Jianying as nominal head of the group, radicals Wang

---

[91] See Yan and Gao, *Turbulent Decade*, pp. 430-32; *Zhou nianpu*, vol. 3, p. 648; *Shanghai minbing douzheng shi ziliao*, vol. 16 (December 1980), p. 13; *Mao zhuan*, vol. 2, p. 1681; Fenwick, "Gang of Four," pp. 237-38; Forster, *Rebellion*, p. 242; *History of Party*, p. 362; *Feiqing nianbao 1974* [Chinese Communism Yearbook 1974] (Taipei: Guofangbu qingbaoju, August 1974), Section 3, pp. 68-69; and "Quarterly Chronicle and Documentation," *CQ*, no. 58 (1974), pp. 407-408. Other indications of the intensity of the effort which unfolded are: in Heilongjiang 300,000 cadres were involved in study classes to mid-March; and in March alone 200 million copies of books on *pi Lin pi Kong* (especially on *pi Kong*) were distributed.

[92] See Zhang Zuoliang, *Zhou Enlai de zuihou shinian*, p. 316, on the January 27 meeting.

Hongwen and Zhang Chunqiao, and Deng Xiaoping, but not to the group's professional military members, Chen Xilian and Su Zhenhua. The events of the 24th unquestionably indicate Mao's fundamental backing of Jiang at this juncture, notwithstanding subsequent complaints that he was not aware of the details, since Jiang's capacity to convene such a meeting on minimal notice without any known PLA resistance, despite her lack of any formal army authority,[93] was unthinkable without the Chairman's support. These events also underlined the crucial—and "legal"—positions of Wang and Zhang for carrying out the campaign in the military. Finally, they suggested that Deng would have some role in the conduct of the campaign, a role that Jiang, and more importantly Mao, surely assumed would be in support of *pi Lin pi Kong*.[94]

The post-Mao narrative of the January 25 meeting unsurprisingly depicts a gathering orchestrated by the "gang of four," with Jiang Qing playing the leading role, in pursuit of their factional interests. According to Mao's secretary, Zhang Yufeng, the Chairman was unaware of the rally beforehand, nor did he know the contents of the speeches to the gathering by Chi Qun and Xie Jingyi. Another aspect of the story is that Jiang tightly controlled Chi and Xie, regarding them as "cannon balls" and herself as a "gunner" when dispatching them to a Zhejiang PLA unit nearly two weeks earlier, and on the 25th providing them with detailed oral instructions for their speeches. A further part of the official picture emphasizes the victimization of senior revolutionary cadres, notably Zhou Enlai and Ye Jianying. Indicative of their high-handedness, the radicals reportedly only informed Zhou of the meeting a few hours before it convened, thus dragging the ill Premier to an intense rally where he was a major if unnamed target, while Jiang allegedly took personal delight that Zhou had no way to defend himself. Ye, moreover, was vulnerable to Chi's strong criticism of "going in through the back door," the practice of senior cadres using their influence to place relatives in universities, PLA units, and official positions, a practice Chi asserted was a betrayal of Marxism-Leninism. When subsequently criticizing developments at the meeting, Mao particularly singled out the emphasis on "going in through the back door" as an error—something treated in official sources as not only a sign of anger with Jiang, but also of his solicitude for revolutionary veterans.[95]

---

[93] Similarly, Jiang was able to impose Xie Jingyi and Chi Qun, young radicals with no military posts, in leading roles at the rally where Chi gave the main address.

[94] See Chen and Du, *Shilu*, vol. 3, part 2, p. 1026; *Mao zhuan*, vol. 2, pp. 1681-82; Yan and Gao, *Turbulent Decade*, pp. 430-31; Perry and Li, *Proletarian Power*, p. 178; Fenwick, "Gang of Four," p. 239; and "Jiang Qing zhi Wang Hongwen, Ye Jianying, Zhang Chunqiao, Deng Xiaoping de xin" [Jiang Qing's Letter to Wang Hongwen, Ye Jianying, Zhang Chunqiao and Deng Xiaoping] (January 24, 1974), in *CRDB*, p. 1.

[95] *Mao zhuan*, vol. 2, pp. 1682, 1684-87; An Jianshe, "Mao Zedong yu 'pi Lin pi Kong' ruogan wenti," pp. 58-59; Chen and Du, *Shilu*, vol. 3, part 2, pp. 1026, 1038-39; Yan and Gao, *Turbulent Decade*, p. 431; Barnouin and Yu, *Ten Years*, pp. 258-59; Forster, *Rebellion*, p. 142; "Zhonggong zhongyang guanyu 'Wang Hongwen, Zhang Chunqiao, Jiang Qing, Yao Wenyuan fandang jituan zuizheng (cailiao zhi yi)'," p. 4; and interview with senior Party historian, February 2000.

While there is some truth in this story, transcripts of the January 25 meeting, including lengthy speeches by Zhou Enlai and Jiang Qing,[96] suggest a more complex situation. Without doubt Zhou was the central target of the meeting, with Jiang Qing explaining this to Chi Qun when instructing him before the rally. Chi and others sharply criticized Lin Biao's [read Zhou's] "doctrine of the mean," and other failings obviously linked to the Premier. Zhou, however, clearly had some forewarning, as indicated by the fact that he came prepared with a lengthy opening address. Moreover, in his speech Zhou commented that *he* had proposed a few days earlier to several Politburo colleagues the convening of a gathering for Party Center and state organs, apologizing for being a day late compared to the military rally, and also late in giving his attention to *pi Lin pi Kong*. Consistent with this alternative scenario, Jiang Qing claimed that she did not wish to attend, but responded to Zhou's invitation. In his speech, Zhou strongly praised Jiang, making clear that Mao had placed her in charge of ideological work. Similarly, Chi and Xie Jingyi emphasized that the whole *pi Lin pi Kong* effort was Mao's idea, while praising Jiang's direct contribution. Of particular note, in his speech, the Premier addressed the question of "going in through the back door" before Chi Qun raised the issue.[97]

At this stage, however much Ye Jianying was vulnerable, the back door issue was nothing new, and in raising it in his talk, Chi Qun criticized the practice in the Foreign Ministry and the First Foreign Languages College attached to the ministry—not the PLA. Meanwhile, Jiang Qing, in her long speech covering the various themes of the criticism of Lin Biao and Confucius, only tangentially addressed the back door issue, and she also seemed reluctant to endorse fully Chi's and Xie Jingyi's attacks. Jiang interrupted the discussion to say she had to speak up as this was a problem affecting only a minority. Beyond this, it appears that there was not a great deal of coordination among the four Politburo radicals at the meeting. Apart from Jiang herself, Yao Wenyuan was the most notable advocate, seemingly in response to her urgings. But Zhang Chunqiao, except

---

[96] A lengthy transcript, "Zhou Enlai, Jiang Qing, Chi Qun, Xie Jingyi, Yao Wenyuan zai zhongyang zhishu jiguan he guojia jiguan pi Lin pi Kong dongyuan dahui de jianghua" [Speeches by Zhou Enlai, Jiang Qing, Chi Qun, Xie Jingyi and Yao Wenyuan at the Mobilization Meeting for Party and State Organs Directly under the Center] (January 25, 1974), is provided in *CRDB*, pp. 1-14, while an abridged version can be found in Wang Nianyi, *Dadongluan*, pp. 480-87. Texts of the speeches by Zhou Enlai and Jiang Qing are in hand-written minutes of the January 25 meeting, among a collection of 1970s documents held at the Menzies Library, the Australian National University (ANU). While the reliability of this collection cannot be completely verified, and its documents vary in credibility, a careful linguistic and contextual analysis of the January 25 document, including cross-checking with other sources, gives us very high confidence in its genuineness.

[97] *Mao zhuan*, vol. 2, p. 1682; "Zhou Enlai, Jiang Qing, Chi Qun, Xie Jingyi, Yao Wenyuan de jianghua," pp. 1-3, 8-10; and minutes of the January 25 meeting in the ANU collection. In his speech, Zhou provided further indication of his awareness before the meeting by referring to his visit, together with Zhang Chunqiao, to Guo Moruo on the eve of the rally, to mobilize Guo to attend.

for one reported jibe at the Premier,[98] does not appear to have participated in the discussion to any great extent. Most striking, according to the meeting's transcript, Wang Hongwen did not make any contribution, apart from leading the singing of the "The Three Main Rules of Discipline and Eight Points of Attention."[99]

The meeting on January 27 appears to have been much more significant in turning the back door question into a loaded political issue. Chaired by Zhou, and attended by Ye Jianying, Jiang Qing, Zhang Chunqiao, Yao Wenyuan (but seemingly not Wang Hongwen), Wang Dongxing and, most surprisingly, the seriously ill Kang Sheng, the gathering had a theoretical bent with Yao frequently called upon by Jiang to elaborate on Confucius, but its political import concerned the PLA. With GPD officials gathered, Jiang questioned GPD Deputy Director Tian Weixin, who effectively ran the department, about the *Communist Manifesto*, abused him when he could not answer the question, and had the military insignia ripped off his uniform. Jiang then turned to Ye, questioning how his son had entered the air force, accusing him of facilitating entry *via* the back door. On the 30th, Jiang pursued the matter with Ye in the Politburo, as well as criticizing the military for being too slow in carrying out *pi Lin pi Kong*. After thanking her for reminding him of the problem, Ye wrote to Mao making a self-criticism on the same day.[100]

Mao soon reacted negatively to these developments. While we have no smoking gun to refute the official claim that Mao had not been specifically informed in advance of the two rallies on the 24th and 25th, this is extremely dubious except in the sense that he may not have approved everything in minute detail beforehand. In the larger sense, there is little doubt that Jiang had received explicit authority from the Chairman to launch the new movement. While criticizing the alleged failure to inform him, Mao also addressed other matters. As in so many other events of the late Mao era, Wang Hairong and Tang Wensheng played an important role. After the January 25 meeting, the "two ladies," whose attendance

---

[98] According to Chen Yonggui, Zhang demanded to know why Zhou had not convened the Politburo Standing Committee to consider launching the movement, reducing the Premier to tears and forcing him to acknowledge yet another mistake. "Hua Guofeng, Ye Jianying deng jiejian Shanghai Ma Tianshui dengren de jianghua" [Speeches by Hua Guofeng, Ye Jianying *et al.* Receiving Shanghai's Ma Tianshui *et al.*] (October 12, 1976), in *CRDB*, p. 1.

[99] Jiang Qing's speech in the minutes of the January 25 meeting, ANU collection; "Zhou Enlai, Jiang Qing, Chi Qun, Xie Jingyi, Yao Wenyuan de jianghua," pp. 10, 13; Chen and Du, *Shilu*, vol. 3, part 2, p. 1026; and Yan and Gao, *Turbulent Decade*, p. 431. However, Chen Yonggui (see the preceding note) refers to a recording of a speech by Wang to the January 25 meeting. Also, Wang later made a self-criticism for his role in convening the two meetings without reference to the *full* Politburo, and for not having reported to Mao in good time. As the ranking Party leader after Mao and Zhou, Wang presumably had some responsibility in this regard, but clearly Jiang was the driving force, and Zhou too had such responsibility—particularly if he indeed took the initiative for calling the meeting on the 25th. See "Zhonggong zhongyang guanyu 'Wang Hongwen, Zhang Chunqiao, Jiang Qing, Yao Wenyuan fandang jituan zuizheng (cailiao zhi yi)'," p. 5.

[100] Zhang Zuoliang, *Zhou Enlai de zuihou shinian*, p. 320; and Fan Shuo, *Ye Jianying zai feichang shiqi*, vol. 2, p. 426.

was surely with his knowledge, reported to Mao who became very dissatisfied with what they related. His focus, however, apparently was less with the content of the meeting than with the plans of Jiang and Yao Wenyuan to disseminate a recording of the gathering to the entire Party, and he immediately ordered that the recording not be issued—instructing Zhou Enlai to enforce his order. Mao also asked to hear the recording himself, listened to a part only, and then convened the Politburo where he criticized Jiang for holding the meeting and distributing materials without authorization. Part of the Chairman's dissatisfaction with the meeting on the 25th was that historian Guo Moruo was criticized by name for past work acknowledging Confucius' contributions and attacking Qinshihuang. In fact, the criticism had been mild and demonstrated a considerable degree of respect, with Jiang interjecting that Guo's achievements were much greater than his shortcomings, but naming Guo was considered excessive, and drew Mao's rebuke. The broader issue of Jiang allegedly acting individually continued to rankle the Chairman, and when he received some *pi Lin pi Kong* materials from her on February 6, he responded a few days later that she should seek out the Politburo on such matters.[101]

The most notable issue to emerge from the late January meetings was the question of "going in through the back door." This was hardly a new issue when addressed by Chi Qun and others on the 25th, or by Jiang Qing on the 27th. Wang Hongwen had attacked the practice in his report to the Tenth Congress as the type of unhealthy tendency and bourgeois ideology that must be overcome, and it was also criticized in the joint New Year editorial. In the post-Congress period, particular attention was given to its manifestation in university admissions, a phenomenon ironically linked to Cultural Revolution reforms that reduced the role of entrance exams. A model case receiving publicity, one raised by Chi Qun on the 25th, was that of Zhong Zhimin, a second-year student whose father had arranged for him to enter a university from the PLA "by the back door," but who repented and left the university and military to work in the countryside. In any case, Ye was known to have engaged in the practice, and thus was vulnerable when Jiang accused him directly. As noted above, it was in this context that Ye wrote Mao on January 30, making a self-examination for his own failings regarding "going in through the back door," but also, and more significantly, for his capitulationist mistakes in the Kissinger talks. It is conceivable that, in offering his self-examination which Zhang Chunqiao later referred to as "a great invention turning self-criticism into a weapon [for a counterattack]," Ye was seeking to reduce the campaign's potential for disrupting the PLA, and the next day Zhou proposed that military organizations should not be subject to the "four

---

[101] See *Mao zhuan*, vol. 2, pp. 1682, 1685; Chen and Du, *Shilu*, vol. 3, part 2, p. 1026; An Jianshe, "Mao Zedong yu 'pi Lin pi Kong' ruogan wenti," pp. 58-59; *Zhou nianpu*, vol. 3, p. 648; *Mao wengao*, vol. 13, pp. 372, 375; "Zhou Enlai, Jiang Qing, Chi Qun, Xie Jingyi, Yao Wenyuan de jianghua," p. 3; and "Zhonggong zhongyang guanyu 'Wang Hongwen, Zhang Chunqiao, Jiang Qing, Yao Wenyuan fandang jituan zuizheng (cailiao zhi yi)'," p. 4.

bigs"[102] during the movement, a view adopted by the Politburo and seemingly accepted by Mao. Interestingly, there are no reports of radical objections to this proposal, and the same Politburo meeting established the seven-person small group to guide *pi Lin pi Kong*, and assigned the MAC small group responsibility for the campaign in the PLA—both measures providing significant radical authority over the campaign.[103]

Ye Jianying's letter led Mao to consider the back door matter. Also of undoubted importance was Zhou Enlai's February 6 letter following the Politburo discussion of the 5th, a discussion which reiterated the non-use of the "four bigs" in the PLA. In his letter, Zhou argued that only focusing on "going in through the back door" was too narrow and limited. On the 15th, Mao declared his position in replying to Ye: the matter had been blown out of proportion, good people entered through the back door while some bad people had entered through the front door, and the speeches of Chi Qun and Xie Jingyi on January 25 contained shortcomings and should not be distributed. While Mao's reaction was perhaps influenced by the fact that he too had engaged in the back door practice,[104] his rationale concerned the aims of the movement. Essentially, the Chairman regarded the back door issue as a distraction. He complained that the back door had become a third arrow, when the movement should only have two—the criticism of Lin Biao, and the criticism of Confucius and the retrogression from the Cultural Revolution that Confucian values represented. It is also likely that Mao believed the issue, which he had surely authorized, had become a distraction from a more important target than Ye—Zhou Enlai. He criticized the attack on the back door practice as metaphysical and one-sided, and demanded that this relatively trivial issue be relegated to investigation and research. This is indeed what happened: while "going in through the back door" remained an item of sporadic public discussion for the remainder of the year, it was no longer a cutting edge for *pi Lin pi Kong*. Meanwhile, Jiang Qing was left speechless by Mao's reaction, and was required, along with at least Wang Hongwen, to offer a self-criticism on this as well as on other issues arising from the January rallies. There was a particular irony here in that Mao had criticized Zhou for dealing with trivial matters rather than big issues going back to the Premier's management of foreign affairs in 1973, a theme picked up in Chi's January 25 speech. But in March 1974 it was Jiang Qing

---

[102] Big character posters, big debates, big blooming and big contending.

[103] *PR*, no. 35-36 (1973), p. 33; Starr, "China in 1974," p. 10n19; Barnouin and Yu, *Ten Years*, pp. 258-59; *Mao zhuan*, vol. 2, p. 1685; *Zhou nianpu*, vol. 3, p. 648; and interview with senior Party historian, February 2000.

[104] For his dancing partners. See "Jizeng huishou: Xie Jingyi, bei Mao Zhuxi fuhua de nühai" [Some Recollections: Xie Jingyi, the Girl Corrupted by Chairman Mao] (December 12, 2004), http://www.peacehall.com/news/gb/pubvp/2004/03/200403120251.shtml. In the Chairman's case, something other than nepotism could be involved. According to an academic in Beida's philosophy department at the time, a young woman, formerly a waitress at the Hangzhou guesthouse where Mao stayed, was admitted to the department on the basis of his casual remark that since her cultural level was low, she should go to university. Interview, January 2005.

who earned the Chairman's biting comment, "You too don't discuss important matters, [but] every day deal with trivial affairs."[105]

The Campaign Unfolds, February-August. While Mao's handling of the back door issue can be seen as reining in the movement in one sense, it more fundamentally reflected his determination to push the effort forward, to prevent it from losing focus and being diluted. In the following months an intense campaign unfolded, reaching a high point by early April when initial attempts to curb Cultural Revolution-style practices were made, decreasing in media intensity from mid-May, yet maintaining momentum into August. Throughout this period, although reportedly offering few concrete opinions, the Chairman engaged in the two-sided process of "emergency salvage." Authoritative official sources emphasize Mao's periodic moderation of *pi Lin pi Kong*, claiming he only sought an ideological education movement, citing his terse comments on official documents to grasp policy and guard against shortcomings, enforce unified Party leadership, and avoid enlarging the movement. These sources also note his criticisms of the radicals in general and Jiang Qing in particular—criticisms culminating in his July 17 declaration that Jiang only spoke for herself, and his simultaneous warning against forming a "small faction of four people." Yet none of these interventions reversed the thrust of the movement, thus indicating Mao's ongoing support, or at least his reluctance to move decisively against its excesses. Significantly, despite Mao's criticisms, Jiang Qing's major role in the Lin Biao-Confucius campaign was largely maintained, and received his encouragement. After his March criticism, the Chairman advised her not to feel pessimistic, waver or retreat. And even in his searching criticism on July 17, Mao again demonstrated indulgence toward Jiang, allowing her leeway as someone with "good" as well as "not so good" aspects.[106]

Given the ambiguities of the situation, the Chairman's elusiveness, and the problems of sources noted at the start of this chapter, no detailed definitive statement of the elite politics of the *pi Lin pi Kong* movement during these months is possible. While we shed light on individual aspects of the campaign below, overall we can only offer the unsurprising conclusion that Zhou Enlai, Ye Jianying and the establishment beneficiaries of the Cultural Revolution had an interest in minimizing the disruption caused by the movement, the radicals —as befit their assigned role—sought to push it forward, while Mao vacillated

---

[105] *Zhou nianpu*, vol. 3, pp. 649, 651-52; *Mao zhuan*, vol. 2, pp. 1682, 1685-86; An Jianshe, "Mao Zedong yu 'pi Lin pi Kong' ruogan wenti," p. 59; "Quarterly Chronicle and Documentation," *CQ*, no. 58 (1974), pp. 414-15, no. 59 (1974), p. 637, no. 60 (1974), p. 832; and *Mao wengao*, vol. 13, p. 372. Mao undoubtedly was not referring solely to the back door question in criticizing Jiang, but it was a trivial matter in his view.

[106] *Mao zhuan*, vol. 2, pp. 1683, 1692-94; An Jianshe, "Mao Zedong yu 'pi Lin pi Kong' ruogan wenti," pp. 58-59; *Zhou nianpu*, vol. 3, pp. 662-65, 667; and *Mao wengao*, vol. 13, pp. 372-75. In his March comment, Mao was apparently responding to Jiang's suggestion that she withdraw from active leadership.

between his aim of reasserting Cultural Revolution values and his wish to avoid the excesses of 1966-68. The contradictions of the unfolding situation mirrored Mao's ambiguity: Party leadership was repeatedly endorsed, but Party authorities were often under attack and even paralyzed; old cadres continued to be liberated, while the recruitment of young rebels who had attacked such veterans increased markedly; social and economic disruption spread, even as directives emphasizing production and banning Cultural Revolution-type activities were issued; and a broad purist policy critique emerged that even touched on areas where Mao had clearly endorsed moderation. But the character and course of *pi Lin pi Kong* was not simply a reflection of elite politics. After years of political mobilization, it was difficult to maintain campaign momentum among a jaded populace, particularly since the allegorical and theoretical messages underpinning the effort were unpersuasive or incomprehensible. To paraphrase Keith Forster's insightful characterization of the campaign in Zhejiang, in political style and thematic substance the Lin Biao-Confucius movement was (to a degree) a rerun of the Cultural Revolution, but with greatly reduced participation and enthusiasm among the masses whom Mao sought to revolutionize.[107]

While varying from place to place and unit to unit,[108] *pi Lin pi Kong* was intense from its launch in January in both massive media attention and the mobilization of work units nationwide. In this initial period and throughout the campaign, esoteric articles targeted Zhou Enlai (even if a large proportion of the population was unaware of this), with a new upsurge of anti-Zhou articles appearing in June under Jiang Qing's direction. February and March also saw intense conflict in key organizations, most notably the central headquarters units of the PLA, as well as conflicts in the localities which would last through the summer and beyond. At the same time, severe disruption developed in economic units, with coal production and transport particularly affected. Zhou Enlai and the SPC attempted to address the problem in April, but, as one source put it, with the movement at its climax there was not much that could be done about it. It took several more months of declining production before the Center, with Mao's endorsement, issued a directive on July 1 that addressed economic issues and related problems of the movement in a thorough fashion. These economic problems and the official response are discussed in detail in Chapter 3.[109]

---

[107] See Barnouin and Yu, *Ten Years*, pp. 258-59, 265-66, 268; Fenwick, "Gang of Four," pp. 247-48, 290n83; and Keith Forster, "The Cultural Revolution in Zhejiang Revisited: The Paradox of Rebellion and Factionalism, and Violence and Social Conflict amidst Economic Growth," in Law, *The Chinese Cultural Revolution Reconsidered*, p. 136.

[108] Despite the chaos created in many places and units, participants in various organizations report little more than boring meetings even during the intense initial phase of the movement. Of particular note, an academic at Beida, the very epicenter of the movement where radical influence was pronounced, recalled many wall posters, but limited disruption, and few attacks on individuals or personnel changes. Interview, January 2005. Cf. above, p. 121n30.

[109] See Liu and Wu, *China's Socialist Economy*, pp. 387-90; Yan and Gao, *Turbulent Decade*,

Notwithstanding these efforts to bring greater order to the situation, in April and lasting into the summer another Cultural Revolution-style phenomenon emerged, wall posters criticizing individual leaders, including Politburo members Li Desheng, Chen Xilian, Xu Shiyou and Hua Guofeng. By the summer, however, similar to the effort to restore economic order, various themes of the movement had moderated.[110]

Throughout this period, a broad-based radical critique mirroring the rhetoric of 1966-68 unfolded, one that went far beyond the superstructure issues emphasized at the Tenth Congress. Naturally those issues, particularly efforts to enforce harsh strictures in culture and the arts[111] and to staunch the erosion of Cultural Revolution education reforms, received intense attention, but the radical perspective extended to virtually all areas that were hotly debated half a dozen years earlier. Ann Fenwick has ably summarized the main contents of this comprehensive, across-the-board critique that included organizational norms and leadership composition, dealing with capitalist roaders in the Party, material incentives, industrial management, national development strategies, and foreign trade.[112] Here we simply note that despite Cultural Revolution-style denunciations of, e.g., worshiping foreign things, placing tonnage (i.e., quota fulfillment rather than politics) in command, and restoring to office those who had fallen into obscurity, the effect on policy—as opposed to disruption in work

---

pp. 450-51; "Zhonggong zhongyang guanyu zhuageming cushengchan de tongzhi" [CCP Central Committee Notice on Grasping Revolution and Promoting Production] (July 1, 1974), in *CRDB*, pp. 1-2; and below, pp. 196ff.

[110] See Starr, "China in 1974," pp. 8-9; Fenwick, "Gang of Four," p. 214; and "Quarterly Chronicle and Documentation," *CQ*, no. 59 (1974), pp. 626-28, 637-38, 644. Examples of moderation included *Red Flag's* praise of an outstanding answer on a chemistry exam by a student who entered college on the recommendation of a PLA unit, a far cry from Zhang Tiesheng's blank paper, and increasing emphasis on study and the training of "worker theorists."

In early April, commenting in the name of the Party Center, Zhou endorsed several provinces' restrictive measures concerning wall posters. *Zhou nianpu*, vol. 3, pp. 663-64. Some sources summarized in Forster, *Rebellion*, p. 290n167, claim that Mao belatedly endorsed the use of wall posters in early May, but the central directive that supposedly reflected his approval did not mention wall posters, although it did declare exposing people involved with Lin Biao was completely necessary. Of the Politburo members attacked, the military figures reflect the ongoing focus on the PLA, while Hua Guofeng was arguably singled out because of the *Song of the Gardener* issue in Hunan. See "Zhonggong zhongyang guanyu pi Lin pi Kong yundong jige zhengzhi wenti de tongzhi" [CCP Central Committee Circular on Some Political Questions in the Lin Biao-Confucius Campaign] (May 18, 1974), in *CRDB*, p. 1; and below, n. 111.

[111] Prominent cases were: 1) controversy concerning Italian director Antonioni's film *China* as slandering the Cultural Revolution (see below); 2) attacks on the Shanxi opera *Going up to Peach Peak Three Times* as attempting to invoke Liu Shaoqi by allegedly recalling the activities of Liu's wife; and 3) criticism of the Hunan opera *Song of the Gardener* for promoting the revisionist line in education by encouraging teachers to act as gardeners and cultivate their students. See *History of the Party*, p. 363; and "Quarterly Chronicle and Documentation," *CQ*, no. 58 (1974), pp. 412-14.

[112] See Fenwick, "Gang of Four," pp. 256ff.

places, bureaucratic units and localities—was very limited. Generally speaking, the critique simply maintained the stalemate on consolidation that took hold in 1973, or at most achieved modest reversals as in education.[113]

Speculatively, the most likely factor underpinning this situation was that Mao probably saw the movement as a rebalancing, a reemphasis on broad values that was not meant to sweep aside necessary policy changes. As a case in point, the radical claim that importing technology benefited capitalists and denigrated China's workers seemingly challenged the import program initiated and authorized by the Chairman in 1971-73, but imports continued to grow in 1974.[114] Similarly, despite their reservations concerning the rehabilitation of cadres, another Mao program, Politburo radicals were at best able to slow the process during *pi Lin pi Kong*. A case in point concerned Chen Pixian, Shanghai's First Party Secretary at the start of the Cultural Revolution. From spring 1973, the question of Chen's rehabilitation dragged on for a year and a half while the "gang" and local Shanghai radicals objected, but in fall 1974 Mao decided the case in Chen's favor.[115] In addition to the constraints created by the Chairman's attitude, another factor for policy continuity was, in sharp contrast to 1966-68, the relative institutional cohesion of the Party and state during the Lin Biao-Confucius campaign. In addition to the emphasis on the principle of unified Party leadership, the Politburo functioned throughout the movement and addressed policy problems, and the State Council provided administrative leadership while suffering only a pale reflection of the disruption of 1966-68. The central if elusive figure in this institutional setting was Zhou Enlai.

Zhou Enlai as Victim and Leader of the Movement. There is no doubt that, together with the PLA, Premier Zhou was one of the two central targets of *pi Li pi Kong*. This is apparent from Mao's discontent with Zhou since late 1972, his being linked to Confucius by the Chairman at various points in 1973, and the vicious criticism on Mao's demand during the November-December Politburo meetings. Although Mao ended the extreme pressure on Zhou by mid-December, the allegorical references to the Premier that had been building since the Tenth

---

[113] E.g., downgrading or discarding entrance examinations in many areas. See *ibid.*, pp. 266-67. Note, however, the case of the chemistry exam cited above, p. 157n110.

[114] See Nai-Ruenn Chen, "China's Foreign Trade, 1950-74," in Joint Economic Committee, Congress of the United States, *China: A Reassessment of the Economy* (Washington DC: U.S. Government Printing Office, 1975), p. 649.

[115] *Mao zhuan*, vol. 2, p. 1698; and Perry and Li, *Proletarian Power*, pp. 182-83. While the radical critique of restoring Confucian families to office has been interpreted as blanket opposition to rehabilitating veteran cadres, and the "gang" in fact made the liberation of individual veterans difficult, the actual situation was more complex. The position articulated by Wang Hongwen in his January 14 speech that was clearly influenced by Mao's stance was that old cadres were the CCP's precious treasures whose talents should be used once they had genuinely reformed. In addition, as in the case of Ma Tianshui, practical support was given to old cadres judged to be politically reformed and supportive of the radical cause. See "Wang Hongwen zai zhongyang dushuban," pp. 3-4; above, p. 117.

Congress intensified during the Lin Biao-Confucius campaign into summer 1974. Many of the characterizations of Confucius, not least repeated references to his position as Prime Minister and personal characteristics associated with Zhou, pointed to the Premier, while the most obvious sign was media criticism of Zhou Gong, the Duke of Zhou.[116] Although claims of ignorance by those involved in writing the historical allegories may be disingenuous, the fact that Chi Qun apparently required briefing before his January 25 speech so that he would fully understand that Zhou was the key target, and Chi's comment not long afterward that "[Confucius] can be whoever you think he resembles," suggest that some uncertainty surrounded Zhou's identity as the sage.[117] The essential point, however, is that those in the inner circle understood fully that Zhou was under attack, they would read the ebb and flow of attacks as some sort of indicator of his political health, and the Premier simply had to put up with it.

Zhou's vulnerability to esoteric media criticism appears to have been more or less continuous regardless of the shifting course of *pi Lin pi Kong*. Unsurprisingly, Jiang Qing was active during the campaign's most intense period at the start of the year in encouraging a series of articles aimed at the Premier. In particular, she directed the *Liang Xiao* group to prepare a treatise, "Confucius the Man," that portrayed Confucius in terms of Zhou's background and work style, even including his serious illness.[118] Also striking was a new upsurge in articles attacking Zhou by analogy in June, the very period in which the overall movement was moderating. In mid-June, Jiang convened a meeting of *Liang Xiao* and urged the group to write articles criticizing "the present-day Confucius." While this terminology had, at least formally, been linked to Lin Biao, she subsequently identified "the target of the current movement [as] the chief Confucian in the Party," and called attention to a foreign news dispatch depicting herself as a "radical" and Zhou as a "moderate." It would seem, then,

---

[116] According to Lin Qingshan in *Mao Zedong sixiang yanjiu* [Research on Mao Zedong Thought], no. 3 (1988), cited in Barnouin and Yu, *Ten Years*, pp. 263-64, in late 1973 Mao commented that "the time is ripe to criticize Zhou Gong." We have reservations, however, about the reliability of Lin's work.

[117] See Yan and Gao, *Turbulent Decade*, pp. 438-39; "Zhonggong zhongyang guanyu 'Wang Hongwen, Zhang Chunqiao, Jiang Qing, Yao Wenyuan fandang jituan zuizheng (cailiao zhi san)' de tongzhi ji fujian" [CCP Central Committee Notice and Attachment concerning "Proof of the Crimes of the Wang Hongwen, Zhang Chunqiao, Jiang Qing, Yao Wenyuan Anti-Party Clique (third batch of materials)"] (September 23, 1977), in *CRDB*, pp. 16, 26; and above, p. 124n35. In addition to obscure historical analogies, there were contemporary themes demonstrating that Zhou was a target, e.g., Wang Hongwen's January and March statements equating criticizing "ultra-leftism" with criticizing the Cultural Revolution. "Wang Hongwen zai zhongyang dushuban," p. 4; and *Zhou nianpu*, vol. 3, p. 657.

[118] See "Zhonggong zhongyang guanyu 'Wang Hongwen, Zhang Chunqiao, Jiang Qing, Yao Wenyuan fandang jituan zuizheng (cailiao zhi san)'," pp. 16, 26. In addition to the articles targeting Zhou, the "gang" assertedly depicted Jiang Qing as the "queen of Legalism" by encouraging a series of articles eulogizing historical female rulers.

that Jiang's writ to attack the Premier was not restricted by overall trends in the campaign. Perhaps also relevant to the June upsurge was the coincidence in timing noted earlier—i.e., Jiang's new involvement in criticizing Zhou came as Mao, for whatever reason, called for a new revision of Yan'an's nine articles that singled out Zhou as the representative of empiricist errors.[119]

Zhou suffered in other respects during the course of *pi Lin pi Kong*. Within the Ministry of Foreign Affairs, where Zhou's reputation had already taken a battering due to Mao's various criticisms in 1973, the more conservative faction that had supported the Premier during the post-1965 upheavals in the ministry began to disintegrate, leaving the "two ladies" with their current critical posture toward Zhou even more dominant.[120] The Premier also had to put up with personal humiliations. For example, in mid-March, shortly after Zhou left his hospital bed following treatment for a relapse, Jiang Qing asked him to go to an exhibit of "black paintings." From 1971 to 1973, the Premier had supervised production of these paintings along nationalistic rather than revolutionary themes for hotels and export. Many were produced in Shanghai, and reportedly had drawn praise from Wang Hongwen, Zhang Chunqiao and Yao Wenyuan, but in the context of the Lin Biao-Confucius campaign they were denounced as a restoration of "the black line in literature and art." With criticism of the paintings growing, and the introduction to the exhibition claiming that they had emerged as a result of "a certain person's encouragement and support," Zhou was pressured into attending.[121] This case and others were clearly made more difficult for the Premier by his deteriorating physical condition. In the most poignant instance, when Zhou was having his first blood transfusion in April, he was summoned to a Politburo meeting by Wang Hongwen. Although Zhou's doctor and Deng Yingchao sought leave for him to be excused, Wang insisted and the Premier was forced to attend.[122]

In addition to such indignities and physical deterioration, Zhou was periodically on the receiving end of Jiang Qing's hectoring within the Politburo. In his recollections, Wu De, the Politburo member nominally responsible for culture, recounted instances of the Premier's difficulties in coping with Jiang on cultural matters. A case in point, one of the most prominent examples of cultural narrowness during the Lin Biao-Confucius campaign, concerned the film *China* by the Italian director Antonioni, made in 1972 with official cooperation that

---

[119] See *History of the Party*, pp. 363-64; Yan and Gao, *Turbulent Decade*, pp. 441-42; and above, pp. 138-39. The possible link between Mao's action and Jiang's activities is speculative, as we have no direct evidence that she was aware that the Chairman had reopened the nine articles issue.

[120] Barnouin and Yu, *Chinese Foreign Policy*, pp. 37-38.

[121] See Yan and Gao, *Turbulent Decade*, pp. 436-38.

[122] See Zhang Zuoliang, *Zhou Enlai de zuihou shinian*, pp. 328-29. While this case paints Wang Hongwen as uncaring, it is unclear precisely what Wang knew of Zhou's condition at that moment, or what pressure he (Wang) was under. There is other evidence suggesting that, overall, Wang was very concerned about the Premier's health. See below, pp. 211n61, 250n19.

reflected the new foreign policy openness to the West. A non-ideological film, it presented a realistic rather than heroic picture of Chinese life. Now, in late January and early February 1974, a fierce outburst of xenophobic criticism denounced Antonioni's creation as failing to reflect China's new born things and new spirit, instead using the camera to slander the Cultural Revolution, insult the Chinese people, and attack the leadership. Apart from the public response, Jiang Qing pursued the question of responsibility for allowing the film to be made. Wu De said he had not seen it, with Jiang responding by telling Wu to view it and find out who was culpable. Wu proposed that the film not be shown in China, but Jiang insisted that it be screened, in Wu's view as part of her effort to get at Zhou. In pressing the investigation Jiang asserted that the affair was not simply a mistake, but treason. In the Politburo she sharply criticized the Premier on the issue, although not by name. Zhou's response, as in other cases of fending off Jiang's attacks, was to claim he was not clear about the matter, and simply to avoid the issue from then on. This was apparently the limit of what the Premier could do in his own defense without Mao's intervention. The Chairman's intervention finally came in July, quietly as he took Yan'an's nine articles off the table, and dramatically as he told the radicals in front of the whole Politburo to stop their criticism of Zhou and Ye Jianying while holding hands with the veteran leaders. After having relentlessly undermined the Premier throughout 1973-74, Mao now provided significant respite.[123]

Even as Zhou endured attacks in the media and Politburo, he performed an important if unclear leadership role in the Lin Biao-Confucius campaign. As Premier, he was necessarily concerned with the impact of the movement in State Council ministries, providing directives on its implementation in at least some cases.[124] As the leader responsible for the daily work of the Party Center and for Politburo meetings, he clearly bore some responsibility for the movement that was frequently on the Politburo's agenda. Zhou's function as ranking member of the seven-person small group is more uncertain. Exceptionally little is known about his involvement with the group, apart from convening a joint meeting with the MAC small group to discuss campaign issues in various departments and localities on February 21, and participating in the group's meeting on May 3. Nor, as indicated earlier, is much known more generally about the group's relationship in practice to the full Politburo to which it was formally subordinate.[125]

---

[123] See Wu De, "Guowuyuan wenhuazu," pp. 79-80; *PR*, no. 5 (1974), pp. 7-10; Starr, "China in 1974," p. 11; "Quarterly Chronicle and Documentation," *CQ*, no. 58 (1974), p. 412; and above, pp. 110, 139.

[124] For example, Zhou issued instructions to the State Physical Culture and Sports Commission in March on carrying out *pi Lin pi Kong*. See Yan and Gao, *Turbulent Decade*, p. 435; and *Zhou nianpu*, vol. 3, p. 655.

[125] See *Zhou nianpu*, vol. 3, pp. 653, 668; and above, p. 116. Arguably, Zhou's role in the group could be seen as analogous to the situation of Deng Xiaoping in 1975, when Deng presided over *ad hoc* small group meetings convened on Mao's orders in November 1975 for the purpose of criticizing

More important than the Premier's formal positions was his interaction with Mao. Although his personal contact was apparently largely limited to nine occasions in the context of the Chairman receiving foreign visitors,[126] this was considerably more than Jiang Qing, who reportedly was banned from seeing Mao, and equal to that of Wang Hongwen, who also attended all the foreign receptions during the Lin Biao-Confucius campaign. The Politburo member, and member of the seven-person *pi Lin pi Kong* small group, who presumably had the greatest access to the Chairman was Wang Dongxing, the Zhongnanhai security chief who was attached to Mao's household. Given Wang's personal inclination to favor Zhou and his difficult relationship with Jiang, this was a potentially advantageous channel for the Premier.[127] Moreover, in one respect, Zhou's formal responsibilities greatly bolstered his interaction with Mao. As convener of the Politburo, Zhou drafted reports on the body's activities and recommendations, reports sometimes, as in the post-Tenth Congress period, cosigned by Wang Hongwen,[128] and sometimes apparently not. While this did not prevent others from writing the Chairman to express their views, it did provide Zhou with a legitimate and regular means that could be used to influence Mao. At the same time, Zhou was often the vehicle through which Mao conveyed important decisions and their political meaning. Thus it was Zhou who not only circulated Mao's decision on the back door issue, but who also informed Chi Qun and Xie Jingyi that this was the Chairman's criticism of Jiang Qing.[129]

How effective was the Premier in using the opportunities provided by his formal positions and channels to Mao? This is particularly difficult to judge given the truncated and distorted record. It is unclear to what extent the proposals Zhou put to Mao were his own or reflected a Politburo consensus, and, in any case, we believe they would have reflected his sense of the Chairman's preferences and tolerances at any given moment. While there can be little doubt that Zhou's fundamental objective was to limit disruption, in cases such as the Physical Culture and Sports Commission, his instructions were for the relevant leaders to acknowledge the attacks of the "masses" and make self-criticisms, an approach that reportedly frustrated the radicals.[130] In other areas, notably his efforts in

---

him; see below, pp. 402ff. This appears unlikely since, unlike Deng whose responsibilities were progressively whittled away, Zhou continued to exercise important functions.

[126] On February 22 and 25, March 25, April 2, and May 7, 11, 18, 25 and 29. In addition, Zhou and most Politburo members attended the July 17 meeting when Mao first raised the "small faction of four" question.

[127] Another link to Mao was the "two ladies." While it is uncertain to what degree they served as a link during the campaign, they clearly played some role. Notwithstanding the tensions created by their actions in enforcing Mao's negative attitudes toward Zhou over the previous year, they at least were established and, we believe, largely accurate purveyors of Mao's wishes.

[128] Such joint reports occurred on January 18 and April 3, but Wang's involvement in Zhou's reports was not otherwise noted. See *Zhou nianpu*, vol. 3, pp. 644, 661.

[129] See *Mao zhuan*, vol. 2, p. 1686; and *Zhou nianpu*, vol. 3, p. 652.

conjunction with the SPC to deal with setbacks to the economy, it took over two months before a sufficiently strong central directive emerged, and another three months or so before a significant improvement in production took hold.[131]

Specific instances suggest the possibilities and limits of Zhou's influence. In the famous "snail incident" of early February 1974, Jiang Qing pursued the xenophobic theme then being spread by criticism of Antonioni's film. The background was similar in that the issue arose out of the post-Lin Biao openness to the West. In 1973, the Fourth Ministry of Machine Building proposed purchasing a production line for color televisions from abroad, a proposal receiving Politburo approval including that of Jiang and her radical colleagues. When ministry representatives went to the US toward the end of the year, each member of the delegation received a small glass snail from their hosts as a gift. When *pi Lin pi Kong* unfolded, however, this was revealed to Jiang, who went to the ministry and characterized the incident as an insult that depicted China as crawling, denounced the plan to introduce the color television production line as "worshiping foreigners" and "knuckling under to imperialist pressure," ordered the snails returned to the US Liaison Office, and declared that the project would be cancelled. Zhou quickly intervened, instructing the MFA to investigate the case, an investigation that concluded that such a gift was common practice and involved no malice. The Premier indicated his agreement with the report, and submitted it to Mao who also agreed. The Politburo then declared Jiang's talk at the ministry erroneous, ordered a halt to its distribution, and recalled those copies already issued. Nevertheless, the contract was in fact cancelled (causing a decade's setback in the introduction of color television to China), and investigations into the affair were conducted. The incident is instructive. Zhou seemingly acted before approaching Mao, perhaps banking on the fact the whole project was pursuant to the policy of importing foreign technology that had been explicitly endorsed—as opposed to unobtrusively accepted—by the Chairman, and that Jiang's demand to return the snails to the US diplomatic mission would have been an unnecessary hiccup in Mao's effort to cultivate the US relationship. Yet Zhou's victory was partial since the contract was cancelled, and Mao allowed the xenophobic features of the movement to continue.[132]

---

[130] See above, p. 161n124. In this case, Zhou advised Minister Wang Meng to welcome the masses' serious attitude in criticizing him.

[131] See below, pp. 198-99.

[132] See Yan and Gao, *Turbulent Decade*, pp. 433-34; and Chen and Du, *Shilu*, vol. 3, part 2, pp. 1036-38. In addition to the Fourth Ministry of Machine Building, the SPC, Ministry of Foreign Trade, and the State Broadcasting Bureau were attacked for their involvement in the affair.

Strikingly, Li Xiannian strongly backed Jiang Qing when the issue surfaced, a demeanor consistent with his opportunistic behavior on other occasions, and one contrasting with that of Zhou in this case. See interview with Sun Shunxing, in Li Zhongqiang, "Yiqi huangtang de woniu shijian" [The Ridiculous "Snail Incident"] (October 14, 2002), http://secretchina.com/news/gb/articles/2/10/14/26598.html; and below, p. 389.

A final case indicates the limits of Zhou's effectiveness. As we have seen, on February 6 Zhou reported the Politburo's (or probably just his own) concern over the emphasis on "going in through the back door," a report which perhaps contributed to Mao's rejection of the issue as an unnecessary "third arrow" detracting from the main objectives of *pi Lin pi Kong*. In the same letter, however, Zhou probably conveyed (for the second time) the Politburo's view that PLA organs should not be subjected to the "four bigs," and thus to the disruption of largely unrestricted debate and criticism. In addition, the Politburo advocated leadership of the movement by military Party committees, and the banning of such Cultural Revolution practices as establishing fighting groups among the troops and linking up with army units in other places. Mao circled Zhou's letter raising the back door issue and reporting on "the Politburo's situation," but there was little to indicate his specific endorsement of the proposals restricting the conduct of *pi Lin pi Kong* in the PLA.[133] In any case, within days major conflict erupted within this second major target singled out by Mao at the end of 1973.

The PLA under Attack. As we have seen, Mao set his sights on the military at the December Politburo meetings. Several issues were involved: returning the army to unambiguous civilian control, further weakening any remnant Lin Biao influence, and countering the dispersion of PLA power to long-ensconced regional commanders. All of these matters were addressed in personnel measures beginning with the rotation of regional commanders. The issue of dispersion was also one of the themes of *pi Lin pi Kong* through demands for centralization and attacks on "big warlords."[134] But for Mao, something even more fundamental was involved, as seen in his warning against the reappearance of revisionism. Significantly, the Chairman raised the danger of revisionism when addressing military leaders on December 21. Wang Hongwen reiterated Mao's warning in his address to the Central Study Class on January 14, when he also criticized unconditional obedience in the army, called for more political work, held that there was nothing to fear from the "four bigs," and advocated appointing a young

---

[133] See *Zhou nianpu*, vol. 3, pp. 648-49. Precisely what happened on this matter is obscure in several regards. 1) Concerning the "four bigs," the Politburo reportedly *decided* (*jueding*) to ban them on January 31, while *believing* (*renwei*) this was the proper course on February 5. 2) At neither Politburo meeting was any radical dissent recorded, while Wang Hongwen joined Zhou in submitting a joint report on February 1, but not on February 6. 3) Zhou's letter of the 6th reported on "the Politburo's situation" in unknown detail, and then went on to raise the back door issue which was not listed as specifically discussed by the body. 4) In both cases, Mao simply circled (*quanyue*) the letters concerned, a procedure strictly meaning that they had been seen, but more broadly suggesting that the recipient had no objection. For Politburo members generally, this was a somewhat fraught situation, since they could be blamed in the future for failing to detect an erroneous political development. For Mao, however, it could simply mean that he had not made up his mind.

[134] See Fenwick, "Gang of Four," pp. 210, 238, 273-74; "Zhonggong zhongyang guanyu 'Wang Hongwen, Zhang Chunqiao, Jiang Qing, Yao Wenyuan fandang jituan zuizheng (cailiao zhi yi)'," p 5; and above, p. 141. The slogan "knock down the big warlords" appeared widely throughout the country in March, reportedly creating serious disorder in PLA units.

military region commander in his thirties to overcome obstacles to cultivating successors in the army. And, as we have seen, some of Jiang Qing's earliest efforts to spread *pi Lin pi Kong* involved military units, while the first major mobilization meeting in the capital on January 24 concerned the army.[135] In short, the earliest efforts of the emerging campaign focused on the military, but it was an effort that met significant resistance.

The most intensive onslaught against the military began in early February and extended into March. It focused on the central departments and service arms of the PLA in Beijing, notably the "three headquarters" (the General Staff Department, General Logistics Department, and GPD) and the navy and air force, as well as extending to military-related organizations such as the PLA's Science and Technology Commission for National Defense. These activities were apparently conducted under the authority and leadership of Wang Hongwen and Zhang Chunqiao, the second and third ranking members of the MAC small group, with Jiang Qing also deeply involved and taking a particular interest in army cultural activities. Of all developments within the PLA during *pi Lin pi Kong*, these are the most frequently discussed, but in a highly limited and partisan fashion to demonstrate the culpability of the "gang." As with the seven-person group responsible for the overall Lin Biao-Confucius effort, the functioning of the MAC small group and its relationship to the full MAC is largely unknown. A number of questions concern Ye Jianying, the head of the group: Was his position entirely nominal, or was he able to exert some influence as Zhou did in the political/administrative sphere? Was he systematically excluded from discussions concerning measures carried out in the three headquarters in February-March, or ignored by the radicals on a more *ad hoc* basis? Was he directly involved as either target or leader in the criticism of the General Staff Department where he served as Party secretary?[136] Questions can also be asked about Deng Xiaoping's definite but elusive role in the movement, questions we address at the end of this chapter. More nuanced information is available on another group member, Su Zhenhua, information we examine after reviewing the post-Mao charges concerning the radicals' activities in this period.

Radical discussions of the need for serious measures at the three headquarters surfaced on February 8, only two days after the Politburo again advocated banning the "four bigs" in the military. According to standard accounts, all of which appear based on the official documents issued in 1976-77 detailing the sins of the "gang," Wang and Zhang convened a meeting where they claimed

---

[135] See "Wang Hongwen zai zhongyang dushuban," pp. 3, 4, 6; and above, pp. 142, 146. Wang's reference to the "four bigs" did not specify PLA units.

[136] Ye's standard biography, *Ye zhuan*, p. 623, devotes a single paragraph short on detail to this period. While its claim that Ye resisted the "gang's" activities is possibly true at some level, no subtle understanding of his actions or the situation is conveyed. Moreover, during a March 8 meeting for which a summary record exists (see above, p. 14n33), Ye reportedly advocated sending people to military bases to "light fires."

the General Staff Department leaders "were so far to the right they could not go any farther," the power of the GPD should be seized, and "the more completely the General Logistics Department collapses the better." On February 23, after receiving a letter addressed to her and Ye, Jiang Qing commented on the need to "light fires" in the logistics department, and passed her comment on to Wang, but not to Ye. Two days later Jiang, based on her reading of letters submitted during the movement, declared the General Staff's problems were so large that lighting fires would be needed there as well. In early March, radical pressure intensified. On the 5th, Jiang and Zhang called a meeting of cultural officials including Chen Yading, deputy head of the GPD's cultural division. Jiang concluded that matters had deteriorated to such an extent that "it seems we must seize power," and nominated Chen Yading to be in charge of army cultural work. In implementing the decision, the masses were aroused to struggle against those who had "committed evils," reportedly resulting in organizational chaos. The next day Wang, after hearing a report by the General Staff, asserted the need to continue to lift the lid to expose the top echelon, smashing it open and even using bombs if necessary. On March 15, Wang visited the General Staff headquarters again, this time allegedly attacking Ye's leadership of the General Staff's combat operations department. In words resonant with Mao's late 1973 criticism of the MAC for neglecting military affairs, and also his aspersions concerning Zhou if the enemy attacked, Wang claimed that if the Soviet revisionists or US imperialists attacked, the operations department would amount to nothing more than the puppet Peace Preservation Association under the Japanese occupation.[137]

What can one make of this? A more subtle appreciation can be gained from examining the performance of Su Zhenhua, political commissar of the navy, member of the six-person MAC small group and alternate member of the Politburo, and—not least—a Mao favorite, in the conduct of *pi Lin pi Kong* in his service. The information is not unbiased, as it comes from the memoirs of Navy Commander Xiao Jingguang who, as we saw in Chapter 1, had been effectively deposed in 1973 and bore animosity toward Su as a result, but it provides revealing insights. The story begins on January 23, 1974, when Jiang Qing, having organized a meeting to launch the Lin Biao-Confucius campaign in the navy, sent Chi Qun and Xie Jingyi to participate, and had them present a handwritten letter and materials to Su. As befit his position, Su declared the navy's stance (*biaotai*)

---

[137] Chen and Du, *Shilu*, vol. 3, part 2, pp. 1042-43, 1048-49; Li Ke and Hao Shengzhang, *"Wenhua dageming" zhong de Renmin Jiefangjun* [The PLA during the "Cultural Revolution"] (Beijing: Zhonggong dangshi ziliao chubanshe, 1989), pp. 170-71, 173; Yan and Gao, *Turbulent Decade*, pp. 434-35; and above, p. 133. Another notable if obscure development was Zhang Chunqiao's March 11 order to the *PLA Daily* to carry only NCNA dispatches, and cease publishing its own articles, a ban which lasted 178 days. See Chen and Du, pp. 1050-51.

Evidence of Mao's awareness and approval of the radicals' activities is indicated by the fact that, when ordering Xie Jingyi and Chi Qun to go to the GPD and "light fires" in early March, Jiang assured them that their safety would be guaranteed because she had already arranged with Wang Dongxing to provide bodyguards for them. Ji Xichen, *Shi wu qianli de niandai*, vol. 2, p. 616.

in favor of Jiang's proposal for active participation in the movement. Others had to *biaotai* as well, including Xiao who admitted to reading too many Confucian books which cast an influence he needed to eliminate. Xiao's account is critical of Su for his willingness to go along with Jiang's desire to make the navy a *pi Lin pi Kong* experimental point, acting in a way that sidelined the navy's Party committee, adopting Wang Hongwen's approach of "lifting the lid," attacking leading cadres (e.g., charging that Xiao had "negated the Cultural Revolution" in a 1972 speech to a *pi Lin zhengfeng* meeting), and catering to whatever Jiang wanted. Yet Xiao admitted it was a situation in which Jiang was able to brandish Mao's flag, with the result that many followed her, and no one, not even those like himself who were ill disposed, could sing a different tune.[138]

Xiao Jingguang's account, taken together with fragments from the official denunciations of the "gang," make some things reasonably clear. First, there can be no doubt about Jiang Qing's authority in the military sphere. Not only did Su Zhenhua allegedly cater to her every wish, but even ordinary cadres apparently understood this was the case. Thus the February letter raising problems in the logistics department, presumably from cadres in that unit, was addressed to Marshal Ye, head of the small group overseeing the campaign in the PLA, and Jiang, who had no formal military role. In addition, Jiang did not feel it necessary to pass on her comments on the letter to Ye. Nearly a month later, when considering the GPD's cultural issues, she almost off-handedly remarked to Zhang Chunqiao that he could "make a suggestion to the MAC of our opinion [to put Chen Yading in charge of PLA culture]," a sign she was informing the notionally top military body of her decision rather than seeking its permission.[139] It hardly requires argument that, the claims of Mao's biographers notwithstanding, none of this was possible without the Chairman's clearly understood backing.

A second, less certain observation is that the radicals' aim, at least in the first instance, may simply have been to achieve full mobilization behind Mao's new movement. Regarded by the radicals as a conservative force, the army had been largely perfunctory in handling propaganda on Confucius in 1973, and now demonstrated little enthusiasm for the new campaign. The three headquarters were, according to Jiang, run by diehard bureaucrats, and Wang and Zhang criticized their passive attitude. Moreover, at a meeting on February 10 concerning the engineering, railway, artillery and second artillery forces, Wang and Zhang complained that there were few wall posters and the movement had not developed. Zhang singled out Engineering Corps Commander Chen Shiju for poor leadership, forcing him to admit he had not firmly grasped the campaign.[140]

Yet the rhetoric of "lighting fires," "lifting the lid," and especially "seizing power from the top down," suggests additional objectives of changing the PLA's

---

[138] See *Xiao Jingguang huiyilu (xuji)*, pp. 337-40; and above, pp. 41-42.

[139] Yan and Gao, *Turbulent Decade*, p. 434.

[140] See Barnouin and Yu, *Ten Years*, p. 260; and Li and Hao, *"Wenhua dageming,"* pp. 170-71.

leadership, and inserting their followers. This is clearly plausible given radical suspicion of military conservatism, as well as personal tensions such as those between Wang and Xu Shiyou. Yet there is little evidence of attempts to force personnel changes,[141] with the Chen Yading affair almost unique as a case where an individual was designated to seize power in a military unit. The Chen affair is also mysterious in that it is unclear from whom power was to be seized, while within the GPD as a whole, if not "seized," power had already been stripped from Li Desheng with his transfer to Shenyang. Who concretely led the department before Zhang Chunqiao's appointment as GPD head in January 1975 is unclear, but given the GPD's ideological functions and the aims of *pi Lin pi Kong*, it was virtually inevitable that the radicals would fill the political vacuum. As for Chen Yading, when he sought to carry out Jiang Qing's instructions on March 17, he did not dare to seek out the Party organization or department heads since the situation was unclear, and there was a danger of contacting the wrong person.[142] In short, whatever larger goals the radicals harbored, there is little indication that much power was "seized" in PLA central organs.

The intentions of the "gang" notwithstanding, disruption within central military organizations soon became unacceptable to Mao. On March 20, the Chairman criticized Jiang Qing while rejecting her request for a meeting. His comments apparently did not specify the chaotic developments in the PLA, instead complaining of her failure to listen to him, assuming special privileges, and not dealing with major matters, but they coincided with the end of excessive measures in the three headquarters and service arms. According to official sources, Mao had detected the radicals' activities not long after Jiang's March 5 talk. The day after Mao's March 20 criticism, moreover, Chen Yading, accompanying Wang Hongwen and Zhang Chunqiao, admitted that in spreading Jiang's talk on the 5th he had spoken irresponsibly, while Jiang herself soon proposed to Mao that she retreat from active duty. Despite having made the PLA a key target, granting Jiang

---

[141] A seeming, if vaguely reported exception was Zhang Chunqiao's alleged big adjustment of responsible personnel in a department under the General Staff on March 18. Chen and Du, *Shilu*, vol. 3, part 2, p. 1049.

[142] Li and Hao, *"Wenhua dageming,"* p. 173. A junior GPD cadre at the time provides an interesting perspective on these events. First, he confirms that the department was indeed thrown into chaos by the campaign, after having gradually reclaimed a degree of normal functions from 1970 following the Cultural Revolution. He further described Chen Yading as very ambitious and advantaged by his participation in a group helping prepare speeches for Jiang on PLA arts issues in 1965-66. In contrast, former deputy head of the unit, Chen Qitong, had both leftist credentials and more substantial accomplishments, but had been criticized and demoted during the Cultural Revolution and mainly just wanted to avoid disruption of GPD work. Both Chens, and many other GPD leaders, pledged loyalty to Jiang, and, according to our source's knowledge, they were not engaged in any kind of power struggle. In general terms, during the post-1966 period department cadres felt orders from Mao or Lin Biao had to be obeyed, but they were uncertain of the authority of Jiang and other actors, and would hedge their bets to the extent possible. In 1974, while some younger cadres sought to use the movement for rapid advancement, most department members were not interested in *pi Lin pi Kong*, sought safety, and simply waited on developments. Interview, January 2005.

authority over the movement in the military, and allowing more than a month of building pressure, Mao now turned against his wife. The timing suggests a link to the excesses in the three departments, even if this is not absolutely certain.[143]

While the overheated activities in central military organizations seemingly stopped, this did not mean that *pi Lin pi Kong* was over in the army. Throughout the first half of 1974 and into the summer, campaign activities were carried out at the military region and provincial military district levels. According to one account, the wall posters that began to appear in April attacked 35 military cadres, including seven military region and six military district commanders.[144] Also, given the still significant if declining political role of PLA officers in the localities, military leaders would be involved in the conduct of the movement in provinces and cities, as leaders as well as targets (see below). The most significant developments concerned the criticism of the rotated military region commanders, both in the regions themselves, and then in August-September at a central conference convened on Mao's orders. Chapter 3 examines the outcome of this critical conference, notably its role in calling a halt to the Lin Biao-Confucius campaign. Here we assess the criticism of these commanders. While not a great deal is known about this criticism, it seemingly was not nearly as harsh as the attacks suffered by many PLA leaders during the Cultural Revolution, yet the process still created considerable anxiety within China's top military elite.[145]

We must again emphasize the limits to what is known about this process, the paradoxes involved, and thus the high degree of uncertainty in any assessment. As indicated previously, the transfer of the commanders encouraged criticism of them by their former subordinates. This situation may have allowed these generals to escape face-to-face criticism, but, in accord with Mao's demand for "back-to-back struggle" (*bei kao bei douzheng*) where higher-level officers criticized each other *in absentia*, it produced considerable material on their pasts that was sent to the Politburo. In some respects, this was worse than face-to-face struggle, since those attacked had no opportunity to refute charges made against them. While clearly flowing from Mao's plan, it is unclear to what degree the *pi Lin pi Kong* campaign in the military regions was centrally managed initially. According to a close student of the period, criticism of the military in the localities was basically carried out by local radicals, while Jiang Qing only set up a few trial points, and did not undertake a comprehensive effort. Xu Shiyou's

---

[143] See Chen and Du, *Shilu*, vol. 3, part 2, p. 1049; *Mao wengao*, vol. 13, pp. 372-75; and above, p. 166.

[144] Dittmer, *Continuous Revolution*, p. 150n18. Dittmer does not provide the original source and only lists four military region commanders: Li Desheng (Shenyang), Zeng Siyu (Ji'nan), Han Xianchu (Lanzhou), and Ding Sheng (Nanjing). Chen Xilian (Beijing) and Xu Shiyou (Guangzhou) were the fifth and sixth, leaving one unidentified. One report, moreover, claims that Ding Sheng, a Fourth Field Army veteran, was ordered to stand aside while being investigated for his ties to Lin following his transfer. See Forster, *Rebellion*, p. 140.

[145] Interview with leading specialist on the period, November 2002; and below, pp.194-95.

former secretary, however, reports that the Politburo radicals were active in the Nanjing Military Region, especially in March-April 1974, encouraging the exposure of region leaders in general, and former commander Xu in particular.[146] Meanwhile, two special case groups were established under Wang Hongwen in May to compile and review materials on the big region commanders. One group was solely devoted to Li Desheng, and the second to the seven other transferred commanders, with Xu, Yang Dezhi, Han Xianchu and Chen Xilian reportedly the most scrutinized. That Chen was included as a subject of investigation, as well as targeted in wall posters, was a major paradox given his recent promotion and emerging signs of Mao's favoritism. Indeed, a senior Party historian specializing on the period speculated that in bringing Chen to Beijing under the rotation plan, Mao was already considering him as a replacement for Ye Jianying, something that eventuated in 1976.[147]

Mao's intention in "back-to-back struggle" was to uncover, as much as possible, any problems with the big region commanders. As suggested by his December comments, this undoubtedly involved all the issues identified previously: high-handed interference in civilian matters, running "independent kingdoms," and questionable loyalty to the Cultural Revolution. In Li Desheng's case, however, GPD leadership was a unique factor, both as a logical source of radical interest and ambition, and, as we have seen, due to vulnerability to charges of insufficiently promoting the Cultural Revolution line. Yet during the criticism of big region commanders, and especially of Li, involvement with Lin Biao, something that, in Mao's mind, was increasingly indistinguishable from "revisionism," became a key issue. In the post-September 13 period, while many former military associates of Lin had been removed from their positions, it was by no means a sweeping purge. Mao had to sort out which of Lin's former subordinates were reliable, and which were not, and *pi Lin pi Kong* in the military regions continued the process. Some, such as Ding Sheng, now in Nanjing, and Zeng Siyu, now in Ji'nan, had apparently earned Mao's high regard, but a full disclosure of any issues was required. The sensitivity of clarifying connections with Lin Biao was seen in loyalty letters discovered after Lin's demise. Such letters from Li Desheng, Xu Shiyou, Yang Dezhi, Chen Xilian and Han Xianchu were reportedly found in Lin's residence during investigations. As a senior specialist on

---

[146] Li Wenqing, *Jinkan Xu Shiyou*, pp. 255-57; and interview, January 2005. It is, of course, possible that "gang of four" interference was limited to the Nanjing Military Region where, according to Wang Hongwen, Xu had tried to use the three surrounding provinces to oppress Shanghai. This was the "gang's" base area, Xu had bad personal relations with Wang, and Zhang Chunqiao was the military region's political commissar. It may also be the case that the Nanjing Military Region suffered a particularly heavy personnel toll during the Lin Biao-Confucius campaign since all of the standing members of its Party committee who attended the Lushan plenum had been removed by November 1974. It is unclear, however, to what extent these removals had happened earlier or during the campaign, but the linkage to Lushan points to Xu's letter, as well as those of others, in support of Lin Biao at Lushan, letters which became a major *pi Lin pi Kong* issue (see below).

[147] Cheng and Xia, *Deng zai yijiuqiwu*, pp. 14-15; interview, January 2005; and below, pp. 445-46.

the period observed, there was nothing special in this; in analogous circumstances, after the arrest of the "gang of four," similar loyalty letters to Jiang Qing were discovered from such unlikely establishment figures as Zhao Ziyang, Hu Qiaomu and Tan Zhenlin. In this scholar's account, Li Desheng's problem was less the existence of such a letter, but more due to Mao's unhappiness with his failure to disclose the fact promptly. Whatever the precise circumstances, Li's letter was known well before the Lin Biao-Confucius campaign and had not prevented his rise, but now the Chairman had lost confidence in him.[148]

The question of Li's link to Lin Biao was especially paradoxical given his role in first curbing Lin's influence after the Lushan plenum, then in securing control of the air force after September 13, and finally in questioning other regional commanders, notably Xu Shiyou, about their loyalty letters at Mao's behest. Most paradoxical of all, of course, was his promotion to Party Vice Chairman after nearly two years of investigations into the Lin affair. Apart from any delayed disclosure, Li's vulnerability differed from that of other commanders in its circumstances. While their loyalty letters were reportedly sent in support of Lin's state chairmanship proposal at Lushan, the key moment in Mao's estrangement from his successor, Li's apparently came earlier and was linked to his appointment as GPD head in 1970. This appointment was recommended by Lin, in a seeming move to prevent Zhang Chunqiao from being named. In his memoirs, without admitting to a letter, Li recalled how Lin told him in May 1970 of the recommendation, and observed that it was hard not to express thanks. When under attack in 1974, with the May 1970 meeting a major issue, Li acknowledged that he had blindly praised Lin, but tried to excuse himself on the grounds that he did not know what kind of person Lin Biao was—in another irony, the same excuse Mao used after September 13. In any case, focusing on Li's May 1970 encounter with Lin Biao underlined the centrality of the GPD to his problem, a problem which became relevant in the context of *pi Lin pi Kong* and the revived onslaught against revisionism.[149]

As the movement unfolded, Li was under immense pressure. Besides his sudden demotion and being singled out in a special case group of his own, Li's children were implicated in criminal investigations, with one son brought to Beijing under criminal escort and held in a small room under close surveillance. Finally, as the August-September conference of military region leaders concluded, Li was compelled to accept the official verdict that he had "carried out Lin Biao's line [and] boarded Lin's pirate ship." In the context of ending the criticism of the commanders, and calling off the entire Lin Biao-Confucius campaign (see Chapter 3), Mao declared Li's self-criticism sufficient. But it would take until 1980 for an official reversal of this verdict.[150]

---

[148] Cheng and Xia, *Deng zai yijiuqiwu*, pp. 14-15; interviews with senior Party and military historians, January 2005; and above, p. 169n144.

[149] *Li Desheng huiyilu*, pp. 391-92, 477; Li Wenqing, *Jinkan Xu Shiyou*, p. 246; and above, p. 145.

Threats to Party Leadership in the Provinces. For all of the pressure on Zhou Enlai and the PLA, the most dramatic threats to the revamped post-Cultural Revolution political structure occurred in the provinces. During the February-August period, significant attacks on the Party leadership or major disturbances occurred in at least 12 provinces.[151] As with *pi Lin pi Kong* as a whole, the intensity of the movement began to decrease in the localities from mid-year and dramatically after August, although not without some significant rearguard struggle. While it is difficult to assess provincial variations in the absence of comparable studies, in the one case where a detailed analysis does exist, Keith Forster's excellent study of Zhejiang, the threat to local Party authority was severe, and probably significantly worse than in other provinces.[152] We shall pay particular attention to Zhejiang in examining the salient issues: the nature and consequences of attacks on Party leaders, the related tensions between veteran cadres and Cultural Revolution rebels, especially as manifested in the *shuangtu* or "double crashthroughs" of organizational norms and conventions in the Party recruitment and promotion of rebels, and the question of the relationship between the Politburo radicals and rebel activity in the localities. In Zhejiang, perhaps even more than elsewhere, the role of PLA officers in provincial Party positions was a central feature of developments. Indeed, as reflected in Wang Hongwen's April 1974 appeal to local rebels to expose the military region's leaders and Xu Shiyou, one could say the Zhejiang issue was simultaneously the issue of the Nanjing Military Region.[153]

Party committee leadership, a central theme of the Tenth Congress, was reiterated throughout the movement. However, particularly in the initial months of the campaign, it coexisted with discordant notes. Party committees were to give free rein to the masses, and not throw cold water on them. Wang Hongwen,

---

[150] Cheng and Xia, *Deng zai yijiuqiwu*, p. 16; and *Li Desheng huiyilu*, pp. 484-85.

[151] Zhejiang, Jiangxi, Shanxi, Fujian, Sichuan, Anhui, Shandong, Hubei, Guangxi, Hunan, Guangdong and Yunnan, as indicated by Politburo discussions or other central measures, or notations in major post-Mao chronologies. See Chen and Du, *Shilu*, vol. 3, part 2, pp. 1046, 1064, 1073-74, 1092, 1096-97, 1103; and *Zhou nianpu*, vol. 3, pp. 650-51, 654, 656-57, 659-65.

[152] In his retrospective reexamination of the period, Forster, "The Cultural Revolution in Zhejiang Revisited," pp. 135, 143, assesses the factionalism and rebellion erupting into violence in the mid-1970s, and observes that it "may well have been much worse [in Zhejiang] than in other areas of China." He speculates that this may have been due in part to ongoing resentment against the almost complete domination of the province by outsiders, and by the protection afforded rebel leaders after the Ninth Congress by central and regional patrons. Based on the fragmentary information we have canvassed, Jiangxi appears to have been closest to Zhejiang in the degree of disruption. See Chen and Du, *Shilu*, vol. 3, part 2, pp. 1046, 1103.

[153] See Li Wenqing, *Jinkan Xu Shiyou*, p. 256. The background to the events discussed below is that before Lin Biao's demise, both the Zhejiang Party Committee and Zhejiang Military District had been led by PLA officers with close links to Lin. In the aftermath of the Lin affair, Xu Shiyou presided over the purge of these officials and the installation of new leaders with ties to himself and/or the Nanjing Military Region. This process also caused tension with rump rebel groups from 1966-68 that had ties to the previous leadership.

in his January 14 speech, not only asserted the Tenth Congress' contrary theme of "going against the tide," he also used the even more provocative Cultural Revolution slogan that "to rebel is justified." While ultimately a pale reflection of events in 1966-68, a dynamic that could reasonably be called a "second Cultural Revolution" quickly emerged. Dissident elements, whether "new rebels" (*xin zaofanpai*) or, seemingly more prevalent, reenergized mass factions that had been disbanded or marginalized since 1968, now moved to the center of the political stage. This involved a replay of battles waged between competing popular factions in the latter half of the 1960s, but more important for our story, it allowed rebel organizations that had been most virulent in attacking the pre-Cultural Revolution political structure to challenge again those in authority. In the new context, this involved conflict between these rebels and veteran cadres who had been attacked during the Cultural Revolution, removed from office but rehabilitated in the post-Ninth Congress period, and, as claimed by Wang Hongwen, in at least some cases were now seeking revenge against their tormentors. Such animosity-fueled challenges undermined the authority of Party committees at various levels and, as we shall see in some detail in Zhejiang, often resulted in a loss of control by, or virtual paralysis of, intimidated leaders. The most provocative notion to emerge in this context was that articulated by Zhang Chunqiao, and seemingly widely believed by rebels—that *pi Lin pi Kong* was a "second seizure of power."[154]

Whatever Zhang may have meant by a new "seizure of power,"[155] in practice most "seizures," i.e., the replacement of existing leaders, appear to have been limited to low-level units such as factories, or to provincial organizations in the cultural sphere where the radicals already held bureaucratic power.[156] At the critical provincial Party committee level, few leaders are known to have been replaced, with only one Party first secretary, Shanxi's Xie Zhenhua, ousted. A Politburo decision replaced Xie, a military man, with Wang Qian, a veteran cadre and pre-Cultural Revolution Shanxi leader, on February 11. Whether this was simply in response to rebel pressure during *pi Lin pi Kong*, or reflected longer-term problems, is unclear, but it does appear that the central leadership was acquiescing to rebel attacks on local leaders to some degree. Over the following

---

[154] See "Wang Hongwen zai zhongyang dushuban," pp. 4-5; Forster, *Rebellion*, p. 143; Fenwick, "Gang of Four," pp. 214, 223-24, 254-55; Perry and Li, *Proletarian Power*, pp. 177-78; and "Quarterly Chronicle and Documentation," *CQ*, no. 58 (1974), pp. 407, 409, no. 59 (1974), p. 627.

[155] In addition to the discussion below, note the lack of clarity concerning "seizures" in the PLA central organs, above. It is also of interest that, even at the height of power seizures in March, the "gang" reportedly pursued such objectives by more regular means. In what would be described as "organizational preparations for seizing power," the "gang" and their Shanghai followers selected young cadres for possible central posts—a move entirely in line with Mao's prescriptions for future leadership—and submitted a list of 88 for consideration as vice ministers to a central study class at the end of April. See Chen and Du, *Shilu*, vol. 3, part 2, p. 1059; Perry and Li, *Proletarian Power*, p. 179; and below, p. 223.

[156] See Perry and Li, *Proletarian Power*, p. 178; and Fenwick, "Gang of Four," p. 292n94.

months, Xie was criticized both by Wang Hongwen in March at a meeting on Shanxi's problems convened by the Politburo, and during a Shanxi Provincial Party Committee plenum in June, for failing to criticize Lin Biao or Confucius, but instead criticizing "ultra-leftism" in order to attack the Cultural Revolution.[157] But with few provincial leaders actually removed, and some redoubtable rehabilitated cadres such as Zhao Ziyang in Guangdong gaining enhanced prominence,[158] the result was that little provincial power was definitively "seized" during the movement. Nevertheless, the great pressure brought to bear on Party committees from early in the year profoundly disrupted regular organizational life and temporarily altered the power equation. Nowhere was this more apparent than in Zhejiang.

From the perspective of the Zhejiang rebels, *pi Lin pi Kong* was indeed about "seizing power" since power was everything. This was bluntly stated in March by Weng Senhe, the most notorious of the province's rebel leaders: "It's already been seven to eight years of the Cultural Revolution, and recently what have we got organizationally?... We must get leadership power."[159] This view, which was undoubtedly widely shared throughout China by the remnants of Red Guard and other Cultural Revolution rebel groups, was fueled not only by the heady days of 1966-68, but arguably even more so by disappointments since 1968 when such groups were marginalized. Now a new opportunity had arisen, and even if the potential for mobilizing mass support from a jaded population was significantly diminished, the experience gained in political struggle, contacts built up with local and central leaders, and greater cynicism made the rebels a formidable force. Contradictory factors in Zhejiang's recent past paradoxically contributed to the intensity of the conflict in the province. On the one hand, rather than simply being dispersed, rebel organizations from 1966-68, notably the radical groups

---

[157] *Zhou nianpu*, vol. 3, pp. 651, 656-67; and Chen and Du, *Shilu*, vol. 3, part 2, pp. 1096-97. Xie's case was perhaps linked to contemporary criticism of a local Shanxi opera (see above, p. 157n111). The apparent accommodation to rebel attacks on local leaders at the time of Xie's replacement is further suggested by a February Party Center circular attacking a Jiangxi secretary by name for allegedly negating the Cultural Revolution. By April, however, there were indications of a more protective approach through central attempts to curb wall poster attacks, and the summoning of Kunming Military Region Commander Wang Bicheng to Beijing in order to protect him from "unexpected developments" in Yunnan. See *Zhou nianpu*, pp. 663-65; and Chen and Du, p. 1046.

[158] At the height of the movement in March, Zhao was appointed head of the Guangdong Revolutionary Committee, and identified as First Party Secretary in April. Zhao had been rehabilitated as a Party secretary in Inner Mongolia in 1971, and transferred to Guangdong in 1972. By the Tenth Congress, when Zhao was elected to the Central Committee, he was identified as a Guangdong Party secretary and had in fact been placed in overall charge of Party work. See Chen and Du, *Shilu*, vol. 3, part 2, p. 1060; Zhang Gensheng, "Hua Guofeng tan fensui 'sirenbang'" [Hua Guofeng Talks about Smashing the "Gang of Four"], *Yanhuang chunqiu* [Chinese Annals], no. 7 (2004), p. 1; and David L. Shambaugh, *The Making of a Premier: Zhao Ziyang's Provincial Career* (Boulder: Westview Press, 1984), ch. 5.

[159] Cited in Forster, *Rebellion*, p. 137. See also idem, "The Cultural Revolution in Zhejiang Revisited," p. 142.

led by the famous trio of Weng Senhe, Zhang Yongsheng and He Xianchun, retained a presence in the local political structure after the Ninth Congress. Undoubtedly due in considerable measure to the support of the Politburo radicals (see below), Weng *et al.* were able to remain active, keep their networks alive, and gain positions in various official bodies. Nevertheless, their position was marginal, constrained first by the military crackdown on disruption after the Ninth Congress, and then, after September 13, by the restoration of orthodox leaders—notably veteran cadre Tan Qilong as First Party Secretary, and local PLA figure Tie Ying as the new number two provincial leader, both figures with historic ties to Xu Shiyou, and in Tie's case a current position under the Nanjing Military Region. Perhaps particularly frustrating, even with the Tenth Congress emphasis on mass representatives and revolutionary successors, there was little significant improvement in the rebels' position. In short, the Zhejiang rebels had charismatic leaders, relative political cohesion, and unrequited grievances as the new movement approached.[160]

As the story of the Lin Biao-Confucius campaign in Zhejiang has been told in exquisite detail by Forster, we only note some key aspects here. One prominent feature was the revival of the conflict between the descendants of the two mass factions of 1966-68, with what was now termed the "mountaintop" faction of Weng, Zhang and He again leading the fight against the provincial authorities, and a more conservative "base of the mountain" faction again more supportive of the official establishment. The "mountaintop" faction not only prevailed over its old enemies, it also brought incessant pressure to bear on the provincial leadership. This pressure did not force a change in the Zhejiang Party leadership as Tan Qilong and the more forceful Tie Ying held their positions, but they were now stripped of whatever protection Xu Shiyou could give them. While the post-Mao claim that Weng Senhe "ruled supreme" in Zhejiang may be overstated, Weng's faction repeatedly humiliated the Party leadership, and left it virtually paralyzed for several months. Even before the movement, with Wang Hongwen's purported backing, at the end of November 1973 Weng *et al.* summoned Tan and other Party leaders to the top of Mt. Pingfang (thus "mountaintop" faction) for four and a half days of questioning, largely about excesses in dealing with rebels. With *pi Lin pi Kong* underway, from February to mid-1974, the "mountaintop" faction basically controlled the movement's course and with it much of Zhejiang's political life. A rally in early February affirmed the "right to rebel against reactionaries," and attacked "responsible comrades of the provincial Party committee" as the source of the "rightist trend" in the province. By March, Tan and Tie no longer presided at rallies, but instead were compelled to attend and listen to denunciations of

---

[160] See Forster, *Rebellion*, chs. 5-6; idem, "The Cultural Revolution in Zhejiang Revisited," pp. 141-42; and "T'ieh Ying—Chairman of the Chekiang Provincial Advisory Commission," *IS*, October 1984.

their leadership as Weng, Zhang and He directed proceedings, while serious self-criticism was still demanded of Tie and others in August. The March-August period also saw an ongoing "three-in-one plenum," a joint meeting of the provincial Party committee, Zhejiang Revolutionary Committee, and Party committee of the Zhejiang Military District, which enabled rebels to attack the departed Xu Shiyou, air grudges and accusations, and exert a degree of control over the local military. The "three-in-one plenum" concluded shortly after the July 17 Politburo meeting on the Party Center's order, presumably conveyed by Wang Hongwen who was in charge of both the Center and the Zhejiang problem, thus marking the winding down of the local movement parallel to national developments.[161]

If lasting "seizures of power" did not eventuate at the provincial level, the position of local radicals was significantly enhanced through lower-ranking appointments and Party recruitment. In Zhejiang, and probably elsewhere, this was sometimes the result of rebels confronting Party authorities, as in March when a group presented a list of 60 names largely from the "mountaintop" faction to the Hangzhou Municipal Party Committee, demanding posts ranging from membership in the city's Party standing committee to positions under its jurisdiction, and the municipal authorities soon capitulated.[162] But more significant was the *shuangtu* program to speed up the promotion of cadres and recruit new Party members. Reportedly promoted by Zhang Chunqiao and carried out, apparently, on a nationwide basis, this approach implemented Mao's demand to promote "little soldiers," and reflected his emphasis on the Party as the core of leadership. As we saw in Chapter 1, Cultural Revolution rebels had been seriously disadvantaged in the rebuilding of political institutions following the Ninth Congress, since a large portion of them were not Party members and thus obstructed from assuming administrative responsibilities. In the post-Mao critique, the *shuangtu* was denounced as reckless, as ignoring proper procedures by admitting candidates without evaluation or training, and even opening prisons to search for new Party members. In any case, the result was dramatic, as seen in the "gang's" Shanghai base where Party recruits in 1973-74 nearly doubled the figure for the previous five years. What should be noted, in any case, is that despite the Politburo radicals' clear interest in the expanded recruitment of rebels, and the fact that they had held key positions in Party reconstruction and personnel matters since the late 1960s, it was only in the context of Mao's renewed attention

---

[161] See Forster, *Rebellion*, pp. 135-36, 143-46, 161-63; *Sirenbang fangeming zuixing cailiao jilu* [Collected Materials on the Counterrevolutionary Crimes of the Gang of Four], internal materials edited by the Library Archive Office of the Institute of Philosophical Studies, Chinese Academy of Social Sciences, May 1977, p. 385; and "Zhonggong zhongyang guanyu 'Wang Hongwen, Zhang Chunqiao, Jiang Qing, Yao Wenyuan fandang jituan zuizheng (cailiao zhi san)'," p. 37.

[162] Forster, *Rebellion*, pp. 149-50; and "Zhonggong zhongyang guanyu 'Wang Hongwen, Zhang Chunqiao, Jiang Qing, Yao Wenyuan fandang jituan zuizheng (cailiao zhi san)'," p. 37.

to cultivating such successors and *pi Lin pi Kong* that extraordinary measures were adopted.[163]

Clearly, developments in China's provinces during the campaign and subsequently cannot be explained without reference to central politics, and equally clearly local rebels were often bolstered by the Politburo radicals to whom they sometimes pledged loyalty. Forster, on the basis of his close examination, concludes that central factional allegiances were crucial to the fortunes of Zhejiang's rebels, while Fenwick argues more broadly that *pi Lin pi Kong* was a case of the "gang" building its factional networks throughout the country in an effort to mobilize a social base that would leave them less dependent on Mao.[164] Yet the situation was more complicated. As noted in the Introduction, for all the presumed and real overlap of the interests of the Politburo radicals and local rebels, their interests diverged in significant ways. The "gang" were central politicians, bound, at least loosely, to the Politburo and its regulations. Even more crucially, they were restricted by Mao, aware of his wishes which were beyond the knowledge of local rebels and often against their interests. A further complication is that leading rebels were judged individually: in Zhejiang's case, where Mao took a special interest, he came to regard Zhang Yongsheng more favorably than Weng Senhe, with consequences for the treatment of each.[165] And shifting national priorities naturally meant changing calculations in Beijing concerning the rebel cause in the localities.

These complications can be seen in the relationship between the Politburo radicals and the Zhejiang rebels. Aside from alleged factional arrangements, as in the reported "underground command center" in Hangzhou linked to a "secret liaison office" in Beijing, Wang Hongwen and Zhang Chunqiao had special local responsibilities by virtue of being leading figures in the East China region, while Jiang Qing had her own local network. Concretely, post-Mao sources cite many examples of "gang" support for the "mountaintop" leaders: e.g., Zhang Chunqiao's praise of Zhang Yongsheng at the Ninth Congress which secured his Party membership, Wang Hongwen's summer 1973 lobbying for Weng Senhe's inclusion in Zhejiang's delegation to the Tenth Congress, and Wang's June

---

[163] See Forster, *Rebellion*, pp. 150-52, 174-75; idem, "The Cultural Revolution in Zhejiang Revisited," pp. 141-42; Perry and Li, *Proletarian Power*, pp. 177-80; Fenwick, "Gang of Four," pp. 255-56; "Zhonggong zhongyang guanyu 'Wang Hongwen, Zhang Chunqiao, Jiang Qing, Yao Wenyuan fandang jituan zuizheng (cailiao zhi san)'," pp. 37-38; *RMRB*, May 17, 1977, in *SPRCP*, no. 6358 (1977), pp. 210-12; and above, pp. 78-79, 142.

In terms of actual numbers of new Party members, the picture is not so clear-cut. In Shanghai, recruits in 1973 before the movement (45,028) exceeded those in 1974 (38,275). In Zhejiang, there was an increase in recruitment in 1974 compared to 1973 (38,005 *v.* 28,950), but the 1974 figure was virtually the same as that in 1971 (38,090).

[164] See Forster, *Rebellion*, pp. 109-10, 173; and Fenwick, "Gang of Four," pp. 203, 220-21, 277-78.

[165] See Wang Ying and Sun Zhongfan, "Yijiuqiwu nian dang zuzhi zhengdun de qianqian houhou" [A Detailed Account of the 1975 Party Organization Rectification], *BNC*, no. 8 (2001), pp. 41, 43; above, p. 18; and below, pp. 276n90, 279n99.

1974 instruction that Zhang, Weng and He be allowed to attend meetings of the Zhejiang Party standing committee. A close reading of developments in Zhejiang, however, indicates a more contingent relationship. At the Tenth Congress, with the radicals notionally in charge of personnel and many "mass representatives" selected, none of the "mountaintop" leaders were elevated to Central Committee status. With conflict escalating between rebels and the provincial leadership, in mid-November 1973 Wang tried to straddle the issue, asking Tan Qilong to make a self-criticism for the leadership's behavior toward the rebels, but also instructing him to dissuade a rebel "complaints delegation" from leaving Hangzhou. And in March 1974, with Zhang, Weng and He stirring up conflict in the Zhejiang Military District and armed struggle erupting in Wenzhou, Zhou Enlai asked Wang Hongwen and Zhang Chunqiao to handle the situation, leading Wang to instruct the provincial authorities to bring the situation under control. In all of these cases, however much the central radicals wished to support the Zhejiang rebels, they were constrained. As we shall see in Chapter 4, by the middle of 1975, the contingent relationship had degenerated into direct conflict, with Wang Hongwen supporting the jailing of Weng Senhe.[166]

Much as in the Cultural Revolution itself the *pi Lin pi Kong* movement provided ample opportunity for the development of radical networks linking Jiang Qing *et al.* and local rebel groups. Such networks, however, were fragile, diverse, often individually based as seen in the conflicts within the strongest radical base in Shanghai,[167] and contingent. Local rebels could not expect unwavering support in their attacks on establishment figures from a "gang" that paradoxically had become part of the official establishment and beholden (at least sporadically) to its procedures, while the actions of such rebels always involved the danger of compromising their ideological soul mates in Beijing. In any case, if the Politburo radicals believed social mobilization and the elaboration of vertical networks of like-minded people would provide political capital that could compensate for a fading Mao, they were sadly mistaken. The twists and turns of the movement indicated just how deep their dependence on the Chairman was. This would soon be even clearer as *pi Lin pi Kong* wound down dramatically from August 1974.

The Ascent of Deng Xiaoping

It can be safely assumed that Mao had a significant future in mind for Deng Xiaoping when he brought him back to office in early 1973, even if a probation period would be required before that future could unfold. During his first eight months back in office, Deng's activities were exceptionally low-key, with even scholars specializing in his career unable to provide much insight into what he was doing. His work apparently was concentrated in foreign affairs, but even

---

[166] See Forster, *Rebellion*, pp. 115-16, 132-33, 135, 147, 160, 183-84; idem, "The Cultural Revolution in Zhejiang Revisited," p. 141; *Zhou nianpu*, vol. 3, p. 656; and below, pp. 277ff.

[167] See above, p. 117. See also Fenwick, "Gang of Four," pp. 220-24.

in this sphere, where Deng had considerable previous experience, his role appeared marginal. By April 1973 he was at the airport to welcome high-ranking foreign guests, attended state banquets, and in the case of the President of Mali accompanied the visitor to Dazhai.[168] But he apparently did not participate in working sessions with the visiting leaders where Zhou Enlai continued to perform as the key interlocutor, and he never attended their receptions with Mao. In addition, there is no evidence that, after their intriguing meeting in early April,[169] and despite common foreign policy duties, Deng had anything more than formal contact with the Premier.

The change, of course, came with the November-December 1973 Politburo meetings to which Deng was specially invited, and the telling incident was Mao's excited summons after Deng criticized Zhou. As we have seen, important positions followed: Politburo and MAC membership during the next phase of the meetings, and membership in the MAC small group responsible for *pi Lin pi Kong* in the PLA as well as professional military affairs in January 1974. Deng's foreign affairs role also increased dramatically. By May, Deng was not only dealing with the business end of state visits together with Zhou, he was also included, along with Zhou and Wang Hongwen, in Mao's receptions of foreign guests.[170] The most obvious increase in both Deng's diplomatic responsibilities and his public stature came with his selection to head China's delegation to the special session of the United Nations in April, a decision, as we shall see, that was Mao's initiative and took not only Jiang Qing, but also Zhou Enlai, by surprise. The blanket media coverage of Deng's trip greatly enhanced his public profile, although as early as the end of January he was placed on official lists of leaders greeting foreign leaders or attending funerals among Politburo members—after the radicals and Li Xiannian, but ahead of establishment beneficiaries Chen Xilian, Ji Dengkui and Hua Guofeng.

If Deng's star was rising, it was not completely clear how this affected his responsibilities outside of foreign affairs. Very little is known concerning his role in domestic policy issues. Regarding economic affairs, over the March 1973-August 1974 period, Deng dealt with such issues as the ten-year plan, annual planning, foreign credit, hydroelectric power, and new technology, but it is unknown with what authority, or what position, if any, he took on contentious issues questions raised by *pi Lin pi Kong* criticism. More indicative of his rising significance, although still saying nothing about his position on contentious matters, together

---

[168] See *PR*, no. 26 (1973), p. 4.

[169] See above, pp. 73-74.

[170] Mao met with foreigners five times in May, and Deng was present on three occasions, compared to the ever present Zhou and Wang. On the two occasions when Deng was not present, Li Xiannian attended. Throughout 1973-74, Li was the only other Politburo member, apart from Zhang Chunqiao and Li Desheng on one occasion in November 1973 (see above, pp. 115n15, 130), to join the Chairman's receptions. From May 1974, Deng and Li Xiannian substituted for the ill Zhou at various formal functions during state visits.

with Li Xiannian he assisted the increasingly ill Premier with State Council daily work, and when Zhou entered the hospital on June 1, it was Deng, rather than the higher-ranking Li, who was given responsibility for government daily work. This can be seen as prefiguring Mao's October decision to name Deng First Vice Premier in waiting, but there is little nuanced information regarding Deng's political or personal relationship with Zhou, and Deng is not known to have visited Zhou's hospital quarters before the new situation created by his October promotion.[171] Indeed, whatever Deng's undoubted private preferences, and despite official distortion, Jiang Qing's claim that she and Deng got along well in this period is basically convincing.[172] Beyond this, it appears that, as of spring 1974, Mao envisioned Wang Hongwen and Deng as embodying his desired melding of Cultural Revolution successors and purified veteran cadres that would see China into a revolutionary yet sufficiently pragmatic future. This, in any case, was the conclusion of Deng's daughter when writing of Mao's receptions with Pakistani President Bhutto, Cypriot leader Archbishop Makarios, and former British Prime Minister Heath in May with Wang and Deng in attendance: "In his heart Mao Zedong hoped that Wang Hongwen and Deng Xiaoping would join together and compose a new work structure."[173]

Deng's role in PLA affairs is particularly elusive, although clearly significant. His new duties must be divided into the strictly military and the political. On the professional side, despite exceptionally sparse information, Deng surely played a major role. Significantly, the MAC small group, where he was the fourth-ranking member, was set up on January 18 to deal with urgent military issues in the midst of a foreign crisis, the confrontation with South Vietnamese forces in the South China Sea. In dealing with the crisis, Deng and Ye Jianying spent two days in a bunker directing military measures. More generally in 1974, according to Deng's daughter, he assisted Ye with a range of military issues including war preparations, training, equipment and military academy affairs, as well as clearing up remaining issues concerning the Lin Biao affair.[174] As suggested earlier, Deng was ideal for this latter task—a figure of great military prestige who was not compromised by career links to Lin.

Although ideal for this role in Mao's eyes, it underlined the complexities of Deng's political situation. While it seems clear that his December 1973 MAC appointment was designed in part to ease any anxieties caused by the rotation of commanders, there is little to suggest that he did much to alleviate such fears once

---

[171] See Mao Mao, "*Wenge*" *suiyue*, p. 315; Cheng and Xia, *Deng zai yijiuqiwu*, p. 25n1; and above, p. 21n59.

[172] See Jiang's 1976 statement, below, p. 186. According to a senior specialist on Deng, Jiang sought to cultivate Deng since her real conflict was with Zhou, and she did not see Deng as Zhou's man. Interview, November 2002.

[173] Mao Mao, "*Wenge*" *suiyue*, pp. 307-308. Cf. Short, *Mao*, pp. 610-11.

[174] Fan Shuo, *Ye Jianying zai feichang shiqi*, vol. 2, pp. 393-96; and Mao Mao, "*Wenge*" *suiyue*, p. 315.

he assumed his MAC duties. The only concrete indication of Deng supporting a moderate position was his reported backing of Zhou and Ye Jianying on January 31 in opposing the "four bigs" in military units, but, as we have noted, there is no evidence that the radicals took a different position on that occasion.[175] More generally, despite their collaboration during the South China Sea confrontation and Deng's assistance with various military tasks, there is little hard evidence of close coordination between Deng and Ye despite their shared responsibilities, especially on political matters. According to a member of Ye's household, there was little Deng-Ye contact in this period.[176] The critical question, however, is the nature of Deng's role in *pi Lin pi Kong* criticism of PLA organizations and leaders.

Deng was clearly involved. He was one of the MAC leaders (along with Ye, Wang Hongwen and Zhang Chunqiao) to receive Jiang's January 24 letter on the movement in the military, a week before the MAC small group formally took responsibility for guiding the campaign in the PLA. Although the evidence is limited, one document reports Deng's criticism, cited in the Introduction, of Tao Lujia, an official who had served in his base area during the revolutionary period. This criticism took place at a meeting convened by the MAC small group and controlled by Wang on March 8, at the height of the disruptive developments in central military organizations, to deal with problems in the PLA's Science and Technology Commission for National Defense. In this meeting, as the commission's leading figure, Tao came under attack for failing to push the *pi Lin pi Kong* effort, with Wang calling the shots and Deng making substantial and frequent interjections. Several things stand out from this account. First, although Wang was clearly in charge and everyone echoed his criticisms, his comments fell short of the vitriol commonly ascribed to the "gang's" activities in this period. Secondly, when Deng did speak, he went further than Wang in attacking Tao by demanding that he "take down [his] trousers" (i.e., engage in a thorough self-criticism), carry out the demands of Jiang Qing, and learn from the Cultural Revolution.[177] There are indications that Deng was also involved in the case of the most vulnerable big region commander—his old Second Field Army subordinate, Li Desheng (see below). But the clearest evidence of his key role in pushing the Lin Biao-Confucius agenda forward came at a Politburo meeting in early February. At that meeting, Deng was entrusted with the task of overcoming resistance to the movement by old cadres who lacked a proper understanding of the Cultural Revolution.[178] Subsequently, in August-September, Deng played a

---

[175] See Chen and Du, *Shilu*, vol. 3, part 2, p. 1030; and above, p. 154.

[176] Interview, March 1997. It is also of interest that the brief coverage of *pi Lin pi Kong* in *Ye zhuan*, p. 623, makes no mention of Deng, while noting that Ye, Li Xiannian and Li Desheng came under Jiang's attack.

[177] The document in the ANU collection summarizing this meeting has stood up to detailed linguistic and contextual analysis. See above, pp. 14n33, 151n96.

[178] See Gao Wenqian, *Wannian Zhou*, p. 500.

role in easing the circumstances of the military region commanders (see Chapter 3), but at the height of *pi Lin pi Kong* he was surely deeply involved in the harsh attacks on army leaders.

Much as we must make assumptions concerning Deng's actions, we can only speculate about his calculations. First and foremost, he would have understood Mao's intent to deal seriously with the PLA generally and the big region commanders in particular. Deng's presumably harsh criticism of old subordinates flowed from political necessity. Moreover, it was also in his interests to root out any remnant influence of Lin Biao, and facilitate the promotion of his own former Second Field Army comrades, even if some had to suffer during the course of the campaign. But arguably, his ultimate objective was to stabilize the PLA's situation, i.e., while it was necessary to go through the criticism process according to Mao's demand, the net result would hopefully satisfy the Chairman and lead him to reduce the pressure on the generals. This is precisely what happened in August-September. While the substance of Deng's criticism of PLA leaders during *pi Lin pi Kong* may not have been too different from that of the radicals, his goal surely was. The radicals wanted to remove as much conservative influence from the army as possible, and, as stated by Wang Hongwen in his January 14 speech, promote young officers to high command posts. Deng, who would be sympathetic toward Li Desheng when Li paid a courtesy call in early 1975, wanted conservative generals to pass through the gate of reform to Mao's satisfaction.[179]

Of all the developments concerning Deng before fall 1974, the most celebrated—and distorted—concerns his selection as leader of the Chinese delegation to the United Nations. In and of itself, the choice of a delegation leader for the General Assembly's special session on problems of raw materials and development starting on April 9 should not have been a major issue. Although many heads of state and government routinely attended such high-profile General Assembly meetings, the PRC had always been underrepresented since joining the UN in 1971. Qiao Guanhua, only a Vice Minister of Foreign Affairs, had led each special delegation, the only tension being internal to the MFA since the sophisticated Qiao had been selected by Mao over Foreign Minister Ji Pengfei. On the surface, the only thing different this time was that Mao's "theory of the three worlds" was now ripe for introduction on the world stage, a matter Mao's biographers plausibly claim was a big issue for the Chairman. In reality, Mao's "theory" only summarized aspects of China's foreign policy over the last few years, and Qiao had articulated its key concepts during previous visits to the UN. As a conceptual overview, however, Mao had only outlined the theory privately in February during a meeting with Zambian President Kaunda. The UN General Assembly, in contrast, was a high-profile international forum where considerable attention would focus on the Chairman's latest theoretical creation.[180]

---

[179] See *Li Desheng huiyilu*, pp. 483-84; and above, pp. 164-65.

It is likely that Mao was at least equally concerned with enhancing Deng's domestic and international profile. Deng was the highest-ranking PRC leader yet dispatched to the UN, both through his state position as Vice Premier and due to his status as a Politburo member. Deng's selection became a source of conflict, and has been routinely presented in post-Mao sources as proof of "gang of four" hostility toward him. Inevitably, the story is more complicated, and in fact reflected a quite different dynamic. It begins with the "two ladies," Wang Hairong and Tang Wensheng, approaching Mao on the matter on behalf of the MFA. The Chairman immediately responded that Deng should head the delegation, with Qiao as his experienced deputy. Mao added that this should not be revealed to the Politburo as his decision, but instead should be presented as a MFA proposal. On March 20, however, Zhou was informed of this on Mao's order by Wang Hairong, and enjoined not to disclose the information. The required Foreign Ministry report appeared on March 22, and was circled by Mao on the 24th. Jiang Qing was unhappy and summoned Wang Hairong to censure the report, allegedly "for no reason," and ordered the ministry to take it back and reconsider the issue. Jiang phoned Wang Hairong again the next day to reaffirm her view. During these exchanges the two women quarreled, something, a senior Party historian observed, that was only possible because of Wang's special status as Mao's relative. When the Politburo approved the report on the 26th, Jiang reserved her opinion, but the next day Mao wrote her to reveal the proposal was his opinion and warn her not to oppose him. When the Politburo met to consider further details of the UN trip on April 2, Jiang, along with Zhang Chunqiao and Yao Wenyuan (but not Wang Hongwen), pleaded illness and did not attend.[181]

While even the bare bones of these events suggest a complex picture, additional factors should also be considered. One central factor was Mao's motivations. His motives concerning Deng seem reasonably straightforward: the UN assignment fit the longer-term project of gradually bringing Deng back into a position of real power. As for Jiang Qing, however, Mao's actions virtually amounted to entrapment, a likely expression of his dissatisfaction with his wife, and/or a test to see if she truly grasped his plans for Deng. Zhou Enlai was informed of the Chairman's view but told to keep quiet on March 20, the very day Mao criticized Jiang seemingly over the chaos in the central military organs. With Jiang having presumably failed her test, Mao sharply criticized her again on the 27th, and it is possible, indeed likely, that Jiang's proposal to withdraw, which took place

---

[180] See Barnouin and Yu, *Chinese Foreign Policy*, pp. 50, 152-53, 214-26; *Mao zhuan*, vol. 2, p. 1688; and above, p. 87n153.

[181] *Mao zhuan*, vol. 2, pp. 1689-90; An Jianshe, "Mao Zedong yu 'pi Lin pi Kong' ruogan wenti," p. 59; *Deng Liqun guoshi jiangtan*, vol. 3, p. 322; Su Caiqing, "'Sirenbang' dui Deng Xiaoping chuxi Lianda zhi jienan" [The "Gang of Four's" Heckling toward Deng Xiaoping Attending the UN Conference], *Zhonggong dangshi ziliao* [Materials on CCP Party History] (hereafter *ZGDSZL*), no. 58 (1996), pp. 197-99; and interview, December 2002.

some time after Mao's March 20 criticism, was actually delayed until after the conflict over the UN delegation.[182] The Premier's reaction illuminates another aspect. Although party to Mao's deception, Zhou sought to limit Deng's time abroad, advocating to the Chairman a one-week trip rather than the three weeks in the MFA proposal. Zhou's argument was intriguing: Deng was needed not only because Ye Jianying was in the hospital, but also to assist Wang Hongwen *in handling the Lin Biao-Confucius movement*. The Premier's position was in fact similar to that of Jiang Qing, who reportedly justified her opposition to Deng going abroad on the grounds that he was needed in China. Jiang averred that she was not opposing Deng, but there was an MAC conference on Li Desheng's case that Deng had to attend. What she expected of Deng at this meeting was left unstated, but she clearly believed he was indispensable. Given that Li was facing severe criticism, it would have been *de rigueur* for those participating to attack strongly, and Jiang's attitude indicated her expectation that he would fulfill this role, as he had earlier concerning Tao Lujia.[183]

Deng's performance at the UN also bears scrutiny. Apart from the theoretical packaging, Deng's speech broke little new ground. Its perceived tough tone caused some concern in Western capitals, notably Washington, but in fact Deng was recycling familiar Chinese rhetoric about great disorder in the world, superpower contention for hegemony, the third world's struggle for political and economic independence, and the need for self-reliance and changed conditions of international trade. The overarching practical foreign policy problem of the period remained the stalled Sino-US relations, which had cooled and showed no sign of progress since Kissinger left Beijing the previous November. In this regard, the most significant event of Deng's trip was his three-hour dinner meeting with Kissinger on April 14, the first of several encounters which left Kissinger disappointed that he no longer had Zhou Enlai as his diplomatic partner. This meeting, however, was less prickly than future encounters, but broke no new ground in substantive terms. What is most interesting from our point of view is that in contrast to his authoritative performance only seven months later, not to mention his no nonsense aura of command in the post-Mao period, Deng appeared ill at ease and short of full confidence. Indeed, Qiao Guanhua provided some of the more incisive comments from the Chinese side. In the final volume of his memoirs, Kissinger claimed that at the April meeting he did not consider Deng a major figure, and described him as "act[ing] as if he were on a training mission on how to deal with Americans." While Kissinger may have overstated the case, his view is consistent with the American transcript. What is striking

---

[182] See *Mao wengao*, vol. 13, pp. 372-74. Even many months later Mao pondered why Jiang had opposed Deng's UN visit, asking Zhou his view in December 1974. *Mao zhuan*, vol. 2, p. 1711.

[183] See Su Caiqing, "'Sirenbang' dui Deng Xiaoping chuxi Lianda," pp. 198-99; and Chen Hongshi, "Tang Wensheng yanzhong de weiren" [Great People in the Eyes of Tang Wensheng], *Wenshi jinghua* [The Cream of Literature and History], no. 1 (1998), p. 13. In the event, Deng was overseas for two and a half weeks.

is that even after being restored to the Politburo, and obviously having the Chairman's confidence, Deng was still feeling his way, apparently unsure of just where he stood in the perilous world of CCP elite politics.[184]

All in all, from the time of his appointment to the Politburo at the end of 1973 through to August 1974, when the *pi Lin pi Kong* movement began to wind down dramatically, Deng Xiaoping maintained a relatively low profile. From the point of view of the historical record, this may in part be due to a deliberate suppression of activities which would reveal support of the Lin Biao-Confucius campaign, a lack of genuine conflict with Jiang Qing and the "gang of four," and possibly an active and cooperative work relationship with Wang Hongwen along the model Zhou Enlai had established. But it also reflected the realities of Deng's situation: his role was gradually being redefined, and while he undoubtedly was no longer on probation, Mao was still observing his performance. Moreover, as one Party historian suggested, it was Deng's practice to mull things over before acting, and given his time in exile, there was much to relearn about Beijing politics.[185] The circumstances shaping Deng's move to the very center of leadership politics began to unfold in August as Mao altered his view of the overall situation, decided eight years of the Cultural Revolution were enough, and set in train developments leading to the Fourth NPC in January 1975.

---

[184] See Burr, *Kissinger Transcripts*, pp. 265-85; and Kissinger, *Years of Renewal*, pp. 163-65. Kissinger's account oddly makes some fundamental factual errors, although his characterization of the encounter appears accurate. In Kissinger's previous memoir volume covering the period in question, *Years of Upheaval*, the meeting with Deng did not even rate a mention. More generally, American diplomats who dealt with Deng in this period commented on his lack of full confidence. Interviews with Chas Freeman (notetaker at the April 1974 meeting) and William Gleysteen, June 1999; and interview with Richard Solomon, November 2003.

[185] Interview, July 2001.

Chapter 3

TOWARD THE FOURTH NATIONAL PEOPLE'S CONGRESS, AUGUST 1974-JANUARY 1975

Some people have made mistakes, and it's good to expose them. Use the "cure the illness to save the patient" method, knocking them over with one blow is not good. Let everyone correct their mistakes, [you] must give everyone the opportunity. When they make self-criticisms, don't interrupt, and applaud when they are finished. From now on emphasize stability and unity. It's time to move on. The Cultural Revolution has already lasted eight years. It is now time to establish stability. The entire Party and the army should unite.

—Mao Zedong, discussing the criticism meeting of military region commanders and political commissars, August 1974[1]

I knew very early from talking with the Chairman that he ... wanted to distinguish Deng Xiaoping from Liu Shaoqi [and protect him]. When [Deng] returned to work, at first he was so kind to me, ... I thought [he] was a reasonable person, someone you could talk to heart to heart. ... At that time the Premier was ill. Originally I was rather anxious about the Premier's position, but afterward I was not too worried. I even believed that [Deng] could be the one to bring stability and unity [to the whole Party]. ... When he came to me and said the most important question was the need for a First Vice Premier [given the Premier's illness], I replied, in that case it should be you. See how stupid I was.

—Jiang Qing, reflecting on her attitude toward Deng Xiaoping in fall 1974, March 2, 1976[2]

Our primary task is to continue to broaden, deepen and persevere in the movement to criticize Lin [Biao] and Confucius. The struggle between the two classes, the proletariat and the bourgeoisie, between the two roads, the socialist and the capitalist, and between the two lines, the Marxist and the revisionist, is long and tortuous and at times even becomes very acute. We must never relax [this] criticism....

—Zhou Enlai's "Report on the Work of the Government," drafted by Deng Xiaoping, to the Fourth NPC, January 13, 1975[3]

While efforts to curb the disruptive aspects of the Lin Biao-Confucius campaign had appeared sporadically since late March 1974, and Mao had articulated a particularly strong criticism of the radicals, including his first recorded reference to "a small faction of four people" at the famous mid-July Politburo meeting, the decisive move effectively ending the *pi Lin pi Kong* movement came with his comment on "stability and unity" in August. Although the movement continued in the media, and was still hailed as the Party's primary task in Zhou Enlai's government work report in January 1975, it was no longer the focus of political activity after summer 1974.[4] Mao's subsequent comment at the end of the year that it was wrong to view the campaign as a second Cultural Revolution further reflected his conclusion that *pi Lin pi Kong* should be wound down, although this hardly affected his underlying view that more Cultural Revolutions would be required in the future.

The effective end of the Lin Biao-Confucius campaign served to reorient Chinese politics toward political stability and economic development, two of the "three directives" from the Chairman in the second half of 1974 that Deng Xiaoping would use as the touchstone of his policy efforts in 1975.[5] Inevitably, this reorientation led to the revival of the effort to hold the Fourth NPC that had been scheduled for fall 1970, but aborted as a result of the dispute involving Lin Biao at that summer's Lushan plenum,[6] and again in October 1973 in the wake of Li Zhen's mysterious death. The project was officially put back on the agenda a year later on October 11, 1974, one week after Mao directed that Deng would become First Vice Premier in the new State Council, as the Party Center

---

[1] Compiled from *Mao zhuan*, vol. 2, p. 1697; *Mao wengao*, vol. 13, p. 402; *Deng Liqun guoshi jiangtan*, vol. 3, pp. 232-33; and Cheng and Xia, *Deng zai yijiuqiwu*, pp. 15-16. Mao's instruction was given sometime after August 1 and before August 18 when it was printed for internal distribution. Cf. below, pp. 194-95.

[2] "Jiang Qing zai dazhaohu huiyi qijian shanzi zhaoji de shier sheng, qu huiyishang de jianghua jilugao" [Draft Record of Jiang Qing's Speech to the Meeting of 12 Provinces and Regions Convened without Authorization at the Time of the Warning Meeting] (March 2, 1976), in *Zhonggong dangshi cankao ziliao* (hereafter *ZGDSCKZL*) [CCP History Teaching Reference Materials], vol. 27 (n.p.: Zhongguo Jiefangjun Guofang Daxue dangshi dangjian zhenggong jiaoyanshi, October 1988), pp. 377, 380.

[3] *PR*, no. 4 (1975), p. 22.

[4] There are some indications that, at least in some more radically-inclined localities, the salience of the campaign lasted longer. For example, Song Ping recalled that the local radical leader in Gansu (Xian Henghan) wanted to turn a spring 1975 conference on learning from Daqing into a *pi Lin pi Kong* meeting. Niu Ying and Peng Xiaozhong, *Song Ping zai Gansu* [Song Ping in Gansu] (Beijing: Zhongyang wenxian chubanshe, 2003), p. 32.

[5] In addition to his August directive on "stability and unity," in November Mao called for "boosting the national economy," and in December he advanced the more radical demand to "study the theory of the dictatorship of the proletariat." On Deng's use of the "three directives" and the related political conflict, see below, pp. 307, 313, 323, 328-29, 337-38, 376ff, 395, 408-409.

[6] See Teiwes and Sun, *Tragedy*, pp. 134ff, for a discussion of the derailing of the Fourth NPC in 1970.

announced that the NPC would convene in the near future, and at the same time conveyed to lower levels Mao's message on the need for stability and unity.[7] Preparing for the NPC and the accompanying formation of a new government hierarchy thus became the central issue of elite politics for the remainder of 1974, one involving a new policy orientation not unlike Zhou's efforts in 1972, the distribution of state power among different individuals and groups, and the replacement of Zhou by Deng as the leading figure of the "old revolutionaries," and of moderate forces more generally. The widely accepted interpretation of the latter part of 1974 posits a fierce struggle over the power inherent in the new state appointments, with the "gang of four" attacking the Premier and seeking to derail Deng as the *de facto* leader of the government. The asserted result, however, was a victory for the moderates at the NPC itself, with the pre-Cultural Revolution elite obtaining a substantial grip on governmental authority, and the Congress introducing a development-oriented program that became known informally as the "four modernizations."[8] While there are elements of truth in this overview, in important respects it distorts the leadership politics of the period.

In certain respects, the accepted view of this period is more at variance with the available evidence than was the case for the Lin Biao-Confucius campaign. In the Lin Biao-Confucius case, the radicals led by Jiang Qing were indeed in the forefront of a movement that threatened moderate policy trends, Party unity, institutional interests and organizational coherence, and the personal interests of other Politburo leaders—above all Zhou Enlai and key PLA commanders. While Chapter 2 demonstrates that the story of *pi Lin pi Kong* was more complicated than this simple overview conveys, the reality of the often sharply clashing interests and behavior of the Politburo radicals and other top leaders is clear. However, in the period from August, and especially after Mao's October 4 designation of Deng as First Vice Premier in waiting, the situation changed not only in terms of overall regime direction, but also in the conduct of elite politics. While tensions and clashes continued, the equation was dramatically altered. Deng's appointment, as one senior Party historian observed, left the radicals few options (*meiyou banfa*) to alter the new political reality.[9] As we discuss in detail below, with Mao having both made the crucial appointment at the start, and requiring unity from the Politburo, the contention over NPC personnel matters, which lasted until the end of 1974, was less confrontational than usually claimed,

---

[7] See *Mao zhuan*, vol. 2, p. 1700.

[8] Although the "four modernizations" have become inextricably linked to the Fourth NPC in PRC and foreign accounts, Zhou's report only referred to the objective of "accomplish[ing] the comprehensive modernization of agriculture, industry, national defense and science and technology before the end of the century"; *PR*, no. 4 (1975), p. 23. Moreover, there is only limited evidence of the "four modernizations" catch phrase being used in public discussion during the remainder of Mao's life, and it only came into widespread use in the post-Mao period. However, it was used as shorthand within elite circles. See *Deng nianpu*, vol. 1, p. 98. Cf. below, p. 467n14.

[9] Interview with a leading scholar in Zhou Enlai studies, January 2005.

with both "sides" holding back to a certain extent, and the Chairman clearly in control of the overall process. Moreover, the result at the NPC, while broadly favoring the moderate forces, was less clear-cut than often assumed.

In the following pages we first examine the unfolding of Mao's major shift, with particular attention to the July 17 Politburo meeting, and his critical August directive that the time had come to wind down the Cultural Revolution. We then turn briefly to the perilous state of the economy that undoubtedly was a major factor in the overall reorientation, and the tentative moves to deal with this situation. Next, Deng Xiaoping's continuing rise is examined, both before and after his nomination as First Vice Premier, with particular attention to his October appointment as PLA Chief-of-Staff and his full assumption of the foreign policy reins as demonstrated during Kissinger's visit in November. This is followed by analyses of the dispute over the Chinese-built ocean freighter *Fengqing* as part of the ongoing conflict over importing foreign technology, including Wang Hongwen's famous trip to Changsha to present the radical view to the Chairman, and of the tug of war over appointments to the new state structure. Finally, we examine the conduct and results of the Fourth NPC itself.

Calling a Halt to *pi Lin pi Kong*

As we saw in Chapter 2, Mao had handed out rebukes to the radicals for their management of *pi Lin pi Kong* from virtually the outset of the campaign, complaining in January-February of their alleged failure to consult him and their use of the "back door" issue. Nevertheless, at this stage the Chairman's complaints did not amount to a call to temper the movement; in fact, Mao regarded the "back door" question as a distraction from his main objectives. Mao's first intervention to curb excesses in the campaign came in the latter part of March, when intense activities in the three PLA headquarters departments threatened to get out of hand. Party Center directives in April and May, which surely had Mao's approval, addressed economic problems (see below) and factional strife, but there were no decisive moves to curb the movement in the localities; wall posters attacked leading figures, including some of Politburo rank, and production losses continued. While a new directive on July 1 dealing with economic problems and factional disruption more generally seemingly had greater bite, in various respects the movement continued unabated. Shortly thereafter, Mao addressed in person matters arising in the course of *pi Lin pi Kong* when the Politburo met on July 17.

The July 17 meeting was the last occasion for nine months when Mao would meet with his top colleagues as a group. The following day he left for a prolonged southern trip, one which saw him reside in Wuhan until early October, then in Changsha for four months, and finally in Hangzhou until he returned to Beijing in April 1975.[10] One of the key consequences of this, as we shall

---

[10] See *Mao zhuan*, vol. 2, pp. 1693-94, 1701, 1715, 1719, 1729.

indicate at greater length subsequently, was that conveying his views became increasingly linked to the visits of foreign leaders who were taken to meet him in the south. This underlined the importance of not only the "two ladies," Wang Hairong and Tang Wensheng, but also of Deng Xiaoping and Li Xiannian, who were the only Politburo leaders accompanying the foreign guests.[11] In any case, having a premonition that this time his stay away from the capital would not be short, and feeling the need to make clear his current views and expectations, the Chairman convened the Politburo collective on the 17th. Notwithstanding his recent surgery, for such an important occasion Premier Zhou left his hospital bed to attend.[12]

In assessing the meaning of the July 17 meeting, as with other occasions centering on Mao, we are faced with major analytic problems. While official sources have made much of this occasion and cite various Mao statements, nothing like a complete record is available. Indeed, a few quotations are repeated over and over again in the sources, with little beyond them. There is also a clear bias, if difficult to judge in terms of its extent, in the heavy emphasis on the Chairman's critical remarks toward the Politburo radicals. In the absence of a complete record, it is difficult to know whether other leaders also suffered Mao's displeasure, or to assess the full context and precise tone of Mao's criticisms of the radicals. Nevertheless, what is known indicates that Mao was chastising the radicals for their stridency in conducting the Lin Biao-Confucius campaign, and, as seen in his dramatic hand holding with Zhou Enlai and Ye Jianying, was also seeking to provide some solace and political cover for these veteran leaders. While the Chairman himself was, of course, ultimately responsible for their—and especially Zhou's—predicament, Mao seems to have decided that enough was enough. Beyond that, even with the limited record, several important deductions can be made about the meeting and the larger nature of elite politics in mid-1974.

First, and largely consistent with Mao's criticisms of the radicals throughout 1974 and subsequently, despite the reference to the "four," the Chairman was primarily—indeed almost solely—addressing the perceived shortcomings of his wife. The involvement of the others was clearly alluded to, but Jiang alone was singled out. Her shortcomings, moreover, were essentially matters of political style. Mao rebuked Jiang, ordering her to "Stop running those two factories, one the iron and steel factory and the other the hat factory, stop slapping big hats on others at will," i.e., to curb her abrasive behavior that could only exacerbate leadership tensions. Mao further warned her of the hostile views she was

---

[11] On the occasion of the visit of Li Xiannian with the Prime Minister of Trinidad in early November, however, Wang Dongxing was present when Li talked with Mao afterward. See below, p. 199. In addition, it is unclear what access Wang Hongwen had as the leader responsible for the Center's daily work, apart from well-documented visits to Changsha in mid-October and late December (see below).

[12] *Mao zhuan*, vol. 2, p. 1695.

engendering among her colleagues: "Others have opinions about you." As Mao's biographers note, these were indeed heavy words and very unusual. While top leaders were aware that this was hardly the first occasion Mao had criticized Jiang, it was the first time he had done so by name in a Politburo meeting.[13] But for all this, there was no indication that Mao raised different policy or theoretical views from those pushed by the radicals during *pi Lin pi Kong*. Moreover, notwithstanding Party Center directives and the Chairman's marginal comments about guarding against shortcomings and avoiding enlargement of the movement during the previous months, the available record does not indicate that Mao now addressed broader issues such as factionalism in official organizations or threats to social order. In particular, while one would expect him to be exasperated with mounting evidence of economic losses, there is no direct evidence that Mao discussed economic issues at this meeting. Thus, while Jiang's rhetoric and actions were undoubtedly one cause of political and economic disruption, Mao apparently did not make—or at least articulate—the connection. Indeed, one could even speculate that his criticisms were as much a product of a long-standing annoyance with Jiang's *modus operandi* at the highest levels as a reaction to the current situation.

While Mao's comments suggested an unusual degree of unhappiness with Jiang, and involved an explicit effort to distance himself from her—"She doesn't speak for me, she only speaks for herself. ... In a word, she represents herself," the whole exchange simply underlined what Party historians frequently refer to as Jiang's special status. After all, Jiang had free rein to criticize Zhou Enlai, and the Premier rarely reacted, while a condition of Deng's return to office was that he not attack her. Mao's warning to Jiang that "others have opinions about you" paradoxically further indicated her status, as he went on to indicate that these others were too intimidated to tell Jiang their opinions face-to-face.[14] The simple fact of the matter was that, since her active role in politics from the onset of the Cultural Revolution, other leaders were deeply inhibited from challenging Jiang because she was the Chairman's wife, and no matter what irritation he might have with her at any particular point, no one could be sure that Mao would not come to her defense if she were under attack. Indeed, Deng's daughter would express the general view that for all his repeated annoyance, Mao did not want to oust Jiang from power.[15] And for all his own efforts and those of later CCP historians to distinguish Mao and his wife, Jiang was truly Mao's creature whose very movements were normally controlled by the Chairman.[16] Of course, when

---

[13] See *ibid.*, p. 1693; and *PR*, no. 35 (1977), p. 26.

[14] *Ibid.* Whether this was strictly true in all circumstances is another matter. See below, p. 213.

[15] Mao Mao, *"Wenge" suiyue*, pp. 309-10.

[16] Of course, Jiang sometimes misunderstood Mao's intentions, overstepped the mark in carrying out his wishes, or was caught out when circumstances changed and Mao altered his view. The Chairman's control of her movements was confirmed by a leading specialist on Mao in an interview, January

Mao was critical of Jiang it could relieve other leaders from exposure to her sharp tongue and give them greater room to maneuver, but this was limited license. In the case at hand, for all his critical words, Mao ultimately provided her with considerable respite by declaring that she had "good" as well as "not so good" qualities, an assessment he would repeat at the end of the year with reference to her performance during the Cultural Revolution and *pi Lin pi Kong*.[17] This hardly provided a great deal of scope for Jiang's enemies, even though the Chairman's dressing down prefigured his demand for "stability and unity" a month later. For Jiang's part, whether or not she avoided further attacks on Zhou and Ye, within days of the Politburo meeting the radicals launched an attack on the opera *Song of the Gardener*, an opera promoted by the Hunan provincial leadership formally led by Hua Guofeng.[18]

As indicated previously, one of the most striking developments at the meeting on the 17th was Mao's introduction of the concept of a four-person faction or "gang." His actual words were ambiguous. In addressing Jiang Qing he asserted that she already was part of a "Shanghai gang"; in addressing the four radicals as a group he enjoined against *forming* "a small faction of four people." As we shall see, this warning against becoming a "gang" would be repeated later in the year, but only in May 1975 did he unambiguously claim the four radicals were consistently behaving as this type of faction.[19] Whether Mao actually thought a four-person "gang" had already formed by mid-1974, or whether he believed Jiang, Wang, Zhang and Yao were equally involved, cannot be determined from his words. Yet whatever Mao's view at the time, he was responsible for the formation of this group going back to the days of the Central Cultural Revolution Group that gave Jiang, Zhang and Yao the task of promoting the movement, and then by bringing Wang to Beijing in 1972. At the time of the Tenth Party Congress he had taken special delight in the four, granted them great power over the Congress, and asked the Politburo as a whole to assist them, to help them grow like "green vegetables." And similar to 1966-68, after the Congress the four were given key responsibilities in pushing *pi Lin pi Kong* forward. Whatever the common interests of the four radicals, or the degree of their cooperation during the Lin Biao-Confucius campaign, the "gang" gained new definition in circumstances where they were required to implement Mao's objective of reviving Cultural Revolution values.

2005. An example during this period was Jiang's request to extend for a few more days her June visit to Tianjin. Such control was not complete, however, as when Jiang ignored Mao's wishes and flew to Changsha to see him in January 1975. See *Mao zhuan*, vol. 2, pp. 1692-93, 1718.

[17] See *Mao zhuan*, vol. 2, pp. 1693-94; and *PR*, no. 35 (1977), pp. 26, 27.

[18] See "Zhonggong zhongyang guanyu 'Wang Hongwen, Zhang Chunqiao, Jiang Qing, Yao Wenyuan fandang jituan zuizheng (cailiao zhi san)'," p. 51. Regarding Zhou, at least one radical attack after July 17 was claimed—Yao Wenyuan's order on August 5 that newspapers reprint an earlier article criticizing the Qin dynasty's Prime Minister. *Ibid.*, p. 16.

[19] See *Mao zhuan*, vol. 2, p. 1693; and *PR*, no. 35 (1977), pp. 26, 27.

If Mao's known words at the July 17 Politburo meeting were largely restricted to commenting on Jiang Qing's responsibility for fractious relations at the highest levels, and perhaps for her actions in such cases as attacks on the three PLA headquarters, there nevertheless were also indications of an intent to ease the Lin Biao-Confucius campaign. As we saw in Chapter 2, at some point shortly after the meeting, Wang Hongwen issued orders winding down the movement in Zhejiang, the most fractious of provinces.[20] Moreover, the very fact of Mao setting off on an extended holiday suggests that, at least in his mind, his intervention in the Politburo would bring matters under control. In any case, Mao's remarks in August went much further, making the new direction obvious. Although again addressing unity within the high-ranking elite, by declaring that eight years of Cultural Revolution were enough, he focused squarely on the key issue affecting the overall functioning of the political system, something only he could do. The fact that it was from August that *pi Lin pi Kong* began to wind down to a significant degree, a process that accelerated in October when Mao's remarks on stability and unity were more widely circulated, clearly indicates that whatever his earlier concerns with elite unity and broader system disruption, it was only now that Mao took the decisive step. This development further indicates that even a brief, but much clearer, comment from the Chairman was sufficient to reorient the body politic.

What was the context of Mao's August intervention? The key situational factor was the Lin Biao-Confucius campaign in the large military regions. Even before his August statement, Mao's attitude toward the PLA was softening. On the eve of the August 1 anniversary of the founding of the PLA, a number of high-ranking officers who had been ousted during the Cultural Revolution reappeared for the first time, notably former Acting Chief-of-Staff Yang Chengwu.[21] In Yang's case, Mao personally took the initiative for his appearance and thus effective rehabilitation. Zhou Enlai confided to Yang that his liberation was particularly difficult, that despite the Premier's three reports urging such an outcome, it was only when Mao became angry with the delay that his return to work was settled. Both the events of Army Day 1974, and the broader policy of cadre liberation discussed in Chapter 1, illustrate some notable aspects of the process. While there can be little doubt that the radicals dragged out the reexamination of many cases, although rarely if ever blocking the "reversal of verdicts," the whole process was inherently difficult and not amenable to quick solutions. As a senior Party historian observed, these were cases originally approved by Mao and the Politburo, and they could not be set aside without careful consideration. However much Mao may have given a green light in principle, in practice that

---

[20] See above, p. 176.

[21] Yang, who had succeeded Luo Ruiqing as the effective Chief-of-Staff at the start of the Cultural Revolution, was himself purged in early 1968, with Jiang Qing playing an important role, but Mao clearly dominating. See Teiwes and Sun, *Tragedy*, pp. 90-102.

light would inevitably be amber, especially in cases such as Yang Chengwu's where Yang's purge had been solely Mao's decision. But with the Army Day celebrations, the Chairman had given the process a new push forward. Another feature, ironic given Mao's doubts about the PLA, was that as a rule high-profile cases in which Mao was personally involved tended to result in army figures returning more quickly to real power than their civilian counterparts. Thus pre-Cultural Revolution Politburo figures Chen Yun and Tan Zhenlin had to settle for marginal positions in low-ranking State Council work and/or NPC posts, while in 1972 Su Zhenhua quickly became the real head of the navy and Yang Chengwu would soon be PLA Deputy Chief-of-Staff.[22]

The immediate context of Mao's altered attitude toward the PLA and his call for stability and unity was *pi Lin pi Kong* criticism directed at military region commanders. As discussed in Chapter 2, following the rotation of these leaders, criticism meetings largely aimed at the departed commanders were held in the regions, and in May two special case groups were set up under Wang Hongwen to investigate Li Desheng and the other seven commanders. Based on criticism by their old subordinates, the regional criticism meetings produced considerable material on the commanders, including bulletins of the meetings, wall posters, and various other exposure materials. These materials were sent to the Center where Wang's special case groups reviewed and organized the documents. In July, Wang, now responsible for Party daily work since the Premier permanently relocated to his hospital quarters in June, as well as for the special case groups, submitted the reorganized material to Mao and circulated it to the Politburo. The Chairman, seemingly relieved that no serious issues were uncovered, noted that the PLA was feeling crestfallen, and, shortly after Army Day, ordered Wang to convene a meeting of large region commanders and political commissars in mid-August to thrash things out. While Mao presumably expected such a meeting would solve ideological problems, Wang allegedly did not pass on his ameliorating comments which included the call for stability and unity, with the result that tension understandably surrounded the gathering. In the post-Mao account, Wang also assertedly used the occasion to stir up attacks on old military cadres, while Deng, when accompanying a foreign leader to see Mao in early September, reported on the proceedings and reassured the Chairman about army reliability. Mao found nothing new in the conference discussions, and declared that "these are all old questions, people shouldn't be so tense." With this, the pressure on the PLA eased.[23]

---

[22] *Mao zhuan*, vol. 2, pp. 1696-97; *Zhou nianpu*, vol. 3, p. 673; interview with leading Party historian on the period, January 2005; and above, pp. 43-49. On the occasion of Yang's reappearance, Zhou informed him of his daughter's death, allegedly caused by Lin Biao, but also admitted his own "excessive words" at the time of Yang's 1968 purge.

[23] *Mao zhuan*, vol. 2, pp. 1696-97; *Zhou nianpu*, vol. 3, p. 674; Cheng and Xia, *Deng zai yijiuqiwu*, pp. 14-16; and interview with senior specialist on the period, November 2002. Organization Department

There are several problems with this version as it reflects on Wang and Deng, although nothing detracts from the central significance of Mao's August comment. First, whatever Wang did or did not withhold of Mao's remarks, and however much he may have criticized the participants, he soon conveyed Mao's central message, including the dramatic statement that eight years of Cultural Revolution were enough, about a week into the conference on August 18. Moreover, it was the materials prepared under Wang's direction that reassured the Chairman concerning the generals in the first place, and in the absence of any convincing information to the contrary, we must assume it was Wang, not Deng, who briefed Mao on the initial developments at the meeting that further reinforced his conclusion that there were no serious problems with the commanders. As for Wang's behavior in chairing the criticism sessions, vague claims about stirring up attacks overlook Mao's (typical) two-sided injunction: while people were not to be "knocked over with one blow," Wang was still required to preside over the exposure of mistakes. While somewhat speculative on our part, it does not appear that Wang—in contrast to Jiang Qing's July emphasis on the seriousness of the generals' problems—sought to exacerbate the situation at the meeting. In any case, even with the reduction of tension that surely flowed from the circulation of Mao's remarks, the conference and criticism continued into early September. It was then, on September 4, that Deng accompanied the President of Togo to see Mao in Wuhan and reported further on the military meeting. Mao now decided to wind down the meeting; he approved Li Desheng's self-examination on the 8th and the conference concluded on the 10th. In other words, while Deng played a part, the basic decision had been taken earlier without his known involvement. Both Wang and Deng had supporting roles as providers of information, but Mao's crucial decision was based on his own reading of the situation.[24]

More important than easing pressure on the generals, the larger political and economic situation was now altered. Although he apparently had not raised key issues facing the Party in his August remarks, Mao soon addressed the question of the organizational arrangements needed to deal with those problems. At their September 4 meeting, he asked Deng whether the Fourth NPC could be held by the end of the year, a clear pointer to Deng's key position in the new State Council to be confirmed at the Congress. While presumably responding positively, Deng observed that personnel issues would be the main problem. Over the following month, Mao reportedly gave particular attention to implementing the Party's traditional workable (luoshi) cadre policy, i.e., the employment of sufficiently experienced cadres, a policy obviously linked to new official appointments. This had been

---

head Guo Yufeng, who had worked with Kang Sheng, was directly responsible for the work of the two special case groups. Cf. below, p. 271.

[24] See Cheng and Xia, Deng zai yijiuqiwu, pp. 15-16, who provide the only (albeit minimally) detailed account of these events. Although Cheng and Xia emphasize Deng's contribution while painting Wang in a negative light, the timing of events supports the interpretation here.

reflected in the Army Day rehabilitations, notably in the quick assignment of Yang Chengwu to the PLA General Staff. With National Day coming, Mao was seemingly even more involved in arranging for the reappearance on October 1 of over 40 old cadres who had not been seen for years. These included key players in Deng's 1975 measures: Hu Qiaomu, the Chairman's former secretary, who would be a lynchpin of the effort, and Li Chang, who would take a leading role in the revived Academy of Sciences. Mao also pushed to a conclusion several key rehabilitation cases that had long been stalled: on the military side, the posthumous reversal of Marshal He Long's verdict, and on the civilian side, the rehabilitation of the pre-Cultural Revolution Shanghai leader Chen Pixian. Meanwhile, the Politburo discussed holding the NPC, and on October 4 Wang Hongwen, as the leader responsible for Party daily work, reported to the Chairman that the Congress could be convened by the end of the year or by spring festival in early 1975. Mao's response was to press for speeding up the process and settling personnel questions, and he had his secretary phone Wang with that message and his proposal that Deng become First Vice Premier. Clearly, while Deng had been earmarked for important duties since his return and was already carrying out major State Council responsibilities, it was the turn away from *pi Lin pi Kong* and the revival of consolidation tasks that placed him at the center of the political equation.[25]

Dealing with Economic Disruption

While political stability was clearly the necessary condition for dealing with a Chinese economy that had markedly deteriorated during the course of the Lin Biao-Confucius campaign, there is little evidence that Mao explicitly addressed economic issues before November 1974. Although he surely approved the April 22 and July 1 directives addressing this situation (explicitly in the latter case), no indication of a personal comment beyond the Cultural Revolution slogan, "grasp revolution and promote production," has been reported. That slogan itself is vague and ambiguous: while it gives priority to "revolution," in practice it was introduced to restrain the movement from totally disrupting economic activity. Moreover, even after his August declaration that eight years of Cultural Revolution was enough, when discussing the general situation on August 20 with the leadership's top economic official, Li Xiannian, from the minimal information available, his remarks dealt with "stability and unity," not with the economy as such.[26] This diffidence, as we shall see, apparently continued until another meeting with Li in early November, with consequences for addressing the problems at issue.

As discussed in Chapter 1, the Chairman's elusiveness on economic issues was hardly new. Simply put, Mao was not indifferent toward the economy —

[25] See *Mao zhuan*, vol. 2, pp. 1695, 1697, 1699; and above, p. 158.

[26] *Mao zhuan*, vol. 2, p. 1695.

he periodically gave economic repair work increased priority, and he certainly wanted to see a prosperous and powerful China—but he was quite prepared to bear enormous economic costs in pursuit of his ideological vision. The priority placed on political goals was not only implicit in "grasp revolution and promote production," but explicitly reiterated in May 1973 when, in objecting to some aspects of planning work, Mao observed that correcting economic problems was all well and good, but more attention should be given to the superstructure. Since the Ninth Congress, with further increments following the 1970 Lushan plenum and the September 13 incident, Mao clearly endorsed efforts to restore economic order, notably by reviving the planning and economic management systems that had collapsed in 1966-68, although the hard work was left to others. The legacy of Cultural Revolution rhetoric inhibited these efforts, and the redefinition of Lin Biao as an "ultra-rightist" at the end of 1972 largely stalled further efforts. Nevertheless, economic conditions improved in 1973, only to suffer a severe setback in 1974. While other problems contributed to poor economic performance (notably dislocations resulting from war preparations, although these had moderated by 1974), the critical factor was the disruption caused by political movements.[27]

The economic performance of the PRC over the entire "Cultural Revolution decade" lagged significantly behind that of the pre-1966 period in terms of gross economic output, the main criterion by which socialist economies measured their success. While afflicted by the normal if intensified socialist pathologies of low quality output, inefficient use of resources, and overemphasis on accumulation in comparison to consumption, the defining feature of poor economic performance during the decade was tremendous fluctuations in production, and these were tightly linked to political disruption. During the Cultural Revolution proper in 1967 and 1968, the value of industrial and agricultural output decreased by 9.6 and 4.2 percent respectively. In 1974, despite moderate to usually substantial increases over the previous five years, output declined over the first three-quarters when *pi Lin pi Kong* dominated, only recovering to a small 1.4 percent increase in output value for the full year. Only 95.6 percent of the planned annual figure was achieved, and production was reduced in a number of key sectors. The key factors in 1974 were the breakdown of management systems, most famously as a consequence of January propaganda against measuring work by tonnage on the Shanghai docks which led to the clogging of ports nationwide, and even more importantly the breakout of factional fighting on the railroads and in productive units.[28] The lesson seemingly was clear to the PRC's economic officials. According to a Party historian specializing on the period, during internal

---

[27] See above, pp. 49-54.

[28] See the 1986 State Statistical Bureau's report concerning economic development in 1966-76, in Schoenhals, *China's Cultural Revolution*, pp. 262-66; Liu and Wu, *China's Socialist Economy*, pp. 387, 389, 391-92; and Ma Qibin, *Sishinian*, pp. 324, 336, 345, 354, 365.

discussions these officials concluded that there was nothing wrong with the economic system *per se*, that poor performance was due to damage caused by rebel activities in the workplace.[29] Indeed, dealing with this issue would be the centerpiece of Deng's approach to the economy well into 1975.

By April 1974, economic losses since the start of the Lin Biao-Confucius campaign could no longer be ignored. Production declined drastically in key industrial sectors, notably steel, chemical fertilizer, and especially coal. Figures subsequently available for January-May showed total output value at only 35.7 percent of the year's planned figure. The most critical problem was transport, with factional fighting and organizational chaos in the railroad sector leading to frequent delays and shortfalls in deliveries, while ports also failed to move goods. Thus, even with decreased production, coal piled up in Shanxi and could not reach places where there were critical shortages. In this context, the SPC held a conference attended by representatives of 15 provinces and municipalities from April 5 to 15 to study how to promote production as quickly as possible, but, as noted in Chapter 2, with little effect. Indeed, the Party Center's transmission of the SPC's report on April 22 was a timid document that only listed the 1974 annual targets decided in October 1973, and noted that due to *pi Lin pi Kong*, a majority of important targets had fallen behind the plan. With apparently few concrete solutions offered, it is hardly surprising that, as subsequently claimed, "there was not much that could be done about [the situation]."[30]

It took several more months with no sign of improvement before more forceful action was taken, culminating in a Party Center circular on July 1, with Mao's endorsement. The politics of this development are obscure, but again the SPC was the body to act by reporting to the Politburo on June 18 concerning further economic deterioration. The SPC report noted that industrial production had declined in many areas, presented the January-May figures noted above, and pinpointed coal production and rail transport as the key problems. The State Council now acted by quickly approving reports on restoring order on the railways and freeing up clogged harbors. But the key measure was the Party Center directive which addressed not only the economic issues, but also the broader problems resulting from *pi Lin pi Kong*. The July 1 document, under the title of "grasping revolution and promoting production," enjoined leaders to carry out policy and not fear the masses, and indicated that factionalism and the inability to resist worker wage demands were widespread. Cadres were not to be arrested or beaten, and those who had left their posts were ordered

---

[29] Interview, April 1999.

[30] See Liu and Wu, *China's Socialist Economy*, pp. 387-90; Chen and Du, *Shilu*, vol. 3, part 2, pp. 1064-65; Gao and Yan, *Turbulent Decade*, p. 450; and "Zhonggong zhongyang tongyi bing pizhuan Guojia jiwei 'Guanyu 1974 nian guomin jingji jihua (caoan) de baogao' (gaiyao)" [CCP Center Agrees with and Transmits the SPC's "Report on the 1974 (Draft) Economic Plan" (Outline)] (April 22, 1974), in *CRDB*, p. 1. According to Liu and Wu, Zhou Enlai adopted "some measures" to deal with these problems, but nothing was specified.

to return. At a more philosophical level, "going against the tide" was declared very different from "rebelling against the leadership," despite the equation of the two earlier in the movement. Concretely, such Cultural Revolution practices as exchanging experiences, fighting civil wars, and spreading the fallacy of "not producing for erroneous lines," were denounced. These were, in the context of mid-1974, strong words, and it is hard to believe there were no indications from Mao that something had to be done. Nevertheless, the Chairman's sole known action was minimalist—reading and circling the Center's notice without apparent comment.[31]

The impact of these measures, countered as they were by continuing radical messages from the Lin Biao-Confucius campaign, was not dramatic, with only a slight economic improvement in August, but no fundamental change. With the Chairman still largely silent, progress would necessarily be slow even if there were more leeway for economic officials to act. One step was the Politburo's order to the SPC to convene a national planning conference on October 6, a meeting that addressed the financial deficit, light industrial shortages, and other problems, as well as setting average daily output targets for key sectors. But the key authority for further progress came in early November when, as one account put it, "The economic situation caught Mao Zedong's attention."[32] In a conversation with Li Xiannian and Wang Dongxing on November 6, a conversation in which Li emphasized absolute support for the Chairman's decisions on "stability and unity" and promoting Deng, Mao highlighted the need to "boost the national economy." The impact of Mao's statement was indicated a few days later when Deng Liqun, recently returned to Beijing from a cadre school and soon to play a key role in Deng Xiaoping's consolidation program in 1975, visited Wang Zhen, his old superior when he worked in Xinjiang in the 1950s. Deng Liqun found Yu Qiuli, one of Party's top economic officials since just before the Cultural Revolution, at Wang's home. Yu expressed great relief over Mao's remarks, noting that he and others had been under huge pressure and criticized as proponents of the "theory of productive forces," but they now felt liberated. Over a month later, on December 17, while briefing Mao on the government work report to be delivered at the NPC, Deng Xiaoping reviewed growth over the past ten years, observed that the speed of foreign trade development was a bit slow, argued the need to use the coming five years to address the situation, and declared construction was impossible without realizing "stability and unity." Mao approved Deng's approach, and asked him to work together with Li Xiannian and Yu Qiuli in handling the problem.[33]

---

[31] Chen and Du, *Shilu*, vol. 3, part 2, pp. 1094-96; Yan and Gao, *Turbulent Decade*, pp. 450-51; and "Zhonggong zhongyang guanyu zhuageming cushengchan de tongzhi," pp. 1-2.

[32] Liu and Wu, *China's Socialist Economy*, pp. 390-92.

[33] See *Mao wengao*, vol. 13, p. 410; *Mao zhuan*, vol. 2, pp. 1706, 1709-10; and *Deng Liqun guoshi jiangtan*, vol. 3, p. 91.

As the Fourth NPC approached, Mao was showing greater attention to the economy, and as a result his associates were feeling greater confidence in addressing economic problems. But this was still a slow process carried out with considerable caution, one marked by references to Mao's August directive. Although Li Xiannian quickly reported Mao's November comment to the Politburo, it was not until February 1975 that it was distributed in a central document. It is unclear how clearly or strongly the message was conveyed, with Jiang Qing in 1976 going so far as to question whether Mao had actually said it.[34] In any case, a further step had been taken by the end of 1974 toward dealing with economic issues, a step that undoubtedly goes some way toward explaining the introduction of the modernization theme at the Congress. But that theme would be encased in radical rhetoric, the immediate post-NPC approach to the economy was largely one of restoring order, and it was only in summer 1975 that an attempt to lay out specific programs was undertaken. It was truly one step at a time.

The Further Emergence of Deng Xiaoping

As we saw in the preceding chapters, Deng's initial role after returning to office in spring 1973 was quite marginal to the end of that year, and while his status and duties were significantly enhanced in 1974, including taking over responsibility for State Council daily work in June, Deng's activities, political clout and leadership relations were elusive prior to his nomination as First Vice Premier in October. In terms of his relations with the radicals and Jiang Qing in particular, there is no evidence of conflict apart from that concerning Deng's assignment to head the Chinese delegation to the UN in April, a case grossly distorted in the post-Mao telling (see Chapter 2). Notwithstanding the tension surrounding this case, none of the available accounts reveal a direct clash between Deng and Jiang, and, as we saw, she wanted him to remain in Beijing to assist with *pi Lin pi Kong* criticism. Of course, Deng had pledged not to oppose Jiang as a condition for his return to work, and he was aware that Mao would be observing him in this and other regards. For her part, Jiang knew of Mao's partiality toward Deng, and if her own account cited at the start of this chapter is to be believed, she supported Deng for the First Vice Premiership even before Mao had made his determination. Deng's rise must also be seen in terms of the Chairman's plans for Wang Hongwen. As we have seen, Deng's daughter believes Mao was contemplating a cooperative relationship between Deng and Wang, yet by the end of 1974, the Chairman's declining confidence in Wang was clear, with implications for Deng's authority.[35]

---

[34] "Zhonggong zhongyang guanyu 'Wang Hongwen, Zhang Chunqiao, Jiang Qing, Yao Wenyuan fandang jituan zuizheng (cailiao zhi san)'," p. 58; and below, p. 338.

[35] See above, p. 180. When Mao lost confidence in Wang is a matter of conjecture. Several senior Party historians speculate that it was as early as the Tenth Congress, a proposition we find dubious given the powers granted Wang at the time. Interviews, January 2005. Our best guess, as discussed

Meanwhile, Deng's relations with Zhou Enlai and other moderate leaders were not as clear-cut as normally assumed. While an underlying common view undoubtedly existed, and Zhou and Deng did have working relations in the State Council and concerning foreign policy, Deng's seeming failure to visit Zhou's hospital room from June to early October is striking.[36]

The area where Deng's activities are most clear is foreign relations. In addition to the UN assignment, by May he was attending Mao's meetings with foreigners (alternating with Li Xiannian whose foreign responsibilities focused on trade), and he joined Zhou for diplomatic exchanges with the visitors. His role increased further from June, with Zhou in the hospital and for that month not receiving foreigners. Zhou resumed seeing foreigners in July, but these appear to have been increasingly courtesy calls, or at least limited exchanges, with business referred to Deng and Li. Somewhat later, after Deng's nomination as First Vice Premier, the new situation was made abundantly, even brutally, clear during Kissinger's visit in November. Reflecting Mao's attitude whereby PRC representatives had treated the Premier as a virtual non-person in their communications with the US since Kissinger's previous visit a year earlier, when the Secretary of State visited his hospital quarters, Zhou avoided substantive discussion, claiming doctors' orders. As noted, a crucial aspect of the situation was that once the Chairman went south, Deng and Li became the top officials accompanying foreign leaders to see Mao. The "two ladies" were again omnipresent, but Wang Hongwen no longer attended these encounters. Thus Deng (and Li) had a first-hand opportunity to gauge Mao's attitude and to test the waters with their own ideas.[37]

Deng's ascent in foreign policy matters, particularly because it signified Mao's confidence, had some important consequences. First, although overstated, in the view of one key Ministry of Foreign Affairs insider, Deng's arrival as the key player in MFA affairs resulted in a new period of peace in the ministry. With Zhou no longer the focus of contention, and leading figures no longer having to navigate Mao's complicated attitudes toward the Premier, the "two ladies," who were "bad to Premier Zhou but good to Deng Xiaoping" in Li Xiannian's view, developed an apparently strong link to Deng, while their potential and eventually actual enemy, Qiao Guanhua, also worked well with him.[38]

The situation also affected Deng's self-confidence, as seen during Kissinger's November 25-29 visit. In contrast to his somewhat hesitant performance at the

---

below, is that it developed in a major way between October and December 1974.

[36] See *Zhou nianpu*, vol. 3, pp. 671ff. A senior figure in Zhou Enlai studies claims that the *nianpu* record of Zhou's visitors is complete, although only a single visit by the "two ladies" on August 16 is recorded before October. Interview, January 2005.

[37] *Zhou nianpu*, vol. 3, pp. 672-74 *et seq.*; *Mao zhuan*, vol. 2, p. 1695; Kissinger, *Years of Renewal*, p. 161; and interview with leading specialist on Deng, November 2002.

[38] Interview, November 2002; above, p. 20; and below, pp. 225-26, 427ff, 433-34.

UN in April, Deng now demonstrated command, a brisk no-nonsense approach to the exchanges, and more than a bit of sarcasm toward the Secretary of State. The rougher edges, of course, were a product of the situation: the stalemate over normalization, uncertainty over the new American administration after Nixon's resignation, and China's unhappiness with the just concluded Vladivostok meeting of Ford and Brezhnev. With Mao declining to meet Kissinger, Deng minced no words, expressing non-belief in détente, raising sharp questions about the Vladivostok meeting, and dismissing the Secretary's excuses regarding normalization, declaring "you owe us a debt." One leading Party specialist on Deng cites his handling of Kissinger as not only creative in putting Kissinger on the back foot, but also as a sign that Deng had a deeper understanding of Mao's intentions than Zhou. Certainly, Mao would have appreciated Deng's combative style, but in substantive terms his position was little different from Zhou's the previous year. While making sure to remind Kissinger of Mao's view that the Taiwan issue could only be settled by force, Deng declared Sino-US relations normal and warned of the "polar bear." In short, while the style was different, the substance was the same as during Kissinger's previous visit, and we can only conclude that Mao's underlying attitudes toward the two men, not policy or even its implementation, were critical in his favorable reaction to Deng's performance.[39]

Deng's confidence in dealing with Kissinger would have been especially bolstered by his unprecedented nomination as First Vice Premier in October. The background to this appointment naturally involved Zhou's health. If Zhou were to continue as Premier, someone else would have to take over the lion's share of State Council duties, something Deng was already doing to a substantial degree since assuming responsibility for daily work in June. The idea of a First Vice Premier was discussed among high-ranking leaders in summer 1974; according to one account, Zhou himself was the first to propose such a post, but with typical caution did not indicate a candidate. It was in this context, as described in Jiang Qing's statement at the start of this chapter, that Deng approached her, arguing the need for such a position, but not making any suggestion concerning the person, and drawing her response that "it should be you." One can only speculate about the motives of both leaders in this exchange. In Jiang's case, it

---

[39] Kissinger, *Years of Renewal*, pp. 868-73; Burr, *Kissinger Transcripts*, pp. 286-88, 296, 298-99, 304, 312; James Mann, *About Face: A History of America's Curious Relationship with China, From Nixon to Clinton* (New York: Alfred A. Knopf, 1999), p. 65; and interview, November 2002. Some American recollections of these meetings depict a less secure Deng, a man "glancing back at his Chinese associates, as if checking that he was saying the right thing"; Burr, p. 287. This was attributed to worry about "dangerous enemies," above all Jiang Qing. While we naturally cannot attest to Deng's glances or what they meant, by late November Deng had little reason to fear Jiang, although, of course, no one could be truly secure at Mao's court. In any case, several interlocutors perceived a more self-assured Deng by 1975, compared to his 1974 UN performance. Interviews with Chas Freeman and William Gleysteen, June 1999.

most likely was her knowledge of Mao's view of Deng, but it could also have involved the belief that he was the best candidate given both his experience and his apparently solicitous behavior toward her since returning to work. Another possibility, again speculative, is that Jiang's position may have reflected tensions between her and Zhang Chunqiao, the radical most commonly considered premier material, even though at some point she had touted Zhang's premiership qualities to the Chairman.[40] In any case, in contrast to claims of fierce contention over the position, for the period leading up to Mao's designation of Deng, there is no evidence of it being a source of significant conflict. According to Wang Hongwen's 1980 confession, moreover, in the two weeks from October 4 to the 17th, when the *Fengqing* incident erupted in the Politburo, the other three radicals seemed unconcerned with Deng's appointment, although Wang acknowledged some reservations on his part given Deng's status as the number two capitalist roader during the Cultural Revolution.[41] It is only in the context of the *Fengqing* question that a case can be made that Deng's promotion *then* became an issue, but as we argue in the following section, this exaggerates and distorts the tensions that emerged as a result of the incident.

The final indication of Deng's rise, his designation by Mao as PLA Chief-of-Staff later in October, is a more complicated story, one that also became entangled in the *Fengqing* incident, and was only settled in its wake. While reserving that discussion for the next section, here we analyze the lead-up to the filling of the post. As with the First Vice Premiership, evidence for radical resistance to Deng assuming the position has not been found. The background to this appointment was the uncertainty concerning top-level PLA posts since the Lin Biao affair: none of the three headquarters departments had heads in 1974. The GPD post was vacant since Li Desheng's sudden departure at the start of the year, while there had been no Chief-of-Staff since Huang Yongsheng's arrest after the September 13 incident. Ye Jianying, as Party first secretary, was the leading figure of the General Staff Department, and conceivably was favored by some as Chief-of-Staff, although this is unlikely given his advanced age, not to mention Mao's criticism of the old marshal.[42] In any case, regularizing military positions at the same time as making State Council appointments made sense, and clearly was on the minds of top leaders. With Mao having decided the NPC would go ahead and designating Deng the new head of government on October 4,

---

[40] See Yan and Gao, *Turbulent Decade*, p. 455; Tong Xiaopeng, *Fengyu sishinian (dierbu)* [Forty Years of Trials and Hardships (second part)] (Beijing: Zhongyang wenxian chubanshe, 1996), p. 534; above, p. 186; and below, p. 221. On Jiang-Zhang tensions, see above, p. 18n51.

[41] Interview with exceptionally well-connected senior Party historian, January 2005. Apart from Deng's classification as the number two capitalist roader, Wang cited his exposure to the negative comments of many old cadres who had worked with Deng as influencing his view.

[42] Concerning the third and least significant headquarters organization, the General Logistics Department, Zhang Zongxun, who was formally appointed in 1975, may have been in effective control earlier.

the Chief-of-Staff position gained enhanced salience. On October 6, Jiang Qing visited Zhou Enlai with her proposal on the position, a proposal left unspecified in the most authoritative sources, undoubtedly because it did not fit the usual radical paradigm. In the same period, Deng also proposed a candidate. At this stage, there was apparently no consideration of Deng himself as the new Chief-of-Staff.[43]

Zhou Enlai, who had already been approached on personnel issues by Deng, did not indicate a preference concerning Jiang's nominee during their lengthy talk, nor, insofar as can be determined, did he make a nomination prior to Mao's decision. But who did Jiang and Deng favor? The best evidence indicates that Deng's nominee was Chen Xilian, his old Second Field Army subordinate and now Beijing Military Region Commander, a man whose fighting abilities he praised when visited by another Second Field Army veteran, Li Desheng, at the end of the year.[44] Jiang's proposal that Yang Chengwu become Chief-of-Staff was more surprising, but in fact neither nomination was easily predictable. In Deng's case, however much he may have been reassured by his past links to Chen, it is simplistic to think this was his primary motive. For one thing, to advocate someone from one's own mountaintop, even given Mao's call at the end of 1973 to promote more people from the Second Field Army, risked the Chairman's suspicion of factionalism. The telling factor, we believe, was Deng's understanding of Mao's own partiality toward Chen. This could already be sensed in the transfer of Chen to Beijing, the most sensitive military region post, in the December 1973 rotation. A more direct indication of Mao's high assessment of Chen would come in May 1975, when he indicated that a greater military role awaited Chen in the future.[45]

In contrast, Jiang's nomination of Yang Chengwu, when suggested to various Party historians, was treated as impossible given her role in attacking Yang in February 1968. Yet it was not only Jiang and Lin Biao who harshly criticized Yang on that occasion: Zhou Enlai also used "excessive words." Whatever their real individual views, they all danced to Mao's tune. The question really becomes the situation surrounding the reversal of Yang's case. While it is

---

[43] We cannot be sure of this since Mao later claimed that Ye Jianying proposed Deng be appointed Chief-of-Staff and First Vice Premier concurrently. *Mao zhuan*, vol. 2, p. 1705. Our judgment, however, is that this most likely came after the stalemate involving Deng's and Jiang's nominees.

[44] See *Zhou nianpu*, vol. 3, p. 677; Li Desheng, "Weiren de danshi yu xionghuai," p. 112; and Tie Ji, "Changsha juece" [Policy Decisions at Changsha], in An Jianshe, *Zhou Enlai de zuihou suiyue*, pp. 380-81. These sources do not stipulate the identities of the nominees, identities we arrived at through a long process of considering possible candidates and a host of contextual factors. A Party historian with close ties to Yang Chengwu's family independently concluded that Jiang proposed Yang; interview, March 2001. Finally, our conclusion was confirmed by a well-connected senior historian who reported seeing a document naming Chen and Yang as Deng's and Jiang's respective nominees; interview, January 2005.

[45] See above, p. 170; and below, p. 295.

well documented that Jiang and the other radicals provided tough and skeptical reviews of military cases, there is no direct information that this applied to Yang's. In presenting Zhou's claim that he had to write three reports before Yang's verdict was reversed, post-Mao sources imply that this was due to the obstruction of the radicals, but they do not state it explicitly, with one reasonably detailed analysis of radical obstruction of PLA rehabilitations failing to mention Yang's case. The most likely explanation for Jiang's apparent support of Yang's rehabilitation is that she was aware of Mao's intent. In this, and in her nomination of Yang for the Chief-of-Staff position, Jiang presumably calculated that Yang would feel gratitude and thus be amenable to her influence.[46] In any case, Mao's selection of Deng is best explained as an inspired intervention to resolve the conflicting proposals of Deng and Jiang, one that gave something to all concerned. Deng, of course, became Chief-of-Staff himself, while Yang Chengwu became the First Deputy Chief-of-Staff responsible for daily work, and thus would run the General Staff under Deng's authority. Meanwhile, Jiang saw her nominee obtain a major military position. Ye Jianying, who seemingly suggested Deng as a way to resolve the matter, gained the Chairman's trust after a period in relative disfavor, while Chen Xilian would soon be rewarded when Mao added his name to the list of vice premiers for the Fourth NPC.

The *Fengqing* Dispute and Wang Hongwen's Trip to Changsha

Mao's October 4 decision to name Deng the presumptive First Vice Premier changed the political equation. While top leaders such as Jiang Qing would have already understood the Chairman's favoritism for Deng, and Deng had been in effect running the government since June, Mao had now made a clear decision. One consequence was an immediate increase in Deng's interaction with Zhou after no known private contact since their meeting in April 1973. With a transition in government leadership and preparations for the coming NPC on the agenda, such enhanced interaction was normal, although the leader most frequently seeing Zhou in the period up to the Congress was Wang Hongwen.[47] It is the contrast of before and after October 4, however, that requires comment, particularly in view of Deng's responsibility for State Council daily work from June 1, the date of Zhou's permanent relocation to the PLA's 305 Hospital. This would suggest the

---

[46] See Xie Guoming, "175 wei jiangjun," pp. 357-70; *Mao zhuan*, vol. 2, pp. 1695-97; and *Zhou nianpu*, vol. 3, p. 673. Although there is little evidence of prior Deng-Yang tension, a possible reason Deng did not support Yang is that Yang had been deeply involved in the purge of Luo Ruiqing in 1965-66, a case concerning which Deng had major reservations. As for Zhou, once Mao's decision was made, he indicated his approval and commented that after Yang matured, Deng could hand the post over to him. Gao Wenqian, *Wannian Zhou*, p. 534.

[47] According to *Zhou nianpu*, vol. 3, pp. 677-86, from October 4 to his departure for Changsha on December 23, Zhou met with Wang Hongwen on 16 occasions, Deng 12, Li Xiannian and Ji Dengkui 11 each, Ye Jianying 10, Zhang Chunqiao 6, Jiang Qing 5, Hua Guofeng and Yao Wenyuan 2 each, and six other leaders one time each. In addition, Zhou saw the "two ladies" 10 times.

need for frequent consultation, but the available information does not bear this out over the first four months. The seriousness of the Premier's health in June, when he received no foreign visitors due to his condition, may go some way to explain this. In addition, the lack of major state visits and receptions of foreign leaders by Mao after late May until early September, when the Chairman was no longer in Beijing, would have reduced the need for interaction. There is also the possibility, despite the claim of a senior scholar with access to Zhou's hospital records that the list of visitors in his official chronology is complete, that for the pre-October period key visits simply went unrecorded or, for some unexplained reason, have been suppressed.[48]

While speculative, the most persuasive explanation for this situation, at least through August, is political. With Zhou under attack during *pi Lin pi Kong*, Deng probably kept his distance, and adopted a low posture on conflicts involving Jiang Qing and the Premier. There is no evidence of Deng springing to Zhou's defense during the campaign, something we could normally count on being documented in post-Mao sources had it happened. Although it is quite likely, as a senior specialist on Zhou has argued, that Zhou would have understood and accepted this without rancor as simply unavoidable,[49] the situation also gave Deng something of a free pass with the radicals. But in his new position, Deng would no longer have such luxury. All Politburo members would be looking for indications of his position on the issues of the day, with the radicals having grounds to believe that Deng would cooperate with them. This was the background to the explosion in the Politburo on October 17 over the *Fengqing*, an explosion which led to Wang Hongwen's hurried trip to see Mao in Changsha the next day, and within a few more days to Deng's nomination to the concurrent post of Chief-of-Staff by a Chairman displeased with the radicals' actions.

In a not unfamiliar pattern, the eruption on the 17th involved both long-standing issues and an almost accidental development. Since the start, the intended target of the *Fengqing* saga, despite the official emphasis on the October 17 incident as aimed at derailing Deng's new appointment, was Zhou Enlai. The long-standing context concerned conflict over importing advanced Western technology, an approach denounced during the Cultural Revolution as slavish worship of foreigners. In 1974, the *Fengqing*, a Chinese designed and constructed ocean-going freighter, became a symbol of the radical claim that native technology could do the job, while upholding national dignity. Zhou Enlai was identified with buying and renting foreign ships, a policy he supported in 1964, but as part of a program linked to developing China's own shipbuilding industry that was approved by Mao. As we have seen, even though the import of foreign technology had been specifically authorized by Mao in 1972 and 1973, the whole issue was again subject to radical rhetoric, but no policy change, during

---

[48] *Zhou nianpu*, vol. 3, p. 672; and interview, January 2005.

[49] Interview, January 2005.

pi Lin pi Kong. In this ideologically-charged atmosphere, the *Fengqing* departed from Shanghai for its maiden voyage in May 1974, and became the subject of media articles in the spring and summer as representing the correct Party line, articles that could also be read as attacks on Zhou. When the ship returned to Shanghai at the end of September, it was again lavishly celebrated, but at the same time Jiang Qing learned of comments by the ship's political commissar and his deputy (both high-level Ministry of Communications cadres who had been seconded to the *Fengqing* for the voyage) in defense of the policy of purchasing foreign ships. Having also read a Shanghai article that used the ship's return to attack the "slavish comprador philosophy," she commented critically on the issue, and her remarks were circulated to the Politburo on October 14.[50]

The *Fengqing* incident originated from a combination of ideological contention, clashing organizational interests, and Jiang Qing's ongoing criticism of the Premier. In terms of concrete interests, the *Fengqing* was the product of the Shanghai shipbuilding industry, but the Ministry of Communications was unhappy with the standard of the local industry's work, while other State Council bodies budgeted for buying ships abroad, budgets that were approved by Zhou. With *pi Lin pi Kong* underway, these concrete disputes were subsumed by large ideological themes, with the Shanghai radicals emphasizing their adherence to Mao's self-reliance injunctions as a correct line in contrast to buying from the capitalist world. In this context, Jiang seemingly felt obliged to push the issue, given both her ongoing license to criticize Zhou and her roving assignment to report on any threats to the Cultural Revolution, an assignment Mao would soon reaffirm when rebuffing her complaint about her lack of specific responsibilities. The problem for Jiang as the *Fengqing* issue unfolded was that she had misread Mao's intentions in the post-August period. During the Lin Biao-Confucius campaign, the Chairman had allowed radical themes to interfere with organizational performance, although not to radicalize policy. Now, although heavy media coverage hailing Shanghai's ocean freighter would continue through November, Mao gave greater attention to pragmatic results, which, as he would put it, reduced the *Fengqing* to a trivial matter. Jiang Qing, however, sought to maintain *pi Lin pi Kong* pressure, and barged ahead.[51]

In her circulated remarks on October 14, Jiang asked, "[since the State Council is an organ of our country's proletarian dictatorship, [how is it that] a

---

[50] See *Mao zhuan*, vol. 2, pp. 1701-1702; Yan and Gao, *Turbulent Decade*, pp. 446-47; Barnouin and Yu, *Ten Years*, pp. 269-70; *RMRB*, January 17, 1977, in *SPRCP*, no. 6269 (1977), pp. 169-72; and above, pp. 157-58. The date of Jiang's remarks is variously given as October 13 or 14, but we take the *Mao zhuan* version of the 14th as more authoritative.

[51] See Su Caiqing, "Weirao 'Fengqinglun wenti' de yichang douzheng" [A Struggle concerning the "Fengqing Discussion Question"], in Zhang Hua and Su Caiqing, eds., *Huishou "wenge": Zhongguo shinian "wenge" fenxi yu fansi* [Recalling the "Cultural Revolution": Analysis and Rethinking of China's Ten Years of "Cultural Revolution"] (2 vols., Beijing: Zhonggong dangshi chubanshe, 2000), vol. 2, pp. 1132-37; and below, pp. 220, 222.

handful of people in the Ministry of Communications who worship ... foreign things ... dictate to us? The Politburo should declare its position and carry out necessary measures." The target was the ministry as well as other concerned government bodies and leaders,[52] and beyond that the State Council and its Premier—not Deng Xiaoping. While the other radicals and Kang Sheng provided support by noting "completely agree" on the document containing her remarks, with Kang's comment the most fulsome, other Politburo members, including Zhou and Deng, simply noted her comment or circled their names, indicating low-key acceptance, or at least an unwillingness to challenge Jiang's position.[53] The Politburo majority may have hoped the matter would rest there, but Jiang pursued the issue further when the Politburo met on the 17th and tried to force Deng to state his position. After more than a year of seemingly cordial relations, and given Deng's active support of the Lin Biao-Confucius campaign, she probably hoped he would back her position. Given Deng's central role in the proposed new government structure, his views would clearly be important to the fate of her policy preferences.

The developments on the evening of the 17th, which Mao came to regard as a confrontation of two "steel companies," i.e., one individual determined to get her way, and another not to be pushed around, almost certainly came as a surprise to both protagonists. With NPC preparations the main agenda of the evening, it is not even clear that Jiang came to the meeting with a firm intention to raise the matter; she only brought the subject up "suddenly" as the meeting was rapidly coming to its conclusion. Jiang articulated the same themes as in her circulated remarks of the 14th, but then demanded that Deng express his attitude on the matter. Deng did not take kindly to the pressure, said he had circled her remarks, but that further investigation was required. With Jiang persisting, Deng rejected her attempt to force her views on him, saying if she behaved like this, it would be impossible for them to cooperate and the work of the Politburo would break down. Deng reportedly initially sat, then stood, and finally, "unable to bear" any more abuse, walked out. Although Mao's official biography claims that Zhang Chunqiao and Yao Wenyuan also "attacked" Deng, other accounts focus solely on Jiang, and in any case it is clear that she was the prime mover in the confrontation. No account, moreover, indicates that Wang Hongwen, who probably chaired the meeting, participated in any criticism of Deng. The result of the evening left the Politburo in disarray, hardly a sustainable situation, particularly with the NPC on the agenda.[54]

---

[52] These included Minister of Foreign Trade Li Qiang, who was responsible for buying foreign ships, and SPC head Yu Qiuli, who was responsible for the budget. See Su Caiqing, "Weirao 'Fengqinglun wenti'," pp. 1131-32. Wang Zhen, who would be named Vice Premier responsible for communications in early 1975, seemingly already had responsibility in this area in fall 1974 and may have been another target, although we have found no direct criticism of him.

[53] See *Mao zhuan*, vol. 2, p. 1702; Yan and Gao, *Turbulent Decade*, p. 447; above, p. 164n133; and below, p. 361n165.

Following the Politburo meeting, the four radicals met at their Diaoyutai residence to discuss the events of the evening.[55] Much as in the Politburo meeting, Jiang Qing was the dominant figure. After considering alternatives, the four decided that Wang Hongwen should travel to Changsha to report to Mao—in the standard view to try to obstruct Deng's appointment as First Vice Premier. In this interpretation, Mao quickly saw through the "plot," backed Deng, rebuked Wang, and two days later added the Chief-of-Staff position to Deng's new powers. The result was also to place Zhou in charge of selecting the new State Council personnel to be confirmed at the NPC, and thus strike a sharp blow to the "gang's" ambitions. As in other cases, this overview identifies key events and provides a plausible interpretation of the meaning of those events, but ignores many nuances and distorts the general picture. These nuances, and their consequences for an overall interpretation, can be elucidated by a detailed reconstruction of events starting the night of the 17th.[56]

Throughout that night the four radicals sought to understand the meaning, as it appeared to them, of Deng's sudden departure from a cooperative or at least non-oppositional stance toward them. While the *Fengqing* question up to that point had focused on the Premier, and Zhou continued to draw radical attacks, in the night's discussion attention now shifted to Deng's unanticipated behavior. Underlining Deng's previous posture, Yao Wenyuan noted that in the [recent] past Deng rarely spoke, but at today's meeting he gave vent to a sudden outburst of high emotion. Yao also indicated doubts about Deng's real unexpressed views, referring to Mao's observation that, if people were on the same line, it was easy to cooperate, but difficulties arose if people were on different lines. Yao thought Deng's behavior was linked to the coming NPC, while Zhang felt it had something to do with the still unsettled Chief-of-Staff position as well as the NPC appointments. But the group's apparent predominant view, one particularly pushed by Jiang, was that Deng's actions confirmed his dissatisfaction with the Cultural Revolution. Indeed, earlier that evening as the Politburo meeting broke up, Zhang reportedly declared he had long known that Deng wanted to "jump out" on this issue. The question became what to do about it, and the decision was made "by the four of us," Wang informed the Chairman the next day, that he should go secretly to Changsha to report to Mao.[57]

What was the precise objective of Wang's trip? While the official claim that the goal was to prevent Deng from assuming his new office, a claim backed by

[54] See *Mao zhuan*, vol. 2, p. 1702; Su Caiqing, "Weirao 'Fengqinglun wenti'," p. 1140; Mao Mao, *"Wenge" suiyue*, pp. 318-19, 323; and Ji Xichen, *Shi wu qianli de niandai*, vol. 2, pp. 641-42.

[55] In addition to the sources cited, the following discussion of the events of that night, Wang's trip to Changsha on the 18th, and developments during the next several days draws heavily on an interview with a senior Party historian familiar with key relevant documents, January 2005.

[56] For a summary of the official view, see Yan and Gao, *Turbulent Decade*, pp. 447-48, 455-56.

[57] See Su Caiqing, "Weirao 'Fengqinglun wenti'," p. 1140; Ji Xichen, *Shi wu qianli de niandai*, vol. 2, p. 643; and Yan and Gao, *Turbulent Decade*, p. 447.

the confessions of the ever cooperative Wang and the somewhat less cooperative Yao at their 1980 trial, cannot be dismissed out of hand, it should be treated with the utmost skepticism. It would have been remarkable if the Chairman could have been persuaded to reverse a decision made only two weeks previously over what he regarded a trivial incident, and surprising if the radicals thought they could achieve such an outcome. More likely, more modest goals were involved, such as securing a favorable verdict on the *Fengqing* issue itself and alerting Mao to Deng's assertedly questionable attitude toward the Cultural Revolution, in the hope that pressure would be brought to bear on him to alter his views, or that a better outcome might be obtained as lesser posts in the new government were filled. Or possibly, indeed probably, the decision to seek out the Chairman was an act of pique and frustration, driven by Jiang, in a situation in which the radicals truly had no *banfa*, no way to reverse the key political appointment in the new State Council. In this regard, it may simply have been, as Zhou Enlai commented privately, a case of complaining to one's superior (*gaozhuang*) as any expectations of cooperation with Deng came into serious question.[58]

If the why of Wang's mission remains uncertain, greater clarity surrounds the who. That is, while all four radicals were involved in the decision, Jiang Qing was the driving force. Jiang was at the center of the confrontation at the Politburo, she was the leading figure in the radical group because of her (however fraught) relationship with Mao, she called the other three radicals together after they had all returned to Diaoyutai following the Politburo meeting, when Wang wrote to Mao in the early morning of the 18th to request a meeting, he attached three written materials selected by Jiang, and at the 1980 trial Wang claimed the idea for the trip was hers. Jiang was concerned that the radical version of events get to Changsha before Deng, who was scheduled to accompany the Prime Minister of Denmark on the 20th, would have a chance to present his account. After apparently discarding the idea of going as a group in order not to alarm other leaders, Wang was selected for the task. Why Wang? Undoubtedly one factor was Mao's sporadic criticism of Jiang throughout 1974, and his previous refusals to see her. Wang, in contrast, was probably still seen favorably by the Chairman as the future successor, and in any case, as the official responsible for the Party Center's daily work, he had an obligation to report on the work of the Politburo, particularly on a major clash such as had occurred on the 17th. But there was something improper in the four deciding among themselves, and not informing Zhou or other Politburo members of Wang's mission. Despite declaring in a mid-1975 self-criticism that he was obligated to report and his fault was "only listening to one side," upon meeting Mao on the October 18, Wang stated he was "taking a risk" in coming after meeting with the other radicals without the knowledge of the wider Politburo. In our view, the "risk" (*fengxian*) Wang sensed was that in deviating from collective

---

[58] See *A Great Trial*, pp. 47-50, 159; *Mao zhuan*, vol. 2, pp. 1702, 1705; and Yan and Gao, *Turbulent Decade*, p. 456.

leadership, he was ignoring Mao's July warning against acting as a "small faction of four."[59]

In his meeting with the Chairman, Wang, arguably a somewhat reluctant messenger,[60] largely appeared to relay accusations advanced by the other three radicals during their all-night meeting of October 17-18. In addition to recounting the incident on the 17th, he repeated Yao Wenyuan's comparison during the previous night's discussion of the current situation in Beijing to the 1970 Lushan plenum. That is, Zhou Enlai and other senior leaders were allegedly behaving as Lin Biao had at Lushan. Not only had the Lushan miscreants engaged in surprise attacks and sought to expand their power, but their ultimate target was the Cultural Revolution itself—the one thing on which Mao had repeatedly shown he would not compromise. Further, echoing private remarks by Jiang Qing and Zhang Chunqiao, Wang reported that, although ill, Zhou summoned people for talks far into the night, notably Deng, Ye Jianying and Li Xiannian, talks that were somehow connected to NPC appointments. Of particular interest, while Wang conveyed these attacks on the Premier, he insisted in his 1980 confession, even as he admitted to attempting to derail Deng, that he had never personally said anything against Zhou in this period and he was mainly concerned with protecting Zhou's health. Wang's personal contribution to the radicals' complaints seemed limited to echoing Jiang Qing's claim that Deng had failed to support the "new born things" of the Cultural Revolution. Mao was unimpressed with all this, and indeed even seemed disinterested, cutting Wang short and redirecting the conversation to general political and economic issues. He chastised Wang for his one-sided behavior, and advised him to talk with Deng if there were disagreements, to increase his contacts with Zhou and Ye, and—in terms that mirrored his July warning—to be careful of Jiang and not get mixed up with her.[61]

There was more to Wang's meeting with the Chairman, however. Wang described Deng's mood as very cocky, and said that this seemed related to the issue of selecting a Chief-of-Staff (as Zhang Chunqiao had suggested on the

---

[59] *Mao zhuan*, vol. 2, p. 1704; *A Great Trial*, p. 47; Yan and Gao, *Turbulent Decade*, pp. 447, 455-56; Ji Xichen, *Shi wu qianli de niandai*, vol. 2, p. 664; and interview with senior Party historian, January 2005.

[60] Although Wang confessed that he had suggested reporting to the Chairman, he also claimed the proposal for the trip was Jiang's (see above). In general terms, during the all-night session after the Politburo meeting, Jiang and Zhang were most forceful in assessing the situation and the need for action, while Wang seemingly made the fewest contributions to the discussion.

[61] See *A Great Trial*, pp. 47-48; *Mao zhuan*, vol. 2, pp. 1700, 1704; Ji Xichen, *Shi wu qianli de niandai*, vol. 2, p. 643; and Su Caiqing, "Weirao 'Fengqinglun wenti'," p. 1140. On how Mao came to see the Cultural Revolution as the key factor at Lushan, see Teiwes and Sun, *Tragedy*, pp. 148-49.

Regarding Wang and the Premier, in response to Mao's query, Wang raised concern about Zhou's health on October 18. He also claimed to have called attention to the need to reduce Zhou's burdens several times at Politburo meetings during the period, and again during his subsequent visit to Changsha in December, although on that occasion Zhou stopped him on the grounds of not bothering the Chairman. Interview with senior Party historian, January 2005. Cf. below, p. 250n19.

night following the Politburo conflict) and a head of the GPD, appointments about which Deng and Jiang Qing had different opinions. Although Jiang had been insistent on Yang Chengwu's selection as Chief-of-Staff the previous night, there is little to indicate that Wang did anything other than simply convey Deng's and Jiang's respective recommendations without offering his own opinion, and Mao apparently gave no clear reply on the issue. Most interesting, Wang reported on a quarrel between himself and Jiang that apparently took place during a Politburo meeting on the 16th, for unexplained reasons.[62] Wang's report of his difficulties with Mme Mao produced laughter and a question from the Chairman: "So you dared to confront her?" Mao seemingly was surprised and a bit incredulous that Wang would stand up to his wife, the fearsome steel factory. Meanwhile, Jiang's dissatisfaction with Wang during the same period further indicated tension within the "gang of four." Apart from Jiang's nomination of Wang to a lesser position in November, in January Mao told the "two ladies" that Jiang not only did not have a high opinion of Zhou, Deng or Ye, but couldn't get along with Wang and was always complaining about him.[63]

Shortly after the arrest of the "gang of four" in 1976, Ye Jianying claimed that the Changsha encounter marked the start of Mao's loss of confidence in Wang Hongwen. Whether completely accurate or not, Ye's observation is credible. Although Wang (and Zhang Chunqiao and Yao Wenyuan) had been caught in the sweep of Mao's complaints about the radicals earlier in the year, the focus had clearly been on Jiang Qing. Although Jiang remained the central culprit in the Chairman's Changsha criticisms, Mao pointedly told Wang that his own actions were unacceptable. While post-Mao accounts emphasize Mao's unhappiness with the attacks on Deng and Zhou, other factors were also involved in his dissatisfaction with Wang. One issue was that, again following Jiang's urging,[64] Wang suggested posting one of his secretaries (who had also worked for Zhang and Yao) in Mao's personal office to boost the household staff and serve as a liaison. Mao rejected this proposal, noting that Wang was naïve to meddle in his domestic affairs. The proposal may also have alienated the "two ladies" who were performing their own liaison function. In any case, while the timing is unclear, hostility was clearly in evidence by the end of the year. Although they undoubtedly were crucially influenced by Mao's disenchantment with Wang, the "two ladies" at some point started giving Mao unfavorable information about his

---

[62] Whatever the cause of the conflict, Wang recalled Ye Jianying calling him afterward, ostensibly to offer support, but Wang regarded this as an attempt to sow discord between himself and Jiang. Interview, January 2005.

[63] Ji Xichen, *Shi wu qianli de niandai*, vol. 2, p. 645; Su Caiqing, "Weirao 'Fengqinglun wenti'," p. 1140; and interview with senior Party historian, January 2005. The question of the GPD head is never mentioned in standard sources, but it is included in Su Caiqing's detailed account. See also below, p. 215n70.

[64] This matter apparently began with Zhang Yufeng's complaints that she faced difficulties in managing Mao's household alone, and Jiang urged Wang to provide his secretary to assist Zhang.

putative successor, e.g., that he had failed to do his homework before meeting foreign guests and could only make small talk. But arguably, Wang's greatest shortcoming in Mao's eyes, as revealed in his skeptical query about confronting Jiang in the context in which Wang was in Changsha at her bidding, were doubts whether his successor had the mettle to stand up to his wife. Mao surely had more in mind than just adding to the radical representation on the Politburo in bringing Wang to Beijing in 1972. A long-term successor would have to have independent substance and not simply submit to hectoring by Jiang Qing.[65]

Whatever Mao's doubts about Wang's specific report concerning his conflict with Jiang on the 16th, or the accuracy of his general sense of Wang's mettle, there is evidence of more frequent clashes between Wang and Jiang and that, at least on one occasion, Wang held his own. Wang Dongxing later reported having seen Wang Hongwen confront Jiang several times. Also, although the timing is unclear, Wang Hongwen submitted to Mao a scathing written criticism of Jiang's many faults, including her lack of strategy and tactics in struggle, her inability to keep a cool head, arbitrary behavior, failing to show respect for Politburo colleagues, a proclivity to lash out at old and new comrades alike, and generally that she engaged in such behavior on matters having little to do with principle. Overall, Wang observed, Jiang's actions since the start of *pi Lin pi Kong* deviated from collective leadership.[66] Whether Wang's criticism was written before or more likely after the Changsha meeting, perhaps during the criticism of the radicals in mid-1975, it echoed the types of criticisms the Chairman had been making of his wife throughout 1974, notably at the July 17 Politburo meeting. In this sense, Wang's critique may not have indicated any special courage, but together with other evidence, it clearly demonstrates significant underlying tensions between himself and Jiang.

While Wang Hongwen was meeting the Chairman in Changsha, in Beijing, in arguably a further indication of her low confidence in and mistrust of Wang, Jiang sought an alternative channel to Mao. With the "two ladies," as well as Deng, scheduled to depart for Changsha in the company of the Danish Prime Minister, Jiang summoned Wang Hairong and Tang Wensheng about noon on

---

[65] See "Zhongyang lingdaoren guanyu sirenbang wenti de jianghua" [Speeches of Central Leaders on the Gang of Four Question] (October 8, 1976), in *CRDB*, p. 2; *Mao zhuan*, vol. 2, p. 1704; Fan Shuo, *Ye Jianying zai feichang shiqi*, vol. 2, p. 447; and Li Xun, *Da bengkui*, p. 493. An indication of at least Wang Hairong's antipathy toward Wang Hongwen was apparent in December at Changsha, when she made it clear she would not go to a party marking Mao's birthday if "the guy from building 3" (Wang Hongwen) attended. See Gao Zhenpu, "Zai Zongli he dajie shenbian chengzhang" [Growing Up by the Side of the Premier and Big Sister (Deng Yingchao)], in Cheng Hua, *Zhou Enlai he ta de mishumen*, p. 458.

[66] See Qing Ye and Fang Lei, *Deng Xiaoping zai 1976, xiajuan: Huairentang shibian* [Deng Xiaoping in 1976, vol. 2: The Huairentang Events] (Shenyang: Chunfeng wenyi chubanshe, 1993), p. 129; and Ji Xichen, *Shi wu qianli de niandai*, vol. 2, p. 649.

the 18th. Jiang asked Wang and Tang to convey her version of the Politburo meeting the previous evening to the Chairman. Similar to Wang in Changsha, Jiang described the row at the meeting, blamed Deng for the contretemps, and attacked Zhou as the "backstage boss" who was colluding with Deng and Ye. On the evening of the 19th,[67] Jiang called the "two ladies" to Diaoyutai a second time. On this occasion, Zhang Chunqiao and Yao Wenyuan—but seemingly not Wang Hongwen—were present, and Jiang asked Zhang to brief the "two ladies" on the current situation. Zhang provided a broader perspective in terms of the country's financial difficulties and the problem of "worshiping foreign things," and concluded it was not accidental that Deng had raised the *Fengqing* issue. Moreover, Zhang described Deng's attitude on the *Fengqing* as similar to the "February adverse current" of 1967, the incident regarded by Mao as the most intolerable attack on the Cultural Revolution since the movement's inception. Jiang, Zhang and Yao then asked them to report this to the Chairman.[68]

By this point, Zhou Enlai had begun a series of consultations on the situation created by the *Fengqing* incident. On the 19th, he called in Hua Guofeng, Ji Dengkui, Li Xiannian and Deng separately to get a complete picture of what had eventuated at the Politburo session. The Premier would soon meet with Wang Hongwen as well. Wang had briefed the other three radicals upon returning from Changsha, although it is unclear whether he fully conveyed the Chairman's instructions, but he also saw Zhou several times over the next ten days. Wang not only reported on his trip, but also made a number of self-examinations before the Premier. Having never appeared enthusiastic about his mission to Changsha, Wang now took Mao's strictures to heart, not only by making contact with Zhou, but also by engaging in self-criticism for his factional activities. Meanwhile, following their meeting with the three radicals at Diaoyutai on the evening of the 19th, the "two ladies" briefed Zhou on their encounters with Jiang *et al*. The Premier told them he was already aware of what had happened in the Politburo, and that the fault lay not with Deng who had been very patient, but with the intention of the radicals to undermine Deng. Zhou also offered advice. After asking the "two ladies" whether they had a duty to report to Mao on Politburo developments and receiving a negative response, he cautioned against "troubling"

---

[67] While most authoritative sources report this meeting taking place on the evening of October 18, the version in *Zhou nianpu*, vol. 3, p. 679, placing it on the 19th, is more credible. The clearest evidence is Jiang's remark to the "two ladies" that Wang Hongwen had brought back the Chairman's gift from Changsha *yesterday*. Cheng and Xia, *Deng zai yijiuqiwu*, p. 29.

[68] See Su Caiqing, "Weirao 'Fengqinglun wenti'," pp. 1141-42; Mao Mao, *"Wenge" suiyue*, p. 321; *A Great Trial*, p. 49; and Yan and Gao, *Turbulent Decade*, pp. 448, 456. While various official sources routinely claim all four radicals were present at the second meeting with the "two ladies," Mao Mao indicates that Wang was not there. On Mao's hypersensitivity to the February adverse current, see Kang Sheng's comment that he had never seen Mao so furious; Zeng Tao, "Zhengyi de kangzheng—suowei 'eryue niliu' de qianqian houhou" [Righteous Resistance—Before and After the So-called "February Adverse Current"], in Zhang and Su, *Huishou "wenge,"* vol. 2, p. 821.

Mao with such a matter and indicated that he had given Deng the same counsel as it was something that could be dealt with after he returned to Beijing.[69]

Once in Changsha on October 20, however, although Deng followed Zhou's advice, Wang and Tang reported the situation to Mao. The Chairman now reacted along the same lines as he had responded to Wang Hongwen two days earlier. Angry at what he heard, he declared that it was pointless for Jiang to make such a big scene, the *Fengqing* issue was a trivial matter that was already being dealt with by Li Xiannian and Ji Dengkui, and the "two ladies" should convey his words to the Premier and Wang Hongwen when they returned to Beijing. Beyond this, Mao made several decisions that had not been reached two days earlier, observing that he had not been so clear when Wang Hongwen was in Changsha. The Chairman now determined that Deng would be Chief-of-Staff, but there is no evidence whether he addressed the issue of the GPD head,[70] the post that would be assumed by Zhang Chunqiao in January. Mao also declared that "the Premier is still our Premier," an ambiguous statement which could not disguise the fact that Deng was *de facto* replacing Zhou in the post. More significantly, Mao formally placed Zhou, his health allowing, in charge of NPC preparations and personnel selection—jointly with Wang Hongwen. This suggests that Mao had not given up on Wang, who was now placed in a potentially key position as the NPC approached. Finally, the "two ladies" were to warn all three of the other radicals not to collude with Jiang and to convey the guideline of "stability and unity" for all work.[71]

When relayed to the central leaders by the "two ladies" on October 22, Mao's decisions of the 20th provided the framework for settling the *Fengqing* question and moving on to dealing with the Fourth NPC. While the decisions favored the moderates, the demand for "stability and unity" within the Politburo required concessions from both sides. No one grasped this more clearly than Zhou Enlai. In an effort to defuse the tensions caused by the issue, in early November the Premier met with all Beijing-based Politburo members (except for the seriously ill Kang Sheng and Liu Bocheng, the elderly Zhu De and Dong Biwu, and Wang Dongxing)[72] in three groups. Of special note, he advised Deng to pay a visit to Jiang in an effort to make peace, and Deng followed Zhou's advice. Deng sought to reduce the conflict to a clash of personalities, observing that they were both "steel companies," i.e., individuals very similar in their determination. Jiang accepted the analogy, although she insisted that while she had probably

---

[69] *Zhou nianpu*, vol. 3, pp. 679-80; Tie Ji, "Changsha juece," p. 384; and Gao Wenqian, *Wannian Zhou*, p. 533. Wang reportedly saw Zhou on October 20, 23 and 28.

[70] Of course, it is possible that Mao considered Zhang Chunqiao as head of the GPD at this time, which would have made for a more "balanced" outcome. It is also possible that Jiang Qing had nominated Zhang as well as Yang Chengwu when visiting Zhou on October 6.

[71] *Mao zhuan*, vol. 2, pp. 1704-1705; and Mao Mao, *"Wenge" suiyue*, pp. 321-22.

[72] Although normally based in Zhongnanhai, Wang undoubtedly was with Mao in Changsha overseeing his security arrangements.

erred in the manner in which she addressed the issue, Deng's problem in the *Fengqing* matter was a question of principle. In any case, Jiang apparently was quite satisfied with what she considered an apology and the relationship seemed to return to a more even keel afterward. Nearly a year and a half later in March 1976, in the course of attacking Deng, Jiang claimed that she still had faith in him following the *Fengqing* affair, because he had taken the initiative to come see her and show friendship.[73] In sum, for all the conflict and drama generated by the incident, it quickly blew over as an issue.

When Deng visited Changsha again on November 12 with another foreign visitor, Mao asked him about the events of October 17. In their long exchange, Deng not only discussed the Politburo meeting and his unwillingness to suffer abuse at Jiang's hands, he also informed Mao that he had gone to visit her subsequently. Mao's response was to approve of Deng's behavior ("I support you"), while at the same time stating that he, and the "two ladies" as well, were unhappy with Jiang. While it is not entirely clear, it appears that Mao's approval related to both Deng's guts in standing up to Jiang on the 17th, probably in contrast to his perception of Wang's behavior, and Deng's willingness to make amends subsequently. During this visit Mao again affirmed Deng's Chief-of-Staff assignment, and, not long after returning to Beijing, Deng moved his household to PLA accommodations.[74] Meanwhile, on the same day that he met Deng, Liao also wrote to Jiang in stern tones: "Don't flaunt yourself in public [or] write instructions on documents. Don't ... organize the cabinet (as the boss behind the scenes). You've already got too many complaints against you."[75]

The reference to "organizing the cabinet" pointed to the central political issue of the period, forming the new government that would be installed at the January NPC. For all the efforts in post-Mao sources to portray the *Fengqing* incident as a central part of the "gang of four's" conspiracy to seize power, in this and other respects it was a sideshow. The dispute was only tangentially linked to NPC preparations, more as a barometer of the overall political climate than anything else. For all the sudden prominence of Deng Xiaoping in the story as a result of the unexpected confrontation on October 17, the *Fengqing* issue had from the outset been targeted at Premier Zhou, who was clearly on the way out before the confrontation erupted. Similarly, the die had been cast in general terms with Mao's August declaration that "stability and unity" would now be the guiding principle, and in specific terms with his October 4 nomination of Deng as First Vice Premier. And for all his sensitivity to ideological issues, particularly those that could be linked to the Cultural Revolution, Mao treated the dispute a

---

[73] See *Zhou nianpu*, vol. 3, p. 681; Mao Mao, *"Wenge" suiyue*, p. 323; Gao Wenqian, *Wannian Zhou*, p. 533; Ji Xichen, *Shi wu qianli de niandai*, vol. 2, p. 647; and "Jiang Qing zai dazhaohu huiyi," pp. 378-79. Of course, it was actually Zhou Enlai's initiative to urge Deng to visit Jiang.

[74] See *Mao zhuan*, vol. 2, pp. 1706, 1708; and Mao Mao, *"Wenge" suiyue*, pp. 323, 326.

[75] *PR*, no. 35 (1977), p. 26.

trivial matter. As for the explosion at the Politburo meeting, it is best seen as a personality clash between two "steel companies" that had hitherto tried to get along, and had succeeded as long as Deng played a subdued role on domestic policy. With that situation ending, the potential for conflict was greatly enhanced, although in the immediate term it was less than usually believed.

Forming a Government

In the standard view, the *Fengqing* affair was merely the first incident in an intense battle over staffing the new government to be ratified at the NPC in January. This conflict presumably raged over the last two months of 1974 until the forces led by Zhou Enlai and Deng Xiaoping emerged victorious, with the result approved by Mao when Zhou and Wang Hongwen visited Changsha at the end of the year. Even though the new allocation of power was naturally of great concern to all parties, this interpretation overstates the intensity of the conflict and oversimplifies the process. Much as with the settlement of the *Fengqing* incident, a degree of compromise was mandated by Mao's insistence on "stability and unity." Concretely, not only was Zhou to share responsibility with Wang, and the two men did meet repeatedly,[76] they were both enjoined to consult with "every side" (*kefang*). The implication, presumably, was that various Politburo members were entitled to propose their own nominees, notwithstanding the effort of post-Mao official sources to paint radical nominations as part of a plan to seize power. As we discuss below, some of the nominees from both moderates and radicals do not fit the usual assumptions. Moreover, our understanding can only be partial since, according to a senior source from the Central Documents Research Office, any actual name lists from the period have not survived. Finally, it is worth noting that the entire process was completed in about two months, as well as recalling that a year earlier personnel appointments were apparently proceeding rapidly before the NPC was suddenly aborted. Whatever the tensions inherent in the division of power, once Mao demanded that the NPC go-ahead, the necessary compromises were made and a slate was presented to the Chairman in late December.[77]

As with all developments in the post-Lin Biao period, the lead-up to the Fourth NPC took place against the background of Mao's and Zhou's poor health. In Mao's case, further deterioration was indicated by his last swim in December, and by his decision at the end of the month that he would no longer receive foreign

---

[76] *Zhou nianpu*, vol. 3, pp. 680-86, records 14 meetings between Zhou and Wang in the period from October 22 to December 22, including five apparently alone, and six more involving one to three additional leaders. The rate of contact increased after November 20, when Mao seemingly bolstered Zhou's individual authority regarding personnel. It is likely that three meetings between the 9th and 14th of December involving Zhou, Wang and Ji Dengkui dealt with personnel matters. Cf. above, p. 205n47.

[77] *Mao zhuan*, vol. 2, p. 1705; interview, January 2005; and above, p. 119.

visitors regularly, with the trademark proviso that he definitely would not see those demanding an audience.[78] As for the Premier, despite post-1976 attempts to dramatize his late December trip to Changsha as courageously disregarding his severe illness for the sake of the nation, it appears Zhou's condition had improved somewhat since the summer. At least, this is what he claimed in a letter to Mao on November 6, and he seemed in good spirits in Changsha in December. In any case, as Zhou would have understood implicitly, for political as well as health reasons he was on the way out, something Mao made explicit at Changsha by saying that after the NPC the Premier should take a rest and turn over State Council work to Deng.[79] Throughout November and December, however, Zhou was at the center of the process of appointing a new government.

While we can be sure that the Premier was central to the selection process, much else is less certain, notably the contributions of others. Mao's directive of October 20 gave Wang Hongwen joint responsibility, and one could speculate about a division of labor whereby Zhou focused on State Council appointments, while Wang dealt with NPC leadership posts and, possibly, Party positions that would be ratified at the Second Plenum of the Central Committee to be held just prior to the Congress. As noted, Wang was active in consulting with Zhou, although the substance of these consultations remains unknown. When, in response to personnel proposals by Jiang Qing (see below), Mao reacted angrily and stipulated that Deng, Zhang Chunqiao and Li Xiannian would be the ranking Vice Premiers, and Zhu De, Dong Biwu and Song Qingling would be the NPC Standing Committee Chairman and ranking Vice Chairs, he also apparently increased Zhou's authority, declaring that the "the Premier will be in charge of deciding the rest through discussion." Others were clearly involved, however. Apart from Wang, Deng would naturally be consulted. Mao's official biography credits Zhou and Deng with the personnel arrangement, while Li Qi, a cadre in the State Council Science and Education Group, claimed Zhou and Ye Jianying were responsible for the outcome in education. It also seems clear that Ji Dengkui, who met frequently with Zhou and held the Politburo portfolio for organization, played a significant role. But for all the uncertainties, a larger political meaning is clear: Mao dominated the process. Whether the claim of one senior Party historian that the Chairman determined the entire personnel arrangement is strictly accurate, Mao made the crucial choice of Deng in early October, set the guidelines for the process on October 20, assigned key positions below Deng on November 20, and, as we shall, determined other significant appointments along the way.[80]

---

[78] *Mao zhuan*, vol. 2, pp. 1709, 1715.

[79] See *ibid.*, p. 1712; *Zhou nianpu*, vol. 3, p. 682; Zhang Zuoliang, *Zhou Enlai zuihou shinian*, p. 343; Xiong Huayuan and Liao Xinwen, *Zhou Enlai zongli shengya* [Zhou Enlai's Career as the Premier] (Beijing: Renmin chubanshe, 1997), pp. 546-57; and Li Ping, *Kaiguo zongli Zhou Enlai* [Founding Premier Zhou Enlai] (Beijing Zhonggong zhongyang dangxiao chubanshe, 1994), pp. 492-93.

Zhou's behavior in carrying out his assignment was typically cautious. He understood that this was not a zero-sum game, and overreaching might be punished by Mao. Thus, far from consistently proposing either old revolutionaries or experienced specialized cadres, the Premier made substantial bows toward Cultural Revolution standards in both concept and specific nominees. In a November letter to Mao, Zhou declared promoting middle-aged and young cadres should be the keypoint in personnel assignments, and during the process he supported younger rebels for government posts. In a particularly high profile case, the Premier pushed for the promotion of Mao favorite Xie Jingyi to NPC Vice Chair. Similarly, although unrelated to the NPC, Zhou had earlier promoted Mao's niece and presumptive new radical, Wang Hairong, from Assistant Minister of Foreign Affairs to Vice Minister in August. While this blatant attempt to curry favor resulted in the Chairman's anger, it underlined Zhou's ongoing calculation concerning Mao's presumed sensitivities. But the most intriguing examples of Zhou's advocacy concerned less prominent figures with no personal connection to Mao—figures who would be quickly ousted after the arrest of the "gang of four." For example, to realize Mao's intention of staffing the State Council to embody fully the sprit of the Cultural Revolution, Zhou urged Wang Hongwen and Zhang Chunqiao to recommend Shanghai radical Zhu Jiayao as Vice Minister of Public Security, from which position Zhu was the person in actual charge of the ministry until his 1976 purge. Another of Zhou's recommendations was to appoint Deng Gang as head of the State Broadcasting Bureau; although an old cadre, Deng Gang was widely considered a die-hard follower of the "gang," and was removed as such. In an even more striking (and tragic) case, Zhou proactively supported Yu Huiyong to head the Ministry of Culture, a case that will be discussed subsequently.[81]

Zhou also consulted widely, and carefully considered various options in order to reach something approaching a consensus. On December 14, after reviewing quota arrangements for the list of NPC delegates, he wrote to Wang Hongwen and the Politburo proposing an increase in the representation of old cadres and people from the foreign affairs and sports sectors. On the 21st, after the famous meeting of nine Politburo members, including the four radicals,[82] when Jiang

---

[80] *Mao zhuan*, vol. 2, pp. 1708-1709, 1710; Zhang Hua, *Deng Xiaoping yu 1975 nian de Zhongguo* [Deng Xiaoping and China in 1975] (Beijing: Zhonggong dangshi chubanshe, 2004), pp. 400-401; interview, January 2000; and above, pp. 205n47, 217n76.

[81] See Gao Wenqian, *Wannian Zhou*, p. 534; Qing and Fang, *Deng zai 1976*, vol. 2, pp. 235, 238; Wu De, "Guowuyuan wenhuazu," p. 81; "Geng Biao guanyu sirenbang qingkuang," p. 2; above, p. 8n19; and below, pp. 228-30. In another case, the Premier persuaded Chen Yonggui to accept a vice premiership. While the peasant leader was not a Cultural Revolution rebel and survived to play a significant role in 1977-78, Chen had been highly praised by Mao for his leftist Dazhai model for agriculture. Wu Si, *Zhongguo touhao nongmin: Chen Yonggui fuchenlu* [China's Number One Peasant: The Rise and Fall of Chen Yonggui] (Hong Kong: Tiandi tushu gongsi, 1993), p. 153. Cf. below, China's Number One Peasant: pp. 232-33.

[82] The others were Deng, Ye Jianying, Li Xiannian, Ji Dengkui and Wu De.

Qing and Zhang Chunqiao pushed their views on appointments for the culture, education and sports ministries (see below), on the basis of further consultation with Li Xiannian and Ji Dengkui, Zhou drew up two lists of candidates for NPC chair and vice chairs and vice premiers, lists which were then given to Deng, Ye, Jiang and Zhang for review. Afterward, the Premier added old revolutionary Chen Yun and Politburo member and Guangxi leader Wei Guoqing to the slate of NPC vice chairs on the first list. The two lists were then discussed at another partial Politburo meeting on the 22nd,[83] and on the basis of the discussion, Zhou drafted a third list that, jointly with Wang, he presented to Mao in Changsha. Another aspect of Zhou's caution was revealed in his preparation of the lists for the meeting on the 21st. After writing these out by hand, he had them printed, and then ordered the hand-written version burned. Prudence meant broad consultation and avoiding confrontation with the radicals, but the Premier was seemingly equally concerned with avoiding leaving evidence that could be utilized by them in the future.[84]

If Zhou Enlai proceeded cautiously with Mao's "stability and unity" directive firmly in mind, Jiang Qing seemingly behaved in a provocative fashion. Here, as in other instances in 1974, evidence of excessive behavior and especially of Mao's negative reaction focuses much more on Jiang personally than on the four radicals collectively. And, as earlier in the year, Mao's complaints had more to do with her political style and personality than anything else. One could go so far as to say that, whatever the implications for the leadership lineup, what eventuated between the Chairman and his wife at the end of 1974 and start of 1975 was as much an ongoing personal as a political drama. On November 6, Mao dismissively referred to her in a conversation with Li Xiannian as "the Daoist goddess (wangmu liangliang), who doesn't listen ... and can't be completely believed." Mao's November 12 rebuke, quoted above, addressed her tendencies to be overbearing in public and provoke widespread resentment. She replied abjectly in a letter on the 19th, expressing shame for "failing to live up to your expectations," as well as admitting serious shortcomings in self-knowledge and the ability to handle situations objectively. But Jiang also used the occasion to note that she held no official duties and was "quite idle at present," which produced Mao's sharp retort that she did have work of major importance—"[the] responsibility ... to study the current situation of China and abroad," i.e., her roving commission to be on the lookout for revisionist threats. Throughout this period, the Chairman also sought detailed information on her behavior, as in asking Deng to describe the confrontation at the October 17 Politburo meeting and quizzing Zhou at Changsha in December on why she had opposed Deng's UN trip. But perhaps

---

[83] On this occasion involving Wang Hongwen, Ye Jianying, Zhang Chunqiao, Ji Dengkui, Hua Guofeng, Chen Yonggui, Chen Xilian, Ni Zhifu and Wu Guixian.

[84] See *Zhou nianpu*, vol. 3, pp. 685-86; Mao Mao, *"Wenge" suiyue*, pp. 328-29; *Mao zhuan*, vol. 2, p. 1710; and Yan and Gao, *Turbulent Decade*, p. 459.

the most poignant expression of his preoccupation and frustration came in the wake of the NPC in January. On that occasion, after listening to the "two ladies" relay Jiang's negative opinions on virtually the entire Politburo, Mao not only expressed unhappiness that "she thinks highly only of herself," he even claimed that she regarded him lightly, and predicted that after he died she would make trouble with everyone.[85]

In any case, Jiang did make proposals concerning NPC appointments, and this contributed greatly to Mao's vexation. The Chairman's November 12 criticism, with its striking demand that Jiang should not "organize the cabinet" came in response to her letter of the same day proposing that Xie Jingyi become NPC Vice Chair, Qiao Guanhua Vice Premier, Chi Qun Minister of Education, and that Mao Yuanxin, Chi Qun and Xie Jingyi all be given the right to attend Politburo meetings as part of cultivating them as successors—appointments that all failed to eventuate, although Xie did attend at least one crucial Politburo meeting, and probably more. In addition to complaining on the 19th about her own lack of work, something relating more to Party than government duties, and ignoring Mao's strictures concerning "forming a cabinet," about the same time she had the "two ladies" convey to Mao her view that Wang Hongwen should be appointed NPC Vice Chairman, ranking after Zhu De and Dong Biwu. It was in response to this proposal that Mao declared: "Jiang Qing has wild ambitions. She actually wants Wang Hongwen to be Chairman of the NPC Standing Committee and herself to be Party Chairman." Mao repeated his comment on Jiang's "wild ambitions" to Zhou and Wang in Changsha at the end of the year, adding that he had instructed her not to participate in the government, and that he knew her better than they did after several decades' experience. In the December meeting in Changsha, when Wang raised the question of Jiang's responsibilities in terms similar to what she had done on November 19, but now specifically in terms of the division of work in the Politburo, this again drew Mao's retort that her job was research, and he added that she should read two of his books. As for leadership of the government, despite implausible post-Mao claims that the radicals had prepared a list with Jiang as Premier, given Mao's designation of Deng as *de facto* Premier in early October, it is most unlikely that the "gang" proposed anything different. Yet Mao did say at Changsha that, presumably at some earlier stage, Jiang had expressed the view that Zhang Chunqiao had the qualities to lead the State Council.[86]

---

[85] See *Mao zhuan*, vol. 2, pp. 1706-1708, 1711, 1717; *Mao wengao*, vol. 13, pp. 374-76, 394-99; Yan and Gao, *Turbulent Decade*, pp. 458-59; An Jianshe, "Mao Zedong yu 'pi Lin pi Kong' ruogan wenti," pp. 59-60; and above, pp. 190-91.

[86] Wu De, "Guanyu fensui 'sirenbang'," p. 52; *Mao zhuan*, vol. 2, pp. 1708, 1711-12; Yan and Gao, *Turbulent Decade*, pp. 458-59; "Geng Biao guanyu sirenbang qingkuang," p. 1; and below, p. 231n108. There are other versions of Jiang's list, notably that it proposed that Shanghai's Jin Zumin be given the right to attend Politburo meetings. Jin allegedly had already been the "gang's" candidate for head of Party organization in place of Kang Sheng's protégé, Guo Yufeng—another suggestion of tension between Kang and the radicals. See Barnouin and Yu, *Ten Years*, p. 271; and "Geng Biao guanyu sirenbang qingkuang," p. 1.

The colorful if inevitably incomplete story of Jiang's efforts to influence personnel appointments at the Fourth NPC involves a number of aspects that may not be obvious. First, it can be argued that what Mao found intolerable was again a matter of *modus operandi*: rather than advance her views in the Politburo as he had repeatedly advised her to do, and which would also have fit his directive to Zhou to consult "every side," Jiang used her personal connection to appeal directly to the Chairman. It is also of note that the proposals she made, i.e., the ones most commonly cited where we can have confidence that she actually made them, dealt with comparatively lesser posts, especially the largely symbolic NPC positions.[87] As emphasized above, the key assignment of Deng had already been made by Mao. Moreover, in addition to her list featuring people with connections to the Chairman (Xie, Chi and Mao Yuanxin), there was an overlap between Jiang's recommendations and what Zhou eventually proposed in the case of Xie Jingyi, and perhaps to some degree concerning Qiao Guanhua and Chi Qun as well (see below). Particularly intriguing was Jiang's nomination of Wang Hongwen as the *third*-ranking NPC official. While undoubtedly related to Mao's discussion of NPC posts at Changsha in October when he apparently mentioned Zhu De and Dong Biwu, but stated that the matter could be considered further, the nomination can be interpreted as another sign of Jiang's low regard for Wang since it placed the second-ranking *Party* Vice Chairman and putative successor in an entirely symbolic post after two elderly and inactive figures. If Mao's assessment that Jiang really wanted to be Party Chairman was accurate, moreover, Wang would become her subordinate in the future. In any case, the idea could not be regarded as a collective "gang" proposal. Not only was Yao Wenyuan surprised when he learned of it, but Wang declined to take up the post.[88] As for Jiang in late 1974, whatever the true extent of her ambition,[89] and whatever the degree of Mao's exasperation, her status, with all its latent power, was essentially unchanged. For all of the Chairman's annoyance over her style, in assigning her a "research" function in domestic and international affairs, Mao preserved Jiang's roving commission to make sure overall trends were compatible with his ideological direction.

Another feature of the available information concerning personnel arrangements for the Fourth NPC is that Jiang's proposals of November 12, and her subsequent recommendation of an NPC post for Wang, are the only clearly documented formal nominations to emerge from the radical camp for leading

---

[87] Note further that Jiang's list on the 12th preceded Mao's decision to name Zhang Chunqiao and Li Xiannian Vice Premiers, yet Qiao Guanhua, who surely would have ranked low on any list of top government leaders, was the only person she nominated for that post.

[88] See *Mao zhuan*, vol. 2, pp. 1705, 1708; Ji Xichen, *Shi wu qianli de niandai*, vol. 2, p. 650; and below, p. 229.

[89] While Jiang undoubtedly expected a major role in China's post-Mao future, and notwithstanding some rebel demands after Mao's death that she assume the Party Chair (see below, p. 556), whether she actually believed she could obtain the position and sought it is an entirely speculative issue.

posts in the critical November-December period, and these were her individual suggestions. While we discuss some less clear-cut cases below, and the collective interest of the radicals in the appointments at the NPC is obvious, attacks on the collective "gang" in this regard are generally vague, and tend to blur the issue by including efforts to promote presumed supporters well before the year-end focus on government appointments. Once again, it is difficult to get a clear indication of Wang Hongwen's involvement. Although attacked in the post-Mao period for seeking to place his Shanghai followers in central positions during *pi Lin pi Kong*, and despite his assignment of leading the process jointly with the Premier, there is little to indicate a major advocacy role on his part in the post-October phase apart from, ironically, his enquiry concerning Jiang's duties that drew Mao's rebuke in December. Of particular note, at the December 21 meeting when Zhou's lists were discussed and the radicals reportedly made demands concerning the culture and education spheres (see below), there is little evidence of Wang being involved in these demands.[90]

The broader context of personnel advocacy by the radicals must also be considered. In developments since spring 1973, the radicals had been given key roles in overall personnel recruitment before and after the Tenth Congress. Developments in the radical citadel of Shanghai are instructive. A special initiative was launched in spring 1974 to send new cadres to central posts, with Wang Hongwen and Zhang Chunqiao playing prominent roles, and in August local Shanghai officials prepared a list of 18 names for high-ranking ministerial appointments. While there was resistance to many of these, and to another 16 subsequent candidates, ten were reportedly appointed. Most importantly, all of this was in accord with directives from Mao and Zhou to recruit worker cadres to be sent to Beijing, Zhou criticized Shanghai for not sending enough, and the arrangements were all done in accord with organizational procedures. In July 1974, moreover, when a request for cadres came from ten ministries, the local Shanghai authorities were unable to fulfill the request.[91] In short, whatever potential political advantage the situation provided, the radicals' role was legitimate, and Zhou Enlai was cooperative in key respects, even pressing the radicals for more action. But the radicals' scope of activity apparently narrowed in the last months of 1974, as seen in the meeting of December 21, when their demands were narrowly focused on culture and education—the area in which Zhang Chunqiao would have direct responsibility as Vice Premier. Further complexities will become apparent as we examine the selection of the leaders of the restored Ministry of Culture and Ministry of Education.

First, however, the Ministry of Foreign Affairs deserves analysis. Jiang Qing's nomination of Qiao Guanhua as Vice Premier in her letter of November 12,

---

[90] See Mao Mao, *"Wenge" suiyue*, p. 328; and "Wang Xiuzhen de jiefa jiaodai" [Wang Xiuzhen's Unmasking Confession] (November 6, 1976), in *CRDB*, p. 6.

[91] See Perry and Li, *Proletarian Power*, pp. 169-71.

taken together with Qiao's "excessive" criticism of the Premier at the November-December 1973 Politburo sessions and developments in 1976 (see Chapters 6 and 7), suggest Jiang's cultivation of Qiao, and led many, but not all, foreign affairs officials to believe that he had developed close ties with the "gang of four."[92] About the time of Jiang's proposal, Qiao, the leading professional in the MFA who, despite only holding vice ministerial rank, was relied on by Mao and Zhou for diplomatic work, was named Foreign Minister, a position confirmed in the NPC appointments in January. The appointment was presumably formally made by Zhou, but there is evidence to indicate that Jiang was aware of the promotion more than a month earlier.[93] It can be assumed, then, that at the very least Jiang was happy with the promotion, and perhaps had a role in bringing it about.[94] On the other hand, it may simply have been a long overdue administrative matter, particularly given Mao's dissatisfaction of more than a year's standing with Minister Ji Pengfei, who in fact had already been transferred to work at the NPC Standing Committee. In any case, a full consideration suggests that Qiao's elevation suited not only Jiang, but Zhou, Deng and—most importantly—Mao as well.

Mao's position, of course, was crucial, and it typically reflected a mix of personal and political considerations. In narrow political terms, Qiao possessed neither the Party status, ideological proclivities, nor symbolic profile to make him a prime candidate for a vice premiership in Mao's eyes, but he did have the diplomatic skills required of a Foreign Minister. For all his periodic raging against MFA professionals, including quixotic calls for Wang Hongwen and Zhang Chunqiao to learn foreign languages, the Chairman clearly valued competence in the area he controlled most tightly. Meanwhile, administrative power in the ministry was exercised by the "two ladies," an arrangement conducive to conflict and distressful for Qiao, but one further enhancing Mao's control. A personal factor, moreover, also came into play through Qiao's new wife, Zhang Hanzhi. Mao had taken a particular interest in Zhang, both as the adopted daughter of his 1920s benefactor, Zhang Shizhao, and as a talented woman whom he wished to appoint as the PRC's first female ambassador. Zhang Hanzhi, who had also

---

[92] Regarding the division of opinion within the MFA over whether Qiao opposed or was linked to the "gang," Chinese officials present at the UN in 1974 (it is unclear whether this was in April or the fall) recall a slightly inebriated Qiao attacking the radicals. On the other hand, Vice Minister Zhang Wenjin and his wife attended a private dinner hosted by Qiao in late 1975 where he and Zhang Hanzhi told the visiting couple about Jiang's high regard for them, something they interpreted as a recruitment effort. Ma Jisen, *The Cultural Revolution in the Foreign Ministry*, pp. 386-87.

[93] According to one source, Jiang Qing revealed Qiao Guanhua's promotion to Zhang Hanzhi on National Day 1974. See Wen Xiang, "Lishi huigu" [Looking Back at History] (March 10, 2004), http://www.comefromchina.com/newbbs/archive/topic/225628-1.html.

[94] Speculatively, another factor in Jiang's cultivation of Qiao may have been the development of tensions between her and the "two ladies." It is difficult, however, to pin down the timing of this deterioration of relations and relate it to Qiao's promotion.

served as Mao's English teacher for several months in 1963, fit Mao's concept of female emancipation. He was delighted when she heeded his advice to divorce her husband from her first failed marriage, but unhappy when she declined the diplomatic posting in order to continue her relationship with Qiao, which led to their marriage at the end of 1973. Indeed, one senior specialist on foreign policy, with personal connections to the MFA, believes there was a link between Mao's critical reaction to the 1973 report on the Nixon-Brezhnev summit, in which Qiao had played a leading role, and his displeasure over Qiao's relationship with Zhang. This displeasure apparently was short-lived, however, and, as we saw in Chapter 1, after a brief bout of severe criticism, Qiao's career was again on the rise with his election to the Central Committee at the Tenth Congress.[95]

While Mao's apparent approval of Qiao would have been crucial for Zhou, other factors were also involved in the Premier's presumed support of Qiao's appointment. In terms of career and personal associations, Qiao was a classic example of the MFA elite. A foreign affairs professional who had been a vice minister since 1964, Qiao had worked with Zhou since their service in Chongqing during the 1940s, developing a personal relationship and, according to Zhang Hanzhi, regarding the Premier as a father figure. Early in the Cultural Revolution, Qiao was among the first leaders singled out for radical attack in the Foreign Ministry, and there is little to suggest any policy tension in the 1970s with Zhou (or with Deng subsequently). From Zhou's perspective, Qiao would have had the appropriate diplomatic skills (as seen in his assignment to draft the 1972 Shanghai communiqué) to implement a foreign policy that would be set by the Chairman in any case. Of course, the Premier might have harbored resentment over Qiao's attacks in late 1973, but no one understood better, or had himself adhered to more strictly, the need to carry out Mao's demands to criticize whomever had been singled out. In this respect, when Qiao visited his hospital room in late 1975 and apologized, Zhou's reported remark that "I too have made mistakes" was no more than the simple truth.[96] In the context of selecting the new State Council in 1974, Qiao was the logical choice, one made easier because it suited Jiang.[97]

For Deng Xiaoping, who by the time of Qiao's promotion was in direct charge of foreign affairs work, the calculation would have been similar to Zhou's. That

---

[95] Zhang Hanzhi, *Wo yu Qiao Guanhua*, pp. 30ff, 42-43; Ma Jisen, *The Cultural Revolution in the Foreign Ministry*, pp. 375-78; interview, July 1997; and above, p. 91. Qiao's distress at the situation in the MFA sometimes made him feel the position wasn't worth it, as in his comments after becoming Foreign Minister on the difficulty of dealing with the "two ladies," and his reported effort to secure an overseas posting; Ma Jisen, pp. 379-80.

[96] See Zhang Hanzhi, *Wo yu Qiao Guanhua*, pp. 84-88; Ma Jisen, *The Cultural Revolution in the Foreign Ministry*, pp. 373-76; and Barnouin and Yu, *Foreign Policy*, p. 39.

[97] This did not mean that the radicals were necessarily satisfied with MFA performance. Wu De, "Guowuyuan wenhuazu," p. 83, recalled a Politburo discussion on an unspecified foreign policy issue in which the "gang" kept pursuing the issue, leading Ji Dengkui to confront Jiang, arguing

is, Qiao's expertise was obvious, and Mao's apparent support was all important. Moreover, Deng, like Zhou, understood that whatever the questionable actions by Qiao in criticizing the Premier and maintaining good relations with Jiang, this was fundamentally a product of the situation created by the Chairman. Indeed, Deng had been in a similar position through his own apparently cordial relations with Mao's wife, and his harsh criticism of the Premier in late 1973. In any case, the true nature of the personal relations between Qiao and Deng is unclear, with Zhang Hanzhi predictably portraying them as quite good, while an American official, recalling Deng contrasting himself as a "country bumpkin" (*tu baozi*) to Qiao's Western sophisticate (*yang baozi*), felt that Deng needled Qiao in front of foreigners. Professionally, in any case, Deng and Qiao apparently worked well together, while given the political situation in 1974 and most of 1975, Qiao would have recognized Deng's power, and presumably have been comfortable with it.[98]

Superficially, given Mao's attitude, Qiao's behavior mirrored that of the "two ladies": however "bad" Qiao might have been to the Premier, he would be "nice to Deng Xiaoping." Yet the situation was different, given Jiang Qing's apparent cultivation of Qiao, which stood in sharp relief to her testy relations with Wang Hairong. In the context of State Council appointments, it was an easy matter for Deng to support Qiao, but questions of ultimate loyalties would have been present. Nevertheless, after Qiao's dismissal and subsequent prolonged interrogation and isolation following the arrest of the "gang of four," on several occasions Deng intervened to mitigate Qiao's situation. But equally if not more telling, Deng intervened more quickly and decisively to ease the situation of Wang Hairong and Tang Wensheng, who had also been subjected to lengthy criticism for their treatment of Zhou, but whose animus toward Jiang was well understood. While we examine the complexities of life in the MFA and the Qiao-"gang" connection in subsequent chapters, perhaps the best judgment at this point is to repeat the observations of CCP leaders in the early 1980s when Qiao's case was finally being rectified shortly before his death. In 1982, Hu Yaobang remarked that "some things [Qiao] did were unavoidable since he was in power," while later in the same year Vice Premier Xi Zhongxun and Chen Pixian advised Qiao that, like almost all veteran comrades, Qiao had endured unjust suffering, and it was best "to let bygones be bygones."[99]

---

that the policy had already been decided and Zhou was handling the matter, so there was no need to pursue it further. When Mao became aware of the conflict, he arranged for Ji to accompany Jiang on a visit to Xiaojinzhuang, her radical model village, in order to give them an opportunity to settle their differences.

[98] Zhang Hanzhi, *Wo yu Qiao Guanhua*, pp. 73-74; and interview with Richard Solomon, November 2003, and personal communication, March 2005.

[99] Ma Jisen, *The Cultural Revolution in the Foreign Ministry*, pp. 389-90, 399-402; interview with foreign policy specialist with close MFA ties, January 2005; and above, p. 20. Ma Jisen, p. 390,

The area where there is the most, albeit contradictory, information concerning conflict over personnel assignments is the culture and education spheres. As noted, this was the area where radical proposals had particular legitimacy given Zhang Chunqiao's responsibilities in the arrangements approved after the Fourth NPC. Whether his specific assignment had already been formally decided, Zhang's status as the second-ranking Vice Premier had been determined by Mao on November 20, and culture and education was clearly the logical area for his oversight. The standard official account depicts a tug-of-war between the radicals and Zhou Enlai in this area, one that supposedly came to a head in the meeting of December 21. In this version, Jiang Qing and Zhang now made demands for placing their trusted followers in the culture, education and sports ministries, but Zhou felt strong enough to resist. During post-meeting consultations with Li Xiannian and Ji Dengkui, the Premier assertedly determined to insist on rehabilitated old cadre Zhou Rongxin as Minister of Education, conceding the other two ministries to the radicals.[100] Other information, however, suggests a more complicated picture for both the Ministry of Education and the Ministry of Culture, which we now address in turn.

A striking feature of the official story is that no radical candidate for Minister of Education is identified in accounts of the December 21 meeting, even though Jiang Qing had proposed Chi Qun for the post in her letter to Mao the previous month. Chi had a definite appeal from the radical perspective, having been a key author of the 1971 "two assessments" that damned the pre-Cultural Revolution educational system, having played an important role in carrying out the *pi Lin pi Kong* campaign, and also due to his links to Mao as a member of his household guard unit whom the Chairman had dispatched to Qinghua University in 1968 to bring the situation there under control. Chi's behavior, however, had caused a lot of discontent in the State Council Science and Education Group where he held a leading post, and when delegates to the NPC were elected by the group, Chi did not get sufficient votes. Only when Xie Jingyi reported this to Mao did Chi become a delegate due to the Chairman's intervention. This seemingly was not enough to become a minister, however, and it may well be the case that by the time of the December 21 meeting the "gang" no longer even attempted to put his name forward.[101]

A further qualification is that even if the Premier decided on the desirability of Zhou Rongxin's appointment, together with Li Xiannian and Ji Dengkui after the meeting of the 21st, or with Ye Jianying at some indeterminate point,

---

claims an initial Deng intervention, or at least an intervention by others using Deng's words, as early as late 1976. While not ruling this out, we believe this is far too early.

[100] See *Zhou nianpu*, vol. 3, p. 686; Mao Mao, *"Wenge" suiyue*, p. 328; and Yan and Gao, *Turbulent Decade*, p. 459.

[101] Zhang Hua, "1975 nian jiaoyujie de douzheng" [The 1975 Struggle in the Educational Sphere], *ZGDSZL*, no. 70 (1999), pp. 147-48; and above, pp. 57-58, 148ff.

it appears he did not bring that view to Mao as a clear preference. According to one plausible source, Zhou Enlai approached Mao with the names of both Chi Qun and Zhou Rongxin. The Premier, probably aware that Mao had been informed that Chi had not even garnered enough votes to be a delegate, first asked whether Chi was fit to be a minister, drawing the Chairman's querulous response of how could someone who had proved unable to do a good job with a small bureaucratic unit be a minister. Zhou then raised Zhou Rongxin's name. While Zhou Rongxin had been close to the Premier as secretary-general of the State Council before the Cultural Revolution, more relevant was Mao's favorable disposition. The Chairman had been impressed with Zhou's performance when he was sent to Zhejiang University in 1958 and, although not highly educated himself, won over the university's intellectuals, producing Mao's statement that on the educational front cadres like Zhou Rongxin were what was needed. That Mao retained a favorable view despite Zhou's disgrace during the Cultural Revolution is suggested by his being among the first cadres liberated after the Lin Biao affair. In any case, notwithstanding the fact that Chi himself secured no position in the reestablished Ministry of Education, Chi Qun's followers gained lesser posts in the ministry, and reported to him after the Congress.[102]

Similarly, the appointment of a Minister of Culture was more complicated than a radical-moderate tussle leading to a strategic decision by the Premier to concede the ministry to the "gang" on the grounds it was less significant than education. The eventual appointee as Minister of Culture, Yu Huiyong, a musician, leftist arts theorist, and creator of model Cultural Revolution stage works, had worked closely with Jiang Qing and Zhang Chunqiao in various capacities, and was indeed one of three presumptive radicals named minister at the NPC.[103] But Yu was not the "gang's" first choice. Instead, they asked Beijing Party leader and Politburo member Wu De to assume the post. A number of factors came into play here. First, Wu's nomination came out of the consultative process mandated by Mao. In October, as Zhou began consulting on personnel issues with groups of leaders, he approached Jiang and Zhang on the culture position, and they proposed Wu. This had a certain bureaucratic logic, since Wu was the head of the State Council Culture Group. It also fit Mao's emphasis on finding people acceptable to all sides, and according to one senior Party historian, even after Wu declined, the effort to find such a person continued. From the narrow perspective of the "gang," Wu was an acceptable although not ideal choice. As we saw in the previous chapters, with little knowledge of culture, Wu had been completely overshadowed by Jiang Qing. While the relationship, particularly in

---

[102] Zhang Hua, "1975 nian jiaoyujie de douzheng," p. 148; Zhou Shaohua, "Zhou Zongli he wode fuqin Zhou Rongxin" [Premier Zhou and My Father Zhou Rongxin], Zhuanji wenxue [Biographical Literature], no. 5 (1993), pp. 16-17; Yan and Gao, Turbulent Decade, p. 460; and interview with specialist on educational history, January 2005.

[103] The others were Zhuang Zedong as head of the Physical Culture and Sports Commission, and Liu Xiangping as Minister of Public Health.

Wu's telling, was full of tension, he basically offered no opposition to her general approach and, as at the start of *pi Lin pi Kong*, gave public voice to her line. But it clearly was an uncomfortable situation for Wu, particularly in instances when Jiang's cultural activities were aimed at the Premier. Of course, from another perspective, the degree of cooperation that Wu did provide could be seen as too accommodating, and in the post-Mao period perceptions of links to the "gang" contributed to Wu's downfall.[104]

Wu, however, did not accept the post. When approached by Zhou, he argued that not only did he not understand culture, but his duties as Beijing's Party First Secretary and Revolutionary Committee head were too demanding for him to take on ministerial responsibilities. Wu's position led to a conflict in the Politburo between Zhang Chunqiao and Ni Zhifu. Although a worker who had risen due to the Cultural Revolution, Ni as a Party secretary in Beijing supported Wu's position, emphasizing the heavy nature of work in the municipality, and, as a result, was rebuked by Zhang as a departmentalist. Zhou Enlai proposed a compromise whereby Wu would remain First Secretary but Ni would take over Revolutionary Committee duties, but Ni refused. After further inconclusive discussion, Zhou dropped the matter. In a seeming final effort to draft Wu, Zhang proposed that Wu be appointed both Vice Premier and Minister of Culture. While all this was going on, Wu consulted Li Xiannian, with whom he was close. Li urged Wu to be resolute in refusing the culture post, and also spoke to the Premier about Wu's situation. Zhou then offered Wu a NPC Vice Chairmanship, commenting that Wang Hongwen and Hua Guofeng had both declined the post, but that there was a precedent to combine the position with the Beijing municipal leadership in Peng Zhen's pre-Cultural Revolution case. Wu, however begged off, earning Li Xiannian's rebuke. Li reasoned that he was foolish since this was the best way for Wu to extricate himself from the radicals' territory and wash his hands of them.[105]

With Wu declining the position, it finally fell to Yu Huiyong, who was Wu's deputy in the State Council Culture Group and the radicals' choice over a famous Shanghai scholar of Chinese literature, Liu Dajie, whom Wu had proposed. While the appointment was widely regarded as a "gang of four" success, this was not strictly the case even though there can be no doubt of Yu's radical ideology. Moreover, it did not mean smooth sailing in the relationship between Yu and the Politburo radicals, particularly Jiang Qing. Yu had previously been appointed to the State Council group by Zhou, and it was the Premier who proposed raising

---

[104] Wu De, "Guowuyuan wenhuazu," pp. 77-81; "Beijing shi 'wenhua dageming' dashiji (1965 nian 11 yue–1976 nian 10 yue)" [Chronology of the "Cultural Revolution" in Beijing Municipality, November 1965-October 1976], *Beijing dangshi ziliao tongxun (zengkan 17)* [Beijing Party History Materials Bulletin, supplement no. 17], May 1987, pp. 27-28, 37; interview, February 2000; and above, pp. 56-57, 160-61. The consequences for Wu's career will be examined in our Volume II.

[105] Wu De, "Guowuyuan wenhuazu," pp. 80-81; and interview with senior Party historian, February 2000.

the status of the group to that of a ministry—over the objections of Jiang and Zhang Chunqiao. Zhou also pushed Yu's appointment as minister, leaving Jiang Qing furious that he was getting the credit, and refusing to congratulate Yu. Once in office, Yu sought direction from the radicals and carried out their line, but the new minister was not immune from Jiang's rebukes, being forced by her on at least four occasions to engage in self-criticism. For his part, it appears that Yu was particularly uncomfortable with attacks on the Premier, to whom he seemingly was genuinely grateful for nominating him to be a minister, and he carried out his "anti-Zhou" activities under pressure from Jiang. After the fall of the "gang," Yu hoped the Party Center would understand his situation, but after being denounced as a "new born counterrevolutionary," he committed suicide.[106]

With the complicated process of producing recommendations for the new government and NPC posts behind him, the Premier set out for Changsha on December 23, with Wang Hongwen taking a separate plane on the same day. Over the December 24-27 period, Mao met with the two leaders on four occasions, three times jointly, and in a particularly significant meeting, with Zhou alone on the 26th, the Chairman's 81st birthday. While the standard story implies that the Chairman accepted Zhou's personnel recommendations, this was not strictly the case, as illustrated by the Ministry of Education appointment. In addition, Mao deleted Xie Jingyi, Qiao Guanhua and economics specialist Fang Yi from the Premier's list of NPC vice chairs and vice premiers, while apparently adding Chen Xilian to the vice premier list. Also, with whatever intent, Mao enquired about Zhou's wife, Deng Yingchao, as NPC Vice Chair, but did not discuss it further after the Premier's explanation, presumably of why such an appointment was inappropriate. Although there is some uncertainty as to whether Mao or Zhou took the initiative, it was decided at Changsha that Deng would be Party Vice Chairman as well as First Vice Premier, and his appointments as MAC Vice Chairman in addition to PLA Chief-of-Staff, apparently proposed by Ye Jianying, were confirmed. Zhou also asked who would be a good GPD head, mentioning three possible choices. Mao responded "Luo Ronghuan," the former head who died in 1963, thus implying none of the three were fully adequate. Nevertheless, Mao did appoint Zhang Chunqiao to the position during Zhou and Wang's December visit.[107]

---

[106] See Dai Jiafang, *Zouxiang huimie: "Wenge" Wenhua buzhang Yu Huiyong chenfulu* [Toward Destruction: Record of the Tide-following "Cultural Revolution" Minister of Culture Yu Huiyong] (Beijing: *Guangming ribao* chubanshe, 1994), pp. 3, 336, 353-56; and Richard Kraus, "Arts Policies of the Cultural Revolution: The Rise and Fall of Culture Minister Yu Huiyong," in William Joseph *et al.*, eds., *New Perspectives on the Cultural Revolution* (Cambridge: Council on East Asian Studies/ Harvard University, 1991).

[107] See *Mao zhuan*, vol. 2, pp. 1711-12; Mao Mao, *"Wenge" suiyue*, pp. 329-30, 519; Barnouin and Yu, *Ten Years*, p. 372; Gao Wenqian, *Wannian Zhou*, p. 537; and Yin Jiamin, *Gongheguo fengyun zhong de Mao Zedong yu Zhou Enlai* [Mao Zedong and Zhou Enlai during the Republic's Tumult]

As repeatedly emphasized in official accounts, Mao used the occasion of the visit to criticize the radicals heavily. As noted above, much of this reflected his ongoing frustration with his wife and her alleged "wild ambitions," but even now he used the "one divides into two" formula to describe Jiang, thus implying there was a good part that had to be acknowledged. Beyond this he coined the phrase "gang of four" for the first time, both warning Wang against participating in such a group, and authorizing the formal relaying of this view to the Politburo. This did not stop him from articulating a favorable opinion of Zhang Chunqiao (see below), but he now emphasized his disenchantment with Wang Hongwen. Although the precise reasons are not entirely clear,[108] Mao not only lectured Wang to "stop carrying on with your 'gang of four'," he also pointed to his notional successor and declared that Deng is "stronger than you in politics and ideology, [and] a rare talent hard to match." By now Wang's star was clearly on the decline while Deng's was on the rise, and the Chairman required that Wang prepare a written self-examination, while also ordering that Jiang make a self-criticism. Yet Mao was not prepared to abandon his successor, and Wang retained his responsibility for the daily affairs of the Party Center. Personal considerations aside, Mao's dressing down of Wang reflected his larger hopes for a united team, for a reconciliation of the factions. He urged Zhou and Wang to have a good talk, observing with regard to the leadership more broadly that "the Center only has these people, they must unite."[109]

The most significant encounter of the visit was Zhou's personal audience with Mao on the 26th, a long four hour meeting lasting into the early morning. The Premier was reportedly pleased with the encounter, feeling that Mao was inclined to listen. But this was a meeting of the two men alone, their last meaningful conversation, and apart from fragments Zhou subsequently revealed, and what can be deduced from an exchange between Mao's and Zhou's secretaries, the

---

(Beijing: Zhonggong zhongyang dangxiao chubanshe, 1999), p. 438. Whether Zhang Chunqiao was among the three candidates for GPD head, or a compromise choice in a manner similar to Deng as Chief-of-Staff, remains a mystery.

Concerning Deng Yingchao, Mao may have been testing Zhou. Alternatively, the Premier's wife may have been on an earlier list, and Mao was enquiring what had happened. In either scenario, Zhou clearly concluded it was not in his interest that she be appointed. That would wait until after his and Mao's deaths.

[108] While the specific trigger could have been Wang's enquiry about Jiang's work, this is unlikely since it apparently came very shortly before the departure of the two leaders. Using a less reliable source, Barnouin and Yu, *Ten Years*, p. 272, claim Wang carried a message from Jiang suggesting that a new premier was required given Zhou's poor health, which arguably led Mao to repeat his statement that "the Premier is still our Premier," and would have angered him given the arrangements he had clearly made, but we regard this scenario as highly unlikely. It is more likely, we believe, that this was a generalized complaint about the "gang's" activities throughout the year, as suggested by Mao's comments on the old issues of the "11th line struggle" and the back door question, and his conclusion that *pi Lin pi Kong* was not a "second Cultural Revolution." It is also likely that, by this stage, Mao was influenced by the negative reports of the "two ladies" concerning Wang. See above, pp. 212-13.

[109] See *Mao zhuan*, vol. 2, p. 1711; Mao Mao, *"Wenge" suiyue*, p. 329; and above, p. 155.

content of the discussion remains unknown to a substantial extent. In general terms, however, Mao picked up on the theme of Party unity. He reemphasized his August message on "stability and unity," a message that Zhou took back to Beijing as the keynote for the Fourth NPC. Mao further called for developing the national economy, and there were also additional discussions of personnel questions, with the Chairman again pointing to the need to speed up the rehabilitation of old cadres.[110] In contrast to these familiar themes, the exchanges between Premier and Chairman also produced two surprising topics that seemingly ran against the general trend of the previous months. These were the "historical problems" of Politburo members, introduced by Zhou, and theoretical issues raised by the Chairman.

Authoritative sources either ignore the "historical problems" issue, or deal with it vaguely: e.g., Zhou "seriously spoke to Mao ... about the historical problems of Jiang Qing and Zhang Chunqiao," while the Chairman indicated that he "already knew the circumstances concerning [their] serious political history issues."[111] More details can be deduced from lesser sources, but it will be useful to note a few general aspects of the "historical problems" question first. One consideration is that "historical problems," issues arising in the pre-1949 revolutionary struggle, encompassed a wide range of behavior from fairly minor violations of organizational procedures, to selling out the Party as a spy or traitor. These latter issues were lethal, beyond forgiveness in a way no political or ideological mistake could be. Another feature of "historical problems" was the vulnerability they created, particularly for those who had worked in "white areas" controlled by the enemy. Given complex revolutionary situations, understandable suspicions, and often rudimentary records, many revolutionary comrades were potentially at risk during post-1949 political campaigns to error or to the unscrupulous settling of old scores. In the Cultural Revolution in particular, the most effective way to get rid of people was to claim they had been traitors. Finally, where the highest levels were concerned, Mao could bend the rules and evidence to suit his wishes. A benign case concerned Chen Yonggui. When selected a delegate to the Ninth Party Congress in 1968, Chen was overwhelmed by the honor, but guilty about some aspect of his past, and confessed to an unspecified "historical problem." Chen's case was downplayed by Zhou Enlai, who, obviously reflecting his understanding of Mao's attitude, commented on the need to uphold "the red flag of [Chen Yonggui's] Dazhai," and counseled leaving the historical issue alone. In the event, Chen not only attended the Congress, but was elected to the Central Committee. The issue resurfaced

---

[110] See *Mao zhuan*, vol. 2, p. 1713; Mao Mao, *"Wenge" suiyue*, pp. 330, 333; and *Zhou nianpu*, vol. 3, p. 689. While we do not doubt Mao's reported comments on liberating veteran cadres, we suspect the need for the promotion of young cadres emerging from the Cultural Revolution, something seen in Zhou's personnel recommendations, would also have been discussed.

[111] Mao Mao, *"Wenge" suiyue*, p. 330. See also *Zhou nianpu*, vol. 3, pp. 687-88.

in 1974 at an enlarged meeting of the Party committee of the Beijing Military Region. Given both clear evidence and Chen's 1968 confession, it was difficult to resolve the question, and the matter was sent to Mao for a decision. The message came back, *via* Military Region Commander Chen Xilian, that the Chairman knew about it, and the case should not be mentioned again.[112]

Concerning Jiang and Zhang in 1974, Kang Sheng appears to have been the driving force in raising the issue. Having cursed them as traitors to Deng after the latter's return to work in early 1973, Kang seemingly now pressed Zhou for direct action. Given his role in cadre investigations during the Cultural Revolution, the fact that his protégé Guo Yufeng headed the Organization Department, and not least that Jiang had previously given him Zhang's file, Kang presumably was well placed to make charges against both Jiang and Zhang. He reportedly approached Zhou with detailed evidence purporting to show that Zhang had been a Guomindang spy and Jiang a traitor, and urged the Premier to raise the matter with Mao. Zhou apparently used some of what Kang had provided when meeting with Mao on December 26, making sure to emphasize Kang's role. In the most detailed account, however, Zhou only relayed accusations against Zhang Chunqiao, steering well clear of Jiang Qing. We find this credible despite the fleeting mention of Jiang in more authoritative sources. Zhou's inherent caution suggests he would not touch Jiang Qing, a step that could lead to political death, whatever the Chairman's current fulminations about his wife. But would a cautious Premier have raised Zhang's historical problems either? A number of Party historians, questioned separately on the issue, concluded that this was credible. The factors they saw coming into play were that, as the responsible figure for the NPC, Zhou was duty bound to report on candidates for leading positions (which included Zhang, but not Jiang), including any problems concerning their past. Related to this, Zhou would be vulnerable for failing to report any relevant information to the Chairman. And since others, notably Kang Sheng, could be cited, Zhou did not have to appear as the primary accuser. Whatever Zhou put to the Chairman, as earlier Mao was not interested in pursuing Zhang's problem, reportedly commenting that Kang Sheng was an "ultra-leftist," that there may have been some problem with Zhang's pre-1949 activities in Shanghai but it was not a case of spying, his problems were the kind of general historical questions

---

[112] See Fan Yinhua, "Chen Yonggui guoguan ji" [An Account of Chen Yonggui Getting Off the Hook], *Yanhuang chunqiu*, no. 5 (1999), pp. 23-24. This complicated case involved conflict between Chen Yonggui and the Shanxi provincial leader, Xie Zhenhua, who had been obliged to report Chen's confession to the Party Center. This conflict developed in the context of the criticism of the "ultra-left" in 1972, with Xie enthusiastic about the effort, while Chen declared that rightism was the main danger. Xie was ousted in the context of *pi Lin pi Kong* in 1974, with a major role played by Jiang Qing; see above, pp. 157n111, 173-74. Xie's successor as leader of the 69th army, however, felt obliged to pursue the matter, leading to a situation in which Mao intervened. Note that in Chen's case, Mao was arguably more cavalier than in dismissing charges against Zhang Chunqiao (see below), given clearer evidence and Chen's confession. Cf. above, p. 74n125.

many cadres had and where no proof existed in any case, and the whole matter should simply be shelved.[113]

The theory question introduced by Mao on the 26th was less of a surprise given his ongoing theoretical preoccupations and firm commitment to the Cultural Revolution, but it was still a different emphasis than Party unity, articulating government structures and staffing, and giving attention to the economy. Here Mao laid down the framework for the campaign to "study the theory of the dictatorship of the proletariat," which we examine in detail in Chapter 4, in both thematic and operational terms. He reminded Zhou of the need to "guard against revisionism," pointing to significant problems in the economic organization of socialism that would lead to backsliding if unchecked, and called attention to his philosophical exchange on the issue with the Prime Minister of Denmark in October. Practically, the Chairman told Zhou to have Zhang Chunqiao and Yao Wenyuan write articles on this theme, articles that became major political events in early 1975 following the NPC, and his extended comments subsequently became the instruction launching the study movement. If Zhang and Yao were uncertain about the task, they could consult his talk with the Danish leader. Moreover, in sharp contrast to his complaints about Wang Hongwen and, above all, Jiang Qing, Mao spoke highly of Zhang's talents in the exchange with Zhou, thus indicating a positive attitude regardless of any "historical problems" or complaints about a "gang of four."[114] More broadly, with the Fourth NPC approaching, the Chairman appeared ready for a more far-reaching reassessment of the 30 percent shortcomings of the Cultural Revolution than in 1972, yet his theoretical concerns remained a powerful constraint.

The Fourth National People's Congress

The stage was now set for the Fourth NPC to finally meet, five years behind its constitutionally stipulated schedule. With Mao having spoken and Zhou and Wang back in Beijing, preparations for the Second Plenum (January 8-10) and the NPC session (January 13-17) proceeded apace, with little further conflict. Deng's elevated position was now even more apparent: on Mao's proposal he attended a Politburo Standing Committee meeting for the first time on December 28, and on January 1 his proposals for (presumably supplemental) State Council appointments were accepted on the principle of "basically don't change, only

---

[113] Lin Qing, *Zhou Enlai zaixiang shengya*, pp. 317-19; Gao Wenqian, *Wannian Zhou*, p. 541; Zhang Zuoliang, *Zhou Enlai zuihou shinian*, p. 344; interviews, December 2002; and above, pp. 73-74. Generally speaking, we have reservations about Lin Qing's work, but the detailed account here appears credible, although the author seemingly got the timing wrong.

[114] *Mao zhuan*, vol. 2, pp. 1712-15; Mao Mao, *"Wenge" suiyue*, p. 330; *Mao wengao*, vol. 13, pp. 413-17; and interview with senior Party historian, January 2000. A further indication of Zhang's standing with Mao at this point is that he had Politburo responsibility for Party affairs and Volume 5 of Mao's *Selected Works*. *Mao zhuan*, vol. 2, p. 1712.

make minor changes." On January 5, the Party Center issued Document no. 1 (1975) formally appointing Deng to his new military posts as MAC Vice Chairman and Chief-of-Staff, while also affirming Zhang Chunqiao's selection as GPD head.[115] This left some ambiguity concerning authority within the MAC, since Deng was formally outranked by not only Ye Jianying, but also by Wang Hongwen on the body's Standing Committee. The best evidence, however, is that Deng quickly exercised the main leadership in running the body.[116] The other major leadership issue to be addressed was Mao's negative views on Jiang Qing and the "gang of four," which he had stipulated should be formally presented to the Standing Committee and Politburo. Before Zhou executed this task on the 28th and 29th, he took Jiang aside to relay the Chairman's views. The next day Jiang again wrote abjectly to Mao, expressing full agreement with his criticisms, lamenting her "perilous brain" that forgot everything, hoping she could leave Beijing after the NPC, and once more seeking permission to see her husband—a request again denied.[117]

The Second Plenum formalized the arrangements for the NPC session. The meeting sanctioned the major documents that would be passed by the NPC: the new state constitution, the report on the revision of the constitution to be delivered by Zhang Chunqiao, and the government work report to be given by the Premier. The latter report, on Mao's orders, had been drafted under Deng's direction since November. Despite some suggestions of tension, with Mao's biographers unconvincingly claiming Deng cut out attempted "gang" insertions in the draft, and insisted that the four modernizations be the report's focal point consistent with the original use of the concept at the Third NPC in 1964-65, there is virtually nothing to suggest serious conflict over the document (see below). The plenum also confirmed Deng's promotion to the Politburo Standing Committee and Party Vice Chairman, as well as accepting Li Desheng's forced resignation from both positions and giving final approval to the NPC and State Council appointments. All in all, it was a cut and dry meeting, with the most interesting development being what did not happen. On January 9, in the midst of the plenum, Zhou Enlai phoned Mao asking that he be authorized to give yet another self-criticism at the conclusion of the meeting. The Chairman refused, instead instructing Zhou to reiterate his demand for "stability and unity." While Mao's order prevented the Premier from undertaking this particular self-criticism, his hand was not stayed for long. On February 1, the last time he chaired a State Council meeting, the

---

[115] Mao Mao, "Wenge" suiyue, pp. 325, 332-33; Zhou nianpu, vol. 3, pp. 688-91; Mao zhuan, vol. 2, p. 1721; and Li Desheng huiyilu, pp. 488-89. The ministry arrangements approved on January 1 were seemingly more detailed than what had been reviewed by Mao in Changsha. The minor changes involved the ministries of communications, petroleum and chemical industries, and commerce. It was also decided not to revisit the issue of the ministries of culture and education, on the grounds of "avoiding unnecessary domestic and foreign comment"; Zhou nianpu, vol. 3, p. 689.

[116] See below, p. 253.

[117] Mao zhuan, vol. 2, p. 1712; and Zhou nianpu, vol. 3, p. 688.

Premier made a self-criticism that highlighted the Chairman's complaints about his alleged tendency to pay attention only to trivial matters.[118]

In broad perspective, the preparations for the NPC reflected the secretive and tightly controlled features of post-1966 major gatherings—albeit not to the extreme of the Tenth Party Congress when new Central Committee members only became aware of the meeting at the eleventh hour.[119] In the NPC case, three months had passed since the Center announced the coming session, but the "election" of delegates seemingly was managed from above, without the local procedures of the pre-Cultural Revolution period. Furthermore, in contrast to the weighty documents of the earlier period, Zhou's government work report, the new state constitution, and Zhang Chunqiao's report on the constitution were all, like similar Cultural Revolution-era documents, no more than one-third the length of their pre-1966 predecessors. While Deng's daughter explains the short work report as a conscious effort to avoid taxing the Premier's frail health, the more fundamental reason for brevity was the lack of clarity concerning future directions, and the danger inherent in being too specific.[120]

Once the NPC was in session, it very much followed Mao's script. This observation is at odds with contemporary (and various later) scholarly accounts which generally saw it as Zhou's Congress, an occasion when "The decisions of the Congress were apparently dominated by the growth-oriented policies of veteran cadres and the ... military which rallied increasingly around [Zhou Enlai and] his chosen lieutenant [Deng Xiaoping]."[121] The dominant view also saw conflicting agendas expressed at the Congress, while Mao, who remained in Changsha, assertedly sought to dissociate himself from proceedings he found less than to his taste and unable to control.[122] In fact, what Zhou Enlai and Zhang Chunqiao each articulated in their reports was an attempt to combine Mao's emphasis on Cultural Revolution concepts and attention to economic development, with a decided priority to the former. Whatever the undoubted different preferences dividing Zhou and Deng from Zhang, or the consequences of their different

---

[118] *Mao zhuan*, vol. 2, pp. 1716-17; *Zhou nianpu*, vol. 3, pp. 690-91; Gao Wenqian, *Wannian Zhou*, p. 542; and above, p. 144. According to the 1976 confession of a Shanghai follower of the "gang," in something less than a major conflict over principle, Zhang Chunqiao successfully objected to including 1980-85 grain and steel targets in the work report. "Ma Tianshui de buchong jiefa jiaodai" [Ma Tianshui's Supplementary Unmasking Confession] (November 21, 1976), in *CRDB*, p. 2.

[119] See above, pp. 93n166, 106.

[120] See Yan and Gao, *Turbulent Decade*, pp. 457-58; and Mao Mao, *"Wenge" suiyue*, p. 325. The NPC documents were published in *PR*, no. 4 (1975), pp. 12-25. For comparisons, see the summary of Zhou's work report to the Third NPC, in *PR*, no. 1 (1965), pp. 6-20, and the reports and new Party constitution at the Tenth Congress, in *PR*, no. 35-36 (1973), pp. 17-33. Moreover, the duration of the Congress, a mere five days, contrasted with the 16-day Third NPC.

[121] Jurgen Domes, "The 'Gang of Four' and Hua Kuo-feng: Analysis of Political Events in 1975-76," *CQ*, no. 71 (1977), p. 479.

[122] See especially Kenneth Lieberthal, "China in 1975: The Internal Political Scene," *Problems of Communism*, May-June 1975, pp. 7-9.

functions of reporting on government work and the new constitution, there was little to choose in basic meaning between the two reports.

Zhou began with a paean of praise to the Cultural Revolution and its new born things, including Jiang Qing's "revolutionary theatrical works," defended the movement against claims that it had disrupted the economy, demanded (à la Jiang in the *Fengqing* incident) criticism of "servility to things foreign," and declared the primary task was to continue the movement to criticize Lin Biao and Confucius. Far from advancing a coherent growth-oriented policy, Zhou only referred to the modernization of agriculture, industry, national defense, and science and technology half way into his report (never using the "four modernizations" catch phrase), and made sure to source the objective to Mao's instruction that the Premier had transmitted at the Third NPC in 1964. While promising a ten-year plan, and laying down the objectives of building a fairly comprehensive national economic system by 1980 and achieving all-round modernization to bring China into the world's foremost ranks by the end of the century, the skimpy discussion of the economy was impeccably referenced to Maoist concepts. For his part, although giving particular attention to the dictatorship of the proletariat issue, Zhang Chunqiao also supported the development of the economic base, including "necessary flexibility" on such matters as private plots and household sideline production.[123]

The paradox, then, was that the essential verbal agreement at the NPC mandated by Mao's views coincided with an underlying tension bordering on hostility between the radicals and virtually everyone else in the top leadership. While somewhat overstated given the tensions within the "gang" and the uncertainty created by Mao, Deng's daughter Mao Mao, writing nearly a quarter of a century later, claimed that "two camps" had already formed and were implacably opposed to one another by the time of the NPC. Mao, she observed, had genuinely hoped for stability and equilibrium, for some form of unity between the two forces, but he didn't realize that after eight years of Cultural Revolution this simply could not be realized. Looking back, moreover, she also recalled great enthusiasm for the modernization goals proffered, however briefly, by Zhou Enlai, a claim difficult to credit on the written record despite present-day claims that the "four modernizations" were the spirit of the work report. While delegates may have seen signs of hope in the tentative reference to modernization, and recalled the much greater emphasis on economic development at the Third NPC, there was little opportunity to explore the possibilities in such a brief, truncated Congress. Most important, as Mao Mao acknowledged, were the limitations of the situation. Given Mao's attitude, *fundamentally* correcting the errors of the

---

[123] See *PR*, no. 4 (1975), pp. 18-25; and above, p. 188n8. For a contemporary account arguing little difference in the NPC reports of Zhou and Zhang, see John Bryan Starr, "From the 10th Party Congress to the Premiership of Hua Kuo-feng: the Significance of the Colour of the Cat," *CQ*, no. 67 (1976), pp. 467-68.

Cultural Revolution remained impossible. The course of consolidation that Mao was now initiating, and Deng would implement, was to be limited to correcting the 30 percent mistakes of the Cultural Revolution. While ending disruption and developing the economy were key goals of the Chairman's directives in the second half of 1974, that he had set limits was understood by Deng and the reconstituted leadership generally.[124]

The State Council appointments ratified by the NPC were regarded then and subsequently as a relatively clear "victory" for veteran officials and their younger establishment associates. This was graphically captured in Chi Qun's reported reaction: "They took up almost all the posts of ministers!"[125] The basis for such conclusions, by official reform-era histories and foreign scholars alike, was the heavy representation of pre-Cultural Revolution State Council officials, including a good number who were severely criticized during 1966-69, in the new ministerial structure (together with presumably like-minded PLA figures) on the one hand, and the small representation of protégés of the radicals on the other. This conclusion, however, must be qualified by a number of considerations. Most basic, as already demonstrated, despite the obvious benefits for the old establishment, the result was essentially Mao's arrangement, bestowed by the Chairman from above to realize his directives on stability and economic development. To be sure, Zhou and Deng had played key roles in the actual selection of officials below the very top positions decreed directly by Mao, but they acted with an understanding of the Chairman's intention, and a wary eye cast in his direction. Indeed, as we have seen, Zhou gave considerable attention to young officials including radicals in preparing personnel appointments, and ministries generally contained Cultural Revolution activists who would complicate the running of these organizations in the future.

Both the extent of the tilt to the pre-Cultural Revolution establishment, and the qualifications involved, can be seen in an analysis of the ministers and vice ministers confirmed at the NPC session. While various data problems exist, especially at the vice ministerial level,[126] Table 5 presents the overall pattern:

---

[124] See Mao Mao, *"Wenge" suiyue*, pp. 333-34, 336, 337; and *Mao zhuan*, vol. 2, p. 1717. Mao Mao identified the two forces as the four radicals and the "old revolutionaries"—Zhou, Deng, Ye Jianying and Li Xiannian—thus ignoring one of the most significant groupings of leaders at the Congress, the establishment beneficiaries of the Cultural Revolution. Compare Zhou's gingerly treatment of economic construction to his 1964 work report, where the subject was the first item discussed. *PR*, no. 1 (1965), pp. 7-10.

[125] Yan and Gao, *Turbulent Decade*, p. 460.

[126] The main problem is the absence of information on vice ministers for various ministries, especially defense-related ministries, and the consequent lack of balance among different sectors. For example, the main source used, He Husheng, *Zhiguanzhi*, lists no vice ministers for nine ministries, including the Defense Ministry and five defense-related machine building ministries, under the Fourth NPC appointments, while as many as 16 vice ministers are listed for Metallurgy and, surprisingly, the First Ministry of Machine Building. Some of the holes can be filled from other sources, but the overall result remains uneven.

Table 5: State Council Appointments—Fourth NPC, January 1975

Ministers—pre-Cultural Revolution posts (3rd NPC, 1/65)	N=29		Ministers—post-Cultural Revolution careers	N=29	
in same/related ministry:[a]	N=13	(45%)	reappointed at 5th NPC 3/78:[b]	N=9	(31%)
in another ministry:	N=2	(7%)	other State Council posts:[c]	N=5	(17%)
			other top posts:[d]	N=1	(3%)
provincial-level Party secretaries:	N=3	(10%)	provincial-level Party secretaries:	N=1	(3%)
PLA posts:	N=8	(28%)	return to PLA:	N=5	(17%)
Cultural Revolution radicals:[e]	N=3	(10%)	ousted for radical links:[f]	N=4	(14%)
			died in 1976:	N=2	(7%)
			unknown:[g]	N=2	(7%)
Vice Ministers—pre-Cultural Revolution posts (3rd NPC, 1/65)	**N=173**		**Vice Ministers—post-Cultural Revolution careers**	**N=173**	
same post:	N=77	(45%)	reappointed 3/78:	N=131	(76%)

Sources: He Husheng, *Zhiguanzhi*; *Lijie Zhonggong zhongyang weiyuan renming cidian*; Lamb, *Directory*; Bartke, *Who's Who in the People's Republic of China*; Wolfgang Bartke and Peter Schier, *China's New Party Leadership: Biographies and Analysis of the Twelfth Central Committee of the Communist Party of China* (London: Macmillan Press, 1985); *Who's Who in Communist China* (Hong Kong: Union Research Institute, 1966); and *Gendai Chugoku Jimmei Jiten* [Modern China Biographic Dictionary] (Tokyo: Gaimusho, 1982).

a. Including Zhou Rongxin, the Minister of Education promoted to State Council Secretary-General at the 3rd NPC, and again appointed Minister of Education at the 4th NPC. Related ministries refer to cases where the amalgamation or splitting of ministries meant the same precise positions did not exist, but the organizational lineage was clear.

b. Including 7 who continued to serve after the 12/78 3rd Plenum, 4 of whom served beyond the 9/80 State Council reorganization.

c. Including Hua Guofeng who served as Premier until 9/80.

d. Minister of Defense Ye Jianying retired from that post in 3/78, but remained CCP and MAC Vice Chairman.

e. The musician Yu Huiyong as Minister of Culture, the table tennis player Zhuang Zedong as head of the Physical Culture and Sports Commission, and Liu Xiangping, widow of former Politburo radical Xie Fuzhi, as Minister of Public Health.

f. The Cultural Revolution radicals (e. above), plus Foreign Minister Qiao Guanhua.

g. Ministers Chen Shaokun of Metallurgy and Li Jitai of the 3rd Machine Building Ministry, both pre-Cultural Revolution military officers who at least formally continued in their posts after Mao's death, but could not be identified after 6/77 and 12/77 respectively.

The results indicate a strong, but by no means sweeping, tendency to "restore" pre-1966 State Council officials to central government posts, notably to the same specific ministries or their descendant organizations. Forty-five percent of ministers appointed in January 1975 had either been vice ministers in the corresponding ministries at the Third NPC in 1965 or, in three cases, ministers (Wang Zheng in the Fourth Ministry of Machine Building, Gu Mu in the State Capital Construction Commission, and Fang Yi in the Commission for Economic Relations with Foreign Countries). In addition, 45 percent of the vice ministers appointed had also served in the same posts in 1965, a figure which undoubtedly understates organizational continuity.[127] In terms of the Congress facilitating "growth-oriented policies," moreover, a more telling indication than the policy line articulated at the Fourth NPC can be inferred from the frequency of reappointments of officials at the March 1978 Fifth NPC, a session conducted under the banner of "socialist modernization": 31 percent of ministers, and 76 percent of vice ministers, were reconfirmed in the same positions. The ministerial figure understates the presumed commitment to modernization, since another 23 percent of the 1975 ministers were promoted or transferred to other key positions during the post-Mao project to reverse the Cultural Revolution.[128]

The other side of the coin, however, is that only roughly half of the new ministerial and vice ministerial appointments represent a restoration of the pre-Cultural Revolution State Council elite. Apart from the three ministries conceded to the radicals,[129] pre-1966 provincial leaders, and especially PLA officers, made up the "other half." While the anti-radical inclinations of these types are clear in broad terms, their collective lack of experience in the central bureaucracy before the Cultural Revolution is also telling.[130] Indeed, the PLA men appointed as ministers in 1975 had been inserted into their respective ministries during or following the upheavals of the late 1960s, often obtaining the title of minister

---

[127] The data for vice ministers included in Table 5 are not as comprehensive as for ministers where past and future careers were closely examined in each case. The procedure for vice ministers was simply to compare vice ministerial personnel appointed in 1975 with that of the same or predecessor/ successor ministries for the 1965 and 1978 NPC sessions, and on into the early 1980s. Thus 1975 vice ministers who held more junior positions in the respective ministries on the eve of the Cultural Revolution were not picked up in the tabulation.

[128] The vice ministerial figure is also an understatement since it would not pick up transfers to other ministries.

[129] Apart from the Ministers of Culture, Public Health, and Physical Culture and Sports being removed shortly after the purge of the "gang of four," the retention rate of vice ministers in these organizations was low in comparison to other ministries.

[130] An exception is Wan Li, the new Minister of Railways, who had served in the State Council in the 1950s before becoming a Beijing municipal Party secretary.

by the early 1970s. Their function was to restore order, but at the same time to enforce the Cultural Revolution line. Thus they reflected conflicting tendencies— undoubtedly respectful of Party status and desirous of order, but of limited non-military expertise, influenced by Cultural Revolution ideology, and above all loyal to Mao. That military men were still relied on to this extent despite Mao's post-Lin Biao effort to reduce the army's role in civilian affairs testifies to the political fluidity of the time. It was only in the post-Mao period when, by the end of 1977, most of the 1975 "PLA ministers" had been transferred back to military duties,[131] that the civilian control disrupted by the Cultural Revolution was fully restored.

More broadly, the very uncertainty of the situation should be emphasized, particularly for those now taking up State Council posts, whether their previous experience was in the central government or elsewhere. Various new ministers such as Ye Fei, the pre-1966 Party leader in Fujian and political commissar of the Fuzhou Military Region now appointed Minister of Communications, were surprised by their appointments and faced difficulties in assuming control, while even figures like Zhou Rongxin with past experience in his Ministry of Education took a considerable period to reorient themselves to their new responsibilities.[132] In short, while the great bulk of ministers and vice ministers came from the Party-state-PLA establishment, the diversity of previous careers, the varying impact of their Cultural Revolution experiences, and the lack of a clear agenda meant the new State Council could only grope its way forward.

Qualifications concerning the personnel outcome of the Fourth NPC can also be seen in the post-Congress assignment of responsibilities to the newly confirmed vice premiers. Reflecting the shift of power from Zhou Enlai to Deng Xiaoping, the allocation of duties was made by Deng, although Zhou stepped forward to make the actual announcement, ostensibly to save Deng "embarrassment."[133] Table 6 on the following page, which lists the vice premiers in rank order, identifies their work responsibilities:

---

[131] Five such ministers were clearly transferred, while Ye Jianying stayed on in the traditionally army-run Ministry of Defense until March 1978, when replaced by Marshal Xu Xiangqian. Chen Shaokun and Li Jitai could not be traced beyond 1977, but it is clear they played no further role in the State Council.

[132] See *Ye Fei huiyilu (xu): zai Jiaotongbu qijian* [Memoirs of Ye Fei, continued: The Period at the Ministry of Communications] (Beijing: Renmin jiaotong chubanshe, 2001), pp. 2, 48; and below, pp. 270, 340ff.

[133] See Mao Mao, *"Wenge" suiyue*, p. 344. While one could speculate that Zhou's action was designed to deflect criticism of controversial decisions away from Deng, there is no hard evidence to back this view. Indeed, our own belief is that, again, the division of work reflected Mao's preferences, and thus was beyond any direct challenge.

Table 6: Vice Premiers' Division of Work, February 1, 1975

Vice Premier	Party status	State Council work responsibilities
Deng Xiaoping	CCP VC	foreign affairs, in charge of meetings and important documents
Zhang Chunqiao	Politburo SC	culture, education
Li Xiannian	Politburo	daily work, finance, trade
Chen Xilian*	Politburo	defense industry, sports
Ji Dengkui	Politburo	daily work, labor and wages, cadre allocation
Hua Guofeng	Politburo	daily work, political and legal work, science
Chen Yonggui	Politburo	agriculture
Wu Guixian	alternate Politburo	health, light industry
Wang Zhen	CC	communications, supply and marketing
Yu Qiuli**	CC	planning, industry
Gu Mu	CC	construction, industry
Sun Jian	alternate CC	industrial production

Source: Chen and Du, *Shilu*, vol. 3, part 2, p. 1181.
Key: *=PLA officer; **=former PLA officer; VC=Vice Chair; SC=Standing Committee; CC=Central Committee.

Several things are immediately apparent. While in terms of future developments it is interesting that Chen Xilian and Ji Dengkui outranked Hua Guofeng at the start of 1975, more significant for the politics of the moment was the appointment of Ji and Hua—establishment beneficiaries who would be viewed as possible successors by *both* Mao and the old guard of Zhou, Deng and Li Xiannian—as Standing Vice Premiers responsible for the daily work of the State Council along with Li. The three Standing Vice Premiers, the cagey veteran Li and the two pre-Cultural Revolution provincial Party secretaries, thus became Deng's closest bureaucratic colleagues in managing State Council business in 1975, and they clearly were active in that role. The specific responsibilities of Ji and Hua further indicate their importance—Ji as responsible for personnel, a responsibility that mirrored his organizational duties on the Party side, and Hua as responsible for political and legal work (also reflected in his appointment as Minister of Public Security) and science (which became a priority in Deng's 1975 efforts, and the portfolio Deng asked for when he returned to work in 1977).

With vice premiers having greater bureaucratic authority and oversight of ministers, it is notable that the restoration of the pre-State Council elite was less pronounced at this level. Only five of the twelve vice premiers had served in the central government before the 1970s, and of this group only Deng and Li had previously held vice premier rank. Indeed, it is striking that most other surviving and not disgraced 1965 vice premiers, all of whom had high Party status as senior revolutionaries as well, were relegated to the largely symbolic positions of NPC vice chairmen[134]—thus limiting the experience and prestige available to facilitate the emerging consolidation program. Of the seven new vice premiers from non-State Council backgrounds, Hua, Ji and Chen Xilian were products of the Party-army establishment, however much their careers had been advanced during the Cultural Revolution, Zhang Chunqiao was the lynchpin of the radical presence in the central government, and the remainder—peasant leader Chen Yonggui and model workers Wu Guixian and Sun Jian—were products of the Cultural Revolution. This, of course, did not mean these representatives of the "masses" would necessarily follow the "gang of four," as the enmity between Chen Yonggui and Zhang Chunqiao soon demonstrated.[135]

While the vice premier selections reflected Mao's commitment to Cultural Revolution symbolism to a greater extent than the ministerial appointments, the question remains to what extent these theoretically higher-ranking officials exerted actual authority. While one might presume that inexperienced representatives of the masses were outmaneuvered by bureaucratic veterans, their very positions (and Mao's presumed patronage) complicated the situation. This was the case with Chen Yonggui, whose formal responsibility for agriculture was clearly overshadowed by the *de facto* authority of Hua in 1975 (as well as by that of Ji in the early post-Mao period), yet in both contexts he advanced positions that had to be taken into account.[136] Even more intriguing was the situation created by Zhang Chunqiao's oversight of education, given that the new Minister of Education, Zhou Rongxin, had been appointed despite Jiang Qing's preference for Chi Qun. As we shall see in Chapter 6, this relationship developed differently from what one might assume from formal bureaucratic responsibilities.

In both ideological and personnel terms, then, the outcome of the Fourth NPC was less clear-cut as a moderate political victory than usually believed. The ideological message of the Congress was more radical than the concrete policy

---

[134] Chen Yun, Ulanfu, Tan Zhenlin and Nie Rongzhen. Two other 1965 vice premiers, Bo Yibo and Lu Dingyi, were also alive, but still in disgrace for their "crimes," while Luo Ruiqing had been rehabilitated, but received no position at the Fourth NPC.

[135] See below, p. 502, on the Chen Yonggui-Zhang Chunqiao relationship. As for textile worker Wu Guixian, she was not linked to the "gang," but was downgraded to Central Committee status at the Eleventh Party Congress in 1977, and seemingly lost any real role as Vice Premier by this time. Sun Jian, however, was declared a follower of the radicals, and purged following their fall.

[136] See below, pp. 352ff. In 1977-78, Chen was the strongest advocate of brigade level accounting in rural communes, eventually coming into conflict with Ji. This is a topic for our Volume II.

settings that soon emerged as consolidation began following the Congress, and as a result hindered the effort. The personnel appointments brought back into the State Council a significant amount of pre-Cultural Revolution bureaucratic experience, but the result was definitely not a government led by prestigious old revolutionaries—Deng, Ye and Li Xiannian aside. To a certain extent, leadership had passed to a younger cohort from the Party establishment, a situation that would only be reversed in the post-Mao period. At the same time, as much due to their own limited capabilities as Mao's unhappiness with them, the radicals had suffered a setback. Whether the "gang of four" as a whole was "especially depressed" (gewai jusang) by the results of the Congress as claimed by Mao's biographers is uncertain, although it would certainly seem to be the case for Jiang Qing.[137] But in Mao's scheme the radicals still had an important function, as quickly became clear even as Deng's consolidation efforts developed following the Fourth NPC.

---

[137] *Mao zhuan*, vol. 2, p. 1717.

Chapter 4

MAO, DENG AND THE POLITICS OF CONSOLIDATION: FROM THE FOURTH NPC TO SUMMER 1975

Comrade Mao Zedong used to criticize the Headquarters of the General Staff for failing to offer advice. This situation should be changed. A lot needs to be done. Problems have piled up. The Headquarters of the General Staff must thoroughly straighten things out according to the military line and the principles for building the army formulated by Comrade Mao Zedong, so that we really can fulfill our advisory function.

— Deng Xiaoping's first talk on consolidation, January 25, 1975[1]

They [the radicals] made contributions in the past, opposing Liu Shaoqi and Lin Biao. [But] now they are not so good, opposing the Premier, Deng Xiaoping, Marshal Ye [and] Chen Xilian. ... The direction of the wind is changing in the Politburo. You [Deng] must take control of [all] work. [Some will oppose you], the tallest tree in the forest will surely face the storm.

— Mao Zedong, speaking to Deng Xiaoping, June 1975[2]

Deng Xiaoping chaired the [May 27 and June 3, 1975, Politburo] meetings [where the "gang of four" were criticized and Wang Hongwen and Jiang Qing were forced to make self-examinations]. He acted like Mr. Dongguo [who was kind to the wolf and was then eaten by the wolf], committing a big mistake [by ending the criticism process]. ... If Deng had held another half month's Politburo meetings, grabbing them like so, then we wouldn't have this mess now.

— Geng Biao, criticizing Deng Xiaoping's "soft" approach in dealing with the "gang of four" in spring 1975, October 16, 1976[3]

While the Fourth NPC produced a less certain outcome than usually believed, the result clearly favored Politburo moderates, both in terms of policy program and political leadership. As in 1972, the program was essentially one of consolidation (*zhengdun*), now drawing its authority from Mao's two directives on "stability and unity" and boosting the national economy. Unity and a calming of the political atmosphere had been Mao's demand since at least the previous August, and it provided the context in which the practical tasks of economic development and other concrete policy problems could be dealt with. This *zhengdun* approach can be rendered as consolidation, readjustment or rectification, and we use each in this and the following chapter. Readjustment emphasizes reorganizing institutions and approaches, while rectification focuses on correcting erroneous behavior and practices. Yet consolidation, the preferred official translation,[4] comes closest to capturing the nature of the program in the context of the times, and certainly its essence as Mao saw it. The essential idea was that after a period of advance, which was Mao's view of the Cultural Revolution, it was necessary to come to a stop, to rest and deal with the unavoidable problems appearing during the victorious advance, before preparing for a further breakthrough. This view was captured in the military imagery used in summer 1975 by Li Chang, one of the key implementers of Deng's program: "My understanding of *zhengdun* is that it is just like our troops resting and regrouping after a big battle in preparation for the next struggle."[5]

The fact that an important figure in the consolidation effort used such language suggests its fragile basis. The policy orientation endorsed by Mao in his two directives of August and November 1974 favored practical work. Yet the Chairman's December directive on the study of theory of the dictatorship of the proletariat, his third chronologically, but the first in pride of place when Deng packaged the three directives together as an overall guideline for Party work in July 1975 (see Chapter 5), provided an ideological orientation of a quite different nature. The problem was not simply that the dictatorship of the proletariat campaign which unfolded in March-April was disruptive, including a new attack on Zhou Enlai *via* criticism of empiricism. It lay fundamentally

---

[1] *Selected Works of Deng (1975-1982)*, p. 13.

[2] Drawn from Chen and Du, *Shilu*, vol. 3, part 2, p. 1234; Mao Mao, *"Wenge" suiyue*, p. 366; and Mao Zedong, "Tong Deng Xiaoping guanyu piping 'sirenbang'," p. 1.

[3] "Geng Biao guanyu sirenbang qingkuang," p. 2. Geng, who soon became impatient for Deng's early return to work, here joined in the critical approach toward Deng adopted by the post-Mao leadership for the benefit of the wider elite in the period immediately after the arrest of the "gang," albeit with this twist. On the two Politburo meetings, see below, pp. 299-301.

[4] This is the predominant but not sole usage in the *Selected Works* translations of Deng's 1975 speeches on the theme. Other translations are "put in order," "reorganize," and, in the context of Party work style, "rectify" (*zhengdun dang de zuofeng*). See *Selected Works of Deng (1975-1982)*, pp. 11, 23, 27, 39, 47.

[5] "Hu Yaobang, Li Chang de jianghua" [Speeches of Hu Yaobang and Li Chang] (1975), documents available at the Fairbank Center Library, Harvard University, items 13-22, p. 33.

in the underlying tension between the two orientations. This tension surfaced not only as a result of the March-April developments, but also subsequently in the context of the *Water Margin* criticism in the summer (again aimed at Zhou Enlai), and finally in Mao's turn against Deng beginning in October. While the tensions between the "two camps" were involved in these developments, the key factor was the contradictions inherent in the three directives—i.e., between Mao's effort to consolidate the Cultural Revolution by rectifying its shortcomings, and his unbending commitment to the movement's fundamental correctness.

Although the view of 1975 prior to November as "Deng Xiaoping's year in charge"[6] has considerable validity, and the themes of consolidation were consistent throughout, two relatively distinct phases can be identified, with the change coming in mid-year. In program terms, the first half of the year involved tending to immediate issues of restoring order and economic activity in key areas. From the middle of the year, the effort became more systematic. This "comprehensive consolidation" (*quanmian zhengdun*) involved a readjustment of underlying ideology and policy approaches. As another major figure in the consolidation effort, Yu Guangyuan, later recalled, in June Deng observed that many problems had been solved in the preceding months, but now "there must be consideration across the board."[7] The key to this change was a shift in political fortunes at the top, as Mao concluded that the radicals had overstepped the mark in carrying out the dictatorship of the proletariat campaign and endangered Party unity in the process, criticized them with more far-reaching consequences than what had resulted from his 1974 complaints, and granted authority to Deng that went further than any similar grant in the post-Ninth Congress period. We analyze these developments below, and in Chapter 5 examine Deng's use of his expanded authority over the three plus months from mid-year.

Organizationally, Deng's role also changed in mid-year. Wang Hongwen was formally in charge of the daily work of the Party Center until July 2, when Deng took over this responsibility, while Wang relocated to Shanghai over the following months.[8] Although, when under pressure at the end of the year, Deng somewhat disingenuously claimed that he was being blamed for too much as he

---

[6] The relevant section heading in MacFarquhar, "Succession," p. 292.

[7] Yu Guangyuan, "Yi Deng Xiaoping he Guowuyuan zhengyanshi" [Recalling Deng Xiaoping and the State Council Political Research Office], *Bainianchao* [The Hundred Year Tide] (hereafter *BNC*), no. 7 (2000), p. 11.

[8] See Cheng Zhongyuan, "Mao Zedong de sanxiang zhishi he Deng Xiaoping zhuchi de 1975 nian zhengdun" [Mao Zedong's Three Directives and the 1975 Consolidation under Deng Xiaoping], *DDZGSYJ*, no. 1 (1997), p. 74; Yu Guangyuan, "Yi Deng Xiaoping he zhengyanshi," p. 4; and *Mao wengao*, vol. 13, p. 497. Various sources, notably in the West, erroneously date Deng's assumption of Party Center authority from January, while the authoritative *Zhou nianpu*, vol. 3, p. 709, in a joint entry for May 27 and June 3, reports Mao and Zhou agreeing that Deng should take charge of Party Center daily work at that point. Inexplicably, *Mao wengao* gives March as well as July as the time of Deng assuming control; see vol. 13, p. 491. In our view, Deng exercised informal authority over the Party Center from the point in June when Mao declared Deng had to take control of all work, but Wang continued handling routine paper work. Cf. below, pp. 248n10, 277n92, 306n5.

had only had overall responsibility for the three months plus since taking over in July,[9] Deng was clearly the most influential first-front leader throughout the first half of 1975. Given Mao's long-standing regard, and his December 1974 judgment that Deng was "stronger in politics and ideology" than Wang, Deng definitely had the upper hand regardless of formal ranking or traditional Party authority over the government. At least equally important was the Chairman's consolidation agenda, which fit Deng's practical talents and made the State Council the center of action. Indeed, the evidence indicates that during the first half of the year Wang supported Deng's efforts, whether actively and willingly, or because, as he reportedly complained later in the year, his responsibilities were routine and entrapped him into Deng's program. Whatever Wang's motivation, he provided Deng with the necessary handling of Party documents, including obtaining Mao's approval. This, of course, also reflected the Chairman's demand for leadership unity.[10]

While Deng was basically "in charge" of consolidation during the first half of 1975, the standard view crediting the readjustment program to him ignores the fact that the initiative and overall concept—not to mention approval of virtually all key measures—came from Mao. Indeed, as one leading Party historian has argued, it was not simply a matter of Mao supporting Deng's effort, but as with Zhou Enlai in 1972, the Chairman's backing was a *prerequisite* before anything could be done.[11] By 1975, moreover, Mao seemed prepared to countenance a more far-reaching consolidation than he had three years earlier. Linked to this was the Chairman's apparent belief that, in contrast to the Premier who had proven too rightist for the task in 1972, Deng had sufficient strength in "politics and ideology," something undoubtedly confirmed for Mao by Deng's performance during *pi Lin pi Kong*. Deng had good access and channels to Mao in this period, whether through reporting mechanisms on State Council work, occasions provided by the Chairman's receptions of foreign visitors (Deng attended five from January to early July), at least one other meeting when the two discussed important issues, or *via* the "two ladies."[12] Mao's support of his consolidation

---

[9] Deng made this claim to Mao Yuanxin on November 2 as the attack on him gathered momentum. *Mao zhuan*, vol. 2, p. 1755.

[10] On Wang's alleged complaint in fall 1975, see Yan and Gao, *Turbulent Decade*, p. 478. Yu Guangyuan, "Yi Deng Xiaoping he zhengyanshi," p. 4, reports Deng writing to Wang seeking Politburo consideration of establishing a State Council Political Research Office on June 15, an indication of the type of routine work involved. For further discussion of Wang's role, including indications of more active cooperation than suggested by his reported remarks, see below, pp. 254, 267, 271, 273-74.

[11] Interview, December 2002. It is also worth noting that the glorification of Deng has resulted in downplaying the contributions of others to consolidation, notably Li Xiannian who oversaw economic work, and especially Hua Guofeng and Ji Dengkui whose roles later became inconvenient for Deng-era orthodoxy.

[12] *Deng nianpu*, vol. 1, pp. 7, 37, 55, 62, 64, 65; and interview with senior Party historian, November 2002. On two other occasions, Li Xiannian accompanied foreigners to see Mao, and on one Ji

efforts, of course, did not mean that Deng could ignore the Chairman's sensitivity concerning the Cultural Revolution, and according to a leading specialist on Deng, throughout 1975 Mao observed his actions closely. Nor did Deng have a free hand with the radicals. Similar to the situation at the time of his return to work in 1973, when Deng took over the State Council in early 1975, Mao again warned him against "causing conflict with Jiang Qing *et al.*"[13]

Mao's advice was one more concrete example of his repeated emphasis on the need for unity. This applied to all sides, and while the struggle of contending forces was never far from the surface, for much of the year it was contained, in no small measure due to Mao's demand. As for the radicals, there were further efforts, after those by Wang Hongwen the previous fall, to conform to Mao's strictures about not being a "gang of four." On February 20, Wang wrote Jiang Qing proposing that they take heed of Mao's criticism, while Zhang Chunqiao observed in June that "we should ... do our best to strengthen unity with others, [and] not add to the Chairman's burden."[14] Whatever the "gang's" intention, however, strains were inevitable given not only their specific responsibility for the dictatorship of the proletariat campaign, but more generally because of their broader ideological duties. Notwithstanding Wang Hongwen's cooperation with Deng on consolidation measures, occasional clashes resulted over the theoretical implications of the program. Thus in early 1975, a draft editorial by Li Xiannian on Mao's three directives was rejected by the *People's Daily*, while Jiang Qing criticized the movie *Pioneers* that praised the disciplined work culture and organization of the Daqing oilfields, an object of emulation as consolidation unfolded.[15]

Leftist ideological posturing was not the sole preserve of the "gang," however. Given Mao's sensibilities, even as the Chairman turned against the radicals in the spring, Deng still spoke of "the revisionist line of Zhou [Enlai] and Ye [Jianying]" in a reference to their 1973 mistakes.[16] For all Mao's emphasis on unity, the Premier was still vulnerable, not simply to radical attacks on empiricism, but also in the sense that Deng felt the need to acknowledge Zhou's alleged sins. What was Zhou's role in this period, and through to his death in January 1976? As Mao had stipulated in December, the Premier no longer played a central role in the government where Deng exercised overall leadership. Beyond that, there was a process of marginalization, with some of Zhou's few recorded directives and

---

Dengkui performed the honors.

[13] Yao Jin, *Yao Yilin baixitan*, p. 185; and interview, November 2002.

[14] "Zhonggong zhongyang guanyu 'Wang Hongwen, Zhang Chunqiao, Jiang Qing, Yao Wenyuan fandang jituan zuizheng (cailiao zhi yi)'," p. 9; and above, p. 214.

[15] See *Deng Liqun guoshi jiangtan*, vol. 3, p. 315; Chen and Du, *Shilu*, vol. 3, part 2, pp. 1186-88; and *RMRB*, December 23, 1976, in *SPRCP*, no. 6253 (1977), pp. 191-93. When Li Xiannian told Deng Liqun about the *People's Daily* incident years later, he only indicated that it happened after Mao's three directives, but we conclude it was most likely in the early months of 1975.

[16] Gao Wenqian, *Wannian Zhou*, pp. 563-64.

comments dealing with matters of limited significance, e.g., extending the Beijing library, united front work, and the reform of the written language. Important issues to engage Zhou were Mao's health, concerning which the Premier chaired an expanded Politburo conference on February 19-22, and cadre rehabilitation, about which he consulted with Ji Dengkui, Hua Guofeng and Wu De, but apparently not Deng, on a number of occasions in February and March. Perhaps his most significant policy involvement concerned dealing with the festering factionalism issue in Zhejiang in mid-year. Meanwhile, through July Zhou chaired nine meetings of the Politburo Standing Committee, although apparently not meetings of the full Politburo where Wang presumably presided until May 27 when Deng took over. The Premier's concrete contributions during the Standing Committee meetings he chaired, in any case, remain largely unknown[17]

In the April-June period, however, as the issue of empiricism came to a head, and a more favorable political environment emerged with Mao's criticism of the "gang," Zhou emerged as a central if cautious player in terms of shaping the Politburo's response to Mao's intervention, and as a political adviser, particularly to Deng. Revealingly, the Premier's contact with Deng increased from April, and throughout the last year of his life, in sharp contrast to the period from spring 1973 through September 1974, Deng was the leader who most frequently visited Zhou in his hospital quarters. Meanwhile, at least according to the official record, Wang Hongwen was a much less frequent visitor than previously.[18] Nevertheless, a senior historian in Zhou Enlai studies claims that Wang, in addition to adopting a respectful posture toward senior leaders generally and the Premier in particular, as a member of the leadership small group responsible for Zhou's medical work demonstrated a sincere concern for his condition not seen in the other radicals, including Zhang Chunqiao who was also on the medical group. This arguably was one factor leading Zhou to appeal to the visiting Wang a month before his death to give heed to Mao's warning concerning becoming entangled with Jiang Qing.[19]

---

[17] See *Zhou nianpu*, vol. 3, pp. 692, 693, 696-97, 698-99, 704, 706, 708-709, 714, 715, 720; *Deng nianpu*, vol. 1, pp. 38, 40-41, 49-50; and below, pp. 270-71, 276-77, 280. While we have located no references to Politburo meetings prior to April 27 when Wang was apparently in charge, we assume that the body was meeting with some regularity over the preceding months.

[18] Of course, Wang was outside of Beijing from July to mid-November. According to *Zhou nianpu*, the visitors were: Deng more than 26 times, Li Xiannian 15, Ji Dengkui 13, the "two ladies" more than 12, Hua Guofeng 8, Wu De 7, Wang Dongxing more than 5, Ye Jianying 5, Wang Hongwen 4, Chen Xilian 3, Jiang Qing, Su Zhenhua and Qiao Guanhua 2 each, and Zhu De, Xu Shiyou, Wei Guoqing, Chen Yonggui and Saifudin one each. Cf. above, p. 205n47.

[19] Interview, January 2005. This scholar reported having seen Wang's comments on Zhou's medical report that indicated genuine concern and worry. Another very well-placed historian, however, while acknowledging Wang's polite demeanor toward old cadres, felt this did not reflect any sincere respect; interview, November 2002. Zhou's medical group consisted of Wang, Ye, Zhang and Wang Dongxing. In the event, it was Zhang rather than Wang who stood vigil during several of the Premier's operations in 1975, together with other leaders who prominently included Deng. See *Zhou nianpu*,

In the remainder of this chapter we deal with both consolidation measures in various areas and the key political developments leading to Deng's enhanced power by mid-year. We begin by examining Deng's initial effort in the PLA, a process beginning in January shortly after the NPC, and extending into mid-year with the convening of a long delayed MAC conference in June-July. We then turn to key domestic issues, notably the efforts of Deng and others in the economic sphere in several major conferences from February to May, and also deal with cadre rehabilitation and education in which Deng's role was less pronounced. Next, the central aspect of the consolidation effort in the first half of 1975, the struggle against factionalism, is analyzed, with particular attention to dramatic developments in Zhejiang that culminated in a military crackdown in the summer. The campaign to study the dictatorship of the proletariat is then examined, together with its critique of empiricism, and thus Zhou Enlai. Finally, the process leading from Mao's dissatisfaction with the radicals' performance during that campaign, and especially the resultant damage to Party unity, to his investing Deng with sweeping authority is analyzed in detail.

Consolidating the Military, January-July 1975

Before the events of the spring led to the mid-year political changes, the consolidation program had already made significant inroads in the PLA, although the army did not avoid the disruption caused by the campaign to study the dictatorship of the proletariat. Military readjustment, which was ordered by Mao at the end of 1974,[20] became the first object of Deng's efforts. The background to Deng's assignment consisted of Mao's various concerns with the army since the Ninth Party Congress. As discussed earlier, these included, *inter alia*, the adequacy of war preparations, the heavy-handed methods of army officers who had been thrust into ruling the localities by the Cultural Revolution, worry over whether the military would return power to civilian authority, anxiety about Lin Biao's PLA following even after the September 13th incident, fear of the localization of political and military power, the need for army stability in the coming succession, and above all, doubt about the military's support of his cherished Cultural Revolution.

As we saw in detail in Chapter 2, having concluded that Ye's performance was inadequate, Mao finally acted decisively to deal with many of these problems in late 1973 by rotating large military region commanders, bringing Deng into the MAC, and then following this up with the Lin Biao-Confucius campaign that made the PLA one of its main targets, most likely even more important in Mao's

---

vol. 3, pp. 695, 716, 721, 722, 723.

[20] According to *Deng Liqun guoshi jiangtan*, vol. 3, p. 322, Mao's intent had been to place Deng in charge of military consolidation at the time of the December 1973 Politburo meeting. An even earlier step can be seen when placing Ye Jianying in charge of the PLA in November 1971 following the Lin Biao affair. See above, p. 37; and below, p. 255n29.

mind than Zhou Enlai. While involving all of the PLA problems that had been vexing Mao since 1969, in the context of *pi Lin pi Kong*, the emphasis was on combating revisionism, and on thoroughly eliminating Lin Biao's influence. The Chairman's ideological worries about the army had been seen earlier, as in his spring 1973 initiative for a Party-controlled militia of working class composition and emphasizing class struggle (see Chapter 1). By 1975, however, befitting the overall thrust of consolidation, Mao was increasingly concerned with the military performance of the PLA, and this became the centerpiece of Deng's efforts. But the Chairman's multiple political and military objectives, and the complexities of the arrangement, can be seen in the revamped MAC leadership, with a new 11-member restored Standing Committee superseding the 1974 six-man small group in February 1975.[21] Table 7 lists the membership of the two bodies in formal rank order.

Table 7: Political Leadership of the PLA, 1974-75

MAC Six-man Small Group, 1/74	MAC Standing Committee, 2/75
* Ye Jianying (MAC Vice Chair, 4/69)	* Ye Jianying (MAC Vice Chair, 4/69)
# Wang Hongwen	# Wang Hongwen
# Zhang Chunqiao	Deng Xiaoping (MAC Vice Chair, 1/75)
Deng Xiaoping	# Zhang Chunqiao
* Chen Xilian	* Liu Bocheng (MAC Vice Chair, 4/69)
* Su Zhenhua	* Chen Xilian
	Wang Dongxing[a]
	* Su Zhenhua
	* Xu Xiangqian (MAC Vice Chair, 4/69)
	* Nie Rongzhen (MAC Vice Chair, 4/69)
	* Su Yu

Sources: *Zhou nianpu*, vol. 3, pp. 644, 695; and Ma Qibin, *Sishinian*, p. 380.

Key: * pre-Cultural Revolution PLA leader; # Cultural Revolution radical.

a. Although holding military rank, Wang's duties were in the Party Center and Mao's household.

---

[21] The February 5 decision formally disbanded the MAC Council established in the wake of the Lin Biao affair, and revived the MAC Standing Committee which had lapsed as an effective organ early in the Cultural Revolution. See Ma Qibin, *Sishinian*, p. 380; and above, pp. 37-39. In fact, the restored body replaced the six-man group as the leading MAC body.

While Wang Hongwen and Zhang Chunqiao retained positions in the leading group, their clout was clearly reduced from what it had been when they oversaw *pi Lin pi Kong* in the PLA, subject to Jiang Qing and with the cooperation of Deng. More significant than losing formal ground to Deng,[22] the influence of Wang and Zhang was diluted as the six-man group was expanded by the addition of four career military men, although Marshal Liu Bocheng was so seriously disabled as to be a symbolic member only, and Wang Dongxing, who again provided a direct link to Mao. Ye Jianying, as before, was formally in charge, as well as the ranking member of the full MAC after Mao, but his role was more significant than under the six-man group which had largely followed a radical agenda, at least during the first half of 1974. Ye seemingly chaired MAC Standing Committee meetings throughout the first half of 1975,[23] played a leading role in drawing up the list for the reshuffle of military leaders announced in August (see below), and gave the concluding speech at the June-July MAC conference. He worked closely with Deng, a relationship Marshal Nie Rongzhen commented on when addressing new air force leaders in October 1975: "Overall, we have to listen to Chairman Mao, but on concrete matters we have to listen to Ye Jianying and Deng Xiaoping as MAC Vice Chairmen. Both are in charge of daily work, and the General Staff is the headquarters of the whole army carrying out the will of the MAC. [We] should listen to the command of the General Staff." But without doubt, Deng, the Chief-of-Staff, was the dominant partner, exercising the main responsibility for PLA daily work, giving directives at Standing Committee meetings, and clearly having the most authoritative voice on key occasions such as the June-July meeting.[24]

The relationship of Deng to the two radicals in this new situation is unclear, due to a paucity of information and the propensity of official sources to avoid any indication of cooperation. The best evidence points to a mixed picture. Leaving until later the disruption caused by the dictatorship of the proletariat campaign, tensions also existed over priorities generally. In February, when the restored Standing Committee considered preparations for the summer MAC conference, Wang proposed that political and ideological work should be the number one agenda item, and Zhang emphasized the theoretical issue. Deng and Ye, however,

---

[22] Deng was now listed higher than Zhang, and although still ranked after Wang, was a MAC Vice Chairman which his junior colleague was not. Wang assertedly resented the fact that he had been denied a Vice Chairmanship. See "Wang Dongxing zai quanguo xuanchuan gongzuo huiyishang de jianghua" [Wang Dongxing's Speech to the National Propaganda Conference] (November 18, 1976), in *CRDB*, p. 2.

[23] Information is sparse on these meetings, largely coming from *Deng nianpu* which simply records him as attending rather than chairing the sessions. It is likely that Ye was in the chair, although possible, given his ranking, that Wang chaired sessions in Ye's absence.

[24] See Wang Nianyi, *Dadongluan*, pp. 524-25; Zeng Qingxiang *et al.*, "1975 nian de jundui zhengdun" [The 1975 Military Consolidation], *DDZGSYJ*, no. 4 (2003), p. 119; *Nie Rongzhen nianpu* [Chronology of Nie Rongzhen] (2 vols., Beijing: Renmin chubanshe, 1999), vol. 2, p. 1129; *Mao zhuan*, vol. 2, p. 1721; and *Deng nianpu*, vol. 1, pp. 18, 24, 26, 29, 31-32, 33-34, 39, 46-47, 59-60.

reportedly rejected the proposal on the grounds that the conference should focus on military problems, notably war preparedness, reorganizing and streamlining army institutions, cadre problems, and the pursuit of army stability and unity.[25] Yet there is also evidence of cooperation. Wang Hongwen in particular performed MAC administrative roles. Several generals recalled being summoned to Beijing in early 1975 to brief central leaders, and to their surprise were told to report to Wang. This meeting was apparently satisfactory for the generals concerned who were not alone in finding Wang helpful, while more generally Wang and Zhang were involved in the personnel decisions determining new appointments, and at least passively gave their backing to Deng in this process. Finally, at the June-July conference, the radicals not only did not oppose the proceedings, but Zhang praised Ye's speech as "excellent" and Deng's as "very good," while Yao Wenyuan also made positive remarks. Of course, by this time the radicals were under pressure and may have felt compelled to be positive; in any case, in early 1976, as the political tide again turned, Ye's and Deng's speeches were withdrawn as official documents. Yet it is worth noting that, notwithstanding the February differences over placing theoretical issues on the agenda, Ye devoted a section of his speech to the theory of the dictatorship of the proletariat, while Deng highlighted the importance of theory to oppose and guard against revisionism. Indeed, from the very outset of his expanded military authority in January, Deng showed a keen appreciation of the need to affirm the radical strain in Mao's line by declaring *pi Lin pi Kong* a long-term task.[26]

Whatever the precise relationship of Deng and Ye on the one hand, and Wang and Zhang on the other, Mao's expectation was that Deng would deal emphatically with PLA shortcomings that were undermining military performance,[27] while also guaranteeing the army's acceptance of the Cultural Revolution and continuing to weed out Lin Biao's remnant influence. From the outset, Deng's focus was on a range of practical problems, including bloated organization, factionalism, poor discipline, lack of combat preparedness, and excessive budget outlays. His first foray was a January 25 speech to officers from the General Staff Department which notionally kicked off army consolidation. While presented in a fairly low-key ("Today I have just come to meet you"), the

---

[25] See Deng Lifeng, "Deng Xiaoping yu yijiuqiwu nian de kuoda junwei huiyi" [Deng Xiaoping and the 1975 Expanded MAC Conference], *BNC*, no. 3 (2001), p. 14.

[26] Hu Shihong, *Zhang Aiping zai 1975* [Zhang Aiping in 1975] (Beijing: Zuojia chubanshe, 1998), pp. 284-85; Chen and Du, *Shilu*, vol. 3, part 2, p. 1232; "Ye Jianying zai Zhongyang Junwei kuoda huiyishang de zongjie jianghua" [Ye Jianying's Summary Speech at the Central MAC Expanded Conference] (July 15, 1975), in *CRDB*, p.1; "Deng Xiaoping zai Junwei kuoda huiyishang de jianghua [Deng Xiaoping's Speech at the MAC Expanded Conference] (July 14, 1975), in *CRDB*, p.1; *Deng nianpu*, vol. 1, p. 6; interview with military historian, January 2005; and below, pp. 419, 449.

[27] One of the charges raised internally against the "gang" immediately following their arrest was that they had removed "emphatically" from a Mao directive on dealing with the 30 percent shortcomings of the movement. While Mao's comment apparently occurred later in 1975, this attitude was clearly in evidence as he launched the consolidation effort in the military. See below, p. 403n48.

issues were clearly laid out, as was Deng's demand that something be done about them. Although surely toned down in the official post-Mao version,[28] a feature of Deng's presentation, as it would be in all areas throughout the year, was to firmly link the program to Mao's recent directives, as well as to traditional CCP methods. Another significant aspect of the speech was its implicit criticism of Ye Jianying's stewardship of the PLA. While the basic problems were slated home to Lin Biao, in a comment reminiscent of Mao's December 1973 complaint that the MAC was not managing army affairs, Deng observed that the General Staff Department, of which Ye was Party first secretary, had allowed a lot of problems to accumulate and was not offering advice—and this had to change. On the next day, whether in response to Deng's criticism or as a result of some arrangement between them, Ye went to Mao with the proposal for reestablishing the MAC Standing Committee. Of course, the real problems were the dislocations caused by the Cultural Revolution and the current constraints on dealing with them, but the implication of Ye's culpability was present.[29]

An insight into not only the relationship of Deng and Ye, but also concerning problems in building support for achieving the *zhengdun* objective, can be seen in the case of Zhang Aiping, a pre-1966 Deputy Chief-of-Staff who had recently been rehabilitated after harsh treatment during the Cultural Revolution, and who would go on to become Minister of Defense in the early 1980s. Zhang, whose previous duties had involved the defense industries, was approached by Ye on three or four occasions after resurfacing on National Day in 1974 to take over the PLA's Science and Technology Commission for National Defense which had been seriously disrupted during the Cultural Revolution. "Gang of four" favorite Chi Qun had played a major role in the commission, while its new leader in 1974, former Shanxi Party First Secretary Tao Lujia who lacked expertise in the area, had been criticized by the radicals and Deng for insufficient attention to the Lin Biao-Confucius campaign. Reluctant to return to duty in light of his Cultural Revolution suffering, Zhang sought out Deng for advice. Zhang had not had a great deal of contact with Deng previously, but Deng's favorable attitude toward

---

[28] Compare the Cultural Revolution rhetoric of Zhou Enlai's NPC report, the drafting of which Deng oversaw, to the undoubtedly sanitized *Selected Works* version of Deng's speech. In contrast to various other Deng speeches in this period, there is no *CRDB* version of the January 25 speech. Cf. below, pp. 258, 274n83.

[29] *Selected Works of Deng (1975-1982)*, pp. 11-13; and Chen and Du, *Shilu*, vol. 3, part 2, pp. 1178-79. Although the notion of Deng starting the readjustment process on January 25 is a staple of official histories, relevant measures had been undertaken earlier. With Mao having ordered a focus on war preparations and military consolidation in October 1971, the effort to develop a more streamlined and professional PLA had been underway throughout the post-Lin Biao period. By 1975, the amount of time devoted to production declined significantly, production corps were shifted from MAC to local government control, responsibility for national defense industry had been moved from the MAC to the State Council, and the bloated defense budget had been significantly cut back. See Zeng Qingxiang, "1975 nian de jundui zhengdun," pp. 117-18; and Fan Shuo, *Ye Jianying zai feichang shiqi*, vol. 2, p. 346.

Zhang's nuclear weapons work in the early 1960s had left a positive residue. This, most likely combined with Deng's new status, made Zhang responsive to Deng's argument that "work is always better than not working," and he took up duties at the commission in early March.[30]

Zhang quickly cast aside his hesitations, and soon was addressing the problems of not only his commission, but also at the military-related Seventh Ministry of Machine Building, a national defense "major disaster area," with particular attention to factionalism. In these efforts Zhang received support from above. On May 19, when the new change in the Politburo leadership equation had begun but was yet to be concluded, Zhang reported to MAC leaders Deng, Ye and Nie Rongzhen. Deng, who apparently was the dominant figure at the meeting, called for strong action against factionalism, said he and Ye would bear responsibility for any backlash, and laid down concrete targets. Reflecting Mao's current priorities and referring to the railroads where factionalism had been effectively attacked, Deng declared that he had given the railroads one month to solve the problem, and he was now giving Zhang and his colleagues until July 1 to bring everything back to normal. With the type of demand for strong action that would produce problems for him later, Deng decreed that anyone continuing factional activities should be dismissed.[31]

Meanwhile, from April through July, the Party Center convened a number of defense-related conferences which addressed disruption caused by the Cultural Revolution in military construction and the army more generally. These gatherings, culminating in a conference on national defense industries from mid-July to the start of August, thus spanned the two stages of consolidation, and would have involved Wang Hongwen's at least routine cooperation during the pre-July period given his responsibilities at the Center. The most important of the meetings was the long-delayed enlarged MAC conference, held from June 24 to July 15 as the pressure on the "gang of four" reached its peak. We shall address at the end of this chapter aspects of the meeting concerning the new vulnerability of the radicals; here we examine in more detail the themes of readjustment now laid out more systematically than previously by Deng in his speech of July 14, and measures taken to deal with them. Ever careful to aver that "all the ideas here are only what Comrade Mao Zedong [has advocated]," Deng laid down the two tasks for MAC work that the Chairman had stipulated—consolidating the army

---

[30] Zhang Hua, "Zhang Aiping Jiangjun zhengdun Guofang kewei" [General Zhang Aiping Consolidates the Science and Technology Commission for National Defense], *BNC*, no. 2 (2001), pp. 9-10; Hu Shihong, *Zhang Aiping zai* 1975, p. 254; and above, p. 181.

[31] Zhang Hua, "Zhang Aiping," pp. 12, 14. In addition to Deng, Ye and other military figures, in this period Zhang also received the backing of Hua Guofeng in his capacity as Vice Premier in charge of science. Interestingly, in early June, Zhang expressed strong support for the personnel practices of Hua's old Hunan boss and now subordinate in the provincial apparatus, Party Secretary Zhang Pinghua, who was taking a tough line against disruptive elements who had entered the CCP during the Cultural Revolution. See Zhang Hua, "Zhang Aiping," p. 16; and below, p. 288.

and preparing for war. He also offered a pithy summary of PLA shortcomings by citing five words from Mao: "bloating, laxity, conceit, extravagance and inertia."[32]

Bloating meant excessive personnel, and organizational streamlining and restaffing became the central task of the meeting. Military personnel had increased greatly during the Cultural Revolution, reaching 6.1 million, including 1.5 million officers—about 600,000 more than was deemed necessary. The meeting decided to cut total personnel to 4.5 million over a three-year period. Extravagance and inertia, as seen in the pursuit of luxuries, appropriation of civilian property, and just going through the motions rather than risk criticism, underlined how unprepared the army was for war. While war was not considered imminent, preparedness had become a top PLA priority, and a "fever" of military training and exercises was the order of the day in 1975. This emphasis was also reflected in strategic doctrine as Deng endorsed an approach moving away from traditional versions of "people's war." In noting that contemporary wars were fought by combined air, ground and naval units, Deng stated that such operations "cannot be conducted by following our old formula of 'millet plus rifles'." While a sensible statement reflecting much actual PLA practice from before the Cultural Revolution, it was a striking break from the rhetoric of the movement. Again, Mao approved this approach, and one can only conclude that it reflected how far he was willing to go to correct the movement's shortcomings as they applied to the army's war fighting capabilities.[33]

According to Deng, shortcomings emerging during the Cultural Revolution were at the root of conceit, as manifested in overbearing behavior toward the population, and of laxity, expressed in often extreme indiscipline where even whole units defied orders, and particularly in rampant factionalism. He argued that these problems, long solved by the Yan'an rectification and subsequent efforts, had reappeared with a vengeance in the late 1960s, particularly as a result of the "support the left" activities which created factions both within army units and in civil society. There is little to fault the analysis, and Deng declared factionalism was "very dangerous" and not to be tolerated. Leading groups were to be adjusted from top to bottom, and in this process an effort to break up "mountain strongholds" formed during the Cultural Revolution would be undertaken. In this respect, Deng relayed Mao's specific instruction to extend the reassignment and

---

[32] Zhang Hua, "Zhang Aiping," p. 13; and *Selected Works of Deng (1975-1982)*, pp. 27, 33, 38. The reference to Mao's five words was to an inscription made during the revolutionary period, but we can be sure it reflected Deng's effort to hew to the Chairman's current thinking. Mao's support was indicated by his approval of the distribution of Deng's speech and other conference documents on July 19. Ma Qibin, *Sishinian*, p. 386. Much as in the case of the NPC, with an eight-year gap since the previous conference in April 1967, there had been an on again off again process concerning convening a large MAC conference to deal with PLA problems. Deng Lifeng, "Deng yu kuoda Junwei huiyi," p. 14.

[33] *Selected Works of Deng (1975-1982)*, pp. 28, 31-34; Barnouin and Yu, *Ten Years*, pp. 278-79; and Li and Hao, *"Wenhua dageming,"* pp. 274-78.

interchange of personnel that had begun with the eight military regions in 1973 to provincial military districts and some PLA departments. While such a broad critique reflected the conference's main thrust of dealing with the 30 percent errors of the Cultural Revolution, the sanitized post-Mao *Selected Works* version does not convey the full flavor of Deng's message or of the meeting as a whole. Ye Jianying's summary speech, in addition to calling attention to the dictatorship of the proletariat and advocating the elimination of "bourgeois right thought," in key respects was a self-criticism as he assumed personal responsibility for army shortcomings and weak leadership. As for Deng, he not only acknowledged the primary accomplishments of the Cultural Revolution, but in stressing the need to race against time to rectify the PLA's problems, cited learning theory as the guiding principle (*gangling*). This provided some basis, apart from political necessity, for Zhang Chunqiao's praise of Deng's and Ye's speeches.[34]

One of the issues faced during military consolidation and at the MAC conference, but one obscured by severe limits on information, was the people's militia. As we saw in Chapter 1, Mao had initiated the idea for a new type of militia in spring 1973, and by the fall a militia building campaign, with Shanghai as the model, was underway nationwide. While having defense functions, some degree of coordination with the army, and, at least in Shanghai, some significant armaments, both the origins of the idea and assigned role of the new militia were primarily political and sought to bolster anti-revisionist forces in society, notably *via* working class leadership. By placing the new force under the direct leadership of local Party committees, the Chairman was expressing his dissatisfaction with the PLA. Little is known in any detail of the subsequent role of the militia in national politics, apart from its role in the April 1976 Tiananmen crisis (see Chapter 7), and accusations that the Shanghai followers of the "gang of four" attempted to use it to stage an armed rebellion after the "gang's" arrest (see Chapter 8). More generally, in usually vague terms post-Mao sources picture the radicals as attempting to build up the militia as part of their plan to seize power, with Wang Hongwen calling for the establishment of a national militia headquarters with himself as its head. To this day leading Party and military historians are unsure whether any such national headquarters actually existed, but they conclude that the militia's role was largely symbolic. Despite PLA leaders from around the country visiting Shanghai to study its militia experience, by late 1974 only half a dozen major cities had clearly functioning militias on the Shanghai model. Badly trained and poorly equipped, Shanghai's armaments notwithstanding, from the PLA's perspective the people's militia was hardly a force to be reckoned with.[35]

[34] *Selected Works of Deng (1975-1982)*, pp. 28-30, 36; "Ye Jianying zai Zhongyang Junwei kuoda huiyishang de zongjie jianghua," p.1; "Deng Xiaoping zai Junwei kuoda huiyishang de jianghua," p.1; and Chen and Du, *Shilu*, vol. 3, part 2, pp. 1239-42.

[35] *A Great Trial*, pp. 217-19; Laszlo Ladany, *The Communist Party of China and Marxism 1921-1985: A Self-Portrait* (Stanford: Hoover Institution Press, 1988), p. 370; interviews, January 2005;

There is, however, a limited amount of information concerning the specific period from late 1974 to mid-1975 that sheds some light on the militia issue in the context of military consolidation. Mao's ongoing interest in the militia, which had been widely celebrated on its first anniversary in September 1974, was suggested by the new state constitution passed at the Fourth NPC which reaffirmed the militia's status by stipulating that both the PLA and people's militia were "armed forces of the people." This, however, fell short of radical advocacy. Over several conferences in September and November 1974, Wang Hongwen and Zhang Chunqiao pushed issues of militia organization and training, and expressed annoyance at army resistance to militia transformation. Meanwhile, at a conference in Shanghai in November attended by representatives of the three central PLA headquarters departments, local leaders proposed that a Ministry of Militia Work (*Minbing gongzuobu*) be established along side the Ministry of Defense at the NPC, in addition to setting up a national militia headquarters along the lines reportedly floated by Wang Hongwen a year earlier. Neither proposal came to pass, certainly in the case of the new ministry, despite the highlighting of the militia in the newly adopted state constitution.[36]

In this period, moreover, despite his continuing interest in the project, Mao gave attention to shortcomings in the actual performance of the militia, in particular the involvement of local militias in factional fighting, which still continued in various places despite his call for "stability and unity." In December, the Chairman issued an "opinion" that militias should not be involved where two factions were in conflict, and in mid-January 1975 this became the basis of a Party Center notice banning such involvement and armed struggle in Zhejiang and Yunnan. A further notice on disbanding three militia headquarters in Zhejiang was issued by the Center on February 20. By this time Mao had relocated to Hangzhou, and could learn first hand about the disruption in Zhejiang. During his two-month stay the Chairman threatened to mobilize the army against local rebels, and, in the crisis of the summer examined later in this chapter, troops were indeed called in to restore order in the factories of Hangzhou over the heads of factory militias. Ironically, Wang Hongwen would play a role in that assertion of PLA authority.[37]

---

above, pp. 81-85; and below, pp. 476ff, 583-85. As the Shanghai model was still in its experimental phase, it is unremarkable that concrete militia building elsewhere was apparently limited, but in 1975 Deng's concerns seemingly sidelined the effort (see below).

As in other respects, Zhejiang appears atypical in the extent and disruptiveness of local militia organizations, but, as indicated below, by the start of 1975 its militias were being brought under control. See Forster, *Rebellion*, pp. 109, 154.

[36] See *PR*, no. 4 (1975), p. 15; *Shanghai "wenhua dageming" shihua*, p. 633; *Shanghai minbing douzheng shi ziliao*, vol. 22, pp. 65, 67; *ZGDSCKZL*, vol. 27, pp. 628, 633; Ladany, *The Communist Party of China*, p. 371; and above, pp. 84-85.

[37] Chen and Du, *Shilu*, vol. 3, part 2, pp. 1176-77; Mao Zedong, "Guanyu minbing bu yao canyu liangpai duili de yijian" [Opinion on the Militia Not Participating in the Opposition of Two Factions] (December 1974), in *CRDB*, p. 1; Forster, Rebellion, p. 187; idem, "The Cultural Revolution in

Thus the role of the militia and its relationship to the PLA was another contentious issue as military consolidation unfolded. Despite or because of its implied equal status in the new constitution, the army establishment was leery of independent militia tendencies, believing military affairs were its business and a separate structure was neither needed nor helpful. A case in point occurred when General Su Yu, a member of the new MAC Standing Committee, inspected the Jiangsu-Anhui area in preparation for the June-July conference at the behest of Deng and Ye. Su, who apparently was particularly concerned with the militia question, visited an old associate in Shanghai, Chen Pixian, and Chen complained about abnormal behavior by the radicals. When Su reported to Deng and Ye, he warned of an "armed separatist regime in southeast China." At about the same time, in this case clearly after Mao's May 3 criticism of the "gang," Zhou Enlai reportedly argued that the regular army should control the militia.[38]

The militia's relationship to the PLA was then discussed at the expanded MAC conference, although there are no references to the issue in any available version of Deng's and Ye's speeches. According to post-Mao sources and charges aired during the criticism of Deng in 1976, however, Deng sharply criticized an independent militia system as "not normal," and asked Fujian's Liao Zhigao to prepare materials to undercut Shanghai's, and also Liaoning's models. This, however, is a partial account which leaves out the crucial factor of Mao's views. We can only conclude that in a period when he had invested maximum trust in Deng, the Chairman was willing to go along with Deng's recommendations given the problems with the militia that he (Mao) had been sensitive to since the winter. In any case, the apparent outcome was to draw the militia back into a more unified military system. At least this is what Wang bitterly complained about during his July-October sojourn to Shanghai and Hangzhou, where militia work was seemingly one of his major activities. Wang reportedly declared that the MAC meeting wanted to make the militia subordinate to the PLA, as in pre-Cultural Revolution (and 1969-72) arrangements, but he would never change his opposition to this proposal as long as he lived.[39]

While the above concerns were being addressed, Mao's call for an extension of the reshuffle of the PLA continued a process that had been developing since mid-1973, and especially since the year-end rotation of military region commanders that Deng now declared the spirit for the current effort. This would be formalized in an August 30 MAC notice listing 85 appointments resulting from the

---

Zhejiang Revisited," p. 143; Cheng Chao and Wei Haoben, eds., *Zhejiang "wenge" jishi (1966.5-1976.10)* [Principal Events of the "Cultural Revolution" in Zhejiang, May 1966-October 1976] (Hangzhou: Zhejiang fangzhi bianjibu, 1989), pp. 232-33; and below, p. 281.

[38] See Fan Shuo, *Ye Jianying zai feichang shiqi*, vol. 2, pp. 478-79; and *Shanghai minbing douzheng shi ziliao*, vol. 16, p. 14.

[39] *Shanghai minbing douzheng shi ziliao*, vol. 16, p. 14; and *Shanghai "wenhua dageming" shihua*, pp. 560-61, 781.

readjustment of personnel over the previous two years.[40] Following the rotation of regional commanders, new appointments began to be made in significant numbers to central military departments, PLA service arms, military academies, defense commissions, and provincial military districts, leading to significant changes by the latter part of 1974 and early 1975. In fact, virtually all of the central departmental and service arms appointments had been effected before the MAC conference convened, while the great bulk of the military district changes, which affected 60 percent of the provincial districts and largely followed a form of rotation, took place about the time of the conference. All in all, from mid-1973 to late 1975, more than 35 top PLA posts of the central department head and commander level were filled by newly appointed officials, with many more officers assigned to somewhat lesser positions.[41]

Undoubtedly the most striking aspect of these personnel changes was the appointment of rehabilitated Cultural Revolution victims to key PLA roles, involving at least three service arm commanders, two military region commanders, the heads of the Science and Technology Commission for National Defense (i.e., Zhang Aiping), the Military Science Academy and the National Defense Political University, and, as seen in Chapter 3, Deputy Chief-of-Staff Yang Chengwu. Also dramatic was the mid-1975 appointment as MAC advisers of two more of the most famous PLA victims of the Cultural Revolution, Luo Ruiqing and Chen Zaidao, while several of the rehabilitated PLA leaders had been denounced as followers of Marshal He Long, the highest-ranking army victim of the late 1960s.[42] While in pragmatic political terms these particular appointments can be regarded as a victory for Deng, such a narrow interpretation ignores the source and motives for the arrangement—i.e., they not only fit into Mao's complex design, but they restored leaders personally rehabilitated by the

---

[40] Chen and Du, *Shilu*, vol. 3, part 2, pp. 1256-57. While the MAC notice, approved by Mao, referred to the readjustment, some of the listed appointments occurred before the reshuffle began to unfold in 1973. The most remarkable case was Navy Commander Xiao Jingguang, who had held the post since 1950, but who had been superseded in the navy's leadership by Political Commissar Su Zhenhua in 1972. Cf. above, pp. 40-42. The list also included some civilian cadres who had been appointed political commissars in the military regions.

[41] For the lesser positions of deputy department heads and political commissars, at least another 80-90 appointments were made. The problem concerning these positions (and to a certain extent military district commanders) is the vagaries in the data in both PRC and Western sources, some of which are clearly wrong, and much of which is incomplete. The military district rotations could be more complicated than the one-for-one exchanges of military region commanders, involving shifts among up to four districts or other military units. The sources consulted were: Chen and Du, *Shilu*, vol. 3, part 2, pp. 1256-57; He Husheng, *Zhiguanzhi*; Lamb, *Directory*; and Bartke, *Who's Who in the People's Republic of China*.

[42] Of the remaining new MAC advisers, Tan Zheng had been removed from his posts in the early 1960s, while the lesser status figures Chen Shiju and Wang Jian'an apparently had served continuously. On the respective travails of Luo Ruiqing, He Long, Chen Zaidao and Yang Chengwu, together with Mao's primary responsibility, see Teiwes and Sun, *Tragedy*, pp. 24-37, 81-85, 90-102. Cf. above, pp. 141-42, 193-94, 204-205.

Chairman, at least in part to assuage his guilt for the excesses of the Cultural Revolution.[43] It was, in effect, a case of Deng arranging appointments from those Mao had provided, with an unknown degree of participation by the Chairman in the assignment of specific jobs.

While the driving force behind the personnel reshuffle, and military readjustment more broadly, was Mao's desire to enhance China's war fighting capabilities, the continuing objective of preventing "revisionism" in the PLA was also evident in military appointments. This, of course, was reflected in the selection of Zhang Chunqiao as GPD head, and Zhang and Wang Hongwen as MAC Standing Committee members. It can also be seen in the appointment of radicals as local political commissars—most notably of the Chairman's nephew, Mao Yuanxin, as a political commissar in the Shenyang Military Region in early 1974, as well as in other appointments such as Zhang Qiuqiao, Zhang Chunqiao's brother, to an MAC post. Equally striking, some of the new commanders would prove susceptible to radical influence, as in the case of Air Force Commander Ma Ning, who was stripped of his position after the arrest of the "gang of four." The case of the air force is revealing. Little is known concerning Ma's appointment, which occurred in spring 1973 at a time of increasing radical influence, or concerning his fall from grace. Ma was a veteran of Deng's Second Field Army, but relatively junior in PLA seniority. In Mao's terms a middle-aged cadre, age 50 or 51 at the time of his appointment, Ma only attained the rank of major general in 1964. While perhaps selected simply on the basis of finding someone to meet Mao's demand for middle-aged leaders, as someone who rose rapidly due to the Cultural Revolution, he seemingly sympathized with the radical position. Whatever the reality of his presumed links with the "gang," Ma was removed shortly after the fall of the radicals and formally replaced as air force commander in spring 1977, although not purged from the CCP.[44]

The appointments of Ma Ning and others demonstrate that the overall result of the personnel reshuffle was mixed, due to some combination of changing political circumstances over the entire 1973-75 period, some degree of radical input into the process, the need for compromise similar to the NPC appointments under Mao's "stability and unity" directive, and the Chairman's preferences for individual officers. This relates to the larger issue of the degree of PLA support for the "gang of four." While Wang Hongwen's purported 1975 lament that "we have no one in the military"[45] was an overstatement, the bulk of the army command, particularly at the highest levels, would side decisively with the moderates after Mao's death. Notwithstanding their membership on the MAC Standing Committee, the clout of Wang and Zhang in the high command was

---

[43] See above, pp. 43ff.

[44] See *Lijie Zhonggong zhongyang weiyuan*, p. 8; He Husheng, *Zhiguanzhi*, p. 272; "Zhongyang lingdaoren guanyu jiejue sirenbang wenti de jianghua," p. 1; and above, pp. 101, 104-105.

[45] See Yan and Gao, *Turbulent Decade*, p. 478; and *A Great Trial*, p. 191.

bound to be limited. As one well-placed Party historian argues, with their lack of military background, they had no basis for influencing army veterans, and there are indications that they lacked confidence in carrying out their MAC duties.[46] Nevertheless, quite apart from any input Wang and Zhang had on personnel appointments, the impact of Cultural Revolution ideology, and above all loyalty to Mao, left a significant radical imprint on the PLA, even at the height of Deng's *zhengdun* efforts. This was evident in resistance that appeared in the wake of the expanded MAC conference.

The air force was one organization where such resistance surfaced. Following the MAC conference, the standing members of the air force Party committee convened an enlarged meeting to convey the spirit of the MAC gathering. Twists and turns marked the proceedings, with proposals for structural change attacked as rightist deviations during the initial 18 days of the meeting. Deng responded by sending Chen Xilian, Su Zhenhua, Yang Chengwu and GPD Deputy Head Liang Biye to enforce the MAC's line, and in the process effect a change in the air force leadership. Ma Ning, whose role in the air force discussions is unclear, was not affected, but Political Commissar Fu Chuanzuo, installed with Ma in spring 1973, was ousted and replaced by Zhang Tingfa who was entrusted by Deng to be the air force's principal leader, an appointment made formal on October 1 with Mao's blessing.[47] Resistance was also apparent in the Wuhan Military Region, where radical influence was strong, to the extent of one PLA division having called for Zhang Chunqiao to replace Zhou as Premier on the eve of the Fourth NPC. Deng and Ye were concerned with the situation in Wuhan, and on August 30 separately called in Wang Ping, a recent rehabilitee who had only been appointed political commissar of the artillery forces in April 1975, to advise him of the complicated situation in the military region before appointing him its political commissar. While Wang was entrusted with carrying out the consolidation agenda, he was also specifically told not to take on some of the most difficult cases which would have to be dealt with later.[48] That such resistance existed within the PLA at the height of Deng's power, and despite his forceful efforts, suggests a greater fluidity in the military than often assumed. Meanwhile, Deng proceeded with readjustment in various civilian spheres, a process that, especially in the first half of 1975, was both bold and limited, and constrained by Mao's ideological proclivities.

---

[46] Interview, November 2002.

[47] Xiao Sike, *Zhiqing zheshuo* [Insiders' Story] (Beijing: Zhongguo qingnian chubanshe, 2004), p. 72; and Zhang Tingfa, "70 niandai zhongqi liangci Junwei huiyi de qian qian hou hou" [Before and After Two MAC Conferences in the Mid-1970s], *DDWX*, no. 4 (1999), p. 66.

[48] See *Wang Ping huiyilu* [Memoirs of Wang Ping] (Beijing: Jiefangjun chubanshe, 1992), pp. 578-79.

Readjusting the Civilian Sector

While Deng's first move in carrying out Mao's design dealt with PLA consolidation, he was soon, and arguably even more deeply, involved in civilian affairs. While not totally eschewing theoretical matters,[49] for the first half of 1975 Deng's focus was on practical issues and the restoration of order. Under his leadership, the Party Center and State Council organs convened meetings to deal with accumulated deficiencies in railroads, industry, economic planning, capital construction, finance, iron and steel, and public security.[50] Deng's personal role at these conferences was apparently limited, but in the high priority areas of railroads and the iron and steel industry he gave major addresses on March 5 and May 29 respectively that laid out the key themes of readjusting the economic situation.

Deng's activities in the civilian spheres mirrored those in the military. Again, he based the legitimacy of his actions on Mao's directives—in this case the two directives to uphold "stability and unity" and to develop the national economy—as well as on the Chairman's specific support of key measures.[51] The two 1974 directives were closely linked in Deng's thinking and advocacy throughout the first half of 1975 and beyond, and eventually became a major issue in his removal from power (see Chapter 6). As we saw in Chapter 3, in December 1974 Deng told Mao that economic progress was dependent on "stability and unity," while the general view of key economic officials was that the economic structure was sound, and the problems faced by the economy (judged more serious in industry than agriculture)[52] were due to disruptions caused by the Cultural Revolution. There was no sense of a need for deep structural reform, although certain measures, such as the importing of foreign technology in 1972-74 that later bloomed into "reform," were affirmed. To put it another way, the approach was to use political means to deal with economic questions. In his key statements on the economy in March and May 1975, Deng's message emphasized the need to exercise strong leadership over the economy, both from central economic bodies and local Party authorities, strengthening organization and discipline, establishing "essential" rules and regulations in the workplace, and—as in the PLA—fighting factionalism.[53] All of this clearly was "restorationist" in the sense that it emphasized the ethos of the pre-1966 system. But from Mao's perspective, it could also be seen as righting the imbalance caused by the 30 percent failures of

---

[49] Notably the preparation of Volume 5 of Mao's *Selected Works*. See below, pp. 270, 321-22.

[50] See Chen and Du, *Shilu*, vol. 3, part 2, pp. 1190-91, 1196-97, 1204, 1205, 1214-15, 1229.

[51] The key decisions on railroads and the iron and steel industry both had Mao's endorsement. See *RMRB*, February 12, 1977, in *SPRCP*, no. 6288 (1977), pp. 1-2; and NCNA, Beijing, February 21, 1977, in *ibid.*, p. 34.

[52] According to Deng in his March 1975 talk at the conference on railroads to provincial Party secretaries responsible for industry; *Selected Works of Deng (1975-1982)*, p. 14.

[53] *Selected Works of Deng (1975-1982)*, pp. 14-22; and above, pp. 197-98, 199.

the Cultural Revolution. As Deng put it when calling for courage in confronting these issues, "Chairman Mao has said that it is necessary to make revolution [and] promote production, [yet] some comrades ... only dare to make revolution but not to promote production, [saying] that the former is safe but the latter dangerous."[54]

As reflected in his major speeches, Deng's key sectoral priorities were railroads and the iron and steel industry. The conference of provincial Party secretaries responsible for industry from February 25 to March 8 focused on railroads, the weakest link in the national economy which had been so disrupted during *pi Lin pi Kong*. At the conference, Deng articulated his message of leadership, discipline, rules and regulations, and combating factionalism. He was also unhappy with the larger state of the industrial economy, refusing to shake hands with the participants and saying he would only do so when production had increased. Deng's demands produced quick results, largely restoring the orderly operation of the railway system, unblocking bottlenecks, and over-fulfilling targets by April. This, in turn, provided the basis for the consolidation of the entire industrial front. The overall result was a 19.4 percent increase in total output value for industry and agriculture for the first quarter compared to the corresponding period in 1974; these results apparently led to a late April report suggesting a ten-year plan and further study of the economic management system—a report endorsed by Mao. As of April, however, results in the iron and steel industry lagged, leading to the May 8-29 forum where Deng delivered an even stronger message against factionalism, as well as a broad appeal for the rehabilitation and encouragement of cadres, technicians and veteran workers.[55]

Steel had been a priority from the outset, with the Ministry of Metallurgy convening a seminar in February to deal with production falling behind targets, with Mao's pronouncements on studying theory and "stability and unity" as guiding directives. Vice Premier Yu Qiuli addressed the seminar, berating the sector for its poor production record despite huge state investment and more than three million workers. Yu's attitude, we would argue, reflected Mao's fixation with steel—a fixation that had such disastrous consequences during the Great Leap Forward—and one seemingly shared by Deng. In any case, Yu called for a series of measures including enforcing a responsibility system, relying on skilled workers, and securing quality coal, while also emphasizing fully mobilizing the masses. The metallurgy seminar overlapped with the conference of industrial secretaries, where steel and coal were on the agenda in addition to railroads, and Ji Dengkui was the first leader to emphasize steel production. With iron and steel lagging behind other sectors, the May conference of leading officials from 17

---

[54] *Selected Works of Deng (1975-1982)*, p. 14.

[55] See Cheng Zhongyuan, "Deng Xiaoping yu 1975 nian tielu zhengdun" [Deng Xiaoping and the 1975 Railway Consolidation], *DDWX*, no. 5 (1996), p. 75; Liu and Wu, *China's Socialist Economy*, pp. 394-97; Yan and Gao, *Turbulent Decade*, pp. 463-64; and *Selected Works of Deng (1975-1982)*, pp. 19-21.

provincial-level bodies and 11 large steel complexes and State Council ministries was convened. With Deng in France during the first part of the conference, Li Xiannian and Vice Premier Gu Mu, who had primary responsibility for steel, set the tone, many proposals were offered to improve performance, and Minister of Metallurgy Chen Shaokun acknowledged the ministry's shortcomings. When Deng returned from abroad, he made two speeches on the issue, first to the State Council on the 21st, and then to the conference on the 29th. On the 21st, he declared that the time was ripe to deal with steel production, all departments were required to assist, everyone should be daring and not fear to touch the tiger's buttocks, and he distinguished the railroads, where close cooperation among the localities was required, and steel, where power had to be concentrated in the Center. On the 29th, Deng elaborated on the need for daring while attacking factionalism, bringing back needed personnel, and establishing essential rules and regulations. Following the meeting, Central Document no. 13 was prepared in the normal bureaucratic manner to summarize the conference results, and approved by Mao on June 4.[56]

Echoing Deng's May 29 speech, Document no. 13 demanded a strengthening of the leadership of the Ministry of Metallurgy and established a new iron and steel industry small group in the State Council headed by Gu Mu, which had an uncertain effect on Minister Chen Shaokun.[57] Deng also sought a steel target of 26 million tons by the end of the year, and a steel production guarantee small group (baogan xiaozu), also headed by Gu Mu, was set up to press for the target. Although the year-end target would not be met as production fell 2.1 million tons short, within one month of the conference iron and steel production had improved and was judged to be providing adequate results. Deng now declared the industry's problems "solved" along with those of the railroads, and official statistics claimed a record monthly output for May and June in various key industrial products.[58] But while Deng had made considerable progress on the

---

[56] See Cheng Zhongyuan, "Yijiuqiwu nian de gangtie zhengdun" [The 1975 Consolidation of Iron and Steel], ZGDSZL, no. 81 (2002), pp. 100-103, 107-22; Deng nianpu, vol. 1, pp. 47-48; Selected Works of Deng (1975-1982), pp. 19-22; and Chen and Du, Shilu, vol. 3, part 2, pp. 1214-15. On steel targets during the Great Leap, and Deng's role in pushing targets generally, see Teiwes with Sun, Road to Disaster, pp. 100ff, 111-12, 117.

[57] See Mao Mao, "Wenge" suiyue, pp. 368-70; and He Yaomin, "Deng Xiaoping lingdao women jinxing zhengdun he gaige—fan Yuan Baohua Tongzhi" [Deng Xiaoping Led Us in Carrying Out Consolidation and Reform—an Interview with Comrade Yuan Baohua], BNC, no. 8 (2004), p. 11. According to Mao Mao, Deng sidelined the responsible officials of the ministry right after the May conference. Chen Shaokun, however, became the second-ranking member of a new industry small group, and was identified as minister as late as 1977. Chen, in any case, was prominent in attacking Deng in 1976, and his career seems to have ended in 1977.

[58] See Mao Mao, "Wenge" suiyue, p. 370; Cheng Zhongyuan, "Gangtie zhengdun," pp. 123-29; Liu and Wu, China's Socialist Economy, p. 397; Yan and Gao, Turbulent Decade, pp. 463-64; and Yu Guangyuan, "Yi Deng Xiaoping he zhengyanshi," p. 10.

domestic economic front, it was not without resistance. In his speech on May 29, Deng noted that his earlier speech on March 5 "was described by some persons as a 'restorationist program'."[59] Deng did not identify to whom he was referring, but other evidence indicates resistance in the localities, with officials in Changsha reportedly refusing to transmit to lower levels Central Document no. 9 on the February-March conference. One can speculate on higher-level backing for such resistance, but on this issue it did not involve Wang Hongwen. Apart from any routine role in arranging for Mao's approval of central documents, Wang apparently played an important and active role in the *zhengdun* efforts on the industrial front. According to a well-placed Party historian who read the text, Wang gave a very strong speech in support of railroad consolidation, calling for a harsh crackdown on rebel factions in terms similar to Deng, even advocating the use of lethal force where necessary.[60]

Deng's priorities, and some of the political considerations involved in implementing consolidation, can be further understood through the recollections of Ye Fei, the new Minister of Communications named at the Fourth NPC. Ye, who had served before the Cultural Revolution as Party First Secretary of Fujian and, for much of the period, concurrently as commander of the Fuzhou Military Region,[61] was purged during the movement only to be rehabilitated and named a Central Committee alternate at the Tenth Congress. In assuming his new post, Ye was part of the process restoring the pre-1966 bureaucratic arrangement of separate ministries of communications and railways, which had been merged during the Cultural Revolution and still shared the same building. A large part of the Ministry of Communications' brief was ocean transport, the contentious area of the *Fengqing* incident, and in a February meeting with Ye and new Minister of Railways Wan Li, Deng directed Wan to set up a system of rules for the railroads, and told Ye shipping and loading were too slow and the existing ocean shipping fleet was inadequate for China's needs. With Wan's ministry making rapid progress, Ye approached Deng after a State Council meeting on March 8, saying he hoped Deng would grasp consolidation of the communications frontline in the same way he had grasped it for the railroads. Deng responded that "For the present, I first want to grasp steel, coal, [and] the defense industry.[62] Don't you

---

[59] See *Selected Works of Deng (1975-1982)*, p. 20; and Cheng Zhongyuan, "Gangtie zhengdun," p. 119.

[60] Zhang Guangyou, "Wan Li zhengdun tielu yu weixing jiantao" [Wan Li's Consolidation of the Railways and His Forced Self-examination]. *Yanhuang chunqiu*, no. 3 (2002), p. 12; and interview, November 2002.

[61] Ye was one of a small number of officials combining local military command and Party leadership positions before the Cultural Revolution, always in defense-sensitive areas. See Frederick C. Teiwes, *Provincial Party Personnel in Mainland China 1956-1966* (New York: Occasional Papers of the East Asian Institute, Columbia University, 1967), p. 46.

[62] Ye reports Deng also listing education as a priority, but we believe Ye's recollection is inaccurate as

wait, don't miss this opportunity. The good thing is that the general policy of *zhengdun* is already clear, you should go to it with a free hand." More concretely, in response to Ye Fei's report that leasing ships was more costly than buying them, Deng lent his support to shifting the emphasis to purchasing. On Deng's instruction, Ye consulted Vice Premier and SPC head Yu Qiuli, who indicated that insufficient state funds existed to meet the objectives sought by Ye and backed by Deng. Ye, supported by Li Xiannian, then developed the idea of borrowing foreign capital through overseas Chinese banks in Hong Kong to purchase the needed ships abroad, and submitted detailed proposals to Li. These in turn were submitted to the Party Center and State Council, and the ministry's formal report of July 31 was endorsed by the Politburo three days later, without opposition from the radicals who circled their approval.[63]

An indication of the still uncertain political situation in the wake of the Fourth NPC was Ye Fei's cautious reception at the Ministry of Communications. Despite his credentials as an old cadre who had suffered at radical hands during the Cultural Revolution, and notwithstanding his efforts for the *zhengdun* agenda, officials at the ministry were not confident of Ye's political color initially.[64] This undoubtedly reflected Ye's lack of previous service in the sector, but it also indicates that the political crosscurrents of the time engendered uncertainty concerning political allegiance regardless of career background. The hesitancy within the ministry may also have been a consequence of the fact that Deng was less hands-on concerning communications than he was for railroads. While this may have simply been a necessary consequence of setting priorities and the crucial role of restoring railway traffic for the national economy, Deng was personally much closer to Wan Li (which possibly explains Wan's posting to the Railways Ministry in the first place) than to Ye, whose revolutionary and post-1949 careers were separate from Deng's.[65] Moreover, the priority areas Deng chose had more straightforward "solutions" than Ye's portfolio: a reassertion of traditional discipline, attention to production, and eliminating factionalism. In comparison, in addition to these tasks Ye had to find additional funding to purchase ships overseas, and came up with the idea of borrowing foreign currency to do it. In one sense this was simply a rational approach. As Li Xiannian commented: "There are some countries that are bowing and scraping everywhere to get loans but nobody gives them; people want to loan to us, and we don't want

---

it would have been a very unlikely focus for Deng in early March. Cf. below, pp. 270, 339ff.

[63] *Ye Fei huiyilu*, pp. 3, 6, 12-13, 54-58.

[64] *Ibid.*, p. 48.

[65] Wan, who had served in the Southwest under Deng in the immediate post-1949 period, appears to have developed a significant personal relationship as Deng's bridge partner in pre-Cultural Revolution Beijing. Ye served in Chen Yi's Third Field Army system before 1949, and thereafter spent his entire career as a Party and military leader in Fujian until the Cultural Revolution. Other ministers in Deng's priority areas of coal and iron and steel did not have close career ties to him, but had been in leading positions in their respective ministries since the early 1970s.

it. Isn't that giving a false impression! What's bad about using foreign capital and technology!"[66] But given the volatile history of the *Fengqing* incident, this was an intriguing step. That the key actors were the cautious Li and comparatively junior Ye adds to the intrigue. Perhaps Mao's reaction to the October 1974 fracas that the *Fengqing* issue was a trivial matter,[67] as well as Deng's broad support, gave Li and Ye courage, but the timing of events here and in other areas should also be considered.

Although the thrust of consolidation had been clear since the start of the year, the key political development in the first half of 1975 was Mao's criticism of the radicals starting in late April which is examined in detail below. With the exception of the high priority railroads,[68] in most relevant sectors (see the discussion of education below) the pace and bite of readjustment apparently picked up from that time. The case of ocean transport is less clear given the gaps in Ye Fei's account. Ye clearly consulted Li Xiannian and Yu Qiuli shortly after his early March exchange with Deng, and a small group on ship purchases was set up in the Ministry of Communications. By proposing borrowing overseas, Li and Ye were going further than the practices of recent years that involved the purchase of foreign complete plants relying on funds from the state budget while only utilizing short-term credit. The national capital construction conference, held from April 5 to 26, affirmed the import of such plants as the first item in the direction of attack on the capital construction front, but it is unclear whether the new borrowing method was considered. Over the following month or so, however, the ministry developed a complete proposal for expanded foreign purchases using Hong Kong capital. While the impetus for the program came substantially before the criticism of the "gang," its full development, together with the radicals' passive acceptance, unfolded in the wake of Mao's late April-early May intervention.[69]

Deng's efforts for most of the first half of 1975 mirrored those of Zhou Enlai in 1972 in that he focused initially on relatively "easy" issues, including combating factionalism and establishing order, matters we deal with in greater detail shortly. Here we examine briefly several more difficult areas which, similar to the Premier's practice in 1972, became more prominent around mid-

---

[66] *Ye Fei huiyilu*, pp. 56-57.

[67] See above, p. 215.

[68] With Mao's approval in early March, railroad consolidation restored traffic and led to arrests of factionalists within one month. Even here, however, Deng's March comments on factionalism were milder than his corresponding comments on the iron and steel industry in May. Compare *Selected Works of Deng (1975-1982)*, pp. 16-17 and 19-20. Cf. Deng's even milder remarks concerning factionalism in the PLA in January; *Selected Works*, pp. 11-12.

[69] See *Ye Fei huiyilu*, pp. 52, 55-59; and Chen and Du, *Shilu*, vol. 3, part 2, p. 1204. On the PRC's conservative foreign financial practices as of early 1975, see David L. Denny, "International Finance in the People's Republic of China," in *China: A Reassessment of the Economy*. See also Reardon, "Learning How to Open the Door," pp. 487-88.

year, specifically with the May-June criticism of the radicals in the Politburo. An exception, albeit one that only gathered force after mid-year, was Deng's gathering of a group of advisers headed by Hu Qiaomu from early January to grapple with theoretical issues, a group which, with Kang Sheng's backing and Mao's approval, would take over preparation of Volume 5 of Mao's *Selected Works* in March. We shall examine the work of this group, which eventually became the State Council Research Office, in Chapter 5.

Other forays into sensitive areas had less clear links to Deng. One such area where Deng does not appear to have been notably active until the second half of the year was education. This, of course, was the sphere in which the radicals had played a leading role since the onset of the Cultural Revolution, and in which Zhang Chunqiao had primary authority under the State Council arrangements confirmed at and after the Fourth NPC. Despite Zhou Rongxin taking charge of the Ministry of Education, little appeared to be done in the name of readjustment over the next two to three months. The activities of the ministry and Zhou Rongxin seemed limited to publicizing radical models, notably Liaoning's Chaoyang model, which had been promoted in contrast to the 17 years of allegedly revisionist education before the Cultural Revolution, with both Chi Qun and Mao Yuanxin prominent backers. As a specialist in education observed, upon assuming his duties as minister, Zhou undertook four to five months of investigations before forming his own views, a process which occurred in a situation whereby Chi Qun's followers retained positions in the ministry and reported to Chi on its internal developments. It was only in May, as criticism of the "gang of four" unfolded within the Politburo, that Zhou began to implement actively *zhengdun* work in education, holding meetings, giving speeches, listening to opinions, emphasizing the importance of education and intellectuals for the economy, and reportedly "pointing the spearhead" at Jiang Qing's and Zhang Chunqiao's disruptive activities.[70]

A final sensitive area was the ongoing process of cadre rehabilitation, particularly of high-ranking victims of the Cultural Revolution. While post-Mao official accounts, as well as Western scholarship, have given credit to Deng in this area, his actual role appears quite limited. Ji Dengkui, Hua Guofeng and Wu De, as they had since 1973, continued to handle rehabilitations, with Mao now entrusting them with 350 additional cases. This resulted in Ji and Wu handling cases of relatively significant leaders such as Song Renqiong, a close historical associate of Deng Xiaoping. As earlier, conflict with the radicals reportedly occurred, leading Ji, Hua and Wu to approach Zhou Enlai—not Deng—for advice. Zhou's counsel was to wind up the cases as quickly as possible, to bring

---

[70] Ma Qibin, *Sishinian*, pp. 383, 384, 385; and interview, January 2005. See also the December 1975 compilation of Zhou Rongxin's "revisionist speeches" dating from May; *Zhou Rongxin Tongzhi jianghua huibian* [Compendium of Comrade Zhou Rongxin's (1975) Speeches], collection available at the Fairbank Center Library, Harvard University. On the Chaoyang model, see Dittmer, *Continuous Revolution*, p. 191n58.

them to the Politburo in batches, rather than as single cases which the radicals could tie up in drawn out consideration.[71] Paradoxically, Wang Hongwen was also drawn into the rehabilitation process. In addition to being involved in handling the issue by virtue of his responsibilities at the Party Center, by being placed in charge of the Party Center Study Class soon after the Tenth Congress, Wang participated in preparing old cadres for their "liberation." Whatever Wang's personal preferences, and he had used the class in launching the Lin Biao-Confucius campaign and for other purposes, given Mao's dictates he could only preside over the graduation of such Cultural Revolution victims as Hu Yaobang, placing them in a position whereby they could be recalled to duty.[72] Moreover, the concrete work was carried out not only by the GPD for military cadres (thus raising the question of the role of newly installed GPD head Zhang Chunqiao for 1975 cases), but also by the Party Center's Organization Department for civilian cases, then under the leadership of Guo Yufeng, who had been nominated for the position by Kang Sheng.[73]

All of this, in any case, was the product of Mao's design. Zhou Enlai, ever since the December meeting in Changsha, had emphasized Mao's instruction on cadre liberation, while after arriving in Hangzhou in February, the Chairman pushed for more rehabilitations. This led the Premier to stress Mao's "urgent" request for action not only in dealing with the 350 cases, but also to release all imprisoned leaders pending a review of their cases, except for a very few who were beyond the pale such as Chen Boda—significantly Lin Biao's ally at Lushan. With this conveyed in early March, the Politburo radicals fell silent. Significantly, the key person in implementing this process was Mao's security chief, Wang Dongxing, who became head of a reorganized special case group that combined the three existing groups established during the Cultural Revolution.[74]

---

[71] *Zhou nianpu*, vol. 3, pp. 696, 697, 698-99; and interview with specialist on the period, February 2000.

[72] The other main function of the study class was to educate new Central Committee members, many of whom were mass representatives. Wang also used the class for factional purposes. According to a senior military historian based on personal knowledge, Wang called in graduates of the study class, and asked them to report back to him on the leaders of their new work units. Fenwick, "Gang of Four," pp. 223-24; interview, January 2005; and above, pp. 110, 147, 164-65.

[73] Although a military man without long-standing career ties to Kang, Guo, a man of cultural standard, came to Kang's attention during the Cultural Revolution, and as a result rose in the organizational area where Kang had an oversight role. Interview with senior Party historian, January 2000.

[74] See *Mao zhuan*, vol. 2, pp. 1722-24; *Zhou nianpu*, vol. 3, pp. 698-99; Wu De, "'Wenhua dageming' houqi zai jiefang ganbu wentishang yichang douzheng" [A Round of Struggle on the Question of Liberating Cadres in the Latter Part of the "Cultural Revolution"], *DDZGSYJ*, no. 2 (2003), pp. 41, 43; and above, p. 232.

There is considerable irony in that Wang Dongxing, who had previously played a significant role by recommending officials for rehabilitation to Mao in 1971-72 following Lin's demise, would be vulnerable in the post-Mao period for his involvement with the special case group, even though its clear function in 1975 was to liberate—not oppress—old cadres. This will be examined in our Volume II.

Against this background, the role of Deng in cadre liberation deserves further examination. As indicated, official histories, and various Western analyses,[75] attribute the continuing rehabilitations in 1975 to Deng, or at least emphasize his role. Of course, this overstates Deng's contribution in the fundamental sense that the initiative came from Mao, as well as ignoring the roles of Ji, Hua, Wu and Wang Dongxing. As for Deng's specific contribution to rehabilitation, in an action foreshadowing his cautious behavior in 1977-78,[76] he passed on to Mao a letter from the daughter of He Cheng, a comparatively minor figure from the PLA's health services, seeking work for her father. The result was that Mao declared He innocent on May 17, and his comment inspired a further burst of freeing detained officials.[77] Significantly, He Cheng's case paled in comparison to Mao's recent actions concerning high profile victims Yang Chengwu and Luo Ruiqing, and his rehabilitation of propagandist Zhou Yang two months later.

What of more prominent cases? One of the most notorious cases from the Cultural Revolution was that of the so-called "61 traitors," high-ranking Party leaders who had been released from prison by the Guomindang in 1936 after renouncing communism on the orders of the Party Center, played major roles after 1949, but were purged along with their patron, Liu Shaoqi, in 1966. In the latter part of May 1975, as criticism of the radicals unfolded but apparently reflecting Zhou's earlier instruction to release everyone but a very few, these figures were released from prison, but were still under investigation and faced demands for confessions to fictitious crimes.[78] While one source credits Deng with pressing for "solving" these cases and those of other significant officials "on many occasions" in 1975, Wu De recalled Deng merely raising the need for reexamining the cases, but then backing off when Jiang Qing berated Wu, who also backed the idea, as wanting "to reverse the verdict on traitors." The recently-published official chronology of Deng's activities, moreover, makes no mention of the "61 traitors" case during the relevant period. In addition, in Deng Liqun's understanding, Mao raised an even more explosive case in this same period, that of the highest-ranking victim of the initial stage of the Cultural Revolution, Peng Zhen. According to Deng Liqun, the radicals strongly opposed any action,

---

[75] For interpretations that new rehabilitations in 1975 were Deng's doing and directly related to his struggle with the radicals, or at least pushed by him, see Lieberthal, *Sino-Soviet Conflict in the 1970s*, p. 123; and Pamela Lubell, *The Chinese Communist Party and the Cultural Revolution: The Case of the Sixty-One Renegades* (Oxford: Palgrave, 2002), p. 166.

[76] Deng's role then was also restricted to less controversial cases; his caution was virtually indistinguishable from that of Hua Guofeng. The initiative on sensitive cases came from others, notably Chen Yun at the work conference preceding the 1978 Third Plenum. This will be examined in our Volume II.

[77] Ma Qibin, *Sishinian*, p. 384; and Chen and Du, *Shilu*, vol. 3, part 2, p. 1217.

[78] Lubell, *Case of the Sixty-One Renegades*, pp. 166-67. Bo Yibo, the most significant of these figures, had actually been released several months earlier and placed under house arrest.

arguing that more investigation was required, and nothing further eventuated. This account does not record any argument against the radicals' position—from Deng Xiaoping or anyone else.[79]

Apart from rehabilitations *per se*, as in PLA consolidation, new personnel arrangements were made which, apart from those undertaken in the revamped State Council, most importantly concerned provincial Party committees. While Deng undoubtedly deserves credit for appointments in 1975, once again this was a process that had been under way well before his return to work as part of Mao's larger design to bring back notionally reformed officials into positions of authority, and it accelerated in 1973-74 predating Deng's involvement in managing Party affairs.[80] Similar to PLA appointments, much of the restaffing of the provincial Party apparatus had been completed by mid-1975, i.e., by the time Deng assumed formal responsibility for the daily affairs of the Party Center. This was overwhelmingly the case for the most powerful local official—the provincial Party first secretary. Of the 17 first secretaries newly identified in 1973-75, only four were appointed while Deng was in charge of Party affairs, seemingly fewer than when Wang Hongwen was responsible, although one can assume Deng had a powerful voice in the selection of the one or two Party leaders named in the first half of 1975. The pattern was similar under both men: new first secretaries were overwhelmingly civilians, and of these, most had been rehabilitated and/or had previously served in the provinces concerned.[81]

Thus it did not matter whether the radical Wang or old revolutionary Deng was notionally in charge—"reformed" civilians were restored to power. The underlying pattern had been set by Mao. Although we may reasonably conclude that the deepest sympathies of most restored cadres lay with Zhou Enlai and Deng, the politics of their appointment was far from clear-cut. While the radicals may have resisted particular rehabilitations and/or new work assignments, in

---

[79] See "Wei 'liushiyi ren an' pingfan" [The Rehabilitation of the "Sixty-One Cadres Case"], in Liao Gailong, ed., *Zhongguo Gongchandang lishi dacidian (zengdingben): shehuizhuyi shiqi* [Chinese Communist Party History Comprehensive Dictionary (Expanded Version): The Socialist Period] (Beijing: Zhonggong zhongyang dangxiao chubanshe, 2001), p. 334; Wu De, "Jiefang ganbu wentishang yichang douzheng," pp. 42-43; *Deng nianpu*, vol. 1, pp. 40-53; and *Deng Liqun guoshi jiangtan*, vol. 3, p. 241.

[80] On the role and background of rehabilitated civilian cadres in the provincial Party committees reestablished from the end of 1970, see Teiwes, *Provincial Leadership*, pp. 96-98, 118-21.

[81] Identifications based on He Husheng, *Zhiguanzhi*; and Lamb, *Directory*. Of the 17 new first secretaries appearing in 1973-75, 13 were civilians, including eight who had been rehabilitated, and an overlapping eight who had served in the same province before the Cultural Revolution. While there are difficulties concerning precise dating (cf. above, p. 261n41), seven were first identified in the period of Wang Hongwen's management of the Party Center, although it is likely some of these were actually appointed when Zhou Enlai still performed the duty. While the data are even less reliable, it is clear that a solid majority of ordinary provincial Party secretaries first identified in 1975 had been appointed before Deng assumed responsibility for the Party Center. On similarities in terms of the types of civilians appointed to provincial leading posts since the late 1960s, see Teiwes, *Provincial Leadership*, pp. 79-81.

his duties at the Party Center in addition to his role in the Central Study Class, Wang Hongwen was involved in facilitating the return and assignment of Cultural Revolution victims. Meanwhile, although Deng was surely aware of potential political benefits from, e.g., recommending Zhao Ziyang who became the new First Secretary of Sichuan in October 1975, this was hardly a case of Deng controlling the process, even during the period of his maximum authority. It is worth recalling that Zhao was initially rehabilitated as a Party Secretary in Inner Mongolia in 1971 *before* the Lin Biao affair, and subsequently appointed to his pre-Cultural Revolution post as First Secretary of Guangdong during *pi Lin pi Kong* in 1974.[82] At root, both rehabilitation and restaffing reflected Mao's unrealistic hope that testing in the fires of the late 1960s and subsequent reform would provide experienced cadres who would join the project of *consolidating* the Cultural Revolution and *preventing* revisionism.

The Struggle against Factionalism

The struggle against factionalism, or "bourgeois factionalism" in the rhetoric of the period,[83] was arguably Deng's number one task in the first half of 1975. The complexity of elite politics is illuminated by considering who played key roles in this struggle extending into the summer and early fall. It is not surprising, given the central importance of railroad consolidation, not to mention his then and later ties to Deng, that Minister of Railroads Wan Li's efforts have drawn much praise in post-Mao accounts. Less congenial to orthodox historiography are the important contributions of leading establishment beneficiaries, Ji Dengkui and Hua Guofeng. Hua gave Wan resolute and enthusiastic support in the summer removal of the radical head of the Zhengzhou Railway Bureau.[84] Even more significant in fighting factionalism and its accompanying disruption was Ji Dengkui, an ironic circumstance given Ji's rise as a consequence of factional battles in Henan in 1966-68, and in view of his post-Mao fall in large part because of the fallout of those Cultural Revolution struggles. The youngest Politburo member apart from Wang Hongwen and Yao Wenyuan, in 1975 Ji both outranked Hua in the State Council and had greater seniority on the Politburo,[85]

---

[82] Zhao's Sichuan appointment was recommended by Deng and Zhou; Yan and Gao, *Turbulent Decade*, p. 469. On Zhao's Inner Mongolia and Guangdong assignments, see above, p. 174n158.

[83] Deng's *Selected Works* always quotes him as referring to "factionalism" rather than "bourgeois factionalism," the term frequently used in the original, in a clear effort to sanitize his speeches of Cultural Revolution usage. Compare, e.g., *Selected Works of Deng (1975-1982)*, p. 19, and "Deng Xiaoping jiejian gangtie gongye zuotanhui daibiao shi de jianghua [Deng Xiaoping's Speech When Receiving Delegates to the Iron and Steel Industry Seminar] (May 29, 1975), in *CRDB*, p. 1.

[84] Zhang Guangyou, "Wan Li zhengdun tielu," pp. 14-15.

[85] Other signs of Ji's special prominence in early 1975 were that on several occasions he attended Politburo Standing Committee meetings, even though he was not a member, and that he was the only leader apart from Deng and Li Xiannian to accompany a foreigner to meet Mao. *Zhou nianpu*, vol. 3, pp. 693, 699; and above, pp. 248-49n12.

as well as having responsibility for the key organizational area. In this period, Ji was both among those considered leadership successors by Mao, and as an alternative to Wang by Zhou, Deng and other senior leaders. Moreover, Ji's work against factionalism was undoubtedly a major factor in both Deng Liqun's praise his of "outstanding" contributions a quarter of a century later, as well as in the contemporary support of veteran revolutionaries. Ji's efforts included strong backing for Wan Li's efforts to overhaul the railway system, notably a visit to Henan in August 1975 to lend his authority to Wan's tough measures against local radical factions. More famously, Ji was sent to Zhejiang in June-July to deal with the year's most serious disruption of social order, the widespread industrial strikes in Hangzhou. Deng would soon be speaking of Ji's efforts as creating a trial point for Party rectification.[86]

Ji's role in combating factionalism illustrates a number of features of the period ignored in conventional accounts: Ji's close cooperation with Deng, his influence in shaping Deng's concept of consolidation, and an importance in restoring organizational discipline that preceded Deng's own contributions. Ji, whose authority in organizational matters can be dated to at least his taking effective charge, under Zhou Enlai, of the post-September 1971 investigations of Lin Biao's "clique,"[87] was asked by Zhou in August 1974 to deal with the deteriorating situation in Inner Mongolia. A major aspect of this situation was the province's completely paralyzed railroads, and in carrying out this assignment, Ji adopted measures at least as tough as those later implemented by Deng and Wan Li. Indeed, Wan's actions in 1975 can be considered to have been modeled on Ji's performance the previous year. Ji had warned then that "whoever stops the wheels [of railway carriages] from turning will be arrested, whether they are rebels or not," thus putting local radical factions on notice that they would suffer quick retribution if they continued to disrupt production.[88] This took place while Deng's role in domestic Party affairs was still unclear. Ji's cooperation with, and influence on, Deng became apparent in the context of dealing with factional strife and labor unrest in Zhejiang and Hangzhou.

The situation in Zhejiang and Hangzhou was not only a test for Ji, it was also a major test for the Party Center as a whole. As we saw in Chapter 2, Zhejiang

---

[86] See Wang and Sun, "Dang zuzhi zhengdun," pp. 41-42; *Deng Liqun guoshi jiangtan*, vol. 3, p. 347; above, pp. 9, 10; and below, pp. 310-11. On Ji in Henan during the Cultural Revolution, see Lampton, *Paths to Power*, pp. 41-47. The role of these 1960s conflicts in Ji's post-Mao fall will be examined in our Volume II.

[87] Ji's key role was emphasized in interviews with a source close to Lin Biao, September 1995, and with a person who worked with Ji, August 2003. Ji's prominence in sensitive political matters came even earlier in his assignments to the MAC Office and the Beijing Military Region (in both cases together with Li Desheng) as part of Mao's anti-Lin moves to "mix in sand" and "uproot the cornerstone" after the 1970 Lushan plenum. See above, p. 80n137.

[88] Wang and Sun, "Dang zuzhi zhengdun," p. 40. Ji was also active in the latter part of 1974 in dealing with factional problems in his home province of Henan, leading to an October provincial document curbing the reckless recruitment of Party members. Wang and Sun, p. 42.

was probably the province most seriously affected by factional strife during the Lin Biao-Confucius campaign. Moreover, while factionalism was brought under relative control in most areas in the last part of 1974 and the first half of 1975, Zhejiang remained seriously affected. It was one of the two provinces singled out in the Center's order banning militia participation in factional conflict, and also one of only two provinces where industrial production over the first five months of 1975 declined relative to the same period in 1974.[89] Zhejiang's situation was special politically as well. Given Wang Hongwen and Zhang Chunqiao's interest in and apparent responsibilities for the province adjacent to their Shanghai base, they had developed significant relations with local rebels, with Wang in particular taking a close interest in the political fortunes of Weng Senhe and Zhang Yongsheng. As argued previously, however, this did not produce a total identity of interests. Finally, Zhejiang's situation was influenced by the fact of Mao's presence in Hangzhou from February to early April 1975. During that time, Mao not only threatened to mobilize troops to remove rebels occupying the Hangzhou Hotel, he received reports from the provincial leadership *via* Wang Dongxing on threats to local order and as a consequence formed increasingly negative opinions of Zhejiang rebel leaders, particularly of Weng Senhe. It was only after the Chairman returned to Beijing, however, that the Party Center began a determined effort to solve the Zhejiang problem.[90]

The initial response occurred in mid-April when Ji and Chen Yonggui were reportedly summoned by Zhou Enlai, who expressed concern with the Zhejiang situation. While Ji was the key figure dealing with the Zhejiang problem as events unfolded, at this point Chen was dispatched to the province where, in a speech on April 15, he sharply criticized "bourgeois factionalism," a theme then picked up by local leaders. It is unclear why the Premier emerged from relative quietude to address such an important issue, but in any case, Chen's mission did not solve the province's factional strife.[91] With the situation continuing to deteriorate, in mid-

---

[89] See Forster, "The Cultural Revolution in Zhejiang Revisited," p. 143. Moreover, between January and August 1975 industrial output in China increased 17.3 percent over the same period in 1974, but decreased 6 percent in Zhejiang. Also, 58 percent of factories in Hangzhou experienced stoppages or semi-stoppages.

[90] See *ibid.*; Wang and Sun, "Dang zuzhi zhengdun," p. 41; Chen Fawen, "Xiaoping Tongzhi zhua zhengdun de yige fanli—huiyi Zhonggong zhongyang 1975 [16] hao wenjian de xingcheng he shishi" [An Example of Comrade Xiaoping Grasping Consolidation—Remember the Formation and Implementation of CCP Central Document No. 16 (1975)], *BNC*, no. 5 (2001), p. 38; Forster, *Rebellion*, pp. 39, 69, 112, 132-33, 157, 183-84, 213, 249, 252; and above, pp. 177-78. While a direct statement from Mao on Weng's evil nature is recorded only in November 1975 (see Forster, p. 212), it is hard to believe, particularly in view of Weng's summer arrest, that the Chairman had not made up his mind during his stay in Hangzhou or shortly thereafter. In any case, during the summer crackdown in Zhejiang (see below) Weng Senhe was identified as a "bad person" (*huairen*), while Zhang Yongsheng and He Xianchun were only said to have made mistakes. Chen Fawen, pp. 38-39.

[91] See Forster, *Rebellion*, pp. 191-94. Of course, the report of Zhou's involvement at this stage may be inaccurate, and *Zhou nianpu* records no such meeting, but he clearly was involved in June. By then, he had been vindicated by the rebuffing of the attack on empiricism, and the radicals were in

June Zhou, whose interaction with Deng had increased markedly in April-May, asked Ji to solve the problem. Ji had already been assigned responsibility for the Zhejiang issue, and his immediate response was to send two leading cadres from the Central Organization Department to the province, significantly telling them that "now with Comrade [Deng] Xiaoping in charge of the Center, you should feel freer in your work [of opposing factionalism]." Ji himself soon followed and, as events unfolded, it was Ji who apparently made the tough decisions on the scene. But when Zhou recommended and Mao approved a central work team headed by Ji, he was not the only central leader dispatched to the province to combat factionalism. The ranking leader in the Party hierarchy, although not of the team, was none other than Wang Hongwen, recently criticized in the Politburo and no longer in charge of Party affairs, but still a figure of significance.[92]

What was Wang Hongwen's role in relation to factionalism generally, and with regard to Zhejiang in particular, and how can we explain it? Although much remains unclear, the available evidence again raises questions concerning the orthodox view of Wang. In general terms, while Wang's activities in the anti-Lin Biao and Confucius campaign in 1974 clearly contributed to the factional disruptions of that year, in early 1975 there is not only little concrete information linking him to the activities of the rest of the "gang" on the theoretical front that briefly threatened consolidation (see below), but in his duties at the Party Center Wang conveyed the directives addressing factionalism in both the railroad and iron and steel sectors to Mao for approval. Moreover, there is nothing to indicate that he expressed any dissent from Deng's position, and, as we have seen, the available evidence indicates he was equally firm in calling for a crackdown.[93] All in all, regardless of his political inclinations, Wang supported the anti-factionalism effort during the conferences of March-May, which makes a reexamination of the summer 1975 Hangzhou case all the more pertinent.

Wang's role in Zhejiang factional politics in the 1970s leading up to the Hangzhou incident is notable from several perspectives.[94] First, as a young Cultural Revolution radical from neighboring Shanghai, Wang had an affinity to and shared interests with radical Zhejiang groups. After his move to Beijing in fall 1972, moreover, both during visits to the province and through associates in Shanghai, Wang supported the remobilization of inactive Cultural Revolution mass organizations. This involved more than factional politics. Most crucially, in supporting the campaign against Lin Biao and Confucius in Zhejiang, Wang

---

retreat.

[92] Wang and Sun, "Dang zuzhi zhengdun," p. 41; and *Zhou nianpu,* vol. 3, p. 712. Wang and Sun's account puts Deng's takeover of Party responsibility somewhat earlier than the formal date of July 2 (see above, p. 247). Author Wang Ying was one of two officials sent by Ji to Zhejiang at the time.

[93] See above, p. 267.

[94] The following draws heavily on the excellent work of Keith Forster, especially his detailed study, *Rebellion,* and the broader overview in "Factional Politics in Zhejiang, 1973-1976," in Joseph, *New Perspectives on the Cultural Revolution.*

was carrying out Mao's wishes. Also, in addition to his duties at the Party Center from June 1974, Wang had specific formal responsibility for Party affairs in East China.[95] The immediate context for his 1975 activities concerning the province was Mao's call for "stability and unity." Thus in December 1974, with Zhejiang's particularly virulent case of factionalism continuing, the province's major factional leaders were ordered to Beijing for a study class and conference, with Wang playing a central role in the month-long negotiations which resulted. While Wang's preferences were undoubtedly with the local radical groups as claimed by hostile post-Mao sources, his actions did not fully back them. He reportedly explained his constraints to the province's most famous radical, Weng Senhe: "I'm not the [Politburo]." Nor was he Mao, whose "latest directive" against militia involvement in factional fights was included in the January Party Center notice which singled out Zhejiang, a notice presumably handled by Wang and issued as the negotiations concluded, or slightly thereafter. Moreover, when Mao stayed in Hangzhou in February-April, he was persuaded by Tie Ying, the second-ranking provincial Party Secretary who had survived heavy attacks during the Lin Biao-Confucius campaign, that local factionalism—especially that caused by the reckless recruitment of new Party members and promotion of cadres during *pi Lin pi Kong*—had gotten out of hand. In addition, the Chairman's increasingly negative view of Weng as an evil doer (*huairen*) created the basis for Weng's arrest in July. In other words, against this background, Wang had no choice but to work to dampen factional strife in Zhejiang.[96]

When Ji Dengkui and Wang Hongwen arrived in Hangzhou around the start of July, the situation was even more conducive to a crackdown on the continuing factionalism in the province, and especially on the related major labor unrest in the city. Despite erroneous reports of Deng's personal involvement in Hangzhou,[97] Ji and Wang were the responsible leaders heading a large delegation of central officials on the scene and making the recommendations which shaped the decision of the Center (now formally under Deng) on July 17. We can only speculate as to the reasons Wang was added to Ji's mission. Formal and pragmatic reasons would include Wang's responsibility for East China and his ties to local radicals, ties which in theory could facilitate bringing them under control, and which were consistent with Mao's ongoing reluctance to make a clean sweep of Cultural Revolution activists. In terms of elite politics, Wang's assignment, which occupied the first month or so of his four months in East China, is subject to varying interpretations. It could be seen as providing a soft landing for Wang following the criticism of the radicals, as well as an opportunity to test his mettle.

---

[95] Chen Fawen, "Xiaoping Tongzhi zhua zhengdun," p. 38. See also Forster, *Rebellion*, p. 199.

[96] See Forster, *Rebellion*, pp. 148-52, 183-87; Ma Qibin, *Sishinian*, p. 379; Chen Fawen, "Xiaoping Tongzhi zhua zhengdun," p. 38; and above, p. 276n90. Cf. above, pp. 174-78.

[97] E.g., Dittmer, *Continuous Revolution*, p. 166. See Forster, *Rebellion*, pp. 198-99, for further discussion.

While there is nothing to indicate that Mao had completely given up on Wang, the Chairman's official biography records him commenting on Wang's deficiencies in political ability and prestige, and deciding to send him to Zhejiang and Shanghai in late June to "help with work." There is, however, an alternative explanation for Wang's extended sojourn that we find more persuasive, one consistent with the evidence and argued by several well-placed senior Party historians. In this view, it was not Mao's initiative to send his successor south for an extended stay, whether to punish him or give him another chance, but rather Wang's own idea. The main consideration reportedly influencing Wang was dissatisfaction with political life in Beijing, a disenchantment involving boredom with official tasks, the loss of Mao's confidence, frustration that his actual power did not match his high station, and especially the difficult relations between himself and Jiang Qing as a result of her overbearing style. Indeed, in June Mao told Deng of Jiang's complaints about Wang.[98]

There is little to indicate how closely or otherwise Ji and Wang cooperated during their two weeks plus in Zhejiang. The inevitably hostile reports on Wang's actions in the province appearing after the fall of the "gang of four" picture him as sympathetic to the local radicals, but they provide little concrete evidence of his support for them during this crucial period.[99] As an outside commentary put it at the time, "his official mission was to restrain and even suppress [the Zhejiang radicals]. The success of his mission will alienate him from the radical Leftists [but its] failure ... will affect his status as a top Party leader."[100] Indeed, when Ji reported to Deng in Shanghai on an uncertain date, but probably preceding the departure of the work team he and Wang headed, he spoke of Wang in conditional terms: "In case Wang Hongwen does not cooperate, we should pursue the method used before [i.e., call the two factions to Beijing for negotiations]."[101] While Ji's remarks indicate a well-founded suspicion of Wang's allegiances, they did not allege non-cooperation. Given that the issue was settled in the province with harsh results for the local radicals, it appears that on this occasion, whatever

---

[98] *Mao zhuan*, vol. 2, p. 1739; Mao Zedong, "Tong Deng Xiaoping guanyu piping 'sirenbang'," p. 1; and interviews, January 2005. Wang possibly used Mao's comments at the May 3 Politburo meeting praising Chen Yonggui's plan to spend most of his time away from Beijing (see below) in arguing for his request. Dispatching Wang along with Ji Dengkui to deal with the urgent Zhejiang problem can be regarded as conceptually separate from Wang's longer-term relocation from the capital.

[99] A rare example of limited support was Wang's reported intervention to have local rebel chieftain Zhang Yongsheng sent to labor in rural Hebei rather than suffer more severe punishment. Wang, however, did not obstruct the arrest of Weng Senhe (see below), or the general undermining of the radical faction in this period. See Forster, *Rebellion*, pp. 211-13.

[100] *China News Summary*, no. 583 (1975), p. 2, as cited in Forster, *Rebellion*, p. 199.

[101] Wang and Sun, "Dang zuzhi zhengdun," p. 41. Wang and Sun incorrectly date this encounter in early July, but Deng was not in Shanghai at the time. Deng was in the city on June 10-12, and the conversation probably occurred then. Ji was already responsible for Zhejiang, he probably made multiple trips to the area in this period, and mid-June was the time he discussed Zhejiang with Zhou. See *Deng nianpu*, vol. 1, pp. 54, 56; and *Zhou nianpu*, vol. 3, p. 712.

differences existed between them, Wang cooperated with Ji on the crackdown.

Whatever the nature of Wang's actual performance in Zhejiang, Ji appears to have been the decisive actor, thus earning the appreciation of Deng and others in Beijing. It was reportedly on Ji's personal order that high profile radical Weng Senhe was arrested on July 9, and Ji also altered local circumstances by revealing to Tie Ying, in a breach of Politburo discipline, Mao's critical opinions concerning the "gang." The astonishment and excitement of Tie, the Zhejiang leader most inclined to crack down on factionalism, is another pointer to the ignorance of even relatively high-ranking elite members concerning the politics of the Center, but in the circumstances it would have bolstered Tie's determination to deal with local radicals.[102] When Ji returned to Beijing on July 15, together with Zhejiang leaders Tan Qilong and Tie Ying and a draft decision jointly prepared by the central delegation and provincial officials on how to deal with the situation,[103] he was summoned from the airport to report directly to Zhou Enlai. After hearing Ji's report, Zhou directed him to brief Deng, and that evening following Tan and Tie's report to the Politburo and Deng's warm praise, the draft proposal was approved, becoming Central Document no. 16. Wang would almost certainly have been present and lent his support at the Politburo meeting; in any event, the document was quickly approved by Mao on the 16th, and issued on the 17th. In addition to addressing the Zhejiang situation, the decision was intended to establish an experimental point that could become a model for the whole nation.[104]

Both Ji and Wang then returned to Hangzhou to implement Document no. 16. Whatever their precise roles during the initial mission to Zhejiang, or in the drafting of the document, the mid-July recommendation to the Center called for strong measures against factionalism. As Keith Forster has detailed, the resulting decision had three major aspects. First, it called for a major reshuffle of the Zhejiang provincial and Hangzhou municipal Party leaderships, as well as that of the Zhejiang Military District. Officials involved in factional disturbances were dismissed, demoted or transferred, with replacements from other provinces

---

[102] Forster, *Rebellion*, pp. 193, 204, 211; and interview with senior Party historian who heard the story of Ji's revelation directly from Tie, November 2002.

[103] There are inconsistencies in the sources concerning this development. According to Wang and Sun, "Dang zuzhi zhengdun," p. 41, Ji arrived in Beijing on July 15 on a flight including Tan and Tie, while Chen Fawen, "Xiaoping Tongzhi zhua zhengdun," p. 39, reports Tan and Tie arriving on the 14th, presumably without any central leaders. Neither version mentions Wang Hongwen, who surely attended the Politburo meeting on the 15th (see below, n. 104). Nor was Wang mentioned with regard to the central delegation and the provincial authorities jointly preparing the draft decision on the 13th, again something which seems unlikely given Wang's assignment and status.

[104] See Wang and Sun, "Dang zuzhi zhengdun," pp. 41-42; and Chen Fawen, "Xiaoping Tongzhi zhua zhengdun," p. 39. Although Wang was not mentioned in these sources, according to *Zhou nianpu*, vol. 3, p. 715, "before and after" July 16 Zhou consulted with Ji, Wang and others. Given Wang's status in the CCP, his responsibility for East China, and his specific assignment in the Zhejiang case, it is extremely unlikely he would not have participated in the Politburo meeting on the 15th. In any case, there are no claims that Wang opposed Document no. 16, something that could be counted on if he had done so.

assuming leading positions. The reshuffle, while including representatives of different factional interests, nevertheless incorporated severe punishment of leading local mass organization radicals with apparent links to Wang Hongwen. One of the striking aspects of this personnel reshuffle was the transfer of Zhang Zishi, Kang Sheng's son, from Shandong to become Party leader of Hangzhou, a decision within the purview of the Central Organization Department led by Guo Yufeng, Kang's protégé who had participated in the initial Ji-Wang mission, in yet another suggestion of Kang's support of Deng's efforts.[105] The second and third aspects dealt with factional disruptions and strikes affecting nearly 60 percent of Hangzhou's factories. The twofold response was to send in over 10,000 troops to pacify the workplaces, perhaps the largest military mobilization for domestic purposes since the late 1960s, and to launch an intensive emulation campaign in Hangzhou factories which repudiated radical behavior and provided guidelines for the restoration of industrial order. Wang Hongwen, based in nearby Shanghai, seems to have been active on the scene, arguably involved in overseeing tough measures in the factories during the remainder of the summer.[106]

With these steps taken and Wang remaining in the area, Ji's value to Deng and his supporters was underlined a short time later when, at the start of August, an upsurge of railway disruption in Zhengzhou caused Li Xiannian to panic. Li declared that it was necessary to use the Zhejiang approach, and Ji was hastily dispatched to deal with the situation. Even more fundamental, the interaction of Deng and Ji later in August profoundly influenced the development of Deng's concept of consolidation. At a Politburo meeting, Deng not only praised Ji's successes in Zhejiang and Henan, he also indicated that they provided a key step in broadening organizational consolidation, leading to a focus on the Party itself.

---

[105] See Forster, "Factional Politics," pp. 114-15; idem, *Rebellion*, pp. 203-14; and Cheng Chao and Wei Haoben, *Zhejiang "wenge" jishi*, p. 235. After a careful review of leadership changes, Forster concluds (*Rebellion*, p. 210) that the new arrangement was indecisive, with increased radical influence actually likely. We believe, however, that with Tie Ying seemingly playing the key local leadership role, and mass organization rebels suppressed, for the following months radical influence in Zhejiang was significantly reduced before resurfacing in the context of the events of late 1975 and 1976.

Zhang Zishi, who emerged early in the Cultural Revolution in Qingdao, was of classic rebel background, but based on the limited evidence available, he upheld Deng's line after his posting to Hangzhou. See *Rebellion*, pp. 207-209, 233, 243.

[106] See Forster, "Factional Politics," p. 114; and idem, *Rebellion*, pp. 214-24. Wang, who had military authority as a MAC Standing Committee member, reappeared in Hangzhou on July 19, the day troops began to move into four key factories. In August, he was back at one of the key points in the factory emulation campaign. Although Dittmer's account, *Continuous Revolution*, p. 166, erroneously places Deng on the scene to rectify Wang's blunders, its claim that Wang "adopted a very hard line" toward strikers is credible. Forster's analysis is superior in almost all respects, but his conclusion that Wang "continued to keep factional cleavages on the boil" in the factories (*Rebellion*, p. 219) appears to give too much credit to fragmentary post-Mao assertions concerning Wang's summer 1975 activities. None of this is to question the conflicting pressures on Wang noted above and emphasized by Forster, but as we have stressed, the circumstances of summer 1975 required Wang to support the intensified attack on factionalism.

The experiences in Zhejiang and Henan, Deng stated, had already achieved an initial Party rectification in those provinces, and could become the basis for a decision on rectification of the entire CCP. But this development is a story for Chapter 5.[107]

Ultimately, Deng, with the backing of Zhou, active implementation by Ji, and the all-important authority of Mao, called the shots in the struggle against factionalism. His rhetoric escalated once the radicals suffered Mao's rebuke, and by early July he further upped the ante by declaring that any ongoing factionalism "would be quite a different matter" from either the "mountaintops" of the revolutionary period, or even the factions of the early stage of the Cultural Revolution, all of which had "formed naturally." Forster's fine analysis, based on provincial commentary over the following months, has illuminated Deng's elusive statement to indicate the nature of the new factionalism. Put simply, rather than the spontaneous small groups of 1966-67, mass organizations whose contradictions presumably were "among the people," the new factionalism involved an antagonistic line struggle, with the implication that these factions were organized and directed from above.[108] Such an interpretation clearly contained potential menace for central radicals like Wang Hongwen whose contacts with the likes of Weng Senhe were well known, even if he did nothing to prevent Weng's arrest in the current situation. Yet there was a paradox, as seen in the stronger, less elusive comments of local leaders than those of Deng himself. Mao's spring intervention to criticize the "gang" had opened the way to an intensification of consolidation, but Mao clearly wished to limit any criticism of the central radicals—something Deng understood and acted upon. But various provincial leaders, undoubtedly ignorant of the fine points of developments in the capital, seemingly grasped the tougher policy toward factionalism to deal harshly with their local enemies. This paradox is another reason for examining the process leading to the temporary curbing of the Politburo radicals.

The Dictatorship of the Proletariat Campaign and the Empiricism Issue

Deng's *zhengdun* efforts took place against the background of, first, the campaign to study the dictatorship of the proletariat, including its divisive ingredient of attacking empiricism, and then Mao's intervention to curb the campaign, criticize the radicals, and place Deng in unambiguous charge of the Party, government and military. According to conventional interpretations of the early post-NPC period,[109] the "gang of four," reflecting the deep split at the Congress and reacting

---

[107] Wang and Sun, "Dang zuzhi zhengdun," p. 42; and below, pp. 344ff.

[108] *Selected Works of Deng (1975-1982)*, p. 25; Forster, "Factional Politics," pp. 108-11; idem, *Rebellion*, pp. 194-97; and above, p. 269n68.

[109] While different works have their own individuality, a common feature is the notion of a radical counter-attack after their NPC setback. For a summary of the orthodox PRC view, see Yan and Gao, *Turbulent Decade*, pp. 461-63. For Western studies at various points in time, see, e.g., Lieberthal,

to their own setbacks and the danger of Deng's succession becoming irreversible, quickly counter-attacked by launching the dictatorship of the proletariat campaign. In this they gained Mao's support, either because he himself had been weakened at the NPC and needed to reassert his own authority, or because he wanted to readjust the balance which had shifted too much in favor of the pre-Cultural Revolution establishment. The radicals, however, overplayed their hand, and in the spring Mao again tilted to the old guard, allowing the veterans to press home their advantage into the fall. As in other cases, this view has some resonance with actual developments in 1975, but in key respects distorts the reality of the period: rather than a "counter-attack," the study of the dictatorship of the proletariat was part of Mao's design since before the Fourth NPC; the radicals did overstep in attacking empiricism, and were duly criticized by Mao, but they had reason to believe they were carrying out his will; Mao's criticism of the "gang" was not as strong as post-Mao official historiography claims; nor did Deng use the new situation to launch as thorough an attack on the radicals as often believed. Here we examine the nature and meaning of the dictatorship of the proletariat campaign, and in the following section analyze the fallout as Mao moved into action.

As discussed in Chapter 3, in his lengthy discussion with Zhou Enlai in December 1974, Mao not only emphasized the danger of revisionism, he also instructed Zhou to tell Zhang Chunqiao to write an article on the dictatorship of the proletariat, and made the statements that would be repeatedly quoted as "Chairman Mao's recent instructions on theory" in the discussions of the coming months. Zhang's article, "On Exercising All-Round Dictatorship over the Bourgeoisie," was published on April 1, one month after Yao Wenyuan's "On the Social Basis of Lin Biao's Anti-Party Clique," which had also been ordered by the Chairman. In addition, Mao had directed Zhang and Yao to search the writings of Marx, Engels and Lenin for appropriate quotations, a project which resulted in the publication of 33 such quotations in the *People's Daily* in late February, and the study of them one by one by the Politburo itself. In all of this, not just the launching of the study campaign in February, but also the major articles by Yao and Zhang and the curriculum of quotations from the classics, several factors in addition to Mao's initiating role were apparent. One was the key role of Zhou Enlai as the purveyor of Mao's wishes. Another was that each major development was discussed and approved by the Standing Committee and/or Politburo. There is no indication of any divisions in these discussions over the two articles which would, in later orthodox histories, be seen as central features of the radical "counter-attack." It was, after all, Mao's agenda, and the theoretical premises were beyond challenge.[110]

"China in 1975," pp. 8-9; Dittmer, *Continuous Revolution*, p. 128; and Huang, *Factionalism*, pp. 345-46.

[110] *Zhou nianpu*, vol. 3, pp. 693, 695-96, 697, 701; Ma Qibin, *Sishinian*, pp. 378, 380, 381-82; Cheng and Xia, *Deng zai yijiuqiwu*, pp. 171-72, 174-75; and *PR*, nos. 7, 9, 10, 14 (1975). In addition

How can the articles by Yao and Zhang be characterized? While one should not overstate their sophistication, these articles can be regarded, as John Bryan Starr has suggested, as a serious effort to lift the level of theoretical discourse, an effort that saw a new explanation for the persistence of the "new bourgeoisie" in socialist society.[111] The analysis offered by Yao and Zhang supplemented the emphasis in Mao's rambling observations since the early 1960s on superstructural factors—specifically the corrosion of bourgeois ideas and the misuse for selfish purposes of official authority—with an economic argument. Following Mao's December comments, this analysis focused on the persistence of "bourgeois right" (inequalities remaining under socialism, particularly in the eight-grade wage system and commodity exchange) which provided the economic basis for possible capitalist restoration. A key function of the dictatorship of the proleta at in these circumstances was to restrict bourgeois right, to prevent existing inequalities from gradually polarizing society and creating the conditions for restoration. But as various analysts noted at the time,[112] the remedies proposed for this situation were mild. The need for theoretical study was emphasized generally, socialist education would be necessary for the masses for several generations, and those infected by capitalist tendencies were to be treated in a manner more lenient than what Deng Xiaoping was advocating for factionalists in the same period.[113] In terms of economic structure, the prescription was relatively status quo. Any changes would be gradual and limited for the time being: "[bourgeois right] should be restricted so that in the long course [major differences] will be gradually narrowed" (Yao); "we will have to continue [for now] with commodity production, exchange through money and distribution according to work" (Zhang). Crucially, none of this was to affect production adversely—the aim remained to "grasp revolution *and* promote production." Indeed, Yao Wenyuan loosely linked the three directives of studying the dictatorship, bolstering the economy, and stability and unity which became such a feature of Deng's program

---

to Zhou, Wang Hongwen, as the responsible person of the Party Center, undoubtedly played a part in conveying the message. Jiang Qing, who visited Changsha in January, apparently carried the instruction that Yao was to write an article. See "Jiang Qing zai dazhaohu huiyi," p. 382.

[111] Starr, "From the 10th Party Congress," pp. 468-72. For a fine comprehensive discussion of theoretical developments on this issue since the 1950s, see Graham Young and Dennis Woodward, "Chinese Conceptions of the Nature of Class Struggle Within the Socialist Transition," in Marian Sawer, ed., *Socialism and the New Class: Towards the Analysis of Structural Inequality within Socialist Societies* (Bedford Park, South Australia: APSA Monograph no. 19, 1978).

[112] E.g., John Bryan Starr, "China in 1975: 'The Wind in the Bell Tower'," *AS*, January 1976, p. 50; and Lieberthal, "China in 1975," p. 9.

[113] Compare Yao's statement whereby even those "who have sunk deep into the quagmire of capitalism" would receive the sharp warning of "*Comrades*, mend your ways right now!" (*PR*, no. 10 [1975], p. 10, emphasis added), with Deng's rather tougher March 5 injunction that one of the worst factional ringleaders be given a month "to mend his ways," or otherwise face criminal treatment (*Selected Works of Deng [1975-1982]*, p. 16).

(and subsequently his fall) later in the year.[114]

In purely theoretical and even programmatic terms, then, the challenge of the dictatorship of the proletariat campaign was limited. So what was the problem? Fundamentally, as previously argued, it lay in the tension among the Chairman's three directives, the conflict between Mao's desire to affirm the 70 percent correct Cultural Revolution, and the need to deal with the 30 percent shortcomings that had damaged the economy and political stability. The very fact of reemphasizing Cultural Revolution objectives created an air of uncertainty that put stress on Mao's other goals. In terms of policy development, the drumbeat of radical themes as magnified in contemporary media comment inhibited implementing even officially endorsed aspects of "bourgeois right"—particularly when rhetoric shifted from careful phrases about gradual changes to full-blooded attacks on material incentives as the devious schemes of Liu Shaoqi and Lin Biao.[115] A case in point concerned agriculture. Against the backdrop of the dictatorship of the proletariat campaign, the Ministry of Agriculture and Forestry reported to Li Xiannian, Hua Guofeng and Chen Yonggui in early May on the question of private plots. Although the tide was already turning against the radicals, in a rare instance of Hua leaning in a leftist direction in 1975,[116] he stressed the need to carry out Mao's directive on theoretical study and to criticize revisionism. More concretely, Hua reportedly said, "Issue an order to stop using [private] markets, and run the collective economy well," to which Li Xiannian rejoined that "This policy of yours won't work! ... The private plot issue has to be treated carefully. When the collective economy has surpassed the individual [economy, only then the peasants] won't engage in [private plots]." Of course, the situation was complex: Li bolstered his views with references to the Chairman, the new state constitution (as well as Zhang Chunqiao's report on the same) permitted small-scale private plots, and the commodity economy was reaffirmed for the present in the two articles. Nevertheless, in the crosscurrents created by the study campaign, opinions remained divided and there was no conclusion concerning detailed policy on private plots.[117]

---

[114] See Yao in *PR*, no. 10 (1975), pp. 6, 8, 10; and Zhang in *PR*, no. 14 (1975), pp. 8, 10. In comparison to Deng, Yao did not explicitly refer to Mao's three directives or describe them as jointly being the key link, but he did paraphrase them together as Party objectives (p. 10). Similarly, Yao endorsed the "three revolutionary movements" of the early 1960s—class struggle, the struggle for production, and scientific experiment (p. 8).

[115] See Yao in *PR*, no. 10 (1975), p. 7; and Zhang in *PR*, no. 14 (1975), p. 10.

[116] Hua apparently continued to lean in this direction in agriculture in the lead-up to the September-October Dazhai conference, although he then veered to a more centrist position. See below, pp. 354ff.

[117] Zhang Hua, "1975 nian nongye xue Dazhai huiyi yu nongye zhengdun de yaoqiu" [The 1975 In Agriculture Learn From Dazhai Conference and the Demand to Readjust Agriculture], *DDWX*, no. 6 (1999), p. 17; and *PR*, no. 4 (1975), pp. 14, 20, no. 10 (1975), p. 6, no. 14 (1975), pp. 7-8. This, at a high level, is akin to what David Zweig has termed "policy winds," that is, the ability of radical public statements (as well as factional lobbying) to skew policy. See Zweig, *Agrarian Radicalism in*

An even more significant issue was the implications of the study campaign for personnel. Zhang Chunqiao's April article included a potentially explosive observation:

There are undoubtedly some comrades among us who have joined the Communist Party organizationally but not ideologically. In their world outlook they have not yet stepped out of the confines of small production and of the bourgeoisie. They do approve of the dictatorship of the proletariat at certain stages and in certain spheres, because these will bring them some gains; once they have secured their gains, they feel it's time to settle and feather their cosy nests.[118]

Zhang went on to note that such communists, "particularly leading cadres," had contributed to the struggle against landlords and capitalists during the revolutionary period, but now engaged in retrograde actions detrimental to the proletarian dictatorship.[119] While less direct, this was a foretaste of the attack on "democrats" during the campaign against Deng Xiaoping in 1976: Party veterans who had contributed to the pre-1949 democratic revolution were unable to keep up with the demands of socialist and communist transformation (see Chapter 6). Similarly, and more famously, veteran Party leaders were the presumed target of a brief reference in Yao Wenyuan's article a month earlier quoting a 1959 remark by Mao: "at present, the main danger lies in empiricism." Although it is conceivable that, in its textual context, this passing reference was only meant to emphasize the need to read theory, a more sinister interpretation is supported by Yao's earlier mention of Lin Biao's alleged "using expertise [the forte of rehabilitated leaders] to cover up politics." Particularly unsettling was the fact that empiricism was one of the key criticisms of Zhou Enlai during the Yan'an rectification in the 1940s, a matter Mao had again highlighted in June 1974.[120] Nevertheless, these statements were accepted by the Politburo without known controversy. The problem came in actions by Zhang, Jiang Qing and, perhaps less importantly, Yao, in the period following publication of Yao's article.

Whatever the meaning of empiricism in Yao's article, it quickly became a centerpiece of the study campaign. Speaking to a meeting of directors of the political departments of large PLA units on the same day Yao's essay was published, Zhang also used Mao's 1959 statement on empiricism and emphasized,

---

China, 1968-1981 (Cambridge: Harvard University Press, 1989), p. 10 and ch. 2.

Another policy area possibly affected was industrial wages policy. While the effect was unclear, it may be that the campaign closed off wage adjustments and the use of bonuses which had been introduced in some local areas in the second half of 1974. See Forster, *Rebellion*, pp. 181-82. Also, although the policy does not appear to have been hindered, the campaign provided the context for complaints that Deng's March 5 speech dealing with railway readjustment was a "restorationist program"; see above, pp. 266-67.

[118] Zhang in *PR*, no. 14 (1975), p. 9.

[119] *Ibid.*, p. 10.

[120] See Yao in *PR*, no. 10 (1975), p. 9; and above, pp. 138-39. Surprisingly, empiricism was not mentioned in Zhang Chunqiao's April 1 article.

which Yao's article had not, that vigilance against the danger was relevant and vital for the current situation. Indeed, Zhang argued that opposing empiricism was the key link in the study of the dictatorship of the proletariat, and for solving the problems of the whole Party and whole army. While there apparently had been no controversy concerning the content of Yao's article when discussed by the Politburo, nor would there be over Zhang's article a month later, this did not mean an absence of conflict over implementation of theoretical study. Specifically, as we have seen, during MAC Standing Committee discussions concerning the summer military conference in February, Zhang and Wang Hongwen had tried to place the theory issue on the conference agenda, but were rebuffed by Deng and Ye Jianying. Thus when Zhang raised empiricism to the army political directors on March 1, it was against a background of differences concerning the study campaign in the PLA.[121]

Remarkably little detail exists on the unfolding of the campaign in March-April, but standard sources depict a number of developments. On March 21, with Yao Wenyuan exercising his authority over propaganda, the *People's Daily* published an editorial which again used Mao's 1959 observation on empiricism, now characterized as the "handmaiden of revisionism." At the same time, Yao ordered a propaganda drive that resulted in articles, news reports and special columns in national and local publications over the following weeks. During this period extending through the first ten days of April, Jiang Qing joined the fray. Jiang visited various places to promote the message that "empiricism is the main danger," a greater danger than doctrinairism, and the "great enemy of the present time." The propaganda campaign, however, may not have been as far reaching or focused as claimed. For example, the March 21 *People's Daily* editorial did not give empiricism the degree of attention implied; as with Yao's article, there was only a single passage, two-thirds into the editorial.[122] Moreover, in post-Mao criticism of the activities of the "gang of four" during March-April, official histories almost uniformly mention Zhang, Jiang and Yao, but Wang Hongwen is rarely cited as involved in attacks on empiricism.

What was the meaning of these developments? Three key matters can be identified: personnel questions, disruption caused by the campaign, and the new round of attacks on Zhou Enlai, all of which related to the larger issue of Party unity. There can be little doubt that personnel matters affecting Cultural Revolution rebels and veteran revolutionary cadres were at issue. The question is at what level. While official sources claim that the target was "veteran comrades represented by Zhou Enlai," there is little to suggest that Zhou or other top Party, government and army cadres were threatened with removal from office. After all,

---

[121] See Chen and Du, *Shilu*, vol. 3, part 2, pp. 1193-94; *Zhou nianpu*, vol. 3, p. 697; Ma Qibin, *Sishinian*, p. 382; *RMRB*, March 3, 1977, in *SPRCP*, no. 6298 (1977), p. 2; and above, pp. 253-54.

[122] See Chen and Du, *Shilu*, vol. 3, part 2, pp. 1198-99, 1203, 1204-1205; *Zhou nianpu*, vol. 3, pp. 701, 702; Ma Qibin, *Sishinian*, p. 382; *RMRB*, March 21, 1975, p. 1; and *RMRB*, March 3, 1977, in *SPRCP*, no. 6298 (1977), pp. 2-3.

Mao had only recently endorsed the personnel arrangements of the Fourth NPC, was the prime mover in the return of key veterans to major PLA posts, and, most of all, had made "stability and unity" a guiding principle. We deal with Zhou's case shortly, but note here that, as with so much of his treatment at Mao's hands, it was more a matter of humiliation than his removal as Premier, with Deng in any case having already taken over the reins of government.

The personnel question more broadly reflected the tension between the contradictory aspects of Mao's cadre policy, the two-sided approach of promoting young Cultural Revolution activists and rehabilitating experienced officials. There was a downside for both groups in Mao's plan: activists who engaged in unbridled factionalism should be disciplined, while veteran cadres truly had to reform before returning to work, and the Party had to be on guard against any restorationist tendencies once they were back at their posts. With organizations being revived and staffing readjusted in 1975, there were opportunities and threats for both sides in the competition for positions. In the spring struggle against factionalism, Hua Guofeng's Hunan associate, provincial Party Secretary Zhang Pinghua, revoked the membership of those who had been recklessly recruited into the Party under the *shuangtu* program, requiring that they be reassessed according to the standards of the Party constitution, while later in the year, Ji Dengkui's proposed organizational readjustment called for sending back to their previous posts those who had received crash promotions in the campaign against Lin Biao and Confucius.[123] In attacking empiricism, the radicals emphasized the other side of the coin. Crucially, in carrying the study movement into specific organizations, as Zhang Chunqiao had with the PLA political directors, a situation was created whereby the bona fides of specific veteran cadres were challenged. While the extent of manipulation from above is unclear, in "some places," alleged "empiricists" were reportedly ferreted out and forced to make self-examinations. In one specific case, allegedly under "the remote control" of Wang Hongwen and Zhang Chunqiao, the anti-empiricism movement in the Shanghai Garrison Command resulted in attacks on various leadership levels and cadres in general, "indiscriminately nam[ing] names and giv[ing] everybody a hard time."[124] Overall, however, there is very little evidence of leading officials being ousted at any level.

Organizational disruption caused by the campaign, rather than theoretical issues *per se*, produced conflict in the Politburo. This can be seen in Zhou Enlai's

---

[123] Zhang Hua, "Zhang Aiping," p.16; and Wang and Sun, "Dang zuzhi zhengdun," p. 43. Zhang Pinghua had been Hua's boss as Hunan First Secretary before the Cultural Revolution, and later served under Hua as a rehabilitated cadre in the restored local Party apparatus. After the fall of the "gang of four," Zhang became the first head of the revived Central Propaganda Department in the new order headed by Hua.

[124] *RMRB*, February 3, 1977, in *SPRCP*, no. 6291 (1977), p. 155, and March 3, 1977, in *SPRCP*, no. 6298 (1977), p. 3. The Shanghai Garrison case was a rare instance of Wang Hongwen being named as directly involved in the events of March-April.

early May criticism of attacks on empiricism as causing incessant conflict in some areas, military units, other official organs and schools. In this atmosphere, Zhou asserted, old cadres didn't dare assume responsibility since they bore their experience as millstones around their necks. Later in May, Zhou turned his attention to Zhang Chunqiao's March 1 address to army political directors, the initial step in creating significant tension in military organs over the following month and a half.[125] While such disruption was an issue for the Politburo, it remains unclear how widespread it was, and it may have been, in fact, exaggerated by Zhou and others. As noted, details on this campaign are sparse in post-Mao sources, with the contrast to *pi Lin pi Kong* especially striking. The absence of such details, together with the admittedly limited recollections of several people who lived through it, suggests that the overall emphasis was on theory, with little evidence of significant organizational dislocation. According to a junior cadre in the GPD at the time, only some unit leaders wanted to implement the campaign, while most cadres did not see it as a serious matter. In another case, an intellectual then in the Beida philosophy department recalls being dispatched to the headquarters of the northern fleet to lead theoretical study over a three to four month period, without any unusual tension.[126] Whatever the precise scale of institutional disruption, it clearly paled in comparison to that created by the Lin Biao-Confucius campaign a year earlier. Nevertheless, there is every reason to believe that Deng, Zhou and other leaders would see the organizational consequences of the movement as inimical to the consolidation project.

A particular source of tension within the top leadership was the renewed attack on Zhou Enlai. While the empiricism issue may be exaggerated in the retelling,[127] it struck a sensitive note as the link between the Premier and empiricism was well understood. This was underlined by the publication of clearly identifiable anti-Zhou articles on the subject, notably reference materials issued on April 7 by the Shanghai *Liberation Daily* which criticized empiricists who had participated in the Northern Expedition of 1926-27, and later, ironically, backed Wang Ming's doctrinaire policies in the early 1930s—a description that clearly fit Zhou. More importantly, the connection was reportedly pressed by Jiang Qing in her dealings with other Politburo members. According to Chen Xilian, in the first part of April she lobbied individual Politburo members "one by one" to oppose the Premier,

---

[125] See *Zhou nianpu*, vol. 3, pp. 705, 707.

[126] Interviews, January 1975. Su Zhenhua, who had actively supported the Lin Biao-Confucius campaign in the navy (see above, pp. 166-67), reportedly was very enthusiastic about the study movement, even wanting the entire Beida philosophy department sent to the northern fleet.

A similar picture of little general impact from the campaign is given by a former trade union cadre who could not recall any tension in the period, remarking it was a relaxed time, with people talking relatively freely among themselves. Personal communication, June 2005.

[127] Note its limited use in Yao's March 1 article and the March 21 *People's Daily* editorial, and Zhang's failure to mention it in his April 1 treatise.

while demanding a formal discussion of empiricism by the body as a whole.[128]

In any case, while it is tempting to see the empiricism issue as a conflict between Zhou Enlai and Jiang Qing and Zhang Chunqiao, the Premier, who only became engaged in a major way *after* Mao's appearance in the Politburo on May 3, was mainly concerned with satisfying Mao's expectations on the matter, addressing broader issues rather than personal matters. Thus on the 21st, when informing all Politburo members of the circumstances of Mao's criticism of the radical attack on empiricism (see below), Zhou submitted a draft letter to Mao for Politburo discussion. In this draft, he directly challenged Zhang's initiative in raising the issue in the PLA on March 1. While the details of Zhou's criticism of Zhang's actions are not clear, given the context of Mao's criticism of the radicals, there was only minimal opposition to passing on Zhou's letter to the Chairman. Jiang Qing and Yao Wenyuan, who were not Standing Committee members and thus not privy to the highest body's discussions on May 4 and 8 concerning how to convey Mao's views, claimed to have no clear understanding of the matter, Wang Hongwen's response was to leave the matter of submitting the letter up to Zhou, and Wang dutifully conveyed it when the Premier decided to proceed. Zhang himself claimed the Premier's account was "not exact," but when challenged by Zhou to offer his own account he withdrew his objection.[129]

While Zhou had embarrassed Zhang in the wash-up concerning the empiricism issue, it is not clear that Mao's position was as firmly opposed to the radicals on empiricism as official histories claim. Indeed, on May 3, he indicated that he owed Zhang an apology for not having noticed empiricism in his draft article.[130] While Mao was perhaps disingenuous on this point,[131] in the general sense it is more than likely that the radicals felt they were carrying out his will in attacking empiricism. In strict theoretical terms, empiricism arguably was the main danger to be emphasized in a campaign to ward off revisionism at a time when practical work was being reinvigorated. In political terms, given Mao's penchant for belittling the Premier, and his reviving of the empiricism question the previous year, such an attack could be presumed to be congenial to the Chairman. For Jiang Qing, it may well have seemed an opportune occasion to indulge in her seemingly never revoked license to criticize Zhou Enlai.

---

[128] See Chen and Du, *Shilu*, vol. 3, part 2, pp. 1204-1205; Gao Wenqian, *Wannian Zhou*, p. 553; and Mao Mao, *"Wenge" suiyue*, p. 354.

[129] See *Zhou nianpu*, vol. 3, pp. 704, 706, 707-708; Mao Mao, *"Wenge" suiyue*, pp. 361-62; and Cheng and Xia, *Deng zai yijiuqiwu*, p. 196. Jiang's and Yao's claims suggest they were not informed of the Standing Committee discussions by Wang and Zhang who presumably upheld the body's confidentiality.

[130] See Chen and Du, *Shilu*, vol. 3, part 2, pp. 1211-12. Mao seemingly confused Zhang's April article, which contained no such reference, with his March 1 speech or, according to the editors of *Mao zhuan*, vol. 2, p. 1731, with Yao's article.

[131] While arguably a case of covering up more direct approval of the critique of empiricism, Mao's claim that he simply missed Zhang's reference gains some credibility from the fact that he was virtually blind pending an operation for cataracts, and documents had to be read to him.

If Zhang's raising of the empiricism issue in the PLA was one factor in bringing the issue to a head, the activities of Jiang Qing were much more significant, and it is striking that the Premier did not dare to challenge her. In major official accounts,[132] Jiang has pride of place over Zhang as the person most culpable. However much her various talks in the 20 days from March 21 exacerbated tensions in subordinate units, the key lay in her actions in the Politburo itself. When Deng approached Mao on April 18 to complain of the anti-empiricism drive, in addition to Zhang's March 1 speech, he specifically cited Jiang's repeated demands in Politburo meetings for a formal discussion of empiricism. Seemingly around April 11,[133] Jiang "again and again (yizai) raised the issue of opposing empiricism," demanding discussion by the Politburo. The issue was Party unity at the highest level. More than Jiang's anti-Zhou lobbying which did not seem to bother Mao or the Premier overly, the crucial factor for the Chairman was the resurfacing of Deng-Jiang tension, much along the lines of the *Fengqing* incident. In the course of her repeated demands, Jiang seemingly again provoked Deng. Although there is less detail available than for the previous October, the claim that Jiang "again and again" pushed the issue and met Deng's abrasive opposition suggests the same sort of personality clash. In this case, while the potential threat of a major anti-empiricism campaign to the implementation of the readjustment program was undoubtedly involved, the difficulties Jiang's disruptions were causing for Politburo business would have been central to Mao, who clearly wanted consolidation to proceed under Deng. In another parallel to October 1974, Zhou Enlai talked with both Deng and Jiang, meeting with Deng on April 11th and 14th, and Jiang on the 12th, apparently again trying to smooth over the situation. In the new circumstances, Deng approached Mao on the 18th, with or without the Premier's advice.[134] The emphasis on Deng in official accounts, however, avoids an intriguing aspect of the situation. Since Wang Hongwen was in charge of the Party Center and chaired Politburo meetings at this juncture, any unwillingness, or at least hesitation, to proceed with Jiang's demands presumably involved him too. In any case, once Deng decided to seek Mao's support, the stage was set for a major change in the radicals' fortunes, including those of Wang.

---

[132] E.g., *Zhou nianpu,* vol. 3, pp. 702, 704.

[133] The timing is given simply as "the middle part of April" (*siyue zhongxu*), which covers the period April 11 to 20; *Zhou nianpu,* vol. 3, p. 702. Since the entry goes on to talk of separate meetings of Zhou with Deng and Jiang over the April 11-14 period, it seems probable that the Politburo incidents started on or about the 11th.

[134] *Zhou nianpu,* vol. 3, p. 702; Gao Wenqian, *Wannian Zhou,* p. 553; Mao Mao, *"Wenge" suiyue,* p. 354; and above, p. 208. Mao Mao described her father's reaction to Jiang's demands as "not at all polite" (*hao bukeqi*).

The Decline of the Radicals

Mao, of course, was the key to unraveling the empiricism issue. As of mid-April, neither Deng nor the radicals could be certain where the Chairman stood on the matter, a situation which persisted even after he began to articulate his views. Mao had, whether by oversight or not, approved the use of his 1959 statement, "at present, the main danger lies in empiricism," in Yao's article and, perhaps, in Zhang's speech to army political directors. Yao Wenyuan, undoubtedly thinking there were no theoretical problems and surely unaware of Deng's exchange with Mao on April 18, attempted to obtain Mao's further endorsement by compiling and sending to the Chairman a report critical of empiricism on the 20th.[135] In these circumstances, Deng's approach to Mao on the 18th was arguably his boldest political move since his return to office. Using the opportunity of seeing Mao following the Chairman's reception of Kim Il Sung, Deng was undoubtedly emboldened by the Chairman's remarks to Kim. Noting that he himself was ill and would be 82 that year, and that the Premier, Kang Sheng and Liu Bocheng were all seriously ill, Mao advised Kim to talk politics with Deng, whom he described as able to fight battles and oppose revisionism, someone who had been purged by the Red Guards, but now was again standing up. After Kim left, in addition to expressing his objections to the actions of Jiang and Zhang, Deng stated he could not agree with the formulation that empiricism was the main danger in the current circumstances.[136]

In contrast to post-Mao depictions of the exchange, Deng probably raised these matters in a low-key manner, seeking guidance on how to proceed. The crucial point, in any case, is that Deng somehow obtained Mao's support, presumably because of the importance the Chairman attached to his consolidation efforts, and due to concern that the radicals were damaging stability and unity. Five days later, on April 23, Mao issued a statement on Yao's April 20 report that clearly, albeit subtly, changed the ideological landscape, and criticized the political and theoretical credentials of the radicals:

> It seems the formulation should be opposing revisionism, including opposing empiricism and dogmatism, since both revise Marxism-Leninism. Don't mention one part, [and] let the other part go. ... In our Party there are not many who truly understand Marxism-Leninism. Some people think they do, but in fact they don't fully understand [even though] they think they are right [and] always lecture others. ... This is a problem for the Politburo to discuss.[137]

Mao's comment changed the political dynamic of elite politics as well as the ideological landscape. In the official account, on the 27th, the Politburo met to study the spirit of his statement, with Deng, Ye Jianying and others using the occasion to criticize Jiang and Zhang sternly for their errors in opposing

---

[135] *RMRB*, March 3, 1977, in *SPRCP*, no. 6298 (1977), p. 3. The degree to which this report actually focused on empiricism, however, is unclear. Cf. above, p. 289n127.

[136] See *Mao zhuan*, vol. 2, pp. 1729-30; and Mao Mao, *"Wenge" suiyue*, p. 354.

[137] *Mao zhuan*, vol. 2, p. 1730.

empiricism. This was then followed by Mao's last appearance at the Politburo on May 3, where he personally criticized the radicals, again raising the "gang of four" issue. Finally, on May 27 and June 3, with Deng now chairing the Politburo, the strong criticism continued, thus forcing radical self-criticisms, and setting the stage for completing the transfer of power to Deng. Once again, there is substantial truth in official claims, but the reality was more complicated.

The meeting on April 27, chaired by Wang Hongwen, intensified conflict within the Politburo. While it is difficult to gauge with any precision the extent of the attacks on the radicals, Jiang found herself at loggerheads with Deng, and in a vulnerable position given Mao's statement of the 23rd. In addition to criticism of her stance on empiricism, Deng and Ye Jianying extended their attacks to Jiang's December 1973 assertion that criticism of Zhou Enlai was the "eleventh line struggle" in CCP history, and to her factionalist activities during *pi Lin pi Kong*, forcing her to make a self-examination. After the meeting, Jiang approached Zhang Yufeng to accuse the Politburo of attacking her in a repeat of the Lushan plenum,[138] obviously hoping that Mao would again come to her rescue. In addition, exercising his responsibility for Party Center work, Wang Hongwen wrote to Mao to report on what had transpired, and reportedly claimed that Ye and Deng sought to reverse the verdict on the December 1973 Politburo meeting, which had been Mao's initiative. Meanwhile, in the immediate aftermath of April 27, "some comrades" (presumably the radicals) complained that the criticism had been excessive and represented a "surprise attack." Jiang would later claim that Deng had launched a struggle against her on April 27 that lasted more than a month, without the Chairman's approval.[139]

All of this, however, seemingly overstates the nature of the criticism, and ignores the fact that Mao's anti-revisionist line was strictly adhered to. In addressing charges of excess and surprise attack a month after the April 27 meeting, Deng argued that the criticism had in fact been limited, not touching on even 40 percent of the radicals' problems, probably not even 20 percent. Even more to the point, their errors were strictly defined as exceeding the Chairman's guidelines, and throughout the entire month plus of attacks, Deng sought to confine criticism to what Mao had actually said. Thus criticizing Zhou and Ye in December 1973, for what Deng still referred to as their "revisionist line," was completely justified, but, as Mao had declared at the time, talking of an "eleventh line struggle" was not. Carrying out the campaign against Lin Biao and Confucius was necessary, but introducing the back door issue and fomenting factionalism violated Mao's intention, just as the focus on empiricism assertedly distorted his call to study the dictatorship of the proletariat. Whatever the actual

---

[138] At Lushan in 1970, Lin Biao's followers attacked Zhang Chunqiao, and by extension Jiang, but Mao intervened to back Zhang and Jiang. See Teiwes and Sun, *Tragedy*, pp. 144-49.

[139] Mao Mao, *"Wenge" suiyue*, p. 355; *Zhou nianpu*, vol. 3, p. 703; Gao Wenqian, *Wannian Zhou*, pp. 554-55; and "Jiang Qing zai dazhaohu huiyi," pp. 374, 377.

extent of the attack on the radicals on April 27, uncertainty remained concerning the parameters of what Mao would allow.[140]

Uncertainty could be seen in various developments after the meeting and into May. Wang Hongwen, who apparently received little if any personal criticism at the meeting on the 27th, seemingly made no objection to Deng and Ye's criticism of the radicals concerning empiricism in his report to Mao. On this and other issues, however, in the plausible view of Gao Wenqian, Wang underestimated Mao's annoyance with the radical position and downplayed the Chairman's objections in leadership discussions, with the result that a dissatisfied Chairman placed Deng in charge of future Politburo meetings criticizing Jiang Qing. But Wang's lack of clarity was not unique. Zhou Enlai, who scrambled to understand what had happened on the 27th,[141] was also unsure how to interpret Mao's opinion on empiricism, even after the Chairman's appearance at the Politburo on May 3, and behaved with typical caution throughout. As indicated above, discussions were immediately held in the Standing Committee on May 4 concerning how to convey Mao's views of April 23 and May 3, and Zhou set about drafting a document on studying Mao's theoretical views, but delayed reporting to Mao. Eleven days later, after consulting with Wang in detail on the situation in the Politburo, the Premier finally submitted a report to the Chairman, apologized for being slow to understand Mao's directives and not acting promptly, and assumed complete personal responsibility. Of course, both Zhou and Wang could be excused for being slow to understand, given Mao's own lack of clarity concerning how far he wanted to go with the matter. Specifically, when Mao instructed Wang to convey his April 23 comments on empiricism to the Politburo, he specified that these not be publicized, thus suggesting a desire to keep criticism of the radicals within bounds.[142]

The meeting on May 3 was not simply significant for deepening the criticism of the radicals which would last until early June.[143] Beyond its immediate effect, the meeting was notable for what it said about the texture of elite politics in the late Maoist era, and concerning the Chairman's attitude toward his leadership colleagues. This was, as noted, the last Politburo meeting Mao attended, the last occasion on which he saw many of his ranking subordinates. The most poignant case concerned Zhou Enlai, a man who had faithfully served Mao for three and a half decades, and who had earlier been solicitous of Mao's sensibilities,

---

[140] See Chen and Du, *Shilu*, vol. 3, part 2, pp. 1219-20; and Gao Wenqian, *Wannian Zhou*, pp. 554-55, 563-64.

[141] Zhou consulted with Deng, Wang, Hua Guofeng, Wu De and Chen Xilian on April 29-30, and also had a secretary gather materials on the anti-empiricism campaign for him to examine. *Zhou nianpu*, vol. 3, pp. 703-704.

[142] See *Zhou nianpu*, vol. 3, pp. 704-707; and Gao Wenqian, *Wannian Zhou*, pp. 560-62.

[143] According to Mao Mao, *"Wenge" suiyue*, p. 356, Wang's report on the April 27 meeting only made Mao more unhappy and determined to prevent the radicals from stirring up further trouble by dealing with them face-to-face.

even when on the other side of political issues and outranking him during the revolutionary period.[144] While Mao had for many years entrusted Zhou with some of the most sensitive tasks, recently including the NPC personnel arrangements and conveying his instructions concerning the study of the dictatorship of the proletariat, over the previous two years the Chairman had initiated or endorsed some of the most searching criticisms the Premier had ever endured. Once Zhou moved into hospital quarters a mere five hundred meters from Mao's residence in mid-1974, Mao never visited him. And when Zhou welcomed Mao at the start of the May 3 meeting, his earnest comment about how he had missed seeing the Chairman was brushed off with a perfunctory "how are you," and Mao then barely responded to the Premier's statement that he had had three operations. During the long meeting itself Zhou was almost an irrelevancy, with virtually his only contribution to call for its conclusion because the Chairman must be tired. In taking his leave of the Premier for the last time, Mao referred to the "three do's and three don'ts,"[145] the warning he laid down after September 13 to avoid the type of traitorous activities engaged in by Lin Biao. Zhou's sad plight simply underscored how even a senior revolutionary, widely respected and, in a real sense, representative of the interests of the most powerful establishment forces, could be reduced to next to nothing in the presence of the great leader. It perhaps was also a factor influencing the Premier's submission to Mao of a review of his "mistakes and crimes" over the previous 40 years little more than a month later.[146]

Other Politburo members received warmer, if sometimes puzzling, greetings from Mao. The Chairman addressed Chen Xilian as "commander," and suggested a greater command role awaited him, as indeed turned out to be the case in early 1976 when Chen assumed Ye Jianying's responsibility for MAC daily work. Mao greeted Wu De with an enigmatic play on his name, "*Wu De you de*" (Wu De is virtuous), an ostensible greeting of praise, but one that left Wu anxious and wondering whether it somehow foreshadowed a new struggle. Wu was only relieved when he approached Zhang Yufeng subsequently and was told that the Chairman's meaning was to rebut complaints Jiang Qing had made against him.[147] To Su Zhenhua, Mao declared that "the navy can only rely on you."[148] He

---

[144] Cf. Zhou's sensitive treatment of Mao in 1932 when Zhou replaced Mao as general political commisar of the Red Army. Teiwes with Sun, *Formation*, pp. 43-44.

[145] "Practice Marxism, and not revisionism; unite, and don't split; be open and aboveboard, and don't intrigue and conspire."

[146] Mao Zedong, "Tong zai jing zhongyang zhengzhiju weiyuan de tanhua" [Talk with Politburo Members in Beijing] (May 3, 1975), in *CRDB*, pp. 1-3. Mao's comments to other participants in the meeting, discussed in the following paragraph, also come from this source. On Zhou's submission, see above, p. 3.

[147] Interview with senior Party historian, February 2000. Mao had previously used the "*Wu De you de*" phrase shortly after the Lin Biao affair, but this apparently did not alleviate Wu's anxieties.

[148] Mao's concern with the navy was seen in his comment that it was very small and did not scare

greeted peasant Politburo member Chen Yonggui with praise for his "wonderful" letter proposing that he (Chen) spend two-thirds of his time away from Beijing, remarking that Chen and alternate member Wu Guixian should move out of Diaoyutai, the state guesthouse where the radicals were based.[149] Wu was a factory worker promoted to great heights under Mao's Cultural Revolution policies, but his comment to her that "I don't know you" indicated decidedly less interest than he had in such military veterans as Chen Xilian and Su Zhenhua, or in Xie Jingyi from his own household unit, whom he addressed as a "big official."[150] In addition to his remark about Wu and Chen Yonggui's living arrangements, Mao jokingly noted that Ji Dengkui, who had temporarily moved into Diaoyutai while his home was being renovated, was in danger of joining a "gang of five." Given Ji's clear antipathy to the radicals in 1975, such a comment arguably indicated that Mao's comments about a "gang of four," which would again be aired at the meeting, were less definitive than post-Mao official commentary has claimed. Above all, Mao's sometimes obscure comments, and the nervous reactions of those present, only emphasized his absolute authority.

Mao's substantive message to the meeting as a whole was detrimental to the radicals, although distinctions must be made among them. Jiang Qing was overwhelmingly his main target, similar to the situation at the July 17 Politburo meeting the previous year. Although described in various accounts as a principal person in the empiricism affair, it is unclear whether Zhang Chunqiao was singled out for criticism by the Chairman who, in fact, apologized to Zhang for overlooking the empiricism issue in Zhang's March 1 speech.[151] Moreover, although Yao Wenyuan could not avoid responsibility for the alleged theoretical mistakes of the March-April period, there is no direct evidence that he was individually criticized by Mao then or later. Most interesting, there is little to suggest that Wang Hongwen, who seemingly had earlier escaped criticism on April 27, was specifically criticized on the 3rd, even though Wang would be forced to undertake a self-examination a month later. This again underlined the vexed situation whereby whatever the faults of the other radicals, they were further damaged by Jiang's excesses—and Mao's fixation with those excesses. Indeed, when Jiang submitted her relatively far-reaching written self-criticism on June

---

any enemies, and something should be done about this. On May 23, he approved a navy proposal for strengthening the service over a ten-year period. See Chen and Du, *Shilu*, vol. 3, part 2, p. 1212.

[149] Although Chen was on exceptionally bad terms with Zhang Chunqiao (see below, p. 502), his reasons for wanting to leave Diaoyutai seemingly had more to do with boredom concerning theoretical study organized by Wang Hongwen. Wu Si, *Chen Yonggui*, p. 156. Chen's proposal was to spend one-third of his time at the Center, another third carrying out investigations, and the final third engaged in labor.

[150] Xie replied that she didn't want such a high office, and Mao told her to "just try." Although not a Politburo member, Xie apparently had the right to attend its meetings. Cf. above, p. 221.

[151] See Chen and Du, *Shilu*, vol. 3, part 2, p. 1212; Cheng and Xia, *Deng zai yijiuqiwu*, p. 195; and above, p. 290.

28, she not only acknowledged that she had to bear the main responsibility for the radicals' mistakes, but also that the other three suffered because of her.[152]

On the theoretical issue, Mao elaborated upon and reinforced his April 23 comment. He remarked that those who only talked about and only hated empiricism while ignoring doctrinairism in fact didn't have much Marxism themselves, since both empiricism and doctrinairism revise Marxism-Leninism. Even more sharply, Mao criticized the radicals for falling prey to empiricism themselves, specifically declaring Jiang Qing a "petty empiricist." Having rejected their theoretical position and directly criticized some of them in front of their Politburo colleagues, the Chairman further undermined the radicals' position by addressing critically, apparently for the first time, developments in the superstructure area where their influence had been most profound. Adopting a posture considerably more positive toward intellectuals than that associated with the radicals (or himself recently, for that matter), Mao noted that in educational, literary and art, journalistic and medical circles, there were some good intellectuals with a bit of Marxism-Leninism. Crucially, and in sharp contrast to the motif of the Cultural Revolution, Mao declared the need for intellectuals, that "'the stinking ninth category' [intellectuals] should not go away." It is no accident that Zhou Rongxin's initial efforts at educational readjustment came shortly thereafter.[153]

The Chairman's most important criticism of the radicals reflected his by now overriding concern with Party unity. In this regard, he lent his voice to the complaints of senior Politburo members at the April 27 meeting. While Mao apparently did not mention the criticism of Zhou Enlai in December 1973, he did weigh in on questions of factional excesses during the Lin Biao and Confucius campaign, particularly the distortion of the movement by introducing the back door theme that threatened Ye Jianying. The factional fighting and lack of Party discipline in early 1974 now retrospectively alarmed Mao, and it was Jiang Qing's undisciplined behavior at that time which drew his pointed rebuke. During that intense phase of the campaign, Jiang had issued documents to PLA and government units in her own name; now Mao attacked the practice of documents being issued in the names of individuals, including his own, and insisted all such documents be distributed in the name of the Party Center. Reemphasizing "stability and unity" and the "three dos and three don'ts," Mao chastised the radicals by demanding that they stop behaving like a "gang of four," asked why they didn't unite with the more than 200 Central Committee members, demanded prudent and disciplined behavior instead of going their own way, and told them to raise their concerns in collective discussions within the Politburo. Apart from his specific criticisms, the Chairman demanded that the Politburo have a good

---

[152] See *Mao zhuan*, vol. 2, p. 1738.

[153] See *Mao zhuan*, vol. 2, pp. 1732-33; Chen and Du, *Shilu*, vol. 3, part 2, p. 1212; Mao Mao, *"Wenge" suiyue*, pp. 356-57; Ma Qibin, *Sishinian*, p. 384; above, p. 270; and below, pp. 341-42.

discussion about what he had said.[154]

The evidence indicates, however, that Mao's position at the May 3 meeting was less one-sided than standard accounts present. Jiang Qing, for one, made precisely this claim when attacking Deng Xiaoping in March 1976, and within limits her version is credible. According to Jiang, Mao had criticized both sides at the meeting, with only 50 percent directed at them, but Deng subsequently depicted the Chairman's views as only directed at the radicals. She asserted that Mao required both sides to read Marxist books, demanded prudence from the military and all Central Committee members, not just the radicals, that he didn't mention a Shanghai gang (she less plausibly denied he spoke of a "gang of four"), but did speak of Guangdong and Hunan factions, and criticized the penchant of intellectuals to think that "foreign moons were rounder than a Chinese one." Even official accounts provide support for Jiang's version, as the Chairman's demands for Party unity had a larger aim than simply to call the radicals to account. The reference to Guangdong and Hunan factions apparently was not a code for any contemporary individuals, but a general plea for everyone to pull together and avoid the situation of the early 1920s when the respective labor movement groups on the Canton-Hankow Railroad shunned people from the other locales. The underlying message was that the Politburo members should seek unity and work out their problems among themselves. Mao said he had spoken to Jiang and Deng once each, and didn't want to be drawn into further discussions. Moreover, Mao's displeasure with the radicals was still limited even as he called for their self-criticism, and he indicated the problem they had caused did not require immediate solution. As he put it, "I don't see this as a big problem, don't make a big fuss. But when there are problems, it is good to make things clear. If they cannot be solved in the first half of this year, then the second half; if not this year, then next year; if not next year, then the year after next."[155]

The situation at and following the meeting was perceptively summarized by Deng's daughter Mao Mao, writing a quarter of a century later. Three things defined her assessment. First, as noted above, Mao's criticism of "Jiang Qing and company" was limited, he didn't fundamentally attack their errors. Second, the Chairman's poor health meant he could not really deal with the situation. And finally, Jiang and the others only feared Mao: secure in the knowledge of his underlying strong backing, they would take no heed of anyone else. As a result, even with Mao's rebukes of May 3, they would only modify their behavior rather than fundamentally change.[156] This is not a completely accurate assessment,

[154] See *Mao zhuan*, vol. 2, pp. 1732-33; Chen and Du, *Shilu*, vol. 3, part 2, p. 1212; Mao Mao, *"Wenge" suiyue*, pp. 356-57; and above, p. 154.

[155] "Jiang Qing zai dazhaohu huiyi," pp. 375-76; Chen and Du, *Shilu*, vol. 3, part 2, p. 1212; Mao Mao, *"Wenge" suiyue*, p. 357; and interview with senior Party historian, January 2005.

[156] Mao Mao, *"Wenge" suiyue*, p. 357.

however, since it was more Mao's contradictory perception of the situation than his health that prevented decisive action, and the radicals did indeed have to take heed of the new circumstances.

The criticism by Mao at his last appearance before the Politburo, although limited, served to erode further the position of the radicals. This could be seen in Zhang Chunqiao's unwillingness to defend himself against Zhou's characterization of his actions at the meeting of army political directors, and in Jiang Qing's subsequent low profile. For the remainder of May, bolstered by Mao's demand that the Politburo deal with the problem, the leadership grappled with the situation, starting with the Standing Committee meeting on the 4th for the purpose of organizing a central document and full Politburo discussions on the issues raised by the Chairman. Despite uncertainty and tardiness in reporting to Mao, this provided an opportunity to bring additional pressure on the radicals. In the document he drafted on May 4-5, Zhou criticized the disruptive effect of the attacks on empiricism, and made detailed suggestions on the proper handling of issues and the issuing of documents. He affirmed the Chairman's demand that the radicals make self-criticisms, but was careful to indicate that he agreed with Deng that these did not have to be pushed to the limit. Further preparations were made at another Standing Committee meeting on the 8th, with agreement reached that the full Politburo meeting would be convened following Deng's return from his May 12-17 state visit to France. Wang Hongwen, given his duties at the Party Center, played a significant part in these preparations, even though Mao judged him too weak in dealing with Jiang Qing and handed responsibility for future Politburo meetings to Deng. In particular, in a long phone call on May 14, Zhou and Wang reviewed in detail the circumstances of the coming Politburo meeting. Following further leadership exchanges from May 21, during which Zhang Chunqiao grudgingly accepted Zhou's version of his March 1 speech to army leaders, and more importantly Deng turned the focus on Jiang Qing's treatment of the empiricism issue in the Politburo, the stage was set for the climactic Politburo meetings of May 27 and June 3, when the radicals were subject to searching criticism.[157]

With Deng Xiaoping in the chair and Zhou Enlai not attending due to his illness, or perhaps out of a desire to avoid a confrontation with Jiang Qing, the agenda of the two Politburo meetings was to study the spirit of the Chairman's opinions at the May 3 meeting and "help" the radicals overcome their shortcomings. This assertedly led to "pointed and sharp" criticism by a range of Politburo members, first by Deng, and subsequently by Ye Jianying, Wu De, Li Xiannian and Chen Xilian, while all those attending undoubtedly participated in the ritual, with varying degrees of intensity. Deng began the process on the 27th by repeating Mao's arguments about unity and the "three dos and three don'ts,"

---

[157] *Ibid.*, p. 358; *Zhou nianpu,* vol. 3, pp. 704-708; Cheng and Xia, *Deng zai yijiuqiwu,* p. 196; and Gao Wenqian, *Wannian Zhou,* p. 561.

with particular reference to the Party life of the Politburo itself, and by refuting the claims that the earlier criticisms of April 27 had been excessive. Li and Chen echoed Deng's arguments, while Wu picked up on his call for vigilance against factionalism and forming a "gang of four" by demanding to know why they continued to act in such a fashion despite Mao having warned them three times against becoming such a "gang." On June 3, the main criticism was made by Ye Jianying, apparently in a harsher tone than that adopted by Deng on the occasion. Ye emphasized the negative effect on Party unity of the radicals acting as a small group, disparaged them for treating the Marxist-Leninist books they had read as private property, criticized their alleged failure to consult Mao, demanded strict organizational discipline, and harked back to the events of late 1973 and early 1974 when he (Ye) had been under attack. Once again, Jiang Qing was the main target of criticism, but an important new stage had been reached in these Politburo sessions since late April in that Mao had, for the first time, authorized the Politburo to criticize Jiang. It was one thing for the Chairman to dress down his wife within the confines of the body, another to extend the right to the collective. By the end of the June 3 meeting, Jiang, as well as Wang Hongwen, was forced to make a self-examination, and each of the radicals was required to prepare a written self-criticism.[158]

Of the two self-examinations on June 3, Jiang Qing's seemed particularly bland. From the available accounts, she merely acknowledged that her earlier self-criticism of April 27 was insufficient, that she would have to understand deeply her new unsuitable behavior and make further self-examination. In contrast, Wang Hongwen's offering was more specific and revealing. Part of his self-criticism dealt with the initial stage of the campaign against Lin Biao and Confucius. While accepting fault in not applying the spirit of the Tenth Party Congress to these developments, including the back door issue, and holding the January 1974 mass rallies without prior notification of the Chairman, Wang suggested a certain distance between himself and the worst excesses of the period. Thus he only "participated" in the January rallies, felt uncomfortable about the excesses, and exchanged views with "certain comrades," but in the end supported them. But perhaps the most important part concerned the period (June 1974-June 1975) "when I was in charge of the Party Center for more than a year." Wang pointed to the *Fengqing* incident, suggesting that he was obliged to go to Changsha to report to the Chairman, but that he had erred by listening only to the opinions of one side, and not listening to Deng Xiaoping. As for the empiricism issue, which ostensibly was the cause of the Politburo discussions, Wang claimed he had little understanding of this issue and had not given it serious attention. More generally, he said he had reservations on some issues, although it is unclear what they were, or what the implications of these reservations were for leadership politics. All in all, Wang seemed to be saying he must assume responsibility for

---

[158] See Mao Mao, *"Wenge" suiyue*, pp. 362-63; *Mao zhuan*, vol. 2, pp. 1731, 1735, 1737-38; Chen and Du, *Shilu*, vol. 3, part 2, pp. 1219-20, 1223-24; and *Zhou nianpu*, vol. 3, p. 709.

mistakes during his watch at the Party Center, but that he was far from deeply involved in all of these.[159]

As in cases of other meetings where the radicals came under fire, it is difficult to know just how tense the May 27 and June 3 Politburo sessions were. That they were unpleasant for the radicals is clear, even if Jiang's subsequent assertion that Deng and company had shat on her for several months is surely exaggerated. That there was a great deal of animus on the part of the establishment types on the Politburo is also clear; Deng reported to Mao in June that there was particular anger at the radicals' claim that they had not formed a "gang of four," and also the feeling that Wang's self-examination was "insincere." With that acknowledged, however, it is equally clear that, as the Chairman had stipulated, there were limits on the attacks the radicals suffered at the meetings. For one thing, since the framework for the sessions was Mao's theoretical demarche, apart from restricting attacks on the radicals to matters explicitly criticized by him, *all* Politburo members were required to undertake self-criticism for their deficiencies in this regard. Ironically, notional empiricists like Deng wound up making self-examinations of their own dogmatism, seemingly with greater enthusiasm than the radicals could muster.[160] But the key was not pressing the radicals to the limit. While, according to Gao Wenqian, all Politburo members were hesitant to launch attacks on the Chairman's wife, with Ye Jianying finally breaking the silence after Deng spoke on the 27th, the guiding hand was that of Deng Xiaoping. As we have seen in the final quotation at the head of this chapter, in the period immediately following the arrest of the "gang of four," with criticism of Deng *de rigueur*, internal discussions (unfairly) targeted his "softness" toward the radicals.[161] In any case, however searching the criticism within the Politburo or low her public profile, Jiang continued to act like a "queen" (*nüwang*) in her interactions with elite personalities—including with Deng's family.[162]

Perhaps the clearest indication of Deng's lenient approach and the circumstances surrounding it, as well as of other aspects of elite politics in mid-1975, came during his remarkable meeting with Mao sometime in June. In his report to Mao, Deng noted that although there was considerable anger among Politburo members, he had laid down that the radicals should not be pursued

---

[159] Chen and Du, *Shilu*, vol. 3, part 2, p. 1224. Wang's claim regarding the empiricism issue is credible in that he appears to have been more involved in the anti-factionalism measures of the period—i.e., activities led by Deng.

[160] See "Jiang Qing zai dazhaohu huiyi," p. 374; Chen and Du, *Shilu*, vol. 3, part 2, p. 1234; and "Geng Biao guanyu sirenbang qingkuang," p. 2.

[161] Gao Wenqian, *Wannian Zhou*, p. 564. In addition to Geng Biao's comment, above, p. 245, Ye Jianying spoke of Deng's efforts to unite with the radicals, while Tan Zhenlin complained that Deng let criticism end when the "gang" refused to admit their mistakes. "Zhongyang lingdaoren guanyu sirenbang," p. 2; and "Li Xiannian, Chen Yun, Tan Zhenlin de jianghua," p.1.

[162] See Mao Mao's account of Jiang's behavior, *"Wenge" suiyue*, pp. 364-65.

to the very end, that a few words of self-criticism would do. Deng apparently further recommended that since the radicals were unwilling to talk, the criticism should be ended. Of course, in doing this Deng was reading Mao's intentions, and his accurate assessment was confirmed when Mao responded that "this is a good method, leave them some leeway, as long as everyone has an idea that's enough." Mao also said that he would call in Wang Hongwen and tell him to seek out and listen to Deng. When Deng noted that Politburo members considered Wang's self-criticism insincere, the Chairman replied that Wang's prestige was not high, and further observed that Jiang did not like Wang and "complains to me about him." Thus while Mao was again advocating that the two sides talk to one another in his pursuit of the elusive Party unity, his remarks also suggest that he had reason to think that any "gang of four" was not set in cement. Finally, and crucially, Mao indicated that Deng, at least for the time being, had his full trust and would be responsible for all work. Deng observed that some might oppose him, leading to Mao's observation (quoted at the start of this chapter) about the tallest tree facing the storm. Deng acknowledged he was being placed on a knife's edge, but pledged to carry out the Chairman's assignment.[163]

As Mao put it to Deng, "the direction of the wind [was] changing in the Politburo." The process of criticizing the radicals finally wound down by the end of June with Jiang's written self-examination and self-criticisms by the others, and Yao, as well as Wang, was dispatched to Shanghai, albeit in Yao's case for only a few weeks. But definite limits remained, as again analyzed by Deng's daughter many years later. In Mao Mao's view, the Chairman's actions were for the purpose of demonstrating his support of Deng, something necessary to further the consolidation agenda, but he "absolutely" did not seek to knock Jiang Qing down. In fact, Mao continued to pursue the unrealistic goal of Party unity. Similar to his prescriptions for Wang Hongwen, Mao directed Jiang to visit Deng, an encounter which was brief and seemingly not satisfactory to either side. His hope was that Jiang and Deng could cooperate, as they had in the recent past, and that the criticism she had endured would both lead Jiang to restrain herself, and satisfy Deng. Zhou Enlai recognized this, and following Jiang's comparatively stringent self-criticism on June 28[164] called in several Politburo members to advise them to let the matter rest, and strive for unity. As for Jiang, she not only emphasized the damage she had done to unity, the overriding theme of the

---

[163] See *ibid.*, p. 366; Chen and Du, *Shilu*, vol. 3, part 2, p. 1234; Mao Zedong, "Tong Deng Xiaoping guanyu piping 'sirenbang'," p. 1; and "Geng Biao guanyu sirenbang qingkuang," p. 2. Cf. *Deng Liqun guoshi jiangtan*, vol. 3, pp. 346-47.

[164] The self-criticisms of Wang, Zhang and Yao were reportedly superficial, with Zhang reportedly only saying he would follow Mao's instruction about not forming a "gang of four," and strive to unite with more comrades. Jiang, however, seemingly was required to go further on the same theme, stating that she had been shocked but helped by the criticism at the Politburo meetings which made her realize the damage the four were causing to Party unity. Yao Wenyuan's self-criticism is not available, but it surely followed the unity theme.

self-criticisms of all the radicals, she also had to moderate her behavior even though she undoubtedly hated the situation—a mood that would not have been improved by rumors resulting from her low profile that she had been deprived of her positions, sent to a labor camp, or had even committed suicide.[165] Meanwhile, the Premier further contributed to unity on June 16 with his grotesque self-examination of 40 years of "mistakes and crimes," an effort which met Mao's demand that everyone engage in self-criticism, while yet again displaying his excessive zeal in self-flagellation.[166]

Despite Mao's demand for unity, no real solution of the underlying conflict between Jiang and Deng, or the radicals and establishment forces more broadly, was possible. The fundamental problem for Deng as the wind changed direction was uncertainty concerning the sustainability of the change. While there is little doubt about Mao's confidence in Deng as of June 1975, several dangers lurked. One was overconfidence by engaging in political struggle despite Mao's call for unity. The radicals had overstepped the line in carrying out the dictatorship of the proletariat campaign a few months earlier, and now, in less blatant fashion, Deng's forces risked a similar mistake. During June-July, Deng and others violated Politburo confidentiality to reveal Mao's criticism of the "gang." As we have seen, Ji Dengkui had done this in Zhejiang by informing Tie Ying of Mao's remarks to bolster local determination to suppress radicalism. Deng had already done the same in Shanghai on June 12, revealing, in an indirect and exploratory manner, Mao's views to Party First Secretary Ma Tianshui. Deng's apparent aim was to win over Ma, an old cadre who had become part of the radical Shanghai establishment during the Cultural Revolution, but Ma quickly informed key local Shanghai radicals and at least Yao Wenyuan and Wang Hongwen (but definitely not Jiang Qing) of the encounter. The most sustained case occurred at the June-July MAC conference, where Ye Jianying called in military region leaders one by one, not only to inform them of the situation in the Politburo, but also to warn them of the need to prevent "plotters like Jiang Qing" from interfering in the PLA. A conference participant worried that this was overreaching, and believes today that Mao became aware of it at some point, leading to Ye's subsequent sidelining.[167] As suggested, Zhou Enlai shared these qualms. During this period,

[165] See Mao Mao, *"Wenge" suiyue*, pp. 363-66; Yan and Gao, *Turbulent Decade*, p. 465; *Zhou nianpu*, vol. 3, p. 713; *Deng Liqun guoshi jiangtan*, vol. 3, p. 347; Gao Wenqian, *Wannian Zhou*, pp. 565, 567-68; Cheng and Xia, *Deng zai yijiuqiwu*, p. 202; Chen and Du, *Shilu*, vol. 3, part 2, p. 1224; and "Jiang Qing zai dazhaohu huiyi," p. 383.

[166] See above, p. 3.

[167] Mao Mao, *"Wenge" suiyue*, p. 365; *Deng nianpu*, vol. 1, p. 56; Chen and Du, *Shilu*, vol. 3, part 2, p. 1242; Sima Dongqu, *Haojie: Shanghaitan, yige Zhongyang gongzuozu chengyuan de erwen mudu* [Catastrophy: Shanghai, as Heard and Seen by a Central Work Team Member] (Beijing: Zhonggong zhongyang dangxiao chubanshe, 1999), pp. 89-91; *Shanghai "wenhua dageming" shihua*, p. 777; Wang Nianyi, *Dadongluan*, p. 525; interviews with senior Party historians, November and December 2002; interview with participant in the MAC conference, January 2005; and above, p. 280. In addition to Ye's case, according to a senior Party historian Mao also became aware of the Deng-Ma

with various Politburo members excited by the criticism of the radicals and hoping to topple Jiang, Wu De sought the Premier's advice. It was now that Zhou offered his previously cited cautionary warning that Mao was still observing and direct confrontation with the radicals should be avoided.[168] Mao's demand for unity called for a cautious approach to the inevitable ongoing struggle, and while these maneuvers were more subtle than the radicals' activities in March-April, they still stretched Party norms.

An even greater danger lurked in the policy realm: Mao's internally contradictory objectives and attitudes, the tension among his three directives, between Cultural Revolution goals and national development. The danger could be seen in the "seven whethers," criteria for assessing progress laid down in the June 4 decision on the iron and steel industry drafted under Deng, and approved by Mao. In listing the "seven whethers," the directive gave pride of place to ideological concerns—whether the ideological and political line is correct, whether the study of the dictatorship of the proletariat has been truly launched—relegating Deng's signature issues of the previous months (strong leadership, combating factionalism, conscientiously implementing Party policies) to lower positions.[169] While this was largely cosmetic, Deng undoubtedly felt it was required by the times. In any case, a new stage, summed up as "comprehensive consolidation," was beginning. The efforts of January-June had been fundamentally piecemeal, dealing with the specific problems of the PLA, railroads, the iron and steel industry, and other areas. Now, as Deng put it to Yu Guangyuan, the time had come for "consideration across the board."[170] But however much the wind had changed, uncertainties and ambiguity remained as the new phase of consolidation began to unfold.

---

exchange, although this seemingly did not take place until early 1976. Interview, January 2005. The complicated politics concerning the handling of Ma Tianshui's exposure of Deng's approach is discussed in Chapter 6.

[168] See above, p. 8. Zhou's advice appears to have been given sometime in May-June after Mao's May 3 criticism of the radicals, but our source could not be more precise. *Zhou nianpu*, vol. 3, p. 706, records Wu meeting Zhou about May 18.

[169] See *RMRB*, February 12, 1977, in *SPRCP*, no. 6288 (1977), pp. 1-2.

[170] See above, p. 247. There are differences concerning when comprehensive consolidation began. Wang and Sun, "Dang zuzhi zhengdun," p. 40, quite inaccurately, place this in January 1975. Mao Mao, *"Wenge" suiyue*, pp. 367ff, more plausibly begins the discussion of it essentially in May, but this too is too early. Comprehensive consolidation can best be regarded as occurring in July-September, the three months when Deng was unambiguously "in charge," and into October when his position began to erode.

Chapter 5

DENG'S PERIOD "IN CHARGE": COMPREHENSIVE CONSOLIDATION, JULY-OCTOBER 1975

Comrade Mao Zedong has recently given us three important instructions. First, study theory and combat and prevent revisionism. Second, achieve stability and unity. Third, boost the economy. These three instructions, being related to one another, form an organic whole and none of them should be left out. They form the key link in our work for the present period.

—Deng Xiaoping's talk to a theoretical study class organized by the Party Center two days after assuming responsibility for CCP daily work, July 4, 1975[1]

[During 1975] Comrade Chen Yun once asked Comrade Xiaoping, "Did you accurately get Chairman Mao's pulse [i.e., understand his meaning] or not?" Deng said, "I did."

—Deng Liqun's report on a 1975 exchange between Chen Yun and Deng Xiaoping[2]

The fifth draft [of the "Outline Report on the Work of the Academy of Sciences," one of the "three poisonous weeds" subsequently attacked during the anti-Deng campaign], was sent to Mao Zedong, and Deng Xiaoping went to report to [Mao] about it [in mid-October 1975]. He never expected that Mao Zedong would not approve it. The "Quotations of Chairman Mao on Science and Technology Work" [included in the draft] used bold type to quote a statement of Mao Zedong's: "Science and technology is a force of production." Mao Zedong said he did not recall saying this. Deng Xiaoping said that Marx also had said something like it, but Mao Zedong still could not recall saying it himself.

—Recollection of Yu Guangyuan, one of the editors of the report[3]

By early July the pieces had fallen into place for Deng Xiaoping. The radicals were on the defensive after two months of criticism, for the first time Deng was responsible for the work of *all* key institutions as he formally took over the Party Center from Wang Hongwen on July 2,[4] and, most importantly, he had received Mao's blessing and trust concerning his expanded authority. Nevertheless, reflecting Chen Yun's warning about misreading the Chairman, Deng's time "in charge" would be limited to three to four months at most,[5] with signs of his being in trouble beginning to appear by mid-October, followed by Mao's clear signal that the situation was serious toward the end of the month. In addition to examining the policy developments Deng oversaw and their attendant politics, this chapter addresses several key questions: what actual authority and direction did Mao provide Deng; what were the circumstances of Deng's miscalculation; and when and why did the Chairman turn against his favorite leader for the second time? The full story of Mao's turn will be completed in the following chapter, but the roots of the Chairman's dissatisfaction lie in the period examined here.

As discussed in Chapter 4, a new stage of consolidation, which had been developing since Mao's April-May criticism of the radicals, emerged by July, a stage marked by a much more comprehensive agenda. This broader agenda was not simply a matter of new projects, or a shift from fixing specific problems to something more systematic. As with so much else, it reflected the changing wind

---

[1] *Selected Works of Deng (1975-1982)*, p. 23.

[2] From *Deng Liqun guoshi jiangtan*, vol. 3, p. 329, and vol. 5, p. 458. Deng Liqun commented that events proved Deng "had not grasped Mao's meaning [at all]." The precise dating of the encounter is unclear, but the official, who is the original source of the report based on information from Chen's family, believes it occurred somewhat earlier than the summer when Deng started to act with full confidence. Interview, January 2005

[3] Yu Guangyuan, "Yi Deng Xiaoping he zhengyanshi," p. 10. In this case Mao was correct in the sense that the remark could not be verified, although his comment in December 1963 conveyed the importance of science and technology to the forces of production. Of particular note is the importance both Mao and Deng attached to the sanctity of the Chairman's words, and the implication of Mao's dissatisfaction with the inaccuracy and by extension with the document. As Yu put it, the incident "brought about trouble." Cf. below, p. 337n97.

[4] Also note that while Ye Jianying was formally responsible for the military, Deng had been exercising the dominant role throughout the first half of 1975; above, p. 253. In addition, Wang Hongwen's departure for Shanghai suspended his responsibilities in this area.

[5] The period of Deng's responsibility for all work is subject to various interpretations, with both Deng and the radicals speaking of the three months from July to September as the height of his authority, although his responsibility certainly extended into October. See Mao Mao, *"Wenge" suiyue*, p. 394; and Ji Zhi [pseud.], *Sirenbang yanxinglu* [Record of the Words and Deeds of the Gang of Four] (Hong Kong: Wenhua ziliao gongyingsi, 1977), pp. 35-36. In strictly formal terms, it extended longer in that it was not until early 1976 that responsibility for State Council affairs was given to Hua Guofeng, and responsibility for Party daily affairs was either given to Hua or left ambiguous. In the same period Chen Xilian took control of MAC daily affairs from Ye Jianying. See below, pp. 440ff. In real terms, however, Deng's control can be considered longer than three months from the other end of the period in that he was seemingly exercising *de facto* control of the Party Center by late May when he chaired the Politburo meetings criticizing the radicals. Cf. above, p. 247n8.

in the Politburo. Previously there had been a more or less clear, although not absolute, division of responsibilities: Deng largely dealt with the economic base, while the radicals concerned themselves with ideology and the superstructure. With the radicals now in temporary retreat, Deng extended his authority into theory and the superstructure, which would soon contribute to his undoing. Signs of the new situation were Deng's formulation (*tifa*), cited above, that "the three directives are the key link of all work," a formulation initially used by him in late May[6] and now developing into a unifying theme, and the advocacy of a *comprehensive* (*quanmian*) understanding of Mao's Thought, as well as a *comprehensive* approach to consolidation.[7] In this Deng was developing his own interpretation of consolidation, one at notable variance from the "one-sided" approach of the radicals, but one whose relationship to Mao's thinking was neither clear-cut nor stable.

The key developments of this period can be divided into two categories: the steps taken by Deng in the development of his interpretation of Mao's consolidation, and events beginning in August that suggested potential conflict and led to or foreshadowed Deng's demise. The MAC meeting which ended in mid-July (see Chapter 4) was clearly part of Deng's effort, but it is arguably better considered the culmination of measures underway in the PLA since January, and in personnel terms for a considerably longer period.[8] More reflective of the new orientation was the establishment of a State Council Political Research Office in late June[9] which, under Hu Qiaomu's direction, answered to Deng and developed theoretical and policy positions over the following months. Another key development was a broad review of economic policy at a State Council theory conference led by Li Xiannian from mid-June to mid-August, a review leading to the drafting by the SPC of "Some Problems in Speeding Up Industrial Development," the 20 articles on industry for short. The 20 articles would be denounced in 1976 as one of the "three poisonous weeds" along with

---

[6] The first recorded occasion was on May 29 in a speech to the forum on iron and steel work; Mao Mao, *"Wenge" suiyue*, p. 370. Deng, when under attack in late 1975 or early 1976, claimed that the formulation was first used by Zhou Enlai and he was merely echoing the Premier. Even if strictly true, use of the *tifa* was a prominent feature of Deng's efforts in 1975. *Deng Liqun guoshi jiangtan*, vol. 3, p. 323. Note also Yao Wenyuan's looser use of the same idea in April; above, p. 284.

[7] In an ostensible refutation of Lin Biao's simplistic understanding of Mao's Thought, but one that clearly applied to the radicals as well, Deng advocated "comprehensively studying, propagating and carrying out Mao Zedong Thought" at a rural work forum in Beijing in September-October. Concerning comprehensive consolidation, Mao Mao regards July-September as the "high tide" of the process, although Deng is not known to have used the term itself. He did, however, beginning with the Dazhai conference in mid-September, speak of consolidation as covering a very extensive range of activities. Mao Mao, *"Wenge" suiyue*, pp. 394, 396, 399-400.

[8] *Ibid.*, p. 373, provides a different perspective by emphasizing the essential role of military consolidation in *quanmian zhengdun*.

[9] While the members of the Research Office were appointed on July 5, Deng had already informed Wang Hongwen of his intention to set up the office on June 15, and it was informally operating toward the end of the month. Yu Guangyuan, "Yi Deng Xiaoping he zhengyanshi," p. 5.

two other draft documents—the "Outline Report on the Work of the Academy of Sciences," initially drafted under Hu Yaobang's leadership of the Academy, and the "General Program for All Work of the Party and Nation," prepared by the Research Office under the primary direction of Deng Liqun. Nor was this the end of programmatic outline reports (*huibao tigang*) under preparation by people linked to Deng, notably a document on education under the direction of Zhou Rongxin, and an outline on Party rectification under Ji Dengkui's auspices. A final document reflecting the drive for comprehensive policy guidelines was Hua Guofeng's report to the September-October Dazhai conference which laid down the direction for agricultural modernization. Of all these efforts, only Hua's report passed draft stage and was issued as an official document. The others were caught up in the new change of wind in the Politburo.

The first suggestion of a possible new change of direction, although one not taken seriously by Deng initially, came with the publication of esoteric articles on the classic novel *Water Margin*. Made possible by a mid-August discussion between Mao and an academic from Beijing University during which the Chairman declared that the novel's major theme, its "negative example," was capitulation, the radicals used their roles in the propaganda sphere to develop a press campaign against "capitulators inside the Party."[10] While, as we shall argue, to the extent there was a target initially, it undoubtedly was the perennial whipping boy, Zhou Enlai, rather than Deng; the significant development was that the radicals were again pressing an aggressive theoretical campaign, with Mao's support. This was followed by Jiang Qing's appearance at the Dazhai conference in September where she pushed the *Water Margin* issue, ominously linking it to "two line struggles" within the CCP. While Mao angrily rejected her comments as "farting," the more important point is that she was there at all. In a system where Mao controlled the appearances of leaders,[11] the crucial fact, as Jiang claimed, was that she had in effect been "confined in a cage [allegedly] by Deng Xiaoping, [but] the Chairman let her out," including permission to attend the Dazhai meeting.[12]

Another, and ultimately much more significant, straw in the wind was the appearance in Beijing of Mao's nephew, Mao Yuanxin, in late September, and his subsequent assignment in October as the Chairman's new liaison to the leadership as a whole, basically replacing the "two ladies," Wang Hairong and

---

[10] Strictly speaking, this was not the first post-spring activity by the radicals as a number of articles continuing the themes of the campaign against Lin Biao and Confucius appeared in July. See Mao Mao, *"Wenge" suiyue*, p. 381.

[11] For example, Mao's approval was required before any leader could receive foreigners. A case of his use of this power was in November 1975 when he vetoed Jiang attending a state banquet. *Mao wengao*, vol. 13, p. 494. See also above, pp. 191-92n16.

[12] See *Mao zhuan*, vol. 2, p. 1751; *HQ*, no. 12 (1977), p. 38; and Qing and Fang, *Deng zai 1976*, vol. 1, p. 83. Of course, Jiang was simply blaming Deng for a situation created by Mao's actions in the spring.

Tang Wensheng, and assuming a more authoritative and influential role. This change should have been a warning in that Mao Yuanxin was an important Cultural Revolution radical who had, to that point, taken a leading role in Liaoning, one of the provinces most badly affected by the movement, and arguably was a future successor in Mao's eyes. Wang and Tang were not completely different, having been Cultural Revolution activists in the Foreign Ministry, albeit with a more "royalist" cast generally in support of Zhou Enlai during the ministry's factional struggles in the late 1960s. Wang, in particular, had assumed a leading role in the ministry, and, like Mao Yuanxin, had a special status as Mao's relative. The crucial difference was the close relationship they had developed to Deng while mirroring the Chairman's attitude of being "bad to the Premier but nice to Deng," whereas Mao Yuanxin would become Deng's most significant critic.

Finally, the August-October period saw the unfolding of a drama centering on Qinghua University that, while initiated on campus as an attempt to attack university radicals with only limited involvement by Deng, wound up affecting negatively Mao's view of Deng. This drama of Qinghua Deputy Party Secretary Liu Bing's two letters, letters passed on to Mao by Deng in August and October, is examined in detail in Chapter 6. For now, we simply note that in allowing himself to be drawn into this affair, Deng was not only entangled in the superstructure generally, but he also intruded into a specific area of Mao's Cultural Revolution experiments, one where the Chairman continued to exercise direct control in the 1970s.[13]

Before turning to the specific developments of the period, several aspects of the leadership equation warrant further examination. First, at least until the *Water Margin* issue, the radicals were in an unprecedented passive position. Jiang Qing virtually disappeared from public life, Wang Hongwen spent most of the summer in Shanghai under unclear circumstances, and Mao's strictures about a "gang of four" left the radicals unwilling to visit one another for fear of appearing to behave like a faction.[14] The situation fed "rumors arising everywhere" during the July-September period—rumors concerning the bad behavior of Jiang in particular, Mao's harsh judgment of her and their separation, and even that she had been exiled or had committed suicide.[15] These rumors undoubtedly had a dynamic of

---

[13] See above, pp. 113, 120; and below, pp. 390-91.

[14] This was normal behavior by leaders from both "camps" when Mao placed them under pressure. Earlier in 1975, following Mao's criticism of the "gang" in 1974, Wang Hongwen wrote to Jiang Qing advising against circulating materials the four had all commented on in identical terms lest the Chairman think they were indeed acting like a faction, while Li Xiannian later described how for a number of months in 1976 he did not dare contact Ye Jianying. *Zhonggong yuanshi ziliao xuanji* [Selection of Original CCP Materials] (Taipei: Zhonggong yanjiu zazhishi, 1981), vol. 2, 1st series, p. 119; *Deng Liqun guoshi jiangtan*, vol. 1, p. 398; and above, p. 249.

[15] See Yan and Gao, *Turbulent Decade*, pp. 471-73; and "Jiang Qing zai dazhaohu huiyi," p. 383. A probably exaggerated post-Mao account claims that the radicals themselves felt their situation was precarious, to the point of saying "I'm ready for the blow from the axe" (Wang Hongwen), "I ... have long been prepared to face the guillotine" (Zhang Chunqiao), and "I'm in a predicament [but] I think

their own, but they were not unrelated to the activities of establishment leaders in leaking information on Mao's May 3 Politburo criticisms of the radicals.[16] Another tactic indulged in by Deng, Hu Qiaomu and Deng Liqun was to encourage and pass on letters to Mao from writers and other creative artists decrying specific instances of the radicals' heavy-handed actions in the literature and art world, letters which—until the somewhat different Liu Bing case—generally received the Chairman's endorsement.[17]

As a result, while they adhered to Zhou Enlai's advice not to confront the radicals, Deng and other ranking leaders participated in a low-level ongoing campaign to undermine their influence. For Deng personally, the events of the spring marked a shift in the nature of his relationship with Jiang Qing. Whereas previously, incidents like the *Fengqing* affair notwithstanding, Deng had carefully followed Mao's injunction not to oppose Jiang and, in return, she had conducted a comparatively cordial relationship with him, now animosity had clearly developed even if it was not displayed openly. From Jiang's perspective, despite her earlier support (based on the fact that she understood Mao's backing of Deng), Deng had betrayed her in the spring, by somehow getting the Chairman's ear and turning him against her.[18] For Deng, the undermining of the radicals had clear advantages in furthering the consolidation program, but his and others' actions ran counter to Mao's basic wish for stability and unity. For the Chairman, the differences of the two sides should somehow be reconciled, not degenerate into a subterranean conflict. Deng's soft approach to the radicals in the spring had secured Mao's approval, but the ongoing anti-radical maneuvers were a potential source of vulnerability. As other factors came to a head in October, when Wang Hongwen complained to Mao late in the month about anti-Jiang rumors, it could not have helped Deng.[19]

Apart from efforts designed to undercut the radicals, another feature of Deng's political plans in summer 1975 was his promotion of alternative future leaders to the "gang." This was clearly the time when Deng and other veteran revolutionaries began to view Hua Guofeng and Ji Dengkui as preferred successors, seemingly

---

I can manage if I had to ... go to the May 7 cadre school" (Yao Wenyuan). *GMRB*, March 24, 1977, in *SPRCP*, no. 6317 (1977), p. 3.

[16] Regarding leaks by Deng, Ji Dengkui and Ye Jianying in the June-August period, see "Jiang Qing zai dazhaohu huiyi," p. 376; Chen and Du, *Shilu*, vol. 3, part 2, pp. 1243-44; and above, p. 303. Cf. Chen Xilian revealing the same criticisms to Xinjiang military commander Yang Yong at the end of September; Yang Qing, *Huiyi Yang Yong Jiangjun* [Remember General Yang Yong] (Hong Kong: Mingbao chubanshe, 1986), pp. 326-27.

[17] Kraus, "The Rise and Fall of Yu Huiyong," pp. 236-39, discusses this process with particular reference to Hu Qiaomu. See also Yu Guangyuan, "Yi Deng Xiaoping he zhengyanshi," p. 13. It is not clear to what extent Deng and company instigated such letters, or to what extent they simply facilitated their being forwarded to Mao.

[18] "Jiang Qing zai dazhaohu huiyi," pp. 375, 377.

[19] On Mao's desire for reconciliation, see Mao Mao, *"Wenge" suiyue*, pp. 363-66. On Wang's late October complaint, see Yan and Gao, *Turbulent Decade*, p. 479.

in response to a reported defiant observation by Wang Hongwen. Deng Liqun recalled the situation:

> In Shanghai [in summer 1975] Wang Hongwen ... said something: Wait and see in ten years. This was reported back to Beijing and Comrade Xiaoping and [other veterans] all knew about it. Comrade Xiaoping said: Sure, they have an age advantage. In discussion with Comrade [Li] Xiannian, [he noted that] we're much more senior than they are in age, about twenty or more years, so they have the advantage. We have to think up a way to support a few people among the comrades younger than us. Among the several who Deng Xiaoping and Xiannian deliberated about supporting, Hua Guofeng was one, and another was Ji Dengkui. At that time Deng and Li went about deliberately supporting Hua Guofeng and Ji Dengkui to handle Wang Hongwen *et al.* and their "wait and see in ten years." Comrades Deng Xiaoping and Xiannian thought, in ten years' time we'll be no good, but there'll be Hua Guofeng and Ji Dengkui and other young comrades to deal with them.[20]

Deng Liqun also indicated that Zhou Enlai was heavily involved in these discussions and the backing of Hua and Ji, and further speculated that Deng had spoken highly of these potential successors to Mao.[21]

Various factors went into the old revolutionaries' preference for Hua and Ji. Their respect for revolutionary status surely was appreciated by Deng and company. Hua and Ji had apparently negotiated smoothly the tricky period from spring to late 1973 when Deng's formal position was not only subordinate to theirs, but his actual responsibilities were more limited during this period of "probation" under Mao's watchful eye.[22] In addition, Ji Dengkui, second only to Wang Dongxing, had responsibility for the household arrangements of Deng and his family. In all this, the two younger leaders apparently managed to show sufficient deference to their revolutionary elder while exercising ostensibly superior authority. In addition, Hua and Ji performed key roles in the consolidation program, in full support of Deng. As we have already seen, and shall see in more detail below, they made critical contributions to some of his most important projects. To quote Deng Liqun again, with specific reference to Ji, "at that time

---

[20] *Deng Liqun guoshi jiangtan*, vol. 3, p. 347.

[21] *Ibid.*, p. 102. In this passage Deng Liqun only mentioned Hua, but we can assume that Ji's name also came up in discussions involving Zhou and in any relevant comments Deng made to Mao. While there is no direct evidence that the issue came up, frequent meetings involving Zhou and Deng and/or Li were held in the June-October period. See *Zhou nianpu*, vol. 3, pp. 710, 712-17, 719-20, 722; and Mao Mao, *"Wenge" suiyue*, p. 380. In all this, if a credible but unconfirmed Hong Kong version of Deng's speech to the July 1977 Central Committee plenum is accurate, Deng took the initiative, and Ye Jianying was also involved. See Sima Changfeng, *Deng Xiaoping fuzhi shimo* [A Comprehensive Account of Deng Xiaoping's Return] (Hong Kong: Bowen shuju, 1980), p. 191.

[22] In 1973, in addition to formal rank, as *de facto* head of the Professional Work Office (*yewuzu*) of the State Council Hua had more administrative functions than Deng, while Ji was responsible for Party organization work. On Hua and Ji's respect for status, see above, p. 13.

[his] performance was outstanding, he handled a few things really well."[23]

But undoubtedly most fundamental was simply that Hua and Ji were well positioned for the assignment as Politburo members and, with Li Xiannian, Deng's ranking subordinates in the State Council responsible for government daily work. The crucial factor in this regard was that they had Mao's favor, and the Chairman had been considering them for future leadership roles since 1971 and 1969 respectively.[24] The point is that Hua and Ji had been handpicked by Mao, and, as in policy matters in 1975, Deng was operating within the Chairman's parameters. A corollary of this was that however much confidence Deng had in Hua and Ji, and however similar their policy preferences to his, it was not necessarily a choice he would have made in other circumstances, or to which he would be irrevocably committed. Simply put, while Deng and other old revolutionaries saw Hua and Ji as the best bet for the future in a complex political environment, this very calculation ultimately derived from Mao's design.

As the above suggests, the key variable inevitably was Mao. The Chairman's propensity to shift positions, to present contradictory and ambivalent views, and to blame others for positions he had endorsed earlier was well understood within the leadership, much as was his absolute authority. This clearly was the basis of Zhou Enlai's caution that "the Chairman is still observing," and Chen Yun's query to Deng Xiaoping concerning whether he had grasped Mao's meaning. It was also seen in the anxiety expressed by Zhou and Ye Jianying that Deng was pressing readjustment too hard, even as they themselves engaged in limited or subterranean attacks on the radicals. Why, then, did Deng—who historically had particularly close relations with Mao—miscalculate and overstep? Ultimately, this is unknowable, although it is clear to us that, contrary to official claims, it was not due to unwavering bravery or a principled refusal to endorse the Cultural Revolution.[25]

One key to Deng's overconfidence, in any case, must have been Mao's unstinting expressed support following their mid-June conversation when

---

[23] *Deng Liqun guoshi jiangtan*, vol. 3, p. 347.

[24] Mao's consideration of Ji and Hua can be dated to 1969 in Ji's case, when he was elevated to alternate membership of the Politburo, and to 1971 in Hua's, when he was called to Beijing in the wake of the 1970 Lushan plenum. Significantly, as had been the case for Zhou Enlai, Deng arranged specific appointments for Mao's young favorites in 1975. In 1969 following the Ninth Party Congress, Zhou proposed that the newly appointed Ji be placed in charge of Party building and rectification as well as labor, youth and women's affairs; *Zhou Enlai junshi huodong jishi* [Chronology of Zhou Enlai's Military Activities] (Beijing: Zhongyang wenxian chubanshe, 2000), vol. 2, p. 694. As we have seen, after the Fourth NPC Deng proposed Hua and Ji as Standing Vice Premiers.

[25] We examine this issue in Chapter 6. Here we simply point out that Deng's various statements in 1975 lauding daring, including the famous claim that he was "not afraid to fall a second time," are better understood as efforts to bolster the determination of subordinates to carry out consolidation after all the uncertainty and insecurity of the Cultural Revolution than as indicating any unwillingness to accept Mao's demands. See *Selected Works of Deng (1975-1982)*, pp. 14, 18, 31-32, 36, 39, 47; Yan and Gao, *Turbulent Decade*, pp. 470, 479-80; and Barnouin and Yu, *Ten Years*, p. 280.

the Chairman declared Deng had to take over all work. This was certainly the perception of other keen observers of Mao, as seen in Zhou Enlai's assertion to a Romanian Communist Party delegation in early September that Deng would succeed him as premier, something the radicals surely expected as well.[26] More dramatic, and an infinitely more weighty indication of the future, was provided by Mao himself during a September 24 meeting with Vietnamese leader Le Duan: "We now have a leadership crisis. The Premier is in poor health, ... Kang Sheng is in poor health, and so is Ye Jianying. I'm 82, and I'm also sick. He [pointing to Deng] is the only one who's in fine fettle."[27] Notwithstanding the Chairman's fluid thinking, or his duplicity, from Deng's point of view Mao's affirmations must have been reassuring well into October. Indeed, even as Mao demanded criticism of Deng in November, he affirmed to an anxious Deng that his work was satisfactory.[28]

But more than a simple affirmation of Deng's work was involved. While sometimes indirect, there can be little doubt that Mao sanctioned Deng's efforts to consolidate the superstructure. In the retrospective assessment of someone who understood how the system worked, Deng Liqun, the battlefront had shifted in mid-1975 to the ideological sphere and, "looking back, if Chairman Mao had not given the signal, Comrade Deng Xiaoping would not have taken it on ..., it was a co-production of the two."[29] More narrowly, the notion of "the three directives as the key link" that Mao later rejected as distorting the fundamental priority to class struggle was never openly questioned by him during the period of comprehensive consolidation. Deng's articulation of the principle in May and July would have been known to the Chairman, and in mid-September he approved a document, probably prepared by Hua Guofeng, on boosting piggery enterprises which used the *tifa*.[30] And as late as October, Mao approved a proposal to publish *Ideological Frontline*, a theoretical magazine to be organized by the State Council Research Office which would clearly reflect Deng's spin on the nature of consolidation.[31] Most significantly, despite official efforts to argue the influence of Deng and others in producing Mao's more liberal view of the superstructure from spring 1975, in fact the influence flowed in the opposite direction.[32]

---

[26] See *Zhou nianpu*, vol. 3, pp. 719-20. Concerning the radicals' perception, note Jiang Qing's subsequent complaint that she felt intimidated when Deng came into the Politburo after seeing Mao and confidently asserted that he had the Chairman's support; "Jiang Qing zai dazhaohu huiyi," p. 379.

[27] Mao Mao, *"Wenge" suiyue*, p. 410.

[28] See below, p. 389.

[29] *Deng Liqun guoshi jiangtan*, vol. 3, p. 315.

[30] See ZGDSCKZL, vol. 27, pp. 304, 546, on the piggery directive. Deng's earlier statements to the forum on iron and steel work and the Party Center's theoretical study class surely would have been submitted to Mao for review.

[31] Yu Guangyuan, "Yi Deng Xiaoping he zhengyanshi," p. 12.

[32] This is not to claim that there was no influence on the Chairman. A case in point where such

The crucial turning point was Mao's statement to his last Politburo meeting on May 3rd. In addition to criticizing the radicals on the empiricism issue and for their factional tendencies, Mao indicated the need for a significant policy revision concerning intellectuals. As we have seen, the Chairman declared that intellectuals in educational, literary and art, journalistic and medical circles weren't all that bad, and they were needed. Clearly the harsh policies of the radicals toward "the stinking ninth category" would no longer do. Further indications from Mao soon followed: in early July Mao disapprovingly told Deng that there was too much fault finding over trifles, the Hundred Flowers were not blooming, and people were unable to express their opinions. At the same time, in the context of the ongoing rehabilitations of senior cadres, Mao called for the magnanimous handling of the case of literary czar Zhou Yang, one of the earliest Cultural Revolution targets of Jiang Qing (and, of course, of himself) in 1966, a further indication of a desire for a more flexible intellectual policy. And on July 14, the Chairman made a longer statement on literary and art policy, affirming the need for adjustment and a step-by-step expansion of output over the next one to three years. Again, he emphasized a lenient approach to writers, citing the traditional "save the patient" approach, and stating that the rebuffing of rightists in 1957 showed there was nothing to fear. These were ideological problems, and there was no need to be anxious.[33]

As Yu Guangyuan recalled more than two decades later with specific reference to the Chairman's early July reference to the Hundred Flowers, all of this "offered an opportunity" for Deng to "open up the field of culture and education."[34] As we saw in Chapter 4 and will examine in greater detail later in this chapter, steps toward educational readjustment began shortly after Mao's May Politburo comments, while Hua Guofeng chaired seminars on the "double hundred" policy shortly after Mao's July remarks, and radical followers of the "gang" such as Yu Huiyong's Ministry of Culture came under intense pressure which forced them to relax policy toward intellectuals. It was also *after* the Chairman's signals on the literary and art front that letters of complaint against the radicals began to appear in July.[35] Nevertheless, for all the opportunity and

---

influence did exist was the Hunanese film, *The Song of the Gardener*. This film had been produced in Hunan at Hua Guofeng's behest. In 1973 the radicals criticized the film as negating the Cultural Revolution, and in 1974 ordered its banning. See above, pp. 157nn110-11, 192. In November 1974, however, when Mao was in Changsha, the Hunan provincial leadership (of which Hua was still First Secretary although based in Beijing) screened it for the Chairman, resulting in his favorable assessment. See Kraus, "Rise and Fall," p. 237; and *RMRB*, November 29, 1976, in *SPRCP*, no. 6250 (1977), pp. 9-12. For a discussion implying Deng's initiative in the ideological loosening generally, see Yan and Gao, *Turbulent Decade*, p. 467.

[33] Chen and Du, *Shilu*, vol. 3, part 2, pp. 1235, 1239. For a contemporary account of the 1966 purge of Zhou Yang, see Merle Goldman, "The Fall of Chou Yang," *CQ*, no. 27 (1966).

[34] Yu Guangyuan, "Yi Deng Xiaoping he zhengyanshi," p. 6.

[35] See *ibid.*, p. 13; Chen and Du, *Shilu*, vol. 3, part 2, pp. 1243, 1246; "Hu Yaobang, Li Chang de jianghua," items 13-22, pp. 36, 40; above, pp. 270, 297; and below, pp. 322-23, 341-42. The "double

opening presented by Mao, his deep ambivalence about intellectuals should have given pause. The reference to the 1957 rightists in July was suggestive, as was the full content of his remarks about intellectuals in May. As Jiang Qing would complain later, Mao's comments about the need for intellectuals were linked to complaints—never circulated by Deng—concerning their feckless lack of national pride, their belief that "the foreign moon is better than the Chinese one."[36] While Mao had given Deng license to correct perceived shortcomings in the superstructure, it was hedged by similar reservations to those that had led him to launch the Cultural Revolution.

The State Council Political Research Office

The background of the formation of the State Council Political Research Office reflects the larger pattern of elite politics in 1975. Initially, as Deng took over prime responsibility for the State Council around the time of the Fourth NPC, he considered gathering a group of advisers. This had not crystallized into a proposal for a formal office, but Deng had in mind a writing group that would consider a range of theoretical issues, even though his activities focused on practical matters during the first half of 1975. Significantly, on January 6 Deng turned to Mao's former secretary, Hu Qiaomu, to canvass the idea. Hu, like the other officials Deng would propose, came from pre-Cultural Revolution establishment theoretical circles. He had been sidelined after the onset of the Cultural Revolution, but received a degree of protection from Mao,[37] and had reappeared at the 1974 National Day celebrations. Indeed, it was Hu's long-time service as Mao's secretary and as drafter of key documents, which gave him the informal title of "the Party's pen," that made him particularly attractive to Deng. Few had as much personal experience with the Chairman, or as great a knowledge of the theoretical complexities of his "thought," or as much skill at mastering the vital task of documentary preparation. Given the pragmatic bent of Deng's immediate tasks and subsequent performance, the need for theoretical backup reflected in his exchange with Hu is particularly striking. Deng told Hu he wanted something along the lines of the pre-Cultural Revolution Diaoyutai writing group, i.e., the theoreticians who wrote a series of "anti-revisionist, anti-imperialist essays" at Beijing's State Guesthouse during the polemical jousting with the Soviet Union in the early 1960s under the direction of Deng and Kang

---

hundred" referred to the policy launched in 1956 of "letting a hundred flowers bloom, and a hundred schools of thought contend."

[36] "Jiang Qing zai dazhaohu huiyi," pp. 375-76.

[37] In a typically bizarre development, in 1967 Mao's car passed by Hu's house and the Chairman noticed anti-Hu wall posters. Although Mao stopped the car, he failed to see the absent Hu, but the incident was seen as a positive gesture which served to shield Hu from mistreatment. Cheng Zhongyuan, "Guowuyuan zhengzhi yanjiushi he 1975 nian de zhengdun" [The State Council Political Research Office and the 1975 Consolidation], *ZGDSZL*, no. 61 (1977), p. 139; and interview with member of the Research Office, February 1998.

Sheng. Deng also named veterans of the Diaoyutai group as possible advisers along with Hu: Wu Lengxi, Hu Sheng and Kang Sheng's secretary, Li Xin, and instructed Hu to find other recruits for the writing team.[38] Apart from the Diaoyutai connection, it is further notable that, like Hu, several of those Deng nominated had direct working experience with Mao in the past, and that they had all been recently rehabilitated by him.[39]

What can be said about Deng's initial idea? First, both the historical reference and related personnel choices suggest a focus on foreign affairs, the area where Deng had been active since his return to work, and for which he would assume formal responsibility in the immediate aftermath of the Fourth NPC. This was further indicated when Deng outlined the issues with which the writing group would deal. These included the delineation of the Third World, the social character of the Soviet Union, the problem of war and peace, and the economic crisis of the capitalist world.[40] Beyond the apparent foreign policy focus, what was involved might be termed mainstream Maoist anti-revisionism, something also linked to work on the projected Volume 5 of Mao's *Selected Works*. While clearly not in the full Cultural Revolution mode, Deng's proposal certainly hewed to the anti-revisionist themes that the Chairman had been pushing since 1960, and, of course, it was compatible with Mao's most recent directive on the study of the dictatorship of the proletariat.[41] Deng's motive undoubtedly involved being in tune with Mao to protect his own interests, but, particularly in view of his committed participation in the earlier anti-Soviet polemics, it is equally plausible that the emphasis reflected his own views in the international area. Moreover, although the radicals were in charge of the major ideological campaign of early 1975, Deng's idea indicated his sensitivity to and need to keep abreast of theoretical concerns at this early stage.

Another point of note is that all of the people mentioned for Deng's think tank were not only orthodox theoreticians in the past, they would also be leading

---

[38] Yu Guangyuan, "Yi Deng Xiaoping he zhengyanshi," p. 4; Cheng Zhongyuan, "Zhengzhi yanjiushi," pp. 137-38; Wu Lengxi, *Shinian lunzhan: 1956-1966 Zhong-Su guanxi huiyilu* [Ten Years' Theoretical Struggle: Recollections of Sino-Soviet Relations in 1956-1966] (Beijing: Zhongyang wenxian chubanshe, 1999), vol. 2, pp. 540, 563; and interview with member of the Research Office, February 1998. Hu himself had not been involved in the Diaoyutai group due to illness. Xiong Fu, who joined the Research Office at its formation, was another member of the group. Cf. below, p. 318n47.

[39] Wu Lengxi in particular had a close relationship with Mao. See Wu Lengxi, *Yi Mao Zhuxi—Wo qinsheng jingli ruogan zhongda lishi shijian pianduan* [Remembering Chairman Mao—Fragments of My Personal Experience with Certain Major Historical Events] (Beijing: Xinhua chubanshe, 1995); and above, p. 47n58. Hu Sheng, moreover, had served as a member of Mao's informal think tank in the early 1960s.

[40] Yu Guangyuan, "Yi Deng Xiaoping he zhengyanshi," p. 4; and Cheng Zhongyuan, "Zhengzhi yanjiushi," p. 138.

[41] This can be further seen in Deng's request that Hu also address issues raised in Mao's recent talks on theoretical issues such as "bourgeois right." Cheng Zhongyuan, "Zhengzhi yanjiushi," p. 138.

conservative ideological advocates in the post-Mao period—men labeled, apart from Hu Qiaomu, as "whateverists."[42] The story of this misunderstood group and the larger clash of theoretical perspectives with the so-called "practice faction" is a matter for our Volume II.[43] In any case, as with the subject matter, the intention to rely on these people suggests a more orthodox orientation than normally associated with the "pragmatist" Deng. Finally, the fact that Deng's idea was not realized in January should be examined. While there is no clear-cut evidence concerning the reason for not following through,[44] one might speculate that with the more concrete immediate tasks in the military, railroad and iron and steel sectors, the idea simply receded to the backburner. But equally if not more plausible is the fact that Deng's power was still limited organizationally to the government and PLA, while ideological authority largely rested with Zhang Chunqiao and Yao Wenyuan who had been designated by Mao to undertake the campaign to study the dictatorship of the proletariat. The time was not quite right for bold forays into the theoretical realm, but the situation had changed by June. As one Party historian put it, the time then was opportune both because the readjustment of the railways and industry provided political momentum, and since the radicals were now out of favor with Mao.[45] In one respect, however, Deng's ideological influence had already increased in March when he was given responsibility for Volume 5 of Mao's *Selected Works* (see below).

On June 8, after discussing the question with Li Xiannian, Deng raised the matter a second time with Hu Qiaomu, this time with a proposal for an office housed in the State Council.[46] There was both continuity and a considerable expansion in the personnel, scope and tasks envisioned for the new organ. Deng again named the theorists he had proposed in January (Wu Lengxi, Hu Sheng and Li Xin, as well as Hu himself), plus another veteran of the pre-Cultural

---

[42] I.e., supporters of the position of upholding "whatever policy decisions Chairman Mao made, and [following] whatever instructions Chairman Mao gave."

[43] Here we simply note that while Deng came to support the "practice" position in summer 1978, the matter was not as clear-cut as generally believed, with Deng's theoretical (as opposed to political) leanings arguably closer to the theory *and* practice view of those criticized as "whateverists."

[44] Yu Guangyuan, "Yi Deng Xiaoping he zhengyanshi," p. 4, states that he did not know the reason for the five-month delay. The Research Office staff member interviewed in February 1998 concluded that the atmosphere at the start of 1975 was not particularly good, so Deng waited.

[45] Cheng Zhongyuan, "Zhengzhi yanjiushi," p. 138.

[46] According to Deng Liqun, both Deng Xiaoping and Li Xiannian, who continued to be involved in the office's affairs, came up with the idea of establishing the Research Office; *Deng Liqun guoshi jiangtan*, vol. 1, p. 415. The location of the new body in the State Council reflected the continuing uncertainty of leadership arrangements, even after the radicals' setback. As Yu Guangyuan explained, it was more "convenient" to locate it in the government where Deng was in charge than in the Party Center where Wang Hongwen was still formally responsible in June; see "Yi Deng Xiaoping he zhengyanshi," p. 4. When Deng did formally take over the Party Center at the start of July, moreover, it was notionally on a temporary basis as Wang retreated to Shanghai.

Revolution theoretical and propaganda establishment, Xiong Fu.[47] Broader objectives were indicated when Hu suggested, and Deng accepted, adding Yu Guangyuan, someone with a quite different background. Although having some links to the propaganda system, Yu's basic pre-1966 experience had been in scientific and academic organizations, including service as Vice Chairman of the State Council's Scientific and Technological Commission in 1964-66. Sidelined for nine years during and after the Cultural Revolution, Yu had done some research work for the SPC on a casual basis since early 1975 when Hu contacted him and requested he participate in "political and ideological theory work" in the new office. Subsequently, after Deng's proposal was submitted to Wang Hongwen and the Party Center on June 15, Deng Liqun, someone with a propaganda background who would play a particularly important role in the months ahead, was added to the list of principal members of the new organ. In the course of discussions, Deng reportedly resolutely rejected the inclusion of any Cultural Revolution rebels (*geming zaofanpai*) in the new body.[48]

The staff of the new office was not limited to the seven leading cadres, but had 30 to 40 junior members in administrative, library, and professional roles. Their functions were broader than the "writing of anti-revisionist essays" (essays that were to be more persuasive than those produced in the radical-controlled media) that Hu mentioned when he conveyed Deng's instructions to a gathering of office leaders in late June. The additional, more significant tasks centered on editing Mao's *Selected Works* and research for and the drafting of documents for the State Council—notably the three documents later denounced as "poisonous weeds," as well as documents for the Chairman, a clear indication of Mao's support for the office. Other functions included taking responsibility for the Philosophy and Social Science Section of the Academy of Sciences, collecting materials on the situation in literature and art, education, science, and publishing, and setting up a theoretical magazine. To carry out these tasks a range of skills was clearly called for, although the staff was basically recruited from the propaganda and theoretical spheres. Taking the leading cadres and staff as a whole into account, a certain common background, as well personal familiarity to at least some degree, can be seen. This involved, apart from the Diaoyutai experience, not only previous service in key establishment organs such as the Central Committee's theoretical magazine, *Red Flag*, the Xinhua News Agency,

---

[47] It is possible that Xiong, who had been another participant in the anti-Soviet polemics of the early 1960s, was on Deng's January list. Cheng Zhongyuan, "Zhengzhi yanjiushi," p. 140, refers to Xiong and the others as those proposed in January. However, neither Cheng nor any other source specifically lists Xiong when directly discussing the January Deng-Hu meeting.

[48] Yu Guangyuan, "Yi Deng Xiaoping he zhengyanshi," p. 4; and Cheng Zhongyuan, "Zhengzhi yanjiushi," pp. 140-41. Deng "did not agree" to Hu's June 8 proposal to seek out rebels, a suggestion perhaps meant to provide some cosmetic cover by including a token radical.

According to *Deng Liqun guoshi jiangtan*, vol. 1, p. 386, the rank order of the office leaders was Hu Qiaomu, Wu Lengxi, Hu Sheng, Xiong Fu, Yu Guangyuan, Li Xin and Deng Liqun.

the Central Party School, and the Ministry of Culture, but also similar fates during the Cultural Revolution, including time spent in the same May 7 cadre school.[49] All of this promoted a common sentiment, but also resulted in a certain naïveté by individuals who had been basically sidelined for an extended period prior to joining the office. As described by Deng Liqun more than two decades later, "we were outraged without limit by the ... activities of the 'gang of four,' and were engaged in resisting them, but ... we were badly lacking an understanding of the complexity of the struggle."[50]

From the outset, Deng not only placed high importance on the Research Office, he also personally directed its activities. Deng conveyed his agenda for the office—an agenda usually sourced to Mao, and in fact accurately reflecting the Chairman's expressed wishes which Deng regularly reported to the staff. Deng also received briefings and encouraged work, read documents and directed important emendations, and conveyed the results of the office's work to Mao. He was the driving force, in Yu Guangyuan's recollection, "directly in charge." Under Deng, day-to-day authority clearly rested with Hu Qiaomu, whose involvement ranged over the full scope of Research Office activities, and who also became involved in the redrafting of documents that originated outside of the office, notably the SPC's 20 articles and Hu Yaobang's Outline Report on the Academy of Sciences (see below). Under Hu, the office was functionally and physically divided into two main sections: the editorial board for Mao's *Selected Works* under Wu Lengxi, Hu Sheng, Xiong Fu and Li Xin, and a policy-oriented section in charge of investigation, research, and other work headed by Yu Guangyuan and Deng Liqun. While both sections were housed within Zhongnanhai, they were in different buildings and the ordinary staff rarely mixed, although the principal leaders often discussed work together.[51]

---

[49] *Deng Liqun wenji* [Collected Works of Deng Liqun] (Beijing: Dangdai Zhongguo chubanshe, 1999), vol. 1, p. 40; Yu Guangyuan, "Yi Deng Xiaoping he zhengyanshi," pp. 4ff; Feng Lanrui, "Zai Guowuyuan zhengzhi yanjiushi de rizi" [Days at the State Council's Political Research Office], *BNC*, no. 3 (2000), p. 5; *Deng Liqun guoshi jiangtan*, vol. 3, p. 340; and interview with member of the Research Office, February 1998.

Moreover, people who might not otherwise have been particularly familiar with one another earlier sometimes became close during their inactivity in the post-1966 period. A case in point, although not strictly within the Research Office, concerned office member Hu Jiwei and Hu Yaobang, who worked closely with the office in 1975 from his assignment at the Academy of Sciences. In the second half of 1974 the two Hus became close as they exchanged views when receiving treatment at the Peking Union Hospital. Hu Jiwei, "Jiehou cheng zhongren yin dui zhuyi cheng—wei Hu Yaobang shishi shizhounian er zuo" [Assuming a Weighty Responsibility after the Calamity out of Loyalty to an Idea—Written for the Tenth Anniversary of the Death of Hu Yaobang], *Shuwu* [Reading Room], no. 4 (2000), p. 4.

[50] *Deng Liqun wenji*, vol. 1, p. 41.

[51] Yu Guangyuan, "Yi Deng Xiaoping he zhengyanshi," pp. 6-12; *Deng Liqun guoshi jiangtan*, vol. 1, p. 389; and Cheng Zhongyuan, "Zhengzhi yanjiushi," p. 141. The division of work between the two sections as it affected the leading personnel was not rigid, as can been seen in the fact that Wu Lengxi participated in the drafting of the 20 articles and was drawn into some late revisions of the General

The division of the Research Office into two sections requires further comment, especially since the individuals Deng had singled out in January were assigned the task of editing Mao's *Works*. This, in one respect, simply underlines the centrality of Mao's authority and thinking to everything that was going on in elite politics. But some history is required. Given their canonical status, the *Selected Works* had always been of critical importance for the Party line. After the fourth and final volume covering the revolutionary period had been published in 1960, work began on a post-1949 compilation with Liu Shaoqi, Deng Xiaoping and Hu Qiaomu all having key roles. This was naturally disrupted by the outbreak of the Cultural Revolution, but by 1969 work had resumed with Kang Sheng and Zhou Enlai responsible. By the end of 1974, with Kang and Zhou gravely ill, the radicals were involved with Zhang Chunqiao holding Politburo responsibility for the project, but in 1975 new arrangements were made for reasons that are not entirely clear. It was in this context that Hu Qiaomu returned to public life as Deng assumed responsibility for the *Selected Works*, perhaps on Kang's recommendation. Hu, who had initially been asked by Kang Sheng to assist Li Xin with the project, was appointed with Mao's endorsement to join the editorial work in March, and in April he received the first batch of the Chairman's manuscripts for editing. At the same time, Deng's theoretical authority was bolstered by Mao's April 18 comment which affirmed his crucial leadership role with the observation that Deng was "able to fight on the battlefield [*and*] oppose revisionism."[52]

A source who worked closely with Hu Qiaomu believes Mao's *Works* was the main reason Deng approached Hu in January, on the assumption that Hu was in a better position than anyone to interpret the Chairman. A case of particular importance was Mao's 1956 speech, "On the Ten Great Relationships." Deng was especially eager to include this talk—a treatise fully in tune with the current tasks

---

Program. Hu Qiaomu's office was located in the *Selected Works* section.

[52] NCNA, Beijing, April 30, 1977, in *SPRCP*, no. 6338 (1977), p. 197; Cheng Zhongyuan, "Zhengzhi yanjiushi," p. 140; *Deng Liqun guoshi jiangtan*, vol. 3, pp. 341, 374; Liu Zhonghai *et al.*, eds., *Huiyi Hu Qiaomu* [Remember Hu Qiaomu] (Beijing: Dangdai Zhongguo chubanshe, 1994), p. 17; Wang Yuxiang, "Hu Qiaomu zai sanzhong quanhui qiande zhongyang gongzuo huiyishang" [Hu Qiaomu at the Central Work Conference Before the Third Plenum], *Zongheng* [Broad Coverage], no. 10 (1998), p. 12; Cao Junjie, ed., *Zhongguo er Qiao—Hu Qiaomu, Qiao Guanhua zhuanlüe* [China's Two Qiaos—Brief Biographies of Hu Qiaomu and Qiao Guanhua] (Nanjing: Jiangsu renmin chubanshe, 1996), p. 123; and Chen and Du, *Shilu*, vol. 3, part 2, p. 1206.

It is unclear precisely when Deng assumed responsibility for Mao's *Works*, but a three-man group of Deng, Hu and Kang appears to have been established to oversee Volume 5 by March. As for the Politburo radicals, there is little evidence of their role apart from Wang Hongwen's December 1974 report to Mao that Zhang Chunqiao had responsibility; see above, p. 103n189. Party historians interviewed on the history of Volume 5 in April 1987, however, claimed the radicals had drafted much of what eventually appeared in the 1977 version. Although there is no documentation to confirm this, Li Xin's concern over radical efforts to control the undertaking (see below) is suggestive. Speculatively, it may be that there was early radical involvement, but a complete transition took place in the context of Mao's criticism of the "gang" in April and May.

of stability and economic development—in the projected fifth volume, and with the establishment of the Research Office he assigned Hu the task of cleaning up the manuscript so it could be published as soon as possible. In July, Deng wrote Mao advocating open publication of "this important essay" once it was ready as a centerpiece of national theoretical study. Mao agreed, although stipulating the publication should be internal. Although both Deng and Mao reportedly admired Hu's revision, with the political turnaround later in the year, it was never published during Mao's lifetime as the whole fifth volume project was sidelined, but in the immediate post-Mao period Deng's beloved "Ten Great Relationships" became a theoretical flagship of the new Hua Guofeng leadership.[53]

In selecting Li Xin for the Research Office and work on the *Selected Works*, Deng further indicated his apparently close relationship with Kang Sheng, as well as the benefit of substantive continuity since Li had exercised operational authority in editing the *Works* under the ill Kang. This in turn related to the hostility between Kang and the "gang." According to Li's Research Office colleague, Yu Guangyuan, although Li was unhappy under the new setup in that he had to play second fiddle to Hu Qiaomu with whom he had substantive differences, on the other hand he was "happy because he sensed that Zhang Chunqiao, Yao Wenyuan and possibly Jiang Qing very much wanted to get their hands on the power to edit the *Selected Works*, and having Deng Xiaoping taking care of this work could add a sense of security."[54] Finally, a brief look into the future of the editorial group is appropriate. The group swung into action after Mao's death, producing the fifth volume of the *Selected Works* in spring 1977, and its members apparently also comprised the newly influential Party Center theory group (*zhongyang lilun xiaozu*). Moreover, as noted above, they were the more conservative (alleged) "whateverists" of the post-Mao theoretical debate which raged in 1978. Again, the full story must be left to our Volume II, but their functional responsibilities and the fact that all of the individuals involved were handpicked by Deng for crucial tasks in 1975 suggests the inadequacy of the conventional interpretation.

The foregoing history, together with the allocation of more leading personnel and apparently more resources to the Mao's *Works* section, indicates that for

[53] Xue Qingchao, *Lishi zhuanzhe guantou*, pp. 413-14; Wang Yuxiang, "Hu Qiaomu zai zhongyang gongzuo huiyishang," p. 12; *Mao wengao*, vol. 13, pp. 444-45; and interview with member of the Research Office, February 1998.

An edited version of "On the Ten Great Relationships" was initially published in December 1976, and in the following spring became a prominent text in the then issued fifth volume of Mao's *Selected Works*. Ironically, the text was one of the two documents singled out for study (along with Hua's December 1976 speech to the second Dazhai conference) in the February 1977 so-called "two whatevers" editorial which, mistakenly, came to be regarded as the platform of neo-Maoism. That, however, is another story for our Volume II.

[54] Yu Guangyuan, "Yi Deng Xiaoping he zhengyanshi," p. 6. According to Yu, unlike other leaders, Li never visited the members of the other section. In the editorial group, Li's role was to provide material for editing to Wu Lengxi, Hu Sheng and Xiong Fu, with Wu the real leader, and then everything was handed to Hu Qiaomu for revision.

all the significance of the "three poisonous weeds" as events unfolded, in the initial concept and actual operations of the Research Office, the *Selected Works* endeavor was considered the top priority. This can be seen in Deng's own schedule: while busy with foreign affairs over the entire period and overseeing (but not continuously involved with) a broad range of domestic policy, Deng carefully vetted the compilation of Mao's Volume 5 line by line, participating in study sessions of Mao's writings on an almost weekly basis. The office's output also reflects this priority. Building on earlier work, the Research Office made substantial inroads into completing a draft of Volume 5 during a period when it could not wind up work on the three contemporary policy documents discussed in the following section. Beyond this, the whole project was seen as relevant to contemporary policy. The Chairman's writings were regarded both as the starting point for current policy directions, and as a necessary theoretical support for any approach taken. This will become clear when we examine the various "weeds" produced with the input and often guiding hand of Deng's think tank.[55]

While the editorial group worked on Mao's manuscripts, the Research Office's section responsible for daily work, i.e., policy-related investigation and research, undertook a range of tasks. Some, involving coordination with State Council vice premiers and other key officials, will be examined shortly. But what is of interest here is how quickly and centrally the office's activities focused on policy toward intellectuals, and how this orientation drew its impetus from Mao. This was clearly the case when Deng first addressed the leaders of the office on July 9. After greeting those assembled, Deng immediately conveyed Mao's latest instructions on letting a hundred flowers bloom and the question of literature and art—the key area of Jiang Qing's activities, and a source of her current vulnerability. Deng then elaborated on the new orientation, calling attention to the need for a hundred schools of thought to contend in scholarship, and for intellectual stultification to end. It was here that he called for gathering material on the implementation of the double hundred policy in culture, education, science, publishing, and other fields, thus making the purview of the office as broad as possible in the intellectual sphere. Even earlier, in his private talks with Hu Qiaomu on June 8 and 29, Deng indicated he wanted the Research Office to exercise direct control over elite academic activity by placing the office in charge of the Studies Department (*xuebu*) of the Academy of Sciences, the forerunner of the post-Mao Chinese Academy of Social Sciences. In all this, Deng was clearly, as Yu Guangyuan put it, seizing "the opportunity opened by Mao's comments," yet the substance of his actions were fully compatible with the Chairman's

---

[55] Yu Guangyuan, "Yi Deng Xiaoping he zhengyanshi," p. 8; *Deng Liqun guoshi jiangtan*, vol. 1, p. 389; Yu Guangyuan, *Wenge zhong de wo* [The Cultural Revolution and I] (Shanghai: Shanghai yuandong chubanshe, 1995), p. 109; and "Hu Yaobang, Li Chang de jianghua," items 13-22, p. 9. According to Deng Liqun, Deng came every week to participate in Mao study, while Yu Guangyuan noted seven occasions over a three-month period. Contrast this to Deng's total absence from the June-August State Council theory conference on the economy.

expressed discontent with the stagnation of intellectual life.[56]

In related respects, the door had also been opened by Mao. As previously noted, it was only after the Chairman's comments on literature and art that the flow of complaints from creative artists began to flow. Mao had indicated his impatience with the overly rigid limitations on cultural output enforced by the radicals since at least the late 1974 case of the *Song of the Gardener*, when Hua Guofeng had pushed the liberalization cause well before Deng.[57] Now, the Chairman's early and mid-July complaints to Deng about the scarcity of artistic output, finding fault over trifles, and the inability of artists to express their opinions, legitimized gathering material on the failure to implement the Hundred Flowers in the arts. The materials gathered included letters of complaint, usually addressed to Deng or Mao, but channeled through the Research Office. In the most famous case, that of the film *Pioneers*, letters written by the scriptwriter on July 18 concerning Jiang Qing's suppression of the film were passed to Hu Qiaomu, then on to Deng who presented them to Mao. Mao responded on the 25th, found nothing seriously wrong with the film, criticized the radicals for their excessive attacks, and again emphasized the need for an adjustment of policy toward literature and art. This, in turn, allowed Deng to bring further pressure on the Ministry of Culture, and undoubtedly furthered the stream of additional letters from oppressed artists to Mao through the auspices of the Research Office (especially Hu Qiaomu and Deng Liqun), and Deng Xiaoping personally.[58]

Mao's authority was also invoked in the move to establish a theoretical journal run by the Research·Office, albeit less directly and *via* a rather creative effort on the part of Deng. When the office was being set up, Deng already proposed that the Studies Department run such a journal, and he emphasized several times subsequently its importance and the need to move quickly. The need for such a publication was clear given that the Central Committee's theoretical organ, *Red Flag*, which remained under radical control, only emphasized the first of Mao's three directives on studying theory, to the neglect of the other two instructions. Preparations began in August, with Hu Qiaomu proposing the title *Ideological Frontline*. In suggesting topics for the magazine in September, Deng singled out (along with Party rectification) the double hundred policy that Mao had highlighted in July. In the spirit of breaking through restrictions, Deng repeatedly

[56] Yu Guangyuan, "Yi Deng Xiaoping he zhengyanshi," p. 6; and Feng Lanrui, "Zhengzhi yanjiushi de rizi," p. 5. Personal responsibility for the Studies Department and several institutes was given to Hu Sheng, while Yu Guangyuan was assigned the tasks of assisting the economics institute and establishing a SPC research institute.

[57] See above, pp. 313-14n32. Although in Beijing, Hua maintained daily contact with Hunan, issuing instructions on the movies and other entertainment to be offered to the Chairman. It could be argued that in raising the *Song of the Gardener* matter, Hua was being bolder than Deng half a year later since, in late 1974, Mao had not yet spoken clearly on the double hundred policy.

[58] Yu Guangyuan, "Yi Deng Xiaoping he zhengyanshi," p. 13; Cheng Zhongyuan, "Zhengzhi yanjiushi," p. 143; *Mao wengao*, vol. 13, pp. 450, 452; Mao Mao, *"Wenge" suiyue*, pp. 376-77; and above, p. 310n17.

called for many journals, declaring that every institute could put one out. Here Deng invoked Mao's authority, citing the Chairman's mid-September support of the paleontological magazine *Fossil*: "[Since] the Chairman cares so much about magazines like *Fossil*, how could he not care about a general theoretical journal." The Studies Department had already prepared a report formally proposing the establishment of *Ideological Frontline* to the Party Center which Mao approved in October, albeit in the minimal manner of circling the document. But despite an elaborate schedule of articles, which included the General Program in the first issue, the magazine never appeared.[59]

The fate of the State Council Political Research Office was closely linked to that of Deng. As Deng came under pressure in November, although the office continued to function, it lost contact with its increasingly passive leader, and it soon became a focus of the criticism campaign. After Mao's death, although the Mao *Works* section became even more important and its members formed the Party Center theory group, the office as a whole was initially slated for winding down, but saved by Deng's intervention around the time he resumed office in 1977.[60] These developments will be examined in the following chapters and in our Volume II. In October 1975, however, the Research Office was still a driving force in developing the consolidation program despite the first signs of serious trouble. Among its key activities was work on the three documents that would soon be attacked as "poisonous weeds."

"The Three Poisonous Weeds": The 20 Articles on Industry, the Outline Report on the Academy of Sciences, and the General Program

Although centerpieces of Deng's effort to advance the consolidation program following Mao's grant of authority in mid-year, the three documents were arguably less significant to the politics of the period or the subsequent reversal of Deng's fortunes than often thought. A key consideration, as we have repeatedly emphasized, is that consolidation was Mao's program, and however forcefully Deng implemented that program, or however much he tried to shape it according to his own policy preferences and political objectives, he was significantly constrained. As a consequence, the interpretation skillfully argued by Kenneth Lieberthal many years ago, that Deng "sought to build bridges to potential allies [including the military, scientists, older cadres, and all leaders anxious for economic development] through a clearly antiradical program, [and the three] documents offered a powerful appeal to [this] range of potential ... supporters in

---

[59] Yu Guangyuan, "Yi Deng Xiaoping he zhengyanshi," pp. 12-13. Concerning circling documents, see above, p. 164n133.

[60] For an overview of these events, see Feng Lanrui, "Zhengzhi yanjiushi de rizi," pp. 5ff. On the situation in November, Yu Guangyuan, "Yi Deng Xiaoping he zhengyanshi," p. 15, commented that "apart from some diplomatic activities, Deng Xiaoping rarely showed his face, and he stopped seeking us out."

the succession"[61] misses the essence of leadership politics in 1975. To be sure, the program Deng developed did appeal to such groups, but it was not necessary to secure their support for several reasons. First, Deng's orientation toward stability and development was assumed on the basis of his pre-Cultural Revolution track record. Even more fundamental was the elite's inherent deference to revolutionary status, and the fact that the radicals were beyond the pale for the vast majority of the old establishment, precisely because they had attacked that establishment so harshly in 1966-68 and subsequently. But whether this support could be fully realized depended on Mao, at least as long as the Chairman lived. To put it another way, this was not in essence the politics of securing the backing of interest groups and their leaders. For Deng, it was a politics of maintaining Mao's trust while carrying out his instructions, and for the radicals one of finding a way to influence the Chairman's views, or simply to survive until he adopted a new tack.

If, as we argue, the three documents and the larger program they embodied were not essential to Deng's support in the larger elite, it is also clear that in and of themselves they were not central to his downfall. Not only had Deng consulted Mao on the policy issues addressed by the documents and reported back that the Chairman was "very concerned" about these issues, but even as Mao withdrew support from Deng he never negated any of the documents. He did not endorse them, but he did not disown them either. More broadly, the Chairman indicated in early 1976 that the Party Center (i.e., Mao himself) must bear responsibility for shortcomings in the consolidation effort. The radicals, moreover, were late in focusing on the "poisonous weeds."[62] As we will see in subsequent chapters, it was only starting in February 1976 that they began to pursue the issue, in April the documents became the focus of a press campaign, and in the summer a new upsurge of attacks on the "weeds" implicated Hua and other active leaders more than Deng. Yet for all this, the three documents were central features of Deng's efforts in June-October 1975, and they provide a window into the politics of the period.

While the State Council Research Office as Deng's think tank played a significant part in each of the documents, government bodies and leaders, notably Standing Vice Premiers Li Xiannian, Ji Dengkui and Hua Guofeng, were also critically involved. The first two documents, the 20 articles, which grew out of the June 16-August 11 State Council theory conference chaired by Li and in which Ji played an important role, and the Outline Report on the Academy of Sciences,

[61] Lieberthal, *Central Documents*, p. 34.

[62] Yu Guangyuan, "Yi Deng Xiaoping he zhengyanshi," p. 12; *RMRB*, July 7, 1977, in *SPRCP*, no. 6384 (1977), pp. 81-82, and July 16, 1977, in *SPRCP*, no. 6389 (1977), pp. 88-90; *GMRB*, August 16, 1977, in *SPRCP*, no. 6428 (1977), p. 230; *Ye Fei huiyilu*, p. 113; "Jiang Qing zai dazhaohu huiyi," p. 383; and Lieberthal, *Central Documents*, pp. 43, 49.

which gained its authorization from Hua, originated outside the Research Office but were revised within the office, particularly by Hu Qiaomu. The General Program was the product of the office, but several vice premiers were apparently called in to review its contents.

The first document undertaken, the 20 articles, was initially drafted from mid-July to early August by the SPC[63] and revised by Ji, with the Research Office (seemingly Deng Liqun and Yu Guangyuan) involved after Deng Xiaoping's August 8 request for its participation. On August 18, this 14-article draft was discussed by the State Council, with Deng confirming its basic correctness and reportedly proposing a number of additional items for inclusion.[64] This resulted in a 20-article second draft on August 22, and a more sharply worded 18-article third draft on September 2,[65] versions apparently overseen by Hu Qiaomu and other members of the Research Office. Hu emphasized that these drafts should be based on all of Mao's relevant statements, and that the "red thread" would be speeding up industrial development to achieve modernization in 25 years. The newly revised version was discussed in the first part of September by 20 enterprise leaders, and in October by 12 provincial-level Party secretaries, and their suggestions were incorporated into further (now again 20-article) fourth and fifth drafts[66] by Hu Qiaomu. This process started around October 8, and the

---

[63] Vice Premier and SPC head Yu Qiuli was reportedly placed in charge of the task although he may not, in fact, have performed the role. See "Deng Xioaping yu yijiuqiwu nian quanmian zhengdun" [Deng Xiaoping and the 1975 Comprehensive Consolidation], in Wu Shihong and Gao Qi, eds., *Deng Xiaoping yu Gongheguo zhongda lishi shijian* [Deng Xiaoping and the Republic's Major Historical Events] (Beijing: Renmin chubanshe, 2000), p. 126; and below, p. 332n83. The SPC's Fang Weizhong was the key planning official involved at every stage of the drafting process.

[64] Remuneration according to labor, emphasis on quality of production, agriculture as the basis of the national economy, strengthening the responsibility system in industry, bringing order to enterprise management, strengthening scientific research in enterprises, establishing a fixed export base, and importing advanced technology. This list combines slightly different items in Yu Guangyuan, "Yi Deng Xiaoping he zhengyanshi," p. 11; and *Selected Works of Deng (1975-1982)*, pp. 43-46. On the political significance of Deng's additions, see below.

[65] The apparent sole PRC reference to the August 22 draft is from the radical Shanghai journal *Xuexi yu pipan* [Study and Criticism], June 1976, in *Selections from People's Republic of China Magazines* (hereafter *SPRCM*), no. 879 (1976), p. 1; it is not mentioned in any post-Mao source we have seen. A definitely genuine text of this draft appeared in *Zhanwang*, no. 372 (1977), pp. 31-36. The differences between the second and third drafts involved a reorganization of material, the exclusion of some relatively minor articles, and the addition of articles on Party leadership and relying on the working class; cf. Lieberthal, *Central Documents*, pp. 46-47. We speculate that the second draft was an immediate response to Deng's comments, while the third involved polishing the text by Hu Qiaomu. All of the points raised by Deng on August 18 remained in the third draft. The important difference was not content, but the much more pointed tone of the third draft, with its sharp barbs against rebels who had undermined industrial production. Ironically, and we again speculate, this seems less the input of Deng than of his "pen," Hu Qiaomu, and it apparently reflected Ji Dengkui's strong criticisms of rebel activities on August 31. In any case, this contrasted with the softening of the Outline Report that Deng and Hu Qiaomu both contributed to in the same period (see below).

[66] Although the discussion is inconsistent in various sources, an October 14 version apparently reflected the views of the 20 enterprise leaders, while the October 25 draft also incorporated the input

document was finally presented on the 25th as the political landscape shifted. These drafts, which may or may not have reached Mao, were substantially different, containing significant political adjustments that will be discussed shortly. Even the softened fifth version quickly came under radical pressure in the Politburo and State Council, leading Hu Qiaomu to produce a sixth draft on November 3. By that time, however, Deng was firmly in Mao's sights, and this draft and yet another subsequent version were shelved.[67]

Meanwhile, on July 18 Hua Guofeng, the Vice Premier responsible for science and technology, dispatched a leadership team of Hu Yaobang, Li Chang and Wang Guangwei to overhaul the Academy of Sciences, improve scientific work, and draft a report as soon as possible after investigation and study.[68] By the end of July, the first of three versions was seemingly prepared by the three new Academy leaders under the title "Some Questions concerning Science and Technology Work," and over the following weeks the second and third drafts were submitted to Deng, while Hu Qiaomu and Yu Guangyuan were consulted on the second draft. Ironically, in view of subsequent developments, it was the first draft at the Academy, before any involvement by Deng, that became the target of radical attack in 1976. After meeting with Hu Qiaomu on August 26, Deng asked for adjustments to soften the tone (to be discussed), a task that engaged Yu Guangyuan and Hu and led to a fourth draft by early September, now retitled "Outline Report on the Work of the Academy of Sciences." With further prodding from Deng, a fifth draft was presented to the State Council on September 26, sent to Mao on the 28th, and personally reported on by Deng "about October 13." This was the precise period that Mao's attitude toward Deng began to change, and in late October the Chairman returned the report with a few

of the 12 provincial secretaries.

[67] Yu Guangyuan, "Yi Deng Xiaoping he zhengyanshi," pp. 10-11; Xue Qingchao, *Lishi zhuanzhe guantou*, pp. 416-18; Fang Weizhong, *Jingji dashiji*, pp. 550-52; Cheng Zhongyuan, "Guowuyuan zhengyanshi zai 1975 nian zhengdun zhong de zhongyao zuoyong" [The Important Function of the State Council Political Research Office during the 1975 Consolidation], in Han Taihua, ed., *Zhongguo Gongchandang ruogan lishi wenti xiezhen* [True Portrait of Some CCP Historical Questions] (Beijing: Zhongguo yuanshi chubanshe, 1998), p. 1189; *Xuexi yu pipan*, June 1976, in *SPRCM*, no. 879 (1976), pp. 1-10; *PR*, no. 42 (1977), p. 7; and Lieberthal, *Central Documents*, pp. 44-48.

Concerning whether the 20 articles ever reached Mao, we have found no explicit statement that they did. Nevertheless, it seems questionable that they would not have, in view of Yu Guangyuan's comment (p. 12) that the Politburo "naturally" could not discuss the Outline Report because Mao had not approved it, and his report (p. 11) that Deng said the General Program could go to the Politburo *if* the Chairman agreed. When taken together with the fact that the 20 articles were discussed in the Politburo in October, this suggests at least some tentative approval by Mao. That Yao Wenyuan expressed reservations about the document during a Politburo meeting may indicate that Mao only called for discussion, or that the Chairman's shifting views were becoming apparent. On the late October Politburo discussion and Zhang Chunqiao's simultaneous objections in the State Council, see below.

[68] See *ZGDSCKZL*, vol. 27, pp. 531-32. Lieberthal, *Central Documents*, pp. 37-38, notes other related activities by Hua in this period, including convening an August conference on science and technology.

instructions for alterations. Deng then arranged for Hu Qiaomu to prepare a sixth draft, but by the time it was ready Deng was under attack, and the new version of the document was never sent to Mao.[69]

While the 20 articles and Outline Report had developed early and were efforts to lay down systematic policy guidelines in specific areas of current concern, the General Program came later and sought to articulate a broad philosophic approach to the Party's work. The basic idea, which reflected Deng's disdain for the "mutilation of Mao's Thought," i.e., the one-sided ideology of the radicals, originated with Hu Qiaomu's September 19 proposal for an article explicating the relationship among the three directives that Deng had decreed were the key link. Deng immediately approved, and asked that the essay be written quickly, indicating that he would call in several vice premiers to vet it so it could then be passed on to Mao. If the Chairman agreed, it could then go to the Politburo for approval. In pushing for action Deng repeated his ideas on comprehensive consolidation that he had articulated at the Dazhai conference five days earlier, and which in fact had stimulated Hu's proposal, and called for completing Party rectification the coming winter and following spring. Hu Qiaomu assigned the task of organizing the essay to Deng Liqun,[70] with several other members of the Research Office doing the actual writing. While others in the office were pleased with the resulting October 7 draft, Hu was dissatisfied with its combative tone and called for a substantial rewriting. This assignment finally fell to Wu Lengxi, but by the time Wu was finished in November, anti-Deng criticism had begun within the top leadership, and Wu's effort was not even read by Hu Qiaomu, much less vetted by Deng or sent to Mao. Indeed, Deng would later claim that he had not even seen the earlier Deng Liqun-organized draft until the post-Mao period in early 1977.[71]

What was the content of these three documents?[72] Although different in

---

[69] Yu Guangyuan, "Yi Deng Xiaoping he zhengyanshi," pp. 9-10; Cheng Zhongyuan, "Guowuyuan zhengyanshi zai 1975 nian zhengdun," p. 1193; and Lieberthal, *Central Documents*, pp. 35-44. In Cheng Zhongyuan's article only the third draft was sent to Deng. As in the case of the 20 articles, Lieberthal's account, based on sources from 1976-77, is basically compatible with post-Mao sources, although there are some differences.

[70] Although commonly referred to as the author of the General Program, Deng Liqun's role was to give oral instructions to others who did the actual drafting. Hu Qiaomu, with a degree of intellectual snobbery, would later comment that Deng Liqun did not really know how to write; see Li Rui, "Hu Yaobang qushiqian de tanhua" [Talks before Hu Yaobang Passed Away], *Xinshiji* [New Century Net] (May 1, 2002), http://www.ncn.org/asp/zwginfo/da.asp?ID=44257&ad=1/5/2002. The actual writing of the draft was done by Hu Jiwei, Yu Zongyan, Su Pei and Teng Wensheng. See Chen and Du, *Shilu*, vol. 3, part 2, p. 1278.

[71] Yu Guangyuan, "Yi Deng Xiaoping he zhengyanshi," pp. 11-12; Zhang Hua, "Yetan Mao Zedong de sanxiang zhishi yu 1975 nian de zhengdun" [A Further Discussion of Mao Zedong's Three Directives and the 1975 Consolidation], *Zhonggong dangshi yanjiu* [Research on CCP History], no. 5 (1997), p. 72; and interview with senior Party historian, January 2000.

[72] The following is largely based on the versions of each document most fully available: the September

focus and detail, they presented a common view and considerable repetition of specific themes. They were all written with an anti-revisionist gloss and repeated citations of the Chairman's words and authority. In particular, ostensible pride of place was given to Mao's directive on studying the theory of the dictatorship of the proletariat: according to the General Program, "the study [campaign] and opposing and preventing revisionism is of prime importance among the three important instructions."[73] Moreover, while no names could be mentioned, the documents represented scathing Cultural Revolution-style attacks on the radicals who, allegedly in Lin Biao like fashion, "[waved] the flag of anti-revisionism to practice revisionism."[74] Even more striking, the Outline Report defined *zhengdun* as deepening the Cultural Revolution ideal of "struggle-criticism-transformation" (*dou-pi-gai*).[75] In practical terms, however, the thrust of the documents was quite different. As Yu Guangyuan recalled, while Deng's assertion was that Mao's three directives were inseparable and together formed the key link, a theme included in each of the documents in one draft or another, in fact "the true focus [Deng] stressed was the latter two instructions [on stability and unity and developing the economy]."[76] One could go even further to say that the thrust was restorationist: not of capitalism, of course, but of orthodox Maoist socialism pre-1966. This did not exclude support of some measures that had been strongly advocated since 1966,[77] but these had pre-Cultural Revolution roots and the orientation was away from the most unique and disruptive features of the 1966-68 movement. There was nothing particularly innovative in all this; it was largely a case of laying out at greater length and with specific application the themes Deng had been

2 draft of the 20 (actually 18 in this version) articles (trans. in Lieberthal, *Central Documents*, pp. 115-40); Hu Qiaomu's early September draft of the Outline Report (trans. in *ibid.*, pp. 141-54); and Deng Liqun's October 7 draft of the General Program (trans. in *IS*, August 1977, pp. 77-99). On the basis of what has been published in the PRC, these translations, based on 1977 Hong Kong and Taiwan sources, are clearly genuine. See *ZGDSCKZL*, vol. 27, pp. 487-98, 507-18, 528-31. In the case of the General Program and the 20 articles, the versions used here are those the radicals seemingly found most offensive and singled out for criticism as "poisonous weeds." In the case of the Outline Report, the third part of Hu Yaobang's initial draft became the "weed"; the translation in *IS*, September 1977, pp. 63-70, is of this version. See Yu Guangyuan, "Yi Deng Xiaoping he zhengyanshi," pp. 10, 12; Lieberthal, *Central Documents*, pp. 46-47; and *RMRB*, July 7, 1977, in *SPRCP*, no. 6384 (1977), p. 81.

[73] General Program in *IS*, August 1977, p. 79.

[74] *Ibid.*, p. 80. Charging opponents with using anti-revisionist slogans as a cover for sinister motives was a game played by both sides. The radicals applied the same logic in 1976 when denouncing the "three weeds"; see Yao Wenyuan's February 1976 comment as reported in *RMRB*, July 7, 1977, in *SPRCP*, no. 6384 (1977), p. 84.

[75] Outline Report in Lieberthal, *Central Documents*, p. 150. This undoubtedly was the contribution of the Research Office. On August 22, Hu Sheng visited the Academy with this message; Cheng Zhongyuan, "Guowuyuan zhengyanshi zai 1975 nian zhengdun," p. 1183.

[76] Yu Guangyuan, "Yi Deng Xiaoping he zhengyanshi," p. 11.

[77] E.g., worker participation in management, cadre participation in labor, and continuing, although modified, decentralization. See the 20 (18) articles in Lieberthal, *Central Documents*, pp. 122-23, 125-27.

articulating since at least March, and driving home the implications of Mao's forceful mid-year endorsement of the Hundred Flowers policy.

Perhaps the most fundamental message of the three documents was simply the need to restore disciplined Party leadership, with its corollary that factionalism would not be tolerated. This was to involve organizational and personnel readjustment, including the Party rectification that Deng had emphasized when approving Hu Qiaomu's proposal for the essay which became the General Program. Order and discipline were endorsed in each document, and the 20 articles highlighted its economic counterpart of unified planning. Notwithstanding specific economic proposals, the essence of the approach to developing the economy was to use political methods to fix it, i.e., there was little wrong with the economy *per se* that could not be set right by eliminating Cultural Revolution indiscipline. This, of course, did not mean that the economy was anything but center stage. Although the revisionist "theory of productive forces" was routinely denigrated, "objective laws of socialist construction" had to be obeyed, and Lenin was quoted that "the result of political education can only be measured by the improvement of economic conditions."[78] The objective, moreover, was the urgent speeding up of development, Hu Qiaomu's "red thread." Despite links to the 70 articles on industry overseen by Deng in 1961 and Deng's assertion that the 20 articles revised rather than abolished the earlier guideline, the spirit of the new document was completely different: it was more in tune with the Great Leap Forward than the retreat from the leap that the 70 articles represented. Indeed, a senior specialist on the period described the State Council theory forum that provided the spirit for the 20 articles as promoting rash advance.[79] Of the concrete economic measures advocated, a number of proposals were endorsed where the radicals had previously advocated clashing views, notably on importing advanced foreign technology, exporting industrial and mining projects to pay for imports of foreign technology and equipment, adopting international trade practices such as deferred payment, and affirming

---

[78] General Program in *IS*, August 1977, pp. 89-90, 92.

[79] Interview, January 2005. The emphasis was on the need to accelerate industrial growth for defense as well as economic purposes; see the 20 (18) articles in Lieberthal, *Central Documents*, p. 116. The link between the 70 and 20 articles has been emphasized by Cheng Zhongyuan, "Guowuyuan zhengyanshi zai 1975 nian zhengdun," p. 267; and Fang Weizhong, "Wo suo zhidao de gongye ershitiao qicao shimo" [What I Know about the Complete Process of the Drafting of the 20 Articles], *ZGDSZL*, no. 3 (2004), p. 80. Fang quotes Deng asking, "how are the 20 articles going now, they are in fact more important than the present briefing [on the 10-Year Plan], basically they replace the 70 articles from the past." There indeed were continuities, especially regarding the need for regulations, responsibility systems and Party leadership, but the two documents had vastly different objectives.

A practical measure reflecting the current emphasis was establishing a State Council steel industry leadership group headed by Gu Mu, with Ji Dengkui as political commissar, on September 21. The new group, with similar functions to the steel guarantee small group set up in March (see above, p. 266), was responsible for overcoming the lag in meeting the steel target of 26 million tons, a situation reminiscent of the production headquarters set up during the Great Leap. See Chen and Du, *Shilu*, vol. 3, part 2, p. 1268.

remuneration according to work.[80]

Concerning science and technology, the Outline Report set an agenda expressing even greater urgency and calling for a ten-year plan to repair the parlous state of Chinese science. Although hedged rhetorically by statements such as "the elite are the most ignorant" and "bourgeois thought [has] exerted a relatively deep influence [in the Academy of Sciences]," the document essentially called for a readjustment of policy toward scientific intellectuals, and laid down concrete if broad tasks for the scientific community. While continuing to insist on politics in command, there were repeated injunctions not to be one sided, and the report called for recognizing the role of specialist scientists and their research organizations, supporting basic research, using intellectuals who had not completed remolding, and abjuring the use of crude ideological interference in academic matters. Three broad objectives for scientific work were laid down: undertaking major research tasks required for economic and defense construction, opening up new areas of science and technology including information theory, new energy sources, and environmental science, and developing research in the basic sciences. All in all, the Outline Report built on Mao's July demands for implementing the double hundred policy, while at the same time carefully taking into account the Chairman's prejudices concerning intellectuals.[81]

What can be said about the politics of drafting the three documents? One aspect, insightfully discussed by Kenneth Lieberthal a quarter of a century ago, was the consultative nature of the process, incremental adjustments in the documents, and the fact that the division of work responsibilities served to limit the radicals' knowledge of developments and their ability to interfere. As Lieberthal observed, the process followed established bureaucratic procedures, notably of the pre-Cultural Revolution period: an initiative from the top, a series of drafts generated by the bureaucracy which were circulated, commented upon and revised, attention to political circumstances in revising language, and a bureaucratic routing of information that kept documents largely bottled up in relevant functional segments of the hierarchy until almost ready for final adoption. In the case at hand, since the radicals had no responsibility for the economy or science (and were not involved in the Research Office), they had no right to know about, and thus little ability to object to, the three documents as they evolved in August-September. It was only in October as the political

---

[80] See the 20 (18) articles in Lieberthal, *Central Documents*, pp. 133-36. On the attendant politics, see below.

[81] Outline Report in Lieberthal, *Central Documents*, pp. 142-44, 146, 148-49. As suggested earlier, however, concerned Party leaders could overestimate Mao's pro-intellectual stance. A case in point was Hu Yaobang's September 23 visit to the Academy of Sciences' printing house when he told the printers that "now intellectuals are moving ahead of the workers," and it was the Chairman's demand that the workers catch up. This was in response to Mao's brief remark concerning the scientific journal *Fossil* (see above, p. 324) on September 16. See *Mao wengao*, vol. 13, p 468; and "Hu Yaobang, Li Chang de jianghua," items 13-22, p. 25.

climate changed, and more particularly in 1976, that they were in a position to raise objections.[82] This very fact, as well as even more striking evidence in the educational sphere where the radicals did have organizational responsibility (see the following section), indicates that while bureaucratic norms played a role, they were far less significant than, and in vital respects a function of, political factors. In short, it was largely because of the political blow suffered by the radicals at Mao's hand in May-June that the bureaucratic rules of handling documents could again function as well as they did, and subsequently due to the Chairman's change of heart in the fall and winter that the process was largely paralyzed.

Apart from bureaucratic procedures, the roles of individual leaders deserve comment. Deng's role, as we have seen in the setting up and operation of the Research Office, was of course vital. However, accounts of the period tend to neglect the contributions of others, while overemphasizing his. The clearest case concerns the economy, an area where Li Xiannian, who personally received the Chairman's directive on boosting the economy, had overall responsibility. Deng apparently never attended the State Council theory conference, which met several times per week over a two-month period. This forum, denounced by the radicals in 1976 as the "high tide of restoration," generated the "spirit" of the 20 articles. Li Xiannian was in charge, and seven other vice premiers, notably Ji Dengkui, Hua Guofeng and Chen Xilian,[83] participated and spoke. The leaders of economic ministries and members of the Research Office also attended. The conference further examined the especially sensitive area of education, something Deng subsequently highlighted in September after the conference wound down. In any case, while the precise details concerning who took the initiative on various specific issues remain unclear, the 20 articles' emphasis on restoring discipline and cracking down on

---

[82] See Lieberthal, *Central Documents*, pp. 39-40, 48-49. The division of work, however, was not airtight in that followers of the radicals within the Academy of Sciences provided the "gang" information concerning the Outline Report, while Yao Wenyuan reportedly obtained a copy of a version of the 20 (18) articles in September, presumably from a follower in a relevant economic unit or someone who had seen a copy of the draft when it was circulated. See *ibid.*, pp. 40-41, 47-48.

[83] The others mentioned were Wu Guixian, Wang Zhen, Gu Mu and Sun Jian. Thus only Deng, Zhang Chunqiao, Chen Yonggui and Yu Qiuli were not listed. The absence of Yu Qiuli from this listing is puzzling, given his leadership of the SPC and reported assignment to oversee the initial draft of the 14-article version. Yu was also apparently absent from other meetings in the period. This was possibly due to illness, or perhaps for political reasons. It is striking that while the Dazhai model for agriculture had high prominence in this period, the Daqing model for industry which was closely connected to Yu received little publicity. Indeed, as noted in Chapter 4, Jiang Qing's early 1975 criticism of the film *Pioneers* about heroic oil workers can be seen as an attack on Daqing. But with the radicals' fortunes in decline in the spring, it may have been Deng's dissatisfaction with Yu over the performance of the steel industry in March that was more telling. See above, pp. 249, 265.

As for Deng, immediately following the purge of the "gang of four" in October 1976, Hua claimed he (Deng) had not attended the theory forum; see below, p. 462. While logically, if inaccurately, absolving Deng of a connection with the "high tide of restoration," it more importantly disassociated the policies of the 20 articles, which the post-Mao leadership would quickly pursue, from Deng, who was still subject to *pro forma* criticism. By mid-1977 official propaganda was fully engaged in refuting the radical critique of the "three weeds."

factionalism in industry had been a Deng theme since at least March.[84]

While exaggerated in post-Mao sources, one can hardly doubt Deng's interest in, and impact on, this area beyond the crackdown on factionalism: it was his proposal in June to convene a theory conference on the long-term economic plan, and his interventions at meetings on August 8 and 18 clearly had an important effect on the evolution of the 20 articles. The latter intervention was particularly revealing about the politics of the period, and somewhat different from his more cautious actions in the case of the Outline Report discussed below. On the 18th, Deng raised a number of items that were reportedly added to the 14-article draft, including the particularly sensitive matters of remuneration according to labor and importing advanced foreign technology. Whether these matters had been discussed at the theory conference is unclear, but apparently they and other issues addressed by Deng were not in the initial document.[85]

At one level, Deng's additions should not have been particularly controversial. For example, notwithstanding the angst of the radicals, importing foreign technology and paying for it with the export of China's energy resources and foreign exchange reserves had been initiated by Mao in 1971-72 and continued to receive his endorsement as necessary policies in 1973-74.[86] Yet in the climate of the time, against the background of Cultural Revolution assaults on "material

---

[84] Fang Weizhong, *Jingji dashiji*, pp. 546-47, 550-52; Chen and Du, *Shilu*, vol. 3, part 2, p. 1228; and below, pp. 342-43. Deng's major speeches on industrial matters in March and May were almost solely devoted to restoring discipline, and it was only in August, as the theory conference moved toward its conclusion and the 14 articles were drafted that he addressed other economic questions. See *Selected Works of Deng (1975-1982)*, pp. 14-22, 40-46.

[85] Accounts of the theory conference indicate that in its second stage from July 2 it addressed specific issues in functional groups, but discussions of matters such as foreign technology and remuneration according to work were not reported. Fang Weizhong, *Jingji dashiji*, p. 547. According to *Xuexi yu pipan*, June 1976, two articles definitely added after Deng's August 18 intervention were those on remuneration according to work and increasing exports of industrial and mineral products, exports which would provide funds for importing technology. Lieberthal, *Central Documents*, p. 46.

[86] See *Weida de renmin gongpu—huainian Li Xiannian Tongzhi* [A Great Public Servant—Cherish the Memory of Comrade Li Xiannian] (Beijing: Zhongyang wenxian chubanshe, 1993), p. 448; and above, p. 51n70.

In the context of both the economic opening to the outside world from early 1972 and the market opportunities due to the fall 1973 international oil crisis, petroleum exports at least doubled each year from 1972 to 1975, clearly with Mao's consent. According to Hua Guofeng, Mao added a zero to the proposed oil exports to Thailand, thus increasing the amount tenfold. It was only during consolidation in 1975, however, that a historic peak was reached, and exports as a percentage of production increased from 10 to 16 percent. When under attack in January 1976, Deng assumed responsibility for increasing exports and cutting fuel supplies to Shanghai and Liaoning. Hua Guofeng's speech of November 7, 1976, handwritten document available at the Menzies Library, the Australian National University; Kenneth Lieberthal and Michel Oksenberg, *Policy Making in China: Leaders, Structures, and Processes* (Princeton: Princeton University Press, 1988), p. 202; and Qing and Fang, *Deng zai 1976*, vol. 1, p. 37. In any case, this policy was under pressure by October, arguably due to Mao Yuanxin's representations to the Chairman, and the article on the issue was dropped from the October 25 version of the document. See Cheng and Xia, *Deng zai yijiuqiwu*, p. 266; and below, pp. 375-76.

incentives" and the recent discussions of "bourgeois right," advocating the socialist principle of distribution according to work during the present historical stage of socialist construction was apparently regarded by the economic specialists as too hot to handle. Indeed, in October 1974 Mao included distribution according to labor among practices he subsequently identified as examples of "bourgeois right." In facing the matter, Deng hesitated, agonizing whether "the time was right," but decided he could not be at ease (*fangxin*) if the matter was left unaddressed. Of course, in dealing with the issue, the relevant article was careful to inveigh against material incentives and bourgeois right, and advocated raising the wages of low-paid workers as part of a gradual reform of the existing wage system. The episode, in any case, sheds light on Deng's acclaimed "courage" in pushing forward the consolidation program in 1975, and the reported concern of Zhou Enlai and Ye Jianying that he was being too bold. While post-Mao views of Deng's boldness have been overstated, here was a case where he took some risks, pushing the envelope a bit further in contrast to restraining others over the Outline Report a week later. This arguably reflected the difference between reviving the economy where his assignment had been clear from the start of 1975, and the more sensitive issues surrounding intellectuals even with Mao's mid-year shift. What is particularly striking was the trepidation surrounding a matter that should not have been so difficult given Mao's current concern with the economy and Deng's newly confirmed authority, not to mention the fact that distribution according to work had been affirmed in the new state constitution only seven months earlier. Nevertheless, the uncertainty surrounding the Chairman's ultimate thinking caused great nervousness.[87]

There are other aspects of Deng's role in pushing forward the program embodied in the three documents to consider beyond his involvement with the documents themselves. The question is: how deeply was he involved in supporting different bureaucracies as they implemented the consolidation program? While our conclusion is impressionistic, apparently many of the old cadres called back to assume leading roles in State Council ministries at the Fourth NPC largely functioned independently of Deng's close attention. They may have taken solace from Deng's clout as *de facto* premier, or even received his encouragement at one point or another, but often they seemed to be on their own. A case in point was Minister of Communications Ye Fei. As we saw in the previous chapter, although Deng certainly backed Ye's efforts, it was more a matter of giving him a "free hand" to build up shipping than providing ongoing close support; Li Xiannian, as was appropriate from his economic portfolio, appears to have been more involved with Ye's work. Indeed, despite the sensitivity of purchasing foreign ships as seen in the *Fengqing* incident, Ye continued to implement this program into 1976 despite attacks on his ministry during the anti-Deng campaign, and his

[87] See Yu Guangyuan, "Yi Deng Xiaoping he zhengyanshi," p. 11; Chen and Du, *Shilu*, vol. 3, part 2, p. 1141; Xue Qingchao, *Lishi zhuanzhe guantou*,, pp. 415-17; Zhang Hua, "Yetan Mao Zedong de sanxiang zhishi," p. 71; *Xuexi yu pipan*, no. 6 (1976), p. 16; *PR*, no. 4 (1975), p. 14; and the 20 articles in Lieberthal, *Central Documents*, p. 135.

defense of his actions is instructive. Ye argued that he had not been carrying out Deng's line, but merely implementing the spirit of central documents approved by Mao in the first half of 1975, documents that had never been revoked.[88]

It is also necessary to consider the personnel on the cutting edge of the three documents. While these individuals are often considered Deng's people, in fact, as we saw in the staffing of the Research Office, the relevance of Mao was more significant. The most striking case is that of Hu Yaobang, the fervent reformer of the post-Mao period who has generally been regarded as Deng's protégé. While Hu's career, particularly after 1949, had links to Deng, he had been rapidly promoted before 1949 by Mao personally, and assigned to his key post-revolution positions by the Chairman.[89] Moreover, after being ousted during the Cultural Revolution, Hu was among four cadres slated by Mao for "liberation" in the immediate post-Lin Biao period.[90] In 1975 he was assigned to the Academy of Sciences shortly after "graduating" from the required study class probably overseen by Wang Hongwen.[91] We do not know the precise circumstances of Hu's appointment to the Academy of Sciences, but in the largest sense, similar to Hua Guofeng and Ji Dengkui albiet different due to the disruption to his career, Hu owed his new prominence to Mao. But more than political obligation or acknowledgment of Mao's power was involved for Hu. By all accounts Hu remained a Mao loyalist: he continued to worship the Chairman both then and in at least the early post-Mao period. A consequence of this was that although Hu demonstrated a degree of anti-radical passion in 1975, as late as 1977 he still expressed belief that the Cultural Revolution had been "ideologically brilliant, [although] mistaken in practice."[92]

---

[88] See *Ye Fei huiyilu*, pp. 110, 112; above, pp. 267-68; and below, p. 457. The central documents in question, nos. 9, 12 and 13, dealt with railroads, suppressing factionalism, and steel production respectively.

[89] After the Long March, Mao assigned Hu a leading role at the Anti-Japanese University despite his youth, a role that then led to promotion in the Yan'an military structure, again at Mao's personal initiative. Hu's key post-1949 assignment as head of the Youth League in 1952 was again made by Mao. See Yang Zhongmei, *Hu Yaobang*, pp. 39-40, 47, 52-53, 83-86.

[90] The others were Lin Hujia, Zhou Rongxin and Su Zhenhua. Fu Yi, "Jiaoyu buzhang Zhou Rongxin de zuihou suiyue" [Minister of Education Zhou Rongxin's Last Years], *BNC*, no. 2 (2002), p. 39. The actual measure was a demand for their self-criticism, a process that would almost certainly lead to rehabilitation.

Interestingly, in 1980 Hu confided that Mao (along with He Long, Lin Biao and especially Luo Ruiqing) understood him well, and drew a contrast to Zhou Enlai and Li Xiannian who didn't understand him. Wang Zhongfang, "Yaobang yu wode liangci tanxin" [(Hu) Yaobang's Two Heart-to-heart Talks with Me (in Jiangxi)], *Yanhuang chunqiu*, no. 7 (2005), pp. 16-17. Hu Yaobang further stated that "of course Comrade Xiaoping understood me."

[91] "Hu Yaobang, Li Chang de jianghua," items 13-22, p. 7. An interesting insight into Mao's dominance of the political process in 1975 was the fact that Hu, like all study class students, was required to write a "thesis" on his ideological understanding and progress before being allowed to graduate. Mao had set a 3,000-character limit, and Hu expended a great deal of anxious energy in getting his essay down to 2,980 characters.

[92] Shen Baoxiang, *Zhenli biaozhun wenti taolun shimo* [The Debate on the Criterion of Truth Issue from Beginning to End] (Beijing: Zhongguo qingnian chubanshe, 1997), p. 24. Hu expressed this

In short, even those deeply involved in the consolidation process were profoundly influenced by Maoist ways of thinking, as graphically illustrated by the comment of Hu's colleague in the new Academy leadership, Li Chang, that consolidation was like resting after a battle while preparing for the next struggle.[93]

Indeed, from start to finish in the drafting of the three documents, Mao's views were of primary concern. The standard operating procedure at the Academy, the Research Office, and the economic departments involved in the 20 articles was to begin by collecting and studying the Chairman's (and the Party Center's) pronouncements on the subject at issue. Even Deng himself, as we have seen, took time every week or two to meet with top Party intellectuals to study Mao's writings in the course of overseeing the *Selected Works*.[94] As drafting proceeded, the need to stay within Mao's parameters was a repeated concern, one apparently better understood by older leaders with more personal experience of the Chairman and his ambiguities than by their more junior colleagues enthused by the battle against the radicals. A case in point was Deng's August 26 reaction to Hu Yaobang's draft of the Outline Report:

> The Academy of Sciences draft touches on too many problems; it's unnecessarily sharp and unsteady. The Academy of Sciences is also a controversial unit; to say so much and to say it sure handedly is very difficult. Say less, and don't put everything so harshly. Make sure to say less among the masses, wait till the outline is properly revised and passed by the State Council and approved by Chairman Mao; let the outline speak for itself, and let the masses speak for themselves when discussing the outline. This document is very important; you must strengthen its ideological content, make it more persuasive, but don't be too sharp. It must be solidly argued and unassailable.[95]

---

opinion in September 1977 to Shen and others at the Central Party School as they undertook the task of liberalizing Mao's Thought. Hu's devotion to Mao has been attested to by various well-placed oral sources.

As for Hu's performance in 1975, on the one hand he oversaw the "too sharp" draft of the Outline Report considered on August 26 (see below), but on the other hand Wang Zhen, well after the fact, regarded Hu's performance at the subsequent September 26 meeting on the next draft of the report as "too cautious." "Wang Zhen Tongzhi zai zhengzhi yanjiushi jianghua" [Comrade Wang Zhen's Talk at the Political Research Office] (December 17, 1976), document available at the Fairbank Center Library, Harvard University.

[93] See above, p. 246.

[94] See Li Chang's speech of September 9, 1975, in "Hu Yaobang, Li Chang de jianghua," items 13-22, pp. 43-44; *Deng Liqun guoshi jiangtan*, vol. 1, pp. 388-89; and above, p. 322n55. In the case of the Academy, it appears the new leadership initially focused on the study of the dictatorship of the proletariat, and it took an impatient Hua Guofeng to get these leaders to embark on *zhengdun*. There is a paradox in that this Academy leadership, which had to be encouraged from above, still produced a draft that Deng considered too sharp (see below).

[95] Yu Guangyuan, "Yi Deng Xiaoping he zhengyanshi," p. 9.

While it is reasonable to speculate that the emergence of the *Water Margin* issue in mid-August influenced Deng's cautious response,[96] we do not believe this was the case at this stage for reasons to be discussed in more detail subsequently. In brief, the *Water Margin* had not yet become a matter of concern to Deng; his caution is better understood as prudent wariness when it came to Mao's sensibilities—particularly concerning intellectuals. In any case, rather than return the draft to Hu Yaobang, Deng assigned the Mao-savvy Hu Qiaomu with the task of revision. Hu Qiaomu shortened the text, inserted some anti-revisionist rhetoric, and added a section of Mao's statements on science and technology for the fourth draft. Deng, apparently seeking even greater ideological cover, then asked for a more thorough compilation of quotations from Marx, Engels, Lenin and Mao on the natural sciences in preparation for the subsequent draft that was submitted to Mao on September 28. This prudence, together with the belief Deng expressed at the time that Mao was extraordinarily interested in the issues the Outline Report was addressing, contributed to his confidence that the Chairman would be fully aboard. But as stated in the final quotation at the start of this chapter, this draft contained the erroneous Mao quotation that "science and technology is a force of production" which drew the Chairman's querulous response, and seemingly contributed to his changing attitude toward Deng in the wake of Mao Yuanxin's late September complaints about Deng (see the concluding section of this chapter).[97]

If Deng's caution on August 26 came at a time when he was still very confident of Mao's support, subsequent politically-inspired revisions of the three documents surely reflected worry over possible danger, although the matter is by no means entirely clear. The intensification of *Water Margin* criticism by the radicals in early and mid-September may have been a factor. Additionally, if our conclusion that Mao's reconsideration of Deng began in the last few days of September is correct (see the concluding section of this chapter), a sense of threat can reasonably be seen in revisions in early to mid-October. With regard to the Outline Report, Deng saw the Chairman "about October 13." Mao's questioning of his alleged statement that "science and technology is a force of production"

---

[96] See Lieberthal, *Central Documents*, p. 37. This was the interpretation of the radicals when they attacked the "three poisonous weeds" in 1976. At the time, on August 26, Deng reassured those present that there was no cause to "imagine that things might go wrong" because of the *Water Margin* question. A month later he still expressed confidence, telling relevant officials they should not be afraid to act boldly in supporting the Outline Report; *ibid.*, p. 39. By this stage, however, there were indications that his confidence had been dented (see below).

[97] Yu Guangyuan, "Yi Deng Xiaoping he zhengyanshi," pp. 9-10; Xue Qingchao, *Lishi zhuanzhe guantou*, p. 422; Chen and Du, *Shilu*, vol. 3, part 2, p. 1271; and below, pp. 375-77. The erroneous quotation was based on unreliable Cultural Revolution period internal materials concerning a 1963 comment. Following Mao's reaction, a thorough check of the occasion revealed that Mao's actual statement was "without doing science and technology, the forces of production cannot be improved." Cf. above, p. 306n3. The claim that "science and technology is a force of production" had also been included in Hu Qiaomu's early September draft (see Outline Report in Lieberthal, *Central Documents*, p. 145). Ironically, in overreaching for Mao's authority, Hu inadvertently undercut Deng's cause.

should have alerted Deng, and it is possible, although by no means certain, that the Chairman used the occasion to convey concern about Deng's slogan that "the three directives are the key link."[98] In any case, when Hu Qiaomu produced the fourth and fifth drafts of the 20 articles between October 8 and 25, he not only virtually doubled the document's length by adding an article on "Carrying out Chairman Mao's line on developing industry in a comprehensive manner," which contained 66 Mao quotations, as well as including Mao's comments on the Cultural Revolution and *Water Margin*, he also substituted "take the Party's basic line as the key link" for "the three directives are the key link." Similarly, in mid-October, the reference to "the three directives [as] the key link" was deleted, presumably by Wu Lengxi, from the October 7 draft of the General Program that had earned Hu Qiaomu's displeasure, a development plausibly linked to Deng's meeting with Mao in the same period.[99]

As the foregoing shows, the importance of Mao's words and perceived attitudes cannot be overstated. A critical aspect of this was that no one could be completely sure of where the Chairman stood—thus Chen Yun's question to Deng whether he accurately understood Mao's meaning. With access to Mao limited (although Deng may have had more in this period than any other top leader apart from Wang Dongxing), not to mention the often Delphic nature of the Chairman's comments, imperfect understanding was hardly surprising. A striking case concerned Mao's "third" directive on boosting the national economy.[100] The radicals might well have been unsure that this was in fact a clear instruction from Mao. Jiang Qing would later claim that she had hardly heard of such a directive, while her doubts about the larger proposition concerning the "key link" seemingly influenced Mao Yuanxin's crucial exchange with the Chairman in late September. In fact, it may have been the case that no clear proof of such a directive was available. Consider CCP Document no. 4 (1975) issued on February 10 and vetted by Mao. In laying out guidelines on economic planning, the document stated that "*we have to insist on revolution, production, work, war preparations,* and boosting the national economy," but only the italicized

---

[98] Notwithstanding his approval of documents carrying this slogan as late as mid-September, at some point in the fall or early winter Mao objected to the formulation as undermining the correct concept that "class struggle is the key link." This occurred during the October-January period, but cannot be pinned down beyond that. See *Mao wengao*, vol. 13, pp. 486, 490-91, 492. The possibility of the Chairman raising the matter with Deng is suggested by the likelihood that Mao Yuanxin discussed the issue with his uncle on September 27; see below, p. 377. In the case of the Outline Report, Hu Qiaomu's early September draft spoke of "penetratingly study[ing] Chairman Mao's three important instructions"; Lieberthal, *Central Documents*, p. 151. While definitive information on the subsequent draft is not available, there is no reason to believe the three directives were not mentioned, perhaps using the offending phrase.

[99] See *RMRB*, July 7, 1977, in *SPRCP*, no. 6384 (1977), p. 82, and July 16, 1977, in *SPRCP*, no. 6389 (1977), pp. 80-81; and Lieberthal, *Central Documents*, p. 48.

[100] It was third in Deng's trilogy, although the second directive chronologically when given in November 1974.

part was rendered in the boldface used to represent Mao's instructions. The radicals might be forgiven for having doubts, and with the wind changing again, began to express their reservations—albeit very cautiously at first. When the 20 articles were considered by the Politburo in late October, Yao Wenyuan opposed presenting the document to the national planning conference on the grounds that it was "not mature," while at a State Council meeting on October 29 Zhang Chunqiao objected that its many quotations only cited Mao's pre-1966 words, ignoring his Cultural Revolution statements. Yet Mao had not clearly rejected the document either, and it was still an unsettled issue in summer 1976. In any case, while the three documents seemingly played some role in the Chairman's turnaround, they were not subjected to open criticism until spring 1976, while other matters were at least equally and probably more significant features of the politics of fall 1975.[101]

The Fourth and Fifth "Poisonous Weeds": Documents on Education and Party Rectification

Education and Party rectification provided two additional major issues in summer and fall 1975. Both of these issues emerged in the same period as the more famous "three weeds," attracted Deng's involvement and encouragement, and resulted in draft documents in the October-November period. In the last days before his arrest in October 1976, Zhang Chunqiao decided to launch an attack on the "four poisonous weeds" including the education document prepared under Minister of Education Zhou Rongxin. Although Ji Dengkui's document on Party rectification did not attain quite the same designation, in 1976 it was criticized as a sequel to the three renowned documents, and thus could be considered the "fifth weed."[102]

The importance of education in the turnaround in Deng's fortunes has long been understood: this was the first area identified in the campaign against the "rightist reversal of verdicts" in December 1975. Education was indisputably one of the most sensitive spheres of the whole post-1966 period, having been, along with culture, central in the unleashing of the Cultural Revolution. Mao pressed for

---

[101] "Jiang Qing zai dazhaohu huiyi," p. 382; Zhang Hua, "Yetan Mao Zedong de sanxiang zhishi," pp. 67-68; *RMRB*, July 16, 1977, in *SPRCP*, no. 6389 (1977), pp. 88-89; Lieberthal, *Central Documents*, pp. 48-49; and below, pp. 376, 497n85, 506ff. Oddly, *Mao wengao*, vol. 13, p. 410, claims that "boosting the national economy" was in boldface in document no. 4, but Zhang Hua's account contains convincing evidence to the contrary.

The complexity of the relationship between things Mao may have said and his "instructions" is further indicated by the fact that on the occasion Mao emphasized "boosting the national economy," he went on to speak of the need to "reduce the national population." Deng Liqun claims that this last matter was of a different order of importance, so it was not considered an instruction. *Deng Liqun guoshi jiangtan*, vol. 3, p. 115. Yet clearly the ability to package Mao's views was a critical political resource. We believe, however, that ultimately this power remained in Mao's hands, certainly concerning central Party documents.

[102] See Fu Yi, "Jiaoyu buzhang Zhou Rongxin," p. 36; and Wang and Sun, "Dang zuzhi zhengdun," p. 43.

educational reforms in the immediate pre-1966 years, but was unhappy with the bureaucracy's response, launched the Cultural Revolution on university campuses, and began a far-reaching "revolution in education" once the dust had settled and classes resumed. As we saw in Chapters 1 and 2,[103] this educational revolution with its emphasis on politics, simplified curricula, and student recruitment based on class rather than entrance examinations, clashed with the imperative of restoring educational quality, producing twists and turns in educational policy in 1972-74. At the end of 1974, however, Mao's selection of Zhou Rongxin, rather than Chi Qun, as Minister of Education enhanced the likelihood of an educational approach consistent with the broader consolidation agenda.

In addition to Zhou Rongxin's selection by Mao, rather than by Zhou Enlai and Deng Xiaoping, in other respects developments on the educational front in 1975 were not entirely as commonly believed. One aspect where conventional wisdom is on the mark, however, concerns the sharp divergence of views between the radicals and the rehabilitated establishment. As had been reflected in the Outline Report on the Academy of Sciences concerning science and technology, Deng and others were deeply concerned about the damage to the quality of education, and believed some Cultural Revolution experiments were worthless. A case in point that became the subject of a national campaign in late 1974 was Liaoning's Chaoyang experience whereby agricultural colleges had no set curriculum, were located in rural areas rather than cities, adapted courses to local agricultural needs, and trained peasants who were to return to their communes after graduation. Chi Qun was a major advocate of the Chaoyang model and, more significantly, Mao's nephew Mao Yuanxin was its key local backer. In fact, central features of the model could be seen in Mao's talks with his nephew in 1964-66, when the Chairman criticized the inadequate political content of education. The Chairman had further declared Mao Yuanxin useless since he could not grow grain or perform labor, and most importantly because he knew nothing of class struggle. The Chaoyang model was designed to overcome these shortcomings not only through its labor orientation, but especially as a political university where the emphasis was placed on struggling against revisionism and capitalist roaders. As 1975 unfolded, however, with Mao now concerned with educational deficiencies, Deng and other veteran leaders became dismissive of the Chaoyang experience. This subsequently became one of the complaints Mao Yuanxin fatefully raised with his uncle in the fall.[104]

Nevertheless, as we saw in Chapter 4, initially such matters did not lead to confrontation. This initial caution on the part of the establishment generally and Zhou Rongxin in particular reflected Mao's mixed signals of early 1975. Thus

---

[103] See above, pp. 56-59, 120-21.

[104] See Chen and Du, *Shilu*, vol. 3, part 2, pp. 1156-57; Mao's 1964-66 talks with Mao Yuanxin in Stuart Schram, ed., *Mao Tse-tung Unrehearsed, Talks and Letters: 1956-71* (Harmondsworth: Penguin Books, 1974); pp. 242-52; and below, p. 376.

when, immediately after his appointment, Zhou Rongxin consulted Chen Yun, his old superior in the 1950s, Chen's advice was to approach things cautiously, and adopt a careful attitude toward Chi Qun who, having previously been Zhou's superior in the educational hierarchy, reportedly harbored resentment over being passed over as minister, had his followers in the new ministry, and remained a key leader at Qinghua University. Chi, Chen advised, was not irrelevant. Similarly, at the end of January Zhou Enlai told Zhou Rongxin not to rush, to sort things out gradually and slowly, and to try to deal properly with people like Chi Qun. Over the next few months, as indicated previously, Zhou Rongxin followed this advice, with the Ministry of Education's activities seemingly limited initially to promoting radical educational models. Strikingly, this included substantial efforts in March and April to study the Chaoyang experience, efforts that appear little different from those carried out under the direction of Mao Yuanxin and Chi Qun in December 1974.[105]

The change in policy orientation, as discussed in the preceding chapter, came with Mao's early May comments criticizing the radicals and indicating the need for a more sympathetic attitude toward intellectuals. It was only now that Zhou Rongxin began to implement *zhengdun* work in education actively, assertedly "pointing the spearhead" at Jiang Qing and Zhang Chunqiao. The change was clearly the result of Mao's reassessment, and it was not linked to any change in bureaucratic responsibilities. Throughout both the pre-May period and in May-October, Zhang Chunqiao remained the leader responsible for education in both the Politburo and State Council, yet in neither period, Zhang complained in November, had Zhou Rongxin reported to him.[106] In terms of substance, the sharpness of the policy shift has arguably been overemphasized, perhaps in no small measure due to Zhou Rongxin's martyr status since he died in 1976, allegedly as a result of "persecution" by the "gang of four." In fact, while Zhou Rongxin, reportedly on the orders of Zhou Enlai and Deng Xiaoping, did embark within a week of the Chairman's May remarks on a series of speeches and meetings that would later be attacked as revisionist, his actions and those of others still paid homage to the "revolution in education." This can be seen in the positive assessment of the Dazhai brigade's educational model, even as the Chaoyang model was now disparaged. The difference was that while the Dazhai

---

[105] See Fu Yi, "Jiaoyu buzhang Zhou Rongxin," pp. 30-32; Ma Qibin, *Sishinian*, pp. 378, 383, 384; and above, pp. 56, 270. While Chi previously had responsibility for science and education in the State Council Science and Education Group, upon his rehabilitation in 1972 Zhou was only in charge of daily work at the Academy of Sciences.

In the double game being played by all sides during the period, however, Zhou Enlai passed on materials about Chi Qun to Ji Dengkui (who had Politburo responsibility for personnel) with a critical comment in March 1975. *Zhou nianpu*, vol. 3, p. 701.

[106] Fu Yi, "Jiaoyu buzhang Zhou Rongxin," p. 36. While Zhou did not report personally to Zhang, his reports were addressed to Zhang as the Vice Premier in charge of education. The lack of personal contact before May is intriguing, but in the circumstances following Mao's criticism of the radicals there was nothing for either man to gain from such contact. Cf. below, pp. 420-21.

approach lauded practical education and participation in labor, it still gave recognition to book knowledge and called for combining theory and practice. The Chaoyang experience, in contrast, gave short shrift to such considerations, regarding politics and "revolutionary practice" sufficient in and of themselves. More broadly, this homage can be seen in continuing genuflection to the 1971 document that provided the "two assessments."[107]

Indeed, one of Deng Xiaoping's earliest known comments on education to an American delegation in early June 1975 echoed traditional Maoist concerns: he cited the need to rectify radically "theory divorced from reality," and for educated people to be in touch with physical labor.[108] Moreover, even as comprehensive consolidation moved further into the superstructure in summer 1975, Zhou Rongxin's approach was circumspect. In late August, after spending a week reviewing Mao's statements, Zhou convened a low-key seminar involving only four provincial-level units. Although urging educational officials not to fear a reversal of policy and privately criticizing Zhang Tiesheng, the hero of the blank university entrance examination paper, the main concern of the seminar was to achieve a thorough understanding of Mao's writings, an understanding which allowed criticism of the radicals' educational approach by using the Chairman's strictures against metaphysics and one-sidedness. It was only in September that readjustment of education took a major step forward at Deng's urging. In early September, he complained in the Research Office that the many problems with education threatened the four modernizations. The crucial impetus, however, came at the September 26 meeting which considered the Outline Report on the Academy of Sciences.[109]

Zhou Rongxin attended this State Council meeting along with most vice premiers and leaders of the SPC, National Defense Science and Technology Commission and National Defense Industry Office. In the course of the discussion, Deng turned the spotlight on Zhou's ministry, speaking sharply of

---

[107] Vice Premier Wang Zhen's July attack on the Chaoyang model and call for emulation of Dazhai's experience is a case in point. Zhou Rongxin assured wider publicity for Wang's remarks by informing a Xinhua reporter, and subsequently propaganda on Chaoyang ceased. Su Donghai and Fang Kongmu, eds., *Zhonghuarenmingongheguo fengyun shilu* [True Record of the PRC's Storms] (2 vols., n.p.: Henan renmin chubanshe, 1993), vol 2, p. 1529; and Chen and Du, *Shilu*, vol. 3, part 2, pp. 1208-1209. On continuing acknowledgment of the 1971 decision, see *Zhou Rongxin Tongzhi jianghua huibian*, pp. 10, 12-14, 28. On Zhou Rongxin's "persecution to death," see below p. 422.

[108] Reported in Zhou Rongxin's speech to Xinhua journalists, July 24, 1975, in *Zhou Rongxin Tongzhi jianghua huibian*, pp. 14-18. The only reference we have found to an earlier comment by Deng is his purported February 1975 statement to Ye Fei that education was one of his priorities, a reference we regard as suspect given the lack of evidence of Deng focusing on education before September. See above, pp. 267-68n62.

[109] See Ma Qibin, *Sishinian*, p. 389; *Zhou Rongxin Tongzhi jianghua huibian*, pp. 24-26; *Zhanwang*, no. 334 (1975), p. 9; and Yu Guangyuan, "Yi Deng Xiaoping he zhengyanshi," p. 14. There is a suggestion, however, that Deng was already raising the profile of education before September in Yu Guangyuan's remark that he had (at some unspecified time before September 3) complained that there had never been a summing up of the educational revolution.

"a crisis in education." Deng demanded that the ministry lift its game, and Zhou (who was also criticized by Deng in the same period for failing to speak out about educational problems) made a self-criticism for failures in controlling factionalism. Whether out of chagrin over Deng's reproaches (which arguably were unjust given Zhou's role in downgrading the sensitive Chaoyang model and the limitations of Deng's own involvement with education hitherto), encouragement due to his leader's willingness to deal with tough issues and admiration of the science and technology document, or simply following orders, Zhou now began to organize an outline report on education modeled on the Academy of Sciences report. It went through three drafts, the first of which, around October 8, was sharpest in tone and expressed the spirit of Deng's efforts. As with the three famous "weeds," there was a softening of the subsequent draft, while the third draft of November 10 did a virtual about-face by emphasizing the great achievements of the revolution in education. By this time, in any case, the report was overtaken by events and shelved.[110]

Party rectification came to a head during the same period as education, with Deng focusing on the issue from August to early October,[111] and Ji Dengkui taking charge of drafting an outline report in September-October before the matter was pushed aside, with Ji exposed to criticism during the subsequent campaign against Deng. As with education, moreover, the Party rectification question was deeply embedded in recent history—specifically, events since the fall of Lin Biao. As we have seen in earlier chapters, soon after Lin Biao's death and the purge of his purported followers, Mao set in motion (or, more precisely, markedly accelerated) the process of rehabilitating civilian and military cadres who had suffered during the Cultural Revolution, notionally at Lin's hands, although the Chairman in fact bore much more responsibility for their victimization.[112] This

---

[110] Fu Yi, "Jiaoyu buzhang Zhou Rongxin," pp. 30, 33-35; Deng Xiaoping's remarks at the September 26, 1975, briefing on the outline report, document available at the Fairbank Center Library, Harvard University, pp. 17-20; Yu Guangyuan, "Yi Deng Xiaoping he zhengyanshi," pp. 10, 14; and above, p. 342n107. Zhou's self-criticism dealt with factionalism in the Academy of Sciences where the Education Ministry had some bureaucratic responsibility. The ministry similarly had responsibility in a variety of spheres where studies were undertaken, including military schools, railway colleges, etc.

[111] Since Deng's highlighting of Party rectification seemingly began in August, and Ji's strong efforts predated Zhou Rongxin's (see below), Party rectification probably preceded education on Deng's agenda although, in another sense, it was the culmination of the entire consolidation effort. Perhaps the first indication of Deng's interest came in his July 4 talk to a theoretical study class that was later retitled "Strengthen Party Leadership and Rectify the Party's Style of Work." *Selected Works of Deng (1975-1982)*, pp. 23-26.

[112] The issue of responsibility for the injustices of 1966-68 is a complicated one that cannot be resolved here. Two general points can be made, however: the whole context for the purges and persecutions of leading cadres was created by Mao alone; and the view that Lin and the "gang of four" persecuted veteran leaders while Zhou Enlai heroically sought to protect them is a distortion. Our own earlier study concluded that while Lin was hardly blameless, there is little convincing evidence that he was a driving force behind the purge of other revolutionary veterans. See Teiwes and Sun, *Tragedy*, especially pp. 22-37, 90-102; and above, p. 49.

rehabilitation process had several purposes from Mao's point of view. As we have emphasized, the Chairman brought back people who would replace Lin Biao's supporters and weaken any remaining sympathizers, as well as counterbalance existing leaders such as Zhou Enlai and Ye Jianying who had earned his displeasure. Perhaps even more important for Mao was his long-held belief in ideological redemption. All of those rehabilitated had to go through a prolonged process of reform that was carefully monitored by Mao; however naïve in the ultimate sense, he seemingly believed these people had returned to his "line." Thus, as argued previously, the rehabilitation of veteran cadres had been a feature of inner-Party life well before Deng assumed responsibility for Party affairs, and the oft-noted new upsurge in the summer and fall of 1975 was the continuation of an existing program rather than the result of a Deng-led offensive against the radicals.[113] Yet in the same post-Lin Biao period, Mao also sought to cultivate Cultural Revolution activists as successor leaders. The contradiction inherent in both restoring Cultural Revolution victims and cultivating the activists of the movement inevitably became a focus of Party rectification.

Well before placing the Party rectification program at the top of the agenda in August-September, Deng's efforts since early 1975 had focused on strengthening Party leadership and combating factionalism—objectives further emphasized in the "three poisonous weeds." As with so much else, this endeavor drew on Mao's authority: cracking down on factionalism in the provinces had been a feature of directives issued or endorsed by the Chairman throughout 1975,[114] and dealing with the critical Zhejiang question followed his concern with developments in the province. In bringing about order in the provinces, the so-called "consolidation of the localities" (difang zhengdun), Ji Dengkui played the key role assisting Deng, not to mention the fact that, as we saw in Chapter 4, his efforts to crack down on local factionalism had significantly predated Deng's own. Not only was the July document on Zhejiang that Ji crafted often considered the start of Party rectification, his continuing importance was clearly seen in Deng's August 18 statement on the need for rectification, when he cited the positive experience of countering the "double crashthroughs" in Party recruitment and promotion of rebels in Zhejiang, i.e., problems Ji had handled to Deng's and Mao's satisfaction over the previous two months.[115]

In fact, Deng began to formulate his conception of Party rectification as the "core" (hexin) of the overall consolidation program while listening to Ji's August briefing on his efforts to curb factionalism in Zhejiang and Henan. In mid-August,

---

[113] See Lieberthal, Sino-Soviet Conflict, p. 123; and Dittmer, China's Continuous Revolution, p. 131, for discussions of these rehabilitations as part of Deng's political struggle. Cf. above, pp. 270-73.

[114] Apparently the earliest such directive was the notice issued on January 17 with special reference to Zhejiang and Yunnan. See above, p. 259.

[115] See Deng Liqun guoshi jiangtan, vol. 1, pp. 385-86; Yu Guangyuan, "Yi Deng Xiaoping he zhengyanshi," p. 11; and above, pp. 275n88, 276ff.

Deng proposed and the Party Center approved conducting Party rectification in the coming winter and following spring, and Deng directed Ji to draw up an outline report for this task based on his successful experiences in the two provinces. Deng reiterated and elaborated upon the message on several further occasions in September and early October[116] in the context of advocating a comprehensive consolidation program involving industry, agriculture, education and culture, and the military. By early October, Deng made it clear that Mao, who had taken the initiative in military consolidation and had approved all other efforts, had also given his approval to the proposal for Party rectification. Meanwhile, Ji proceeded to carry out his brief, calling in Organization Department leaders on August 24 to organize local investigations in preparation for the winter-spring effort. Subsequently, in mid-September, the Central Organization Department convened a meeting of six provincial departments, and then started drafting the outline report.[117]

What was the vision of Party rectification articulated by Deng and Ji from mid-August to mid-October which shaped the new outline report?[118] As with all consolidation efforts under Deng's leadership, there was due obeisance to Mao. Not only was the need to adhere to Mao's Thought emphasized, albeit a comprehensive understanding of that thought, but the Cultural Revolution and the importance of studying the dictatorship of the proletariat were upheld. Naturally, the main features of Deng's efforts since early in the year were strongly affirmed: discipline, Party leadership, and opposition to factionalism. The question was how to do it, with Deng observing that the method would be different from the past, and requiring each province to draw up a plan. At root, the issue was, as Ji put in August, what types of people to rely on in rebuilding a seriously threatened Party in which, in some areas, one-third of its organizations were "impure." The answer was two-fold. First, reflecting the lesson of the "double crashthroughs," it involved rejecting the unsystematic recruitment and promotion of rebels who had achieved little, but had caused disruption. Rapidly rising "helicopters" would not be dismissed, but they would be sent to lower levels to accumulate experience. The second factor was to rely even more on veteran and middle-aged cadres for the leadership core, especially at the key

---

[116] Whether Deng's urgings actually extended into early October is not completely clear, but his important remarks on Party rectification to a rural work forum were part of comments identified as being given on September 27 and October 4. See *Selected Works of Deng (1975-1982)*, pp. 47-49.

[117] Yu Guangyuan, "Yi Deng Xiaoping he zhengyanshi," pp. 11-12; and Wang and Sun, "Dang zuzhi zhengdun," pp. 39-43.

[118] The following is based on reports concerning, and edited versions of, Deng's remarks at or about the time of the September-October rural work forum, and comments by Ji in August-October. See *Jiang Weiqing huiyilu* [Memoirs of Jiang Weiqing] (Nanjing: Jiangsu renmin chubanshe, 1996), p. 566; "Jiang Weiqing Tongzhi zhuanda zhongyang lingdao tongzhi jianghua jingshen" [Comrade Jiang Weiqing Relays the Spirit of Talks by a Central Leading Comrade], October 26, 1975, document available at the Fairbank Center Library, Harvard University; *Deng sixiang nianpu*, p. 19; *Selected Works of Deng (1975-1982)*, pp. 47-49; and Wang and Sun, "Dang zuzhi zhengdun," pp. 42-43.

provincial level. Such cadres had of course risen through the ranks in contrast to the sudden ascent of the "helicopters." This amounted to Deng's "ladder theory" (*taijielun*) which he articulated in late September or early October. While endorsing the Cultural Revolution "three-in-one combination" (*sanjiehe*) of old, middle aged and young cadres and the need to promote younger officials, Deng noted that too rapid promotion produced poor results: the desired method was to climb step by step as on a ladder rather than rocket upwards. Despite the call for new methods, Deng's theory and Ji's measures were in fact quite traditional, and Deng claimed it would not be difficult to find Party secretaries among cadres who had undergone self-criticism. But given the uncertain atmosphere created by the unfolding *Water Margin* campaign, Deng found it necessary to advise people to banish worries that the program was one of restoration.

With this orientation for Party rectification laid down by early October, there is no evidence of Deng speaking further on the matter, or indeed on other domestic issues, after October 4. In contrast, Ji Dengkui, dissatisfied with the initial draft of the outline report, continued to press for a clear statement of objectives at an Organization Department meeting on October 20, emphasizing Party discipline, unity, combating factionalism, and dealing with "helicopters" who had risen during the Lin Biao-Confucius campaign by sending them back to their pre-campaign posts. Ironically, given Ji's subsequent neo-Maoist reputation, his actions appeared to uphold the consolidation faith in the same period that other draft documents were undergoing prudent revision. In any case, in the rapidly changing political climate, and notwithstanding Ji's attempt to stand firm, plans for the winter-spring rectification were put on hold, the organization work group that had been sent to Henan was forced to retreat, Ji eventually came under radical attack, and the outline report was shunted aside much as Zhou Rongxin's effort and the more famous "three poisonous weeds" had been.[119] What went wrong?

Apart from simply being caught up in events, the underlying factor was the tension between Mao's two projects: cultivating Cultural Revolution activists, and restoring "reformed" veteran cadres. The Chairman's support of the latter project as Deng pressed ahead with plans for the winter-spring rectification cannot be doubted. Mao proposed the September-October rural work forum that placed Party rectification high on the agenda, and assembled veteran first secretaries from 12 provinces, many of whom were recently rehabilitated according to Mao's plan.[120] Yet the Chairman hoped this emphasis would not

---

[119] Wang and Sun, "Dang zuzhi zhengdun," p. 43. While it is difficult to find explicit criticism of Ji, and one historian familiar with his career believes he was not too badly affected by attacks in 1976, criticism of the Central Organization Department and the compilation of material on the eight vice premiers, among other indications, demonstrate that he was under some pressure. Interview, November 2002; and below, pp. 411, 442, 506, 511ff.

[120] The 12 provinces were Fujian, Guangdong, Guangxi, Guizhou, Hebei, Henan, Jiangsu, Jiangxi, Sichuan, Yunnan, Zhejiang and Hubei. All of the first secretaries were veteran cadres, and half had been ousted in 1966-68 and subsequently rehabilitated.

negate the role of rebel activists or undermine Party unity, that his warnings against "settling old accounts" of the late 1960s would be obeyed. This would leave room for these activists, notwithstanding his sanctioning since early in the year of anti-factionalism measures including clamping down on the *shuangtu*. Typically, Mao was ambiguous on the basic issue, as expressed in a December 1975 comment addressing the tension between the two groups. While affirming the role of young rebels and warning against kicking them aside, he also cautioned against belittling veteran officials, observing that "I am the oldest."[121] Both were required, but Mao provided little meaningful guidance for managing the tensions between them that his policies had created.

In the summer and fall, in any case, Cultural Revolution activists could hardly have been sanguine about either the sending down of "helicopters" or the restoration of veteran leaders whose ideological orientation they questioned. In a fundamental sense, this was a rerun in reverse of the radicals' failed effort to extend the study of the dictatorship of the proletariat into an attack on established cadres. That threat to Party unity was a factor in Mao's turn against Jiang Qing and company in the spring. Now, as Deng's rectification effort increasingly targeted Cultural Revolution activists, it posed a threat to unity and to the most basic interests of both the activists and the Politburo radicals. But, notwithstanding the fundamental interests involved, the influence of the Party rectification issue on Deng's fall remains unclear. As we shall see later in this chapter, it is very likely that the matter came up in late September when Mao Yuanxin reported on the complaints of Liaoning rebels concerning Deng's *zhengdun* measures. Certainly something happened in the period between mid-September when, if not earlier, Mao approved Deng's rectification plans, and the shelving of those plans a month or so later.[122] Yet, as with the "three weeds," open attacks on Deng's "ladder theory" did not begin until *pi Deng* was launched in 1976.[123]

While the outline reports on education and Party rectification were prepared in the same period in response to Deng's urgings, and suffered the same fate as the political tide turned, there were significant differences in the circumstances and performance of the two responsible leaders—Zhou Rongxin and Ji Dengkui respectively. First of all, Ji had considerably higher rank, and as a result a better understanding of the inner state of politics at the very top, something further enhanced by his apparent relatively frequent interaction with Mao. Secondly, Ji was much more active earlier than Zhou; in fact, he was one of the figures most prominent on the cutting edge of anti-radical efforts throughout 1974-75.

---

[121] Zhang Hanzhi, *Wo yu Qiao Guanhua*, pp. 83-84; and *Mao wengao*, vol. 13, p. 488.

[122] While rectification was one of the four main agenda items for the rural work forum, it was not thoroughly considered as a wait and see attitude emerged. Shortly after the October 20 meeting when Ji attempted to push rectification work forward, the outline report and the proposed winter-spring effort were shelved. See "Jiang Weiqing zhuanda jianghua jingshen"; and Wang and Sun, "Dang zuzhi zhengdun," p. 43.

[123] E.g., *HQ*, no. 4 (1976), p. 30. Cf. below, p. 411.

While Deng's reprimand was required before Zhou swung into full action on the educational front, Deng cited Ji's actions in Zhejiang as a model for Party rectification. Yet, in what should be a caution for analysts of CCP elite politics, it is Zhou Rongxin who is today regarded both within and outside China as the fighter for Deng's cause, while Ji Dengkui carries the stigma of a neo-Maoist. Zhou's historical reputation, bolstered by being a victim of the Cultural Revolution, was further sanctified by his death in 1976, assertedly due to radical "persecution."[124] Ji's case is more complicated, and clearly a function of developments in the 1977-78 period which will be examined in our Volume II. For now, we simply say that the neo-Maoist label strikes us as unjust. But as a junior figure rising to high office as a result of the Cultural Revolution, and as the leader responsible for organizational matters at the end of the Maoist era, Ji would inevitably be vulnerable to the accumulated discontents of veteran cadres. Nevertheless, during the 1975 consolidation he was arguably Deng's most important collaborator.

The First Dazhai Conference on Agriculture, September-October 1975

If one were to extend the idea of additional "poisonous weeds" concocted by Deng Xiaoping and his allies in August-October 1975, Hua Guofeng's report to the "learn from Dazhai in agriculture" conference on October 15 could be considered the sixth such document. The State Council Research Office was deeply involved in its preparation, and the policies it advocated were fully in line with the consolidation program and, equally significant, Deng's own ideological universe as of the second half of 1975. This has not been generally understood in analyses influenced by conventional post-Mao views of the alleged clashing political orientations of Deng and Hua. In the present context of agricultural policy in 1975, such interpretations have pictured Hua as a "soft radical" standing between the "hard radicals" of Jiang Qing et al. and Deng's moderate position. Hua's motivation assertedly was to build a winning political coalition, but Deng's presence prevented him from advocating an even more radical program.[125] The reality, and the political significance, was quite different.

---

[124] We are skeptical that Zhou was actually "persecuted to death," both since the pressure brought on leading cadres in late 1975 and 1976 was, as a rule, far milder than the treatment handed out in 1966-68, and because Zhou suffered from a preexisting heart condition. See below, p. 422.

On Ji Dengkui's interaction with Mao, a senior Party historian with excellent access to leading figures of the period claims that Ji had more contact with Mao over the 1972-76 period, including fairly regular theoretical discussions, than any other Politburo member except Wang Dongxing. Interviews, January and February 2000. Ji's theoretical exchanges with Mao sit uncomfortably with his description in Lampton, *Paths to Power*, p. 24, as "crude, xenophobic, and scarcely educated." An oral source with significant personal experience with Ji strongly disputes this assessment. Interview, November 2002.

[125] The terminology is adopted from Zweig, *Agrarian Radicalism*, pp. 34-35, 65-69. See also Dali L. Yang, *Calamity and Reform in China: State, Rural Society, and Institutional Change Since the Great Leap Famine* (Stanford: Stanford University Press, 1996), p. 124.

The Dazhai conference, and the overlapping agricultural forum,[126] canvassed issues beyond agriculture, including comprehensive consolidation and Party rectification as noted above, and the emerging *Water Margin* campaign. The latter matter, which involved a significant degree of tension and uncertainty, was quite separate from the concrete agricultural issues discussed at the meetings, but assessments of Dazhai developments have gone beyond this tension to posit a sharp Jiang Qing-Deng Xiaoping clash over agricultural policy *per se*. We shall examine the *Water Margin* issue in the following section. Here we only note that although Jiang reviewed rural issues going back to the "high tide" of cooperativization in 1955 and placed current rural policy in the context of opposing revisionism and restricting bourgeois right, the contentious matters she raised at Dazhai were basically limited to the *Water Margin* question and related ideological questions, not agriculture. Moreover, Jiang pressed for the distribution of her views, although at one point she reportedly sought to limit publicity concerning her *Water Margin* comments, worrying that they might be seen as interfering with the agricultural agenda of the State Council. The content of her address to the opening plenary session of the conference on September 15 has never been officially revealed. A well-placed oral source, however, reports that it largely consisted of impromptu remarks on the *Water Margin*, as well as complaints that provinces were not giving attention to agriculture by only sending second Party secretaries (which was what the central directive on conference organization stipulated), but nothing significant on agricultural policy questions.[127] Setting the *Water Margin* issue aside for the moment, the following analysis focuses on the agricultural issues addressed at the conference.

---

[126] The "learn from Dazhai in agriculture" conference was held from September 15 to October 19 in two segments, the first near Dazhai, and the second in Beijing. This gathering of 3,700 participants was the largest work conference held in the PRC since the famous 7,000 cadres conference in 1962. The small agricultural forum, held in Beijing from September 23 to October 21 and chaired by Li Xiannian, involved 17 leaders, including central officials responsible for agriculture and 12 provincial secretaries. See Chen and Du, *Shilu*, vol. 3, part 2, pp. 1263-65, 1269.

[127] Feng Dongshu, *Wenmang zaixiang Chen Yonggui* [Illiterate Minister Chen Yonggui] (Beijing: Zhongguo wenlian chubangongsi, 1998), pp. 222, 237; and interview with scholar with access to key participants at the conference, November 2002.

The matter is complicated by a purported text of Jiang's September 15 speech from a Taiwan source that has been used in existing analyses to demonstrate radicalism; see Zweig, *Agrarian Radicalism*, pp. 66-67. This text (which can be found in *CRDB*, and in translation in *Chinese Law and Government*, Spring 1977, pp. 12-16) called for vigilance against rural capitalist restoration, but this does not indicate the distinctive radicalism claimed (see below). In any case, despite a certain plausibility of its content, the use of untypical language for a PRC document strongly suggests it is a fabrication. A related, clearly fabricated case using a similar non-PRC source is Jiang's alleged July 2, 1975, letter to an agricultural conference urging the delegates to keep class struggle alive and avoid the revisionist policies of Khrushchev- and Malenkov-type leaders (Zweig, p. 66). Not only does this document also fail the linguistic test of contemporary PRC usage, but the imperial tone adopted is something we regard as virtually unthinkable given her abject self-criticism only four days earlier and Mao's apparent advice that she adopt a low profile. See above, p. 302. Finally, consulting multiple PRC chronologies fails to identify the conference to which the letter was supposedly addressed.

These agricultural issues must be seen in the context of developments since 1970 when steps were first taken to bring some order to rural policy after the disruption of the Cultural Revolution. The key elements—agricultural mechanization, learning from Dazhai, and the 60 articles on agriculture—can all be traced to Mao and, unsurprisingly, contained contradictions among themselves. The process began in April 1970 with the Chairman proposing to the Politburo revisions of the 60 articles that he had overseen in 1961-62, a document that, in the context of the rural crisis of the time, stabilized the three-level structure of the communes with accounting (and thus the distribution of income) at the team level, and provided limited guarantees of private economic activities. What, if anything, Mao proposed *specifically* is unknown. While any revisions could reasonably be expected to strengthen the collective economy in comparison to the 1962 document, the very fact of placing the 60 articles on the agenda was a reaffirmation of the Party's "established policies" (*luoshi zhengce*), i.e., guarantees to the peasants against radical change. This was followed by the establishment of the Ministry of Agriculture and Forestry in June 1970,[128] and the August-October northern region agricultural conference, which focused on concrete economic problems and emphasized implementation of the 60 articles. But the conference also called for learning from (albeit without indiscriminately copying) the Dazhai experience, Mao's favored agricultural model from the mid-1960s with its emphasis on brigade-level accounting and ideological incentives. On the eve of the conference, moreover, the *People's Daily* quoted Mao: "If Xiyang [county, the locale of Dazhai] can do it, why can't you do it? If one year isn't enough, isn't three years enough? Four or five years should surely be long enough." As a post-Mao PRC analyst has noted, the Chairman's sentence "placed a lot of pressure [on Party organs] everywhere."[129]

The northern region conference also called for increased investment in agricultural mechanization, another of Mao's passions. The Chairman's interest can be traced to 1955 during the agricultural cooperativization movement when

[128] Combining the previously separate Ministries of Agriculture and Forestry, and at the same time normalizing organization after the bureaucratic disruption since 1966.

[129] Wu Xiang, *Zhongguo nongcun gaige shilu* [A True Account of China's Rural Reforms] (Hangzhou: Zhejiang renmin chubanshe, 2001), p. 54; Ji Yecheng, "Dui nongcun gaige chuqi liangjianshi de huiyi" [Memories of Two Events from the Early Period of Rural Reform], in Du Runsheng, ed., *Zhongguo nongcun gaige juece jishi* [A Record of the Policies of Chinese Rural Reform] (Beijing: Zhongyang wenxian chubanshe, 1999), p. 98; and Ma Qibin, *Sishinian*, p. 333. For overviews of developments in 1970, see Zweig, *Agrarian Radicalism*, pp. 58-61; and Yang, *Calamity*, pp. 103-104. On Mao and the Dazhai model before the Cultural Revolution, see Teiwes, *Politics and Purges*, pp. 404-405, 431-33, 505n104; and Richard Baum, *Prelude to Revolution: Mao, the Party, and the Peasant Question, 1962-66* (New York: Columbia University Press, 1975), pp. 117-22.

In addition to the specific issues cited here, Mao's influence can be seen in the recurrent drumbeat of pro-collective and anti-capitalist themes during the rather amorphous "line education" campaign that ran from summer 1973 to summer 1977; see Zweig, *Agrarian Radicalism*, pp. 44, 46, 47, 51, 64, 67. While such emphases might be assumed to be congenial to the radicals, in fact they strongly criticized the line education effort in 1976 for reasons to be explored subsequently.

he called for basically achieving nationwide mechanization in 20 to 25 years, a timetable he reaffirmed on the eve of the Cultural Revolution in 1966. Now, in August-September 1971, Hua Guofeng convened a national conference on farm mechanization,[130] and in early 1972 he directed the Ministry of Agriculture and Forestry to prepare for a national conference on learning from Dazhai, a conference that would revise the 60 articles. This undertaking was repeatedly postponed, but in July 1974 the ministry convened a preparatory meeting for a learn from Dazhai conference that would also take up mechanization. A year later in mid-August 1975, the preparatory small group for the conference led by Hua and Chen Yonggui reported to the State Council on a proposed agenda: exchanging experiences on learning from Dazhai, especially concerning constructing Dazhai-type counties, further developing the Dazhai campaign and rapidly transforming the face of poor production teams, and exchanging experiences on agricultural mechanization while discussing reaching Mao's goal by 1980. Surprisingly, revising the 60 articles apparently was no longer an explicit agenda item. Three days later, Deng approved and issued instructions on the report, thus setting the stage for the conference in September-October.[131]

What is the political meaning and significance of the five-year delay from when Mao raised the Dazhai experience to the convening of the 1975 conference? First and foremost is the fact that, the Chairman's interest notwithstanding, agriculture was not a priority issue in policy or elite politics during this period. None of the key turning points, or Mao's displeasure with various of his colleagues, had much if anything to do with rural policy: not the late 1972 redefinition of Lin Biao as an ultra-rightist rather than an ultra-leftist, not the December 1973 criticism of Zhou Enlai and Ye Jianying largely over matters of foreign and military policy, not the August 1974 declaration that eight years of Cultural Revolution was enough, nor the spring 1975 turn against the radicals for their excesses in the campaign to study the dictatorship of the proletariat. Even when agriculture was placed prominently on the agenda, as when listed first among the four modernizations at the Fourth NPC, which also endorsed the 1980 mechanization target, in fact it did not compare to other areas in terms of leadership attention as Deng unfolded the consolidation program.

This, of course, did not mean that there was no diversity of views on rural matters. A PRC analyst has identified three tendencies within the leadership that mirror David Zweig's "hard" and "soft" radicals and moderates, but in a manner indicating a less conventional individual lineup and a more complicated political process. One tendency was a radical posture identified with "Jiang Qing and

---

[130] According to an early post-Mao source, Hua prepared a *People's Daily* editorial on the conference that called for basic implementation of mechanization by 1980, the end date of Mao's 20 to 25 years. Yao Wenyuan, however, assertedly killed the editorial, arguing that such a firm target should not be declared without prior investigation. *RMRB*, December 23, 1976, in *SPRCP*, no. 6251 (1977), p. 85.

[131] *GMRB*, January 12, 1977, in *SPRCP*, no. 6291 (1977), p. 157; Ma Qibin, *Sishinian*, pp. 266, 333; and Zhang Hua, "1975 nian nongye xue Dazhai huiyi," p. 16.

others." For our immediate purposes, the striking thing is how amorphous this tendency was, defined as simply "[paying] no attention to the backwardness of the countryside and the interests of the peasants."[132] Here Zweig's insightful concept of "policy winds" is relevant. In a context where no clear-cut agricultural policy was developed, and Mao's contradictory positions including opposing rural capitalism, rapid development of the countryside, and continuing to guarantee concessions to the peasantry restricted all central actors,[133] the emphasis placed on conflicting themes in the media, which largely remained in the hands of the radicals, profoundly affected local leaders as signals of what was politically safe, thus encouraging leftist practices in different places at different times. (Importantly, however, the breakdown of disciplined Party rule that Deng so abhorred allowed other local officials and peasants to opt for practices weakening the collective system.) But what is also striking is how limited the periods of "radical winds" emanating from the organs controlled by the "gang" in Beijing were in 1970-75. These periods were largely restricted to late 1973-early 1974 at the time of launching *pi Lin pi Kong*, and to the early 1975 dictatorship of the proletariat drive—again, developments having little to do with agriculture *per se*. The general leftist themes of these periods could be extended to rural issues, but there is little to suggest that the radicals, who had no bureaucratic responsibilities in this area, had any serious program for agriculture. Indeed, they were largely passive observers as agricultural policy unfolded in 1975.[134]

The key debate of 1975 involved the other two tendencies. One, roughly equivalent to Zweig's "soft radicalism," favored a rapid raising of the accounting level within the communes from production team to production brigade and other pro-collective measures, while the other adopted a more cautious approach

[132] Zhang Hua, "1975 nian nongye xue Dazhai huiyi," pp. 16-17. This is not to deny specific radical policy preferences such as Mao Yuanxin's Heertao model launched in Liaoning in January 1975 which experimented with eradicating the private market. In terms of national trends, however, it should be noted that this did not receive national publicity until the changed circumstances of 1976. See Zweig, *Agrarian Radicalism*, pp. 39, 65; and Fang Weizhong, *Jingji dashiji*, pp. 565-66.

[133] While Zweig's conclusion that "Mao never openly supported the radicals' rural program" yet "prevent[ed] the modernizers from controlling rural policy making" (*Agrarian Radicalism*, pp. 8-9) addresses the ambivalence of Mao's views, in our analysis it misses the reality of the situation by picturing the Chairman as "relatively inactive" on rural policy while letting contending forces fight in order to bolster his threatened personal power, or balance their competing preferences. This clearly was not the essence of elite politics in this period generally, and, as we argue, the contending groups could only act within whatever parameters Mao chose to give them.

[134] See Zweig, *Agrarian Radicalism*, ch. 2 and pp. 50-69, 223-24n3, 228n73; see also Yang, *Calamity*, pp. 115-19. Zhang Hua, "1975 nian nongye xue Dazhai huiyi," p. 16, supports the idea of "policy winds" by noting that "shifts in political trends" were a key factor in the prolonged preparation for the Dazhai conference. It is worth noting, in this regard, that Zweig's research into *People's Daily* articles on rural issues revealed not only very few articles advocating radical policies outside of the two periods identified, but also that only a handful of articles critical of radical policies appeared in 1975 when Deng controlled the policy agenda (subject, of course, to Mao). The latter development, we believe, had far less to do with radical control of the media than with the constraints of Mao's views.

to these questions.[135] Before examining the substance of this debate, a brief consideration of the major actors is in order. The "soft radical" approach was reportedly "represented by Chen Yonggui and others." Chen, of course, was the peasant leader of Dazhai who won Mao's heart before the Cultural Revolution and was raised to the Politburo in 1973. Apart from Chen's on the ground experience and the Chairman's infatuation with Dazhai, Chen's right to speak on rural issues was clear in his position as the Vice Premier in charge of agriculture. In this, however, he was clearly less important in rural policy than Hua Guofeng, and possibly Ji Dengkui, with whom he reportedly had good personal relations.[136] As we have seen, Hua had undoubtedly been playing the key rural policy role since 1971.[137] Beyond this was the fact that the peasant leader was not taken seriously by leaders schooled in the ways of higher-level Party politics. Notwithstanding his relatively radical policy preferences, moreover, Chen was reportedly disdained by the "gang," with their followers in Shanghai reportedly telling him he "knew only how to work hard and sweat and knew nothing about the political line." Indeed, it appears that some radicals were most hostile to Chen of the relevant central leaders, and unimpressed with the relatively "soft" radicalism of Dazhai. In sum, while Chen had a place at the table given Mao's support, his limited political skills and influence inevitably compromised his policy effectiveness.[138] As for the more cautious moderate tendency, this was identified with Zhou Enlai and Li Xiannian, although by 1975 Zhou's illness significantly limited his input.

What is striking from this PRC account is the absence of the two key players in Western analyses: Deng Xiaoping and Hua Guofeng. As we shall argue below, in Deng's case we believe this is largely due to his relatively small role in rural policy, but it may also reflect views at some variance from an unambiguously moderate approach. Indeed, the PRC analyst who identified the three tendencies questioned the common Chinese view that, at the Dazhai conference, Deng sought to break through the thinking of the "three red banners" and bring about

---

[135] The two tendencies and their representatives are discussed in Zhang Hua, "1975 nian nongye xue Dazhai huiyi," p. 17.

[136] Perhaps in part because all three were Shanxi natives. Ji Dengkui, who had overseen a regional learn from Dazhai conference in 1970, apparently had Politburo-level responsibility for overseeing Shanxi affairs. See Feng Dongshu, *Wenmang zaixiang*, p. 282.

[137] Indicatively, Deng's daughter referred to Hua as the Vice Premier responsible for agriculture despite Chen's formal assignment at the Fourth NPC; Mao Mao, *"Wenge" suiyue*, p. 398. Ji Dengkui had been involved with agriculture earlier (see n. 136), and later exercised the main responsibility for agriculture in the initial post-Mao period. However, there is no concrete evidence of Ji having a major agricultural role in 1975, and he apparently did not attend the first stage of the Dazhai conference, although he was present for Hua's report in Beijing.

[138] Chen Yonggui's December 20, 1976, speech to the second Dazhai conference, in *SPRCP*, no. 6252 (1977), p. 131; and interview with senior Party historian specializing on the period, February 2000. The radicals' disdain for Dazhai, while perhaps exaggerated in the post-Mao retelling, did become a particular issue in 1976. See below, pp. 499ff.

the reform and development of agriculture, stating that a review of conference documents and interviews with participants indicated that "these views are not accurate enough and are open to dispute."[139] As for Hua, his position is difficult to characterize due to contradictory behavior, something arguably due to his primary functional responsibility which required him to juggle Mao's conflicting attitudes. In 1974-75, Hua resisted radical disruption of rural industry, yet, as we saw in Chapter 4, took a restrictive stance toward rural markets.[140] According to a specialist on Chen Yonggui, as the Dazhai conference approached, Hua generally supported Chen's advocacy of brigade accounting, but shifted his position as events unfolded.[141]

One final observation before turning to the events of August-October 1975: no one could oppose the Dazhai model, the only issue was to what extent and how rapidly it could be implemented. In part, of course, this was simply a political fact of life, a requirement of political survival.[142] But it would be shortsighted to ignore the significant degree of elite belief in the model and collective agriculture more generally, a belief going far to explain the reluctance of many leaders and groups to abandon the model, and especially to adopt the heretical household responsibility system in the post-Mao period. Of particular note was the support of military leaders. In summer 1975 the navy's political department called for learning from Dazhai and set up a Dazhai study group, top navy leaders Xiao Jingguang and Su Zhenhua attended the conference, and representatives of various PLA units made the pilgrimage to Dazhai, an affinity even more dramatically revealed in 1977 when Ye Jianying made his own pilgrimage to the brigade and famously wrote a poem in its praise.[143] Whatever the precise mix of belief, calculation, or simply following orders, this reflected a broad elite predisposition to accept the legitimacy of the Dazhai model.

From mid-August 1975, two related processes unfolded: the drafting of reports to the Dazhai conference, and the debate over the level of accounting within the people's communes. While Hua Guofeng and Chen Yonggui may have jointly presented the agenda for the conference that Deng endorsed on behalf of the State Council, different approaches were soon apparent. In addition, it

---

[139] Zhang Hua, "1975 nian nongye xue Dazhai huiyi," p. 16.

[140] In December 1974, Hua wrote to the Hunan provincial Party committee complaining of efforts to suppress rural industries; see *Mao wengao*, vol. 13, pp. 470-71. On his May 1975 attempt to close markets, see above, p. 285. Around the time of the Dazhai conference, Hua also politely reprimanded a mid-level official for free market activity; see *Women zhongxin aidai yingming lingxiu Hua Zhuxi* [We Sincerely Love and Support the Wise Leader Chairman Hua] (Beijing: Renmin chubanshe, 1977), p. 129.

[141] Interview, January 2005.

[142] Thus Jiang Qing, notwithstanding her dismissive attitude toward Chen Yonggui, made sure to demonstrate her "concern" for Dazhai when visiting the brigade by bringing gifts of sweets "from Chairman Mao." Feng Dongshu, *Wenmang zaixiang*, p. 235.

[143] *Ibid.*, pp. 158, 225-27.

appears that Chen and Hua relied on different resources to draft documents for the conference. Within two weeks of Deng's go-ahead, Chen wrote to Mao on August 24 proposing a rapid transition from the team to brigade level as the basic accounting unit within the communes, advocating widely implementing Dazhai workpoints which emphasized "politics in command," and calling for reducing "present disparities in the countryside." Additionally, in two drafts of speeches being prepared for the conference, the Dazhai brigade and Xiyang county committees trumpeted their own experience in continuing the revolution in the relations of production, e.g., curbing private plots and privately owned housing as well as implementing brigade accounting, restricting bourgeois right by such measures as abolishing quota work, and emphasizing the collective spirit through public assessment of work points and grain allocations. These recommendations and other proposals attacking bourgeois right, which did not come from the Politburo radicals, attracted Mao's interest and led him to instruct the Party Center to discuss them. As one PRC specialist has put it, "the considerable attention of Mao Zedong [to these proposals] inevitably led the ... Dazhai conference in a leftist direction."[144]

In this context, Hua Guofeng could not be expected to deviate sharply from Chen's direction, and seemed genuinely inclined toward it in any case. Nevertheless, although the timing is unclear,[145] the preparation of Hua's key report took place in a setting far different from the model Dazhai brigade and Xiyang county. The players in this process were "some big talents" from the State Council's rural and agricultural departments,[146] key figures from Deng's Research Office, i.e., Hu Qiaomu and Yu Guangyuan, and Hua himself. Hua personally oversaw the drafting, and the framework and main guiding ideas were determined in discussions involving him, Hu and Yu. Hu and Yu then supervised different sections of the document. Hua was intimately involved throughout. According to Yu Guangyuan, Hua attended State Council and Party Center meetings in the day, and gathered the drafters together after dinner and worked with them to early morning. Not only was Hua reportedly very satisfied with the result, but "many people who read it said it was infinitely better than the stuff

---

[144] Zhang Hua, "1975 nian nongye xue Dazhai huiyi," pp. 17-18. The major proposal, apart from Chen's recommendations, was a May letter to Mao by a PLA political cadre, Bai Yuntao, advocating adopting different grain purchasing prices in different areas to provide greater income equality regardless of productivity. See also *Mao wengao*, vol. 13, pp. 436-37.

[145] Since Hua's report was given at the end of the conference, it is logical that its drafting extended well into the meeting and related agricultural forum, thus reflecting the debate at these meetings. Some of the anti-capitalist rhetoric, moreover, may have been a consequence of the shifting political atmosphere in October, much as other documents became more ideological in the same period. In contrast, the Dazhai brigade and Xiyang county presentations would have come early in the Dazhai gathering. Unfortunately, no information has been found on the preparation of Chen Yonggui's speeches to the opening (September 15) or closing (October 19) sessions.

[146] Xue Ju, Xie Hua and Yu Guohui were identified as the main people from these departments involved in the drafting.

that had been published during the Cultural Revolution." Writing 20 years later as a committed reformer, Yu Guangyuan said he never read the report again, "but I believe that if I did I would not feel as self-satisfied as I did then." The point, however, is that in the context of 1975, Hua's report was both as much as was politically possible, and was put forth with considerable enthusiasm by leading figures of Deng's think tank.[147]

Before examining the resolution of the different viewpoints, it is first necessary to recount the core elements of the Party line reflected in Hua Guofeng's report. These elements are consistent with what little we know of Chen Yonggui's opening and closing speeches, and with Deng Xiaoping's opening address on September 15 and his two talks to the agricultural forum (see below).[148] Naturally, Hua stayed within Mao's ideological parameters, defining the objective of Dazhai-type counties as preventing revisionism, urgently pushing the national economy forward, and preparing against war. More specifically, the Dazhai standards to which counties were to aspire were: a united county Party committee; the dominance of poor and lower middle peasants to enable them to wage resolute struggles against rural capitalism; regular cadre participation in productive labor; rapid progress in farmland capital construction, mechanization, and scientific farming; steady expansion of the collective economy; and all-round development of farming and related endeavors, with considerable increases in output, big contributions to the state, and steady improvement in peasant living standards. Within these broad objectives, and reflecting the overall anti-revisionist gloss of the report, attention to class struggle and combating "fairly serious spontaneous capitalism" was a significant feature, but not one overwhelming concrete agricultural tasks. The measures called for, moreover, were relatively restrained, focusing on "education in the Party's basic line," while limiting the "spearhead of struggle" to the handful of class enemies who had engaged in sabotage, and inveighing against the summary dismissal of cadres. And notably, of the issues that had bedeviled policy makers in the spring, private plots were allowed within the limits of existing policy, i.e., the 60 articles, while rural markets were not raised.[149]

The real heart and soul of Hua's report concerned the two themes that had been central to Deng's efforts throughout the year: organizational rectification and economic development. Indeed, the key to building Dazhai-type counties was

---

[147] See Yu Guangyuan, *Wenge zhongde wo*, p. 117.

[148] For the full text of Hua's report, see *HQ*, no. 1 (1977), in *SPRCM*, no. 910 (1977), pp. 44-63. For brief summaries of Chen's speeches, see *PR*, no. 38 (1975), pp. 3-4, no. 44 (1975), p. 3. Deng's September 15 speech has only been summarized briefly in official sources, notably *Deng nianpu*, vol. 1, pp. 97-99, while the available versions of his September 27 and October 4 talks to the agricultural forum tell us very little about his position on rural issues. Below we examine his views from other sources concerning the forum. As for Jiang Qing, while we believe the only available version of her September 15 speech is a forgery, if it were genuine it would not be inconsistent with the policies adopted at the conference, even if more anti-revisionist in tone. See above, p. 349n127.

[149] Hua's report, in *SPRCM*, no. 910 (1977), pp. 44, 50, 53-55; and above, p. 285.

said to lie in the county Party committee, and careful attention had to be given to placing suitable people in the first and second positions. Hua echoed Deng's remarks concerning other areas by complaining of "soft, lax and lazy" leading groups, and similarly called for promptly transferring anyone who stubbornly persisted in bourgeois factionalism. While the county Party committee was the key, provincial, municipal and prefectural Party committees were to pay close attention to the organizational revamping. Although Hua did not explicitly call for work teams, his injunction that provincial, prefectural and county committees "must send large numbers of cadres to the basic levels" resulted in these levels dispatching work teams made up of something on the order of 1.6 million cadres to overhaul the communes and boost production. The fundamental message was the same as Deng's: only when Party discipline and leadership were restored could progress be made. And while such toughened leadership would be responsible for enforcing the ideological line, the pressing concerns were clearly economic.[150]

Hua's report called for a multi-faceted approach to increasing production and long-term rural development. It endorsed Mao's declaration that "the fundamental way out for agriculture lies in mechanization," as well as the Chairman's long-standing target of basically achieving mechanization by 1980. Another strand harked back to the early and mid-1960s before the Cultural Revolution: Mao's eight-point charter for agriculture[151] which pragmatically focused on inputs needed to increase production. Linked to that, and also reflective of Mao's current 1975 emphasis on tapping available intellectual talent, were early 1960s-style measures to promote scientific research in agriculture, strengthen scientific organizations from the county to basic levels, and fully utilize professional scientific and technical personnel. Rural industrialization also featured, with emphasis on expanding commune and brigade industries an extension of trends since the early 1970s, and a more restrained version of developments during the Great Leap Forward. Indeed, the overall tone of urgency, as reflected in the revived Great Leap slogan of "more, better, faster and more economically," like the summer's State Council theory conference, carried a distinct whiff of the late 1950s. The leap forward imprint was also seen in the proposal for mass mobilization for farmland capital construction over the coming winter, something that continued unabated on a massive scale even with the change in the political wind. All of this was part and parcel of the ambitious goal for one-third of all counties to reach the Dazhai standard by 1980, something further reminiscent of the top-down pressure of the Great Leap and consistent with Mao's current plan, however much the radicals grumbled *sotto voce* that this was a production-

---

[150] See Hua's report, in *SPRCM*, no. 910 (1977), pp. 50-53, 55-56, 61-62; Barnouin and Yu, *Ten Years*, p. 279; and Zweig, *Agrarian Radicalism*, p. 67.

[151] The charter called for soil improvement, rational application of fertilizer, water conservancy, improved seed strains, rational close-planting, plant protection, field management, and innovation in farming implements.

oriented program that ignored revolution.[152]

The above themes were the basic parameters of policy leading into and at the Dazhai conference and the related agricultural forum. Simply put, there was no moderate alternative program to that offered by Hua, nor did the central radicals offer anything concrete on agricultural policy. Jiang Qing, apart from her *Water Margin* sallies which are discussed subsequently, did make a nuisance of herself, interrupting Deng perhaps five times during his opening speech, reportedly disputing his account of grain production in some prefectures and counties not reaching pre-1949 levels. But none of this amounted to a programmatic challenge, and was notable more for its manner than for any substance.[153] As previously indicated, this did not mean that there was no policy debate. The key issue was the level of accounting within the communes and related aspects of the Dazhai model as reflected in Chen's August 24 letter to Mao. Within days of Chen's letter, "the leader of the Ministry of Agriculture [and Forestry]," presumably Minister Sha Feng, objected that Dazhai methods could not be implemented nationwide, and that in the present stage the main thing was to carry out the Party's established rural policies, i.e., the (apparently unnamed) 60 articles. This reaffirmed the existing three-level ownership with the team as the basic accounting unit, and such resistance reportedly "led to an 'evening up' [of forces] prior to the ... Dazhai conference, and to a certain containment of voices favoring a 'transition' [to brigade accounting]."[154]

The issue was apparently joined less during the initial phase of the Dazhai conference in Shanxi[155] than at the much smaller agricultural forum in Beijing, starting on September 23, which discussed Chen Yonggui's letter.[156] The forum, attended by a few central agricultural officials and 12 provincial leaders, brought together a small high-level group responsible for implementing rural policies— officials who were clearly aware of the practical difficulties that would result

---

[152] See Hua's report, in *SPRCM*, no. 910 (1977), pp. 46-49, 56-61; and above, p. 330. According to a March 1976 NCNA report, in seven provinces alone 130 million people worked on capital construction projects, with more turning out for winter field work than ever before, while a post-Mao report spoke of 150 million people being involved at one time. See Zweig, *Agrarian Radicalism*, pp. 67, 229n102; and *HQ*, no. 1 (1977), p. 98.

[153] *Deng nianpu*, vol. 1, p. 99; Long Pingping, *Xishuo Deng Xiaoping* [A Detailed Account of Deng Xiaoping] (Beijing: Hongqi chubanshe, 1997), p. 148. The manner, together with her *Water Margin* comments, was of course significant as it dramatized her reinsertion on the political stage after the Chairman "let her out of the cage."

[154] Zhang Hua, "1975 nian nongye xue Dazhai huiyi," p. 18. This, of course, was not the only or first sign of resistance to such trends. Li Xiannian, in addition to his May objections concerning restrictions on private plots and markets, reportedly contradicted Bai Yuntao's letter on the grain purchasing price in June. Cf. above, pp. 285, 355n144.

[155] According to Zhang Hua, "1975 nian nongye xue Dazhai huiyi," p. 18, at Dazhai, Deng only mentioned Chen's policy views briefly, saying that many issues required study.

[156] Presumably Chen's August 24 letter to Mao, although it was not identified as such. See Mao Mao, *"Wenge" suiyue*, p. 398. Mao, of course, had instructed the Party Center to consider Chen's recommendations.

from Chen's proposals. A few participants supported Chen's formulation, but the majority, "who engaged in practical work," was opposed, and a "massive rift" developed from the very start of the meeting. Several provincial leaders strenuously objected, notably Guangdong's Zhao Ziyang, an official with positive historical links to Hua in the agricultural sphere,[157] and Zhejiang's Tan Qilong. They did not attack the Dazhai model as such, which they acknowledged was worthy of admiration, but in their view nationwide implementation would be disruptive given the great diversity of local conditions. Chen Yonggui reportedly lost his temper in an argument that degenerated into a shouting match. In these circumstances no agreement could be reached on Chen's proposals for a "transition," so the matter was shelved, thus affirming existing policy on three-level ownership with the team as the basis. In this context, the drafting of Hua's report, which stipulated a step-by-step transition to brigade accounting, but emphasized that in the main current arrangements were still in harmony with the growth of rural productive forces, was completed. Additionally, in finalizing the speeches of Dazhai brigade and Xiyang county leaders to the initial stage of the conference, Hua excised their leftist recommendations from the published versions. The result of these developments, as Deng's daughter would shrewdly observe, was "a procrastinating approach to roll back and resist the leftist method."[158]

Where did Deng Xiaoping stand in these developments? There can be little doubt that he backed the approach adopted in Hua's report. At the same time, as suggested, it must be questioned how deeply he was involved in agricultural policy. He certainly gave it much less time and attention than he gave to combating factionalism, industrial development, the PLA, or moderating policy toward intellectuals. Indeed, Deng reportedly only decided to participate in the Dazhai conference a few days before it opened (or, more likely, Mao decided for him),[159]

---

[157] Hua and Zhao developed cordial relations when both were provincial leaders responsible for agriculture in Hunan and Guangdong respectively before the Cultural Revolution; interview with Party historian specializing on the period, February 2000. Despite conventional views to the contrary, there is also evidence of similarities in their views on the role of household responsibility systems in the late 1970s. This will be addressed in our Volume III.

[158] Mao Mao, "Wenge" suiyue, pp. 398-99; Chen Dabin, Ji'e yinfa de biange: yige zishen jizhe de qinshen jingli yu sikao [The Revolution Sparked By Famine: The Personal Experiences and Reflections of a Senior Journalist] (Beijing: Zhonggong dangshi chubanshe, 1998), pp. 40-41; and Hua's report, in SPRCM, no. 910 (1977), p. 60. Over the coming year and through 1977, brigade-level accounting nationwide did increase modestly from 6.4 percent of all brigades in 1975, to 9.7 percent in 1978. See Jianguo yilai nongye hezuohua shiliao huibian [Collected Historical Materials on Agricultural Cooperativization Since the Founding of the State] (Beijing: Zhonggong dangshi chubanshe, 1992), pp. 1388-89.

[159] While Zhang Hua's account implies it was Deng's decision, we find this unlikely given Mao's control of the movements of his colleagues. In the case at hand, since Mao apparently arranged for Jiang Qing to attend the conference to indicate that she was not a spent force (see below), he arguably sent Deng in order to reaffirm that no drastic political change was then considered. Without Deng's presence, Jiang would have been the ranking Politburo member present. In any case, whoever took

and spoke off the cuff, not having prepared a lengthy speech, the result being largely hortatory in demanding great efforts to meet four modernization goals in agriculture and on other fronts.[160] All in all, Deng apparently made only three substantive appearances[161] in the nearly five weeks devoted to the conference and forum, a period when he was involved with at least a couple of the "three weeds" and carried out heavy foreign affairs duties. With regard to substance, the available truncated versions of Deng's addresses indicate a focus on wider matters—notably the need for comprehensive consolidation, understanding Mao's Thought as a comprehensive system, and Party rectification. When his comments on agriculture were recorded, they were mostly very broad: Mao's concept of "agriculture as the foundation" was necessary for realizing the four modernizations, Chinese agriculture was still very poor and backward, great efforts were required to change this, the meeting should develop into a mass campaign to learn from Dazhai, and consolidating and developing the collective economy was essential.[162]

Beyond these general propositions, a number of additional features of Deng's talks can be identified. From the outset, he clearly was against the universal implementation of the Dazhai model, arguing in his September 15 speech that mechanization had to be carried out according to the conditions in different localities, not strictly by the methods used in Dazhai. But on the more contentious issue of the transition to brigade accounting, during the initial stage of the conference Deng apparently sidestepped the issue, saying only that Chen's proposals required study. Twelve days later, however, presumably in response to the "massive rift" that had developed at the forum, Deng articulated essentially the same position that would be set down in Hua's report, albeit in different language: "The pace [of the transition] can vary from place to place, it must be taken fairly steadily. ... Revising the 60 articles would be a basis." Deng, like Hua, affirmed that the direction was toward brigade accounting and ownership, but there was no rush. Yet if Deng backed the effort to resist leftism, he also spoke in the manner of orthodox pre-Cultural Revolution Maoism. This was more than endorsing long-standing goals such as mechanization. While undoubtedly opposed to a radical onslaught against the private sector in the countryside, Deng

---

the initiative for Deng to attend, the last minute nature of the decision emphasizes that this was not an area in which he was deeply involved.

[160] Zhang Hua, "1975 nian nongye xue Dazhai huiyi," p. 18; and *Deng nianpu*, vol. 1, pp. 97-99.

[161] That is, on September 15 when he gave his "important speech" at the conference opening, and in his talks to the forum on September 27 and October 4. Deng was also present at the October 15 plenary session when Hua delivered his report. In the assessment of Deng Liqun a quarter of a century later, Deng attended Hua's October report in order to support Hua as part of his general promotion of his younger colleague in this period; *Deng Liqun guoshi jiangtan*, vol. 3, p. 102. We doubt the accuracy of this observation given that the entire top leadership, except Wang Hongwen who was in Shanghai, attended. We believe the near complete attendance would have been Mao's arrangement.

[162] See *Selected Works of Deng (1975-1982)*, pp. 47-50; *Deng nianpu*, vol. 1, pp. 98-99; *Deng sixiang nianpu*, pp. 17-18; and Zhang Hua, "1975 nian nongye xue Dazhai huiyi," p. 18.

still spoke of "grasping the main contradiction in the villages between socialism and capitalism, focusing efforts on sorting out the two classes and two roads, and cracking down wherever capitalism was rampant." Finally, as with Hua's report, there was also more than a whiff of the Great Leap. Indeed, Deng went further than Hua by adopting some of the extreme rhetoric of the earlier period, arguing that if the target of one-third of all counties attaining Dazhai status was achieved, then the rural areas would have so much food they wouldn't know where to store it.[163]

With Hua's report the contentious issues of the conference were settled, and, alone among the "poisonous weeds" and potential "weeds," the report was promptly published and widely disseminated in the media, producing a quick burst of national publicity. The Politburo radicals were reportedly not happy, and, despite their lack of an explicit alternative policy, sought to curb that publicity. On October 27, Yao Wenyuan scuttled plans to publish the speech in *Red Flag*, arguing that since it was a Party document, such publication was unnecessary. This mirrored Yao's actions after the opening of the conference in mid-September when, after several days of reports on Dazhai dominating newspapers, he declared the coverage excessive and distracting attention from the *Water Margin* campaign.[164] Yet no obvious public criticism of the approach advocated by the conference and Hua's report emerged until spring 1976, when the campaign against Deng intensified, and virtually everything was open to attack. Direct criticism of Dazhai and the September-October conference was, however, voiced internally or privately. These objections will be examined in detail in our later analysis. For now, we simply note the radicals' major complaints. In October, Jiang Qing told Hua his report was revisionist without explaining her objections,[165] and the radicals subsequently succeeded in preventing its proposed reaffirmation in April 1976. More generally, the radicals viewed the Dazhai emphasis on production, capital construction, and mechanization as carrying out the reviled "theory of productive forces." In addition, implementation of the Dazhai conference agenda

---

[163] Chen and Du, *Shilu*, vol. 3, part 2, p. 1264; Zhang Hua, "1975 nian nongye xue Dazhai huiyi," p. 18; Feng Dongshu, *Wenmang zaixiang*, p. 222; and "Jiang Weiqing zhuanda jianghua jingshen," p. 8. Jiang Weiqing's account simply referred to a "central leading comrade," but textual comparisons of various sections of this leader's comments with authoritative accounts of Deng's statements indicate that he was the leader in question.

[164] *Zhonggong yuanshi ziliao xuanji*, vol. 1, 2nd series, p. 537; and Zweig, *Agrarian Radicalism*, p. 67.

[165] See Chen Yonggui's speech to the second Dazhai conference, in *SPRCP*, no. 6252 (1977), pp. 129-31. Jiang's remark, which was stated directly to Hua and Chen immediately after the report, might be interpreted as reflecting a position to the "left" of Chen Yonggui, not to mention Hua, since she was cultivating the highly collectivist Xiaojinzhuang model. Nevertheless, there is no evidence that she argued this view in the context of the Dazhai conference, and on this point her views were apparently quite different from those of other radicals (see below). Overall, there is little doubt of the radicals' generally dismissive attitude toward the report and the Dazhai model generally. Moreover, the radicals claimed that even if Mao had circled Hua's report, it did not necessarily mean he approved it, and it was necessary to wait and see.

by sending work teams to lower levels was attacked as an effort to divert attention from the essential anti-revisionist task. Finally, some radicals, including Zhang Chunqiao, were unenthusiastic about Dazhai's emphasis on brigade accounting and preferred to develop their own models, and the transition lagged in Shanghai and Liaoning where radicals largely or to a significant degree held sway.[166]

The Dazhai conference and resulting policies fell well within Mao's stated preferences. The left-leaning (or "soft radical") aspects owed nothing to the "gang of four" who, notwithstanding Jiang Qing's "important speech" at the conference opening, were basically excluded from agricultural policy making. Nor did they reflect a policy push by Hua Guofeng who, along with Deng Xiaoping, Li Xiannian, and various responsible officials in Beijing and the provinces, contributed to derailing the most threatening proposals: Chen Yonggui's call for a rapid transition to brigade accounting and nationwide implementation of the Dazhai model. Although Chen was not taken seriously as a politician, his proposals were because of Mao's decade-long endorsement of the Dazhai model, and the Chairman's August 1975 instruction to consider them. Deng was seemingly less involved with agricultural policy than any other aspect of the overall consolidation program, although as the leader in overall charge of work his backing for Hua and the others was certainly important. Yet the reason why comparative moderation prevailed remains obscure. The strong advocacy of provincial leaders Zhao Ziyang and Tan Qilong at the agricultural forum and Deng's subsequent support undoubtedly played their part, but where did Mao stand in all this? Did he simply remain aloof while others discussed the issue as per his instruction, or did he give a decisive nod, or even take the initiative, when meeting with Deng on September 24,[167] three days before the latter indicated his position at the forum? While the evidence is skimpy, and it seems Hua was moving toward the moderate position during the drafting of his report, in the view of a scholar with close knowledge of the Dazhai conference, it was Mao's caution concerning brigade accounting that led Hua to dilute his earlier support of Chen Yonggui's policy.[168]

In any case, the policies endorsed by the conference were carried out well after Deng was in trouble, albeit with varying outcomes. The transition to brigade accounting was gradual, as called for in Hua's report. The massive drive for farmland capital construction, dismissed by the radicals as using production to subvert revolution, continued apace in winter 1975-76. Sending work teams to

---

[166] See Chen Yonggui's speech to the second Dazhai conference, in *SPRCP*, no. 6252 (1977), pp. 130-31, 134-35; *Chedi jiefa pipan 'sirenbang' cuandang duoquan de taotian zuixing* [Thoroughly Expose and Criticize the Monstrous Crimes of the "Gang of Four" in Overthrowing the Party and Seizing Power] (Beijing: Renmin chubanshe, 1977), p. 189; *GMRB*, January 12, 1977, in *SPRCP*, no. 6291 (1977), p. 158; Zweig, *Agrarian Radicalism*, pp. 67-69; and below, pp. 499ff.

[167] It is possible that Deng had cleared his position with Mao, or even received Mao's instructions, following a meeting with Vietnamese leader Le Duan on September 24, the day after the transition issue initially exploded at the forum.

[168] Interview, January 2005.

conduct line education and rectification in the villages continued into the winter, but in the first half of 1976 various provinces withdrew the teams under radical pressure.[169] These developments are examined in Chapter 7. The decisions of the Dazhai conference thus continued to be a source of conflict until the purge of the "gang of four." Ironically, in the process, Mao's favorite left-leaning rural model became a rallying symbol for anti-radical forces.

Gathering Clouds: The *Water Margin* and Mao Yuanxin's Assignment in Beijing

Deng Xiaoping was clearly in the driver's seat in elite politics into fall 1975. Recalling the time 20 years later, Deng's daughter observed that her father had Mao's support until September. As previously noted, toward the end of that month Mao approvingly told the visiting Vietnamese leader Le Duan that of the old line leaders only Deng was fit, clearly suggesting that Deng was the answer to the current leadership crisis. A few days earlier, when receiving former British Prime Minister Heath, the Chairman told his visitor he was anxious to increase the speed of China's economic development, precisely the policy orientation he had entrusted to Deng. In this period the Chairman was reportedly in a very good mood when meeting foreigners in Deng's presence, on one occasion being photographed in jovial spirits with Deng, Wang Dongxing and his medical staff after the visitor left.[170] Yet shortly thereafter the climate began to change. After early October, Deng was no longer making major domestic policy statements, and the "three weeds" were being revised in a more strident ideological direction, with Deng's trademark slogan of "the three directives as the key link" being excised from the various drafts. While the signals from the Chairman remained mixed, a shift was taking place which made Deng and his supporters more nervous, and the radicals more willing to raise queries about, without yet launching a frontal attack on, the measures he had been pushing.

What went wrong? The answer ultimately lay in Mao's mind, surely involving a mixture of personal and political factors, and thus is forever elusive. Clearly, however, a number of developments introduced uncertainty into elite politics, beginning well before the late September-October shift. Some of these, notably the *Water Margin* issue which unfolded from the second half of August, were poorly understood by important participants in elite politics at the time,[171] much less by contemporary or later outside analysts. As the following discussion

---

[169] See *Zhonggong yuanshi ziliao xuanji*, vol. 1, 2nd series, p. 540; above, p. 358n152; and below, pp. 502-03.

[170] See *Zhou Rongxin Tongzhi jianghua huibian*, p. 29; Mao Mao, *"Wenge" suiyue*, pp. 410-11; and above, p. 313. The photograph probably occurred after the meeting with Le Duan on the 24th, but it could have taken place after Mao received Heath on the 21st.

[171] Deng Liqun, in *Deng Liqun guoshi jiangtan*, vol. 4, pp. 170-71, declared to scholars at his institute that he had never understood aspects of the *Water Margin* issue, and praised the research of a young scholar that had enlightened him on these matters.

will explain, we believe that, despite the elite anxiety it caused, the *Water Margin* campaign had little to do with Deng's demise, although it was profoundly revealing of the state of leadership politics. Another straw in the wind was the reemergence of Jiang Qing on the political stage at Dazhai—her escape from her "cage" that produced concern or delight in different elite circles. The most significant development for the ultimate outcome, however, was the appearance in Beijing of Mao's nephew, Mao Yuanxin, and then his taking up the role, at least partially,[172] of the Chairman's liaison to the rest of the leadership by mid-October. His nephew's views clearly had an important influence on Mao, but this should be distinguished from the radicals (or other leadership groupings) manipulating the Chairman. Mao was never a "soft ear," although he certainly could be receptive to messages confirming his preconceptions or calling his attention to matters of concern. In this sense, much as Deng had been able to bring the excesses of the dictatorship of the proletariat campaign to the Chairman's attention in April, Mao Yuanxin now had a major impact on the change in Deng's fortunes. But the event which became the pretext for Mao's decision to criticize his favorite colleague was the arrival of Liu Bing's second letter in mid-October. We touch on this complicated matter at the end of this chapter, but the full story must wait until Chapter 6.

These specific developments took place against the background of potentially counterproductive political moves by Deng and his supporters in leaking information that contributed to anti-radical rumors. The spate of rumors attacking Jiang Qing in particular, rumors that circulated in the July-September period, proved detrimental to Deng's cause. Whatever the involvement of moderate leaders in these rumors, Mao's reaction when he learned of them was anger. The Chairman had deliberately knocked the radicals, and his wife in particular, down a peg in the spring, and directed her to take a low profile. But it is clear that he did not want to drive her from the political stage, and would not allow others to pursue that objective. As he put it, "I have criticized Jiang Qing, but how does that mean they have the right to knock her down?"[173] Toward the end of August Mao's attitude toward Jiang warmed considerably, as seen in an incident concerning Jiang's passion for designing ladies' fashions, an incident perhaps also suggesting a relaxation of previous limits on her access. Jiang had designed a new outfit for Chinese women, and when she took it to Mao he was favorably impressed and had his secretary Zhang Yufeng model the outfit; around this time or slightly later Jiang also regained her voice in the Politburo.[174] Mao's more positive

---

[172] See below, p. 374n195, for a discussion of the likely overlap between Mao Yuanxin and "the two ladies," Wang Hairong and Tang Wensheng, in this role.

[173] Gao Wenqian, *Wannian Zhou*, p. 583. Gao places this remark in August, and declares that Mao had already decided to criticize Deng, something we believe at variance with the evidence.

[174] See "Zhang Hanzhi jiaodai cailiao (zhaiyao)" [Zhang Hanzhi 's Confession Material (summary)], handwritten document available at the Fairbank Center Library, Harvard University, p. 2; and Mao Mao, *"Wenge" suiyue*, p. 364. While official sources consistently play down Jiang's access to Mao

attitude, together with his anger over the rumors and his dismissive response to Kang Sheng's allegations against her (see below), was apparently responsible for Jiang's presence at the Dazhai conference—i.e., as graphic evidence that she was not a spent force. Indeed, when Jiang reported to Mao before departing, he had his staff prepare a Song dynasty poem enjoining her to lift her spirits and be brave. Not only did Jiang appear with a large retinue claiming Mao sent her, she was the second ranking leader present after Deng,[175] like him gave what would be described as an "important speech," and had the temerity to interrupt him. This led to concern in establishment circles that a new inner-Party struggle might be on the cards, while Wang Hongwen in Shanghai and the city's radical leaders were greatly heartened by Jiang's reappearance, in Wang's view a sign that the Chairman was starting to take action against the rumors.[176]

Whether or to what degree Mao connected the anti-Jiang rumors to Deng at this time, or had any knowledge of the leaking of his spring criticisms of the radicals, is unclear, although a senior oral source believes that Mao at some point became aware of, and uncomfortable with, Deng's June approach to Ma Tianshui, something that definitely eventuated by January 1976. Certainly such activities flew in the face of the Chairman's desire for unity within the Politburo, and Deng's role is perplexing given his avoidance of harsher criticism of the radicals in the spring, and especially his understanding of Mao's wish for conciliation within the leadership. In any case, there is little to indicate, even in Wang Hongwen's late October complaint to Mao about the rumors, that they were presented as Deng's doing. By early 1976, however, the radicals were indeed claiming that the rumors were organized and not accidental—in Jiang Qing's words that Deng was "the general manager of a rumor company"—while, more broadly, Jiang complained bitterly that Deng had turned on her in 1975, thus dashing her (Mao-induced) expectation that Deng would unite the Party.[177] But as the situation changed in October 1975, there was no clear indication that the unity issue was used against Deng, or cited by Mao. Nevertheless, the Chairman's sensitivity to the attacks on Jiang and his ongoing concern with Party unity suggest it was unlikely to have

---

throughout the post-Lin Biao period, the senior historian cited claims that it was much more frequent than Party historians themselves had believed, although he did not pinpoint this precise period. Given Mao's restrictions on her visits since 1972, and his absence from Beijing from July 1974 to April 1975, the timing seems to fit. See above, p. 116n17.

[175] Thus further suggesting that she was sent by Mao to demonstrate her continuing political importance. While Jiang's formal rank was second among those present, the fact that others of higher rank—e.g., Wang Hongwen and Zhang Chunqiao—were not dispatched, only highlighted her significance. Cf. above, p. 359n159.

[176] See *Deng Liqun zishu: shierge chunqiu (1975-1987)* [Deng Liqun's Self-statement: 12 Years, 1975-1987], internal publication available at the Fairbank Center Library, Harvard University, pp. 31-32; Yang Qing, *Huiyi Yang Yong*, p. 321; and "Ma Tianshui de buchong jiefa jiaodai," p. 3.

[177] "Jiang Qing zai dazhaohu huiyi," pp. 374, 377; and interview, January 2005. On the Deng-Ma exchange, see above, p. 303. *Deng nianpu*, vol. 1, p. 146, reports that Wang Hongwen wrote Mao concerning the matter on January 24.

been an insignificant factor.

In this context, a striking if elusive example of both Deng's willingness to be involved in anti-Jiang activities, and of his good relationship with the subsequently reviled Kang Sheng, unfolded in August. As we saw in Chapter 1, Kang had confidentially denounced Jiang Qing and Zhang Chunqiao to Deng shortly after the latter's return to Beijing in early 1973. Then at Changsha in December 1974, while making clear Kang's support, Zhou raised Zhang Chunqiao's "historical problems"—but apparently not those of Jiang Qing[178]—although the Chairman did not take up the matter. In any case, by mid-1975, presumably because of the diminished political position of the radicals, and arguably since, in the terminal months of his life, he had less to lose than in normal circumstances, Kang decided to push his vendetta against Jiang and Zhang one more time. With Jiang Qing as his main target, Kang again accused both Jiang and Zhang of being traitors to the Party during the revolutionary period. Ironically, the materials damning Zhang had been given to Kang at an earlier stage by none other than Jiang Qing herself.[179]

Kang first attempted to enlist Zhou in the new effort to approach Mao, but as with the Witke issue, the Premier avoided the matter, thus earning Kang's disdain for his lack of guts. He then approached Deng, who presumably had some idea of what Kang intended, even if he had not been explicitly informed. Deng told the "two ladies," the most convenient channel to Mao, that Kang wanted to see them, and after securing the Chairman's approval they went, seemingly in the latter part of August. Kang asked them to report to Mao on the traitorous activities of Jiang and Zhang. When Wang Hairong and Tang Wensheng reported the matter to Mao, he dismissively responded that Kang had dealt with spies for so long that "he suspects everyone."[180] As for Deng, Mao knew that, at the

---

[178] See our earlier argument that, despite the claim in authoritative sources that Zhou had also raised Jiang Qing's "historical problems," the official assertions on this point are unconvincing; above, pp. 232-33.

[179] Chen and Du, *Shilu*, vol. 3, part 2, p. 1373.

In addition, although the incident cannot be verified and we believe that in all likelihood it was merely a rumor, in July 1975 Kang allegedly urged Zhou Enlai to make use of the Chairman's anger over the interviews Jiang had given the American scholar, Roxane Witke, and carry out Mao's stated wish to "kick her out of the Politburo," but the Premier demurred. Even if genuine, this strange development was not actually about Witke's book subsequently published in 1977. Instead, a Hong Kong book lauding Jiang, *Hongdu nü wang* [Empress of the Red Capital], was confused with Witke's work, but Mao's anger reportedly was real and he called for Jiang's ouster. Zhou, however, concluded this was simply passing outrage rather than a serious order, and did not act. See Gao Wenqian, *Wannian Zhou*, pp. 577-79; Lin Qing, *Zhou Enlai zaixiang shengya* pp. 334-35; and Chen and Du, *Shilu*, vol. 3, part 2, pp. 850-51.

[180] This account is largely based on "Zhang Hanzhi jiaodai cailiao," i.e., her April 1976 letter to Mao explaining the circumstances surrounding the visit of the "two ladies" to herself and her husband, Qiao Guanhua, immediately after they had seen Kang, in *Zhonggong yuanshi ziliao xuanji*, vol. 2, 1st series, pp. 145-47; and interview with person close to Kang Sheng's household, September 2002. See also Chen and Du, *Shilu*, vol. 3, part 2, p. 1373; Lin Qing, *Zhou Enlai zai zaixiang shengya*,

very least, he had been a facilitator in the affair. The outcome was paradoxical. On the one hand, Jiang's emergence from her "cage" shortly after the incident indicates that the accusations not only did not have the desired effect, but in fact, like the anti-Jiang rumors of the period, may have contributed to Mao's decision to place her back on the public stage. On the other hand, there were no immediate repercussions for Deng: until the end of September every indication was that he continued to have the Chairman's full backing. The final twist, in even more mysterious circumstances, occurred two to three months later when Kang conveyed a message to Mao attacking Deng for still opposing the Cultural Revolution (see Chapter 6).

If the details and reverberations of this development remain unclear, the political calculations of the anti-radical forces are also elusive. Deng Xiaoping, if not as circumspect as the Premier and Ye Jianying wished, had also been wary of confrontation as seen in the spring Politburo meetings, an undoubted consequence of Mao's stipulation that he must not oppose Jiang Qing. While the prudent course would have been simply to focus on meeting Mao's work requirements even though, as events would prove, this was hardly foolproof, arguably Deng was tempted by the possibility of finishing off Jiang and Zhang once and for all with evidence of their betraying the revolution. Or perhaps the goal was more limited: to use accusations about the past to induce the radicals to retire from politics. This was suggested by Wang Hairong's observation immediately after seeing Kang that veteran leaders would not be too harsh in dealing with Jiang, but she should withdraw from politics.[181] Yet everything was dependent on Mao's unpredictable reaction, making the risk for all concerned, including the dying Kang,[182] seem excessive to the outside analyst. While hatred of Jiang Qing in particular, self-delusion concerning the Chairman's meaning since May, and genuine revulsion on the part of veteran leaders over what they believed was a betrayal of their revolutionary cause were all likely factors, we can offer no satisfactory explanation for this potentially explosive gambit.

Against this background, the *Water Margin* issue had been evolving for nearly a month by the time Jiang Qing arrived in Dazhai in September and raised the matter in strident fashion. In standard post-Mao accounts, once Mao commented on the novel on August 13, the radicals quickly seized upon the question to attack Party veterans, with Zhou Enlai the most prominent target, and to use it to

---

pp. 337-39; Li Zhisui, *Private Life*, p. 600; and below, pp. 517-18. Li Zhisui's account, in our view, confuses the sequence and details of these events.

[181] Chen and Du, *Shilu*, vol. 3, part 2, p. 1373.

[182] Although both Kang Sheng and Zhou Enlai were in the terminal stages of their respective illnesses, they still had much to lose in terms of their revolutionary reputations. Thus Zhou went into surgery on September 20 famously shouting that he was "loyal to the Party," after signing a statement affirming that he was not "Wu Hao," the alias of an apostate to the CCP's cause in the 1930s, while Kang, in making his accusations against Jiang and Zhang, asserted that *he* was not a traitor. *Zhou nianpu*, vol. 3, p. 721; and Chen and Du, *Shilu*, vol. 3, part 2, p. 1258.

undermine Deng Xiaoping, while some contemporary foreign scholars speculated that the episode was a possible early sign of Mao's displeasure with Deng.[183] The reality was more complex. Initially, the issue emerged in a casual, almost benign fashion. With Mao virtually blind before his operation for cataracts, arrangements were made for a young Beijing University Chinese literature instructor, Lu Di, to read classical works to the Chairman starting in May.[184] During these encounters Mao commented on various novels, including the *Water Margin*, in response to the questions of his young reader. Of course, although casual, Mao's remarks were not without political significance, both due to who he was and because they reflected his ongoing concern with revisionism. And given the radicals' leftist perspective, the Chairman's comments were obviously of potential benefit to their cause. Even if Mao's initial raising of the matter was accidental, their pursuit of it was not. Nevertheless, at first there were no sharp differences over the substance of Mao's remarks or the need circulate them. Moreover, as the matter unfolded it only gradually, and unclearly, took on anti-Deng meaning, and the evidence indicates it was something less than a common "gang of four" project.

A significant factor in this story was recent political history concerning the *Water Margin*. Mao had spoken of the *Water Margin* as early as 1964, and according to the recollection of Zhang Yufeng, his August 1975 comments expressed exactly the same view a decade later. But more recent history in 1973 was crucial. After some musings earlier in 1973, the Chairman intensified leadership tension in December of that year when he declared the lesson of the novel was the danger of capitulationism, as exemplified by the peasant leader Song Jiang refusing to carry through rebellion against the emperor. In the context of intense criticism of Zhou for his alleged concessions to Kissinger a few weeks earlier, mistakes characterized by the Chairman as "right capitulationism," a link between the Premier and the *Water Margin* had been established.[185] When Mao again singled out capitulationism in his August 1975 comment, it naturally had potential implications for the Premier, even if the casual, responsive nature of the remarks suggest they were directed at revisionism in a generic sense rather than representing a premeditated rebuke of the Chairman's favorite target. Moreover, contrary to official claims of a sinister Yao Wenyuan maneuver to seize the issue

---

[183] Yan and Gao, *Turbulent Decade*, pp. 473-75, faithfully rehash orthodox histories which posit Deng as the ultimate target, although they go beyond those histories to suggest Mao's anti-Deng intent. The identity of the target(s) varied in official accounts depending on the timing. In the early post-Mao period, the emphasis was on Zhou Enlai and Hua Guofeng. See, e.g., *GMRB*, March 24, 1977, in *SPRCP*, no. 6317 (1977), pp. 6-8. For a sophisticated Western account suggesting that Mao lent his support to the radicals' onslaught against Deng, see Merle Goldman, "The Media Campaign as a Weapon in Political Struggle: The Dictatorship of the Proletariat and *Water Margin* Campaigns," in Godwin C. Chu and Francis L.K. Hsu, eds., *Moving a Mountain: Cultural Change in China* (Honolulu: University Press of Hawaii, 1979), pp. 191-202.

[184] Mao's surgery was on July 23, but the reading sessions continued into August. See *Mao zhuan*, vol. 2, pp. 1747-48.

[185] *Ibid.*, pp. 1747-49; and *Deng Liqun guoshi jiangtan*, vol. 3, p. 121.

for inner-Party struggle, the emergence of the matter from casual comment to public campaign further suggests a largely unthreatening context in the first instance, even though this did not prevent many in the elite from seeing a threat as events unfolded.

The impetus for the circulation of Mao's remarks is best seen as a manifestation of the imperial tradition whereby the emperor's statements were regarded as precious wisdom. In a context where a new edition of the *Water Margin* was being prepared, Lu Di showed her notes to Zhang Yufeng who had attended the reading, and who apparently suggested they would make a good preface to the new edition. After Mao vetted the notes, he turned the matter over to Wang Dongxing to handle. Since it was a literary matter, Yao Wenyuan was informed, he immediately proposed widespread propaganda on Mao's remarks in the context of the ongoing campaign to study the dictatorship of the proletariat, and Mao quickly approved. In the same period Deng, presumably informed by Wang Dongxing,[186] proposed that the Chairman's comments be circulated as an internal Party Center document (there is no evidence that he opposed Yao's request for publicity), but Mao demurred on the grounds that such a document was unnecessary given the public media campaign. On August 28, *Red Flag* published a series of articles on the issue, and on September 4 the *People's Daily* editorialized on the significance of the *Water Margin* for opposing revisionism and capitulationism. Thereafter, the press campaign escalated, producing considerable nervousness, perhaps creating fears that this might be another *Hai Rui*, the literary issue that preceded the turmoil of the Cultural Revolution. Nevertheless, despite post-Mao characterizations of Yao's efforts, there is no hard evidence that he had picked out any specific leadership targets, his obvious interest in the anti-revisionist theme notwithstanding. In any case, whatever Mao's intent, approving Yao's media campaign rather than Deng's Party document had the effect of spreading the issue to wider, non-Party audiences, but with less authority and clarity as to the "line" than a central document would have conveyed.[187]

---

[186] Recall Wang's important role as the link between Mao and Deng during the latter's internal exile, and his efforts to ease Deng's lot. Wang would again act to protect Deng's interests in 1976. See above, p. 69; and below, pp. 490-91.

[187] See *Deng Liqun guoshi jiangtan*, vol. 4, pp. 170-71; *Mao wengao*, vol. 13, pp. 457-60; Shui Luzhou, "Du *Mao Zedong zhuan* biji" [Notes on Reading *Biography of Mao Zedong*], *Zhongguo yu shijie* [China and the World] (special issue, July 2005), p. 10, http/www.zgysj.com; Barnouin and Yu, *Ten Years*, pp. 283-84; Yan and Gao, *Turbulent Decade*, p. 474; and *HQ*, no. 9 (1975), pp. 5-32. On the *Hai Rui* case in 1965-66, see Teiwes, *Politics and Purges*, pp. lx-lxi, 460-62; and MacFarquhar, *Origins 3*, pp. 439ff. An alternative account has Mao deciding against Deng's proposal on the grounds it was a literary issue; *Deng Liqun zishu*, p. 30.

An insight into the importance of having a campaign backed by a Party document is provided by developments surrounding 1975 National Day celebrations in Xinjiang. At that juncture, old cadres and local officials were concerned and confused by the *Water Margin* campaign; they could only read about it in the press but had no authoritative central document. When a central delegation led by Chen Xilian and including Mao Yuanxin arrived in Xinjiang, local military commander Yang Yong arranged for a private discussion with Chen to find out what it all meant. Other revealing aspects were

Regardless of any possible intent on the part of Mao and/or Yao, in the early stage of the drama Deng Xiaoping appeared confident that the Chairman was not signaling a reversal of course, or that he was a target. Deng not only proposed a Party Center document, he articulated the key themes of the contemporary relevance of the novel, and that in criticizing capitulationism, the main task was criticizing revisionism and capitalist restoration. Apparently seeing no threat, he reassured officials discussing the Outline Report on August 26 that they should not "imagine that things might go wrong" because of the *Water Margin*. But the significance was different for Zhou Enlai given the history of 1973, and the fact that in late August Jiang Qing was claiming within her circle of supporters at the Ministry of Culture that the key issue of the novel was Song Jiang making Chao Gai, the leader of the bandit group, i.e., Mao, a figurehead in order to seize power himself, even though it is unlikely Zhou was aware of her activities at this stage. The issue of marginalizing Mao was dangerous for Zhou, notwithstanding the Chairman's December 1973 rejection of Jiang Qing's claim that the Premier was impatient to replace him. In any case, Zhou was clearly worried. He ordered his secretary to compile materials on the issue on September 2, and declared later in the month that "I am not a capitulationist" as he entered the operating theater for critical surgery. About this time Zhou also wrote Mao, in effect offering his resignation by asking that Deng take over his Party and state responsibilities, a further indication that he believed the *Water Margin* critique was aimed at him. Deng was informed of the Premier's letter, but Mao never responded.[188]

Deng, meanwhile, continued to downplay the disruptive potential of the new campaign. In comments on September 5, he echoed the radical theme of the contemporary relevance of the novel and its importance for learning theory, but qualified this with the assertion that "the Chairman's remarks are definitely not aimed at inner-Party struggle." Significantly, when attacking these observations by Deng in July 1976, the radicals compared them to Peng Zhen's 1966 February Outline. The logic apparently was that both were cases of an overconfident leader attempting to derail class struggle by shielding guilty individuals. In Peng's case the guilty were his subordinates within the Beijing municipal apparatus; in Deng's it presumably was Premier Zhou.[189]

While the *Water Margin* issue was already causing uncertainty in elite circles, a significant increase in tension resulted from Jiang Qing's performance at Dazhai. As previously indicated, her activities had little to do with agriculture.

Yang's elaborate plan to send Mao Yuanxin away while having his talk with Chen, and his dismissal of his wife's reservations about even discussing the matter with Chen on the grounds that as a veteran military leader, "deep in his heart he won't follow the Shanghai gang." Yang Qing, *Huiyi Yang Yong*, p. 327. Cf. below, p. 562.

[188] See *HQ*, no. 12 (1977), p. 38; *Zhou nianpu*, vol. 3, pp. 719, 721; Gao Wenqian, *Wannian Zhou*, p. 586; and above, p. 337n96.

[189] *HQ*, no. 7 (1976), p. 36. On the February Outline, see Teiwes, *Politics and Purges*, pp. 461-63; and MacFarquhar, *Origins 3*, pp. 452ff.

Instead, arriving before other leaders, she addressed the *Water Margin* question in a talk on September 12, and with the conference underway again on the 17th. In one sense she was clearly justified; not only was the *Water Margin* now part of Mao's overriding directive to study the theory of the dictatorship of the proletariat, but official conference documents included material on the new campaign. Yet Jiang overstepped whatever leeway Mao had granted her. On the 12th, in what was very much her own rather than a common "gang of four" initiative, she addressed the Dazhai masses and developed her late August theme that a key lesson of the novel was kicking Chao Gai upstairs, something that had not been part of Mao's August comments, and placed the campaign in the tradition of "line struggles" in the top leadership. It was probably this aggressive talk that Dazhai Party secretary Guo Fenglian later claimed had made her flesh crawl. On the 17th, Jiang went even further in a talk restricted to propaganda officials, claiming explicitly that some people planned to make Mao a figurehead, Politburo members resisted studying theory, and she had been struggling for more than half a year against revisionists in Beijing. Meanwhile, as noted previously, her speech to the conference's opening session on the 15th, which had not been scheduled but which she insisted on giving, also focused on the *Water Margin*. Jiang had already demanded that a recording of her first speech be broadcast to the conference, and now wanted the text of her opening session remarks published as a conference document, leading Hua Guofeng, as conference chairman, to approach Mao concerning her demand. The Chairman, presumably feeling she was undermining the main focus of the conference, declared her views "farting," and ordered that they were not to be circulated.[190]

These developments unsurprisingly produced contradictory reactions. On the one hand, some leaders were encouraged by Mao's "farting" comment; thus participants at the agricultural forum took solace and argued against leftist rural policies. The more telling reaction, however, was enhanced concern. While Deng continued in his efforts to reassure, arguing at the forum that Mao's remarks on the *Water Margin* had been casual even though "some people" had made a big issue of them, and there was no reason to be afraid

---

[190] *Mao zhuan*, vol. 2, p. 1751; Chen and Du, *Shilu*, vol. 3, part 2, pp. 1265-67; *HQ*, no. 1 (1977), p. 98; Yan and Gao, *Turbulent Decade*, pp. 474-75; Barnouin and Yu, *Ten Years*, p. 285; and interview with specialist on Dazhai conference, November 2002.

There is a divergence in the sources concerning the circumstances of Mao's "farting" comment, with Chen and Du, p. 1267, and *RMRB*, August 11, 1978, p. 1, reporting it as his response to Hua, while *Mao zhuan*, p. 1751, and *Deng nianpu*, vol. 1, p. 103, claim it occurred on September 24 when Deng reported following a reception of Vietnamese leader Le Duan. Of course, it is possible that Mao made the comment on more than one occasion, or that Deng conveyed Hua's concern. In any case, it is likely that Mao first heard of Jiang's activities at Dazhai from Xie Jingyi, whom he had dispatched to the conference along with other radicals from the "two schools." See Fan Daren, *"Wenge" yubi chenfulu: "Liang Xiao" wangshi* [The Rise and Fall of the "Cultural Revolution's" Imperial Pens: The Past Events of *Liang Xiao*] (Hong Kong: Mingbao chubanshe, 1999), p. 100.

since "we're not Song Jiangs," to some degree a heightened sense of danger was emerging at the highest levels. Thus, although clear signs that Deng was being fitted for the Song Jiang mantle only came much later, according to one report, when meeting with Deng and Wu Lengxi the day after Jiang's first talk on September 13, Hu Qiaomu told Deng that, in his view, Deng was Jiang's implicit target—the "you know who" she had attacked in private discussions, which had been leaked to Hu by Xinhua News Agency reporters through the organization's chain of command. While the "you know who" was more likely to have been Zhou Enlai, Hu's assessment was credible given the animosity Jiang bore toward Deng for the events of the spring. But Jiang would have to be cautious, in that Deng was still the Chairman's man as far as anyone could reasonably see, and, interruptions during his speech aside, at Dazhai she displayed cordiality toward Deng, photographing him and his family. In any case, Deng responded to Hu's assessment by observing that the situation was serious, and it was necessary to raise the matter with Mao. A striking aspect of this development was that both the Xinhua reporters who leaked information on Jiang's activities and Deng wanted the information to reach Mao, an apparent indication that whatever level of threat they thought existed, they believed the Chairman still backed Deng's efforts.[191]

Whether or not he felt personally threatened at this stage, Deng was clearly concerned with Jiang's activities, notwithstanding his reassuring statements to different leaders. He noted that Jiang had her own agenda, there was urgency concerning informing the Chairman, but as this would be difficult for him to do, another channel would have to be found. The obvious choice, the "two ladies," were recruited for the task. Following Mao's reception of former British Prime Minister Heath on September 21, Tang Wensheng gave the Chairman a copy of one of Jiang's Dazhai speeches, while in the most detailed account Deng remained silent. Three days later on the 24th, after Mao received Le Duan, Deng did speak up and raised Jiang's behavior, producing, perhaps for the second time, the famous comment that she was farting, to which Mao added that she was ignorant

---

[191] "Deng Xiaoping 1975 jiu, shi yue jian zai nanfang shiersheng shengwei shuji huiyishang de jianghua zhailu" [Abridged Record of Deng Xiaoping's Speeches in September-October 1975 at the Conference of 12 Southern Provincial Party Secretaries], pp. 10, 12, 21, document available at the Fairbank Center Library, Harvard University; Zhang Huifang and Wang Fang, *Renmin jizhe Mu Qing* [People's Reporter Mu Qing] (Zhengzhou: Henan renmin chubanshe, 2003), pp. 82-83; Mao Mao, *"Wenge" suiyue*, pp. 398-99; *Deng nianpu*, vol. 1, pp. 96-97; and Du Xiuxian, *Hongzhaopian* [Red Photos] (Xi'an: Shaanxi shifan daxue chubanshe, 1999), vol. 2, p. 232. The discussion here of Jiang's activities conflates her late August complaints in cultural circles (above, p. 370) when she apparently referred to "you know who," and her sharp talk to propaganda officials at Dazhai. That Deng *was* "you know who" gains support from Jiang's reported Dazhai remark that Song Jiang had been an exiled government official sent to a region that was present-day Jiangxi—the area where Deng had been exiled in 1969-72; *ZGDSCKZL*, vol. 27, p. 300. Descriptions of Song Jiang in the national media as "a short, dark, and faithful 'number three,'" cited in various sources (e.g., Yan and Gao, *Turbulent Decade*, p. 475) as proof that Deng was the target of the *Water Margin* campaign, did not begin until well after Deng was clearly in trouble, and Deng was explicitly denounced as the "modern Song Jiang" only after the 1976 Tiananmen crisis (see *ZGDSCKZL*, vol. 27, p. 300).

and few people believed her. Thus, at one level, Deng gained reassurance that Jiang's views were her own, but at another he was treading into the territory of opposing her that Mao had demanded he not enter. In any case, in Gao Wenqian's assessment, Deng's complaints were one factor in altering Mao's attitude toward his hitherto favored colleague. Meanwhile, Xinhua officials prepared a more extensive report on Jiang's activities at Dazhai which they passed on to Wang Hairong most likely on October 8, but which never reached the Chairman. In November, Ji Dengkui informed the officials that the climate had changed and they should put on more clothes, while Wang Hairong returned the report saying she could not transmit it to Mao.[192]

In considering the *Water Margin* affair, it is important to distinguish among the so-called "gang of four." Despite Yao Wenyuan's documented role in advocating and organizing the media campaign, the abrasive edge, the overstepping of the mark was the apparent work of Jiang Qing alone. While she had been developing the theme of kicking Mao upstairs since late August, Yao seemingly became deeply involved with the figurehead issue only in late December, with the major commentary on the *Water Margin* in Yao's *Red Flag* at the start of November making no mention of kicking anyone upstairs. Moreover, there is evidence of different behavior toward Zhou Enlai by Jiang in contrast to the other three radicals, and of a different assessment on Zhou's part of these three in this period. With Zhou suffering from terminal cancer and the end clearly in sight in September-December, Wang Hongwen, who had demonstrated particular concern for the Premier's health, Zhang Chunqiao and Yao Wenyuan joined other Politburo members in visiting the Premier in hospital, but Jiang apparently never went. On one of these occasions Zhou tried to convince Zhang and Yao that they should support Deng, and in early December he reminded Wang of Jiang's ambitions at his (Wang's) expense. While probably a futile project, Zhou's effort indicated a variegated view of the radicals, even if in the larger policy sense their different orientation from the veteran leaders was well understood by all concerned. In any case, before late October, any effort to attack Zhou or Deng using the *Water Margin* was seemingly carried out by Jiang on her own.[193]

---

[192] *Mao zhuan*, vol. 2, p. 1759; Zhang and Wang, *Renmin jizhe Mu Qing*, pp. 80-83; Gao Wenqian, *Wannian Zhou*, p. 591; and Cheng and Xia, *Deng zai yijiuqiwu*, p. 518. According to *Deng nianpu*, vol. 1, p. 102, Deng reported (*huibao*) to Mao concerning Jiang following the meeting with Heath on the 21st, but there is no indication what if anything Deng said, nor of Mao's response except that he reportedly issued directives. Thus it would appear that Deng's effort on this occasion was tentative, with Tang Wensheng playing the largest role.

[193] Qing Ye and Fang Lei, *Deng Xiaoping zai 1976, shangjuan: Tiananmen shijian* [Deng Xiaoping in 1976, vol. 1: The Tiananmen Incident] (Shenyang: Chunfeng wenyi chubanshe, 1993), p. 114; *HQ*, no. 11 (1975), pp. 5-7; *Zhou nianpu*, vol. 3, pp. 721-23; and interview with senior Party historian, February 2000. In this context, we note that accounts in the immediate post-Mao propaganda campaign claiming that the radicals had tormented the terminally ill Zhou in his hospital bed (see the faithful recycling in Yan and Gao, *Turbulent Decade*, p. 482) are not credible. There are no such claims in later, more reliable accounts from Zhou's medical staff; see Zhang Zuoliang, *Zhou*

Regardless of the intentions and calculations of the various actors, there is little to indicate that the *Water Margin* issue had much if any role in Mao's changing attitude toward Deng. The Chairman not only did not apply the capitulationist label to his colleague, but in January 1976 he explicitly rejected Jiang Qing's argument that Deng, akin to Song Jiang, wanted to kick him upstairs.[194] Although the campaign continued in the media, it was soon overtaken as a political issue in late October by Liu Bing's letters, a saga going back to Liu's first, seemingly uneventful letter to Mao in August, but which rapidly came to the fore in the process of the Chairman's reassessment once a second letter was received about October 15 or shortly thereafter. This story is told in detail in the following chapter.

A crucial intervening development, in our view the most significant of all, was the arrival of Mao Yuanxin in Beijing and his assignment as liaison between Mao and the top leadership. The Chairman met with his 36-year-old nephew on September 27, prior to the latter's departure on a delegation to celebrate National Day in Xinjiang, but Mao Yuanxin apparently was just passing through, with no arrangement for his assuming a liaison role yet made. When he returned to Beijing on October 10, he soon began functioning in this role, although perhaps initially sharing the function with Wang Hairong and Tang Wensheng.[195] Although reportedly not formally endorsed by the Politburo, Mao Yuanxin's status was institutionalized to a degree considerably greater than that of the "two ladies," and involved much more ongoing and intense interaction with the top leadership. Personal and political factors were involved in this development. Mao Yuanxin was not only Mao's nephew (and in the view of both Deng's daughter and Yao Wenyuan, the Chairman only fully trusted his relatives), he had a family relationship as well with Jiang Qing. The nature of that relationship is uncertain, however. Some sources describe it as close—Mao Yuanxin reportedly called Jiang Mom—but a senior Party historian specializing on the period claims a considerable degree of tension existed between them, with the Chairman ordering Mao Yuanxin to address Jiang as Mom after a row during the Cultural Revolution. In any case, Jiang apparently lobbied for such an appointment,[196]

Enlai de zuihou shinian. Moreover, such treatment of Zhou made no political sense regardless of the differences between the Premier and the "gang." Cf. above, p. 250n19, on Wang Hongwen's concern for the Premier's health.

[194] See the discussion of Jiang's attempt to make this case against Deng and Mao's rejection, below, p. 415.

[195] Apart from the "two ladies'" liaison duties in their MFA roles and at key political moments, such as the late 1973 Politburo criticism of Zhou Enlai, Wang Hairong accompanied Mao on his travels in south China in 1973-74. Jiang Qing later claimed that after summer 1975, Mao no longer saw them very much. But even after Mao Yuanxin's arrival, both continued to be present at meetings with foreigners into 1976, with Wang Hairong lasting somewhat longer in this role. Subsequently, Zhang Hanzhi and Ji Chaozhu took over the translation function. Mao Yuanxin had no foreign affairs role and did not accompany foreigners to see Mao, but he did attend Politburo meetings, which the "two ladies" may have done on a more *ad hoc* basis.

[196] With her relationship deteriorating with both Deng and Wang Hairong, in the latter case arguably

but it was the Chairman's decision to make Mao Yuanxin the liaison between himself and the Politburo, a measure predicated on his worsening health. This step brought not only a relative, but a still young Cultural Revolution activist into a vitally important position. Moreover, as someone from the localities, i.e., the type of person the Chairman regarded as closer to reality than officials in Beijing, Mao Yuanxin had additional credibility. With Jiang often denied access to the Chairman, Mao Yuanxin was the most effective vehicle for raising radical concerns. But as we shall see subsequently, Mao Yuanxin played an individual role that did not necessarily work in favor of the "gang of four," and at critical junctures worked against them.[197]

Whatever the underlying explanation of Mao Yuanxin's appointment, he began to air a series of complaints to his uncle even before the arrangement was fixed. It is difficult to be precise about the evolution of these complaints and his interaction with the Chairman: the authoritative summary of Mao's comments during these exchanges only refers to them being made over the October-January period, while his official biography discusses their meetings of September 27 and November 2 without distinguishing between them.[198] By extension, even allowing for the possibility that Jiang was already targeting Deng, it is unclear whether Mao Yuanxin's initial intention was to undermine Deng who, after all, to all visible signals still had the Chairman's confidence in late September, or whether it was simply a case of raising a number of troubling concerns in the hope of policy changes. But whatever Mao Yuanxin's objectives, his complaints, when combined with unfolding events, notably Liu Bing's letters, had a profound impact on the Chairman. Indeed, when Yao Wenyuan subsequently attempted to understand Mao's sudden turn against Deng, he concluded that, while no answer was entirely satisfactory, the change must have been linked to Mao Yuanxin.[199] Yao's observation, moreover, further suggests that this crucial development unfolded without any unified "gang of four" input.

In any case, the initial meeting between the Chairman and his nephew on September 27 seems crucial. It appears that Mao Yuanxin briefed his uncle on conditions in his home province of Liaoning. He was particularly upset with the economic situation in his province, especially fuel shortages. These shortages, which also produced complaints from the other leading radical locality, Shanghai,

---

the result of both jealousy over the access of the "two ladies" to Mao, and the fact of their cooperative relations with Deng, Jiang seemingly suggested to Mao that relying exclusively on the two women was not a good arrangement, although she claimed it was Mao's idea. "Zhang Hanzhi jiaodai cailiao (zhaiyao)," p. 2.

[197] *Mao zhuan*, vol. 2, pp. 1752-53; "Zhang Hanzhi jiaodai cailiao," pp. 145-47; Qing and Fang, *Deng zai 1976*, vol. 1, p. 114; Mao Mao, *"Wenge" suiyue*, p. 413; Qing and Fang, *Deng zai 1976*, vol. 1, p. 115; interview with senior Party historian, November 2002; above, p. 309; and below, pp. 442-43, 496.

[198] *Mao wengao*, vol. 13, pp. 486-93; and *Mao zhuan*, vol. 2, p. 1743.

[199] Qing and Fang, *Deng zai 1976*, vol. 1, p. 114.

naturally affected the well-being of the masses, as well as at the same time relating to the ongoing radical position on economic relations with the capitalist world. In the context of the 1973 Middle East oil crisis, petroleum production was diverted from domestic supply to export markets, thus allowing China to cash in on the drastically increased international market price. The resultant domestic shortages now dovetailed with the more ideologically driven radical claim that this policy subordinated national self-reliance to world capitalism. Evolving economic policy seemingly came into play as well, with Mao Yuanxin expressing his doubts concerning the speeches of eight vice premiers to the June-August State Council theory conference that had been brought home by Liaoning's delegates, and asking the Chairman for his views. Apparently on this occasion, Mao Yuanxin also complained of the attacks by Zhou Rongxin and others on the Chaoyang educational model that he had pioneered in Liaoning. Even allowing for the fact that the Chairman had selected Zhou Rongxin over the radical Chi Qun to be in charge of education in the NPC appointments, this was clearly a volatile area, and as we have seen an area where the Chairman had engaged Mao Yuanxin as early as 1964.[200]

Undoubtedly most pregnant in terms of implications for the larger situation were matters centrally related to Deng's comprehensive consolidation effort, and its relationship to the Cultural Revolution. While the details are unclear, Mao Yuanxin relayed the discontent of Liaoning rebels with the whole *zhengdun* process.[201] These rebels were under threat from the rectification in the localities pushed by Deng and Ji Dengkui, and in raising their unhappiness Mao Yuanxin presumably confronted the Chairman with evidence that all was not well with his plan to integrate large numbers of revolutionary successors into leadership roles. Although there is no direct evidence that Mao Yuanxin raised it before November, it is likely that he also broached a second issue at this juncture—the "three directives as the key link" formula. As indicated previously, by September Jiang Qing, not without reason, was questioning the genuineness of the directive on the national economy, something which by extension led to doubts about the "key link." According to Jiang in March 1976, she had discussed the matter with Mao Yuanxin in September:

> … I only heard about "the three directives as the key link" at the start of September. I said what is this business, it's not clear. … I felt this three directives was strange, but I didn't dare make use of it. The Chairman had warned me not to make noise or speak rashly. … At this time Mao Yuanxin returned [to Beijing]. He also had misgivings. … I told him, you've come back now, you must clarify this matter.[202]

---

[200] See Cheng Zhongyuan, "Mao Zedong sanxiang zhishi he Deng Xiaoping," p. 75; *Deng Liqun guoshi jiangtan*, vol. 3, p. 240; *Mao zhuan*, vol. 2, p. 1753; and above, pp. 227-28, 333n86, 340.

[201] *Deng Liqun guoshi jiangtan*, vol. 3, p. 240.

[202] "Jiang Qing zai dazhaohu huiyi," p. 382. Jiang's comments, together with the evidence of Chen Xilian's National Day speech in Xinjiang (see below), suggest that Mao Yuanxin in all likelihood raised the issue on September 27.

Apart from her claim of being unaware of the slogan before September, Jiang's account is credible and revealing. Given the downturn in her fortunes from May 1975 (and it was only in late May that Deng started to use the concept of three directives), and the intimidation she felt when Deng confidently strode into the Politburo to relay the Chairman's views, her lack of an earlier response becomes understandable. In any case, Mao Yuanxin seemingly did take up the issue with his uncle in September, setting in train a complex process affecting the "three weeds," the larger consolidation project, and ultimately Deng's fate.

Beyond these matters, it appears that Mao Yuanxin directly raised the more sweeping question of Deng's attitude toward the Cultural Revolution on September 27. While the standard view is that his famous claim that Deng "hardly [ever] mention[ed] the achievements of the Cultural Revolution, [or] criticized Liu Shaoqi's revisionist line," an assessment reportedly endorsed by the Chairman, occurred on November 2, Mao Yuanxin himself asserted this took place at the September meeting.[203] In any case, whatever the Chairman's state of mind when his nephew visited in September, Mao Yuanxin's complaints produced a new alertness on his part. The encounter arguably elevated the Chairman's sense that something might be amiss when he received the draft Outline Report on the 28th, with its erroneous claim that he had endorsed science and technology as part of the forces of production, and it is conceivable that the document's possible use of "the three directives as the key link"[204] now had a significance he had not noticed throughout the May-September period. When Mao Yuanxin returned from Xinjiang on October 10 and began to function in the liaison role, such issues came up in ongoing discussions between Mao and his nephew. The Chairman asked Mao Yuanxin to look further into the "three directives," and his nephew reported back in November.[205] The Chairman's reassessment of Deng was well and truly under way.

---

[203] See Zhang Haini, "Wo wei Mao Yuanxin bianhu" [I Defend for the Plaintiff, Mao Yuanxin], *Zhonghua ernü*, May 1999, pp. 17-18, an account based on an interview with Mao Yuanxin's lawyer at his 1986 trial. For the standard account, see Mao Mao, *"Wenge" suiyue*, p. 415. Although succinctly capturing Deng's focus on practical issues, Mao Yuanxin's claims were not strictly correct. Even a few days later, Deng praised the Cultural Revolution, as well as the campaign to criticize Lin Biao and Confucius and the study of the dictatorship of the proletariat; see Deng's National Day speech in FBIS-PRC, no. 192 (1975), p. D2. In addition, the various "poisonous weeds" contained ritual attacks on Liu's revisionism and praise of the Cultural Revolution, and Deng's own rhetoric was clearly stronger than what has been released in post-Mao versions of his comments.

[204] While it is unclear whether this fifth draft of the Outline Report contained the offending slogan, it is likely; see above, p. 338n98. On the forces of production issue itself, it is also unclear what might have upset Mao apart from the misquotation of his views. It is conceivable that he had become aware of Li Chang's talk at the Academy of Sciences in late August, when Li contentiously argued that for a long time science and technology had been "wrongly treated as part of the superstructure." "Hu Yaobang, Li Chang de jianghua," items 13-22, p. 40. Although there is no evidence that Mao knew of Li's remark by the time he queried Deng on the forces of production in mid-October, such a view could be taken as critical of the Cultural Revolution.

[205] See Zhang Hua, "Yetan Mao Zedong de sanxiang zhishi," p. 73.

Of the specific issues relating to consolidation and its relationship to the Cultural Revolution, the question of "the three directives as the key link" most clearly illustrates the apparent early impact of Mao Yuanxin's views, the nature of Deng's efforts, and the general complexity of elite politics. While the precise circumstances of why the "key link" formula was dropped from the various "weeds" in October remain obscure, the first obvious departure from Deng's formula came in Chen Xilian's National Day speech in Xinjiang which did not mention a "key link," but enjoined everyone to carry out *a series of Mao's important instructions* which included learning theory and stability and unity, but substituted "speeding up socialist construction and creating the material basis of the dictatorship of the proletariat" for "boosting the national economy." The key factor here was Mao Yuanxin's presence on Chen's delegation, and we can speculate that the new phraseology reflected this fact, most likely having been vetted by Mao himself.[206] But at this point there was no concerted radical effort on the matter: the National Day edition of Yao Wenyuan's *Red Flag* repeated Deng's theme of the "three directives," including "boosting the national economy," being interrelated, and even as late as November 1 a document issued by Zhang Chunqiao's GPD paraphrased Deng's slogan.[207] In late October, moreover, Yao initially approved a report to the Center using Deng's *tifa*, only crossing it out on a second reading, while it took until February before the *People's Daily* openly attacked the slogan.[208] The whole issue, since Deng first articulated the slogan in May, went to the heart of the politics of consolidation: while the program was Mao's, there was inevitably room for interpretation, and Deng sought to promote his own spin. As there were any number of Mao instructions that could be highlighted, the choice of the three oriented the overall effort. This was fine as long as Mao approved, but once he began to focus on the inherent contractions among the three directives, specifically the degree to which stability and unity and

---

[206] See *RMRB*, October 2, 1975, p. 2. While in reality Chen was hardly sympathetic to the radical cause, the Xinjiang visit and, more importantly, his earlier association with Mao Yuanxin in Liaoning led to suspicions concerning Chen in the post-Mao period that contributed to his political demise. Given Chen's reported slavish behavior toward Mao Yuanxin (as reported in an interview with a senior Party historian, April 2001), as well as his actual performance as Party and PLA leader in Liaoning until 1974, this was not unreasonable, but it reflected an inadequate understanding of the situation. This question will be taken up in our Volume II.

[207] *HQ*, no. 10 (1975), p. 65; and *RMRB*, November 2, 1975, p. 1.

The circumstances in both cases are unclear. The *Red Flag* article could have been prepared before September 27, or even if after that date, Yao may have been unaware of Mao's exchange with his nephew. The GPD document might have been a consequence of lower-level decisions initiated earlier that did not come to Zhang Chunqiao's attention; alternatively, it may simply have been an indication that even if "Deng's camp" nervously excluded the slogan, Mao still had not authoritatively decreed against it (see above, p. 338n98). In any case, there were a variety of public expressions broadly consistent with Deng's approach concerning what composed the "key link" in the pre-November-December period before Mao's "class struggle is the key link" became *de rigueur*.

[208] Qing and Fang, *Deng zai 1976*, vol. 2, p. 341; and *RMRB*, February 20, 1976, p. 1.

boosting the economy impinged on Cultural Revolution values, the entire project entered uncertain waters.

Against the background of the Chairman's exchanges with Mao Yuanxin, the receipt of Liu Bing's letter in mid-October was the apparent catalyst or excuse for the dramatic changes that emerged at the end of the month and the start of November, a matter we examine in detail in Chapter 6. For Mao Yuanxin, the letter's attack on his ally in promoting the Chaoyang experience, Chi Qun, amounted to an attack on his own views and connections. For the Chairman, it involved an intrusion into educational policy and a disruption of his own experimental point at Qinghua University. Although his concern with Deng's direction had been developing since September 27, or possibly earlier,[209] Mao arguably might have been prepared to let matters proceed more or less as they had been for the time being, but Liu Bing's letter confirmed his fears and provoked him to act. In late October, Wang Hairong, after another liaison task with the Chairman, privately revealed to her Foreign Ministry colleague, Qiao Guanhua's wife, Zhang Hanzhi, that Mao wanted to criticize Deng over Liu Bing's letter.[210] By early November Deng's vulnerability on this matter became crystal clear, and firmly entangled with the larger question of his attitude toward the Cultural Revolution.

How do we assess Deng Xiaoping's performance during his three to four months "in charge"? We have emphasized Mao's central role in setting the policy framework and creating political constraints throughout our account of consolidation in 1975. Even at the height of his authority during July-September, Deng was severely limited in his options. Despite post-Mao orthodoxy claiming great bravery on the part of Deng and associates, in fact theirs was a cautious performance. Sometimes Deng demonstrated a modest degree of policy courage, as in the case of the 20 articles; on other occasions he showed great attention to avoiding possible offense to Mao's sensibilities, as in the softening of the Outline Report. The most he could do was shape the program at the margins, to put his own spin on the Chairman's directives, and

---

[209] While speculative on our part, Mao's displeasure with the anti-Jiang Qing rumors and Kang Sheng's accusations *could* have started a process of reassessment by the time of the Dazhai conference in mid-September. Deng's curious reference to the Dazhai gathering in his September 15 speech as the most important meeting of leading cadres from various levels since the 1962 7,000 cadres conference, a conference that criticized the excesses of the Great Leap and that Mao later cited as giving him food for thought about the loyalty of Liu Shaoqi, conceivably also set off alarm bells in the Chairman's mind; see *Deng sixiang nianpu*, p. 18. Another possible factor in a longer-term build-up of Mao's concern was Liu Bing's first letter in August, which also dealt with Qinghua affairs, although there was no immediate response from him (see Chapter 6).

[210] Zhang Hanzhi, *Wo yu Qiao Guanhua*, p. 82; and interview with MFA insider, November 2002. Zhang dated this conversation as taking place on October 12, but Mao had not yet received the letter. October 21, following Mao's meeting with Kissinger, is almost certainly the date. Cf. below, p. 388.

Another factor at this time, one ignored in post-Mao historiography and running against the grain of the virtuous old revolutionary theme, is that Li Xiannian spoke to Mao about Deng's alleged efforts to negate the Cultural Revolution. This is discussed in Chapter 6.

push the envelope cautiously. This, in fact, was the judgment of Deng Liqun many years later when reviewing the period with Party historians from his institute. Stressing that the 1975 program, including ideological consolidation from mid-year, was Mao's initiative, Deng Liqun concluded that it was hard to say Deng Xiaoping had achieved any policy breakthroughs. In this view, Deng Xiaoping "did a good job in implementing the three directives, but it is very difficult to say that [his work] was ground breaking."[211]

Indeed, when the Chairman launched criticism against Deng in November, he still affirmed that his lieutenant's work was acceptable, and many if not most of the policies developed in 1975 were left in place rather than countermanded. Deng had, in fact, focused on the task Mao had set for him: rectifying the 30 percent shortcomings of the Cultural Revolution. It was Deng's political skill that let him down even as he worked within Mao's parameters, something striking in a perceptive leader who had worked closely with the Chairman over a long period, and who had suffered from his unpredictable change of course a decade earlier. As events subsequently unfolded in the fall, it became clear that the central problem was Mao's judgment that Deng remained insufficiently committed to the Cultural Revolution. To put it another way, Deng had paid inadequate lip service to the movement, and, in correcting its mistakes, had impinged on the notionally predominant positive features that Mao cherished. There was no easy way to avoid this conundrum given the contradictions among Mao's three directives, and whatever Deng's private views on the Cultural Revolution, it was not his intention to overstep the Chairman's guidelines. As Yu Guangyuan observed concerning the Outline Report, Deng "never expected that Mao Zedong would not approve" his efforts.[212] Even as anxiety appeared in the wake of the *Water Margin* campaign, considerable confidence was still exhibited by Deng's "camp": on September 28 Li Chang attacked mass-oriented "open door" practices in a talk at the Academy of Sciences, on October 8 Zhou Rongxin set about drafting a fairly sharply worded outline report on education, and at both the start and end of October Hu Yaobang emphasized professional rather than political work at the Academy.[213]

We should not be too harsh concerning Deng's political judgment, or that of his supporters. Mao's repeated green light over the summer surely contributed to Deng getting somewhat carried away, albeit still cautiously, and even as the Chairman's attitude shifted, his intentions remained clouded well into the latter part of October. Indeed, according to Deng Liqun's recollection, Mao had given his full backing to Deng Xiaoping's 1975 measures (and equally so to Zhou Enlai's

---

[211] *Deng Liqun guoshi jiangtan*, vol. 3, pp. 326-27.

[212] See above, p. 305.

[213] Zhang Hua, "Zhongguo kexueyuan 1975 nian de zhengdun" [The 1975 Consolidation at the Chinese Academy of Sciences], *Zhonggong dangshi yanjiu*, no. 1 (1996), pp. 56-58; and above, p. 343. In addition, confidence that even Liu Bing's letter would not derail Deng's work was expressed by Wan Li later in October; see below, p. 396.

1972 efforts). Moreover, the Chairman's secretary, Zhang Yufeng, recalled that about September 1975, in a precursor to his famous statement concerning Hua Guofeng, Mao commented when Deng proposed Zhao Ziyang as the new leader of Sichuan that "with you in charge, I'm at ease."[214] Equally, on the other side of the political equation, there is little to suggest that the Politburo radicals had any particular sense that Deng was vulnerable before the middle of the month, and they moved cautiously even then. Even Jiang Qing, generally an exception, having been active and sometimes abusive since let out of her "cage" in late August, is not known to have taken a bold step at this crucial juncture. In any case, undoubtedly influenced by Mao Yuanxin's complaints, and in the narrow sense responding to Liu Bing's letter, in the latter part of October the Chairman initiated steps against Deng that he seemingly was very reluctant to undertake.

---

[214] Qing and Fang, *Deng zai 1976*, vol. 1, p. 50; and interview with senior Party historian, January 2005. Mao had, in fact, used the phrase on many earlier occasions with regard to both Deng and Zhou Enlai. Cf. below, p. 492.

Chapter 6

THE UNFOLDING OF A NEW LEADERSHIP EQUATION: THE TURN AGAINST DENG AND THE ASCENT OF HUA, NOVEMBER 1975-MARCH 1976

Mao Zedong was giving Deng Xiaoping a chance, allowing Deng Xiaoping to change his views. One truly should say, Mao Zedong was "exhausting all magnanimity" (*renzhi yijin*) toward Deng Xiaoping. Analyzing Mao Zedong's inner state, he both sincerely valued Deng Xiaoping's ability and character, and also abominated Deng Xiaoping's attitude toward the Cultural Revolution. Time and again he showed mercy toward Deng Xiaoping, hoping that Deng Xiaoping would compromise and abide with his final wishes. Mao Zedong was really too old, too exhausted. The "stable and unified" political setting was a choice he had made after long consideration; unless there was absolutely no other choice, he did not want to shift it again.

—Deng Xiaoping's daughter's assessment of Mao's attitude toward her father in November 1975[1]

Hua Guofeng's [theoretical] standard (*shuiping*) is not high, but he is kind and honest (*zhonghou laoshi*), does not engage in plots or factionalism, [and] letting him be Premier puts me at ease (*fangxin*).

—Mao Zedong, explaining his choice of Hua as Acting Premier to his nephew, Mao Yuanxin, late January 1976[2]

Deng Xiaoping: The Politburo has virtually stopped my work, my estimate is that Chairman Mao has made up his mind and is about to "change horses."
Ye Jianying: My estimation is that it is not easy to "change horses." If it happens, there are two possibilities. One is to push you off the political stage (*xiatai*). A second is to "criticize and protect," to use you for a period of time because there are some things [to do]. The Chairman won't give them [the radicals] the entire power, he wouldn't be at ease.
Deng Xiaoping: [Yes,] but I'm prepared for the worst.

—Reported conversation between Deng Xiaoping and Ye Jianying during the early months of 1976[3]

By the start of November 1975 Mao's reassessment of Deng Xiaoping had evolved into a determination to subject Deng to serious criticism. The focus of that criticism quickly became clear: Deng's role in Liu Bing's letter in the first instance, his perceived lack of enthusiasm for the Cultural Revolution in a more fundamental sense. Yet many things remained unclear as this criticism slowly unfolded over the following five months. Most importantly, what were the Chairman's intentions for Deng: criticism followed by a resumption of full or substantial authority, a major reduction of responsibilities and marginalization of power, or a more sweeping "second purge"[4] of his long-standing close comrade-in-arms? Related to this were the matters of who else would be affected by the criticism of Deng, how disruptive the process would be, and the extent of any policy reorientation. Finally, on the likely—although by no means certain—prospect that Deng would not recover his July-September preeminence, how would the power equation within the top CCP leadership be reshaped?

That none of this was clear from the outset can be seen in the behavior of various actors. Many of those deeply involved in the *zhengdun* effort remained in the dark or optimistic well into the criticism of Deng. Thus Yu Guangyuan, from his position in the State Council Research Office, had no sense whatsoever of anything unusual in October, and only in November developed a vague feeling that "there were problems again, but I did not know the details." Zhou Rongxin, one of the earliest targets in the "consolidation camp" as education quickly became the first policy area under systematic scrutiny, was not overly concerned with his situation despite initial indications of his vulnerability in November, and even in December apparently believed that demotion would be the worst outcome. Deng himself made repeated self-criticisms in the apparent hope that they would suffice, only gradually coming to the conclusion that his political days were numbered. Meanwhile, leading figures such as Hua Guofeng, who were thrust into high-level meetings criticizing Deng, as well as other *ad hoc* gatherings reviewing the actions of "erring" subordinates, temporized, sympathetic toward Deng above and lesser officials below, but uncertain of what was required by Mao. For their part, the Politburo radicals were unsure how far Mao was prepared to take the

---

[1] Mao Mao, *"Wenge" suiyue*, p. 426.

[2] Qing and Fang, *Deng zai 1976*, vol. 1, p. 46. Qing and Fang record Mao's comment as occurring on January 29, but the 21st, or perhaps the 28th, is more likely. See *Mao zhuan*, vol. 2, pp. 1766-67; and below, p. 443.

[3] Fan Shuo, *Ye Jianying zai feichang shiqi*, vol. 2, p. 530. Fan Shuo places this conversation in the second half of February, while Yin Jiamin, *Jiangjun buru shiming* [The General Does His Job Well] (Beijing: Jiefangjun wenyi chubanshe, 1992), p. 341, places the encounter around mid to late March. Deng's official chronology, *Deng nianpu*, vol. 1, makes no reference to any meeting between Deng and Ye in this period.

[4] Deng's eventual ouster in April 1976 has been commonly considered his "second purge" at Mao's hands, but this is imprecise in that although he was removed from office, in neither 1967 nor 1976 was Deng technically purged since he never lost his Party membership, and on both occasions he received Mao's protection.

criticism of Deng, and to varying degrees held back. Perhaps most indicative was Yao Wenyuan's hesitation to commit himself strongly against Deng out of fear of repeating the mistake of overstepping the mark as the radicals had done during the campaign to study the dictatorship of the proletariat earlier in the year. Indeed, according to Yao, initially the "gang" hesitated to speak out in the Politburo against Deng, leading Mao Yuanxin to convey the Chairman's message that they should speak out. Clearly, the orchestration of the campaign against Deng, its gradual expansion involving a mixture of pressing the case against him while at the same time protecting him, came from the Chairman. Mao Yuanxin, as we argued in Chapter 5, played a vital role in influencing the Chairman's views, but both the necessary authority and the design of the unfolding events, at least initially, came from Mao alone.[5]

If Mao both controlled the process and was uncertain at the outset as to how far he wanted to push measures against Deng, what explains his deepening antipathy? Much remains shrouded in mystery. The official view, suggested by his daughter's observation in the first quotation at the head of this chapter, and then made explicit in her account, and that of many additional sources, is that the decisive element was Deng's refusal to compromise and bow to Mao's assessment of the Cultural Revolution.[6] This question cannot be decided beyond any doubt; due to the sensitivity of the matter for Deng's reputation and his subsequent role as the godfather of the regime's post-Mao reform orientation, much of Deng's actual behavior in this period has been suppressed. Yet, as suggested previously, we do not believe the characterization of a brave Deng refusing to toe Mao's line on the Cultural Revolution: such a view does not correspond to Deng's earlier behavior, or to the political logic of late 1975 and Deng's actions as events unfolded. We shall present more detailed commentary on this critical matter as we proceed.

In the analysis which follows, we first address the matter which provided the immediate context for criticism of Deng—Liu Bing's letters which raised personnel and policy issues at Qinghua University. This discussion involves both the lower-level factional politics behind the affair, and Mao's seizing on the matter as having wider implications. It is followed by an examination of the gradual expansion of the criticism, both in terms of Mao-stipulated participants and the issues raised, during the remainder of the year and into January 1976. After considering developments centering on Deng, we then examine specific

---

[5] Yu Guangyuan, "Yi Deng Xiaoping he zhengyanshi," p. 15; Fu Yi, "Jiaoyu buzhang Zhou Rongxin," pp. 37-38; Qing and Fang, *Deng zai 1976*, vol. 1, pp. 112, 114; and below, pp. 405, 407-409. Concerning Mao Yuanxin's message that the radicals should speak out in the Politburo, Yao only mentioned himself, Jiang and Wang as specifically cited. Yao Wenyuan's version of events in Qing and Fang here and elsewhere comes from Yao's interrogation during the 1980 trial of the "two cliques." Although his testimony may be regarded as self-serving, it is broadly credible given what is known of his actions and the general situation in late 1975.

[6] Mao Mao, *"Wenge" suiyue*, pp. 426-27.

individuals and areas that came under scrutiny: Zhang Aiping in the military science and technology sector, Zhou Rongxin in the crucial educational sphere, and Hu Qiaomu who performed ubiquitous roles in the State Council Research Office. In addition, we devote separate attention to the Ministry of Foreign Affairs where, despite few meaningful policy differences, the ministry became one of the earliest organizations embroiled in the attack on rightism, in the process providing a particularly fascinating window into the curious world of elite politics.

Major changes were apparent by the end of 1975: education was under public attack, propaganda themes had become more radical, and, while formally retaining his existing responsibilities, Deng's actual role was now limited to foreign affairs.[7] But further changes were imminent, fueled by Mao's determination to press on with the question of the Cultural Revolution and made unavoidable by the death of Zhou Enlai on January 8. We analyze the politics of the period following Zhou's death that culminated in the unexpected appointment of Hua Guofeng as Acting Premier. Contrary to what might seem obvious given Hua's emergence in the post-Mao period as the successor, this appointment was limited in contemporary powers and thus future prospects, carrying far less authority than what Deng had exercised in July-September 1975. Hua now held clear government responsibility only, with his Party status enhanced but ambiguous, and no military authority conveyed. If, as often claimed, Zhang Chunqiao was bitterly disappointed that he did not become premier, he accepted Mao's decision and, at least at one level, worked to support Hua. Meanwhile, Wang Hongwen, back at the Center since mid-November and, with Zhou's death, the ranking figure in the Party structure after Mao, now played a role in the PLA as a MAC Standing Committee member, chaired various Party meetings, and, by early 1976, arguably was more vigorous in pushing the radical cause than at any time since the Lin Biao-Confucius campaign. Primary responsibility for MAC daily affairs, however, was now—if not earlier—vested in Chen Xilian as Ye Jianying was pushed aside. All of these matters will be discussed in detail later in this chapter.

Finally, we will examine the escalation of the campaign to criticize Deng (*pi Deng*) and the increasingly fractious leadership politics of February-March following Hua's elevation, a process undoubtedly linked to Mao's increasingly declining health. Internally, information on Deng's case was made available to broader Party audiences, although it had not officially reached below the

---

[7] Even here other leaders began to play more prominent roles, with Hua Guofeng increasingly active in receiving foreign delegations from mid-October and Zhang Chunqiao involved in Burmese leader Ne Win's November visit on Mao's instruction (see *Mao wengao*, vol. 13, p. 494), including accompanying Ne to see Mao along with Deng. During President Ford's early December visit, Li Xiannian as well as Deng accompanied Ford to see Mao, although the business end of the American visit, as had been the case with Ne Win, was conducted by Deng (and Foreign Ministry officials) alone.

provincial level by the start of April. While Deng would not be named in the public media until after the Tiananmen incident, the euphemism of "unrepentant capitalist roader" and much media commentary during February-March pointed clearly at Deng. Thematically, the areas subjected to sharp public criticism expanded, with science and technology designated the target of "the second heavy artillery attack" (education being the first) at the start of February, while in inner-Party circles radicals denounced virtually everything Deng had done. In this period Deng lost even his foreign affairs duties, with the unlikely figure of Jiang Qing now assuming overall responsibility in this area.[8] Thus Deng's pessimism, as reflected in the final quotation at the start of this chapter, was justified, even as he and Ye Jianying held out hope for the Chairman's continued magnanimity.[9] In the event, it took the unprecedented circumstances of the first Tiananmen incident before Deng was publicly named and formally dismissed from his posts. Yet, as we examine in detail in Chapter 7, even in those extreme circumstances Mao's partiality toward his favorite colleague would again be in evidence: Deng was allowed to keep his Party membership, and thus the ability to fight another day.

If uncertainty surrounded Deng and Ye's assessment of Mao's intentions, as already suggested, this applied to the radicals as well. In addition, taking the November-March period as a whole, several previously noted features of the so-called "gang of four" and radical forces generally were again in evidence. First, signs of tension among the four Politburo radicals, which continued to involve their respective followers in Shanghai,[10] were apparent, as strikingly indicated by a worried exchange between Zhang and Yao over excessive attacks on Deng in February by Jiang Qing and Wang Hongwen, attacks leading Zhang to conclude that "in the end we will be implicated." In addition, the gap in information and perception between central and local radicals was again seen with Zhang Chunqiao and Mao Yuanxin chastising and restraining their regional followers. But perhaps most striking was the role and impact of the younger radicals—above all, but not limited to, Mao Yuanxin. Not only had Mao Yuanxin been critically influential in setting the Chairman on his new path, but he, Xie Jingyi and Chi Qun were generally more prominent than

---

[8] See "Zhang Hanzhi jiaodai cailiao," pp. 145-47; Yin Jiamin, *Jiangjun buru shimin*, pp. 338-40; and "Zhang Hanzhi jiaodai cailiao (zhaiyao)."

[9] Ye's thinking is suggested in the cited quotation. As for Deng. in the conversation with Ye, he concluded that if worse indeed came to worst, the outcome would be like that of Li Weihan, who had been in limbo since 1964. When Li wrote to the Party Center in early November 1975 seeking a conclusion on his case, the Politburo considered two options, one involving expulsion from the Party, and one allowing him to retain his membership. While the Politburo voted for the harsher option, Mao reversed the decision and allowed Li to retain his Party ticket. See Fan Shuo, *Ye Jianying zai feichang shiqi*, vol. 2, p. 529; and *Mao wengao*, vol. 13, pp. 498-500.

[10] Note the squabbling among these followers during *pi Lin pi Kong* (see above, p. 117). Also, in March 1975, Shanghai Second Party Secretary Xu Jingxian wrote to Zhang Chunqiao and Yao Wenyuan exposing Wang Hongwen for his lavish life style. Xu Jingxian, *Shinian yimeng*, pp. 424-28.

the "gang," Jiang Qing excepted, in pushing forward the anti-Deng movement in February-March. Earlier, Chi and Xie were the main protagonists in the Qinghua conflict producing Liu Bing's letters that contributed to, and provided the pretext for, Mao's change of course. Overall, as Mao Yuanxin later claimed at his 1986 trial, "my behavior had an impact that the Jiang Qing clique couldn't achieve." This, of course, included his role as liaison between the Chairman and the Politburo, a role in which he was the key purveyor of his uncle's instructions and meaning. And, in the opinion of several senior historians, as well as major participants on both sides of the political divide during the period, the Chairman was cultivating his nephew as the eventual successor.[11]

All of this took place against the background of a further precipitous worsening of Mao's health. As we saw previously, by the end of 1974 the Chairman's physical activities were extremely limited, and the decline continued apace in 1975. Speaking became increasingly difficult for Mao, his neck could hardly support his head, and he increasingly talked about meeting god. When Kissinger visited in October after nearly a year's absence, he found Mao "very ill," and communication was conducted through the Chairman's barely intelligible grunts, followed by the "two ladies" repeating what they understood him to have said to obtain confirmation, as supplemented by brief written notes. Yet Kissinger not only found Mao mentally alert, but also exuding the willpower that had so impressed the Secretary of State since their first encounter, and which now left him marveling at the "unbelievable" force of will that sustained the Chairman through a two hour meeting (subsequently repeated with President Ford in December) despite his condition. There apparently was a further deterioration of Mao's condition from about January 1976, yet he persisted in receiving foreigners until late May 1976 when, with no one daring to suggest the obvious themselves, the Chairman finally called a halt to such encounters.[12] Yet as his condition worsened, by 1976 severely reducing his capacity to manage affairs, Mao still remained the central, decisive actor in elite politics.

---

[11] Qing and Fang, *Deng zai 1976*, vol. 1, pp. 112-13, 115; Zhang Haini, "Wo wei Mao Yuanxin bianhu," p. 16; and interviews, April 1986, November 2002, and January 2005. Cf. below, pp. 444, 496, 517.

Many examples of different understandings and interests between radicals in Beijing and those in the localities could be cited. For example, in February 1976 Mao Yuanxin deleted a part of a Jiangxi document which attacked the PLA before it was circulated to the Politburo, while in the same period he ordered his Liaoning subordinates to recall Zhang Tiesheng who had been making speeches attacking "democrats" in various places. "Xu Jingxian de buchong jiefa jiaodai" [Xu Jingxian's Supplementary Unmasking Confession] (November 21, 1976); in *CRDB*, p. 2; and Zhang Haini, "Wo wei Mao Yuanxin bianhu," p. 19. Thus even the most significant younger radical at the Center, precisely because he had an understanding of the limits of the Chairman's wishes, took a more restrictive stance than many local rebels.

[12] See Zhang Yufeng's account of Mao's declining health from 1971, "Anecdotes of Mao and Zhou," in FBIS-CHI-89-017, pp. 16-19 and 89-019, pp. 30-37; "Wang Dongxing zai quanguo xuanchuan gongzuo huiyishang de jianghua," p. 1; Burr, *Kissinger Transcripts*, pp. 389, 402, 418; interview with Richard Solomon, November 2003; interview with person with access to Mao in 1975, November 2002; and above, pp. 217-18.

The Precipitating Factor: Liu Bing's Letters, August and October 1975

Despite much angst among those directly concerned, and support from several high-ranking figures, Liu Bing's first letter about problems at Qinghua University in August was a political non-event, with the letter read by Mao, but drawing no response from him. However, when Mao received the second letter *via* Deng about October 15, a very different situation existed as a result of Mao Yuanxin's advocacy since late September. The Chairman now ordered his secretary to find the first letter, and seemingly quickly concluded that, much like the 1970 events in Lushan, the whole affair reflected unhappiness with the Cultural Revolution. He first commented on it on October 19, asking Li Xiannian to stay following a meeting with the Prime Minister of Mali. Speaking with Li, Wang Dongxing, the "two ladies" and Zhang Yufeng, Mao again referred to his displeasure over the rumors concerning his wife—"a gust of wind that I was critical of Jiang Qing," but then addressed Liu Bing's letter in startling terms:

> The Qinghua problem is not an isolated matter, [but] a reflection of the current two line struggle. ... Liu Bing and others at Qinghua University sent letters complaining about Chi Qun and Little Xie [Xie Jingyi]. The motives behind the letters are impure. They want to knock down Chi Qun and Little Xie. The spearhead of their letters is [actually] pointed at me.[13]

The Chairman then added that Chi could be criticized but not knocked down, declared that "Xiaoping is taking sides with Liu Bing," and asked Li *et al.* to warn Deng not to be fooled by Liu Bing. Mao further asked that Li, Wang, Xie, Chi and Wu De meet with Deng to discuss the situation, something which transpired on the 23rd, with two sets of minutes prepared, one by young radicals Xie and Chi, and the other by Li and Wang, and the Chairman signing off on the Li-Wang version. Finally, on the 27th, Deng, Li, Wu and Wang wrote a report to Mao advocating that the Chairman's criticisms of Deng *and Jiang Qing* should not be transmitted to lower levels, and Mao agreed the next day. Mao's criticisms of Jiang, however, were a passing remark, while Deng was clearly the main target of his remarks.[14]

---

[13] See *Mao zhuan*, vol. 2, pp. 1753-55; and Mao Mao, *"Wenge" suiyue*, pp. 414-16. Prior to the publication of *Mao zhuan*, authoritative sources placed Mao's remarks on November 2, but October 19 is much more credible. In the quotation cited, *Mao zhuan* does not include the first sentence on the problem not being an isolated matter, but this is treated by Mao Mao as part of a single series of comments by the Chairman, although she places it on November 2, as does *Mao zhuan*. Given Mao's propensity to repeat key assertions, it is likely that he included the thought on both October 19 and November 2.

On the link between Lin Biao's activities at Lushan and dissatisfaction with the Cultural Revolution, see Teiwes and Sun, *Tragedy*, pp. 148-49.

[14] See *Mao zhuan*, vol. 2, p. 1754; and Cheng Zhensheng, "Li Xiannian yu fensui 'sirenbang'" [Li Xiannian and the Smashing of the "Gang of Four"], *Zhonggong dangshi yanjiu*, no. 1 (2002), pp. 45-46. While we must speculate, we believe Mao was attempting to provide balance by criticizing both Deng and Jiang, thus, as with so much other evidence, suggesting he had not yet determined to oust Deng. Cf. the exchange between Mao and Wang Dongxing in early November in which Mao affirms

One question which cannot be definitively resolved, but which at the very least sheds light on the escalating tension caused by the situation, concerns Li Xiannian's role. In the Li-friendly work of his biographical writing group, Li was shocked and bewildered by Mao's comments. Other evidence, however, suggests that however surprised he was, Li responded by casting doubts on Deng's fidelity to the Cultural Revolution, the precise position already raised by Mao Yuanxin. This, in any case, was the claim of Wang Hongwen, who told Xu Jingxian that Li was the first person to alert Mao that Deng's *zhengdun* effort was negating the Cultural Revolution. While this was surely inaccurate in terms of who was first, it is an entirely credible claim as to substance.[15] Thereafter events unfolded quickly, with an anxious Deng seeking a meeting with Mao to explain himself and seek reassurance. When the meeting eventuated on November 1, Deng inquired whether the guiding principles and policies of central work under his stewardship were correct, the Chairman, somewhat lukewarmly, replied that Deng's performance was "OK" (*dui*). And on November 3, the matter was brought to Qinghua where Wu De conveyed the spirit of Mao's critical message, although seemingly not naming Deng, and daily criticism of Liu Bing and his collaborators in the letter ensued. Meanwhile, as we examine in the following section, high-level meetings focusing on Deng's errors began to unfold.[16]

First, however, an examination of the curious matter of the letters and the political factors involved is in order. This complicated affair involved personal tensions at Qinghua, accidents of personnel movements, the involvement of Politburo members who were *not* driving forces in the drama, considerations of organizational procedures and the facilitating possibilities of personal career ties, and clashing policy and ideological views. Of particular note was the contradictory mix of a belief that the radicals were in eclipse since the spring and an overhang of caution even as Deng appeared to be in charge, and a political

---

that his aim was only to correct mistakes and achieve Party unity; above, p. 3. Mao's criticism of Jiang referred to her failure to heed his earlier criticisms.

[15] See Cheng Zhensheng, "Li Xiannian yu fensui 'sirenbang'," p. 45; and Xu Jingxian, *Shinian yimeng*, p. 376. Xu claimed that Wang told him of Li's action "around National Day." This is not impossible since Li could have been informed of Mao Yuanxin's arguments by Chen Xilian, who was accompanied by Mao Yuanxin to Xinjiang in this period. October 19 is more likely, however, in the context of being confronted by the Chairman's sharp remarks. On Li's propensity to adopt radical positions when required, see above, p. 163n132; and below, p. 418.

[16] Mao Mao, *"Wenge" suiyue*, pp. 413-18; and Liu Bing, *Fengyu suiyue: Qinghua Daxue "wenhua dageming" yishi* [Times of Tumult: A Memoir of Qinghua University in the Cultural Revolution] (Beijing: Qinghua Daxue chubanshe, 1998), pp. 232-39. In early November, Mao referred to having spoken to Deng twice on the Liu Bing issue. One of those times might have been on October 21 following Mao's reception of Kissinger, but there is no clear evidence that this was the case.

Concerning Wu De's November 3 talk at Qinghua, although Mao Mao, p. 418, clearly suggests Wu cited Mao's comment on Deng, as noted above Mao had agreed not to reveal this remark. Moreover, Wu claimed to have only conveyed the spirit of Mao's comments, something supported by Liu Bing's relatively calm reaction on November 3 compared to his thunderstruck panic on the 15th when hearing Mao's full remarks. Liu Bing, pp. 232-33, 243.

culture where matters great and small were pushed upward to the Chairman for resolution. Apart from the overall turn in the fortunes of Deng and the radicals since May, an important contextual precedent was the series of letters sent to Mao by intellectuals and creative artists complaining of excesses by Jiang Qing and company, letters that combined elements of large policy (the Hundred Flowers) and personal bitterness about excessive behavior by the radicals. In this regard, in the context of July 1975, there was nothing out of the ordinary for either Liu Bing, Qinghua Deputy Party Secretary, and his associates at the university, writing to Mao, or in Deng passing their efforts on. Liu Bing's two letters, however, were different in character from one another in two vital respects. The August letter, while having a larger background, was limited to issues of personal work style only, and had only one target: Qinghua Party Secretary Chi Qun. The second letter in mid-October, in contrast, significantly expanded the attack, both in terms of issues which now dealt with educational policy, and in terms of individual targets by including Xie Jingyi as well as Chi Qun. While only Chi's deputy at the university, Xie was a more significant figure than her superior on the university Party committee.

As with so much else, analysis of this affair requires an understanding of the political situation emerging at the end of the Cultural Revolution. As we saw in Chapter 2, Qinghua was no ordinary university: it was one of the "six factories and two schools" singled out as models for the new, purified post-Cultural Revolution era in 1969. These organizations continued to have a special interest for Mao over the following years. As Deng Liqun observed a quarter of a century later, "[In 1975] Chairman Mao fully handed over ... all Party, government and military [power] to Comrade Deng Xiaoping, and he only kept [for himself] the six factories and two schools [Qinghua and Beijing Universities]."[17] Indeed, when Mao remarked to Nixon in February 1972 that "I've only been able to change a few places in the vicinity of Beijing, he was referring to these "six factories and two schools." Nevertheless, it appears that insufficient attention was given to this fact in fall 1975, even though Hu Qiaomu was warned by Li Xin against interfering on this sensitive turf. In addition, the key personnel, Chi and Xie, came from the central guard unit and bureau of confidential matters respectively in Zhongnanhai, virtually Mao's extended household, and acted on his instructions and reported to him. As we have seen, in addition to Qinghua duties, Chi had played a key role in science and education before the Fourth NPC, although passed over for Minister of Education on that occasion. Xie was even more important. Earmarked by Mao as a future leader, she was elected to the Central Committee in 1973 at

---

[17] *Deng Liqun guoshi jiangtan*, vol. 3, p. 328. These experimental points for Mao's Cultural Revolution ideas included six factories in Beijing that became models for the "struggle-criticism-transformation" process in 1969, an approach emphasizing class struggle, but also offering a second chance for intellectuals and technical personnel. See Su and Fang, *Fengyun shilu*, vol. 2, p. 1199.

age 34 and the NPC Standing Committee in January 1975, and more significantly served as a Beijing Municipal Party Secretary, and had the right to attend Politburo meetings. Most significantly, like the "two ladies," she had "access to heaven" and could convey the Chairman's instructions before they appeared in official Party documents. Finally, it should be noted that for all the radical provenance of the "two schools," their experiments also involved a method for reintegrating intellectuals and cadres who had been attacked and confined during the Cultural Revolution back into educational institutions, a facet that would lead Deng Liqun, no friend of radicalism, to reflect on their positive contribution. With no small irony, a concrete example of this process was the resurrection of Liu Bing after suffering at the hands of the Red Guards—by none other than Chi Qun and Xie Jingyi.[18]

While the two letters became known as Liu Bing's letters, Liu did not initiate the project, nor was he the main drafter of the first letter. Instead, the initiator and real author was a PLA cadre, Liu Yian, who had served as part of the leadership structure imposed on Qinghua after the Cultural Revolution, but who had been sent by Chi Qun, in his leadership capacity at the State Council Science and Education Group, to work at the Studies Department of the Academy of Sciences in late 1974, although retaining his Qinghua posts. Tensions over Studies Department work led Liu Yian, who had been having personal and political problems with Chi since at least 1973, to consider (together with two other military cadres, Hui Xianjun and Lu Fangzheng) what action could be taken against him. They decided on a letter to Mao exposing Chi's problems, and in late July approached Liu Bing, telling him that as an old Qinghua cadre they wished to hear his views, and Liu, who apparently also did not get along with Chi, promptly supported the project and agreed to take the lead. This was not simply a matter of offering to support three disgruntled soldiers in intra-organizational infighting, however. The broader context was that since January 1975, Chi and Xie, whose approval was required to communicate the speeches of central leaders within the university, allegedly had been obstructing the transmission of Deng's speeches. Liu Bing and his allies at Qinghua, however, worked to see that Deng's message got through, either using meetings authorized by the Party Center or the Beijing Municipal Party Committee, or through informal means. In the first half of August, Liu Bing convened a meeting while Chi and Xie were away to convey Deng's August 3 remarks on scientific and technical personnel policy, a step that led Xie to berate him the next day.[19]

---

[18] See *Deng Liqun guoshi jiangtan*, vol. 3, pp. 328-29; Xue Qingchao, *Lishi zhuanzhe guantou*, p. 464; Liu Bing, *Fengyu suiyue*, pp. 192, 202, 248; *Mao zhuan*, vol. 2, p. 1754; Burr, *Kissinger Transcripts*, p. 60; and above, pp. 221, 296. Chi and Xie's rescue of Liu Bing occurred in 1968 after Mao sent them to Qinghua to curb factionalism. As the affair of the letters blew up in November 1975, Liu Bing's driver rebuked him for a lack of conscience since Chi and Xie had been kind to him and saw to his liberation (Liu Bing, p. 244).

[19] Liu Bing, *Fengyu suiyue*, pp. 201-208; and Zhang Hua, "1975 nian jiaoyujie de douzheng," p. 148. Relations between Chi and the three military cadres further deteriorated when, as part of Hu Yaobang's

In this context, planning for the proposed letter resumed. In the retelling of the story by Liu Bing more than two decades later, a deliberate decision was taken to avoid raising educational issues and to laud the progress made in Qinghua's educational revolution. Instead, the focus was on Chi Qun's leadership style, and his personal life style. Even here the letter was constructed carefully, with due acknowledgment given to Chi's accomplishments since arriving in 1968. The message, however, was that Chi had degenerated since becoming a leader, falling prey to the attitudes of a big official with growing ambition. He assertedly had become domineering, and would only allow his own voice to be heard. In addition, he developed an increasingly serious bourgeois life style, including a lazy attitude toward work, drinking and smoking too much, and engaging in sexual harassment, behavior that was specified in a detailed appendix. The writers claimed they had tried to help Chi to mend his ways, and significantly claimed that Xie Jingyi had also been offering "stern and conscientious criticism," but all to no avail. In this they had carefully distinguished between Xie, a Mao favorite, and Chi, concerning whom the Chairman had expressed reservations after hearing reports of bad behavior, notably during the deliberations preceding the Fourth NPC, although in the end Mao intervened at Xie's behest to secure Chi's delegate status at the Congress. Moreover, as Xie's "stern criticism" would imply, according to a specialist on the period, Xie and Chi had their own conflicts.[20]

With the letter completed on August 13, the next order of business was to find a way to get the letter to Mao. The authors feared it might simply be pigeonholed and fail to reach its destination, or, even worse, fall into the hands

---

personnel reshuffle at the Academy, they were sent back to Qinghua in August but Chi was unwilling to accommodate them. This, however, appears to have occurred after the first letter was prepared.

The issue of obstruction, and the related question of who was bending Party procedures, is a complex one. One issue is the degree to which Chi and Xie were obliged to convey Deng's speeches. While Qinghua was under both the Ministry of Education and Beijing Municipal Committee, since it was one of the "two schools" directly controlled by Mao, Chi and Xie may have had considerable authority to make judgments without reference to their notionally superior bureaucratic masters. Yet by acting while Chi and Xie were away which was often the case, Liu Bing as the Qinghua leader responsible for daily work (Liu Bing, p. 202) appeared to have the authority to relay Deng's speeches according to normal bureaucratic procedures.

[20] Xue Qingchao, *Lishi zhuanzhe guantou*, pp. 458-59, 464; Liu Bing, *Fengyu suiyue*, pp. 203, 207, 302-308; interview, January 2005; and above, pp. 227-28. With regard to Mao's connection to Xie, two oral sources with some personal experience with Xie claim she was Mao's mistress. We are skeptical, and can only offer the Scottish verdict of "not proven" on this claim. As for Chi, Mao disingenuously claimed on October 19 not to know him, despite his duties in the Chairman's guard unit and his Qinghua assignment on Mao's orders; *Mao zhuan*, vol. 2, p. 1754. Whatever Liu Bing *et al.* actually knew or believed, they clearly viewed Xie and Chi differently.

The spin put on these and subsequent developments by Liu Bing's memoir arguably exaggerated the policy component of an essentially personal conflict. While not questioning that policy differences probably existed, they appear to be a minor part of the story. Certainly in mid-August, educational policy had not yet become a key part of Deng's agenda, and it is unlikely that the low-ranking authors of the initial letter would have been particularly focused on the issue, even if only in the sense of a "deliberate decision" not to raise it.

of Xie Jingyi,[21] unless special measures were taken. The basic idea was to get the letter to Deng for forwarding to the Chairman, but an intermediary was needed. Liu Bing decided to seek out Hu Yaobang for this role. Liu had worked under Hu in the Communist Youth League's General Office between 1953 and 1956, and the two reportedly became firm friends. Moreover, Hu was aware of the problems with Chi and Xie, having asked about them when he saw Liu in 1974. Liu now brought a copy of the letter to Hu's home, and, despite reservations concerning the accuracy of its claims, Hu indicated his support and willingness to help. But Hu was unwilling to serve as a personal conduit, citing internal Party procedures as a handy excuse: since they were in different organizational systems (Hu at the Academy of Sciences, Liu at Qinghua), it was inappropriate for him to pass on the letter. Instead, Hu said he knew Deng's home address, so Liu could send it directly using the post. Liu had concerns with this method, and Hu then gave him the phone number of Deng's secretary, Wang Ruilin. After Wang advised posting the letter to the State Council, Liu still equivocated, returning to an exasperated Hu Yaobang who now gave him Deng's home address. Further hesitation ensued, with Liu fearfully turning back after one approach to Deng's house, but finally the letter was delivered to the commander of the regiment guarding Deng's residence, who was known to Hui Xianjun. Seemingly thinking it dealt with personal matters only, Deng then passed the letter on to Mao, commenting to Research Office leaders that it denounced Chi's "drunken troublemaking."[22]

The paradoxical political crosscurrents of the time could be seen in the determination, as Liu Bing put it in October, to "light a fire in [Chi Qun and Xie Jingyi's] backyard," which, given the significance of the "two schools," was *Mao's* backyard, yet at the same time in the exercise of caution reflected in the letter itself and the elaborate dance concerning its delivery. With the letter delivered, Liu Bing *et al.* awaited some response from Mao, and ostensibly followed organizational principles by reporting on and providing a copy of the letter to their local superior, Wu De, after a week or so.[23] After nine days, with no reply from Mao, Liu and Hui Xianjun went to the offices of the municipal committee where subordinate officials simply listened to their report and accepted the copy for Wu De. The basic consideration was that Mao had expressed no reaction to the letter, so nothing further could be done. This did not, however, mean that officials at the highest level were unsympathetic to its aims. In September, as

---

[21] See Liu Bing, *Fengyu suiyue*, p. 208. Liu's memoir also mentions concern that the letter might fall into Mao Yuanxin's hands, but this must be a case of faulty memory since, unlike in October, in August Mao Yuanxin was not stationed in Zhongnanhai, and thus not in a position to intercept the letter.

[22] *Ibid.*, pp. 208-13; and Yu Guangyuan, "Yi Deng Xiaoping he zhengyanshi," p. 15.

[23] That a copy of the letter was provided to the Beijing Municipal Committee a week *after* its dispatch to Mao suggests, along with other maneuvers in this process, that fidelity to organizational principles was hardly a controlling factor. Nevertheless, as with Hu Yaobang's unwillingness to cross system boundaries, organizational understandings did play a role as actors attempted to limit their vulnerabilities.

the anxiety of Liu Bing and associates over the lack of news grew, Liu received a message from an old colleague in Henan during the 1950s, Ji Dengkui. Ji's responsibility for organizational matters probably obliged him to have a view on the type of issues raised in the letter, but it did not require him to act. The message came via a visit from Ji's daughter: "Chi Qun and Xie Jingyi do not represent Chairman Mao." Less direct and more implicit support came from Wu De who, a subordinate indicated in a talk with Liu, would deal with the difficult Qinghua issue. More telling than this vague promise, Wu had passed his copy of the letter to the sympathetic Ji, rather than to either the Politburo radicals or to Xie, his direct subordinate in the Beijing apparatus with responsibilities at Qinghua. Nevertheless, by the end of September there still was no response from Mao.[24]

While Liu Bing and the other letter writers were frustrated by the lack of a response, they took heart from several developments in September and early October. Ji Dengkui's message led them to believe they had not only Ji's backing, but that they would receive Mao's as well, thus increasing their fighting spirit *vis-à-vis* Chi and Xie. Further encouragement came from Deng's speeches at the Dazhai conference elaborating on the themes of comprehensive consolidation, including the consolidation of culture and education, leading them to conclude that Deng was speaking for Mao, and thus educational line issues could be raised in the Qinghua context. Moreover, despite Chi's efforts to block the transmission of Zhou Rongxin's speeches to Qinghua, in this period they also began to learn of Zhou's increasingly forthright comments on education. At the same time, their determination was raised in another sense when Chi, possibly having become aware of the first letter, suddenly convened a university Party secretariat meeting on October 5, which aggressively attacked "capitalist roaders" within the Party committee who allegedly pretended to be revolutionary but in fact engaged in plots. The confluence of three factors, then, arguably contributed to the decision for a second letter: anger at the attacks of October 5, the belief that the consolidation program was becoming even more dominant, and frustration that as yet there had been no Party document conveying Deng's Dazhai remarks which they hoped to use to influence Qinghua developments, nor any response to their own August letter.[25]

In these circumstances, Liu Bing and his three collaborators considered what should go into the new effort. They concluded that there had been too many

---

[24] Liu Bing, *Fengyu suiyue*, pp. 214, 218-19, 225, 227. That Wu was doing more than simply acting according to Party principles by handing over the letter to Ji, whose organizational duties would have included any disciplinary issues resulting from the case, was suggested by Ji's emissary to Liu in October (see below). In noting Wu's possible sympathy, we do not deny that once Mao had taken a stance, Wu's attitude toward Liu was colder than that of Ji in particular, nor that Wu was reluctant to reverse Liu's verdict in the post-Mao period and resented by Liu as a result. See *Ibid.*, pp. 233-34, 295-96.

[25] See *ibid.*, pp. 219-24.

gaps in the August letter that would now have to be filled to make matters more concrete. One decision was no longer to avoid mention of Xie Jingyi's role at Qinghua, but instead to point out that she had supported Chi and covered up for him. Still, a distinction was maintained between the two, even while calling attention to Xie's "problems." Even more significant, the second letter was no longer restricted to issues of personal behavior. With Liu Bing the drafter, this letter related Chi Qun's shirking of his duties over the two months since August to an unwillingness to carry out Deng's policies. Specifically, it attacked Chi's refusal to attend mid-September meetings convened by the Beijing Municipal Committee to study Deng's signature concept of implementing Mao's three directives, his indifference to the spirit of these meetings, and his shelving of the report by Liu Bing *et al.* on them. The irony, of course, was that just as the authors pointed to the three directives in their indictment of Chi Qun, Mao was assessing the deeper (negative) meaning in Deng's promotion of them as the key link, and Deng's own close collaborators were backing off from the concept.[26]

With the letter completed on October 13, the problem again became getting it to Deng for passing on to Mao. The previous method of using the military personnel at Deng's residence did not work this time, as the chief guard, on Wang Ruilin's orders, refused to accept the letter, indicating that it should be sent to the State Council instead.[27] Liu Bing and associates then decided to try Vice Minister of Education Li Qi, who had been Liu's intimate friend during the anti-Japanese war although seldom seen since, was well connected with central leaders, and had been criticized over personal matters by Chi Qun. Li, who had been unaware of the first letter when Liu approached him, was delighted to find someone within Qinghua willing to stand up to Chi, and offered his support, saying he could pass the letter to Wang Ruilin at a State Council meeting. The encounter ended with Liu asking Li to keep the matter secret, only informing Zhou Rongxin since Zhou was his superior within the education system. Thus again, there was a peculiar mix of operating in secret, drawing on old career connections, yet also attempting to invoke organizational principles.[28]

Li Qi did arrange for the second letter to reach Deng, not through Wang Ruilin, but instead *via* Hu Qiaomu, and Deng again passed it on to Mao. In the period after dispatching the letter, there were some positive signals for the authors. A few days later, Ji Dengkui sent an official to see Liu who informed him not only of Ji's support concerning Chi Qun, but who also concluded that

---

[26] *Ibid.*, pp. 224, 308-14.

[27] *Ibid.*, pp. 224-26. While it might seem that greater caution was being exercised by Wang Ruilin than in the case of the first letter, in fact Wang had also directed the letter writers to send the earlier missive to the State Council, but the authors had circumvented his wishes. Thus it may simply have been a case of the guards being put on notice in August not to repeat their action, or that when the new situation came up Wang insisted that his previous wishes be followed.

[28] See *ibid.*, pp. 224-26, 305.

Ji and Wu De had the same view of the matter.[29] Thus encouraged, the authors sent a copy of the second letter to Wu. But still anxious, Liu phoned Wan Li on October 26, here relying on work ties during Wan's posting as a Beijing Party secretary before the Cultural Revolution, and again in 1973-74, when Wan took an interest in Qinghua affairs. They arranged to meet, and Wan revealed that he was already aware of the second letter. Although Wan was somewhat guarded about the outcome of the Qinghua struggle, and indicated that they had to wait to see what the Chairman's reaction was, he seemed optimistic. But as we have seen, by that point Mao had already decided to act. At the meeting stipulated by him on the 23rd, Deng, Li Xiannian, Wu De and Wang Dongxing met with Chi and Xie and showed them the second letter. On the 25th, a letter was sent to Mao from a Qinghua Party official attacking Zhou Rongxin's "very bad" influence on education, and strongly defending Chi as a paragon of the educational revolution; Mao's comment on this letter was that the matter should be investigated and then discussed by the Politburo. And on the 27th, Wu De called in Chi and Xie to discuss how to debate Liu's letter, and proposed that Chi chair a mass meeting on the topic at Qinghua. Liu Bing *et al.* were still in the dark, but their vulnerability became more apparent on November 3 when the Qinghua meeting was convened, with not only Chi and Xie in charge, but also with Wu De conveying the spirit although not the detail of Mao's assessment of Liu's letter and the struggle at Qinghua.[30]

What can we make of this curious affair? Perhaps the most incontrovertible conclusion is that, despite understandable speculation,[31] this was not an affair stage managed from above. Neither Deng nor subordinate officials such as Hu Yaobang or Hu Qiaomu played any part apart from their roles in passing the letters upward until they reached Mao. The impetus came from below, initially not even involving Liu Bing, and reflected personal tensions more than different political views. Liu Bing *et al.* to a large extent operated in the dark, attempting to assess trends in the opaque world of Chinese elite politics, and seeking help from old career contacts, but they were essentially on their own. Those contacts were supportive of the position staked out by the writers and willing to help, but only in a cautious manner. Hu Yaobang would provide Deng's address and telephone number, but would not deliver the first letter himself. Ji Dengkui sent informal messages of support, but did little more. Meanwhile, Liu's local superior, Wu De, while seemingly sympathetic, did nothing. Of course, they were all constrained, as Wan Li observed, by the need to wait for Mao.

---

[29] While this can be considered the official's speculation (cf. above, p. 394n24), an exceptionally well-placed oral source reports a very good Wu-Ji relationship. Interview, November 2002. Ji's support, as relayed by his emissary, seemingly referred only to the first letter as there was no indication that Ji was yet aware of the second letter.

[30] Liu Bing, *Fengyu suiyue*, pp. 226-29; Chen and Du, *Shilu*, vol. 3, part 2, p. 1285; Ji Xichen, *Shi wu qianli de niandai*, vol. 2, p. 722; "Beijing 'wenge' dashiji," pp. 14-15; and above, p. 389n16. We deduce that the meeting with Wan Li took place on the 26th from the context.

[31] See MacFarquhar, "Succession," p. 296.

This was the crux of the matter. For Liu Bing and the others the problem could only be solved by an appeal to the Chairman. It apparently never occurred to them to attempt some maneuver within Qinghua to overturn the authority of Chi and Xie, or to seek action by Zhou Rongxin and the responsible Ministry of Education, or even to appeal to Deng Xiaoping for anything more than conveying their letters to Mao. Moreover, for all their hesitancy and anxiety, the logic of their actions was that they believed Mao would back them, or, if not, they would avoid serious consequences. In this, as we saw in Chapter 5, they were not alone: well into October important players in the consolidation effort continued to push aggressively in this policy direction. Moreover, in passing on letters critical of important if junior radicals as late as mid-October, Deng still seemed to believe, as he averred to Chen Yun in the summer, that he had basically understood Mao's meaning. In the specific case, Deng presumably thought Liu's second letter did not create problems for him or the consolidation program, and might even further progress in the educational sphere through a favorable response from the Chairman. Yet, in the new context created by the stepped up consolidation efforts in September, Liu Bing's second letter succeeded in dragging policy issues (and thus Deng himself) into the predominantly personal conflict with Chi and Xie, something that seemingly did not sit well with Deng in the post-Mao period when he had time to reflect on what had gone wrong.[32]

Nevertheless, Deng's decision to pass on the second letter remains something of a puzzle. Since the first letter only targeted Chi Qun and didn't raise policy issues, passing it on might have been routine in the circumstances of summer 1975. The second letter, however, was a different matter, especially as it came in mid-October when there were some straws in the wind to give pause.[33] Deng, after all, had not been adverse to caution or careful attention to Mao's sensibilities while pushing consolidation forward. Why risk the progress being made by "lighting a fire in Mao's backyard" where one of the Chairman's handpicked future leaders, Xie Jingyi, was now criticized? And strategically, with the radicals in retreat and the Chairman's days obviously numbered, there was no need for unnecessary controversy. Yet, remarkably, Deng and his closest associates did not sufficiently grasp Mao's meaning, whether due to overconfidence or carelessness. Thus Hu Qiaomu seemingly ignored Li Xin's warning against interfering in the "two schools." An even more remarkable instance of non-comprehension occurred subsequently when Deng and Hu Qiaomu discussed the meaning of what was going on, and Deng concluded the problem for him was simply that he had

---

[32] Unlike other noted victims of the 1975-76 anti-rightist campaign, Liu Bing did not prosper in the post-Mao period. He did not regain a leading post at Qinghua, but was instead sent to Lanzhou University. Moreover, he apparently was never granted an audience with Deng.

[33] How much pause should have been taken is unclear, because the timing of events around October 13-15 is uncertain. If Deng passed on the letter after learning of Mao's unhappiness with the forces of production question, and possibly concerning the three directives slogan, the act would have been particularly fraught with potential danger. See above, pp. 305, 337-38, 377.

relayed the letter. But by then Hu knew better, telling Deng that "it's not just about transmitting Liu Bing's letter, the Chairman has [critical] opinions about [your] comprehensive consolidation methods."[34] While Hu drew on his long understanding of Mao in making this assessment,[35] the Chairman's reaction to the second letter followed a familiar pattern that should have been more widely understood.

This pattern involved more than Mao's ambiguous policy positions and unpredictability. As emphasized throughout our analysis, it reflected the tension inherent in the consolidation effort, between affirming the Cultural Revolution and correcting its excesses. On key occasions since 1966 Mao called for rectifying the movement's faults, but then reacted sharply when others picked up on his theme in ways he felt undermined the movement's essence and challenged its leading supporters. The most recent case concerned another letter to Mao, Wang Ruoshui's late 1972 appeal against the harshly critical views of Zhang Chunqiao and Yao Wenyuan concerning the *People's Daily's* repudiation of anarchy. As we saw in Chapter 1, rather than back Wang's interpretation of the existing anti-leftist trend, the Chairman declared his views incorrect and defined Lin Biao's political line as "ultra-rightist." Five years before that, in early 1967, high-ranking old revolutionaries drew encouragement from Mao's criticism of the excesses of the leaders of the new Central Cultural Revolution Group to attack them sharply during the so-called "February adverse current," but only succeeded in enraging the Chairman, leading him to see the attacks as aimed at the Cultural Revolution itself, and warn that whoever opposed the Cultural Revolution Group would have to answer to him. And at the pivotal 1970 Lushan plenum that was critical to Lin Biao's fall, although the ostensible issues were different, the reality was that the onslaught orchestrated by Lin Biao's supporters on Zhang Chunqiao gained its emotional support from elite resentments concerning the Cultural Revolution. This was understood by Mao, and proved crucial for his support of Zhang, as seen in a comment that would resonate with his October 1975 remark concerning Chi Qun [and Xie Jingyi]: "Opposition to Zhang Chunqiao is opposition to me."[36] The identification was not with any individual as such, but with the fact that they represented Mao's treasured Cultural Revolution, and attempts to finish them off politically would not be tolerated. In yet another familiar pattern, Mao threatened

---

[34] Mao Mao, *"Wenge" suiyue*, p. 425. Mao Mao reports this exchange as taking place on November 10, a date we regard as too late, even though *Deng nianpu*, vol. 1, p. 128, also uses it. Having been subjected to three "help" meetings, as well as Mao Yuanxin's accusations concerning the Cultural Revolution by the 10th (see below), Deng surely knew that something more than passing on the letter was at issue. A more credible time would be between October 19 when Mao first raised the issue, and the start of the "help Deng" sessions in early November.

[35] As Mao's secretary before the Cultural Revolution, Hu Qiaomu had a demonstrated propensity to sense Mao's changing attitudes, and to warn other leaders accordingly. See Teiwes, *Politics and Purges*, pp. xxx, xxxiv.

[36] On the "February adverse current," Lushan, and Wang Ruoshui cases, see Teiwes and Sun, *Tragedy*, pp. 75-76, 144-49; and above, pp. 63-64.

that "if Chi Qun is forced out [by people who don't dare to attack me], there will be a second Cultural Revolution."[37] But if Chi was now safe, many other issues arising from Liu Bing's letters remained.

Evolving Criticism: The Issues and Participants Expand, November 1975-January 1976

As the criticism sessions against Liu Bing unfolded at Qinghua during the first two weeks of November, a more significant set of meetings of high-level leaders evolved under Mao's direct orchestration. In this process, and the larger pattern of elite politics surrounding it, Mao Yuanxin played a central, if somewhat contentious, role. Over the weeks and months which followed, the Chairman relayed both his specific instructions and general attitudes to his top colleagues and wider circles of the elite through Mao Yuanxin, and Mao Yuanxin reported back to his uncle concerning what transpired at the meetings Mao had ordered convened. Thus a key question was the degree to which Mao Yuanxin was a faithful purveyor of the Chairman's views, or conversely the extent to which he inserted his own views in both delivering messages and reporting back.

While the judgment of a senior historian that Mao Yuanxin did not distort his uncle's meaning, but nevertheless had great influence by organizing and making logical the Chairman's ideas carries weight, actors on both sides of the political divide suspected that Mao Yuanxin was more than a mere liaison officer. Both Ye Jianying and Yao Wenyuan later claimed that Mao Yuanxin provided a one-sided version of events that reflected his own input. As Yao recalled, Mao Yuanxin did much more than convey the Chairman's views to the Politburo, instead providing his own elaboration, and declaring that Mao agreed. Yet there is little evidence of anyone challenging Mao Yuanxin's version of the Chairman's instructions or the general thrust of his presentations to the Politburo. The only recorded resistance came early in the piece, notably on the evening of November 2 during the first meeting Mao had organized to "help" Deng, when Deng rejected Mao Yuanxin's opinion (apparently not attributed to Mao) that the Party Center was implementing a revisionist line. Significantly, Deng's rejection was based on the fact that the previous night he had heard from Mao's own mouth that the guiding principles and policies of Party work were "OK," so "[how can you say] the Center with Chairman Mao at its head is carrying out a revisionist line?" When Mao Yuanxin reported this development the next day, the Chairman said a clash was not unexpected as Deng had been taken by surprise, but his nephew must continue to confront Deng as he had right on his side, and this is what helping Deng was all about. Even on the 2nd, in any case, Deng had already offered a

---

[37] Hu Shihong, *Zhang Aiping zai 1975*, p. 254; and Xu Jingxian, *Shinian yimeng*, p. 377. The classic example of Mao raising the dire consequences of failing to bend to his will occurred at the 1959 Lushan conference when he threatened to organize a new Red Army and overthrow the government if the PLA supported Peng Dehuai. See Teiwes, *Politics and Purges*, p. 325.

self-criticism in response to Mao Yuanxin's assertions. And as events unfolded thereafter, no one was game to question Mao Yuanxin's version of the emperor's words, regardless of private doubts.[38]

Clearly, as we saw in Chapter 5, Mao Yuanxin played a critical part in his uncle's initial reassessment of Deng, and his role remained vital as Deng's position unraveled from November. Official histories, pointing to the Chairman's declining health and dependence, emphasize his nephew's sinister impact. Although far less evidence is available, in this same period another "evil influence" has been cited by official sources as corrupting Mao's view of Deng—Kang Sheng. Even Deng's daughter, a source generally eschewing vilification of Kang, highlights Kang's alleged contribution to the "dramatic turn" in Deng's fortunes: "Kang Sheng [like Mao Yuanxin] also leapt at the opportunity to spread his slanders to Mao Zedong, saying that 'Deng Xiaoping wants to overturn the case of the Cultural Revolution.'"[39] Very little is clear about this incident, including whether Kang still attempted to attack Jiang Qing and Zhang Chunqiao in the same message, how the message was conveyed to Mao, or precisely when the incident occurred. Thus any discussion must be highly speculative, and much hinges on when Kang actually acted. Although mid-November seems most likely, some sources indicate that it happened earlier, even as early as mid-October. Simply put, a mid-October intervention by Kang *before* Mao's new concern with the Cultural Revolution was revealed to top-level leaders on the 19th could indicate an important input into Mao's evolving thinking, but it would have been out of character with Kang's past and current partiality toward Deng, and even more clearly with his hostility toward Jiang and Zhang, for him to have acted at that point. While late October is plausible, mid-November, as implied by Deng's daughter, is more likely as Mao's aims became clearer.[40] Whenever he acted, one

---

[38] "Zhongyang lingdaoren guanyu sirenbang wenti de jianghua," p. 1; Qing and Fang, *Deng zai 1976*, vol. 1, p. 112; Mao Mao, *"Wenge" suiyue*, pp. 417-18; *Mao zhuan*, vol. 2, pp. 1755-56; and interview, November 2002. In addition to the November 2 incident, another instance of Deng-Mao Yuanxin acrimony occurred when the Chairman sent Mao Yuanxin to Deng's home for a discussion. Mao Mao (p. 424) overheard a heated argument, but could not make out its substance. This clash possibly occurred earlier, although the context suggests it took place once criticism of Deng had started. Of note on this occasion was that Deng had only recently moved into this new, larger residence that had been renovated for Zhou Enlai, a move (that would have been arranged by Wang Dongxing) indicating ongoing elite expectations of his preeminence. Deng left this residence in March 1976.

[39] Mao Mao, *"Wenge" suiyue*, p. 426. Apart from the fact that Mao Mao only refers critically to Kang twice, a more telling point is the absence of her father's criticisms of Kang even after he was posthumously expelled from the CCP. See above, p. 15.

[40] The November dating is suggested by the sequence of events in Mao Mao's account which would place it between November 15 and 20. She also suggests that the message was carried by Wang Hairong and Tang Wensheng, and included attacks on Jiang and Zhang; *"Wenge" suiyue*, pp. 425-26, 433-34. Concerning dates in October, Long Pingping, *Deng Xiaoping yu tade shiye* [Deng Xiaoping and His Endeavors] (Fuzhou: Fujian jiaoyu chubanshe, 1997), p. 144, declares Kang personally saw Mao "in mid-October," and made no mention of either the "two ladies" or criticism of Jiang and Zhang. Fan Shuo's account, *Ye Jianying zai feichang shiqi*, vol. 2, pp. 501, 504, suggests Kang's

motive for Kang's two-faced behavior was presumably to guarantee an honored place in Party history by backing Mao. Another, arguably more important motive, one which would also have gained impetus from an understanding of Mao's position, was Kang's genuine identification with the Cultural Revolution, the event which most defined his position in CCP history and was again being placed front and center by the Chairman. In any case, whatever Kang's intervention may have added to Mao's shifting attitude, it could not have been decisive in undermining Deng as the Chairman continued to hold out hope for him beyond mid-November.

Whatever the precise influence of Mao Yuanxin or Kang Sheng, the Cultural Revolution quickly became the centerpiece of the Mao-directed elite discussions which unfolded in November.[41] By November 2 at the latest, if not on October 19,[42] the Chairman had made his two critical assertions: Liu's Bing's letter was ultimately aimed at himself, and it was not an isolated matter, but instead a manifestation of a "two line struggle." In the November 2 exchange with his uncle, if not already in September, Mao Yuanxin reportedly argued that the situation was now worse than the 1972 criticism of the "ultra-left" that negated the Cultural Revolution, many people had a fundamentally negative view of the movement, thinking it was 70 percent erroneous, and there was a danger of a reversal at the Party Center. What was significant was Mao's seeming agreement with these assessments, particularly by picking up on attitudes toward the Cultural Revolution. The Chairman complained of two types of negative attitudes, dissatisfaction and wanting to settle accounts with the movement, and went on to elaborate pointedly: "Some comrades, especially old comrades, have ideologically stopped at the stage of the bourgeois democratic revolution, they do not understand the socialist revolution, resist it, even to the point of opposing it." It was in this context that Mao seemingly again addressed Liu Bing's letter, and Deng's role in delivering it.[43]

In recounting this exchange between the Chairman and his nephew, and

---

intervention took place before November 2, and was encouraged by the radicals' lobbying. Lin Qingshan, *Fengyun shinian yu Deng Xiaoping* [Deng Xiaoping and the Ten-year Storm] (Beijing: Jiefangjun chubanshe, 1989), pp. 369-76, places the event in September-October, but his book is careless with dates. Long Pingping is the only source we have seen claiming that Mao gave Kang a personal audience, while a Party historian claims there is no record of such an encounter. Interview, December 2002.

[41] Apart from the issues of what was said on September 27 and October 19, as opposed to November 2, there are slight disparities in the dating of the November meetings among the four authoritative sources we have largely relied on: *Mao zhuan*, vol. 2, pp. 1753-61; Mao Mao, *"Wenge" suiyue*, pp. 414ff; Chen and Du, *Shilu*, vol. 3, part 2, pp. 1289-93; and Ma Qibin, *Sishinian*, pp. 392-93. After comparing these sources and consulting others, we have adopted what appears most credible.

[42] See above, p. 388n13.

[43] *Mao zhuan*, vol. 2, pp. 1754-55; Mao Mao, *"Wenge" suiyue*, pp. 414-16; and *Mao wengao*, vol. 13, pp. 486-87. If *Mao wengao* is correct, Mao's comment on old comrades stopping ideologically at the bourgeois democratic revolution occurred in October-January, and thus not on September 27.

further developments in subsequent weeks as well, Deng's daughter and other sources have emphasized two somewhat contradictory factors. The first was Mao's unbending commitment to, worry over, and anger concerning any perceived effort to undermine his Cultural Revolution. But at the same time he assertedly did not want to upset the "stable and unified" political order he had invested in so heavily: he wanted to criticize, but not "knock over," Deng or the bulk of revolutionary veterans. This latter claim seems supported by various of Mao's actions in pursuing the Cultural Revolution issue. Two meetings were held in rapid succession on November 2 and 3 to focus on a unified understanding of the Cultural Revolution. While the first led to a sharp exchange with Deng when Mao Yuanxin, following Mao's orders to come straight to the point in articulating his views (but seemingly not identifying them as the Chairman's),[44] after the second meeting Mao Yuanxin indicated his understanding of the Chairman's objective by asking his uncle whether "the goal is to arrive at unity and doing work well through discussion [of the Cultural Revolution]," to which Mao responded in the affirmative.[45]

The effort to keep things low-key and relatively positive can be seen in the selection of leaders to participate in the meetings. The November 2 meeting was limited to four people, with Chen Xilian and Wang Dongxing joining Deng and Mao Yuanxin. While no senior revolutionaries were included, the additional participants can be considered broadly sympathetic to Deng, although completely loyal to Mao and his position.[46] More to the point, none of the Politburo radicals were included, a step Deng's daughter specifically attributed to Mao's desire to avoid a heating up of the discussion, but one which distinguished the "gang" from younger radicals Xie Jingyi and Chi Qun who had already met Deng on the Chairman's order, not to mention Mao Yuanxin. The November 3 meeting, which followed Mao's reported dissatisfaction with Mao Yuanxin's report on the first meeting, was expanded to eight people: the original four, plus Li Xiannian, Ji Dengkui, Hua Guofeng and Zhang Chunqiao. This enlarged group was still weighted toward leaders sympathetic to Deng, although now, in the person of Zhang, a radical was included, and, as we have suggested, Li Xiannian's position may have been ambiguous, or even ostensibly severe toward Deng. Moreover, Mao specifically instructed that Jiang Qing not be informed of the two meetings,

---

[44] This is our conclusion, based on the fact that there is no explicit statement that Mao Yuanxin made such a claim on the 2nd, Deng's rebuttal by citing Mao's words of the previous night, and our belief that Deng would have behaved far differently if the opinions had been identified as Mao's. Even so, Deng still offered a self-criticism; see above, pp. 399-400.

[45] See Mao Mao, *"Wenge" suiyue*, pp. 415-17, 419.

[46] Moreover, Wang Dongxing in particular could be considered sympathetic to Chi Qun's situation at Qinghua, given that Chi had served under Wang in Zhongnanhai and that Wang was heavily involved in supervising Chi at the university. See Liu Bing, *Fengyu suiyue*, p. 159. Similarly, Mao would have expected Li Xiannian's strong support when the group was expanded to eight people, given Li's earlier criticism of Deng.

another apparent attempt to keep the temperature down by preventing her from meddling and rocking the boat. Jiang's absence also indicates that, in contrast to earlier occasions when she led attacks on senior leaders, she had no role in the emergence of the critical attack on Deng. In any case, when reporting to his uncle on the 4th, Mao Yuanxin indicated that all those in attendance had expressed strong opinions about Deng's performance, while Wang Dongxing, who sat in on the report, gained Mao's assent to the proposition that the aim of these sessions was unity. The eight-person meeting resumed for a second session on November 7.[47]

During Mao Yuanxin's briefing on either the 3rd or the 4th, the Chairman offered his famous assessment of the Cultural Revolution as fundamentally correct, with achievements (70 percent) clearly outweighing mistakes (30 percent). It is important to note the limits in Mao's assessment: he was far from demanding indiscriminate affirmation of the movement. Not only was 30 percent a far higher ratio of errors than Mao had acknowledged early in the movement (1 finger to 9 at the time of the "February adverse current" in 1967), but he specifically called for consideration of the movement's shortcomings since a consensus had not been reached—i.e., precisely the focus he had assigned to Deng in 1975. This was a double-edged sword for Deng, in that the Chairman affirmed the need to deal with shortcomings, yet at the same time indicated differences over how to approach those deficiencies. In any case, Mao did not seem particularly distressed with the results of the November 3 gathering, notwithstanding a purportedly hostile reporter in his nephew. He largely went along with the meeting's distinction of positive and negative results, while adding his own 70/30 assessment. If this view was transmitted back to Deng, it may go some way to explain his apparent underestimation of his personal problem.[48] In any case, the matter clearly was far from finished, and indications of change were quickly apparent. On November 8, the *People's Daily* gave maximum publicity to a speech on the 7th (the day the eight-person meeting resumed) by an unspecified "State Council leader"—none other than Deng himself.[49] In this speech Deng completely dropped the rhetoric

---

[47] Mao Mao, *"Wenge" suiyue*, pp. 416, 419; *Mao zhuan*, vol. 2, p. 1756; interview with senior Party historian specializing on the period, November 2002, and above, p. 3. Before settling on the composition of the November 2 meeting, Mao also considered involving Li Xiannian, Ji Dengkui and Hua Guofeng.

[48] See Mao Mao, *"Wenge" suiyue*, p. 419; *Mao zhuan*, vol. 2, pp. 1755-56; and above, p. 3. To further confuse matters, *Deng nianpu*, vol. 1, p. 127, claims the first eight-person meeting took place on the 4th.

It may be the case that Mao's remarks on studying the movement's faults were even stronger than the version recorded in *Mao wengao*, vol. 13, p. 488. At least this was apparently suggested by Hua Guofeng in the immediate post–Mao period, when he charged that the radicals had deleted "emphatically" from Mao's comments on the 70/30 assessment; "Zhongyang lingdaoren guanyu sirenbang wenti," p. 1. Also, ambiguity was created in that Mao was both summarizing the views of the eight-person meeting and expressing his own opinion, but the point is that there does not appear to have been a sharp disparity between the two.

[49] While the identity of the leader was not revealed, after investigation well-situated oral sources

of *zhengdun*, instead emphasizing the achievements of the Cultural Revolution. Also on the 8th, Zhang Chunqiao called in and criticized Zhou Rongxin, indicating that education policy was very much in the firing line. And about the same time Zhang Aiping was summoned to a "help" session on Mao's initiative. These developments, together with Zhang Chunqiao's public prominence during the visit of Burmese leader Ne Win starting on the 11th, were taken by Wang Hongwen and his associates in Shanghai as promising signals. Most tellingly, Wang advised the local radicals to pay close attention to positive signs emerging from the "two schools" in Beijing. Under these circumstances, Wang returned to Beijing by November 15, most likely on Mao's orders.[50]

When the Politburo met on the evening of November 15, the situation was looking grimmer for Deng. Following the reception of Ne Win on the 13th, Mao gave Deng and Zhang Chunqiao instructions for the Politburo session. There may have been a deliberate delay of a day in convening the meeting to allow Wang Hongwen to return; in any case, the atmosphere was tense. Deng chaired the meeting, but reportedly said little apart from opening the meeting, indicating that the Chairman had issued new instructions including summoning Hu Yaobang, Hu Qiaomu, Zhou Rongxin, Li Chang and Liu Bing to participate as a means of helping them, and closing the session. Deng tried to avoid reporting on Mao's remarks, saying he was hard of hearing and didn't understand everything, and asked Zhang Chunqiao to summarize, but Zhang dismissed the request on the grounds that he had not taken notes. The summoning of the five officials, in at least Liu Bing's case in sudden, alarming fashion, added to the tension. They were clearly in some sort of serious trouble. Also apparently in trouble was Ye Jianying, who remained silent throughout, taking notes and drinking tea. With Deng and Zhang avoiding relaying Mao's instructions, Mao Yuanxin again took

---

confirmed that he was Deng. One senior Party historian, who had not previously noticed this matter, concluded that the use of the "State Council leader" label was a way to downgrade Deng's prominence at this early stage. Interview, December 2002.

[50] See *RMRB*, November 8, 1975, p. 1; Fu Yi, "Jiaoyu buzhang Zhou Rongxin," p. 36; *Shanghai "wenhua dageming" shihua*, p. 763; Xu Jingxian, *Shinian yimeng*, pp. 377-78; Hu Shihong, *Zhang Aiping zai 1975*, pp. 259-62; and Chen and Du, *Shilu*, vol. 3, part 2, p. 1292. Wang reportedly was aware of critical remarks by Mao on the Ministry of Education (Zhou Rongxin) and the Seventh Ministry of Machine Building (Zhang Aiping), something undoubtedly due to his receiving Party documents as CCP Vice Chairman. We speculate that Mao's remarks on education that Wang referred to may have been those in response to the Qinghua letter attacking Zhou Rongxin on October 25, which would have also alerted Wang to the drama unfolding at the "two schools"; see above, p. 396. The Shanghai material also claims that Wang suddenly decided to return to Beijing. We find this difficult to believe given Mao's control of leadership movements, and think it much more likely that Mao summoned Wang back to the capital. For more details on the Zhou Rongxin and Zhang Aiping cases, see the following section.

Concerning the Ne Win visit, Deng indicated his new vulnerability when writing Mao on November 5 by asking whether he or Zhang should host the visit. Mao responded that Deng would be the host, and at the same time crossed out MFA proposals for Jiang Qing to met Ne. *Mao wengao*, vol. 13, p. 494.

up this role, and reported the Chairman's remarks on Qinghua. Wang Hongwen reportedly spoke next, claiming that while in Shanghai he had heard a lot of criticism "from below" of Hu Yaobang and Zhou Rongxin, particularly blaming the Ministry of Education for focusing on traditional education and not carrying out the educational revolution. Zhang Chunqiao added that this was all rightist stuff, and Zhou Rongxin had never listened to him. Clearly, some radicals were making aggressive noises, but it was far from an organized or premeditated attack. Yao Wenyuan seemed little different from most Politburo members in saying little beyond a few interjections, while Jiang Qing walked around making occasional comments, but saying nothing substantial. Indeed, it may have been this haphazard performance that led Mao Yuanxin to convey Mao's instruction that Jiang, Yao and Wang should do more than interject, and make considered speeches in the Politburo.[51]

At this juncture on the 15th, whether before or after the Politburo meeting, Deng proposed that Wang, whom he technically was replacing only while Wang was away from the capital, resume responsibility for the work of the Party Center, and also chair an imminent expanded 17-person Politburo meeting that Mao had stipulated. Mao refused the request, saying that Deng should continue to bear these tasks for the time being, a step viewed by Deng's daughter as a further indication that the Chairman had not decided to remove her father, but was "still observing, still making up his mind."[52] Deng's request, however, clearly indicated a sense of vulnerability, and it may be at this point or a few days later that Deng prepared for the prospect that he would lose power. At some point in fall 1975, he told Li Xiannian and Wu De that he was prepared to resign his posts "one by one" (indeed, his proposal concerning Wang may have been the first step), and advised them that if it came to that, they should make an accommodation and avoid confrontation in order to survive.[53] In any case, most of Deng's authority outside the foreign affairs realm appears to have dissipated after mid-November.

The Politburo meeting resumed the next evening. Deng was again in the chair but immediately called on Mao Yuanxin to convey the Chairman's comments after receiving his nephew's report on the previous night's session. Mao Yuanxin proceeded to provide a 40-minute summary which included praise of Zhang

---

[51] Liu Bing, *Fengyu suiyue*, pp. 239-44; and Qing and Fang, *Deng zai 1976*, vol. 1, p. 112.

[52] Mao Mao, *"Wenge" suiyue*, p. 425.

[53] This encounter, which we cannot pin down more precisely, was revealed by a senior Party historian who had access to the principals involved; interview, July 1999. We are unable to support this claim through written sources. Mao Mao, *"Wenge" suiyue*, p. 423, indicates visits by Li among others in this period of increasing nervousness for work purposes, but does not record the incident, while *Deng nianpu* provides no record of such meetings. Nevertheless, we have great confidence in the historian who provided the information. If his account is accurate, it suggests a belief on Deng's part that whatever posture Li Xiannian felt obliged to adopt as events unfolded in October-November, Li (and Wu De) were on the moderate side of politics, and their self-preservation was important to the larger cause.

Tiesheng, Liaoning's (and thus Mao Yuanxin's) model who had turned in the blank college entrance examination paper. Once Mao Yuanxin finished, Deng asked the five people summoned for "help" what they had to say for themselves. Hu Yaobang tried to defend himself against Wang Hongwen's allegations the previous night, averring that he never said what was claimed, and also sought to explain his role concerning Liu Bing's first letter. Hu Qiaomu explained his role in relaying the second letter to Deng, earning Jiang Qing's scorn over how the Chairman's former secretary could do such a thing to oppose him. Liu Bing himself made a self-examination, saying he only saw the trees, i.e., the personal issues, rather than the larger situation at Qinghua, admitted mistakes of false accusation, asked for punishment, and promised his loyalty and future efforts to the Party and Mao. Zhou Rongxin spoke last, and his talk was repeatedly interrupted by the four radicals with sharp charges such as "carrying out bourgeois education," "revisionism," and "restoration." Liu Bing later reported that he could see dissatisfaction in the faces of other Politburo members, but no one resisted. Deng simply closed the meeting, and said everyone would be informed of the next session.[54]

The onslaught continued on November 18 on several fronts. Chi Qun convened a large-scale "big debate" meeting at Qinghua, where Wu De again relayed Mao's remarks on Liu Bing, and extensive criticism of the four letter writers followed. While this meeting focused on the problems of Liu *et al.*, on the same day Mao Yuanxin called in Chi and Xie Jingyi, telling them that Liu Bing had already made a self-criticism and now instead of just harping on the two letters, the target should shift to Zhou Rongxin whose attitudes had encouraged Liu, a shift which was duly implemented when the Qinghua "debate" meeting resumed on the 19th. But this rapid shift from Liu Bing's letter to the educational issue was not the limit of the expansion of targets. In the Politburo, also on the 18th, Zhang Chunqiao declared that focusing on Zhou Rongxin was unfair and insufficient, that Zhou had drawn his inspiration from Deng's speeches, and therefore Deng was the root of the "wind of rightist reversal."[55]

Events moved rapidly over the next week with two meetings, the 17-person Politburo meeting on November 20,[56] and a 130 plus person "warning" (*dazhaohu*) meeting on the 24th, both convened at Mao's behest, and a Party Center notice conveying Mao's comments on Liu Bing, his warning that the Qinghua events were a "wind of rightist reversal," and his reassertion that "class struggle is the key link," which was sent on the 26th to all provincial-level and military region Party

---

[54] Liu Bing, *Fengyu suiyue*, pp. 247-49. Liu mentioned that Li Chang also spoke, but did not provide any details.

[55] *Ibid.*, pp. 250ff, 257; and "Beijing 'wenge' dashiji," p. 16.

[56] The full list of participants is unknown, but it presumably included the dozen or so healthy Politburo members in Beijing, plus Xie Jingyi and others. The striking contrast with the earlier four- and eight-person meetings was the full participation of the Politburo radicals.

first secretaries and other top CCP, government and military leaders. This period, especially the 17-person Politburo meeting on November 20, has been presented in official histories as a key development in Mao's estrangement from Deng. In his instructions for this meeting, Mao asked that the Politburo draw up a resolution formally evaluating the Cultural Revolution, and that Deng be in charge of this task. Deng declined, which has been taken as staunch resistance; in his daughter's words, "he completely refused to make a concession" on Mao's assessment of the Cultural Revolution. Following this ostensibly unsatisfactory outcome, the Chairman enlarged the matter by calling for the 130-person meeting, reportedly to involve all Politburo members then in Beijing,[57] responsible old cadres of Party, government and military organs, as well as some youthful responsible comrades (although Mao quickly decided these younger figures should not attend). This meeting, together with the November 26 notice, had the effect of greatly expanding elite knowledge that serious problems had emerged within the top leadership, albeit still limiting this knowledge to a tiny segment of the elite. Strikingly, however, the version of Mao's comments made available at this point did not include his linking of Deng to Liu Bing. While this reconstruction is broadly accurate concerning events, their meaning—particularly the explanation of Deng's behavior—requires further analysis.[58]

The lead-up to the 17-person Politburo meeting clearly indicated Mao's preoccupation with the Cultural Revolution. In Deng Liqun's assessment, "Chairman Mao had to make a political testament (*jiaodai*), and thus had to make an examination (*jiancha*) and summing up of the Cultural Revolution." In calling for a resolution it was clear that, while mistakes had to be acknowledged, Mao wanted the Party Center to endorse his 70/30 overall assessment of the Cultural Revolution. There was no problem with affirming such a broad judgment, but the resolution he called for would presumably have had to go into some detail about both the achievements and shortcomings of the movement. While the accepted story focuses on Deng, in fact Mao's assignment also involved Zhang Chunqiao who would obviously be the main drafter of any document, and who was instructed by Mao to lecture Deng on the necessity and significance of the Cultural Revolution. This, however, gave Deng an excuse for declining the task precisely because he had been on the sidelines, out of the political loop, during the crucial years of 1967-69 and beyond. In giving his reasons, Deng said, "It would be inappropriate for me to oversee the writing of this resolution. '[I] have lived in the peach blossom grove, and did not know of the Han dynasty, let alone the Wei and the Jin eras'." More than providing a classical reference

---

[57] This should not be taken literally since the terminally ill Zhou Enlai and Kang Sheng surely, and other aging leaders possibly, did not attend.

[58] See Chen and Du, *Shilu*, vol. 3, part 2, pp. 1293-95; Mao Mao, *"Wenge" suiyue*, pp. 426-29; *Deng nianpu*, vol. 1, pp. 132-33; and below, p. 409n60. In addition, on November 22, Chi and Xie compiled Zhou Rongxin's speeches and submitted them to Jiang Qing; Chen and Du, p. 1293.

(arguably beyond Deng's own knowledge) for his position, the significance of Deng's statement was that it echoed Mao's comment on the peach blossom grove only a week earlier when the Chairman gave a warning to old cadres. Far from being the defiant leader who "admitted no wrongdoing and upheld his position on matters of principle" portrayed in official Party histories, Deng was in effect acknowledging Mao's criticism of veteran figures like himself who had been attacked during the Cultural Revolution, even as he sought to avoid responsibility for a resolution on the movement on grounds of his unsuitability.[59]

There were other indications that Deng's unwillingness to assume responsibility for the resolution amounted to less than a decisive watershed. The whole idea was quietly dropped; there is no indication that Mao continued to push the matter, or that the radicals—including Zhang Chunqiao who shared the assignment—either pursued Deng over it, or volunteered to draft a resolution in his absence. The Chairman's apparent indulgence was also seen in the fact that his critical comment linking Deng to Liu Bing was not conveyed to the 130-person meeting, thus trying to keep this damaging assertion strictly within the highest circles, in a manner strikingly similar to his effort concerning his May 3 criticism of the radicals. In addition, when Deng wrote to Mao on the 21st advising him of preparations and talking points for the large meeting, the Chairman's response was "very good," and Mao went on to reduce somewhat the pressure on veteran leaders by indicating that warnings were also necessary for middle-aged and especially young cadres. Most tellingly, at the meeting convened on the 24th, after conveying Mao's comments on the talking points, Deng made

---

[59] Deng Liqun guoshi jiangtan, vol. 3, p. 327; Mao Mao, "Wenge" suiyue, pp. 426-27; Long Pingping, Deng Xiaoping yu tade shiye, p. 145; Mao wengao, vol. 13, p. 495; and "Xu Jingxian de chubu jiefa jiaodai" [Xu Jingxian's Preliminary Unmasking Confession] (November 5, 1976), in CRDB, p. 4. Note that on the 15th, Deng had already indicated his unsuitability for such a task by proposing that Wang Hongwen resume responsibility for the Party Center. Indeed, it is conceivable that Deng genuinely felt that his distance from events meant he would be unable to fulfill satisfactorily the Chairman's desire for a comprehensive assessment—a posture of modesty rather than defiance. We acknowledge, in any case, that a strong preponderance of Party historians questioned on the matter support the Deng resisting view. While we tend to believe this reflects a genuine belief rather than simply parroting an official line, our own analysis as discussed here is that the evidence points in a different direction. For a Western interpretation claiming Deng's resistance in order to maintain broad elite support, see Huang, Factionalism, p. 349.

In early December, Mao again raised the peach blossom grove where remnants of the Qin dynasty escaped after its fall, thus leaving them largely ignorant of successor dynasties, in a more detailed, but still limited criticism of old cadres: "Don't belittle the old comrades. I'm the oldest. The old comrades still have some use. Don't be harsh on the rebels [either], don't get rid of them at the drop of a hat. Sometimes they make mistakes. And so don't we old comrades make mistakes? We also make them. Pay attention to the three-way integration of young, middle-aged and elderly. Some old comrades haven't managed affairs for seven or eight years, and there are many things they don't know. They have lived in the peach blossom grove, and did not know of the Han dynasty, let alone the Wei and the Jin eras. Some people have been attacked and don't feel happy. They have anger in their hearts. That's excusable. But that anger can't be directed at the majority, or directed at the masses, standing at odds with them and condemning them." Mao wengao, vol. 13, p. 488.

his own elaboration—in effect a sweeping self-criticism—which affirmed the importance of a correct attitude toward the Cultural Revolution, endorsed Mao's insistence that class struggle was the key link, and acknowledged that his own formulation of the three directives as the key link was incorrect. Of course, as we have argued previously, Deng had never been shy about bending to Mao's will, including repeated instances concerning the Cultural Revolution since 1966, notably his famous pledge never to reverse verdicts on the movement. There was nothing different now, and in three self-criticisms which followed in December and January, Deng accepted that the essence of his problem was indeed his attitude toward the Cultural Revolution. Finally, even during the anti-Deng campaign's most intense phase from about March 1976, when Deng was accused of virtually *everything*, the radicals did not raise his asserted flouting of Mao's will over the resolution.[60]

What, then, explains Deng's avoidance of the proposed resolution, given that he was in fact willing to affirm the Cultural Revolution and admit his own shortcomings in that regard? A Party historian specializing on the period has offered a subtle alternative explanation to brave resistance, or simply accepting Mao's already stated verdict on people in Deng's position. In this view, Deng parroted Mao's words as a way of deflecting the demand as delicately as possible, thus undermining the Chairman's attempt to use Deng's endorsement as a way to persuade old cadres to accept the permanent legacy of the Cultural Revolution. Mao was not seeking to dramatize why Deng had to go, but was making a genuine effort to cement his and other older generation leaders' acceptance of the Cultural Revolution, but once Deng refused the Chairman simply ditched the idea.[61]

There is much to recommend in this view, particularly in terms of Mao's likely motivation, but also given Deng's past record of, while never opposing the Chairman, sometimes distancing himself from Mao's impractical projects.[62] But this interpretation, which suggests subtle rather than confrontational resistance on Deng's part, still does not explain why he would resist at all, or convince us that he did indeed resist.[63] Certainly, there was no danger of losing the support of his core backers who fully understood the need to appease Mao, and with the Chairman clearly in the twilight of his life, a probably short period of compromise

---

[60] See Mao Mao, *"Wenge" suiyue*, pp. 427-29; above, pp. 14, 20, 70; and below, pp. 413ff. In addition to preventing disclosure of his comment on Deng's partiality to Liu Bing, Mao further limited disclosure by reversing himself and excluding young cadres from the meeting.

[61] Interview, September 1999. See also Mao Mao, *"Wenge" suiyue*, p. 426.

[62] This seemingly was the case in the immediate pre-Cultural Revolution years when Deng focused on practical issues while leaving others to cope with Mao's problematic concerns in the superstructure. See Teiwes, "Mao and His Lieutenants," pp. 68-69.

[63] In addition to the following considerations, it is worth questioning whether Deng was as relentlessly opposed to the Cultural Revolution as commonly believed. That is, as a political matter, even in the post-Mao period he often wanted to soft-pedal criticism of the movement when others in the leadership were much more inclined to open up the issue. This is a matter for our Volume III. Cf. above, pp. 69-70.

would have been inherently rational. But Deng may have regarded drafting the resolution as a poisoned chalice, a task (as Chen Boda found out with the political report for the Ninth Congress)[64] full of dangers in attempting to achieve a consensus within a divided leadership, and most crucially a verdict satisfying Mao. While no one would challenge the Chairman's 70/30 assessment, analyzing specific developments and tendencies could be fraught with peril. Sidestepping the task by using the Chairman's authority might have seemed the best way out of a difficult situation, something that may, or may not, have been a miscalculation. All that can be said with certainty is that, despite both the clever use of the peach blossom grove *and* his acceptance of the Chairman's criticisms, Deng's position continued to erode in December and January despite some desperate attempts to obtain Mao's forgiveness.

An indication of the further deterioration of Deng's position was the publication in *Red Flag* on December 1 of an article by "mass criticism groups" from Qinghua and Beijing Universities upholding the revolution in education, and attacking the "strange theory" that it had been a flop, things had gone too far, and the orientation should be reversed. Appearing after a set of quotations from Mao setting out the educational principles of the Cultural Revolution—serving proletarian politics, combining education with productive labor, shortened schooling, selecting students from the workers and peasants, and the return of students to production after study—the article systematically defended these features and denounced revisionist efforts to negate them. Now the issue that had been brewing for a month was made public, gaining further attention when republished in the *People's Daily* on December 4.[65] No one was named, certainly not Deng who was not even named in internal documents restricted to high-ranking circles, but the issue was now exposed in the media, and at the same time internal criticism of Zhou Rongxin's (and thus Deng's) educational policies developed further.[66] All this indicated that Mao intended to press further on at least the educational issue, while the concept of a "rightist reversal" that had been aired in top-level internal meetings since mid-November was now in the public realm.

While education was basically the only issue receiving media coverage as a case of "rightist reversals of verdicts" in December and January, other issues were surfacing internally. A key area concerned the economy. The venue for this development was the national planning conference held in Beijing from October 26 to January 23. When the meeting convened in October with the agenda of

---

[64] See Teiwes and Sun, *Tragedy*, pp. 106-108.

[65] See Mao's quotations, the two universities' article, and another article on education from *HQ*, no. 12 (1975), in *SPRCM*, no. 852 (1975), pp. 1, 2-11, 32-37.

[66] On December 8, Wu De attacked Zhou Rongxin at a meeting of the Beijing Municipal Committee, which was responsible for Qinghua, and on December 14 the Party Center approved and circulated a Qinghua report on Liu Bing's letters and, more importantly, the revolution in education. "Beijing 'wenge' dashiji," p. 19; and Chen and Du, *Shilu*, vol. 3, part 2, p. 1300.

discussing the 1976 annual plan and the ten-year plan, the task must have seemed largely professional to the participants, although the sidelining of the 20 articles undoubtedly gave cause for concern. Targets for the 1976 plan were agreed to, including an ambitious 7 to 7.5 percent overall growth target. Moreover, based on a three to four month seminar held by the SPC, and feedback from the regions and ministries, principles for the ten-year program were discussed when the conference convened, once Mao approved the draft plan. By late December, moreover, the Politburo accepted the revised outline draft with only slight changes. Nevertheless, at some point, presumably in January, the "counterattack on the rightist wind of reversing verdicts" disrupted discussions of readjusting economic work system reform. It was also in this period that "gang of four" followers in Shanghai collected the speeches of eight vice premiers, including Hua Guofeng, to the summer 1975 State Council theory conference, and discussed energy problems, in both respects more than three months after Mao Yuanxin raised these matters with his uncle. The latter question, whose salience increased during the winter due to fuel shortages exacerbated by petroleum exports, was both a genuine policy dilemma and provided a platform for attacks on Deng, by young radicals in particular, during February-March.[67]

In another crucial area, Party organization, internal criticism of the proposed Party rectification and Deng's "ladder theory" surfaced in January, with Ji Dengkui now apparently coming under attack, although the theory was only openly criticized in April, and then without explicit reference to Deng. This matter, however, illustrated another feature of the period—the hesitancy of at least some Politburo radicals to engage in a wholehearted attack on Deng. Thus with regard to the April 1 *Red Flag* critique of the "revisionist organizational line" and the "ladder theory" at the very time the Tiananmen crisis unfolded, Yao Wenyuan credibly claimed he had toned down the draft, deleting a lot of excessive language pointing to Deng.[68] In any case, January also saw the start of efforts, reportedly directed by the same Yao Wenyuan, to use the *People's Daily* network to collect material on rightist tendencies, with the alleged aim of

---

[67] See Chen and Du, *Shilu*, vol. 3, part 2, pp. 1285-87; "Hua Guofeng jiejian Shandong Hubei deng Nanjing budui deng lingdao tongzhi de jianghua" [Hua Guofeng's Speech Receiving Leading Comrades from Shandong, Hubei etc. (Provinces) and the Nanjing Troops etc.] (October 7, 1976), in *CRDB*, p. 1; "Ma Tianshui de buchong jiefa jiaodai," p. 3; Qing and Fang, *Deng zai 1976*, vol. 1, p. 121; and above, pp. 333n86, 375-76.

Among those under attack during the February-March warning meetings were leading economic officials Li Xiannian and Gu Mu. In an interesting development, in fall 1975 Wang Hongwen, followed by Zhang Chunqiao in February, talked of Ma Tianshui being transferred to Beijing to take charge of economic work, a development that never eventuated. See "Xu Jingxian de chubu jiefa jiaodai," p. 6; and Xu Jingxian, *Shinian yimeng*, pp. 356, 387.

[68] See Qing and Fang, *Deng zai 1976*, vol. 1, pp. 30-31; "Ma Tianshui, Xu Jingxian zai Fudan Daxue de jianghua" [Ma Tianshui's and Xu Jingxian's Speeches at Fudan University] (January 8, 1976), in *CRDB*, p. 1; and above, pp. 343ff. As noted later in this chapter and discussed more extensively in Chapter 7, the Central Organization Department (and by implication Ji Dengkui) came under attack in March; below, pp. 447, 513.

"framing leading cadres."[69]

As these policy issues unfolded, life within the Politburo became increasingly tense, with the radicals now adopting a more aggressive stance in criticizing Deng's consolidation work. Although nominally in charge of these meetings, Deng, with probably some overstatement, told his daughter that he just sat silently through them, only declaring the sessions open and finished. Yet even in this tense atmosphere, there were still suggestions that the Chairman might relent. One instance came early in December following Mao's meeting with US President Ford. In a small group including Deng, Li Xiannian, Foreign Minister Qiao Guanhua and the "two ladies," Mao called on old cadres to be tolerant of rebels who had criticized them during the Cultural Revolution, but also indicated that such veterans weren't all that bad, and, in fact, he was the oldest. The effect of this message of mutual tolerance was to relieve the anxiety on all sides of the conflict in the Ministry of Foreign Affairs (see below): Qiao Guanhua, as an old cadre, as well as Wang Hairong and Tang Wensheng, "rebels" in the context of ministry strife, could all take heart. Significantly, when Qiao and his wife, Zhang Hanzhi, who was also present at the meeting, reviewed the significance of Mao's remarks, they concluded not only that they would be OK after making self-criticisms, but also that Deng should be OK too. Indeed, according to a participant, at the meeting following Ford's reception Deng attempted to seize the moment and offer a self-criticism, but did not succeed in engaging Mao's attention.[70]

This turn of events possibly explains some ostensibly optimistic developments over the next week or so as seen in Zhou Enlai's exchanges with other leaders. Zhou offered moral support to Deng, perhaps encouraged Ye Jianying to be steadfast against the radicals, and sought to wean Wang Hongwen away from Jiang Qing—all steps that can be read as reflecting a belief that all was not lost and matters would not necessarily deteriorate further for Deng and his supporters.[71]

---

[69] See *A Great Trial*, pp. 172, 225.

[70] Mao Mao, *"Wenge" suiyue*, p. 431; Zhang Hanzhi, *Wo yu Qiao Guanhua*, pp. 83-84; and interview, November 2002. Zhang Hanzhi misdates the event as occurring on December 12, rather than December 2.

[71] This observation must be speculative since so little is known beyond tantalizing tidbits from these encounters at a time when Zhou was apparently saying goodbye to a larger number of leaders. Regarding Deng, Zhou reportedly asked Deng on December 8 whether he would ever change his attitude, and was extremely happy when Deng said "never." While often taken as a sign of Deng's steadfastness concerning the Cultural Revolution, it could equally be seen as indicating that Deng would play out his cards prudently, loyal to Mao and hoping to survive. In his famous injunction to Ye not to allow the radicals to seize power (which may or may not have taken place at this time—the authoritative *Zhou nianpu* only says "this year [1975]," while Mao Mao, *"Wenge" suiyue*, p. 437, places it in December), the implication was that Ye would be in a position to prevent such an outcome. And in reminding Wang of Jiang's late 1974 dismissive attitude toward him, Zhou arguably hoped he could encourage Wang to keep his distance from the rest of the "gang." See *Zhou Enlai nianpu*, vol. 3, pp. 723-24; and Mao Mao, *"Wenge" suiyue*, pp. 430-31.

In addition to Zhou's activities, optimism could be read into Deng's action in arguing against Lu

Mao's radical themes did not fade, however. When China successfully launched a satellite in mid-December, it was hailed as a result of taking class struggle as the key link and consolidating the Cultural Revolution. Yet some ambiguity was introduced by a favorable reference to Mao's three directives—although not as the "key link." Ye Jianying's memorial speech for Kang Sheng on December 21 again highlighted class struggle as the key link, as would Deng's own memorial speech for Zhou Enlai in January. Shortly before, on December 18, Mao Yuanxin gained his uncle's approval for organizing his various instructions, instructions that were apparently taking on an increasingly anti-Deng tone, into a document that could be circulated within the elite.[72]

The clearest sign that the tide was running against Deng was his oral self-examination before the Politburo on December 20. While Deng clearly was not prone to the excessive long-winded self-criticisms so typical of Zhou Enlai, as we have indicated he was perfectly willing to perform the ritual when necessary—something earning him Mao's disingenuous comment that he was different from Liu Shaoqi and Lin Biao, precisely because he was willing to undergo self-criticism.[73] On this occasion, after thanking the Chairman and "especially young comrades for their help," Deng explained how he had only gradually come to understand his errors. The crux of the self-examination was his acknowledgment not only that his attitude toward the Cultural Revolution was the essence of his problem, but that the reason for this error was not that he had been in the peach blossom grove, thus not having worked for eight[74] years, but rather due to his own ideological shortcomings. If Deng had metaphorically attempted to hide in the grove to avoid responsibility for a resolution on the Cultural Revolution in November, he now in effect acknowledged that such a ploy had lost its utility. After the meeting, Deng sent a transcript of his self-examination to Mao, along with a cover note expressing his hope that he could receive face-to-face instructions from the Chairman. Mao did not reply, meetings to criticize and

---

Dingyi being stripped of his Party membership when his case came before the body on December 13. Deng arguably could have been encouraged by not only Mao's December 2 remarks on old comrades, but also by the Chairman's somewhat sympathetic reaction to a recent request by Lu's children. See Chen Qingquan and Song Guangwei, *Lu Dingyi zhuan* [Biography of Lu Dingyi] (Beijing: Zhonggong dangshi chubanshe, 1999), pp. 535-36; and *Mao wengao*, vol. 13, p. 472.

[72] *RMRB*, December 18, 1975, p. 1; *PR*, no. 52 (1975), p. 8, no. 4 (1976), p. 8; and Chen and Du, *Shilu*, vol. 3, part 2, pp. 1301-1303. After Mao's instructions were distributed to the Politburo later in December, additional comments by Mao in January were subsequently added to form a Party document issued in March 1976. *Mao wengao*, vol. 13, pp. 490-91.

[73] Despite Mao's claim, Liu clearly did offer self-criticisms during the Cultural Revolution. As for Lin, there is evidence not only that he did make a self-criticism after the 1970 Lushan plenum, but that he repeatedly sought an audience with Mao. Similar to Deng's situation in December 1975-January 1976, however, the Chairman refused to meet him. Interview with specialist on Lin Biao, September 1994.

[74] Actually, Deng's period of not working was more like six years, but here he was echoing Mao's reference to seven or eight years; see above, p. 408n59.

"help" Deng continued, and Deng never saw the Chairman again.[75]

While Deng would make further self-criticisms, and Mao continued to distinguish him from Liu Shaoqi and Lin Biao, the cutting off of contact was a sign that a reprieve was very unlikely. How had matters reached this impasse, particularly in view of the plausible observations of Deng's daughter that the Chairman was reluctant to oust Deng and only acted after "exhausting all magnanimity"? This, of course, is ultimately unknowable, but it surely centered on the Cultural Revolution. For all Mao's favoritism toward Deng, and Deng's apparent begging for forgiveness before contact was cut off,[76] it appears the Chairman finally lost patience with him on the Cultural Revolution issue, not because of any principled resistance, but rather due to a (correct) judgment that his priorities lay elsewhere. Thus, at some point in late 1975, Mao reportedly chastised Deng for having promised to uphold the Cultural Revolution, but not being "up to scratch" concerning the movement in practice. This fell short of declaring that Deng was an "unrepentant capitalist roader," a phrase coined by Chi Qun and apparently tacitly approved by Mao, but from the Chairman's perspective it was a harsh enough conclusion.[77]

As 1976 began, a further decline in Deng's fortunes was evident. The joint New Year editorial of the *People's Daily*, *Red Flag* and *PLA Daily* highlighted Mao's dictum to "never forget class struggle," and again stated that it was the key link. Of course, in itself none of this was new in the context, but Mao's "recent teaching" that "Stability and unity do not mean writing off class struggle, ... everything else hinges on it" was a clear rebuke to Deng's formulation of the key link. Even more significant than the editorial itself was that it represented a last minute change from the draft agreed to by the Politburo, presumably including the radicals. On New Year's eve, Wang Dongxing called Deng and asked him to look at the editorial. When asked why it replaced the one approved by the Politburo, Wang simply said the final version was approved by Mao, leaving Deng with nothing further to say.[78] In the wake of this, Deng spent New Year Day composing a new self-examination, which he read to the Politburo on January 3. In this he acknowledged that his earlier self-criticism had been insufficient, and

---

[75] See Mao Mao, *"Wenge" suiyue*, pp. 431-33; and *Deng nianpu*, vol. 1, pp. 136-37. Deng was now excluded from meetings between Mao and foreign leaders, beginning with the visit of the President of Sao Tome and Principe on December 23. Although still formally in charge of foreign affairs, Deng apparently also no longer handled substantive negotiations with such visitors. He did, however, briefly, still perform ceremonial functions, receiving Julie Nixon Eisenhower on December 30, and bidding farewell to Prince Sihanouk on December 31.

[76] See above, p. 70n116. While this comes from a source which cannot be absolutely vouched for, we regard it as credible. It is our supposition that any such begging by Deng would have occurred at this juncture.

[77] Chen and Du, *Shilu*, vol. 3, part 2, pp. 1339, 1346; *Sirenbang fangeming zuixing cailiao jilu*, pp. 41-42; and interview with senior Party historian, February 2002. While no evidence has been found that Mao used the "unrepentant capitalist roader" label himself, he clearly allowed its use in the campaign against Deng.

[78] *PR*, no. 1 (1976), p. 9; and Ji Xichen, *Shi wu qianli de niandai*, vol. 2, pp. 723-74.

that he had benefited from the "stern analysis" of his mistakes by comrades in the ongoing criticism meetings which should continue, but especially from the Chairman's instructions conveyed by Mao Yuanxin. Clearly, Deng's new effort responded to those instructions, most notably by repeating Mao's complaint that he had not sought the Chairman's prior approval or Politburo discussion of the "three directives as the key link" formulation. Deng concluded by expressing his wish to enunciate his understanding before Mao and receive the Chairman's instructions. Mao did not grant the wish, but instead instructed on January 14 that both of Deng's self-examinations be printed and distributed to the Politburo for discussion, a clear sign that he was still dissatisfied.[79]

As bleak as the situation looked, Mao still had not indicated a determination to oust Deng completely. When informed that Jiang Qing, seemingly sometime in January, portrayed Deng at a Politburo meeting as wanting to kick Mao upstairs, the Chairman, after noting that (the supposedly unyielding) Deng was willing to admit to the charge under pressure, rejected the view, declaring, "it's too excessive, he has some ambition, but not to the point of kicking me upstairs."[80] Nevertheless, Deng had by now concluded that time was running out and made a third self-examination to another Politburo criticism session on January 20, held after a delay caused by Zhou Enlai's death. He now carried through the step he had apparently been contemplating since mid-November, stating he was unsuited to principal leadership work since he was bound to make mistakes in concrete tasks given his fundamentally incorrect standpoint, in effect requesting to be relieved of his posts. That evening he again wrote to Mao, submitting a copy of his Politburo speech and once more requesting a face-to-face meeting to discuss his work, and proposing to end his responsibility for the daily work of the Party Center. When Mao Yuanxin reported on the Politburo meeting and relayed Deng's requests the next day, Mao declared the issue was an internal contradiction among the people, Deng was different from Liu Shaoqi and Lin Biao in his willingness to make self-criticism, and his request concerning work could be dealt with later: "I mean his work can be reduced, but he cannot leave work, that is, he should not be killed with one blow." For all the ambiguity of the statement, a watershed had been reached. In the same conversation Mao indicated for the first time that Hua Guofeng would assume Deng's leading role and Zhou's vacant position.[81]

---

[79] Mao Mao, "Wenge" suiyue, pp. 436-37.

[80] Qing and Fang, Deng zai 1976, vol. 1, p. 44. The dating in Qing and Fang is sometimes unreliable, and this incident could have happened earlier. The judgment that as of mid-January Mao still had not made up his mind about Deng was given by one of best informed Party historians on the period. Interview, October 1994.

[81] See Mao Mao, "Wenge" suiyue, pp. 446-49; Deng nianpu, vol. 1, pp. 145-46; and Mao zhuan, vol. 2, pp. 1765-66.

Leaders under Attack: Zhang Aiping, Zhou Rongxin and Hu Qiaomu

As the above discussion indicates, while the drama surrounding Deng Xiaoping unfolded, various sub-Politburo-level leaders who had played prominent roles in Deng's consolidation effort became targets of criticism. Apart from the considerably lower ranking Liu Bing, Hu Yaobang and Li Chang from the Academy of Sciences, Hu Qiaomu from the Research Office, and Minister of Education Zhou Rongxin had been summoned to the Politburo to make an accounting of their actions on November 15. In addition, Zhang Aiping, who was responsible for military science and technology, had been called to his own personal "help" meeting about a week earlier. These five figures had not merely served Deng in developing the consolidation program, they were involved in the key superstructure areas of science and technology, education, and overall theory. Moreover, several of them—Zhang Aiping, Hu Yaobang and Li Chang—had initiated personnel cleanouts that threatened the interests of young rebels who had risen in their organizations as a result of the Cultural Revolution, precisely the "constituency" of Mao Yuanxin. They were thus doubly vulnerable.[82]

Here we examine events surrounding three of these leaders—Zhang Aiping, Zhou Rongxin and Hu Qiaomu—where available material provides another window into the confused politics of the period. These cases not only illuminate the circumstances, false hopes, and varying reactions of the principals, they also shed light on the responses of other individuals within their respective organizations, and of Politburo members forced to cope with a fast changing situation.

Zhang Aiping. As we saw in Chapter 4, after his rehabilitation in fall 1974, Zhang was approached by Ye Jianying to take over the PLA's National Defense Science and Technology Commission (*Kewei*), finally accepting after encouragement from Deng Xiaoping. Zhang's new role also included dealing with factionalism at the military-related Seventh Ministry of Machine Building (*Qijibu*) which managed China's nuclear weapons program, a task he carried out enthusiastically. At the *Kewei*, he joined (and

---

[82] A sixth figure, Minister of Railways Wan Li, was mentioned in popular rumors at the time as one of Deng's four "Buddhist guardians" along with Hu Yaobang, Zhang Aiping and Zhou Rongxin, and Zhang reportedly understood that he and the other three were major targets. Hu Shihong, *Zhang Aiping zai 1975*, p. 269; and interview with specialist on the period, November 2002. However, we have no evidence of Wan being subjected to special criticism before February 1976. His situation was different from those under attack in fall 1975 in that his work did not focus on the superstructure, although it did involve tough action against rebels within the railways sector. In addition, in a perplexing November 13 comment, Mao added former Sichuan leader Li Jingquan to the two Hus, Zhou Rongxin, Li Chang and Liu Bing as among the several tens of old comrades requiring a warning. Unlike the others, Li Jingquan had no known active role in the consolidation process, despite being a Central Committee member. *Mao wengao*, vol. 13, p. 492. Speculatively, this may have been due to Mao becoming aware that Deng entertained the "three generations of Sichuan leaders," Li (the first generation), Liao Zhigao (the second generation and now Fujian leader), and current Party First Secretary Zhao Ziyang, during the September-October agricultural forum. See Xu Jingxian, *Shinian yimeng*, p. 379; and "Jiang Qing zai dazhaohu huiyi," p. 378. In 1976 Mao Yuanxin pursued the matter, demanding to know why Deng hosted the three figures in his home. Qing and Fang, *Deng zai 1976*, vol. 1, p. 36.

effectively replaced as the number one leader) another old cadre who had suffered grievously during the Cultural Revolution, Tao Lujia. Tao now became the commission's political commissar and second secretary, while Zhang was named its director and first secretary. The relationship, however, would not prove to be a happy one.[83]

The first sign of anything wrong came when Zhang received a phone call from Chen Xilian about November 5 advising caution: "Comrade Xiaoping wants me to convey to you that you should not talk too much in public." Apparently a few days later, Zhang was summoned by a PLA deputy chief-of-staff to a small auditorium in Zhongnanhai where he met with a five-man group set up to "help" him: Politburo members Li Xiannian (who chaired the meeting), Hua Guofeng, Ji Dengkui and Chen Xilian, as well as another "old comrade" who, although unidentified, was clearly Tao Lujia. As Zhang later observed of the assembled Politburo leaders, although he did not have deep historical ties with any of these figures, they had been giving him very good support in 1975, yet now the atmosphere at the meeting was suddenly not good. Only Chen greeted Zhang, while Li quickly assumed an accusatory stance, telling Zhang that in his work during the recent period he had not only committed mistakes, but they were mistakes in line. The seriousness of the situation was further revealed when Li showed Zhang two letters of complaint, one from a rebel leader in the Seventh Ministry of Machine Building, Shu Longshan, and the other of uncertain but clearly significant authorship—"someone with access to heaven," that is, to the Chairman himself. Most unnerving, the letters bore Mao's supportive comments.[84]

The issue raised by the first letter, which had been written on October 1, was the issue that Mao Yuanxin had apparently first broached with Mao a few days earlier: the question of the Cultural Revolution. It seized on remarks Zhang had made about the situation he found at the *Qijibu*, i.e., that the situation was getting worse, an attitude assertedly negating the achievements of the movement. Most important was Mao's comment, not only that the letter should be circulated to the Politburo and dealt with by the PLA's GPD, a clear sign of a significant issue, but also his pointed judgment that "this person [Shu Longshan] is a leftist." All we know of the second letter is the Chairman's comment to "let Zhang Chunqiao read and deal with it," which probably simply reflected Zhang's organizational position as GPD head, but in the process provided "gang" involvement in the matter. As to whom the "someone with access to heaven" was, the most likely candidate is Mao Yuanxin, not only because of his role as the Chairman's liaison

---

[83] Dongfang He, *Zhang Aiping zhuan* [Biography of Zhang Aiping] (Beijing: Renmin chubanshe, 2000), p. 928; interview with Party historian familiar with Tao Lujia's career, July 1997; and above, pp. 255-56. Tao, Shanxi Party First Secretary before the Cultural Revolution, assumed a leading post at the Commission by January 1974 after a period of solitary confinement.

[84] See Hu Shihong, *Zhang Aiping zai 1975*, pp. 263-64. As Hu's book is often careless with dates, the timing of these events, while credible, must be regarded with some reservation. Much of the assessment of the various leaders present presumably was Zhang's own view, since Hu's account was largely based on interviews with Zhang.

officer, but also given his background as a graduate of the Harbin Science and Technology University and as a former cadre in the Science and Technology Commission. A less likely possibility is Chi Qun, who previously had oversight responsibilities in this area and was now considered by Mao as a surrogate target for himself by people opposing the Cultural Revolution. In any case, the fact that the Chairman himself had in effect endorsed the criticisms shaped everything. Li Xiannian sternly demanded to know what Zhang had to say about Mao's comments, and when Zhang replied that he didn't know what to say, Li angrily wanted to know how he could remain speechless when faced with the Chairman's views.[85]

The behavior of the leaders nominated to "help" Zhang at this awkward meeting is of interest both in terms of the character of the individuals concerned, and regarding larger features of contemporary political dynamics and future orthodox interpretations. Of the four Politburo members in attendance, Li Xiannian was the most rigid in dealing with Zhang. While arguably a function of his role as chair, Li's posture is somewhat at odds with what might be expected from not only a key figure in the consolidation process, but even more significantly from a senior old cadre who is given credit for his steadfast opposition to the "gang of four" in Deng-era Party histories. As we have discussed, however, both during the Lin Biao-Confucius campaign, and a few weeks earlier on October 19, Li had been quick to adopt a leftist stance when required. The other especially harsh critic at the encounter was none other than Zhang's partner at the Kewei, Tao Lujia. Whether due to fear of again being caught up in another anti-rightist campaign, as he had been during *pi Lin pi Kong*, and perhaps embittered over Deng's role on that occasion, or simply following an opportunistic reading of the political wind at the moment, Tao aligned himself with the radical position by criticizing consolidation in the science and technology spheres, despite the fact that many of the matters under attack had been joint decisions by Zhang and Tao. As a senior Party historian observed with regard to a related case, this type of behavior was considered worse than attacks on comrades during the chaotic period of the late 1960s, since the situation was less immediately threatening, and viable half-measures were available. In Tao's case, he would lose his Central Committee membership in 1977, and seemingly was never forgiven by Deng Xiaoping for his excesses in 1975-76.[86]

Of the others present, at the other extreme was Chen Xilian. Described as "simple and honest" (*dunhou*), Chen was the only person attending to greet Zhang at the start of the meeting, in contrast to the cold faces displayed by everyone else. In his uncomplicated manner, Chen tried to help Zhang, who was known for not easily conceding mistakes, by cajoling him to say simply that he was wrong, and

---

[85] *Ibid.*, p. 267.

[86] *Ibid.*, pp. 269-70; Dongfang He, *Zhang Aiping zhuan*, p. 931; interview, November 2002; and above, pp. 163n132, 181, 389. Tao held no positions of significance in the post-Mao period after being dropped from the Central Committee at the 11th Congress, only serving for a brief period as an ordinary member of the low-significance Chinese People's Political Consultative Conference.

observing that everyone including Chen himself made mistakes in line, so what did it matter. While Chen's aim seemed clear, perhaps the most contradictory picture was that of Ji Dengkui. On the one hand, Ji's thinking was described as "slightly leftist" compared to others, and he was unhappy with Zhang's response. Ji harshly criticized Zhang's remarks that the situation was getting worse which had been raised in Shu's letter, demanding to know whether this meant Zhang was "completely negating the Cultural Revolution," and suggesting Zhang was "a major villain in the rightist reversal of verdicts." Nevertheless, Zhang apparently believed that Ji was "very honest and loyal to the Party," and felt sympathy for him as someone in a difficult situation given his responsibility for planning work. Finally, Zhang also seemingly regarded Hua Guofeng as honest and a nice person. Largely silent during the encounter, and apparently uneasy with the situation where he himself was vulnerable given his own responsibilities in science and technology, Hua still had to say something, and finally suggested a solution providing Zhang with some respite. Hua's proposal was that Zhang be given Mao's remarks to take away and study, and once he had thought things over they could all talk about it later, a proposal that Li Xiannian accepted as the meeting broke up.[87]

Any respite was short lived. As the anti-rightist struggle unfolded in the *Kewei* and *Qijibu* in January, with Tao Lujia in charge of struggle sessions and providing a keynote speech, Zhang was forced to disclose his work relations with Deng and his other alleged "backstage bosses": Ye Jianying and Hua Guofeng. Meanwhile, an interesting development occurred in early December when Zhang was summoned to another "help" session which was now joined by Wang Hongwen. While this meeting had soft as well as hard aspects, Wang, using "typical rebel language," characterized Zhang's mistakes as dismissing the Cultural Revolution, and focused on Zhang's "tongue lashing of all factional heads [as] bastards," noting that he (Wang) was a factional head too. Interestingly, however, Zhang did not enter the meeting with an unfavorable impression of Wang. Since Wang was a MAC Standing Committee member, they had met several times in 1975, and Zhang had found Wang very helpful with his work. In addition to that, Zhang held great respect for Wang as a Party Center leader, i.e., someone handpicked by Mao. In the ambiguous and opaque world of CCP politics in 1975, this was not a unique case of elite perceptions not quite fitting the stereotypes of reform-era Party history.[88]

Zhou Rongxin. As we have seen in the preceding chapters, the case of Zhou Rongxin is more complicated than that of a martyr to Deng's cause who was "persecuted to death" by the radicals. Zhou had indeed been placed on a crucial

---

[87] See Hu Shihong, *Zhang Aiping zai 1975*, pp. 270-72, 313-15.

[88] See *ibid.*, pp. 277, 284-88, 313-15; and Dongfang He, *Zhang Aiping zhuan*, pp. 118-19. Cf. the complaints of military leaders criticized after the fall of the "gang" for their deference to Wang on the grounds that he had been introduced to them as a successor by none other than Ye Jianying; above, p. 96.

front of the consolidation effort as Minister of Education, although ultimately by Mao's decision, rather than by Zhou Enlai or Deng Xiaoping. As education chief, his efforts for much of 1975 reflected the changing political climate, cautious for the first four months as *per* the Premier's advice, then stepping up his consolidation efforts, and finally becoming notably aggressive after Deng's prodding in September. By late September Zhou was engaged in preparing an outline report addressing the negative consequences of the Cultural Revolution, which unavoidably questioned aspects of the revolution in education. The sensitivity of the area, in a sense the jewel of the Cultural Revolution, naturally created vulnerability. As matters unfolded, there was a certain inevitability in the escalation of themes from the Qinghua issue to the revolution in education to the Cultural Revolution as a whole, and in targets from Liu Bing to Zhou Rongxin to Deng Xiaoping.

Pressure on Zhou intensified between the draft of the outline report on October 8, with its first sometimes sharply critical assessment of the state of education, and the third draft on November 10, which lauded the great achievements of the revolution in education. As we have seen, in the context of the Qinghua conflict, on October 25 a Qinghua official wrote to Mao not only defending Chi Qun's role at the university, but denouncing Zhou's "very bad" influence on education more generally, and Mao's comment on the letter called for investigation and Politburo discussion. Whether before or after this letter, a second draft of the outline report appeared that dropped sharply critical references, but still advocated various consolidation themes such as greater respect for teachers and rectifying past mistakes of slighting professional studies. Clearly things were becoming more difficult for Zhou, but their meaning was still unclear. A more immediate indication of Zhou's personal vulnerability came when he was called in for a talk on the educational situation by Zhang Chunqiao on the evening of November 8.[89]

The exchange between Zhang and Zhou was notable for several reasons. Although Zhou had been Minister of Education since the Fourth NPC, and Zhang was the Vice Premier responsible for education, this was the first and only time Zhang summoned Zhou for a talk. Zhang complained that when Zhou wrote reports, he did not direct them to his immediate superior, but instead to the State Council. This, however, distorted reality: Zhou's reports had been directed to "Comrade Zhang Chunqiao and the State Council," and Zhou now angrily rejected Zhang's assertion.[90] Clearly, although at least from late September, Zhou was taking his orders directly from Deng, it was Zhang who had failed to utilize his bureaucratic authority over Zhou. We can speculate about the reasons. Before May, Zhang may have been satisfied that Zhou's ministry was carrying

---

[89] Fu Yi, "Jiaoyu buzhang Zhou Rongxin," pp. 35-36; and interview with specialist in educational history, January 2005.

[90] Fu Yi, "Jiaoyu buzhang Zhou Rongxin," p. 36.

out policies consistent with the revolution in education, he possibly relied on radicals within the ministry for information (there is evidence that both Chi Qun and Jiang Qing received reports from such sources), or he may simply have been preoccupied with other matters—notably the theory of the dictatorship of the proletariat campaign. From May through mid-October, a single explanation seems most persuasive: given Mao's early May criticism of the radicals and Deng's subsequent enhanced authority, there was simply no point in trying to interfere. Now, however, in the changing political circumstances, there was an opportunity to reverse the emerging educational policies and bring Zhou Rongxin to heel.

The other main point of note from this encounter was that, notwithstanding mutual aggravation and clashes over educational policy, Zhang was, in a sense, trying to win Zhou over, i.e., to offer him a way out of his predicament. The price would be exposing his superiors, i.e., Zhou Enlai and Deng Xiaoping. This, however, Zhou Rongxin would not do, even though the third draft of the outline report two days later in effect conceded the policy issues. In particular, Zhou Rongxin had been very close to the Premier while serving in the State Council before the Cultural Revolution, and he now made very clear that he assumed full responsibility for whatever was judged wrong. Having stood firm, Zhou was among those summoned to the Politburo meeting on the 15th when, as previously indicated, Wang Hongwen and Zhang Chunqiao attacked him for ignoring the revolution in education, emphasizing old feudal ideas, and practicing "rightist stuff." Of particular moment was Wang's assertion that the real problem at issue was less Liu Bing's letter than educational policy. Even more unsettling would have been Mao's comment, conveyed by Mao Yuanxin the next day, in praise of Zhang Tiesheng, whose blank exam paper represented the disdain for learning that Zhou was attempting to overcome. Later that day Zhou had his opportunity to respond, but the only available account focuses on the hostility of the radicals toward his efforts, rather than on anything he may have tried to say. In any case, neither the argumentative encounter with Zhang on the 8th, nor the unpleasant developments at the Politburo on the 15th and 16th, seem to have unduly concerned Zhou. He departed for a two-week trip to Africa on November 18, and made little attempt to follow closely what was happening back home while abroad. When he returned in early December, moreover, he still appeared quite comfortable with his situation.[91]

By the time of Zhou's return, however, things had become worse. On November 30, Zhang Chunqiao told an Albanian Communist delegation that there was a serious debate concerning education and the Cultural Revolution and named Zhou as having problems in this regard. More visible were the open polemics launched by the December *Red Flag* article concerning the alleged "two line struggle" in education. When Zhou enquired about the situation,

---

[91] *Ibid.*, pp. 36-37; Chen and Du, *Shilu*, vol. 3, part 2, p. 1292; Liu Bing, *Fengyu suiyue*, pp. 243, 247, 249; and above, pp. 405-406.

his secretary hesitated, but Zhou's daughter showed him the media attacks on educational policy. Zhou was surprised, and defiantly declared that, like Deng, he was not afraid to be knocked down, but he now sensed a serious problem. This concern would have been intensified by a wall poster campaign against him, and especially by the Party Center's circulation on December 14 of the Qinghua Party committee's report on the "great debate concerning education," a report asserting there had been an attempt in August-September to attack and split the Party Center led by Mao, and which named Zhou as opposing Mao's educational line. Thus the issue had been made public, and Zhou had been named in a Party document. Nevertheless, even as the public campaign gathered momentum, and Chi Qun orchestrated the establishment of a special case group within the ministry to deal with his case, Zhou remained fairly optimistic. If he really was in serious trouble and could no longer be minister, he reportedly reasoned, at worst he could still pick up an ambassadorial post somewhere.[92]

Although under heightened criticism at the ministry from the start of February, Zhou continued to defend himself against Zhang Chunqiao's charges. His power was formally stripped away on February 24 when, as in other ministries where the anti-rightist struggle was intense, a provisional leading group was set up, in this case headed by a former Shanghai worker and militia leader, Zhou Hongbao. Struggle sessions continued after the change, but the implication that these resulted in Zhou Rongxin's "persecution to death" is, at best, exaggerated, particularly with regard to the "gang of four." Zhou had a heart condition, and Hua Guofeng ordered that he receive medical attention. While it is likely that the campaign interfered with his treatment, in one report Zhou's condition was seemingly worsened by his insistence on attending criticism sessions in order to refute the case against him, even though he had permission to stay at home. A more direct culpability apparently occurred in the wake of the Tiananmen incident as the special case group pursued links between Zhou and Deng. At that time Zhou was under hospital care, but this did not prevent lengthy interrogations, leading him to leave the hospital in anger shortly before his death on April 13. When Zhou then collapsed during a struggle session on the 12th, his demise was more the product of bureaucratic red tape than evil design.[93] In any case, in

---

[92] Chen and Du, *Shilu*, vol. 3, part 2, pp. 1294, 1300; Fu Yi, "Jiaoyu buzhang Zhou Rongxin," pp. 37-38; and above, p. 312n25.

[93] See Fu Yi, "Jiaoyu buzhang Zhou Rongxin," p. 38; and NCNA, Beijing, September 17, 1977, in *SPRCP*, no. 6431 (1977), pp. 89-90.

The circumstances of Zhou's inadequate treatment on the 12th were that, as a minister, his hospitalization required State Council approval. Minister of Health Liu Xiangping would not act until authorization had been given by the Council or by a Politburo member. Li Xiannian reportedly passed the issue on to the Education Ministry, where Zhou Hongbao sought Zhang Chunqiao's approval, which was apparently given but came "too late." Ji Dengkui also approved, and finally Hua instructed that every measure be taken to save Zhou Rongxin. Altogether three and a half hours were lost, which apparently were decisive. Li Jing, "Dongluan zhong de Jiaoyu buzhang Zhou Rongxin" [Minister of Education Zhou Rongxin in the Midst of Chaos], *Zhonghua ernü*, no. 5 (2003), p. 19, no. 6 (2003),

comparison to 1966-68, the assault on even highly vulnerable elite members like Zhou Rongxin was more limited, and the possibilities of deflecting the process were much greater. Even as the anti-Deng campaign took off from February, there was no mass movement; rather than being "dragged out," leading cadres in Beijing formally retained their posts, and, however unpleasant, face-to-face criticism was largely kept within the confines of the concerned units.

Hu Qiaomu. Hu Qiaomu's situation was different from those of Zhang Aiping and Zhou Rongxin in several regards. First, in the consolidation effort Hu headed a small think tank that was newly created, not a large bureaucratic organization with a history of sharp internal conflict since the onset of the Cultural Revolution. As a result, notwithstanding personnel changes since the January NPC, organizations like the *Qijibu* and Ministry of Education contained rebel elements profoundly out of sympathy with the new trend, while such 1960s rebels had been explicitly excluded from the State Council Research Office. Another contrast was the considerably greater interaction Hu had with Deng Xiaoping: Deng's visits to the Research Office were frequent, while evidence of actual face-to-face contact with Zhang Aiping, Zhou Rongxin and other bureaucratic leaders of the consolidation effort is comparatively scarce. This in turn reflected the centrality of Hu's functions as Deng saw them in 1975: the need to provide theoretical justification, the ability to both prepare Party documents and skillfully interpret Mao's thought, and a broader capacity, honed from years as the Chairman's secretary, to read Mao politically. Finally, in comparison to so many other old cadres who returned to power in the post-Lin Biao period, Hu had, because of Mao's chance intervention, largely avoided the traumas of 1966-68.[94]

When Hu was called to the November 15 Politburo meeting, the ostensible issue was his role in passing on Liu Bing's second letter. Hu had barely acknowledged that he had indeed passed Liu's letter to Deng when Jiang Qing interrupted, demanding to know why he had engaged in this anti-Mao act. Hu tried to explain, indicating that by reputation he had a more favorable impression of Liu as compared to Chi Qun. Given Mao's view of the letter, it was hardly surprising that this explanation did not satisfy, with Jiang Qing waxing indignant over how a former secretary could oppose the Chairman.[95] Nevertheless, as with Zhou Rongxin, Hu's case did not seem desperate. When the 130-person warning meeting was held on November 26, three members of the Research Office attended: Hu Qiaomu, Hu Sheng, and a young librarian, Nong Weixiong. When they returned to the Office they were quizzed in great detail concerning what had transpired: who walked in first followed by the others?—Deng Xiaoping; who chaired the meeting?—Deng; who gave the speech?—Deng. Considering all this, the consensus was that the situation was not so serious, Deng's leadership was still stable, and once self-criticisms had

---

p. 80.

[94] See above, p. 315n37.

[95] See Liu Bing, *Fengyu suiyue*, pp. 248-49.

been offered, that would be the end of the matter.[96]

It is unclear how much pressure Hu was under over the next two months, but apparently there was comparatively little conflict within the Research Office, whether because (unlike Zhou Rongxin's ministry) its performance had not been subjected to sustained public criticism, or simply because of the relative homogeneity of the unit's personnel. The situation changed, however, once the anti-Deng campaign was formally launched in February. On February 3, Nong Weixiong responded to the new situation with a letter to the Chairman exposing the office's errors, asking Yao Wenyuan, ironically in the tradition of Deng and Hu Qiaomu, to pass it on to Mao. Yao passed on the letter with his own, which pointed to the link of the Research Office to the 20 articles on industry and the Academy of Sciences' Outline Report. Mao's instruction to circulate Nong's letter to the Politburo and especially to Hu indicated the Chairman's backing, and the radicals dispatched Xinhua reporters to the office to collect intelligence and regularly report to them. On February 19, Hu and Nong were summoned to an informal meeting of the Center where Nong was warmly received by Yao and Jiang Qing, and encouraged to "get the campaign going in the Research Office." Following this meeting, the office, like most central organs, was reorganized, with an anti-rightist leading group established and paradoxically headed by Hu, with Nong as his deputy. In fact, Hu was the main target of the unfolding campaign, while Nong not only was the real leader of the leading group for the campaign, but also the new holder of Party and administrative power within the unit.[97]

What were the dynamics of the situation within the Research Office as criticism of Deng and Hu unfolded, and the unit itself became a major target as "the source of the rightist wind"? Clearly, the assault was led by low-ranking figures in the office—the so-called "three young and one old" activists."[98] As for the main leaders of the office, all had to make an accounting of their own actions as well as participate in the criticism of Deng and Hu. Exposing Deng was a major objective of the exercise, and Hu, of course, was the main responsible figure of the unit singled out for attack. While available accounts leave various matters murky, several things seem clear. First, with regard to Deng, the office leaders, with varying degrees of firmness, seem to have fundamentally held the line, i.e., while everyone had to go through the motions of criticizing the office's ultimate boss, truly sensitive matters, such as Deng's critical remarks concerning the radicals, were not revealed.[99] Second, a similar solidarity which

---

[96] *Deng Liqun zishu*, pp. 62-63, 78-79; and interview with specialist on the period, November 2002.

[97] *Deng Liqun zishu*, pp. 78-79; *Deng Liqun guoshi jiangtan*, vol. 3, p. 340; Feng Lanrui, "Zhengzhi yanjiushi de rizi," p. 5; interview with contemporary member of the Research Office, February 1998; and interview with senior Party historian specializing on the period, November 2002.

[98] The "three young" were Nong Weixiong, Zhao Qiande and Zhou Xirong, and Wang Fei was the "one old." All were support staff in the operations of the office. Interview with Party historian specializing on the Research Office, November 2002.

[99] *Deng Liqun zishu*, pp. 81, 83, 89.

initially existed regarding criticism of Hu Qiaomu soon dissipated. The division appears to have been between those adopting the same attitude toward Hu as all had displayed toward Deng—i.e., "criticize and protect"—and those who simply criticized, or in fact sought to "criticize and knock [Hu] down." While the precise positions of various individuals are unclear,[100] there can be little doubt that Deng Liqun, one of the most influential voices on the current policy side of the office, was most protective of Hu, while Li Xin, who had been downgraded as a result of Hu assuming leadership of the editorial group for Mao's *Selected Works*, was particularly harsh in denouncing him. Indeed, a Party historian with excellent knowledge of Research Office affairs regards the division between "criticize and protect" and "criticize and knock down" as virtually mirroring the organizational divide between the policy and Mao *Works* branches of the office, although he viewed the others on the theoretical side as largely following Li Xin's lead rather than having any real animus toward Hu.[101]

What of Hu Qiaomu himself in this threatening situation? During the period itself there was controversy over Hu's performance, and aspects of it remain in dispute today. After two months of intense pressure, Hu produced a "10,000 character" self-criticism, a confession that provided information concerning Deng, although whether this went beyond what was already known by the radicals is unclear.[102] Hu also wrote what came to be regarded as a "loyalty letter" to Jiang Qing, seemingly in the context of a failed attempt to secure official participation at Mao's memorial service in September. As Deng Xiaoping subsequently observed, all this might have been understandable, but when Deng Liqun and Yu Guangyuan presented Deng with Hu's letter of apology in April 1977, it is clear that Deng (and many others) viewed Hu's actions as politically weak, the typical performance of a bookish intellectual.[103] The sharp contrast was with the other "conservative reformer" Deng Xiaoping came to rely on in the late 1970s and early 1980s—Deng Liqun. Deng Liqun had been particularly firm in dealing with

---

[100] While the interview source cited below, n. 101, seems to suggest that as many as four office leaders engaged in harsh criticism of Hu, various participants in the events only speak of one or two leaders overstepping the mark. See Feng Lanrui, "Zhengzhi yanjiushi de rizi," pp. 5-6; Yu Guangyuan, "Yi Deng Xiaoping he zhengyanshi," p. 15; and *Deng Liqun guoshi jiangtan*, vol. 3, p. 340.

[101] Interview with senior Party historian specializing on the period, November 2002. Cf. *Deng Liqun guoshi jiangtan*, vol. 3, p. 340; and above, p. 321.

[102] According to Yu Guangyuan, "Yi Deng Xiaoping he zhengyanshi," p. 15, "To begin with Hu Qiaomu did not reveal anything of substance, but after the exposures and denunciations [by] one or two leaders, he happily revealed the circumstances of talks he had had with Deng Xiaoping." However, according to Feng Lanrui, "Zhengzhi yanjiushi de rizi," p. 8, the 18 points "exposing" Deng that Hu confessed to only provided information that had already been seized by Research Office radicals.

[103] Deng, however, returned Hu's letter unread as a sign of trust, and indicated that, as "the Party's number one pen," Hu had an important role to play. See Feng Lanrui, "Zhengzhi yanjiushi de rizi," p. 9; and *Deng Liqun guoshi jiangtan*, vol. 3, p. 345. Interestingly, another intellectual who over the long term adopted a much more thoroughgoing reformist stance than Hu, Yu Guangyuan, was also disdained by a participant in the 1976 events as (in contrast to Deng Liqun) "no good, … a scholar [who was] not skilled at toughing it out." Feng Lanrui, p. 6.

the pressure he was placed under, only giving out dribs and drabs of information to frustrate his attackers, thus earning Deng's praise as a "strong shoulder," the only Research Office leader to have fully resisted the tide in the tumultuous days of 1976. As for Hu, apart from his bookish proclivities, another factor cited by those involved was precisely his easy time in the Cultural Revolution. Whereas others had been hardened by those events, Hu lacked the experience to cope with the much less testing circumstances of this period and, at least to some degree, panicked.[104] One of the ironic outcomes was that when pressure built up for disbanding the Research Office in the first half of 1977, what was largely at issue was not a conservative effort to undermine support for the returning Deng Xiaoping, but, on the contrary, resentment over the perceived weakness toward, or betrayal of, Deng's cause by Hu Qiaomu, the office's leader, during the anti-rightist campaign in 1976. But that is another story for our Volume II.

Taken together, the cases of Zhang Aiping, Zhou Rongxin and Hu Qiaomu suggest a number of things about the attack launched against the "rightist wind" in late 1975. First, for a considerable period of time there was not only uncertainty about Mao's intent as it affected both Deng Xiaoping and senior cadres generally, but there was also a considerable degree of optimism by figures singled out for attack that matters would turn out reasonably well. Moreover, even as the situation deteriorated in early 1976, for these figures it never reached anything like the chaos of 1967-68, and establishment leaders deflected the attacks on Deng and themselves as best they could with a degree of success. Of course, different individuals responded with varying degrees of courage, as seen in the contrasting cases of Deng Liqun and Hu Qiaomu in the Research Office, and senior cadres generally were unable to withstand the takeover of organizational power by radical-dominated leading groups. Yet these cadres by and large remained in place, positioned for the new situation following Mao's death. As for those who sided with the radical cause, whether an old cadre like Tao Lujia or a young rebel like Nong Weixiong, they were different from the destructive rebels of the Cultural Revolution, largely limiting their activities to attacks on prominent targets in their own units. While arguably disdained all the more for such opportunistic behavior, such figures do not appear to have been unduly punished in the post-Mao period, with a few exceptions.[105] For all the hyper-charged ideological atmosphere, a certain restraint operated in 1976 which would become a more profound feature of the new period following Mao's death.

---

[104] Apart from the written sources cited above, p. 425n100, the above draws on interviews with a relative of Hu Qiaomu (October 1994), a contemporary member of the Research Office (February 1998), and a senior Party historian with excellent connections to leading players in the period (January 2000).

[105] E.g., if Tao Lujia never held significant power again, he continued to live the life of a retired high-ranking cadre, while Nong Weixiong reportedly holds a position in the Chinese Academy of Social Sciences.

The Strange Case of the Ministry of Foreign Affairs

While the crucial issues leading Mao to change course were domestic in nature, as before, foreign affairs was quickly involved in a critical political turning point, this time the mounting attack on Deng. The MFA became the first ministry, even before the Ministry of Education, to launch criticism of the "rightist wind of reversing verdicts" in late November.[106] This occasion was different from Zhou Enlai's travails in 1973 in that the Premier's problems, however unfairly, were linked to foreign affairs performance, while Deng's, notwithstanding accusations of rightist policy errors as the MFA criticism unfolded, were not. The telling similarity is that, similar to Zhou during the period of Sino-US rapprochement in 1971-72, with Mao's backing Deng had been able, since taking the reins in 1974, to impose a degree of unity and hierarchical order on the fractious strains within the ministry. As we have seen, these included tensions between senior diplomatic staff and young Cultural Revolution rebels, conflicts among senior professionals themselves, and the complicated relationship of Foreign Minister Qiao Guanhua and his wife Zhang Hanzhi with the "two ladies" who had access to "heaven." With Deng in trouble, however, these strains came increasingly to the fore and became intertwined with attacks on him.

The one thing missing from the multiple sources of conflict within the ministry had been and remained genuine divisions over substantive policy. In the present context, despite MFA criticism of Deng's rightist mistakes, when attempting to make a case against his foreign policy errors in March 1976, Jiang Qing was forced to admit that Deng could not do much damage since this was an area that "the Chairman grasps tightly."[107] A further reflection of this situation was that the "two ladies" had little input into policy. Their clout within the MFA was manifested in their dominance of personnel and routine management decisions, something that led Qiao Guanhua to feel he had no power. This, in turn, was of course based on their close ties to Mao, which allowed them to rebut any challenge to their decisions as amounting to disrespect of the Chairman, leaving others with no viable recourse. Policy, however, proceeded in another sphere. A case in point was the process leading to establishing diplomatic relations with Thailand and the Philippines in the first half of 1975, a process involving the delicate matter of finessing China's ties to the armed Philippine communists in particular. The matter was dealt with in a professional manner, involving a small circle including Deng, Qiao Guanhua, Vice Minister Han Nianlong, the responsible negotiator, Ke Hua, and, of course, Mao as the ultimate decision maker. Nowhere were the "two ladies" or ministry rebels to be seen.[108]

---

[106] See Zhang Hanzhi, *Dahongmen*, p. 156. Cf. below, p. 428n110.

[107] "Jiang Qing zai dazhaohu huiyi," p. 378.

[108] Xu Huangang and Li Zhaoxiang, *Ke Hua Dashi de waijiao shengya* [Ambassador Ke Hua's Foreign Affairs Career] (Beijing: Zhongguo qingnian chubanshe, 2001), pp. 97-104; and interview with involved MFA cadre, November 2002. While Zhou Enlai was fully briefed and participated in

The major substantive issue facing Chinese foreign policy in this crucial period, as throughout the post-Lin Biao years, was Sino-US relations. Kissinger made yet another visit to Beijing from October 19 to 23, the very period when Mao had begun to express his discontent with Deng, and this was followed by President Ford's December 1-5 state visit, when Deng was clearly in serious trouble. The Americans had no sense of Deng's difficulties, as he appeared both authoritative and abrasive in his dealings with them. From the US point of view, the question was to what degree the relationship was in trouble. The problem, of course, was the inherent difficulty of getting beyond common anti-Soviet views and managing the increasingly vexed process of moving toward the normalization of relations, matters made increasingly difficult by US domestic politics. With Ford facing a challenge from Ronald Reagan for the 1976 Republican nomination, no movement was feasible, a situation China had to live with. While the Chinese leaders accepted the situation, they were not happy about it, which resulted in Kissinger's least cordial PRC reception in October, one he characterized as "insolent behavior and self-righteous lack of responsiveness." This involved Deng's aggressive questioning and references to appeasement [of the Soviets], and Mao's assertions that Kissinger's words were "not reliable," the US was simply "standing on our shoulders" to gain an advantage with Moscow, but gave less priority to China than to the Soviet Union, Europe and Japan. When Ford arrived, the atmosphere was milder, even though the PRC had refused to agree to a communiqué, but the content of the visit was inconsequential, as seen in the fact that Ford's meeting with Deng disposed of business in half an hour, and was only extended for appearances' sake.[109] In sum, Sino-US relations had stalled more or less at the point they had reached following Kissinger's ill-fated visit (for Zhou) two years earlier, but with the atmospherics having deteriorated. In terms of basic policy, however, there was no sign of the radical postures that were articulated as criticism of Deng unfolded in the MFA during this period.

Undoubtedly, the early emergence of anti-rightist criticism in the MFA had little to do with foreign policy *per se*, but much to do with the continuing if diminished liaison role of the "two ladies." They were among the first to know of Mao's intent to criticize Deng over Liu Bing's letter, and the letter and Deng's domestic policies featured strongly in the unfolding criticism within the ministry. But bureaucratic responsibilities meant that foreign affairs matters inevitably became involved. When the ministry's Party group met to study Mao's remarks,[110]

---

the signing ceremonies, the actual negotiations were under Deng's direction.

[109] Burr, *Kissinger Transcripts*, pp. 371, 373-75, 381-88, 391, 400-401; Kissinger, *Years of Renewal*, pp. 868-94; and interview with Richard Solomon, November 2003. On Ford's domestic problems, see Tyler, *A Great Wall*, pp. 201-204, 214-15.

[110] The timing of this meeting is uncertain, but it could have been in late October. While Zhang Hanzhi is often inaccurate, her report that it took place on October 25 is plausible given the liaison role of the "two ladies" and their recent exposure to Mao's criticism of Deng, even though systematic criticism within the MFA apparently did not begin until the latter part of November.

someone attacked Qiao Guanhua for alleged mistakes committed during the September-October United Nations session. These "mistakes" concerned negotiations for a peace treaty with Japan and discussions with the US, areas Jiang Qing subsequently identified as examples of Deng's errors according to "[the little] I know based on the MFA material I've seen." Apparently reflecting Mao's remarks, Qiao was criticized for weakness in both cases, although in fact his sins seem to have been more procedural. In the negotiations concerning the treaty with Japan, Qiao may have indicated too much flexibility regarding the emphasis on opposing hegemonism in the document, something the Japanese sought to water down, but which Mao regarded as essential given its anti-Soviet meaning. Qiao, moreover, seemingly was at least as vulnerable because he had been authorized to hold a (single) meeting with the Japanese, but when, sensing progress, he scheduled a follow-up session, this was interpreted as exceeding his instructions. While Qiao had informed Beijing and received no objection, he was now attacked for having failed to obtain Mao's prior approval. Even more dubious was criticism of Qiao for his behavior during his meeting with Kissinger at the UN. Mao had warned of a possible US-Soviet Munich, the appeasement theme Deng would raise with the Secretary of State in Beijing, but Qiao addressed the Chairman's assessment only after Chinese UN Ambassador Huang Hua had already quoted Mao. More generally, Qiao was soon under attack for allegedly carrying out a rightist line that continued Zhou Enlai's foreign policy, and which was supported by Deng.[111]

While charges of major policy errors, much less opposition to Mao's diplomatic line, were patently absurd, they were also highly ironic given both the context of the time and Deng's negotiating style, as well as Qiao's actual performance. Not only had Deng been very tough in dealing with Kissinger in October (and Kissinger perceived Qiao as even more hard line), but as previously suggested, Deng's performance played to some of Mao's deepest instincts. While Mao had certainly been willing to soft-pedal differences with the US in order to achieve rapprochement, he had shown displeasure at the conciliatory aspects of Zhou's style. The contrast with Zhou that so vexed Kissinger should have gratified the Chairman: the suave, discursive and conceptual discussions of the Premier had given way to Deng's sarcastic comments and no-nonsense approach. Yet Deng's performance in the crucial foreign affairs area did not stay Mao's hand as the Chairman increasingly focused on domestic issues, although it arguably

---

[111] Zhang Hanzhi, *Dahongmen*, pp. 149-50; Ma Jisen, *The Cultural Revolution in the Foreign Ministry*, pp. 383-84; Pei Hua, *Zhong-Ri waijiao fengyun zhongde DengXiaoping* [Deng Xiaoping in the Storm of Sino-Japanese Relations] (Beijing: Zhongyang wenxian chubanshe, 2000), pp. 36-45; "Jiang Qing zai dazhaohu huiyi," p. 378; and interview with leading MFA player at the time, November 2002. Jiang Qing's brief comment claimed that Deng was willing to compromise on the hegemony issue with Japan but Mao intervened, and that Deng had "flattered" US representative George Bush during a discussion concerning Taiwan. Concerning the latter charge, it is of interest that during his December reception of Ford, Kissinger and Bush, Mao remarked that Bush could be president. Burr, *Kissinger Transcripts*, p. 398.

contributed to his decision to continue Deng's oversight of this sphere well into December.[112]

Notwithstanding accusations of policy error, the real factors driving conflict within the MFA before and during the anti-rightist drive involved power, personnel, and personality. The most obvious division was between the "two ladies," who had organizational power in the ministry and the ability to control appointments, and Qiao Guanhua, who was frustrated by the resulting limitations on his ability to be an effective minister. In the present context, Wang Hairong and Tang Wensheng organized the ministry's anti-rightist campaign, while Qiao was required to make a self-criticism. An angry Qiao, urged on by Zhang Hanzhi, decided to fight back. After deciding against approaching the terminally ill Premier, and being deflected by Deng who indicated there was little he could do, Qiao settled on Zhang Hanzhi writing to Mao, who had both periodically shown favoritism toward him in the past and had taken a close interest in his wife's career, with complaints of Qiao's treatment. Deng's deflection of Qiao further underlined the complexity of the situation, particularly as it concerned the new movement and Deng. The movement, of course, was ultimately aimed at Deng, and given their leading organizational role in the ministry and direct links to Mao, Wang and Tang were under heavy pressure and had no option but to push the *pi Deng* thrust forward. Yet at the same time they had cooperated closely with Deng on Mao's orders since he effectively took over the management of foreign affairs in 1974, and they even continued to maintain sympathetic contact with him, perhaps into early 1976. These factors, as well as the perception that Qiao had ties to Jiang Qing, arguably contributed to Deng's unwillingness to side with Qiao against the "two ladies," even though Qiao's management of policy had clearly been in accord with Deng's views, and the criticism of Qiao inevitably attempted to tar him as an advocate of the Zhou-Deng "line." More likely, Deng was simply stating the obvious: he had no authority to protect Qiao, even if he wished to do so. In any case, as events unfolded, both the "two ladies" and Qiao were forced into positions critical of Deng, even as those same events placed them at each others' throats.[113]

The clash of Wang Hairong and Tang Wensheng against Qiao and his wife was not the only source of tension in the MFA. In addition to Qiao, the "two ladies" targeted Huang Zhen, the head of the PRC's liaison office in

---

[112] Kissinger, *Years of Renewal*, pp. 868-94; interview, November 2002; and above, pp. 201-202. Years later, Kissinger, p. 875, erroneously attributed Qiao's hard-line stance to casting his lot with the "gang of four."

[113] Zhang Hanzhi, *Dahongmen*, pp. 150-51; Mao Mao, *"Wenge" suiyue*, p. 424; interview with leading MFA figure at the time, November 2002; and above, p. 86. The timing of these events is again uncertain, with Zhang Hanzhi, *Dahongmen*, p. 150, placing Qiao's self-examination on October 27. While this is feasible if Qiao had been criticized on the 25th (see above, p. 428n110), it more likely occurred once the campaign was underway in the MFA in late November. Ma Jisen, *The Cultural Revolution in the Foreign Ministry*, p. 384, also reports Qiao's self-examination on October 27, but Ma's book follows Zhang's dating, including some of the most obvious errors.

Washington.[114] Huang's situation was complicated. For one thing, Huang was a former military subordinate of Deng during the revolution and remained close to him, something which opened Huang to attack as the representative of the right wing in China's overseas missions. But Huang had also been handpicked by Mao for the US position, and the Chairman appeared eager to keep him at his post. Huang's problems, moreover, predated the turn against Deng and grew out of conflicts with young rebels on the liaison office staff. By August 1975, Huang was so fed up with the situation, as the rebels argued officials over 60 should retire, that he sent a resignation request to Mao and Zhou, something which angered Qiao as going over his (Qiao's) head. The case was referred to Deng who was deeply unimpressed with Qiao's handling of the matter, commenting that if the MFA could not accommodate Huang, he (Deng) would find a place for him as PLA deputy chief-of-staff. Deng, however, advised Huang to stay at his post for the time being, but with the anti-rightist developments Huang was again under pressure.[115]

Whatever tensions may have existed between Qiao Guanhua and Huang Zhen over Qiao's less than supportive posture earlier in the year, the anti-rightist campaign placed them both in the line of fire, and reinforced their common ties as senior foreign affairs cadres. While Qiao attempted to fight back against the "two ladies," Huang resisted their pressure to convene a meeting to deal with the problems of the Washington liaison office. The tension, however, was briefly reduced by Mao following his meeting with Ford on December 2. All the key MFA actors were present: Wang Hairong, Tang Wensheng, Qiao Guanhua, Zhang Hanzhi, Huang Zhen and, of course, Deng Xiaoping. This was the occasion of Mao's famous call for better mutual understanding between rebels and old cadres, tellingly punctuated by his reminder that "I am the oldest." Beyond the general sentiment, which apparently was greeted with some relief by all present, the Chairman addressed the specific conflicts within the MFA. Concerning the

---

[114] A third targeted figure was Vice Minister He Ying, who was criticized for opposing the Cultural Revolution. This apparently was on the basis of some critical remarks by He's son which were presumed to be linked to him. Interview with participant in the criticism sessions, November 2002.

[115] See Ma Jisen, *The Cultural Revolution in the Foreign Ministry*, pp. 381-83; and idem, *Waijiaobu wenge jishi*, p. 344. Apart from personal friction between young rebels and the old general, and generational conflict generally, Huang's attackers in the liaison office raised minor matters such as whether Huang had paid too much for the office premises in Washington, and that he was spending too much time cultivating bourgeois politicians, notably Senator Ted Kennedy. These issues had already been raised at the time of the Fourth NPC, but Zhou assured Huang that he had Mao's as well as the Premier's own trust.

Another incident of conflict between leading MFA professionals involved Qiao Guanhua and UN Ambassador Huang Hua. This case concerned Huang's awareness of a Hong Kong book, *Empress of the Red Capital*, which as previously noted reflected badly on Jiang Qing, and became confused with Roxane Witke's as yet unpublished book based on her interviews with Jiang. When Huang reported the matter to Qiao, the Foreign Minister, seemingly fearing Jiang's ire if he pursued the issue, effectively pigeon-holed Huang's report to the latter's discontent. Interview with MFA insider, April 2001; and above, p. 366n179.

main conflict of the "two ladies" against Qiao and his wife, Mao instructed "you four" to get together and resolve the differences that were dividing the ministry, including Huang Zhen's "problem." As for Huang, Mao had already told Ford that he would be returning to Washington, and observed that while some young people had strong opinions about him, they would be advised not to offend the old general. Given these comments and the optimism the encounter engendered that life would soon return to normal, December was a relatively peaceful period in the MFA.[116]

This was, of course, a false dawn. With Mao's attitude having hardened toward Deng, following Zhou Enlai's funeral full-scale anti-rightist mobilization began in the MFA, with the "two ladies" assuming an organizing role despite their closeness to Deng. Similar to the case of Hu Qiaomu in the Research Office, they wanted Qiao to criticize Deng at the initial meeting, but to their frustration Qiao, and several other leading officials, retreated to hospital quarters or otherwise claimed illness. As the struggle pitting MFA rebels, supported by Wang and Tang, against Qiao Guanhua, attacked as Zhou and Deng's man in the ministry, and senior cadres generally intensified, at least some old cadres including a few vice ministers and ambassadors decided to resist during meetings held at Qiao's house. The strategy adopted was to try and cut the link between the "two ladies" and the Chairman, and the method was to send letters and materials to Mao exposing their behavior in the MFA. Under this strategy, the question of a channel to Mao became crucial. The choice was Mao's secretary, Zhang Yufeng, one of four young women along with Wang, Tang and Zhang Hanzhi who were Mao's favorites, but who sometimes had sharp conflicts among themselves. Clearly hoping that Zhang Yufeng's own differences with the "two ladies" would come into play, Zhang Hanzhi approached Zhang Yufeng with a letter and documents in late January or early February, and obtained her agreement to pass them on. This could hardly be a comprehensive response to the dilemma facing senior MFA officials, since they were expected to participate in a Mao mandated campaign against Deng, and it is unclear which old cadres supported the stratagem, but the effort indicated who was seen as the immediate threat.[117]

This already complex situation was further complicated by the entry of Jiang Qing into the foreign affairs realm. What was important here was less her attacks on Deng, which were particularly virulent concerning foreign trade,[118] than her seizing on the intra-ministry conflict involving the "two ladies" to pursue

---

[116] Zhang Hanzhi, *Dahongmen*, p. 151; Kissinger, *Years of Renewal*, pp. 891-92; interview with leading MFA figure at the time, November 2002; and above, pp. 408n59, 412.

[117] Zhang Hanzhi, *Dahongmen*, pp. 158-59; Ma Jisen, *The Cultural Revolution in the Foreign Ministry*, pp. 385-86; and interview with key MFA player in the events, November 2002.

[118] See "Jiang Qing zai dazhaohu huiyi," p. 378, when she attacked Deng as a comprador for foreign capitalists. In addition, Jiang and other radical leaders attacked Deng on, *inter alia*, the Japan and US issues, and his preference for dealing with first and second world countries at the expense of the third world.

her own resentment of Wang and Tang. About February 20, at the time of the visit of former President Nixon, Jiang summoned Qiao and Zhang Hanzhi, not simply to circumvent the "two ladies" regarding translation arrangements for Nixon, but crucially to let Qiao and Zhang know that she had seen their letter "at the Chairman's place," and that further communications should be sent *via* her since Mao had decided she should take charge of foreign affairs matters. This was apparently the first step in Jiang exercising oversight responsibility for foreign relations, and displacing Wang and Tang's authority in the MFA, a situation lasting until May when Hua assumed control. This development created a major quandary for Qiao and other senior leaders. They risked being drawn into Jiang's maneuvers, but she provided the necessary channel for them to resist the campaign within the ministry and strike back at the "two ladies." After further discussions at Qiao's house, the decision was made to go along with Jiang, to use "poison to attack poison," to invoke a "big turtle egg" to overcome "small turtle eggs." They reportedly consoled themselves that they were not turning the MFA over to Jiang, on the not unreasonable assumption that she was so ignorant of foreign affairs that they would be able to retain control of actual diplomatic matters. Whether this fateful decision was a joint determination of the ministry's top leaders, as sources sympathetic to Qiao claim, or essentially the Foreign Minister's own doing, must remain uncertain on the available evidence. In any case, other MFA leaders were happy to let the blame fall on Qiao in the post-Mao period. It may also be the case that some leaders consciously sided with the "two ladies," either to resist Jiang's influence in the ministry, or as a consequence of accumulated grievances against Qiao. Whatever the reality, letters and material were passed to Mao *via* Jiang from February to April.[119]

The dangers of this approach were several. For Qiao and Zhang Hanzhi, they were seemingly being drawn more deeply into Jiang's social circle at Diaoyutai, perhaps being exposed to additional political machinations on those occasions.[120] But apart from the inherent dangers of association with Jiang Qing, another conundrum was how to handle the Deng Xiaoping issue which, of course, was an overriding priority for Jiang. This was not limited to the old cadres' side of the MFA conflict. Deng's daughter would many years later praise Wang Hairong and Tang Wensheng for being the last significant figures to visit Deng before

---

[119] "Zhang Hanzhi jiu Qiao Guanhua yu Jiang Qing de guanxi suoxie de jiaodai cailiao" [Zhang Hanzhi's Written Explanation Material concerning the Relations of Qiao Guanhua and Jiang Qing] (1976), in *CRDB*, p. 1; Ma Jisen, *The Cultural Revolution in the Foreign Ministry*, pp. 385-86; "Waijiaobu dangzu guanyu Qiao Guanhua de wenti qingshi baogao" [The MFA Party Group's Report Seeking Instructions on the Qiao Guanhua Question], *Zhanwang*, no. 361 (1997), p. 15; and interview with key MFA player in the events, November 2002. In the post-Mao wash-up, other MFA leaders claimed they had been "kept in the dark" by Qiao concerning this matter.

[120] According to a well-placed and reliable, but nevertheless second-hand source, Qiao and Zhang joined Jiang for movie nights during this period; interview, November 2002. These social occasions, however, may have started earlier, as suggested by Jiang's nomination of Qiao as a vice premier in late 1974.

the Tiananmen events, although any such visits probably ceased in January.[121] As for Qiao and senior cadres including Huang Zhen, Han Nianlong and Vice Minister Zhong Xidong, while Jiang sought information against Wang and Tang, she also pressed them to expose Deng and provide any information they may have gleaned concerning Mao's attitude to Deng when the Chairman received foreigners. Huang, Han and Zhong reportedly resisted such pressure to some extent; it may be that Qiao's "second great mistake" of involvement with Jiang Qing that Zhang Hanzhi acknowledged decades later included less resistance on this score.[122] In any case, the senior leadership of the MFA appeared to be more successful in retaining its authority and deflecting rebel criticism than their counterparts in other central ministries. But the perception that Qiao had been drawn into the "gang of four's" camp would result in his dismissal as Minister of Foreign Affairs as one of the first acts of the new leadership after the "gang's" arrest in October.

The conflict between Qiao and Zhang Hanzhi against the "two ladies" continued after Tiananmen; the dramatic developments affecting both sides are examined in Chapter 7. But a tentative judgment of the two sides, the surviving principals who remain strongly hostile to this day, can be offered here. From the perspective of post-Mao political probity, both sides made mistakes, particularly through actions inimical to Zhou Enlai and Deng Xiaoping. In this, however, they were caught by the circumstances of the time and the need to implement Mao's purpose—a factor particularly constraining on the "two ladies" given their liaison role. Qiao, in particular, may have gone further than necessary, notwithstanding Zhou's reported understanding of Qiao's predicament before his death—and both sides were heavily criticized after Mao's passing. Yet in the longer term they lived comfortable lives, including holding minor official positions. Whatever their faults and weaknesses, the ultimate judgment was that neither the "two ladies" nor Qiao and Zhang were followers of the "gang of four," they had all displayed a great deal of respect toward Zhou and other senior leaders, and their errors largely stemmed from following Mao's orders.[123]

---

[121] See Mao Mao, "Wenge" suiyue, p. 424. For her part, "Jiang Qing zai dazhaohu huiyi," p. 378, lumped the "two ladies" with Hu Qiaomu, Hu Yaobang and Li Jingquan as frequent visitors to Deng's home. A source unfriendly to the "two ladies," however, claims that Deng himself commented that he knew they played both sides; interview, November 2002.

[122] Zhang Hanzhi, Wo yu Qiao Guanhua, pp. 65-66. As Zhang Hanzhi was vague about the nature of this mistake, we can only speculate that Qiao and Zhang were less firm on the Deng question than others. However, one account of an exchange between Jiang and Zhang Hanzhi allegedly has Jiang pressing Zhang to go beyond exposing the "two ladies" and revealing Deng as the "backstage boss" in the MFA, but with Zhang attempting to avoid the issue on the grounds that the Center had not named Deng. See Qing and Fang, Deng zai 1976, vol. 1, p. 52.

[123] The summary here closely follows the assessment of a leading Party historian specializing on Mao and Zhou during this period; interview, December 2002. This assessment was echoed by a number of other historians interviewed in November-December 2002. It is further consistent with the previously discussed views of Qiao by post-Mao leaders; above, p. 226.

The Death of Zhou Enlai and a New Leadership Equation

In and of itself, the death of Zhou Enlai on January 8, 1976, was not a crucial development in the evolving power equation in the Chinese leadership. While, in Mao's words, "still our Premier," Zhou was not a central player in forces that rallied around Deng's consolidation efforts. In fact, it is difficult to assess Zhou's role after Deng took over as *de facto* premier following the Fourth NPC. Although chairing at least some Politburo Standing Committee meetings in the first half of 1975, playing a seemingly significant part in the maneuvers surrounding the criticism of the radicals in the spring and early summer, and throughout the year receiving senior leaders in his hospital quarters—old revolutionaries and radicals alike—being briefed on important developments, giving advice to Deng and others, and receiving foreign leaders,[124] there is little to indicate that Zhou exercised authority. Indeed, the *Water Margin* campaign indicated that he was as vulnerable as ever, even while Deng held Mao's trust. This, of course, was linked to Mao's attitude: the Chairman's preference for Deng, and his coolness toward the Premier as Zhou's life ebbed away. Throughout all this, Mao inflicted personal cruelties such as the virtual snubbing of Zhou during their last meeting at the Politburo in May 1975, and his failure to undertake the short trip from Zhongnanhai to the 305 Hospital to visit the Premier.[125] Clearly, Zhou's role in shaping political events had been exhausted well before he passed away.

Notwithstanding interpretations to the contrary,[126] Deng Xiaoping's fall was basically unrelated to Zhou's death, even if Mao only moved unambiguously

---

[124] For example, Philippine President Marcos in June, and a Romanian Communist Party delegation in September. *Zhou Enlai nianpu*, vol. 3, pp. 710, 719.

[125] See above, pp. 294-95. Mao's loyal secretary, Zhang Yufeng, tried to paint a very different picture of a "profound friendship" between Mao and Zhou, citing such unconvincing details as Mao's gift of a sofa and his reading of reports on the Premier's condition. In fact, she underlines the one-sidedness of the relationship by reporting how Zhou left his sickbed in August 1975 to attend in the anteroom while Mao was operated on for cataracts. See Zhang's "Anecdotes of Mao and Zhou," in FBIS-CHI-89-019, pp. 32, 35.

An opposite but also unsustainable view claims that both Mao and especially the "gang of four" participated in indifference bordering on physical persecution of the Premier over the last years of his life. See Gao Wenqian, *Wannian Zhou*, pp. 378, 509ff; and Yan and Gao, *Turbulent Decade*, p. 482. Apart from the additional physical strain placed on Zhou during the late 1973 Politburo criticism and the Lin Biao-Confucius campaign (see above, pp. 134, 160), there is little concrete evidence to back this up in the testimony of Zhou's medical staff and other sources. See Zhang Zuoliang, *Zhou Enlai de zuihou shinian*, pp. 277, 323, 327, 328, 345; and above, p. 250.

[126] The view advanced in, e.g., Teiwes, *Leadership*, pp. 74-75, that Zhou's presence may have provided a degree of protection for Deng is not credible given the information now available. It is plausible, however, that awareness of Zhou's impending death stayed Mao's hand given the inevitable public grief that would greet the Premier's passing. On the other hand, it is also plausible that the outpouring of public grief for the Premier and Mao's fears that this might be used to undercut criticism of Deng may have further stiffened the Chairman's determination to act against him. See Gao Wenqian, *Wannian Zhou Enlai*, pp. 591, 603. The basic point, however, is that Zhou's death simply interrupted a process that was well underway as Mao's attitude toward Deng hardened in November-December, and had little impact on the basic dynamic.

toward the end of January. Despite some mixed signals on the Chairman's part and wishful thinking by moderate leaders, Deng's situation worsened steadily since early November. Formal responsibility for foreign affairs, and seemingly even the Party Center at the start of 1976, could not hide the reality that Deng no longer had power or function. When Deng made a new self-criticism less than a week before Zhou's passing, Mao again brushed it aside and refused Deng's renewed plea for an audience. The Chairman may well have been uncertain of his final verdict on Deng—something which would only be crystallized by the unprecedented Tiananmen events in the spring—but there is nothing to suggest that as of early 1976 that he could play more than a supporting role in some new arrangement. What Zhou's death did do, once the domestic mourning and international attention subsided, was to clear the decks for a political campaign against the "rightist reversal of verdicts" that had been brewing since early December at the latest. And by creating a vacancy in the premier's position, Zhou's passing forced a personnel decision that would both confirm Deng's decline and define a new leadership equation.

Before these matters could unfold, Zhou's funeral and associated developments amounted to a major domestic and international event. Zhou was, after all, one of the most prominent and popular public faces of the regime. Whatever the complex reality of his actions during the Cultural Revolution, Zhou was widely perceived within the elite and by the *laobaixing*, China's ordinary people, as, in MacFarquhar's words, the embodiment of "rationality and restraint."[127] Internationally, Zhou had been key negotiator with the outside world for nearly all of the life of the People's Republic, and was seen as a critical figure in bringing about the startling reorientation of China's foreign policy in the 1970s, notwithstanding his virtual non-person status in recent diplomatic exchanges with the United States. Thus the outpouring of internal grief and foreign condolences was entirely to be expected. Given these factors, although there was contention over the arrangements (see below), in narrow formal terms the memorial activities provided all the respect the Premier was due, including a state funeral, massive publicity, and a nationwide moment of silence. One notable exception was the decision to reject foreign participation, normal in international practice for a head of government, even after some foreign leaders were setting out. In this the Politburo affirmed Mao's plan of "no invitations without exception."[128] Yet this could be interpreted as simply the appropriate way to honor an old revolutionary: eight months later foreign dignitaries were also excluded from Mao's memorial ceremony.

---

[127] MacFarquhar, "Succession," p. 297. For an argument that Zhou was at least as subservient as Lin Biao in backing Mao's demands during the Cultural Revolution, see Teiwes and Sun, *Tragedy*, *passim*. Of course, the question is whether Zhou (or for that matter Lin) had any option except, as Deng later asserted, to do things against his will in order to survive and exert a moderating influence. See *Selected Works of Deng (1975-1982)*, pp. 329-30.

[128] See Mao Mao, *"Wenge" suiyue*, pp. 439-40.

Despite the formal proprieties, and the essentially tangential impact on Deng's fate at best, the question of Zhou's funeral and associated activities became a major issue both within the elite and for the general public. As we shall see in further detail in Chapter 7, public dissatisfaction from the outset over the Premier's treatment, together with the sense that the Politburo radicals were to blame in some vaguely perceived struggle over his reputation, contributed to the developments that exploded on Tiananmen Square in April. In the period immediately following Zhou's death, attempts to place constraints on honoring him, most notoriously the poorly observed five no's—no black armbands, no wreaths, no mourning halls, no memorial meetings, and no handing out of photos of the Premier—caused great resentment, and the Party Center's decision to prohibit further displays of mourning following the memorial ceremony on January 15 only added to popular discontent. In the orthodox account, these developments were attributed to the "gang of four" who allegedly tried every means possible to limit publicity and public expressions of grief. This is at once exaggerated, true, and misleading. It is exaggerated in that, e.g., the "gang's" Shanghai base was fully mobilized to honor Zhou on the day of the memorial meeting, while media attention matched or exceeded in extent and duration the considerable attention that had been given to Kang Sheng following his death in December. It is true in that radicals did seek to dilute the attention to Zhou and shift it to the developing anti-rightist struggle. Thus, the day after Zhou's death at Qinghua, Chi Qun and Xie Jingyi asserted that the replacement of the old by the new should be seen as a victory of dialectics, and energy should be put into criticism of Deng. Particular anger was created by Yao Wenyuan's order to the *People's Daily* to reprint an article concerning the "rightist wind of reversals" in education on page one the day before Zhou's memorial service. As will become clear below, what is misleading is the focus on the "gang of four." In both their self restraint in view of public sentiment, and in their efforts to downplay the commemoration of Zhou, the Politburo radicals were basically reflecting Mao's attitude.[129]

While these developments undoubtedly caused tension within the Politburo, other matters required attention. In discussing arrangements for Zhou's memorial ceremony on the 15th, there was no controversy concerning the chairing of the meeting: as the ranking Party Vice Chairman, that task would fall to Wang Hongwen as it had at Kang Sheng's funeral three weeks earlier. On the earlier occasion, Ye Jianying, the next ranking Vice Chairman, had delivered the memorial speech; now Zhang Chunqiao proposed that Ye undertake the task again. Ye, however, demurred, and insisted that the speech be given by the next

---

[129] See Yan and Gao, *Turbulent Decade*, pp. 483-85; Roger Garside, *Coming Alive!: China after Mao* (New York: McGraw-Hill, 1981), pp. 7-13; and Mao Mao, *"Wenge" suiyue*, p. 441.

Concerning media attention, using *Renmin ribao suoyin 1946-1995* [Index to *People's Daily*, 1946-1995] (Beijing: Beijing Daxue tushuguan, 1996) [electronic resource] as an indicator, 183 articles commemorating Kang Sheng appeared between December 17 and January 9, while 311 articles on Zhou Enlai appeared between January 8 and February 23.

ranking Vice Chairman after himself—Deng Xiaoping. This arguably was meant to bolster Deng's position, and any arrangement would have to be approved by Mao, which it was. While logically a step against the interests of the radicals, there is little to indicate any strong resistance on their part. In the event, Deng's speech repeated the key slogan of "class struggle as the key link" that Ye had articulated at Kang Sheng's ceremony in full accord with the anti-rightist rhetoric of late 1975-early 1976, a slogan which had become a pointed expression of Mao's discontent with Deng.[130]

If this much was relatively straightforward, key issues remained: the historical assessment of the Premier and Mao's presence at the ceremony. These questions, as was well understood by high-ranking members of the leadership, would ultimately be determined by the Chairman and reflect his complicated view of Zhou. Despite the widespread elite view that the Premier should receive full honors, even leaders strongly critical of the Cultural Revolution were wary of Mao's feelings. With Xinhua compiling large volumes on the domestic and international reaction to Zhou's death on a daily basis, Vice Premier Wang Zhen, one of the leaders most hostile to the "gang of four," expressed uneasiness concerning Mao's reaction if these materials were sent to him for vetting. Still, there was hope that Mao would attend the Premier's service, much as he had done unexpectedly during another period of exceptionally poor health for Chen Yi in January 1972. According to one report, when the Politburo discussed the matter, Ye Jianying, Deng, Li Xiannian and Zhu De proposed asking Mao to attend, Jiang Qing, Zhang Chunqiao and Wang Dongxing opposed the suggestion, while Hua Guofeng, Ji Dengkui, Chen Xilian, Wu De, Wang Hongwen and Yao Wenyuan advocated leaving it to Mao to decide. Outside the Politburo, 40 marshals and generals reportedly proposed that Mao make a brief appearance at the funeral. In any case, Mao, who could be exceptionally emotional, reacted without emotion to the news of Zhou's passing. Zhang Yufeng tried to put the best face on this as due to exhaustion, but the tears did not flow as they had for other fallen comrades in recent years. Nor did Mao respond to her coaxing that he attend, and his only contribution to the praise of Zhou was to circle the official condolence document for the Premier—a reaction considered too weak by many. And when Zhang Yufeng herself considered attending Zhou's service, she was reminded by another of Mao's personal staff that her place was taking care of the Chairman. What is particularly striking in these developments is the apparent willingness of those who knew full well of Mao's attitude toward the Premier, and who—like Deng—had participated in sharp attacks on Zhou on the Chairman's demand, were now willing to attempt to prod him to attend and honor one of the most

---

[130] Mao Mao, *"Wenge" suiyue*, p. 443; *Mao wengao*, vol. 13, p. 515; and *PR*, no. 52 (1975), pp. 7-8, no. 4 (1976), pp. 5-8. After the arrest of the "gang of four," in contrast to Mao Mao's account, Hua Guofeng claimed that Zhang Chunqiao himself proposed that Deng give the memorial speech; "Hua Guofeng jiejian lingdao tongzhi jianghua," p. 2.

senior and prestigious contributors to the CCP's cause.[131]

Mao not only failed to contribute any personal praise to the assessment of the Premier, but on the contrary served to restrict the historical verdict on his achievements. Famously, Mao denied Zhou the status of a "great Marxist," and in the process zeroed in on the overriding issue of his last years: the Cultural Revolution. According to one report, when confronted with the request from the 40 marshals and generals to appear at the funeral, Mao observed that in asking him to attend, they were "imploring me to rethink the Cultural Revolution."[132] He further revealed his fixation on the Cultural Revolution in attacking the proposal to declare Zhou a great Marxist, expressing bitterness over Zhou's alleged opposition and influence over others in recent years: "The Premier opposed me over launching the Cultural Revolution, [and] not a small batch of veterans all listened to him [although] on the surface they supported me ... because there was nothing they could do about it. I clearly understand that there is no way to bridge the gap between me and the Premier." But the future was of even greater concern than past resentments, with Mao declaring that "mourning activities are in fact only a cover for restoration." So that no one could be uncertain of his attitude, he instructed Mao Yuanxin, his nephew and liaison officer, to convey this latter comment to the Politburo.[133]

Whatever Mao's feelings about Zhou, the focus of elite politics quickly returned to Deng. On the 20th, Deng submitted his third self-criticism and request for an audience. As previously indicated, the difference from the first two attempts was Deng's full recognition that the game was up, and he now produced a clear statement that he was unsuited to principal leadership work in view of

---

[131] *Deng Liqun guoshi jiangtan*, vol. 1, p. 396; Luo Bing, "Yao Wenyuan xie Mao Zedong neimu" [Yao Wenyuan Reveals the Inside Story of Mao Zedong] (December 19, 2003), http://www.ncn. org/asp/zwginfo/da.asp?ID=55956&ad=12/19/2003; "Zhang Yufeng jie Mao wannian mimi cailiao" [Zhang Yufeng Brings to Light Secret Materials on Mao's Later Years] (May 22, 2004), http://www. secretchina.com/new/articles/4/5/22/65524.html; and Zhang Yufeng, "Anecdotes on Mao and Zhou," in FBIS-CHI-89-017, pp. 17-18 and 89-019, pp. 35-36. According to a source who had personal contact with Mao in these years, he frequently broke into tears. In one instance in January 1975, when Mao prepared to receive a foreign visitor, his staff withheld news of Li Fuchun's death for fear that he would be unable to maintain his composure, and once informed he did indeed cry. Interview, November 2002. Cf. above, p. 32.

Several of the claims here, specifically concerning the views expressed in the Politburo and the proposal of the 40 senior PLA officers, cannot be fully verified. In the case of the PLA leaders, a senior Party historian denies that any such proposal existed; interview, January 2005. On balance, however, the claims, if not precisely accurate, credibly reflect significant sentiment within the high-ranking elite. See also below, n. 133, concerning a key source on the events.

[132] "Zhang Yufeng jie Mao wannian mimi cailiao." Cf. above, n. 131.

[133] Gao Wenqian, *Wannian Zhou Enlai*, pp. 601-604. Of course, Zhou's "opposition" was marked by the same ostensible support as that shown by others. Gao, as a former deputy head of the Zhou Enlai section of the Central Documents Research Office, had access to many sensitive materials, although his book is poorly referenced, making it difficult to be completely certain of his specific claims. We are, however, satisfied concerning the general validity of what is presented here. Cf. the discussion of Gao's work in the Preface, above, pp. xvii-xviii.

his fundamentally incorrect standpoint. The next day, Mao declared Deng was an internal contradiction, should be dealt with on the rectification principle of "curing the illness to save the patient," and still had useful work to perform. It was also about this time, although perhaps a week later, that Mao rejected Jiang Qing's claim, and Deng's forced admission, that Deng had sought to kick the Chairman upstairs. But the issue had become who would assume Zhou's position and Deng's leadership role, at least as far as the State Council was concerned. Mao Yuanxin not only understood this, but he undoubtedly had some inkling of the Chairman's thinking when he asked which of three vice premiers—Hua Guofeng, Ji Dengkui or Chen Xilian—should take over. This list excluded both Zhang Chunqiao, the only radical vice premier, and Li Xiannian, the third-ranking vice premier who was in charge of State Council daily work along with Hua and Ji, and an old revolutionary. Mao reportedly replied, "then ask Hua Guofeng to take charge. He's someone who believes his political level is not high. Xiaoping will take charge of foreign affairs only." The final comment was empty in the sense that Deng's foreign policy role had withered to virtually nothing by the end of 1975, but still significant by implying that Deng could assist Hua in an area where Hua had virtually no experience. In a week's time, Mao confirmed his choice of Hua, and it was quickly endorsed by the Politburo.[134]

Relatively little is known about the process leading to the choice of Hua. Given the small number of people involved, and the sparse discussion of the Mao-centered events in authoritative sources, conflicting claims are hard to assess, and, however plausible, views on the reasons for Mao's decision are ultimately speculation. Contrary to some assessments,[135] the one thing that is certain is that the decision was entirely Mao's own. The Politburo, as on all other matters, simply ratified the Chairman's diktat. This did not, of course, mean that Mao was oblivious to opinion in the Politburo or the broader elite. With his own life ebbing away, he had to be concerned with the viability of his choice for a future in which he would no longer be present. In this restricted sense, the choice of Hua can be considered a compromise; in the view of a senior Party historian, Mao had no choice (meiyou banfa) but to select Hua as someone acceptable to both sides if he wanted a semblance of unity. Yet this did not mean that Hua was the only option. Leaving aside Ji Dengkui, another favored establishment beneficiary of the Cultural Revolution, but one who may have been too forceful in pushing Deng's agenda for the radicals' taste, Li Xiannian was an obvious alternative. In addition to being bureaucratically next in line—and as such suggested by Hua, Ji and Chen Xilian, Li was someone clearly acceptable to old revolutionaries and reportedly nominated by Ye Jianying, and also someone who arguably had

---

[134] Mao zhuan, vol. 2, p. 1766; Mao Mao, "Wenge" suiyue, pp. 446-49, 451-52; and above, p. 415. Chen Xilian, as a military man, was clearly an unlikely choice. The remaining vice premier who also had Politburo status was Chen Yonggui.

[135] See, for example, Dittmer's claim in China's Continuous Revolution, p. 130, that with the Politburo deadlocked, Hua emerged as a compromise candidate.

toed the radical line sufficiently to be somewhat attractive to the other side. The reaction of the leading local Shanghai radical was revealing in this respect. Ma Tianshui, Zhang Chunqiao's Shanghai supporter, later confessed that although he had strongly favored Zhang, he realized Zhang was not suited to the role given his administrative deficiencies, and, after taking seniority into account like the three vice premiers, felt Li was "the next ideal person." Ma was shocked when Hua's was announced, but, upon reflection, thought it was not a bad idea since Hua represented the middle.[136]

One potential key to the outcome lay with the people with access to the Chairman, and thus in a position to influence him, a group ever more restricted with his deteriorating health. As suggested by the exchange on January 21, undoubtedly most important among them was Mao Yuanxin, given his liaison role and ability to report, and perhaps distort, developments in the Politburo. Undoubtedly others in the immediate household also had the opportunity for input, with Zhongnanhai security chief and Politburo member Wang Dongxing probably the most significant. An important unknown is precisely what access Jiang Qing had in this crucial period. While there is no concrete evidence of Jiang having a role in the consideration of alternatives, well-placed Party historians believe her access to Mao was significantly greater than they previously believed.[137]

While the evidence is sketchy, what is known, or seemingly known, about attempts to influence Mao and the Chairman's reactions? Although Li Xiannian's promotion would have both provided administrative experience and economic expertise, as well as acknowledging the broad elite preference for revolutionary status, Ye Jianying's proposal that Li be named premier was reportedly deflected by the Chairman. The more indirect suggestion of Hua, Ji and Chen Xilian that they could handle concrete work, but a "main responsible person" (i.e., Li) was needed to oversee the State Council, was also ignored, with Mao instead responding by naming Hua. The Chairman's unwillingness to countenance Li probably reflected his assessment of Li's personal qualities and political orientation, his general discontent with the lukewarm attitude of old revolutionaries toward the Cultural Revolution, and his desire to blood younger leaders for the long haul. In contrast to his fluctuating admiration of Deng, Mao viewed Li as soft politically. The fact that of all Politburo members Li had been closest to Zhou Enlai arguably also counted against him with Mao,

---

[136] "Ma Tianshui de buchong jiefa jiaodai," p. 4; Qing and Fang, *Deng zai 1976*, vol. 1, pp. 43, 46; and interview, January 2005. Ma's support of Li, which apparently led him to consider writing to Mao's proposing Li's appointment, caused conflict with Xu Jingxian and Wang Xiuzhen who presumably favored Zhang's elevation. "Xu Jingxian de chubu jiefa jiaodai," p. 7. The available versions of Ma's and Xu's confessions delete Li's name, but they clearly were referring to him.

[137] This view was expressed in an interview with two such historians in December 2002. Corroborative evidence can be seen in Jiang's claims made to Zhang Hanzhi that her relations with Mao had improved significantly since mid-1975, and that she had seen Zhang and Qiao's letter "at the Chairman's place." See above, p. 433.

notwithstanding Li's propensity for supporting radical policies when required. And, by January at the latest, the Chairman pointedly criticized "old comrades whose thinking is still mired at the stage of the bourgeois democratic revolution," a view he seemed to believe applied to Li.[138]

If a choice from the ranks of the old revolutionaries was unacceptable, what about a radical? Logically, Zhang Chunqiao was a strong possibility, not only given his State Council position, but due to the fact that, as early as 1969, he had been viewed by Mao as a possible successor. Compared to other possible candidates such as Hua and Ji, Zhang had much stronger credentials in theory and as a Cultural Revolution advocate, the very area where Deng fell short in the Chairman's eyes. The strong indications are that the radicals had hopes that Zhang would be named, and that at the same time Wang Hongwen would resume his responsibility for the work of the Party Center. Indeed, there were signs of concerted efforts to promote Zhang's cause as wall posters proposing him as the new premier quickly appeared in Shanghai after Zhou's death. Beyond that, the radicals assertedly prepared to undermine other contenders by gathering speeches by eight vice premiers to the 1975 State Council theory conference, i.e., including possible candidates Hua and Ji, which could be criticized from the current anti-rightist perspective. The wall posters, at least, earned Mao's displeasure, and on his instruction Zhang Chunqiao ordered the painting over of the Shanghai slogans.[139]

Mao's reaction to such maneuvers notwithstanding, the evidence suggests he regarded Zhang as a serious possibility, and perhaps the candidate he would have favored without the consideration of Party unity. Moreover, in his subsequent confessions, Mao Yuanxin claimed an important role in his uncle's decision to bypass Zhang. Combining information from Party historians familiar with Mao Yuanxin's confessions, together with a brief discussion in his uncle's official biography, a sketchy picture emerges of the Chairman's interest in Zhang, Mao Yuanxin's (and Wang Dongxing's) opposition, and the selection of Hua. One well-placed historian claimed that the Chairman had raised, in a casual manner,

---

[138] See Qing and Fang, *Deng zai 1976*, vol. 1, pp. 43, 46; Chen and Du, *Shilu*, vol. 3, part 2, p. 1321; *Mao wengao*, vol. 13, p. 487; and above, p. 37n34. Mao's observation concerning old comrades could have been made as early as October as part of his "important directives." One such observation concerning the failure to understand what was required after socialist transformation appears to have been in part targeted at Li, or at least Li perceived it necessary to make a self-criticism on this point. Qing and Fang, p. 112.

[139] See Wang Nianyi, *Dadongluan*, pp. 387-88; Yan and Gao, *Turbulent Decade*, pp. 485-86; *RMRB*, November 7, 1976, in *SPRCP*, no. 6220 (1976), p. 68; "Hua Guofeng jiejian lingdao tongzhi jianghua," p. 1; "Wang Dongxing xuanchuan gongzuo jianghua" p. 1; Wu De, "Guanyu fensui 'sirenbang'," p. 53; and "Xu Jingxian de chubu jiefa jiaodai," p. 2.

The Shanghai wall poster question again illustrates the fractured communication and lack of cohesion within the radical "camp." Zhang Chunqiao revealed Mao's attitude to Ma Tianshui at the time, but Ma never relayed Zhang's message to his Shanghai colleagues Xu Jingxian and Wang Xiuzhen, who only learned of the matter in September.

Zhang's name within his immediate household, but Mao Yuanxin objected on the grounds that Zhang was not upright, and Wang Dongxing also indicated opposition. While there apparently was no love lost for Zhang, this historian believes Mao Yuanxin's reasoning was more complex, reflecting a calculation that Zhang, and also Jiang Qing, had made too many enemies to survive. How much influence the views of Mao Yuanxin and Wang Dongxing had on the Chairman is unknowable, but he obviously decided to look elsewhere. Perhaps the most plausible explanation of the Chairman's decision was offered by another senior Party historian: while Zhang would have been canvassed as a possibility, Mao was after all a politician who understood that Zhang would be seriously undermined by his lack of respect within the elite. Moreover, Mao knew that Zhang also lacked the broad administrative experience necessary to run a large country, that he was a man of talk rather than action. The Chairman, however, still held Zhang in high esteem, and sent Mao Yuanxin to Zhang and Wang Hongwen to convey his choice of Hua, ask them to give way and support Hua, support which was immediately offered, and, in at least one version, to console Zhang that his time might yet come. According to Mao's biography, once having decided against Zhang on January 21, the Chairman counted off the remaining Politburo members on his fingers before declaring that Hua was comparatively the best, and should be asked to take the job even though he [Hua] didn't think his political standard was high.[140]

With Zhang Chunqiao passed over, and old revolutionaries apparently not considered, the choice effectively, we presume, was between Hua Guofeng and Ji Dengkui. But apart from the fact that Mao Yuanxin mentioned Ji together with Hua, and the unsuited Chen Xilian, as a possible premier, there is virtually no evidence to suggest that Ji was in fact given serious consideration—something of a surprise given that Ji outranked Hua as a vice premier, and seemed to have better theoretical credentials than Hua.[141] In any case, Hua was chosen on January 21, confirmed by Mao on the 28th, and announced to the Party on February 2. The question remains why? Mao's stated reasons, focusing on Hua's honesty and modesty, tell us little except that Hua was unlikely to have many enemies in the non-radical part of the elite, and perhaps even among the Politburo radicals. One line of speculation, adopting a cynical interpretation of Mao's motives, is that

---

[140] *Mao zhuan*, pp. 1766-68; Qing and Fang, *Deng zai 1976*, vol. 1, p. 47; and interviews with Party historians, October 1994 and November-December 2002. According to Zhang, the Chairman also conveyed his wishes to Zhang personally. "Xu Jingxian de chubu jiefa jiaodai," p. 2.

Mao Yuanxin reportedly also argued against Zhang in the context of naming a successor after the Tiananmen incident, and there is some possibility of the two cases being conflated in the discussion here. See below, p. 496.

[141] See above, p. 348n124, on Ji's apparent theoretical credentials. A possible explanation of the apparent lesser consideration of Ji was his sometimes abrasive relations with Jiang Qing, and especially his heavy involvement in Deng's organizational rectification in 1975. This latter factor was unlikely to have earned him any support from Mao Yuanxin in particular. See above, pp. 225-26n97, 274ff, 343-47.

he saw Hua as merely a short-term stopgap, someone who was not particularly capable but was obedient, and could pave the way for a full-scale radical takeover, in one version with Hua serving under Jiang Qing as Party leader.[142] A more persuasive view is that Mao would have expected Hua, as a beneficiary of the Cultural Revolution, to uphold his basic political line and, in the process, protect the position of the "gang of four."[143] Beyond that, it is plausible, as widely believed in Party history circles, that the Chairman hoped Hua would eventually be succeeded by his nephew, Mao Yuanxin.[144]

Whatever his long-range hopes for his nephew, Mao would certainly have banked on Hua's political loyalty. Our interpretation, however, emphasizes several additional factors. Perhaps most important was the Chairman's hope that, as someone who "does not engage in plots or factionalism," Hua could help unify the Party. This, as events would soon demonstrate, was a delusion, much as Mao's earlier hope that Deng and the radicals could provide a sustainable political balance had proven, but the objective had been and remained a major consideration for the Chairman. Another undoubted critical factor, one for which explicit evidence exists in the context of Hua's further elevation in April following the Tiananmen incident, was that Hua could provide the generalist administrative experience that Zhang could not: he had served at all levels of the regime and had accumulated hands-on experience in working with the masses at the grass roots, as well as in running a large province and being responsible for crucial State Council functions.[145] Perhaps the great irony was that in selecting Hua the Chairman was choosing someone who had not simply played a key role in Deng's consolidation efforts, but who actually had a profile reminiscent of Deng. While lacking Deng's revolutionary credentials, deep experience at the Center, and, or so it seemed, a tough, decisive personality, Hua like Deng was essentially a man of practical works, someone aware of the theoretical line and concerned with staying within it, but ultimately most comfortable with the concrete tasks of building a stronger China.

The one missing thing in Hua's credentials was theoretical accomplishment, but even here the situation was not entirely clear-cut. All important was Mao's evaluation, and this can be read several ways. Clearly, although impressed with Hua since the mid-1950s, the Chairman felt he needed more than administrative capabilities. As Mao put it in 1971, Hua needed to develop his "political nose." That the Chairman saw positive signs in this regard was evident from his

---

[142] This view was put particularly strongly by a Party historian in an interview, December 2002, and has been advanced in different variants in interviews over the years. The problem with such interpretations positing Mao's dismissive view of Hua is both that Mao had been cultivating Hua as a future leader for years, and that when the Tiananmen crisis exploded in April the Chairman unambiguously made Hua his successor.

[143] See MacFarquhar, "Succession," p. 298.

[144] See above, p. 387; and below, p. 496.

[145] See below, p. 493.

important political assignments in investigating the Lin Biao affair and asserting control over the MAC immediately after the September 13 incident, and in his 1975 appointment as Minister of Public Security. On the narrower question of theoretical abilities, despite declaring at the time of Hua's appointment as Acting Premier that his "standard is not high," according to one report, Mao also saw signs of improvement in his theoretical efforts.[146] Nevertheless, it was clear that Hua's theoretical sophistication fell far short of Zhang Chunqiao's, and Mao's reference to Hua's "standard" implied that Zhang was still needed to supplement and assist Hua.

Although now the most prominent official of the regime after Mao himself, Hua's selection as *Acting* Premier was hardly decisive. Not only was Hua's new status in the State Council not a full appointment, but in other respects he clearly fell well short of Deng's previous positions. Hua's formal Party status was not elevated: he neither became a vice chairman as Deng had at the time of assuming the *de facto* premiership in January 1975, nor was he elevated to the Politburo Standing Committee. Thus in nominal terms, he was outranked by not only Vice Chairman Wang Hongwen and Standing Committee member Zhang Chunqiao, but, if the Politburo pecking order had not changed since Zhou's memorial service, by five full members including Jiang Qing and Yao Wenyuan. Nor did Hua assume *any* military role, again in sharp contrast to Deng who had become both PLA Chief-of-Staff and MAC Vice Chairman at the time of the Fourth NPC. Thus, at least in terms of formal positions, he had no authority in an area where MAC Standing Committee members Wang Hongwen and Zhang Chunqiao had significant clout, clout which Wang at least exercised in the following months (see below). In any case, Document no. 1 (1976), which announced Hua's appointment, also conferred responsibility for the daily work of the MAC on Chen Xilian in place of Ye Jianying who went on sick leave. In this decision, where Mao Yuanxin reportedly supported Chen, the Chairman again went against the interests of the Politburo radicals. While there were proposals that Wang Hongwen and/or Zhang Chunqiao assume responsibility, Mao placed question marks on their names, instead opting for Chen as someone with battlefield experience.[147]

---

[146] Wen Xiang, "Mao Zedong wannian de chongchen—Hua Guofeng" [Mao Zedong's Favorite Official in His Later Years—Hua Guofeng] (July 16, 2005), http://www.ncn.org/asp/zwginfo/da.a sp?ID=64834&ad=7/16/2005; and above, pp. 37-38. Wen Xiang claims that Mao was impressed with both Hua's report to the Dazhai conference, and a talk criticizing Deng for failing to praise the Cultural Revolution. Wen does not specify the timing of the criticism of Deng, which conceivably came after Hua's promotion, but it presumably was sometime in early 1976.

[147] Chen and Du, *Shilu*, vol. 3, part 2, p. 1324; "Zhongyang lingdaoren guanyu sirenbang wenti de jianghua," p. 1; and interview with Party historian familiar with Mao Yuanxin's file, November 2002. In this case, Mao Yuanxin was arguably influenced by Chen's careful (even slavish) treatment of him when they both served in the Northeast. See above, p. 378n206. The general question of the relationship of Chen and Mao Yuanxin, and its connection to Chen's fall in the post-Mao period, will be examined in our Volume II.

Apart from the specific decisions of Document no. 1, much is unclear about the new leadership equation that emerged at this time. Chen Xilian's MAC appointment was murky in several senses. Some anecdotal evidence suggests that Chen was already in charge of daily work in fall 1975 when Ye Jianying . was coming under pressure.[148] Well-placed oral sources, moreover, claim that Ye himself proposed Chen for the job, Chen was very reluctant to take up the post, leading Wang Dongxing to ask whether he wanted to "let them [Wang and Zhang] be in charge," and that in the event Chen remained deferential toward Ye and sought his counsel.[149] In any case, the evidence suggests that although Ye (like Li Xiannian, who similarly went on sick leave in early March) may have had some slight health problems and took the initiative to ask to be relieved of duty, the illness was fundamentally political, and Ye (and Li) were simply brushed aside as attacks on old revolutionaries as mere "democrats" escalated.[150] With Deng's Chief-of-Staff position vacant, and the most senior revolutionaries sidelined in the PLA structure, military power essentially fell to lower-ranking veterans of the armed struggle, veterans who would surely side with their former superiors in any showdown with the radicals.

The most confusing situation concerned the Party, with the formal pecking order remaining confused,[151] even though Hua has been variously reported in authoritative sources as placed in charge of the Politburo and the Party Center by Mao in his comments on January 21 and 28 respectively. The former clearly was the case, but the latter is more problematic. According to one specialist on the period, there is no available archival evidence that Deng was stripped of formal responsibility for the daily work of the Center prior to the Tiananmen events. As we have seen, when Deng tried to pass authority back to Wang Hongwen after Wang returned to Beijing in November, Mao rejected the request, although it is

---

[148] "Zhongyang lingdaoren guanyu sirenbang wenti de jianghua," p. 1; interview with Party historian, December 2002; and above, p. 404. That Ye was still at least formally in charge at the end of 1975, however, is indicated by his December letter to Mao on a military matter; *Mao wengao*, vol. 13, p. 512.

[149] Interviews with oral sources with access to key players, July 1997, July 1999 and December 2002. Cf. Qing and Fang, *Deng zai 1976*, vol. 1, p. 57.

[150] Well-placed oral sources report that both Ye and Li had mild heart problems, and that at least Ye proposed his own rest period. All tend to agree, however, that the real problem was political. Interviews, April 1986, July 1999, February 2000 and December 2002. For the decision which saw Li replaced by NPC Standing Committee Vice Chairman Li Suwen, a former vegetable seller, as the person in charge of finance and foreign economic relations, see Chen and Du, *Shilu*, vol. 3, part 2, p. 1335.

Regarding Li Xiannian, this may be another case where his actual power was in decline well before he went on sick leave. According to one source, Li Suwen had already replaced him as head of the Party Center's finance and economics work in late November 1975; *Mao wengao*, vol. 13, p. 496. See also *Deng Liqun zishu*, p. 74.

[151] This situation continued right up to the April 7 decision appointing Hua CCP First Vice Chairman. Throughout February and March, Hua, Wang Hongwen and Zhang Chunqiao never appeared together in public, thus avoiding the need to list them in rank order. Cf. below, p. 478.

plausible that Wang resumed some of these duties on a *de facto* basis, despite the claim in Mao's biography that Wang never again held responsibility for Party Center work after heading south in mid-1975. On January 31, at any rate, halfway between Mao's formal decision to appoint Hua Acting Premier and the official Party notice affirming the fact, Wang drafted a speech on behalf of the Center. Document no. 1, moreover, seemingly made no mention of Party responsibilities. It appears that, although the leadership generally interpreted Hua's promotion as involving a substantial degree of authority at the Party Center, this was not clearly spelled out perhaps as a consequence of Mao's illness, but arguably because the Chairman wanted to assess Hua's performance before fully formalizing arrangements. To this end, and apparently because he believed Hua capable of providing a degree of unity, Mao placed Hua in charge of the critical Party task of the moment—the *pi Deng* campaign (see below). Hua's authority was thus bolstered but still unclear, and he very much remained on trial.[152]

As a result of this lack of clarity, a messy situation existed over the following two months. One indication was the post-Mao accusation that the radicals addressed their official reports to Wang rather than Hua; another was their alleged complaints over being excluded when foreign guests were received, since they outranked Hua who was neither a Party vice chairman nor a Standing Committee member.[153] Moreover, while Hua as a rule presided at Politburo meetings from the time he became Acting Premier, Wang Hongwen nevertheless chaired important meetings, such as the warning meeting on February 14 when Hua was forced to defend himself over his report to the Dazhai conference.[154] Wang was also active in the affairs of the Central Organization Department, the area of Ji Dengkui's responsibility. As examined in more detail in Chapter 7, in March he criticized the department for carrying out Deng's revisionist line.[155] Meanwhile, although apparently less authoritative than Chen Xilian, Wang was active in military affairs, calling for a change in the air force leadership in early 1976, criticizing Marshal Nie Rongzhen (although reportedly less strongly than "a responsible comrade of the MAC"—presumably Chen Xilian) at an MAC report meeting in March for interfering in the anti-rightist movement in military-related institutions, and chairing various meetings on military matters during the period.[156] Beyond the lack of clarity concerning authority, the basic contradiction

---

[152] *Mao zhuan*, vol. 2, pp. 1737, 1766-67; Chen and Du, *Shilu*, vol. 3, part 2, p. 1324; Ma Qibin, *Sishinian*, p. 396; Mao Mao, *"Wenge" suiyue*, p. 450; and interview, November 2002. Concerning Document no. 1, responsibility for the Center's daily work is not included in available versions of the document. Moreover, when addressing the background to Document no. 1, *Mao wengao*, vol. 13, pp. 518-19, made no mention of this matter.

[153] See "Wang Dongxing zai quanguo xuanchuan gongzuo jianghua," p. 2; and "Hua Guofeng, Ye Jianying deng jiejian Shanghai Ma Tianshui dengren de jianghua," p. 1.

[154] Qing and Fang, *Deng zai 1976*, vol. 1, pp. 82-87.

[155] Wang and Sun, "Dang zuzhi zhengdun," p. 43; and below, p. 513.

[156] See Zhang Tingfa, "70 niandai zhongqi liangci Junwei huiyi de qian qian hou hou," p. 66;

between Mao's radical goals and less than radical leaders, similar to the underlying tension throughout the post-Lin Biao period, deepened. The Chairman now endorsed a new campaign that attacked much of what he had endorsed in 1975, with the Center deciding on January 31 to convene a (seemingly ongoing) "criticize Deng, beat back the wind of rightist reversal" warning meeting.[157] But at the same time, Mao placed effective power, certainly in the government and army, predominantly in the hands of leaders who had been identified with Deng's project and/or had ties of historical loyalty to him. While Hua and Chen lacked the experience and prestige of Deng and Ye, they represented the same Party establishment, and, in the broadest sense, the same approach to China's future.

Intensifying Attacks: February-March 1976

By the start of February a number of key matters had been clarified: Deng would be thoroughly marginalized within the leadership while younger establishment figures assumed key posts, the anti-rightist themes that had emerged since the previous fall would be deepened by a systematic effort to oppose the "rightist wind of reversing verdicts," various radical activities such as collecting incriminating material, developing critiques, and reinvigorating factional links that had surfaced in January now had new scope to develop, and the emerging mobilization carried with it the potential to disrupt official organizations throughout the country. Important benchmarks included: opening up another front of criticism (after education) with the "the second heavy artillery attack" targeting science and technology in *Red Flag* on February 1; takeovers of troubled ministries by new "temporary leading groups" (*linshi lingdao xiaozu*) by the latter part of February; the convening of a warning meeting of provincial and military region leaders on February 25, which extended criticism of Deng beyond the Politburo to a forum of key local leaders; the issuing of a central document on March 3 compiling "Chairman Mao's important instructions" criticizing Deng since October (albeit without naming him); and, by early March, the formal launching of the criticize Deng campaign throughout the Party, naming him in internal discussions, and shifting the rhetorical focus from "rightist reversal" to "that unrepentant capitalist roader."[158]

Mao Mao, *"Wenge" suiyue*, pp. 457-58; Hu Shihong, *Zhang Aiping zai 1975*, pp. 284-88; and *Nie Rongzhen nianpu*, vol. 2, pp. 1131-32. Another indication of Wang Hongwen's clout in the PLA occurred in January-February when General Yang Yong's associates warned Yang against preparing materials on the militia for fear of offending Wang. Yang Qing, *Huiyi Yang Yong*, pp. 331-32. Jiang Qing, although lacking military posts and speaking in a non-MAC forum, also brought pressure on the air force leadership; "Jiang Qing zai dazhaohu huiyi," p. 382. Chen Xilian, however, apparently exercised MAC authority, as in granting Nie's request for sick leave in early April. Chen's criticism of Nie was arguably another source of suspicion of him both immediately after Mao's death and in the following post-Mao period. On Chen Xilian, see above, p. 378n206; and below, p. 549.

[157] Mao Mao, *"Wenge" suiyue*, p. 450.

[158] See *HQ*, no. 2 (1976), in *SPRCM*, no. 859 (1976), pp. 2-12; Chen and Du, *Shilu*, vol. 3, part 2, p. 1323ff; *Mao wengao*, vol. 13, pp. 490-91; Mao Mao, *"Wenge" suiyue*, p. 453; *A Great Trial*, pp.

Yet uncertainties and important questions remained apart from the ambiguities surrounding leadership authority. As reflected in the conversation between Deng and Ye Jianying around this time cited at the start of this chapter, the question concerning Deng personally was whether he would be "criticized and protected," or "pushed off the political stage." Even when Jiang Qing spoke of Deng as a traitor in early March, she acknowledged that Mao was still protecting him. In this period Deng could be named, but only in documents issued to the county and PLA regiment levels, and not in the media. It was only at the start of April, in the context of the Nanjing incident (see Chapter 7), that the Politburo recommended transmitting the Chairman's "important instructions" critical of Deng more widely to Party branches.[159] More broadly, what degree of disruption would be tolerated, both within official organizations and in society, as public and internal rhetoric heated up? Which 1975 policies were still in effect, even as Deng was criticized? For example, PLA cadres must have been perplexed by the February 16 central document affirming the military readjustment measures of the previous summer's MAC conference, while at the same time withdrawing from study the speeches of Deng and Ye to that conference which advocated those measures.[160] In addition, major dilemmas faced the key players. How would Hua and other establishment beneficiaries manage the fraught task of pursuing the anti-Deng campaign to Mao's satisfaction, while keeping things under control? As for the radicals, while in our view any lasting alliance with Hua was beyond their grasp,[161] they still had choices as to how hard to push the campaign against Deng, and whether or not to seek some sort of *modus vivendi* with Hua and others. Finally, perhaps the greatest uncertainty concerned Mao himself. With the Chairman's health in accelerated decline,[162] his grip on proceedings appeared more problematic than ever before. There was no doubt about Mao's continuing authority, but in contrast to November when he micromanaged the evolving criticism of Deng, initiative now often seemed to drift into the hands of others.

172-73, 181, 225; and Yan and Gao, *Turbulent Decade*, pp. 485-88. The use of "unrepentant capitalist roader" first appeared in mid-February, but it became dominant after Hua's February 25 speech to the warning meeting of provincial and military region leaders. Both "reversal of verdicts" and "unrepentant capitalist roader" clearly pointed to Deng in any case, although the latter was arguably more severe. Regarding temporary leadership groups, according to Zhang Guangyou, *Gaige fengyun zhong de Wan Li* [Wan Li in the Reform Storm] (Beijing: Renmin chubanshe, 1995), p. 71, such a group was already operating in the Ministry of Railways by January 21.

[159] See "Jiang Qing zai dazhaohu huiyi," p. 380; *Mao wengao*, vol. 13, p. 453; and Chen and Du, *Shilu*, vol. 3, part 2, p. 1356.

[160] See Chen and Du, *Shilu*, vol. 3, part 2, pp. 1328-29.

[161] See MacFarquhar, "Succession," pp. 299-300, for the contrary view that the Politburo radicals and Hua were potential allies who were both threatened by Deng, but the possible alliance was scuttled by the political ineptitude of the "gang."

[162] See above, p. 387n12, for sources concerning a worsening of Mao's health about January. Also, according to Mao Mao, *"Wenge" suiyue*, p. 452, the Chairman's condition had already taken a major change for the worse by February.

How did the Politburo radicals react to Hua's appointment? While some disappointment would have been natural, particularly on Zhang Chunqiao's part, after the arrest of the "gang" the new leadership went to great lengths to portray deep hostility and opposition toward the newly selected Acting Premier. Two pieces of "evidence" were most frequently cited. The first, a diary entry by Zhang Chunqiao on February 3, referred to the formal decision of the previous day: "Here is another Document no. 1. There was one last year too. The more they achieve, the more unrestrained they become. But the faster and more ferociously they come, the quicker their downfall." The second proof was the publication, in the *People's Daily* on February 24, of a new article by the *Liang Xiao* writing group on "Confucius the man," a piece allegedly attacking Hua. In draft form, this article contained references to Confucius' positions as both Minister of Justice (said to equate to Hua's position as Minister of Public Security) and Acting Prime Minister, references cited as clear evidence of the radicals' intent to attack Hua.[163]

Neither of these matters is convincing as an indication of opposition to Hua. The article on Confucius in all likelihood had been prepared at the "two schools" in January, before anyone could have known of Hua's surprising promotion. Moreover, the references to Confucius' positions were standard in earlier allegorical writings, as in a January 1974 *People's Daily* article on the eve of the Lin Biao-Confucius campaign in which the target was Zhou Enlai, who had been neither Minister of Public Security nor Acting Prime Minister. When the article was considered following Hua's appointment, Yao Wenyuan ordered these references deleted—thus clearly and intentionally eliminating any easy connection between Confucius and Hua.[164] As for Zhang Chunqiao's diary entry, a strict textual reading strongly suggests that it was a reflection on Deng, who rose rapidly in 1973-74, had now fallen precipitously in late 1975-early 1976, and who was doomed to fail for pursuing a mistaken line, rather than distress at Hua's rise or an expression of determination to bring about his downfall.[165]

In the event, the Politburo radicals fell quickly into line behind Mao's selection of Hua. This involved more than simply offering support for the Chairman's decision, as Zhang and Wang Hongwen did when informed by Mao Yuanxin.

---

[163] See Chen and Du, *Shilu*, vol. 3, part 2, pp. 1324, 1330; NCNA, Beijing, December 13, 1976, in *SPRCP*, no. 6244 (1976), pp. 69-70; and *RMRB*, December 30, 1976, in *SPRCP*, no. 6261 (1977), pp. 68-70.

[164] See Yan and Gao, *Turbulent Decade*, p. 438; "Zhonggong zhongyang guanyu 'Wang Hongwen, Zhang Chunqiao, Jiang Qing, Yao Wenyuan fandang jituan zuizheng (cailiao zhi san)'," pp. 18-19; and *RMRB*, December 30, 1976, in *SPRCP*, no. 6261 (1977), p. 70. Other post-Mao claims that the radicals used allegorical attacks to liken Hua to Song Jiang, Yuan Shikai and other "disreputable" figures in Chinese history are equally dubious. See *GMRB*, March 17, 1977, in *SPRCP*, no. 6330 (1977), p. 12.

[165] When questioned on this issue, a senior Party historian argued that Zhang's diary entry could have reflected both delight at Deng's fall and disappointment over Hua's appointment. Interview, January 2005.

It also involved some of the strongest vocal support of Hua's elevation, and an apparent effort to assist Hua in his new role. At least, when asked to come to Shanghai by his local supporters later in February, Zhang declined on the grounds that Hua had just taken up his duties and needed help, and he (Zhang) would stay in Beijing to provide support. Zhang's action adhered to Mao's instruction to assist Hua, specifically by providing the kind of theoretical expertise the Chairman felt Hua lacked. This, of course, did not mean the absence of conflict. In addition to the inevitable problems caused by varying interpretations of the new campaign (see below), such matters as Jiang Qing's (accurate) charge at the February 14 meeting that Hua's Dazhai report reflected Deng's views, or her March 2 criticism of Zhang Pinghua, and thus the Hunan leadership that Hua formally led, over the *Song of the Gardener*, as well as the ongoing "second heavy artillery attack" on science and technology which targeted a key area of Hua's responsibility in 1975, could only heighten tension. There were also background factors in that during the period preceding Hua's promotion, his speeches to the summer 1975 State Council theory conference were among those of the eight vice premiers being collected as evidence of rightist errors, and in Wang Hongwen's reported claim during his period in Shanghai in 1975 (although Wang Xiuzhen was probably the real author of the comment) that Hua was a "branch manager" in Deng's restorationist program. Yet in February 1976, with the Chairman having spoken, the "gang" in Beijing by and large supported Hua rather than challenge him. Thus for Hua, the ironic effect of his promotion was largely to insulate him from direct attacks in the Politburo, attacks to which he would have been much more vulnerable as part of Deng's team had he remained in a lower position. It is also worth noting that, in a familiar pattern, it was Jiang Qing—who single-handedly convened the March 2 meeting where she engaged in extreme criticism of Deng without the support of the other Politburo radicals—rather than the "gang" as a whole, who particularly made life difficult for Hua.[166]

In a not unfamiliar pattern, various lower-ranking radicals were not on the same page as the "gang." Perceiving a close Deng-Hua relationship, but removed

---

[166] See *Mao zhuan*, vol. 2, pp. 1767-68; "Hua Guofeng, Ye Jianying deng jiejian Shanghai Ma Tianshui dengren de jianghua," p. 3; Qing and Fang, *Deng zai 1976*, vol. 1, pp. 56-58, 84-85, 120; "Jiang Qing zai dazhaohu huiyi," p. 381; Mao Mao, *"Wenge" suiyue*, pp. 429-30; and above, pp. 314n32, 411, 442, 448. Concerning the "second heavy artillery attack," while post-Mao sources, e.g., *RMRB*, March 9, 1977, in *SPRCP*, no. 6300 (1977), pp. 71-75, claim that the "gang of four" attacked Hua on science and technology, highlighting issues central to both the Academy of Sciences' Outline Report and the February 1, 1976, *Red Flag* critique, it is likely that the decision to launch this "artillery attack" was taken well before Hua's promotion. Of course, it is possible that Yao Wenyuan, who was responsible for the media, knew of the promotion before the publication of the attack, although it is not completely clear that Zhang Chunqiao and Wang Hongwen knew much before January 31; see *Mao zhuan*, p. 1767. It is also likely that Ji Dengkui, who had been asked by Deng for advice on a theoretical point concerning science and technology, was more of a target than Hua. For this and other evidence of attacks on Ji by radicals, although never publicly, see "Xu Jingxian de chubu jiefa jiaodai," pp. 5, 6; "Xu Jingxian de buchong jiefa jiaodai," p. 8; and Hu Shihong, *Zhang Aiping zai 1975*, p. 268. Cf. above, p. 346n119.

from politics at the top, Liaoning's Zhang Tiesheng of blank examination paper fame declared that "the new premier is a rightist."[167] In Beijing, however, better connected junior radicals such as Chi Qun joined the chorus of support for Hua. Yet while not opposing Hua, they complicated his efforts through their vigorous activities at the forefront of the criticize Deng campaign. In early February, Chi Qun named Deng five times to Qinghua's Party standing committee, about two months before official authorization for such naming. Then, Mao Yuanxin and Xie Jingyi addressed the Shanghai delegation to the February warning meeting, attacking various vice premiers and remarking critically on the performance of Politburo members in the *pi Deng* effort. Xie and Chi led resistance at Qinghua in early March to Document no. 5 that set restrictions on the movement, a document largely based on Hua's February 25 speech (see below). While based on scattered evidence, during February and March, it appears that young radicals Mao Yuanxin, Xie and Chi were more active in pushing the anti-rightist project than any of the "gang of four" other than Jiang Qing, even allowing for the activities of Wang Hongwen in the MAC and concerning the Central Organization Department. In this, the telling figure was Mao Yuanxin, as befit his influence since the previous fall and his ongoing status as the Chairman's liaison officer. Several ironies surrounded Mao Yuanxin's activities in this crucial period. While seemingly more forceful in pushing the radical cause than any of the "gang" save Jiang, his role in opposing Zhang Chunqiao to head the State Council worked against that cause. Concerning Hua, despite claiming after the arrest of the "gang of four" that he had done much to secure Hua's position, Mao Yuanxin's activities only made the Acting Premier's task more difficult. A final irony came after the Chairman's death and the arrest of the Politburo radicals. According to a senior Party historian, a deal was struck with Mao Yuanxin, probably about the time of the 1980 resolution on Party history, whereby he attributed the excesses and disruptions of the Cultural Revolution and late Maoist era to the "gang," thus absolving his uncle, the real driver of events, and in the process supporting the legitimacy of the new leadership as it overturned the Chairman's most cherished goals.[168]

The activities of the young radicals further illustrated the complexity of anti-Deng politics. As discussed above, in this period key younger figures Mao Yuanxin, Xie Jingyi and Chi Qun were both more aggressive and influential than at least three of the "gang of four." In this, several aspects stand out. One was the Chairman's favoritism toward these figures, not only his nephew, but also Xie and Chi who represented his personal experimental point of the "two schools." In February, he had Hua invite visiting former President Nixon to go

[167] See *ZGDSCKZL*, vol. 27, p. 546.

[168] "Wang Xiuzhen de jiefa jiaodai," p. 2; "Hua Guofeng jiejian lingdao tongzhi jianghua," p. 1; Mao Mao, *"Wenge" suiyue*, p. 458; Qing and Fang, *Deng zai 1976*, vol. 1, p. 120; and interview, January 2005.

to Qinghua to witness China's current political debate. Another aspect was the interaction of Jiang Qing, but not necessarily other members of the "gang," with Mao Yuanxin and the Qinghua radicals. In mid-March, Jiang complained to Mao Yuanxin that while criticism of Deng was very vigorous at the two universities, it was cold and quiet in the Politburo. A few days later during a Politburo meeting, she said the Chairman wanted central and provincial leaders attending the current warning meeting to go to Qinghua and Beida, and more generally large numbers of officials went to "seek inspiration" during this period. But no Politburo members went, which led to Jiang's proposal, subsequently approved by Mao, that representatives of the "two schools" come to the Politburo to report on their experiences. This led to the enlarged meeting of March 26 where, allegedly following secret preparations in which Jiang and Mao Yuanxin incited Chi and Xie, representatives from the two universities dominated with strong attacks on Deng, apparently with limited contributions from the "gang," Jiang included. In this specific case, the radicalism of these younger figures, abetted by the Chairman's patronage, received critical support from Jiang Qing, but it is difficult to generalize how close these links were in the critical February-March period.[169]

With the formal launching of the new campaign in February, the intensity and scope of radical criticism intensified. Many issues that had been cautiously criticized in the fall, and/or canvassed among themselves by radicals in the winter, now were subject to sustained attack—not only revisionism in science and technology, but such matters as Deng's alleged waste of funds on foreign purchases, his purported distortion of Mao's directive on boosting the economy, and (somewhat later) his "ladder theory" for promotions, among many others. During the first six days of February, Jiang Qing and Zhang Chunqiao directed the Ministry of Culture to produce works attacking "capitalist roaders," and throughout February and March articles on various anti-rightist themes appeared in the media on an intensified basis.[170] Another feature of the new situation was efforts to uncover evidence of deviation that had hitherto escaped the radicals. Thus Zhang Chunqiao quizzed provincial leaders such as Zhao Ziyang during the February-March warning meeting concerning their interaction with Deng at the previous fall's agriculture forum, and it was only now that the "gang" became aware of the existence of Deng Liqun's General Program, which eventually led to attacks on the "three poisonous weeds."[171] By March, with Mao's newly issued

---

[169] See Qing and Fang, *Deng zai 1976*, vol. 1, pp. 119-24; and Fan Daren, *"Wenge" yubi chenfulu*, pp. 98, 100. Concerning the secret meeting involving Mao Yuanxin, Xie and Chi, Qing and Fang refer to the "gang of four" participating, but there is no concrete evidence that this extended beyond Jiang Qing.

[170] See Chen and Du, *Shilu*, vol. 3, part 2, p. 1323; and Mao Mao, *"Wenge" suiyue*, pp. 450, 457-58.

[171] See Qing and Fang, *Deng zai 1976*, vol. 1, pp. 103-104; and Cheng and Xia, *Deng zai yijiuqiwu*, pp. 556-57.

"important instructions" pointing squarely at such hallmark Deng apostasies as "taking the three directives as the key link" and "so long as it catches mice, whether black or white it's a good cat" virtually everything Deng ever did in a policy or personal sense was subjected to withering attack. Perhaps the high point was Jiang Qing's March 2 address to provincial and military region leaders at the ongoing warning meeting. Jiang not only criticized Deng on a wide range of policy issues, she also bitterly complained of his treatment of her since spring 1975, used extreme terms like "counterrevolutionary commander" and "Han traitor," and raised trivial matters while engaging in ludicrous posturing. Jiang's tirade reflected the atmosphere of the time, but it was hardly smart politics.[172]

While we have argued that there was little prospect for a substantive alliance between the radicals and Hua and other Party machine types in any case, the excesses in Jiang's speech undoubtedly increased the latter group's hostility toward her. Moreover, it hardly impressed Mao who complained that she had gone too far, even though the Chairman was apparently content to let the harsh criticism of Deng run its course.[173] Moreover, there are indications that Jiang's excesses caused nervousness among other Politburo radicals. It was at this point, during the February-March warning meetings, that Zhang Chunqiao reportedly expressed concern at Jiang's (and Wang Hongwen's) activities to Yao Wenyuan, saying that Jiang and Wang were making a lot of claims against Deng, but in the end they (Zhang and Yao) would also suffer as a result.[174]

Another indication of wariness toward Jiang Qing on the part of the other Politburo radicals, as well as of a more general lack of coordination among them and of the importance of Party procedures at this time of high conflict, came in the same meetings. This related to Deng's approach to Ma Tianshui in June 1975. As briefly noted in Chapter 4, Ma revealed the encounter to several of his local Shanghai colleagues, and Yao Wenyuan and Wang Hongwen were informed soon after, but apparently no further steps were taken. While there is no evidence of Zhang Chunqiao being informed at this juncture, Jiang was deliberately not informed—in all likelihood due to fears that her impetuous tendencies might cause further damage to the radical cause at a time when it was already in retreat. With Deng in trouble by late 1975, however, his approach to Ma became something that could be added to the charges against him as a violation of Party unity and Politburo confidentiality. In late January, after being

---

[172] See *Mao wengao*, vol. 13, p. 486; and "Jiang Qing zai dazhaohu huiyi," pp. 374-84. Mao's criticism of Deng's "cat theory" and other personal attacks were not included in the authoritative *Mao wengao* version of Mao's instructions, but they were almost certainly in the original. See Wang Nianyi, *Dadongluan*, pp. 559-61.

Examples of trivial matters and silly posturing by Jiang on March 2 included her attack on Deng for failing to stay with the masses when he visited Dazhai in September 1975, and her claim to be poor while displaying an empty purse.

[173] See Mao Mao, *"Wenge" suiyue*, p. 454; and *Mao wengao*, vol. 13, p. 527.

[174] Qing and Fang, *Deng zai 1976*, vol. 1, pp. 112-13; and above, p. 386.

urged by a local Shanghai leader, Wang wrote to Mao revealing the incident, although it is unclear what, if any, response came from the Chairman. At the warning conference in February, Zhang Chunqiao, who may have only then or recently become aware of the matter, now took up the issue. Zhang pressed Ma to disclose Deng's approach openly, arguing that under Party norms only those with direct knowledge could expose questionable behavior.[175]

Meanwhile, although the activities of the radicals and Jiang Qing in particular undoubtedly hardened attitudes toward them, both old revolutionaries and younger officials who had climbed the ladder of the Party-state were faced with serious dilemmas concerning how to respond to Mao's latest campaign. By March, senior revolutionaries were under particular pressure as the radicals drew on Mao's criticism of veteran comrades whose thinking "is still in the stage of the bourgeois democratic revolution, [and who] have a poor understanding of socialism, ... even opposing it," to claim such people had morphed into capitalist roaders intent on overturning the dictatorship of the proletariat. The main strategy adopted by veteran revolutionaries, as seen in the cases of Deng, Ye Jianying and Li Xiannian, was inactivity, with or without the cover of sick leave. Li would remark after the arrest of the "gang" that in this period the pressure was so great he didn't dare to make contact with Ye.[176]

More junior figures with lesser revolutionary credentials had difficult choices of their own. As we have previously seen, whether under attack themselves, or forced to participate in ritual attacks on Deng or their immediate colleagues, such officials reacted in a variety of ways: Deng Liqun resisted steadfastly, Zhou Rongxin was combative, Hu Qiaomu was uncertain and "soft," and Qiao Guanhua and Tao Lujia provided varying degrees of cooperation with the radicals. While clearly not universal,[177] the predominant approach of leaders of

---

[175] *Shanghai "wenhua dageming" shihua*, pp. 777, 783; Xu Jingxian, *Shinian yimeng*, pp. 355-56; *Deng nianpu*, vol. 1, p. 146; and above, p. 303.

[176] See *Mao wengao*, vol. 13, p. 487; *HQ*, no. 3 (1976), in *SPRCM*, no. 863 (1976), pp. 2-9; Mao Mao, *"Wenge" suiyue*, pp. 452-55; and *Deng Liqun guoshi jiangtan*, vol. 1, p. 398. Li's comment was unspecific as to the precise period he referred, but it is likely to have begun in February or March.

In strictly formal terms, unrepentant capitalist roaders were openly said to be only a small number of all bourgeois democrats and were to be dealt with by "curing the illness to save the patient" (see *HQ*, no. 3 [1976], in *SPRCM*, no. 863 [1976], pp. 8-9), but the violence of the language and parallels to Liu Shaoqi, Lin Biao and others suggested the possibility of a more sweeping purge.

[177] Most analysts paint a picture of widespread resistance to the anti-Deng campaign, with some especially emphasizing resistance at the provincial level and in the PLA. While broadly accurate, this somewhat overstates the case. In circumstances suggesting that the concerned officials had not sufficiently distanced themselves from the radicals, the top Party secretaries were changed in seven provinces, mostly involving military cadres, while the commander of the Nanjing Military Region was also removed, before the 11th Party Congress in mid-1977. As for ministers, apart from the three radicals appointed at the Fourth NPC, Qiao Guanhua and Minister of Metallurgy Chen Shaokun, who had apparently cooperated with the "gang" (see Qing and Fang, *Deng zai 1976*, vol. 1, p. 81), were formally removed in October 1976 and June 1977 respectively. From another angle, resistance was largely successful in that, from February to Mao's death, Wan Li was the only minister

central and regional organizations was to participate in a formalistic way, not giving anything significant away. This could be seen in a conversation during the period between Hu Yaobang, who was now under strong attack, and Sichuan leader Zhao Ziyang, who was not under any special pressure, over how to deal with the criticism of Deng. They agreed the best approach was to keep all criticisms on a general and theoretical level, while steering clear of disclosing any personal exchanges with Deng. This approach, of course, reflected both the more restrained conduct of this anti-rightist campaign compared to during the Cultural Revolution, and the learning experience gained from that movement.[178] To reiterate an earlier observation, while elite sentiment could excuse a degree of cooperation or capitulation in the unprecedented circumstances of 1966-68, conceding to the "gang of four" in 1976 was far less forgivable.

Arguably the most complicated dilemma, and certainly the most important for future outcomes, was that facing Hua Guofeng. Under pressure from the radicals pushing Mao's campaign, and charged with leadership of *pi Deng* by the Chairman, whom he apparently saw infrequently, Hua had to judge how strongly to pursue criticism of Deng, old revolutionaries generally, and vulnerable younger members of the Party machine. In general terms, Hua adopted a middle course concerning Deng: sternly criticizing his errors, but avoiding extreme attacks. Even more crucial were his efforts to prevent the anti-Deng campaign from expanding into a broad purge. According to post-Mao sources, beyond criticizing old revolutionaries as a group, the radicals attempted to "ferret out" capitalist roaders in the government and army, with Jiang Qing reportedly claiming over 75 percent of veteran State Council leaders had so degenerated, and Zhang Chunqiao going to PLA units in search of such deviants.[179] To the extent he had the authority, this was something Hua would not allow.

Undoubtedly Hua's most important statement of the middle position came with the convening of the warning meeting of provincial and military region leaders on February 25. Hua's speech on that day, a speech approved by Mao and reflecting the Chairman's current thinking, addressed the key issues. Deng was placed in a higher degree of vulnerability, but with some limits: his errors were now formally placed before leaders of this level, he could be criticized by name internally, but he would not be named in the media, and wall posters attacking him would not be allowed. In any case, criticizing Deng was the main task: Hua called for a "deep-going exposure ... of Comrade Deng Xiaoping's revisionist line errors." Hua quoted Mao that "for any mistakes [in 1975] the [whole] Center

---

actually removed from office as opposed to being pushed aside or dying in office (in addition to Zhou Rongxin, Minister of the Coal Industry Xu Jinqiang died in July, presumably unrelated to the political situation), while overall the radicals achieved only very limited organizational gains. Cf. Dittmer, *China's Continuous Revolution*, pp. 194-95.

[178] Interview with former associate of Hu Yaobang, May 2000.

[179] See *GMRB*, December 23, 1976, in *SPRCP*, no. 6203 (1976), p. 155; and *RMRB*, January 27, 1977, in *SPRCP*, no. 6281 (1977), p. 46.

[i.e., including the Chairman himself] is responsible," but said that the Politburo believes the main responsibility lay with Deng. This formulation had the effect of not being excessively harsh on Deng, but at the same time focusing the attack on him so that others could distance themselves from his mistakes. The aim of restricting the fallout to Deng was reflected in a further comment of Mao's relayed by Hua: "we should not go too far in dealing with Deng's protégés at various levels." Building on this, Hua emphasized there should be no attempt to "ferret out" Deng's agents in various places, and the movement should be carried out under the unified leadership of Party committees. How resilient or successful Hua was in this effort is uncertain, but it was clearly the main thrust of his handling of the situation.[180]

If laying down the middle course was not, because of Mao's backing, particularly difficult in principle, complexities arose in practice. An indication at the policy level concerned the ship buying efforts of Minister of Communications Ye Fei. Ye defended these efforts in the face of sharp radical attacks on the basis that the policy had been approved by the Party Center and Mao and had never been revoked, and orders for new ships actually stepped up even as the anti-Deng campaign intensified in February and March. But Hua apparently bent under the pressure of the radicals' criticism of this "revisionist" policy, and on March 20 phoned Ye to notify him that the State Council had formally decided to cease buying ships for the time being. The immediate effect of this was not to stop imports, however, since orders that had already been signed went ahead. The halt to purchases only took effect from August 1976, by which time China's ocean-going shipping fleet had nearly doubled in size from the previous year.[181]

A more detailed insight into the complexities of the situation can be gained from the situation affecting the Ministry of Railways and its leader, Wan Li. Wan Li and his ministry, of course, had been at the forefront of one of the signature features of Deng's consolidation program, the attack on factionalism. In that effort, an even more significant figure was Ji Dengkui, who would now, along with Hua, be dragged into the consequences of the anti-rightist upsurge for Wan's ministry. Wan, a particularly combative personality, had been seen as a close follower of Deng, but when the first moves against Deng unfolded the previous November and issues were raised concerning the railroad sector, there is little to indicate that he was under any particular pressure. In late January, however, railway cadres who had been ousted in the struggle against factionalism under

---

[180] "Hua Guofeng Tongzhi de jianghua" [Comrade Hua Guofeng's Speech] (February 25, 1976), in *ZGDSCKZL*, vol. 27, p. 385; *Mao wengao*, vol. 13, pp. 525-26; Chen and Du, *Shilu*, vol. 3, part 2, p. 1331; and Chen Yonggui's December 20, 1976, speech to the second Dazhai conference, in *SPRCP*, no. 6252 (1977), pp. 130-31. Chen Yonggui's account claims that despite Hua's efforts, the "gang of four's" attempt to overthrow a large number of leading cadres resulted in paralyzing Party and government organizations. Cf. below, pp. 460-61.

[181] Ye Fei, *Ye Fei huiyilu*, p. 71. Ye's account only mentions a phone call from "the leader of the State Council," but this surely was Hua.

Wan's leadership took advantage of the new circumstances to press their cases. Hua quickly ordered the newly formed temporary leading group of the ministry to listen to the complaints and criticisms of the Zhengzhou and Lanzhou Railway Bureaus, and of Henan and Gansu provinces, on the "rightist wind" theme. Further to this, the State Council and Party Center ordered the ministry to unify its thinking with that of Henan and Gansu, write two reports on the respective problems of the two bureaus and submit them to the Center after gaining the approval of the two provincial committees. A standoff of about a week resulted, but on February 8 the Henan and Gansu provincial leaders submitted opinions to the Center attacking the leaders of the two bureaus for carrying out the "wind of rightist reversals" that had overturned the verdicts of the Cultural Revolution, opinions that secured Mao's agreement.[182]

This situation led to conflict between Wan Li and his superiors, Hua and Ji. Hua, as State Council leader, clearly had to be involved. While Ji's portfolio did not include railroads, an area under the crusty old general, Wang Zhen, Ji was responsible for Party organization, and had been directly involved in supporting Wan in his earlier struggles against factionalism in the railway sector. In addition, there was a personal revolutionary connection in that Ji (and Zhao Ziyang) had served *under* Wan in the Hebei-Shandong-Henan Border Region. In the current circumstances Hua and Ji were bound to support criticism of the "rightist wind," but Wan strongly objected to the specific requests of the Center, arguing, much as Ye Fei had done, that they contravened central Document no. 9 (1975) on railway consolidation that Mao had approved. Another issue was Wan's objection to naming the secretaries of the two bureaus in the required report, declaring he would assume total responsibility: "If you want names, then name me, otherwise I won't sign!" In a tense evening meeting on February 9, Hua and Ji criticized Wan for procrastinating, with Ji declaring "whoever is named depends on the views of the Center, you can keep your opinions to yourself!" Under such pressure, Wan reportedly had no choice but to sign against his will.[183]

Subsequently, on the evening of February 14, Hua, Ji, Wang Hongwen and Wu De met with Wan, the leaders of the ministry's newly established temporary leading group, Henan and Gansu leaders, and leaders of the Zhengzhou and Lanzhou bureaus. The meeting predictably fol!owed the current campaign agenda, with Hua stressing that problems could be solved by counterattacking

---

[182] Zhang Guangyou, *Gaige fengyun zhong de Wan Li*, pp. 69-73; Wang Lixin, *Yao chi mi zhao Wan Li: Anhui nongcun gaige shilu* [For Rice to Eat, Find Wan Li: True Record of Anhui's Rural Reform] (Beijing: Beijing tushuguan chubanshe, 2000), p. 25; and above, pp. 274-75, 416n82. There are some differences in detail and the sequence of events between the accounts of Zhang Guangyou and Wang Lixin. We have preferred Zhang's account.

[183] Zhang Guangyou, *Gaige fengyun zhong de Wan Li*, p. 73; Wang Lixin, *Yao chi mi zhao Wan Li*, p. 25; and interview with person assigned to the Ministry of Railways at the time and subsequently close to Wan Li, November 2002. According to Party historians specializing in Wang Zhen, Wang assumed responsibility for both Ye Fei and Wan Li when they came under criticism. Interview, November 2002.

the "rightist wind" and rousing the masses to expose the errors of the leaders of the two bureaus. After the meeting, Hua kept the ministry's leading group, including Wan, back for further instructions. In his exposition, Hua said Wan had committed many errors and had a wrong view of the situation, but that the main responsibility lay with Deng, and he should both examine his own errors and criticize Deng.[184] While probably broadly accurate, this account from post-Mao published sources at the very least does not give a sympathetic account of Hua and Ji's predicament. Such a perspective, and further insights into the politics of the period, has been provided by an oral source who was present in the Ministry of Railways as a Xinhua reporter during this period, subsequently developed close ties to Wan Li and also established cordial relations with Ji Dengkui. According to this source, a special cause of tension was the refusal of Hua and Ji to let Wan be named, something he wanted as a badge of honor. Wan was apparently particularly unhappy with Ji, complaining that Ji was once his subordinate (during the revolution), but now "he lords it over me, and refuses to see me." Of course, objectively, by refusing to name Wan, Hua and Ji were in effect protecting him. But the crucial point, our source emphasized, was that Hua and Ji had no choice in the matter. The "Center," i.e., Mao, had decided, and Hua and Ji simply had to follow orders. Whatever their past connections, Ji would have to follow the script in meetings in which other leaders were present, and could not afford to grant a private audience to Wan. Our source, a committed reformer as Chinese politics unfolded over the following period, concluded that Ji was a fair-minded and capable official, but one compromised by the blight of the system—following orders.[185]

In the event, Wan Li was the only minister formally removed from office during the anti-rightist upsurge. More broadly, as we have observed, while power was lost to temporary leading groups within central organs, Cultural Revolution-style seizures of officials and parading in the streets were banned, and struggles in Beijing were confined to the concerned units. This, however, did not translate into social and political calm across China. Both of the conflicting political tendencies were involved in the unrest. Starting in February, students and workers put up wall posters in various cities attacking the Politburo radicals, especially Zhang Chunqiao but seemingly not Wang Hongwen, notably in the south. In a potentially ominous development, workers from Guizhou traveled to Zhengzhou and Changsha to put up wall posters there. Other popular protests against the radicals included a letter to Mao from workers in a Guangdong county, denouncing Zhang

---

[184] Zhang Guangyou, *Gaige fengyun zhongde Wan Li*, pp. 73-75; and Wang Lixin, *Yao chi mi zhao Wan Li*, p. 25.

[185] Interview, November 2002. Ironically, this source was dispatched from Xinhua at the behest of the radicals to keep tabs on developments in the Ministry of Railways, in effect to spy for them. But, as with others sent on similar missions, he was not a follower of the "gang of four," and developed views supportive of Wan Li.

Chunqiao.[186]

In certain localities, greater problems were caused by rebel activities that damaged social order and disrupted local elite politics. Major incidents and disorder that erupted in Sichuan, Yunnan and Henan in March had a number of features. Notwithstanding Hua's injunction not to "ferret out" Deng's followers, radical "factionalists" in these provinces used conferences convened to carry out the anti-Deng campaign to attack responsible officials at the provincial, municipal and special district levels as "capitalist roaders," force them to make self-examinations, and try to replace them. Part of this strategy involved rehabilitating those who had been removed during Deng's consolidation effort in 1975 and organizing them to resume work. And, unlike developments in Beijing, violent Cultural Revolution-style activities occurred: entering and occupying Party compounds, attacking public security organs, assaulting meeting places, and seizing leading officials at different levels. In Yunnan, where a provincial secretary as well as lower-level leading cadres were seized, the local radicals invoked Cultural Revolution and *pi Lin pi Kong* rhetoric in calling for a "second seizure of power." The impetus for these developments was surely local, but in a few cases (arguably tangential) "gang of four" involvement has been alleged. In Sichuan, "factionalists" seized provincial Party Secretaries Duan Junyi and Xu Mengxia and took them to Beijing. Once in the capital, these rebels reportedly made contact with the "gang," demanded that the Center express its attitude and reorganize the provincial leadership, and proposed two leading local radicals to take charge of the province's work; these demands, however, were apparently rebuffed. Meanwhile, Henan "factionalist" Tang Qishan assertedly held "secret talks" with Jiang Qing during the February-March central warning meeting and secured her promise that he could be provincial first secretary and also the Center's representative in handling situations in neighboring Hubei. Thus emboldened, Tang went to various places in Henan to mobilize the masses against "capitalist roaders," allegedly declaring that the guiding principle of this effort was "chaos" (*luan*).[187]

It is unclear how widely or over what precise time frame such developments unfolded, whether local rebels in fact received any meaningful support from the Politburo radicals, or how the central authorities responded, but in Sichuan, Yunnan and Henan the March disruptions clearly reverberated for many

---

[186] See Mao Mao, *"Wenge" suiyue*, p. 459. While presumably a partial list since she claimed unrest was found "all over China," Mao Mao cites incidents initiated by groups in Fujian, Guizhou, Guangdong and Hubei.

[187] Chen and Du, *Shilu*, vol. 3, part 2, pp. 1341, 1342-43, 1347-48. In Sichuan, a province apparently severely affected by factional strife in 1976, the leaders proposed by the rebels to take over the province were the famous husband and wife pair, Liu Jieting and Zhang Xiting, who had been arrested by the Party establishment before the Cultural Revolution. Liu and Zhang took leading roles in attacking that establishment in 1966-67, were placed in leading positions in the new provincial Revolutionary Committee in 1968, but were apparently swept aside during the 1969-70 reaction against extreme leftism. See Teiwes, *Provincial Leadership*, pp. 37, 78.

months with deleterious effects on political stability, economic production, and an increasingly chaotic social order.[188] Into this deteriorating mix another explosive element was added, one also reflecting the actions of both political tendencies. This, of course, was the symbolic treatment of Premier Zhou Enlai with the approach of the *Qingming*, the sweeping of the graves festival, a potent occasion for honoring the dead. Against a background of popular resentment over the restrictions on honoring the late Premier, and in a context in which wall posters had already appeared attacking the "gang of four," the stage was set for intensified conflict as widespread public support of the Premier's memory unfolded. The result, of course, was the last great crisis of the Maoist era, the Tiananmen demonstrations and their suppression in early April.

---

[188] See Chen and Du, *Shilu*, vol. 3, part 2, pp. 1343, 1348, which includes statistics on production losses in Yunnan and Henan. We have not made an effort to determine how extensive disorder was in other parts of China, but national statistics indicate that in 1976 the overall value of industrial and agricultural growth increased by an anemic 1.7 percent, while the key steel and railways sectors actually declined. Ma Qibin, *Sishinian*, p. 408. See also below, pp. 498, 513.

Chapter 7

THE TIANANMEN INCIDENT AND MAO'S LAST DAYS, APRIL-SEPTEMBER 1976

Crushing the Tiananmen incident was personally grasped by the Chairman. ... Initially the Beijing militia refrained from striking back, nor did they engage in cursing back [at the rioters]. ... [But when the rioters] used counterrevolutionary violent force, we then wanted to use revolutionary violent force to deal with them. This is a basic Marxist-Leninist principle. Later [we] took up clubs [but not tanks and live ammunition—the authors], the Center [Mao] clearly conveying that we could strike back.

—Yao Wenyuan, discussing the Tiananmen incident, April 26, 1976[1]

At this year's planning seminar [in July-August 1976] criticizing Deng was correct ..., but they [the "gang of four"] used criticizing Deng to engage in plots. At the meeting they incited people by saying openly that the source of last year's rightist wind of reversing verdicts was the State Council's [June-August 1975] theory conference. [But] Deng Xiaoping did not participate [in this conference], Li Xiannian was in charge, and other comrades attended. [The "gang's"] goal was not to criticize Deng, it was to purge [other] people, to get at [current] Politburo comrades.

—Hua Guofeng on leadership conflict in summer 1976, October 7, 1976[2]

"Spare the rats because of the precious dish (*tou shu ji qi*)." It's not good to do things [in a way that would imperil Mao]. But not solving [the problem of the "gang of four"] is also unacceptable. [We] have to think of a method.

—Ye Jianying, using a Chinese saying to oppose action against the radicals before Mao's death, late summer 1976[3]

The final five months plus of Mao's life, together with the month of conflict following the Chairman's death that culminated in the arrest of the "gang of four" in early October, encompassed some of the most dramatic events in the history of the People's Republic. The first Tiananmen crisis in early April, coming 13 years before the even more dramatic and much more violent Tiananmen events in 1989, resulted in the disposition of Deng Xiaoping's case. More significant in the context of the period, it also resolved all ambiguity concerning the post-Zhou Enlai political equation, by clearly designating Hua Guofeng as Mao's successor. The demonstrations and their suppression also marked a major escalation of tension for both the elite and populace, and the resulting suppression would become a *cause célèbre* in the post-Mao period. Following the disturbances, leadership conflict reflected the contradiction that marked the entire post-Lin Biao period: upholding the Cultural Revolution legacy *v.* pragmatic efforts to correct the movement's shortcomings, now in the midst of the ongoing anti-Deng campaign. This naturally complicated Hua's situation since attacks on Deng and his policies touched directly on the efforts of Hua and other establishment beneficiaries who had implemented Deng's measures. In the midst of this continuing conflict, one of the great natural disasters of recent Chinese history occurred—the late July earthquake centered on Tangshan east of Beijing which took more than 242,000 lives. Managing this crisis was another test of Hua's new leadership. Finally, dealing with the death of the Great Helmsman and structuring a decisive outcome to the simmering divisions within the leadership was a further test, one that Hua would pass with flying colors. This last crisis will be examined in Chapter 8; here we deal with developments up to the Chairman's passing.

All of this took place against the background of Mao's rapidly deteriorating health, which again worsened in June. As we shall see in detail, during the Tiananmen crisis the Politburo acted with unusual initiative, although contact with the Chairman through Mao Yuanxin was critical, and ultimately the Chairman's perceived interests and actual decisions were decisive. Much as had been the case since January, over the next two months, while still holding final authority, Mao's grip on developments was even more reactive, and less in control. As an indication of his declining condition, the Chairman received a foreign leader

---

[1] "Yao Wenyuan dui *Hongqi* zazhi bianjizu zhaojiren" [Yao Wenyuan's Talk to the *Red Flag* Magazine Editorial Staff] (April 26, 1976), in *CRDB*, p. 1. We have inserted the reference to tanks and live ammunition since they had been discussed by the Politburo during the crisis (see Qing and Fang, *Deng zai 1976*, vol. 1, p. 177), but strongly argued against by Wang Hongwen, Zhang Chunqiao and Yao Wenyuan, and ruled out by Mao. The contrast to 1989 is striking.

[2] "Hua Guofeng jiejian lingdao tongzhi de jianghua," pp. 1-2.

[3] *Ye zhuan*, p. 638. According to this source, the saying was used in a conversation between Ye and Nie Rongzhen. Wang Nianyi, "'Wenhua dageming' cuowu fazhan mailuo" [Thoughts on What Led to Mistaken Developments in the "Cultural Revolution"], *Dangshi tongxun* [Party History Newsletter], October 1986, however, reports Ye using the phrase in reply to Wang Zhen's proposal to move against the radicals.

for the last time on May 27, seemingly taking the initiative himself to no longer meet such visitors.[4] Shortly afterward, in early June, he suffered a heart attack. Mao made his last politically relevant statement on June 25,[5] and two days later the Center informed the Party of the gravity of Mao's medical condition, while planes were dispatched to bring various Politburo members back to Beijing in view of a further ominous turn in his condition. From that time until his passing in September, the Chairman was "in a semi-conscious state for most of the time," and "often in a coma," although this did not prevent periods when he could read, including the pursuit of some of his preoccupations, notably by reviewing the nine articles critical of Zhou Enlai, or a brief improvement shortly before his death.[6]

With the final drastic turn in Mao's health at the end of June, a new dynamic had to come into play, but what was it? Previously, the Chairman, not only exercising unchallenged authority, but beyond that providing the impetus for major changes of direction, was the reference point for all leaders in their calculations concerning what could be attempted, and regulated the acceptable degree of conflict within the Politburo. Even with his health deteriorating and his control slipping since January, this situation broadly applied. Now, however, only fitfully conscious, Mao was no longer directing political affairs—although his "line" remained crucial to the equation. The Chairman does not appear in any of the political dramas of the summer. His sole recorded act, apart from pursuing the nine articles, was to read and approve Hua's report on the Tangshan earthquake on August 18, the last official document he dealt with.[7] In this uncharted situation, the Tiananmen crisis had given Hua the vital authority of the successor, a degree of legitimacy and clout that he would use in both the last two months of Mao's life and in the crucial month after his death. Hua's use of that power in the former period is a central concern of this chapter.

Other issues are central as well. Clearly a great deal of top-level conflict on policy and broader ideological issues, involving Hua and other establishment beneficiaries against the Politburo radicals, existed both before Mao's effective removal from the equation at the end of June and after, but its ultimate meaning is uncertain. In the accepted view, both Chinese and Western,[8] the period saw the

---

[4] Although the government issued a notice that Mao would no longer receive foreigners, Barnouin and Yu, *Ten Years*, p. 291, credibly claim this was the Chairman's own decision since "Nobody in the Politburo or in the State Council dared" to make such a proposal.

[5] This instruction, "pay attention to domestic problems," was given to Hua. See *Mao wengao*, vol. 13, pp. 538-39. This collection records only five other political statements from April, all in that month and related to Tiananmen. In addition, there are three formal diplomatic telegrams to foreign governments, the last one on July 10. See *ibid.*, pp. 530ff.

[6] See *Mao zhuan*, vol. 2, pp. 1781, 1783-84; Perry and Li, *Proletarian Power*, p. 184; above, pp. 138-39; and below, p. 503.

[7] *Mao zhuan*, vol. 2, p. 1783.

[8] See, e.g., Yan and Gao, *Turbulent Decade*, pp. 511ff; MacFarquhar, "Succession," pp. 365-67; and

radicals intensify their aggressive activities as a prelude to their bid for power after Mao's death. Meanwhile, while Hua attempted to resist, in the prevailing interpretation, old revolutionaries out of formal power—notably Ye Jianying— began to plot for a decisive showdown with the "gang." These claims will be tested in the subsequent analysis. To what extent did the radicals have a coherent, unified strategy? Did their activities build to a crescendo as Mao's life ebbed away? How did Hua respond to radical challenges? How significant were the activities of the veteran revolutionaries? What was the balance of power on the eve of Mao's death?

Understanding these crucial events is exceptionally difficult. In many respects, gaining an accurate sense of the meaning of these developments is more problematic than for any other period covered in this volume. Fundamentally, this is due to the comparative paucity of sources available, and to the frequent gaps in the narrative of events or the activities of key figures. In particular, important claims concerning Mao's last wishes for the leadership structure after his death are highly contentious and basically undocumented, and often no more than mere rumors. Memoir reflections on these months are sparse, Party historians in interviews note the difficulty of accessing material on the period, the more detailed sources—including one of the most important on the period[9]— are of the reportage literature genre, and thus less than completely reliable, and even major, widely acknowledged events are poorly documented.[10] Behind the limitations on sources stands a political fact: both sides of the political conflict in April-September 1976 suffer from unsympathetic treatment in official PRC historiography. Of course, this has been consistently the fate of the so-called "gang of four," whether during the initial post-Mao period when the radicals' clashes with Hua were emphasized, or later when Deng was pictured as their main antagonist along with Zhou Enlai. Arguably more important than any exaggeration or demonization concerning the "gang" has been diminution of Hua's historical role. This has inhibited detailed historical enquiry into the careers of Hua *et al.*, to a certain extent has denied these leaders a voice in shaping perceptions of them,[11] and limited the nuanced insights that can be derived from

---

Richard Baum, *Burying Mao: Chinese Politics in the Age of Deng Xiaoping* (Princeton: Princeton University Press, 1994), pp. 37-40.

[9] Qing and Fang's two-volume *Deng zai 1976*, on which we rely heavily. For the reasons we discuss in the Preface, above, p. xviii, we grant considerable credibility to this source, while approaching its specific claims cautiously and critically.

[10] E.g., Mao's famous assessment that he accomplished two things in his life (see below, p. 595), the victory of 1949 and the Cultural Revolution, is normally recorded as having taken place on June 15, 1976 (e.g., Ma Qibin, *Sishinian*, p. 402), but there is no solid evidence as to timing. No documentary record exists, and the source appears to be a March 1977 statement by Ye Jianying, who was not present, which provided no further details. Fan Shuo, *Ye Jianying zai feichang shiqi*, vol. 2, p. 580; *Mao zhuan*, vol. 2, pp. 1781-82; and interviews with specialists on the period, November 2002 and January 2005.

[11] No official biography of Hua has appeared, and at different points, projects on Wu De and Ji

many reform-era studies.

The analysis below first examines the dramatic Tiananmen crisis—the events leading up to the demonstrations, developments on the Square, and the politics of the regime's response, followed by an analysis of the consequences of the outcome for leading political figures. We then turn to major cases of policy conflict during the late spring and summer, particularly those involving agriculture and economic planning—issues which both bore the imprint of Deng's consolidation effort and Hua's direct input in 1975. Next, we resume the story of divisions within the Ministry of Foreign Affairs with another round in the conflict between the "two ladies" and Qiao Guanhua, a conflict which (along the responsibilities of his new position) now drew Hua into a sector where he lacked meaningful experience. This is followed by a discussion of the crisis created by the Tangshan earthquake, including Hua's response and the actions of the radicals. We conclude with an assessment of the situation on the eve of Mao's death: the nature of the activities of the various political forces in the preceding weeks, the preparations in place for dealing with the inevitable public shock, and possible political calculations within the Politburo.

The First Tiananmen Incident

In various respects, the circumstances leading to the remarkable and almost certainly spontaneous popular demonstrations in Tiananmen Square in early April, demonstrations that amounted to the first challenge to the regime from below, are relatively clear. As we noted in Chapter 6, the critical context was the sense among large sections of the urban public that Zhou Enlai had not been adequately honored after his passing. The tension originated in the period immediately following the Premier's death, with such constraints on honoring him as the notorious five no's, and was further exacerbated by the Party Center's decision to prohibit further displays of mourning following the Premier's memorial ceremony.[12]

Popular resentment was inevitably linked to distaste for the anti-rightist campaign that had been unfolding against Deng Xiaoping since late 1975 and, more broadly, for the entire Cultural Revolution experience, resentment which resulted in a significant if hard to measure loss of faith in Mao.[13] The desire of radicals at

---

Dengkui were vetoed by higher authorities at various stages of preparation. Interview with senior Party historian, January 2000. This situation has ameliorated with the recent publication of Chen Xilian's memoirs, *Chen Xilian huiyilu* [Memoirs of Chen Xilian] (Beijing: Jiefangjun chubanshe, 2004), and most importantly Wu De's recollections, *Wu De koushu*, which are relied on heavily in this chapter. Wang Dongxing's recollections and diaries have also been published, but they do not relate to the period of this study.

[12] See above, p. 437.

[13] While, as we shall see, Mao was attacked indirectly on Tiananmen Square during the April events, the attitude of the population, or particular segments thereof, toward the great leader is difficult to grasp clearly. Of particular interest is the testimony of one intellectual who worked in a factory in the

high and low levels to get on with the criticism of Deng's "rightist deviations" clashed with genuine grief at the loss of a leader widely seen as representing moderation and justice. Ironically, the key radical concern was less the reputation of the dead Premier than that his death was an inconvenient distraction from the anti-Deng movement. As the campaign accelerated in February-March, it naturally became possible to read criticisms of Deng's 1975 policies as criticisms of Zhou as well—notwithstanding the fact that Zhou had not played a leading policy role, or that Deng's initiatives had been authorized or even initiated by Mao. The extent to which informed publics actually connected the relatively infrequent criticism assertedly targeting the unnamed Premier to Zhou is unclear, as is the degree to which, if any, said criticism was in fact intended to blacken his reputation,[14] but certainly radicals associated Zhou with Deng's "rightist" measures, and many people would have seen Zhou's reputation as vulnerable to the radical onslaught. While the primary force in the unfolding events leading to Tiananmen was undoubtedly the popular urge to express the grief that had been prematurely halted in January, this quickly became entangled in the factional conflict surrounding the anti-rightist campaign, with expressions of opposition to the Politburo radicals beginning to surface in various places following Zhou's

---

Beijing suburbs at the time, and periodically went to Tiananmen during February-March to honor the Premier. According to this source, the general attitude at the time was anger at the unfair treatment of Zhou, antipathy toward the Politburo radicals, and difficulty in comprehending the government's behavior, although little concern with Deng's situation. But he found it hard to describe sentiment toward the Chairman himself, noting dissatisfaction and anger over his support for the "gang" and the treatment of Zhou, but at the same time a continuing deep faith in Mao. Interview, January 2005.

[14] For example, the *People's Daily's* February 6 attack on "capitalist roaders" charged that "a complete set of revisionist programs and lines was hidden behind the four modernizations." See Garside, *Coming Alive*, pp. 17-18. But how widely this would have been perceived as referring to Zhou's report to the Fourth NPC is uncertain, given that the term was not used in Zhou's speech and rarely if ever used as a public slogan in 1975; cf. above, p. 188n8. Moreover, a page one *People's Daily* critique by "Beida revolutionary teachers and students" on February 15 claimed to support production and the four modernizations, only objecting to rightist methods. In any case, Garside, pp. 119, 124, 128, reports frequent mentions of the four modernizations during the Tiananmen demonstrations, although this may have been a consequence of further and more focused radical attacks on the concept in March; see *RMRB*, March 1, 21, 1976. As to the extent of other alleged media allusions to Zhou, which were mostly centered in Shanghai, sources intent on emphasizing attacks on the Premier only specified six critical articles. See Gao and Yan, *Shinianshi*, p. 581; and Gao Wenqian, *Wannian Zhou*, p. 605.

Popular perceptions were clearly complex. David Zweig's perceptive account of his days in Beijing during this period, "The Peita Debate on Education and the Fall of Teng Hsiao-ping," *CQ*, no. 73 (1978), p. 146, notes how students objected to Zhou Rongxin's membership on the Premier's funeral committee, as if the participation of such a rightist would besmirch Zhou Enlai's memory. That is, these students apparently accepted the rightist label on someone now conventionally seen as the Premier's man, and that Zhou Enlai's legacy had to be defended in terms of the proletarian rhetoric of the period. The bottom line was protecting the Premier's reputation, rather than defending any particular policy orientation. Others, however, clearly saw grief for the Premier as an opportunity to express anti-Cultural Revolution sentiments.

funeral.[15] At the leadership level, much of the tension concerned how to pursue the anti-Deng campaign, and on March 24, Mao endorsed the majority view of dissuading Cultural Revolution-style student travel to Beijing and keeping the movement under Party control.[16] This was the very day that the so-called Nanjing incident, which would have a significant impact on the subsequent Tiananmen events, began to unfold.

On the 24th, the Nanjing Medical Institute laid the first wreath locally to honor Zhou in the Revolutionary Martyrs Cemetery near Nanjing. There was nothing unique in this development: mourning activities had started in Beijing in mid-March. The fact that a photographer, reportedly innocently, had removed the elegiac couplet from the wreath, led to rumors that this was the work of the "Shanghai gang," with the result that students put up a slogan to "Defend Zhou Enlai with our lives" in the city's downtown area the next day. Coincidentally, also on the 25th, in nearby Shanghai the *Wenhui bao*, a leading newspaper under radical control, published a page one article that, although not by name, was universally—but mistakenly (see below)—taken as pointing to Zhou as "the capitalist roader inside the Party [who] wanted to help the unrepentant capitalist roader [assumed to be Deng] regain power." This inflamed opinion in Nanjing at the same time as an order was issued banning further pilgrimages to the Martyrs Cemetery. Over the next few days, students organized and carried out a march to the cemetery, posters appeared attacking the *Wenhui bao* article, and starting on March 28, Zhang Chunqiao and Jiang Qing were denounced by name. Moreover, news of these developments and similar incidents began to spread to other areas, particularly in East China. By March 30 Wang Hongwen, who had special responsibility for the region and seemingly still at least shared in managing the daily work of the Party Center after Hua Guofeng's elevation to Acting Premier, learned of escalating protests in Nanjing and nearby areas, and, after nearly two days of monitoring the situation, on April 1, the Party Center ordered the Jiangsu provincial authorities to tear down the offending posters and warn against counterrevolutionary opinion. By April 4 order was largely restored, in part by allowing people to go to the cemetery and lay wreaths, while more momentous events were unfolding in Beijing.[17]

The stage was thus set for the Tiananmen crisis as news of the Nanjing events,

---

[15] Wall posters and letters attacking the Politburo radicals appeared on a significant scale starting in February. See Li Naiyin, "Cong Yao Wenyuan de zhaji kan 'sirenbang' fumeiqian de zui'e xintai" [The Criminal Psychology of the "Gang of Four" before Its Collapse as Seen from Yao Wenyuan's Notes], *Yanhuang chunqiu* [Chinese Annals], no. 9 (1997), pp. 36-37; and above, pp. 459-60.

[16] See *Mao wengao*, vol. 13, p. 529.

[17] For summaries of these events, see Yan and Gao, *Turbulent Decade*, pp. 489-92; Chen and Du, *Shilu*, vol. 3, part 2, pp. 1349-50; Garside, *Coming Alive*, pp. 110-14; Qing and Fang, *Deng zai 1976*, vol. 1, pp. 124-25, 128-34; and Genny Louie and Kam Louie, "The Role of Nanjing University in the Nanjing Incident," *CQ*, no. 86 (1981). By the end of the *Qingming* festival and the disturbances in Beijing, such protests had appeared in virtually all provinces and major cities. See Gao and Yan, *Shinianshi*, pp. 641ff.

notwithstanding a media blackout, reached Beijing and other places by word of mouth and through slogans painted on buses and railway carriages. But what exactly were the implications of the situation that had been reached by the start of April, and who was responsible for it? One aspect was that the March 25 *Wenhui bao* article seemingly established an unambiguous link between Zhou and the alleged transgressions of Deng, and in the process contributed to the (erroneous) notion of a close Zhou-Deng relationship and the Premier's alleged initiative in restoring Deng to office. This perception added to the explosive potential of the situation. As we shall see, at the elite level Deng became central to assessments of Tiananmen, even though he had no direct input into those events. At the popular level, Deng's precarious situation was clearly a factor, but one which resulted in limited overt activity. Deng apparently was only sporadically mentioned explicitly in Nanjing, the subsequent events in Beijing, or during similar protests in virtually all provinces and major cities,[18] undoubtedly because his official disfavor was so clearly understood. The main thrust of popular sentiment focused on Zhou, and was in essence an emotional protest over the Premier's mistreatment by Mao and the radicals. For large numbers of people the hostility of the Politburo radicals toward Zhou was clearly demonstrated, and earned them stinging rebukes, ironically often using Cultural Revolution language. The scope of anti-Zhang Chunqiao and Jiang Qing slogans and demonstrations in Nanjing went well beyond the scattered anti-radical wall posters and letters of the previous few months. This was hardly something that could be ignored by the central leadership, including those who had no love lost for the "gang." As Wang Dongxing observed after their arrest, at the time the four were still in power, and attacks on them were hard to distinguish from attacks on the Party.[19]

Who was responsible for this fraught situation? The standard understanding,

---

[18] In their extensive review of the *Qingming* protests nationwide, Gao and Yan, *Shinianshi*, pp. 595-96, 645-46, 649-51, only report pro-Deng slogans or the playing of recordings of Deng's memorial speech for Zhou in Changzhou, Wuxi, Hangzhou, Hefei and Tianjin, while Chen and Du, *Shilu*, vol. 3, part 2, pp. 1354-55, 1358, note instances of pro-Deng sentiments in Hangzhou and Xi'an during this period. Regarding Nanjing, Qing and Fang, *Deng zai 1976*, vol. 1, pp. 137, 143-44, claim pro-Deng actions not reported in other sources. As for the developments in Beijing, Garside, *Coming Alive*, p. 136, based on his own experience in the Square, noted "the absence of any mention of Deng" during the demonstrations, a view seconded by David Zweig based on his experience (personal communication, January 2004). George Black and Robin Munro, *Black Hands of Beijing: Lives of Defiance in China's Democracy Movement* (New York: John Wiley & Sons, 1993), p. 24, however, based on information from Chinese protestors, claim that "some openly chanted support" for Deng, while Chen and Du, *Shilu*, vol. 3, part 2, pp. 1358-59, report the playing of Deng's memorial speech for Zhou and a handbill containing praise of Deng on April 4. Perhaps most indicative of the low profile accorded Deng at Tiananmen, when Wu De reported to the Politburo on April 4 concerning reactionary speeches, posters, etc., he did not note support for Deng apart from the general statement that these activities amounted to a deviation from the main direction of the "criticize Deng" campaign. It was during this report, however, that Wu referred to Deng's influence on these developments over a long period of time (see below). *Wu De koushu*, pp. 207-208.

[19] "Wang Dongxing zai guanguo xuanchuan gongzuo jianghua" p. 2. Wang's remark specifically referred to the Tiananmen crisis.

in both Chinese and Western interpretations, points squarely to Jiang Qing and company in Beijing. In this view, through the *Wenhui bao* article, as well as earlier disrespect toward the Premier and their subsequent performance during the Tiananmen crisis, the "gang" polarized the political atmosphere, whether due to strategic incompetence or as a calculated effort to create a crisis that would finally eliminate Deng from the political stage.[20] At one level, the Politburo radicals clearly must bear major responsibility: they pushed the anti-Deng campaign, sometimes more stridently than Mao wished, and they showed little sensitivity to popular attitudes concerning Zhou. But despite the contemporary view that Zhang Chunqiao was the backstage backer of *Wenhui bao*, the weight of evidence argues against Zhang's responsibility, or that of any other member of the "gang," for the most explosive development, the March 25 article. One indication is that there is no claim of Zhang's involvement in the late 1976 confessions of local Shanghai radicals, nor in Xu Jingxian's memoirs three decades later. Moreover, a generally reliable detailed chronology points to the Shanghai leadership and middle levels of the city's propaganda apparatus as responsible for the *Wenhui bao* piece. A further suggestion of its likely local origins quickly surfaced in Hangzhou, the locale of arguably the most important protests outside of Nanjing and Beijing over the April 1-4 period. For our purposes here, the key factor in Hangzhou was that popular distaste for radicalism centered on regional leaders, especially Shanghai's Ma Tianshui, the ultimate boss of *Wenhui bao*. In any case, the offending article was not reprinted in the national press, a strong indication that the fateful step was local in origin, or at least that the Politburo radicals were unwilling to exacerbate the situation.[21]

As suggestive as the above considerations are, there is much more definitive evidence absolving the "gang of four," and in the process revealing the affair as a screw-up where *no one* intended to attack the dead Premier. The evidence comes in a recent article by a *Wenhui bao* chief editor at the time, an account which presents the results of extensive post-Mao investigations involving more

---

[20] See, e.g., Yan and Gao, *Turbulent Decade*, p. 489; MacFarquhar, "Succession," pp. 299-301; and Garside, *Coming Alive*, p. 109.

[21] See Su and Fang, *Shilu*, vol. 2, p. 1570; and Chen and Du, *Shilu*, vol. 3, part 2, pp. 1354-55. Ma Tianshui's November 21 confession only stated that *after* the "Nanjing incident" emerged, Zhang Chunqiao ordered the Shanghai radicals to keep him informed of critical letters received by *Wenhui bao*. "Ma Tianshui de buchong jiefa jiaodai," p. 5. Zwieg, "The Peita Debate," p. 154, reports that students in Beijing became aware of the *Wenhui bao* article from rumors.

Popular sentiment in Hangzhou had perhaps more focus on Deng than elsewhere, as in posters demanding that he must not fall, and references to his signature policy of carrying out Mao's three directives. Also, one of the demands concerning Ma called for investigating him for spreading political rumors—a possible reference to his revelation of Deng's June 1975 approach to him. See above, pp. 303, 365. Interestingly, Wang Hongwen termed the Hangzhou events a "counterrevolutionary incident," but apparently only from April 7, i.e., once the official counterrevolutionary verdict on Tiananmen was determined. For a detailed account of the Hangzhou events, their background and subsequent fallout, see Keith Forster,"The 1976 Ch'ing-ming Incident in Hangchow," *IS*, April 1986.

than 2,000 interviews by the authorities. The conclusion drawn was that the whole matter was a case of poor drafting with no evil intent as far as Zhou Enlai was concerned. The "capitalist roader inside the Party [who] wanted to help the unrepentant capitalist roader regain his power" was not meant to be Zhou, but rather Deng himself as the initial draft clearly indicated, while the (in fact plural) "unrepentant capitalist *roaders*" was intended to point to "little Deng Xiaopings" who had been brought back to power during Deng's period in charge. Although the belief that the Premier was being attacked is more than understandable, it was not the case. The catastrophic mistaken version of the incident further provides a much better fit with the logic of the situation: even a severely weakened Deng was still a potential threat, while attacks on the sainted Premier could only guarantee a popular backlash.[22]

If the incendiary effect of the March 25 article was an accident, it could only have happened because of the larger climate since January. And here ultimate responsibility lay with a familiar source: Chairman Mao. Simply put, the Chairman's well-understood reservations concerning Zhou encouraged leaders critical of his legacy and eager to get on with the anti-Deng campaign, while inhibiting others who would have preferred a more unambiguously positive treatment of the Premier. As we saw in Chapter 6, Mao was directly responsible for denying Zhou the accolade of a "great Marxist," and his concerns about mourning for the Premier being a cover for opposing the Cultural Revolution were conveyed to the Politburo, with clear implications for the official treatment of Zhou. In this context, it was the failure to honor Zhou adequately, rather than radical attacks on him, that fueled popular grievances, but at the same time produced an atmosphere where a clumsy article could be misinterpreted and greatly intensify public anger.

The Events on Tiananmen Square. The Tiananmen crisis thus developed against this background of popular determination to honor Zhou Enlai, Mao-generated constraints on such activities, broad discontent with the new leftist upsurge, a more long-term if indeterminate erosion of Mao's authority with the public, and escalating anger against the Politburo radicals who were seen as the Premier's opponents. Here we first review the events on the Square, and then turn to the main focus of our analysis, the reconstruction of the elite politics underpinning the response of the authorities. The events themselves are reasonably clear. Signs of preparations for the *Qingming* festival appeared as early as March

---

[22] Shen Guoxiang, "Qinli 1976 nian 'san.wu': 'san.erwu' shijian" [Personal Experience of the 1976 "March 5" and "March 25" Incidents], *BNC*, no. 3 (2005), p. 37. This report, which was not available at the time of our summer 2004 *Pacific Affairs* article, "The First Tiananmen Incident Revisited: Elite Politics and Crisis Management at the End of the Maoist Era," allows us to move beyond the argument in that analysis to an even stronger exoneration of the "gang of four" for the Nanjing incident. An earlier, less detailed claim along these lines, one noting that the failure to designate "unrepentant capitalist roader" in the plural led to misunderstanding, was Xu Jingxian's post-Mao confession in which he also claimed that he and Ma Tianshui were deeply upset by the blunder at the time. "Xu Jingxian de buchong jiefa jiaodai," pp. 6-7.

19, with a wreath to Zhou placed on Tiananmen Square by an elementary school. This and several subsequent wreaths were removed, and the city's public security bureau was ordered to compile records of whoever brought such memorials to the Square. Beijing's public security head, Liu Chuanxin, in a comment reflecting Mao's January remarks, reportedly expressed official nervousness by commenting that "these wreaths reflect severe class struggle." By March 30-31, with news on the "Nanjing incident" reaching the capital, wreaths began to proliferate, anti-radical sentiments were aired in poems posted in Tiananmen, and the number of people visiting the Square started to increase dramatically, reaching a total of more than one million from the end of March to April 3, the day before *Qingming*. In this period, the authorities proceeded cautiously, on the one hand, setting up on April 2 a joint command of Beijing public security personnel, the local workers' militia and the Beijing PLA Garrison on one corner of the Square, and issuing directives that *Qingming* was an outdated custom, that work units should prevent their workers and staff from going to Tiananmen, and declaring the Nanjing events had been a "reactionary incident," yet taking little action against people on the Square apart from a limited number of discreet arrests, and the removal of some wreaths. For all the actual and potential tension, on Saturday April 3 order prevailed at Tiananmen.[23]

On the day of the festival itself, coincidentally the one non-work day of the week, vast numbers came to the Square, perhaps one to two million people. With them came many more wreaths, poems, handbills and small character posters, as well as verbal declarations and outbursts. Tension grew during the day, with sporadic fighting breaking out among the crowd, and public security personnel were injured while attempting to maintain order. Many of the sentiments aired were simple if emotional eulogies to the Premier, but significant numbers carried a political sting. Some linked Zhou to policies under attack in the current anti-rightist campaign, although overall denunciations of the radicals focused on their alleged evil actions against the Premier rather than on policy issues. Although alluded to by the appearance of strings of little bottles (*xiaoping*), Deng Xiaoping was mentioned rarely, apparently to an even lesser extent than elsewhere in China, an indication that despite popular support for his policy approach in 1975, there were limits that even this emotional crowd observed. Of particular sensitivity, as in Nanjing, were sharp attacks, sometimes explicit, sometimes by allusion, on three of the Politburo radicals—especially Jiang Qing and Zhang Chunqiao, and also Yao Wenyuan, but seemingly never including Wang Hongwen. One handbill that particularly drew Jiang Qing's anger depicted an "11th line struggle" between Jiang and the Premier, a struggle allegedly decided in favor of Zhou with Mao's 1975 criticism of Jiang and the further elevation of Deng.[24]

[23] See Yan and Gao, *Turbulent Decade*, pp. 492-95; Garside, *Coming Alive*, pp. 115ff, 123, 128-29; *Wu De koushu*, p. 205; and Chen and Du, *Shilu*, vol. 3, part 2, pp. 1348, 1356, 1358.

[24] See Yan and Gao, *Turbulent Decade*, p. 495; *Wu De koushu*, pp. 206-207; Garside, *Coming Alive*,

Far more sensitive than any of this was the sense of defiance directed at Chairman Mao himself. Not only were many of the sentiments aired on the Square at variance with Mao's new campaign, and more fundamentally with his treasured Cultural Revolution, but additionally, although short of actually naming him, Mao was obliquely attacked in a small number of posters and speeches. This was strikingly seen in a slogan linking feelings for Zhou Enlai, disgust with the radicals, and defiance of the Chairman: "We want Premier Zhou, we don't want Franco [i.e., Mao], and even less the Empress Dowager [Jiang Qing]." As night fell, a confrontation between the Chairman and the Premier, never possible while Zhou lived, now appeared symbolically in the rows upon rows of wreaths to Zhou on the Square facing Mao's portrait on the Gate of Heavenly Peace itself. It was a serious challenge that the Politburo could not afford to overlook. As Wang Dongxing indicated more than seven months later, while there was nothing wrong with the masses coming to Tiananmen to honor Zhou, attacking sitting Politburo members was a problem, and attacks on the Chairman simply could not be tolerated.[25]

With the Politburo deciding after midnight that the wreaths would have to be removed, the Square was cleared and the small number of people remaining were detained during the night, and by early morning of the 5th all wreaths and writings were gone. With no explanation given for the removal of the wreaths, word spread rapidly as small numbers of people visited the Square, and by 8 a.m. 10,000 agitated people had gathered, later multiplying by several fold during the day. Confrontations quickly emerged: people massed on the steps of the Great Hall of the People and demanded the return of their wreaths, a police van that had broadcast loudspeaker messages against class enemies was overturned, and by late afternoon the joint command post was overrun and set alight. Throughout all this, according to the firsthand testimony of Roger Garside, the police and militia were very restrained, and even in the late afternoon no arrests had been made. The crowd became significantly smaller after the lights in the Square went on around 6.30 p.m. and Beijing Mayor Wu De's recorded message declared that a handful of bad elements had used *Qingming* to deceive people, and called on those remaining to leave Tiananmen. With Wu's speech played over and over again, the crowd dwindled further, with several hundred remaining around the monument, and sometime approaching 11 p.m. militiamen and police finally rushed the rump crowd, engaging in a brief spasm of violent beatings before

---

pp. 117ff; Chen and Du, *Shilu*, vol. 3, part 2, pp. 1358-60; Mao Mao, *"Wenge" suiyue*, pp. 466, 469; and above, p. 469n18.

[25] *Wu De koushu*, p. 207; Garside, *Coming Alive*, pp. 126-28; Ji Xichen, *Shi wu qianli de niandai*, p. 745; and "Wang Dongxing zai guanguo xuanchuan gongzuo jianghua," p. 2. The characterization of a confrontation between Mao and Zhou comes from Garside, p. 128. While it should not be overstated, and various memorials to Zhou carefully linked him to not only Mao, but even to the Cultural Revolution (see Zweig, "The Peita Debate," pp. 155-56), the combination of distinctly anti-Mao overtones and the palpable sense of a wronged Premier did amount to a confrontation of sorts.

carting off the victims. Although the Square was then cordoned off, this was not strictly enforced and perhaps several thousand people went to Tiananmen the next day to affirm their loyalty to Zhou, including the laying of a wreath that was respected by the militia throughout the day. While some in the crowd denounced Jiang, Zhang and Yao (but not Wang), the mood was somber, and there was no further suppression. The popular resistance had been broken, and normal order returned quickly to Tiananmen and its environs.[26]

Before turning to the elite politics of the Party's response, it is necessary to consider briefly the issue of what social and political forces actually drove developments on the Square, actions characterized by Garside as a heady mix of anger over the treatment of Zhou, revolt against Mao, apprehension for China's future, and defiance of those who would seek to punish the demonstrators. Garside and other observers at Tiananmen noted that all levels of society, including the poorest of peasants, were represented, while wreaths from ministries and central PLA organs and the presence of cadres in expensive clothes suggested the possibility of high-ranking influence on what unfolded.[27] Indeed, Yao Wenyuan, speaking to his *Red Flag* staff three weeks later on April 26, voiced precisely this view: "Even without the pretext of mourning the Premier things were bound to explode ... because deepening the *pi Deng* campaign gives a hard time to inner-Party capitalists [and] threatens the interests of big officials." He went on to say that despite the high profile of workers on the Square, intellectuals had been the most active and the real troublemakers, especially those from the Academy of Sciences, the Seventh Ministry of Machine Building, and the Ministry of Foreign Affairs, and he particularly cited the children of high-ranking cadres.[28] Apart from social origins, the mix on the Square, and indeed in other places such as Nanjing, involved both people without any real knowledge of elite politics and those, like the children of high-level cadres, who had some, however limited and distorted, inside information. But the net result was that both types were deeply committed to the Premier's memory and hostile to the radicals.

Whatever the precise contributions of workers and intellectuals to the Tiananmen events, Yao's assessment that something similar was "bound to happen" is questionable. Without the excuse, legitimacy and energizing factor provided by defending Zhou's reputation, it is unlikely that a similar popular outburst

---

[26] See Yan and Gao, *Turbulent Decade*, pp. 495-500; *Wu De koushu*, p. 216; Garside, *Coming Alive*, pp. 128-32, 134-35; Mao Mao, *"Wenge" suiyue*, p. 473; and Chen and Du, *Shilu*, vol. 3, part 2, pp. 1363-64. Yao Wenyuan also indicated initial restraint; see the quotation at the head of this chapter. Most accounts claim the violent beatings took place between 9:35 and 9:45 p.m., but according to Wu De, the action took place more than an hour later. Cf. below, p. 484.

[27] Garside, *Coming Alive*, pp. 123, 125, 126. Black and Munro, *Black Hands*, p. 23, claim that the predominant protesters were ordinary citizens, especially workers, with university students "all but invisible." Zweig, "The Peita Debate," p. 156, reports the majority of the crowd on April 4 as made up of workers and low-level cadres.

[28] "Yao Wenyuan dui *Hongqi* zazhi," p. 2. See also *Wu De koushu*, p. 207.

would have occurred even given the festering dissatisfaction with the Cultural Revolution, at least without some other unusual combination of circumstances. In particular, as we explore in the following section, the unexplained removal of wreaths violated an understanding that the wreaths would be allowed to remain for a few days. Moreover, the limited willingness of angry people on the Square to take up Deng's cause explicitly suggests the centrality of the emotional link to the Premier's reputation and treatment, notwithstanding that this provided an excuse for many to vent their frustration with the regime. As for the role of middle to higher-ranking cadres from official organizations, what is striking is the gradual escalation of units involved in mourning activities, from elementary schools to middle schools to central government bureaucracies, a process suggesting a cautious reading of what was being tolerated by the authorities. Crucially, there is virtually nothing to suggest manipulation from the very top echelons. This was truly a threat to the Party from below, what Zhang Chunqiao called a "Hungarian incident," in which no top leader had an interest. High leaders knew in their bones that action in support of what was going on in Tiananmen Square was political death. No one understood this better than Deng Xiaoping, who not only stayed away from the Square, but also ordered his children to do likewise. And when Jiang Qing *et al.* charged that Deng had indeed gone to the Square to command the scene, Hua and Wang Dongxing were skeptical, and Mao clearly agreed with their skepticism.[29]

Coping with the Crisis: Decision Making in the Politburo, April 1-6. Less can be said with complete confidence concerning the politics of the regime's response to the unprecedented crisis, given gaps in the available material (including in key sources that are less than completely reliable), misleading pictures of some actors, not to mention fanciful inventions, clashing accounts of important factual matters such as who attended Politburo meetings[30] and especially the

---

[29] Mao Mao, *"Wenge" suiyue*, pp. 467-68, 474-77. The issue of Deng's alleged visit to Tiananmen is discussed further below, pp. 482, 490. (For a fanciful account of a purported Deng visit to the Square on April 3, see Qing and Fang, *Deng zai 1976*, vol. 1, pp. 163-69.) This did not mean that important figures were completely aloof. Ye Jianying reportedly sent people to the Square every day to observe developments, and was even driven to the area to see for himself. Fan Shuo, *Ye Jianying zai feichang shiqi*, vol. 2, p. 535; and *Ye zhuan*, p. 636. According to a source close to Ye's family, however, while Ye's son and grandson went to the Square, this was without his approval, and he remained silent when they discussed what was going on; interview, March 1997. To the extent accurate, Ye's reported interest in Tiananmen indicates little more than seeking to keep abreast of events or, at best, private sympathy for aspects of the demonstrations. Similarly, even the aggressive Wang Zhen, who also sent a secretary to Tiananmen, did not go himself. *Wang Zhen zhuan* [Biography of Wang Zhen] (2 vols, Beijing: Dangdai Zhongguo chubanshe, 2001), vol. 2., p. 167.

[30] For example, the crucial Politburo meeting of April 4 which considered removing the wreaths. According to several authoritative sources (e.g., Mao Mao, *"Wenge" suiyue*, p. 471), Li Xiannian did not attend, assertedly claiming poor health, while Qing and Fang, *Deng zai 1976*, vol. 1, p. 171, less reliably report Li participating. There are also different claims concerning whether Zhu De attended, and various sources neglect to mention that Deng was there, which certainly was the case. On Deng, see *Deng nianpu*, vol. 2, p. 149.

timing of events, and unanswered basic questions. The accepted interpretation of
a process "dominated by the [cooperative] combined forces of the loyalists [Hua
and other establishment beneficiaries of the Cultural Revolution] and the Left"[31]
is accurate only insofar as these were the only forces in the Politburo with the
ability to act. Prior to April 7, with the apparent exception of the largely silent
Deng Xiaoping on April 5, and perhaps Li Xiannian or even less likely Zhu De,
the surviving old revolutionaries simply were not there.[32] But the interests of
Hua et al. and the radicals were hardly identical, and the individual behavior
of all participants bears scrutiny. Apart from attitudes and advocacy concerning
events on the Square, the relative authority of key actors is also at issue. Some
accounts picture Jiang Qing as controlling Politburo power at this juncture and,
as we shall see, her influence was great. According to Yao Wenyuan, Wang
Hongwen, perhaps as national militia commander, oversaw the response on the
Square,[33] and indeed the evidence suggests he was active in that respect and
exerted a major moderating influence. Wu De, as the local Party leader in Beijing,
played an even more central role in managing and implementing the response
at the Square, although Wu had less clout within the Politburo. Hua Guofeng
chaired the Politburo meetings throughout, was Minister of Public Security, and
emerged as Mao's unambiguous choice as successor by the end of the crisis,
yet the available evidence concerning the actual events does not picture Hua
as exercising particularly forceful leadership. Finally, there is the question of
Mao himself. Considerable evidence points to a reactive figure limited by ill
health in his ability to control events, yet the initiative in at least the most critical
decision came from the Chairman.[34] In this context, Mao Yuanxin, who provided
the Chairman with information on what was happening on the Square and in the
Politburo, and who conveyed his orders to the leadership, played a vital if often
overlooked role.

---

[31] Baum, Burying Mao, p. 33. The quotation specifically refers to the Politburo meeting of April 4,
but can be taken to characterize the entire crisis. See also MacFarquhar, "Succession," p. 303.

[32] We reach this conclusion largely on the basis of Wu De koushu, pp. 206, 212, 217. There is no
source indicating that Ye Jianying was involved in any Politburo discussions before April 7. Cf.
above, p. 475n30.

[33] "Yao Wenyuan dui Hongqi zazhi," p. 1, states that "All the major maneuvers [in dealing with the
matter] were decided by the vice chairman." The vice chairman in question must be Wang Hongwen,
since he was the only vice chairman at the time apart from Ye Jianying, who was excluded from any
role apparently on Mao's orders, and Deng Xiaoping. That Yao was not speaking of Hua is clear since
he immediately goes on to refer to Hua as the new First Vice Chairman. While it is unclear whether
a national militia headquarters was ever established, a development we doubt (see above, pp. 84-85,
258-59), as we have seen Wang was later accused of aspiring to the national militia commander
position. Interestingly, Beijing deputy militia head Ma Xiaoliu reportedly referred to Wang by this
title when recounting events on the morning of April 5 (see below).

[34] Mao zhuan, vol. 2, pp. 1775-76, based on the testimony of his secretary, Zhang Yufeng,
misrepresents the situation by picturing Mao as so ill that he was virtually passive throughout the
crisis. While accurately describing the seriousness of Mao's condition, this ignores his decisive role
in dealing with the critical events of the 5th.

Although piecing together the specifics of the unfolding drama is fraught with difficulty,[35] it is clear that the Politburo as a collective body was faced with a serious challenge requiring a response of some firmness. Not unlike the situation at Tiananmen 13 years later, the front-line leadership was faced with an unfolding and unpredictable situation on the Square, and a supreme leader whose will and sensibilities could not be ignored. For all the preexisting tensions within the top elite, and different preferences for handling the crisis, no one—including Deng Xiaoping—had an interest in the palpable challenge to the Chairman continuing.

The first Politburo consideration of the escalating crisis came deep into the night of April 1, with an emergency meeting focusing on the Nanjing developments, which were correctly seen as having national rather than just local significance. The meeting was attended by only six members: Hua, Wang, Jiang, Yao Wenyuan, and two unidentified others,[36] but not including Zhang Chunqiao. As in all meetings during the crisis, it was chaired by Hua, undoubtedly according to the Chairman's instruction. Mao Yuanxin called the meeting as well as taking notes, but there is no explicit evidence that he conveyed instructions from the Chairman. The meeting dealt with three matters, most importantly the Nanjing incident in the context of other developments around the country involving mourning for Zhou, and attacks on the three Politburo radicals. An intense discussion ensued on a handbill circulated in Nanjing purporting to convey Zhou Enlai's last will, a fake document highly critical of Jiang Qing while praising Deng. A proposal emerged to issue a formal circular to the whole nation warning people not to be taken in by such enemy slanders. Other issues considered were arrangements for May Day activities, including making sure Deng did not attend, and transmitting to the Party's grassroots Mao's October-January instructions, which made clear his dissatisfaction with Deng. Mao Yuanxin prepared a written report to the Chairman on the Politburo discussions before dawn on the 2nd, but it was only on the 3rd that Mao expressed his agreement. The reasons for the delay and why, if indeed it were the case, Mao Yuanxin presented a written report instead of engaging in a personal exchange with the Chairman remain unknown, with Mao's health one likely explanation. Another possibility is that Mao

---

[35] In the following discussion, we have had to make judgments based on the weight of evidence, linguistic analysis, and political logic, concerning the credibility of various sources. Of particular note in this regard is the most detailed account of events, Qing and Fang, *Deng zai 1976*, vol. 1. While parts of this book are clearly unreliable (cf. above, p. 475n29), we include information from it, particularly from purported documents such as Mao Yuanxin's notes, that we believe credible on the basis of analysis of the specific items, supporting documentation when available, and our knowledge of the authors. On this source, see the Preface, above, p. xviii.

[36] Our deduction is that these two, whose identity was "inconvenient to reveal," were Chen Xilian and Ji Dengkui. See Qing and Fang, *Deng zai 1976*, vol. 1, p. 144.

delayed while mulling over the leadership implications of the May Day proposal (see below).[37]

Less is known about the April 1 meeting than any of the other Politburo sessions during the crisis. While the handling of the Nanjing issue has been portrayed as a radical initiative, it almost certainly reflected the consensus of the small Politburo gathering. Furthermore, the conduct of the meeting suggests a different meaning than radical dominance. The striking features were: 1) Zhang Chunqiao did not attend, while Wang Hongwen reportedly remained completely silent; and 2) Hua assumed the chair, compared to six days earlier, when Wang reportedly chaired the March 26 expanded Politburo meeting on the anti-Deng campaign. The meeting thus reflected an ongoing shift of authority to Hua that was only completed after the crisis on April 7. As emphasized in Chapter 6, before the crisis the leadership pecking order was confused, with Hua prominent as Acting Premier, but outranked by Wang and others in the Party, while responsibility for the daily work of the Center unclear. The discussion of May Day arrangements further underlined the ambiguity: rather than the traditional practice of assembling the leadership in rank order, a proposal to divide the leadership into three smaller groups at different venues finessed the problem. This probably indicates that Mao had not finally made up his mind about Hua, and certainly that the Politburo was uncertain of the Chairman's intentions. As for Zhang's absence and Wang's silence on the 1st, we can only speculate that a possible consideration was that, given their East China responsibilities, and especially Zhang's role as the main target of protests in Nanjing, they were not considered sufficiently disinterested to take charge. Arguably related to this was Mao's ongoing preoccupation with Party unity, a repeated feature of his thinking since the Lin Biao affair, and his apparent belief that Hua had the qualities of a unifying figure. In the absence of direct information, we cannot be sure that Mao ordered this arrangement, but it is a logical conclusion, particularly in view of the fact that Mao Yuanxin proposed the meeting. A final aspect of the emergency meeting, and a pointer to subsequent developments at Tiananmen, was the absence of any order for a physical crackdown in Nanjing, nor did the meeting classify the developments there as a "*counterrevolutionary* incident."[38]

---

[37] Chen and Du, *Shilu*, vol. 3, part 2, pp. 1353, 1355-56; Qing and Fang, *Deng zai 1976*, vol. 1, pp. 144-46; and Yan and Gao, *Turbulent Decade*, p. 491. Regarding Mao Yuanxin's written reports, there is considerable uncertainty as to precisely what was involved. Had they been vetted by the Politburo before being presented to Mao? Were they sometimes/always/never accompanied by Mao Yuanxin's oral comments, or did these occur separately? While guesswork on our part, we believe it most likely that any written report, whether vetted or not, would have largely reflected actual Politburo discussions and decisions, while Mao Yuanxin probably provided his own emphases in any oral exchanges.

[38] See Qing and Fang, *Deng zai 1976*, vol. 1, pp. 123, 125, 144-46, 207; and above, pp. 445-47. While initially, the less pejorative "reactionary" label was applied to the Nanjing events, in one respect the Politburo on April 1 used "counterrevolutionary" to describe the claims concerning Zhou's alleged will. Chen and Du, *Shilu*, vol. 3, part 2, p. 1353.

The Politburo next met during the evening of the *Qingming* festival itself to discuss developments at Tiananmen. Before dawn on the previous day, April 3, Wang Hongwen visited the Square, examining wreaths and memorial poems by flashlight. Although hostile post-Mao accounts report Wang demanding to know why reactionary poems had not been taken down, an apparent outcome of Wang's visit was that restraint was observed on the 3rd, and indeed, in different forms, well into the evening of the 5th. On the 4th, Mao Yuanxin was again present taking notes when the Politburo convened, and—as on April 1—there is no report that he conveyed any message from Mao before the session, something more certainly the case on this occasion. The first item of business was to hear a report on Tiananmen developments from Wu De who, as the local Party leader and mayor of Beijing, had direct management responsibilities for handling the situation, and who would be forever linked to and blighted by the events of this and the following day. Wu gave a detailed report on the numbers of wreaths and units involved, as well as the types of people who came to Tiananmen. While acknowledging the presence of reactionary sentiments and making remarks linking Deng to the events on the Square, Wu advocated further investigation, saying it was not a big deal, we should do work among the masses, and the wreaths could soon be transferred to the Babaoshan Revolutionary Cemetery. Indeed, Wu's subordinates had earlier made a tacit agreement with "mass representatives" that wreaths could remain until the 6th. In Wu's subsequent recounting, his proposal gained everyone's agreement, and, similar to Nanjing, at this stage, while some spoke of "counterrevolutionary activities" at Tiananmen, no one said this was a "counterrevolutionary incident."[39]

At about 10 p.m., a report received by Yao Wenyuan from *People's Daily* reporters on the Square dramatically changed the atmosphere. This report emphasized anti-Jiang Qing sentiments, resulting in Jiang's ire and demands for the immediate arrest of the offenders. Others, reportedly including Chen Xilian, Ji Dengkui and Chen Yonggui, also called for action. Jiang further berated Wu De as an "old rightist deeply affected by Deng Xiaoping's poison," and angrily rejected his plan to let matters rest for a couple more days. Wu was forced to make a self-criticism, and then checked with Beijing Garrison Commander Wu Zhong about the feasibility of arrests. Wu Zhong argued that this would be provocative, but when Wu De conveyed this to the Politburo, the body insisted

---

Qing and Fang, p. 123, report Wang chairing the March 26 meeting, while *Deng nianpu*, vol. 1, p. 148, records Deng attending, but does not indicate who presided. As for the May Day arrangements, similar arrangements were used for major holidays in 1972 and 1973 following the Lin Biao affair, but more orthodox appearances of a (largely) full leadership had resumed by October 1974. See above, p. 31n18.

[39] *Wu De koushu*, pp. 206, 208-209; Qing and Fang, *Deng zai 1976*, vol. 1, pp. 170-72, 178-79, 227; and Chen and Du, *Shilu*, vol. 3, part 2, p. 1360. Defining the protests as a "counterrevolutionary incident" would be a significant escalation from simply noting counterrevolutionary aspects of the events, an escalation indicating the need for more forceful action. Note also that at this stage, neither had the events in Hangzhou been described as a "counterrevolutionary incident"; above, p. 470n21.

on proceeding and the arrests were made. With this settled, the question of what forces should be mobilized as a precautionary measure was discussed. Jiang Qing, supported by the ranking military man present, Chen Xilian, called for the dispatch of troops, but Wang Hongwen, Zhang Chunqiao and Yao Wenyuan, with Hua's agreement, insisted that any force should be limited to public security forces and especially the militia.[40]

The key issue, however, was the fate of the wreaths. Wu De continued to argue for his proposal to continue mass work for another two days, with Jiang angrily claiming this was giving counterrevolutionaries more time. When the meeting passed midnight, she demanded removing the wreaths before dawn, saying there was no longer any justification for delay since *Qingming* was over. Wu tried to argue against this with flimsy excuses that there were insufficient trucks and workers for the task, leading to a standoff and silence. Finally, Hua asked Wu to do his best and see whether he could handle the matter that night. Many years later, Wu reflected that if Hua had supported him, the Tiananmen incident might have been avoided. But on the night, Wu De had to carry out the Politburo decision, ironically adapting words from his report earlier in the evening, to deal with what was now declared a "counterrevolutionary incident [that had] developed out of long preparations by Deng Xiaoping."[41]

During the Politburo meeting of April 4, both Hua and Wu De made statements that would later be used against them. In Hua's case, apparently in response to the changed mood following the *People's Daily* report concerning sentiment on the Square, he declared that "a batch of bad people have jumped out, written things unmistakenly attacking the Chairman, [made] very many attacks on the Party Center, inciting the masses, [and are] very vicious." This statement, of course, was understandable in terms of both the general situation facing the leadership, and the specific dynamics of the meeting. It is, however, virtually the only aspect of Hua's performance during the entire crisis that has been prominently criticized from a post-Mao perspective. Even when Hua was subject to blatantly distorted criticism in the early 1980s, hardly anything of substance was said concerning his Tiananmen performance, which had tended to veer toward moderation when the option existed. Wu De would be more harshly dealt with in the future on the Tiananmen issue, and indeed his statements on April 4 went much further than Hua's. Wu's great sin retrospectively was to attack Deng directly, seemingly introducing what became the Politburo conclusion by linking the events on the Square to Deng's activities over a long period going back to 1974, and involving his attacks on certain people [i.e., the radicals] for their opposition to Zhou Enlai. What is somewhat puzzling is that Wu's remarks occurred during his initial report, i.e., before Jiang Qing's accusations concerning how deeply he had been affected

---

[40] Qing and Fang, *Deng zai 1976*, vol. 1, pp. 160, 172-77, 227; *Wu De koushu*, p. 209; and Mao Mao, *"Wenge" suiyue*, p. 471.

[41] *Wu De koushu*, pp. 209-11.

by Deng's poison. We can only speculate that Wu felt obliged to make some critical comments given the situation on the Square, the heightened "criticize Deng" campaign, and above all his understanding of Mao's increasingly negative attitude toward Deng. Particularly suggestive is the fact that, in this context, Wu declared the events on the Square "the biggest adverse current since the start of the Cultural Revolution"—thus homing in on the Chairman's greatest preoccupation and fear. When added to the events of the following day, the ultimate result was disastrous for Wu's career.[42]

What is particularly striking about the leadership politics of April 4 is that, according to all available accounts, not only had no message from Mao preceded the Politburo discussion, but in addition, the decisions to remove the wreaths and writings, send the militia (the main component) and public security personnel to the vicinity of the Square as a precaution, and mobilize garrison troops in reserve, were taken by the Politburo without reference to the Chairman. As following the April 1 meeting, Mao Yuanxin prepared a written report for the Chairman before dawn on the 5th. While at some point Mao circled the report, moves to clear the Square of wreaths were clearly underway earlier, and in all likelihood Wang Hongwen had already visited the Square at 5:10 a.m. to instruct the combined security forces on how to deal with the situation during the coming day.[43]

Wang Hongwen's pre-dawn visit requires analysis. Various post-Mao sources imply a close relationship between Wang and the deputy head of the Beijing militia, Ma Xiaoliu, who was further denounced for his role in the violence late on April 5. This greatly overstates the significance of any Wang-Ma connection, as well as exaggerating Ma's culpability in simply carrying out orders from the Politburo as a whole on the night of the 5th. A quite different picture is given by Wang's early morning inspection. After checking on the removal of the wreaths, Wang proceeded to the joint headquarters on the edge of the Square to give his instructions for the day. Finding that people who had been arrested during the night were being mistreated, Wang intervened to stop the beatings and ordered the restraint that marked the performance of the militia throughout the chaotic events of the day. In chastising Ma and other personnel, Wang reportedly both affirmed the political role for the militia laid down by Mao as the "advanced armed force of the working class," and demanded the highest standards in dealing with the masses.[44]

The removal of the wreaths was a rare instance, arguably the first time in

---

[42] Qing and Fang, *Deng zai 1976*, vol. 1, pp. 178, 180; *Wu De koushu*, p. 208; and Chen and Du, *Shilu*, vol. 3, part 2, p. 1360. See Tan Zongji, "The Third Plenum of the Eleventh Central Committee is a Major Turning Point in the History of the Party Since the Founding of the People's Republic of China," *Chinese Law and Government*, May-June 1995, for a comprehensive hatchet job on every imaginable failing of Hua, but one which steers clear of Tiananmen.

[43] See Chen and Du, *Shilu*, vol. 3, part 2, pp. 1361-63; *Wu De koushu*, pp. 206-11; and Qing and Fang, *Deng zai 1976*, vol. 1, pp. 180-83.

[44] See Qing and Fang, *Deng zai 1976*, vol. 1, pp. 184-87.

the history of the PRC, when a major political decision was taken without the decisive input of the Chairman. It might be said, nevertheless, that however fateful the removal of the wreaths turned out in the event, from the perspective of the Politburo at the time, it must not have seemed so critical as to require disturbing a seriously ill Mao, and there may also have been a general assumption that removing the offending wreaths was the least he would expect. While Politburo members undoubtedly believed the decision was not as momentous as eventuated, it is extremely unlikely that the body would not have referred a decision on a major crisis in the heart of Beijing to a well Mao. In any case, the political process quickly returned to a more familiar path as the next, far more fateful step, that of moving against people in Tiananmen Square on the night of April 5, once again reflected the hand of the Chairman. According to Qing Ye and Fang Lei, following a Politburo meeting on the morning of the 5th, Mao met with Mao Yuanxin to discuss developments at Tiananmen after Hua had asked Mao Yuanxin to seek instructions as popular anger escalated on the Square.[45] In this context, it is important to emphasize that Mao, whose access to information had become increasingly restricted with the worsening of his health over the past year, at this critical juncture was to a large extent, though not solely, dependent on his nephew, his liaison officer, for an understanding of developments beyond the walls of Zhongnanhai, and particularly of the Politburo's handling of the crisis. Indeed, elite suspicions since the previous fall that Mao Yuanxin was distorting information must have been present even if, as previously, there is no evidence of anyone challenging the veracity of his communications.[46]

In any case, in his face-to-face encounter with the Chairman on the morning of April 5, Mao Yuanxin presented accusations against Deng, and reported that the Politburo was not unanimous about what to do as disturbances grew on the Square.[47] Concerning Deng, when Mao Yuanxin claimed that he had single-handedly planned and incited the counterrevolutionary incident on the Square, the Chairman seemed less than convinced, and asked for proof. He also rejected Zhang Chunqiao's claim at the morning's Politburo session that Deng was China's Imre Nagy and had caused a "Hungarian incident." The crux of the

---

[45] Qing and Fang, *Deng zai 1976*, vol. 1, pp. 197-98.

[46] Certainly Hua had no access to Mao in these crucial days, as affirmed by Deng in 1978; see Garside, *Coming Alive*, p. 207. According to Zhang Yufeng's testimony in 1980, Jiang Qing did see Mao at least once in this period, but members of Mao's work staff were forbidden by Jiang and Mao Yuanxin to leave Zhongnanhai; Qing and Fang, *Deng zai 1976*, vol. 1, pp. 219-20. As both Zhongnanhai security chief and a Politburo member, Wang Dongxing also had access to the Chairman, as vividly demonstrated on April 7 (see below). In addition, a potentially important source of information was *People's Daily* internal reports edited by Yao Wenyuan that allegedly "cheated Chairman Mao." See Yu Huanchun, "*Renmin ribao* yu 1976 nian Tiananmen shijian" [The *People's Daily* and the 1976 Tiananmen Incident], *BNC*, no. 2 (1998), p. 44.

[47] The differences largely centered on the degree of force to be used, with Jiang Qing calling for the option of machine guns, but Hua and especially Wang Hongwen and Zhang Chunqiao objecting (see below).

encounter, however, was the Politburo's request for instructions. This produced three directives from Mao: 1) an affirmation that the Tiananmen disturbances were indeed an organized "counterrevolutionary rebellion"; 2) authorization for the Politburo to use necessary force, but not firearms or combat troops; and 3) stipulating that Deng, whose bearing of responsibility for the counterrevolutionary incident could not be denied, be placed under investigation. While these directives limited both the extent of force and any immediate purge of Deng, they marked a clear decision that force would be used if required. In seeking clarification on this point, Mao Yuanxin asked whether the Chairman was approving the use of force, and Mao reportedly answered: "Right, a gentlemen uses his mouth [persuasion] but also uses his fists" (*junzi dongkou ye dongshou*), a sentence Qing and Fang claim pushed the Tiananmen incident toward the bloodshed of that evening. When Mao Yuanxin conveyed Mao's message to the Politburo as it reconvened in the early afternoon, the predictable response was unanimous support by all members present, apparently including Deng Xiaoping.[48]

There was, however, a tension between using the mouth and using the fists in the Politburo's effort to carry out Mao's orders. As soon as Mao's instructions were received, Wang Hongwen, with his experience in developing the Shanghai militia if not a national militia command, advocated mobilizing 100,000 militiamen. Wu De and alternate Politburo member Ni Zhifu, the commander of the Beijing militia, argued against such numbers, citing the possibility of chaos and offering the excuse that the Beijing militia wasn't as good as Shanghai's. Wu, and seemingly Hua, hoped that persuasion would work, and they gained crucial support from Zhang Chunqiao, who suggested using a radio broadcast. Jiang Qing accepted the idea, although in the process she confronted Wu with the accusation that he was afraid of the masses, and demanded that he undertake the task and do it at the Square itself. Wu then drafted the speech, which was vetted by Hua and unanimously approved. Using the radical rhetoric of the moment in warning of counterrevolutionary sabotage, calling for the defense of Mao and the Party Center, and attacking the revisionist line of the unrepentant capitalist roader (but not mentioning Deng by name),[49] the speech would create anger as well as an incentive to leave the Square. Recorded by Wu De, the speech was played starting at 6:30 p.m.[50]

Over the next few hours the crowd on the Square dwindled as Wu's speech

---

[48] Qing and Fang, *Deng zai 1976*, vol. 1, pp. 215-19, 223-24; and *Wu De koushu*, p. 212. Qing and Fang is the only source we have seen that refers specifically to Mao Yuanxin's morning talk with Mao or cites the Chairman's words, but Wu De's account confirms the essence of Mao Yuanxin conveying orders that involved the use of restrained force. As for Deng's presence, *Deng nianpu*, vol. 1, p. 149, confirms his attendance at the morning session, but does not mention the afternoon.

[49] When Wu's speech was published after the decision to strip Deng of his posts, Deng's name was added. See *Wu De koushu*, p. 214; and Chen and Du, *Shilu*, vol. 3, part 2, p. 1364.

[50] *Wu De koushu*, pp. 212-14; Qing and Fang, *Deng zai 1976*, vol. 1, pp. 225-26, 227; and Li Naiyin, "Yao Wenyuan de zhaji," p. 38.

was broadcast over and over again. The decision to begin broadcasts at 6:30 also stipulated that forceful clearing of the Square would start at 8 p.m. Wu De and Ni Zhifu went to the Beijing Garrison Command headquarters to consult with Wu Zhong, and the three leaders, fearing bloodshed, decided to stall as long as possible to reduce the crowd to a minimum, with Wu Zhong then departing for the Revolutionary History Museum on the edge of the Square to coordinate action at Tiananmen. Hua and Chen Xilian phoned shortly after 8 to enquire why no action had been taken, but the three continued to stall, inventing various excuses. The Politburo was impatient, undoubtedly mindful that Mao had ordered "fists" when "mouths" no longer worked. Finally, about 10:30, Hua and Chen rang again, and force could no longer be delayed. Wu Zhong's last maneuver was to turn on the lights and play Wu De's speech one final time to scare people away, and once the majority left, around 11 p.m. the brief spasm of violence occurred. The violence was not only brief, lasting no more than 10 to 15 minutes, it also involved only clubs and no deadly force, and was limited in physical consequences. Despite popular rumors, no one died, and arrests were relatively few. But blood had been shed, and the image of the suppression would become a major problem for Mao's successors, despite the efforts of those directly concerned to keep matters as restrained as possible.[51]

No one, of course, would be more tainted than Wu De. We have argued that Wu was thrust into a leading role by virtue of his job, and had more or less consistently advocated a soft approach to events on the Square. He did misstep by criticizing Deng at the April 4 Politburo meeting, and possibly on the 5th as well, but this can perhaps be explained, if not necessarily excused, by the pressure of events and the existing anti-Deng campaign, as well as by the fact that as the responsible leader for the capital he could not adopt a lower profile. It is also of interest that Wu had good working relations with Deng before the Cultural Revolution, and had been—along with Li Xiannian—advised by Deng in fall 1975 to keep his distance in order to survive as the anti-rightist movement began to unfold.[52] In this respect, what might be termed the Deng family verdict on Wu by Deng's daughter, Mao Mao, a quarter-century later, is revealing. Mao Mao ignores Wu's remarks of the 4th, and makes only one brief reference to Wu, a reference indicating the belief that he was acting against his will on April 5: "[At 6:30 p.m.] Beijing First Secretary Wu De *acting under orders* (*fengming*) gave a

---

[51] *Wu De koushu*, pp. 214-16; Qing and Fang, *Deng zai 1976*, vol. 1, pp. 227-28, 232; interview with Party historian specializing on the period, November 2002; and above, p. 474n26. Concerning the extent of violence, post-Mao investigations conducted by Peng Zhen confirmed Wu De's claim that there were no deaths (p. 219), while Ma Qibin, *Sishinian*, p. 400, reports only 38 people arrested, as well as another 39 three days earlier. Overall, including people rounded up as a result of investigations after the demonstrations, 388 were arrested, most of whom were released shortly after the fall of the "gang." For rumors of deaths and many more arrests on April 5, see Garside, *Coming Alive*, pp. 132-33n; and Baum, *Burying Mao*, p. 402-403n30.

[52] See above, pp. 405.

broadcast speech, declaring the Tiananmen incident was a 'counterrevolutionary incident,' [and] demanded that the masses in the Square leave immediately."[53] Another major actor, and long-standing Deng associate, who would suffer as a Mao-loyalist in the post-Mao period, Chen Xilian, also drew no criticism (or praise) in Mao Mao's book. Chen, however, did have some guilt concerning the events of early April, although not over developments on the Square. Years later he reflected that there was only one thing for which he owed Deng an apology, and that was his failure to refute charges against Deng during the heated discussions of early April 1976.[54] As we shall explore in our Volume II, the subsequent demise of Wu, Chen and other alleged "neo-Maoists" was a complex process involving some genuine Cultural Revolution excesses, elite misperceptions, and, it would appear, a willingness on Deng's part to sacrifice them, rather than being a consequence of opposition to Deng during the Tiananmen crisis or later.

If Wu De and Chen Xilian had felt the need to attack or simply not defend Deng due to the weight of circumstances, the radicals consistently pushed the case against him. The most significant instance apparently took place during the late afternoon of the 5th as events headed toward the violence of the evening. Jiang Qing went to see the Chairman and, in view of Mao's conclusion that Deng bore responsibility for the "counterrevolutionary rebellion" on the Square, proposed that Deng be expelled from the Party. Mao did not respond immediately, but later decided that Deng would retain his Party membership, a decision formalized on April 7. While this turn of events surprised Deng and elicited his profuse thanks, the incident indicates more than Jiang's implacable hostility toward Deng. For Mao, the issue at Tiananmen, and indeed for the entire post-Lin Biao period, was defending *his* Cultural Revolution. As he put it shortly thereafter, the events on the Square were a case of "firing at me, [and] all in all repudiating the Cultural Revolution." Mao understood that Deng, as Zhou before him, was completely loyal politically and personally, but he had concluded that Deng could not be relied upon ideologically to stay true to the Cultural Revolution vision. Deng's responsibility lay not in organizing protests, which would have merited expulsion, but in Mao's belief that his implementation of policies in 1975 had strayed from the vision. From this perspective, the assertion in the *People's Daily* the next day that the ongoing campaign aimed at Deng was "the continuation and deepening

---

[53] Mao Mao, *"Wenge" suiyue*, p. 472 (emphasis added). This echoes Wu's own claim that he had been forced to read out what had been prepared by the "gang of four." Fan Shuo, *Ye Jianying zai feichang shiqi*, vol. 2, p. 538.

[54] Interview with an exceptionally well-connected senior Party historian, July 1999. Another Party historian detected guilt when interviewing Chen, but was unable to determine the reason; interview, December 2002. Chen's overall performance during the crisis is somewhat difficult to characterize. On the 4th, Chen supported Wu on the issue of letting the wreaths remain for a few days, but subsequently backed Jiang Qing's call for their removal. As a military man, he was concerned with the positioning of PLA forces and offered to provide troops if needed. And on the evening of the 5th, he pressed Wu *et al.* for action once the deadline passed. See Qing and Fang, *Deng zai 1976*, vol. 1, pp. 172, 175, 177.

of the Cultural Revolution" was the essence of the matter.[55]

With Tiananmen forcibly cleared, the Politburo met again in night session on April 5-6. The meeting heard Beijing public security chief Liu Chuanxin report on the day's events, and also outline preparations for preventing new outbreaks. Liu reported that nine battalions of garrison troops were ready, but indicated that the militia and public security personnel were completely capable of handling the situation as long as they were authorized to use clubs. This can be interpreted as another sign of restraint from Wu De's municipal apparatus, in that it served to fend off recourse to firearms. The Politburo authorized the mobilization of additional militia on standby, but also stipulated that the militia should not lightly decide to appear on the Square. While Hua articulated the meeting's view that an "outright counterrevolutionary incident" had occurred, he added a calming note, observing that victory would be easily achieved if everyone settled down and looked at things accurately. Finally, Hua proposed a notice to the whole nation explaining the nature of the previous two days' events, a document that would be submitted to the Chairman for his approval. Mao Yuanxin prepared another detailed written report for his uncle on the meeting and the day's developments at 3 a.m. Later on the 6th, a reportedly pleased Chairman wrote on Mao Yuanxin's report: "Morale is buoyant, good, good, good." That evening, the Politburo authorized drafting the notice to the nation, including a report by the Beijing Party committee, and the next morning Mao approved publication of a *People's Daily* report on events in the Square and Wu De's speech—but not the Beijing Party report. What remained to be settled on April 7 was a revised leadership arrangement that fixed Hua's status as the successor.[56]

What can be said about the political dynamics of this intense period? There is little to suggest that the crisis was the result of any clear "gang of four" strategy to attack Zhou, with the key factor of the March 25 *Wenhui bao* article a clumsy mistake rather than a provocation. Although the "gang's" impatience to focus on the criticism of Deng and regard memorializing Zhou as an insidious distraction was a contributing factor, it was less significant than Mao's grudging attitude toward the late Premier and his specific assessment of mourning activities. As events unfolded at Tiananmen, the Politburo was faced with an unprecedented and fast-moving situation with uncertainties concerning both the population

---

[55] Qing and Fang, *Deng zai 1976*, vol. 1, p. 220; *Mao zhuan*, vol. 2, pp. 1776-77; Mao Mao, "*Wenge*" *suiyue*, pp. 482-84; "Zhang Yufeng jie Mao wannian mimi cailiao"; and Chen and Du, *Shilu*, vol. 3, part 2, p. 1367. We have deduced the timing of Jiang's visit from the context, as the several times given in the sources are either implausible or unlikely.

[56] See Chen and Du, *Shilu*, vol. 3, part 2, pp. 1364-67; Qing and Fang, *Deng zai 1976*, vol. 1, pp. 228-33; and Mao Mao, "*Wenge*" *suiyue*, p. 473. Regarding the precise timing of Mao's "good, good, good" comment, the sources differ. Clearly erroneous is the claim of Ma Qibin, *Sishinian*, p. 400, placing it on the 4th. Several sources, e.g., Qing and Fang, p. 232, place it at 11 a.m. on the 6th, while Chen and Du, p. 1367, give the time as 6 p.m. on the same day. According to "Yao Wenyuan dui *Hongqi zazhi*," p. 1, the comment came as Mao watched a film of the militia finally using force against the remaining demonstrators on the Square.

below and the Chairman above. While there were well-established predilections on issues such as dealing with Deng which reflected the divisive politics of the entire "Cultural Revolution decade," responses in the heat of the moment were very much *ad hoc*, diverse, and to an extent unpredictable. In terms of the decisions actually taken, for all of the missteps—none greater than removing the wreaths on the night of April 4-5—restraint was the dominant tendency. This certainly appears to have been the case with leading establishment beneficiaries Hua Guofeng and Wu De, although Hua's willingness to bend on the issue of removing the wreaths, and to apply pressure on Wu as the deadline for violent action passed on the 5th, demonstrated some weakness in resisting Jiang Qing's hard-line demands.[57]

In fact, notwithstanding understandable inconsistencies, restraint was the dominant tendency for virtually the entire Politburo, with Jiang Qing the only member clearly arguing more or less consistently for harsh action. The Politburo radicals, while emphasizing the reactionary nature of events on the Square and attempting to use the situation against Deng, were divided over the use of force, with Jiang Qing agitating for strong action, while Zhang Chunqiao, Wang Hongwen and Yao Wenyuan counseled restraint. A purported exchange between Jiang and Wang on the morning of April 5 expresses these differences in striking terms:

> Wang Hongwen: "We can dispatch a few more militia and soldiers, but without exception there must be no weapons."
>
> Jiang Qing: "Not carry weapons, aren't you hindering our militia and soldiers in wiping out counterrevolution?"
>
> Wang Hongwen: "If you want to carry weapons you can! If you want to open fire you can do that too! In any case, I will not be responsible for this crime."[58]

Notwithstanding the reference to soldiers, this exchange reflected Wang's (and Zhang and Yao's) more general position during the crisis of consistently favoring the use of the militia over the PLA, something which could be attributed in part to Wang's role in developing the Shanghai militia, as well as to an awareness based on Cultural Revolution experience of the danger inherent in the army confronting the people.[59] Moreover, while Wang may have been quick to call for mobilizing a

---

[57] As for other leading beneficiaries, see above, p. 485n54, on Chen Xilian. There is remarkably little evidence concerning Ji Dengkui in the detailed account of Qing and Fang, *Deng zai 1976*, vol. 1, although they do report one striking statement by Ji accusing Deng of crimes on April 5 (p. 196).

[58] Qing and Fang, *Deng zai 1976*, vol. 1, p. 197. While it is possible that Qing and Fang, the sole source for the exchange, have embellished it, it is broadly consistent with the account in *Wu De koushu*, which presents an aggressive Jiang, but is more restrained concerning Wang, Zhang and Yao, not picturing them as eager to use force. In addition, a number of senior Party historians were specifically questioned about this passage, and found it credible. Interviews, January 2005.

[59] For other instances of Wang and Zhang opposing the use of troops and deadly force, see Qing and Fang, *Deng zai 1976*, vol. 1, pp. 132, 177, 187. In 1974, Zhang reportedly reflected on Shanghai's January 1967 "revolutionary storm," and commented that if the military handled security, "there

huge militia force on the afternoon of the 5th, that morning he had ordered militia restraint. And as the situation deteriorated in the late afternoon, Zhang proposed the use of broadcasts that potentially could delay and reduce the consequences of using such force. In any case, Wang, Zhang and Yao's sharp differences with Jiang Qing over the appropriate level of force to deal with events on the Square again raise questions about the very notion of a "gang of four."[60]

As asserted in critical post-Mao accounts, responsibility lay with "the Politburo of the time." But, as Qing and Fang ask rhetorically, "Whose decision did Hua Guofeng and the Politburo carry out [on April 5]? Mao Zedong's? The 'gang of four's'? Or Mao Yuanxin's? [This is] very hard to say clearly."[61] A tentative answer might be that the pressure created by Jiang Qing's demands and the disturbances on the Square, possible distortions in Mao Yuanxin's two-way reporting, but ultimately Mao's perceived and actually expressed wishes changed the nature of the situation from a threatening challenge that would hopefully have faded away as the *Qingming* festival receded into memory into a full-blown "incident" that would intensify popular anger with the regime in the short run, and dog elite politics for several years to come thereafter.

Indeed, what is most striking about the Tiananmen events is the degree to which the crisis was dominated by the Chairman, even as ill health limited his ability to control events, and despite the fact that the Politburo, in a largely unprecedented manner, took critical decisions without Mao's direct approval, especially the removal of the wreaths. Mao's attitude toward Zhou was crucial in shaping the prelude to the crisis, and anticipation of his sensibilities certainly weighed on the minds of Politburo members during the unfolding events on the Square. An instinctive sense of the need to protect the Chairman's prestige arguably drove what turned out to be the fateful decision to remove the wreaths on April 4, and Mao himself took the even more fateful decision to authorize force on the 5th which, despite the prohibition on deadly weapons, undercut efforts to avoid the spilling of blood. That Mao's "line" was sacrosanct throughout the crisis, and upholding it was second nature to Politburo members, is hardly surprising. As we have repeatedly seen, it was, in fact, the essential requirement of elite politics during all phases, moderate as well as radical, at the end of the Maoist era.

---

will come a day when the masses will be unhappy." *Shanghai minbing douzheng shi ziliao*, vol. 17 (1980), p. 59.

[60] In addition to the discussion of the use of force above, other indications of differences among the four include the absence of any charges against Wang Hongwen concerning the Tiananmen incident during the 1980 trial of the "gang." See *A Great Trial, passim*. From the different perspective of popular perceptions, throughout the entire period beginning with scattered attacks on the radicals following Zhou Enlai's death, through the Nanjing and Tiananmen incidents, and extending to the days and weeks following the crackdown of April 5, denunciations were apparently directed solely at a "gang of three": Jiang Qing, Zhang Chunqiao and Yao Wenyuan. Notably, two days after the crackdown on the 7th, students in Beijing attacked the "three family village" of Jiang, Zhang and Yao. Gao and Yan, *Shinianshi*, pp. 660-61.

[61] Qing and Fang, *Deng zai 1976*, vol. 1, p. 228.

Deng's Fate and the Revised Political Equation

When Mao Yuanxin briefed his uncle on the events of April 5 and 6 for a bit more than an hour from about 8 a.m. on the morning of the 7th, the key issues mirrored those of late January following the death of Zhou Enlai: the handling of Deng Xiaoping's case, and clarification of power and status within the leadership. While Mao had been unimpressed with Mao Yuanxin's claims on the 5th that Deng had organized the Tiananmen disturbances, he now responded to his nephew's exaggerated emphasis on popular support for Deng on the Square. Mao Yuanxin claimed that the "counterrevolutionary political incident … publicly unfurled and embraced the banner of Deng Xiaoping [and] furiously pointed its spearhead at the great leader Chairman Mao." Noting that the nature of the problem had changed, the Chairman instructed that, "based on this, throw [Deng] out, retain his Party membership, and see how he behaves," and then added that "Hua Guofeng becomes [full] Premier." In dispatching Mao Yuanxin to inform the Politburo of these decisions, he further stipulated that, in addition to Deng, Zhu De, Ye Jianying, Li Xiannian and, rather mysteriously, Su Zhenhua should be excluded from the meeting to ratify his orders. While subsequently modified to exclude only Su, this was still an indication that old revolutionaries would remain on the sidelines until the Chairman's death. In the afternoon, as the Politburo convened, Mao, apparently finally realizing that the Party could no longer put up with an ambiguous leadership arrangement, sent another directive that Hua should also be designated CCP First Vice Chairman, an unprecedented title which now (despite post-Mao attempts to deny such a clear designation) unambiguously placed Hua in the successor role. The meeting dutifully endorsed Mao's instructions, and at 8 p.m. two resolutions were announced to the nation, the first appointing Hua to his new posts, the second declaring that the nature of Deng's contradiction had become antagonistic, and removing him from office on precisely the terms the Chairman had decreed.[62]

---

[62] See Mao Mao, *"Wenge" suiyue*, pp. 473-74, 478; Qing and Fang, *Deng zai 1976*, vol. 1, pp. 232-34; *Wu De koushu*, p. 217; and Chen and Du, *Shilu*, vol. 3, part 2, p. 1368. Party historians today are unable to understand Su Zhenhua's exclusion, much as Wu De and Wang Dongxing reportedly could not understand it at the time. Although someone who had resisted the Cultural Revolution, Su historically had been close to Mao, being responsible for his security on the Long March, and, as we have seen, had been among the first of the old.revolutionaries rehabilitated after the Lin Biao affair, and was raised more rapidly to Politburo status (as an alternate) than anyone else in his situation. Mao also placed particular importance on Su's role in reviving China's navy, evaluating his work highly in May 1975. *Mao wengao*, vol. 13, pp. 290, 434; interviews, February 2000 and November 2002; and above, pp. 41, 295. A possible explanation is that Mao's order, rather than reflecting a negative view of Su, was an indication that he had been assigned important duties at this critical juncture.

As for the old revolutionaries as a group, while many would soon appear in public as a symbol of Party unity, notably on May Day, there is nothing to indicate they exercised any power after the Tiananmen incident. The May Day leadership list was largely identical to the previous year's National Day list, with the notable exceptions of the absence of Deng, the placement of Hua at the top, and the reappearance of Wang Hongwen, who had been in Shanghai in October 1975, in the number two position. Also, Chen Xilian, who had been in Xinjiang in October, was now listed

Deng Xiaoping's fate was entirely in Mao's hands, and once again the Chairman opted for mercy by allowing him to retain his Party membership. Despite the new categorization as an antagonistic contradiction, Deng would still have a chance to mend his ways under observation. But Mao's protection of Deng went beyond this. When the Politburo met on the 7th, Jiang Qing and Zhang Chunqiao took up Deng's case. They spoke of the possibility of the masses trying to "storm" and seize Deng, and raised the accusation that he had gone to Tiananmen to command the scene. Hua, arguably seeking to protect Deng, deflected these claims by saying it was necessary to ask Deng himself to be sure of the facts. No one offered to undertake the task of quizzing Deng, so Jiang nominated Wang Dongxing. Wang, reminiscent of his crucial role in guaranteeing Deng's security in Jiangxi on Mao's orders, was concerned that there really would be an attempt to seize Deng, and went directly to Mao for instructions. When Wang recounted the Politburo discussion, Mao apparently again took little interest in claims of Deng's active role on the Square, instead harking back to Liu Bing's letter, that is, the events of fall 1975 that left him so disappointed in his colleague. On the matter of Deng possibly being attacked or seized, Mao declared it could not be allowed, and asked Wang what could be done. Wang proposed moving Deng's residence to a new location, and the Chairman agreed.[63]

Wang Dongxing quickly implemented Mao's instructions. He also asked Deng about the accusations concerning the Square, which Deng denied, claiming he had only gone to the nearby Beijing Hotel for a haircut. Wang then returned to the Politburo and repeated Deng's account, but kept secret that Deng had been moved. During subsequent Politburo meetings, Jiang Qing complained that Deng had disappeared, but seemingly was powerless to do anything about it. Meanwhile, on April 8, Deng wrote to Wang both expressing his gratitude at being allowed to retain his Party membership, and affirming that he embraced Hua's new appointments as First Vice Chairman and Premier. While hardly anything else could have been expected, decades later Deng's daughter claimed he had been completely sincere in supporting this decision that was so important to the fate of China, a clear indication of the underlying coincidence of interests of the old revolutionaries and establishment beneficiaries. Thereafter, contrary to rumors of Deng being taken to south China under the protection of old revolutionaries such as Xu Shiyou,[64] Deng lived in Beijing in semi-isolation, unable to play any political role until after the arrest of the "gang of four." Under this tight

---

according to his Politburo rank.

[63] Mao Mao, *"Wenge" suiyue*, pp. 474-75. Cf. above, p. 69.

[64] This fiction has appeared in various scholarly sources including Teiwes, *Leadership*, p. 75; and Baum, *Burying Mao*, p. 36. Baum also reports another inaccurate account that placed Deng in Beijing, but under a looser control regime than was in fact the case.

control, he continued to be dependent on Wang Dongxing for everyday needs as well as security.[65]

At the same time that Deng was removed from any residual power as well as being protected, Hua clearly became *the* leader on the "first front" rather than occupying an ambiguous position as previously—a fundamental change in the Party's power equation. The new arrangements strengthened Hua's position in other ways than simply identifying him as the putative successor. As First Vice Chairman, Hua for the first time outranked Wang Hongwen and Zhang Chunqiao in the Party structure. Whether he now became, if he had not been earlier, responsible for the daily work of the Center is not entirely clear, but even if Wang retained some administrative responsibility in this area, he presumably would have been subject to Hua's directives. In the event, in the immediate wash-up of the Tiananmen incident, *both* Hua and Wang took charge of telegraphing to the localities directives dealing with the dissemination of the official interpretation of the Tiananmen events, and the organization of celebrations concerning the "victory" achieved. This, however, was a two-edged sword: while perhaps involving a degree of cooperation between the two men, it also continued ambiguity concerning responsibility for Party affairs that arguably intensified distrust, especially in the period after Mao's death.[66]

Hua's increased status in the government structure was more straightforward: he no longer held a notionally temporary acting appointment. Politically, it also meant that any hope Zhang Chunqiao might still have harbored for the position would have dissolved; in any case, there was no indication of the bitter reaction conventionally (but we believe falsely) ascribed to Zhang after Hua's initial promotion in February. The one area where Hua did not gain enhanced formal power was the military. He was, in fact, left without *any* organizational authority over the PLA, a situation that would not be remedied until after the arrest of the "gang of four." Here Hua presumably had to rely on the principle of "the Party controls the gun," as well as personal relations with Chen Xilian, relations that were apparently marked by mutual trust, and would facilitate close cooperation in the purge of the "gang of four" in October. As the responsible official in charge of MAC daily work, Chen was the key figure in securing army support for the new successor.[67] Finally, a bit belatedly in mid-May, Hua took over responsibility

[65] Mao Mao, *"Wenge" suiyue,* pp. 475ff.

[66] See Qing and Fang, *Deng zai 1976,* vol. 1, p. 237. An indication that Hua took over responsibility for Party Center work at this time, albeit not from the most reliable source, is the report that shortly after Mao's death Zhang Chunqiao said to Hua that "From April on the Chairman clearly said you are in charge of the Center." Xia Chao and Yang Fengcheng, *Longnian zhibian—Zhongguo 1976 nian jishi* [Transformations in the Year of the Dragon—Record of Events in China in 1976] (Shijiazhuang: Hebei renmin chubanshe, 1994), p. 333. On the uncertainty concerning who was responsible for Party daily work preceding the Tiananmen crisis, see above, pp. 446-47. On the distrust following Mao's death, see below, p. 558.

[67] Although oral sources believe Chen was respectful to Ye throughout 1976, there is little concrete evidence of Ye exercising PLA authority before Mao died. Cf. above, pp. 445-46.

for foreign affairs, an area in which he had very limited experience, and in which Jiang Qing had oddly been playing a leadership role since February.[68] There were other clear indications of Mao's intent to strengthen Hua's position. The Chairman ordered that Hua receive publicity in the media, even though Hua was reportedly reluctant to receive such glorification and sought to limit the propaganda, while Yao Wenyuan allegedly attempted to undercut the effort.[69] Mao's most famous endorsement came after receiving New Zealand Prime Minister Muldoon on April 30, when he wrote out and gave to Hua several comments including the soon to be famous, "With you in charge, I'm at ease" (ni banshi, wo fangxin).[70] Hua did not reveal this comment immediately, but instead held it back until after the arrest of the "gang of four," when it was used within the leadership and then massively with the public to bolster the legitimacy of his succession. When Hua was eased from power in the early 1980s, it was claimed that Mao's statement had no broad political meaning for the succession, but was merely the Chairman's approval of Hua handling an administrative matter. In one sense, there is some substance to this claim since Mao had apparently used the fangxin phrase many times when approving the work of Deng Xiaoping and Zhou Enlai, but dismissing the significance of this occasion distorts the situation in April 1976. For one thing, the matter Hua had reported on to Mao was not a secondary administrative matter, but rather the central political issue of the time—the conduct of the anti-Deng campaign which Hua had described as uneven. When combined with the increased organizational authority bestowed on Hua, and the Chairman's concern for his public standing, there can be little doubt that, for whatever reason, Mao had made his final choice of a successor.[71]

[68] "Zhang Hanzhi jiu Qiao Guanhua yu Jiang Qing de guanxi," p. 1. As we have seen, when Hua became Acting Premier, Deng, who had previously been responsible for foreign affairs, was still formally assigned to assist in this area, but in fact had already ceased to have any real function. Shortly afterward, Mao ordered that Minister of Foreign Affairs Qiao Guanhua and his wife Zhang Hanzhi should report via Jiang, although this apparently involved internal ministry politics more than substantive policy. See Mao Mao, "Wenge" suiyue, p. 449; and above, pp. 432-33, 440.

[69] See "Hua Guofeng jiejian lingdao tongzhi de jianghua," p. 2; Wang Dongxing zai guanguo xuanchuan gongzuo jianghua," p. 2; GMRB, November 30, 1976, in SPRCP, no. 6251 (1977), p. 76; and RMRB, March 3, 1977, in SPRCP, no. 6298 (1977), p. 6.

[70] Mao wengao, vol. 13, p. 538. Mao's other comments on the occasion were also supportive: "Take your time, don't be anxious"; and "Act according to past principles." According to Wu De koushu, p. 217, Mao Yuanxin had earlier conveyed the Chairman's fangxin comment to the Politburo on April 7. On the "past principles" question as a major issue between Hua and the "gang" in September, see below, pp. 563ff.

[71] See "Hua Guofeng jiejian lingdao tongzhi de jianghua," p. 2; Deng Liqun, cited in Baum, Burying Mao, pp. 38, 391n39; Andres Onate, "Hua Kuo-feng and the Arrest of the 'Gang of Four'," CQ, no. 75 (1978), p. 550; Geng Biao huiyilu (1949-1992) [Memoirs of Geng Biao, 1949-1992] (Nanjing: Jiangsu renmin chubanshe, 1998), p. 288; and above, p. 381n214. The information that the relevant issue was the anti-Deng campaign, and that Hua reported it was proceeding unevenly in different provinces, comes from Onate based on credible reports from a Guangdong cadre. Geng Biao confirmed that Hua reported on the situation in the provinces, without stipulating that the anti-Deng campaign was the issue.

We are left with the question of why Mao chose Hua for elevation to new heights. In a reported conversation with Wang Dongxing on April 7, the Chairman indicated a number of considerations involving both Hua's credentials and the shortcomings of the radicals, sentiments mirroring his apparent rationale for Hua's original promotion in January.[72] Concerning Hua, Mao noted his broad work experience in industry, agriculture and finance at the county, provincial and central levels, that he was honest and generous, that he was not stupid or selfish, and he was loyal to the Party and people. Echoing his earlier January comment,[73] Mao said "some people think his [theoretical] standard is not very high, but I just want to choose someone who thinks he is of low standard"—an observation perhaps acknowledging reservations about Hua's abilities, and one also consistent with the theory that the Chairman still considered this a stopgap appointment over the longer run. Mao reportedly then commented disparagingly on the radicals. Regarding Wang Hongwen, to that moment the ranking Party figure after the Chairman and an earlier choice as successor, Mao scoffed that "if we allow Wang Hongwen to be in command, no one will be able to eat well except him," a reference to investigations showing that the previous summer in Shanghai Wang had spent over Y20,000 on himself. The Chairman further remarked that Zhang Chunqiao never took responsibility, being "very active with his mouth but not with his hands," questioned Yao Wenyuan's ability to do anything practical, and similarly commented that Jiang Qing "loves to purge people and give them a hard time," but didn't know anything about industry or agriculture. In comparison, Hua must have seemed a good bet.

Beyond these assessments of individuals, some further considerations can be discussed, albeit speculatively. Apart from the need to clarify the leadership arrangement, a strong possibility is that Mao had already made his choice of successor in January, but left it ambiguous in order, as had been his wont in the entire post-Lin Biao period, to observe the performance of his subordinates before fully committing himself. Logically, if Hua had been on trial, then the decision of April 7 reflected the Chairman's satisfaction with his performance—both over the February-March period, and during the Tiananmen crisis itself. Naturally, part of Mao's satisfaction would have been because Hua was pursuing the anti-Deng campaign, but it also was arguably a consequence of Hua's relative balance and restraint in carrying out that campaign. In contrast to his annoyance with

---

[72] The following account of this exchange is based on an interview with an exceptionally well-connected senior Party historian, October 1994. While the degree of coherence attributed to Mao's remarks gives pause in view of his physical condition, this historian has interviewed Wang Dongxing, and probably Zhang Yufeng, who was reportedly present during the conversation, and thus the account has considerable credibility. Mao's key references to Hua were also reported by Wang Dongxing in an interjection during a post-Mao speech by Hua; "Hua Guofeng jiejian lingdao tongzhi de jianghua," p. 2. Of course, distortion by Wang Dongxing or Zhang Yufeng is possible given their animosity toward Jiang Qing, and Wang's interest in justifying the October 1976 coup against the radicals. See above, pp. 441-45, on Mao's January decision.

[73] See above, p. 443.

Jiang Qing for pushing things too far, Mao both before and after the Tiananmen crisis opted for control and avoiding unnecessary exacerbation of the situation, an approach Hua seemed to embody. As we have seen, on March 24 Mao approved the Party Center's notice calling for Party committee control of the *pi Deng* effort, while on April 13 he rejected a proposal brought to him by Mao Yuanxin to publish a collection of so-called counterrevolutionary poems from the Square on the grounds that the incident had already been solved, and this would needlessly expand the problem. The seeming approval of Hua's cautious approach was reflected not only in Mao's April 30 comment that he was "at ease" with him, but also in his advice to Hua on the same occasion to take his time and not give in to anxiety.[74]

It is important to emphasize the transformative impact of the Tiananmen crisis on the power equation in broader perspective. As intimated previously, without the death of Zhou and the subsequent Tiananmen events, it is possible that, as one of the key figures carrying out Deng's agenda in 1975, Hua himself could have been heavily attacked during the escalating anti-Deng campaign.[75] Zhou's death, however, created the need to designate a new State Council leader, and Mao opted for Hua as someone with the necessary administrative experience, while still retaining doubts about Hua's theoretical abilities and continuing to observe his performance. Tiananmen, however, demonstrated the necessity for decisive action on the leadership. Moreover, in addition to his long-standing reservations concerning the radicals as conveyed to Wang Dongxing on the 7th, the events on the Square, however distasteful, would have underlined for the Chairman just how unpopular the "gang" was, and how unsustainable they would be as dominant leaders.

While Hua's organizational and political position was decisively strengthened by Mao's April 7 decision, this still leaves the question of the remaining power of the Politburo radicals. In the aftermath of their "victory" over Deng, the "gang's" power seemed enhanced to many observers within and outside China. With Jiang Qing particularly active, the radicals played a prominent role in propagating the official interpretation of the Tiananmen events and pushing forward the anti-Deng campaign. Given the centrality of these issues and the "gang's" influence over the media, there is little surprise that they had a strong platform for their views, and an ability to bolster support in sympathetic circles inside and outside the Party. But their real power was significantly constrained. They did not have a controlling voice in any of the key institutions of the Party-state. Large segments of society were unsympathetic to their message, while all the railing against the "capitalist class within the Party" in the media did not result in a large-scale mass movement. And at the top, they had few friends in the Politburo. The fact that Jiang Qing could not get information about Deng's whereabouts is indicative, as

---

[74] See *Mao wengao*, vol. 13, pp. 527-28, 529, 533-34; and above, pp. 456-57, 468.

[75] See above, p. 451.

was Wang Dongxing's refusal to cave in to Zhang Chunqiao's demand to put in writing his report on Deng's claim not to have visited the Square.[76] While Jiang in particular had to be taken seriously as the Chairman's wife, and during the unprecedented Tiananmen crisis her demands had a disproportionate influence, she and her fellow radicals were clearly the lesser force in the conflicts that unfolded in the remaining period to Mao's death.

The key clearly was Mao, yet much remains uncertain about his attitude toward Jiang and the other radicals. There can be little doubt of the significance of his sporadic criticisms going back to 1974, and, at least as far as Jiang was concerned, the Chairman continued to criticize her excesses during the anti-Deng campaign.[77] Yet for all his dissatisfaction and doubts about the radicals' capacity to deal with practical matters, there can equally be little doubt that he saw them as a valued force to keep alive the ideals of the Cultural Revolution, as well as providing the theoretical ballast that Hua lacked. There are some arguments, however, that Mao intended much more, including Jiang Qing as the real power after his death. The most frequently cited evidence for this view is the rumor that began to circulate about the time of the trial of the "two cliques" in 1980, reportedly based on Jiang's testimony, that Mao had given Hua additional advice on April 30 that was subsequently suppressed: if there were important matters, he should "consult Jiang Qing."[78] In our view, while Mao may have uttered such an injunction to Hua on April 30 or at another point, it probably had no greater meaning than the Chairman's desire that Hua be attentive to Cultural Revolution values. Similarly, various claims that the Chairman proposed a leadership team for the period after his death with a strong radical representation, to the extent credible, most likely had a balancing objective, rather than reflecting a wish to see the "gang of four" assume power.[79] The overriding factor was that in early April, as a consequence of the Tiananmen crisis, Mao transformed the political equation so that, at a moment of fluidity, the deck was restacked against Jiang Qing and company.

---

[76] See Yan and Gao, *Turbulent Decade*, pp. 509ff; Mao Mao, *"Wenge" suiyue*, pp. 477, 479-81; and Garside, *Coming Alive*, p. 137.

[77] See "Wang Dongxing zai guanguo xuanchuan gongzuo jianghua," p. 2; and above, p. 454.

[78] See John Gardner, *Chinese Politics and the Succession to Mao* (London: Macmillan, 1982), pp. 112-13; and Xing Ziling, *Lin Biao zhengzhuan* [Lin Biao's True Story] (Hong Kong: Liwen chubanshe, 2002), pp. 616-17. Xing makes further claims, e.g., in June Mao advised that Jiang should guide Party affairs, since "someone very bold" was required, that cannot be confirmed. Onate, "Hua Kuo-feng and the Arrest," pp. 547-48, discusses another uncertain Mao injunction that the Politburo should "help Jiang Qing carry the red banner."

[79] We have found three versions of such a team: Hua, Mao Yuanxin, Wang Hongwen, Zhang Chunqiao, Chen Xilian and Ji Dengkui (Qing and Fang, *Deng zai 1976*, vol. 2, p. 306); Jiang Qing (as Party chair), Hua (as Premier), Wang Hongwen, Mao Yuanxin (Wang or Mao as NPC chair), and Chen Xilian (as MAC head) (Luo Bing, "Yao Wenyuan xie Mao Zedong neimu"); and Mao Yuanxin, Hua, Jiang Qing, Chen Xilian, Ji Dengkui, Wang Dongxing and Zhang Yufeng ("Zhang Yufeng jie Mao wannian mimi cailiao"). These purported teams are of varying credibility in our judgment, but the presence of Chen Xilian on all the teams is credible, as is that of Mao Yuanxin.

Yet, as in other respects, in focusing on the "gang of four" as the standard bearers of radicalism at the end of the Maoist era, attention has been shifted from another actor whose role was more crucial in the Chairman's last lurch to the left since fall 1975, and arguably in his hopes for the future: Mao Yuanxin. According to a key player in the period, in the wake of the Tiananmen crisis, Mao Yuanxin, presumably for the second time, raised doubts about the suitability of Zhang Chunqiao for leadership. While this cannot be confirmed, and perhaps conflates Mao Yuanxin's arguments against Zhang in January with the situation in April, this source also expressed the view that the Chairman wanted Mao Yuanxin as his successor, but concluded that at 36, his nephew was insufficiently mature for leadership. Again, this cannot be confirmed, although the belief has substantial backing in Party history circles, and Mao Yuanxin was a constant on the leadership lists allegedly promoted by the Chairman. Whatever the reality, in the last months of the Chairman's life, Mao Yuanxin remained a potent figure, even as the Chairman slipped in and out of a coma, often pushing the same issues as the "gang," but remaining his own man.[80]

Political and Policy Conflict, Spring and Summer 1976

Notwithstanding Hua's greatly enhanced status, conflict was inevitable within the post-Tiananmen Politburo. This, as we have frequently emphasized, was a consequence of the fundamental contradiction in Mao's objectives of reaffirming and correcting the Cultural Revolution, and the presence on the top body of forces with very different ideas of how to deal with the contradiction. Arguably, each side believed it was more faithful to Mao's vision of China's future. Conflict was also a product of the ongoing campaign to criticize Deng, which continued at a high pitch from the conclusion of the Tiananmen crisis to Mao's death.[81] This intensified the shrill ideological atmosphere in which politics was conducted, and also created a constant source of division over how the movement should be conducted. Moreover, as various policy issues were considered, the attacks on Deng's program continued, but as Hua later noted, sitting members of the Politburo who had implemented Deng's approach, himself included, were vulnerable. Personal friction also came into the mix, undoubtedly with Jiang Qing in particular. Hua would claim it was very hard to deal with the radicals, that they simply didn't listen to him. According to Hua, it was after hearing this complaint on April 30 that Mao bolstered his successor with the famous statement about being "at ease" while Hua was "in charge."[82] Finally, in their disparate ways, Zhou Enlai's death and Mao's fading from the scene removed

---

[80] Interview, January 2005; and above, p. 495n79.

[81] An indication of the intensity of the campaign can be seen in the number of articles promoting it in the *People's Daily*. According to *Renmin ribao suoyin*, 452 articles criticizing Deng were published over this period, reaching an average of over 100 per month from June through early September.

[82] *Geng Biao huiyilu*, p. 290.

inhibitions to confrontation. The Premier was no longer present as a conciliator,[83] while Mao, although the ultimate source of conflict, had also repeatedly reined in the contending groups in his quixotic demands for unity. By the end of June, however, although the Chairman seemingly desired the consolidation of Hua's position, he was in no condition to impose restraint on any upsurge in conflict.

With so many factors conspiring to intensify conflict, and repeated conflict being a defining feature of the period, the question remains concerning the actual meaning of these developments. In the standard official view shared by various observers,[84] the radicals were attacking Hua as part of stepped up preparations for a bid for power. Indeed, post-Mao hyperbole aside, there was palpable distrust on the part of other leaders that such an objective may have been on the radical agenda. The use of the eight vice premiers' 1975 speeches at the July-August planning seminar (see below), makes plausible Hua's claim cited at the start of this chapter that the aim was to oust sitting Politburo members. Moreover, media attention to the "three poisonous weeds" inevitably involved Hua, particularly because of his contribution to the Outline Report on the Academy of Sciences.[85] Yet while preparations for a post-Mao showdown is plausible, the precise strategic goals of the radicals remain unclear. Somewhat lesser objectives, such as mobilizing support for their Cultural Revolution agenda and their own continuing role *within* the leadership, are more likely than a full-blooded bid for power. We examine this question further at the end of this chapter, and in our analysis of the decisive events of September-October in Chapter 8. For now, we only note that, like the period after Hua's appointment as Acting Premier in January, the Politburo radicals apparently supported his position even as they clashed with him on a variety of issues.[86]

In any case, the scope for contention was vast. As suggested, a critical area was sharply contrasting attitudes toward the anti-Deng campaign. For Hua and those associated with him, the approach was to toe the line and criticize Deng, but with restraint, and indeed as much avoidance as the circumstances would allow, whereas the radicals used the media to project a disruptive message. A

---

[83] Although often bearing the brunt of radical attacks himself, the Premier had repeatedly sought to ameliorate leadership differences, for example, attempting (without success) to reconcile the bitterly antagonistic Zhang Chunqiao and Chen Yonggui. See Wu Si, *Chen Yonggui*, p. 158; and below, p. 502.

[84] See, e.g., Baum, *Burying Mao*, pp. 37-39; and below, p. 525.

[85] While various themes advocated in the three "weeds" had been previously criticized, especially those raised in the Outline Report, it was seemingly only from April that the label "three poisonous weeds" was widely applied, and each of the documents subjected to systematic criticism, with a new upsurge of criticism in August. See *RMRB*, July 7, 1977, in *SPRCP*, no. 6384 (1977), p. 81; *RMRB*, May 31, 1976, p. 2; *HQ*, August 1, 1976, in *SPRCM*, no. 886 (1976), pp. 43-50; Chen and Du, *Shilu*, vol. 3, part 2, pp. 1379, 1403-1404; above, p. 451; and below, pp. 506ff.

[86] Cf. above, pp. 450-51. Also, Zhang Chunqiao now advised Shanghai to no longer criticize other provinces, advice suggesting a concern with stability and unity as Hua assumed his new position. "Wang Xiuzhen de jiefa jiaodai," p. 2.

case in point, which underlined the poisonous distrust, occurred in April when an article appeared in the *People's Daily* on the conduct of *pi Deng* at Dazhai. Hua was disturbed by this development, and rang Dazhai's ultimate leader, Vice Premier Chen Yonggui, to ask what was going on. Chen, who had advised his subordinates back at the brigade and Xiyang county that "these things are too complicated," and the best course was to keep a low profile, was nonplussed, and phoned the leader in Dazhai, Guo Fenglian. Guo also had no idea of the matter, and enquiries showed that the report had originated with a low-level journalist without the knowledge of the brigade or county authorities.[87] The incident demonstrated the preferences of Hua and Chen among others, but equally the difficulties of navigating a nationwide ideological campaign.

The impact, as Hua reported to Mao on April 30, and Wang Hongwen complained in a (probably undelivered) draft letter to the Chairman in July,[88] was uneven. Many individual work units simply went through the motions, and many ministerial-level organizations apparently weathered the storm with limited disruption. There were exceptions, however, for example, in the large numbers of leaders and cadres in the Academy of Sciences reportedly labeled "capitalist roaders," and in the complete reshuffle of leadership groups under the Seventh Ministry of Machine Building.[89] Moreover, many localities were deeply affected, with social disorder, strikes, economic losses, and attacks on leaders and cadres, along the pattern of February-March, apparently accelerating during the spring and summer. But while the machinations of local followers of the "gang" were cited, even in comparison to March when elusive claims were made concerning Sichuan and Henan, there were only minimal suggestions of any direct input by the Politburo radicals into these disorders—except, of course, that created by the environment of the anti-Deng campaign.[90]

Meanwhile, disputes were rife in various functional spheres as relevant bodies held meetings to determine policy and set agendas. Mao's ambiguous policy legacy left ample room for conflict: the anti-rightist themes since the previous fall undercut many of Deng's policies, but as we have seen, few if any of these had been formally withdrawn by the Chairman. In at least one area, education, where the radicals not only had the advantage of the anti-rightist campaign since the previous December, but also bureaucratic authority *via* Zhang Chunqiao, they

---

[87] See Wu Si, *Chen Yonggui*, pp. 205-206.

[88] See Chen and Du, *Shilu*, vol. 3, part 2, p. 1399. Wang reportedly wrote to the Chairman "in July" complaining of the unevenness of the anti-Deng campaign, and recommending dismissals of leading figures in ministries and MAC organs that were seriously lagging. It is unclear whether this letter was actually delivered.

[89] Chen and Du, *Shilu*, vol. 3, part 2, p. 1318; Yan and Gao, *Turbulent Decade*, pp. 511-12; and interviews with former trade union cadre, May and June 2003.

[90] See Chen and Du, *Shilu*, vol. 3, part 2, pp. 1375, 1380-81, 1401-1402, 1404; Garside, *Coming Alive*, pp. 138-39; and above, pp. 460-61. The great majority, if not all, of China's provinces were affected. The most spectacular incident was the August kidnapping of Shanxi's top leaders.

were able to set the agenda.[91] In other areas, including foreign trade (where the issue would again be taken up at the July planning seminar),[92] public security,[93] and the military,[94] the "gang" assertedly interfered, but apparently without achieving major policy changes. In the railroad sector, however, where Wan Li had been pushed out as minister, significant economic setbacks occurred.[95] But for our purposes, the best insights into the dynamics of top-level elite politics are found in three areas: agriculture and rural policy, economic planning, and personnel and organization issues.

Agriculture and Rural Policy. Somewhat ironically, conflict over agriculture and broader rural policy must be traced back to the October 1975 Dazhai conference. As we saw in Chapter 5, at the time of the conference, the radicals had very little input into the agricultural policy debate, and their main impact on the meeting was Jiang Qing's disruptive talks on the *Water Margin* issue—talks that earned Mao's displeasure. Instead, the key advocate of "leftist" policies was Chen Yonggui, who pushed for a higher level of collectivism, notably by raising the level of accounting within the communes to the brigade, an approach sidelined through the efforts of provincial leaders, Li Xiannian, Deng and Hua. In the post-Dazhai period, however, radicals, notably including their Shanghai followers as well as the "gang" itself in Beijing, crossed swords with both Hua and Chen on rural issues. This involved policy questions and personality clashes, but perhaps most fundamentally it reflected the fact that as the anti-rightist campaign evolved into the anti-Deng movement, the organizational approach of

---

[91] From May 6 to June 23, the Ministry of Education convened seminars for all provincial-level units in three groups to promote radical enrollment policies trialed in Liaoning in 1975. Chen and Du, *Shilu*, vol. 3, part 2, p. 1376.

[92] See NCNA, Beijing, January 14, 1977, in *SPRCP*, no. 6265 (1977), pp. 22-26; and *Sirenbang fangeming zuixing cailiao jilu*, p. 526. These sources refer to three conferences from March to June where the radicals launched attacks on the "comprador" Ministry of Foreign Trade.

[93] In June, the Ministry of Public Security held a national seminar on security work under the control of radicals from the ministry's Party core group, who seemingly followed instructions given by Wang Hongwen in March. The seminar drafted an outline calling for strong measures against inner-Party capitalists and other enemies. The outline, however, was rejected by Hua and was never issued. Chen and Du, *Shilu*, vol. 3, part 2, pp. 1386-87; and *RMRB*, January 3, 1977, in *SPRCP*, no. 6259 (1977), p. 240.

[94] Although apparently not occurring at any national conference, from June through August, the "gang," especially MAC Standing Committee members Wang Hongwen and Zhang Chunqiao, reportedly attacked PLA performance in carrying out the still in force decisions of the 1975 MAC conference. Wang allegedly emphasized the need for personnel changes at the higher levels of the military. While reportedly causing disruption in some lower-level units, these efforts seemingly did not alter the basic orientation and personnel stability of the PLA. See Chen and Du, *Shilu*, vol. 3, part 2, p. 1382; and *RMRB*, January 27, 1977, in *SPRCP*, no. 6281 (1977), pp. 46-51.

[95] See Chen and Du, *Shilu*, vol. 3, part 2, pp. 1400-1401; and above, pp. 457-59. Strikingly, in July the "gang's" followers in the Ministry of Railways attacked the policy guideline of March 1975 as a "restorationist program," boldly asserting that "Central Document no. 9 [1975], which was circled by Chairman Mao, has errors and can be criticized." Nevertheless, there is no indication that this document was revoked.

the Dazhai conference toward the countryside was clearly at variance with the new radical upsurge.

As suggested by Yao Wenyuan's efforts to downplay publicity on the conference, China's radicals had little time for its policy directions; indeed, Shanghai's Xu Jingxian would later confess, "we [in Shanghai] always opposed Hua's report," and Zhang Chunqiao allegedly prevented transmission of the spirit of the conference to the city. But despite objections voiced internally or privately, such as Jiang Qing's comment directly after its delivery, that Hua's report was revisionist, no obvious criticism of the conference or report emerged until spring 1976, when the anti-Deng campaign gathered momentum. Even then the sacred Dazhai was never openly disparaged. Instead, an alternative emphasis on the positive role of Dazhai in promoting class struggle and the restriction of bourgeois right was trumpeted in the media. But with Deng sidelined and then ousted, Hua and Chen Yonggui were the active officials most vulnerable to complaints about the conference's policy directions.[96]

At its most basic level, the radicals' objections to the Dazhai conference orientation had less to do with agricultural policy *per se* than with the broader political issues they reflected: the consolidation emphasis on developing the national economy and combating factionalism. As noted in Chapter 5, while not openly linked to Dazhai, the model brigade's promotion of production, capital construction and mechanization assertedly amounted to practicing the "theory of productive forces," an effort to use modernization to negate revolutionization. In contrast, radical models focused on political culture and the superstructure, such as the Xiaojinzhuang brigade near Tianjin, cultivated by Jiang Qing, which emphasized female literacy and combating bourgeois thinking.[97] On another key issue, in an accusation reminiscent of Cultural Revolution attacks on Liu Shaoqi's performance in sending work teams to the countryside during the Socialist Education Movement in 1964,[98] the radicals dismissed the Party line education campaign which carried official propaganda and leadership reorganization to the villages. Notwithstanding the campaign's anti-capitalist themes, it was denounced as "pointing the spearhead down," i.e., directing rectification efforts against large numbers of low-level cadres, many of whom were promoted during the Cultural Revolution, in order to protect revisionists at higher levels. As Shanghai's Ma

---

[96] Wu Si, *Chen Yonggui*, pp. 173-74; *Sirenbang fangeming zuixing cailiao jilu*, p. 449; *Zhonggong yuanshi ziliao xuanji*, vol. 1, 2nd series, p. 537; *GMRB*, January 12, 1977, in *SPRCP*, no. 6291 (1977), p. 158; Zweig, *Agrarian Radicalism*, pp. 67-68; Chen Yonggui's December 1976 speech to the second Dazhai conference, in *SPRCP*, no. 6252 (1977), pp. 129-31; and above, p. 361.

[97] On the Xiaojinzhuang model, see Edward Friedman, "The Politics of Local Models, Social Transformation and State Power Struggles in the People's Republic of China: Tachai and Teng Hsiao-p'ing," *CQ*, no. 76 (1978), pp. 875ff; and Dittmer, *Continuous Revolution*, p. 191. Cf. the Chaoyang educational model linking the Cultural Revolution approach to education and agricultural needs; above, p. 340.

[98] For allegedly "hitting hard at the many in order to protect the few." See Richard Baum and Frederick C. Teiwes, "Liu Shao-ch'i and the Cadre Question," *AS*, April 1968.

Tianshui put it in summer 1976, provincial Party committees and the Party Center had problems, so why should the campaign focus on the county level and below. Specific agricultural policies were also involved, however, albeit in a relatively secondary sense. Thus in May 1976, the *People's Daily* briefly publicized another alternative radical agricultural model: the Heertao experience launched by Mao Yuanxin in Liaoning in January 1975, which experimented with eradicating the private market, and this model was introduced in a number of scattered localities. Another issue still percolating was the question of brigade accounting, an issue that produced conflict between Chen Yonggui and Zhang Chunqiao.[99]

While arguably one of the least significant members of the Politburo, someone explicitly disdained by the radicals for having no understanding of politics, Chen Yonggui did bear administrative responsibility for agriculture, and became centrally involved in conflict over rural policy. Ironically, at the most general level, i.e., the applicability of the Dazhai experience, Zhang Chunqiao's position was similar to the reservations expressed by Zhao Ziyang and other provincial leaders the previous fall. The core question was how widely or rapidly the whole package of practices summarized as the Dazhai model, practices developed in a small and poor mountainous brigade, could be adapted to often vastly different areas. Zhang's reported remark that "we don't have mountains to remove in Shanghai," was a sentiment that could easily have been echoed figuratively although not literally by Zhao with regard to agricultural conditions in Sichuan. On the specific aspect of the Dazhai model that had been the center of intense dispute in September-October 1975, Chen Yonggui's proposal to speed up the transition to brigade-level accounting, Zhang echoed the provincial skeptics in opposing such a move, and in fact Shanghai (and Liaoning) lagged in implementing this policy. In actual policy terms, as we have seen, Chen's proposals were derailed, although a gradual move toward brigade accounting was endorsed, and probably implemented to some limited degree in 1976.[100] The cool attitudes of Zhang Chunqiao and local Shanghai radicals toward Dazhai, however, stood at variance with Jiang Qing's even more collectivist Xiaojinzhuang model

---

[99] See Chen Yonggui's speech to the second Dazhai conference, in *SPRCP*, no. 6252 (1977), pp. 130-31, 134-35; *Chedi jiefa pipan sirenbang zuixing*, p. 189; *GMRB*, January 12, 1977, in *SPRCP*, no. 6291 (1977), pp. 158-59; Fang Weizhong, *Jingji dashiji*, pp. 565-66; *Zhonggong yuanshi ziliao xuanji*, vol. 1, 2nd series, p. 540; and Zweig, *Agrarian Radicalism*, pp. 39, 65, 67-69.

[100] Wu Si, *Chen Yonggui*, pp. 177; *Sirenbang fangeming zuixing cailiao jilu*, p. 447; interview with specialist on Chen Yonggui, November 2002; and above, p. 359n158. The degree of progress in brigade accounting in 1976 is unclear, since it is impossible to disaggregate the very modest growth reflected in the figures for 1975 and 1978. Shanghai, and certainly the equally lagging Liaoning, apparently continued to drag their feet in 1976, although the evidence is not as clear-cut for Shanghai. Both trailed the national average of brigades practicing brigade accounting in 1975. In 1978, when the response to the issue after both the first and second (December 1976) Dazhai conferences would be reflected in the figures, and thus also involve non-radical post-Mao local leaderships, Liaoning was still well behind the national average, while Shanghai had drawn level. See *Jianguo yilai nongye hezuohua shiliao huibian*, pp. 1388-89.

that dissolved private plots while implementing brigade accounting. Although neither the general issue of Dazhai's model, nor brigade accounting, were at the core of rural policy contention in 1976, the simmering brigade issue fueled the existing bad blood between Chen and Zhang.

The origins of the feud between Chen and Zhang had nothing to do with agriculture, instead growing out of a seemingly trivial incident, but one reflecting deep leadership tensions. At the reception on the eve of National Day in 1974, Chen caught Zhang's attention with his enthusiastic applause of Zhou Enlai. At a subsequent Politburo meeting, probably in the context of discussing Fourth NPC appointments, Chen objected to Zhang's proposal for a new position for Xie Zhenhua, Chen's bitter enemy in Shanxi during the Cultural Revolution, who ironically had been removed as leading provincial Party secretary when the Politburo radicals pushed *pi Lin pi Kong*. In the ensuing argument, Zhang referred to Chen's vigorous applause as a kind of illicit activity, and Chen angrily responded that Zhang had no authority to reprimand him. The efforts of both Zhou, with whom Chen had developed very close ties, and Wang Hongwen, who had quite amicable relations with Chen, could not assuage the peasant leader's hostility toward Zhang—a hostility manifested in Chen's refusal to face Zhang in Politburo meetings on the excuse of a twisted neck, an ailment that miraculously disappeared after the arrest of the "gang of four." Against this background, and Zhang's fall 1975 opposition to Chen's brigade accounting proposal, relations were further embittered after the Dazhai conference when Zhang sent a representative to Dazhai to collect material on the brigade. Whatever Zhang's intention, Chen reacted with anger when informed, eventually concluding that Zhang wanted to "steal our scriptures" and develop an alternative Shanghai model of brigade accounting for promotion in China and throughout the world.[101]

While the brigade accounting question further exacerbated tensions between Chen Yonggui and Zhang Chunqiao, the central rural issue as the post-Tiananmen period unfolded was the use of work teams, an issue encompassing both specific village-level policies and the broader political direction. This conflict mirrored the controversy over the Socialist Education Movement in ways beyond the similarity to the attacks on Liu Shaoqi. As in 1964, the attempt to bring ideological indoctrination and organizational change to the countryside led to considerable grassroots resentment and resistance. Under pressure from below, several provinces, notably Yunnan, Henan and Ningxia, withdrew the teams.

---

[101] Wu Si, *Chen Yonggui*, pp. 151, 160, 178, 234; and interview with specialist on Chen Yonggui, November 2002. On Xie Zhenhua's fate during the Lin Biao-Confucius campaign and the Chen-Xie relationship, see above, pp. 173, 174n157, 233n112.

Chen's good relations with Wang Hongwen apparently grew out of theoretical study classes they both attended in April 1973. Subsequently, they both resided in Diaoyutai. They seemingly had a good deal of worker-peasant sympathy for each other, and there were no indications of any problems between them. In fact, on a visit to Shanxi, Wang criticized Chen's *bête noir* Xie Zhenhua, suggesting Xie should pay a visit to Dazhai. This yet again suggests the need to distinguish among the so-called "gang" in terms of their political roles and relationships. Wu Si, p. 142.

This naturally brought pressure on Hua and Chen as key figures in framing and implementing the 1975 decisions, and by the same token provided the radicals with a potent weapon. As the matter drew attention at the Center, the Ministry of Agriculture and Forestry under Sha Feng proposed to Chen convening a meeting to clarify the situation by reaffirming Document no. 21 [1975] which transmitted the Dazhai conference results to the Party, and also by backing the work teams. Chen agreed and took the proposal to Hua, who also saw the need for action. Hua, however, concluded that the ministry, as well as the State Council, lacked sufficient clout to deal with the issue, so the Party Center would have to consider it. When the Politburo met sometime in April, Chen proposed that the Center issue telephone instructions backing Document no. 21 and the work teams, but Zhang Chunqiao objected, cited basic-level opposition, and damned the teams for persecuting people who had the right to rebel. Given the Politburo divisions, no reaffirmation of the Dazhai decisions was made, and more work teams were called back from the villages.[102]

With the issue still unsettled, the Ministry of Agriculture and Forestry convened two meetings to review agricultural policy in late May and late June, the first in Shijiazhuang, to deal with the problems of the northern wheat areas, and the second in Wuxi, concerning the southern rice-growing areas. Li Xiannian and Ji Dengkui nominated Chen to preside at Shijiazhuang, while the radicals increased their pressure on him in an attempt to prevent any distraction from the anti-Deng campaign. At the meeting itself, divergent views were expressed by Dazhai's representatives who naturally defended their own model, and by the delegates from Mao Yuanxin's Liaoning who hardly referred to Dazhai. Sha Feng tried to reach a consensus, and Chen urged the Dazhai people to accept a compromise, commenting that the clash left him in an awkward position and it was better for him not to be involved. In his own concluding speech, Chen made his own compromise by making anti-Deng comments while warning against disrupting agricultural production. Overall, despite the clear differences, the Shijiazhuang conference was relatively low-key and avoided heated debate.[103]

The Wuxi conference, which convened on June 30 just after the final dramatic turn in Mao's health, saw a similar straddling of the issues, but with considerably more tension. In the lead-up to the meeting, Chen proposed to Hua and Ji Dengkui that he attend, but expressed uncertainty about what he should say under the circumstances. Both Hua and Ji encouraged Chen to talk about whatever he wanted. In the event, with the anti-Deng campaign raging, Chen attempted to separate Dazhai from Deng. He affirmed the correct decisions of the fall 1975 conference and Hua's report, including the dispatch of work teams,

---

[102] See Wu Si, *Chen Yonggui*, pp. 216-17; and Zweig, *Agrarian Radicalism*, p. 68. On the parallel 1964 experience, see Baum and Teiwes, "Liu Shao-ch'i"; Baum, *Prelude to Revolution*, chs. 4-5; and Teiwes, *Politics and Purges*, pp. 422-39.

[103] Wu Si, *Chen Yonggui*, pp. 218-21.

and argued that the apparently ongoing recall of the teams was not in line with Mao's teachings. But he condemned Deng's role at the Dazhai conference as disruptive and leading to a dead end, declared the necessity of negating the influence of Deng's Dazhai speech, and called for criticism of the theory of productive forces. Yet, Chen argued, such criticism did not mean giving no attention to boosting farm production. This did not satisfy the (non-Politburo) radicals in attendance, and a big character poster denouncing Chen for using productivity to disrupt the *pi Deng* campaign appeared following his talk. Shortly thereafter in early July, Ma Tianshui in nearby Shanghai read Chen's speech and called in his immediate subordinates, Party Secretaries Xu Jingxian and Wang Xiuzhen. Ma declared Chen's speech problematic, that it still carried the tone of the Dazhai conference, questioned the Dazhai decision to focus on county-level committees when provincial committees and the Center had problems, and flatly contradicted Chen's assessment of the work teams by saying the decision to send them last year was wrong, and their withdrawal this year was correct. For his part, Chen, didn't dare to express his Wuxi opinions at Politburo meetings once back in Beijing.[104]

There is little evidence concerning any further conflicts over agriculture in the remaining months before Mao's death. The net political result of the conflicts described above seems to have been a standoff, with the pressures created by the anti-Deng campaign preventing any systematic reaffirmation of the Dazhai conference results, different localities reacting according to their circumstances and persuasions, and the more mundane aspects of agricultural policy, which did not particularly interest the central radicals, presumably left to the Ministry of Agriculture and Forestry. Perhaps symbolic of this situation were Jiang Qing's visits to Xiaojinzhuang and Dazhai in late August and early September shortly before Mao's death. Jiang undertook the trips when the Chairman's condition briefly improved, and almost certainly did not exhibit the callous unconcern for his health depicted in post-Mao accounts of her time in Dazhai.[105] At Xiaojinzhuang her focus apparently was on women's equality and the anti-Deng campaign, while at Dazhai, where she was careful to show concern for the brigade which remained one of Mao's treasured models, Jiang emphasized criticizing Deng, but neither raised specific agricultural questions nor the larger issues that had marked

---

[104] *Ibid.*, pp. 221-22, 224; "Zhonggong zhongyang guanyu 'Wang Hongwen, Zhang Chunqiao, Jiang Qing, Yao Wenyuan fandang jituan zuizheng (cailiao zhi san)'," p. 60; Zweig, *Agrarian Radicalism*, p. 68; and interview with specialist on Chen Yonggui, November 2002.

[105] Yan and Gao, *Turbulent Decade*, p. 518, parrot the official claim that Jiang unfeelingly continued to play poker at Dazhai when informed of Mao's turn for the worse. While coming from a source of questionable reliability, a credible alternative picture has Jiang, although indeed continuing to play poker while travel arrangements were made, in a state of great anxiety when news of Mao's sudden deterioration reached her. This Internet source purports to be a May 1989 interview with Chen Yonggui. While the timing of the interview is impossible (Chen died in 1986) and some of the content is highly dubious, in other respects it has the ring of truth. Chen Yonggui, "Wo mengjian Mao Zhuxi le" [I Dream of Chairman Mao] (June 5, 2003), http://www.peacehall.com/forum/lishi/246.shtml.

the Shijiazhuang and Wuxi conferences. At Dazhai, moreover, Jiang expressed anger over various trivial and personal matters, such as when she berated brigade leaders because a trench she had dug for an air-raid shelter on her previous visit was no longer there and had been subsumed in a piggery allegedly built on Deng's orders.[106] The paradox is that at this crucial juncture Jiang chose to visit two agricultural models, even though she apparently had limited interest in rural policy issues. In any case, much more important for the radicals in summer 1976 was the overall direction of national economic policy.

Economic Planning. The most serious confrontation between the radicals and Hua *et al.* took place at the national planning work seminar from July 6 to August 1. While many of the specific issues had been aired in attacks by the radicals since before the Tiananmen incident, the seminar provided a setting for a systematic policy review. As with the agricultural meetings in Shijiazhuang and Wuxi, this conference involved both concrete economic issues and the pressures created by the anti-Deng campaign. Its specific content derived from the 1976 plan targets set at the October 1975-January 1976 national planning conference. As we saw in Chapter 6, that conference, which followed a three to four month SPC seminar, began with a professional agenda which also included principles for a ten-year economic program and readjusting the economic work system. The Politburo and Mao endorsed the conference's ambitious 1976 annual plan for 7 to 7.5 percent growth, but by the end of the meeting attacks on the "rightist wind" disrupted discussions of system reform. By spring 1976, moreover, in large part due to the fallout of the continuing anti-Deng campaign, economic results were well behind the plan, with notable shortfalls in steel, chemical fertilizer and cotton, and it became clear that revisions for targets in the second half of the year would be required. As a result, on May 31 the Politburo decided (and Mao approved) to convene the planning seminar with two agenda items, the readjustment of the plan and criticism of dictatorship by central ministries (*tiaotiao zhuanzheng*) in economic management. Such criticism, while consistent with the radicals' objections to overly centralized bureaucratic control, was also a perennial issue of economic management that policy makers dealt with since well before the Cultural Revolution, had been highlighted by Mao's May 1973 criticism of planning work, was again on the agenda at the summer 1975 theory conference when Deng's consolidation efforts were in full flight, and would be reaffirmed by Hua after the arrest of the "gang."[107]

---

[106] See *RMRB*, December 15, 1976, in *SPRCP*, no. 6252 (1977), pp. 149-52; and Yan and Gao, *Turbulent Decade*, pp. 517-18.

[107] See Chen and Du, *Shilu*, vol. 3, part 2, pp. 1228, 1285-87; Fang Weizhong, *Jingji dashiji*, pp. 547, 566-67; Yan and Gao, *Turbulent Decade*, p. 513; *GMRB*, February 16, 1977, in *SPRCP*, no. 6291 (1977), pp. 152-53; Lieberthal, *Central Documents*, pp. 125-27; Jonathan Unger, "The Struggle to Dictate China's Administration: The Conflict of Branches v Areas v Reform," *The China Journal*, no. 18 (1987); and above, pp. 52, 410-11.

Despite the Politburo- and Mao- approved agenda, leadership tensions over economic issues burst to the fore on June 25 when the Politburo discussed the SPC's June 13 report shortly before the seminar convened. The SPC reported on economic performance in the first half of the year and plans for the second half, recommending reduced targets as well proposing management changes to increase local control. The specific issue setting off the outburst was foreign trade policy: specifically the importing of chemical fertilizer and exporting crude oil, a policy the "gang" denounced as "selling out the country." In the sharp debate, Jiang Qing, Zhang Chunqiao, Wang Hongwen and Yao Wenyuan all attacked various foreign trade measures, but the language of Jiang and Zhang was particularly harsh, citing "Han traitors" and "slaves of foreigners." When Wang claimed that the Ministry of Foreign Trade contained a group of people who betrayed the nation, Zhang reportedly declared: "It's not just the Ministry of Foreign Trade, … in our Party, and first of all in the Politburo, the bourgeois class exists." Another feature of this tense meeting, at a time when Mao was about to lapse into a critical state, Hua defended the policy by noting that all the imported items had been approved by the Chairman. Zhang, in a response reminiscent of Jiang's complaint over how Deng cut off debate by claiming Mao's support in 1975, immediately objected, saying "you always use the Chairman to oppress people."[108]

Against this background of conflict at the very top, the broad-based economic conference convened, involving provincial-level representatives as well as State Council leaders and top ministerial officials, usually the number two figures, perhaps reflecting the discreet withdrawal of the ministers themselves during the anti-Deng campaign.[109] This provided a forum where a wide range of criticisms could be aggressively pushed. Regarded in post-Mao commentary as an important step by the "gang of four" in its attempt to seize power, radicals did use the seminar to attack economic organizations and responsible officials. Radicals at the Center and in the localities had long been suspicious of the economic policies implemented in 1975, and by early 1976 were gathering material on alleged mistakes committed by State Council bodies and their leaders. Thus, in February Zhang Chunqiao received material from local radicals in Shanghai that compiled speeches by central leaders for internal criticism in the municipal organization. Among the most prominent speeches printed for such criticism in this period, speeches which spread to various units locally and in Beijing, were those previously noted by the eight vice premiers at the summer 1975 State Council theory conference, the conference that comprehensively reviewed economic policy and initiated the process leading to the 20 articles on industry. As the

---

[108] Chen and Du, *Shilu*, vol. 3, part 2, pp. 1227, 1385-86; and above, p. 499n92.

[109] Ye Fei, *Ye Fei huiyilu*, p. 117, notes that the ministerial representatives were most often the second in command. In this period, many ministers, the key targets of intra-organization criticism, stayed away from their duties by feigning illness.

July seminar approached, radical attention to economic issues and vulnerable leaders in this sphere seemingly intensified, and at Wang Hongwen's urging Shanghai representatives brought 20 documents to the meeting concerning the State Council and 12 ministries and commissions, including the SPC, State Capital Construction Commission, Ministry of Foreign Trade, and Ministry of Communications. But these preparations, according to Shanghai leader Ma Tianshui, were not designed to launch an indiscriminate attack. Rather, they were to be carefully organized with the aim of winning over ministries with acceptable political leanings.[110]

While radical attacks at the seminar would be framed in harsh ideological terms, it is important to note that concrete political and economic interests were at issue, particularly for local representatives who played a prominent part in the proceedings. This was nothing new, with Shanghai's local interests providing a major context for the *Fengqing* affair in 1974, and perceived economic disadvantages for Liaoning having been among the complaints Mao Yuanxin raised with the Chairman in their critical September 1975 conversation. With the anti-rightist *cum* anti-Deng campaign developing in 1976, complaints about the performance of central economic bodies intensified. Ma Tianshui noted the tension between Shanghai and the SPC, claiming that the responsible comrade of the SPC, presumably Yu Qiuli, always opposed his city, while other Shanghai officials continued to collect materials on State Council leaders. Meanwhile, Mao Yuanxin also complained that the budgetary policies of State Council economic departments were giving the provinces a hard time.[111]

In the preparatory stage before the seminar and during the meeting itself, a particularly important role was reportedly played by Wang Hongwen, somewhat unusual for him in alleged "gang" maneuvers until recently, although also one apparent on organizational issues (see below). Zhang Chunqiao was also involved to some degree, although there is little indication of significant roles by Yao Wenyuan or Jiang Qing. Another figure, rarely noted in accounts of the conference but arguably very important, was Mao Yuanxin, who presumably acted in his own right since the Chairman was incapable of playing any role. The charges constructed against Wang after the arrest of the "gang" highlight his purported activities in inciting local radical representatives from Shanghai and Liaoning to launch attacks on the economic establishment. On the eve of the conference, in reaction to the Politburo contretemps of June 25, he circulated material prepared in Shanghai attacking the work of the Ministry of Foreign Trade, and commented that after the recent internal publication of Mao's 1964 comments on socialist education, big officials were already alarmed. He reportedly also enjoined "his

---

[110] *Ibid.*, p. 116; Chen and Du, *Shilu*, vol. 3, part 2, p. 1333; "Zhonggong zhongyang guanyu 'Wang Hongwen, Zhang Chunqiao, Jiang Qing, Yao Wenyuan fandang jituan zuizheng (cailiao zhi yi)'," pp. 13-14, 19; and "Hua Guofeng jiejian lingdao tongzhi jianghua," p. 1.

[111] "Ma Tianshui de buchong jiefa jiaodai," pp. 3, 4; and above, pp. 206-207, 375-76.

cronies": "Don't be polite toward the old cadres, ... seize their mistakes and criticize them, and when the time comes oust them." Once the meeting was under way, Wang allegedly engaged in irregular activities, on four occasions visiting the Jingxi Guesthouse where the Shanghai and Liaoning delegations were housed, to seek information on the seminar proceedings and give instructions. Among his instructions and comments were a call for criticism of the comprador philosophy, and, apparently in response to reports that some ministries were airing "unwholesome" opinions at the seminar, the observation that "once Deng is criticized in some ministries and commissions, then the criticism will come down on their own heads."[112]

Whatever the instigating role of Wang and other central radicals, the locus of the attacks on existing economic policy was the regional group sessions. As in regular CCP practice, following the opening speech by Gu Mu, the Vice Premier responsible for industry and construction and now apparently also for planning,[113] the seminar began with the participants broken up into regional groups for wide-ranging discussion of the agenda. The relevant groups were the East China group where Shanghai participated, with municipal Party standing committee member Huang Tao the main spokesperson, and the Northeast group with Liaoning Party Secretary Yang Chunfu the key advocate. As both delegations were staying at the Jingxi Guesthouse, there was clearly an opportunity for coordination, with Huang and Yang allegedly "conducting north-south concerted operations." The main thrust of the attack, at least in the very sparse post-Mao accounts, was not on policy issues *per se*, but on the two key economic conferences of 1975 and their alleged relationship to the "rightist wind" and "restorationist high tide" of the period: the summer State Council theory conference and the end of year national planning conference. On July 13 or 16,[114] Huang Tao addressed the East China group and declared that the theory conference had been under Deng's direction, and while in name it was making long-term plans for the national economy, in fact it was scheming to promote the rightist reversal of verdicts. The theory conference, then, was the source of the rightist reversal which followed. Speaking to the Northeast group on the 20th, Yang Chunfu further attacked the theory conference as awash with capitalism, and went on to depict the national planning conference as providing a cover for Deng's retreat. In a further comment unrelated to economic matters, a comment which pointed to the gap

---

[112] See Chen and Du, *Shilu*, vol. 3, part 2, pp. 1384, 1392; Ye Fei, *Ye Fei huiyilu*, p. 116; and "Zhonggong zhongyang guanyu 'Wang Hongwen, Zhang Chunqiao, Jiang Qing, Yao Wenyuan fandang jituan zuizheng (cailiao zhi yi)'," pp. 17-20.

[113] Gu Mu's keynote role further underlines the apparent mysterious sidelining since 1975 of Yu Qiuli, the Vice Premier formally responsible for planning. Gu also relayed the Politburo's instructions on July 25; "Zhonggong zhongyang guanyu 'Wang Hongwen, Zhang Chunqiao, Jiang Qing, Yao Wenyuan fandang jituan zuizheng (cailiao zhi yi)'," p. 18. Cf. above, p. 332n83.

[114] Chen and Du, *Shilu*, vol. 3, part 2, p. 1392, places Huang's talk on the 13th, while Ma Qibin, *Sishinian*, p. 403, places it on the 16th.

in understanding between local and central radicals, Yang asked why Deng had been selected to give the memorial speech for Zhou Enlai, suggesting this move was engineered by those under Deng's influence, when it appears to have been Zhang Chunqiao's proposal.[115]

By raising the issue of the two conferences, Huang and Yang appeared to be aiming higher than the 12 ministries. This was certainly how it was interpreted by Hua and others in the leadership, as seen in Hua's explanation immediately after the arrest of the "gang." While Hua was disingenuous in denying the link of the theory conference to Deng on the grounds that Deng never attended the meeting, with the speeches of the eight vice premiers, four of whom currently sat on the Politburo, circulated for criticism, the "spearhead" could justifiably be considered directed at them. Yet several problems exist with the sparse story of the first two weeks of the seminar.

As already suggested, the prominent role depicted of Wang Hongwen is puzzling on the surface, both given his less aggressive role than Jiang Qing or Zhang Chunqiao in the alleged activities of the "gang" generally and at the June 25 Politburo meeting, and his lack of expertise or bureaucratic responsibility for economic matters. In fact, according to the recollection of Wang Xiuzhen, Wang Hongwen's active role during the seminar was a consequence of his role as the representative of the workers on the highest Party body. In any case, while Wang was accused of instigating both the attacks on the two conferences and the tough treatment of old cadres, some evidence suggests a somewhat more restrained approach. Thus, with regard to "the problems of various ministries," just before or during the seminar Wang referred to the example of discharging *Comrade Wan Li* and the assignment of two young cadres to the Ministry of Railways core group, and stated this experience needed summing up and application in other ministries in *gradual* steps. As for the attacks on the two conferences, Wang's most concrete specified involvement came *after* Yang's speech on the 20th, when he praised the effort, observed that the theory conference and its links to the 20 articles were worth studying, and offered encouragement about the necessity to struggle, since without struggle revisionist lords would defeat them. This, together with subsequent developments, suggests the possibility that the line of argument about the two conferences originated with the local radicals. Another intriguing aspect is that while the post-Mao accounts paint Shanghai as the key local group, in some respects Liaoning's representatives appear to have been more aggressive at the seminar and elsewhere. In all likelihood this was related

---

[115] See Chen and Du, *Shilu*, vol. 3, part 2, p. 1392; Fang Weizhong, *Jingji dashiji*, p. 567; and "Zhonggong zhongyang guanyu 'Wang Hongwen, Zhang Chunqiao, Jiang Qing, Yao Wenyuan fandang jituan zuizheng (cailiao zhi yi)'," pp. 17, 20. While other scenarios are possible, Hua claimed after the arrest of the "gang" that Zhang Chunqiao proposed Deng to give Zhou's memorial speech, thus suggesting poor communication between the Politburo radicals and their local followers, and the possibility of the latter overreaching at the meeting without prior "gang" knowledge. On alternative versions of Deng's nomination for the January speech, see above, pp. 437-38.

to Mao Yuanxin's role going back to September 1975 in raising economic issues with the Chairman, including questions about the vice premiers' speeches to the 1975 theory conference. Moreover, for all the emphasis on Wang, Yang Chunfu felt it necessary to report on developments, including Wang's involvement, to his provincial boss: Mao Yuanxin.[116]

Whatever the precise input of Wang Hongwen and other individuals, or the relative initiative of central and local radicals in the unfolding events, two weeks into the seminar, and after at least one week of attacks on the two conferences, the disruption caused in the regional groups led to Politburo intervention. Meeting on the evening of the 20th, following Yang Chunfu's speech in the Northeast group and Wang Hongwen's afternoon visit to the Jingxi Guesthouse, the Politburo heard reports on the situation at the seminar and decided to proceed according to the original plan. This apparently meant that while a broad-ranging policy debate was authorized in the initial stage of the meeting, a debate that would inevitably involve pointed criticism given the ongoing anti-Deng campaign, the time had now come to move on to the second stage of revising targets for the second half of the year. In the immediate context, this meant that pursuing the theory conference issue was no longer allowed, and from the 21st, the direction of the seminar changed. During the Politburo meeting on the 20th, Hua clashed with Zhang Chunqiao who advocated letting the local radicals continue talking and issuing the conference bulletin which included their views. Hua rejected this course as further disrupting the seminar, and the bulletin was not released. For all the efforts of the radical forces, the tide was turned by Hua's action and a Politburo decision.[117]

Hua followed his decisive action with a speech to the conference which, along the lines of his February 25 talk that laid down guidelines for the emerging anti-Deng campaign, again sought to restrict inner-Party struggle. Hua's speech left a bitter taste in the mouths of local radicals, with Huang Tao objecting to preparing minutes of the talk, and Liaoning's Zhang Tiesheng later complaining that Hua's talk failed to highlight the Party's basic line, did not mention the Cultural Revolution or deepening the *pi Deng* campaign, and failed to criticize bourgeois right or uphold class struggle.[118] The most interesting aspect of the

---

[116] See Chen and Du, *Shilu*, vol. 3, part 2, pp. 1392-93; Li Xun, *Da bengkui*, p. 484; Yan and Gao, *Turbulent Decade*, p. 513; "Zhonggong zhongyang guanyu 'Wang Hongwen, Zhang Chunqiao, Jiang Qing, Yao Wenyuan fandang jituan zuizheng (cailiao zhi yi)'," pp. 19, 56-60; Shui Luzhou, "Du *Mao Zedong zhuan* biji"; and above, p. 376. Wang's comment concerning Wan Li was only dated as occurring "in July."

[117] See Chen and Du, *Shilu*, vol. 3, part 2, pp. 1393; "Hua Guofeng jiejian lingdao tongzhi jianghua," p. 2; and "Zhonggong zhongyang guanyu 'Wang Hongwen, Zhang Chunqiao, Jiang Qing, Yao Wenyuan fandang jituan zuizheng (cailiao zhi yi)'," p. 19.

[118] See *GMRB*, March 29, 1977, in *SPRCP*, no. 6319 (1977), p. 82; "Zhonggong zhongyang guanyu 'Wang Hongwen, Zhang Chunqiao, Jiang Qing, Yao Wenyuan fandang jituan zuizheng (cailiao zhi yi)'," p. 20; and "Zhang Tiesheng, Liu Jiye Tongzhi tanhua qingkuang jilu" [Record of Conversation of Comrades Zhang Tiesheng and Liu Jiye] (September 9, 1976), *ZGDSCKZL*, vol. 27, pp. 545-

turn in the proceedings, however, was the hasty retreat of both central and local radicals once the Politburo acted. When informed of the Politburo decision by Gu Mu on July 25, Huang Tao sought instructions from Wang Hongwen, Zhang Chunqiao and Yao Wenyuan, specifically asking about how to deal with the issue of the theory conference, and indicating a willingness to revise Shanghai's summary report. Especially revealing was Wang's reply to Huang's nervous request for guidance on revising the report:

> I have consulted with Zhang Chunqiao about a revision on the problem of the "source of the wind." Its wording is not exact. It is advisable that the passage concerning the theory conference be deleted. Let others raise this question. Let those from Liaoning do it. The passage "the minority headed by Deng Xiaoping" should also be revised for its target is too large and it will do harm to us.

Apart from trying to shift the burden to Mao Yuanxin's Liaoning, Wang's advice is revealing in that it shows, for all their ability to encourage radical themes in at least two regional groups, the "gang" was outgunned in the Politburo and saw no option save retreat. It further suggests that whatever role Wang Hongwen in particular played in stimulating radical activities at the conference, local leaders drove the criticism and, in the process and not for the first time, created difficulties for the Politburo radicals who faced different constraints.[119]

Personnel and Organizational Issues. While developments at the national planning seminar marked the sharpest confrontation between radicals and the dominant forces around Hua, another issue in summer 1976 was arguably even more central to the interests of radicals from the Politburo to basic levels: personnel and organizational policy. Relatively little is known of developments in this area, even in comparison to the limited information concerning agriculture and planning, but the importance of the question demands attention. This, of course, goes back to the inherent tension between the two projects pushed by Mao since the Lin Biao affair: the rehabilitation of cadres attacked during the Cultural Revolution, and the cultivation of activists in the movement for official positions. While in Mao's vision this could somehow be dialectically managed under such concepts as the "three-in-one combination" of old, middle aged and young cadres, sharp conflicts of interest and animosity existed between the rebels of 1966-68 and officials who had suffered at their hands. The issue was made more explosive by the recurring changes in emphasis initiated by Mao. As we have seen in previous chapters, both from August 1974 preceding Deng's

---

46. While no date for Hua's speech has been given, it is logical that it occurred after the Politburo decision.

[119] See "Zhonggong zhongyang guanyu 'Wang Hongwen, Zhang Chunqiao, Jiang Qing, Yao Wenyuan fandang jituan zuizheng (cailiao zhi yi)'," pp. 18-20. With the reorientation of the seminar after June 20, the SPC proposed significant reductions in key targets. However, due to the Tangshan earthquake, a simple discussion of the plan revisions was hurriedly concluded, and the revisions were not well implemented. Chen and Du, *Shilu*, vol. 3, part 2, p. 1393.

leadership of the "first front," and as part of his consolidation program in 1975, rehabilitations of pre-Cultural Revolution leaders accelerated, while cracking down on factionalism resulted in the demotion or ousting of young rebels. This became a major focus of Deng's effort, culminating in Ji Dengkui's abortive organizational outline and unfulfilled plans for Party rectification.[120]

As we have also seen, while factionalism was a serious problem throughout China, two of the most seriously affected provinces, where Ji Dengkui's efforts to bring the problem under control became the model for Deng's (Mao-approved) Party rectification proposal, were Henan and Zhejiang—especially Zhejiang. In bringing the Zhejiang situation under control, Ji was joined by Wang Hongwen, whether reluctantly or not. Their efforts produced a strict program for solving local factionalism in July's Party Center Document no. 16 [1975]; local radicals who had been Wang's allies earlier were severely dealt with, and the "double crashthroughs" in the Party recruitment and promotion of rebels, which had been extensively carried out in the province, was systematically criticized. But with Mao's attitude toward Deng shifting from October on, a new dynamic fitfully emerged in both central policy, and in localities such as Zhejiang.[121]

In Zhejiang, the provincial leadership underwent a *de facto* change as First Secretary Tan Qilong and, even more significantly, Secretary Tie Ying, who had carried out the attack against the "double crashthroughs" since early in 1975, disappeared from public view by the end of the year, seemingly on the excuse of poor health. By January 1976, Lai Keke, one of the few pre-Cultural Revolution provincial leaders supporting the rebel faction in 1966-67, who was promoted in the July 1975 leadership reshuffle overseen by Ji Dengkui and Wang Hongwen, had assumed the actual leadership of the province. As Lai took over, local pressure built against the anti-rebel actions of the previous period. In an odd initiative, Lu Xun's brother, the pre-Cultural Revolution ostensibly non-Party Zhejiang Governor Zhou Jianren (but who was in fact a CCP member), wrote to Mao appealing on behalf of one of the key local rebel leaders who had been ousted in the summer, Zhang Yongsheng. This resulted in the Chairman's comment that Zhang's living conditions should be improved. Cadres in the Central Organization Department were unhappy with this development, believing the decision taken in this case was correct, but since Mao had commented they had no option but to obey. However, as their own research indicated no basis to reverse Zhang's verdict, and crucially because Mao presumably had not asked for that, the department made arrangements for him at a Tianjin convalescent hospital, but left the status of his case unchanged. While in December and January Wang Hongwen continued to support the tough decision on Zhang and other Zhejiang rebel leaders that he had played an apparently significant role in formulating, following Mao's action he shifted

---

[120] See above, pp. 270-73, 274ff, 343ff.

[121] See Forster, *Rebellion*, pp. 219, 224, 229, 232; and above, pp. 278-81.

to attacking the position of the Organization Department. The "gang of four" reportedly brought Zhang Yongsheng to Beijing where he was received by Wang and Jiang Qing, who encouraged him to expose Ji Dengkui and Tan Qilong for oppressing Zhejiang's rebels and carrying out Deng's revisionist line. It may also have been about this time that the "gang" allegedly tampered with an earlier comment of Mao's by excluding the name of Weng Senhe, the most notorious of the Zhejiang rebels, from a list of those the Chairman criticized as unsuitable to serve as part of the mix of young, middle-aged and old officials.[122]

The conflict was further joined in a more direct fashion in March as the anti-Deng campaign escalated. In the context of emerging public criticism of the "three poisonous weeds," Wang Hongwen visited the Organization Department and commented on its study bulletin, noting the influence in the department of Deng's "counterrevolutionary revisionist line," and especially his organizational line, and stressing the need to expose and criticize any manifestation in the department's practice. Wang reportedly was particularly unhappy with the measures (that he had contributed to) to solve the "double crashthroughs" in Zhejiang, but because Mao had criticized these practices, there was nothing he could do about it, and the "gang" could only bear grudges over the matter. At a Politburo meeting Wang accused the department of carrying out Deng's revisionist line, and called for a thorough putting in order of its affairs. The "gang" also instigated criticism of the stalled organizational outline as a companion volume to the "three poisonous weeds," something they could do because the draft had not been formally put in place."[123]

As we have seen, from March into summer 1976 the conflict between established cadres and rebels surfaced in local areas throughout China. But as also noted, despite the almost ritual attribution of radical attacks on provincial authorities to followers of the "gang," there is little concrete evidence linking the Politburo radicals in Beijing to specific disruptions in the localities. By similar token, there are few indications of anti-radical forces at the Center intervening decisively to bolster the established leadership in the provinces. The impression, rather, is of local rebels using the anti-Deng campaign, sometimes citing the specific words of Politburo radicals such as Zhang Chunqiao, but essentially acting on their own. In turn, provincial leaders, where they had not retreated as in Zhejiang, seemingly relied on their official appointments, only occasionally supported by the Center, but they were nevertheless relatively secure as long as their commission was not withdrawn. This is, clearly, a

---

[122] Forster, *Rebellion*, pp. 237-39; Wang and Sun, "Dang zuzhi zhengdun," p. 43; NCNA, Beijing, January 6, 1977, in *SPRCP*, no. 6260 (1977), p. 32; "Zhongyang lingdaoren guanyu sirenbang wenti de jianghua," p. 3; and personal communication from Keith Forster, January 2006.

[123] Wang and Sun, "Dang zuzhi zhengdun," p. 43.

speculative conclusion, but one based on the limited information available short of detailed investigations of individual provinces.[124]

In August 1976, however, Hua's Center did act decisively to rebuff a move by Zhejiang rebels, apparently on their own initiative without reference to the Politburo radicals, to demand the reversal of the previous July's Document no. 16 which had led to the crackdown on rebel activities, and a review of Weng Senhe's case. On August 23, the Center reaffirmed the correctness of Document no. 16, rejected attempts to overturn the negation of the "double crashthroughs," declared there would be no reversal of Weng's verdict, and also banned the restoration of a Red Guard organization and a militia commander.[125] Given the sparseness of information on this decision, much remains uncertain, but several intriguing patterns exist for both the organizational issue since the launching of the anti-rightist campaign, and for other areas. First, much of the initiative for specific radical challenges came from below, notwithstanding the general coincidence of interests with the Politburo radicals. Both the attempt to challenge the crackdown on Zhejiang rebels at the turn of the year, while Wang Hongwen still endorsed the 1975 anti-factional measures, and the challenge to Document no. 16 in August seemingly originated in the province itself, even if, at least in the first case, the "gang" quickly adopted the issue. Similarly, in rural policy it apparently was basic-level opposition to the disruption caused by work teams that placed the matter on the Politburo's agenda, and the case against the Dazhai policies at the Shijiazhuang and especially Wuxi conferences, was made by provincial representatives in the absence of "gang" participation. At the national planning seminar, where the interests of the Politburo radicals were much more focused, there was a close interaction of Wang Hongwen in particular with local radicals, but it is at least possible that the most destabilizing themes at the forum were the creation of provincial and municipal delegations.

A second pattern concerned the significance of official documents, and especially Mao's imprimatur. In the organizational sphere, the organizational outline was vulnerable because it had not been formally promulgated, and thus

---

[124] See Chen and Du, *Shilu*, vol. 3, part 2, pp. 1375, 1380-81, 1401-1402, 1404; *RMRB*, May 17, 1977, in *SPRCP*, no. 6358 (1977), pp. 214-15; and above, pp. 460-61. Even less than in March when concrete "gang" links to disruptions were alleged in two cases, accounts of incidents in April, June and August in Hubei, Hunan, Jiangsu and Shanxi make no such claims. According to Gao and Yan, *Shinianshi*, pp. 681-82, however, Fujian rebels had direct means to communicate with the "gang" in Beijing.

In Hunan, there was a particularly strong attack in July on Zhang Pinghua, the ranking leader on the scene. Since Hua was the formal provincial first Party secretary, such attacks could be seen as also targeting Hua. But as in other cases, there is no convincing evidence linking the "gang of four" to these attacks. See Chen and Du, p. 1381; and "Zhonggong zhongyang guanyu 'Wang Hongwen, Zhang Chunqiao, Jiang Qing, Yao Wenyuan fandang jituan zuizheng (cailiao zhi yi)'," p. 66.

[125] Cheng Chao and Wei Haoben, *Zhejiang "wenge" jishi*, p. 258. One other case of a documented central response backing the local Party leadership occurred at the same time with regard to Shanxi. Following a report on the kidnapping of First Secretary Wang Qian and other violent action, the Party Center ordered the arrest of those responsible. Chen and Du, *Shilu*, vol. 3, part 2, p. 1404.

had not received Mao's blessing. In contrast, Mao's comment on improving conditions for Zhang Yongsheng frustrated the Organization Department, while on the other side of the argument the Chairman's views on Weng Senhe, the "double crashthroughs," and Document no. 16 left radicals with little hope of success. In agriculture, the situation was somewhat different, in that Document no. 21 transmitting the Dazhai decisions, which Mao had simply circled, was not reaffirmed in April given considerable grassroots objections, but neither was it reversed. As for the national planning seminar, the approach of the previous year's theory conference and the resultant 20 articles on industry had neither been endorsed nor rejected by Mao, and thus were potentially fair game for criticism. But it is not too fanciful to argue that the fact that Mao had approved the seminar's agenda gave extra weight to Hua's reassertion of that agenda after the sharp attacks of the first part of the meeting. The point is that even as his physical decline progressed, including during the period from late June when his ability to act was virtually nil, Mao's stated positions carried enormous clout. But it may also be that the comparative boldness of Hua and company in reasserting control over the planning seminar in July, and reaffirming Document no. 16 in August, reflected an awareness that Mao's days were very numbered, and with it his capacity to reverse course on the issues at hand.[126]

The Continuing Conflict in the Ministry of Foreign Affairs

As we saw in Chapter 6, tensions within the Foreign Ministry festered indecisively in the period before the Tiananmen crisis. From what is known, the "two ladies" apparently directed the anti-Deng campaign within the ministry, subjecting Qiao Guanhua and other old cadres to criticism in the process. Wang Hairong and Tang Wensheng, however, had their authority diminished with Jiang Qing's oversight of the MFA from February, and by that time had lost Mao's favor as a consequence of his changing attitude toward Deng, while senior officials on the whole emerged relatively unscathed. Meanwhile, Qiao and Zhang Hanzhi funneled materials critical of the "two ladies" to Mao through Jiang, materials that perhaps included accusations against Wang and Tang for their personal closeness to Deng, a closeness Jiang attacked in early March.[127] While the above is true in broad outline, the gaps in the record, no doubt in part due to the sensitivity of foreign affairs, suggest it is an oversimplified picture, one that does not capture adequately the complexity of a ministry rent by numerous factions and suffering from tensions among its senior officials. Similar gaps in information, together with the ongoing complexity of intra-organizational conflicts, limit our ability to elucidate the post-Tiananmen politics of the ministry and their relationship to the

---

[126] On Mao's circling of the Dazhai documents, see above, p. 361n165. More generally, none of the documents approved by Mao in 1975 were revoked, even if in some cases, notably Documents nos. 9 and 21, controversy concerning them erupted in 1976. Cf. above, p. 499n95.

[127] "Jiang Qing zai dazhaohu huiyi," p. 378.

larger drama of elite politics, but they do not prevent the effort.

In the new circumstances following the Tiananmen incident, there was one clear continuity: the lack of any significance of the ongoing struggle in the MFA for actual foreign policy, as opposed to sweeping claims that Qiao Guanhua represented the "rightist line" that had been promoted by Zhou and Deng.[128] What did change was the passing of formal responsibility for foreign affairs to Hua in mid-May on Mao's orders, although this may not have completely eliminated Jiang Qing's activities in this area.[129] As we shall see, Hua's new role would create further problems for Qiao Guanhua. But the most dramatic developments affecting the ministry concerned the shifting fortunes of the main protagonists—the "two ladies" v. Qiao and Zhang Hanzhi. Initially, apparently in April and most of May, Wang Hairong and Tang Wensheng suffered a major setback. But by the end of May, the issue of conflict in the MFA was reopened from above by the Party Center, and an organized debate unfolded that resulted in a loss of power for Qiao, although he continued to serve as minister. Wang and Tang were vindicated to some degree, but the major shift in power placed an outsider, Liu Zhenhua, a military man who had been serving as ambassador to Albania, in an important role in the MFA. While Liu's actual clout as a newly appointed vice minister, and his policy relevance given his inexperience, should not be overstated, he probably served as the main link to higher authority as Qiao's role faded. These events can be reconstructed, although various aspects remain murky.

As in the MFA story throughout, the key factor was Mao's shifting attitudes—attitudes based on deeply personal perceptions of individuals rather than on specific policy positions. His attitude toward the "two ladies," and thus his own niece, had clearly soured by April. Whether Mao was influenced by Jiang Qing's claims or the material from Qiao Guanhua and Zhang Hanzhi, or simply as a consequence of the redefinition of Deng as an antagonistic contradiction, Wang and Tang were no longer welcome in the Chairman's inner sanctum when he received foreign leaders. Although performing other foreign affairs duties for a period, the last time they accompanied a visitor to see Mao was on February 23

---

[128] Ross, "From Lin Biao to Deng Xiaoping," pp. 283, 294-95, while describing any earlier radical influence as "imperceptible," identifies a limited "radical input" into foreign policy in July when the PRC raised the Taiwan issue with the US. We have no concrete information on the politics behind this development, and can only observe that there is no reason to ascribe this to radical forces either in the Politburo or MFA, and the change itself was marginal in the scheme of things. Our analysis does not claim that there were no incidents that could be presented as matters of policy "line," only that these were distorted out of all relevance to actual policy. On the attacks on Qiao for his "rightist" policies, see above, pp. 91, 429; and below, p. 520.

[129] On Jiang Qing's role prior to mid-May, see above, pp. 432-33. As for her connection to the foreign affairs sector after May, the fact that she demanded to be included on a list of representatives from these units to pay respect to Mao after his death, even though she did not in fact participate in the group, suggests that there was some ongoing connection, at least in her own mind. See "Geng Biao guanyu sirenbang qingkuang," p. 1.

with former US President Nixon.[130] At some point in April, Mao declared he no longer wanted Tang Wensheng to translate for him, and Qiao and Zhang arranged for Ji Chaozhu, who had been dispatched to the countryside, to return to Beijing as a potential replacement. And indeed Ji (with Zhang Hanzhi apparently not present) was the translator when Mao received New Zealand Prime Minister Muldoon on April 30, Singapore Prime Minister Lee Kuan Yew on May 12, and Pakistan Prime Minister Bhutto on May 27. After the meeting with Lee, Mao told Qiao that from then on he should report to Hua. On the next day, Mao Yuanxin conveyed further instructions from the Chairman: in addition to Hua, Chen Xilian, Wang Dongxing, Zhang Chunqiao and Mao Yuanxin should receive Qiao's reports. While this left two radicals in the foreign affairs loop, as well as being another indication of the Chairman's effort to cultivate Mao Yuanxin, it meant that Jiang Qing's role was diminished. Qiao subsequently neither reported to her nor, apparently, had further contact. At the same time, Mao Yuanxin informed Qiao of the Chairman's anger with Wang and Tang: "I have now seen the true nature of [these] two people, these two rats thought our boat would sink and quickly jumped onto Deng Xiaoping's ship."[131]

If this appeared a victory for Qiao and Zhang Hanzhi in the conflict with the "two ladies," the situation was more complicated. Ironically, one of their exposures of Wang and Tang conveyed to Mao, presumably *via* Jiang Qing, damaged the minister's cause. On April 25, Zhang Hanzhi wrote the Chairman to reveal the role of the "two ladies" in "trumped-up charges" against Jiang and Zhang Chunqiao, charges allegedly stage managed by Deng Xiaoping. In her letter Zhang detailed the summer 1975 events outlined in Chapter 5: how Wang and Tang came to her and Qiao one evening the previous August with news of their visit to Kang Sheng, the visit arranged by Deng, where Kang laid out his accusations that Jiang and Zhang Chunqiao had been traitors during the revolutionary period, and asked the "two ladies" to convey his concerns to Mao. Kang further wanted them to seek out two comrades who had information to

---

[130] Both when Mao received Nixon, and earlier on December 31, when he received Nixon's daughter and son-in-law, Wang, Tang, Qiao and Zhang were all present.

[131] *RMRB*, May 1, 13, 28, 1976, all reports on p. 1; "Zhang Hanzhi jiu Qiao Guanhua yu Jiang Qing de guanxi," p. 1; and interview with MFA insider, November 2002. Qiao was present at Mao's meeting with Lee, but apparently not at the meetings with Muldoon and Bhutto, or the Chairman's receptions of Laotian and Egyptian leaders on March 17 and April 20 respectively.

No reason was given for Mao assigning Politburo responsibility for foreign affairs to Hua. Most likely it was simply filling out Hua's duties as the successor. Another possibility is that, since Jiang's role since February was a byproduct of the *de facto* removal of Deng from his remaining responsibility, the apparent good relations of Jiang and Qiao around the time of the Fourth NPC if not earlier meant this seemed a useful temporary reporting channel, but it had now outlived its usefulness. To the extent this was the case, it is intriguing that Mao's decision came in mid-May, i.e., after his discontent with Zhang Hanzhi's letter of April 25 (see below). This suggests that Mao may also have been angry with Jiang for her role in the matter. Also note the similarity of the new group receiving foreign affairs reports to the "teams" Mao reportedly considered for taking over after his death; above, p. 495n79.

prove his claims. Wang and Tang wanted advice and information from Qiao concerning the two comrades and other matters, thus indicating that at this stage their relationship was still more one of cooperation than conflict. Qiao and Zhang Hanzhi advised the "two ladies" not to convey Kang's accusations, arguing that Kang had his own means to communicate with the Chairman, with Zhang especially emphasizing that nothing to do with Jiang should be relayed. Whether the "two ladies" adopted the advice at the time is unknown, although we believe it unlikely that they would have said nothing to Mao since he had given permission for the visit to proceed. Now, in spring 1976, Jiang Qing claimed that this exposure showed Wang and Tang's activities were no different from those of Lin Biao. But more significantly, when the Chairman received Zhang Hanzhi's letter, his reaction was anger, and he scrawled on it, "this is using [Jiang Qing's] knife to kill people [i.e., Wang and Tang]." Mao had seen through Qiao and Zhang's attempt to attack Deng in name, and use the incident to further their struggle with the "two ladies." Qiao and Zhang, however, were unaware of Mao's comment until they were confronted with it after the arrest of the "gang of four."[132]

With Mao displeased with both sides of the conflict in the MFA, and the "two ladies" apparently having a particularly tough time, in late May the Foreign Ministry issue came up at a meeting of the Party Center. Following Mao's lead, the "gang of four" effectively abandoned Qiao Guanhua.[133] Jiang Qing and Zhang Chunqiao held Qiao responsible for shortcomings in the conduct of the anti-Deng campaign and disunity in the ministry, and called for an investigation. Qiao was surprised by this sudden attack since, in Zhang Hanzhi's somewhat distorted account, before this Mao had "many times" said the MFA's problem was the rebels' wish to purge a group of old cadres. In any case, to "solve" the ministry's problem, Hua set up a central five-person group of himself, Wang Hongwen, Wang Dongxing, Mao Yuanxin and one other person to deal with the issue. To illuminate the situation, each side would have an opportunity to make its case, and both Qiao and the "two ladies" formed their own five-person groups to make their arguments.[134]

---

[132] Chen and Du, *Shilu*, vol. 3, part 2, p. 1373; "Zhonggong zhongyang guanyu 'Wang Hongwen, Zhang Chunqiao, Jiang Qing, Yao Wenyuan fandang jituan zuizheng (cailiao zhi yi)'," pp. 15-16; "Li Xiannian, Chen Yun, Tan Zhenlin de jianghua," p. 1; interview with source close to Qiao Guanhua, November 2002; interview with Party historian specializing on the period, December 2002; and above, pp. 86, 366-67.

[133] This, however, did not mean that individual members of the "gang" were ill-disposed to each side equally. Thus Wang Hongwen, who had tense relations with Wang Hairong (see above, pp. 212-13), criticized both sides, but reserved special venom for the "two ladies." See "Xu Jingxian de chubu jiefa jiaodai," p. 1; and below, p. 577.

[134] Zhang Hanzhi, *Dahongmen*, p. 159; and interview with key player in the MFA, November 2002. Mao, in fact, had called on both sides to resolve their differences; see above, pp. 431-32.

While supposition on our part, we believe that the picture painted by those close to Qiao of a conflict of the "two ladies" v. old cadres is overstated given various tensions between Qiao and other

Before the meeting convened, the complicating factor of uneasy Hua-Qiao relations came to the fore. The occasion was the visit of Nepalese King Birendra to China in early June. Hua was scheduled to meet the King in Chengdu, with Qiao as Foreign Minister to accompany him, and with both Zhang Hanzhi and Ji Chaozhu in tow as translators. On such occasions previously, Qiao had always flown on the same plane as Zhou or Deng. Now, however, to Qiao's consternation, Hua notified Qiao that he and other MFA personnel should fly out first on June 1 on a separate aircraft. To make matters worse, once in Chengdu a number of miscalculations, together with Hua arriving ahead of schedule, meant that Qiao was not at the airport or guesthouse to greet Hua. This was understandably, if inaccurately, taken as a sign of disrespect, something consistent with Qiao's apparent opinion of the new successor. Qiao had privately complained that he was forced to "accompany the [ignorant] crown prince as a tutor" (*peitaizi dushu*), and his seeming disdain for the foreign affairs neophyte, if Lee Kuan Yew's memoirs a quarter of a century later are to be believed, was easily observed by others, and undoubtedly sensed by Hua himself, who later complained of Qiao's arrogance.[135]

While Zhang Hanzhi's memoirs dwell on the question of perceived disrespect, other factors were more likely relevant to Hua's distrust of Qiao, the actions taken against him in June, and especially in his sacking in October immediately after the arrest of the "gang." In the interpretation of an oral source close to Qiao, Hua needed someone in the ministry who could pose as the revolutionary faction and who had links to Mao: that is, the "two ladies."[136] More likely, from Hua's perspective Qiao must have seemed too close to Jiang Qing. As a Politburo member, Hua was undoubtedly aware of Qiao's apparent cooperation with her since late 1973, as well as Jiang's nomination of Qiao as a vice premier in 1974. Moreover, given his central role in 1976, Hua presumably had some knowledge of the Jiang-Qiao link in February-April. As for the Politburo radicals, by this time they were distancing themselves from Qiao, perhaps due to Mao's new attitude, but apparently also because, in the

---

senior MFA figures, and that some old cadres probably aligned with Wang and Tang. Cf. above, pp. 431, 433.

[135] Zhang Hanzhi, *Dahongmen*, pp. 159-60; *Memoirs of Lee Kuan Yew: From Third World to First, The Singapore Story: 1965-2000* (Singapore: Singapore Press Holdings, 2000), pp. 647, 650; Wen Xiang, "Mao Zedong, Qiao Guanhua, Zhang Hanzhi, Zhou Enlai"; interview with Party historian specializing on the period, February 2000; interview with source close to Qiao Guanhua, November 2002; and interview with MFA insider, August 2003.

Hua, with his lack of experience, did not impress foreign interlocutors. In addition to Lee Kuan Yew's particularly dismissive assessment, which even pictured Hua as a mere "thug" (p. 681), Stephen Fitzgerald, Australia's ambassador who accompanied Prime Minister Fraser to a meeting with Hua in June, described Hua as wooden, forgettable, and not engaging with his visitor's agenda. Personal communication, August 2005.

[136] Interview, November 2002.

"gang's" view, both sides in the MFA were "Deng's people."[137]

Nevertheless, as the debate of the contending groups in the MFA began, even though wall posters had appeared attacking his "serious mistake" in Chengdu, Qiao had some reason to feel confident given Mao Yuanxin's mid-May revelation of Mao's comments on the "two rats." Exactly why the situation changed so dramatically remains unclear, but June 7 was a turning point. On that day the Politburo convened to consider the issue, with Jiang Qing, Zhang Chunqiao and Mao Yuanxin severely criticizing the ministry for engaging in "civil war" to the detriment of the anti-Deng campaign. In the debate of the two sides within the MFA, Qiao came under serious attack for carrying out a right wing policy, with charges of being too soft on the US and Japan again raised, and for resisting self-criticism. Despite their disadvantages going into the meeting, the "two ladies" were apparently able to muster enough detail concerning Qiao's cooperation with Zhou and Deng to paint him as their man and carry the day. On the evening of the meeting, a totally confused Qiao rang Mao Yuanxin to ask what happened, saying "I thought the Chairman supported us, why the change?" Mao Yuanxin's response was both formal and cold, reminding Qiao that he was the minister and the first person responsible for his organization's shortcomings. Qiao, Mao Yuanxin instructed, should engage in self-criticism, and not criticize others.[138]

It was shortly afterward that Liu Zhenhua was recalled from Albania to assume a leading role in the ministry. From this perspective, a source close to Qiao has argued, it was in June, not October after the arrest of the "gang," that Qiao fell from grace. In any case, the situation in the ministry was confusing to the observer in summer 1976: Qiao remained minister and participated in every meeting Hua held with major foreign leaders from June to early September, the "two ladies" emerged from the shadows but seemingly without their former clout, and significant if indeterminate power within the ministry was purportedly now exercised by Liu. The political background was also perplexing. Despite Hua's presumed distrust of Qiao as a backer of the radicals, the radicals seemed to have jettisoned their support for Qiao. While Jiang Qing in particular had sought to discredit Wang and Tang, they appear to have made a partial recovery, but without developing any known ties to Hua despite speculation in Qiao's camp to that effect. And Liu Zhenhua, despite his ambassadorial service since 1971, was a MFA outsider, with no known ties to any of the major factions in the ministry. But it is suggestive, although no more than that, that Liu had been a political commissar in the Shenyang Military Region, where Mao Yuanxin also served in the same position.[139]

---

[137] "Ma Tianshui de buchong jiefa jiaodai," p. 5.

[138] Zhang Hanzhi, *Dahongmen*, pp. 160-61; and interview with source close to Qiao Guanhua, November 2002.

[139] *RMRB*, June 12, 21, July 27, 28, September 3, 4, 1976, all reports on p. 1; and interview with source close to Qiao Guanhua, November 2002. There is no evidence of concrete links between Liu Zhenhua and Mao Yuanxin, but both worked in Liaoning in the late 1960s, although Mao Yuanxin's

The final episode in Qiao's travails before Mao's death came with the Tangshan earthquake. Shortly after the quake struck on July 28, Wang Dongxing received a report of a follow-up earthquake of even greater proportions. Qiao (not Liu Zhenhua, although reportedly the decision was formally taken by the ministry's Party committee)[140] acted on this information, and made arrangements to disperse foreign diplomats given the ministry's responsibility for the safety of embassy personnel. The new quake did not eventuate, but the outcome left Qiao vulnerable. The next day Hua called to rebuke the ministry for acting independently of the Center, although in fact the MFA had passed on its proposal for evacuation to Hua's secretary, and then proceeded when there was no immediate reply. Hua equated the ministry's actions to a lack of discipline and panic, which caused damage to national dignity. Two days later, the MFA began daily criticism of Qiao's new "serious mistake." At this point, in a Politburo meeting, Jiang Qing reportedly demanded that Qiao make a self-criticism over the matter, while Zhang Chunqiao commented that this was not an isolated matter, but was linked to the MFA's inadequate performance in the anti-Deng campaign. The *coup de grâce* came a few days later when, with wall posters calling for Qiao's ouster already put up, Hua arrived at the ministry unannounced to criticize his minister. Qiao continued to serve until Mao's death and then until the fall of the "gang of four," but by the start of August his power in the ministry was well and truly marginalized.[141]

The Tangshan Earthquake

Adding to the uncertainty of the political situation, the Tangshan earthquake disrupted the CCP agenda in summer 1976. The readjusted planning targets could not be discussed systematically at the national planning seminar, nor could they be comprehensively implemented. As for the impact on the Foreign Affairs Ministry, while Hua's criticism of Qiao Guanhua may have been unfair and seen as such within the ministry, his assertion that national dignity was at stake reflected a general hypersensitivity to international image. A particularly perverse manifestation of this was the "polite decline" by the PRC, which routinely provided aid to stricken lesser countries, of offers of foreign assistance to cope with the enormous humanitarian problems created by the quake. This attitude would eventually be regarded as a consequence of the discredited "closed

---

military appointment apparently came later. Liu, in any case, stayed in the MFA until 1979, well after the arrest of Mao Yuanxin.

[140] Qiao's leading role apparently was a product of two factors. First, whatever the internal politics of the MFA, he was still minister in the eyes of the outside world. Also, Wang Dongxing's news of the expected second quake was relayed to Ji Dengkui at a state dinner on the 30th, and Ji passed the information on to Qiao. See Zhang Hanzhi, *Dahongmen*, p. 163.

[141] Zhang Hanzhi, *Dahongmen*, pp. 161, 163-65; and interview with MFA insider, November 2002. Although publicly performing as minister until early October, according to Zhang Hanzhi, p. 161, in early August, Qiao was released from his position (*weizhi*) by the Center.

door" approach of the Maoist era, but in 1976 it was *de rigueur* for any Chinese leader.[142]

The responsibility for dealing with the crisis fell on Hua. Although Mao read at least one report on the situation during a conscious moment, approving a document on August 18, there is no indication that he had any effective input into the regime's response. Indeed, when the earthquake struck on July 28, the Chairman was carried out of his quarters apparently unaware of what was happening. Hua was involved throughout August and into September in managing relief and reconstruction efforts, but the only activities known in any detail were his leadership of the comfort delegation to the Tangshan area in early August, and his leading role at the Beijing conference of representatives of advanced units in anti-quake and relief work at the start of September. It is unclear how effective Hua's efforts were, with the actual toll arguably much higher than the 242,000 deaths eventually acknowledged, and disorganization and delays apparently considerable, but the very fact of taking charge in handling a serious crisis by practical means undoubtedly enhanced his reputation. In the accepted view, moreover, Hua's activities built up his public profile to the consternation of the radicals who sought to undermine the effort, and thus Hua's position, by pushing the *pi Deng* agenda regardless. In addition to the Tangshan situation, when a less severe earthquake struck Sichuan on August 16, the "gang of four" allegedly again used the situation for political purposes, in this case by slandering Zhao Ziyang's anti-quake efforts as hiding from the priority task of opposing Deng.[143]

In actual fact, the political fallout of the Tangshan earthquake was less dramatic. As far as Hua was concerned, the boost to his public profile was both restricted to the August comfort mission and the September conference, and was relatively modest even in these contexts. For example, in the *People's Daily*, Hua's visit to the quake area received prominent but not excessive coverage, as seen in the fact that only two photos of Hua conducting comfort activities were published, and little attention was given to any directives or statements he may have issued. In official pronouncements, the leader assertedly showing most concern was the critically ill Chairman. At the conference convened on September 1, Hua was more prominent. For the first time since his elevation, a substantial speech by him on a domestic matter was not only published, but also received substantial publicity. The photos of the conference, moreover, pictured him as the ranking leader, with the entire Beijing-based Politburo following in his wake. Nevertheless, the conference was presented as an occasion of collective Politburo support for relief efforts, with one headline actually mentioning Hua, as

---

[142] See Zhang Hanzhi, *Dahongmen*, p. 165; Chen and Du, *Shilu*, vol. 3, part 2, p. 1397; Yan and Gao, *Turbulent Decade*, p. 514; and above, p. 511n119.

[143] See *Mao zhuan*, vol. 2, p. 1783; Chen and Du, *Shilu*, vol. 3, part 2, pp. 1397, 1403; Ma Qibin, *Sishinian*, p. 404; Yan and Gao, *Turbulent Decade*, pp. 514-16; and Baum, *Burying Mao*, pp. 38-39. While Hua was the leader of the comfort delegation from August 4, he was actually preceded to the scene several days earlier by deputy head Chen Yonggui.

speech giver, after Wang Hongwen who chaired the meeting. Moreover, this was a brief spasm of publicity, and by September 4 all references to the conference and Hua's role had disappeared from the pages of the *People's Daily*.[144]

As for the Politburo radicals, while they clearly pursued the anti-Deng campaign throughout August and up to Mao's death, particularly by intensifying attacks on the "three poisonous weeds," they appeared relaxed about the efforts to deal with the Tangshan crisis. To be sure, the overarching theme, familiar since early in the year that nothing must deflect people from criticizing Deng, was central in media reports, but there was only limited criticism of people allegedly using relief work to subvert Mao's line. In relatively few instances could statements reflecting the radical view be seen as potentially targeting those like Hua in charge of anti-quake work. The most famous occurred in an August 11 *People's Daily* editorial: "Chieftains of opportunist lines in the Party always try to take advantage of temporary difficulties brought on by natural disasters to divert the revolution from its course and restore capitalism." Whether this was in fact an allusion to Hua is unknown; an explicit reference to Deng's alleged use of the disasters of 1959-61 to advance his pernicious theory of "white and black cats" followed the quoted sentence. Overall, even the August 11 editorial was relatively moderate in the context of the times. Moreover, there were few other indications of possible criticism of Hua in the context of anti-quake work. Indeed, after Hua's September 1 speech, Jiang Qing reprimanded Wang Hongwen for showing too much respect to Hua on the occasion, a remark that earned Mao Yuanxin's rejoinder that it wasn't a question of respecting Hua, but instead a matter of respect to the Chairman since he had anointed Hua his successor.[145]

Rather than pushing a confrontational message, official propaganda concerning the earthquake took on a more positive, if still radical, note, one that saw anti-quake work and the anti-Deng campaign as compatible endeavors. Of course, in good Maoist terms, politics assumed command, and the anti-Deng campaign was said to provide the motive force for combating the effects of the earthquake. Various related themes were repeated *ad nauseum* as a virtual mantra, including deepening the anti-Deng movement, affirming class struggle as the key link, urging quake victims to study Mao's important directives, and ascribing successes in anti-quake work to tempering in the Cultural Revolution and the campaign against Lin Biao and Confucius. These repeated references, however, had an air of ritual about them, and they were accompanied by other themes which, while impeccably Maoist, had a pre-Cultural Revolution lineage: praise of the revolutionary heroism and optimism of the masses, the importance of the

---

[144] See *RMRB*, August 5, p. 1, August 6, p. 4, September 2, 1976, pp. 1, 3, 4. Apart from the two cases, Hua was hardly mentioned in the *People's Daily* during this period except for his role in receiving foreign visitors. A similar pattern in the media more generally was apparent in items surveyed in FBIS-PRC, August to mid-September 1976.

[145] See *RMRB*, August 11, 1976, p. 1; and Xia Chao and Yang Fengcheng, *Longnian zhibian*, p. 324.

human factor over material constraints, the powerful strength of self-reliance, and the important role of Party committees. There was, inevitably, a tension between themes deriving from the 1966-76 period, and those emerging earlier. Indeed, attacks on Deng for allegedly claiming that "the present is not as good as the past" suggest a defensiveness against public opinion that current conditions, as symbolically reflected in the Tangshan disaster, could not match the pre-Cultural Revolution situation.[146]

How did Hua negotiate this issue? In his September 1 speech, he repeated the key tasks of using the criticism of Deng as the motive force in anti-quake work and taking class struggle as the key link, but overall his remarks were moderate despite numerous references to radical themes. He avoided the harsher phrases appearing in some media reports on the relief efforts that attacked "capitalist roaders" and "bourgeoisie in the Party," and much of the speech dealt with the practical measures that had been undertaken to deal with the situation. Hua did address sabotage and interference with the relief efforts, but notwithstanding a ritual denunciation of interference by Deng's revisionist line, the practical target was "class enemies" in society who spread rumors and disrupted public order. Hua's basic message was that much had been accomplished by the efforts of the Party and people, while his goal was to restore confidence for the rebuilding tasks which remained.[147]

In sum, several observations can be made about the elite politics surrounding the effort to deal with the Tangshan earthquake. First, there is no evidence of any division over the actual relief measures. Beyond that, while it is reasonable to assume different tendencies, with Hua playing down the ideological themes that the Politburo radicals sought to emphasize, the public discourse was not sharply confrontational. Indeed, compared to issues such as agriculture and especially the national planning seminar, there was little evidence of conflict over the earthquake. It may even have been the case that the sharpest discontent with the "gang" in this context concerned their alleged disinterest, as well as Jiang Qing's personal foibles. Specifically, during Politburo discussions, the radicals reportedly did not attend briefings on the Tangshan situation, while Jiang assertedly insisted on bringing up the alleged bourgeois nature of rarv

---

[146] The themes cited here are based on a survey of reports compiled in FBIS-PRC in August and early September 1976. On the question of current conditions compared to the past, a *Red Flag* article on "the two-line struggle in China's history of earthquakes" assessed reactions to earthquakes from the Song dynasty to the present, arguing the reactionaries always used quakes to claim that reformers were incapable of proper rule. *HQ*, no. 9 (1976), in *SPRCM*, no. 891 (1976), pp. 85-91. While used against Deng, "the present is not as good as the past" charge more specifically targeted one of his key supporters in 1975, Zhang Aiping. See above, p. 417.

[147] See the NCNA account of Hua's speech in FBIS-PRC, September 2, 1976, pp. E2-5; and the AFP assessment of Hua's status at the time of the conference in FBIS-PRC, September 7, 1976, pp. E1-2. For a similarly moderate albeit very brief statement by Hua during the early August comfort mission, see NCNA, Beijing, August 7, 1976, in FBIS-PRC, August 9, 1976, p. E3.

hats, causing Su Zhenhua to grumble, "how can you deal with this woman?"[148] But perhaps the most striking aspect of the episode is how closely the public discussion of the situation followed the rhetoric of the anti-Deng campaign. That campaign had been mandated by Mao, and even as he lay dying and unable to influence events, his authority remained so great that no leader could depart from that framework.

Political Calculations on the Eve of Mao's Death

Given ten years of conflict and enmity between the Politburo radicals and representatives of the political establishment, indications of private discussions since at least 1973 of ways to get rid of at least two (Jiang Qing and Zhang Chunqiao) of the so-called "gang of four," and, not least, the initial moves toward an anti-radical coup within 48 hours of Mao's death, it is logical to believe that the arrest of the "gang" in early October was inevitable. Beyond this, the dominant view of the final stage of Mao's illness from late June depicts the opposing forces "jolted … into action, [with] the plotting for ascendancy in the post-Mao era commenc[ing] in earnest."[149] In this interpretation, the radicals, for their part, "had evidently decided to confront [their enemies] by military force if necessary," while "The generals [associated with Ye Jianying], too, were preparing."[150] But as indicated at the outset of this chapter, less attention has been given to the activities and calculations of the leader with the greatest formal authority, Hua Guofeng. In Chapter 8 we address the issue of inevitability and the dynamics of the crushing of the radicals. Here, despite severe limitations on sources and distortions in the available material, we assess in turn the circumstances and calculations of the three forces, and conclude with a brief review of events at the very end of Mao's life.

The relentlessly negative picture of the "gang of four" in Chinese sources involves claims which range from the crudely distorted[151] to those undoubtedly true in the narrow sense, but open to interpretation. Any assessment of the radicals' activities at the end of Mao's life must take into account the overall political situation in August and early September 1976, a situation which calls into doubt the logic of heightened preparations by the "gang" for "seizing power." As indicated previously, the April decisions had placed the bulk of executive authority in the hands of Hua Guofeng, while immediate military

---

[148] "Geng Biao guanyu zhua sirenbang qingkuang," p. 1; and "Zhongyang lingdaoren guanyu sirenbang wenti de jianghua," p. 3.

[149] Keith Forster, "China's Coup of October 1976," *Modern China*, July 1992, pp. 273-74.

[150] MacFarquhar, "Succession," p. 306.

[151] Relevant here are claims of Jiang Qing's cavalier attitude toward the dying Mao, something unimaginable both in terms of elite political culture, or any possible calculation of political advantage. See Yan and Gao, *Turbulent Decade*, pp. 518-19; Fan Shuo, *Ye Jianying zai feichang shiqi*, vol. 2, pp. 578-81; and above, p. 504n105.

power rested with Chen Xilian as the official responsible for MAC daily work, and Yang Chengwu as the *de facto* PLA Chief-of-Staff.[152] While there were complexities in this situation, complexities reflected in the advocacy of some military officers after Mao's death that Jiang Qing become the new head of the Party and MAC, overall both the top command's inclinations and the corporate interests of the military as an institution were unsympathetic or hostile to the radicals.[153] Similarly, although radical sympathizers were spread throughout the ministries in Beijing and local Party and state organs, these again appear to have been a distinct minority, with only Shanghai and Mao Yuanxin's Liaoning comparatively firm "base" areas for the radical cause. Moreover, as we have suggested in earlier contexts, ideological sympathy and common interests on the part of local officials thrust into official positions by the Cultural Revolution did not necessarily mean a tightly integrated factional system organized from Beijing. The excesses of lower-level sympathizers not only sometimes embarrassed the Politburo radicals, and on occasion, as in the case of Wang Hongwen and the Zhejiang rebels, brought them into direct conflict, but there is little concrete evidence to suggest a direct "gang of four" hand in the factional fighting in the localities in summer 1976. Moreover, the intensified social and economic disruption which accompanied such factional conflicts could only have served to heighten opposition to the "gang" within the top elite.[154]

Given this decidedly weak position, the most sensible radical strategy arguably would have been to avoid confrontation—something which can indeed be seen in their reaction to the Tangshan earthquake following the rebuff at the national planning seminar. Indeed, the strongest factors for the radicals' survival in the post-Mao era were their legal position as Politburo members, and Jiang

---

[152] As Deputy Chief-of-Staff, Yang took over the leading role in the General Staff Department when Deng was set aside and then formally dismissed in April. While Yang had been Jiang Qing's preferred choice as Chief-of-Staff in 1974, he was party to Ye Jianying's discussions concerning the radicals in summer 1976. See above, pp. 204-205; and below, p. 531.

[153] See Wang Dongxing's claim that some people in the PLA supported not only Jiang, but also other members of the "gang" for high posts, including Zhang Chunqiao as premier; "Wang Dongxing zai quanguo xuanchuan gongzuo jianghua," p. 3. Alan P. L. Liu, "The 'Gang of Four' and the Chinese People's Liberation Army," *AS*, September 1979, while placing too much weight on comparative military studies which did not adequately grasp the PRC situation, provides a broadly accurate picture of the conflict between the radicals' activities and PLA interests and traditions. In the event, with the arrest of the "gang" in October, only a small number of high-ranking military leaders were dismissed, notably Air Force Commander Ma Ning and Nanjing Military Region Commander Ding Sheng, although significantly more were reshuffled in 1977.

[154] See above, pp. 178, 278ff, 460-61, 498. The disadvantage of economic disorder to the radical cause was well understood, as seen in the early 1976 comments of radical Shanghai leader Ma Tianshui. Ma observed that the Party Center [i.e., Mao] was worried about economic chaos, and if they did not do good work in this area, they would hand an advantage to their political enemies; interview with senior Party historian, January 2000. If Mao was unimpressed with economic disruption, Hua, the Politburo majority, and the old cadres in the wings would have been even less impressed during the deteriorating situation in the summer.

Qing's "special position" as Mao's wife, factors suggesting the desirability of a wait and see approach. Of course, given the "gang's" demonstrated history of less than skilful politics, not to mention Jiang's apparent exaggerated sense of herself, nothing can be ruled out. Desperate measures in anticipation of forceful action against them, such as what eventually happened, could also have had a logical appeal. One of the problems, however, is that for all the effort to depict evil plotting by the "gang" in these last days, hardly any evidence has been presented of the four, or a sub-grouping of the four, coming together to adopt a strategy for the coming political transition. Indeed, we see this as further evidence, however limited, of the proposition that the whole notion of a "gang of four" is greatly overstated. As one senior Party historian put it when discussing this period, "the evidence suggests they were not a highly organized or coordinated group."[155] In any case, the fragmentary information available addresses two types of activities by the "gang of four": 1) political measures designed to highlight the radical agenda and maintain at least Jiang's profile, a quite natural effort to consolidate their position at a time of uncertainty; and 2) claims of illicit plans to prepare for a showdown, claims which are very weak.

We have already noted the radicals' main political activity: the ongoing pursuit of the anti-Deng campaign in the media. This, of course, was an activity authorized by Mao. The centerpiece of this effort in August and early September, the attack on the "three poisonous weeds," could, however, be seen as a criticism of Hua in addition to Deng, given Hua's involvement in the 20 articles and Outline Report, much as the attack on the 1975 State Council theory conference at the planning seminar potentially threatened him and other leaders.[156] At the least, these media attacks would have been designed to create pressure against the policy approach advocated in the three documents, and to bolster support from like-minded people in the Party including substantial numbers of presumptive radical sympathizers in the Central Committee. A less well-known, but subsequently criticized activity was Jiang Qing's several inspections at the end of August and start of September. On August 26, she visited the Xinhua printing factory in Beijing, as well as Qinghua and Beijing Universities, ostensibly to examine anti-earthquake measures. During these inspections Jiang declared that she was representing Chairman Mao and the Party Center. Chi Qun organized a report on these visits, and Yao Wenyuan demanded that the Beijing Municipal Committee arrange for its publication in the *Beijing Daily*. But when Wu De saw the front page layout with a banner heading emphasizing Jiang as the representative of Mao and the Center, he decided publication without referral to the Center would violate organizational principles. Wu consulted Hua on the matter, noting that an excuse

---

[155] Interview, December 2002.

[156] Similarly, Wang Hongwen's summoning "in August" of State Council and MAC documents and meeting records for the June 1975-January 1976 period, allegedly to provide a basis "to attack Party Center and State Council responsible comrades," could be seen as targeting Hua. See Chen and Du, *Shilu*, vol. 3, part 2, p. 1405.

for not publishing the piece should be concocted for Yao's benefit. In the end, Hua simply sat on the article, and it was never published.[157] About the same time, Jiang obtained permission from Mao, whose condition had fleetingly improved, to leave Beijing and visit Tianjin and the Xiaojinzhuang agricultural model, troops in the Ji'nan command, and finally Dazhai. While hostile post-Mao reports dwell on Jiang's self-promotion, female chauvinism, and petty complaints on these trips, they were clearly legitimate tours undoubtedly designed to demonstrate support for the concerned areas, and to promote the anti-Deng campaign.[158]

Notwithstanding the anti-Hua implications of the campaign to criticize Deng, or Jiang's presumption in claiming to represent Mao and the Party Center, these political activities were broadly legitimate in the context of the time. Military developments, however, raise more serious questions. Apart from vague accusations that the "gang" and their agents agitated for insubordination in the ranks in the months before the Chairman's death,[159] innuendo concerning military preparations in East China form the concrete basis for the idea of serious planning for a seizure of power. Yet the record is hardly substantial. One incident stands out. On August 8, Nanjing Military Region Commander Ding Sheng reportedly held secret talks with the ranking (radical) leaders of the Shanghai Municipal Party Committee, Ma Tianshui, Xu Jingxian and Wang Xiuzhen. Ding allegedly expressed his unease with a certain unit under his command and was very worried about its deployment, telling the Shanghai leaders they should make preparations. Soon afterward, Ma Tianshui ordered the immediate issuing of a report concerning the distribution of arms to the Shanghai militia. A meeting of the militia command on August 11 and 13 considered arrangements for issuing weapons in order to strengthen border and air defenses in the area, and these were presented to the municipal committee on August 31. Finally, on September 3 Ding had further consultations on military matters with Shanghai leaders. In addition to these local activities, another post-Mao report has Wang Hongwen visiting Shanghai "sometime between July and August" when he "expressed hopes" for the transfer of arms and ammunition to Shanghai's "second army," i.e., the people's militia. These reports represent the extent of concrete claims backing the notion that the radicals sought to deploy the militia in preparation for Mao's death, with the goal of "seizing power."[160]

---

[157] See *ibid.*, pp. 1404-1405; and Wu De, "Guanyu fensui 'sirenbang'," p. 53.

[158] See Yan and Gao, *Turbulent Decade*, pp. 517-18; and *RMRB*, December 24, 1976, in *SPRCP*, no. 6272 (1977), p. 96.

[159] See Liu, "Gang of Four," pp. 819, 824.

[160] See Chen and Du, *Shilu*, vol. 3, part 2, p. 1405; Gao and Yan, *Shinianshi*, p. 688; MacFarquhar, "Succession," p. 306; Liu, "Gang of Four," pp. 823, 829-33; and below, pp. 530-31. Ding and the three Shanghai leaders also met on August 13, when Ding spoke on "the bourgeoisie in the army" to a unit of the Shanghai Garrison. While this reportedly generated heated objections from some of the officers present, it was clearly a propaganda effort that had no illicit connotations; Chen and Du, pp. 1402-1403.

What can be said about these claims? First, given the general lack of detail concerning these developments, to assume they involved active preparations for an armed "seizure of power" is an act of faith. A more restrained interpretation would focus on the inevitable tension between Ding Sheng, who was sent to the Nanjing Military Region in 1974 with a brief to preside over criticism of the shortcomings of the similarly transferred Xu Shiyou, and the military region's troops (notably including the unit that particularly concerned Ding) which had long served under Xu. This was undoubtedly complicated by Ding presumably cooperating to some indeterminate degree, as *per* CCP procedures, with the local Party authorities, as well as with MAC Standing Committee members Wang Hongwen and Zhang Chunqiao (Zhang also being the military region's political commissar), and further complicated by the fact that Xu was a bitter foe of Wang and Zhang.[161] Moreover, a more detailed account (see below) both gives support to this consideration and suggests a quite different perspective on Ding's involvement from the official innuendo. Second, the moves to distribute arms to the militia, even as depicted in hostile sources, were explicitly defensive in intent. Such measures most likely reflected in part fears that others might act against the radicals, fears which of course proved correct in October. Third, reports of Wang Hongwen's role notwithstanding, the key actors involved in the East China measures, on the available evidence, were the local Shanghai radicals and Ding Sheng, the PLA leader responsible for the area. Again, evidence of an integrated radical system extending downward from Beijing is weak. Fourth, the effort to paint the whole issue of the "second army" of the people's militia as an illegitimate device to further the factional ends of the radicals overlooks one central fact: as we saw in Chapter 1, the militia and its role as a separate force from the PLA (seemingly modified in 1975) was Mao's creation. It may have been a resource the radicals could use, but its existence, ideological orientation, and Wang Hongwen's involvement, were all matters determined by the Chairman, and legitimate under the arrangements of the period. Notably, the charge of planning to use the militia to seize power was the only matter the normally cooperative Wang would not fully accept at the 1980 trial of the "gang of four."[162]

Finally, the circumstances of the August developments point to a broad-based concern of the elite as a whole that Mao's death would set off social instability, such as had occurred at the time of the *Qingming* festival. Drawing on

---

[161] The animosity of Xu as well as that of Ye Jianying, together with the general suspicion and guilt by association rife in leadership circles at the time, probably explains why Ding was sacked from his military region post after the arrest of the "gang." He was expelled from the CCP in 1982.

[162] See Qing and Fang, *Deng zai 1976*, vol. 2, p. 280; *A Great Trial*, pp. 78-79; and above, pp. 81ff, 145-46, 260. Wang admitted under sharp questioning that building up the militia provided the basis for the alleged "rebellion" in Shanghai after the arrest of the "gang," and that his advocacy of using the militia against revisionist attempts to seize power, since "the army is not in our hands," was actually aimed at veteran cadres who had been overthrown during the Cultural Revolution. However, Wang in effect denied the latter admission with a statement that his remark about the army was directed at Lin Biao's influence in the military.

the lessons of Tiananmen, Wu De and Chen Xilian, as officials responsible for security in the capital, had drafted contingency plans designed for three levels of disturbances: less than, equal to, and greater than what had occurred during *Qingming*. Once Mao passed away, these plans were implemented on a standby basis. In the meantime, the evidence indicates that the entire military apparatus was placed on alert in August, an alert that was apparently suspended when the Chairman's condition took a momentary turn for the better in late August and early September, but was then restored as he relapsed on September 5. In terms of the distribution of arms to the Shanghai militia, Wang Hongwen called for its enhanced readiness immediately following the Center's announcement of Mao's grave medical condition at the end of June, but major steps apparently were only taken from mid-August with central PLA backing, including approval by the General Staff and Logistics Departments.[163]

Of special interest, and indicative of the overly glib treatment of individuals in official sources, Ding Sheng's face-to-face involvement with the Shanghai radicals seems to have only begun in the context of the national, Beijing-authorized alert. Although posted to nearby Nanjing at the start of 1974, rather than developing close ties with the Shanghai leadership, Ding visited Shanghai *for the first time* in August 1976, staying for a month until after Mao's death.[164] All of this strongly indicates that militia activities in Shanghai in the summer and into the period following Mao's death should be viewed more in terms of a generalized anxiety about the wider consequences of the Chairman's passing than as part of a plan to seize power. This, plus the influence of Xu Shiyou's former troops, is further indicated by a credible Internet source. This source claims that the meeting on August 8 dealt with a planned military exercise near Shanghai in the context of the general mobilization, and the agenda with local leaders concerned such prosaic matters as logistic support and traffic management while the exercise was in progress, not politics. Ding's reported concern regarding "a certain unit," in fact the 60th Army stationed in Jiangsu, in this version was not expressed on August 8, but instead on September 3 in response to Ma Tianshui. On that occasion Ma passed on a letter from Xu Shiyou's son, an officer in the 60th Army, a letter that predicted a civil war after Mao's death. This led to Ding's expression of unease about having little control over this unit, an unease which, rather than resulting in intense plotting with the Shanghai leadership,

---

[163] See "Beijing 'wenge' dashiji," p. 42; Qing and Fang, *Deng zai 1976*, vol. 2, p. 144; Chen and Du, *Shilu*, vol. 3, part 2, p. 1388; "Ma Tianshui de buchong jiefa jiaodai," p. 5; Li Xun, *Da bengkui*, pp. 554-55; *Shanghai shehuizhuyi jianshe wushi nian* [Fifty Years of Shanghai's Socialist Construction] (Shanghai: Shanghai renmin chubanshe, 1999), p. 414; *Shanghai minbing douzheng shi ziliao*, vol. 22, p. 88; *Shanghai "wenhua dageming" shihua*, p. 727; and Perry and Li, *Proletarian Power*, p. 184. We have not located a precise source pinpointing a national alert, but the weight of the evidence and the logic of the situation strongly indicate that there was one in August.

[164] Li Xun, *Da bengkui*, p. 545.

led him to report through formal military channels to Chen Xilian, the official in charge of the MAC.[165]

The other significant feature of much wisdom on the period posits active preparations by the old revolutionaries, particularly veteran military figures led by Ye Jianying, for the eventual purge of the "gang of four." This view, based to a large extent on memoirs and biographies of senior PLA leaders, basically ignores Hua Guofeng's role in the whole process leading to the demise of the "gang," and gives virtually sole credit to the older generation. Clearly something was going on in summer 1976 involving these senior figures, many of whom had no formal power or, as in the case of Ye, significantly limited authority. Again, given the limited information available, it is difficult to be categorical about the activities of the old guard, but on the available evidence the emphasis on the role of these revolutionaries is greatly overstated, certainly as far as any specific preparations were concerned.

Memoirs and biographies report discussions centering on Ye, in his Western Hills residence outside Beijing, in the two months plus preceding Mao's death, discussions which explicitly or indirectly touched on the "problem of the gang of four." These exchanges involved an array of PLA veterans: Nie Rongzhen, Xu Xiangqian, Chen Xilian, Yang Chengwu, Su Zhenhua, Wang Dongxing and, most notably, Wang Zhen. How frequently these encounters occurred is unclear. For example, claims that Ye and Nie "many times" addressed the issue of stopping the "gang" are not confirmed in other sources or in much detail.[166] The people involved represented, broadly speaking, three types of situations: 1) those like Nie and Xu, who had no official positions apart from membership on the Central Committee; 2) Chen, Yang, Su, Wang Dongxing and Wang Zhen who held active portfolios; and 3) Ye, who sat on the Politburo but seemingly remained

---

[165] Yu Ruxin, "Wei Ding Sheng bian" [In Defense of Ding Sheng] (June 2005), http://blog.wenxuecity.com/blogview.php?date=200506&postID=1975. An indication that Ding did not feel that he was compromised by any radical connections is found in the recollection of General Liao Hansheng of Ding's relaxed manner on the eve of the meeting of Party and military leaders in Beijing immediately after the arrest of the "gang." *Liao Hansheng huiyilu, xu* [Memoirs of Liao Hansheng, continued] (Beijing: Jiefangjun chubanshe, 2003), p. 394.

[166] Compare Nie Rongzhen, "[Ye] Jianying was in Fact a Proletarian Lu Duan," NCNA, October 31, 1986, in British Broadcasting Corporation: Summary of World Broadcasts, Far East/8409/BII/6 (November 6, 1986), which makes the claim, with his memoirs, *Nie Rongzhen huiyilu* [Memoirs of Nie Rongzhen] (Beijing: Jiefangjun chubanshe, 1984), vol. 3, p. 867, his biography, *Nie Rongzhen zhuan* [Biography of Nie Rongzhen] (Beijing: Dangdai Zhongguo chubanshe, 1994), pp. 689-90, and *Nie Rongzhen nianpu*, vol. 2, p. 1132, none of which mention such discussions. *Ye zhuan*, p. 638, however, confirms talks between the two marshals on how to solve the problem of the "gang."

It is also unclear to what extent if any Xu Xiangqian was involved in discussions with Ye since these are not explicitly mentioned. The only information on Xu is the claim in his biography, *Xu Xiangqian zhuan*, p. 546, that he sometimes secretly discussed his anxiety about the situation with his "comrades-in-arms." Wang Dongxing did not appear to have had direct contact with Ye, but probably talked to Wang Zhen.

under some cloud and may formally still have been on sick leave. Indeed, in one discussion with Wang Zhen, Ye commented that it was difficult for him to be more active in light of "my present status," while Ye's biography refers to his degraded "military leading power that was still not completely stripped away." More broadly, all of this took place in an atmosphere of great tension and uncertainty, which contributed to indirection as well as evasiveness on the part of some participants. The actual situation of these senior figures was apparently somewhat less restrictive than that of at least some Politburo members who, according to Li Xiannian, feared even to talk to one another outside of formal meetings. In any case, on the existing record, Li does not appear to have engaged in similar discussions. For those who did participate, the utmost discretion was *de rigueur*.[167]

What was the content of these discussions which required such discretion? From the sketchy accounts available, their essence was mainly expressions of anxiety about the future of the Party and country, not to mention the futures of the veteran leaders themselves. Rather than deciding on particular measures, it apparently was at most a case of tossing ideas around. For the time being, the conclusion apparently was that nothing could be done as long as an even incapacitated Chairman survived, action against the "gang" being simply unthinkable while they retained his support, with Jiang Qing's "special status" as Mao's wife cited as a particular impediment. It would be necessary to wait for an appropriate opportunity, Ye told Nie Rongzhen, but most accounts give no indication of what might have been considered.[168] The exception, but one ultimately consistent with this picture, was Wang Zhen. In accounts based in significant part on his own testimony, Wang has been portrayed as an active and aggressive player who initiated contact with Ye, pushed for drastic action, and served as a liaison between Ye and a broader range of senior cadres. In the classic, repeatedly cited, exchange, Wang asked Ye why the problem of the "gang" couldn't be solved by simply arresting them, while Ye responded with hand gestures. Ye's gestures, much like his comment about "sparing the rats to save the precious dish,"[169] meant that while Mao was around it was inappropriate to act, but afterward an opportunity would present itself. The fact that Ye's response went no further than inconclusive hand gestures underlines the strong

---

[167] See *Ye zhuan*, p. 638; Fan Shuo, *Ye Jianying zai feichang shiqi*, vol. 2, pp. 574-77; Fan Shuo, *Ye Jianying zai 1976* [Ye Jianjing in 1976] (Beijing: Zhonggong Zhongyang dangxiao chubanshe, 1995), pp. 224-25; and *Wang Zhen zhuan*, vol. 2, p. 169. On Li Xiannian's comment, see above, p. 455.

[168] See *Ye zhuan*, pp. 637-38; Fan Shuo, *Ye Jianying zai feichang shiqi*, vol. 2, pp. 574-77; and Nie Rongzhen, "[Ye] Jianying was in Fact a Proletarian Lu Duan."

[169] While some sources claim Ye's remark was directed at Wang, others report it was said to Nie; see above, p. 463n3. Deng Liqun (cited in Baum, *Burying Mao*, p. 40) records Ye conveying the same message to Wang: "the old man [is] still around, ... [would] he approve [arresting the 'gang'] or not?" Some Party historians interviewed, however, believe Ye never went beyond hand gestures on such a delicate subject. Indeed, Deng Liqun's account may simply verbalize Ye's presumed intent.

likelihood that nothing concrete was planned in these last weeks of Mao's life, that the rational approach was to sit tight and avoid doing anything silly, while the question of whether Ye had a firm intent for forceful action after the Chairman's death remains open. As for Wang Zhen, in discussing his role, Party historians specializing in Wang's career explained his comparative boldness not simply in terms of his aggressive personality, but also because Mao's high degree of trust in Wang inhibited the radicals from confronting him. Most tellingly, they believe that Wang's actions in this period were nevertheless significantly constrained. He may have gone further than others, but the sum of the evidence suggests Wang's role was mainly limited to canvassing seemingly diffused opinion. Overall, the picture emerging from these discussions is of leaders unwilling to act while Mao lived, great animosity toward and considerable fear of the radicals, and indecisiveness regarding any future strategy. All of this, moreover, took place on the sidelines, well removed from official power.[170]

And what of Hua in these fraught circumstances? Although, as we shall see in the following chapter, Hua was the first to act after Mao's death, there is no evidence indicating active preparations on his part for a showdown with the radicals before Mao passed away. This, of course, could be a function of the concerted effort since the early 1980s to minimize Hua's role.[171] What we do know, however, is that Hua used his authority as the Party's chief executive officer to rebuff the political maneuvers of the "gang of four" and other radicals. This can be seen in his rejection of the program put forward by radicals in the Ministry of Public Security in June, in stopping the radical agenda at the July

---

[170] *Ye zhuan*, pp. 637-38; *Wang Zhen zhuan*, vol. 2, pp. 168-69; and interview, November 2002. *Wang Zhen zhuan*, p. 168, has Wang advocating guerrilla war to other old revolutionaries staying in hospital accommodations after the Tiananmen incident, but this surely was an emotional outburst rather than a serious proposition.

In the earliest exchange we have found on the matter, on February 2, Wang Zhen reportedly visited Nie Rongzhen, complaining bitterly of the radicals' treatment of Zhou Enlai, and declaring that he would fight them to the death. Nie reportedly replied that dealing with them was inevitable, but you should be careful about strategy and not act on your own. No indication of anything more concrete is recorded. *Nie Rongzhen nianpu*, vol. 2, p. 1131.

[171] While the official 1981 Historical Resolution gives Hua primary credit for "smashing" the "gang" (see below, p. 591), the only reference to Hua during the period immediately before Mao's death we have seen in memoirs, biographies and quasi-journalistic accounts, is a mention of his September 1 speech to the Beijing earthquake conference. Fan Shuo, *Ye Jianying zai feichang shiqi*, vol. 2, p. 578. By noting his advocacy of the anti-Deng campaign, Fan distorts Hua's actual circumstances and position on that occasion.

A rare suggestion of possible preparations by those in charge of the official apparatus, although not specifying Hua, is a report that in summer 1976 Yao Wenyuan received information claiming that Ji Dengkui's son had been involved in discussions with Henan officials canvassing a bloody crackdown after Mao's death. See Qing and Fang, *Deng zai 1976*, vol. 2, p. 300. If this account is true, what is also striking is that although Ji's son allegedly singled out Zhang Chunqiao as a traitor, Yao, who could not quite believe the report, kept the information to himself. This further suggests the looseness of the "gang of four," and is particularly notable in that Yao and Zhang appear to have been the closest of the four.

national planning seminar, in excising the "gang's" claim that Mao's health was improving from a Party Center notice in July,[172] presumably in rebuffing the Zhejiang rebels' attempt to reverse the mid-1975 document denouncing factionalism in their province in August,[173] and in quashing publicity for Jiang Qing later that month. More generally, according to Wang Dongxing, the leadership, presumably Hua and Ji Dengkui, "did not let [the radicals] have their way in personnel deployment."[174] These steps notwithstanding, Hua, as was seemingly the case for both the Politburo radicals and old revolutionaries, for the time being acted within the framework set by the dying Mao, despite the intense suspicion and concern for the future that were rife within the top elite. The campaign against Deng was not questioned: even senior figures clearly sympathetic to Deng are not recorded as directly addressing the issue. Leaders placed on the Politburo by Mao retained their positions, even as those who had earned his disfavor such as Ye Jianying and Li Xiannian were largely denied executive authority.[175] While Hua, as the designated successor, was able exercise a decisive voice on contentious issues, he was careful to adhere to the *pi Deng* iine. The degree to which this reflected loyalty to the dying Chairman, or a political calculation that while Mao lived any bolder action would be counterproductive, is unknowable. But everyone understood that a new situation would be created once Mao passed from the scene.

It was against this background that the final scenes of Mao's life were played out. While the brief improvement in the Chairman's condition at the end of August and start of September allowed Jiang Qing to ask for, and receive, Mao's permission for her trips outside of Beijing, he took a turn for the worse on September 5, when Jiang was summoned back from Dazhai. The intense distrust within the highest circles could be seen at Mao's deathbed. A system had been established whereby, according to Mao's wishes, Politburo members Hua, Wang Hongwen, Zhang Chunqiao and Wang Dongxing took turns in standing vigil, and before leaving for Dazhai, Jiang asked Wang and Zhang to pay attention to what others were doing when they were at Mao's side.[176]

---

[172] At a July Politburo meeting, a conflict developed over a statement concerning Mao's heaith. Hua rejected the "gang's" proposal to say that Mao's health was improving, and he would return to work before long. In the contentious argument, Ye Jianying reportedly joined Wang Dongxing in rebutting Jiang Qing and Zhang Chunqiao. Chen and Du, *Shilu*, vol. 3, part 2, p. 1399.

[173] Hua's personal role in this matter is not known, and Ji Dengkui as the leader primarily responsible for Party organization may have been the key actor. It is virtually certain that Hua would have been consulted in any case, and likely that he had a major input as well as final authority.

[174] "Wang Dongxing zai quanguo xuanchuan gongzuo jianghua," p. 1.

[175] Evidence in Li's case consists of his remark that he was pushed aside for eight months (see "Zhongyang lingdaoren guanyu sirenbang wenti de jianghua," p. 3), and the lack of any indication that he participated in the national planning seminar, the area of his expertise. Regarding Ye, see below, p. 547.

[176] See Fan Shuo, *Ye Jianying zai feichang shiqi*, vol. 2, pp. 579-80. Apart from being alert to what was going on at Mao's bedside, the discussion allegedly called for criticizing Deng, toppling Ye

The most celebrated event during the deathbed vigil occurred late at night on September 8, only hours before the Chairman's death just after midnight on the 9th. The Politburo members were called in to bid farewell to Mao in small groups, with Ye Jianying, Li Xiannian and Wu De in one group. Mao appeared able to recognize the names of his colleagues as they reported, but he was unable to say anything. This, of course, reflected his inability to communicate clearly throughout 1976, and on this evening even his closest personal staff could not understand his wishes. On this occasion, when the three leaders turned to leave, Mao gestured that Ye should come back. They clasped hands, and Mao seemed to be trying to convey a message. Afterward Ye pondered what that message might be, and quickly concluded, as reported by Deng Liqun, that "Chairman Mao's meaning was that he had to bolster (*fuzhu*) Hua Guofeng well. This was tantamount to ... I'm entrusting Hua Guofeng to you."[177] Whether or not this was an accurate interpretation of the Chairman's intent, and whether or not it was truly needed, Mao's final "message" served to enhance further Hua's position as the PRC entered a new period totally unlike anything it had faced since the establishment of the regime.

Jianying, and winning over and then overturning Hua, but no details were indicated. Fan Shuo, vol. 2, p. 579.

[177] *Deng Liqun guoshi jiangtan*, vol. 3, p. 348. For the full quotation, see below, p. 595. Other accounts of the Mao-Ye exchange include: Wu De, "Guanyu fensui 'sirenbang'," pp. 53-54; *Ye zhuan*, pp. 639-40; Fan Shuo, *Ye Jianying zai feichang shiqi*, vol. 2, pp. 582-83, 589; and Chen and Du, *Shilu*, vol. 3, part 2, p. 1406. On Mao's staff, see Guo Jinrong, *Mao Zedong de huanghun suiyue* [The Twilight of Mao Zedong's Life] (Hong Kong: Tiandi tushu youxian gongsi, 1990), p. 249.

Chapter 8

THE PURGE OF THE "GANG OF FOUR," SEPTEMBER-OCTOBER 1976

Zhang Chunqiao: Now there is no one who can be compared to Chairman Mao in ability and prestige. From now on the Center can only rely on collective leadership. ... Who do you think is suitable [to be Party Chair]?
Yao Wenyuan: Naturally it [will be] Comrade Hua Guofeng. He is the successor chosen by the Chairman.
Zhang Chunqiao: The key is to see what line he follows...

— Reported conversation between Zhang Chunqiao and Yao Wenyuan, September 25, 1976[1]

[After the death of Mao] we felt outraged at the "gang of four" ... and were worried about the wild ambition of Jiang Qing and others. We hoped that Marshal Ye and other old comrades would be able to come forward to solve the "gang of four" problem and foil their conspiracy to seize Party power. But we also felt that for a matter of such importance, if Hua Guofeng, who was First Vice Chairman at the time and in charge of the Center's work, came forward it would make it fully proper. At that time I had no idea that Hua Guofeng, Ye Jianying and other old comrades were occupied with finding a way to solve the "gang of four" problem. ... There are now all manner of stories around about the relationship between Hua Guofeng and Marshal Ye. Some are at variance with the facts.

— Geng Biao's recollection concerning September-October 1976[2]

I remember that Hua Guofeng said [at a meeting with Li Xiannian, Chen Xilian, Ji Dengkui and myself sometime in mid-September]: "Chairman Mao put forward the 'gang of four' problem, [the issue now is] how to solve it?" I remember that Ji Dengkui said that he thought [we] had better make distinctions in how these people are treated. None of us said anything, and the discussion didn't go any further. I think that at that time Comrade Hua Guofeng was sounding out our attitudes, and preparing for the task of smashing the "gang of four." Later, Hua Guofeng told me that at that time he had already determined to solve the "gang of four" problem.

— Wu De's recollection of events in mid-September 1976[3]

The death of Mao Zedong created an unprecedented political situation, one which reached a dramatic denouement with the purge of the "gang of four" less than a month later. The extra-legal nature of that denouement, rightly termed "China's [October] coup" by Keith Forster, has understandably contributed to the widely accepted view of a bitter political conflict over that month culminating in the arrest of Jiang Qing, Zhang Chunqiao, Yao Wenyuan and Wang Hongwen on the evening of October 6. While various analysts have shown a healthy skepticism about certain official claims, distinguishing political agitation from violent action, and concluding that the "gang" was more in a defensive mode than planning an outright "seizure of power,"[4] accepted wisdom nevertheless pictures a harsh struggle during the September 9-October 6 period that almost inevitably led to the "solution" of the incarceration of the "gang." Given the legacy of tension between the radicals and establishment figures detailed throughout this study, as well as palpable suspicion over big and small matters following Mao's passing, this is a reasonable view. But it greatly oversimplifies and distorts the politics of this fraught period.

In many respects, we will never know the full story of these critical weeks. Many of the key players are dead, and central players still with us—above all Hua Guofeng—have said little.[5] Whatever documentary record exists of, e.g., Politburo meetings, has been highly restricted, with even senior Party historians and high-ranking political figures barred from access. Moreover, as we saw in the case of Mao's assessment of his two major accomplishments,[6] sometimes there was no immediate record of major events, a problem magnified by the confidential,

---

[1] Qing and Fang, *Deng zai 1976*, vol. 2, p. 200.

[2] *Geng Biao huiyilu*, pp. 285, 287. The "we" referred to by Geng included Xiao Jingguang and Wang Zhen, as well as himself.

[3] Wu De, "Guanyu fensui 'sirenbang'," pp. 56-57. While Wu simply refers to this meeting as taking place in mid-September, the precise date appears to be September 16, and to have also included Chen Yonggui; see below, p. 569. It is of interest that several Party historians, including one who had earlier contributed to a Ye Jianying-centered account of the purge of the "gang," accept the basic veracity of Wu's recollections. Interviews, December 2002.

[4] Such skepticism marks the two best reconstructions of the fall of the "gang of four," each largely based on quite different sources more than a decade apart: Onate, "Hua Kuo-feng," especially, pp. 541, 559-61; and Forster, "China's Coup," especially pp. 289-90. For other cautionary comments, see MacFarquhar, "Succession," p. 309; and Baum, *Burying Mao*, p. 39.

[5] Hua reportedly spoke to a group of Party historians in the mid-1990s on his period in power, but it apparently was a disjointed performance that was not followed up despite the hopes of the historians involved. Interview, August 2000. In a recent personal exchange summarized by an old associate, Hua reviewed the events of September-October 1976, confirming the following analysis which was constructed on the basis of other sources. See Zhang Gensheng, "Hua Guofeng tan fensui 'sirenbang'," pp. 2-4.

Apart from Hua, of the other figures downgraded in the Deng era version of Party history, Wu De's recollection, "Guanyu fensui 'sirenbang'," is most relevant in this regard. Cf. above, pp. 465-66n11. Of course, apart from what was reported of their defense at the 1980-81 trial, the Politburo radicals, who are now all dead, were completely denied an opportunity to argue their case.

[6] See above, p. 465n10.

indeed illicit discussions of September-October. Beyond this, it is inevitably the case that subsequent reconstructions, whether by official propaganda, serious PRC historians, or outside scholars, give more form to the events than was actually the case. Given the fundamental secrecy of elite politics, many vitally concerned at the time had little sense of what was happening, and, as reflected in Geng Biao's comment above, rumors bearing little relation to fact circulated widely and affected subsequent assessments. And even those at the center of the action acted in the equivalent of the "fog of war," uncertain of the meaning of events and affected by emotions of genuine distress at Mao's passing, deep anxiety about the future, and suspicions that applied not only to the "other side," but also to people in one's own presumptive "camp."

Another crucial problem, as also noted in Chapter 7, is that material released by the CCP, on which analysis ultimately depends, both contains major gaps in the record and is severely biased. The actions of the "gang of four," of course, have consistently been portrayed in the most negative light possible, thus distorting both specific events and the larger dynamics of elite politics. There has been a major shift, moreover, in how events have been presented from the period of Hua's leadership to the Deng era, centering on the question of who deserves credit for "smashing" the "gang." Naturally, in the first year or so after October 1976 the focus was on Hua, albeit in a propagandistic and usually undiscriminating manner. By the early 1980s, with Hua virtually a non-person, credit for taking the initiative in the action and kudos for the result were increasingly given to veteran revolutionaries and especially Marshal Ye Jianying, particularly in reportage literature that provided insights into, although not necessarily accurate accounts of, the maneuvers preceding the arrest of the radicals.[7] But the problem does not

---

[7] The outstanding proponent of this literature and the glorification of Ye's role is Fan Shuo, especially *Ye Jianying zai 1976*, and *Ye Jianying zai feichang shiqi*. A researcher at the Academy of Military Science, Fan had access to many people round Ye and Ye himself, and much of his analysis is based on these sources. Although himself critical of errors in reportage literature, Fan, as Forster, "China's Coup," pp. 287-88, has observed, is representative of the genre, differing only in the official privileges and access granted to him.

With regard to accuracy, many events cited in reportage literature are dubious at best, e.g., the claim that, on September 16, Deng visited Ye to express his concern over the intentions of the radicals; Qing and Fang, *Deng zai 1976*, vol. 2, p. 107. This claim is at considerable variance with the picture provided by Deng's daughter, Mao Mao, *"Wenge" suiyue*, pp. 522-23, of her father as totally isolated in this period. Moreover, although there are differences of opinion, some Party historians express great doubt that, given the close scrutiny of Deng's activities at the time, he could have made such a visit, or given his understanding that such an attempt would have been counterproductive, that he would have undertaken such an effort. Moreover, one highly-placed specialist on Deng insists that Ye and Deng did not meet before February 1977. Interviews, November-December 2002. More generally, the problem of assessing such claims and contradictory information, sometimes within the same source, remains vexed. In particular, problems of dating during this period are even more severe than for other periods, with even leading scholars such as Cheng Zhongyuan making clearly erroneous claims. See Cheng's claim that Wang Hongwen was in Shanghai from September 17 to 23, when in fact Wang played his role as the number two Party leader at Mao's memorial ceremony in Beijing on the 18th; "Liangge Zhongguo zhi mingyun quezhan--1976 nian cong Tiananmen

end with biased overall interpretations. On the issue of who should reap the glory, specific accounts have been altered to reflect the changing official view. Thus the November 1976 confessions of two of the "gang's" followers in Shanghai, Xu Jingxian and Wang Xiuzhen, indicated that, in their initial confusion as to who might have acted against the four, they concluded that Hua and Wang Dongxing must have played central roles, although they also saw possible involvement by the old marshals. In their testimony at the trial of the "gang" in 1980, however, a new version highlighting Ye and other old marshals who allegedly mobilized the military replaced their earlier accounts.[8] More broadly, in contrast to the immediate post-Mao claims of "wise leader" Hua accomplishing what even Mao could not with regard to the radicals, the Deng era version has pictured an indecisive leader who had to be prodded into action by Ye. According to one suspect account, Ye responded to a comrade's concern by complaining that "[Hua] has not expressed an attitude, so what can I do? ... This person is soft and weak, hesitant and indecisive, so that he can hardly achieve anything significant." Whether or not intended by the authors of this account, Ye's purported comment, if it were genuine, would also raise questions about *his own* decisiveness.[9]

The above problems notwithstanding, we address several key issues in this chapter. First, what did the activities of the Politburo radicals amount to? If we can dismiss the weakly documented claim of a plan for a violent seizure of power, was there a political strategy for attaining the leading positions of the Party and state? Second, can we resolve the question of where the credit for the demise of the "gang" justly belongs: with Hua Guofeng, with Ye Jianying and other old revolutionaries, or some combination of the two? More broadly, was the denouement of October 6 inevitable, or were alternative outcomes in the immediate post-Mao period viable? And finally, at a more conceptual level, was the outcome "decided by ... political actors whose power resided chiefly in their connections, revolutionary service, and prestige rather than in the formal position they occupied,"[10] or were formal positions of power decisive in this case?

We pursue these issues through a detailed examination of the unfolding drama following Mao's death just after midnight on September 9. First, however,

shijian dao fensui 'sirenbang'" [The Decisive Battle in the Fate of Two Possible Chinas--From the Tiananmen Incident to the Smashing of the "Gang of Four" in 1976], *DDZGSYJ*, no. 1 (2005), p. 77. We can only say that a careful consideration of each specific claim, the nature of the source, and the fit with the larger pattern of events provide a strong likelihood, albeit not absolute certainty, that the following interpretation of events is broadly accurate. See also below, n. 9.

[8] Compare "Xu Jingxian de chubu jiefa jiaodai," in *CRDB*, p. 9, and "Wang Xiuzhen de jiefa jiaodai," p. 4, with Xu's 1980 confession in Qing and Fang, *Deng zai 1976*, vol. 2, p. 144.

[9] Qing and Fang, *Deng zai 1976*, vol. 2, p. 161. We regard this as a dubious quotation, but as with vol. 1 of of Qing and Fang's work (see above, p. 477n35), we rely heavily on their overall account, despite reservations about various specific claims. In this case, it is plausible that the authors deliberately produced a bogus account to cast doubt subtly on the conventional view of Ye. Cf. the Preface, above, p. xviii.

[10] Forster, "China's Coup," p. 296.

we review the resources and perspectives of the main actors in the drama—Hua and other active non-radical members of the Politburo, the "gang of four," and Marshal Ye and other old revolutionaries with limited formal authority. This is followed by an examination of events in the initial period after Mao's death up to the massive memorial meeting in Tiananmen Square on September 18, together with an assessment of the mood among top leaders, the first instances of friction, and the politics of decisions taken during this ten-day period. We then turn to an examination of the curious affair of the "principles laid down," a slogan allegedly concocted by the radicals as Mao's last testament and used by them as a political program for attacking Hua and, in the most fevered official accounts, as a signal to launch a violent "seizure of power." The following section reviews events beginning in the latter part of September and culminating in the arrest of the radicals on October 6, including alleged preparations by the "gang" for a showdown, and the much more real plotting undertaken by Hua, Ye and an assortment of other figures. Before concluding with an overall assessment of the politics of the coup, we also examine the efforts of the new leadership over the next several weeks, first to bring to heel the largest radical base, Shanghai, where an "armed rebellion" was assertedly planned, and secondly, to provide a convincing rationale to the broader central, provincial and military elites for an illegal, totally unprecedented "solution" to the problem presented by the "gang of four"—and more poignantly by Mao's legacy.

The Contending Forces: Resources and Perspectives

At one level, when Mao died the basic division within the Chinese polity from the Politburo to the grass roots was obvious. On one side stood the radical adherents of the Cultural Revolution, those who benefited from the movement and/or believed in its ideological message. At the apex, of course, stood the so-called "gang of four" who had been catapulted to their elevated positions from the margins of the elite in a process quite different from the Party's traditional ladder of promotion. In opposition were a variety of individuals and groups identified with the establishment: officials who had directly suffered at the hands of rebels during the movement, others dismayed by the political and economic disruption associated with the Cultural Revolution, and a broad range of people who objected to the whole process as an inversion of proper status within the CCP. As noted in Chapter 7, pride of place in this oppositional coalition in both official and Western scholarly accounts has been given to the "old revolutionaries," the leading veterans of the pre-1949 struggle who had, to varying degrees, been marginalized even when they survived the traumas of 1966-69. Finally, as also noted throughout this study, accepted wisdom posits a third force, represented by Hua Guofeng at the top of the system, our establishment beneficiaries of the Cultural Revolution. These leaders have usually been regarded as Maoist loyalists and often as potential allies of the radicals, i.e., as a group that could have sided with either the "gang" or veteran leaders as late as September 1976, or alternatively as one forced into an alliance with the old revolutionaries only because of the radicals' political ineptitude.[11]

The above overview gives more form to the situation at Mao's death than was in fact the case. This relates only in part to our argument that Hua and other establishment beneficiaries, because of policy preferences, specific conflicts with the "gang" in the post-1972 period, and different socialization as members of the Party apparatus, almost certainly would not have formed a meaningful alliance with the radicals despite the accommodation they had to make while Mao lived, and might have been expected to continue for a limited period after his passing. A fundamental consideration, as we detail below, is that none of the three broad forces were as coherent as implied.[12] Tensions and suspicions existed within each "camp" as well as between the contending forces, and the situation was exacerbated by the tight controls in place in the period around and following Mao's death, a period perceived as a potential crisis along the lines of what happened five months earlier at Tiananmen, and by anxiety on all sides for the future of individuals and the nation. All of this inhibited or slowed down communication among presumed principal collaborators,[13] with the particular result that discussions of possible action and especially plans for the actual coup of October 6 were kept in the narrowest circles possible. The level of fear concerning what the other side might do was palpable, as seen in Nie Rongzhen's purported warning that the radicals might attempt to place Ye Jianying under house arrest or assassinate Deng Xiaoping,[14] and by Zhang Chunqiao's efforts to divorce his wife who represented his greatest vulnerability to charges of treason against the revolution.[15]

While this tension-filled, fearful elite politics was part of Mao's legacy, it was also the case that *all* elite actors capable of influencing the situation were Mao's beneficiaries. This was even the case for the old revolutionaries despite their comparatively marginalized position: Ye Jianying remained Party and MAC Vice Chairman, other old marshals Nie Rongzhen and Xu Xiangqian had Central Committee status, and the prickly Wang Zhen possessed a certain leeway because

---

[11] See MacFarquhar, "Succession," pp. 299-300, 306-307; Baum, *Burying Mao*, pp. 37-40; and Forster, "China's Coup," p. 276. The differences among these accounts concern whether the claimed potential alliance with the radicals was still possible at the time of Mao's death.

[12] To be accurate, the literature canvasses differences within the establishment beneficiaries group by speculating on the tendencies of specific individuals, even to the point of arbitrarily assigning individuals from this category to the old revolutionaries camp on the basis of presumed sympathies. See above, pp. 12-13n28. With regard to the "gang of four" and old revolutionaries, however, a basic unity of purpose and action is generally assumed.

[13] The reported concern of Ye Jianying that his conversations were being recorded is a case in point, as is the three-day delay before Li Xiannian visited Ye in mid-September. See Forster, "China's Coup," p. 298; and below, pp. 561-62.

[14] Yan and Gao, *Turbulent Decade*, p. 524.

[15] See Qing and Fang, *Deng zai 1976*, vol. 2, p. 215; and above, p. 74n125.

of Mao's favoritism.[16] By the same token, the political framework in which all forces had to operate was Mao's: his ideological line which included the campaign to criticize Deng, his succession arrangements, and his paradoxical demand for Party unity. In the weeks following Mao's death, there was little sign of anyone departing in a significant way from the contemporary orthodoxy emphasizing class struggle as the key link, the dangers posed by the bourgeoisie in the CCP, continuing the anti-Deng struggle, and consolidating the Cultural Revolution. Moreover, as suggested by the conversation between Zhang Chunqiao and Yao Wenyuan cited at the start of this chapter, despite claims of plots to seize power, there is little to indicate any serious questioning of Hua as the chosen successor within the Politburo. And while it was something that could not last, at some point before his death the Chairman again emphasized unity, reportedly telling Mao Yuanxin that he wanted five people to do a good job of Party unity: "[Hua] and [Wang] Hongwen should be in charge of the overall situation, [Zhang] Chunqiao should be mainly responsible for Party affairs, and military work can be handed over to Chen Xilian and [Mao] Yuanxin."[17] Mao's repeated calls for unity were a potential restraint, or at least a complicating factor, in the calculations of all sides, yet in a further manifestation of its paradoxical nature, the potential strength this "unified" lineup could give the radical cause may have underlined the urgency of "solving the 'gang of four' problem."

Clearly, the greatest assets of the Politburo radicals derived from Mao's direct legacy. They had been the most forceful advocates of the Chairman's Cultural Revolution ideological line, as well as having been regarded by Mao as guardians of that line, and no one was game to challenge this political orientation directly. They also held critical positions and responsibilities. In Wang Hongwen and Zhang Chunqiao they occupied half of the seats on the Politburo Standing Committee, the most authoritative body. And although the radicals were outnumbered on the larger Politburo, their opponents feared the "gang" might have a majority in the Central Committee and, like Khrushchev in the Soviet Union in 1957, be able to reverse an unfavorable vote in the higher body.[18] In terms of responsibilities, Wang Hongwen retained a key if unclear role in Party affairs, while Yao Wenyuan oversaw the media. This did not equate with control in either case, but it provided the capacity and legitimacy for major influence. Above all this was the "special status" of Jiang Qing as Mao's wife,

---

[16] On Wang Zhen, see above, pp. 531-33.

[17] Qing and Fang, *Deng zai 1976*, vol. 2, p. 306. Whether this account of Mao's wishes, disclosed by Jiang Qing, is accurate cannot be determined, but it is plausible. In addition, while not listing him among the five, Mao also reportedly nominated Ji Dengkui to run the State Council. For other purported lists of Mao's preferred leadership team, see above, p. 495n79.

[18] This possibility, and the Khrushchev parallel, was considered by both establishment beneficiaries and old revolutionaries; see below, pp. 569-70. The uncertainty was created especially by the large numbers of worker and peasant representatives elected to the 10th Central Committee in 1973, although there is no clear indication that they would have necessarily supported the radicals. See above, pp. 105-106.

something seen as an obstacle in the ruminations of old revolutionaries both during the summer and following the Chairman's death. Even apart from her legal position as a Politburo member, how could one act against the great leader's widow? Finally, as suggested above, no matter how ironic, given the actions of the "gang" and more importantly Mao himself, the dictates of Party unity argued for the radicals' continued presence on the top body, however much their actual clout might be diluted once a new leadership was formed.

Other support for the radicals came from Cultural Revolution rebels throughout the system from the central to basic levels. These largely younger, radically-inclined cadres by and large shared the "gang's" ideology and benefited from the same type of rapid elevation in the post-1966 period. The importance of such support, and the awareness that it was lacking at the highest level, was reflected in Yao Wenyuan's comment on the need to recruit revolutionary intellectuals into the Politburo during the anticipated Central Committee plenum to confirm the new leadership.[19] Moreover, despite successes in the Ministry of Culture, Shanghai, Liaoning and elsewhere, organizational control in the great majority of cases was elusive. Indeed, radical efforts to place people in effective positions in Beijing yielded such limited benefit that, in February 1976, Zhang Chunqiao instructed his Shanghai followers to refuse requests from the Central Organization Department to transfer cadres for vice ministerial and SPC appointments, on the grounds that once such people arrived in the capital they were given nothing to do.[20] Another indication of the limited utility of the "gang's" wider following is that, despite official efforts to paint a nationally coordinated faction, this network was loosely integrated at best despite obvious common interests. For one thing, even the closest local followers of the Politburo radicals in Shanghai were often ignorant of the "gang's" situation in Beijing, the interests of central and local radicals could sometimes directly clash as in the case of Wang Hongwen and the Zhejiang rebels, and, as previously argued, there is little indication of the Politburo radicals' hand in provincial rebel activity in 1976. This was confirmed at the trial of 1980-81 when, for all the prosecution's effort to make the connection, all that was demonstrated was that local radicals drew inspiration from the "gang" in Beijing.[21]

All of the above points to the precarious nature of the radicals' circumstances. While considerations of formal positions, the existing ideological line, Jiang Qing's "special status," and Party unity all argued for their continuing in office, with their essential supporter—Mao—no longer on the scene, the remaining sources of support, while not inconsiderable, were essentially scattered and not open to easy mobilization. Moreover, while organizational norms served to protect them as Party leaders, the same norms restricted their freedom of action,

---

[19] Qing and Fang, *Deng zai 1976*, vol. 2, p. 296.

[20] See "Wang Xiuzhen de jiefa jiaodai," p. 6; and above, p. 223.

[21] Interview with participant in the trial, January 2005.

particularly since Hua clearly had the authority to control the agenda. In this context, the "gang" had three fundamental weaknesses. First, as often noted, the radicals lacked adequate military support, as expressed in the famous lament that they had "only the pen, but no gun." This is somewhat overstated. As one high-ranking Party historian observed, apart from the Shanghai militia, various PLA officers who had not personally suffered during the Cultural Revolution, and who tended to worship Mao blindly, were to a degree willing to follow the radicals. But this suggests only tentative and diffuse support, and there can be no doubt of the "gang's" fundamental military weakness, while the militia was at best a defensive instrument, vastly outgunned by the PLA, with even the Shanghai militia having only modestly increased in size compared to its pre-Cultural Revolution force.[22]

Second, the internal tensions among the four seemingly prevented any coordinated planning. Throughout this study we have addressed tensions within the "gang" in terms of the different backgrounds of the principals, various clashes of interest, and signs of mistrust; ample additional instances are documented below as we trace developments up to October 6. Indications that they were less than a unified "gang of four," the term Mao apparently used only twice, can be seen in Zhang Chunqiao's concern during this period that Yao Wenyuan improve his relations with Jiang Qing. Moreover, the establishment beneficiaries, or at least Ji Dengkui, were not entirely clear on whom to arrest, and subsequently they had to persuade the broader elite that there were indeed four, not two, deserving incarceration. And when informed of the arrests, Shanghai's Party leader Ma Tianshui was able to accept that Jiang Qing and Wang Hongwen might have a case to answer, but resisted the notion that Zhang Chunqiao and Yao Wenyuan were guilty of anything more than "internal contradictions."[23]

Finally, more than anything else, the radicals were vulnerable because of their leading roles in the Cultural Revolution, and the (sometimes unnecessary) hatred they engendered in the process. The particular focus of visceral distaste was Jiang Qing, pointedly designated the "ringleader" of the "gang" at the 1980-81 trial, whether due to simple annoyance, such as over Jiang's insistence in talking about naval uniforms at the Politburo meeting in the wake of the Tangshan earthquake, incidents of personal rudeness, such as her refusal to shake Geng Biao's hand during ceremonies following Mao's death, or wild charges against sitting leaders as in her claims that Ji Dengkui was a Soviet spy, Wang Dongxing

---

[22] Yan and Gao, *Turbulent Decade*, p. 476; Forster, "China's Coup," pp. 293-94; Perry, *Patrolling the Revolution*, pp. 242, 339; interview with senior Party historian, December 2002; and interview with leading military historian, January 2005. The two areas seen as potential "gang" military resources, Mao Yuanxin's Shenyang Military Region as well as the Shanghai militia, did not produce in the end.

[23] See Qing and Fang, *Deng zai 1976*, vol. 2, p. 295; "Wang Dongxing zai quanguo xuanchuan gongzuo jianghua," p. 3; "Ma Tianshui de buchong jiefa jiaodai," p. 3; above, p. 536; and below, p. 586.

was also a spy, and Wu De had been a Guomindang member.[24] Yet as infuriating as such personal excesses may have been, it was undoubtedly the excesses of the Cultural Revolution itself that had fixed the animosity of the old revolutionaries and establishment beneficiaries alike against the radicals. While these strongly-held sentiments throughout key segments of the elite did not foreordain the specific outcome of October 6, in all likelihood they guaranteed at the very least the marginalization of the Politburo radicals.

Although this tenuous situation might arguably have encouraged the radicals, as "gamblers with only one card," to challenge Hua,[25] there is little evidence that this was the case. Their latent fears reflected in Zhang Chunqiao's divorce action notwithstanding, overall they appear to have adopted an overly optimistic perspective, one centering on the late Chairman and their tentative assessment of Hua. The radicals clearly saw their duty as holding firm to Mao's political direction, and appear to have naïvely overestimated the staying power of the still officially endorsed Cultural Revolution ideology. Perhaps this was most poignantly put by Zhang Chunqiao who, after reflecting on the strong sense of loss caused by Mao's death, declared that "[although] Chairman Mao is no longer here, he is still everywhere…, [his] line, system and policies will all remain," and predicted that once the loss was absorbed the future would be brighter.[26]

As for Hua, the radicals apparently anticipated that he would be the new leader, but that collective leadership would prevail. This must be seen against the larger pattern of cooperation *cum* conflict which existed since Hua's appointment as Acting Premier. Despite distortions such as the official view of Zhang Chunqiao's February diary entry, the radicals appear to have given a modicum of support to Hua as directed by Mao. This, of course, did not mean that there were no doubts about the new leader. As Zhang Chunqiao observed, it would be necessary to see what line he took. But in the days leading up to their arrest, Zhang and Yao Wenyuan still anticipated cooperation. Zhang told Yao that, his reservations about Hua's commitment to the anti-Deng campaign notwithstanding, he was generally cooperating well with Hua, while Yao affirmed that they should help Hua, that this was the big picture.[27] A much more skeptical view was expressed by the Liaoning model rebel Zhang Tiesheng the day after Mao's passing: "I think this man's political color is rightist, his general line conservative, and he doesn't have a genuine understanding of the Cultural Revolution."[28] In any case, while attacks on such policies as the Dazhai work teams and the 1975 State Council theory conference for much of 1976 could be seen as attacks on Hua

---

[24] "Geng Biao guanyu zhua sirenbang qingkuang," p. 1; Wu De, "Guanyu fensui 'sirenbang'," p. 58; and above, pp. 524-25.

[25] Garside, *Coming Alive*, pp. 142-43.

[26] Qing and Fang, *Deng zai 1976*, vol. 2, pp. 123-24.

[27] Qing and Fang, *Deng zai 1976*, vol. 2, p. 295. As this information comes from Yao's testimony to the 1980 trial, we regard it as having a high degree of credibility.

[28] "Zhang Tiesheng, Liu Jiye Tongzhi tanhua qingkuang jilu," p. 544.

and other establishment beneficiaries, and indeed they were regarded as such by the notional targets, they could also have been efforts to affirm the radical interpretation of Mao's line, to force the leadership to uphold the Chairman's course, rather than a frontal assault. The same motivation (together with fears that Deng might reemerge in the new circumstances) could be seen in continuing the anti-Deng campaign after Mao's death, even as new criticism of the "three poisonous weeds" inevitably reflected on Hua. The apparent assumption was that Hua's position was legitimate, but that he could be pressured within the new collective leadership. As with their belief in the appeal of the Cultural Revolution, this would soon be revealed as a gross miscalculation.

Turning to the old revolutionaries, Chinese and foreign accounts have muddied the waters, placing under this label a range of usually military leaders who differed in age, rank and current responsibilities. Old revolutionaries in the context of 1976 could be most usefully categorized as very senior leaders who largely lacked operational authority. Confusion enters the picture when an officer such as Yang Chengwu is treated as one of the old leaders. Not only was he junior in age and rank to Marshals Ye Jianying, Xu Xiangqian, and his wartime leader Nie Rongzhen,[29] but after Deng's removal he held a critical active post as Acting PLA Chief-of-Staff. To add to the complexity, as we saw in Chapter 3, in 1974 he had been Jiang Qing's nominee for Chief-of-Staff. Yet, of course, there is a rationale for including figures such as Yang. The closeness of bonds, based on shared battlefield service during the war years that were so pronounced in the military, created a degree of trust between sidelined superiors and active duty subordinates that could not be replicated between similarly sidelined civilian leaders and the establishment beneficiaries holding formal authority in Party and government bodies.

The glorification of the old revolutionaries also obscures some inconvenient facts: the very limited numbers of those involved in any significant way, and the seeming hesitation of some who were approached. As in the period before Mao's death, only about two dozen plus old revolutionaries, even under the expanded definition, have been identified as participating in discussions in September and early October concerning how to "solve the 'gang of four' problem." These were all military figures, with the exception of one civilian figure of enormous prestige, former CCP Vice Chairman and current Central Committee member Chen Yun, another former Politburo member, Tan Zhenlin, one current (but basically sidelined) Politburo member, Li Xiannian, the widows of Zhou Enlai and Zhu De, Deng Yingchao, Kang Keqing and a few others.[30] Also, while the

---

[29] To use the Yang-Nie case, General Yang (b. 1914) was 15 years younger than Marshal Nie (b. 1899).

[30] The military figures explicitly identified as involved in September-October are: Marshals Ye Jianying, Nie Rongzhen and Xu Xiangqian, and Generals Xiao Hua, Yu Lijin and Wu Kehua, as well as Chen Xilian, Li Desheng, Yang Chengwu, Su Zhenhua, Xiao Jingguang, Su Yu, Song Shilun, Wu Zhong, Liang Biye, Wei Guoqing, Fu Chongbi, Zhang Tingfa, Liu Zhijian, Wu Fushan, Wu

information is understandably much vaguer, various senior figures who were sounded out apparently avoided any involvement.[31] As we examine the actual unfolding of events over the four weeks after Mao's death, a greater sense will emerge of how important the contributions of these few old revolutionaries were to the outcome. In any case, as reflected in the quotation from Geng Biao at the start of this chapter, there definitely was within the broader elite the hope, even the expectation, that such senior figures would somehow deal with the threatening situation.

This very hope reflected the major resources at the disposal of the true old revolutionaries: their prestige and status. This was the meat of the pre-1966 system when such status largely corresponded to formal office, and reports that people as varied as Hua, who had limited although seemingly very positive personal experience with Ye Jianying, and Wang Zhen, who also had not been close to Ye despite their common background as revolutionary army leaders, greatly respected the old marshal are completely credible.[32] This, of course, provided influence on those who actually held legal authority, and thus served as a link between informal and formal power. The key individual in this context was obviously Marshal Ye, who had both great personal prestige and an indeterminate degree of official power. Ye retained his formal posts as a Party and MAC Vice Chairman, third in the official pecking order, yet in the summer the most that could be said was that his military power had not been "completely stripped away," and in September people placed their hopes in Ye even though he reportedly had been "excluded from the leadership core."[33] Indeed, this seems the case since, although (like Li Xiannian) he had been attending Politburo meetings, there is no evidence that he

---

Lie, Shi Jingqian, Hua Nan, Xiang Shoufa, Geng Biao, Zhang Aiping and Xiong Xianghui who held formal executive positions. See Zhang Jiangming, *Lishi zhuanzhe guantou de Ye Jianying* [Ye Jianying at the Historical Turning Point] (Beijing: Zhonggong dangshi chubanshe, 1997), pp. 141-42; and Yin Yungong, "Lun chenggong fensui 'sirenbang' de guanjian qunti" [On the Key Group in the Successful Smashing of the "Gang of Four"], in *Collected Papers of the 'International Forum on the Contemporary History of China'* (Beijing: Contemporary China Institute, September 2004), p. 114. Although Chen Xilian, as the top military official, clearly played a key role in the coup and talked to at least Yang Chengwu and Wu Zhong, we have found only one vague reference to any Chen-Ye contact in this period. In addition, Wang Dongxing and Wang Zhen could be considered in this category because of their military backgrounds, although they had long been working outside the PLA. On the non-military side Deng Xiaoping was also cited, but we are deeply skeptical on this point; see above, p. 538n7.

[31] According to Fan Shuo, unnamed individuals responded to Wang Zhen's approaches by shaking their heads, behaving in a shifty manner, or avoiding giving an opinion or participating in the plot, although it is unclear how much of this occurred before Mao's death. Forster, "China's Coup," p. 297, speculates that this referred to waverers in the Politburo, but since Wang's only known approach to a Politburo member was to Wang Dongxing, this is unlikely. More likely candidates are old revolutionaries, or at least senior military figures.

[32] See *Ye zhuan*, p. 649; *Wang Zhen zhuan*, vol. 2, p. 168; and below, p. 549.

[33] See Fan Shuo, "The Tempestuous October—A Chronicle of the Complete Collapse of the 'Gang of Four'," *Yangcheng wanbao* [Canton Evening News], February 10, 1989, in FBIS-CHI-89-029, February 14, 1989, p. 17; and above, p. 532.

regained any of the executive authority he gave up when he went on sick leave in February, his position as Minister of Defense being particularly opaque.[34] How all this played out for Ye and other old revolutionaries will be explored below, but clearly their power and influence were largely informal, although Ye's high formal positions crucially enhanced his authority.

The limited numbers of old revolutionaries involved, as well as many of their generational and senior PLA colleagues, had every reason to disparage the radicals and the excesses of the Cultural Revolution. Most had suffered in position and reputation during this period, found the disruption of the country—and especially of the army—deeply distressing, and acutely felt the inversion of proper status since they regarded themselves as the makers of China's real revolution. Ye Jianying, although holding prominent positions throughout, had not only come under criticism in the late 1960s, but also suffered from the "gang's" attacks during the anti-Lin Biao and Confucius campaign, and took advantage of the changed circumstances in 1975 to attack them in turn, at least privately. This did not necessarily mean that the old revolutionaries, much less the establishment beneficiaries, had totally rejected Mao's last great project,[35] but they certainly placed the 30 percent mistakes that the Chairman acknowledged at the feet of the "gang of four." Clearly, significant old revolutionaries regarded the "gang" as presenting a problem to be "solved," but the vague discussions in the summer, scathing comments about "the actress" [Jiang Qing] and "glasses" [Zhang Chunqiao],[36] and Ye Jianying's hand gestures did not amount to serious contributions to a "solution," or indicate that any consensus had been reached by the time Mao died.

Distaste for the radicals aside, several other considerations most likely impinged on the considerations of Ye Jianying and other senior revolutionaries. For one thing, loyalty to the dead Chairman was a real consideration, notably for Ye. Whether his interpretation of his last encounter with Mao accurately relayed the Chairman's meaning or not, the very fact that he considered that interpretation as a duty to fulfill underlines that loyalty. In this context, it is hard to imagine

---

[34] Apart from responsibility for the daily work of the MAC which remained with Chen Xilian, it is unclear who exercised authority over the Ministry of Defense after Ye went on sick leave, but the old marshal did make public appearances as Defense Minister at Hua's urging during the summer, and this continued after Mao's death. Ding Jiaqi, "Fensui sirenbang douzheng zhong de jiangshuaimen" [Generals and Marshals during the Struggle against the Gang of Four], part 1, *Guofang* [National Defense], no. 1 (2005), p. 83. Hua similarly urged Li Xiannian to keep up his public profile, as well as consulting him, particularly on foreign affairs issues. Cheng Zhensheng. "Li Xiannian yu fensui 'sirenbang'," p. 47.

[35] The degree of belief by various leaders is a complex, and probably unknowable issue, one that was played out in the early post-Mao period and will be addressed in our Volume II. For now, we simply note that remarks by Deng during his exile in Jiangxi, and by Hu Yaobang during the early post-Mao period, fell well short of a total rejection of the Cultural Revolution. See above, pp. 69-70, 335. Cf. below, pp. 623ff.

[36] See, e.g., Fan Shuo, *Ye Jianying zai 1976*, p. 211.

that arresting Mao's wife would have been an easy position to come to, however much hatred existed at a personal level. Another complicating factor was Party organizational principles, principles which argued against what happened on October 6 and led the old revolutionaries to consider legal methods, and also led them, as articulated by Geng Biao and others, to understand that Hua Guofeng's cooperation would be essential for any "solution." It is clear, however, that the old revolutionaries had limited knowledge of, and less historical connection with, Hua and the other non-radical civilians on the Politburo. Ye himself had no functional connection to Hua, although he had easy contact with Hua when he was sent to Hunan in 1969 during the war scare at the time, and subsequently Ye asked Hua to join in his reception of cadres from his native county in 1975. Although such contact seemingly bespoke of good relations, it surely was Mao's designation of Hua as the successor that guaranteed Ye's support, and later sympathy, well into the post-Mao period. Ye apparently was more uncertain concerning other establishment beneficiaries, as seen in his query to Li Xiannian concerning the attitudes of Chen Xilian, a military figure but one whose career had never been closely tied to Ye, and Wu De (see below). Of all the relevant old revolutionaries, Li Xiannian, through his overlapping work experience on the State Council of the 1970s, had the best insight into the beneficiaries.[37] Yet for all the personal and professional distance, the old revolutionaries clearly determined that the cooperation of Hua *et al.* was not only desirable and necessary, but also that they would support these younger figures as the core of the CCP's new leadership.

Hua and other establishment beneficiaries had the same broad perspective as the old revolutionaries concerning the radicals, even if they were undoubtedly more accepting of the Cultural Revolution in the broadest sense. Since their main task was the actual running of the Party and state, the disruption to concrete policies caused by radical positions, and the sheer difficulty of working with the "gang" on the top bodies, and thus in any prospective new collective leadership, would have been of great concern to Hua and his Politburo colleagues. They also had their personal tensions with the "gang," whether it was attacks on policies that Hua was identified with, clashes with Ji Dengkui in the organizational sphere, or Jiang Qing's charges concerning spying or Guomindang membership directed at Ji, Wang Dongxing and Wu De. Yet, as was the case with senior revolutionaries, there is little to indicate that plans for a final showdown were afoot at the moment of Mao's death, or that Hua anticipated a challenge to his position, even though events at the July national planning seminar would have given him cause to ponder.[38] In any case, establishment beneficiaries like their elders had to consider

---

[37] Zhang Gensheng, "Hua Guofeng tan fensui 'sirenbang'," p. 2; Ji Xichen, "Fensui 'sirenbang' quanjing xiezhen, xia" [The True Full Story of the Overthrow of the "Gang of Four," part 2], *Yanhuang chunqiu*, no. 11 (2000), p. 8. On the circumstances of the 1969 war scare and the dispersal of Ye and other veteran leaders, see Teiwes and Sun, *Tragedy*, pp. 111-15.

[38] Analysts sometimes posit that the establishment beneficiaries saw a potential threat in the possible

loyalty to Mao, organizational principles, and the "special status" of Jiang Qing as they coped with the new situation. The following sections examine the process of how key figures among them moved from a probably uncertain initial position, to the decisive action of October 6.

Obviously, the great resource brought to the situation by Hua and other establishment beneficiaries was their formal power: a majority on the Politburo, the leader-designate in Hua, the highest authority in military affairs in Chen Xilian, backed by Yang Chengwu as Acting Chief-of-Staff and Su Zhenhua as the political commissar and effective leader of the navy, Wang Dongxing's control of the security forces responsible for the central leadership, and a monopoly of key posts in the State Council. Overall, in the official lineup as late as National Day 1976, the leadership group was essentially unaltered from that of the previous National Day celebration when Deng Xiaoping was dominant, except of course for Deng's absence and Hua's elevation. Moreover, as we shall see, it was largely Hua's decisions that decided key issues and reversed "gang" initiatives over the month after Mao's passing. This, of course, did not mean that formal norms were rigorously adhered to, with the Politburo as such ignorant of the critical and inherently illegal decision to act against the "gang." But in the overall authority of Hua and security responsibilities of Wang Dongxing in particular, formal authority was central to the outcome. The extent to which Ye Jianying was also able to exercise direct authority will be examined in our analysis of events, but broadly speaking, from the perspective of the establishment beneficiaries, the significance of the old revolutionaries was their influence in helping frame the issue, and in serving as a barometer of wider elite views, particularly military sentiment.

While we can assume, and the evidence seems to support, that the establishment beneficiaries basically had a common attitude toward the radicals, this does not mean that there was a unified position, extensive consultation, or deep trust among these leaders. This must be understood in terms of both the limited shared working experience of this group, and the larger fragmentation and suspicion within the leadership created by the elite culture of the entire "Cultural Revolution decade." In 1976 in particular, as exemplified by Li Xiannian's comment that Politburo members did not dare to visit one another, easy private communication, even between officials with related responsibilities, would not have been easy. An intriguing, if somewhat mysterious suggestion of limited trust is the apparent fact that Ji Dengkui was excluded from direct involvement in the demise of the "gang," an involvement which might have been expected given both his history of conflicts with the radicals and his responsibility for

---

return of Deng, and there is some (weak) evidence suggesting this may have been the case. Chen Yonggui reportedly spoke of the existence of people wanting Deng to return in September 1976, and a dubious source claims Hua himself had expressed concern to Chen on the matter. See Wu Si, *Chen Yonggui*, p. 230; and Chen Yonggui, "Wo mengjian Mao Zhuxi le." Overall, however, there is little evidence to suggest that this was a significant consideration within the top elite, apart from possible fears by the radicals that it might take place.

Party organization. Ji's unawareness was indicated by his surprise at the absence of the "gang" as the Politburo met after their arrest. Ji's exclusion was possibly a reflection of unhappiness over his expressed reservations about treating the four equally, or even suspicion due to such insubstantial matters as Mao's comment that Ji should move out of Diaoyutai lest he become part of a "gang of five," or an occasion when Jiang Qing held Ji's arm. Alternatively, it may have been a case of simple prudence, the logic of keeping knowledge of the actual coup on a minimal need-to-know basis, something which apparently delayed Ye Jianying receiving concrete details of the plan. But the basic fact was that, despite presumed generalized hostility toward the radicals, the crucial act was taken without reference to the Politburo as a whole, which was only subsequently informed of the *fait accompli*.[39]

Coping with the Passing of the Great Leader, September 9 to 18, 1976

In a fundamental sense, the immediate activities of the top elite following Mao's passing were much like what would be expected in any country on the death of its preeminent leader, particularly one who had served for a long period with a major influence on his or her people. Two broad processes are involved in such situations. One is making necessary arrangements for a state funeral and associated political measures, particularly in creating a sense of continuity where there could be none. Many concrete tasks would have to be dealt with in a fast moving, stressful context. Second, political maneuvering naturally intensifies. This need not result in a destabilizing "power struggle," but in the Chinese context of September 1976, given the sharp ideological edge of leadership conflict throughout CCP history, the particular bitterness of the preceding ten years, and individual animosities within the current Politburo, the possibility of such maneuvering escalating out of control was obviously high. In the PRC version, virtually from the moment of the Chairman's death the "gang of four" began their activities to "seize power," while the old revolutionaries intensified their planning to "solve" the problem, and Ye Jianying began his efforts to stiffen Hua Guofeng's backbone. But while tensions were there from the outset, it apparently was only after Mao's memorial ceremony in Tiananmen on September 18 that the tempo of conflict picked up, and political plotting on the anti-radical side took on concrete form.[40]

Although Mao's imminent passing had been clear to the top leaders and preparations were made since at least late June, the actual event ten minutes past midnight on September 9 still came as a shock. Hua was reportedly rendered

---

[39] Qing and Fang, *Deng zai 1976*, vol. 2, p. 177, 268; interview with senior Party historian, February 2000; above, pp. 296, 536; and below, p. 581.

[40] Onate observed long ago that "during the first five days of the mourning period, [various public activities] revealed nothing out of the ordinary," and he also debunked several allegations against the radicals concerning this initial period. See "Hua Kuo-feng," pp. 544-45.

inarticulate, a general atmosphere of panic prevailed, and it was left to Wang Dongxing to take charge of the initial practical arrangements such as notifying the Politburo and arranging for a meeting.[41] In this emotional setting, a photo was taken of eight particularly concerned people around Mao's body: Zhang Chunqiao, Wang Hongwen, Jiang Qing, Hua, Mao Yuanxin, Yao Wenyuan, Chen Xilian and Wang Dongxing. Deplorably, this would later be used in 1980 by Chen Yun and the liberal *People's Daily* editor, Hu Jiwei, to paint Hua as an ally of the radicals—something for which Hu expressed remorse in the 1990s. In all likelihood, the photo had been intended as a statement of shared grief and respect, and of Party unity at this critical juncture.[42] But this display of unity in grief did not prevent immediate tension. Wang Hongwen was accompanied by two secretaries rather than the apparently agreed upon one, something Wang's enemies regarded as suspicious behavior.[43] At the same time, pre-planned moves to place the armed forces on alert were implemented in Beijing as *per* Wu De and Chen Xilian's plans for three levels of disturbances, while a nationwide alert had apparently been restored a few days earlier. As previously argued, with similar measures undertaken by non-radical forces in the capital, the mobilization of the militia in Shanghai at this juncture and earlier should be seen in this context of anxiety concerning possible social disorder.[44]

When the Politburo met in the early hours of September 9 there were many issues to deal with. Although Jiang Qing proposed expelling Deng Xiaoping from the Party (see below), immediate practical matters were at the forefront of the discussion: informing the Chinese people and the world of the Chairman's death, handling the international repercussions, arrangements for the mourning period and memorial ceremony, the ideological line and Hua's speech to the memorial meeting, and the disposition of Mao's body. The key documen: issued on September 9 was a message to the Party, army and people announcing Mao's passing and affirming his ideological line. It was accompanied by an announcement of mourning services at the Great Hall from September 11 to 17, followed by the mass ceremony at Tiananmen on the 18th that would be broadcast to the entire nation. This announcement also relayed the Center's decision, similar

---

[41] Qing and Fang, *Deng zai 1976*, vol. 2, pp. 3ff. The reality of grief among top leaders who had been vulnerable to Mao's unpredictability is entirely credible. Consider the case of Soviet leaders, who had been much more exposed to life-threatening peril by Stalin. According to Khrushchev, "it was a great shock [for us in the leadership]. ... Personally, I took his death hard. I wept for him. I sincerely wept." Talbott, *Khrushchev Remembers*, p. 193.

[42] See Hu Jiwei, *Cong Hua Guofeng xiatai dao Hu Yaobang xiatai* [From the Fall of Hua Guofeng to the Fall of Hu Yaobang] (New York: Mingjing chubanshe, 1997), pp. 71-73, 77-80 and back cover. Hua, Wang Hongwen, Zhang and Wang Dongxing had shared responsibility for the vigil at Mao's deathbed, while Jiang and Mao Yuanxin, of course, were family. Chen had overall military responsibility, while Yao would have the task of conveying the news to the public.

[43] "Hua Guofeng jiejian Shandong, Hubei deng Nanjing budui deng lingdao tongzhi de jianghua," p. 2.

[44] See above, pp. 529-30.

to the case of Zhou Enlai, not to invite representatives of foreign governments and fraternal parties to participate, although during the week Beijing-based foreigners did pay their respects. In regard to foreign policy aspects more generally, the reactions of foreign governments raised some issues—particularly the response to the condolences of the Soviet "modern revisionists." On this specific matter, Zhang Chunqiao reportedly demanded that the Ministry of Foreign Affairs reject the Soviet goodwill message, a position that does not appear to have been contentious.[45]

In addition, a funeral committee was announced which adhered to protocol in listing the four surviving Standing Committee members in rank order—Hua, Wang Hongwen, Ye Jianying and Zhang Chunqiao—followed by the remaining Politburo members in stroke order. After that came a long list of luminaries and officials with pride of place going to a small number of old revolutionaries headed by Xu Xiangqian, Nie Rongzhen and Chen Yun, an ordering mirroring that at other large gatherings throughout 1976. The 377 members of the funeral committee represented the key central Party and state, military and provincial organizations of the regime, but for the individuals involved it was much more than that. Beyond recognition of their personal loyalty to Mao, membership on the committee was validation of their life's work as dedicated servants to the CCP's cause. Thus the blow of being excluded was significant, even if it fell predictably on such prominent targets of the anti-Deng campaign as Hu Qiaomu, Zhang Aiping, Wan Li and Hu Yaobang, and less predictably on Mao's niece, Wang Hairong, although not on the other half of the "two ladies," Tang Wensheng. Probably most disheartened were those not even allowed to pay their respects to Mao's body, and thus reduced to standing among the masses at Tiananmen on the 18th, including Research Office leaders Deng Liqun, Yu Guangyuan and, most poignant of all, the Chairman's long time loyal secretary, Hu Qiaomu.[46]

Undoubtedly the most crucial task concerned how to represent the Chairman's career, and thus how to present the surviving leadership's ideological line. This would be accomplished by two documents, the message to the nation on the 9th, and Hua's memorial speech on the 18th. For all the potential division, not to

---

[45] See PR, no. 38 (1976), pp. 14-15; and Qing and Fang, Deng zai 1976, vol. 2, pp. 124-25.

[46] See PR, no. 38 (1976), pp. 12-14; and Feng Lanrui, "Zhengzhi yanjiushi de rizi," p. 6. The funeral list was almost completely based on official rank, with all Central Committee members except NCNA director Zhu Muzhi included. Zhu's omission was arguably linked to his role in passing on critical information about Jiang Qing's performance at the Dazhai conference. See "Hua Guofeng jiejian Shandong, Hubei deng Nanjing budui deng lingdao tongzhi de jianghua," p. 3; and Onate, "Hua Guofeng," p. 543. While Wang Hairong's case perhaps reflected Jiang Qing's animosity toward her, Wang was not a Central Committee member (while Tang Wensheng was an alternate member), and in strict family terms was arguably not related closely enough to Mao to be included. Cf. above, p. 12n25. Another interesting case, one indicating that it was not only "rightists" who were excluded, concerns Liaoning rebel Zhang Tiesheng who, although not on the funeral committee, had been proposed by the provincial authorities to attend the memorial rally, but was rejected by the Party Center. Qing and Fang, Deng zai 1976, vol. 2, p. 153.

mention implications for any "power struggle," the drafting of these documents passed seemingly without major incident between the radicals and establishment beneficiaries. Specific responsibility for drafting these documents had been assigned on an urgent basis in July to Li Xin (the memorial speech) and Zhou Qicai (the announcement)—officials working in Wang Dongxing's General Office-- by Yao Wenyuan and Ji Dengkui who exercised overall authority, with Yao in charge. At the hastily convened Politburo meeting on September 9, the two drafts were read out. Apparently there was little conflict over the documents, although in one account the conflict which did occur on the announcement featured Jiang Qing *against* Yao Wenyuan and Wang Hongwen. Jiang was reportedly critical of the draft for failing to mention the campaign against Lin Biao and Confucius, or the criticism of Deng (both of which were in the end included), and emphasized alleged efforts to reverse the verdict on the Cultural Revolution. Wang reacted by telling her not to have such a big head and stop throwing labels around, and Hua defused the argument. In another version, at this Politburo meeting Jiang argued for including a sentence in the announcement on continuing the criticism of Deng, a proposal which was agreed to by Zhang Chunqiao and several other Politburo members—including Ye Jianying.[47] As for Hua's speech, a significant issue only arose when the Politburo subsequently met on September 16, a matter which placed the radicals in an essentially passive position (see below).

The message in the two documents was essentially the same, one which repeated the then orthodox position of ongoing class struggle and continuing both the criticism of Deng and the consolidation of the Cultural Revolution. Nevertheless, the position conveyed was broader than just a focus on the themes of the Cultural Revolution. Portraying Mao as "the greatest Marxist of the contemporary era," the documents reviewed his entire career, noting his successful "line struggles" from the 1920s against the "opportunist" Chen Duxiu to the recent victory over the "counterrevolutionary revisionist" Deng. Moreover, the main aspects of Mao's approach over different phases of the Party's history were sketched, including (in the September 9 message) the comparatively moderate early 1960s emphasis on "the three great revolutionary movements of class struggle, the struggle for production and scientific experiment." Still another theme was Party unity, a key aspect of the "three do's and three don'ts,"[48] an injunction that was only included in the memorial speech. Another feature was praise of Mao's international role, his leadership in the struggle against "modern revisionism" and the "hegemonism of the two superpowers." A striking feature of both documents was the attention to the Chairman's military theories and to army building, most prominently in Hua's citing of his famous dictum that

---

[47] See Qing and Fang, *Deng zai 1976*, vol. 2, pp. 9, 301; Ji Xichen, *Shi wu qianli de niandai*, v. 2, p. 775-76; and Zhou Qicai, "Mao Zedong daoci xingcheng qianhou" [Before and after the Drafting of Mao Zedong's Memorial Speech], http://book.sina.com.cn/nzt/his/wode1976/11.shtml.

[48] "Practice Marxism, not revisionism; unite, and do not split; be open and aboveboard, and do not foment intrigue and conspire." Cf. above, p. 295.

"political power grows out of the barrel of a gun." While it might be tempting to see this as an appeal for PLA support, it more tellingly reflected the reality of CCP traditions and the perceived internal and external threats facing the country at this critical moment.[49]

While the unity theme was broadly uncontroversial, the "three do's and three don'ts" formula had negative implications for the "gang" that were well understood within the Politburo. Not only had Mao's main and repeated criticism of the radicals focused on their activities that damaged Party unity, but in his critical rebuke of the radicals at the May 3, 1975, Politburo meeting, after invoking the "three do's and three don'ts," the Chairman immediately followed with his warning about not behaving as a "gang of four." When the Politburo met on the afternoon of September 16 to finalize the memorial speech, the issue was injected into the proceedings by Wang Dongxing. Wang could not attend due to duties involving Mao's body, but he sent a message suggesting that the "three do's and three don'ts" be included in the speech. Chen Xilian also advocated this inclusion, Ye Jianying and Li Xiannian added their voices in support, and Hua approved. Crucially, even though adding the injunction to the memorial speech was aimed at them, the Politburo radicals were largely silent. In one report, they only objected to including the "three do's and three don'ts" on the grounds that the speech was already too long, and in any case when Hua settled the matter Zhang Chunqiao went along with the addition. Subsequent criticism following the "gang's" purge was directed at their *failing* to present their own views in the discussion, particularly by not advocating the slogan "act according to the principles laid down" which, as we shall discuss, emerged in the media on the same day as the Politburo discussion. The key consideration, of course, was that the "three do's and three don'ts" were Mao's words, and as such were beyond challenge.[50]

The final practical issue facing the leadership was the arrangements for the Chairman's corpse. Given Mao's 1956 initiative for all top leaders to have their remains cremated, and the precedent set by Zhou Enlai's case in January, cremation might have been adopted, but the possibility of preserving the body of the great leader also existed. Again, whatever divisions existed do not appear to have been overly confrontational. According to one account, Hua wished to preserve the body so that people could pay their respects during the memorial rally on the 18th, while the radicals pushed for adhering to the 1956 understanding.

---

[49] See *PR*, no. 38 (1976), pp. 6-11, no. 39 (1976), pp. 12-16. The tendency to over-interpret Hua's speech can be seen in treating his statement that "anyone who tampers with Chairman Mao's directives ... is bound to fail" as "[laying] down the gauntlet for the ['gang']"; Baum, *Burying Mao*, p. 39. The same theme of the inviolability of Mao's instructions was a staple of articles identified with the radicals in this period.

[50] See Zhou Qicai, "Mao Zedong daoci xingcheng qianhou"; Mao Zedong, "Tong zai jing zhongyang zhengzhiju weiyuan de tanhua," p. 1; "Hua Guofeng jiejian lingdao tongzhi jianghua," p. 2; and *RMRB*, December 17, 1976, in *SPRCP*, no. 6247 (1976), pp. 3-4, 10.

With Hua insisting, both Jiang and Wang Hongwen assertedly refused to assume responsibility for the remains, leading Hua to take complete responsibility. Jiang then wanted Hua to make the decision public, allegedly preparing the ground for an attack on Hua for ignoring Mao's wishes. The undoubtedly more reliable recollection of Wu De paints a somewhat different picture, with Wu claiming the "gang" avoided any involvement in the issue, while Wang Dongxing organized experts to study how to preserve the corpse. Of course, Wu also assigned a sinister intent to the radicals, claiming they would have attacked Hua if the body were not preserved, but also if it were preserved and something went wrong with the process. But neither account of the issue indicates a sharp clash.[51]

In the official narrative, which has been repeated to varying degrees in foreign scholarship, the "gang of four" was engaged in aggressive political activity from the outset. Indeed, a number of developments occurred which were not entirely devoid of political purpose, although far less calculated or coherent than generally assumed. The key instances cited for this initial period are: Jiang Qing's effort to have Deng expelled from the Party at the first Politburo meeting after Mao's passing, Wang Hongwen's purported attempt to monopolize communications between the Center and the provinces, Jiang's efforts to gain access to and tamper with the Chairman's documents, the "gang's" alleged efforts to organize a petition campaign seeking the Party chair for Jiang and high posts for the other three, the launching of an attack on Hua by spreading "the principles laid down," and a wide-ranging propaganda effort to promote Jiang through messages and photographs.[52] In every case, these claims were either factually distorted, or failed to take into account the larger meaning of the situation.

Leaving aside the "principles laid down" issue until the following section, and beginning with the most general assertion of rampant publicity for Jiang Qing, Andres Onate long ago detailed how messages of condolence from local and military organs only mentioned Jiang in a distinct minority of cases, and photos published in the media did not feature Jiang beyond her official status. There was, understandably, some attention to Jiang as the Chairman's wife, as seen in particular mention of her wreaths to Mao both during the week of mourning and at the memorial rally. But overall, there was nothing beyond what could be reasonably expected under the circumstances.[53] The one case where the official version was unambiguously factual, Jiang's demand for Deng's

---

[51] Onate, "Hua Kuo-feng," p. 542; and Wu De, "Guanyu fensui 'sirenbang'," p. 54.

[52] See, e.g., Yan and Gao, *Turbulent Decade*, pp. 519-21; MacFarquhar, "Succession," pp. 307-308; and Baum, *Burying Mao*, p. 40.

[53] See Onate, "Hua Kuo-feng," pp. 543-45; and *PR*, no. 39 (1976), pp. 7, 18. Nevertheless, some members of the public clearly did view the publicity Jiang received as signs of her political ambition. The clearest case came later on October 1, when *RMRB*, p. 4, published a photo of a National Day forum with Jiang in the center, leading ordinary cadres to fear that this meant she would take over top power; interview with former trade union cadre, June 2003. The visual impression notwithstanding, Jiang was simply in a line starting with Hua from the right which followed strict rank order, and was captioned as such.

expulsion, still distorted the situation. At the September 9 Politburo meeting, an emotional Jiang claimed that Mao's death was due to the anger Deng had caused him, and not only called for a continuation of the criticism campaign, but also demanded that Deng be immediately expelled from the CCP. Accounts differ on precisely what happened next, with writers friendly to Ye Jianying emphasizing the old marshal's resolute rebuff of Jiang by arguing that Mao had settled the question of Deng being allowed to retain his Party card, while Wu De recalled Hua taking no notice of Jiang's demand. The striking thing, however, was that Jiang apparently gained no support, with Wang Hongwen, Zhang Chunqiao and Yao Wenyuan seeing her histrionics as a distraction when pressing matters concerning the funeral had to be settled. The clear picture is of Jiang, not simply because of the stress of the circumstances, but in a familiar pattern, acting in a manner widely unpopular in the top echelon.[54]

Another feature of the September 9 Politburo meeting concerned the call for Party unity behind Hua. While various sources emphasize Ye Jianying as the proponent of this position, in fact Jiang Qing took the lead. In response to Hua's statement that with Mao gone the leadership should be even more united, Jiang vociferously called for backing Hua, stating that anyone disrupting unity should stand aside. This provoked Xu Shiyou who stood up and demanded to know whom she was trying to sideline, while others at the meeting tried to calm things down. In exasperation, Yao Wenyuan even advised the older cadres present to save themselves the aggravation and leave, and "just let her talk."[55] Overall, while it is difficult to obtain a clear sense of the atmosphere of this first Politburo gathering after the Chairman's death, it appears that Jiang's well-known emotionalism served to cause tension with both enemies such as Xu Shiyou and members of her own "gang."

Following the events of September 9, the next *cause célèbre* occurred on the 10th when, apparently using the second secretary who accompanied him to Zhongnanhai without clearing the matter with Hua, Wang Hongwen set up an office within the Central Committee's General Office with instructions to contact all provincial-level units and advise them that, if any major problems arose during the mourning period which they could not solve, they should contact this special office directly for guidance. During September 11 and 12, phone calls were made to the various provinces conveying this directive. Hunan Party leader Zhang Pinghua, who had been Hua's boss before the Cultural Revolution

---

[54] See Qing and Fang, *Deng zai 1976*, vol. 2, p. 9; *Ye zhuan*, p. 645; Wu De, "Guanyu fensui 'sirenbang'," p. 54; and "Hua Guofeng, Ye Jianying deng jiejian Shanghai Ma Tianshui dengren de jianghua," p. 2.

[55] Wu De, "Guanyu fensui 'sirenbang'," pp. 54–55; Qing and Fang, *Deng zai 1976*, vol. 2, pp. 221-23, 227; and interview with Party historian studying the events, July 1997.

The Jiang Qing-Xu Shiyou conflict illustrates the problem with dating, as various sources place it at the Politburo meeting of September 29. Xu, however, was definitely at the meeting on the 9th, staying in Beijing through Mao's memorial ceremony on the 18th, while in all likelihood he was in Guangzhou on the 29th before presiding over National Day activities the following day.

and then worked under him when new governing structures were set up in the late 1960s and early 1970s, and who had been given a particularly rough time by local rebels in summer 1976, felt this violated organizational principles, suspected something was amiss, and informed Hua of the development. Hua then checked into the matter, discovered that other provinces had also received phone calls, reportedly consulted Ye, who also felt something fishy was going on, and determined that any reports to the Center would come directly to him.[56]

As Forster has demonstrated, the official story has distorted the situation by portraying Wang's action as beginning almost immediately after Mao's death, thus suggesting an impatience to "seize power," and by treating his directive as a more or less permanent order when in fact it was explicitly limited to the mourning period when a great deal of disorientation and uncertainty could be expected throughout the Party. Moreover, although taken without consultation "behind the back" of the Politburo, there was nothing secretive about Wang's moves within the General Office headed by Wang Dongxing, nor was it a totally unreasonable act for someone who was, after all, the second-ranking figure in the Party Center, and who had for considerable periods been responsible for CCP daily work. This, of course, is not to deny that Wang may have been seeking political advantage by his move, but it falls well short of any plot to usurp power. Perhaps most telling is that it was politically inept in raising unnecessarily the suspicions of Hua and his Politburo colleagues. While undoubtedly exaggerated by the official view of the "gang," Wu De's characterization of Wang's action 20 years later as evidence that the radicals were "already adopting measures to make [Hua] a figurehead under their control, [and] attempting to gain immediate command everywhere across the country," suggests that similar dark thoughts had been provoked within the Politburo at the time. The crucial point, in any case, is that the evidence suggests that at the time Hua saw Wang's action as directed at his authority. It was apparently shortly after being tipped off by Zhang Pinghua that Hua took the first step to set in motion the decisive sequence of events discussed below to "solve the 'gang of four' problem" by summoning Li Xiannian to serve as his messenger to Ye Jianying. Li began the encounter with Ye by referring to the setting up of the special office, observing that struggle was now inevitable, and it was time to deal with the problem.[57]

At the same time that Wang Hongwen sought to manage contacts with the provinces, radicals at Beijing and Qinghua Universities, led by Xie Jingyi and Chi Qun, were organizing a petition drive to the Party Center calling for top positions for the "gang of four." The focus was on Jiang Qing, with oaths of loyalty sent to her, and the Center was asked to name Jiang as the new head of both the Party and MAC. In addition, these petitions called for Zhang Chunqiao to become

---

[56] See Chen and Du, *Shilu*, vol. 3, part 2, p. 1412; Yan and Gao, *Turbulent Decade*, pp. 521-22; Wu De, "Guanyu fensui 'sirenbang'," p. 55; and above, p. 514n124.

[57] See Forster, "China's Coup," p. 277; MacFarquhar, "Succession," p. 308n240; Wu De, "Guanyu fensui 'sirenbang'," p. 55; and Cheng Zhensheng, "Li Xiannian yu fensui 'sirenbang'," p. 48.

Party and MAC vice chairman, and Wang Hongwen MAC first vice chairman. In the official view, the petition drive was organized by Xie and Chi on orders from Yao Wenyuan, but the actual story seems different: Yao and Zhang Chunqiao apparently sought to suppress these activities, as they were causing problems for the Politburo radicals with their colleagues. This reflected a fundamental problem in the larger radical camp we have repeatedly emphasized—the different perspectives of the Politburo radicals and rebels scattered throughout the system. Important actors such as Xie and Chi, and lesser figures like Zhang Tiesheng in Liaoning, often articulated a more extreme line than the "gang" themselves. Both on the day of Mao's death, and in the following days, they spoke of "preparations for war" and not being afraid to die, and, at least in Zhang Tiesheng's case, virtually consigned Hua to the revisionist camp. The need to cool such passions was nothing new for the "gang"; indeed, there was an eerie parallel to earlier in the year that would have impressed itself on Zhang Chunqiao. In January, with Deng in retreat but Hua not yet selected, wall posters called for Zhang to succeed Zhou Enlai as premier, something Zhang moved to suppress when informed that Hua would be named. In September, with Hua's selection to the highest office virtually guaranteed, lower-level enthusiasm could only result in similar problems, and thus required a similar response.[58]

A final matter to consider is Jiang Qing's efforts to secure Mao's personal documents. This apparently began shortly after the Chairman's death when Jiang went "every day" to Mao's residence, asking his secretary, Zhang Yufeng, who basically would not cooperate, to turn over various of his manuscripts and papers, and continued past Mao's funeral. In the post-Mao version of the "gang's" transgressions, Jiang was accused of trying to find some indication of Mao designating her to take over supreme power, or to remove any incriminating information about her past. Jiang secured "by deception" transcripts of two talks Mao held in 1974 with regional military leaders Yang Dezhi and Wang Liusheng, as well as a record of her own interview with Roxane Witke. The transcripts of Mao's 1974 talks were reportedly tampered with, seemingly through writing on the documents. When Wang Dongxing learned of this, he demanded the return of the documents, while Jiang allegedly insisted she and Mao Yuanxin should have responsibility for Mao's papers. On September 21, after sharp debate, Hua determined that the Chairman's papers would be sealed under Wang Dongxing's care. Jiang continued to argue bitterly with Hua face-to-face and over the telephone, but the matter had been settled. When Hua reviewed the incident with Wu De, their conclusions were somewhat milder, but not inconsistent with later official claims: Jiang wanted to control the papers in order to find stray words and phrases that could be distorted for personal advantage, or to threaten some military and local leading comrades. Yet again, the lesson of this episode is how

---

[58] See Chen and Du, *Shilu*, vol. 3, part 2, pp. 1412-13; Forster, "China's Coup," pp. 277-78; and interview with senior Party historian, January 2000. Cf. above, p. 442.

Jiang's excesses simply enhanced the suspicion and animosity toward her in the highest circles.[59]

Apart from the picture of aggressive actions by the radicals, the second part of the dominant narrative concerning the initial period after Mao's death focuses on the efforts of the old revolutionaries to "solve" the problem of the "gang." Some sources are quite specific, such as the claim that Chen Yun went to Ye Jianying as soon as Mao passed away with materials exposing Jiang Qing as a traitor, a claim that probably confuses Chen's visit 10 days or more later, but most are much vaguer, for example simply claiming Chen, Nie Rongzhen, Li Xiannian, Deng Yingchao and (despite our skepticism) Deng Xiaoping exchanged views through their aides or held direct talks with Ye during the mourning period. As in the summer, Wang Zhen is given particular prominence in visiting old comrades to canvas the issue. Particular emphasis, of course, is given to Ye Jianying as standing at the center of this network, and also in rebuffing the "gang" as in the case of Jiang's demand to expel Deng at the September 9 Politburo meeting, as well as calling for unity around Hua's Party Center on the same occasion—even though, as we have seen, Jiang Qing was the first to call for such unity and the other radicals gave no support to her proposal on Deng. Most crucial for this version of events is that Ye is pictured as taking the initiative *vis-à-vis* Hua from the very outset, urging him to fulfill his leadership obligations and not let Mao down by dealing with the radicals, and giving his unconfident younger colleague promises that the old revolutionaries and army would provide support if he acted. One of the major problems with this version, apart from its general vagueness, is that there is virtually no evidence of any of the old revolutionaries proposing a concrete solution to the problem at this early stage.[60]

The larger problem with the above story, as with accounts of events at the September 9 Politburo meeting, is that on the best evidence it is a distortion. This is not to claim that Ye was anything other than anxious about the "gang of four" problem, and desirous of dealing with it as soon as feasible, or that he did not express to Hua at least some of the sentiments attributed to him. But on the central

---

[59] See Chen and Du, *Shilu*, vol. 3, part 2, p. 1415; Yan and Gao, *Turbulent Decade*, p. 520; Forster, "China's Coup," pp. 279-80; and Wu De, "Guanyu fensui 'sirenbang'," p. 54. As in other cases, Ye-friendly sources picture the old marshal taking a leading role in rebuffing Jiang on this matter; see Fan Shuo, "The Tempestuous October," p. 17. There are also, we believe erroneous, claims that Jiang fabricated a document claiming that Mao instructed the Politburo to "help [Jiang Qing] carry the red banner," and that she tampered with Mao's April 30 three directives to Hua. See Onate, "Hua Kuo-feng," pp. 547-51. Finally, there are assertions that on September 19, as the documents issue seemingly came to a head, Jiang demanded a Politburo Standing Committee meeting be held on the matter to which she, Mao Yuanxin and Yao Wenyuan would be invited, but Ye would be excluded, and subsequently demanded that the documents be handed over to Mao Yuanxin for sorting, a claim we find largely implausible and weakly documented. Cf. MacFarquhar, "Succession," p. 309; and Forster, "China's Coup," p. 279.

[60] See Ding Jiaqi, "Fensui sirenbang douzheng zhong de jiangshuaimen," part 2, *Guofang*, no. 2 (2005), p. 78; *Ye zhuan*, p. 645; Fan Shuo, "The Tempestuous October," p. 17; Mao Mao, *"Wenge" suiyue*, pp. 519-20; Forster, "China's Coup," pp. 276, 280; and below, pp. 569-70.

issue of who took the initiative, the evidence clearly points to Hua, not only in the recollections of Wu De who might be considered friendly to Hua,[61] but also through careful reconstructions by Party historians many years after the fact, who drew not only on Hua's own recollections, but on the statements of one of the key old revolutionaries in the process: Li Xiannian. Much of the historical enquiry originated over questions concerning the dating of when Hua took the initiative to approach Li to ask the latter to contact Ye, but the resultant story reveals much about the dynamics of elite politics during the mourning period for Mao.[62]

Whatever contact Hua and Ye had at or around the Politburo meeting of September 9, Hua apparently felt the need to establish a secure line of communication to the old marshal, and concluded that Li would be the most likely channel. On the 11th, most probably in late evening, Hua excused himself when standing vigil at Mao's coffin by claiming to be ill, and ostensibly set out to the hospital. In fact, he went to Li's residence instead. Li was still officially on sick leave, his attendance at Politburo meetings notwithstanding, and had previously received permission to leave Beijing for recuperation, something that presumably would now happen after Mao's funeral. Hua persuaded Li not to go through with this plan, given the threat posed by the radicals, and the need to solve swiftly the potential damage to the Party, country and Hua himself. In Li's recollection of this encounter in May 1981, a time when Hua was being denigrated in preparation for his removal as Party Chairman, Hua had declared that a struggle with the "gang" could not be avoided, while four years earlier Li made the general observation that arresting the radicals was Hua's proposal. At this point in September 1976, however, Hua does not appear to have advanced a specific proposal for solving the problem, and wanted Li to visit Ye to explore the matter. The extreme caution being exercised was further revealed by the plan Li devised with Hua as a cover for his approach to Ye. Under this scheme, Li would head to the Fragrant Hills botanical gardens to the west of Beijing, purportedly for sightseeing, and if he was not followed, he would then go on to Ye's residence in

---

[61] While the common interests of Hua and Wu are generally assumed, some sources, albeit of suspect nature, claim Wu felt betrayed by Hua when he was removed from power in the 1978-80 period. See Chen Yonggui, "Wo mengjian Mao Zhuxi le." On balance, we believe Hua and Wu had common interests and sympathies, as reflected in Hua rushing to Wu's home when he died in 1995 and staying for a number of hours reminiscing. Interview with source close to Wu's family, June 1999.

[62] The point at issue was whether the dates of Hua's approach to Li and Li's visit to Ye were September 21 and 24, as claimed in *Li Xiannian wenxuan (1935-1988 nian)* [Selected Works of Li Xiannian, 1935-1988] (Beijing: Renmin chubanshe, 1989), p. 518n157, or earlier. The investigations in "Yize zhongyao kaoding—youguan Hua Guofeng, Li Xiannian, Ye Jianying shangtan jiejue 'sirenbang' wenti de liangge guanjian shijian" [An Important Verification—Concerning Two Critical Moments in the Discussions of Hua Guofeng, Li Xiannian and Ye Jianying on Solving the "Gang of Four" Problem], *DDWX*, no. 3 (2001), pp. 73-75, conclusively demonstrate that these visits occurred on September 11 and 14, or at least very close to those dates. Zhang Gensheng, "Hua Guofeng tan fensui 'sirenbang'," p. 2, gives the timing as September 10 and 13. The other key source demonstrating the initiative of Hua is Cheng Zhensheng, "Li Xiannian yu fensui 'sirenbang'," pp. 45-51.

the Western Hills. Once the two old revolutionaries met on the 14th for apparently the first time in many months, similar caution was seen in Ye enquiring whether Li came under orders (from Hua), and the two leaders largely communicated in writing. Under these circumstances, Ye reportedly did not advance any specific proposals for dealing with the radicals, and was described by Hua (presumably on the basis of Li's report) as extremely cautious.[63]

In contrast to Ye and Li's caution, several other leaders whose roles in the whole process were significant, Wang Dongxing and Chen Xilian, were already indicating strong support for whatever action was required. According to Hua, on the 11th he also approached Wang Dongxing whose "attitude was very clear," and indicated staunch support for Hua. Chen Xilian has long been one of the most under-acknowledged players in the drama, one who only received due if muted recognition for his contribution to the demise of the "gang" at the time of his death in 1999. Apart from Wang Zhen who was more marginal in terms of formal position and real power, Chen was perhaps the earliest leader to speak of dealing with the "gang," although, like Wang in the summer, this could hardly be regarded a considered proposal. During the vigil at the dead Mao's bedside, while on a toilet break, Chen made hand gestures to Li indicating that the radicals should be arrested, but Li indicated this was not something that could be addressed. Of course, caution was the sensible approach under the circumstances, and both Li and Ye were wise enough to recognize it at the time, even if their actual behavior is in some tension with subsequent efforts to lionize the old revolutionaries.[64]

A final revealing aspect of the Ye-Li meeting was Ye's distrust of at least some establishment beneficiaries. This was the occasion when Ye cautiously enquired about the reliability of Chen Xilian and Wu De, raising the issue by writing question marks next to their names on a list of the leadership. Here we focus on Chen, and Li Xiannian quickly sprang to his defense, asserting that he was completely reliable, and Ye should be at ease.[65] While Ye was reassured, the likely reasons for the mistrust are instructive. Of course, Chen had taken over responsibility for the daily affairs of the MAC when Ye was forced to step aside early in the year. But beyond that was the fact that shared military backgrounds notwithstanding, Ye and Chen had no particular career ties, with Chen belonging to the PLA mountaintop associated with none other than Deng Xiaoping. But

---

[63] See "Yize zhongyao kaoding," p. 74; Cheng Zhensheng, "Li Xiannian yu fensui 'sirenbang'," pp. 48-49; and Wu De, "Guanyu fensui 'sirenbang'," p. 56. Geng Biao, *Geng Biao huiyilu*, p. 286, claims that Ye visited Hua two days later and explained his reticence, and the two men then engaged in a discussion of the "gang" problem. We believe, however, that Geng's version places the Ye-Hua discussion too early.

[64] See Wu De, "Guanyu fensui 'sirenbang'," pp. 56-57; *RMRB*, June 22, 1999, p. 4; and Cheng Zhensheng, "Li Xiannian yu fensui 'sirenbang'," p. 49.

[65] See Cheng Zhensheng, "Li Xiannian yu fensui 'sirenbang'," p. 49. Strictly speaking, Cheng Zhensheng only mentions a question mark by Chen's name. As with the other so-called neo-Maoists effectively dismissed at the time of the 1978 Third Plenum, Chen's case had much to do with elite perceptions of his role during the Cultural Revolution. We examine this in our Volume II.

arguably the greatest source of mistrust, one that would come back to haunt Chen in the subsequent period, was the fact that until 1974 he had been responsible for one of the most radical provinces in China, Liaoning, and had been associated with Mao Yuanxin in that province and the Shenyang Military Region. Like many officers who had served throughout the "Cultural Revolution decade," Chen had been caught in the vortex of Mao's demands which required support of radical policies and, in this case, of an especially favored relative of the Chairman. Against such background, the inclinations of even high-ranking veterans of the revolutionary battlefield could not be taken for granted. While ultimately, as Ye claimed, the army could be relied on, it was not something that could be taken lightly.

In this early period up to the memorial ceremony at Tiananmen, distrust and anxiety existed on all sides. A consensus among the establishment beneficiaries and old revolutionaries, albeit one that was not being articulated openly, seemed to exist on the need to do *something* to deal with the Politburo radicals, perhaps most fundamentally because of the uncertainty for both individuals and the system as a whole if the "gang" continued to have a major say concerning the CCP's future. But there is little to indicate serious planning at this stage concerning how to "solve" the issue. The significance of Hua's initiative on September 11 was his apparent commitment to move toward real action—whatever that might ultimately be. This was a clear step beyond the kind of diffuse expressions of unease that had marked the conversations of the old revolutionaries in the summer and earlier. This new determination was further fueled by the counter-productive actions of the radicals and their followers: Jiang Qing's demand for Deng's expulsion, her efforts to obtain Mao's documents, petitions asking that the "gang" receive high positions, and especially Wang Hongwen's special office for communicating with the provinces, could be and were seen as concerted political acts, perhaps to turn Hua into a figurehead, or even to "seize power" for themselves. Arguably, although understandably in the circumstances, in each case this involved reading more into the incidents than what was in fact there. A similar case can be made for the well-known curious matter of "acting according to the principles laid down."

Much Ado about Nothing: Tensions over "Act according to the Principles Laid Down"

The saga of the "principles laid down" began shortly before Mao's memorial service, and continued right up to the arrest of the "gang of four." The basic facts are beyond dispute. On September 16, a *People's Daily* editorial introduced Mao's purported "exhortation" (*zhufu*) to "act according to the principles laid down" (*an jiding fangzhen ban*). Although not included in Hua's memorial speech, this phrase became a feature of massive publicity over the next two to three weeks. It featured in coverage of the memorial activities with, for example, the Beijing militia pledging to follow the injunction. It was also included in the speeches of leaders of all provincial-level units on the 18th, thus indicating that a central propaganda directive to emphasize the saying had been circulated. In addition to several hundred articles in key publications featuring the "principles laid down" in the bold type usually reserved for Mao's words, the prominence of the concept was dramatically seen by its appearance every day from September 22 to 30 in the box on the masthead of the *People's Daily* used for the Chairman's sayings, either alone or in conjunction with such Mao classics as "class struggle is the key link." In addition, other notable pieces using the "principles laid down" in the national press included a September 29 article in the *People's Daily* by two Qinghua University officials, the *People's Daily's* National Day editorial on October 1, and, most famously, an October 4 article by the *Liang Xiao* writing group in *Guangming Daily*.[66]

In the official interpretation, the promotion of the "principles laid down" was a surprise attack and a continuing onslaught to challenge Hua and further the "gang's" aim of "seizing power." By pushing what they allegedly presented as the Chairman's "deathbed injunction" (*linzhong zhufu*)—although in fact Yao Wenyuan excised this reference from the draft of the September 16 editorial —the radicals reportedly were attempting to picture themselves as the only true bearers of Mao's behests. But more was supposedly involved: the "principles laid down" were a fabrication that tampered with Mao's actual instruction to Hua on April 30 to "act according to past principles" (*zhao guoqu fangzhen ban*). At yet another level, the radicals were assertedly attempting to replace the "three do's and three don'ts" (as we have seen, a concept hostile to their interests) with the "principles laid down" as the central ideological yardstick of the new period. By late September-early October, however, Hua rebuffed the "gang's" efforts, making them more desperate. In this context, the October 4 *Guangming Daily* article was allegedly more than another shot in the ideological war. According to the overheated official reconstruction, it was nothing less than a signal for concrete measures to "seize power," a veritable mobilization order for a coup.[67]

Before turning to the actual events, an examination of the concepts at issue is in order. But even before that, it is necessary to acknowledge that in all likelihood Mao authored both "past principles" and the "principles laid down." There can be little doubt concerning Mao's written message to Hua on April 30. As for the "principles laid down," Jiang Qing credibly claimed that Mao verbally conveyed this version to her and Zhang Chunqiao at some point before his death, but for unclear reasons forbid her to inform the Politburo until after

---

[66] See *RMRB*, September 16, 1976, p. 1, September 29, 1976, p. 2, October 1, 1976, p. 2; *PR*, no. 39 (1976), pp. 10, 22-23, 26, 34-35, no. 40 (1976), pp. 5-17, no. 41 (1976), pp. 12-13; *GMRB*, October 4, 1976, in *SPRCP*, no. 6202 (1976), pp. 49-55; Yan and Gao, *Turbulent Decade*, pp. 522-23; and Onate, "Hua Kuo-feng," pp. 545-47.

[67] See *RMRB*, December 17, 1976, in *SPRCP*, no. 6247 (1976), pp. 1-11; *GMRB*, December 24, 1976, in *SPRCP*, no. 6256 (1977), pp. 68-75; and Qing and Fang, *Deng zai 1976*, vol. 2, p. 91.

he passed away.[68] As we shall see, there is also reason to believe this version had been given to others in the summer. In any case, notwithstanding efforts to see distinctions between the two versions of "principles," there is little to choose between them in terms of Mao's intent. Although some Chinese writers and Western analysts have argued that the "principles laid down" implied very specific support for the type of Cultural Revolution activities promoted by the radicals, while "past principles" had a broader reference to Party procedures and policies, thus conveying a vague sense of continuity, others such as the eminent historian of the period, Wang Nianyi, more persuasively dismiss the difference as insignificant. There can be little doubt that Mao's preeminent concern was that his Cultural Revolution project would not be reversed after his death, whatever formula concerning "principles" he advanced to different colleagues at different times in 1976. Moreover, according to one account, as late as October 1, Hua himself said the difference was only in phrasing, not in meaning. In the immediate post-arrest period, the most precise official explanation claimed the "principles" the Chairman was concerned about were those expressed in his own "important instructions" of late 1975-early 1976 compiled by none other than Mao Yuanxin, and the views expressed by Hua in his February 25 speech to provincial leaders. In other words, these "principles" strongly affirmed the Cultural Revolution and the criticism of Deng, but in the more measured approach of Hua rather than the "gang's" alleged attempt to expand the anti-Deng campaign into a sweeping purge of old revolutionaries. But at root, once the issue surfaced within the leadership, it was more a question of ownership and mutual antagonism than any profound ideological confrontation.[69]

The clearest evidence that this whole episode was, in a sense, "much ado about nothing," is precisely that it took almost two weeks for the issue to attract serious attention at the top despite massive publicity for the "principles laid down," reportedly organized by Yao Wenyuan through directives to Xinhua on September 17, 20 and 23, and including page one highlighting in the *People's Daily* as a Mao quotation for eight consecutive days. The absence of a sense that anything much was wrong can also be seen in the routine mouthing of the slogan by provincial leaders on September 18—including by Hunan's Zhang Pinghua who had been so alarmed by Wang Hongwen's special office only a

---

[68] See Qing and Fang, *Deng zai 1976*, vol. 2, p. 247.

[69] See *RMRB*, December 17, 1976, in *SPRCP*, no. 6247 (1976), pp. 2, 7-8; Qing and Fang, *Deng zai 1976*, vol. 2, p. 244; Gardner, *Chinese Politics and the Succession*, pp. 111-13; and Forster, "China's Coup," pp. 279, 300n9.

This is not to argue that different emphases more generally were insignificant. Statements linked to the radicals, particularly by lower-level radicals, such as those at Qinghua University and in Shanghai, were more focused on the achievements of the Cultural Revolution. See the article by Qinghua leaders in *RMRB*, September 29, 1976, p. 2; and *Xuexi yu pipan*, September 30, 1976, in *SPRCM*, no. 897 (1976), pp. 1-8. Ironically, the Shanghai article (pp. 5, 7) demonstrated its fidelity to the "principles laid down" by affirming the "three do's and three don'ts," and by citing the city's reported doubling of steel output during Mao's mourning period.

week earlier. Wang Dongxing would later claim that initially he was at a loss, and thought that Mao might indeed have written a note on the "principles laid down," and only subsequently realized this was a distortion of the Chairman's April 30 note to Hua. The matter only gained traction toward the end of the month when some Politburo members complained, *not* about the "principles laid down" as such, but concerning the fact that it was given excessive propaganda emphasis compared to the "three do's and three don'ts." Again, leaving aside the pointed implications concerning acting as a "gang," there was not a huge difference in concept: the "three do's and three don'ts" had an impeccable anti-revisionist component; and while they also emphasized Party unity, that too was endorsed by the radicals in general terms. In any case, while the "principles laid down" had clear pride of place, by the start of October, probably reflecting Hua's belated concern, they were often linked to the "three do's and three don'ts," as in the National Day editorial where the latter phrase had greater prominence. By that time, however, Hua was noticing the differences between the two versions of "principles." The crux of the matter was authority — Hua now insisted that *his* version be the official *tifa*.[70]

From the available accounts, criticism of excessive propaganda on the "principles laid down" was first raised in the Politburo by Wang Dongxing on September 29, when the discussion focused on the use of the phrase in Foreign Minister Qiao Guanhua's address to the United Nations scheduled for the first week in October. Wang felt the emphasis should be on the "two documents," the message to the nation on Mao's death and Hua's funeral speech, but he didn't indicate any basic problem with the slogan as such. In the inconclusive discussion which followed, Yao Wenyuan said nothing and later claimed that he only had a vague sense that anything significant was at issue, and felt the matter could be dealt with by adding references to the "two documents." After examining the draft of Qiao's speech at the Foreign Ministry on the 30th, two days later on October 2, Hua wrote to Politburo Standing Committee members Ye Jianying, Wang Hongwen and Zhang Chunqiao that he had checked the phrase against the note Mao had given him, and three characters (*an jiding*) were wrong, declared that the "principles laid down" *tifa* was erroneous and he had excluded it from the draft, and recommended that the matter be explained to the Politburo. Ye, Wang and Zhang all indicated agreement, but Zhang proposed that Hua's comment not be distributed to lower levels to avoid unnecessary confusion, thus leaving the larger issue of propaganda using the formulation unclear. As for the UN speech, Hua was unsure how to proceed and consulted Geng Biao who, as a leading cadre of the Party Center's International Liaison Department, had foreign affairs expertise, and MFA Vice Ministers Han Nianlong and Liu Zhenhua, and they

---

[70] Yan and Gao, *Turbulent Decade*, p. 522; "Wang Dongxing zai quanguo xuanchuan gongzuo jianghua," p. 2; *RMRB*, December 17, 1976, in *SPRCP*, no. 6247 (1976), p. 4; *PR*, no. 40 (1976), pp. 10-11, no. 41 (1976), pp. 12-13; and Onate, "Hua Kuo-feng," p. 552.

advised simply sending a message to New York to drop the offending phrase.[71]

But uncertainty existed within the ranks of the top elite itself. Although Yao had again urged Xinhua to promote the "principles laid down" on September 30, the Politburo discussions of late September, and particularly Hua's intervention about the erroneous version of the "principles," led to changes in the propaganda sphere. For his own part, Hua eschewed the "principles laid down" in his very brief talk to the National Day commemoration on September 30, while, as noted above, the October 1 *People's Daily* editorial gave pride of place to the "three do's and three don'ts." Hua's October 2 comment produced an even greater effect, but with it more confusion and suspicion. Rather than defy Hua, on October 3 Yao Wenyuan summoned *People's Daily* editor Lu Ying to discuss the situation. On the one hand, Yao wanted to clarify the actual story of the different versions of the "principles," and asked Lu to investigate. These investigations, calling on the memories of people who attended the July national planning seminar, produced a conclusion, contrary to the subsequent official story, that on that occasion Hua himself had actually used the "principles laid down" *tifa*. On the other hand, Yao ordered the Party's daily to stop using the "principles laid down" in view of Hua's position. But, in a display of political ineptitude, Yao sought a compromise position between Hua's view and that of Zhang Chunqiao by authorizing the continuing use of the slogan in the other national paper, the *Guangming Daily*.[72]

This led to the notorious article by *Liang Xiao* on October 4, an article which praised the "principles laid down" as essential for the victory of Mao's line, denounced revisionism from Bernstein and Kautsky to Khrushchev to the CCP's own "revisionist chieftains," declared "revisionist chieftains" in the future would not come to a good end, and emphasized the importance of "revolutionary successors," i.e., the young rebels who emerged in the Cultural Revolution. Nevertheless, rallying around the Party Center was emphasized and, in a classic compromise gesture, "acting according to the principles laid down" was defined

---

[71] See Qing and Fang, *Deng zai 1976*, vol. 2, pp. 226, 243-46; "Hua Guofeng jiejian lingdao tongzhi jianghua," p. 2; *Geng Biao huiyilu*, pp. 287-88; and Chen and Du, *Shilu*, vol. 3, part 2, p. 1418. Qiao's actual speech to the UN on October 5 largely concerned the international situation, with the most significant domestic references addressing the "two documents" and deepening the criticism of Deng. *PR*, no. 42 (1976), pp. 12-15. The UN speech question was clearly linked, in perception in any case, to Qiao's past links to the "gang." It seemingly played a role in Qiao's dismissal as soon as the radicals were arrested, and those links arguably heightened Hua's concern about the "principles" issue. Hua had UN Ambassador Huang Hua, who had his own problems with Qiao and who would soon replace him as Foreign Minister, informed of the matter.

More generally, the case against the "gang" for fabricating the "principles laid down" argues that they had taken notes on the "past principles" when Hua revealed Mao's injunction to the Politburo, and Yao had actually seen the original. Moreover, Yao assertedly initially tampered with the phrase in mid-August, although, as noted below, there is evidence that Hua himself used "principles laid down" in the summer. See *RMRB*, December 17, 1976, in *SPRCP*, no. 6247 (1976), pp. 2-3; and *GMRB*, December 24, 1976, in *SPRCP*, no. 6256 (1977), p. 69.

[72] See Chen and Du, *Shilu*, vol. 3, part 2, p. 1417; *PR*, no. 41 (1976), pp. 5-6, 12-13; Qing and Fang, *Deng zai 1976*, vol. 2, pp. 249-50, 292-93; and Onate, "Hua Kuo-feng," pp. 549, 553-54.

as carrying out the "three do's and three don'ts." The subsequent claim that Hua was the new "revisionist chieftain" in the radicals' sights is supposition at best, with no justification from the text itself, while the view of the article as a mobilization order for a *coup d'état* is sheer fantasy. As Onate has observed, the only meaningful target of any *Liang Xiao* mobilization order was to arouse public opinion. Yet even in this respect the article focused on a longer-term and continuing effort, one involving 20 to 30 "line struggles," rather than an imminent showdown, notwithstanding Yao working on another article for publication on the 8th. But for the establishment beneficiaries and old revolutionaries, the article and the broader "principles" issue became another source of suspicion. While not crucial for the plans to eliminate the "gang," the October 4 treatise intensified suspicion, as dramatically seen in Hua summoning Chen Xilian on the 5th to return immediately to Beijing from Tangshan, and it reportedly resulted in plans to arrest the "gang" being brought forward by four days. The radicals might have been preparing for the long haul, but their enemies were not prepared to wait.[73]

Indeed, the whole episode of the *Guangming Daily* article was, much like the case of the March 25 *Wenhui bao* article that was widely seen as an attack on Zhou Enlai, a case of misperception and jumping to erroneous conclusions. As on the earlier occasion, the "gang of four" was only involved in the sense of general propaganda directives, not specifically concerning the October 4 piece, and certainly not as any call to arms. The leading group of the paper was simply carrying out the general ideological line of the moment including the earlier emphasis on "principles laid down," and the article was finalized on September 30, two days before Hua's October 2 comment on using "past principles." While subsequent intensive post-Mao investigations concluded that the paper had acted innocently, and there was no connection to any "gang" plot, in the heated atmosphere of the time, the appearance of the article was seen as a threatening move, even a mobilizing order, by Hua and others.[74]

---

[73] See *GMRB*, October 4, 1976, in *SPRCP*, no. 6202 (1976), pp. 49-55; Onate, "Hua Kuo-feng," pp. 554, 559-61; Cheng Zhensheng, "Li Xiannian yu fensui 'sirenbang'," p. 51; Forster, "China's Coup," p. 288; and *Chen Xilian huiyilu*, pp. 480-81. Another problem with the October 4 article as a mobilization order is that, according to one of the writers, it was written without prior consultation with any member of the "gang," although Yao would have approved its publication; see MacFarquhar, "Succession," p. 310n249.

The projected October 8 article was to be published in *RMRB* and was described as "even more crafty," but despite innuendo it is unclear whether the "principles laid down" would have been used after Yao's three revisions. *RMRB*, December 17, 1976, in *SPRCP*, no. 6247 (1976), pp. 1-2. In any case, two articles by the *Liang Xiao* writing group appearing the morning after the arrest of the "gang" did not contain the slogan. See *RMRB*, October 7, 1976, in *SPRCP*, no. 6200 (1976), pp. 223-30; and *GMRB*, October 7, 1976, in *SPRCP*, no. 6199 (1976), pp. 141-49.

[74] Fan Daren, *"Wenge" yubi chenfulu*, p. 138; and *Shanghai "wenhua dageming" shihua*, p. 965.

Toward the Arrest of the Radicals, Late September-October 6, 1976

As we have argued, in the period up to Mao's funeral, discussions concerning "solving the 'gang of four' problem" were tentative at best. This was seen in Ye Jianying's cautious response to Li Xiannian. Ye's circumspection was further seen around the time of the funeral in his talk with fellow Politburo member and Shenyang Military Region Commander Li Desheng, a conversation that was apparently indirect, but still led the old marshal to turn up the radio to counter any listening devices. Similar caution was seen at the State Council meeting on September 16 involving Hua, Li Xiannian, Chen Xilian, Ji Dengkui, Wu De and Chen Yonggui, the meeting where Ji observed that the four radicals should be treated differently, an idea that was greeted with silence. While Ji seemingly did not stipulate what different treatment he had in mind, a senior Party historian believes that, notwithstanding his sometimes sharp conflict with Jiang Qing, his meaning was that due to her "special status" as Mao's wife, she should be treated leniently. No further exchanges on the radicals ensued, and Hua's reaction to this inconclusive discussion was that it was best to avoid the issue in such settings, restricting any consideration to individual contacts.[75] But once the ceremony honoring Mao was completed, the pace of events in the conflict of the radicals against the establishment beneficiaries and old revolutionaries intensified. One immediate manifestation was the resolution, over September 19-21, of the Mao documents issue discussed above. Other conflicts followed, with the final Politburo meeting before the coup on September 29 being particularly significant, albeit not quite in the way commonly understood. Meanwhile, the radicals engaged in various activities, including exchanges with their followers in Shanghai, although these were hardly the threats later claimed by official accounts. The most significant development was that the anti-radical forces quickly moved from generalized concern to concrete consideration of how to "solve the 'gang of four' problem."

While we cannot be completely confident of the dates, over the week or so after the funeral, various actors turned their minds toward the issue of how to repel the perceived radical threat. Of course, given the general bias of PRC sources, much attention has been given to the initiatives of the old revolutionaries, but the bias does not mean that specific events did not happen. In one account, Chen Yun was summoned to Ye Jianying's residence in the Western Hills on September 19, although this could have happened as much as two weeks later. Ye revealed Mao's comments designating the radicals a "gang of four" to Chen, while perhaps on this occasion or in discussions with Wang Zhen, Chen offered his analysis of the options available. Despite a preference for legal means, Chen

---

[75] Fan Shuo, "The Tempestuous October," p. 19; Cheng Zhensheng, "Li Xiannian yu fensui 'sirenbang'," p. 49; interview, January 2005; and above, pp. 13n30, 225-26n97, 536. According to Fan Shuo, in his talk with Li Desheng, Ye only spoke of the relative urgency of the "organizational problem" as opposed to "problems in production," leaving it to Li to interpret his meaning.

concluded that after a careful examination of Central Committee membership, the anti-radical forces could not be confident of a vote in the body.[76] Two days later, on the 21st, Nie Rongzhen famously called in Yang Chengwu, his old subordinate during the revolutionary struggle, and asked him to convey a message to Ye. While expressing alarmist concerns over Ye's possible arrest and Deng's possible assassination, Nie argued that "normal procedures for inner-Party struggle" were useless, and advocated preemptive action before the "gang" could strike.[77]

If these accounts concerning the old revolutionaries are accurate, they are strikingly similar to what reportedly was considered separately by Hua. According to Wu De, on the evening of September 26 or 27 (it was almost certainly the 26th), Hua met with Li Xiannian and himself to discuss the issue. Hua observed that a struggle with the radicals was unavoidable, saying, in terms like Nie Rongzhen's, that he didn't know how many people would lose their heads if they didn't act. Wu, after observing that some of the "gang's" recent activities were "abnormal," expressed support for Hua, and said there were only two ways to deal with the situation: to arrest them, or to convene a meeting of the Politburo and vote to remove them from their posts. Wu recalled that he inclined toward a meeting, and calculated that "we would have the support of the majority, [while] they had four and a half votes, [the half being alternate member] Wu Guixian." Wu De also alluded to the fundamental change in the situation: "In the past they stole Chairman Mao's name, but now they didn't have the circumstances to do that." Li Xiannian interrupted to ask if Wu knew how Khrushchev won out over the so-called "anti-Party group" in the Soviet Union in 1957 after being in the minority in the Politburo. Of course, Wu was well versed in how Khrushchev relied on the military to assemble the Central Committee and secure a majority there. The three leaders, much as Chen Yun reportedly had done, then examined the Central Committee and estimated its likely vote, similarly concluding that the outcome of such a vote would not be certain. But the difference from the Soviet situation, they decided, was that the radicals had no support among the masses or in the military. Nevertheless, they were given pause by the fact that it was still soon after Mao's death, and Jiang's status as Mao's wife remained potent, so that the radicals retained a capacity to whip up public opinion. Hua *et al.* felt the "gang's" activities were becoming more dramatic, and there was

---

[76] Chen's visit, as with the activities of the old revolutionaries generally, is very hard to pin down. According to Zhu Jiamu, Chi Aiping and Zhao Shigang, "Chen Yun" [Chen Yun], *Zhonggong dangshi renwu zhuan* [Biographies of Personalities in CCP History], vol. 71 (Beijing: Zhongyang wenxian chubanshe, 2000), p. 140, Chen was secretly brought to Ye's residence on September 19 and told of Mao's comments, while the ostensibly authoritative *Chen Yun nianpu, 1905-1995, xia juan* [Chronology of Chen Yun, 1905-1995, vol. 3] (Beijing: Zhongyang wenxian chubanshe, 2000), p. 204, places this meeting in early October. Chen's assessment of the Central Committee could have taken place at the meeting with Ye, or conceivably during his "many" discussions with Wang Zhen from the latter part of September, if not earlier. See also Forster, "China's Coup," p. 284.

[77] See Fan Shuo, "The Tempestuous October," p. 19; and Nie Rongzhen, "[Ye] Jianying was in Fact a Proletarian Lu Duan."

no telling what they might do. After discussions lasting to 5 a.m. in the morning of the 27th, Li and Wu agreed to Hua's proposal that dealing with the problem would be "better earlier than later, and the earlier the better." Both Hua and Li subsequently told Wu that these discussions were the definitive moment when Hua decided to arrest the radicals.[78]

This account raises the question of the role of Ye Jianying, who was not involved in the apparently decisive discussions of September 26, in reaching the ultimate determination. While we believe the glorification of Ye in CCP sources has exaggerated his contribution, and even more to the point unfairly diminished Hua's, we do not gainsay that Ye played a very important role. In general terms, this can be seen in the simple fact that Hua's first move was to send Li Xiannian to sound out Ye, a step that undoubtedly had much to do with Ye's prestige and PLA connections, but probably more with his formal position as a Party Vice Chairman and the only member of the Politiburo Standing Committee from whom Hua could expect support. Yet for all Ye's loathing of the radicals, and notwithstanding claims of the need for him to stiffen Hua's spine from the outset, as we have seen the most persuasive sources indicate that it was Hua who took the initiative. The dating of Ye's direct approaches to Hua in response, as with so much else in this period, is uncertain, but the best evidence indicates this occurred on September 21.[79] According to Hua, this was one of only two occasions when Ye visited his home, with the other probably happening in early October, although there presumably would have been other opportunities in Zhongnanhai after Politburo meetings, although Ye apparently did not attend all of them. In Hua's memory, the exchange on the 21st involved their joint research on how to solve the "gang" issue. Ye also reportedly visited Wang Dongxing in Zhongnanhai on several unspecified occasions, as well as phoning him concerning Mao's documents and dispatching Wang Zhen, who had very good historical relations with the younger Wang. Whatever the precise accuracy of these details, Ye's counsel undoubtedly was an important factor in Hua's decision to opt for the "quick and clean" solution which drew Deng Xiaoping's praise shortly after the coup.[80]

In the absence of truly satisfactory information on Ye's activities, it is still possible to reconstruct an overview, both as it applies to this crucial period just after Mao's funeral as well as earlier, and to early October when concrete plans

---

[78] Wu De, "Guanyu fensui 'sirenbang'," pp. 57-58.

[79] "Yize zhongyao kaoding," p. 74. Other accounts place Ye's visit to Hua as early as September 16 (see above, p. 562n63), or on the 25th, when Ye assertedly told Hua that the conflict with the "gang" was a life and death struggle, advised him to talk to more old comrades, and promised their support and that of the military. In this version, Ye visited Hua again the following day, and the two men discussed the state of the struggle, agreed the "gang" was a "counterrevolutionary clique," and Ye proposed arresting them and placing them under investigation. See Ji Xichen, "Fensui 'sirenbang' quanjing xiezhen," p. 10.

[80] See Wu De, "Guanyu fensui 'sirenbang'," pp. 57, 64; and Fan Shuo, "The Tempestuous October," pp. 16-17, 19.

to arrest the "gang" were put in place. Despite some dubious claims that Ye issued orders in specific situations (see below), in general his role was offering advice, somewhat in the tradition of a mafia *consigliari*. This goes to the heart of the question of formal *v.* informal power. In the military system in particular, procedures were so highly centralized that any unit larger than a company (*lian*) could not be moved without the permission of the MAC—and Chen Xilian, with whom Hua consulted four times on the "gang" issue, had authority over that body. Indeed, as we shall see, in the critical days before October 6 it was Chen, not Ye, who authorized the decisive arrangements concerning the PLA securing the Beijing area. Ye Jianying was identified in his MAC role as Vice Chairman, as well as Minister of Defense, when meeting former US Defense Secretary James Schlesinger on September 27, a meeting specifically arranged by Hua, but it was unclear whether he was actually functioning in these roles. As *consigliari*, Ye's contribution was to encourage and support Hua in his determination to "solve" the question of the radicals, consider various concrete measures, and reassure him of the broad support he could expect from the military and the senior generation of Party leaders generally. The old army veterans were important, but, as a senior Party historian put it, less for anything they actually did during the process of purging the "gang" than because Hua could have confidence in their support. The outcome, in any case, relied more importantly on the actual PLA command structure, which was not in Ye's hands, acting in a supportive manner. There were certainly enough military officers with intense loyalty to Mao who might have behaved differently under conflicting orders, but they were not put to the test. Meanwhile, with the seemingly single exception of Ye, the cream of the older generation of military leaders knew nothing of what was afoot apart from soothing words from the old marshal, such as he conveyed to Nie Rongzhen, that they should relax.[81]

As the anti-radical forces moved into serious plotting mode, what was the "gang of four" up to? Of course, in the official version they were frantically planning for a showdown, but in fact their activities amounted to uncertain reflections on

---

[81] See Wu De, "Guanyu fensui 'sirenbang'," p. 60; Qing and Fang, *Deng zai 1976*, vol. 2, p. 205; Fan Shuo, "The Tempestuous October," pp. 18-19; *RMRB*, September 28, 1976, p. 1; and interview, November 2002. An indication of Ye's informal rather than executive role was his sending a staff member after Mao's death to Air Force Deputy Commander Zhang Tingfa, who was in the hospital, to advise Zhang to "look after his troops." Zhang interpreted this as a warning against possible radical action, but it clearly was not an order for any concrete action. Zhang went on to say that a short while later the MAC convened a meeting, and Chen Xilian announced the "smashing of the 'gang of four'." Zhang Tingfa, "70 niandai zhongqi liangci junwei huiyi," p. 68.

On the Ye Jianying-Chen Xilian relationship, the evidence is mixed. A well-placed oral source claims Chen greatly respected Ye, and even deferred to him during 1976. Interview, July 1997; and above, p. 446. While we do not doubt the respect, our general impression is of limited Chen-Ye contact throughout this crucial year, and Ye's question to Li Xiannian concerning Chen's reliability clearly indicates distance on the old marshal's part. According to Li, however, Chen did pay a visit to Ye at Li's urging sometime after September 14. Cheng Zhensheng, "Li Xiannian yu fensui 'sirenbang'," p. 49.

what was going on around them, pushing the propaganda themes of the Cultural Revolution and the anti-Deng campaign—both still official Party policy—and a number of foolish self-indulgences that could only harm their cause. In the period after Mao's funeral to the end of September, the Politburo radicals engaged in conversations with, or conveyed messages to, their followers in Shanghai on at least six occasions. While excerpts from these exchanges, largely based on confessions and interrogations of these local radicals, are undoubtedly genuine, the reported content of the "gang's" messages consists of general exhortation and assessments of the current situation, rather than any action plan. A sampling of these exchanges includes Xu Jingxian reporting to Zhang Chunqiao on the 21st the concerns of Nanjing Military Region Commander Ding Sheng, raised by Ding *in August*, and also that the local radicals in Shanghai had been speculating among themselves who would get what in the expected leadership reorganization in Beijing. Zhang's reported contribution to the conversation was simply to warn the Shanghai comrades to be careful and pay attention to class struggle. In another instance, Wang Hongwen phoned the Shanghai leaders on the 23rd, calling on them to increase their vigilance and musing that there were some in Beijing who wanted to bring Deng back. And on the 28th, in a development that, similar to the October 4 *Guangming Daily* article, would come to be attacked as a signal for an armed seizure of power, Zhang reportedly dispatched Wang's secretary to Shanghai with warnings that the city might come under attack, that they must be ready to fight, and the question was who would win.[82]

These messages—actually, carefully culled excerpts of messages—did indicate anxiety and the need for vigilance, but almost entirely against vaguely defined revisionist forces in the Party Center rather than specific individuals, and were basically devoid of concrete proposals. Moreover, specific complaints, for example by Wang on September 21, concerned differences over matters such as the disposal of Mao's body, rather than fundamental issues. Overall, the attitude of the "gang" seemed somewhat less tense than that conveyed by the rhetoric recycled by the post-purge authorities. Thus, in Zhang's conversation with Xu Jingxian on the 21st, an occasion when Xu came to Beijing for a health conference rather than to plot with the "gang," Xu enquired whether any major meetings would be convened soon, a clear reference to the Central Committee's Third Plenum that would have to be called to ratify new leadership arrangements. Zhang simply replied that none were presently scheduled, arguably an indication that the Politburo radicals were not at that point pushing for such a potentially divisive encounter. Similarly, on the 27th, Zhang wrote to Shanghai noting that at present the Center had a collective leadership, and pending a decision on the fifth volume of Mao's *Selected Works*, they might proceed with a separate selection of their own that would emphasize the five requirements for (younger)

---

[82] See Chen and Du, *Shilu*, vol. 3, part 2, pp. 1415-17; Qing and Fang, *Deng zai 1976*, vol. 2, pp. 140-42; *A Great Trial*, pp. 77, 80-82, 192; and Forster, "China's Coup," p. 283.

successors. Perhaps most revealing of the "gang's" state of mind was the private exchange on September 25 between Zhang and Yao Wenyuan quoted at the start of this chapter. Zhang and Yao not only considered that the leadership would be collective and Hua, at least for the time being, would be the leader, it was against a background in which they both rejected Wang Hongwen's leadership pretensions as simply unsustainable given his lack of ability and morals. All of this hardly suggests a close knit group ready to make a bid for power.[83]

If, in fact, the "gang's" activities were not immediately threatening, a series of actions on their part contributed to the alarms and sheer annoyance of Hua and his Politburo colleagues. It is difficult to underestimate the antagonism created by Jiang Qing's overbearing manner, something other leaders had put up with for a decade, and which was now typified by her continuing recriminations against Hua for his sealing of Mao's documents. Other developments, even political activities the radicals presumably were entitled to undertake, e.g., visits to PLA units in the Beijing area over the September 26-28 period by Wang, Zhang (both members of the MAC Standing Committee), and Politburo member Jiang, were undoubtedly looked upon with great suspicion. Even arguably innocent developments, such as Wang Hongwen moving his residence to the Western Hills, were regarded as suspect, in this case as a move to spy on Ye, who reportedly then moved his own residence as a result. On top of this, the continuing drumbeat of official propaganda, as in several prominent articles denouncing the "three weeds," would also have sustained unease, notwithstanding the fact that these efforts were still in line with the Party's declared ideology.[84]

Against this background, the Politburo met for the last time before the arrest of the "gang" on September 29. Official accounts give this meeting a special place both in terms of the aggressive behavior of the radicals, and, by implication, in firming up Hua's determination to act. Indeed, according to one account, Hua claimed that the wrangling with Jiang Qing on the 29th led him to conclude that the "gang" was making it impossible for work to continue. Yet if Hua is to be believed, he had already decided to act during his discussions with Li Xiannian and Wu De on the 26th. A closer scrutiny of the meeting itself, moreover, indicates that the accepted descriptions of its content, and especially the radicals' actions, are also seriously flawed. In the standard retelling, several contentious issues dominated the meeting: the radicals' insistence that Mao Yuanxin not be sent back to Liaoning, but instead remain in the capital to use the Chairman's papers to prepare a report for the coming plenum; Mao's "deathbed exhortation" concerning the "principles laid down"; (to a lesser extent) how to celebrate National Day; and, most explosively, the issue of the new leadership

[83] See Chen and Du, *Shilu*, vol. 3, part 2, pp. 1415-17; "Xu Jingxian de chubu jiefa jiaodai," p. 8; Qing and Fang, *Deng zai 1976*, vol. 2, pp. 139ff, 200-201; and Forster, "China's Coup," pp. 281-82.

[84] See Ji Xichen, "Fensui 'sirenbang' quanjing xiezhen," p. 10; Forster, "China's Coup," p. 283; *RMRB*, September 28, 1976, in *SPRCP*, no. 6198 (1976), pp. 82-84; and *GMRB*, September 29, 1976, in *SPRCP*, no. 6198 (1976), pp. 79-81.

of the Center, with Zhang Chunqiao demanding that Jiang Qing's "working position be settled," and in some versions that she become the new Party leader. According to this story, Hua repulsed the "gang's" demands with the staunch backing of Ye, Li and Wang Dongxing. In each respect, however, the implication of a confrontation of opposing forces was exaggerated or completely distorted, as we have already seen in the case of the "principles laid down." In the case of the National Day celebrations, there were indeed different opinions, with radicals arguing for a study forum on Mao's works in the hall on top of Tiananmen gate, against the general preference for a more orthodox ceremony in the Great Hall, but with the Politburo majority conceding to the "gang's" wishes on this issue. The renowned conflicts, though, reportedly concerned Mao Yuanxin's assignment and Jiang Qing's work.[85]

The evidence indicates that the question of Mao Yuanxin's role did produce conflict at the meeting, but the issue was more complicated than that provided in standard accounts. First, it is necessary to understand that the proposal for Mao Yuanxin to return to Liaoning was his own request, not something initially decreed by Hua, and thus something suggesting Mao Yuanxin's less than total identification with the "gang." When the matter was initially proposed, Hua solicited Jiang Qing's view, and she agreed to Mao Yuanxin's request. Subsequently, however, Mao Yuanxin put his request in writing on September 28 (something that led Jiang to rebuke him for not consulting with her first), and on the 29th, Jiang Qing, with the support of Zhang Chunqiao but apparently not Wang Hongwen or Yao Wenyuan, now demanded that Mao Yuanxin remain in the capital to help prepare for the Central Committee plenum and sort the Chairman's documents, as well as to deal with Mao's domestic affairs. Despite their common position, during the discussion Zhang reminded Jiang that she had agreed to Mao Yuanxin's return to Liaoning. In any case, the remaining members of the Politburo unanimously supported Hua's proposal that Mao Yuanxin should still return to Liaoning, but he could return to Beijing for central meetings if the Center "needs him to participate in work." But Jiang typically could not let the matter rest, saying it was a question for the Chairman's family, and continuing to argue with Hua. In pursuing the issue Jiang said others could leave if they wanted, but Wang Dongxing stayed behind. Far from Jiang ordering others from the meeting as sometimes claimed, it was apparently another case of Jiang trying the patience of all concerned. Once again, this included Jiang's radical colleagues. At their last Politburo meeting, as events headed toward the dramatic denouement of October 6, there was no unified radical force.[86]

---

[85] See Ji Xichen, "Fensui 'sirenbang' quanjing xiezhen," p. 11; Fan Shuo, "The Tempestuous October," p. 19; Yan and Gao, *Turbulent Decade*, p. 521; Qing and Fang, *Deng zai 1976*, vol. 2, pp. 222-23, 225; *PR*, no. 41 (1976), p. 5; Forster, "China's Coup," pp. 284-85; MacFarquhar, "Succession," p. 309; and Onate, "Hua Kuo-feng,", p. 551.

[86] Wu De, "Guanyu fensui 'sirenbang'," pp. 54-55; Ji Xichen, *Shi wu qianli de niandai*, vol. 2, p. 798; Qing and Fang, *Deng zai 1976*, vol. 2, pp. 221-23, 227; "Jianzheng Zhuxi zuihou shike, Mao

The even more serious, but less sustainable accusation was that the radicals attempted to secure Jiang's leadership of the Party at this time, much as they allegedly had done by encouraging petitions shortly after Mao's death. Apparently the issue of her work was raised, but not in such dire terms, and perhaps without formal Politburo discussion. It should be kept in mind that Jiang had no concrete portfolio, that she had basically served as a roving gadfly for Mao when he allowed her to carry out this function, and that the Chairman had generally denied her more specific responsibilities. If the issue went beyond this to an attempt to claim the leadership of the CCP as asserted by Fan Shuo, one would have expected it to have been emblazoned on the memories of those participating in the meeting. On the contrary, two leaders with deep antipathy to the "gang" made no reference to any such bid for power in their recollections. Interviewed in 1984, Wang Dongxing recalled the differences of opinion on the relatively low-tension question of how to celebrate National Day, but did not mention any attempt to nominate Jiang as Party leader. Wu De, in his posthumously published recollections, discussed the Mao Yuanxin conflict, but, like Wang Dongxing, had nothing at all to say concerning a new work assignment for Jiang Qing. We can only conclude that whatever transpired on this question was not of great moment, and, as with so much else, has been distorted to paint a picture of wild, impatient ambition on the part of the radicals.[87]

By National Day, plotting for the coup picked up momentum, while the radicals continued to blunder with inept political moves. In addition to Yao Wenyuan's attempted compromise by restricting the "principles laid down" to media outside the *People's Daily*, activities by Jiang Qing and Wang Hongwen in particular seemingly raised concern, and were certainly depicted in a sinister light following the arrest of the radicals. Jiang, as official propaganda would

---

Yuanxin yuanhe bei baohu shencha" [Having Witnessed the Chairman's Last Moments, Why Mao Yuanxin Was Put under Protective Custody], http://1000site.com/75/19207.html; and interview with Party historian studying the events, July 1997.

The question of Mao Yuanxin's return to Liaoning raises perplexing questions regarding the late Chairman's apparent wish for his nephew to play a key role in the new leadership (see above, p. 496). If this was the case, why did Mao Yuanxin propose to return to the Northeast, and the "gang," at least initially, raise no objections? We can only speculate. One possibility is that the Chairman's wishes were only expressed within his household, perhaps to Zhang Yufeng individually, and never presented to the Politburo. Even if Politburo members were aware of them, Mao Yuanxin's position more properly would have been a matter for a Central Committee plenum. From Mao Yuanxin's perspective, his proposal may have reflected the need for a break after an exhausting and emotional year, with the expectation that he would soon return to Beijing, while by the end of September Jiang and Zhang may have expected that the plenum would soon be upon them, thus requiring Mao Yuanxin's presence. Alternatively, Mao Yuanxin may have genuinely desired to return to his home and family, given that his main task as his uncle's liaison had now lapsed.

[87] See Fan Shuo, "The Tempestuous October," p. 19; Qing and Fang, *Deng zai 1976*, vol. 2, pp. 224-25; Wu De, "Guanyu fensui 'sirenbang'," p. 55 and *passim*; and "Hua Guofeng, Ye Jianying deng jiejian Shanghai Ma Tianshui dengren de jianghua," p. 1. We believe it is likely that the matter was raised more informally outside of the Politburo despite Fan Shuo's claim, and that it reflected Jiang's frustration after Hua denied her access to Mao's documents.

colorfully put it, "could not sit still, ran up and down and around to sell her ideas, … and even told others to save their rolls of film [of her visits] and apples for her 'extraordinary happy news' [of becoming Party leader]." Indeed, Jiang did visit universities and factories, especially Qinghua University where she made five visits around National Day, attacked Deng, declared that she would not let Chairman Mao down in the fight against capitalist roaders, and approvingly referred to powerful women in Chinese history. Wang, for his part, after having an official portrait allegedly prepared for his expected appointment as head of the NPC, went to Pinggu county outside Beijing on October 3, assertedly attacked Hua by asking what people should do if revisionists seized power at the Center, observing that more Deng Xiaoping types would emerge in the future, and answered his own question by declaring such figures must be overthrown.[88]

However much such activities may have alarmed Hua and others, post-Mao accusations clearly distorted their reality. When Jiang Qing spoke of a coming happy event, it apparently was the anticipated Central Committee plenum that would affirm the post-Mao leadership. She seemingly expected a place in that leadership, but her remark at Qinghua that Hua was Party Vice Chairman and Premier according to Mao's "crystal clear" suggestion, far from indicating that she was preparing to leapfrog over Hua to the top post, suggested precisely the opposite succession arrangement. And Wang Hongwen, in reciting the standard radical warning against revisionism at the Center, pointed a finger, but not at Hua. The new Deng Xiaopings he referred to were "Tang Xiaoping and Wang Xiaoping," i.e., none other than the "two ladies," Tang Wensheng and Wang Hairong—Wang Hairong being the subject of particular hatred on his part. In this light, in yet another instance of "gang" ineptitude, Wang Hongwen seemingly used the occasion not as a part of a bid to "seize power," but to vent his ill feelings toward relatively low-ranking, and now basically powerless figures. Settling old scores and advancing personal hobby horses, such as the role of women, added little to the radicals' cause, while their generally shrill tone heightened animosity toward them.[89]

Charges against the radicals for military measures would be far more compelling if true. In fact, they are not true, and the actual significance of these pseudo-events is the alarm caused among the establishment beneficiaries and old revolutionaries, as well as the light shed on elite perceptions more generally. Two (perhaps conflated) incidents were reported: an alleged October 2 order from Mao Yuanxin, now back at his post in the Shenyang Military Region, to send an armored division under another rapidly promoted young officer, Sun Yuguo,

---

[88] See *RMRB*, December 17, 1976, in *SPRCP*, no. 6247 (1976), p. 6; NCNA, Beijing, December 25, 1976, in *SPRCP*, no. 6253 (1976), p. 238; Yan and Gao, *Turbulent Decade*, pp. 521, 523-24; and Chen and Du, *Shilu*, vol. 3, part 2, pp. 1417-18.

[89] See Yan and Gao, *Turbulent Decade*, p. 521; and Chen and Du, *Shilu*, vol. 3, part 2, p. 1418. On hostility between Wang Hongwen and the "two ladies," see "Xu Jingxian de chubu jiefa jiaodai," p. 1; and above, pp. 212-13.

to the capital, and maneuvers of tank units near Beijing, allegedly threatening a pincer movement on the city.[90] In both instances, Ye Jianying purportedly played an important role in foiling the radicals, in the Shenyang case by countermanding Mao Yuanxin's order, and in the Beijing case through alerting Hua.

The threat from the Shenyang troops is most easily dismissed as mere rumor. According to a Party historian who questioned Shenyang Military Region Commander Li Desheng, Li denied that any such thing happened. Subsequently, however, Sun Yuguo was relieved of his command, although not expelled from the Party. What apparently was the cause of this career setback was less anything he did in the immediate post-Mao period than the contacts he had developed with the radicals over the previous few years. A hero of the Zhenbao Island clash with the Soviet Union in 1969, Sun was promoted to the Central Committee by Mao, was an activist in the PLA General Staff Department during the campaign against Lin Biao and Confucius, and subsequently participated in the study class run by Wang Hongwen. These connections were undoubtedly the source of any suspicion concerning Sun in October 1976, and arguably contributed to the rumor of the planned attack from Shenyang.[91] The case of the tank units near Beijing has more substance, at least in terms of causing an identifiable reaction by Ye, Hua and others. According to Wu De, Hua told him on October 3 or 4 that Ye was worried about a tank division at Changping in the suburbs of Beijing. The source of this worry was that Zhang Chunqiao's brother, Zhang Qinqiao, who held a position in the PLA's GPD, frequently visited this unit. This was his practice going back a number of years, but in current circumstances it was enough to raise the old marshal's concern, even though investigations after the arrest of the "gang" found that this was an imaginary threat. In contrast to the false rumor concerning the Shenyang troops which claimed Ye had issued an order to stop their march, Ye did go to Hua, who in turn consulted Wu De about the capacity and reliability of the Beijing Garrison forces to repel any threat from the tank units. Wu assured Hua that Garrison Commander Wu Zhong was reliable, and undertook to check with him concerning capacity. Ye Jianying thus only brought the matter to the attention of the formal authorities, rather than dealing with it himself.[92]

[90] See Yan and Gao, *Turbulent Decade*, p. 522; Fan Shuo, "The Tempestuous October," p. 21; Forster, "China's Coup," pp. 283, 287; and Onate, "Hua Kuo-feng," p. 555.

[91] Interview, November 2002. This is supported by the fact that the most reliable chronologies make no reference to this incident. See Chen and Du, *Shilu*, vol. 3, part 2, p. 418; and Ma Qibin, *Sishinian*, pp. 405-406. On Sun Yuguo, see Liu, "Gang of Four," p. 819. An improbable account of an alleged September 21 conversation among Mao Yuanxin, Wang Hongwen and Xu Jingxian concerning the use of Shenyang troops is given in Qing and Fang, *Deng zai 1976*, vol. 2, p. 156.

[92] Wu De, "Guanyu fensui 'sirenbang'," p. 59; and interview with specialist on the period, November 2002. Concerning Ye issuing formal orders or otherwise, the most authoritative claim of any such instance concerns an October 5 directive (*zhishi*) to the army to raise its vigilance and obey orders. This directive was reportedly given to GPD deputy head Liang Biye and Acting Chief-of-Staff Yang Chengwu. From the description, this directive was general in nature, rather than related to the actions

As the "gang of four" indulged in acts that antagonized their enemies, did little to build support beyond their dedicated followers, and, rhetorical assertions of the need to be ready for class struggle notwithstanding, remained totally unprepared for the coup against them, Hua, Ye and others prepared for the decisive moment. Clearly a decision to arrest the "gang" and place them in isolation had been reached sometime in the last ten days of September after discussions between Hua and Ye on the 21st, and among Hua, Li Xiannian and Wu De on the 26th. While the precise timing, sequence and participants cannot be stated with certainty, and some improbable claims exist in the literature, by the start of October planning began among a small group of officials including Hua, Ye, probably Li Xiannian, Wang Dongxing, Wu De, Chen Xilian, Su Zhenhua, Wu Zhong, Yang Chengwu, and Wang Dongxing's subordinates in the Center's General Office and security forces, Li Xin and Wu Jianhua, while still others, including Geng Biao and Liang Biye, were essentially told to be on notice for something important. What is notable about this list is that while it encompassed veteran PLA officials, all held executive power rather than being old revolutionaries on the sidelines—the partial exceptions being Ye and Li who had current Politburo status as well as historical prestige.[93]

A key arrangement was the establishment in the General Office of two groups personally chosen by Wang Dongxing, one under Li Xin to prepare relevant documents, and the other to be in charge of placing the "gang" under investigation. Another important step occurred on October 2, when Hua approached Wu De concerning the security of the capital, and asked about the radicals' followers in the city. Wu noted Chi Qun, Xie Jingyi and others, and they agreed these people would also be seized. Hua further warned that Beijing must not fall into chaos, and assigned Wu responsibility for ensuring stability. In another discussion, Hua told Wu the Beijing Garrison would have to secure the Xinhua News Agency, the People's Radio Station, the *People's Daily*, the airport and other important units, and that he (Wu) would take charge of the Garrison Command, an order effected by Chen Xilian using his authority in the MAC. Meanwhile, Hua told Geng Biao, who had been recommended by Ye, to be ready for an important assignment and wait at home for his personal orders.[94]

While the general planning for the arrest was kept within a narrow circle, the specific measures adopted for October 6 were kept within an even narrower group. While Ye is often given credit for moving the arrest forward during a visit to Hua following the *Guangming Daily* article on the 4th, the actual scenario

---

on the 6th, and it may in fact have been no more than informal urgings to more junior officials. Chen and Du, *Shilu*, vol. 3, part 2, p. 1420.

[93] Despite his important role earlier, Li Xiannian is listed only as probable since the sole concrete claim of his close involvement at this late stage is dubious in its details. On improbable claims concerning events in early October, see below, p. 580n95.

[94] See Wu De, "Guanyu fensui 'sirenbang'," pp. 58-60; Ji Xichen, "Fensui 'sirenbang' quanjing xiezhen," pp. 11-13; and *Geng Biao huiyilu*, pp. 289-90.

was apparently tightly held by Hua and Wang Dongxing, with Ye—rather than personally directing the arrests as sometimes claimed—only informed very late in the piece for security reasons, and others involved in the arrest only informed at the last moment. The ruse that was used, a plan to "take them by cunning," was to announce on the morning of the 6th a Politburo Standing Committee meeting for that evening to examine the final proof of Volume 5 of Mao's *Selected Works*, and to review plans for Mao's memorial hall, and subsequently, after the arrest of Standing Committee members Wang Hongwen and Zhang Chunqiao, invite Yao Wenyuan to participate on the pretext of his propaganda responsibilities, then arresting him. This scheme was proposed by Li Xin, who reportedly had already made clear to Wang Dongxing his advocacy of quick action against the radicals during the vigil following Mao's death. Li's role is yet another suggestion of Kang Sheng's hatred of Jiang Qing and Zhang Chunqiao in particular. Kang had told his then secretary Li in 1975 what others had now concluded in September-October 1976: that the "gang" issue could not be solved by normal means. In the event, Wang, Zhang and then Yao were lured to the meeting where the arrest was organized by Wang Dongxing, and the charges against them read by Hua, at least in the cases of Wang and Zhang. Shortly afterward Mao Yuanxin and finally Jiang Qing were arrested separately in their residences, and within the next 24 hours Chi Qun and Xie Jingyi were similarly placed in custody. Within an hour of the arrest of the four and Mao Yuanxin, Geng Biao was ordered to take control of the central media and communications organs. The decisive action had taken no more than 35 minutes.[95]

A striking feature of these events was the differing treatment of Mao Yuanxin from that of the "gang of four." While the very fact of Mao Yuanxin's arrest at the earliest stage indicates his importance as a target for the coup plotters, from the outset he was treated more gently than the Politburo radicals. While the "gang" was placed under isolation and investigation (*geli shencha*), Mao Yuanxin received the much milder sanction of protective custody (*baohu shencha*). Moreover, when arrested Mao Yuanxin was not subject to a bill of charges as were the four who were accused of splitting the Party.[96] Subsequently in the mid-1980s, he was released while the Politburo radicals continued to serve their long

---

[95] See Chen and Du, *Shilu*, vol. 3, part 2, p. 1420; Fan Shuo, "The Tempestuous October," pp. 21-22; Mao Mao, *"Wenge" suiyue*, p. 520; Ji Xichen, "Fensui 'sirenbang' quanjing xiezhen," p. 11; Qing and Fang, *Deng zai 1976*, vol. 2, pp. 264, 268-69; Yan and Gao, *Turbulent Decade*, p. 525; and interview with senior Party historian, February 2000. There are alternative versions of the arrests as well as various fanciful stories of other alleged events on October 5-6, including Jiang demanding the Party leadership from Hua, a mini-Politburo meeting being convened a day before the arrests, and Ye immediately notifying Deng of the outcome. See, e.g., Forster, "China's Coup," p. 288; Onate, "Hua Kuo-feng," pp. 562-63; Baum, *Burying Mao*, pp. 41, 404n50; and Garside, *Coming Alive*, pp. 153-54. Also, Wu De, "Guanyu fensui 'sirenbang'," p. 59, flatly denies reports that Ye organized the arrests through the Zhongnanhai security forces (Wang Dongxing's organization) and the Beijing Garrison Command (then under Wu).

[96] "Jianzheng Zhuxi zuihou shike, Mao Yuanxin yuanhe bei baohu shencha."

sentences. The irony, of course, is that Mao Yuanxin's influence was much more important in the Chairman's turn against Deng Xiaoping, with all the threat to elite interests that it involved. As with other matters, we can only speculate why this was so. Jiang Qing, Zhang Chunqiao and Yao Wenyuan had been centrally involved in the bitter battles of the Cultural Revolution at the Center, while Mao Yuanxin, although very radical in Liaoning, had been removed from the capital for all but the last year of the Chairman's life. The "gang of four" including Wang Hongwen were the public face of radicalism, as well as participating in the key radical developments of 1972-76, while again Mao Yuanxin's less visible role in national affairs was restricted to less than a year. But Mao Yuanxin's treatment may also have reflected a belief that he was basically the Chairman's liaison, carrying out his uncle's wishes with minimal personal animus toward establishment leaders, as well as having his own conflicts with the "gang." It might further have been the case that his status as a member of the Chairman's family protected him—something which did not work in Jiang Qing's case given the enormous personal hostility she engendered, despite some evidence that leniency was also considered in her case. Whatever the actual considerations, the fact remains that in October 1976 and subsequently Mao Yuanxin received markedly lenient treatment in comparison to that of the Politburo radicals.

With the arrests effected about 8 p.m., an emergency Politburo meeting was convened at 10 p.m. at Ye's residence at Mount Yuquan. Only some of the members filing in would have known what had happened, with Ji Dengkui, depicted by Wu De as "not understanding the circumstances of solving the 'gang of four' problem," particularly in the dark. Even Li Xiannian showed signs of surprise, whether feigned or not.[97] Hua and Ye reported on what had happened, and developed the theme that would be emphasized to the wider elite in the coming days: Mao had taken several steps against the "gang of four," but did not have time to accomplish their downfall, leaving the task for his successors to complete. In the discussion which followed, Ji asked whether the issue of the shortcomings of the Cultural Revolution that Mao had raised should be addressed in the document to explain the outcome. Ye, however, strongly opposed this idea as too dangerous at a time of instability, and also because it would touch on the question of evaluating Mao, a position he would maintain in many subsequent Politburo meetings while affirming the need to hold the Chairman's banner even higher. When the meeting broke up, the Politburo members were ordered to stay in Ye's compound, where they celebrated. In the case of roommates Chen Xilian, Ji Dengkui and Chen Yonggui, their joy at the outcome was expressed in excited jumping about and punching one another. Meanwhile, Politburo members

---

[97] See Wu De, "Guanyu fensui 'sirenbang'," p. 58; Cheng Zhensheng, "Li Xiannian yu fensui 'sirenbang'," p. 51; and Qing and Fang, *Deng zai 1976*, vol. 2, p. 348. Wu De (p. 62), however, claims that Hua, Ye and Li had informed an "absolute majority" of members of the arrest prior to the meeting. In addition, Wang Dongxing and Wu De gave conflicting stories to Party historians on whether Li knew of the arrest arrangements beforehand; interview, February 2000.

based outside of the capital were informed by phone, and measures were taken to inform important departments and selected old revolutionaries. On the 7th, Chen Yun reportedly was told by Wang Zhen, who had himself been informed by Hua that morning, but claims of Ye immediately informing Deng are clearly false. Rather than receiving a message from Ye, according to Deng's daughter, Deng first heard of the news as a rumor from family connections on the 7th, and the Deng household retreated to the toilet for security, excitedly discussing the news over the noise of cautionary flushing. Only after ascertaining confirmation several days later was Deng completely convinced, and he then penned his first letter of fealty to Hua on October 10. Not long afterward, Deng expressed his appreciation of Hua's decisive action to Li Xiannian, Wu De and Chen Xilian: "This was a good way [to deal with the "gang of four"], quick and clean!"[98]

The celebrations and relief could not obscure the daunting tasks ahead. Neutralizing the radicals' strongest base in Shanghai was an immediate priority. Even more fundamental was creating a coherent story to explain to the broader elite and general populace such an unprecedented event: the arrest of fully a quarter of the sitting full Politburo members, including the late Chairman's wife. However widespread and intense the distaste for the radicals as individuals and for their political program, significant segments of both the leadership at all levels and the public would be hostile, dubious, or simply confused by what had been done. It would be no easy task.

The Aftermath: Stabilizing Shanghai and Producing a Rationale

After hearing Hua and Ye report on the arrest of the "gang," the Politburo meeting on the night of October 6-7 unanimously decided that Hua would be the new Party and MAC Chairman. Although this was only publicly confirmed at the time of the mass rally to celebrate the "smashing of the 'gang of four'" on October 24, the signs were apparent almost immediately. On October 8, the decision was taken to proceed with the publication of Volume 5 of Mao's *Selected Works* (the agenda item that drew the three radicals to their fateful encounter, along with the construction of the Chairman's memorial hall in Tiananmen Square which was also authorized on the 8th) under the "direct leadership of the [Politburo] headed by Comrade Hua Guofeng," while on October 10 the formula "the Central Committee headed by Comrade Hua Guofeng" appeared in the authoritative joint editorial of the *People's Daily*, *Red Flag* and the *PLA Daily*. While Hua's

---

[98] "Hua Guofeng, Ye Jianying zai Zhonggong zhongyang zhengzhiju huiyishang de jianghua" [Speeches of Hua Guofeng and Ye Jianying at the CCP Politburo Meeting] (October 6, 1976), in *CRDB*, p. 1; Wu De, "Guanyu fensui 'sirenbang'," pp. 62, 64; Ji Xichen, "Fensui 'sirenbang' quanjing xiezhen," p. 18; Fan Shuo, "The Tempestuous October," p. 21; *Chen Yun nianpu, xia juan*, pp. 204-205; Mao Mao, *"Wenge" suiyue*, pp. 523-24; and interview with historian close to Chen Yonggui, November 2002. According to Hua's recollection, Ji Dengkui did not immediately inform the State Council, earning Ji the new leader's criticism. Zhang Gensheng, "Hua Guofeng tan fensui 'sirenbang'," p. 3.

elevation was undoubtedly a foregone conclusion, according to one source, Hua offered the Party chairmanship to Ye Jianying, but Ye declined, observing that he was merely a soldier and not suited to handling civilian affairs. Ye's modesty was undoubtedly genuine, as well as an accurate reflection of his abilities, but surely, as with so much else, Mao's decisions throughout 1976 had determined the outcome.[99]

With these decisions made, the new leadership moved quickly to deal with the two key immediate challenges: to mop up the "gang's" following, and to provide an explanation for the stunning dispatch of the radicals. The latter undertaking, which we examine subsequently, began with a week-long meeting from October 7 to 14 which summoned key provincial and military region leaders to Beijing where, along with leading officials from central Party, government and PLA organs, they were briefed by Hua, Ye and others. In one account, in addition to placing Mao Yuanxin, Chi Qun and Xie Jingyi in custody, the former task saw the arrest of 30 "close followers of the 'gang'" including members of the *Liang Xiao* writing group and Minister of Culture Yu Huiyong in the next few days following the seizure of the Politburo radicals. But the critical task would be to deal with the key local base of the "gang," Shanghai, although, as far as we can tell, the other locality regarded as a radical stronghold, Liaoning, did not cause the same level of concern. The relative monopoly of municipal power by local radicals in Shanghai meant simple strategic arrests were not an option, and, in Garside's words, Hua opted for a more subtle strategy of "deception, cajolery, and ... half-promises," a strategy which once again demonstrated the less than total community of interests between the "gang" in Beijing, and their followers in Shanghai. Indeed, according to one often reliable source, in late September Hua identified Shanghai radicals Ma Tianshui and Xu Jingxian, as well as Nanjing Military Region Commander Ding Sheng, in a group of people who could be neutralized, as opposed to Mao Yuanxin, Chi Qun and others who had to be attacked. This indeed was the approach to Ma who was immediately summoned to the October 7-14 meeting, along with top local leaders from other areas.[100]

Once the "gang" had been arrested, the inability of the Shanghai group to contact them or find out about their situation caused alarm and panic, but with news of the arrest filtering back from sources in Beijing, various plans were drafted over the following week, including the mobilization of the militia. This

---

[99] Chen and Du, *Shilu*, vol. 3, part 2, pp. 1420-21; Forster, "China's Coup," pp. 288-89; *PR*, no. 42 (1976), pp. 3-4, 6-7; Fan Shuo, *Ye Jianying zai 1976*, pp. 393-94; interview with scholar specializing on Ye, July 1977; and interview with person close to Ye's family, March 1997.

[100] See Chen and Du, *Shilu*, vol. 3, part 2, p. 1422; Garside, *Coming Alive*, p. 155; and Qing and Fang, *Deng zai 1976*, vol. 2, p. 194. Concerning the apparent lack of any drama in Liaoning, we can only speculate that the key factor was the ultimate dominance of military power in the province as reflected in the positions of Politburo member and Shenyang Military Region Commander Li Desheng, and Liaoning Party First Secretary and Shenyang Military Region Political Commissar Zeng Shaoshan, and perhaps most of all through the ongoing influence of former long-serving region commander Chen Xilian.

formed the basis of the claim that an armed rebellion had been initiated in the city, a charge that was in effect pre-dated to include activities concerning militia affairs by Wang Hongwen and Zhang Chunqiao before their arrest. Eventually, of all the evil deeds the "gang" were accused of for the 1972-76 period, only Shanghai's "armed rebellion" remained as a "major crime" in the accusations brought at the 1980-81 trial of the "two cliques," and Wang and Zhang were convicted of this charge. While Zhang maintained his posture of refusing to speak on this as well as other matters throughout the trial, Wang, who as we have seen, was willing to admit virtually anything else and acknowledged statements linking the militia to fighting revisionists, denied involvement in any plot for an uprising. For his part, Yao Wenyuan's defense was to deny any role in such activities which, he implied, were the business of Wang and Zhang. But more telling than denials of guilt are both the ample evidence canvassed earlier that the whole militia issue was created by Mao, and that any mobilization after Mao's death was part of a national alert. Moreover, for all the rhetoric of preparing for class struggle, Shanghai's leaders were totally unprepared for the situation which emerged on October 6. Despite the infusion of weapons since 1973 and local bravado after the arrest, the Shanghai militia was in disarray, with concrete preparations severely hobbled by, for example, out-of-date local maps unable to serve a useful purpose.[101]

This does not gainsay that some Shanghai leaders and their radical followers prepared for a showdown, apparently believing that revisionists had seized control of the Party Center, and fidelity to Mao required resistance whatever the cost. The activities of these local radicals have been well chronicled elsewhere, and it is only necessary to note here some of the major resistance activities. On October 8, with Ma Tianshui in Beijing, Xu Jingxian and Wang Xiuzhen convened an emergency meeting that decided to mobilize the militia. On October 12, some Shanghai officials decided to publish a message to the city and whole country outlining the radical case, and on the same day others planned strikes, parades and demonstrations, even threatening to blow up bridges and fight in the manner of the Paris Commune. But all of this petered out without significant disruption, in large part because the key local leaders had indeed been neutralized or cowed. In addition to the pressure brought on Ma in Beijing, on the 9th he was induced to summon Xu and Wang to the capital, where all three were then subjected to the Center's persuasion. When the three leaders returned to Shanghai on the 13th, they adopted an evasive posture concerning what had happened to the "gang" rather than mobilize resistance, and by that evening, as the city's Party committee absorbed the gist of the meeting in Beijing, the consensus was that "everything

---

[101] See *A Great Trial*, pp. 18ff, 78-82, 108-10, 113, 114-15, 224, 226; Qing and Fang, *Deng zai 1976*, vol. 2, pp. 280, 356ff; Garside, *Coming Alive*, pp. 155ff; Forster, "China's Coup," pp. 289-90; Perry, *Patrolling the Revolution*, p. 255; "Wang Xiuzhen de jiefa jiaodai," p. 4; and above, pp. 83-84, 258, 529-30.

is over and finished."[102]

Meanwhile, the response of the local population in Shanghai to the uncertain situation was generally wait and see, neither supporting resistance, nor displaying a hopeful anticipation that the radicals had fallen. When news of the demise of a "gang of four" was broadcast on October 14, people reportedly were puzzled by the still unexplained reference. But by the 15th, with wall posters naming the four, all resistance activities seemingly stopped, popular enthusiasm for the coup emerged, and on the 21st the new local leadership of Su Zhenhua, Ni Zhifu and Peng Chong arrived to take effective control. Su represented military control, Peng, the Party leader from neighboring Jiangsu, provided local knowledge, and Ni, as a worker on the Politburo and the head of the Beijing workers militia, offered a bridge to the Shanghai working class, part of which proved reluctant to denounce Wang Hongwen. This team, probably deliberately, also represented the Cultural Revolution three-way alliance of the PLA, revolutionary cadres and mass representatives. Moreover, in accord with the sophisticated handling of the situation, Ma Tianshui *et al.* did not immediately disappear. Confessions concerning their involvement in radical activities and what they could reveal about the "gang" were required in inner-Party forums in November, but it was only in mid-December that they disappeared from the public stage.[103]

Beyond illuminating the events in Shanghai after October 6, the confessions of the local radicals are revealing for what they tell us about the larger pattern of relations between the Politburo radicals and their supporters in China's largest city. Despite the obvious ideological sympathies and overlapping interests, the sense of distance between the two groups we have seen in other contexts is reinforced by these confessions, as well as by the persuasion (including assurances that they continued to be trusted by the Center) directed at Ma, Xu and Wang Xiuzhen during the October 7-14 meeting. A major factor, as previously indicated, was the lack of full understanding on the part of the Shanghai leaders of the highly secretive politics at the Center. According to the Shanghai group, "in front of us [the 'gang'] displayed great respect for the Premier," and led us to believe they supported Hua, behavior the city's leaders now dutifully declared "two faced." While local radicals had followed the ups and downs of the four as best they could, they, like ordinary people, claimed to have never heard of a "gang of four," and were only now told that Mao had coined this term for Jiang Qing *et al.* The Shanghai leaders were also shown distorted "evidence" in the form of Zhang's February diary note that, contrary to their own understanding, was presented as proving Zhang's bitter opposition to Hua's initial elevation to Acting Premier. As

[102] See *A Great Trial*, pp. 192-95; Chen and Du, *Shilu*, vol. 3, part 2, p. 1423; Yan and Gao, *Turbulent Decade*, pp. 526-28; Garside, *Coming Alive*, pp. 156ff; Forster, "China's Coup," pp. 289-92; and Onate, "Hua Kuo-feng," pp. 556-58.

[103] See Onate, "Hua Kuo-feng," pp. 557-58; Forster, "China's Coup," p. 292; Perry, *Patrolling the Revolution*, p. 256; and Garside, *Coming Alive*, pp. 164-65. At the popular level, similar ignorance of who the "gang of four" could be was also evident in Beijing; see Baum, *Burying Mao*, pp. 41-42.

we have seen, for their own part, the Shanghai radicals, or at least Ma Tianshui, had preferred Zhang for the job, but concluded that, as a representative of the "middle," Hua was not a bad choice, an attitude they had reason to believe was Zhang's own.[104]

Their limited understanding of Politburo politics meant the Shanghai leaders were confused initially concerning what had happened in Beijing, and then skeptical about the explanations they were being given. One critical aspect, an aspect we have repeatedly emphasized in this study, was differentiation among the four Politburo radicals. In their initial alarm over what was going on, the local radicals speculated that Jiang Qing and Wang Hongwen might be in trouble, but they did not extend this to Zhang Chunqiao and Yao Wenyuan. With Jiang, the apparent calculation was that her excesses and trouble making had finally led to retribution. With Wang, his wastefulness, lack of diligence, and generally perceived low moral standard was telling. As noted earlier, when it became clear that all four had been arrested, the actions against Jiang and Wang were more or less accepted by these leaders who seemed to believe they probably deserved it, but they doubted the culpability of Zhang and Yao, as seen in Ma Tianshui's view that their contradictions should be treated differently. Of particular interest is the continued reluctance to accept the guilt of Zhang, clearly the most hated figure in the inner circle in Beijing after Jiang. Certainly Ma had special reason to be loyal, since Zhang had rescued him during the early stages of the Cultural Revolution when he, like most old cadres in the municipal apparatus, came under harsh attack. But it is also probably the case that Ma and the others had no evidence of any illicit acts by Zhang, thus believing only that he held fast to his understanding of Mao's line. According to one report, it was only when Chen Xilian, Su Zhenhua and Ni Zhifu came to Ma on October 11 with Zhang's February note that Ma dropped his support of Zhang.[105]

If there were problems in persuading the Shanghai radicals concerning justification for what had transpired on October 6, there were also difficulties in presenting a coherent explanation to the wider high-ranking elite who had been equally, if not more, ignorant of internal politics in Zhongnanhai. Providing such an explanation was the main task of the October 7-14 conference of leading central, provincial, and regional military officials. However little love lost there was for the "gang" among these officials, we must again emphasize that the

---

[104] "Hua Guofeng, Ye Jianying deng jiejian Shanghai Ma Tianshui dengren de jianghua,"pp. 1, 3; "Ma Tianshui de buchong jiefa jiaodai," p. 4; Forster, "China's Coup," p. 291; and above, p. 441. The claim of no knowledge of a "gang of four" may also be suspect in view of Deng's approach to Ma in June 1975, but that approach was cautious, and there is no evidence that Deng revealed Mao's use of the concept. See above, p. 303.

[105] "Ma Tianshui de buchong jiefa jiaodai," pp. 1, 3, 7; "Ma Tianshui de jiefa jiaodai," p. 3; Forster, "China's Coup," p. 291; and above, p. 117. In addition to the meeting on the 11th, on the next day Hua, Ye and others, including Chen, Su and Ni, pressed the case against the "gang" to Ma, Xu, Wang Xiuzhen and Shanghai Garrison Commander Zhou Chunlin; "Hua Guofeng, Ye Jianying deng jiejian Shanghai Ma Tianshui dengren de jianghua," pp. 1-3.

radicals had at least a modicum of support on the basis of their appointment by Mao, and their plausible claims to represent the Chairman's line. During the week-long meeting, several lines of argument were advanced by Hua, Ye, Wang Dongxing, Li Xiannian and others. These developed the apparently brief remarks by Hua and Ye on the night of the 6th, while spreading the secrets of the Party Center much more widely than what organizational principles had tolerated over the preceding years. Perhaps most basic was simply the argument that there had been a need to act, to prevent both a Party split and disaster for the country. The emphasis was on the disruption caused by the radicals to leadership cohesion, with Mao's "three do's and three don'ts" cited prominently. Prefiguring the coming public propaganda campaign, the Politburo leaders accused the "gang" of repeatedly disrupting leadership unity, opposing Zhou and (more incredibly) Mao, preparing to seize power, and "pointing the spearhead" directly at Hua. Moreover, heavy emphasis was placed on Hua as Mao's personal choice as successor—a proposition now bolstered by Hua revealing for the first time Mao's April note that he was "at ease" with Hua in charge.[106]

Clearly, what was being invoked was the late Chairman's authority, both with regard to Hua's succession, and through claiming that Mao's alleged efforts to "solve the 'gang of four' problem" had been foiled by ill health and death. But notwithstanding the recitation of Mao's criticisms of the radicals, the Chairman's rarely articulated concept of the "gang of four" must have left the assembled leaders as confused and uncertain as the Shanghai radicals or ordinary people. If we recall the anti-radical posters at the time of the Tiananmen crisis, only three people were cited—Jiang Qing, Zhang Chunqiao and Yao Wenyuan. Indeed, one can wonder to what extent, if any, the establishment beneficiaries on the Politburo or old revolutionaries actually used the term "gang of four" in their anxious discussions since the summer. In any case, it was a convenient stick that could now be used to beat the radicals, and to try to convince skeptical leaders that Mao had indeed been intending to take measures against the four. But as with the local Shanghai radicals, there was some explaining to do to convince everyone that, as Wang Dongxing put it in November, it was necessary to arrest four, not two.[107]

There were various considerations, different from the assessment of the local Shanghai radicals, as to who might be culpable, or alternatively who should be spared from incarceration, that apparently had to be overcome. In fact, the strongest justification, as opposed to political motive, was simply Mao's "gang of four" designation, notwithstanding that the claimed need to "solve" the problem clashed with the Chairman's repeated call for unity among the factions. According

---

[106] These themes appear in "Hua Guofeng jiejian lingdao tongzhi jianghua"; "Zhongyang lingdaoren guanyu jiejue sirenbang wenti de jianghua"; and "Hua Guofeng, Ye Jianying deng jiejian Shanghai Ma Tianshui dengren de jianghua."

[107] "Hua Guofeng jiejian lingdao tongzhi jianghua," p. 1; "Wang Dongxing zai quanguo xuanchuan gongzuo jianghua," p. 3; and above, p. 488n60.

to a Party historian specializing on the period, one current of thought was that only three should be held in custody, while Jiang Qing should be spared on the basis of her "special status" as Mao's wife.[108] Another tendency pointed to the arrest of Jiang and Zhang Chunqiao, on the basis of charges raised behind the scenes since 1973 by Kang Sheng and Zhou Enlai that they had been traitors to the revolution during the pre-1949 struggle. One of the most serious possible accusations against any CCP member, the traitor charge was a significant feature of elite sentiment against the radicals in the early post-arrest period, although it would not be a feature of either public propaganda or the 1980-81 trial, and was in any case exaggerated at best. But by the same token, if Jiang and Zhang were traitors, then how could Wang and Yao, where no such evidence existed, be subject to the same treatment?[109] Whatever the force of these views, two considerations probably drove the decision to arrest all four: resentment over the various indignities of the Cultural Revolution the radicals had instigated or exacerbated, and the wish to remove from the Politburo all voices likely to introduce discordant extremist views. With Mao's "gang of four" justification in hand, Hua could play on the impulse to obey organizational discipline and accept the Party Center's *fait accompli*, even by those unconvinced by the stated rationale.

From what we know from the available extracts of the proceedings at the October 7-14 meeting, most of the discussion focused on the asserted radical threat to the post-Mao leadership and broader elite unity, and on a detailed, if highly selective, account of the "gang's" disruptive behavior over the "Cultural Revolution decade," and especially the previous few years. Here again, the influence of Mao was primary in how this story was told. Much as in the period immediately after the Chairman's death, continuity was the order of the day. This meant repeated praise for the Chairman's Cultural Revolution program, and in delicious irony, framing the radicals' sins as an attempt to overturn Mao's revolutionary line from the right. Party unity would be forged around steadfast adherence to Mao's line, and thus another continuity was calls for continuing the criticism of Deng. Thus general and specific criticism of Deng was a common feature of the meeting, drawing the endorsement of Hua and Ye, but seemingly most strongly articulated by Li Xiannian who referred to both Deng and the "gang" as "insufferably arrogant" (*buke yishi*).[110] The radicals were being denounced, but in Mao's terms, and Deng was still treated as having serious problems, with the result that the ideological line remained firmly in Cultural Revolution mode.

---

[108] Interview, November 2002.

[109] See "Hua Guofeng, Ye Jianying deng jiejian Shanghai Ma Tianshui dengren de jianghua," p. 3; and "Wang Dongxing zai quanguo xuanchuan gongzuo jianghua," p. 2. On Jiang Qing's and Zhang Chunqiao's alleged traitorous activities, see above, p. 74n125.

[110] "Zhongyang lingdaoren guanyu jiejue sirenbang wenti de jianghua," pp. 1, 3. Interestingly, if the transcripts are accurate, only Hua (once) referred to Deng as "comrade"; "Hua Guofeng jiejian lingdao tongzhi jianghua," p. 1. Cf. Li's early criticism of Deng in 1975, but also Deng's advice to Li that he should keep his distance in order to survive; above, pp. 389, 405.

What is arguably most striking is that the same type of exaggerated, often falsified material and leftist rhetoric that would be put to the public over the coming year were considered both necessary and sufficient at this critical juncture for the highest-ranking members of the elite below the very top.

Yet an unavoidable contradiction, a contradiction that would plague Hua's leadership over the next two years up to the Third Plenum at the end of 1978, was already emerging. While continuity was indeed the order of the day, the new leadership, as both past performance and future events indicated, was determined to move in new directions. Some signs can be vaguely seen at the meeting itself, with its "guiding principle" of both solving problems and stabilizing the situation implying not only leadership unity, but also social order and economic revival. The specific attack on the "gang" for disrupting the August planning forum, together with the implicit defense of the 1975 State Council theory conference, amounted to a quiet endorsement of the economic policies developed under Deng's aegis. Meanwhile, in the public realm, a similar movement and thus contradiction was developing, as seen in Wu De's speech to the rally celebrating the downfall of the "gang" on October 24. Wu rehearsed the key features of the leadership conference — the threat from the "gang's" plan to seize power, Mao's designation of Hua as his successor, due deference to Cultural Revolution rhetoric, and the imperative of unity, but gave renewed emphasis to promoting production while grasping revolution. And even while Wu reaffirmed the need to criticize Deng, in fact the campaign was quickly becoming a pale ritual, significantly decreasing in scope and intensity of media coverage. Finally, according to Wu De's testimony, at some point not too long after the arrest of the radicals, Li Xiannian, Chen Xilian and Wu visited Deng and conveyed that he would be returning to office in "at least" his previous positions. This, however, had not been canvassed at the October 7-14 meeting, and indeed was little known even at very high levels, thus contributing to the uncertainties and conflicts surrounding Deng's return in the months ahead.[111]

Over the following year, with many details of the radicals' alleged dastardly actions provided in the ongoing media onslaught, the inherent contradiction of official adherence to Cultural Revolution ideology while systematically reversing the movement's fundamental orientation deepened with ultimately disastrous

---

[111] See Chen and Du, *Shilu*, vol. 3, part 2, p. 1422; "Hua Guofeng jiejian lingdao tongzhi jianghua," pp. 1-2; *PR*, no. 44 (1976), pp. 12-14; and Wu De, "Guanyu fensui 'sirenbang'," p. 64. A survey of the media, using *SPRCP* reports and the *Renmin ribao suoyin*, revealed a sharp drop in the number of references to criticizing Deng following the purge of the "gang," particularly in central publications. The paradoxes of the process of Deng's return to work are examined in our Volume II.

An example of the contradiction in a specific policy sphere is that despite efforts to paint the "gang" as worshiping foreign things and to affirm self-reliance, propaganda guidelines stipulated acknowledging a supplementary role for imports, and avoiding criticism of Deng for selling China's resources to foreigners. See Wu De's October 24 speech in *PR*, no. 44 (1976), p. 13; and "Diantai dangqian xuanchuan koujing" [Current Propaganda Formulas for Broadcasting], handwritten document available at the Fairbank Center Library, Harvard University.

consequences for Hua. But that is a story for our Volume II. In October 1976, such a contradiction was necessary to sell the drastic measures of the 6th, and it was a contradiction readily accepted by the elite as a whole.[112]

Assessing the Politics of the Coup

After a decade of radical politics, the CCP elite, or at least a decisive majority of it, entered the post-Mao period acutely aware that (whether or not the term was actually used) there was a "gang of four" problem that somehow had to be dealt with. This did not mean that the arrest of the four Politburo radicals on the evening of October 6 was foreordained, even if it had been tentatively broached in the summer and earlier. Given the gaps and contradictions in the available sources, we cannot be confident of precisely what happened over the dramatic month following Mao's death. But, on balance, we believe the account above makes more sense of that evidence than the long-accepted narrative, and is more consistent with the logic and constraints of the fractured condition in which Mao had left Chinese politics.

One aspect of the conflict in September-October is abundantly clear: there was no attempt by the radicals to seize power. In the narrow sense, skepticism concerning a radical coup has long been expressed by observers who have noted the "gang's" military weakness and the defensive nature of their activities,[113] but the issue goes considerably beyond that. Despite the tensions of the four weeks after September 9, there is no convincing evidence that the radicals had developed *any* plan to challenge Hua's position as successor, or aspire to anything more than their current positions in the hierarchy, plus some concrete duties for Jiang Qing. Of course, as Zhang Chunqiao reportedly said on September 25, it would be necessary "to see what line [Hua] follows." But this, like proclamations of determination to oppose revisionists if they appeared in the Party Center, was a declaration of an attitude rather than an even remote indication of any plan. In addition to the absence of truly concrete preparations, the simple fact is that during this month the Politburo radicals demonstrated little fundamental solidarity, despite common positions on various issues. In contrast, the available record indicates many instances of internal bickering, as in the impatience of the other three with Jiang's initial attempt to expel Deng from the Party, or disdain as in Zhang and Yao's attitude toward Wang Hongwen's leadership pretensions. Simply put, mutual suspicions and tensions meant the "gang" was too divided to contemplate any serious threat. Similarly, although lower-level

---

[112] Most likely, the contradiction was not managed as cynically as this might imply, with Hua and others having some loyalty to Cultural Revolution ideals. This too, however, is a matter for our Volume II. For an insightful overview of the post-Mao treatment of the Cultural Revolution, see Lowell Dittmer, "Learning from Trauma: The Cultural Revolution in Post-Mao Politics," in Joseph, *New Perspectives on the Cultural Revolution*. Dittmer (pp. 21-24) describes the initial period lasting into 1978 as "tacit discontinuation, overt defense."

[113] E.g., Onate, "Hua Kuo-feng," pp. 560-61; and Forster, "China's Coup," pp. 282-83, 289-90, 294.

radicals throughout China, and especially in Shanghai, had overlapping interests with the Politburo radicals, the bonds were loose, individual tensions existed, and there was no coherent organization that could make such forces a reliable asset. In this context, the most the "gang" could do was to attempt to promote their understanding of Mao's Cultural Revolution line from within an emerging collective leadership, in the naïve expectation that this line would ultimately prevail.

As to who deserves credit for "solving the 'gang' problem," the answer is somewhat more elusive and, in particular, complex. Our verdict, as argued in the foregoing analysis, is that primary credit must go to Hua Guofeng. This is seen in the fact that, on the most reliable evidence, rather than being an indecisive leader who had to be cajoled or pressured into acting against the radicals,[114] Hua took the initiative to raise the issue with old revolutionaries Li Xiannian and Ye Jianying. It is also because, as the holder of the highest formal office, only Hua was in the position to issue orders that would be unquestionably accepted within the very limited circles involved in planning for the coup, and again the most reliable sources point to Hua's decisions on the crucial steps taken. This does not denigrate the role of Ye Jianying as adviser and presumably forceful advocate of strong action. And it is necessary to acknowledge that there is divided opinion among Party historians today as to who deserves most credit for the defeat of the radicals, with a considerable body of opinion giving priority to Ye. In our view, however, historians emphasizing Hua's role have the stronger case. To combine the observations of two senior historians: while Ye played a major role, Ye, Li Xiannian and Wang Dongxing all listened to Hua, and only Hua had the authority to order Wang's actions. In their opinion, Hua was decisive because of his position as the number one leader, and it would have been impossible to arrest the radicals if he were opposed.[115] But perhaps most persuasive in confirming Hua's primary contribution to the "smashing of the 'gang of four'" was the official 1981 Historical Resolution's ranking of the heroes of the venture as Hua, Ye and Li. While arguably unfair to Wang Dongxing,[116] the very fact that Hua retained pride of place at a time when he was being removed from the Party Chairmanship and falsely accused on all sorts of issues suggests that denying him rightful credit for his crucial role at this seminal juncture in CCP history involved more distortion than even his enemies could countenance.

[114] E.g., see Fan Shuo, "The Tempestuous October," pp. 18-19; MacFarquhar, "Succession," p. 310; and above, p. 539.

[115] Interviews, November and December 2002. In these as other interviews, scholars offered their best assessments while normally acknowledging inadequate information.

[116] Wang's role in the actual implementation of the arrest and his firm support of Hua throughout were arguably more important than Li's contribution as a messenger and adviser. One senior Party historian said his order of importance would be Hua, Ye, Wang and Li; interview, December 2002. Whatever the relative merits of Wang and Li, we believe that the official assessment of Li's role was significantly enhanced by his status as a leading old revolutionary. For the Historical Resolution's verdict, see *PR*, no. 27 (1981), p. 23.

In an important sense, the argument over assigning individual credit misses a larger story. Whatever the precise interaction between Hua and Ye and the evolution of their views on how to deal with the "gang," and despite signs of suspicion such as in Ye's enquiry concerning the reliability of Chen Xilian and Wu De, there was an essential unity of attitude toward the radicals and recognition of the need to curb their influence in elite politics. While it would have been different had Hua indeed been indecisive, once Hua and Ye clearly understood one another, it was simply a matter of considering the options, and then organizing the coup. In this, formal authority was primary, not only in that Hua could give orders to those wielding the crucial instruments of power, notably Wang Dongxing and Chen Xilian, but also in the sense that, under these circumstances, there was no need to draw on the informal power of the old revolutionaries. The PLA veterans in the Western Hills and elsewhere, except for those with active responsibilities, essentially lived in a parallel universe. Like the establishment beneficiaries, they too worried about what the radicals might do, considered "legal" options, and so forth, but there is little to suggest that any of this had a major, much less decisive, input into the plotting centering on Hua, Ye and Wang. Ye served as a link between the two groups, but his concrete role seems to have been to reassure the old revolutionaries in non-specific terms, while reassuring Hua that these influential figures of enormous Party prestige would back him. More broadly, the military was a crucial part of the equation, but only in the sense that Hua could count on the support of specific units, the active high command, and these prestigious senior revolutionaries. If Hua had refused to face up to the problem, if the radicals remained on the highest bodies for an extended period and caused ongoing political disruption, it is conceivable that the informal authority of the old revolutionaries might have come into conflict with Hua's formal authority. But since none of this transpired, the old revolutionaries were not only not called upon to exercise their informal power, they quite gratefully accepted the actions and legitimacy of the new formal leader, Hua Guofeng. The real test of formal *v.* informal authority would come with the return of Deng Xiaoping—yet another story for our Volume II.

This leaves the question of the inevitability of what eventuated on October 6. As the preceding indicates, the situation would have been very different had Hua not taken the initiative since, in the words of one of the senior Party historians cited above, it would have been impossible to arrest the "gang" in the face of Hua's opposition, or at the very least it would have led to a more protracted, divisive and perhaps bloody process. But since Hua did decide virtually immediately to confront the problem, some outcome involving at the very least the marginalization of the radicals became essentially inevitable. It is possible to imagine a minimum solution—the four radicals would hold their formal positions or something similar, but be denied any real power or functions. There were precedents for this: after the 1959 Lushan conference Peng Dehuai was dismissed from his executive posts, but was not attacked by name and continued to be listed as a Politburo member, although he was never allowed to attend the body's meetings. This would have had the benefit of presenting a façade of continuity, avoiding the problem of violating the "special status" of Mao's wife, and observing in a pale form Mao's instructions for unity.[117] But whether this was ever seriously considered, it was not practical given the unlikelihood that the radicals would have accepted such an outcome quietly, and that even their symbolic presence on the Politburo would have complicated efforts to bring order to lower levels of the Party and to the polity generally. Moreover, if there ever was a window of opportunity for such a restrained solution, it was probably lost almost immediately due to the combination of Jiang Qing's shrill demands in the Politburo,[118] petitions demanding that Jiang become the new Party leader, and particularly Wang Hongwen's duty office. As we have argued, none of this was as sinister as later asserted, but against the background of a decade of tension, it was more than understandable that Hua and others would take these developments as signs that bold action was required.

The only viable options actually considered seem to have been calling a Central Committee meeting to remove the radicals legally, or to arrest them. The only other consideration known to have been raised, and we have no indication that this ever went beyond Ji Dengkui's tentative remark on September 16, was whether all four should receive the same treatment. While we suspect that when faced with the endorsement of Hua and a solid Politburo majority, the Central Committee would have endorsed a "legal" solution, as Hua, Li and Wu De, as well as Chen Yun independently concluded, there could be no certainty concerning the outcome, and significant conflict in a divided Party would have been a likely consequence in any case. In any case, there would be a need for extensive efforts to explain the charges against the radicals whatever method was used, and given a situation in which there had been no previous opportunity to make the case, there were overwhelming attractions for initially using a carefully selected forum such as that held from October 7 to 14. The arrest of the "gang" was probably not strictly inevitable from the outset, but given both the long festering tensions within the elite, and the continuing mix of abrasive and inept behavior by the radicals over the weeks following Mao's death, the desirability of what Deng later praised as a "quick and clean" solution soon assumed an overwhelming logic.

Despite the irrefutable fact that the outcome was diametrically opposed to

---

[117] As we have seen, some Chinese officials indeed believed that if Zhou Enlai had lived, he would have opted for such a solution; above, p. 23n65.

[118] We do not underestimate the degree to which Jiang's behavior throughout this period, whether it be the initial demand to expel Deng, continued wrangling with Hua over the sealing of Mao's documents, or the sharp exchanges at the September 29 Politburo meeting, may have pushed the "solution" in ever harsher directions.

what Mao had desired, the Chairman's influence hovered over the entire process leading to the arrest of the "gang," and then over the new leadership's attempt to explain it and to chart a new course. Ultimately, the most decisive factor was that Mao had vested formal power in Hua. Over the tumultuous weeks after Mao's death, when Hua did make a decision as on the sealing of Mao's documents, it was obeyed, and as indicated, key holders of power such as Chen Xilian and Wang Dongxing looked to Hua for direction. At another level, Mao had left a time bomb of pronounced personal dislikes and conflicting political tendencies at the heart of the system, thus creating the very problem that had to be "solved." He also left an ideological line that could not be challenged, certainly not in any explicit manner. This probably contributed to both the radicals' sense that they were duty bound to persist in that line, and to a naïve sense, notwithstanding trepidations concerning their own vulnerability, that somehow this line would prevail. Once Hua *et al.* did act, the coup had to be justified in Mao's terms, with an essentially false story concocted to demonstrate that the "gang" had opposed Mao, that only ill health had prevented the Chairman from acting against them, and that they were rightists: indeed, the "bourgeoisie right in the Communist Party." This in turn meant the contradiction between emerging new policy tendencies and the perceived need to justify everything in terms of the Chairman's wishes, while all the while upholding the sanctity of the Cultural Revolution. As we shall see in Volume II, even as the overt endorsement of Mao's Cultural Revolution line faded in the coming years, the contradiction would complicate leadership politics, with the need—for Deng Xiaoping as well as Hua Guofeng—to find ultimate justification in Mao never far from the surface.

CONCLUSION

I have accomplished two things in my life. First, I fought Chiang Kai-shek for a few decades and drove him to a few islands. After eight years of war against the Japanese, they were sent home. We fought our way to Beijing, at last entering the Forbidden City. There are not many people who do not recognize these achievements. Only a few talked into my ears, urging me to recover those few islands. The other matter you all know about. It was to launch the Cultural Revolution. On this matter few support it, many oppose it. But it is not finished, and its legacy must be handed down to the next generation. How to do this? If not in peace, then in turmoil. If it is not done well, then there will be bloodshed. Only heaven knows how you are going to handle it.

— Mao's assessment of his life's work, probably in summer 1976[1]

Marshal Ye [Jianying] said that before Chairman Mao passed away he wanted to see the Politburo members in Beijing for a last time. The Politburo members in Beijing met with him one at a time, and then Chairman Mao wanted Comrade Ye Jianying to come back for another time. Marshal Ye said that by the time he went back to see Chairman Mao, Chairman Mao could no longer speak, and Chairman Mao could only fix his eyes on Marshal Ye. Ye Jianying sensed that Chairman Mao's meaning was that he had to bolster (*fuzhu*) Hua Guofeng well. This was tantamount to ... I'm entrusting Hua Guofeng to you.

— Deng Liqun's account of the last meeting between Mao and his Politburo colleagues, September 8, 1976[2]

The draft [of Ye Jianying's 1979 National Day speech] doesn't say enough about Chairman Mao's achievements. ... [All] lines, principles and policies formulated by Chairman Mao were correct, our mistakes came from not insisting on Chairman Mao's line, principles and policies. ... We all know Premier Zhou protected old cadres, but if the Chairman didn't speak Zhou couldn't protect anyone. If [Mao] didn't protect me, I wouldn't be alive [today].

— Deng Xiaoping, September 4, 1979[3]

In a fundamental sense, it comes as no surprise that following the Lin Biao affair to his own death, CCP politics from the Politburo to basic levels were shaped to a decisive degree by the purposes, attitudes and interventions of Mao Zedong. This, after all, had been the basic pattern of Party politics since the founding of the PRC in 1949, albeit with significant variations from period to period. In the early years of the regime to the onset of the Great Leap Forward, Mao's absolute authority was leavened by a real degree of "collective leadership," at least as far as policy debate before the Chairman made up his mind was concerned.[4] With the Great Leap, however, Mao no longer allowed any real debate, even denying Zhou Enlai the "right to speak" on economic issues, and subsequently when the disaster caused by the leap was apparent, it required a shift in Mao's attitude before serious measures to deal with the crisis could be undertaken by others.[5] While seemingly somewhat chastened, and allowing his Politburo colleagues to shape policy in various areas from the early 1960s, Mao retained overall control, created an ideological atmosphere in tension with pragmatic policies he now endorsed, and on occasion astounded his associates by rejecting policies they had arrived at by consensus, on the assumption these measures would be acceptable to him. This not only made life difficult for the Politburo, it also reflected the Chairman's growing discontent with both his colleagues and trends in the Chinese polity and society generally, resulting in, for the various reasons noted in the Introduction, his decision to launch the Cultural Revolution.[6]

The Cultural Revolution marked an unprecedented development in the conduct of elite politics that underlined Mao's dominance while taking it to a new level. Top leaders, and leading figures at various subordinate levels, were removed on a scale not previously seen in the PRC, and in many cases suffered grave psychological and physical abuse. Perhaps even more remarkable, the core institutions of the regime that these leaders headed experienced, virtually without exception, massive disruption that severely weakened their ability to carry out their designated functions.[7] Yet throughout all this, similar to the pre-1966 period, there is little evidence, apart from what we believe are bogus

---

[1] Wang Nianyi, *Dadongluan*, pp. 600-601. There is no documentary record of this statement or other clear evidence concerning timing, but most accounts place it on June 15, 1976, although some place it earlier in January 1976. Cf. above, p. 465n10.

[2] *Deng Liqun guoshi jiangtan*, vol. 3, p. 348. The precise date is given in Chen and Du, *Shilu*, vol. 3, part 2, p. 1406. Cf. above, p. 535

[3] "Deng Xiaoping guanyu qicao guoqing sanshi zhounian jianghuagao de tanhua jiyao," p. 1.

[4] The classic example was Zhou Enlai's May 1956 private argument to Mao concerning excessive targets, an appeal that resulted in the Chairman's anger, but soon his acceptance of the Premier's position. See Teiwes with Sun, *China's Road to Disaster*, pp. 27-28.

[5] See *ibid.*, pp. 92, 112, 213ff.

[6] See above, p. 7. For another discussion of why Mao decided to launch the Cultural Revolution, see MacFarquhar, *Origins 3*, pp. 469-73.

[7] For an overview, see Teiwes, "The Chinese State during the Maoist Era," pp. 143-48.

charges against Lin Biao, not only of any political challenge to Mao, but even of any serious self-defense by those singled out for demotion or worse by the Chairman. This reflexive obedience to a more enfeebled and more remote leader continued following the dramatic flight and death of his hand-picked successor, notwithstanding the new questions Lin's demise raised concerning the Cultural Revolution. Mao fundamentally shaped the twists and turns of the post-Lin Biao period. To a degree, he was reacting to developments he did not control, but in the largest sense Mao was attempting to set a contradictory course that upheld his 70 percent "correct" Cultural Revolution, while rectifying its 30 percent mistakes. The task was inherently impossible, and the internal tensions exploded less than a month after his passing with Hua Guofeng's decisive illegal solution. But while he lived, the Chairman could enforce a political environment in which those contradictions remained inviolate as central features of his "line."

If the underlying passivity of the top-level elite during the Cultural Revolution was astonishing to outsiders, in a sense the conduct of leadership politics during the last stage of Mao's life was even more remarkable. The Chairman's authority remained undiminished even as his health and ability to function and communicate deteriorated. As we have seen, throughout this period Mao suffered from severe ill health, although no apparent loss of mental acuity,[8] with his condition in 1972 and, of course, 1976 being particularly dire. In addition to this, he was unusually remote, being away from Beijing for eight months in 1974-75, rarely attending Politburo meetings, including none after May 1975, often communicating through family members carrying out liaison duties, and providing crucial advantages to those leaders, notably Zhou Enlai and especially Deng Xiaoping, who were able to see him in the context of accompanying foreign visitors. Beyond this, the Chairman generally chose to avoid detailed statements on issues,[9] adding to the uncertainty over what he wanted, and particularly concerning the limits of his tolerance as Politburo leaders attempted to shape policy in an environment where he only provided vague general directions. For all that, not only were all of Mao's explicit orders accepted without question, his general orientation set the

---

[8] Whatever one may think of the intellectual coherence of Mao's overall thinking during the "Cultural Revolution decade" (see above, p. 7), there is no evidence of senility. The transcripts of his meetings with Kissinger and other US leaders demonstrate command of information, and clear, logical thinking. Note especially the long encounters with Kissinger and Ford in October and December 1975 when Mao's physical deterioration was far advanced; above, p. 387.

[9] Perhaps the outstanding case is the claim of Mao's biographers that he never specifically endorsed the Lin Biao-Confucius campaign, and only provided brief and fundamentally moderate comments on its progress. While we do not challenge this assessment in the sense that the lack of a paper trail is likely, as we argued in Chapter 2, there can be no doubt that *pi Lin pi Kong* grew out of Mao's general and specific concerns as expressed in 1973, or that the radicals orchestrating its mobilization believed they were implementing his wishes.

stage for policy and political developments, leaders of all stripes felt inhibited when his views seemed to go against their interests, and everyone placed great import on reading the Chairman's intent.

Examples abound. At the onset of the *pi Lin pi Kong* movement in early 1974, the navy fell into line with Jiang Qing's instructions for the conduct of the new campaign, even though she had no military position, on the grounds that she invoked "Mao's banner," and this, together with her relationship to the Chairman, was apparently enough to convey an irresistible force for obedience. A year and a half later, in mid-1975, as Deng Xiaoping was in the process of receiving full authority from Mao, Chen Yun voiced a cautionary note, enquiring of Deng whether he was sure he understood the Chairman's meaning. For his part, Deng, as well as other leaders involved in the consolidation effort, devoted considerable time out of a busy schedule to study Mao's works, by way of seeking guidance to viable policy. Meanwhile, in the same period, Jiang was frustrated by Deng's access to Mao which allowed him to come into the Politburo and speak authoritatively, leaving her with little recourse. But when the tide turned in fall and winter 1975-76, Deng himself had little recourse but to throw himself on the Chairman's mercy, accept his mistakes (notwithstanding the misleading post-Mao effort to portray him as resisting approval of the Cultural Revolution), and prepare for his removal from the political stage. Finally, during the Tiananmen crisis, the new emerging leader, Hua Guofeng, and his Politburo colleagues, not only implemented Mao's directive to turn to "fists" to clear the Square, but throughout the crisis made decisions on the basis of protecting the Chairman's prestige.[10]

This, of course, did not eliminate all initiative by other leaders. What is striking, however, is how limited such initiative was with regard to altering overall regime direction. The overwhelming factor determining that direction was Mao's assessment of the situation. Much of the initiative exercised by others came in implementing, and sometimes overstepping, the imprecise limits of Mao's policies. The "gang of four" was particularly prone to dangerous excesses, as seen in *pi Lin pi Kong* in 1974, the dictatorship of the proletariat campaign in 1975, and *pi Deng* in 1976. However excessive the radicals' specific actions may have been—and it is usually difficult to get a precise fix on their excesses—in the broadest perspective the "gang" can be seen as fundamentally carrying out the Chairman's design. In this sense, rather than a "gang of five" including Mao and the four, at best we might speak of a "gang of one" and his loyal followers. But for the Party establishment the situation was similar, if more subtle in execution. Zhou Enlai played a particularly subtle game, always seeking to be on side with the Chairman, making discreet moves to further a trend once he understood the drift in Mao's thinking, as in encouraging He Long's widow to write to the Chairman in late 1971, and seeking to move cautiously into sensitive areas such

---

[10] See above, pp. 149-50, 166-67, 305, 322, 377, 407-409, 413-15, 481ff.

as education during the anti-"ultra-left" phase in 1972, while generally avoiding unnecessary slogans and ideological pretensions. Deng Xiaoping, perhaps misled by a broader mandate and better personal relationship with the Chairman, was less subtle, but still studied Mao's works, and was completely surprised when confronted by Mao's late 1975 judgment that he had gone too far, and was in effect negating the Cultural Revolution.[11]

In three cases, however, actors took steps designed to alter the Party's direction, and in each case had an impact on Mao that contributed to a course adjustment.[12] In the first instance, in the latter part of 1972, the Politburo radicals reacted to what they saw as excesses in attacks on "ultra-left" phenomena, especially anarchism, which they correctly interpreted as an attack on methods adopted during the Cultural Revolution. As we saw in Chapter 1, this complicated case grew out of *People's Daily* staff resistance to the views of Zhang Chunqiao and Yao Wenyuan that were hampering the anti-leftist trend, with no convincing evidence of a direct instigating role by Zhou. For their part, the radicals dealt with the matter through articles in their Shanghai publications and investigations within the *People's Daily*, and the matter came to a head only when leading *People's Daily* theory department staff member Wang Ruoshui wrote to Mao seeking guidance on the dispute. Even at this moment the radicals were fairly restrained in their position, but Mao famously decided that Lin Biao's mistakes had been "ultra-rightist," thus setting in train a gradual shift to the left. The second case, Deng's direct appeal to the Chairman in April 1975 against the disruption caused by the Mao-mandated dictatorship of the proletariat campaign and especially by Jiang Qing's behavior in the Politburo, was a somewhat bolder if arguably less important initiative,[13] and clearly influenced Mao's criticism of the radicals which began only a week later. The final, most significant initiative came not from any Politburo member, but from the Chairman's nephew in September-November 1975. In questioning Deng's commitment to the Cultural Revolution, Mao Yuanxin addressed his uncle's overriding concern, and seemingly persuaded the Chairman to review his support of Deng as the most influential "first-front" leader, and of consolidation as the Party's guiding program. While one cannot know what Mao would have done in the absence of these initiatives, it is telling that in the latter two cases

---

[11] See above, pp. 45, 56ff, 305.

[12] It could be argued that Jiang Qing's aggressive promotion of the *Water Margin* issue before and at the September 1975 Dazhai conference was another effort to influence the Chairman to alter course. In this case, however, our judgment is that her initiative had little effect, and in fact annoyed Mao, while it was only following Mao Yuanxin's initiative in late September that the Chairman started to reconsider the overall situation.

[13] While boldness can be seen in Deng's direct approach to Mao, his action took place not only against the background of the Chairman's repeated praise since late 1973, but also immediately after Mao lauded him to Kim Il Sung. See above, p. 292. Deng's action was less important in the sense that Mao had placed consolidation at the top of the agenda. Thus Deng's action served less to redirect the overall orientation than to remove impediments that had arisen, and in the process advance the new direction.

he had an unusual degree of trust in the people concerned—Deng as his favorite lieutenant at a time of particularly high regard, and Mao Yuanxin—a family member for whom he harbored long-term leadership ambitions.

In critical respects, this Mao-dominated universe can be considered the Chairman's extended family. Mao's patriarchal approach to rule was, of course, reflective of a deeply patriarchal society, but it was even more fundamentally a consequence of a long and successful revolutionary struggle. As with all other founders of indigenous communist regimes,[14] after achieving power Mao's position was unchallengeable until his death: he was truly the father of his country in the eyes of his followers. We shall return to this issue at the end of this Conclusion, but here our focus is on the relationships Mao developed with important elite figures and their implications for leadership dynamics. As noted in the Introduction, Mao's relationships with key players in the 1970s, above all Zhou Enlai and Deng Xiaoping, went back five decades. In contrast to institutionalized systems where leaders sometimes make key appointments of people they barely know,[15] the top CCP leadership in the Cultural Revolution, and only to a somewhat reduced degree thereafter, was made up almost exclusively of people with whom Mao was familiar, in key cases very familiar. This allowed all kinds of personal assessments, recollections of past services and failings, and resentments on the part of a highly judgmental Chairman, something we have repeatedly seen in the cases of Zhou and Deng. In the context of his long-standing view of Zhou's ideological weakness and contemporary jealousy of Zhou's high regard domestically and especially internationally, in 1972-74 Mao relied heavily on the Premier, never once doubted his loyalty, but treated him abominably, particularly in forcing a seriously ill Zhou to endure repeated attacks from his Politburo colleagues, including Deng. In contrast, Deng, notwithstanding the paradox of his dismissal during the Cultural Revolution and again in 1976, was by all evidence, along with Lin Biao, one of the Chairman's most favored lieutenants, admired for his toughness and military as well as administrative skills, and viewed not simply as loyal, but possessing a loyalty based on close personal

---

[14] The cases are few, encompassing Lenin, Ho Chi Minh, Tito and Castro, with the latter, of course, still to meet the "to death" criterion. Two further partial cases, partial given foreign (Soviet and Yugoslav) assistance in revolutionary success, were Kim Il Sung and Enver Hoxha. In these cases, notably, the leader was challenged and violence used to settle the issue. The most instructive comparison is with Stalin who, while not a founding leader, achieved a similar degree of dominance to Mao, but only after extended political struggle in the Soviet era, and the physical elimination of many leading Bolshevik revolutionaries.

[15] The clearest case is the US system where top-level executive posts are staffed by officials drawn largely from outside the legislative branch and civil service. An outstanding example was President-elect Kennedy's selection of his cabinet which included, in Robert McNamara as Secretary of Defense, an appointee to a key position whom he had never met. The general situation was summed up by Kennedy's pithy comment, "People, people, people! I don't know any people. I only know voters. How am I going to [staff my administration]." See Arthur M. Schlesinger Jr., *A Thousand Days: John F. Kennedy in the White House* (London: Andre Deutsch, 1965), pp. 108, 115-16, 119-20.

experience and reflecting a student-teacher relationship that was impossible for more senior figures such as the Premier. When Mao saw the task as correcting the shortcomings of the Cultural Revolution, it was not only logical to turn to Deng, but a step Mao could take with emotional satisfaction.[16]

Although many of the most senior surviving old revolutionaries were reduced to largely symbolic positions on the Politburo,[17] the great bulk of Mao's last Politburo elected at the Tenth Congress, and then supplemented by Deng, were people well known to the Chairman. Of the active senior figures apart from Zhou and Deng, Ye Jianying had demonstrated vital loyalty at the time of Zhang Guotao's mortal threat to Mao during the Long March,[18] and his subsequent loyalty was repeatedly demonstrated as in his active role in the purge of Luo Ruiqing on the eve of the Cultural Revolution,[19] and in his ultimately failed effort to support Hua Guofeng after the Chairman's passing. The remaining senior revolutionary, Li Xiannian, who seemingly only gained the last Politburo place in 1956 as a representative of the Fourth Front Army, did not have similar credentials with Mao who in fact regarded Li as weak, but loyal subservience was beyond doubt.[20] Of the establishment beneficiaries who played important roles in the politics of the period, virtually all had earned Mao's approval during the pre-1966 period: the Chairman considered Wu De one of the four outstanding provincial leaders, he had singled out "my old friend from Guangxi" Wei Guoqing on several key occasions, was favorably impressed by more junior local leaders Hua Guofeng and Ji Dengkui on his tours of the provinces since the 1950s, while Chen Xilian and Xu Shiyou had long received his admiration for their military achievements, and Wang Dongxing had of course long served as Mao's chief

---

[16] While the circumstances were different, i.e., in the context of Deng criticizing Zhou which would be followed by Deng's support of *pi Lin pi Kong*, Mao's excitement in December 1973 demonstrated the emotional bond which would reinforce the pragmatic fall 1974 decision to place Deng in charge of the State Council.

[17] For health and/or age reasons. These were: Zhu De, Dong Biwu, Liu Bocheng and Kang Sheng. Kang Sheng, of course, was different from the others because of his active role during the Cultural Revolution, but by 1973 he was basically inactive.

[18] See Harrison E. Salisbury, *The Long March: The Untold Story* (New York: Harper & Row, 1985), pp. 274-78. Ye's great contribution to Mao in September 1935 came when Red Army forces were divided, with Zhang Guotao having a decided preponderance of force, there were sharp divisions between Zhang and Mao over the destination of the communist armies, and fears were rife of an armed clash of the two forces. Ye fortuitously intercepted a message intended for one of Zhang's subordinates temporarily assigned to Mao's forces that called for "struggle," took the message to Mao, and then facilitated the escape of Mao's troops in the middle of the night.

[19] See Teiwes and Sun, *Tragedy*, pp. 30-31, 64; and MacFarquhar. *Origins 3*, pp. 450, 460.

[20] See above, pp. 37, 389. According to an authoritative Party historian, Li, who had also ranked comparatively low on the 1945 Central Committee, was basically selected to give the Fourth Front Army a representative on the Politburo. Interview, April 1986. Other Fourth Front Army veterans were subsequently appointed to the body: Xu Shiyou, Chen Xilian and Li Desheng in 1969, and Xu Xiangqian, briefly in 1966-69, and then after Mao's death in 1977.

security official in Zhongnanhai.[21] Of the establishment beneficiaries, only Li Desheng, who ironically received the biggest promotion at the Tenth Congress, lacked a long-standing association with Mao.[22] Perhaps most remarkable in Mao's selections for the Politburo and other leading positions, notwithstanding his real and presumed tendencies toward paranoia, was the confidence he showed that he could count on the loyalty of those who suffered during the Cultural Revolution, but were now summoned back to work. Deng, of course, was the pre-eminent case, but appointing Su Zhenhua, his Long March security chief, to take virtual immediate control of the navy following the Lin Biao affair was in some respects even more striking.[23]

Even more paradoxical than Li Desheng's appointment as CCP Vice Chairman in 1973, was, Jiang Qing excepted, Mao's *lack* of personal contact with the "gang of four" before 1966. While he had admired Zhang Chunqiao's theoretical abilities from a distance since 1958, his reliance on these radicals, and especially his choice of Wang Hongwen as the long-term successor, demonstrated a priority to his ideological vision over long-tested loyalty, and in Wang's case, an odd fidelity to the abstract categories of worker, peasant and soldier. Yet in other regards, Mao's personal connection to the larger radical camp was important. Xie Jingyi and Chi Qun came from Mao's personal office, and while they took some direction from Jiang Qing during leftist upsurges, they seemingly sometimes acted independently at key junctures, and their background

---

[21] See Mao Zedong, "Zai Changsha yu Liu Xingyuan, Ding Sheng, Wei Guoqing, Wang Dongxing de tanhua" [Talk with Liu Xingyuan, Ding Sheng, Wei Guoqing and Wang Dongxing at Changsha] (August 28, 1971), in *CRDB*, p. 1; Xu Yong, "Wei Guoqing tusha Guangxi 'sierer' pai" [Wei Guoqing Slaughters Guangxi's "422" Faction], http://museums.cnd.org/CR/ZK03/cr168.hz8.html; "Mao Zedong he Xu Shiyou" [Mao Zedong and Xu Shiyou], http://www.china-shaoshan.com/ bbs/showtopic.asp?TOPIC_ID=7011&Forum_ID=12; *Chen Xilian huiyilu*, p. 474; and above, pp. 10n23, 295. The same historian cited in the preceding note also commented on Xu Shiyou's heartfelt conversion to Mao's cause following his arrest with other Fourth Front Army cadres, and Mao's personal visit to release him. Interview, March 1986. Also note Mao's language in 1971 and 1973 to complain of a perceived decline in Xu's "affection" (*ganqing*). Li Wenqing, *Jinkan Xu Shiyou*, pp. 210, 248.

[22] Li caught Mao's eye for his efforts during the Cultural Revolution, notionally to "support the left"; see above, p. 102. Li's physical bravery in dealing with Cultural Revolution chaos in Anhui, together with the fact that his actions could be interpreted as supporting the movement, probably explains Mao's partiality despite limited personal knowledge of Li. A bizarre additional factor was conceivably involved in Li gaining the Chairman's attention: during the revolutionary period Mao used an English version of the same name (Victor Li) as an alias.

Mao also had limited knowledge of various Politburo members who were basically symbolic appointments: Chen Yonggui, Ni Zhifu and Wu Guixian, as well as Saifudin as a national minorities representative. Chen Yonggui was something of an exception since he had been known to Mao since 1964 when he played an important role in the reversal of Socialist Education Movement policies, but Chen's personal relations with Mao seem limited from that point on, although he continued to receive favor as the representative of the Dazhai model. See Teiwes, *Politics and Purges*, pp. 432-33; and above, pp. 232-33.

[23] See above, pp. 41-42.

undoubtedly magnified their influence in the conflicts of the period. In addition, the Chairman's niece, Wang Hairong (not a genuine radical, but someone who conveyed Mao's radical wishes) and his nephew, Mao Yuanxin (arguably the most significant radical of all at the end of the Maoist era) exercised enormous influence as his liaisons to the top leadership.

For all the importance of Mao's interactions with senior members of his extended revolutionary family over five decades, his scrutiny of the political and work performances of more junior Party officials since 1949, and his interaction with young functionaries in his Zhongnanhai office, no relationships—apart from Zhou and Deng—were more crucial in the developments of the 1972-76 period than those with key family members: Jiang Qing, Wang Hairong and Mao Yuanxin. Much remains unclear about the nature of the Chairman's relationship with his wife for the period at hand, especially concerning the degree of her access which was clearly variable, but may be understated in official sources. On Jiang's part, whatever her excesses, clumsy politics, and personal vendettas, there can be no doubt that she believed she was carrying out Mao's "line." Leaving aside her well-known tendency to histrionics, her shrieks of loyalty to the Chairman to her jailors shortly after her arrest, and her defense at the 1980 trial that she did everything according to Mao's wishes, that, as she famously put it, she was his dog, were surely heartfelt.[24] On Mao's part, the picture is more complex, indeed more obscure. Despite his confidence in bringing back leaders who had suffered badly during the Cultural Revolution, it appears that ultimately he only trusted members of his own family. For such a momentous project as the Cultural Revolution, Mao seemingly felt only Jiang, not Lin Biao who sought to avoid successor status, not Zhou Enlai who undoubtedly would have carried out his orders unquestioningly,[25] could be relied on from the start. Correctly identified as the "ringleader" of the "gang" at the time of the 1980 trial, she could be counted on to push forward the movement, as well as subsequent efforts like the "second Cultural Revolution" of the *pi Lin pi Kong* campaign, and if she overstepped, she could be hauled back into line, with groveling self-criticisms provided as necessary.

But if Mao could force self-criticism from Jiang, others had to be wary given her "special status" as the Chairman's wife—a status which even led some leaders to question the wisdom of arresting her after his death. There were specific warnings from Mao not to criticize Jiang, most notably as a condition of Deng's return to work, and when Mao did mandate Politburo criticism of his wife, other leaders, as in Deng's chairing of criticism meetings in May-June

---

[24] See Sidney Rittenberg and Amanda Bennett, *The Man Who Stayed Behind* (New York: Simon & Schuster, 1993), p. 428; *A Great Trial*, p. 102; and Qing and Fang, *Deng zai 1976*, vol. 2, p. 323.

[25] On Lin and Zhou, see Teiwes and Sun, *Tragedy*, pp. 7, 47-48, 57-65, 78-79, 92, 98 and *passim*. With regard to a hypothetical role for Zhou in 1965, apart from the Premier's total subservience to Mao, note that it was unclear to anyone, Jiang Qing included, what would come out of the steps Mao initiated in 1965-66. Cf. Teiwes, *Politics and Purges*, pp. lx-lxi.

1975, sensibly kept the process restrained, although their private attacks on Jiang left them vulnerable to Mao's displeasure.[26] But overlaid with this clear protection of Jiang was the Chairman's repeated criticism of her; indeed, his criticism of the "gang" as a group overwhelmingly focused on Jiang. Clearly there was a political aspect in that her excesses and blunders complicated Mao's objectives. But by the same token, he would have known well that his main complaint, Jiang's harsh treatment of colleagues and her inability to cooperate with the broader collective, was simply inherent in her political style, and while she might pull her head in when under criticism, fundamental change was nigh on impossible. Yet Mao seemingly never considered removing her from office. Here considerations of face would be all important: face in the sense that Jiang's identification with the Cultural Revolution meant any downgrading of her status would raise questions about the movement, and in the sense of her "special status" which, particularly in the context of the time, meant any diminution of her role was a blow to the Chairman's prestige. Yet at the same time, the focus on Jiang and the nature of Mao's often biting criticism, as well as reported disputes over money and whether she would be allowed to see him,[27] pointed to a vexed personal relationship. While we can only guess what might have been involved for the Chairman, it appears long-standing marital tensions added a sharpness to cases where genuine political matters were at issue, but regardless Mao was unwilling to initiate more than half-measures against his wife.

Wang Hairong was a lesser player than Jiang Qing in the events of the period, but nevertheless someone, together with Tang Wensheng, entrusted with very significant tasks by the Chairman. Undoubtedly the most important was the leading role the "two ladies" played in shaping the searing criticism of Zhou Enlai in November-December 1973. This at once indicated their importance, and the limits of their role. They were "bad to the Premier" on Mao's orders, but were authoritative precisely because they were the bearers of those orders. While conceivably, as charged by their enemies, they worsened Zhou's situation by exaggerating his "mistakes" to placate Mao, the overwhelming evidence is that they simply reflected Mao's shifting attitudes. This did not diminish their influence, by virtue of access, in furthering Mao's inclinations, e.g., *via* Wang Hairong's complaints concerning Jiang and Wang Hongwen. Other actors understood the potency of a relative with access to Mao, not only in the case of Wang Hairong, but as also seen in Zhou and Wu De's initiative to add Wang Hairong's aunt, Wang Mantian, to the State Council Culture Group as a way of diluting Jiang's dominance of the body. The "two ladies," in any case, eventually ran afoul of the Chairman when he perceived their links to Deng, which they had

---

[26] See above, pp. 245, 301-302, 364ff.

[27] See "Zhonggong zhongyang guanyu 'Wang Hongwen, Zhang Chunqiao, Jiang Qing, Yao Wenyuan fandang jituan zuizheng (cailiao zhi yi)'," p. 25; and above, pp. 115-16, 220-21, 235. While we believe post-Mao claims of Jiang demanding money are blown out of proportion, the apparent vexation that this caused Mao reflected the larger fraught relationship.

developed according to his wishes and attitudes in the first place, as opposing his new negative assessment of Deng that emerged in late 1975.[28]

Mao Yuanxin was infinitely more important and influential concerning Mao's leftist project than Wang Hairong, or for that matter Jiang Qing, at least in the crucial year from fall 1975 to the Chairman's death when, in his own words, he achieved "an impact [beyond the capability of] the Jiang Qing clique."[29] We have emphasized in the preceding analysis the importance of Mao Yuanxin's presentation to his uncle, starting in late September 1975, of complaints about the direction of policy under Deng's stewardship. While it is impossible to know whether the Chairman would have continued to approve Deng's leadership of consolidation without Mao Yuanxin's intervention, on the face of the evidence it appears that Mao Yuanxin's arguments had a more profound effect on him than those by any other figure over the entire 1972-76 period. The result was to cut short the consolidation efforts that Mao had approved for many months, shift the propaganda message to the left in a major way, start disruptive internal criticism in official institutions, and place in jeopardy and subsequently remove a trusted colleague who had been cultivated for more than two and a half years for precisely the purpose, as the Chairman saw it, of consolidating the gains of the Cultural Revolution. From that point on, Mao Yuanxin performed the critical liaison role between the Chairman and Politburo in a much more official if not strictly formal manner than that ever exercised by Wang Hairong and Tang Wensheng, and, given the further decline in his uncle's health and the issues raised by Zhou Enlai's death and the Tiananmen crisis, he exercised great influence in an absolutely critical context.

While the evidence is less than ironclad, on balance it strongly points to Mao in 1976 considering his nephew as an ultimate successor, although not quite ready in the present context. Moreover, the Chairman apparently designated Mao Yuanxin as someone who would have an important role to play in the period following his death, presumably assuming an ongoing role. There is little direct indication that he considered his nephew a possible successor earlier, even though Mao Yuanxin was obviously a significant radical force in the Northeast, and had sponsored models with nationwide ramifications. Indeed, one could ask why the Chairman passed over Mao Yuanxin when selecting Wang Hongwen, who was only a few years older—a desire to avoid the appearance of nepotism being the most plausible explanation. But perhaps the more relevant question is why Mao *now* contemplated his nephew as a successor. The dependence on Mao Yuanxin at a time of critical political decisions and the approach of death undoubtedly were important, as was his nephew's manifest commitment to the

---

[28] See "Hua Guofeng jiejian Shandong, Hubei deng Nanjing budui deng lingdao tongzhi de jianghua," p. 1; Quan Yanchi, *Zouxia shengtan de Zhou* Enlai, p. 357; and above, pp. 56-57, 89n157, 91, 127, 131, 133ff, 212-13, 216, 517.

[29] See above, p. 387.

Cultural Revolution and, of course, the familial tie. But also weighing on the Chairman's mind throughout the entire period was the succession issue that he regarded as crucial to the revolution, and each approach he had attempted since 1966 had failed. Following the Lin Biao affair, Wang Hongwen failed to live up to Mao's expectations, although the evidence of 1976 suggests the Chairman had not completely given up on Wang as part of a future leadership. While Deng was never designated as the ultimate successor, by early 1974 he had been clearly earmarked as part of a "unified team" where he would provide expertise and experience in whatever arrangement prevailed, and as Wang's star faded, Deng was clearly emerging as the pre-eminent figure in any arrangement. But with Deng under attack for rightism, this was no longer viable. In selecting Hua Guofeng as the new successor, Mao drew from the existing Politburo, in the first instance reportedly counting off the members on his fingers. The status conveyed to Hua was crucial and, from April 1976, clear, but the choice could hardly have been totally reassuring to the Chairman. He again sought a "unified team" and, with his life ebbing away, seemingly sought to insure that his nephew was part of that team.[30]

A corollary to this highly personalized, quasi-family politics at the highest levels was the weakness of institutional interests and bureaucratic and sectional politics. As formal institutions were restored and strengthened following the Ninth Congress, and then on an accelerated basis after the Lin Biao affair, bureaucratic objectives inevitably played a more significant role. What is striking, however, is the tentativeness of this process, and the constraints concerned leaders imposed on themselves in pursuing their organizations' interests. We have already highlighted the close attention placed on Mao's views by Zhou Enlai and Deng Xiaoping in 1972 and 1975 respectively, the years when the pursuit of organizational interests was most pronounced. The Premier, as noted, eschewed a bold conceptual approach, instead opting to advance gingerly specific approaches that had already been endorsed before Lin's demise, and when relatively bold steps were taken, as concerning revitalizing basic research, attention was given to obtaining some sign of support from Mao.[31] More striking was the consolidation effort of 1975 when, with Mao's blessing, institutions and experts developed programs on a much more thorough and vigorous basis. Even then, however, contrary to the view that this represented an effort by Deng to build a broad coalition of interests to oppose the Politburo radicals and their followers,[32] this was by far a secondary concern for Deng, not least because

---

[30] On Mao's preferences concerning Mao Yuanxin, see above, p. 496.

[31] In this case, Beida scientist Zhou Peiyuan obtained a November 1972 audience with Mao that resulted in the Chairman's remark that his views should be considered. While this did not prevent the radicals from seeing revisionist intent in the effort to strengthen basic research, the point is that even an amber light from Mao was seen as critical for advancing a project that had significant support both within the educational sector and the leadership. See above, p. 59.

[32] As best argued in Lieberthal, *Central Documents*. Cf. above, pp. 524-25.

the vast majority of institutional, sectoral groups and leadership factions would inevitably be on his side in any showdown with Jiang Qing *et al*. Rather, the main objective was to carry out Mao's immediate goal of correcting (the 30 percent) Cultural Revolution shortcomings, which would by definition garner the support of that vast majority, while at the same time avoiding overreaching. Thus Deng studied the Chairman's writings, while even more telling was his hesitation before endorsing remuneration according to work, a standard socialist principle that had been written into the new state constitution in January. Even with basic Marxism and a recent key Mao-endorsed document in support, Deng apparently had to overcome anxiety that this step clashed with the Chairman's Cultural Revolution ideology.[33]

The most dramatic example of the tepid pursuit of institutional interests, and of the comparatively passive role of organizations generally, concerned the institution usually regarded as the ultimate arbiter of power in this period—the PLA.[34] The most vigorous pursuit of core PLA interests, as with other organizations, occurred in 1975, in the effort to streamline and reorganize the military so that it could adequately perform its basic national defense tasks—a program mandated by Mao and implemented by Deng according to the Chairman's specifications. As for the army more generally, it either meekly accepted orders inimical to its interests, or at least to the interests of its leading commanders, or basically stood on the sidelines as the most dramatic episodes of leadership politics were played out. The classic example of the former occurred at the start of 1974 when eight military region commanders were rotated on short notice with negligible support staff, and then the entire army was subject to strong criticism during the *pi Lin pi Kong* campaign. There were no murmurs of dissent from the rotated commanders, nor was Deng's contemporary appointment to the MAC a *quid pro quo* for accepting the rotation plan, and in the event Deng undoubtedly played a key role in the harsh criticism of leading PLA figures as the movement unfolded.

Although unquestioning acceptance of direct orders from Mao is unsurprising, given the tensions and uncertainty concerning the country's future and the army's

---

[33] See above, p. 334.

[34] There is a parallel in the basic non-involvement of the PLA in key decisions concerning the Great Leap Forward, despite the major impact of that movement on the peasant-based army. See Teiwes with Sun, *China's Road to Disaster*, pp. 198-99. The situation was of course different during the Cultural Revolution, but only in the sense that the PLA was drawn into that movement against its will, with major damage to its basic function.

Of course, the nature of institutional interests lies in the eye of the beholder. Thus, with regard to the PLA, it could be argued that the retreat from political leadership in the post-Lin Biao period amounted to a setback to military interests. In our view, however, "true" organizational interests are linked to the primary functions of the concerned institutions, in the PLA's case its national defense capabilities. For an extended discussion of institutional functions and interests, see David Bachman, *Bureaucracy, Economy, and Leadership in China: The Institutional Origins of the Great Leap Forward* (Cambridge: Cambridge University Press, 1991), ch. 3.

role in that future, the military's basic non-involvement in the key political decisions of the late Mao era is striking. Not only is there, understandably, no evidence of PLA input into decisions inimical to its position, e.g., launching the Lin Biao-Confucius campaign, there are also no indications of any lobbying for developments supportive of army interests such as criticism of the "ultra-left" in 1972, or the emergence of Deng as the successor to Zhou in 1974. Moreover, with the future of the Party at stake following Deng's sidelining, on the basis of existing evidence, there was no PLA advocacy not only concerning filling the premiership after Zhou Enlai's death, but even regarding the new functional head of the military with Ye Jianying's sidelining, i.e., the leader responsible for MAC daily work, who turned out to be Chen Xilian. Nor was there any known army input three months later when Hua Guofeng's succession was decisively settled. Similarly, in the following months leading up to Mao's death, there is little indication of serious preparations for the post-Mao period by the existing high command, apart from measures to guard against feared social disorder. In terms of the post-Mao political equation, all that is known is that several active military leaders participated to some indeterminate extent in vague discussions that primarily involved sidelined senior PLA figures.

Even more telling, during the tense period following the Chairman's death, when the matter was finally settled by physical force, the army was essentially a reserve force, mobilized on the orders of the highest political authority (Hua Guofeng) as channeled through the formal chain of command (Chen Xilian at the MAC), while the key measures, both political and operational, were largely initiated and executed by others. During these critical weeks Ye Jianying functioned basically as an adviser, the prestigious senior old army leaders were broadly supportive of doing something to "solve the 'gang of four' problem," but in the dark as to what was going on, while the actual commanders at various levels simply followed orders coming through the formal command structure. What would have happened in other circumstances is anyone's guess, but given the substantial numbers of military officers with "blind belief" in Mao, any move against his widow without the "legal" authorization of the Party Center would have been fraught with even more uncertainty than what was actually faced. In short, despite the damage to PLA interests represented by the radical program, not to mention the threat to national and Party interests perceived by the great majority of inactive senior army leaders and ranking active officers,[35] the army not only was not a central player in the resolution of arguably the most pivotal moment in the history of the PRC, but its leaders apparently did not even formulate a vague position concerning the unfolding situation. The PLA was clearly an important factor in the minds of those orchestrating the showdown, but

---

[35] While there can be little doubt that the most senior old revolutionaries and top-ranking central and regional officers were mostly hostile to the "gang," it is more difficult to assess the attitudes of military commanders generally. Deng subsequently commented that one-third of PLA commanders supported leftist ideology; interview with senior Party historian, June 1999.

it was a force in the wings that took no initiative for its own interests.

While politics where even the notionally most powerful institutions only cautiously, if at all, formulate and argue for their own interests is by most measures abnormal,[36] the 1972-76 period was similarly abnormal in terms of formal CCP organizational norms. These norms, developed during the revolutionary period, and more or less applied, with significant lapses, before the Cultural Revolution, were shattered by that movement. Key principles either explicitly rejected, or more often brushed aside in actual practice, included democratic centralism requiring obedience to higher-level Party decisions, collective leadership in formulating policy, and minority rights whereby leaders unconvinced of a policy could "reserve [their] opinions" as long as they implemented the Party's decision. All of this was swept away by assertions that only Mao's "highest instructions" were legitimate, and true revolutionaries had the "right to rebel" against any illegitimate orders inconsistent with the Chairman's thought, a position which invalidated the defense of carrying out authorized directives once those directives were declared suspect *ex post facto*, thus leaving virtually the entire establishment vulnerable. In the post-Lin Biao period, however, there was a half-hearted effort to restore these norms, which were all reaffirmed in the 1973 Party constitution, and more significantly by the heavy emphasis on the leadership of Party committees, the basic infrastructure of democratic centralism. Yet this effort was repeatedly under pressure, whether through Mao's new directive publicized at the Tenth Congress that "going against the tide is a Marxist-Leninist principle," new campaigns, notably *pi Lin pi Kong*, where Party committees came under sharp attack to the point of being pushed aside in a pale reflection of the Cultural Revolution, or by Jiang Qing's behavior in disrupting Politburo discussions and repeatedly attacking Zhou Enlai, while remaining to a substantial degree untouchable because of her "special status" as Mao's wife.[37]

A paradoxical feature of this period of uncertainty and inconsistent implementation of basic CCP organizational principles was that many specific Party procedures were broadly adhered to, and often provided opportunities for non-radical forces to advance or defend their interests. A case in point was the highly segmented bureaucratic arrangement whereby information and policy planning was largely segregated within different functional systems on a need to know basis. Thus in 1972-73, economic readjustment was carried out by relevant specialist departments, with the Politburo radicals largely restricted to

---

[36] The articulation of interests is not only a feature of institutionalized systems, it was clearly a key feature of CCP politics through 1957, although it was then distorted during the Great Leap before recovering in the years before the Cultural Revolution. See Teiwes with Sun, *China's Road to Disaster*, especially pp. 188-98.

[37] On Party norms in the pre-1966 period, see the detailed discussion in Teiwes, *Politics and Purges*, especially part III on "The Norms Under Stress" from 1957 to 1965, as well as the brief sketch of the norms as a post-Mao issue in 1976-78 (pp. 487-91). See also the overview of Party norms in idem, *Leadership*, ch. 3.

knowledge garnered from Politburo documents, and Zhang Chunqiao reduced to complaining about planning documents on technical grounds separate from actual policy.[38] Similarly, the radicals were excluded from the development of major policy documents under Deng in 1975, apparently only learning of their content by leaks from low-ranking figures, initially objecting only on limited grounds as Mao's larger dissatisfaction with Deng gradually emerged, and finally pursuing knowledge of developments in these functional areas as the *pi Deng* campaign unfolded. Even then, moderate officials were able to defend themselves, as *per* the basic logic of democratic centralism, on the basis that their efforts in 1975 had been authorized by a Party Center document, i.e., a document approved by Mao and never revoked. This not only notionally absolved them of blame, it even provided some scope to continue to carry out those policies in the face of radical attack. In other contexts, the *absence* of a Party document, again, of a policy position approved by the Chairman, allowed moderate actors to complain about radical actions, as in Zhou Enlai's objections to the number of articles criticizing Confucius shortly after the Tenth Congress, or influenced their assessments of the state of play, as in Chen Xilian's reassurance to Yang Yong in October 1975 that the *Water Margin* issue need not cause anxiety since no Party document had been issued on the matter.[39]

Other Party procedures of particular note were Politburo confidentiality and the sanctity of the formal chain of command. We have already noted the priority of formal authority over the informal prestige of the old revolutionaries in the purge of the "gang of four," and will return to this issue when we discuss the importance of Party status and the role of old revolutionaries subsequently. As for Politburo confidentiality, ironically, on the basis of the available evidence, it appears the radicals followed this procedure more faithfully than their opponents. A case in point was Wang Hongwen's complaints to Shanghai leaders on the eve of the Tenth Congress over their failure to understand that his requests for lists of worker-peasant cadres were meant for prospective Central Committee members, something he indicated he had been unable to reveal openly because of Party discipline. More generally, while the "gang's" Shanghai followers had

---

[38] Specifically, on the grounds that one document was too long, and that the second had not been unanimously passed; see above, pp. 52-53. On the effects of functional systems, see Lieberthal, *Central Documents*, pp. 40ff. For further political implications of these systems, see above, pp. 498-99.

Of course, the political context could override any formal procedures, something dramatically reflected on the educational front in 1975. As we saw in Chapter 6, although Minister of Education Zhou Rongxin submitted reports to Zhang Chunqiao as the responsible Vice Premier, Zhang apparently did not engage Zhou for most of 1975, undoubtedly as a result of Zhang falling out of favor in the spring.

[39] See above, pp. 98, 325ff, 331-32, 369n187, 453, 457. Of course, Party documents were not permanently binding given Mao's propensity to change his mind, and on occasion radicals at various levels questioned whether his minimal approval by circling a document fully reflected his views, or even whether such approval was sufficient to provide lasting validity. See above, pp. 361n165, 499n95.

a reasonable understanding of the tensions at the Party Center, something that could be grasped to a considerable degree from the open media but which was undoubtedly enhanced by frequent communication with their patrons in Beijing, at the same time there is little evidence of their having detailed knowledge of specific events within the Politburo. Instead, a repeated pattern was for the Politburo radicals to steer the Shanghai group away from excessive radicalism and toward the formal Party position, whether it be to dampen down local opposition to Deng Xiaoping's return in 1973, to counsel support of Hua following his promotions in February and April 1976, and finally to convey a similar message in September 1976 at the very time Hua et al. were plotting against them.[40] In contrast, Deng, Ye Jianying and Ji Dengkui all violated Politburo confidentiality by revealing Mao's May 1975 criticism of Jiang Qing et al., whether in a tentative effort to win over Shanghai's Ma Tianshui, as part of an attempt to firm up resistance to radical influence in the PLA, or as encouragement to Zhejiang leaders as they faced local rebel disruption.[41]

For all the complications of partially restored institutions, restored but frayed Party norms, procedures that constrained but could not fully contain conflict, and above all Mao's shifting positions, elite interaction in 1972-76 was most fundamentally a politics of animosity, fear and distrustful ignorance. Two camps[42] clearly existed by the time of the Fourth NPC as claimed by Deng's daughter, and in fact throughout the entire post-Lin Biao period, however inchoate and submerged at various points. Yet this did not equate to unremitting conflict, as seen in Deng's "kind relations" and cooperation with Jiang in 1973 and most of 1974, and in Wang's support of Deng's consolidation program in the first half of 1975. As with so much else, conflict surfaced as Mao shifted course and turned against one group or another. Despite Mao's forlorn hope and repeated demands for unity, the combination of fundamentally different world views, resentment over the prominence of figures with no marked contribution to the real pre-1949 revolution, and bitter memories of Cultural Revolution clashes, meant that any civility between the two groups was little more than adhering to the Chairman's demands as long as he lived. The searing conflicts, attacks and punishments of 1966-68 left indelible memories, and the radicals' pursuit of

---

[40] See above, pp. 72n122, 106, 451, 497, 573. In an even more striking indication of discipline, the evidence suggests that Politburo Standing Committee members Wang Hongwen and Zhang Chunqiao upheld the confidentiality of that body and did not inform Jiang Qing and Yao Wenyuan of key discussions in May 1975; above, p. 290n129.

[41] In at least the cases of Deng and Ye, there is evidence that at some point Mao was displeased when he became aware of their actions. See above, pp. 303, 365.

[42] "Two camps" is always a simplification, and we use it differently from Mao Mao, "Wenge" suiyue, p. 334, who presents the conflict as between the "gang of four" and old revolutionaries headed by Zhou, Deng, Ye Jianying and Li Xiannian. Leaving aside individuals such as Qiao Guanhua who dabbled with the "gang," the bulk of high-level central officials, most notably the establishment beneficiaries on the Politburo, were clearly opposed to the radicals, although constrained by Mao's shifting policies and demands for unity.

Cultural Revolution objectives, the use of similar if toned-down methods during the Lin Biao-Confucius campaign, and personal tensions exacerbated by Jiang Qing's excesses in particular, created a poisonous sense of them and us which repeatedly bedeviled politics at the highest level. A partial exception concerned Wang Hongwen, who had not been party to the bitter Beijing conflicts of 1966-68, notably in providing cooperation while carrying out his responsibilities for Party Center work in the first half of 1975. More generally, Wang usually displayed respect for senior figures, above all for the Premier.[43]

Fear was another constant feature of the period. In large part, this was fear of being at odds with the Chairman's wishes and "line," with its inherent danger of career setbacks, including banishment from political life. Such fear was undoubtedly a factor leading Deng to join in attacks on his old revolutionary subordinates during *pi Lin pi Kong*, causing both Zhang Chunqiao and Wang Hongwen to propose that the radicals modify their behavior once Mao had voiced his displeasure concerning a "gang of four," and producing a tacit understanding between Ye Jianying and Li Xiannian to avoid contact with one another during the anti-Deng campaign.[44] At the end of this Conclusion, we shall return to this "fear of Mao" factor, which was central and enduring, but in some senses reduced during these years. Arguably of greater concern to Chinese leaders as the Chairman's life drew to an end were fears of possible post-Mao outcomes. In the anxiety-filled oblique discussions of senior revolutionaries in summer 1976, such worries not only concerned political outcomes, but also reflected a sense of mortal danger if the radicals gained power. Deng's claim cited at the start of this Conclusion that he would not have been alive without Mao's protection may have primarily referred to the Cultural Revolution itself, but it was also on Wang Dongxing's mind following the Tiananmen crisis as he sought Mao's permission to protect Deng anew. Ironically, the radicals, who had more to fear both in terms of the resources at their disposal and the actual outcome, were apparently more sanguine. Although clearly aware of the dangers of the situation, and despite rhetoric about the threat of revisionist restoration,[45] they took few practical precautions before their arrest.

Beyond the animosity between the two camps and fears on all sides about the future, throughout the entire period there was a distrust based on ignorance that enveloped the top leadership more generally. Even in the heyday of Party unity in the 1950s, the greatest trust among leaders was reserved for those with long-standing personal and work relationships, while beyond that, respect was extended to a large extent on the basis of individuals' contributions to the pre-

---

[43] While the genuineness of Wang's respect for senior leaders is controversial, it is at least arguable that his personal relations with other members of the "gang" were more tense than those with Zhou, Deng or establishment beneficiaries. See above, pp. 116-17, 213.

[44] See *Deng Liqun zishu*, p. 105; and above, pp. 181-82, 249.

[45] See, e.g., *A Great Trial*, pp. 77, 79-82, 192.

1949 revolution and their Party status. As a result of the Cultural Revolution, the top leadership no longer had the same degree of cohesion and shared experience, while everyone was required to endorse the radical ideology of the post-1966 period. Even with shared work relations during the post-Lin Biao period, personal interaction appeared limited,[46] and doubts, particularly over general political orientation and what others did during the Cultural Revolution and why, existed even among officials deeply involved in supporting Deng's consolidation efforts in 1975.

This can be seen in the case of Hua Guofeng and Ji Dengkui, major contributors to Deng's program as standing vice premiers responsible for key areas, who performed in a manner that earned Deng's support as possible future successors.[47] Yet in the crisis period of September-October 1976, Hua kept Ji, who had particularly testy relations with Jiang Qing, out of the critical planning for the arrest of the "gang of four," perhaps on the basis of Ji's mid-September view that it was necessary to distinguish among the four, which seemingly suggested lenient treatment for Jiang as Mao's wife, or for even less substantial reasons. Similarly, despite shared Politburo status since 1969, as well as leading positions on the MAC since 1974, Ye Jianying needed to be reassured concerning Chen Xilian in the critical period following Mao's death even though Chen bore great hostility toward the radicals. Speculatively, Ye's reservations about Chen may have reflected a lack of historical relations during the revolutionary period, even though Chen's primary ties were to Deng, but probably more relevant was Chen's period in Liaoning before 1974, where he inevitably had contact with Mao Yuanxin in one of the most radical regions during the Cultural Revolution. Misleading perceptions concerning Chen, as was the case with other more junior Politburo figures of the 1970s, would come back to haunt them in the post-Mao period, but even at the decisive moment at the end of the Maoist era lack of knowledge about fellow leaders, and assumptions based on superficial considerations, complicated top-level politics.

As suggested, a key source of the distrust and ignorance at the highest levels was the distortion of proper status within the CCP due to the Cultural Revolution. From 1949 to 1965, power and position in the PRC largely reflected

---

[46] This is our subjective judgment based on limited concrete information. Of particular interest is the apparent minimal private contact between Zhou and Deng in 1973 and most of 1974, as well as limited contact between Deng and Ye Jianying in the same period. See above, pp. 73, 180, 181, 201. We believe such contact across the status divide between old revolutionaries and establishment beneficiaries would have been even less.

[47] See above, pp. 310-12. Additionally, Hua and Ji reportedly had good personal relations, perhaps partially on the basis of their common Shanxi origins, and lived in the same compound. Interviews with a senior historian, November 2002, and an associate of Hua, January 2005. Of course, sharing residences did not guarantee good relations, and another resident in Hua's compound was Qiao Guanhua, with whom strained relations developed. Even more dramatic were the tensions among the various residents at the Diaoyutai State Guesthouse, including the "gang of four," Kang Sheng and Chen Yonggui, among others. See above, pp. 74, 75n126, 233, 501-502.

the status secured by contributions to the revolutionary struggle. While those closely associated with the "erroneous lines" of Wang Ming and the Returned Student faction naturally were reduced to minor positions, others who had not always sided with Mao but were major figures, most notably Zhou Enlai, gained top-level posts, while the various major constituencies, or "mountaintops," of the armed struggle were represented on peak bodies.[48] Thus informal prestige and official posts were married, but at the same time the formal division of labor generally prevailed. While fully one-third of the 1956 Politburo represented the PLA, the impact of these figures on non-military affairs was limited, as policies were generally dominated by the responsible bureaucratic organs and their leaders—and of course by Mao. In any case, all leaders heading key institutions had made major contributions to the pre-1949 revolution.[49]

All this changed with the Cultural Revolution. As institutions disintegrated into chaos, their leaders were usually removed and replaced by figures not only of often dubious expertise, but also of much reduced prestige—whether these were lower-ranking cadres, youthful rebels, or military officers brought in to restore order. As a result, revolutionary status was out of joint with official positions, a situation that continued at the highest levels with the Politburos elected at the Ninth and Tenth Congresses. Although a group of senior revolutionaries was selected at both congresses, these included elderly and even seriously ill figures who clearly had only a symbolic role. Clearly the Politburo radicals were regarded with the most disdain, but there inevitably was also unease with junior figures such as Hua, who only joined the CCP in 1938, but now held major operational power. Thus when Hua and Ji Dengkui, dutifully carrying out Mao's line, criticized Wan Li in early 1976, Wan's anger went beyond the issue at hand to the fact that Ji had been his subordinate during the revolution, but was now telling him what to do. Yet, as we have discussed previously, Hua, Ji and others in their position were apparently more comfortable in serving under a senior revolutionary, something suggested by their initiative in carrying out the consolidation program under Deng's aegis in 1975, and their proposal in early 1976, in the context of filling Zhou Enlai's position, that they serve under Li Xiannian in the State Council. All of this, of course, came in the context of the Mao-mandated leadership arrangement, where Zhou, Deng and Li cultivated Hua and Ji as desirable successors, i.e., as promising candidates from those the Chairman had made available, despite the lack of long-term familiarity.[50] The problem would come in the future when Mao was no longer around, and Hua's role as successor represented a status inversion at the very apex of the system.

As we shall argue in Volumes II and III, post-Mao politics initially centered on a gradual reassertion of proper status. As the Deng era flowered in the 1980s,

---

[48] See Teiwes with Sun, *Formation*, pp. 20-23, 40-52.

[49] See Teiwes, "The Chinese State during the Maoist Era," pp. 120-25.

[50] On these several matters, see above, pp. 13, 103, 310-12, 458.

this involved a rewriting of the history of 1972-76 to emphasize the role of senior revolutionaries. The grossest distortion, analyzed in detail in Chapter 8, gives credit to Ye Jianying and the old revolutionaries more broadly for purging the "gang of four," while shamelessly marginalizing the role of Hua Guofeng and other establishment beneficiaries in the process. But the broader effort to depict the political conflicts of the period in terms of old revolutionaries *v.* radicals also distorts the situation. The only truly senior revolutionaries holding key positions in Beijing were Zhou, Deng, Ye and Li Xiannian. Zhou and Deng were of course special, being given large grants of authority in periods when Mao focused on Cultural Revolution errors and saw the need to rely on their talents and experiences, but many sensitive political tasks were carried out by establishment beneficiaries in the immediate post-Lin Biao period,[51] such leaders became important architects of the consolidation program in 1975, and with both Zhou and Deng—and to a lesser degree Ye and Li—removed from the political stage in early 1976, it fell to Hua and his fellow beneficiaries to navigate the political crosscurrents of the last months of Mao's life.

The exaggeration of the veteran revolutionaries' role, however, reflected more than an effort to rewrite history in a way congenial to Deng and other senior figures. It also reflected widespread assumptions at the time that veteran revolutionaries somehow held the key to the political situation. In Geng Biao's words, "We hoped that Marshal Ye and other old comrades would … come forward to solve the 'gang of four' problem,"[52] even though in fact these senior figures except for Ye Jianying did no more than talk among themselves, while Ye was drawn into the decisive process by Hua. Apart from exaggerated expectations at the time, senior figures also received a degree of leeway that would not be granted to their junior colleagues as the post-Mao era unfolded. In particular, Li Xiannian, perhaps the first Politburo member to express reservations to Mao about Deng's performance in fall 1975, and alone among the old revolutionaries to earn Jiang Qing's praise at the start of the Lin Biao-Confucius campaign, escaped unscathed in the post-Mao wash-up, while establishment beneficiaries, alleged neo-Maoists Wang Dongxing, Ji Dengkui, Chen Xilian and Wu De, and eventually Hua, were eased from power.[53]

---

[51] Notably Hua, Li Desheng, Ji Dengkui, Wang Dongxing and Wu De in investigating the Lin Biao affair, securing the military after September 13, and overseeing the liberation of cadres. See above, pp. 38-39, 46, 49n65, 71-72, 119nn25-26.

[52] See above, p. 536.

[53] Jiang's praise of Li came in her January 25, 1974, speech to the PLA mobilization meeting, recorded in the meeting minutes in the ANU collection. In March 1974 Li also voiced strong support of Jiang in the snail incident which targeted Zhou Enlai. We further note Mao's apparent low opinion of Li's political strength, and Li's apparent intent to go on sick leave after Mao's death rather than take any initiative in dealing with the "gang of four." See above, pp. 37n34, 163n132, 389, 561. The point is not to paint Li in a negative light, especially since neither Zhou nor Deng could claim clean hands, but to argue that Li's apparent immunity was based less on actual performance than on the fact of his higher status.

The so-called "gang of four" naturally was the least acceptable group to the broad elite in terms of their marginal revolutionary status. As we have argued, these radicals were totally dependent on Mao and fundamentally carried out his wishes, in turn generating deep animosity as a consequence of their Mao-directed activities, while most of the elite nevertheless saw them as different from the Chairman.[54] Moreover, their influence was limited to particular spheres,[55] periods and leftist projects as determined by Mao. They did not initiate major action, but often caused havoc in carrying out the Chairman's design. From the outset of this study, moreover, we have questioned to what extent there actually was a "gang of four" in the sense of a coherent political force: there certainly were four radicals on the Politburo, but the extent to which they amounted to an integrated "gang" is problematic. Their common interests are indisputable: a commitment to Cultural Revolution ideology, specific assignments from Mao to protect the legacy of that movement, a shared (if conflicted) Shanghai base, and the fact of their isolation within the Politburo, not to mention the inherent threat that posed to their viability as leaders. Yet Wang Dongxing's claim shortly after their arrest that the radicals "were united in seeking political power and only differed over the division of that power"[56] overstates the case. Not only is there no evidence of squabbles over the division of the spoils, but Wang's claim implied a degree of cohesion that did not exist.

There is no need to repeat the various instances of personal tensions and different views within the "gang" that have filled these pages. Some general points are worth emphasizing, however. In the "gang's" base, Shanghai, where there had been conflicts between the radical intellectual followers of Zhang Chunqiao and Wang Hongwen's worker activists since the start of the Cultural Revolution, such different perspectives continued throughout period, especially during the leftist upsurges of 1974 and 1976. Thus even at times of maximum opportunity and danger, the Politburo radicals could not pull their supporters together, and apparently could only try to minimize the damage.[57] Within the "gang" itself in Beijing, moreover, although the evidence is limited, Jiang Qing's abrasive personality inevitably raised the hackles of the other radicals—something that was clearly the case with Wang Hongwen. Beyond sheer personality, the fact of Jiang's "special status" as Mao's wife, frustrating as it was to non-radicals in the leadership, presumably was also grating on the other three by giving her

---

[54] According to a senior Party historian from a high-ranking elite family, at the time he and his circle believed the "gang" wanted to oust Zhou, but that Mao had concern for the Premier. Interview, January 2005.

[55] Apart from the obvious education, culture and propaganda spheres where specific responsibilities were more or less constant, unusual duties such as Zhang Chunqiao's oversight of the navy in 1972 further conveyed clout. See above, pp. 40-42.

[56] "Wang Dongxing zai quanguo xuanchuan gongzuo huiyishang de jianghua," p. 3.

[57] Note particularly developments during *pi Lin pi Kong* when followers of different members of the "gang" fought among themselves. See above, p. 117.

"ringleader" authority within the "gang." Thus in the judgment of the 1980 trial, Jiang was declared "directly or indirectly responsible for all offenses," while Zhang was simply designated her "collaborator," and Wang and Yao Wenyuan rated no special category.[58] At the other extreme from Jiang, Wang Hongwen was not only the most cooperative of the radicals with moderate leaders, even, in the view of one very well-placed source, particularly respectful of and concerned about the Premier, he also suffered from the low regard of the other radicals, something that was apparently a major—if not *the*—factor in his retreat to Shanghai in summer 1975. Indeed, one senior Party historian, a relative hardliner when it comes to assessments of the radicals, went so far as to describe Wang, who apparently had no great ambition, as a victim in the elite politics of the period. Victimhood could also be seen in the 18-year sentence Wang received at the 1980 trial following his extensive cooperation with the authorities, a result which both greatly surprised him, and left him in a state of emotional collapse.[59]

Given the odd combination of fundamental common interests and significant internal distrust, either close relations or conflict can be shown according to the situation. The crucial factor was that the divisions among the four, plus the limitations of their basic approach, deeply undercut their ability to function as a coherent group or develop a viable strategy. The most dramatic manifestation occurred in the weeks following Mao's death, precisely the period when cohesion and a realistic assessment of options were most needed. Apart from differences and sharp exchanges on some issues at this crucial juncture, to the extent the radicals could agree on a strategy, it amounted to waiting for the confirmation of their positions when the new leadership lineup was determined, continuing to push the anti-Deng campaign and broader Cultural Revolution themes that were, after all, the official Party line, and placing their hopes in some vague sense that Mao's "spirit" would somehow prevail. In truth, it was already too late. The whole radical approach, as Ann Fenwick has observed, had "its *raison d'être* in political struggle," which resulted in "seeking purity rather than [political] alliances."[60] This was not strictly true in the sense that there were efforts to woo particular individuals,[61] but it reflected the general situation whereby the

---

[58] See *A Great Trial*, p. 129.

[59] Interview, January 2005. See also Wang Wenfeng, *Cong "Tonghuai Zhou" dao shen Jiang Qing* [From the Birth of "Tonghuai Zhou" to the Trial of Jiang Qing] (Beijing: Dangdai Zhongguo chubanshe, 2004), p. 11. Wang was, by all reports, not only not taken seriously by other members of the "gang," but also by the moderate members of the Politburo and broad sections of the elite.

Another indication of the need to eschew lumping the four together was raised by another senior historian based on his own experience. This military historian, who dealt with Yao Wenyuan on an article concerning the PLA, came away with a good impression, concluding that Yao showed no inclination to interfere in army affairs—one of the major charges against the "gang." Interview, January 2005.

[60] Fenwick, "Gang of Four," pp. 6, 8.

[61] Notably Yang Chengwu and Wu De. See above, pp. 204-205, 228-29. But in both cases a history of past conflict meant any such approaches were unlikely to prevail, except in the limited sense that

animosity generated by radical activities meant that no genuine alliance was possible. Although Fenwick further argues that the "gang of four" did have a plan for avoiding over-dependence on the Chairman by mobilizing a mass factional following, with the "socialization of conflict" as a master strategy, there is little evidence that the Politburo radicals systematically tried to mobilize the undoubted rebel forces that might have flocked to their banner, outside of Mao-mandated campaigns.[62] More generally, it is doubtful the "gang" had *any* political strategy beyond implementing Mao's leftist policies, attacking moderate figures when possible, supporting sympathetic groups *to the extent feasible* during windows of opportunity, and hoping for the best.

The Cultural Revolution produced large numbers of young rebel activists, many of whom held largely lower-level positions after the Ninth Congress, and there were efforts to cultivate and promote such rebels in the 1972-76 period. These efforts reflected half of Mao's personnel policy, which also called for liberating cadres criticized during 1966-68, and they involved a complex situation rather than a consistent "gang" initiative.[63] For all their general support of local rebels, the Politburo radicals were required to carry out central policies, something which could lead to sharp conflicts of interest, most notably in Wang Hongwen's significant role in the summer 1975 crackdown in Zhejiang. More broadly, there is little concrete evidence outside of Zhejiang of direct "gang of four" involvement in rebel challenges to local authorities, and even there during the leftist mobilizations of 1974 and 1976 it was far from unconstrained.[64] Common ideology notwithstanding, the "radical camp" from the Politburo to basic levels embodied contradictory interests and was hardly integrated. The Politburo radicals retained their positions regardless of shifts in direction, while lower-level rebels, less attuned to Mao's subtleties and prone to greater excesses than even Jiang Qing, were often bloodied when the tide turned.

The Chairman, in addition to an abstract commitment to young rebels whom he sometimes discarded in practice, also placed hopes in younger figures whom he knew personally: Xie Jingyi, Chi Qun, Wang Hairong and especially Mao Yuanxin. These "new radicals," real and presumptive, were surely seen by Mao as people who, along with Wang Hongwen, could carry the Cultural Revolution torch into the future beyond the life spans of Jiang Qing, Zhang Chunqiao and

---

Mao-mandated policies required a degree of cooperation.

[62] See Fenwick, "Gang of Four," pp. 44, 203-204, 220-21, 255-56, 277-79. This is not to ignore that factional connections were cultivated with lower-level rebels, although as Fenwick (p. 220) observes, these tended to be between rebels and individual Politburo radicals, that such rebels looked to the "gang" as representing the true path at the Center, or that there were significant exchanges of information and documents among radical forces throughout China. The point, as elaborated below, is that such networks were fragile, often ignored or downplayed by the Politburo radicals, and certainly not controlled by them in a manner producing a reliable political resource.

[63] Note particularly Zhou Enlai's role in urging and facilitating rebel promotions, and the "gang's" doubts concerning the value of such assignments. See above, pp. 219, 223, 227-30, 543.

[64] See above, pp. 177-78, 460, 514n124.

Yao Wenyuan. To an indeterminate degree they were independent actors, and it is clear that the Chairman saw at least Mao Yuanxin and Xie Jingyi as figures with a big leadership future.[65] The precise relationship of the "new radicals" to the "gang of four" is unclear. On some occasions, they worked closely with Jiang, notably in following her orders at the time of launching *pi Lin pi Kong*. Even in this context, however, there was little indication of involvement with the other three Politburo radicals, and during the preparatory developments during the "three-month movement" in late 1973, Chi Qun performed a dynamic leading role of his own.[66] At other times, as in early 1976, there was little indication of direct subordination, and the younger radicals tended to be harsher in pushing the anti-Deng campaign than any of the "gang" apart from Jiang. The most significant indication of distance from, and indeed conflict with, "gang" interests was Mao Yuanxin's performance in 1976. We need not place too much weight on Mao Yuanxin's denial at his 1986 trial of links to the "gang of four" given that his radical ideology was fully congruent with theirs, and, as their effort to have him remain in Beijing in September 1976 to deal with Mao's papers suggests, the radicals, or at least Jiang, anticipated his support. Nevertheless, likely personal tension between Mao Yuanxin and Jiang, and especially evidence that he opposed Zhang Chunqiao's appointment as premier, strongly suggest a less than total identity of interests and actions between the Politburo radicals and the Chairman's nephew.[67] These were further indications of the unintegrated nature of radical forces at the end of the Maoist era.

In the end, it was left to the final broad grouping, the establishment beneficiaries, and Hua Guofeng in particular, to deal with the fatally flawed efforts of the "gang of four." While broadly aligned with the old revolutionaries by temperament, policy preferences, and respect for Party status, these leaders, as was the case with Zhou and Deng, tacked as necessary to meet Mao's demands. In terms of implementing the moderate program, of the leading beneficiaries, Hua and especially Ji Dengkui took prominent and vigorous roles, while Wu De, his persistent efforts to avoid bloodshed at Tiananmen notwithstanding, and probably Chen Xilian were seemingly less forthright in resisting radical pressures. By virtue of Mao's belated appointment as the successor, Hua became the center of the resistance. As our detailed examination of his handling of the "gang" after Mao's death demonstrates, Hua was not the weak leader depicted

---

[65] See above, pp. 296, 496. While, in contrast, Mao dismissed Chi Qun's suitability for a minister's position; he had placed Chi in the leading role at Qinghua University, one of the "six factories and two schools" the Chairman personally controlled, and in October 1975 declared an attack on Chi was an attack on himself. Clearly, Chi was a mainstay of the "new radicals."

[66] Regarding the "three-month movement," *pi Lin pi Kong*, and subsequent developments, the *Liang Xiao* writing group confessed that their relationship to the "gang" was remote except for that with Jiang. Apparently, dealings with Yao concerned routine propaganda matters, while there was virtually no contact with Zhang and Wang. Fan Daren, *"Wenge" yubi fuchenlu*, p. 22. Cf. above, pp. 120ff.

[67] See above, pp. 374, 442-43, 496.

by Deng-era orthodoxy, whose backbone had to be stiffened by Ye Jianying. Hua took the initiative at the outset, brought Ye and Li Xiannian into the equation, made the crucial decision on how to "solve the 'gang of four' problem," and orchestrated the key measures carrying out his decision. But if Hua was not Deng's ineffective leader, neither was he the "kind and honest" official Mao thought he was appointing in January 1976, an official who would adhere to the Cultural Revolution line and protect the radicals' position in the post-Mao leadership. Although arguably too weak in handling the wreaths issue during the Tiananmen crisis, overall Hua proved shrewd and decisive in dealing with difficult issues during the last months of the Chairman's life. He read Mao's wishes correctly in pursuing the *pi Deng* campaign in a centrist manner, rebuffed the radicals on various measures when Mao was no longer able to intervene, particularly concerning the summer planning conference, and then moved steadily toward settling the leadership crisis after the Chairman's passing. He emerged from this performance both widely accepted as Mao's legitimate successor, an acceptance graphically seen in Ye Jianying assuming responsibility to "bolster" Hua, and admired for his "quick and clean" solution to the crisis. But this was a situation that could not last once the complexities of the post-Mao era began to unfold.

What explains the obedience Mao received from the elite during the last years of his life, an obedience that extended beyond carrying out explicit orders inimical to elite interests to shaping positions according to expectations of the Chairman's wishes, and holding sacrosanct his "line" even as he slipped into a coma? The answer lies in a combination of fear, belief, and moral authority, with both fear and belief basically reflecting moral authority. Fear was at root a fear of being off side with Mao, with possible consequences, varying by period, of loss of influence and position, or of mortal threat under the most dire circumstances, as well as of personal inadequacy in not being able to keep up with the Chairman's thinking. In the period from the consolidation of Mao's leadership in the 1940s to the launching of the Great Leap, notwithstanding excesses such as the salvation campaign in the context of the Yan'an rectification,[68] for the upper echelons of the elite fear could be palpable, but nevertheless comparatively restrained. After all, part of Mao's platform as he gathered support for his leadership was to attack the earlier organizational approach of "ruthless struggle and merciless blows" and replace it with "persuasive" rectification methods. However much Mao's approach still resulted in frightening experiences for lower-level Party members, higher-level elite figures basically emerged unscathed for most of the 1950s.[69] Indicative cases involved Bo Yibo, criticized in early 1953 by

---

[68] See Teiwes with Sun, *Formation*, pp. 52-59. Of particular note here is that Mao quickly reversed himself as he became aware of the salvation campaign's excesses, and undertook a rare self-criticism concerning the campaign to appease elite opinion.

[69] On Mao's Yan'an platform, see Teiwes, *Politics and Purges*, pp. 46-50. The exception in the 1950s before the Great Leap was the Gao Gang case in 1953-54, but even here Mao offered self-criticism and demotion as a way out. See Teiwes, *Politics at Mao's Court*, pp. 122, 124.

Mao for his tax system that allegedly favored the bourgeoisie, and Deng Zihui whose objections to speeding up collectivization in 1955 earned him the "right opportunist" label. In Bo's case, he seemingly was as much distressed by his serious ideological shortcomings, his lagging behind the Chairman, as by the possible career implications of the incident, which in any case led to a relatively minor setback. Two years later, Deng Zihui astonished his subordinates in the rural work sector by continuing to argue once Mao had made his position clear, and suffered a more significant career setback, but he still held high-ranking positions until 1962. Perhaps most revealing of the limited scope of fear was Zhou Enlai, completely aware of the circumstances of both the Bo and Deng cases, approaching Mao in spring 1956 to persuade him to change his mind on excessive economic growth—and succeeding.[70]

All of this changed with the Great Leap, which saw Zhou denied his "right to speak" at the outset, and the even more momentous watershed of Peng Dehuai's dismissal as Minister of Defense for his clumsy attempt to broaden the discussion of leap shortcomings at the summer 1959 Lushan plenum. These and other developments had a chilling effect on debate as Mao's colleagues became ever more wary of his increasingly unpredictable reactions, but in the period through 1965 a large degree of normal practice, and thus contained fear, prevailed.[71] Understandably, the Cultural Revolution produced a quantum jump in fear as even Politburo-level leaders were marched through the streets in dunce caps, and three—Liu Shaoqi, He Long and (eventually) Peng Dehuai— died of abuse during the movement.

Yet for our purposes, what is striking is the degree to which unmitigated fear declined in elite circles during the post-Lin Biao period. A number of reasons can be identified. First, the top elite generally appeared willing to give the Chairman the benefit of the doubt, to attribute the excesses of the Cultural Revolution to others, whether Lin Biao or the "gang of four," and accept at face value signs of Mao's remorse, as most dramatically seen in his sudden appearance at Chen Yi's funeral—a gesture gratefully accepted by Chen's family as a great honor. Linked to this was the policy of cadre liberation, a policy consistently (at least until fall 1975) if selectively implemented, which saw many of the pre-1966 elite restored to at least honorable positions, and in significant cases to real power. Beyond that, the actual treatment of those deemed to have "erred" was relatively restrained,

---

[70] See Bo Yibo, *Huigu*, vol. 1 (1991), pp. 234-35; Teiwes, *Politics and Purges*, pp. xvii-xx; Teiwes and Sun, *Politics of Agricultural Cooperativization*, pp. 13, 15; and above, p. 596n4.

[71] For an overview of these developments, see Teiwes, *Politics and Purges*, pp. l-lxii. An indication of the chilling effect occurred in spring 1959, before Lushan, when Mao complained that even Liu Shaoqi was unwilling to be completely frank with him; Teiwes with Sun, *China's Road to Disaster*, p. 153. On a more anecdotal level, a senior Party historian reported that in 1963 Party elder Wu Yuzhang was at Zhongnanhai to meet Premier Zhou, but took a wrong turn and found himself face-to-face with Mao. Wu hastily excused himself, not daring to stay and run the risk of saying something wrong. Interview, April 1986.

particularly at the Center, and certainly compared to the Cultural Revolution. Deng Xiaoping was the sole Politburo member removed from office, but at the same time protected by Mao.[72] Suggestive of Mao's direct hand, and thus of the limits of his magnanimity, was that Zhou Enlai suffered most of all top-level leaders—remaining in office to the time of his passing, but subjected to repeated political and psychological stress, and denied full honors in death. Meanwhile, at a practical level, leading figures were better prepared to handle leftist attacks than they had been when the Cultural Revolution descended on the elite as a bolt from the blue in 1966. As a result, high-ranking officials generally gave away as little as possible in criticism meetings, retreated to hospital quarters when necessary, and basically waited out the storm.[73]

It is necessary, however, to distinguish between fear engendered by actual outcomes, where the suffering of those under attack was far less than what had happened earlier in the "Cultural Revolution decade," and fear of being out of step with Mao. As indicated, whether due to a change in Mao's attitude or his failing physical condition, including his inability to attend to the details of cases where individuals were in trouble, political attacks never carried quite the same threat, although anxiety over what the "gang of four" might do after the Chairman's death clearly indicated that fear of dire consequences remained. At the same time, the fate of Lin Biao reemphasized Mao's awesome power, as evidenced by the reported words of Lin's son that "the Chairman commands such high prestige that he need only utter one sentence to remove anybody he chooses,"[74] while Mao's ruminations about future Cultural Revolutions served as a further warning. Thus fear and awe remained, as seen not only in Zhou's and Deng's caution, but also as reflected in Deng's resigned attitude once the Chairman's new attitude became clear in 1975-76, and in his delighted surprise when he was allowed to retain his Party card after the Tiananmen incident. Yet wishful thinking also marked the period, as when leaders supported Deng's 1975 efforts on the basis of their perception that Mao was fully behind him. Courage flowed from the belief that the tide had turned according to Mao's diktat. Something further was involved as well. As in the very early stages of the Cultural Revolution, when Mao initiated criticism of the "rightist wind" in late 1975 many officials could not quite believe that Mao would push matters to a new drastic purge. Whether in the cases of Zhou Rongxin, cadres in the State Council Research Office, or Qiao Guanhua and his wife, there was a sense, or at least hope, that all would turn out well, that after being exposed to criticism,

---

[72] Lower-ranking figures were less insulated, with various ministers subject to criticism and set aside, but only Wan Li was removed from office. Provincial-level leaders were still more subject to rough treatment, but there were few cases of such leaders being ousted. See above, pp. 172ff, 460, 512ff.

[73] See above, pp. 424-26, 432.

[74] "Outline of 'Project 571'," in Michael Y. M. Kau, ed., *The Lin Biao Affair: Power Politics and Military Coup* (White Plains: International Arts and Sciences Press, 1975), p. 92.

everything would be all right.[75] In 1966, this was a vain hope. In 1976, the issue was moot, first because the declining Chairman was in no condition to drive the process, and then because Hua and his establishment associates put a quick end to the threats Mao left behind on his deathbed.

Beyond and even more profoundly than fear, belief in Mao had underpinned his leadership since the 1940s, a belief that was enormously enhanced by the victory of 1949. That victory solidified forever Mao's status as a charismatic leader, a leader who had to be obeyed because he held the keys to success.[76] A palpable sense of this was conveyed in an interview with the widow of Deng Tuo, a prominent victim of the coming storm who committed suicide on the eve of the Cultural Revolution. Whatever she may have thought about her husband's demise, this lady, a Yan'an veteran herself, gave a heartfelt verdict on the revolutionary Mao: he was the only leader capable of avoiding reckless optimism or succumbing to pessimism in the face of overwhelming odds, the indispensable architect of victory.[77] Such widely shared faith was reinforced well into the PRC period when, in the two major decisions in which Mao essentially enforced his view over a Politburo consensus, Chinese entry into the Korean War and speeding up agricultural collectivization in 1955, the Chairman's position, in the *ex post facto* judgment of the elite, appeared to demonstrate again his superior insight. It was especially during this "golden age" that leaders with different opinions from Mao tended to ask themselves where they had gone wrong, why they couldn't keep up with the Chairman.[78]

As with fear, the Great Leap marked a significant but partial change in terms of belief. Belief, of course, was always linked to a suspension of disbelief, and this was clearly at play as various leaders accepted policies at sharp variance with their previous views, in this case when the PRC embarked on a totally unprecedented approach to economic development. This was graphically indicated in the recollections of a vice minister-level official who had significant access to Mao in 1958-59. This official, relatively pragmatic at the time, and a severe critic of the Chairman in the post-Mao period, admitted to believing in the leap against his instincts well into 1958.[79] Moreover, even as problems

---

[75] See above, pp. 412, 422, 423-24. On the eve of the Cultural Revolution, the sentiment that all would be well after criticism (*pipan, pipan, jiu haole*) was expressed by the wife of Wu Han, the first target of the movement. See Teiwes, *Politics and Purges*, p. lxi.

[76] For a discussion of Mao as a charismatic leader, see Teiwes, *Leadership*, pp. 46-49. Note that Mao's continuing authority beyond 1949, at least from the late 1950s, was not technically charismatic since his policies were no longer invariably successful, but had a quasi-charismatic status based on the magnitude of the victory resulting in the establishment of the PRC.

[77] Interview with the late Ding Yilan, April 1987.

[78] See Frederick C. Teiwes, "The Establishment and Consolidation of the New Regime, 1949-57," in MacFarquhar, *The Politics of China*, pp. 11-12; and idem with Sun, *China's Road to Disaster*, p. 13.

[79] Interview, April 1993. There are many other cases of people who should have known better, seemingly believing in the miraculous claims for the movement. See, e.g., Teiwes with Sun, *China's Road to Disaster*, p. 138.

became apparent, in ironic fashion Mao's credibility was sustained by the fact that he was the first leader to point out these shortcomings openly, as others were inhibited by a combination of fear and belief. As much as this distorted the Chairman's responsibility for the horrific consequence of the leap, for Bo Yibo, writing more than four decades later in a likely mixture of sincerity and obligation to uphold Mao's prestige, this was another indication of the inability of others to match him.[80] Of course, as matters deteriorated further and evidence of failure accumulated, a sweeping credulity could no longer be maintained, and by January 1962 Mao not only made a rare self-criticism, but Peng Zhen came as close as any leader ever did in the 1949-76 period to suggesting openly in an inner Party forum that the Chairman could indeed make mistakes.[81]

Nevertheless, Mao's authority was undiminished, and even following the Cultural Revolution, his next major blunder that affected elite prerogatives and interests more directly than the Great Leap, signs of suspension of disbelief endured. We have cited two particularly striking examples: Deng Xiaoping chiding his children when they joined him in his Jiangxi exile for their negative view of the Cultural Revolution, telling them to have faith in the Chairman; and Hu Yaobang, a year after Mao's death, telling his associates at the Central Party School that the concept of the Cultural Revolution was brilliant, but things went wrong in its implementation.[82] Beyond these particular statements, it is possible to see the wholehearted efforts of many leaders in the 1975 consolidation effort in particular as not simply reflecting their own policy preferences, or a calculated assessment of what they could get away with, but also the view that they were implementing an accurate interpretation of the Chairman's "line" of the moment. Whatever Deng actually thought of the Cultural Revolution in 1975, what is striking is his apparent complete surprise when Mao concluded that his efforts were undermining the current aim of consolidating the movement. Notwithstanding the doublethink involved, the overwhelming evidence is that the elite *wanted* to believe in Mao, even if various of his policies were barely credible. As demonstrated by memoir after memoir in the post-Mao era, elite loyalty to Mao was intense. He was indeed, in Ye Jianying's term, a "precious dish" to whom obedience was second nature.

As Mao's life ebbed away, there was still plenty to fear, but less from a fading Chairman himself than there was a decade earlier, as his approach to erring

---

[80] See Bo Yibo, *Huigu*, vol. 2, pp. 807, 817-18; and Teiwes with Sun, *China's Road to Disaster*, pp. 119ff.

[81] See MacFarquhar, *Origins 3*, pp. 156-58.

[82] See above, pp. 70, 335. Hu Yaobang's view of the Cultural Revolution and Mao altered over the years, however. According to Li Rui, shortly before Hu's death in 1989, he had an extended talk with Li, and claimed that all of China's problems under CCP rule stemmed from Mao's "imperial tyranny and the Stalinist dictatorship of the proletariat." See "Li Rui jilu de Hu Yaobang zhengzhi yiyan" [Li Rui's Notes of Hu Yaobang's Political Testament] (November 13, 2005), http://www1. chinesenewsnet.com/MainNews/Forums/BackStage/2005_11_12_22_7_29_741.html.

leaders moderated and his declining physical vitality reduced the likelihood of dramatic action on his part. There was also less reason to believe in Mao's insight, with the shock of the Lin Biao affair intensifying elite doubts about the Cultural Revolution. Yet opposition to the Chairman was simply unthinkable. Even after his death, one of the cruelest blows that Party leaders could experience, including those who had suffered during the Cultural Revolution, was exclusion from his memorial ceremony,[83] and initially it was an unquestioned duty to uphold his "line" in name, even as it was quickly reversed in practice. For the top elite, as well as the vast majority of Party members, Mao exercised a moral authority that eclipsed, and indeed was the basis of, both fear and belief. This moral authority had many aspects that reflected cultural values and revolutionary aspirations. The key consideration was that the elite by and large saw these aspects in the Chairman; whether, or to what extent, they existed in fact is a secondary matter.

One factor was Mao's intellectual stature, both as a presumed Marxist philosopher, and as someone with a deep knowledge of Chinese history, politics and literature, an erudition that left his leadership colleagues overwhelmed, as in the cases of Zhou Enlai and Lin Biao seeking out scholars to interpret what they regarded as his profound statements.[84] Another factor, however ironic, was life style and personal sacrifice. Mao had cultivated a puritan ethos for the Party and a self-sacrificing image for himself. In reality, the Chairman's real living habits were probably a state secret not widely known outside his household, although rumors of his sexual indulgences existed, while his many villas and other special prerogatives were well known by the higher-ranking leadership but considered entirely appropriate to his status. In any case, such considerations seemingly paled in elite consciousness compared to the loss of Mao's children and other hardships during the revolutionary struggle, and to the death of his favorite son during the Korean War.[85] The perception was crucial, and the Chairman was clearly given the benefit of any doubts by his comrades. In certain respects and contexts, moreover, Mao may have lived up to the image, as in his decision not

---

[83] Note especially Hu Qiaomu's distress at being excluded; above, p. 553. This loyal secretary was more affected by the loss of his link to Mao at the Chairman's death than by any possibility that the new situation might improve his then perilous political situation.

A similar yet different reaction can be seen in the experience of Sidney Rittenberg, one of the few foreigners to gain admission to the CCP and someone familiar with Mao. Imprisoned for eight years at the time of Mao's death, Rittenberg recalled a sense of loss at "the great Chairman Mao's" passing, but found himself, inexplicably he thought at the time, unable to shed tears. Rittenberg and Bennett, *The Man Who Stayed Behind*, p. 427.

[84] Zhang Yunsheng, *Maojiawan jishi: Lin Biao mishu huiyilu* [True Account of Maojiawan: Memoirs of Lin Biao's Secretary] (Beijing: Chunqiu chubanshe, 1988), p. 396; *Zhou nianpu*, vol. 3, p. 717. Of course, the possible political implications of what Mao said were ever-present in such seeking of meaning, but the view of the Chairman's exceptional knowledge was genuine.

[85] On the death of Mao Anying and the Chairman's reaction, see the account of Mao's bodyguard, Li Yinqiao, in Quan Yanchi, *Mao Zedong: Man Not God* (Beijing: Foreign Languages Press, 1992), pp. 171-72.

to eat meat during the Great Leap famine. But again, what is important is the perception, and in this case the Premier lauded Mao's action, saying that if the Chairman was making the sacrifice, all leaders should follow suit.[86]

Fundamental to Mao's moral authority was the belief that his animating purpose was to benefit the revolution, socialism, the country and the Chinese people. Mao's stated goals and grand visions were fully in tune with the larger leadership's desires: building socialism, creating an egalitarian society, advancing toward communism, and fulfilling the dream of a rich and powerful China. As a consequence of his leadership in achieving the initial revolutionary victory, the Chairman was seen by the elite as embodying those goals, someone not only owed obedience as the Party's leader, but also as the dynastic founder who had led the CCP to the Promised Land, and who had a vision for an even more glorious future. Given these considerations, CCP leaders, many of whom were swept up in the insanity of the Great Leap precisely because they shared Mao's objective of rapid growth to benefit both national power and popular livelihood,[87] could forgive Mao's failures since his intentions were good. Tragically, the same Chairman, who cried on the eve of the Great Leap when shown a hard, virtually inedible bun poor peasants were condemned to eat,[88] would give up eating meat several years later when becoming aware of the vast starvation his policies had wrecked on the peasantry, even though he never truly accepted responsibility. But in the special world of the Party leadership and broader CCP, even an unmitigated disaster such as the leap could be forgiven, and, as seen in Hu Yaobang's 1977 reflections, the subsequent disaster of the Cultural Revolution could also be rationalized in terms of Mao's claimed intent of attacking bureaucracy and Party privilege.

Perceptions of good intentions, personal sacrifice, intellectual erudition, and a grand vision of commonly held goals could not have sustained Mao's moral authority against the catastrophic failures after 1957 without the elite's belief that the Chairman was inseparable from the revolutionary success of 1949. As Mao put it when assessing his life's work, few would not recognize his achievements in defeating Chiang Kai-shek and establishing the People's Republic. While a detached observer might include such factors as Japanese over-extension in World War II, or Guomindang incompetence, for the CCP elite Mao's leadership was the *sine qua non* of achieving their lifetime mission. For revolutionaries whose task must have seemed distant and at times hopeless over several decades of struggle, to stand on the Tiananmen rostrum in 1949 as the rulers of a proud and great nation was an unimaginable accomplishment. To turn against Mao would

---

[86] Li Yinqiao, *Zai Mao Zedong shenbian shiwunian* [Fifteen Years at the Side of Mao Zedong] (Shijiazhuang: Hebei renmin chubanshe, 1992), p. 230. While Zhou may have been motivated in part to flatter Mao, there is little doubt that Mao made the gesture and that this was seen as reflecting his dedication to the people.

[87] See Teiwes with Sun, *China's Road to Disaster*, pp. 86ff. Also note the enthusiasm of Zhou Enlai and others two years earlier at the start of the 1956 "little leap forward." *Ibid.*, p. 23.

[88] See Quan Yanchi, *Mao Zedong*, p. 48.

have amounted to rejecting their own life's endeavors, as much as their leader. Due to the victory of the real revolution, Mao Zedong was not only obeyed, but forgiven for grave errors that damaged China, the CCP, and leading comrades who had suffered grievously despite unbending loyalty to their leader. It was a moral obligation that could not be denied.

BIBLIOGRAPHY

Chinese Language Sources

Books

An Jianshe, ed. *Zhou Enlai de zuihou suiyue 1966-1976* [Zhou Enlai's Last Years, 1966-1976]. Beijing: Zhongyang wenxian chubanshe, 2002.

Bo Yibo. *Ruogan zhongda juece yu shijian de huigu* [Reflections on Certain Major Decisions and Events]. Vol. 1, Beijing: Zhonggong zhongyang dangxiao chubanshe, 1991; vol. 2, 1993.

Cao Junjie, ed. *Zhongguo er Qiao—Hu Qiaomu, Qiao Guanhua zhuanliie* [China's Two Qiaos—Brief Biographies of Hu Qiaomu and Qiao Guanhua]. Nanjing: Jiangsu renmin chubanshe, 1996.

Chedi jiefa pipan 'sirenbang' cuandang duoquan de taotian zuixing [Thoroughly Expose and Criticize the Monstrous Crimes of the "Gang of Four" in Overthrowing the Party and Seizing Power]. Beijing: Renmin chubanshe, 1977.

Chen Dabin. *Ji'e yinfa de biange: yige zishen jizhe de qinshen jingli yu sikao* [The Revolution Sparked By Famine: The Personal Experiences and Reflections of a Senior Journalist]. Beijing: Zhonggong dangshi chubanshe, 1998.

Chen Qingquan and Song Guangwei. *Lu Dingyi zhuan* [Biography of Lu Dingyi]. Beijing: Zhonggong dangshi chubanshe, 1999.

Chen Shiqu. *Cong Jinggangshan zoujin Zhongnanhai: Chen Shiqu huiyi Mao Zedong* [From Jinggangshan to Entering Zhongnanhai: Chen Shiqu Remembers Mao Zedong]. Beijing: Zhonggong zhongyang dangxiao chubanshe, 1993.

Chen Xilian. *Chen Xilian huiyilu* [Memoirs of Chen Xilian]. Beijing: Jiefangjun chubanshe, 2004.

Cheng Hua, ed. *Zhou Enlai he ta de mishumen* [Zhou Enlai and His Secretaries]. Beijing: Zhongguo guangbo dianshi chubanshe, 1992.

Cheng Zhongyuan. *Deng Xiaoping de ershisici tanhua* [Deng Xiaoping's 24 Talks]. Beijing: Renmin chubanshe, 2004.

_____ and Xia Xingzhen. *Deng Xiaoping yu 1975 zhengdun* [Deng Xiaoping and the 1975 Consolidation]. Beijing: Renmin chubanshe, 2004.

_____ and Xia Xingzhen. *Lishi zhuanzhe de qianzou: Deng Xiaoping zai yijiuqiwu* [The Prelude to the Historical Turning Point: Deng Xiaoping in 1975]. Beijing: Zhongguo qingnian chubanshe, 2004.

Dai Jiafang. *Zouxiang huimie: "Wenge" Wenhua buzhang Yu Huiyong chenfulu* [Toward Destruction: Record of the Tide-following "Cultural Revolution" Minister of Culture Yu Huiyong]. Beijing: *Guangming ribao* chubanshe, 1994.

Deng Liqun. *Deng Liqun guoshi jiangtanlu* [Record of Deng Liqun's Lectures on National History]. 5 vols., Beijing: Zhonghua Renmin Gongheguo shigao bianweihui, 2000.

_____. *Deng Liqun zishu: shierge chunqiu (1975-1987)* [Deng Liqun's Self-statement: 12 Years, 1975-1987]. Internal publication available at the Fairbank Center Library, Harvard University.

Ding Kaiwen, ed. *Chongshen Lin Biao zuian* [The Lin Biao Case Reassessed]. New York: Mingjing chubanshe, 2004.

Dongfang He. *Zhang Aiping zhuan* [Biography of Zhang Aiping]. Beijing: Renmin chubanshe, 2000.

Du Runsheng, ed. *Zhongguo nongcun gaige juece jishi* [A Record of the Policies of Chinese Rural Reform]. Beijing: Zhongyang wenxian chubanshe, 1999.

Du Xiuxian. *Hongjingtou—Zhongnanhai sheying shiyan zhong de guoshi fengyun* [Red Camera—National Affairs Storms in the Eyes of a Zhongnanhai Photographer]. Vol. 1, Shenyang: Liaoning renmin chubanshe, 1998.

_____. *Hongzhaopian* [Red Photos]. Vol. 2, Xi'an: Shaanxi Shifan Daxue chubanshe, 1999.

Fan Daren. *"Wenge" yubi chenfulu: "Liang Xiao" wangshi* [The Rise and Fall of the "Cultural Revolution's" Imperial Pens: The Past Events of *Liang Xiao*]. Hong Kong: Mingbao chubanshe, 1999.

Fan Shuo, *Ye Jianying zai feichang shiqi 1966-1976* [Ye Jianying in an Extraordinary Period, 1966-1976]. 2 vols., Beijing: Huawen chubanshe, 2002.

_____. *Ye Jianying zai 1976* [Ye Jianying in 1976]. Beijing: Zhonggcng zhongyang dangxiao chubanshe, 1995.

Feng Dongshu. *Wenmang zaixiang Chen Yonggui* [Illiterate Minister Chen Yonggui]. Beijing: Zhongguo wenlian chubangongsi, 1998.

Gao Gao and Yan Jiaqi. *"Wenhua dageming" shinianshi, 1966-1976* [A Ten-year History of the "Great Cultural Revolution," 1966-1976]. Tianjin: Tianjin renmin chubanshe, 1986. Trans. as *Turbulent Decade: A History of the Cultural Revolution*, by Yan Jiaqi and Gao Gao. Honolulu: University of Hawaii Press, 1996.

Gao Wenqian. *Wannian Zhou Enlai* [The Later Years of Zhou Enlai]. New York: Mingjing chubanshe, 2003.

Gao Yi. *Lishi xuanze le Deng Xiaoping* [History Chose Deng Xiaoping]. Wuhan: Wuhan chubanshe, 1999.

Geng Biao. *Geng Biao huiyilu (1949-1992)* [Memoirs of Geng Biao, 1949-1992]. Nanjing: Jiangsu renmin chubanshe, 1998.

Guan Weixun. *Wo suo zhidao de Ye Qun* [Ye Qun according to My Knowledge]. Beijing: Zhongguo wenxue chubanshe, 1993.

Guo Dehong and Tang Yingwu, eds. *Zhonggong dangshi gaoceng renwu pingzhuan, shang juan* [Critical Biographies of Senior Figures in CCP Party History, Volume 1]. Changchun: Jilin wenshi chubanshe, 2000.

Guo Jinrong. *Mao Zedong de huanghun suiyue* [The Twilight of Mao Zedong's Life]. Hong Kong: Tiandi tushu youxian gongsi, 1990.

Han Taihua, ed. *Zhongguo Gongchandang ruogan lishi wenti xiezhen* [True Portrait of Some CCP Historical Questions]. Beijing: Zhongguo yuanshi chubanshe, 1998.

Hao Jiansheng *et al. Yang Gui yu Hongqiqu* [Yang Gui and the Red Flag Irrigation Canal]. Beijing: Zhongyang bianyi chubanshe, 2004.

Hao Mengbi and Duan Haoran, eds. *Zhongguo Gongchandang liushinian* [Sixty Years of the CCP]. 2 vols., Beijing: Jiefangjun chubanshe, 1984.

Hu Jiwei. *Cong Hua Guofeng xiatai dao Hu Yaobang xiatai* [From the Fall of Hua Guofeng to the Fall of Hu Yaobang]. New York: Mingjing chubanshe, 1997.

Hu Sheng, ed. *Zhongguo Gongchandang qishinian* [The CCP's Seventy Years]. Beijing: Zhonggong dangshi chubanshe, 1991.

Hu Shihong. *Zhang Aiping zai 1975* [Zhang Aiping in 1975]. Beijing: Zuojia chubanshe, 1998.

Hua Guofeng Tongzhi shi Mao Zhuxi geming luxian de zhuoyue jichengzhe [Comrade Hua Guofeng Is the Brilliant Inheritor of Chairman Mao's Revolutionary Line]. Beijing: Renmin chubanshe, 1977.

Huiyi Deng Xiaoping [Remember Deng Xiaoping]. Vol. 1, Beijing: Zhongyang wenxian chubanshe, 1998.

Ji Xichen. *Shi wu qianli de niandai: yi wei "Renmin ribao" laojizhe de biji* [An Unprecedented Era: The Notes of an Old *People's Daily* Reporter]. 2 vols., Beijing: *Renmin ribao* chubanshe, 2001.

Ji Zhi [pseud.]. *Sirenbang yanxinglu* [Record of the Words and Deeds of the Gang of Four]. Hong Kong: Wenhua ziliao gongyingsi, 1977.

Jiang Weiqing. *Jiang Weiqing huiyilu* [Memoirs of Jiang Weiqing]. Nanjing: Jiangsu renmin chubanshe, 1996.

Jin Chongji, ed., *Zhou Enlai zhuan 1949-1976* [Biography of Zhou Enlai, 1949-1976]. 2 vols., Beijing: Zhongyang wenxian chubanshe, 1998.

Jin Chunming. *Jin Chunming zixuan wenji* [Jin Chunming's Self-selected Collected Works]. Chengdu: Sichuan renmin chubanshe, 2002.

Li Desheng. *Li Desheng huiyilu* [Memoirs of Li Desheng]. Beijing: Jiefangjun chubanshe, 1997.

Li Ke and Hao Shengzhang. *"Wenhua dageming" zhong de Renmin Jiefangjun* [The PLA during the "Cultural Revolution"]. Beijing: Zhonggong dangshi ziliao chubanshe, 1989.

Li Lianqing. *Waijiao yingcai Qiao Guanhua* [Foreign Affairs Bright Talent Qiao Guanhua]. Nanjing: Jiangsu renmin chubanshe, 2000.

Li Ping. *Kaiguo Zongli Zhou Enlai* [Founding Premier Zhou Enlai]. Beijing: Zhonggong zhongyang dangxiao chubanshe, 1994.

Li Wenqing. *Jinkan Xu Shiyou (1967-1985)* [A Close Look at Xu Shiyou, 1967-1985]. Beijing: Jiefangjun wenyi chubanshe, 2002.

Li Xun. *Da bengkui: Shanghai gongren zaofanpai xingwangshi* [The Great Collapse: The Rise and Fall of Worker Rebels in Shanghai]. Taipei: Shibao wenhua chubanshe, 1996.

Li Yinqiao. *Zai Mao Zedong shenbian shiwunian* [Fifteen Years at the Side of Mao Zedong]. Shijiazhuang: Hebei renmin chubanshe, 1992. Abridged trans. by Quan Yanchi. *Mao Zedong: Man Not God.* Beijing: Foreign Languages Press, 1992.

Li Zhonghai *et al.*, eds. *Huiyi Hu Qiaomu* [Remember Hu Qiaomu]. Beijing: Dangdai Zhongguo chubanshe, 1994.

Liao Hansheng. *Liao Hansheng huiyilu, xu* [Memoirs of Liao Hansheng, continued]. Beijing: Jiefangjun chubanshe, 2003.

Lin Qing. *Zhou Enlai zai zaixiang shengya* [Zhou Enlai's Career as Prime Minister]. [Hong Kong:] Changcheng wenhua chuban gongsi, 1991.

Lin Qingshan. *Fengyun shinian yu Deng Xiaoping* [Deng Xiaoping and the Ten-year Storm]. Beijing: Jiefangjun chubanshe, 1989.

_____. *Kang Sheng zhuan* [Biography of Kang Sheng]. Changchun: Jilin renmin chubanshe, 1996.

Lishi de shenpan (xuji) [A Historical Trial, continued]. Beijing, Qunzhong chubanshe, 1986.

Liu Bing. *Fengyu suiyue: Qinghua Daxue "Wenhua dageming" yishi* [Times of Tumult: A Memoir of Qinghua University in the Cultural Revolution]. Beijing: Qinghua Daxue chubanshe, 1998.

Long Pingping. *Deng Xiaoping yu tade shiye* [Deng Xiaoping and His Endeavors]. Fuzhou: Fujian jiaoyu chubanshe, 1997.

_____. *Xishuo Deng Xiaoping* [A Detailed Account of Deng Xiaoping]. Beijing: Hongqi chubanshe, 1997.

Ma Jisen. *Waijiaobu wenge jishi* [True Record of the Foreign Affairs Ministry during the Cultural Revolution]. Hong Kong: Zhongwen Daxue chubanshe, 2003. Trans. as *The Cultural Revolution in the Foreign Ministry of* China. Hong Kong: The Chinese University Press, 2004.

Mao Mao [Deng Rong]. *Wode fuqin Deng Xiaoping, shangce* [My Father Deng Xiaoping, vol. 1]. Beijing: Zhongyang wenxian chubanshe, 1993. Trans. as *Deng Xiaoping, My Father*, by Deng Mao Mao. New York: Basic Books, 1995.

_____. *Wode fuqin Deng Xiaoping: "wenge" suiyue* [My Father Deng Xiaoping: The "Cultural Revolution" Years]. Beijing: Zhongyang wenxian chubanshe, 2000. Trans. as *Deng Xiaoping and the Cultural Revolution: A Daughter Recalls the Critical Years.* New York: Bertelsmann, 2005 and Beijing: Foreign Languages Press, 2002.

Mao Zedong zhuan (1949-1976) [Biography of Mao Zedong, 1949-1976]. 2 vols., Beijing: Zhongyang wenxian chubanshe, 2003.

Nie Rongzhen. *Nie Rongzhen huiyilu* [Memoirs of Nie Rongzhen]. 3 vols., Beijing: Jiefangjun chubanshe, 1984.

Nie Rongzhen zhuan [Biography of Nie Rongzhen]. Beijing: Dangdai Zhongguo chubanshe, 1994.

Niu Ying and Peng Xiaozhong. *Song Ping zai Gansu* [Song Ping in Gansu]. Beijing: Zhongyang wenxian chubanshe, 2003.

Pei Hua. *Zhong-Ri waijiao fengyun zhong de Deng Xiaoping* [Deng Xiaoping in the Storm of Sino-Japanese Relations]. Beijing: Zhongyang wenxian chubanshe, 2000.

Qing Ye and Fang Lei. *Deng Xiaoping zai 1976, shangjuan: Tiananmen shijian* [Deng Xiaoping in 1976, vol. 1: The Tiananmen Incident]. Shenyang: Chunfeng wenyi chubanshe, 1993.

————. *Deng Xiaoping zai 1976, xiajuan: Huairentang shibian* [Deng Xiaoping in 1976, vol. 2: The Huairentang Events]. Shenyang: Chunfeng wenyi chubanshe, 1993.

Quan Yanchi. *Zouxia shengtan de Zhou Enlai* [Zhou Enlai Down to Earth]. Hong Kong: Tiandi tushu youxian gongsi, 1993.

Shen Baoxiang. *Zhenli biaozhun wenti taolun shimo* [The Debate on the Criterion of Truth Issue from Beginning to End]. Beijing: Zhongguo qingnian chubanshe, 1997.

Sima Changfeng. *Deng Xiaoping fuzhi shimo* [A Comprehensive Account of Deng Xiaoping's Return]. Hong Kong: Bowen shuju, 1980.

Sima Dongqu. *Haojie: Shanghaitan, yige Zhongyang gongzuozu chengyuan de erwen mudu* [Catastrophy: Shanghai, as Heard and Seen by a Central Work Team Member]. Beijing: Zhonggong zhongyang dangxiao chubanshe, 1999.

Song Renqiong. *Song Renqiong huiyilu: xuji* [Memoirs of Song Renqiong, continued]. Beijing: Jiefangjun chubanshe, 1996.

Sun Yeli and Xiong Lianghua. *Gongheguo jingji fengyun zhong de Chen Yun* [Chen Yun in the Storms of the Republic's Economy]. Beijing: Zhongyang wenxian chubanshe, 1996.

Tian Guoliang *et al. Hu Yaobang zhuan* [Biography of Hu Yaobang]. Beijing: Zhonggong dangshi ziliao chubanshe, 1989.

Tong Xiaopeng. *Fengyu sishinian (dierbu)* [Forty Years of Trials and Hardships (second part)]. Beijing: Zhongyang wenxian chubanshe, 1996.

Wang Dongxing. *Wang Dongxing huiyi—Mao Zedong yu Lin Biao fangeming jituan de douzheng* [Wang Dongxing Remembers—The Struggle between Mao Zedong and the Lin Biao Counterrevolutionary Clique]. Beijing: Dangdai Zhongguo chubanshe, 1997.

Wang Li. *Wang Li fansi (xia)* [Wang Li's Reflections, vol. 2]. Hong Kong: Beixing chubanshe, 2001.

Wang Lixin. *Yao chi mi zhao Wan Li: Anhui nongcun gaige shilu* [For Rice to Eat, Find Wan Li: True Record of Anhui's Rural Reform]. Beijing: Beijing tushuguan chubanshe, 2000.

Wang Nianyi. *1949-1989 nian de Zhongguo: Dadongluan de niandai* [China 1949-1989: The Years of Great Turmoil]. Henan: Henan renmin chubanshe, 1988.

Wang Ping. *Wang Ping huiyilu* [Memoirs of Wang Ping]. Beijing: Jiefangjun chubanshe, 1992.

Wang Ruoshui. *Xin faxian de Mao Zedong: puren yanzhong de weiren* [Newly Discovered Mao Zedong: A Great Man in the Eyes of Slaves]. Hong Kong: Mingbao chubanshe, 2002.

Wang Wenfeng. *Cong "Tonghuai Zhou" shen: dao shen Jiang Qing* [From "Tonghuai Zhou" to the Trial of Jiang Qing]. Beijing: Dangdai Zhongguo chubanshe, 2004).

Wang Zhen zhuan [Biography of Wang Zhen]. 2 vols., Beijing: Dangdai Zhongguo chubanshe, 2001.

Weida de renmin gongpu—huainian Li Xiannian Tongzhi [A Great Public Servant—Cherish the Memory of Comrade Li Xiannian]. Beijing: Zhongyang wenxian chubanshe, 1993.

Women zhongxin aidai yingming lingxiu Hua Zhuxi [We Sincerely Love and Support the Wise Leader Chairman Hua]. Beijing: Renmin chubanshe, 1977.

Wu De. *Wu De koushu: shinian fengyu wangshi—wo zai Beijing gongzuo de yixie jingli* [Wu De's Oral Account: Past Events during the Ten Years' Storm—Some Experiences from My Work in Beijing]. Beijing: Dangdai Zhongguo chubanshe, 2004.

Wu Lengxi. *Shinian lunzhan: 1956-1966 Zhong-Su guanxi huiyilu* [Ten Years' Theoretical Struggle: Recollections of Sino-Soviet Relations in 1956-1966]. 2 vols., Beijing: Zhongyang wenxian chubanshe, 1999.

_____. *Yi Mao Zhuxi—Wo qinsheng jingli ruogan zhongda lishi shijian pianduan* [Remembering Chairman Mao—Fragments of My Personal Experience with Certain Major Historical Events]. Beijing: Xinhua chubanshe, 1995.

Wu Shihong and Gao Qi, eds. *Deng Xiaoping yu Gongheguo zhongda lishi shijian* [Deng Xiaoping and the Republic's Major Historical Events]. Beijing: Renmin chubanshe, 2000.

Wu Si. *Zhongguo touhao nongmin: Chen Yonggui chenfulu* [China's Number One Peasant: Chen Yonggui's Rise and Fall]. Hong Kong: Tiandi tushu youxian gongsi, 1993.

Wu Xiang. *Zhongguo nongcun gaige shilu* [A True Account of China's Rural Reforms]. Hangzhou: Zhejiang renmin chubanshe, 2001.

Xia Chao and Yang Fengcheng. *Longnian zhibian—Zhongguo 1976 nian jishi* [Transformations in the Year of the Dragon—Record of Events in China in 1976]. Shijiazhuang: Hebei renmin chubanshe, 1994.

Xiao Jingguang. *Xiao Jingguang huiyilu (xuji)* [Memoirs of Xiao Jingguang, continued]. Beijing: Jiefangjun chubanshe, 1988.

Xiao Ping and Wang Sheng, eds. *Junshi jiemi* [Exposing the Secrets of Military History]. Heilongjiang: Heilongjiang renmin chubanshe, 1992.

Xiao Sike. *Chaoji shenpan: Tu Men Jiangjun canyu shenli Lin Biao fangeming jituan qinliji* [The Super Trial: General Tu Men's Account of the Trial of the Case of the Lin Biao Counterrevolutionary Clique]. 2 vols., Jinan: Jinan chubanshe, 1992.

_____. *Zhiqing zheshuo* [Insiders' Story]. Beijing: Zhongguo qingnian chubanshe, 2004.

Xing Ziling. *Lin Biao zhengzhuan* [Lin Biao's True Story]. Hong Kong: Liwen chubanshe, 2002.

Xiong Huayuan and Liao Xinwen. *Zhou Enlai zongli shengya* [Zhou Enlai's Career as the Premier]. Beijing: Renmin chubanshe, 1997.

Xu Huan'gang and Li Zhaoxiang. *Ke Hua Dashi de waijiao shengya* [Ambassador Ke Hua's Foreign Affairs Career]. Beijing: Zhongguo qingnian chubanshe, 2001.

Xu Jingxian. *Shinian yimeng: qian Shanghai shiwei shuji Xu Jingxian wenge huiyilu* [Ten Years One Dream: Cultural Revolution Memoirs of Former Shanghai Municipal Secretary Xu Jingxian]. Hong Kong: Shidai guoji chuban youxian gongsi, 2004.

Xu Xiangqian zhuan [Biography of Xu Xiangqian]. Beijing: Dangdai Zhongguo chubanshe, 1991.

Xue Qingchao. *Lishi zhuanzhe guantou de Deng Xiaoping* [Deng Xiaoping at the Turning Points of History]. Zhengzhou: Zhongyuan nongmin chubanshe, 1996.

Yang Qing. *Huiyi Yang Yong Jiangjun* [Remember General Yang Yong]. Hong Kong: Mingbao chubanshe, 1986.

Yang Shangkun *et al. Wo suo zhidao de Hu Qiaomu* [The Hu Qiaomu I Knew]. Beijing: Dangdai Zhongguo chubanshe, 1997.

Yao Jin, ed. *Yao Yilin baixitan* [Evening Chats with Yao Yilin]. Beijing: Zhongguo shangye chubanshe, 1998

Ye Fei. *Ye Fei huiyilu (xu): zai Jiaotongbu qijian* [Memoirs of Ye Fei, continued: The Period at the Ministry of Communications]. Beijing: Renmin jiaotong chubanshe, 2001.

Ye Jianying zhuan [Biography of Ye Jianying]. Beijing: Dangdai Zhongguo chubanshe, 1995.

Ye Yonglie. *Cong Hua Guofeng dao Deng Xiaoping: Zhonggong shiyijie sanzhong quanhui qianhou* [From Hua Guofeng to Deng Xiaoping: Before and After the CCP's Third Plenum of the 11th Central Committee]. Hong Kong: Tiandi tushu youxian gongsi, 1997.

_____. *Jiang Qing zhuan* [Biography of Jiang Qing]. Beijing: Zuojia chubanshe, 1993.

_____. *Rongru gongguo* [Glory, Humiliation, Achievements and Mistakes]. Beijing: Zhonggong dangshi chubanshe, 2004.

_____. *Wang Hongwen zhuan* [Biography of Wang Hongwen]. Changchun: Shidai wenyi chubanshe, 1993.

_____. *Wannian Mao Zedong* [The Later Years of Mao Zedong]. Beijing: Zhonggong dangshi chubanshe, 2004.

_____. *Yao Wenyuan zhuan* [Biography of Yao Wenyuan]. Changchun: Shidai wenyi chubanshe, 1993.

_____. *Ye Jianying zai 1976* [Ye Jianying in 1976]. Beijing: Zhonggong dangshi chubanshe, 2004.

_____. *Zhang Chunqiao zhuan* [Biography of Zhang Chunqiao]. Changchun: Shidai wenyi chubanshe, 1993.

Yin Jiamin. *Gongheguo fengyun zhong de Mao Zedong yu Zhou Enlai* [Mao Zedong and Zhou Enlai during the Republic's Tumult]. Beijing: Zhonggong zhongyang dangxiao chubanshe, 1999.

_____. *Jiangjun buru shiming* [The General Does His Job Well]. Beijing: Jiefangjun chubanshe, 1992.

Yu Guangyuan. *Wenge zhong de wo* [My Cultural Revolution]. Shanghai: Shanghai yuandong chubanshe, 1995.

Yu Shicheng. *Deng Xiaoping yu Mao Zedong* [Deng Xiaoping and Mao Zedong]. Beijing: Zhonggong zhongyang dangxiao chubanshe, 1995.

Zhang Guangyou. *Gaige fengyun zhong de Wan Li* [Wan Li in the Storm of Reform]. Beijing: Renmin chubanshe, 1995.

_____ and Ding Longjia. *Wan Li* [Wan Li]. Beijing: Zhonggong dangshi chubanshe, 2000.

Zhang Hanzhi. *Kuaguo houhou de dahongmen* [Stepping into the Large Scarlet Gate]. Shanghai: Wenhui chubanshe, 2002.

_____ et al. *Wo yu Qiao Guanhua* [Qiao Guanhua and I]. Beijing: Zhongguo qingnian chubanshe, 1994.

Zhang Hua. *Deng Xiaoping yu 1975 nian de Zhongguo* [Deng Xiaoping and China in 1975]. Beijing: Zhonggong dangshi chubanshe, 2004.

_____ and Su Caiqing, eds. *Huishou "wenge": Zhongguo shinian "wenge" fenxi yu fansi* [Recalling the "Cultural Revolution": Analysis and Rethinking of China's Ten Years of "Cultural Revolution"]. 2 vols., Beijing: Zhonggong dangshi chubanshe, 2000.

Zhang Huifang and Wang Fang. *Renmin jizhe Mu Qing* [People's Reporter Mu Qing]. Zhengzhou: Henan renmin chubanshe, 2003.

Zhang Jiangming. *Lishi zhuanzhe guantou de Ye Jianying* [Ye Jianying at the Historical Turning Point]. Beijing: Zhonggong dangshi chubanshe, 1997.

Zhang Tingdong. *Wo pei Yeshuai zuowan zuihou shiqinian: yi wei shenbian mishu de huiyi* [I Accompanied Marshal Ye during His Final 17 Years: Recollections of a Secretary at His Side]. Beijing: Zhonggong dangshi chubanshe, 1999.

Zhang Yunsheng. *Maojiawan jishi: Lin Biao mishu huiyilu* [True Account of Maojiawan: Memoirs of Lin Biao's Secretary]. Beijing: Chunqiu chubanshe, 1988.

Zhang Zuoliang. *Zhou Enlai de zuihou shinian: yiwei baojian yisheng de huiyi* [Zhou Enlai's Last Ten Years: Recollections of a Medical Care Doctor]. Shanghai: Shanghai renmin chubanshe, 1997.

Zhong Kan. *Kang Sheng pingzhuan* [Critical Biography of Kang Sheng]. Beijing: Hongqi chubanshe, 1982.

Major Party History Journals

Bainianchao [The Hundred Year Tide]. Beijing: Zhonggong zhongyang dangshi yanjiushi, 1997- .

Dang de wenxian [The Party's Documents]. Beijing: Zhongyang wenxian chubanshe, 1988-.

Dangdai Zhongguoshi yanjiu [Contemporary China History Studies]. Beijing: Dangdai Zhongguo chubanshe, 1994-.

Dangshi tongxun [Party History Newsletter]. Beijing: Zhongyang dangshi yanjiushi, 1983-87.

Dangshi yanjiu [Research on Party History]. Beijing: Zhonggong zhongyang dangxiao chubanshe, 1980-87.

Wenxian he yanjiu [Documents and Research]. Beijing: Renmin chubanshe, 1982-87.

Yanhuang chunqiu [Chinese Annals]. Beijing: Zhonghua yanhuang wenhua yanjiuhui, 1992-
.

Zhonggong dangshi yanjiu [Research on CCP History]. Beijing: Zhonggong dangshi chubanshe, 1988-.

Zhonggong dangshi ziliao [Materials on CCP Party History]. Beijing: Zhonggong dangshi ziliao chubanshe, 1981-.

Zhonghua ernü [Sons and Daughters of China]. Beijing: Zhonghua zazhishe, 1995-.

Articles

An Jianshe, "Gaoju pipan jizuo sichao de qizhi" [Hold High the Banner of Criticizing the Ultra-left Ideological Trend]. In An Jianshe, ed. *Zhou Enlai de zuihou suiyue 1966-1976* [Zhou Enlai's Last Years, 1966-1976]. Beijing: Zhongyang wenxian chubanshe, 2002.

———. "Mao Zedong yu 'pi Lin pi Kong ruogan wenti kaoshu" [Commentary on Certain Questions concerning Mao Zedong and "Criticizing Lin Biao and Confucius"]. *Dang de wenxian* [The Party's Documents], no. 4 (2000).

Chen Fawen. "Xiaoping Tongzhi zhua zhengdun de yige fanli—huiyi Zhonggong zhongyang 1975 [16] hao wenjian de xingcheng he shishi" [An Example of Comrade Xiaoping Grasping Consolidation—Remember the Formation and Implementation of CCP Central Document No. 16 (1975)]. *Bainianchao* [The Hundred Year Tide], no. 5 (2001).

Chen Hongshi. "Tang Wensheng yanzhong de weiren" [Great People in the Eyes of Tang Wensheng]. *Wenshi jinghua* [The Cream of Literature and History], no. 1 (1998).

Chen Xiaoya. "Mao Zedong gei Jiang Qing de xin zhenwei bian" [Is Mao's Letter to Jiang Qing Authentic or Fake?]. In Ding Kaiwen, ed. *Chongshen Lin Biao zuian* [The Lin Biao Case Reassessed]. New York: Mingjing chubanshe, 2004.

Cheng Zhensheng. "Li Xiannian yu fensui 'sirenbang'" [Li Xiannian and the Smashing of the "Gang of Four"]. *Zhonggong dangshi yanjiu* [Research on CCP History], no. 1 (2002).

_____. "Li Xiannian yu qishi niandai chu de daguimo jishu shebei yinjing" [Li Xiannian and the Large-scale Importation of Technology and Equipment in the Early 1970s]. *Zhonggong dangshi yanjiu* [Research on CCP History], no. 1 (2004).

Cheng Zhongyuan. "Deng Xiaoping yu 1975 nian tielu zhengdun" [Deng Xiaoping and the 1975 Railway Consolidation]. *Dang de wenxian* [The Party's Documents], no. 5 (1996).

_____. "Guowuyuan zhengyanshi zai 1975 nian zhengdun zhong de zhongyao zuoyong" [The Important Function of the State Council Political Research Office during the 1975 Consolidation]. In Han Taihua, ed. *Zhongguo Gongchandang ruogan lishi wenti xiezhen* [True Portrait of Some CCP Historical Questions]. Beijing: Zhongguo yuanshi chubanshe, 1998.

_____. "Guowuyuan zhengzhi yanjiushi he 1975 nian de zhengdun" [The State Council Political Research Office and the 1975 Consolidation]. *Zhonggong dangshi ziliao* [Materials on CCP Party History], no. 61 (1997).

_____. "Liangge Zhongguo zhi mingyun quezhan--1976 nian cong Tiananmen shijian dao fensui 'sirenbang'" [The Decisive Battle in the Fate of Two Possible Chinas--From the Tiananmen Incident to the Smashing of the "Gang of Four" in 1976]. *Dangdai Zhongguoshi yanjiu* [Research on Contemporary Chinese History], no. 1 (2005).

_____. "Mao Zedong de sanxiang zhishi he Deng Xiaoping zhuchi de 1975 nian zhengdun" [Mao Zedong's Three Directives and the 1975 Consolidation under Deng Xiaoping]. *Dangdai Zhongguoshi yanjiu* [Contemporary China History Studies], no. 1 (1997).

_____. "Yijiuqiwu nian de gangtie zhengdun" [The 1975 Consolidation of Iron and Steel]. *Zhonggong dangshi ziliao* [Materials on CCP Party History], no. 81 (2002).

Deng Lifeng. "Deng Xiaoping yu yijiuqiwu nian de kuoda junwei huiyi" [Deng Xiaoping and the 1975 Expanded MAC Conference]. *Bainianchao* [The Hundred Year Tide], no. 3 (2001).

"Deng Xiaoping yu yijiuqiwu nian quanmian zhengdun" [Deng Xiaoping and the 1975 Comprehensive Consolidation]. In Wu Shihong and Gao Qi, eds. *Deng Xiaoping yu Gongheguo zhongda lishi shijian* [Deng Xiaoping and the Republic's Major Historical Events]. Beijing: Renmin chubanshe, 2000.

Ding Jiaqi. "Fensui sirenbang douzheng zhong de jiangshuaimen" [Generals and Marshals during the Struggle against the Gang of Four]. *Guofang* [National Defense], nos. 1-3 (2005).

Fan Yinhua. "Chen Yonggui guoguan ji" [An Account of Chen Yonggui Getting Off the Hook]. *Yanhuang chunqiu* [Chinese Annals], no. 5 (1999).

Fang Weizhong. "Wo suo zhidao de gongye ershitiao qicao shimo" [What I Know about the Complete Process of the Drafting of the 20 Articles]. *Zhonggong dangshi ziliao* [Materials on CCP Party History], no. 3 (2004).

Feng Lanrui. "Zai Guowuyuan zhengzhi yanjiushi de rizi" [Days at the State Council's Political Research Office]. *Bainianchao* [The Hundred Year Tide], no. 3 (2000).

Fu Yi. "Jiaoyu buzhang Zhou Rongxin de zuihou suiyue" [Minister of Education Zhou Rongxin's Last Years]. *Bainianchao* [The Hundred Year Tide], no. 2 (2002).

Gao Zhenpu. "Zai Zongli he dajie shenbian chengzhang" [Growing Up by the Side of the Premier and Big Sister (Deng Yingchao)]. In Cheng Hua, ed. *Zhou Enlai he ta de mishumen* [Zhou Enlai and His Secretaries]. Beijing: Zhongguo guangbo dianshi chubanshe, 1992.

He Libo. "Li Desheng ciqu Zhonggong zhongyang fuzhuxi qianhou" [Li Desheng around the Time of His Resignation from the CCP Vice Chairmanship]. *Dangshi bocai* [Abundant Materials on Party History], no. 6 (2005).

He Yaomin. "Deng Xiaoping lingdao women jinxing zhengdun he gaige—fan Yuan Baohua Tongzhi" [Deng Xiaoping Led Us in Carrying Out Consolidation and Reform—an Interview with Comrade Yuan Baohua]. *Bainianchao* [The Hundred Year Tide], no. 8 (2004).

Hu Jiwei. "Bingxue qiqing, jinshi qijian: zhuisi Wang Ruoshui Tongzhi" [As Pure as Ice and Snow, as Strong as Metal and Stone: Reminiscences of Comrade Wang Ruoshui]. *Zhengming* [Contention], April 2002.

———. "Jiehou cheng zhongren yin dui zhuyi cheng—wei Hu Yaobang shishi shizhounian er zuo" [Assuming a Weighty Responsibility after the Calamity out of Loyalty to an Idea—Written for the Tenth Anniversary of the Death of Hu Yaobang]. *Shuwu* [Reading Room], no. 4 (2000).

Ji Xichen. "Fensui 'sirenbang' quanjing xiezhen, xia" [The True Full Story of the Overthrow of the "Gang of Four," part 2]. *Yanhuang chunqiu* [Chinese Annals], no.11 (2000).

Ji Yecheng. "Dui nongcun gaige chuqi liangjianshi de huiyi" [Memories of Two Events from the Early Period of Rural Reform]. In Du Runsheng, ed. *Zhongguo nongcun gaige juece jishi* [A Record of the Policies of Chinese Rural Reform]. Beijing: Zhongyang wenxian chubanshe, 1999.

Jin Chunming. "Mao Zedong zhi Jiang Qing de bingfei jielu Lin Biao" [Mao Zedong's Letter to Jiang Qing Does Not Really Expose Lin Biao]. In Ding Kaiwen, ed. *Chongshen Lin Biao zuian* [The Lin Biao Case Reassessed]. New York: Mingjing chubanshe, 2004.

Li Da'nan. "Wo suo zhidao de Zhou Enlai yu shinian haojie zhong de waijiao" [What I Know about Zhou Enlai and Foreign Affairs during the 10-year Calamity]. *Bainianchao* [The Hundred Year Tide], no. 1 (2003).

Li Desheng. "Weiren de danshi yu xionghuai" [The Guts and Heart of a Great Man]. In *Huiyi Deng Xiaoping* [Remember Deng Xiaoping]. Beijing: Zhongyang wenxian chubanshe, 1998.

Li Jing. "Dongluan zhong de Jiaoyu buzhang Zhou Rongxin" [Minister of Education Zhou Rongxin in the Midst of Chaos]. *Zhonghua ernü*, nos. 5 and 6 (2003).

Li Liangyu. "Dui '1976 nian "Nanjing shijian" shimo' yiwen jige zhongyao shishi de dingzheng" [Rectifying Some Important Historical Facts Concerning the Article "A Comprehensive Account of the 1976 'Nanjing Incident'"]. *Bainianchao* [The Hundred Year Tide], no. 9 (2003).

Li Naiyin. "Cong Yao Wenyuan de zhaji kan 'sirenbang' fumeiqian de zui'e xintai" [The Criminal Psychology of the "Gang of Four" before Its Collapse as Seen from Yao Wenyuan's Notes]. *Yanhuang chunqiu* [Chinese Annals], no. 9 (1997).

Lin Qingshan. "Sirenbang zuguo meng de pomie" [The Failure of the Gang of Four to Seize Power]. *Mao Zedong sixiang yanjiu* [Research on Mao Zedong Thought], no. 3 (1988).

Shen Guoxiang. "Qinli 1976 nian 'san.wu': 'san.erwu' shijian" [Personal Experience of the 1976 "March 5" and "March 25" Incidents]. *Bainianchao* [The Hundred Year Tide], no. 3 (2005).

Su Caiqing. "'Sirenbang' dui Deng Xiaoping chuxi Lianda zhi jienan" [The "Gang of Four's" Heckling toward Deng Xiaoping Attending the UN Conference]. *Zhonggong dangshi ziliao* [Materials on CCP Party History], no. 58 (1996).

————. "Weirao 'Fengqinglun wenti' de yichang douzheng" [A Struggle concerning the "Fengqing Discussion Question"]. In Zhang Hua and Su Caiqing, eds. *Huishou "wenge": Zhongguo shinian "wenge" fenxi yu fansi* [Recalling the "Cultural Revolution": Analysis and Rethinking on China's Ten Years of "Cultural Revolution"]. Beijing: Zhonggong dangshi chubanshe, 2000. Also in *Zhonggong dangshi ziliao* [Materials on CCP Party History], no. 59 (1996).

Sun Wanguo [Warren Sun]. "Gu you Dou'e, jin you Lin Biao" [There Was Dou'e in the Past, There Is Lin Biao in the Present]. *Mingbao yuekan* [Ming Pao Monthly], no. 7 (1996). Also in Ding Kaiwen, ed. *Chongshen Lin Biao zuian* [The Lin Biao Case Reassessed]. New York: Mingjnig chubanshe, 2004.

Tie Ji. "Changsha juece" [Policy Decisions at Changsha]. In An Jianshe, ed. *Zhou Enlai de zuihou suiyue 1966-1976* [Zhou Enlai's Last Years, 1966-1976]. Beijing: Zhongyang wenxian chubanshe, 2002.

"Waijiaobu dangzu guanyu Qiao Guanhua de wenti qingshi baogao" [The MFA Party Group's Report Seeking Instructions on the Qiao Guanhua Question]. *Zhanwang* [Outlook] (Hong Kong), no. 361 (1997).

Wang Nianyi. "'Wenhua dageming' cuowu fazhan mailuo" [Thoughts on What Led to Mistaken Developments in the "Cultural Revolution"]. *Dangshi tongxun* [Party History Newsletter], October 1986.

———— and He Shu. "'She guojia zhuxi' wenti lunxi" [Discussion and Analysis of the "Establishing a State Chairman" Question]. In Ding Kaiwen, ed. *Chongshen Lin Biao zuian* [The Lin Biao Case Reassessed]. New York: Mingjing chubanshe, 2004.

Wang Xueliang. "Mingren Wu Guixian de gushi" [Stories of Celebrity Wu Guixian]. *Dangshi wenyuan* [Party History Literary Gallery], no. 11 (2005).

Wang Ying and Sun Zhongfan. "Yijiuqiwu nian dang zuzhi zhengdun de qianqian houhou" [A Detailed Account of the 1975 Party Organization Rectification]. *Bainianchao* [The Hundred Year Tide], no. 8 (2001).

Wang Yuxiang. "Hu Qiaomu zai sanzhong quanhui qian de zhongyang gongzuo huiyishang" [Hu Qiaomu at the Central Work Conference Before the Third Plenum]. *Zongheng* [Broad Coverage], no. 10 (1998).

Wang Zhongfang. "Yaobang yu wode liangci tanxin" [(Hu) Yaobang's Two Heart-to-heart Talks with Me (in Jiangxi)]. *Yanhuang chunqiu* [Chinese Annals], no. 7 (2005).

"Wei 'liushiyi ren an' pingfan" [The Rehabilitation of the "Sixty-One Cadres Case"]. In Liao Gailong, ed., *Zhongguo Gongchandang lishi dacidian (zengdingben): shehuizhuyi shiqi* [Chinese Communist Party History Comprehensive Dictionary (Expanded Version): The Socialist Period]. Beijing: Zhonggong zhongyang dangxiao chubanshe, 2001.

Wu De. "Cong Guowuyuan wenhuazu dao sijie Renda" [From the State Council Culture Group to the Fourth NPC]. *Dangdai Zhongguoshi yanjiu* [Contemporary China History Studies], no. 1 (2002). Also in *Wu De koushu: shinian fengyu wangshi—wo zai Beijing gongzuo de yixie jingli* [Wu De's Oral Account: Past Events during the Ten Years' Storm—Some Experiences from My Work in Beijing]. Beijing: Dangdai Zhongguo chubanshe, 2004.

_____. "Guanyu fensui 'sirenbang' de douzheng" [On the Struggle to Smash the "Gang of Four"]. *Dangdai Zhongguoshi yanjiu* [Contemporary China History Studies], no. 5 (2000). Also in *Wu De koushu: shinian fengyu wangshi—wo zai Beijing gongzuo de yixie jingli* [Wu De's Oral Account: Past Events during the Ten Years' Storm—Some Experiences from My Work in Beijing]. Beijing: Dangdai Zhongguo chubanshe, 2004.

_____. "Lushan huiyi he Lin Biao shijian" [The Lushan Conference and the Lin Biao Affair]. *Dangdai Zhongguoshi yanjiu* [Contemporary China History Studies], no. 2 (1995). Also in *Wu De koushu: shinian fengyu wangshi—wo zai Beijing gongzuo de yixie jingli* [Wu De's Oral Account: Past Events during the Ten Years' Storm—Some Experiences from My Work in Beijing]. Beijing: Dangdai Zhongguo chubanshe, 2004.

_____. "'Wenhua dageming' houqi zai jiefang ganbu wentishang yichang douzheng" [A Round of Struggle on the Question of Liberating Cadres in the Latter Part of the "Cultural Revolution"]. *Dangdai Zhongguoshi yanjiu* [Contemporary China History Studies], no. 2 (2003). Also in *Wu De koushu: shinian fengyu wangshi—wo zai Beijing gongzuo de yixie jingli* [Wu De's Oral Account: Past Events during the Ten Years' Storm—Some Experiences from My Work in Beijing]. Beijing: Dangdai Zhongguo chubanshe, 2004.

Xie Guoming, "175 wei jiangjun jiefang neimu" [The Inside Story of the Liberation of 175 Generals]. In An Jianshe, ed. *Zhou Enlai de zuihou suiyue 1966-1976* [Zhou Enlai's Last Years, 1966-1976]. Beijing: Zhongyang wenxian chubanshe, 2002. Also in Xiao Ping and Wang Sheng, eds. *Junshi jiemi* [Exposing the Secrets of Military History]. Heilongjiang: Heilongjiang renmin chubanshe, 1992.

Yang Chengwu. "Danxin xiangdang, gongbing qianqiu" [Loyal to the Party, Splendid Merit for a Thousand Years]. In *Zhonggong dangshi cankao ziliao* [CCP History Teaching Reference Materials]. Vol. 27, n.p.: Zhongguo Jiefangjun Guofang Daxue dangshi dangjian zhenggong jiaoyanshi, October 1988.

Yin Yungong. "Lun chenggong fensui 'sirenbang' de guanjian qunti" [On the Key Group in the Successful Smashing of the "Gang of Four"]. In Collected Papers of the *'International Forum on the Contemporary History of China'*. Beijing: Contemporary China Institute, September 2004.

"Yize zhongyao kaoding—youguan Hua Guofeng, Li Xiannian, Ye Jianying shangtan jiejue 'sirenbang' wenti de liangge guanjian shijian" [An Important Verification—Concerning Two Critical Moments in the Discussions of Hua Guofeng, Li Xiannian and Ye Jianying on Solving the "Gang of Four" Problem]. *Dang de wenxian* [The Party's Documents], no. 3 (2001).

Yu Guangyuan. "Yi Deng Xiaoping he Guowuyuan zhengyanshi" [Recalling Deng Xiaoping and the State Council Political Research Office]. *Bainianchao* [The Hundred Year Tide], no. 7 (2000).

Yu Huanchun. "*Renmin ribao* yu 1976 nian Tiananmen shijian" [The *People's Daily* and the 1976 Tiananmen Incident]. *Bainianchao* [The Hundred Year Tide], no. 2 (1998).

Yu Ruxin. "Zheyiduan lishi de 'Cheng Shiqing shuo'" [This Historical Period "According to Cheng Shiqing"]. In Ding Kaiwen, ed. *Chongshen Lin Biao zuian* [The Lin Biao Case Reassessed]. New York: Mingjing chubanshe, 2004.

Zeng Qingxiang *et al.* "1975 nian de jundui zhengdun" [The 1975 Military Consolidation]. *Dangdai Zhongguoshi yanjiu* [Contemporary China History Studies], no. 4 (2003).

Zeng Tao. "Zhengyi de kangzheng—suowei 'eryue niliu' de qianqian houhou" [Righteous Resistance—Before and After the So-called "February Adverse Current"]. In Zhang Hua and Su Caiqing, eds. *Huishou "wenge": Zhongguo shinian "wenge" fenxi yu fansi* [Recalling the "Cultural Revolution": Analysis and Rethinking of China's Ten Years of "Cultural Revolution"]. Beijing: Zhonggong dangshi chubanshe, 2000.

Zhang Gensheng. "Hua Guofeng tan fensui 'sirenbang'" [Hua Guofeng Talks about Smashing the "Gang of Four"]. *Yanhuang chunqiu* [Chinese Annals], no. 7 (2004).

Zhang Guangyou. "Wan Li zhengdun tielu yu weixing jiantao" [Wan Li's Consolidation of the Railways and His Forced Self-examination]. *Yanhuang chunqiu* [Chinese Annals], no. 3 (2002).

Zhang Haini. "Wo wei Mao Yuanxin bianhu" [I Defend for the Plaintiff, Mao Yuanxin]. *Zhonghua ernü*, May 1999.

Zhang Hua. "Yetan Mao Zedong de sanxiang zhishi yu 1975 nian de zhengdun" [A Further Discussion of Mao Zedong's Three Directives and the 1975 Consolidation]. *Zhonggong dangshi yanjiu* [Research on CCP History], no. 5 (1997).

_____. "1975 nian jiaoyujie de douzheng" [The 1975 Struggle in the Educational Sphere]. *Zhonggong dangshi ziliao* [Materials on CCP Party History], no. 70 (1999).

_____. "1975 nian nongye xue Dazhai huiyi yu nongye zhengdun de yaoqiu" [The 1975 Agriculture Learn From Dazhai Conference and the Demand to Rectify Agriculture]. *Dang de wenxian* [The Party's Documents], no. 6 (1999).

_____. "Zhang Aiping Jiangjun zhengdun Guofang kewei" [General Zhang Aiping Rectifies the Science and Technology Commission for National Defense]. *Bainianchao* [The Hundred Year Tide], no. 2 (2001).

_____. "Zhongguo kexueyuan 1975 nian de zhengdun" [The 1975 Consolidation at the Chinese Academy of Sciences]. *Zhonggong dangshi yanjiu* [Research on CCP History], no. 1 (1996).

Zhang Tingfa. "70 niandai zhongqi liangci Junwei huiyi de qian qian hou hou" [Before and After Two MAC Conferences in the Mid-1970s]. *Dang de wenxian* [The Party's Documents], no. 4 (1999).

Zhou Shaohua. "Zhou Zongli he wode fuqin Zhou Rongxin" [Premier Zhou and My Father Zhou Rongxin]. *Zhuanji wenxue* [Biographical Literature], no. 5 (1993).

Zhu Jiamu, Chi Aiping and Zhao Shigang. "Chen Yun" [Chen Yun]. *Zhonggong dangshi renwu zhuan* [Biographies of Personalities in CCP History]. Vol. 71, Beijing: Zhongyang wenxian chubanshe, 2000.

Zhu Ruiai. "Wo wei Zongli fei zhuanji" [I Flew the Premier's Charter Plane]. In Cheng Hua, ed. *Zhou Enlai he ta de mishumen* [Zhou Enlai and His Secretaries]. Beijing: Zhongguo guangbo dianshi chubanshe, 1992.

Zong Daoyi. "Wang baqi jianghua yu Waijiaobu duoquan naoju" [Wang's August 7 Speech and the Farce of Usurping Power in the Foreign Ministry]. *Zhonghua ernü* [Sons and Daughters of China], December 2001.

_____. "153 qi Xinqingkuang he Ji Xinge diliuci laifang gei Zhou Enlai dailai de zhengzhi zainan" [Zhou Enlai's Political Disaster Due to (Foreign Ministry Bulletin) No. 153 on the New Situation and Kissinger's Sixth Visit to China]. *Zhonghua ernü* [Sons and Daughters of China], September 2001.

_____. "1973 nian Zhou Enlai shenbian de shitai yanliang" [Zhou Enlai's Fickle Fortunes in 1973]. *Zhonghua ernü* [Sons and Daughters of China], October 2001.

Chronologies, Documentary Collections, Personnel Directories, etc.

"Beijing shi 'wenhua dageming' dashiji (1965 nian 11 yue—1976 nian 10 yue)" [Chronology of the "Cultural Revolution" in Beijing Municipality, November 1965-October 1976]. *Beijing dangshi ziliao tongxun (zengkan 17)* [Beijing Party History Materials Bulletin, supplement no. 17], May 1987.

Chen Donglin and Du Pu, eds. *Zhonghuarenmingongheguo shilu* [True Record of the PRC]. Vol. 3, part 1, *Neiluan yu kangzheng—"wenhua dageming" de shinian (1966-1971)* [Civil Disorder and Resistance—The "Cultural Revolution" Decade, 1966-1971]. Changchun: Jilin renmin chubanshe, 1994.

_____. *Zhonghuarenmingongheguo shilu* [True Record of the PRC]. Vol. 3, part 2, *Neiluan yu kangzheng—"wenhua dageming" de shinian (1972-1976)* [Civil Disorder and Resistance—The "Cultural Revolution" Decade, 1972-1976]. Changchun: Jilin renmin chubanshe, 1994.

Chen Yun nianpu, 1905-1995, xia juan [Chronology of Chen Yun, 1905-1995, vol. 3]. Beijing: Zhongyang wenxian chubanshe, 2000.

Chen Yun wenxuan, disanjuan [Selected Works of Chen Yun, Volume 3]. Beijing: Renmin chubanshe, 1995.

Cheng Chao and Wei Haoben, eds. *Zhejiang "wenge" jishi (1966.5-1976.10)* [Principal Events of the "Cultural Revolution" in Zhejiang, May 1966-October 1976]. Hangzhou: Zhejiang fangzhi bianjibu, 1989.

Dang de xuanchuan gongzuo huiyi gaikuang he wenxian (1951-1992 nian) [Survey and Documents of the Party's Propaganda Work Meetings, 1951-1992]. Beijing: Zhonggong zhongyang dangxiao chubanshe, 1994.

Deng Liqun wenji [Collected Works of Deng Liqun]. 3 vols., Beijing: Dangdai Zhongguo chubanshe, 1999.

Deng Xiaoping nianpu (1975-1997) [Chronology of Deng Xiaoping, 1975-1997]. 2 vols., Beijing: Zhongyang wenxian chubanshe, 2004.

Deng Xiaoping sixiang nianpu (1975-1997) [Chronology of Deng Xiaoping's Thought, 1975-1997]. Beijing: Zhongyang wenxian chubanshe, 1998.

Deng Xiaoping wenxuan (yijiuqiwu—yijiubaer nian) [Selected Works of Deng Xiaoping, 1975-1982]. [Vol. 2], Beijing: Renmin chubanshe, 1983. Trans. as *Selected Works of Deng Xiaoping (1975-1982)*. [Vol. 2], Beijing: Foreign Languages Press, 1984.

Fang Weizhong. *Zhonghuarenmingongheguo jingji dashiji (1949-1980 nian)* [Chronology of Economic Events in the People's Republic of China, 1949-1980]. Beijing: Zhongguo shehui kexue chubanshe, 1984.

Feiqing nianbao [CCP Yearbook]. Taipei: Guofang qingbaoju, 1968-. From 1977 renamed *Zhonggong nianbao* [CCP Yearbook].

Gu Longsheng. *Mao Zedong jingji nianpu* [Chronicle of Mao Zedong on the Economy]. Beijing: Zhonggong zhongyang dangxiao chubanshe, 1993.

Guanyu jianguo yilai dang de ruogan lishi wenti de jueyi zhuyiben (xiuding) [Revised Notes on the Resolution on Certain Questions in the History of Our Party since the Founding of the State], compiled by Zhonggong zhongyang wenxian yanjiushi. Beijing: Renmin chubanshe, 1985.

He Husheng *et al.*, eds. *Zhonghuarenmingongheguo zhiguanzhi* [Directory of PRC Officials]. Beijing: Zhongguo shehui chubanshe, 1993.

Jianguo yilai Mao Zedong wengao [Mao Zedong's Manuscripts since the Founding of the State]. 13 vols. (September 1949-July 1976). Beijing: Zhongyang wenxian chubanshe, 1987-98.

Jianguo yilai nongye hezuohua shiliao huibian [Collected Historical Materials on Agricultural Cooperativization Since the Founding of the State]. Beijing: Zhonggong dangshi chubanshe, 1992.

Li Xiannian lun caizheng jinrong maoyi (1950-1991) [Li Xiannian on Finance, Banking and Trade, 1950-1991]. Vol. 1, Beijing: Zhongguo caizheng jingji chubanshe, 1992.

Li Xiannian wenxuan (1935-1988 nian) [Selected Works of Li Xiannian, 1935-1988]. Beijing: Renmin chubanshe, 1989.

Liao Gailong, ed. *Xin Zhongguo biannianshi* [Chronicle of New China]. Beijing: Renmin chubanshe, 1988.

_____. *Zhongguo Gongchandang lishi dacidian (zengdingben): shehuizhuyi shiqi* [Chinese Communist Party History Comprehensive Dictionary (Expanded Version): The Socialist Period]. Beijing: Zhonggong zhongyang dangxiao chubanshe, 2001.

Lijie Zhonggong zhongyang weiyuan renming cidian 1921-1987 [Dictionary of Successive CCP Central Committee Members, 1921-1987]. Beijing: Zhonggong dangshi chubanshe, 1992.

Ma Qibin *et al.*, eds. *Zhongguo Gongchandang zhizheng sishinian (1949-1989)* [The CCP's Forty Years in Power, 1949-1989]. Revised edition, Beijing: Zhonggong dangshi chubanshe, 1991.

Mao Zedong sixiang wansui [Long Live Mao Zedong Thought]. 2 vols., [Taipei]: 1967, 1969. Red Guard collection of Mao's talks and speeches.

Mao Zedong, Zhou Enlai, Liu Shaoqi, Zhu De ji xianren dang he guojia zhuyao lingdaoren zhuanlüe [Brief Biographies of Mao Zedong, Zhou Enlai, Liu Shaoqi, Zhu De and Current Important Leaders of the Party and State]. [Beijing]: Zhonggong zhongyang wenxian yanjiushi, September 1984.

Nie Rongzhen nianpu [Chronology of Nie Rongzhen]. 2 vols., Beijing: Renmin chubanshe, 1999.

Renmin ribao banmian beiyao [*People's Daily* Page Layouts]. Beijing: *Renmin ribao* chubanshe, 1997.

Renmin ribao suoyin 1946-1995 [Index to *People's Daily*, 1946-1995]. Beijing: Beijing Daxue tushuguan, 1996 [electronic resource].

Shanghai minbing douzheng shi ziliao [Materials on the History of the Shanghai Militia Struggles]. Vols. 16-22, Shanghai: Shanghai minbing douzheng shi ziliao, 1980-81.

Shanghai shehuizhuyi jianshe wushi nian [Fifty Years of Shanghai's Socialist Construction]. Shanghai: Shanghai renmin chubanshe, 1999.

Shanghai "wenhua dageming" shihua [Historical Narrative of the "Great Cultural Revolution" in Shanghai]. 3 vols., Shanghai: 1992.

Sirenbang fangeming zuixing cailiao jilu [Collected Materials on the Counterrevolutionary Crimes of the Gang of Four]. Internal materials edited by the Library Archive Office of the Institute of Philosophical Studies, Chinese Academy of Social Sciences, May 1977.

Song Yongyi, chief ed. *The Chinese Cultural Revolution Database CD-ROM.* Hong Kong: The Chinese University Press, 2002.

Su Donghai and Fang Kongmu, eds. *Zhonghuarenmingongheguo fengyun shilu* [True Record of the PRC's Storms]. 2 vols., n.p.: Henan renmin chubanshe, c. 1993.

Wang Jianying. *Hongjun renwuzhi* [Red Army Personnel Records]. Beijing: Jiefangjun chubanshe, 1988.

_____. *Zhongguo Gongchandang zuzhishi ziliao huibian* [Compilation of Materials on CCP Organizational History]. Beijing: Hongqi chubanshe, 1983. 2nd revised edition, from the 1st to 14th Party Congresses, Beijing: Zhonggong zhongyang dangxiao chubanshe, 1995.

Ye Jianying xuanji [Selected Works of Ye Jianying]. Beijing: Renmin chubanshe, 1994.

Zheng Zhongbing, ed. *Hu Yaobang nianpu ziliao changbian* [A Chronological Record of Hu Yaobang's Life]. 2 vols., Hong Kong: Shidai guoji chuban youxian gongsi, 2005.

Zhonggong dangshi cankao ziliao [CCP History Teaching Reference Materials]. Vol. 27, n.p.: Zhongguo Jiefangjun Guofang Daxue dangshi dangjian zhenggong jiaoyanshi, October 1988.

Zhonggong dangshi dashi nianbao [Chronology of Major Events in CCP History]. Beijing: Renmin chubanshe, 1987.

Zhonggong dangshi renwu zhuan [Biographies of Personalities in CCP History]. Vols 1-60, Xi'an: Shaanxi renmin chubanshe, 1980-96. Vols 61-, Beijing: Zhongyang wenxian chubanshe, 1997-.

Zhonggong Shanghai shiwei dangshi yanjiushi, ed. *Zhongguo Gongchandang zai Shanghai 80 nian (1921-2001)* [The CCP's 80 Years in Shanghai, 1921-2001]. Shanghai: Shanghai renmin chubanshe, 2001.

Zhonggong yuanshi ziliao xuanji [Selection of Original CCP Materials]. Taipei: Zhonggong yanjiu zazhishi, 1981.

Zhongguo Gongchandang lishi dashiji (1919.5-1987.12) [History of the Chinese Communist Party: A Chronology of Events, May 1919-December 1987]. Beijing: Renmin chubanshe, 1989. Trans. as *History of the Chinese Communist Party: A Chronology of Events (1919-1990)*. Beijing: Foreign Languages Press, 1991.

Zhongguo Renmin Jiefangjun zuzhi yange he geji lingdao chengyuan minglu [The Organizational Evolution and Name Lists of Various Levels of Leading Members of the Chinese PLA]. Beijing: Junshi kexue chubanshe, 1990.

Zhonghuarenmingongheguo dang zheng jun qun lingdao renminglu [Name Lists of PRC Party, Government, Military and Mass Organization Leaders]. Beijing: Zhonggong dangshi chubanshe, 1990.

Zhou Enlai junshi huodong jishi [Chronology of Zhou Enlai's Military Activities]. 2 vols., Beijing: Zhongyang wenxian chubanshe, 2000.

Zhou Enlai nianpu 1949-1976 [Chronicle of Zhou Enlai, 1949-1976]. 3 vols., Beijing: Zhongyang wenxian chubanshe, 1997.

Zhou Enlai xuanji [Selected Works of Zhou Enlai]. Vol. 2, Beijing: Renmin chubanshe, 1984. Trans. as *Selected Works of Zhou Enlai*. Vol. II, Beijing: Foreign Languages Press, 1989.

Zhou Rongxin Tongzhi jianghua huibian [Compendium of Comrade Zhou Rongxin's (1975) Speeches]. Collection available at the Fairbank Center Library, Harvard University.

Zhu De nianpu [Chronology of Zhu De]. Beijing: Renmin chubanshe, 1986.

CCP Leaders' Speeches, Draft Manuscripts, and Official Party Documents

(a) Leaders' Speeches

Deng Liqun. "Deng Liqun zai zhu Beijing budui shiyishang ganbu dahuishang de jianghua" [Deng Liqun's Speech to Beijing Troops at the Division Level and Above] (July 7, 1981). In Song Yongyi, chief ed. *The Chinese Cultural Revolution Database CD-ROM*. Hong Kong: The Chinese University Press, 2002.

Deng Xiaoping. "Deng Xiaoping gei Mao Zedong de xin" [Deng Xiaoping's Letter to Mao Zedong] (August 3, 1972). In Song Yongyi, chief ed. *The Chinese Cultural Revolution Database CD-ROM*. Hong Kong: The Chinese University Press, 2002.

_____. "Deng Xiaoping guanyu qicao guoqing sanshi zhounian jianghua gao de tanhua jiyao" [Summary of Deng Xiaoping's Talk on the Draft Speech for the 30th Anniversary National Day Celebration] (September 4, 1979). In Song Yongyi, chief ed. *The Chinese Cultural Revolution Database CD-ROM*. Hong Kong: The Chinese University Press, 2002.

_____. "Deng Xiaoping jiejian gangtie gongye zuotanhui daibiao shi de jianghua" [Deng Xiaoping's Speech When Receiving Delegates to the Iron and Steel Industry Seminar] (May 29, 1975). In Song Yongyi, chief ed. *The Chinese Cultural Revolution Database CD-ROM*. Hong Kong: The Chinese University Press, 2002. Edited version trans. in *Selected Works of Deng Xiaoping (1975-1982)*. [Vol. 2], Beijing: Foreign Languages Press, 1984.

_____. "Deng Xiaoping jiejian guofang gongye zhongdian qiye huiyi daibiao shi de jianghua" [Deng Xiaoping's Speech When Receiving Delegates to the National Defense Industry Key Enterprises Conference] (August 3, 1975). In Song Yongyi, chief ed. *The Chinese Cultural Revolution Database CD-ROM*. Hong Kong: The Chinese University Press, 2002. Edited version trans. in *Selected Works of Deng Xiaoping (1975-1982)*. [Vol. 2], Beijing: Foreign Languages Press, 1984.

_____. "Deng Xiaoping xiegei Zhonggong zhongyang de 'wode zishu' (zhailu)" [Extracts from Deng Xiaoping's "My Self-statement" Written to the CCP Center] (June 20, 1968). In Song Yongyi, chief ed. *The Chinese Cultural Revolution Database CD-ROM*. Hong Kong: The Chinese University Press, 2002.

_____. "Deng Xiaoping 1975 jiu, shi yue jian zai nanfang shiersheng shengwei shuji huiyishang de jianghua zhailu" [Abridged Record of Deng Xiaoping's Speeches in September-October 1975]. Document available at the Fairbank Center Library, Harvard University.

_____. "Deng Xiaoping zai Guowuyuan bangong huiyishang de jianghua" (May 21, 1975) [Deng Xiaoping's Speech to the State Council Work Meeting]. In Song Yongyi, chief ed. *The Chinese Cultural Revolution Database CD-ROM*. Hong Kong: The Chinese University Press, 2002.

_____. "Deng Xiaoping zai Guowuyuan lingdao tongzhi tingqu Hu Yaobang huibao de chahua" (September 26, 1975) [Deng Xiaoping's Remarks during Hu Yaobang's Report to State Council Leading Comrades]. In Song Yongyi, chief ed. *The Chinese Cultural Revolution Database CD-ROM*. Hong Kong: The Chinese University Press, 2002. A more extensive version available at the Fairbank Center Library, Harvard University. English extract as "Priority Should be Given to Scientific Research." In web version of *Selected Works of Deng Xiaoping (1975-1982)*. [Vol. 2], Beijing: Foreign Languages Press, 1984. http://english.peopledaily.com.cn/dengxp/contents2.html.

_____. "Deng Xiaoping zai Junwei kuoda huiyishang de jianghua" [Deng Xiaoping's Speech at the MAC Expanded Conference] (July 14, 1975). In Song Yongyi, chief ed. *The Chinese Cultural Revolution Database CD-ROM*. Hong Kong: The Chinese University Press, 2002. Edited version trans. in *Selected Works of Deng Xiaoping (1975-1982)*. [Vol. 2], Beijing: Foreign Languages Press, 1984.

_____. "Deng Xiaoping zai nanfang shier sheng shengwei shuji huiyishang de jianghua zhailu" [Extracts from Deng Xiaoping's Speech at the Conference of Provincial Secretaries from 12 Southern Provinces] (September 1975). In Song Yongyi, chief ed. *The Chinese Cultural Revolution Database CD-ROM*. Hong Kong: The Chinese University Press, 2002.

_____. "Deng Xiaoping zai zhongyang shouzhang jiejian zhongyang dushuban quanti tongzhi de jianghua" [Deng Xiaoping's Speech When Central Leaders Received All the Central Study Class Comrades] (July 4, 1975). In Song Yongyi, chief ed. *The Chinese Cultural Revolution Database CD-ROM*. Hong Kong: The Chinese University Press, 2002. Edited version trans. in *Selected Works of Deng Xiaoping (1975-1982)*. [Vol. 2], Beijing: Foreign Languages Press, 1984.

_____. Summary of Speech at the Dazhai Conference (September 15, 1975). In *Deng Xiaoping nianpu (1975-1997)* [Chronology of Deng Xiaoping, 1975-1997]. Vol. 1, Beijing: Zhongyang wenxian chubanshe, 2004.

Geng Biao. "Geng Biao guanyu zhua sirenbang qingkuang de jianghua" [Geng Biao's Speech concerning the Circumstances of Seizing the Gang of Four] (October 16, 1976). In Song Yongyi, chief ed. *The Chinese Cultural Revolution Database CD-ROM*. Hong Kong: The Chinese University Press, 2002.

Hu Yaobang and Li Chang. "Hu Yaobang, Li Chang de jianghua" [Speeches of Hu Yaobang and Li Chang] (1975). Documents available at the Fairbank Center Library, Harvard University.

Hua Guofeng. "Hua Guofeng jiejian Shandong, Hubei deng Nanjing budui deng lingdao tongzhi de jianghua" [Hua Guofeng's Speech Receiving Leading Comrades from Shandong, Hubei etc. (Provinces) and the Nanjing Troops etc.] (October 7, 1976). In Song Yongyi, chief ed. *The Chinese Cultural Revolution Database CD-ROM*. Hong Kong: The Chinese University Press, 2002.

_____. "Hua Guofeng Tongzhi de jianghua" [Comrade Hua Guofeng's Speech] (February 25, 1976). In Zhonggong dangshi cankao ziliao [CCP History Teaching Reference Materials]. Vol. 27, n.p.: Zhongguo Jiefangjun Guofang Daxue dangshi dangjian zhenggong jiaoyanshi, October 1988.

_____. Speech of November 7, 1976. In handwritten document available at the Menzies Library, the Australian National University.

_____ et al. "Hua Guofeng he zhongyang lingdao tingqu Caizhengbu huibao shi de zhishi" [Directives by Hua Guofeng and Central Leaders When Listening to the Report of the Ministry of Finance] (November 5, 1976). In Song Yongyi, chief ed. The Chinese Cultural Revolution Database CD-ROM. Hong Kong: The Chinese University Press, 2002.

_____ et al. "Hua Guofeng, Ye Jianying deng jiejian Shanghai Ma Tianshui dengren de jianghua" [Speeches by Hua Guofeng, Ye Jianying et al. Receiving Shanghai's Ma Tianshui et al.] (October 12, 1976). In Song Yongyi, chief ed. The Chinese Cultural Revolution Database CD-ROM. Hong Kong: The Chinese University Press, 2002.

_____ and Ye Jianying. "Hua Guofeng, Ye Jianying zai Zhonggong zhongyang zhengzhiju huiyishang de jianghua" [Speeches of Hua Guofeng and Ye Jianying at the CCP Politburo Meeting] (October 6, 1976). In Song Yongyi, chief ed. The Chinese Cultural Revolution Database CD-ROM. Hong Kong: The Chinese University Press, 2002.

Ji Dengkui. "Ji Dengkui zai Guowuyuan huibao ganbu huiyishi de jianghua jingshen" [The Spirit of Ji Dengkui's Speech at the Time of the State Council Report-back Cadre Conference] (March 31, 1972). In Song Yongyi, chief ed. The Chinese Cultural Revolution Database CD-ROM. Hong Kong: The Chinese University Press, 2002.

Jiang Qing. "Jiang Qing jiejian Dazhai dadui ganbu he sheyuan shi de jianghua lugao" [Record of Jiang Qing's Talk When Receiving Cadres and Members of the Dazhai Brigade] (September 12, 1975). In Zhonggong dangshi cankao ziliao [CCP History Teaching Reference Materials]. Vol. 27, n.p.: Zhongguo Jiefangjun Guofang Daxue dangshi dangjian zhenggong jiaoyanshi, October 1988. Also in Song Yongyi, chief ed. The Chinese Cultural Revolution Database CD-ROM. Hong Kong: The Chinese University Press, 2002.

_____. "Jiang Qing zai dazhaohu huiyi qijian shanzi zhaoji de shier sheng, qu huiyishang de jianghua jilugao" [Draft Record of Jiang Qing's Speech to the Meeting of 12 Provinces and Regions Convened without Authorization at the Time of the Warning Meeting] (March 2, 1976). In Zhonggong dangshi cankao ziliao [CCP History Teaching Reference Materials]. Vol. 27, n.p.: Zhongguo Jiefangjun Guofang Daxue dangshi dangjian zhenggong jiaoyanshi, October 1988. Also in Song Yongyi, chief ed. The Chinese Cultural Revolution Database CD-ROM. Hong Kong: The Chinese University Press, 2002.

_____. Speech to Criticize Lin Criticize Confucius Mobilization Meeting on January 25, 1974. In handwritten minutes of the meeting available at the Menzies Library, the Australian National University.

_____ et al. "Jiang Qing, Yao Wenyuan, Chi Qun deng zai zhongyang zhishu jiguan he guojia jiguan pi Lin pi Kong dongyuan dahuishang de jianghua" [Speeches by Jiang Qing, Yao Wenyuan and Chi Qun et al. at the Criticize Lin Criticize Confucius Mobilization Meeting for [Party] Center and State Organs] (January 25, 1974). In Song Yongyi, chief ed. The Chinese Cultural Revolution Database CD-ROM. Hong Kong: The Chinese University Press, 2002.

Jiang Weiqing. "Jiang Weiqing Tongzhi zhuanda zhongyang lingdao tongzhi jianghua jingshen" [Comrade Jiang Weiqing Relays the Spirit of Talks by a Central Leading Comrade] (October 26, 1975). Document available at the Fairbank Center Library, Harvard University.

Li Xiannian *et al.* "Li Xiannian, Chen Yun, Tan Zhenlin zai sijie Renda Changwei disanci huiyishang de jianghua" [Speeches of Li Xiannian, Chen Yun and Tan Zhenlin at the Third Meeting of the Fourth NPC Standing Committee] (December 2, 1976). In Song Yongyi, chief ed. *The Chinese Cultural Revolution Database CD-ROM.* Hong Kong: The Chinese University Press, 2002.

Ma Tianshui. "Ma Tianshui de buchong jiefa jiaodai" [Ma Tianshui's Supplementary Unmasking Confession] (November 21, 1976). In Song Yongyi, chief ed. *The Chinese Cultural Revolution Database CD-ROM.* Hong Kong: The Chinese University Press, 2002.

_____. "Ma Tianshui de jiefa jiaodai" [Ma Tianshui's Unmasking Confession] (November 5, 1976). In Song Yongyi, chief ed. *The Chinese Cultural Revolution Database CD-ROM.* Hong Kong: The Chinese University Press, 2002.

_____ and Xu Jingxian. "Ma Tianshui, Xu Jingxian zai Fudan Daxue de jianghua" [Ma Tianshui's and Xu Jingxian's Speeches at Fudan University] (January 8, 1976). In Song Yongyi, chief ed. *The Chinese Cultural Revolution Database CD-ROM.* Hong Kong: The Chinese University Press, 2002.

Mao Zedong. "Guanyu dajunqu silingyuan dui tiaodeng wenti de tanhua yaodian" [Main Points of Talks on the Question of Transferring Military Region Commanders] (December 12, 1973 [sic]). In Song Yongyi, chief ed. *The Chinese Cultural Revolution Database CD-ROM.* Hong Kong: The Chinese University Press, 2002.

_____. "Guanyu minbing bu yao canyu liangpai duili de yijian" [Opinion on the Militia Not Participating in the Opposition of Two Factions] (December 1974). In Song Yongyi, chief ed. The Chinese Cultural Revolution Database CD-ROM. Hong Kong: The Chinese University Press, 2002.

_____. "Tong Deng Xiaoping guanyu piping 'sirenbang' de yici tanhua (jielu)" [Extract from a Talk with Deng Xiaoping concerning Criticizing the "Gang of Four"] (June 1975). In Song Yongyi, chief ed. *The Chinese Cultural Revolution Database CD-ROM.* Hong Kong: The Chinese University Press, 2002.

_____. "Tong Wang Hongwen, Zhang Chunqiao de tanhua jiyao" [Summary of a Talk with Wang Hongwen and Zhang Chunqiao] (July 4, 1973). In Song Yongyi, chief ed. *The Chinese Cultural Revolution Database CD-ROM.* Hong Kong: The Chinese University Press, 2002.

_____. "Tong zai jing zhongyang zhengzhiju weiyuan de tanhua" [Talk with Politburo Members in Beijing] (May 3, 1975). In Song Yongyi, chief ed. *The Chinese Cultural Revolution Database CD-ROM.* Hong Kong: The Chinese University Press, 2002.

_____. "Zai Changsha yu Liu Xingyuan, Ding Sheng, Wei Guoqing, Wang Dongxing de tanhua" [Talk with Liu Xingyuan, Ding Sheng, Wei Guoqing and Wang Dongxing at Changsha] (August 28, 1971). In Song Yongyi, chief ed. *The Chinese Cultural Revolution Database CD-ROM.* Hong Kong: The Chinese University Press, 2002.

Wang Bicheng. "Wang Bicheng zai Yunnan shengwei he Kunming junqu dangwei ganbu xuexiban shangde jianghua" [Wang Bicheng's Speech at the Cadre Study Class of the Yunnan Provincial Committee and the Party Committee of the Kunming Military Region] (February 6, 1972). In Song Yongyi, chief ed. *The Chinese Cultural Revolution Database CD-ROM.* Hong Kong: The Chinese University Press, 2002.

Wang Dongxing. "Wang Dongxing zai quanguo xuanchuan gongzuo huiyishang de jianghua" [Wang Dongxing's Speech to the National Propaganda Conference] (November 18, 1976). In Song Yongyi, chief ed. *The Chinese Cultural Revolution Database CD-ROM.* Hong Kong: The Chinese University Press, 2002.

Wang Hongwen. "Wang Hongwen zai zhongyang dushuban de baogao" [Wang Hongwen's Report at the Central Study Class] (January 14, 1974). In Song Yongyi, chief ed. *The Chinese Cultural Revolution Database CD-ROM*. Hong Kong: The Chinese University Press, 2002. Trans. in *Issues & Studies*, February 1975.

Wang Xiuzhen. "Wang Xiuzhen de jiefa jiaodai" [Wang Xiuzhen's Unmasking Confession] (November 6, 1976). In Song Yongyi, chief ed. *The Chinese Cultural Revolution Database CD-ROM*. Hong Kong: The Chinese University Press, 2002.

Wang Zhen. "Wang Zhen Tongzhi zai zhengzhi yanjiushi jianghua" [Comrade Wang Zhen's Talk at the Political Research Office] (December 17, 1976). Document available at the Fairbank Center Library, Harvard University. Also in Song Yongyi, chief ed. *The Chinese Cultural Revolution Database CD-ROM*. Hong Kong: The Chinese University Press, 2002.

Wu De. "Wu De zai shoudu qingzhu dahuishang de jianghua" [Wu De's Speech at the Capital's Celebration Rally] (October 24, 1976). In Song Yongyi, chief ed. *The Chinese Cultural Revolution Database CD-ROM*. Hong Kong: The Chinese University Press, 2002. Trans. in *Peking Review*, no. 44 (1976).

_____. "Wu De zai Tiananmen guangchang guangbo jianghua" [Wu De's Broadcast Speech at Tiananmen Square] (April 5, 1976). In Song Yongyi, chief ed. *The Chinese Cultural Revolution Database CD-ROM*. Hong Kong: The Chinese University Press, 2002. Trans. in *Peking Review*, no. 15 (1976).

Xu Jingxian. "Xu Jingxian de buchong jiefa jiaodai" [Xu Jingxian's Supplementary Unmasking Confession] (November 21, 1976). In Song Yongyi, chief ed. *The Chinese Cultural Revolution Database CD-ROM*. Hong Kong: The Chinese University Press, 2002.

_____. "Xu Jingxian de chubu jiefa jiaodai" [Xu Jingxian's Preliminary Unmasking Confession] (November 5, 1976). In Song Yongyi, chief ed. *The Chinese Cultural Revolution Database CD-ROM*. Hong Kong: The Chinese University Press, 2002.

Yao Wenyuan. "Yao Wenyuan dui *Hongqi* bianjizu zhaojiren tan pi Deng" [Yao Wenyuan Talks to the *Red Flag* Editorial Staff about Criticizing Deng] (February 6, 1976). In Song Yongyi, chief ed. *The Chinese Cultural Revolution Database CD-ROM*. Hong Kong: The Chinese University Press, 2002.

_____. "Yao Wenyuan dui *Hongqi* bianjizu zhaojiren tan pi Kong ji zhuanda Zhuxi zhishi" [Yao Wenyuan Talks to the *Red Flag* Editorial Staff about Criticizing Confucius and Conveying the Chairman's Directives] (December 3, 1973). In Song Yongyi, chief ed. *The Chinese Cultural Revolution Database CD-ROM*. Hong Kong: The Chinese University Press, 2002.

_____. "Yao Wenyuan dui *Hongqi* zazhi bianjizu zhaojiren de tanhua" [Yao Wenyuan's Talk to the *Red Flag* Magazine Editorial Staff] (April 26, 1976). In Song Yongyi, chief ed. *The Chinese Cultural Revolution Database CD-ROM*. Hong Kong: The Chinese University Press, 2002.

Ye Jianying. "Ye Jianying zai Zhongyang Junwei kuoda huiyishang de zongjie jianghua" [Ye Jianying's Summary Speech at the Central MAC Expanded Conference] (July 15, 1975). In Song Yongyi, chief ed. *The Chinese Cultural Revolution Database CD-ROM*. Hong Kong: The Chinese University Press, 2002. Edited version in *Ye Jianying xuanji* [Selected Works of Ye Jianying]. Beijing: Renmin chubanshe, 1994.

Zhang Tiesheng and Liu Jiye. "Zhang Tiesheng, Liu Jiye Tongzhi tanhua qingkuang jilu" [Record of Conversation of Comrades Zhang Tiesheng and Liu Jiye] (September 9, 1976). In *Zhonggong dangshi cankao ziliao* [CCP History Teaching Reference Materials]. Vol. 27, n.p.: Zhongguo Jiefangjun Guofang Daxue dangshi dangjian zhenggong jiaoyanshi, October 1988.

"Zhonggong zhongyang zhuanfa de Zhongyang Changwei zai shiyijie liuzhong quanhui qijian zhaokai gezu zhaojiren huiyishang de jianghua" [CCP Center Transmits Talks of the Central Standing Committee at the Meeting of Group Conveners at the Time of the Sixth Plenum of the 11th Central Committee] (June 23, 1981). In Song Yongyi, chief ed. *The Chinese Cultural Revolution Database CD-ROM*. Hong Kong: The Chinese University Press, 2002.

"Zhongyang lingdaoren guanyu sirenbang wenti de jianghua" [Speeches of Central Leaders on the Gang of Four Question] (October 8, 1976). In Song Yongyi, chief ed. *The Chinese Cultural Revolution Database CD-ROM*. Hong Kong: The Chinese University Press, 2002.

Zhou Enlai. Speech to Criticize Lin Criticize Confucius Mobilization Meeting on January 25, 1974. In handwritten minutes of the meeting available at the Menzies Library, the Australian National University.

_____. "Zhou Enlai zai Zhengzhiju Changwei huishang zhuanda de Mao Zedong tanhua yao dian (jielu)" [Extract from Zhou Enlai's Transmission at a Meeting of the Politburo Standing Committee of the Main Points of Mao Zedong's Talk] (the end of 1974 to the start of 1975). In Song Yongyi, chief ed. *The Chinese Cultural Revolution Database CD-ROM*. Hong Kong: The Chinese University Press, 2002.

Zhou Rongxin. "Zhou Rongxin dui Xinhuashe jizhe de tanhua" [Speech to Xinhua Journalists] (July 24, 1975). In Song Yongyi, chief ed. *The Chinese Cultural Revolution Database CD-ROM*. Hong Kong: The Chinese University Press, 2002.

(b) Draft Manuscripts, Official Party Documents, and Other Written Material

"Diantai dangqian xuanchuan koujing" [Current Propaganda Formulas for Broadcasting]. Handwritten document available at the Fairbank Center Library, Harvard University.

"Guanyu jiakuai gongye fazhan de ruogan wenti" [Some Questions Concerning Accelerating the Development of Industry" (The 20 Articles on Industry)] (draft of September 2, 1975). In *Zhonggong dangshi cankao ziliao* [CCP History Teaching Reference Materials]. Vol. 27, n.p.: Zhongguo Jiefangjun Guofang Daxue dangshi dangjian zhenggong jiaoyanshi, October 1988. Trans. in Kenneth Lieberthal, with the assistance of James Tong and Sai-cheung Yeung. *Central Documents and Politburo Politics in China*. Ann Arbor: Michigan Papers in Chinese Studies no. 33, 1978. Also trans. in *Issues & Studies*, July 1977.

"Guanyu keji gongzuo de jige wenti (jielu)" [Several Questions Concerning Science and Technology Work (extracts)] (first draft of Outline Report, August 11, 1975). In *Zhonggong dangshi cankao ziliao* [CCP History Teaching Reference Materials]. Vol. 27, n.p.: Zhongguo Jiefangjun Guofang Daxue dangshi dangjian zhenggong jiaoyanshi, October 1988. Trans. in *Issues & Studies*, September 1977. Subsequent draft trans. in Kenneth Lieberthal, with the assistance of James Tong and Sai-cheung Yeung. *Central Documents and Politburo Politics in China*. Ann Arbor: Michigan Papers in Chinese Studies no. 33, 1978.

"Guowuyuan, Zhongyang Junwei zhuanfa 'Shanghai chengshi minbing qingkuang diaocha' de tongzhi" [The State Council and Central MAC Issue a Notice on "Investigation of the Circumstances of the Shanghai Urban Militia"] (November 19, 1973). In Song Yongyi, chief ed. *The Chinese Cultural Revolution Database CD-ROM*. Hong Kong: The Chinese University Press, 2002.

Jiang Qing. "Jiang Qing zhi Wang Hongwen, Ye Jianying, Zhang Chunqiao, Deng Xiaoping de xin" [Jiang Qing's Letter to Wang Hongwen, Ye Jianying, Zhang Chunqiao and Deng Xiaoping] (January 24, 1974). In Song Yongyi, chief ed. *The Chinese Cultural Revolution Database CD-ROM.* Hong Kong: The Chinese University Press, 2002.

"Liuzhong quanhui chuanda tigang fulu: Hua Guofeng Tongzhi de zhuyao cuowu" [Appendix to Transmission of Outline of the Sixth Plenum: Comrade Hua Guofeng's Main Mistakes] (July 7, 1981). In Song Yongyi, chief ed. *The Chinese Cultural Revolution Database CD-ROM.* Hong Kong: The Chinese University Press, 2002.

"Lun quandang quanguo gexiang gongzuo de zonggang" [On the General Program for the Work of the Whole Party and Whole Country] (October 7, 1975). In *Zhonggong dangshi cankao ziliao* [CCP History Teaching Reference Materials]. Vol. 27, n.p.: Zhongguo Jiefangjun Guofang Daxue dangshi dangjian zhenggong jiaoyanshi, October 1988. Trans. in *Issues & Studies*, August 1977.

Zhang Hanzhi. "Zhang Hanzhi jiu Qiao Guanhua yu Jiang Qing de guanxi suoxie de jiaodai cailiao" [Zhang Hanzhi's Written Explanation Material concerning the Relations of Qiao Guanhua and Jiang Qing] ([late] 1976). In Song Yongyi, chief ed. *The Chinese Cultural Revolution Database CD-ROM.* Hong Kong: The Chinese University Press, 2002. Other versions: "Zhang Hanzhi jiaodai cailiao" [Zhang Hanzhi's Confession Material]. In *Zhonggong yuanshi ziliao xuanji* [Selection of Original CCP Materials], vol. 2, 1st series. Taipei: Zhonggong yanjiu zazh:shi, 1981. "Zhang Hanzhi jiaodai cailiao (zhaiyao)" [Zhang Hanzhi's Confession Material (summary)]. Handwritten document available at the Fairbank Center Library, Harvard University.

"Zhonggong zhongyang guanyu huifu Deng Xiaoping Tongzhi de dang de zuzhi shenghuo he Guowuyuan fuzongli de zhiwu de jueding ji fujian [1. Deng Xiaoping Tongzhi de xin; 2. Derg Xiaoping Tongzhi de 'Wo de zishu' (zhailu)]" [CCP Center's Decision on Restoring Comrade Deng Xiaoping's Party Organizational Life and State Council Vice Premier Duties and Appendices [:. Comrade Deng Xiaoping's letter; 2. Comrade Deng Xiaoping's 'Self-statement' (extracts)]] (March 10, 1973). In Song Yongyi, chief ed. *The Chinese Cultural Revolution Database CD-ROM.* Hong Kong: The Chinese University Press, 2002.

"Zhonggong zhongyang guanyu pi Lin pi Kong yundong jige zhengzhi wenti de tongzhi" [CCP Central Committee Circular on Some Political Questions in the Lin Biao-Confucius Campaign] (May 18, 1974). In Song Yongyi, chief ed. *The Chinese Cultural Revolution Database CD-ROM.* Hong Kong: The Chinese University Press, 2002.

"Zhonggong zhongyang guanyu 'Wang Hongwen, Zhang Chunqiao, Jiang Qing, Yao Wenyuan fandang jituan shijian' de tongzhi" [CCP Central Committee Notice concerning the "Wang Hongwen, Zhang Chunqiao, Jiang Qing, Yao Wenyuan Anti-Party Clique Incident"] (October 18, 1976). In Song Yongyi, chief ed. *The Chinese Cultural Revolution Database CD-ROM.* Hong Kong: The Chinese University Press, 2002. Trans. in *Issues & Studies*, July 1979.

"Zhonggong zhongyang guanyu 'Wang Hongwen, Zhang Chunqiao, Jiang Qing, Yao Wenyuan fandang jituan zuizheng (cailiao zhi er)' de tongzhi ji cailiao" [CCP Central Committee Notice and Materials concerning "Proof of the Crimes of the Wang Hongwen, Zhang Chunqiao, Jiang Qing, Yao Wenyuan Anti-Party Clique (second batch of materials)"] (March 6, 1977). In Song Yongyi, chief ed. *The Chinese Cultural Revolution Database CD-ROM.* Hong Kong: The Chinese University Press, 2002.

"Zhonggong zhongyang guanyu 'Wang Hongwen, Zhang Chunqiao, Jiang Qing, Yao Wenyuan fandang jituan zuizheng (cailiao zhi san)' de tongzhi ji fujian" [CCP Central Committee Notice and Attachment concerning "Proof of the Crimes of the Wang Hongwen, Zhang Chunqiao, Jiang Qing,

Yao Wenyuan Anti-Party Clique (third batch of materials)"] (September 23, 1977). In Song Yongyi, chief ed. *The Chinese Cultural Revolution Database CD-ROM*. Hong Kong: The Chinese University Press, 2002. Trans. in *Issues & Studies*, July-November 1977, January-May 1978.

"Zhonggong zhongyang guanyu 'Wang Hongwen, Zhang Chunqiao, Jiang Qing, Yao Wenyuan fandang jituan zuizheng (cailiao zhi yi)' de tongzhi ji fujian" [CCP Central Committee Notice and Attachment concerning "Proof of the Crimes of the Wang Hongwen, Zhang Chunqiao, Jiang Qing, Yao Wenyuan Anti-Party Clique (first batch of materials)"] (December 10, 1976). In Song Yongyi, chief ed. *The Chinese Cultural Revolution Database CD-ROM*. Hong Kong: The Chinese University Press, 2002. Trans. in *Issues & Studies*, September-November 1977.

"Zhonggong zhongyang guanyu zhuageming cushengchan de tongzhi" [CCP Central Committee Notice on Grasping Revolution and Promoting Production] (July 1, 1974). In Song Yongyi, chief ed. *The Chinese Cultural Revolution Database CD-ROM*. Hong Kong: The Chinese University Press, 2002. Trans. in *Issues & Studies*, January 1975.

"Zhonggong zhongyang tongyi bing pizhuan Guojia jiwei 'Guanyu 1974 nian guomin jingji jihua (caoan) de baogao' (gaiyao)" [CCP Center Agrees with and Transmits the SPC's "Report on the 1974 (Draft) Economic Plan" (Outline)] (April 22, 1974). In Song Yongyi, chief ed. *The Chinese Cultural Revolution Database CD-ROM*. Hong Kong: The Chinese University Press, 2002.

Internet Sources

Chen Yonggui. "Wo mengjian Mao Zhuxi le" [I Dream of Chairman Mao] (June 5, 2003). http://www.peacehall.com/forum/lishi/246.shtml.

Fan Shidong. "Qiliu nian Beijing gongting zhengbian zhenxiang" [The Truth about the 1976 *Coup d'Etat* in Beijing]. http://www.boxun.com/hero/fansidong/24_1.shtml.

Ji Pomin. "Ting fuqin Ji Dengkui tan wangshi" [Listening to My Father Ji Dengkui Talk on Past Events] (November 6, 2003). http://www.nanfangdaily.com.cn/zm/20031106/ji/jswshb/200311060680.asp.

"Jianzheng Zhuxi zuihou shike, Mao Yuanxin yuanhe bei baohu shencha" [Having Witnessed the Chairman's Last Moments, Why Mao Yuanxin Was Put under Protective Custody]. http://1000site.com/75/19207.html.

"Jizeng huishou: Xie Jingyi, bei Mao Zhuxi fuhua de nühai" [Some Recollections: Xie Jingyi, the Girl Corrupted by Chairman Mao] (December 12, 2004). http://www.peacehall.com/news/gb/pubvp/2004/03/200403120251.shtml.

Li Rui. "Hu Yaobang qushiqian de tanhua" [Talks before Hu Yaobang Passed Away]. *Xinshiji* [New Century Net] (May 1, 2002). http://www.ncn.org/asp/zwginfo/da.asp?ID=44257&ad=1/5/2002.

"Li Rui jilu de Hu Yaobang zhengzhi yiyan" [Li Rui's Notes of Hu Yaobang's Political Testament] (November 13, 2005). http://www1.chinesenewsnet.com/MainNews/Forums/BackStage/2005_11_12_22_7_29_741.html.

Li Zhongqiang. "Yiqi huangtang de woniu shijian" [The Ridiculous "Snail Incident"] (October 14, 2002). http://secretchina.com/news/gb/articles/2/10/14/26598.html.

Luo Bing. "Yao Wenyuan xie Mao Zedong neimu" [Yao Wenyuan Reveals the Inside Story of Mao Zedong] (December 19, 2003). http://www.ncn.org/asp/zwginfo/da.asp?ID=55956&ad=12/19/2003.

"Mao Zedong he Xu Shiyou" [Mao Zedong and Xu Shiyou]. http://www.china-shaoshan.com/bbs/showtopic.asp?TOPIC_ID=7011&Forum_ID=12.

Shui Luzhou. "Du *Mao Zedong zhuan* biji" [Notes on Reading *Biography of Mao Zedong*]. *Zhongguo yu shijie* [China and the World] (special issue, July 2005). http://www.zgysj.com.

Wang Ruoshui. "Zhou Enlai jiuzuo douzheng de shibai" [Zhou Enlai's Defeat in His Effort to Rectify Leftist Excesses] (January 22, 2001). http://www.cnd.org/HXWZ/ZK01/zk247.gb.html.

Wen Xiang. "Lishi huigu" [Looking Back at History] (March 10, 2004). http://www.comefromchina.com/newbbs/archive/topic/225628-1.html.

_____. "Mao Zedong, Qiao Guanhua, Zhang Hanzl.i, Zhou Enlai" [Mao Zedong, Qiao Guanhua, Zhang Hanzhi and Zhou Enlai]. *Boxun* [Well-informed News] (March 9, 2004). http://www.peacehall.com/news/gb/pubvp/2004/03/200403090141.shtml.

_____. "Mao Zedong wannian de chongchen—Hua Guofeng" [Mao Zedong's Favorite Official in His Later Years—Hua Guofeng] (July 16, 2005). http://www.ncn.org/asp/zwginfo/da.asp?ID=64834&ad=7/16/2005.

Xu Yong. "Wei Guoqing tusha Guangxi 'sierer' pai" [Wei Guoqing Slaughters Guangxi's "422" Faction] (March 21, 2003). http://museums.cnd.org/CR/ZK03/cr168.hz8.html.

Yu Ruxin. "Wei Ding Sheng bian" [In Defense of Ding Sheng] (June 2005). http://blog.wenxuecity.com/blogview.php?date=200506&postID=1975.

"Zhang Yufeng jie Mao wannian mimi cailiao" [Zhang Yufeng Brings to Light Secret Materials on Mao's Later Years] (May 22, 2004). http://www.secretchina.com/new/articles/4/5/22/65524.html.

Zhou Qicai. "Mao Zedong daoci xingcheng qianhou" [Before and After the Drafting of Mao Zedong's Memorial Speech]. http://book.sina.com.cn/nzt/his/wode1976/11.shtml.

Primary Chinese Sources in English

Translation Series

British Broadcasting Corporation: Summary of World Broadcasts, Far East. Caversham Park, Reading: Monitoring Service of the British Broadcasting Corporation, 1959-.

Chinese Law and Government. White Plains/Armonk: M.E. Sharpe, 1968-.

Foreign Broadcast Information Service. Daily Report on China [variously Communist China, People's Republic of China, China]. Springfield, Virginia: 1958-.

Selections from People's Republic of China Magazines. Formerly *Selections from China Mainland Magazines*. Hong Kong: United States Consulate General, 1955-77.

Survey of People's Republic of China Press. Formerly *Survey of China Mainland Press*. Hong Kong: United States Consulate General, 1950-77.

Books and Monographs

Deng Mao Mao [Deng Rong]. *Deng Xiaoping, My Father*. New York: Basic Books, 1995. Trans. of Mao Mao. *Wode fuqin Deng Xiaoping, shangce* [My Father Deng Xiaoping, vol. 1]. Beijing: Zhongyang wenxian chubanshe, 1993.

Li Zhisui. *The Private Life of Chairman Mao: The Memoirs of Mao's Personal Physician*. London: Chatto & Windus, 1994.

Liu Suinian and Wu Qungan, eds. *China's Socialist Economy: An Outline History (1949-1984)*. Beijing: *Beijing Review*, 1986.

Ma Jisen. *The Cultural Revolution in the Foreign Ministry of* China. Hong Kong: The Chinese University Press, 2004. Trans. of *Waijiaobu wenge jishi* [True Record of the Foreign Affairs Ministry during the Cultural Revolution]. Hong Kong: Zhongwen Daxue chubanshe, 2003.

Mao Mao [Deng Rong]. *Deng Xiaoping and the Cultural Revolution: A Daughter Recalls the Critical Years*. Beijing: Foreign Languages Press, 2002 and New York: Bertelsman, 2005. Trans. of *Wode fuqin Deng Xiaoping: "wenge" suiyue*. Beijing: Zhongyang wenxian chubanshe, 2000.

Quan Yanchi. *Mao Zedong: Man Not God*. Beijing: Foreign Languages Press, 1992. Abridged trans. of Li Yinqiao. *Zai Mao Zedong shenbian shiwunian* [Fifteen Years at the Side of Mao Zedong]. Shijiazhuang: Hebei renmin chubanshe, 1992.

Yan Jiaqi and Gao Gao. *Turbulent Decade: A History of the Cultural Revolution*. Trans. and ed. by D. W. K. Kwok. Honolulu: University of Hawaii Press, 1996. Trans. of Gao Gao and Yan Jiaqi. *"Wenhua dageming" shinianshi, 1966-1976* [A Ten-year History of the "Great Cultural Revolution," 1966-1976]. Tianjin: Tianjin renmin chubanshe, 1986.

Yang Zhongmei. *Hu Yaobang: A Chinese Biography*. Armonk: M.E. Sharpe, 1988.

Yu Guangyuan. *Deng Xiaoping Shakes the World: An Eyewitness Account of China's Party Work Conference and the Third Plenum (November-December 1978)*. Edited by Ezra F. Vogel and Steven I. Levine. Norwalk: EastBridge, 2004.

Yue Daiyun and Carolyn Wakeman. *To the Storm: The Odyssey of a Revolutionary Chinese Woman*. Berkeley: University of California Press, 1985.

Chronologies, Documentary Collections, Personnel Directories, etc.

Collected Works of Liu Shao-ch'i 1958-1967. Hong Kong: Union Research Institute, 1968.

A Great Trial in Chinese History: The Trial of the Lin Biao and Jiang Qing Counter-revolutionary Cliques, Nov. 1980-Jan. 1981. New York: Pergamon Press, 1981.

History of the Chinese Communist Party: A Chronology of Events (1919-1990). Beijing: Foreign Languages Press, 1991. Trans. of *Zhongguo Gongchandang lishi dashiji (1919.5-1987.12)* [History of the Chinese Communist Party: A Chronology of Events, May 1919-December 1987]. Beijing: Renmin chubanshe, 1989.

Kau, Michael Y. M., ed. *The Lin Biao Affair: Power Politics and Military Coup*. White Plains: International Arts and Sciences Press, 1975.

Schram, Stuart, ed. *Mao Tse-tung Unrehearsed, Talks and Letters: 1956-71*. Harmondsworth: Penguin Books, 1974.

Selected Works of Deng Xiaoping (1975-1982). [Vol. 2], Beijing: Foreign Languages Press, 1984. Trans. of *Deng Xiaoping wenxuan (yijiuqiwu—yijiubaer nian)* [Selected Works of Deng Xiaoping, 1975-1982]. [Vol. 2], Beijing: Renmin chubanshe, 1983.

Selected Works of Zhou Enlai. Vol. II, Beijing: Foreign Languages Press, 1989. Trans. of *Zhou Enlai xuanji* [Selected Works of Zhou Enlai]. Vol. 2, Beijing: Renmin chubanshe, 1984.

Articles, Documents, Speeches, etc.

"CCP Central Committee Document: Chung-fa No. 21 (1974)" (July 1, 1974). *Issues & Studies*, January 1975. Trans. of "Zhonggong zhongyang guanyu zhuageming cushengchan de tongzhi" [CCP Central Committee Notice on Grasping Revolution and Promoting Production]. In Song Yongyi, chief ed. *The Chinese Cultural Revolution Database CD-ROM*. Hong Kong: The Chinese University Press, 2002.

Chen Yonggui. "Report at the Second National Conference on Learning from Tachai [Dazhai] in Agriculture" (December 20, 1976). *Hongqi* [Red Flag], no. 1 (1977). In *Selections from People's Republic of China Magazines*, no. 910 (1977).

Deng Xiaoping. "The Army Needs to be Consolidated" (January 25, 1975). In *Selected Works of Deng Xiaoping (1975-1982)*. [Vol. 2], Beijing: Foreign Languages Press, 1984.

_____. "On Consolidating National Defense Enterprises" (August 3, 1975). In *Selected Works of Deng Xiaoping (1975-1982)*. [Vol. 2], Beijing: Foreign Languages Press, 1984. Extract from original version in Song Yongyi, chief ed. *The Chinese Cultural Revolution Database CD-ROM*. Hong Kong: The Chinese University Press, 2002.

_____. "Priority Should be Given to Scientific Research" (September 26, 1975). In web version of *Selected Works of Deng Xiaoping (1975-1982)* [Vol. 2]. http://english.peopledaily.com.cn/dengxp/contents2.html. Other extracts from Deng's comments on September 26, 1975 in Chinese: "Deng Xiaoping zai Guowuyuan lingdao tongzhi tingqu Hu Yaobang huibao de chahua" (September 26, 1975) [Deng Xiaoping's Remarks during Hu Yaobang's Report to State Council Leading Comrades]. In Song Yongyi, chief ed. *The Chinese Cultural Revolution Database CD-ROM*. Hong Kong: The Chinese University Press, 2002. Also in version available at the Fairbank Center Library, Harvard University.

_____. "Some Comments on Industrial Development" (August 18, 1975). In *Selected Works of Deng Xiaoping (1975-1982)*. [Vol. 2], Beijing: Foreign Languages Press, 1984.

———. "Some Problems Outstanding in the Iron and Steel Industry" (May 29, 1975). In *Selected Works of Deng Xiaoping (1975-1982)*. [Vol. 2], Beijing: Foreign Languages Press, 1984. Extract from original version in Song Yongyi, chief ed. *The Chinese Cultural Revolution Database CD-ROM*. Hong Kong: The Chinese University Press, 2002.

———. "Strengthen Party Leadership and Rectify the Party's Style of Work" (July 4, 1975). In *Selected Works of Deng Xiaoping (1975-1982)*. [Vol. 2], Beijing: Foreign Languages Press, 1984. Original version in Song Yongyi, chief ed. *The Chinese Cultural Revolution Database CD-ROM*. Hong Kong: The Chinese University Press, 2002.

———. "The Task of Consolidating the Army" (July 14, 1975). In *Selected Works of Deng Xiaoping (1975-1982)*. [Vol. 2], Beijing: Foreign Languages Press, 1984. Original version in Song Yongyi, chief ed. *The Chinese Cultural Revolution Database CD-ROM*. Hong Kong: The Chinese University Press, 2002.

———. "Things Must be Put in Order" (September 27 and October 4, 1975). In *Selected Works of Deng Xiaoping (1975-1982)*. [Vol. 2], Beijing: Foreign Languages Press, 1984.

———. "The Whole Party Should Take the Overall Interest into Account and Push the Economy Forward" (March 5, 1975). In *Selected Works of Deng Xiaoping (1975-1982)*. [Vol. 2], Beijing: Foreign Languages Press, 1984.

"A Document of the Central Committee of the Chinese Communist Party: *Chung-fa* (1976) No. 16" (October 18, 1976). *Issues & Studies*, July 1979. Trans. of "Zhonggong zhongyang guanyu 'Wang Hongwen, Zhang Chunqiao, Jiang Qing, Yao Wenyuan fandang jituan shijian' de tongzhi" [CCP Central Committee Notice concerning the "Wang Hongwen, Zhang Chunqiao, Jiang Qing, Yao Wenyuan Anti-Party Clique Incident"]. In Song Yongyi, chief ed. *The Chinese Cultural Revolution Database CD-ROM*. Hong Kong: The Chinese University Press, 2002.

"Document of the Central Committee of the Chinese Communist Party: *Chung-fa* (1976) No. 24" (December 10, 1976). *Issues & Studies*, September-November 1977. Trans. of "Zhonggong zhongyang guanyu 'Wang Hongwen, Zhang Chunqiao, Jiang Qing, Yao Wenyuan fandang jituan zuizheng (cailiao zhi yi)' de tongzhi ji fujian" [CCP Central Committee Notice and Attachment concerning "Proof of the Crimes of the Wang Hongwen, Zhang Chunqiao, Jiang Qing, Yao Wenyuan Anti-Party Clique (first batch of materials)"]. In Song Yongyi, chief ed. *The Chinese Cultural Revolution Database CD-ROM*. Hong Kong: The Chinese University Press, 2002.

"Document of the Central Committee of the Chinese Communist Party: *Chung-fa* (1976) No. 37" (September 23, 1977). *Issues & Studies*, July-November 1977, January-May 1978. Trans. of "Zhonggong zhongyang guanyu 'Wang Hongwen, Zhang Chunqiao, Jiang Qing, Yao Wenyuan fandang jituan zuizheng (cailiao zhi san)' de tongzhi ji fujian" [CCP Central Committee Notice and Attachment concerning "Proof of the Crimes of the Wang Hongwen, Zhang Chunqiao, Jiang Qing, Yao Wenyuan Anti-Party Clique (third batch of materials)"]. In Song Yongyi, chief ed. *The Chinese Cultural Revolution Database CD-ROM*. Hong Kong: The Chinese University Press, 2002.

Fan Shuo. "The Tempestuous October—A Chronicle of the Complete Collapse of the 'Gang of Four'." *Yangcheng wanbao* [Yangcheng Evening News], February 10, 1974. In Foreign Broadcast Information Service-China-89-029, February 14, 1989.

Hua Guofeng. "Political Report to the 11th Natinal Congress of the Communist Party of China" (August 12, 1977). *Peking Review*, no. 35 (1977).

_____. Speech at the Second National Conference on Learning from Tachai [Dazhai] in Agriculture (December 25, 1976). In Foreign Broadcast Information Service-People's Republic of China, no. 250 (1976).

_____. Summing-up Report at the National Conference on Learning from Tachai [Dazhai] in Agriculture (October 15, 1975). *Hongqi* [Red Flag], no. 1 (1977). In *Selections from People's Republic of China Magazines*, no. 910 (1977).

"Interviews with Ji Dengkui." *Liaowang* [Outlook], overseas ed., February 6-13, 1989. In Foreign Broadcast Information Service-China-89-029, February 14, 1989.

Liao Kai-lung [Liao Gailong]. "Historical Experiences and Our Road of Development" (October 25, 1980). *Issues & Studies*, October-December 1981.

Nie Rongzhen. "[Ye] Jianying was in Fact a Proletarian Lu Duan." New China News Agency, October 31, 1986. In British Broadcasting Corporation: Summary of World Broadcasts, Far East/8409/BII/6 (November 6, 1986).

"On Questions of Party History—Resolution on Certain Questions in the History of Our Party Since the Founding of the People's Republic of China" (June 27, 1981). *Beijing Review*, no. 27 (1981).

"On the General Program for All Work of the (Whole) Party and (Whole) Country" (October 7, 1975). *Issues & Studies*, August 1977. Trans. of "Lun quandang quanguo gexiang gongzuo de zonggang." In *Zhonggong dangshi cankao ziliao* [CCP History Teaching Reference Materials]. Vol. 27, n.p.: Zhongguo Jiefangjun Guofang Daxue dangshi dangjian zhenggong jiaoyanshi, October 1988.

"Outline of 'Project 571'." In Michael Y. M. Kau, ed. *The Lin Biao Affair: Power Politics and Military Coup*. White Plains: International Arts and Sciences Press, 1975.

"Outline Summary Report of the Work of the Academy of Sciences" (early September 1975). In Kenneth Lieberthal, with the assistance of James Tong and Sai-cheung Yeung. *Central Documents and Politburo Politics in China*. Ann Arbor: Michigan Papers in Chinese Studies no. 33, 1978.

"Several Questions Concerning the Work of Science and Technology: Excerpts of the First Draft for Discussion of the Briefing Outline" ([August 11, 1975]). *Issues & Studies*, September 1977. Chinese text in *Zhonggong dangshi cankao ziliao* [CCP History Teaching Reference Materials]. Vol. 27, n.p.: Zhongguo Jiefangjun Guofang Daxue dangshi dangjian zhenggong jiaoyanshi, October 1988.

"Some Questions on Accelerating the Development of Industry" [The 20 Articles or Industry] (September 2, 1975). In Kenneth Lieberthal, with the assistance of James Tong and Sai-cheung Yeung. *Central Documents and Politburo Politics in China*. Ann Arbor: Michigan Papers in Chinese Studies no. 33, 1978. Chinese text in *Zhonggong dangshi cankao ziliao* [CCP History Teaching Reference Materials]. Vol. 27, n.p.: Zhongguo Jiefangjun Guofang Daxue dangshi dangjian zhenggong jiaoyanshi, October 1988.

Tan Zongji. "The Third Plenum of the Eleventh Central Committee is a Major Turning Point in the History of the Party Since the Founding of the People's Republic of China." In *Chinese Law and Government*, May-June 1995.

Wang Hongwen. "Comrade Wang Hung-wen's Report at the Central Study Class" (January 14, 1974). *Issues & Studies*, February 1975. Chinese text in Song Yongyi, chief ed. *The Chinese Cultural Revolution Database CD-ROM*. Hong Kong: The Chinese University Press, 2002.

_____. "Report on the Revision of the Party Constitution" (August 28, 1973). *Peking Review*, no. 35-36 (1973).

Wu Teh [Wu De]. "Comrade Wu Teh's Broadcast Speech at Tien An Men Square" (April 5, 1976). *Peking Review*, no. 15 (1976). Chinese text in Song Yongyi, chief ed. *The Chinese Cultural Revolution Database CD-ROM*. Hong Kong: The Chinese University Press, 2002.

_____. "Comrade Wu Teh's Speech at the Celebration Rally in the Capital" (October 24, 1976). *Peking Review*, no. 44 (1976). Chinese text in Song Yongyi, chief ed. *The Chinese Cultural Revolution Database CD-ROM*. Hong Kong: The Chinese University Press, 2002.

Yao Wenyuan. "On the Social Basis of the Lin Biao Anti-Party Clique" (March 1, 1975). *Peking Review*, no. 10 (1975).

Zhang Chunqiao. "On Exercising All-Round Dictatorship Over the Bourgeoisie" (April 1, 1975). *Peking Review*, no. 14 (1975).

_____. "Report on the Revision of the Constitution" (January 13, 1975). *Peking Review*, no. 4 (1975).

Zhang Yufeng. "Anecdotes of Mao Zedong and Zhou Enlai in Their Later Years." *Guangming ribao* [Brightness Daily], December 26-27, 29-30, 1988, January 1-6, 1989. In Foreign Broadcast Information Service-China-89-017 and 89-019.

Zhou Enlai. "Political Report to the Tenth National Congress of the Communist Party of China" (August 28, 1973). *Peking Review*, no. 35-36 (1973).

_____. "Report on the Work of the Government" (January 13, 1975). *Peking Review*, no. 4 (1975).

Secondary Sources

Books and Monographs

Bachman, David M. *Bureaucracy, Economy, and Leadership in China: The Institutional Origins of the Great Leap Forward.* Cambridge: Cambridge University Press, 1991.

_____. *Chen Yun and the Chinese Political System.* Berkeley: China Research Monographs, 1985.

Barnett, A. Doak. *The Making of Foreign Policy in China: Structure and Process.* Boulder: Westview Press, 1985.

Barnouin, Barbara, and Yu Changgen. *Chinese Foreign Policy during the Cultural Revolution.* London: Kegan Paul International, 1998.

_____. *Ten Years of Turbulence: The Chinese Cultural Revolution.* London: Kegan Paul International, 1993.

Baum, Richard. *Burying Mao: Chinese Politics in the Age of Deng Xiaoping.* Princeton: Princeton University Press, 1994.

_____. *Prelude to Revolution: Mao, the Party, and the Peasant Question, 1962-66*. New York: Columbia University Press, 1975.

Black, George, and Robin Munro. *Black Hands of Beijing: Lives of Defiance in China's Democracy Movement*. New York: John Wiley & Sons, 1993.

Bonavia, David. *Verdict in Peking: The Trial of the Gang of Four*. New York: G.P. Putnam's Sons, 1984.

Brugger, Bill, ed. *China: The Impact of the Cultural Revolution*. Canberra: Australian National University Press, 1978.

Burr, William, ed. *The Kissinger Transcripts: The Top Secret Talks with Beijing and Moscow*. New York: The New Press, 1998.

Byron, John, and Robert Pack. *The Claws of the Dragon: Kang Sheng—The Evil Genius Behind Mao—and His Legacy of Terror in People's China*. New York: Simon & Schuster, 1992.

Camilleri, Joseph. *Chinese Foreign Policy: The Maoist Era and its Aftermath*. Oxford: Martin Robertson, 1980.

Chan, Anita, Richard Madsen, and Jonathan Unger. *Chen Village under Mao and Deng*. Expanded and updated edition, Berkeley: University of California Press, 1992.

Chang, Jung, and Jon Halliday. *Mao: The Unknown Story*. London: Jonathan Cape, 2005.

Cheek, Timothy, and Tony Saich, eds. *New Perspectives on State Socialism in China*. Armonk: M.E. Sharpe, 1997.

Chu, Godwin C., and Francis L. K. Hsu, eds. *Moving a Mountain: Cultural Change in China*. Honolulu: University Press of Hawaii, 1979.

Dittmer, Lowell. *China's Continuous Revolution: The Post-Liberation Epoch, 1949-1981*. Berkeley: University of California Press, 1987.

Domes, Jurgen. *China after the Cultural Revolution: Politics between Two Party Congresses*. London: C. Hurst & Co., 1975.

Forster, Keith. *Rebellion and Factionalism in a Chinese Province: Zhejiang, 1966-1976*. Armonk: M.E. Sharpe, 1990.

Gardner, John. *Chinese Politics and the Succession to Mao*. London: Macmillan, 1982.

Garside, Roger. *Coming Alive!: China after Mao*. New York: McGraw-Hill, 1981.

Goldman, Merle. *China's Intellectuals: Advise and Dissent*. Cambridge: Harvard University Press, 1981.

Goodman, David S. G. *Deng Xiaoping and the Chinese Revolution: A Political Biography*. London: Routledge, 1994.

Harding, Harry. *China's Second Revolution: Reform after Mao*. Washington: The Brookings Institution, 1987.

Howe, Christopher, ed. *Shanghai, Revolution and Development in an Asian Metropolis*. New York: Cambridge University Press, 1981.

Huang, Jing. *Factionalism in Chinese Communist Politics*. Cambridge: Cambridge University Press, 2000.

Jain, J. P. *After Mao What? Army Party and Group Rivalries in China*. London: Martin Robertson, 1976.

Jin, Qiu. *The Culture of Power: The Lin Biao Incident in the Cultural Revolution*. Stanford: Stanford University Press, 1999.

Johnson, Chalmers, ed. *Ideology and Politics in Contemporary China*. Seattle: University of Washington Press, 1973.

Joseph, William A. *The Critique of Ultra-Leftism in China, 1958-1981*. Stanford: Stanford University Press, 1984.

_____, Christine P. W. Wong and David Zweig, eds. *New Perspectives on the Cultural Revolution*. Cambridge: Council on East Asian Studies/Harvard University, 1991.

Kissinger, Henry. *Years of Renewal*. New York: Simon & Schuster, 1999.

_____. *Years of Upheaval*. London: Weidenfeld and Nicholson and Michael Joseph, 1982.

Ladany, Laszlo. *The Communist Party of China and Marxism 1921-1985: A Self-Portrait*. Stanford: Hoover Institution Press, 1988.

Lampton, David M., with the assistance of Yeung Sai-cheung. *Paths to Power: Elite Mobility in Contemporary China*. Ann Arbor: Michigan Monographs in Chinese Studies, 1986.

Law, Kam-yee, ed. *The Chinese Cultural Revolution Reconsidered: Beyond Purge and Holocaust*. Basingstoke, Hampshire: Palgrave Macmillan, 2003.

Lee, Hong Yung. *From Revolutionary Cadres to Party Technocrats in Socialist China*. Berkeley: University of California Press, 1991.

Lee Kuan Yew. *Memoirs of Lee Kuan Yew: From Third World to First, The Singapore Story: 1965-2000*. Singapore: Singapore Press Holdings, 2000.

Lieberthal, Kenneth. *Governing China: From Revolution Through Reform*. New York: W.W. Norton, 1995.

_____. *Sino-Soviet Conflict in the 1970s: Its Evolution and Implications for the Strategic Triangle*. Santa Monica: Rand Report R-2342-NA, July 1978.

_____ and Michel Oksenberg. *Policy Making in China: Leaders, Structures, and Processes*. Princeton: Princeton University Press, 1988.

_____ with the assistance of James Tong and Sai-cheung Yeung. *Central Documents and Politburo Politics in China*. Ann Arbor: Michigan Papers in Chinese Studies no. 33, 1978.

Lindbeck, John M. H., ed. *China: Management of a Revolutionary Society*. Seattle: University of Washington Press, 1971.

Lubell, Pamela. *The Chinese Communist Party and the Cultural Revolution: The Case of the Sixty-One Renegades.* New York: Palgrave, 2002.

MacFarquhar, Roderick. *The Origins of the Cultural Revolution 1: Contradictions among the People 1956-1957.* New York: Columbia University Press, 1974.

_____. *The Origins of the Cultural Revolution 3: The Coming of the Cataclysm 1961-66.* New York: Columbia University Press, 1997.

_____, ed. *The Politics of China, Second Edition: The Eras of Mao and Deng.* New York: Cambridge University Press, 1997.

_____ and John K. Fairbank, eds. *The Cambridge History of China*, vol. 14, *The People's Republic, Part 1: The Emergence of Revolutionary China, 1949-1965.* Cambridge: Cambridge University Press, 1987.

_____ and John K. Fairbank, eds. *The Cambridge History of China*, vol. 15, *The People's Republic, Part 2: Revolutions within the Chinese Revolution.* Cambridge: Cambridge University Press, 1991.

Mann, James. *About Face: A History of America's Curious Relationship with China, From Nixon to Clinton.* New York: Alfred A. Knopf, 1999.

Mozingo, David P. *China's Foreign Policy and the Cultural Revolution.* Ithaca: Cornell International Relations of East Asia Project, 1970.

Perry, Elizabeth J. *Patrolling the Revolution: Worker Militias, Citizenship, and the Modern Chinese State.* Lanham: Rowman and Littlefield, 2006.

_____ and Li Xun. *Proletarian Power: Shanghai in the Cultural Revolution.* Boulder: Westview Press, 1997.

Pye, Lucian W. *Mao Tse-tung: The Man in the Leader.* New York: Basic Books, 1976.

Rittenberg, Sidney, and Amanda Bennett. *The Man Who Stayed Behind.* New York: Simon & Schuster, 1993.

Robinson, Thomas W., ed. *The Cultural Revolution in China.* Berkeley: University of California Press, 1971.

Salisbury, Harrison E. *The Long March: The Untold Story.* New York: Harper & Row, 1985.

Sawer, Marian, ed. *Socialism and the New Class: Towards the Analysis of Structural Inequality within Socialist Societies.* Bedford Park, South Australia: APSA Monograph no. 19, 1978.

Schlesinger, Arthur M. Jr. *A Thousand Days: John F. Kennedy in the White House.* London: Andre Deutsch, 1965.

Schoenhals, Michael, ed. *China's Cultural Revolution, 1966-1969: Not A Dinner Party.* Armonk: M.E. Sharpe, 1996.

Schram, Stuart R., ed. *Authority, Participation and Cultural Change in China.* Cambridge: Cambridge University Press, 1973.

_____. *The Political Thought of Mao Tse-tung.* Revised and enlarged ed., New York: Praeger Publishers, 1969.

_____. *The Thought of Mao Tse-tung.* New York: Cambridge University Press, 1989.

Shambaugh, David L. *The Making of a Premier: Zhao Ziyang's Provincial Career.* Boulder: Westview Press, 1984.

_____, ed. *The Modern Chinese State.* Cambridge: Cambridge University Press, 2000.

Short, Philip. *Mao: A Life.* New York: Henry Holt, 2000.

Talbott, Strobe, trans. and ed. *Khrushchev Remembers: The Last Testament.* Boston: Little, Brown and Company, 1974.

Teiwes, Frederick C. *Leadership, Legitimacy, and Conflict in China: From a Charismatic Mao to the Politics of Succession.* Armonk: M.E. Sharpe, 1984.

_____. *Politics and Purges in China: Rectification and the Decline of Party Norms 1950-1965.* 2nd edition, Armonk: M.E. Sharpe, 1993.

_____. *Politics at Mao's Court: Gao Gang and Party Factionalism in the Early 1950s.* Armonk: M. E. Sharpe, 1990.

_____. *Provincial Leadership in China: The Cultural Revolution and Its Aftermath.* Ithaca: Cornell East Asian Papers, 1974.

_____. *Provincial Party Personnel in Mainland China 1956-1966.* New York: Occasional Papers of the East Asian Institute, Columbia University, 1967.

_____ and Warren Sun, eds. *The Politics of Agricultural Cooperativization in China: Mao, Deng Zihui, and the "High Tide" of 1955.* Armonk: M. E. Sharpe, 1993.

_____ and Warren Sun. *The Tragedy of Lin Biao: Riding the Tiger during the Cultural Revolution, 1966-1971.* London: C. Hurst & Co., 1996.

_____ with Warren Sun. *China's Road to Disaster: Mao, Central Politicians, and Provincial Leaders in the Unfolding of the Great Leap Forward, 1955-1959.* Armonk: M.E. Sharpe, 1999.

_____ with Warren Sun. *The Formation of the Maoist Leadership: From the Return of Wang Ming to the Seventh Party Congress.* London: Contemporary China Institute Research Notes and Studies, 1994.

Terrill, Ross. *Mao: A Biography.* Stanford: Stanford University Press, 1999.

_____. *The White-Boned Demon: A Biography of Madame Mao Zedong.* London: Heinemann, 1984.

Ting Wang. *Chairman Hua: Leader of the Chinese Communists.* London: C. Hurst & Co., 1980.

Tyler, Patrick. *A Great Wall: Six Presidents and China, An Investigative History.* New York: Public Affairs, 1999.

Unger, Jonathan, ed. *The Nature of Chinese Politics: From Mao to Jiang*. Armonk, M. E. Sharpe, 2002.

Walder, Andrew G. *Chang Ch'un-ch'iao and Shanghai's January Revolution*. Ann Arbor: Michigan Papers in Chinese Studies no. 32, 1978.

White, Lynn T. III. *Unstately Power, Volume I: Local Causes of China's Economic Reforms*. Armonk: M.E. Sharpe, 1998.

_____. *Unstately Power, Volume II: Local Causes of China's Intellectual, Legal and Governmental Reforms*. Armonk: M.E. Sharpe, 1998.

Witke, Roxane. *Comrade Ch'iang Ch'ing*. Boston: Little, Brown and Company, 1977.

Wong, John, and Zheng Yongnian, eds. *China's Post-Jiang Leadership Succession: Problems and Perspectives*. Singapore: Singapore University Press, 2002.

Yang, Benjamin. *Deng: A Political Biography*. Armonk: M.E. Sharpe, 1998.

Yang, Dali L. *Calamity and Reform in China: State, Rural Society, and Institutional Change Since the Great Leap Famine*. Stanford: Stanford University Press, 1996.

Zweig, David. *Agrarian Radicalism in China, 1968-1981*. Cambridge: Harvard University Press, 1989.

Articles

Baum, Richard. "China: Year of the Mangoes." *Asian Survey*, January 1969.

_____ and Frederick C. Teiwes. "Liu Shao-ch'i and the Cadre Question." *Asian Survey*, April 1968.

Chang, Parris H. "The Anti-Lin Piao and Confucius Campaign: Its Meaning and Purposes." *Asian Survey*, October 1974.

_____. "The Rise of Wang Tung-hsing: Head of China's Security Apparatus." *The China Quarterly*, no. 73 (1978).

Chen, Nai-Ruenn. "China's Foreign Trade, 1950-74." In *China: A Reassessment of the Economy*, a compendium of papers submitted to the Joint Economic Committee, Congress of the United States. Washington DC: U.S. Government Printing Office, 1975.

Denny, David L. "International Finance in the People's Republic of China." In *China: A Reassessment of the Economy*, a compendium of papers submitted to the Joint Economic Committee, Congress of the United States. Washington DC: U.S. Government Printing Office, 1975.

Dittmer, Lowell. "Bases of Power in Chinese Politics: A Theory and an Analysis of the Fall of the 'Gang of Four'." *World Politics*, October 1978.

_____. "Learning from Trauma: The Cultural Revolution in Post-Mao Politics." In William A. Joseph, Christine P. W. Wong and David Zweig, eds. *New Perspectives on the Cultural Revolution*. Cambridge: Council on East Asian Studies/Harvard University, 1991.

Domes, Jurgen. "The 'Gang of Four' and Hua Kuo-feng: Analysis of Political Events in 1975-76." *The China Quarterly*, no. 71 (1977).

Fogel, Joshua A. "Mendacity and Veracity in the Recent Chinese Communist Memoir Literature." In Timothy Cheek and Tony Saich, eds. *New Perspectives on State Socialism in China*. Armonk: M.E. Sharpe, 1997.

Forster, Keith. "China's Coup of October 1976." *Modern China*, July 1992.

_____. "The Cultural Revolution in Zhejiang Revisited." In Kam-yee Law, ed. *The Chinese Cultural Revolution Reconsidered: Beyond Purge and Holocaust*. Basingstoke, Hampshire: Palgrave Macmillan, 2003.

_____. "Factional Politics in Zhejiang, 1973-1976." In William A. Joseph, Christine P. W. Wong and David Zweig, eds. *New Perspectives on the Cultural Revolution*. Cambridge: Council on East Asian Studies/Harvard University, 1991.

_____. "The 1976 Ch'ing-ming Incident in Hangchow." *Issues & Studies*, April 1986.

_____. "The Repudiation of the Cultural Revolution." *Journal of Contemporary Asia*, vol. 17, no. 1 (1987).

_____. "Spontaneous and Institutional Rebellion in the Cultural Revolution: The Extraordinary Case of Weng Senghe." *The Australian Journal of Chinese Affairs*, no. 27 (1992).

Friedman, Edward. "The Politics of Local Models, Social Transformation and State Power Struggles in the People's Republic of China: Tachai and Teng Hsiao-p'ing." *The China Quarterly*, no. 76 (1978).

Gardner, John, and Wilt Idema. "China's Educational Revolution." In Stuart R. Schram, ed. *Authority, Participation and Cultural Change in China*. Cambridge: Cambridge University Press, 1973.

Goldman, Merle. "China's Anti-Confucian Campaign, 1973-74." *The China Quarterly*, no. 63 (1975).

_____. "The Chinese Communist Party's 'Cultural Revolution' of 1962-64." In Chalmers Johnson, ed. *Ideology and Politics in Contemporary China*. Seattle: University of Washington Press, 1973.

_____. "The Fall of Chou Yang." *The China Quarterly*, no. 27 (1966).

_____. "The Media Campaign as a Weapon in Political Struggle: The Dictatorship of the Proletariat and *Water Margin* Campaigns." In Godwin C. Chu and Francis L. K. Hsu, eds. *Moving a Mountain: Cultural Change in China*. Honolulu: University Press of Hawaii, 1979.

Goodman, David S. G. "The Shanghai Connection in National Politics." In Christopher Howe, ed. *Shanghai, Revolution and Development in an Asian Metropolis*. New York: Cambridge University Press, 1981.

Guo, Xuezhi. "Dimensions of *Guanxi* in Chinese Elite Politics." *The China Journal*, no. 46 (2001).

Gurtov, Melvin. "The Foreign Ministry and Foreign Affairs in the Chinese Cultural Revolution." In Thomas W. Robinson, ed. *The Cultural Revolution in China*. Berkeley: University of California Press, 1971.

Harding, Harry, Jr. "China: The Fragmentation of Power." *Asian Survey*, January 1972.

———. "China: Toward Revolutionary Pragmatism." *Asian Survey*, January 1971.

Joseph, William A., Christine P. W. Wong and David Zweig. "Introduction: New Perspectives on the Cultural Revolution." In William A. Joseph, Christine P. W. Wong and David Zweig, eds. *New Perspectives on the Cultural Revolution*. Cambridge: Council on East Asian Studies/Harvard University, 1991.

Kau, Michael Y. M. "Introduction." In Michael Y. M. Kau, ed. *The Lin Biao Affair: Power Politics and Military Coup*. White Plains: International Arts and Sciences Press, 1975.

Kraus, Richard. "Arts Policies of the Cultural Revolution: The Rise and Fall of Culture Minister Yu Huiyong." In William A. Joseph, Christine P. W. Wong and David Zweig, eds. *New Perspectives on the Cultural Revolution*. Cambridge: Council on East Asian Studies/Harvard University, 1991.

Lieberthal, Kenneth. "China in 1975: The Internal Political Scene." *Problems of Communism*, May-June 1975.

Liu, Alan P. L. "The 'Gang of Four' and the Chinese People's Liberation Army." *Asian Survey*, September 1979.

Louie, Genny, and Kam Louie. "The Role of Nanjing University in the Nanjing Incident." *The China Quarterly*, no. 86 (1981).

MacFarquhar, Roderick. "The Succession to Mao and the End of Maoism, 1969-82." In Roderick MacFarquhar, ed. *The Politics of China, Second Edition: The Eras of Mao and Deng*. New York: Cambridge University Press, 1997. Also in Roderick MacFarquhar and John K. Fairbank, eds. *The Cambridge History of China*, vol. 15, *The People's Republic, Part 2: Revolutions within the Chinese Revolution*. Cambridge: Cambridge University Press, 1991.

Naughton, Barry. "The Third Front: Defence Industrialization in the Chinese Interior," *The China Quarterly*, no. 115 (1988).

"Ni Chih-fu—Member of the CCPCC Politburo." *Issues & Studies*, January 1978.

Oksenberg, Michel, and Sai-cheung Yeung. "Hua Kuo-feng's Pre-Cultural Revolution Hunan Years: The Making of a Political Generalist." *The China Quarterly*, no. 69 (1977).

Onate, Andres. "Hua Kuo-feng and the Arrest of the 'Gang of Four'." *The China Quarterly*, no. 75 (1978).

"Organizing China's Peasants: A Rural Upsurge?" *Current Scene*, September 1974.

Pollack, Jonathan D. "The Opening to America." In Roderick MacFarquhar and John K. Fairbank, eds. *The Cambridge History of China*, vol. 15, *The People's Republic, Part 2: Revolutions within the Chinese Revolution*. Cambridge: Cambridge University Press, 1991.

Reardon, Lawrence C. "Learning How to Open the Door: A Reassessment of China's 'Opening' Strategy." *The China Quarterly*, no. 155 (1998).

Robinson, Thomas W. "China Confronts the Soviet Union: Warfare and Diplomacy on China's Inner Asian Frontiers." In Roderick MacFarquhar and John K. Fairbank, eds. *The Cambridge History of*

China, vol. 15, *The People's Republic, Part 2: Revolutions within the Chinese Revolution.* Cambridge: Cambridge University Press, 1991.

_____. "China in 1972: Socio-Economic Progress Amidst Political Uncertainty." *Asian Survey*, January 1973.

_____. "China in 1973: Renewed Leftism Threatens the 'New Course'." *Asian Survey*, January 1974.

Ross, Robert S. "From Lin Biao to Deng Xiaoping: Elite Instability and China's U.S. Policy." *The China Quarterly*, no. 118 (1989).

Schoenhals, Michael. "The Central Case Examination Group, 1966-79." *The China Quarterly*, no. 145 (1996).

_____. "Why Don't We Arm the Left? Mao's Culpability for the Cultural Revolution's 'Great Chaos' of 1967." *The China Quarterly*, no. 182 (2005).

Schram, Stuart R. "Introduction." In Stuart R.Schram, ed. *Authority, Participation and Cultural Change in China.* Cambridge: Cambridge University Press, 1973.

Starr, John Bryan. "China in 1974: 'Weeding Through the Old to Bring Forth the New'." *Asian Survey*, January 1975,

_____. "China in 1975: 'The Wind in the Bell Tower'." *Asian Survey*, January 1976.

_____. "From the 10th Party Congress to the Premiership of Hua Kuo-feng: The Significance of the Colour of the Cat." *The China Quarterly*, no. 67 (1976).

Sun, Warren. "The National Defense University's *Teaching Reference Materials.*" In Timothy Cheek and Tony Saich, eds. *New Perspectives on State Socialism in China.* Armonk: M.E. Sharpe, 1997.

_____. Review of Gao Wenqian. *Wannian Zhou Enlai* [The Later Years of Zhou Enlai]. New York: Mingjing chubanshe, 2003. *The China Journal*, no. 52 (2004).

_____. Review of Song Yongyi, chief ed. *The Chinese Cultural Revolution Database CD-ROM.* Hong Kong: The Chinese University Press, 2002. *The China Journal*, no. 50 (2003).

Teiwes, Frederick C "Before and After the Cultural Revolution." *The China Quarterly*, no. 58 (1974).

_____. "The Chinese State during the Maoist Era." In David Shambaugh, ed. *The Modern Chinese State.* Cambridge: Cambridge University Press, 2000.

_____. "A Critique of Western Studies of Chinese Elite Politics." *IIAS Newsletter* (Leiden), Summer 1996. Expanded version trans. as "Xifang de dangdai Zhongguo yanjiu" [Western Research on Contemporary China]. *Dangdai Zhongguoshi yanjiu* [Contemporary Chinese History Studies], no. 6 (2004).

_____. "The Establishment and Consolidation of the New Regime, 1949-57." In Roderick MacFarquhar, ed. *The Politics of China, Second Edition: The Eras of Mao and Deng.* New York: Cambridge University Press, 1997. Also in Roderick MacFarquhar and John K. Fairbank, eds. *The Cambridge History of China*, vol. 14, *The People's Republic, Part 1: The Emergence of Revolutionary China, 1949-1965.* Cambridge: Cambridge University Press, 1987.

_____. "Interviews on Party History." In Timothy Cheek and Tony Saich, eds. *New Perspectives on State Socialism in China*. Armonk: M.E. Sharpe, 1997.

_____. "Mao and His Lieutenants," *The Australian Journal of Chinese Affairs*, no. 19-20 (1988).

_____. "Mao Texts and the Mao of the 1950s." *The Australian Journal of Chinese Affairs*, no. 33 (1995).

_____. "The Paradoxical Post-Mao Transition: From Obeying the Leader to 'Normal Politics'." *The China Journal*, no. 34 (1995). Also in Jonathan Unger, ed. *The Nature of Chinese Politics: From Mao to Jiang*. Armonk, M. E. Sharpe, 2002.

_____. "Peng Dehuai and Mao Zedong." *The Australian Journal of Chinese Affairs*, no. 16 (1986).

_____. "Politics at the 'Core': The Political Circumstances of Mao Zedong, Deng Xiaoping and Jiang Zemin." *China Information*, no. 1 (2001).

_____. "The Politics of Succession: Previous Patterns and a New Process." In John Wong and Zheng Yongnian, eds. *China's Post-Jiang Leadership Succession: Problems and Perspectives*. Singapore: Singapore University Press, 2002.

_____. "Provincial Politics in China: Themes and Variations." In John M. H. Lindbeck, ed. *China: Management of a Revolutionary Society*. Seattle: University of Washington Press, 1971.

_____. "Seeking the Historical Mao." *The China Quarterly*, no. 145 (1996).

_____ and Warren Sun. "The First Tiananmen Incident Revisited: Elite Politics and Crisis Management at the End of the Maoist Era." *Pacific Affairs*, Summer 2004.

"T'ieh Ying—Chairman of the Chekiang Provincial Advisory Commission." *Issues & Studies*, October 1984.

Tsou, Tang. "The Historic Change in Direction and Continuity with the Past." *The China Quarterly*, no. 98 (1984).

Unger, Jonathan. "The Struggle to Dictate China's Administration: The Conflict of Branches v Areas v Reform." *The Australian Journal of Chinese Affairs*, no. 18 (1987).

"Urban Militia—A New Force?" *Current Scene*, January 1974.

Wang, James C. F. "The Urban Militia as a Political Instrument in the Power Contest in China in 1976." *Asian Survey*, June 1978.

Wang, Shaoguang. "Between Destruction and Construction: The First Year of the Cultural Revolution." In Kam-yee Law, ed. *The Chinese Cultural Revolution Reconsidered: Beyond Purge and Holocaust*. Basingstoke, Hampshire: Palgrave Macmillan, 2003.

_____. "The Structural Sources of the Cultural Revolution." In Kam-yee Law, ed. *The Chinese Cultural Revolution Reconsidered: Beyond Purge and Holocaust*. Basingstoke, Hampshire: Palgrave Macmillan, 2003.

Wich, Richard. "The Tenth Party Congress: The Power Structure and the Succession Question." *The China Quarterly*, no. 58 (1974).

Young, Graham. "Party Building and the Search for Unity." In Bill Brugger, ed. *China: The Impact of the Cultural Revolution*. Canberra: Australian National University Press, 1978.

_____ and Dennis Woodward. "Chinese Conceptions of the Nature of Class Struggle Within the Socialist Transition." In Marian Sawer, ed. *Socialism and the New Class: Towards the Analysis of Structural Inequality within Socialist Societies*. Bedford Park, South Australia: APSA Monograph no. 19, 1978.

Zweig, David. "Agrarian Radicalism as a Rural Development Strategy, 1968-1978." In William A. Joseph, Christine P. W. Wong and David Zweig, eds. *New Perspectives on the Cultural Revolution*. Cambridge: Council on East Asian Studies/Harvard University, 1991.

_____. "The Peita Debate on Education and the Fall of Teng Hsiao-ping." *The China Quarterly*, no. 73 (1978).

Biographical Directories

Bartke, Wolfgang. *Who's Who in the People's Republic of China*. Armonk: M.E. Sharpe, 1981.

_____ and Peter Schier. *China's New Party Leadership: Biographies and Analysis of the Twelfth Central Committee of the Communist Party of China*. London: Macmillan Press, 1985.

Gendai Chugoku Jimmei Jiten [Modern China Biographic Dictionary]. Tokyo: Gaimusho, 1982.

Klein, Donald W., and Anne B. Clark. *Biographic Dictionary of Chinese Communism 1921-1965*. 2 vols., Cambridge: Harvard University Press, 1971.

Lamb, Malcolm. *Directory of Officials and Organizations in China: A Quarter-Century Guide*. Armonk: M.E. Sharpe, 1994.

Who's Who in Communist China. Hong Kong: Union Research Institute, 1966.

Unpublished Ph.D. Dissertations

Fenwick, Ann Elizabeth. "The Gang of Four and the Politics of Opposition: China, 1971-1976." Stanford University, 1984.

Fox, Galen Wheeler. "Campaigning for Power in China during the Cultural Revolution Era 1967-1976." Princeton University, 1978.

INDEX

About the Authors

Frederick C. Teiwes is Emeritus Professor of Chinese Politics at the University of Sydney. He received his B.A. from Amherst College and his Ph.D. in political science from Columbia University, and subsequently taught and conducted research at Cornell University and the Australian National University before joining the University of Sydney in 1976. He is the author of various books on Chinese elite politics including *Politics and Purges in China* (1979, 1993), *Leadership, Legitimacy, and Conflict in China* (1984), and *Politics at Mao's Court* (1990).

Warren Sun is Senior Lecturer in the Chinese Studies Department at Monash University, which he joined in 1996 after a decade as Senior Research Fellow at University of Sydney. Originally from Taiwan, he received his B.A. in English Literature from Taiwan National University and his Ph.D. in modern Chinese intellectual history from the Australian National University. Apart from ongoing work on Chinese Communist Party history, he has published on the life and works of Zhang Binglin, the last master of classical Chinese learning. Until recently he was head of the Chinese Studies Department at Monash.

Over the past decade and a half Professor Teiwes and Dr Sun have jointly produced numerous publications including *The Politics of Agricultural Cooperativization in China: Mao, Deng Zihui, and the "High Tide" of 1955* (1993), *The Tragedy of Lin Biao: Riding the Tiger during the Cultural Revolution, 1966-1971* (1996), and *China's Road to Disaster: Mao, Central Politicians and Provincial Leaders in the Emergence of the Great Leap Forward, 1955-1959* (1999).